SANDERS'
ENCYCLOPÆDIA OF GARDENING

The Late T. W. SANDERS, F.L.S., F.R.H.S.
Author of the Original Edition of the Encyclopædia of Gardening

SANDERS'
ENCYCLOPÆDIA
OF GARDENING

A DICTIONARY OF CULTIVATED PLANTS, ETC., GIVING
IN ALPHABETICAL SEQUENCE THE CULTURE AND
PROPAGATION OF HARDY AND HALF-HARDY PLANTS,
TREES AND SHRUBS, ORCHIDS, FERNS, FRUIT, VEGE-
TABLES, HOTHOUSE AND GREENHOUSE PLANTS, ETC.,
INCLUDING THEIR SPECIFIC AND COMMON NAMES

Revised by A. J. MACSELF

LONDON
W. H. & L. COLLINGRIDGE LIMITED
2-10 TAVISTOCK STREET, COVENT GARDEN, W.C.
NEW YORK: TRANSATLANTIC ARTS INC.

1st Edition by the late T. W. Sanders published 1895
Subsequently a further 20 Editions were published up to 1930
22nd Edition Revised and Enlarged by A. J. Macself 1931
Reprinted 1934
Reprinted 1938
Reprinted 1942
Reprinted 1945
Reprinted 1946
Reprinted 1947
Reprinted 1949
Reprinted 1950

PRINTED IN GREAT BRITAIN BY ROBERT MACLEHOSE AND CO. LTD.
THE UNIVERSITY PRESS, GLASGOW

FOREWORD

FOR the twenty-second time a new edition of this "Encyclopædia of Gardening" is necessary—a wonderful record which needs no comment. After the appearance of the twentieth edition its author, Mr. T. W. Sanders, passed away and a new and revised edition was undertaken by his successor to the Editorial chair of "Amateur Gardening." This edition rapidly became exhausted and is succeeded by the present volume.

The work has been by no means light, for horticulture has progressed at a rapid pace during the past few years, and necessary additions of new plants proved to be very numerous, introductions from foreign countries being supplemented by achievements of plant breeders in our own country. Indeed, the greatest satisfaction attending the laborious task of bringing this work up-to-date has been the proof positive it has afforded that the pace of progress in every branch and phase of horticulture has been increasingly rapid during the years succeeding the great war which for a while threatened to shatter everything that appertained to culture and artistry.

In the present volume some items appear for the first time which have owed their development to the science and skill of great horticulturists of Britain, various European nations and America, but even greater in influence upon the handicraft of garden making and furnishing have been the invaluable additions to the range of available subjects for cultivation resulting from the expeditions of plant collectors in hitherto unexplored regions of China, Tibet and the Himalayas.

It is a strange coincidence, that whilst the collection and importation of exotic orchids, ferns and stove plants has been waning, great increase has been witnessed in introduction of new plants from the higher altitudes of hot countries which are sufficiently hardy to withstand the rigours of a British winter. Not only have these recent introductions from other lands themselves enriched our gardens, but they have provided precious new material which our hybridists have put to good use with highly gratifying results. This new volume of the "Encyclopædia of Gardening" includes many additional items in consequence of these facts. This work, from the first, has endeavoured to make itself a reliable and complete book of reference for those who required a ready and simple guide to cultivated plants, their characters, purposes and distinctions. The necessity for brevity and compactness precludes the possibility of dealing exhaustively and in detail with the individual requirements of particular plants, but in the comprehensive library of practical works on various branches of horticulture issued from the office of " Amateur Gardening " the specialist, connoisseur or veriest novice in gardencraft may find every assistance he requires in the successful pursuit of his hobby or calling. Finally, let it be said, that with all its difficulties and exacting labour the task of revising this volume has been pursued with a feeling that it is a privilege and honour to have been entrusted with it, and our hope is that those for whom the effort has been made will pronounce the result to be entirely satisfactory.

A. J. MACSELF.

INTRODUCTION

GARDENCRAFT, either as a means of livelihood or as a source of recreation and enjoyment, engages the attention of every civilized nation in the World, and it is by reason of its international character that a universal system of scientific nomenclature and description of cultivated plants is essential and indispensable. Advocates of the substitution of popular or common names for the botanical, disregard the fact that even though the English-speaking race might make themselves acquainted with such nomenclature, speakers of other tongues would be entirely mystified and needlessly embarrassed. That would be a more serious matter than may be apparent to those whose horticultural interests are limited to their own gardens. Commercial growers and the curators of botanical gardens are compelled to have dealings with suppliers of plants, seeds, bulbs, etc. in all parts of the world, and without a uniform and generally recognized nomenclature it would be practically impossible to make known to foreign correspondents exactly what is required, and confusion and errors would be rife.

Realization of these facts will, surely, carry conviction that botanical names are really necessary, and it is remarkable how quickly even a novice will surmount the difficulty of memorizing and pronouncing the correct names of plants.

Toward this end careful study of this encyclopædia will prove to be immensely helpful. The student will soon discover that scientific names are not given to plants in a haphazard or casual manner, but that a cleverly conceived system is observed and maintained.

Ere long it will be seen that usually a perfectly sound reason exists for the application of a name to a particular plant. In a large proportion of cases the words used indicate some distinctive feature or characteristic in the foliage, flowers or habit of growth, and in some cases the name has a direct reference to some peculiarity in the roots. It has frequently been remarked that it would enhance the value of this work to supply a guide to correct pronunciation of all the names quoted. This, however, would be a task that would so greatly increase cost of production that a higher price for the volume would be imperative. The need for a glossary of this character is now, however, fully met by publication of a separate work entitled " Plant Names Simplified." That book supplies much information upon the derivation and meanings as well as pronunciation of both generic and specific names, and with its aid, in conjunction with the encyclopædia, the student, professional or amateur, will be thoroughly well equipped so far as works of reference are concerned.

Horticulture has achieved a pace of progress during the past few years which has had a tremendous influence upon the range of plants which demand recognition and inclusion in any work which claims to be recognized as an encyclopædia of cultivated plants. During the last quarter of a century a number of men, who combine the know-ledge of expert botanists and horticulturists with the courage of intrepid travellers and explorers, have scoured hitherto unknown tracts of vast extent in China, the Himalayas, and the mountain regions of other countries in Europe and Asia in search of new trees, shrubs, and plants of many kinds for cultivation in flower borders and rock gardens. Very important additions have been made to such families as primulas, meconopsis and gentians, which have already estab-lished themselves in a secure position among the highly appreciated treasures of British gardens. In regard to trees and shrubs, longer periods of time are involved in bringing to maturity, or a stage of effective serviceability, new species or varieties which had for the most part to be introduced by means of seeds. Hence, it is only of very recent years that the results of the earlier of this cen-tury's plant-hunting expeditions have revealed their full value, and there are greater numbers which are still in comparatively juvenile stages of development and have yet to make their way into general cultivation.

The plants sent home by E. H. Wilson, George Forrest, Reginald Farrer and Kingdon Ward, have provided a great deal of new material to be added to this revised edition of the " Encyclopædia of Garden-ing." They comprise remarkably fine rhododendrons, lovely ber-berises, climbing plants of many kinds and deciduous trees and shrubs of distinctive merit. Rock plants and border perennials are also numerous among the newcomers from the Far East, and there have also been striking additions to hardy and half-hardy annuals and to bulbous plants from Africa, America and from Southern Europe.

During the same period of time hybridists and plant breeders have been incessantly active and surprisingly successful. Many of their achievements have been of sufficient distinction to warrant inclusion in this work, although, of necessity, it has still remained the rule that ordinary garden varieties of florists' flowers, domestic fruits and vegetables must be excluded from notice.

The authorities and experts who make it their business to exert an influence upon the botanical classification of plants, are constantly deciding upon transference of some plant from the genus, or family in which it has lived, perhaps for generations, to some other family. Names which have become familiar as belonging to certain plants have been pronounced to be incorrect, and the edict has gone forth that henceforth they must be called by some other name, the one in general use being styled a synonym. Some authority must be recognized in such matters, and although, at times, it may seem that the changes have been unwarranted and are calculated to create the confusion they are supposed to remedy, it behoves us, so far as possible, to follow the leaders and adopt the course they direct.

The basis of nomenclature followed in this work is that of Kew, and it will be found that considerable differences arise between this edition and former editions, as a result of obeying the ruling of the Kew handbooks and the Index Kewensis. In a few instances, however, where other modern and up-to-date works of reference have adhered to a well established name and there seems to be no serious intention to depart from it, we have allowed that name to stand. Such a course has only been adopted when there seemed sound reason to believe that change would only vexatiously lead to difficulty. In this connection it may be remarked that even the Index Kewensis is sometimes at variance with the handbooks issued by Kew itself.

Thanks, largely, to the wide expansion of the range of available plants for cultivation in gardens or under glass, noteworthy changes have been effected in the style and fashion of British gardens. Another great factor in the advancement of gardencraft is the acquisition of greater knowledge of the cultural requirements and capabilities of many subjects which to-day play a more important part in the furnishing and cropping of gardens than ever before. Among many things which gardeners of to-day have learned is the fact that a great many plants can not only exist but thrive more vigorously with a deal less artificial heat and freer ventilation than our forebears considered essential.

Many plants which years ago were kept in stove houses are now grown in moderately warm greenhouses. Other plants which used to be afforded artificial heat have proved to be satisfactory occupants of unheated glasshouses. Furthermore, experiment has proved, in numerous cases, that plants which had long been confined to glasshouses are capable of making themselves quite at home in wall-sheltered corners, or even in open situations in favourably placed gardens. The question of hardiness of plants was long considered to be dependent upon the latitude of the district in which it might be grown. Closer observation has led to the conclusion that longitude may very well have as great or even greater influence in this matter than latitude. In gardens near the western seaboard, even though far north, plants will thrive and survive our British winters which are killed in gardens of the counties of Oxford, Berkshire or Surrey.

These, and various other cultural changes, have had a great effect upon the general trend of British horticulture, and it may be affirmed without fear of refutation that the gardens of Great Britain are, to-day, more interesting, beautiful and productive than in any previous era.

The old formality and artificiality in design of gardens have been effectively displaced by a more natural and artistic style of planning and planting. The vogue of the rock and water garden has transformed many an uninviting and unimpressive enclosure of ground into a paradise of never waning charm and delight. The wonderfully free and continuous hybrid tea and pernetiana roses, the rampant and gay ramblers and the dwarf bedding polyantha varieties, have bestowed upon the rosary a loveliness that never belonged to the old rose gardens tenanted by hybrid perpetuals and their confrères.

In the branches of horticulture which are concerned with utility rather than ornamentation, progress may be less spectacular than in the branches above referred to, but it has been no less commendable. Developments in potatoes have engaged the attention of both scientists and practical men. Immunity from serious diseases has been partially secured in the majority of varieties of recent introduction, and cropping capacity has been greatly increased while improvement in texture and flavour has by no means been ignored. New tomatoes appear on the market in adequate numbers and essential qualities are brought to a high standard in all that secure a footing among the generally grown kinds. Edible peas, beans and most of the everyday vegetables and salads have likewise been improved and are still annually taking further strides forward. The fruit grower has been placed in possession of improved varieties of most kinds of fruits, and where due attention is given to keeping insect pests and fungoid diseases at a distance, by systematic spraying, sound crops are more regularly assured than could be relied upon in bygone years with older and somewhat erratic varieties. Here, again, scientists have rendered invaluable assistance to the gardener, and it is only the obstinately prejudiced among cultivators who are not reaping immense benefits from the help the chemists and pathologists have offered.

All this progress has broadened the field to be covered by the " Encyclopædia of Gardening," and, furthermore, increases the necessity for such a work. Of weekly literature on gardening matters there is a plenitude, some at least of which fulfils a great mission. Of textbooks, handbooks and monographs there is no dearth ; nevertheless, everyone who controls a garden, be he professional or amateur, and whether the garden under his charge is large or small, finds himself in constant and urgent need of a book of ready reference. But the serviceability of the work is entirely dependent upon its comprehensiveness and accuracy. That is why the exhaustive task has been grappled with to bring this new edition of Sanders' Encyclopædia up-to-date, and to eliminate errors that, during the years of continuous perusal, have been detected but that had evaded the eye of even so able an editor as the originator of the work.

In order to accommodate all the new matter it was necessary to add, but at the same time to avoid unduly enlarging the bulk of the volume, certain less important portions of the original had to be deleted. These, for the most part, were details affecting only the commercial side of horticulture. Costs of materials, labour, etc., and market values of crops are matters subject to such spasmodic fluctuations due to outside causes that it appeared unwise to include them in a work of so permanent a character.

Another deciding factor concerning the suitability or otherwise of entering into costs and values is that, although primarily published for British horticulturists, this book is sought and bought by garden lovers in all parts of the world, and none of such details as relate to garden finance could be of the slightest practical service to the ever widening circle of foreign and colonial readers.

Values of timber, which were quoted in earlier editions of the work, had a certain amount of significance when demand and supply were steady, transport slow and labour cheap, for there was little, under such conditions, that could rapidly upset standard prices. All this has so greatly been affected by improved means of communication, speedy transport and new machinery, that the ruling figures of one week appear ludicrous the next. By saving space hitherto occupied by such unstable information other essentials have been benefited.

The review of the ancient history of horticulture has been omitted from this edition. That topic is possessed of its own interest, but it must be considered secondary in practical importance to descriptions and cultural details of cultivated plants of the present day. It is common knowledge that there was a time when beautiful gardens in this country were a luxury enjoyed by only the aristocracy and the merchant princes. Tribute has been deservedly paid to the monks of bygone centuries who made a great study of horticulture, and by whose untiring efforts very many plants of economic value or superb beauty were introduced to this country permanently to enrich British gardens. A bibliography of works on gardening matters would bear striking testimony to the learned abilities of past generations of gardeners and botanists, British and foreign. The monumental works of Evelyn, Gerard and Parkinson formed a basis for study and teaching, and are still reckoned among the most highly prized treasures of the best of horticultural libraries. It is, however, to the great men of the nineteenth century that we owe a debt of everlasting gratitude for the manner in which they carried the craft along the road of progress with rapid strides

Thomas Andrew Knight, J. C. Loudon, Dr. Lindley were men of great achievements who used their talents and opportunities for the general good of the calling they espoused. It was largely due to these men that gardeners acquired remarkable skill in the propagation and cultivation of good trees, beautiful flowers and choice fruits and vegetables.

During the middle and latter part of last century, the cult of florists' flowers and of specimen stove and greenhouse plants were prominent and strong features of British horticulture. Later developments have changed the character of gardens and set up new ideals, and it has become the habit of the younger generation to speak patronizingly and somewhat contemptuously of what is called the old school of florists. The truth is they were the men whose patient labours and appreciation of good quality in the subjects they cultivated gave us the stock material from which has been evolved the finest races, strains and varieties of the most beautiful and popular flowers that fill our gardens to-day. The old florist was not a gardener, but a cultivator and critical expert in the particular plant he made his speciality. It mattered little to him whether the quarters in which his picotees and carnations, laced pinks and polyanthuses, French marigolds and show pansies grew deserved the term picturesque ; the aim and object was not a prettily arranged garden, but the production of blossoms that conformed as nearly as possible to the accepted standard of points which meant perfection in the flower. In all probability the plants were grown in narrow beds and straight lines for convenience of attention, and as buds commenced to open, all manner of temporary shades and protectors were fixed up, regardless of appearances, because the only thing that mattered was the full and unblemished development of the flowers.

Gardening proper, at that period, concerned itself with elaborate and intricate bedding schemes, the planting and trimming of specimen trees, shrubs and hedges, whilst glasshouse plants were staked, tied and pinched to form specimens of geometrical accuracy.

Then came a great reaction, and the modern school took up the idea that gardens should be laid out and planted in an artistic manner, plants, trees and bulbs being distributed in a free and informal manner, to be allowed to grow in whatever form they chose, in order to produce natural effects. To meet the requirements of that style of gardening, a great many hitherto neglected plants of hardy character and free growth were sought and planted in borders and masses of irregular outline, and the vogue of hardy perennials came into the forefront, pushing the cult of the florists' flower aside and, ultimately, behind. Many flowers which the florist would discard unceremoniously met with rapturous welcome from a race of garden lovers who had new and entirely different ideals. Gardens became gay with blazes of colour provided by plants which depended upon massed planting rather than individual perfection, from the old standpoint. One result of this great change was that thousands of town dwellers as well as countrymen who had never previously attempted to make and keep gardens, found that they could indulge in an occupation which proved to be a delightful hobby. Thus it is that during the past forty or fifty years the whole of the British Isles have become world famous for their multitude of home gardens, ranging in size from plots of two rods of ground, or less, to delightful enclosures embracing acres of land. Rock gardens multiplied at a rate almost equal to herbaceous borders, and as greater knowledge of the requirements of mountain plants was acquired, moraines and scree drifts were provided for those kinds that cannot make themselves happy in close, retentive soil.

Demand creates supply, and it is the vast increase in border and rock plants, flowering shrubs and outdoor climbing plants that is very largely responsible for the necessity which arose for this thoroughly revised edition.

During the period when national needs drained large gardens of their labour, and scarcity of fuel prevented glasshouses being maintained at high temperature, the cultivation of ornamental plants suffered a great set-back. Many choice subjects were all but lost, and for awhile it was opined that they would nevermore be seen in cultivation. The last few years have, happily, witnessed a great revival of interest in this phase of horticulture. Not only have stove plants and orchids been brought into greater prominence, but an enormous number of small greenhouses have been erected in amateurs' gardens of moderate size, and such things as begonias, gloxinias, streptocarpuses and various types of primulas are everywhere grown. Entirely new species of some of these popular genera have found inclusion in this volume, but garden varieties and select strains claim greater attention from most cultivators.

It may be claimed that the main principles of propagation and cultivation remain practically unchanged. The clever gardeners of last century were skilled in their craft. Pupils were well trained by able masters, and knowledge was obtained in the hard but excellent school of practical experience. Radical changes in methods thus learned are difficult to effect, nor is there much wisdom in endeavouring to change that which proves itself by success to be satisfactory. Nevertheless, there must be some alteration where progress and not stagnation prevails. In the case of hothouse and greenhouse plants, it is customary to-day to maintain lower temperatures and give freer ventilation than was usual in pre-war days. Enforced necessity to economize fuel taught cultivators that many plants are not only capable of existing but actually grow more healthily in a moderate and buoyant atmosphere instead of excessive and sultry heat. Some plants which were formerly kept true by persistent propagation from cuttings, are now raised from seeds, liability to variation having been almost eliminated by extremely careful roguing and re-selection of seed stocks. Hollyhocks and antirrhinums may be instanced as two notable examples of so welcome a change. Continuous propagation by cuttings had told upon the constitution of the old florists' varieties of these two subjects to such an extent that their popularity waned. The development of new strains, reproducible from seed, restored vigour and greatly enhanced the serviceability of the plants, with the result that they are more largely grown and highly prized than ever before. In many other cases plants, of which seeds were at one time available only in uncertain mixture, may now be procured in separate distinctive colours, a fact that facilitates their being used in carefully planned schemes where ordinary mixtures would be of little use and would probably wreck the scheme entirely. These possibilities are the outcome of great triumphs on the part of a very important section of the commercial growers whose particular business is the production of improved and reliable stocks of seed. Their work is every bit as difficult, important and beneficial as that of the hybridist who produces wonderful crosses between distinct species.

All along the line of progress which is so well trodden, the worker in every branch of horticulture is handicapped by insect pests and troublesome diseases that attack plants. It seems to be an inexorable rule that the more highly developed an individual plant or a strain becomes, the more it shall be menaced by enemies. In this connection chemists, entomologists and pathologists have rendered services that have in more than one direction been so helpful, that it is not too much to say they have saved the situation. There are some troubles which seem to baffle all efforts to conquer them, but on the whole, successful gardening is within range of possibility for all who will make persevering effort. Study is as necessary as practical work to ensure that the latter is well directed and performed in proper season. The cultivator must know his plants and make himself well informed concerning their requirements. It is in this direction the new edition of this encyclopædia will prove its utility, for strenuous effort has been exerted to ensure that it shall, in all essential details, live up to its claims to efficiency.

"Plant Names Simplified" referred to in the preceding pages *is issued* by the Publishers of this work, price 8/6 net.

ENCYCLOPÆDIA OF GARDENING

ENCYCLOPÆDIA OF GARDENING

Aaron's Beard (*Hypericum calycinum*)—See Hypericum.

Aaron's Rod (*Verbascum Thapsus*)—See Verbascum.

Abaca (*Musa textilis*)—See Musa.

Abchasian Hellebore (*Helleborus abchasicus*)—See Helleborus.

Abele Tree (*Populus alba*)—See Populus.

Abelia—Ord. Caprifoliaceæ. Half-hardy flowering shrubs. Evergreen and deciduous. First introduced 1842.
CULTURE : Compost, equal parts peat, loam, sand. Position, warm, sheltered walls outdoors. Plant, April or Oct. Prune slightly after flowering.
GREENHOUSE CULTURE : Compost, equal parts loam, peat, leaf-mould and silver sand. Position, well-drained pots in sunny, cold house. Pot in Oct. Store in cold frame till Jan. Water moderately at first, freely when in full growth. Give little water during winter. Prune straggly growths after flowering. Stand outdoors during summer.
PROPAGATION : By layers in March, or cuttings of firm shoots in cold frame in July.
SPECIES CULTIVATED : A. chinensis (Syn. A. rupestris), white, fragrant, Sept., to 6 ft., deciduous, China ; floribunda, rosy-purple, June, to 6 ft., evergreen, Mexico ; grandiflora, pink, July to Oct., to 6 ft., semi-evergreen, hybrid ; Schumanni, pink, Aug., to 5 ft., deciduous, China ; triflora, cream and pink, June, to 12 ft., deciduous, Himalayas ; uniflora, pinkish-white, summer, to 6 ft., evergreen, China. A. grandiflora is the hardiest of the family.

Abies (Silver Fir)—Ord. Coniferæ. Hardy coniferous evergreen trees. First introduced 1603.
CULTURE : Soil, sandy loam. Position, high, dry, open from sea coast. Plant, Oct. or April. A. pectinata (Common Silver Fir or Deal Tree), a good species to plant in mixed woods as shelter for game. Timber valuable for joists, rafters, and floor boards. Tree grows rapidly after first few years.
PROPAGATION : By seeds sown $\frac{1}{4}$ in. deep in sandy loam in a temp. 55°, March, or outdoors in April.
SPECIES CULTIVATED : A. amabilis (White Fir), 100 to 250 ft., British Columbia ; balsamea (Balsam Fir), 70 to 80 ft., N. America ; balsamea hudsonia, 2 ft. ; brachyphylla, 120 ft., Japan ; bracteata, 100 to 150 ft., California ; cephalonica, 80 to 100 ft., Greece ; cilicica, 100 ft., Asia Minor and Syria ; concolor, 80 to 100 ft., Colorado, New Mexico, Arizona ; firma, 120 to 150 ft., Japan ; Fraseri, 30 to 40 ft., rarely taller, Carolina ; grandis, 200 to 300 ft., California ; lowiana (Low's Silver Fir), 200 ft., Sierra Nevada and Oregon ; magnifica (Red Fir), 200 ft., Vancouver Island to California ; Mariesi, 40 to 50 ft., occasionally more, Japan ; nobilis, 200 ft., California ; nordmanniana (Caucasian Fir), 100 to 200 ft., Caucasus ; pectinata, 100 to 120 ft., Central and Southern Europe ; Pinsapo, 60 to 100 ft., Spain ; Pinsapo glauca, bluish foliage ; sachalinense, 130 ft., Isle of Sachalin ; Veitchi, 50 to 70 ft., Japan ; webbiana, 80 to 150 ft., Himalayas. See also Picea.

Abobra (Cranberry Gourd)—Ord. Cucurbitaceæ. Half-hardy climbing, tuberous-rooted perennial. Deciduous. Fruit, egg-shaped, scarlet ; Sept. and Oct.
CULTURE : Soil, sandy. Position, south wall. Plant, June ; lift tubers Oct. and store in frost-proof place.
PROPAGATION : By seeds sown in leaf-mould, loam and sand, temp. 65°, March, also by division or by cuttings in spring.
SPECIES CULTIVATED : A. viridiflora, green, fragrant, summer, 6 ft., S. America.

Abroma—Ord. Sterculiaceæ. Stove-flowering plants. Evergreen. First introduced 1770.

CULTURE : Compost, equal parts loam, peat, sand. Pot and prune, March. Water freely in summer, moderately in winter. Temp., March to Sept. 70° to 80° ; Sept. to March 60° to 65°.

PROPAGATION : By seeds sown $\frac{1}{16}$ in. deep, or cuttings of firm shoots, in fine sandy soil, March, temp. 65° to 75°.

SPECIES CULTIVATED : A. augusta, purple, Aug., 8 to 10 ft., Asia ; orbicularis, purple, June.

Abronia (Sand Verbena)—Ord. Nyctaginaceæ. Half-hardy trailing plants. First introduced 1823. Flowers fragrant.

CULTURE : Soil, sandy loam. Position, exposed rockery or elevated warm border. Plant, June. A. umbellata, good greenhouse plant.

PROPAGATION : By seeds sown $\frac{1}{16}$ in. deep in sandy soil, temp. 55° to 65°, March ; perennials by cuttings of young shoots in similar soil and temp.

SPECIES CULTIVATED : A. latifolia (Syn. A. arenaria), lemon-yellow, July, 9 to 18 in. ; umbellata, rosy-pink, June and July, 6 to 18 in. Natives of California.

Abrus (Paternoster or Rosary Pea ; Crab's Eyes ; Weather Plant)—Ord. Leguminosæ Stove climber. Orn. foliage. Deciduous. First introduced 1680.

CULTURE : Compost, two parts loam, one part peat and sand. Pot and prune March. Water freely spring and summer, moderately in autumn and winter. Temp., March to Sept. 70° to 80° ; Sept. to March 60° to 65°.

PROPAGATION : By seeds sown $\frac{1}{4}$ in. deep, or cuttings of firm shoots in sandy loam, temp. 75° to 85°, Feb.

SPECIES CULTIVATED : A. precatorius, pale purple, May, 9 to 12 ft., E. Indies. Seeds scarlet and black.

Absinthium (*Artemisia absinthium*)—See Artemisia.

Abutilon (Indian Mallow)—Ord. Malvaceæ. Greenhouse and half-hardy evergreen shrubs.

CULTURE : Compost, two parts loam, one peat and sand. Position, sunny greenhouse. Pot and prune March. Temp., March to Sept. 55° to 65° ; Sept. to March 50° to 55°. Water freely in spring and summer, moderately in autumn and winter. May be used for bedding in summer. A. vitifolium is hardy in the open in mild districts.

PROPAGATION : By seeds sown $\frac{1}{8}$ in. deep, or cuttings in light rich soil, temp. 70°, March.

SPECIES CULTIVATED : A. aurantiacum, orange, spring and summer, 3 to 6 ft., Brazil ; bedfordianum, red and yellow, autumn, 3 to 6 ft., Brazil ; Darwini, orange, April, 4 ft., Brazil ; esculentum, yellow, summer, 3 to 6 ft., Brazil ; floribundum, orange-red, summer, 5 ft. ; graveolens, orange-red, Asia ; insigne, white and carmine, Jan., 5 ft., New Granada ; megapotamicum (Syn. vexillarium), yellow and scarlet, summer, 4 to 8 ft., Brazil ; pæoniflorum, pink, Jan., 5 ft., Brazil, pulchellum, white, May, 3 to 4 ft., N.S. Wales ; striatum, orange-red, all year round, 6 to 10 ft., Brazil ; sellovianum marmoratum, mottled foliage, Brazil ; Thompsoni, mottled leaves ; venosum, orange-red, July, 3 to 4 ft. ; vitifolium, blue, July, Chile, nearly hardy. Popular varieties : Boule de Neige, white ; Delicatum, rose, Louis Van Houtte, purple ; Queen of Yellows, yellow. These are garden hybrids.

Abyssinian Banana (*Musa ensete*)—See Musa.

Abyssinian Primrose (*Primula verticillata*)—See Primula.

Acacallis—Ord. Orchidaceæ. Stove epiphytal orchids. Culture and propagation as advised for Agansia.

SPECIES CULTIVATED : A. cyanea, light blue, summer, 1 ft., Brazil.

Acacia (Wattle ; Gum Tree ; Popinac)—Ord. Leguminosæ. Greenhouse flowering plants. Evergreen. First introduced 1656.

CULTURE : Compost, equal parts peat, loam, sand. Pot and prune, Feb. or March.

Water freely in spring and summer, moderately in autumn and winter. Temp.,
March to Sept. 55° to 65° ; Sept. to March 50° to 55°.
PROPAGATION : By seeds sown ⅛ in. deep, March, or cuttings of half-ripened shoots,
in sandy peat, well-drained pots, under close frame, June-July.
SPECIES CULTIVATED : A. armata (Kangaroo Thorn), yellow, spring, 6 to 10 ft.,
Australia ; baileyana, yellow, late winter, 15 to 20 ft., Australia ; cordata, yellow,
spring, 12 to 18 in., Australia ; cultriformis, yellow, early spring, 6 to 8 ft., Aus-
tralia ; cyanophylla (Blue-leaved Wattle), golden yellow, early spring, 18 ft.,
Australia ; dealbata (Mimosa), yellow, spring, 50 ft., Australia ; decurrens (Green
Wattle), yellow, early spring, 50 ft., Australia ; Drummondii, yellow, April, 10 ft.,
Australia ; elata, yellow, autumn and winter, 50 to 60 ft., Australia ; Farnesiana
(Popinac, Cassie), deep yellow, July, 6 to 10 ft., Tropics ; juniperina, yellow, late
spring and early summer, 8 to 12 ft., Australia ; leprosa, yellow, April, 6 to 10 ft.,
Australia ; lineata, yellow, spring, 6 ft., Australia ; longifolia (Sydney Golden
Wattle), yellow, March, 10 to 15 ft., Australia ; longifolia floribunda, whitish yellow,
early spring, a very distinct type ; melanoxylon (Blackwood Acacia), cream, early
spring, evergreen, 20 to 30 ft., Australia ; pendula (Weeping Myall), grey foliage,
pendulous branches, 15 to 20 ft., Australia ; neriifolia (Syn. retinodes), yellow,
spring, 15 to 20 ft., Australia ; pubescens, yellow, April, 6 to 12 ft., Australia ;
pulchella, yellow, March, 3 to 6 ft., Australia ; pycnantha (Golden Wattle), yellow,
early spring, 15 to 20 ft., Australia ; riceana, yellow, May, 20 ft., Tasmania ; saligna,
yellow, spring, Australia ; verticillata, yellow, March, 6 to 20 ft., Australia.   See
also the genus Albizzia and Robinia.

Acæna (New Zealand Burr)—Ord. Rosaceæ. Hardy trailing perennials.
Evergreen.   First introduced 1828.
CULTURE : Soil, sandy loam. Position, moist, open, or shady rockery.   Plant,
Oct. to April.
PROPAGATION : By seeds sown 1/18 in. deep in March, temp. 65° ; cuttings in cold
frame in Aug. ; division of roots in April ; all in sandy soil.
SPECIES CULTIVATED : A. adscendens, purple, summer, Patagonia ; argentea,
metallic bronze foliage, red burrs, Chile ; Buchanani, silvery green foliage, red
burrs, N. Zealand ; glabra, smooth shining foliage, N. Zealand ; laevigata, strong,
distinct, almost shrubby, glaucous, Magellanica ; microphylla, crimson burrs,
N. Zealand ; microphylla inermis, khaki coloured, loose habit ; myriophylla,
green, feathery foliage, densely tufted ; Novæ Zealandiæ, trailing, bronze foliage,
purple burrs, N. Zealand ; ovina, erect, 9 in., green foliage, purple burrs on spikes ;
pulchella, bronzy foliage, N. Zealand ; sanguisorbæ, large silky leaves, rounded
burrs, purple ; sericea, greenish, Chile ; splendens, hairy foliage, Chile.

Acalypha (Three-sided Mercury ; Copper-leaf)—Ord. Euphorbiaceæ. Stove
plants. Orn. foliage. Evergreen. First introduced 1866. Leaves, orange, red,
green, crimson.
CULTURE : Compost, equal parts leaf-mould, peat, loam, sand. Pot and prune,
Feb. or March.   Water freely in spring and summer, moderately in autumn and
winter. Temp., March to Sept. 70° to 80° ; Sept. to March 60° to 65°. Suitable
for summer or subtropical bedding.
PROPAGATION : By cuttings in sandy soil, temp. 80°, Feb. or March.
SPECIES CULTIVATED : A. hispida (Syn. A. Sanderi), 6 to 10 ft., New Guinea ;
musaica, 6 to 10 ft., Polynesia ; godseffiana, 1 to 3 ft., New Guinea ; wilkesiana
(Syns. A. illustris and A. tricolor), 3 to 4 ft., Fiji , macafeana, macrophylla, marginata and obovata are varieties of the last-named.

Acantholimon (Prickly Thrift)—Ord. Plumbaginaceæ. Hardy perennials.
Evergreen.   First introduced 1851.
CULTURE : Soil, sandy loam. Position, sunny rockery or warm border. Plant,
Oct. to April.
PROPAGATION : By cuttings in cold frame in Sept., or division.
SPECIES CULTIVATED : A. aceroseum, rose, July-Aug., 6 in., A. Minor ; glumaceum,
rose, July, 6 in., Armenia ; Kotschyi, white, July, Asia ; venustum, pink, summer,
A. Minor.

Acanthopanax—Ord. Araliaceæ. Hardy ornamental-leaved evergreen shrubs formerly included in the genus Aralia.
CULTURE : Soil, rich, well-drained loam. Position, warm, sheltered shrubberies, or corners of lawns. Plant in Sept. or April.
PROPAGATION: By seeds sown in heat in spring ; cuttings of ripened shoots in autumn ; suckers at any time.
SPECIES CULTIVATED : A. Henryi, finely toothed foliage, Central China ; pentaphyllum (Syn. A. spinosum), elegant foliage, Japan ; pentaphyllum variegatum, leaved edged creamy white ; ricinifolium (Syn. Aralia · Maximowiczii), leaves castor-oil like, elegant, Japan ; sessiliflorum, leaves wrinkled, large, Japan.

Acanthophœnix (Prickly Date Palm)—Ord. Palmaceæ. Stove palms. Orn. foliage. Evergreen. First introduced 1861.
CULTURE : Compost, two parts peat, one part loam and sand. Repot, Feb. Water freely in summer, moderately other times. Temp., March to Sept. 70° to 85° ; Sept. to March 60° to 65°.
PROPAGATION: By seeds sown 1 in. deep in light soil, temp. 80°, Feb. or March.
SPECIES CULTIVATED : A. crinita, 6 to 10 ft., Seychelles ; rubra, 6 to 12 ft., Madagascar.

Acanthorhiza—Ord. Palmaceæ. Stove palms. Orn. foliage. Evergreen. First introduced 1864.
CULTURE : Compost, two parts loam, one part leaf-mould and sand. Repot, Feb. Water moderately in summer, very little other times. Temp., March to Sept. 70° to 85° ; Sept. to March 60° to 65°.
PROPAGATION : Like Acanthophœnix.
SPECIES CULTIVATED : A. aculeata, Central America.

Acanthus (Bear's Breech ; Bear's Foot)—Ord. Acanthaceæ. Hardy herbaceous perennials. Orn. foliage. First introduced 1548.
CULTURE : Soil, sandy loam. Position, warm sheltered border. Plant, Oct. to April.
PROPAGATION: By seed sown ¼ in. deep in light soil ; division of roots in Oct. or March.
SPECIES CULTIVATED : A. longifolius, rosy-purple, June, 3 to 4 ft., Dalmatia ; candelabrum, purple, July, 3 ft. ; hirsutus, rose, July, 2 to 3 ft., Orient ; mollis, white, rose, lilac, 3 to 4 ft., S. Europe ; mollis latifolius, a superior variety ; spinosus, purplish, July, 2 to 4 ft., Levant ; spinosus spinosissimum, rosy-flesh, July, 3 ft., Dalmatia.

Acer (Maple)—Ord. Aceraceæ. Hardy trees. Orn. foliage. Deciduous or semi-evergreen.
CULTURE : Soil, well-drained loam. Position, shrubberies or open spaces ; Japanese kinds in warm borders or in pots in cool greenhouse. Plant, Oct. to March.
PROPAGATION: By seeds sown ¼ in. deep in sheltered position Oct. ; grafting March ; budding Aug. for choice Japanese and variegated kinds ; layering Oct.
USEFUL DATA : Common Maple (Acer campestris) will grow to an altitude of 1,200 ft., and the Sycamore (Acer pseudo-platanus) to 1,500 ft. above sea-level. Timber reaches maturity at 40 years of age. Life of trees, 500 to 700 years. Timber of Sycamore used for making pattern moulds, stair rails, turnery, etc. ; that of common species and Sugar or Bird's Eye Maple (A. saccharinum) for cabinet work. Quantity of Maple seeds required to plant an acre of ground, 14 lb. ; Sycamore, 30 lb. Sycamore best tree for hilly exposed positions.
SPECIES CULTIVATED : A. argutum, to 25 ft., Japan ; campestre (Common Maple), to 50 ft., Britain ; campestre variegatum, leaves white and yellow, Britain, 20 ft. ; carpinifolium, 50 ft., Japan ; circinatum, leaves scarlet in autumn, 5 to 6 ft., N.W. America ; creticum (Syns. A. heterophyllum and A. orientale), semi-evergreen, 10 to 15 ft., E. Mediterranean ; dasycarpum, 90 to 120 ft., N. America ; dasycarpum aureo-marginatum, leaves mottled yellow ; guinala, 10 to 15 ft., China, Japan, Manchuria ; japonicum, 20 ft., Japan, and its varieties aureum (golden leaved), and laciniatum (Syn. filicifolium), finely cut leaves ; Negundo (Box Elder), 40 to

70 ft., N. America, and its varieties californicum (more vigorous and rapid-growing), crispum (curled leaves), laciniatum (finely cut leaves), and variegatum (silvery leaves) ; palmatum, 10 to 20 ft., Japan, and its varieties aureum (yellow and scarlet-tinted foliage), atropurpureum (bronzy-purple leaves), septemlobum atropurpureum (purple foliage), septemlobum bicolor (leaves carmine tinted), septemlobum elegans (leaves finely cut, red and bronze tinted), dissectum ornatum (leaves fern-like and bronzy-purple tinted), and dissectum roseo-marginatum (leaves tinted with rose and white) ; pictum, 60 ft., Japan ; platanoides (Norway Maple), 50 ft., Europe, and its varieties aureo-variegatum (leaves blotched with yellow), laciniatum (leaves finely cut), Rectenbachi (beautiful in autumn tints), and Schwedleri (young foliage brilliantly coloured red) ; pseudo-platanus (Sycamore), 100 ft., Central Europe, and its varieties albo-variegatum (leaves green and white), brilliantissimum (young foliage tinted pink), and corstorphinense (young leaves pale yellow, deepening to golden shades) ; rubrum (Red Maple), 80 to 100 ft., Canada, scarlet flowered ; saccharinum (Bird's Eye or Sugar Maple), 40 to 100 ft., N. America, var. nigrum (Black Maple) has darker coloured bark ; tataricum, 20 to 30 ft., S.E. Europe, Asia Minor.

Aceras (Green-man Orchis)—Ord. Orchidaceæ. Hardy terrestrial tuberous-rooted orchid. Deciduous. Nat. Britain.
CULTURE : Soil, chalky loam. Position, open and dry. Plant, Oct. to March.
PROPAGATION : By division of tubers Oct. or March.
SPECIES CULTIVATED : A. Anthropophora, green, June, 6 to 10 in.

Achillea (Milfoil; Yarrow; Sweet Maudlin)—Ord. Compositæ. Hardy herbaceous perennials.
CULTURE : Soil, ordinary. Position, dwarf species on rockery, tall ones in open borders. Plant, Oct. to April.
PROPAGATION : By seeds sown ¼ in. deep outdoors April ; division of roots autumn or spring.
SPECIES CULTIVATED : A. ægyptica (see A. taygetea) ; Ageratifolia, close mounds, silvery leaves and stems, white flowers, July-Aug. ; Ageratum (Sweet Maudlin), white, summer, 6 in., Greece ; atrata, white, Aug., 6 in., Austria ; Clavennæ, white, summer, 6 in., Austria ; Eupatorium (see A. filipendulina) ; filipendulina, yellow, June to Sept., 4 ft., Caucasus ; Parker's var., a superior form of filipendulina with convex corymbs of bright yellow flowers ; grandiflora, cream, May-June, 5 to 6 ft., strong, downy cut leaves ; Herba-rota, neat, aromatic rock plant, white, May-June ; Huteri, dwarf silvery-leaved alpine, white, May-June, Switzerland ; millefolium roseum, rose, summer, 1 to 3 ft., Britain ; ptarmica, " The Pearl," white, double, 2 ft., summer, Britain ; rupestris, white, May, 3 in., Italy ; serbica, white flowers, silvery stems and foliage, May to Aug., 1 ft., a choice and distinct Servian rock plant ; siberica (Syn. mongolica), white, large flower heads on long stems, narrow foliage, May to Aug., Mongolia ; tanacetifolia, yellow, summer, 2 ft., Europe ; taygetea (Syn. aegyptica), yellow, 1½ ft., summer, silvery leaves, Egypt ; tomentosa, yellow, summer, 8 to 12 ins., Europe ; umbellata, white, June, 4 in., silver foliage, Greece.

Achimenes—Ord. Gesneraceæ. Greenhouse tuberous-rooted perennials. Deciduous. First introduced 1778.
CULTURE : Compost, two parts peat and loam, one part leaf-mould, and sand. Pot tubers in Feb., 1 in. apart, 2 in. deep, in pots, pans, or baskets. Water moderately at first, freely when in growth. After flowering gradually withhold water from roots, and when foliage dies place pots on their sides in greenhouse, letting them remain till Feb.
PROPAGATION : By seeds sown ⅛ in. deep in light soil, temp. 70° to 80°, March ; cuttings of young shoots and leaves April ; division of tubers Feb.
SPECIES CULTIVATED : A. coccinea, scarlet, Aug., 1 ft., W. Indies ; grandiflora, crimson, Oct., 18 in., Mexico ; heterophylla, scarlet, July, 1 ft., Brazil ; longiflora, violet, Aug., 1 ft., Mexico, and its varieties alba and major ; patens, violet, June, 1 ft., Mexico. A number of still prettier hybrids and varieties will be found in trade lists. See also Næglia.

Achras—Ord. Sapotaceæ.   Tree native of Central America.   Cultivated for their edible fruits.   First introduced 1731.
CULTURE :   Rich, loamy soil.   Position, borders in warm greenhouse.   Temp. March to Sept. 75° to 90° ;   Sept. to March 65° to 70°.
PROPAGATION :   By cuttings in spring or early summer in temp. 75° to 85°.
SPECIES CULTIVATED :   A. sapota (Marmalade Plum, Sapodilla Plum), russet-brown fruits, 3 to 6 in. long, 65 ft.

Acidanthera—Ord. Iridaceæ.   Tender bulbous plants.   First introduced 1893.
CULTURE :   Compost, equal parts sandy loam and leaf-mould.   Position, pots in cool greenhouse for A. bicolor, warm house for other species.   Water freely during growing period, little at other times.
PROPAGATION :   By offsets treated as advised for bulbs.
SPECIES CULTIVATED :   A. æquinoctialis, white and crimson, Nov., 1½ ft., Sierra Leone ; bicolor, white and purple, 1 to 1½ ft., Abyssinia ; candida, white, 1 to 1½ ft., E. Trop. Africa.

Acineta—Ord. Orchidaceæ.   Stove epiphytal or sub-terrestrial orchids.   Evergreen.   First introduced 1837.   Flowers fragrant.
CULTURE :   Compost, equal parts sphagnum moss and peat.   Position, suspended baskets.   Pot after flowering.   Water freely when growing, little when at rest. Temp., March to Sept. 70° to 75° ; Sept. to March 60° to 65°.   Resting period, winter.
PROPAGATION :   By division of pseudo-bulbs Feb.
SPECIES CULTIVATED :   A. Barkeri, yellow and crimson, May, 2 ft., Mexico ; chrysantha, yellow, May, 2 ft., Colombia ; densa, yellow and red, Oct., 18 in., Central America ; Humboldtii, crimson, May, 2 ft., Colombia ; sulcata, yellow, May, 1 ft., Ecuador.

Acis—See Leucojum.

Aciphylla (Spear-grass or Bayonet Plant)—Ord. Umbelliferæ.   Hardy perennials. Evergreen, forming handsome masses of spiny foliage in rosettes.   Nat. N. Zealand. First introduced 1875.
CULTURE :   Soil, sandy.   Position, large open rock gardens and beds.   Plant, October to April.
PROPAGATION :   By seeds sown ½ in. deep in pans in cold frame, or warm position outdoors April ; division of roots March.
SPECIES CULTIVATED :   A. Colensoi, white, summer, 4 to 6 ft. in Britain, 8 to 9 ft. in native haunts ; Lyallii, 2 ft., sometimes more ; squarrosa, white, summer, 4 to 6 ft.

Acmena—Ord. Myrtaceæ.   Greenhouse flowering shrubs.   Evergreen.   First introduced 1790.
CULTURE :   Compost, equal parts peat and loam, little sand.   Pot, March.   Water moderately spring and summer, little other times.   Temp., March to Sept. 55 to 60° ;   Sept. to March 45° to 50°.
PROPAGATION :   By cuttings of half-ripened shoots in sandy peat under bell-glass, temp. 55°, March.
SPECIES CULTIVATED :   A. floribunda, white, April to Aug., 4 ft., New Zealand ; ovata, white.

Acokanthera (Winter Sweet)—Ord. Apocynaceæ.   Greenhouse evergreen flowering shrubs.   First introduced 1787.
CULTURE :   Compost, two parts light loam, one part leaf-mould, and well-decayed manure, one part sand.   Position, well-drained pots in light part of greenhouse. Water freely March to Sept., sparingly Sept. to March.   Temp., March to Sept. 60° to 70° ; Sept. to March 45° to 55°.
PROPAGATION :   By cuttings of young shoots in April and May, under bell-glass in gentle bottom heat.
SPECIES CULTIVATED :   A. spectabilis (Winter Sweet), white, fragrant, spring, 8 to 10 ft., S. Africa ; venenata (Bushman's Poison), white, fragrant, 6 to 7 ft., S. Africa. Juices of both species are very poisonous.

Aconite (*Aconitum Napellus*)—See Aconitum.

Aconitum (Wolf's-bane; Monk's-hood)—Ord. Ranunculaceæ. Hardy herbaceous perennials.

CULTURE: Soil, ordinary. Position, partially shaded borders. Plant, Oct. to March.
PROPAGATION: By seeds sown ½ in. deep in warm position outdoors April, or in boxes of light soil in cold frame in March; division of roots in autumn or spring.
SPECIES CULTIVATED: Anthora, yellow, July, 2 to 4 ft., Pyrenees; biflorum, blue, June, 6 in., Siberia; Cammarum, purple, July-Sept., 4 ft., Europe; Delavayi, lavender-purple, Aug., China; Fischeri (Syn. autumnale), bluish lilac, July to Oct., Europe and N. America; japonicum, deep violet, Sept.-Oct., 3 ft., Japan; Lycoctonum, purple, July and Aug., 4 to 6 ft., Europe; Lycoctonum ochranthum, yellow, autumn; Lycoctonum pyrenaicum, yellow, late-flowering; Lycoctonum septentrionale, wine purple; Napellus, blue, July to Sept., 4 to 6 ft., England; Napellus albus, white, 3 to 4 ft.; Napellus longibracteatum, rich blue, 4 to 6 ft.; uncinatum (Syn. volubile), climber, dark blue, 5 to 8 ft., autumn, suitable for pillars, arbours, etc., N. America; variegatum, blue and white, July and Aug., 3 to 5 ft., Europe; Wilsonii, pale blue or violet, Sept., 6 ft., China.

Acorus (Sweet Flag; Myrtle Grass)—Ord. Araceæ. Hardy aquatics. Evergreen. First introduced 1796. Leaves and roots fragrant.
CULTURE: Soil, muddy. Position, margins of ponds. Plant, March.
PROPAGATION: By division of roots, March.
SPECIES CULTIVATED: A. Calamus, 3 ft., N. Hemisphere; Calamus variegatus, leaves striped, golden yellow; gramineus, 2 ft., Japan; gramineus variegatus, leaves variegated.

Acroclinium—See Helipterum.

Acrophorus—See Davallia.

Acrophyllum—Ord. Saxifragaceæ. Greenhouse flowering shrub. Evergreen. First introduced, 1838.
CULTURE: Compost, equal parts peat and loam, little sand. Pot and prune, Feb. Water freely spring and summer, moderately other times. Temp., March to Sept. 55° to°60°; Sept. to March 45° to 50°.
PROPAGATION: By cuttings of firm shoots in sandy peat under bell-glass in a cool house in summer.
SPECIES CULTIVATED: A. venosum, pink, May, 6 ft., Australia.

Acrostichum (Elephant's Ear Fern)—Ord. Filices. Stove and greenhouse fern. Evergreen. First introduced 1793.
CULTURE: Compost, equal parts peat, loam, and leaf-mould, sand and charcoal. Pot, Feb. or March. Water freely spring and summer, moderately other times. Temp., stove species, March to Sept. 70° to 85°, Sept. to March 60° to 65°; greenhouse species, March to Sept. 55° to 60°, Sept. to March 45° to 50°.
PROPAGATION: By division of roots at potting time, or by spores in spring.
SPECIES CULTIVATED: Stove—A. acuminatum, 1 to 2 ft., Brazil; apiifolium, 2 to 6 in., Philippine Islands; appendiculatum, 6 to 18 in., India; Aubertii, 1 ft., Natal, Guatemala, etc.; aureum, 1 to 2 ft., Tropics; auritum, 1 to 2 ft., Philippine Islands; cervinum, 2 to 4 ft., Tropical America; conforme, 6 in., Tropics; crinitum (Elephant's Ear Fern), 4 to 18 in., West Indies; decoratum, 1 ft., W. Indies; drynarioides, 1 to 2 ft., Penang; flagelliferum, 1 ft., Tropics; Herminieri, 1 to 2 ft., W. Indies; magnum, 1 to 2 ft., British Guiana; muscosum, 6 to 12 in., Tropical America; nicotianæfolium, 1 to 2 ft., Cuba; osmundaceum, 2 to 3 ft., Ecuador; peltatum, 2 to 6 in., Tropical America; scandens, 1 to 3 ft., China, Ceylon, etc.; scolopendrifolium, 1 ft., Brazil; squamosum, 8 to 12 in., Sumatra, Sandwich Islands, Azores, etc.; virens, 1 ft., Tropical Asia; viscosum, 6 to 12 in., Cuba, Tropical America.
GREENHOUSE SPECIES: A. blumeanum, 4 to 6 in., Assam; canaliculatum, 3 to 4 ft., climbing, Venezuela; Cænopteris, 2 to 3 ft., climbing, Mexico.

Actæa (Toad-root; Bane-berry; Herb Christopher)—Ord. Ranunculaceæ. Hardy herbaceous perennials. Berries, red, white, or black, poisonous.
CULTURE: Soil, ordinary. Position, shady border. Plant, Oct. to March.

7

PROPAGATION: By seeds sown in garden April; division of roots March.
SPECIES CULTIVATED: A. alba, white, May, berries white 12 to 18 in., N. America; spicata, white flowers, May, black berries, 1 ft., Britain; spicata rubra, white flowers, red berries.

Actinella (Pigmy or Dwarf Sunflower)—Ord. Compositæ. Hardy herbaceous perennial.
CULTURE: Soil, light, sandy. Position, rockery or open sunny border. Plant, Oct. to March.
PROPAGATION: By division of roots in March.
SPECIES CULTIVATED: A. grandiflora, yellow, summer, 6 in., Rocky Mountains; odorata, yellow, July-Sept., 9 in., fragrant; scaposa, yellow, foliage silvery, July-Sept., 9 in.

Actinidia—Ord. Ternstrœmiaceæ. Hardy climbing shrubs. Deciduous.
CULTURE: Soil, ordinary. Position, wall, trellis or tree stumps. Plant, Oct. to March.
PROPAGATION: By seeds sown in pots in cold frame April; layering shoots in Nov.; cuttings of half-ripened shoots in close frame.
SPECIES CULTIVATED: A. arguta, white, fragrant, June, Japan; chinensis, white, changing to buff, China and Japan; Kolemikta, white, Manchuria, China, Japan, June; polygama, white, fragrant, summer, Japan.

Actiniopteris—Ord. Filices. Stove and greenhouse ferns. Evergreen.
CULTURE: Compost, equal parts peat, loam, charcoal, potsherds, and silver sand. Pot, Feb. or March. Good drainage and clean pots essential. Water moderately all seasons and keep atmosphere moist. Temp., March to Sept. 70° to 80°; Sept. to March 60° to 70° for A. radiata; and 60° to 70° March to Sept., and 55° Sept. to March for P. radiata australis.
PROPAGATION: By spores similar to Adiantum.
SPECIES CULTIVATED: A. radiata, 3 in., India, requires stove treatment; radiata australis, 6 in., Mascarene Islands, greenhouse kind.

Actinomeris (North American Sunflower)—Ord. Compositæ. Hardy herbaceous perennial. First introduced 1640.
CULTURE: Soil, ordinary. Position, open border. Plant, Oct. to April.
PROPAGATION: By seeds sown ¼ in. deep outdoors April; division of roots March.
SPECIES CULTIVATED: A. squarrosa, yellow, July, 3 ft., N. America.

Actinotus (Flannel Flower)—Ord. Umbelliferæ. Greenhouse or half-hardy herbaceous perennial.
INDOOR CULTURE: Compost, equal parts loam and peat, with a liberal addition of silver sand. Position, sunny part of cool greenhouse. Pot, March or April. Water freely March to Oct.; moderately afterwards. Temp., March to Sept. 55° to 65°; Sept. to March 45° to 55°.
OUTDOOR CULTURE: Soil, ordinary. Position, sunny. Sow seeds in temp. of 65° in March or April. Harden off seedlings gradually, and plant out at the end of May.
PROPAGATION: By seeds sown in a temp. of 65° in spring; or by division of the roots at potting time.
SPECIES CULTIVATED: A. Helianthi, white, June, 2 ft., Australia.

Ada—Ord. Orchidaceæ. Greenhouse orchid. Evergreen. First introduced 1863.
CULTURE: Compost, equal parts peat and sphagnum moss. Position, pots in shade. Repot when new growth begins. Water freely during season of growth moderately afterwards. Resting period, none. Temp., March to Sept. 55° to 60°; Sept. to March 45° to 50°.
PROPAGATION: By dividing plant at potting time.
SPECIES CULTIVATED: A. aurantiaca, orange, Jan., 1 ft., Colombia; Lehmanni, red, 1 ft., Colombia.

Adam's Apple (*Tabernæmontana coronaria*)—See Tabernæmontana.

Adam's Laburnum (*Laburnum Adamii*)—See Laburnum.

8

Adam's Needle (*Yucca gloriosa*)—See Yucca.

Adder's Fern (*Polypodium vulgare*)—See Polypodium.

Adder's-tongue Fern (*Ophioglossum vulgatum*)—See Ophioglossum.

Adder's Violet (*Goodyera pubescens*)—See Goodyera.

Adelia—See Forestiera.

Adenandra—Ord. Rutaceæ. Greenhouse flowering shrubs. Evergreen. Nat. Cape of Good Hope. First introduced 1720.
CULTURE : Compost, equal parts loam, peat and sand. Pot, March. Water moderately Sept. to April, freely afterwards. Temp., Sept. to March 50° to 55° ; March to Sept. 55° to 65°.
PROPAGATION : By cuttings of young shoots in sandy peat under bell-glass, March ; also by seeds sown in similar soil at any time.
SPECIES CULTIVATED : A. amœna, red, June, 2 ft. ; fragrans, pink, June, 2 ft. ; coriacea, pink, June, 18 in. ; marginata, flesh, June, 18 in. ; umbellata, pink, June, 2 ft. ; uniflora, white and pink, June, 18 in.

Adenanthera (Barbados Pride)—Ord. Leguminosæ. Stove evergreen flowering shrubs. First introduced 1759.
CULTURE : Compost, equal parts peat and loam, with a little silver sand. Position, well-drained pots in light part of stove. Pot, March. Water freely in spring and summer, and moderately in autumn and winter. Temp., March to Oct. 65° to 75° ; Oct. to March 55° to 65°.
PROPAGATION : By cuttings of side shoots removed with a base of old wood and inserted in sand under bell-glass in spring.
SPECIES CULTIVATED : A. bicolor, yellow, July, Ceylon ; pavonina, yellow and white, July, 5 ft., China.

Adenophora (Gland Bell-flower)—Ord. Campanulaceæ. Hardy perennials. First introduced 1783.
CULTURE : Soil, ordinary. Position, sunny, well-drained border. Plant, Oct. to March.
PROPAGATION : By seeds sown in March, in pots or pans in cold frame ; division in spring.
SPECIES CULTIVATED : A. denticulata, blue, July, 18 in., Dahuria ; Lamarckii, blue, June, 1 to 2 ft., Transylvania ; latifolia, blue, July, 18 in., Siberia ; lilifolia, whitish blue, fragrant, Aug., 18 in., Europe ; polymorpha, pale blue, Aug., 1½ ft., China ; Potanini, pale blue, Aug., 2 ft., Turkestan ; stylosa, blue, May, 1 ft., Asia ; verticillata, blue, June, 2 to 3 ft., Japan.

Adiantum (Maidenhair Fern)—Ord. Filices. Stove, greenhouse, and hardy ferns. Evergreen and deciduous.
CULTURE : Compost, two parts peat, one part loam, silver sand, charcoal. Pot, March. Water moderately Sept. to March, freely afterwards. Position, shady at all times. Plant hardy species in April in equal parts peat and loam in shady position. Temp., stove species, Sept. to March 60° to 70°, March to Sept. 70° to 80° ; greenhouse species, Sept. to March 50° to 55°, March to Sept. 55° to 65°.
PROPAGATION : By spores sown on fine sandy peat kept moist and shaded under bell-glass.
STOVE SPECIES : A. æmulum, 8 to 12 in., Brazil ; æthiopicum, 12 to 18 in., Tropics, South Africa, Madagascar, New Zealand ; Bausei, 18 in. to 2 ft., hybrid ; Birkenheadii, 18 in., hybrid ; caudatum, 6 to 15 in., Tropics ; caudatum Edgeworthii, 6 to 15 in. ; Collisii, hybrid ; colpodes, 18 in., Tropical America ; concinnum, 12 to 18 in., Tropical America ; concinnum latum, 18 in., E. Indies ; cristatum, 18 in. to 3 ft., W. Indies ; cuneatum, 9 to 18 in., Tropical America, and its varieties deflexum, dissectum, elegans, gracillimum, grandiceps, lawsonianum, luddemannianum, mundulum ; curvatum, 12 to 18 in., Brazil ; cyclosorum, Brazil ; decorum, 8 to 12 in., Peru ; farleyense (see tenerum) ; Fergusoni, 2 to 3 ft., Ceylon ; fragrantissimum, hybrid ; Ghiesbreghtii, probably a hybrid ; henslovianum, 12 to 18 in., Peru ; Lathomii (garden origin) ; lucidum, 12 in., W. Indies ; lunulatum,

12 in., Tropics; macrophyllum, 12 in., W. Indies; Moorei, 12 in., Peru; palmatum, 10 in., Peru; peruvianum, 16 in., Peru; rhodophyllum, 6 in., hybrid; rubellum, 6 in., Bolivia; Seemannii, 18 in., Brazil; tenerum, to 3 ft., W. Indies; tenerum farleyense (Syn. farleyense), 12 to 15 in., Barbados; tenerum scutum, garden origin; tenerum Victoriæ (Syn. A. Victoriæ); tetraphyllum, 12 to 18 in., W. Indies; tetraphyllum acuminatum; tetraphyllum gracile; tinctum, 6 to 12 in., Peru; trapeziforme, 9 to 18 in., W. Indies; trapeziforme Sanctæ-Catherinæ, Brazil; veitchianum, 12 in., Peru; Weigandii, 6 to 10 in., garden origin. GREENHOUSE SPECIES : A. æthiopicum assimile, 8 in., Australia; æthiopicum chilense, 8 in., Chile; æthiopicum emarginatum, 6 in., California; æthiopicum scabrum (Silver Maidenhair), 6 in., Chile; æthiopicum sulphureum (Golden Maidenhair), 6 in., Chile; affine, 12 in., New Zealand; capillus-veneris (Common Maidenhair), 6 in., Temperate Zone, and its varieties, cornubiense, daphnites, grande, imbricatum, Mairisii, magnificum, and Moritzianum; diaphanum, 6 in., Java; excisum, 3 to 6 in., Chile; excisum multifidum, garden form; formosum, 12 in., Australia; fulvum, 9 to 12 in., Fiji; hispidulum (Syn. A. pubescens), 12 in., New Zealand; reniforme, 6 in., Madeira; Williamsii, 12 in., Peru.
HARDY SPECIES : A. pedatum, 1 to 3 ft., N. America.

Adlumia (Climbing Fumitory; Alleghany Vine)—Ord. Papaveraceæ. Hardy biennial. Climber. First introduced 1788.
CULTURE : Soil, light, rich. Position, warm border against south wall, or trellis in open garden. Plant, May.
PROPAGATION : By seeds sown ¼ in. deep in border in April, or in pots in temp. 55° to 65°, March.
SPECIES CULTIVATED : A. cirrhosa, white, Aug., 10 to 15 ft., N. America.

Adonis (Pheasant's Eye; Ox-eye)—Ord. Ranunculaceæ. Hardy annuals and perennials.
CULTURE : Soil, ordinary, rich. Position, open border for annuals, and rockeries for perennials. Plant, Oct.
PROPAGATION : Annuals by seeds sown shallow in borders in March; perennials by division of roots in Oct. and by seeds sown as directed for annuals.
SPECIES CULTIVATED : A. æstivalis (Pheasant's Eye), crimson, June, 1 ft., S. Europe (annual); amurensis, yellow, Jan., 1 ft., China (perennial); autumnalis (Red Chamomile), scarlet, May to Sept., 1 ft., Britain (annual); distorta, yellow, May, 12 in., Alps (perennial); pyrenaica, yellow, July, 1 ft., Pyrenees (perennial); vernalis (Ox-eye), yellow, March to May, 18 in., S. Europe (perennial).

Adonis Flower (*Adonis autumnalis*)—See Adonis.

Æchmea—Ord. Bromeliaceæ. Evergreen stove-flowering plants. First introduced 1824.
CULTURE : Compost, equal parts of fibrous loam, rough peat, leaf-mould. Pot, March. Water freely always. Good drainage essential. Temp., Sept. to March 60 to 70°; March to Sept. 70° to 80°.
PROPAGATION : By offshoots inserted in small pots at any time.
SPECIES CULTIVATED : Æ. bracteata (Syn. Æ. Barleei), yellow, July, 2 ft., W. Indies; cœlestis, blue, July, 18 in., Brazil; drakeana, rose and blue, 1½ ft., Ecuador; fasciata, pink and blue, Aug., 18 in., Brazil; fulgens, scarlet, Aug. and Sept., 18 in., French Guiana; fulgens discolor, scarlet and purple, June, 2 ft., Brazil; Lindenii, scarlet and purple, Aug., 2 ft., Brazil; Mariæ-Reginæ, violet and crimson, Aug. to Dec., 2 ft., Costa Rica; Ortgiesi (Syn. Ortgiesia tillandsoides), red, 6 to 8 in., Brazil; Veitchii, red, July to Sept., 18 in., Colombia. See also Canistrum.

Ægle—Ord. Rutaceæ. Hardy deciduous shrub.
CULTURE : Deep, loamy soil. Position, sunny shrubberies or as a hedge plant.
PROPAGATION : By seeds sown ¼ in. deep in a frame or greenhouse in March; cuttings of half-ripened wood inserted in a close frame in June or July.
SPECIES CULTIVATED : Æ. sepiaria, fruits like a small orange, 8 to 12 ft., Japan and China.

Æranthus—See Angræcum.

10

Ærides (Air-plant)—Ord. Orchidaceæ. Stove-flowering orchids. Evergreen. First introduced 1800.
CULTURE : Compost, sphagnum moss, charcoal, broken potsherds. Position, pots, hanging baskets, or pieces of wood. Pot, after flowering. Water moderately in winter, freely at other times. Shade from sun. Temp., Sept. to March 65° to 75°; March to Sept. 75° to 85°. Flowers appear in axil of third or fourth leaf from top of stem. Resting period, winter.
PROPAGATION : By division of plant with roots attached.
SPECIES CULTIVATED : Æ. affine, deep rose, 3 ft., India ; ballantineanum, white and orange, summer, 2 to 3 ft., East Indies ; crassifolium, purple, May and June, 2 ft., Burma ; crispum, white and rose, June and July, 4 ft., S. India ; Feildingii, white, brown and rose, May and June, 3 ft., Assam ; houlletianum, buff and magenta, May, 2 ft., Cochin China ; japonicum, green, white, and purple, July, 6 in., Japan ; Lawrenceæ, green, yellow, and purple, Sept., 3 ft., Philippines ; Lawrenceæ sanderianum, yellow and purple ; Lobbii, white and purple, July, 18 in., India ; odoratum, white and lilac, July, 2 ft., Trop. Asia ; quinquevulnerum, pink, July, 3 ft., Philippines ; suavissimum, white and lilac, Aug., 2 ft., Malacca ; Vandarum, pure white, dwarf, autumn and winter.

Æschynanthus (Blush-wort)—Ord. Gesneriaceæ. Stove trailing and flowering plants. Evergreen. First introduced 1838.
CULTURE : Compost, equal parts fibrous peat, sphagnum moss, charcoal. Position, hanging baskets, pots, or on blocks of wood or tree fern stumps. Plant, March. Water feely in summer, moderately in winter. Temp., Sept. to March 60° to 70° ; March to Sept. 70° to 80°.
PROPAGATION : By cuttings 3 in. long of firm shoots, inserted in pots of above compost mixed with sand in temp. 85°, Feb.
SPECIES CULTIVATED : Æ. atrosanguineus, red, July, 1 ft., Guatemala ; bracteatus, scarlet and yellow, Aug., 18 in., India ; fulgens, scarlet and yellow, June, 1 ft., E. Indies ; grandiflorus, scarlet, Aug., 5 ft., India ; Hildebrandii, scarlet, July, 10 in., Burma ; lobbianus, scarlet, June, 1 ft., Java ; pulcher, scarlet, June, Java ; purpurescens, purple and yellow, March, 1 ft., Java ; tricolor, red and yellow, July, 1 ft., Borneo.

Æsculus (Horse Chestnut ; Buck-eye)—Ord. Sapinadaceæ. Hardy deciduous flowering trees and shrubs. The genus Pavia (Buck-eye) is now merged in the present one. First introduced 1629. Timber not of much value. Used chiefly for making packing cases, carving, etc. Deer are fond of the nuts.
CULTURE : Soil, ordinary, deep. Position, shrubberies, woods, lawns, parks. Plant, Oct. to March. Prune away dead wood in winter.
PROPAGATION : By seeds sown 3 in. deep in open border soon as ripe ; layering, Feb. ; grafting, choice varieties in March, or budding in July.
SPECIES CULTIVATED : Æ. californica (Syn. Pavia californica), white, July, 20 ft., California ; carnea (Red Horse Chestnut), pink, June, 30 to 50 ft., hybrid (floribunda, rubicunda, and spectabilis are synonyms) ; chinensis, white, May or June, 80 to 90 ft., N. China ; glabra, yellow, May, 30 ft., occasionally taller, United States ; Hippocastanum (Horse Chestnut), white, May, 30 to 100 ft., S.E. Europe, and its varieties, crispa, flore pleno, foliis aureis variegatis, laciniata and pyramidalis ; indica, white, blotched yellow and rose, June-July, up to 100 ft., N.W. Himalayas ; octandra (Syn. flava) ; (Sweet Buck-eye), yellow, May, 30 to 90 ft., S.E. United States ; parviflora (Syn. Pavia alba), white, May, 8 ft., United States ; Pavia (Red Buck-eye) (Syn. Pavia rubra), red, June, 10 to 20 ft., United States ; plantierensis, pink, May, to 40 ft., hybrid ; turbinata, Japan, creamy, June, to 100 ft., Japan.

Æthionema (Candy Mustard ; Lebanon Candytuft)—Ord. Cruciferæ. Hardy perennials. Evergreen. First introduced 1778.
CULTURE : Soil, ordinary, light. Position, sunny rockery, well drained. Plant, Oct. or March.
PROPAGATION : By cuttings of shoots inserted in pots of sandy soil in cold frame, July or Aug.
SPECIES CULTIVATED : Æ. armenum, pink, June, 6 in., Armenia and Palestine ;

coridifolium (**Lebanon** candytuft), rose, June, 6 to 9 in., Orient; grandiflorum, rose, May, 1 ft., Persia; iberideum, white, sometimes flushed lilac, June, 6 in., Levantine Alps; pulchellum, rosy purple, June, 6 in., Armenia.

African Blue Lily (*Agapanthus umbellatus*)—See Agapanthus.

African Corn Flag—See Antholyza.

African Corn Lily—See Ixia.

African Cypress (*Widdringtonia Whytei*)—See Widdringtonia.

African Hare-bell (*Roella ciliata*)—See Roella.

African Harlequin Flower—See Sparaxis.

African Hemp (*Sparmannia africana*)—See Sparmannia.

African Lily—See Agapanthus.

African Marigold (*Tagetes erecta*)—See Tagetes.

African Rag-wort—See Othonna.

African Steel Bush (*Diosma ericoides*)—See Diosma.

African Tea Tree (*Lycium afrum*)—See Lycium.

African Violet (*Saintpaulia ionantha*)—See Saintpaulia.

Agalmyla (Scarlet Root-blossom)—Ord. Gesneriaceæ. **Stove trailing plant** Evergreen. First introduced 1846.
CULTURE : Compost, equal parts peat, sphagnum moss, and charcoal. Position, hanging baskets. Plant, March. Water freely March to Sept., moderately Sept. to March. Temp., Sept. to March 60° to 70° ; March to Sept. 70° to 80°.
PROPAGATION : By cuttings of firm shoots under bell-glass, in temp. 80°, July or Aug.
SPECIES CULTIVATED : A. longistyla, crimson, July, 1 ft., Java ; staminea, scarlet, June, 6 in., Java.

Aganisia—Ord. Orchidaceæ. Stove epiphytal orchids. First introduced 1836.
CULTURE : Compost, fibry peat, charcoal. Position, pots well drained, blocks or wood. Require exposure to sun. Water freely when growing, moderately when at rest. Resting period, winter. Flowers appear at base of new pseudo-bulb. Temp., Sept. to March 65° to 70° ; March to Sept. 75° to 85°.
PROPAGATION : By division of pseudo-bulbs when new growth begins.
SPECIES CULTIVATED : A. ionoptera, white and violet, July, 1 ft., Peru ; lepida, white, purple and chocolate, summer, Tropical America.

Agapanthus (African Lily)—Ord. Liliaceæ. Cool greenhouse herbaceous plant. Hardy S. England, Ireland. Evergreen. Nat. Cape of Good Hope. First introduced 1692.
CULTURE : Compost, two parts loam, one part leaf-mould, dried cow manure, river sand, pots or tubs, greenhouse ; sunny. Position, well-drained border or rockery outdoors. Pot or plant, March. Water freely March to Sept., moderately afterwards. Temp., Sept. to March 32° to 40° ; March to Sept. 45° to 55°.
PROPAGATION : By division of plant in March.
SPECIES CULTIVATED : A. umbellatus, blue, April, 3 ft., and its varieties albus (white), flore pleno (double), Leitchlinii (blue), maximus (blue), minor (blue), mooreanus (blue, hardy), and variegatus (leaves variegated).

Agaricus (Mushroom)—Ord. Fungi. Hardy esculent vegetable.
CULTURE : INDOOR : on prepared beds in cellars, sheds, or other completely darkened buildings where an even temperature may be maintained. OUTDOOR : on steeply-ridged beds in the open or against sun-warmed wall. Mushrooms may also be cultivated with variable success in pasture grass.
PREPARING BEDS : Collect fresh straw manure of horses. Remove long straw, retaining short, urine-stained straw and droppings. Place loosely in conical heap and turn repeatedly for nine or ten days. Protect from rain during this period. For indoor beds the breadth should be about a yard wide, depth nine inches, composed of the manure and straw, evenly mixed, and trodden or beaten thoroughly firm. For outdoor beds should have 3 ft. base, 2½ ft. height with ridge **not wider**

than 6 in. Test daily with thermometer thrust into middle of bed, and spawn when heat steadies to 77° Fahr.

SPAWNING : Break brick of spawn into eight pieces. Bury pieces 2 in. deep at intervals of 9 in. all over bed. Three days later cover with 1 to 2 in. of fine loamy soil, and finish with straw covering. A loose 2 or 3 in. thickness of straw will suffice, indoors, but outdoor beds must be well thatched to 6 in. thickness in summer, 1 ft. in winter. Outdoor beds in July, Oct., or Jan. Indoor beds any time between midsummer and March. Avoid watering if possible, but in event of bed becoming very dry water with tepid water. Bearing should commence about six to eight weeks after spawning, and continue for three months or longer. Gather mushrooms by pulling the stalk from the bed ; never by cutting.

CULTURE IN GRASS : Cut out pieces of turf 6 to 12 in. square, 1 in. thick, and 3 ft. apart. Stir soil below and press into it three or four lumps of spawn, about the middle of June. Replace turf and water occasionally if dry. Best results obtained where herbage is short, soil loamy and dry, and position sunny.

Agathæa (Blue Marguerite ; Cape Aster)—Ord. Compositæ. Greenhouse herbaceous perennial. First introduced 1753.

CULTURE : Compost, sandy loam two parts, leaf-mould, and sand one part. Position, pots, sunny greenhouse, or warm beds outdoors, May to Sept. Pot, March. Water freely in summer, moderately other times.

PROPAGATION : By cuttings of young shoots March or Aug., in sandy soil, temp. 55° to 65°.

SPECIES CULTIVATED : A. cœlestis, blue, June to Aug., 12 to 18 in., S. Africa.

Agave (American Aloe; Century-plant; Mexican Soap-plant)—Ord. Amaryllidaceæ. Greenhouse plants. Ornamental foliage and flowering. Evergreen. Nat. Mexico. First introduced 1640. Flowers, yellowish green or red, borne on spikes 1 to 40 ft. high when plants attain 10 to 60 years of age, in some cases the plant dies after flowering.

CULTURE : Compost, two parts loam, one part old mortar and river sand. Position, pots or tubs in greenhouses ; may be stood outside June to Sept. Water moderately April to Aug., little afterwards. Pot, every five or six years ; good drainage essential. Temp., winter 50° to 55° ; summer 55° to 65°.

PROPAGATION : By offsets inserted in small pots at any time.

SPECIES CULTIVATED : A. albicans, 3 to 4 ft., Mexico ; americana, 30 to 40 ft., Tropical America, and its varieties medio-picta (leaves yellow, edged green) and variegata (leaves dark green and yellow) ; atrovirens, 20 to 30 ft., S. Mexico ; attenuata (Syn. A. glaucescens), 6 to 10 ft., Mexico ; dasylirioides, 10 ft., Guatemala ; ferox, 20 to 30 ft., Mexico ; filifera (Syn. A. filamentosa), 10 to 15 ft., Mexico ; fourcroydes (Syns. A. ixtli, A. ixtlioides, and A. rigida) ; horrida, 8 ft., Mexico ; ingens, 20 to 30 ft., Mexico, and its variety picta (leaves yellow margined) ; Kerchovei, 12 to 18 ft., Mexico ; lophantha, 12 to 15 ft., Mexico, and its varieties cærulescens (glaucous leaved) and Poselgeri (leaves striped) ; maculata, 3 ft., Texas ; polyacantha, 10 to 15 ft., Mexico ; potatorum (Syn. A. Scolymus), 12 ft., Mexico ; salmiana, 30 ft., Mexico ; Shawi, 8 to 10 ft., California ; sisalana (Sisal Hemp), 15 to 20 ft., Yucatan ; striata, 12 ft., Mexico ; stricta (Syns. A. hystrix and Bonapartea hystrix), 10 to 12 ft., Mexico, and its variety glauca (glaucous leaved) ; utahensis, 5 ft., Utah, Arizona ; Victoriæ-Reginæ, 10 to 12 ft., Mexico ; vivipara, 8 ft., Curacoa, and its variety variegata (leaves margined white) ; yuccifolia, 20 ft., Mexico. There are many more species. We only give the most attractive ones.

Ageratum (Bastard Agrimony ; Floss-flower)—Ord. Compositæ. Half-hardy annuals. First introduced 1822.

CULTURE : Soil, ordinary. Position, sunny beds or borders. Plant 6 to 8 in. apart in June.

PROPAGATION : By seeds sown in light soil in temp. 65° to 70° in March, or by cuttings of young shoots from plants preserved for stock by growing in pots, pinching periodically to prevent flowering, and wintering in greenhouse temperature 50°.

SPECIES CULTIVATED : A. mexicanum, blue, summer, 18 in. to 2 ft., Tropics. Numerous dwarf forms and white varieties will be found in seed lists.

Aglaonema (Poison-dart)—Ord. Aroideæ.   Stove perennials.   First introduced 1863.   Flowers, arum-shaped.   Leaves, variegated, green, blotched with grey.
CULTURE: Compost, two-thirds loam, one-third leaf-mould, river sand.   Position, well-drained pots, shady.   Water freely when growing, little afterwards.   Syringe foliage daily.   Pot, March.   Temp., Sept. to March 60° to 70° ;   March to Sept. 70° to 80°.
PROPAGATION: By division of roots in March.
SPECIES CULTIVATED : A. angustifolium, greenish white, July, 18 in., Straits Settlements ;   commutatum, white, July, 1 ft., Manila ;   costatum, white, July, 6 in., Perak ;   Mannii, greenish white, July, 18 in., Tropical Africa ;   oblongifolium, crimson, July, 4 ft., and its variety Curtisii, greenish white, Malaya ;   pictum, white, Aug., 18 in., Malaya ;   simplex, white, July, 18 in., Java.

Agrostemma—See Lychnis.

Agrostis (Cloud-grass)—Ord. Gramineæ.   Hardy annual-flowering grasses. Inflorescence light and graceful and valuable for cutting for mixing with flowers in summer ;   or drying for winter decoration.
CULTURE: Soil, ordinary.   Position, sunny border.
PROPAGATION: By seed sown 1-16 in. deep April in open borders where plants are to grow.
SPECIES CULTIVATED : A. alba (Fine-top Grass), July, 2 ft., Europe ;   nebulosa (Cloud Grass), July, 18 in., Spain ;   pulchella, July, 1 ft., Sicily.

Ailanthus (Tree of Heaven ;   Tree of the Gods)—Ord. Simarubaceæ.   Handsome hardy deciduous trees.   Ornamental foliage.   First introduced 1751.
CULTURE: Soil, light, rich.   Position, sheltered, moist.   Plant, Nov.
PROPAGATION: By inserting portions of roots in pots of light soil in March.   They should be kept close in a pot, frame or cloche until growth advances, then expose to air.   Transplant following spring.
SPECIES CULTIVATED : A. glandulosa, flowers white, leaves pinnate, 30 to 60 ft., China, and its variety pendula (weeping) ;   vilmoriniana, to 50 ft., China.

Aira (Hair Grass)—Ord. Gramineæ.   Hardy ornamental grass.
CULTURE: Soil, ordinary.   Sow seed in April, where plants are required.   Position open.   May be grown in pots in the cold greenhouse.
SPECIES CULTIVATED : A. capillaris pulchella, 12 to 18 in., S. Europe.

Air-plant (*Ærides odoratum*)—See Ærides.

Ajuga (Bugle ;   Gout Ivy)—Ord. Labiatæ.   Hardy perennials.
CULTURE: Soil, ordinary.   Position, margins of shady beds or borders.
PROPAGATION: By seeds sown outdoors in April ;   division of roots Oct. or March.
SPECIES CULTIVATED : A. genevensis, blue, June, 6 in., non-trailing, Europe, and its varieties Brockbankii (dwarfer and slightly spreading), and crispa (curiously curled foliage of bright metallic tints) ;   orientalis, blue, June, 12 to 18 in., E. Europe ;   reptans, blue, white, or rose, June, 6 in., Britain, and its varieties atropurpurea (purple leaves) and variegata (leaves variegated pale pink and cream).

Akebia—Ord. Berberidaceæ.   Half-hardy climbing flowering shrubs.   Evergreen.   First introduced 1845.
CULTURE: Soil, loam, peat, and sand in equal parts.   Position, south wall in S. England and Ireland ;   cool greenhouse other parts.   Plant, Oct., Nov., in border. Prune straggling shoots after flowering.
PROPAGATION: By cuttings, inserted in sandy soil in gentle heat or by layers in autumn.
SPECIES CULTIVATED : A. lobata, vigorous climber, flowers purple, followed by pale violet-tinted sausage-shaped fruits, China and Japan ;   quinata, violet or purple, fragrant, May and June, 30 to 40 ft., China and Japan.·

Akee (*Blighia sapida*)—See Blighia.

Alabama Snow Wreath (*Neviusa alabamiensis*)—See Neviusa.

14

Albizzia—Ord. Leguminosæ. Greenhouse evergreen flowering shrub. First introduced 1803. Formerly included in the genus Acacia.
CULTURE : Compost, equal parts loam, peat, leaf-mould and sand. Position, pots, or in a bed with shoots trained up wall or roof of greenhouse ; in beds outdoors during summer. Pot in March. Water freely during spring and summer, moderately at other seasons. Prune straggly growths in Feb. Temp., Sept. to March 55° to 65° ; March to Sept. 55° to 65°.
PROPAGATION : By seeds sown in sandy peat, leaf-mould and sand in a temp. of 75° in spring.
SPECIES CULTIVATED : A. lophantha (Syn. Acacia lophantha), 10 to 29 ft., yellow, spring, Australia, leaves fine, fern-like.

Albuca—Ord. Liliaceæ. Half-hardy bulbous plant. Nat. S. Africa. First introduced 1880.
INDOOR CULTURE : Compost, two parts loam, one part of equal proportions of peat, leaf-mould, and silver sand. Position, cool greenhouse. Pot in Nov., placing five bulbs 3 in. deep in a 4½ in. pot. Cover pot with cocoanut-fibre refuse until growth begins, then expose to light. Water freely from time bulbs begin to grow until flowers fade, after which keep dry until Nov.
OUTDOOR CULTURE : Soil, light ordinary. Position, well-drained border at base of south greenhouse or hothouse wall. Plant 6 in. deep in Oct.
PROPAGATION : By seeds or offsets in spring.
SPECIES CULTIVATED : A. Nelsonii, white and red, fragrant, June, 2 to 3 ft., Natal.

Alchemilla (Lady's Mantle)—Ord. Rosaceæ. Hardy evergreen perennials.
CULTURE : Soil, ordinary. Position moist, well drained, in shade or partial sun. Herbaceous border or rock garden. Plant autumn or spring.
PROPAGATION : By division of roots Oct. or Feb.
SPECIES CULTIVATED : A. alpina, flowers green, foliage silvery, 6 in., Britain ; pentaphylla, a Swiss species with five-fingered foliage, 6 in ; vulgaris (Great Sanicle), flowers and foliage green, 9 in., Britain.

Alder (*Alnus glutinosa*)—See Alnus.

Alder-Buckthorn (*Rhamnus Frangula*)—See Rhamnus.

Alecost—See Tanacetum.

Alexandrian Laurel (*Danæ racemosa*)—See Danæ.

Algerian Iris (*Iris unguicularis*)—See Iris.

Algerian Wax-Bean (*Phaseolus vulgaris*)—See Phaseolus.

Alisma (Water Plantain ; Deil's Spoons)—Ord. Alismaceæ. Hardy aquatic perennials.
CULTURE : Soil, ordinary. Position, margins of shallow lakes, ponds, ditches. Plant, March.
PROPAGATION : By seeds sown ½ in. deep in March in a pan of sandy peat, plunged below the surface of the water, or by division of roots in April.
SPECIES CULTIVATED : A. Plantago (Water Plantain), pink or rose, summer, Britain ; ranunculoides, purple, May to Sept., Britain.

Alkanet (Anchusa)—See Anchusa.

Allamanda—Ord. Apocynaceæ. Stove climbing plant. Evergreen. First introduced 1785.
CULTURE : Compost, two parts fibry loam, one part leaf-mould, charcoal, and coarse sand. Position, pot, tub, or planted in prepared border ; shoots to be trained close to roof. Pot, Feb. Water freely April to Aug., then moderately. Temp., Sept. to March 60° to 70° ; March to Sept. 70° to 80°. Prune shoots, in Jan., to within one joint of main branch.
PROPAGATION : In Jan., by cuttings of shoots of previous year's growth, 3 in. long, inserted in pots of sandy soil, temp. 80°.
SPECIES CULTIVATED : A. cathartica, yellow, July, 5 to 10 ft., Trop. America ; Chelsoni, yellow, summer, hybrid ; grandiflora, yellow, June, 6 to 10 ft., Brazil ;

neriifolia, golden yellow, streaked orange, June, 3 ft., Tropical America ; nobilis, deep yellow, July, Brazil ; Schottii, yellow, Sept., 8 to 10 ft., Brazil, and its varieties, Hendersoni and magnifica ; Williamsii, yellow, summer, hybrid.

Alleghany Vine (*Adlumia cirrhosa*)—See Adlumia.

Alligator Apple (*Anona palustris*)—See Anona.

Alligator Pear (*Persea gratissima*)—See Persea.

Allium (Chives ; Leek ; Onion ; Shallot)—Ord. Liliaceæ. A genus of hardy and greenhouse bulbous-rooted perennials.

CULTURE OF HARDY FLOWERING SPECIES : Soil, sandy loam. Position, sunny borders or rockeries. Plant bulbs 3 in. deep and 4 in. apart in Oct. or Nov.

CULTURE OF GREENHOUSE SPECIES : Compost, two parts loam, one part leaf-mould, and a little silver sand. Plant six bulbs in a 4½ in. pot in Oct. Cover pots with cocoanut-fibre refuse or ashes in a cold frame till growth begins, then remove to a cool greenhouse. May be flowered in a cold house, or forced into flower in a temp. of 55° to 65°. Water freely whilst growing. After blooming gradually withhold water and keep dry and cool till new growth begins. Repot annually in Oct.

PROPAGATION : By seeds in cold frame or cool house in spring ; offsets after flowering.

CULTURE OF ONION : Soil, rich, porous, deeply dug. Position open to sunshine. Manure from farmyard, stable or fowl run, to be dug in during autumn. Bone meal, superphosphate of lime, Kainit, basic slag, dried or crystallised blood may be used as substitutes for animal manures or supplementary thereto. The last-named may be applied in small doses at intervals during growth, the others before sowing or planting takes place. For exhibition or early maturity sow Jan. or Feb. in warm greenhouse, using boxes 3 to 4 in. deep, filled with good compost. Cover seeds ¼ inch deep. Prick out into boxes 6 in. deep, or on a hotbed as soon as second leaf develops. Harden off gradually and transplant in April. Distance apart for rows 1 ft., plants in rows 1 ft. asunder. Hoe continuously, and feed regularly, but avoid cold tap water. Sow in open ground for main crop March or April, rows 9 in. apart, cover ¼ inch or slightly more. Tread firmly unless soil wet and heavy. Scatter old soot over bed after sowing, and again when seedlings are well up. Seeds may be sown in autumn—Sept. or early Oct. Thin out seedlings when growth is vigorous, leaving plants 6 to 8 in. apart. Gaps may be filled in with care- fully lifted seedlings from crowded parts. Bend over tops when growth slackens, to encourage further swelling of bulbs. Lift, ripen and store when dry. Crops take six months to mature. Seeds retain germinating vigour for two years. Ger- mination takes place in from 7 to 14 days according to conditions of soil and atmosphere. ¼ oz. seed sows 50 ft. row.

CULTURE OF GARLIC : Soil, light, rich. Position, sunny spot. Plant bulbs (cloves) 2 in. deep and 6 in. apart in Feb. Lift and store July or Aug. Increase by division of bulbs Feb.

CULTURE OF CHIVES : Soil, ordinary. Plant 6 in. apart each way in March. Lift, divide, and replant every third year. Used for salads and seasoning.

CULTURE OF POTATO ONION : Soil, ordinary. Plant bulbs 1½ in. deep, 10 in. apart in rows 15 in. asunder in March. Lift and store bulbs in Aug. Used like ordinary onions. Increased by offsets at planting time.

CULTURE OF TREE ONION : Soil, ordinary. Plant bulbs borne on top of stems 1 in. deep and 4 in. apart, in rows 8 in. asunder in March ; or root bulbs 1 in. deep and 12 in. apart each way. Support stems by stakes. Gather stem bulbs when fully grown and store in cool, dry place. Used for pickling.

CULTURE OF ROCAMBOLE : Soil as for garlic. Plant cloves 6 in. apart each way, and similar depth to shallots, in Feb., March, or April. Lift and store in Aug. Bulbs in soil and on stem used for similar purpose to garlic, but milder in flavour. Use soil bulbs only for planting.

HARDY FLOWERING SPECIES : A. acuminatum, rose, July, 9 in., N. America ; albo- pilosum, violet, July-Aug., 2 ft., Asia ; cæruleum (Syn. A. azureum), blue, June, 2 ft., Siberia ; cyaneum, blue, July-Aug., 6 in., China ; giganteum (Syn.

A. nobile), greyish-lilac, 3 ft., Central Asia; Karataviense, white or lilac, 9 to 12 in., Turkestan; Moly, yellow, May, 2 ft., Europe; ostrowskianum, rose, July, 1 ft., Turkestan; neapolitanum (Daffodil Garlic), white and green, June, 1 ft., S. Europe; rosenbachianum, rose purple, May, 3½ ft., Bokhara; roseum, rose, June, 1 ft., S. Europe; triquetrum, white, June, 15 in., Europe; Schubertii, lilac, June, Orient; sphærocephalum (Syn. A. descendens,) maroon, Aug., 1½ ft., Europe and Orient.

EDIBLE BULBOUS-ROOTED SPECIES: A. ascalonicum (Shallot), Palestine; Cepa (Onion), Central or Western Asia; Cepa aggregatum (Potato Onion); Cepa proliferum (Tree or Egyptian Onion); fistulosum (Welsh or Ciboul Onion), Siberia; Porrum (Leek), native country not known; Schœnoprasum (Chives), N. Hemisphere; sativum (Garlic), S. Europe; Scorodoprasum (Rocambole; Spanish Garlic; Sand Leek), flesh, July, Denmark.

Allosorus—See Cryptogramme.

Allspice—See Calycanthus and Pimenta.

Almond (*Prunus Amygdalus*)—See Prunus.

Almond-scented Orchid (*Odontoglossum madrense*)—See Odontoglossum.

Alnus (Aar; Alder)—Ord. Betulaceæ. Hardy trees and shrubs. Deciduous. Timber of little value, except for making charcoal for gunpowder.
CULTURE: Soil, ordinary. Position, damp places for A. glutinosa; drier spots for the others. Plant, Nov.
PROPAGATION: By seeds sown 1 in. deep in damp soil in March, transplanting the seedlings when a year old; or by suckers springing from the roots in Nov., or cuttings of firm wood after fall of leaf, inserted in open ground.
SPECIES CULTIVATED: A. glutinosa, 50 to 90 ft.; Britain, Europe, N. Africa and Asia, and its varieties aurea (golden-leaved), laciniata (cut-leaved), and quercifolia (oak-leaved); incana, 50 to 70 ft., N. Temperate Zone, and its varieties aurea, pendula nova and pinnatifida. There are others, but they are of no special interest.

Alocasia—Ord. Aroideæ. Stove plants. Orn. foliage. First introduced 1854.
CULTURE: Compost, equal parts peat, sphagnum moss, fibry loam, with a little silver sand and charcoal. Pot, March, keeping base of plant above rim of pot; good drainage essential. Position, pots, shady. Water freely March to Sept., moderately afterwards. Temp., Sept. to March 60° to 70°; March to Sept. 70° to 80°.
PROPAGATION: By division of rhizomes in March.
SPECIES CULTIVATED: A. augustiana, Papua; argyrea, 1½ ft., Tropical Asia; chantrieriana, hybrid; cuprea, 18 in., Borneo; gigas, 5 ft., hybrid; illustris, 2 ft., India; indica, 4 to 6 ft., Malaya, and its varieties metallica and variegata; longiloba, 1 ft., Malaya; Lindenii, 2 ft., New Guinea; Lowii, 2 ft., Borneo; Marshalli, India; macrorhiza, to 15 ft. Trop. Asia; Putzeysi, Sumatra; sanderiana, 18 in., Philippines; thibautiana, Borneo; zebrina, 4 ft., Philippines.

Aloe (Medicinal Aloes)—Ord. Liliaceæ. Greenhouse succulent plants. Orn. foliage. Evergreen. Leaves fleshy and more or less prickly or spiny. First introduced 1596.
CULTURE: Compost, two parts loam, one part peat, old mortar, river sand. Position, pots or tubs, sunny greenhouse. Water moderately April to Aug., little afterwards. Pot, March; good drainage indispensable. Temp., winter 50° to 55°; summer 55° to 65°.
PROPAGATION: By seeds sown in well-drained pans of sandy soil, temp. 70°.
SPECIES CULTIVATED: A. abyssinica, Abyssinia; arborescens, S. Africa; ciliaris, S. Africa; humilis, and its varieties, echinata, incurva, and subtuberculata, S. Africa; mitræformis, and its varieties albispina, flavispina and spinulosa, S. Africa; striata, S. Africa; succotrina, S. Africa; variegata, a favourite window plant, S. Africa; vera, Mediterranean Region. There are very many more species, but the foregoing are the most attractive ones. The flowers are red or yellow, and borne on slender spikes.

Alonsoa (Mask-flower)—Ord. Scrophulariaceæ. Half-hardy shrubby perennials. First introduced 1790.
CULTURE : Compost, two parts loam, one part leaf-mould and sand. Position, pots, greenhouse, windows, or sunny beds outdoors, May to Sept. Water moderately always. Pot, March. Plant, May. Temp., Sept. to May 50° to 55°.
PROPAGATION : By seeds sown 1-16 in. deep, March, temp. 60°, in sandy soil ; cuttings, in pots of sandy soil, Aug.
SPECIES CULTIVATED : A. albiflora, white and yellow, summer, 1 ft., Mexico ; incisifolia, scarlet, summer, 18 in., Chile ; linearis, scarlet, summer, 1 to 2 ft., Peru ; linifolia, scarlet, summer, 1 to 2 ft., Mexico ; myrtifolia, scarlet, and its variety, alba, white, 2 to 3 ft., Mexico ; Warscewiczi, summer, 18 in. to 2 ft., Chile.

Aloysia—See Lippia.

Alpine Azalea (*Loiseleuria procumbens*)—See Loiseleuria.

Alpine Bladder Fern (*Cystopteris alpina*)—See Cystopteris.

Alpine Catch-fly (*Silene alpestris*)—See Silene.

Alpine Currant (*Ribes alpinum*)—See Ribes.

Alpine Eryngo (*Eryngium alpinum*)—See Eryngium.

Alpine Forget-me-not (*Myosotis alpestris*)—See Myosotis.

Alpine Pink (*Dianthus alpinus*)—See Dianthus.

Alpine Polypody (*Polypodium alpestre*)—See Polypodium.

Alpine Poppy (*Papaver alpinum*)—See Papaver.

Alpine Rose (*Rhododendron ferrugineum* and R. *hirsutum*)—See Rhododendron.

Alpine Strawberry (*Fragaria vesca*)—See Fragaria.

Alpine Toad-flax (*Linaria alpina*)—See Linaria.

Alpine Wallflower—See Erysimum.

Alpine Wind-flower (*Anemone alpina*)—See Anemone.

Alpinia (Indian Shell-flower)—Ord. Zingiberaceæ. Stove herbaceous perennials. First introduced 1792.
CULTURE : Compost, equal parts peat, leaf-mould and loam. Position, large pots, tubs, or beds. Plant, March. Temp., March to Sept. 55° to 65° ; Sept. to March 70° to 80°. Water freely March to Aug., moderately other times.
PROPAGATION : By division of roots in March.
SPECIES CULTIVATED : A. allughas, red, Feb., 3 to 6 ft., India ; mutica, white, red, and yellow, July and Aug., 5 ft., Malaya ; rafflesiana (Syn. A. vittata), 2 to 3 ft., Malay Peninsula ; Sanderæ, 8 in., horticultural variety ; speciosa (Syn. A. nutans), white, purple and yellow, fragrant, to 12 ft., China and Japan.

Alsophila (Grove Fern ; Norfolk Island Fern)—Ord. Filices. Stove and greenhouse tree ferns. First introduced 1833.
CULTURE : Compost, two parts peat, one part loam, silver sand and charcoal. Pot, March. Water freely March to Sept., moderately afterwards. Position, pots or tubs, shady. Temp., stove 60° to 70° Sept. to March, 70° to 80° March to Sept. ; greenhouse 50° to 55° Sept. to March, 55° to 60° March to Sept.
PROPAGATION : By spores, similar to Adiantum.
STOVE SPECIES : A. aspera, 20 to 30 ft., W. Indies ; atrovirens, 60 ft. or over, Brazil ; infesta Van Geertii, 3 to 4 ft., Trop. America.
GREENHOUSE SPECIES : A. australis, 15 to 20 ft., Tasmania ; Colensoi, 4 to 5 ft., New Zealand ; Cooperi, 20 to 30 ft., Queensland ; excelsa, 60 to 80 ft., Norfolk Island ; pruinata, 3 to 6 ft., W. Indies ; Rebeccæ, 8 ft., Queensland.

Alstromeria (Herb Lily)—Ord. Amaryllidaceæ. Hardy and half-hardy tuberous-rooted perennials. First introduced 1754.
CULTURE : Compost, sandy loam, peat, leaf-mould, equal parts. Plant, Oct. Position, sunny, well-drained border ; or pots in cool greenhouse. Water freely in summer, moderately in winter.

PROPAGATION : By seeds sown ¼ in. deep, in sandy soil, in pans in cold frame, March; division of roots, April or Oct.

SPECIES CULTIVATED : A. aurantiaca, orange, red, and carmine, summer, 2 to 3 ft., Chile ; braziliensis, red, yellow, and brown, summer, 3 to 4 ft., Brazil ; chilensis, orange red, summer, 2 to 3 ft., Chile ; hæmantha, red, green, and purple, summer, 2 to 3 ft., Chile , Ligtu (Syn. A. pulchra), pale lilac or red and purple, 1½ to 2 ft., Chile , pelegrina (Lily of the Incas), lilac, red and purple, summer, 1 ft., Chile, and its variety alba (pure white); pulchella (Syn. A. psittacina), red, green and brown, summer, 2 to 3 ft., Brazil; versicolor, purple, maroon and green, summer, 2 to 3 ft., Peru.

Alternanthera—See Telanthera.

Althæa (Hollyhock)—Ord. Malvaceæ. Hardy perennials. Hollyhock first introduced 1573.

CULTURE OF HOLLYHOCK : Soil, ordinary mould, not too light. Trench three spits deep in Oct. and work in plenty of decayed manure. Plant singly 3 ft. apart each way, or in groups of three, 12 in. from plant to plant, at wide intervals, in April. Mulch surface of soil. Support with stakes standing 6 ft. out of ground. Water copiously in dry weather. Apply liquid manure from May until blooms expand. Remove flowers directly they fade. Cut off tops of spikes where fine blooms are required for exhibition as soon as lower blooms show signs of expanding. Offshoots should be removed from base of plants in June. Young plants yield finest flowers for exhibition. Cut down to within 6 in. of soil after flowering. Manures, ¼ oz. nitrate of soda, ¼ oz. each of superphosphate, kainit, and sulphate of iron to 2 gallons of water, applied to the roots at intervals of a month from May to Sept. ; or liquid drainings or solutions of animal manures, applied in a diluted state occasionally during summer.

CULTURE OF OTHER SPECIES : Soil, ordinary. Position, sunny borders. Plant, Oct. or March.

PROPAGATION: Hollyhocks by seeds sown 1 in. deep and 12 in. apart on a south border in June. Thin seedlings to 6 in. apart in July. On warm soils seedlings may be transplanted direct into flowering positions in Sept. In cold districts or on wet soils pot in autumn and winter in frames, planting in April. Sow seeds in good soil in temp. 55° to 65° in Jan. or Feb., grow in pots, harden off in April, and plant out in May. Increased also by cuttings of young shoots growing out of base of flower stems inserted singly in small pots plunged in a gentle hotbed in spring. Likewise by cuttings of young shoots consisting of two joints with lower leaves removed, inserted in small pots placed in a close frame in Aug. Other species by seeds sown outdoors in April.

SPECIES CULTIVATED : A. cannabina, rose, June, 6 ft., Europe, and its variety narbonensis, red ; ficifolia (Fig-leaved Hollyhock), yellow, June, 6 ft., Siberia; officinalis (Marsh Mallow), rose, July-Aug., 3 to 4 ft., Britain ; rosea (Hollyhock), rose, 5 to 6 ft., summer, China. Many single and double flowered varieties of garden origin, for which see trade catalogues. See also Hibiscus.

Althæa frutex—See Hibiscus.

Alum-root—See Heuchera.

Alyssum (Madwort ; Gold-dust ; Golden-tuft ; Gold Basket ; Sweet Alyssum) —Ord. Cruciferæ. Hardy annuals and perennials. First introduced 1710.

CULTURE : Soil, ordinary. Position, open border or rockery. Plant, Oct. or April.

PROPAGATION : Annual and perennial species by seeds sown ¼ in. deep outdoors in April ; perennial species by cuttings of young shoots inserted in sandy soil in cold frame April and May.

ANNUAL SPECIES : A. maritimum, white, fragrant, summer, 6 to 10 in., Britain and Europe. Compactum is a dwarf and variegatum a variegated variety. Strictly this species is a perennial.

PERENNIAL SPECIES : A. alpestre, yellow, June, 3 in., Europe ; argenteum, flowers yellow, leaves green, slightly silvered, May-July, 1 ft. ; gemonense, yellow, spring, 1 ft., Europe; idæum, soft yellow, trailing, May-June, Crete; mœllendorfianum, flowers yellow, foliage silver, June-July, 6 in., Bosnia ; montanum, yellow, fragrant, summer, 2 to 4 in., Europe ; orientale, yellow, May, 1 ft., Greece ; pyrenaicum, white, summer, 8 to 10 in., Pyrenees ; saxatile, yellow, May, 1 ft., E. Europe, and its varieties, compactum, variegatum, sulphureum, flore pleno (double) ; serpyllifolium, yellow, June, 3 in., S. Europe ; spinosum, white, June, 4 to 6 in., S. Europe ; spinosum roseum, a pretty pink form; wulfenianum, golden yellow, summer, 3 in., E. Europe.

Amaranth Feathers (*Humea elegans*)—See Humea.

Amaranthus (Love-lies-Bleeding ; Prince's Feather ; Velvet-flower)—Ord. Amarantaceæ. Half-hardy annuals. First introduced 1596. Foliage, orange-red, crimson, green.
CULTURE : Soil, ordinary. Position, sunny bed. Plant, June.
PROPAGATION : By seeds sown ⅟₁₆ in. deep, in temp. 65° to 70°, March; seedlings must be hardened off by easy stages, first on greenhouse shelf, then in frame, increasing ventilation until plants are well hardened before planting out.
SPECIES CULTIVATED : A. caudatus (Love-lies-Bleeding) (Syns. A. paniculatus and A. sanguineus), crimson-purple, summer, 2 to 3 ft., Tropics ; hypochondriacus (Prince's Feather), crimson, summer, 4 to 5 ft., Tropics ; tricolor, leaves carmine and yellow, India, less hardy than others ; tricolor splendens, fine crimson foliage, best suited for pot culture in greenhouse ; tricolor salicifolius, leaves willow-like.

Amaryllis (Belladonna Lily ; Daffodil Lily)—Ord. Amaryllidaceæ. Hardy bulbous plant. Deciduous. First introduced 1712.
CULTURE : Compost, sandy loam, enriched with leaf-mould and cow manure. Position, well-drained border foot of south wall. Plant bulbs 9 in. deep and 12 in. apart in September. Water freely in dry weather whilst growing. Mulch with decayed manure in spring.
PROPAGATION : By offsets.
SPECIES CULTIVATED : A. Belladonna, rose, fragrant, Aug. and Sept., 18 in., Cape Colony. Blanda, pale rose, and pallida, flesh, are varieties of it. The flowers appear before the new leaves. For greenhouse amaryllis see Hippeastrum. See also Lycoris Sprekelia and Sternbergia.

Amasonia—Ord. Verbenaceæ. Stove evergreen flowering perennial.
CULTURE : Compost, equal parts loam and leaf-mould, little silver sand. Pot, March. Position, in small pots near glass, well exposed to light ; shade in summer. Water freely in spring and summer, moderately other times. Temp., March to Sept. 70° to 85° ; Sept. to March 58° to 65°.
PROPAGATION : By division of the plants in March.
SPECIES CULTIVATED : A. calycina (Syn. A. punicea), yellow and red, Sept., 12 to 18 in., British Guiana ; erecta, white and pink, July, 18 in., S. America.

Amazon Lily (*Eucharis grandiflora*)—See Eucharis.

Ambyolepis—See Helenium.

Amelanchier (Grape-pear ; Snowy Mespilus ; June-berry)—Ord. Rosaceæ. Hardy spring-flowering trees and shrubs. Deciduous. First introduced 1596.
CULTURE : Soil, ordinary. Position, open shrubbery. Plant, Nov. Prune after flowering. The leaves are prettily tinted in autumn.
PROPAGATION : By seeds or layers in spring and cuttings in autumn.
SPECIES CULTIVATED : A. alnifolia, white, April, 10 to 20 ft., N.W. America ; canadensis (June-berry), white, April, 20 to 30 ft., N. America ; lævis, white, May, 30 to 40 ft., N. America ; oblongifolia, white, April, 6 to 20 ft., Eastern N. America ; vulgaris (Syn. rotundifolia), white, April, 15 to 20 ft., Europe.

American Aloe (*Agave americana*)—See Agave.

American Bell-bind (*Ipomæa pandurata*)—See Ipomæa.

American Blackberry (*Rubus laciniatus*)—See Rubus.

American Black Currant (*Ribes americanum*)—See Ribes.

American Black Larch (*Larix pendula*)—See Larix.

Abutilon hybrida
(Indian Mallow)

Acacia cordata
(Wattle, Gum Tree)

Achimines longiflora

Ærides Sanderianum
(Air-plant)

Agapanthus umbellatus
(African Lily)

Allium Moly

Aloe variegata
(Medicinal Aloes)

Amaranthus caudatus
(Love-lies-Bleeding)

Amaryllis Belladonna
(Belladonna Lily)

Anemone japonica
(Japanese Wind-flower)

Anœctochilus regalis
(King-plant)

Antholyza crocosmioides
(African Corn-flag)

Anthurium Scherzerianum
(Flamingo-plant)

Aphelandra aurantiaca

Aquilegia hybrida
(Columbine)

Araucaria excelsa
(Norfolk Island Pine)

Arbutus Unedo
(Strawberry Tree)

Arctotis stœchadifolia

American Centaury (*Sabbatia campestris*)—See Sabbatia.
American Cowslip (*Dodecatheon Meadia*)—See Dodecatheon.
American Cranberry (*Oxycoccus macrocarpus*)—See Oxycoccus.
American Cress—See Barbarea.
American Cud-weed (*Anaphalis margaritacea*)—See Anaphalis.
American Elm (*Ulmus americana*)—See Ulmus.
American False Heath (*Hudsonia ericoides*)—See Hudsonia.
American Fox-grape (*Vitis Labrusca*)—See Vitis.
American Gooseberry (*Pereskia aculeata*)—See Pereskia.
American Ground Laurel (*Epigæa repens*)—See Epigæa.
American Laurel (*Kalmia latifolia*)—See Kalmia.
American Maidenhair Fern (*Adiantum pedatum*)—See Adiantum.
American May Apple—See Podophyllum.
American Meadow Sweet (*Spiræa salicifolia*)—See Spiræa.
American Plane Tree (*Platanus occidentalis*)—See Platanus.
American Sanicle—See Heuchera.
American Star Grass—See Hypoxis.
American Summer Vine (*Vitis æstivalis*)—See Vitis.
American Swamp Laurel (*Kalmia glauca*)—See Kalmia.
American Wild Pink (*Silene pennsylvanica*)—See Silene.
American Witch Elder (*Fothergilla Gardeni*)—See Fothergilla.
American Wood Lily (*Trillium grandiflorum*)—See Trillium.
American Wych Hazel (*Hamamelis virginica*)—See Hamamelis.
Amethyst Hyacinth (*Hyacinthus amethystinus*)—See Hyacinthus.
Amethyst Speedwell (*Veronica amethystinus*)—See Veronica.
Amethyst Squill (*Scilla amethystina*)—See Scilla.

Ammobium (Everlasting Sand-flower)—Ord. Compositæ. Half-hardy annual. First introduced 1822. Flowers valuable for cutting and drying for winter decoration. Gather when fully grown and hang heads downwards in a cool place.
CULTURE : Soil, light, rich. Position, warm border. Plant, May, 6 in. apart.
PROPAGATION : By seeds sown ⅛ in. deep in light soil, temp. 65°, March ; or outdoors early in May.
SPECIES CULTIVATED : A. alatum, white, summer, 2 ft., Australia. Grandiflorum is a variety with larger flowers.

Amorpha (Bastard Indigo)—Ord. Leguminosæ. Hardy deciduous-flowering shrubs. First introduced 1724.
CULTURE : Soil, ordinary. Position, in the mixed shrubbery. Plant, Oct. to Feb. Prune after flowering, thinning shoots that have borne blossoms.
PROPAGATION : By cuttings in autumn ; layering in summer ; suckers in winter ; seeds sown in cold frame.
SPECIES CULTIVATED : A. canescens (Lead Plant), blue, July, 3 ft., Missouri ; fruticosa, bluish purple, July, 6 ft., Carolina.

Amorphophallus—Ord. Aroideæ. Stove tuberous-rooted perennials. Flowers with purple or white spathes and brown spadices ; fœtid ; appearing before leaves.
CULTURE : Compost, equal parts turfy loam, peat, leaf-mould, decayed manure and silver sand. Position, well-drained pots in shade. Pot moderately firm in pots just large enough to take tubers in Feb. to March, transfer to larger pots in April or May. Water moderately Feb. to April and Sept. to Nov. ; freely April to Sept. ;

B 2

keep quite dry Nov. to Feb. Temp., Feb. to Sept. 70° to 80°; Sept. to Nov. 65° to 75°; Nov. to Feb. 55° to 65°.
PROPAGATION: By dividing the tubers in Feb. or March.
SPECIES CULTIVATED: A. campanulatus (Syn. A. virosus), purple spathe, India; Rivieri, purple spathe, Cochin China; Titanum, purple spathe, very large, Sumatra.

Ampelopsis—See Vitis.

Amphicome—Ord. Bignoniaceæ. Half-hardy perennial herbs. Closely allied to the genus Incarvillea.
CULTURE: Compost, two parts loam, one part of equal proportions of leaf-mould, decayed manure, and silver sand. Position, pots in cool greenhouse. Pot in Oct. or March. Water freely in summer; keep nearly dry in autumn and winter.
PROPAGATION: By seeds sown in a temp. of 55° in spring; cuttings of half-ripened shoots in summer.
SPECIES CULTIVATED: A. arguta, red, Aug., 1 ft.; Emodi, rose and orange, Aug. to Oct., 1½ ft., Himalayas.

Amygdalus—See Prunus.

Anacampseros—Ord. Portulacaceæ. Greenhouse succulent-leaved plant. Nat. S. Africa.
CULTURE: Compost, two parts sandy loam, one part of equal proportions of old mortar, small brick rubble and sand. Position, in not too large pots on shelves near the glass; no shade. Water moderately in spring and summer; keep nearly dry in autumn and winter. Dry atmosphere needed. Repot in March. Temp., 45° to 50° in winter; 50° to 60° in summer.
PROPAGATION: By seeds sown in a mixture of fine rubble and sandy loam, in heat, in spring; by cuttings, exposed to the air for a few days after removal from the plant, then inserted in fine sand in a gentle heat.
SPECIES CULTIVATED: A. arachnoides, pink, July, 12 to 18 in.; filamentosa, pink, Sept., 1 ft.; telephiastrum, pink, summer, 1 ft.

Anacardium (Cashew Nut)—Ord. Anacardiaceæ. Stove evergreen tree widely cultivated in Tropics for its edible nuts. First introduced 1699.
CULTURE: Soil, light, loamy. Position, borders in warm house. Temp., March to Sept., 75° to 85°; Sept. to March 65° to 75°. Water freely during summer.
PROPAGATION: By cuttings of ripened wood, in sandy soil, under hand glass, in warm house.
SPECIES CULTIVATED: A. occidentale, yellow and red fruit with edible kernel, 30 to 40 ft., Trop. America.

Anagallis (Pimpernel)—Ord. Primulaceæ. Hardy annuals and perennials. Trailing.
CULTURE: Soil, light, rich. Position, sunny, well-drained borders for annuals; moist and boggy places for perennials.
PROPAGATION: Annuals by seeds sown ¼ in. deep in temp. 65° March, transplanting seedlings outdoors in June; perennials by division of roots in March, or by seeds sown outdoors in April.
ANNUAL SPECIES: A. fruticosa, vermilion, May to Aug., 2 ft., Morocco; indica, blue, July, 1 ft., India.
PERENNIAL SPECIES: A. linifolia (Syn. A. grandiflora), blue, July, 1 ft., Europe, and its varieties collina and Monelli; tenella, rosy, July and Aug., Britain.

Ananas (Pine-apple)—Ord. Bromeliaceæ. Stove plants, bearing the well-known fruit—pine apples. Orn. foliage. Evergreen. First introduced 1690.
CULTURE: Compost, two parts decomposed fibry loam, one part well-decayed manure, another part ½ in. bones and pounded oyster shells. Position, pots plunged in a tan hotbed in stove facing south. Temp., Sept. to March 65° to 75°; March

to Sept. 75° to 90°. Full exposure to sun essential. Water moderately in winter, freely in summer. Moist atmosphere most essential in spring and summer, and a slightly dry one in winter. When fruit begins to ripen withhold water. Supply freely with liquid manure plants in fruiting pots. Plants come into bearing when two years old.
PROPAGATION : By suckers, or crowns of fruit inserted in small pots in temp. 80°, spring.
SPECIES CULTIVATED : A. sativus, 3 ft., Trop. America, and its varieties variegatus (leaves striped) and porteanus (leaves with central yellow band).

Anaphalis (Pearly Everlasting or Immortelle)—Ord. Compositæ. Hardy perennials. Flowers, white, useful for cutting in August and drying for winter use.
CULTURE : Soil, ordinary. Position, sunny borders. Plant in Oct. or March.
PROPAGATION : By division in autumn or spring ; seeds sown outdoors in April.
SPECIES CULTIVATED : A. cinnamomea, white flowers and foliage, cinnamon scented, July-Sept., 1 to 2 ft., shrubby, China and Japan ; margaritacea, white, July and Aug., 1 ft., N. America ; nubyana, pearl white, July-Aug., 1 ft.

Anastatica (Rose of Jericho ; Resurrection Plant)—Ord. Cruciferæ. Half-hardy annual. Possesses the peculiar property in its native country of withering up in dry weather, and when rain comes of spreading itself out again, as though alive.
CULTURE : Soil, ordinary. Sow seeds in a cold frame in spring and plant in sunny border in May.
SPECIES CULTIVATED : A. hierochuntica, white, summer, 1 ft., Orient.

Anchor Plant (*Colletia cruciata*)—See Colletia.

Anchusa (Alkanet ; Sea Bugloss)—Ord. Boraginaceæ. Hardy biennials and perennials.
CULTURE : Soil, ordinary. Position, sunny borders. Plant, Oct. or March.
PROPAGATION : Biennials by seeds sown ⅛ in. deep in March in pans or boxes of sandy soil, temp. 55° to 65°, or outdoors in April ; perennials by division in Oct.
SPECIES CULTIVATED : A. angustifolia, deep blue, June-Sept., 3 ft., perennial ; Barrelieri, blue and white, June, 2 ft., Europe, perennial ; capensis, blue, July, 12 to 18 in., S. Africa, biennial ; italica, blue, July, 3 to 4 ft., S. France, perennial, and its varieties Dropmore (deep blue) and Opal (Cambridge blue) ; myosotiflora, blue, April to June, 1½ ft., Siberia, Caucasus ; officinalis, rich blue, 1 to 2 ft. (British or Common Alkanet), biennial or perennial ; sempervirens, blue, June, 2 ft., Europe, perennial.

Ancistrochilus—Ord. Orchidaceæ. Stove terrestrial orchid. First introduced 1866.
CULTURE : Compost, good fibrous peat, sphagnum moss and broken leaves. Position, well-drained pots or hanging baskets. Water freely from time new growth commences until leaves fall off, very little at other times. Temp., March to Sept. 65° to 85° ; Sept. to March 60° to 65°.
PROPAGATION : By division at potting time.
SPECIES CULTIVATED : A. thomsonianus (Syn. Pachystoma thomsoniana), white and purple, Oct.-Nov., 6 in., West Tropical Africa.

Anderson's Speedwell (*Veronica Andersoni*)—See Veronica.

Andre's Flamingo-plant (*Anthurium andreanum*)—See Anthurium.

Andromeda (Marsh Rosemary ; Wild Rosemary)—Ord. Ericaceæ. Hardy flowering shrub. Evergreen.
CULTURE : Soil, boggy peat. Position, moist, shady borders or beds. Plant, Oct. No pruning required except to cut away dead wood.
PROPAGATION : By layering shoots in Sept.; seeds sown in peaty soil in a cold frame.
SPECIES CULTIVATED : A. polifolia, pink, June, 1 ft., North Temperate Regions. Angustifolia, rosmarinifolia and major are varieties. See Pieris, Cassandra, Leucothoë and Zenobia for other species formerly included in this genus.

Andropogon—Ord. Gramineæ.   Hardy ornamental flowering grass.
CULTURE: Soil, ordinary, light, and dry.   Position, sunny border.   Plant, Oct.,
March, and April.   Apply liquid manure occasionally in summer.
PROPAGATION: By division.
SPECIES CULTIVATED: A. furcatus, 18 in., N. America.   For the plant formerly
known as A. Schœnanthus see Cymbopogon Martinii.

Androsace (Rock Jasmine)—Ord. Primulaceæ.   Hardy perennial alpine plants.
First introduced 1755.
CULTURE: Soil, sandy peat and loam, with small pieces of limestone.   Position,
sunny rockeries, in fissures of stones or under ledges of rock.   Plant, March or
April.
PROPAGATION: By seeds sown ⅟₁₆ in. deep, in sandy peat in cold frame; cuttings in
pots of sandy soil in frames in Sept. and Oct.; division of roots in April; seeds in
pots in cold frame.
SPECIES CULTIVATED: A. arachnoidea, white, June-July, 3 in., Eastern Europe;
carnea, pink, July, 3 in., Europe; Chamæjasme, white, May-June, 3 in., Europe and
N. America; ciliata, rose pink, June, 3 in., Pyrenees; cylindrica, milk white, June,
2 in., Pyrenees; foliosa, flesh, June, 4 in., W. Himalayas; helvetica, pink fading
white, June-Aug., 1 in., European Alps; imbricata, white, June, 2 in., Alps;
lactea, white and yellow, June-Aug., 6 to 8 in., Switzerland, Transylvania; lactiflora (Syn. coronopifolia), bluish white, biennial, June-Aug., 6 in., Siberia; Laggeri,
pink, March, 3 in., Transylvania; lanuginosa, rose, July, 8 to 9 in., Himalayas,
var. Leitchlini has white, crimson-centred flowers; pyrenaica, white, May-June,
1 in., Pyrenees; sarmentosa, rose, May, 3 in., Himalayas, var. Chumbyi has
brighter flowers; sempervivoides, purple, May, 3 in., Himalayas; villosa, rose,
May, 3 in., Europe; wulfeniana, bright rose, April-June, 2 in., Eastern Alps.   See
also Douglasia.

Anemia (Flower-fern; Ash-leaf Fern)—Ord. Filices.   Stove and greenhouse
ferns.   First introduced 1793.
CULTURE: Compost, equal parts loam, peat, leaf-mould, sand, and charcoal.
Position, shady, moist; useful for wardian cases.   Pot, Feb., March.   Water
freely spring and summer, moderately other times.   Temp., stove, March to Sept.,
70° to 85°, Sept. to March 60° to 65°; greenhouse, March to Sept. 55° to 60°,
Sept. to March 45° to 50°.
PROPAGATION: By spores similar to Adiantum.
STOVE SPECIES CULTIVATED: A. adiantifolia, 12 to 18 in., Trop. America; collina,
8 to 12 in., Brazil; dregeana, 9 in., Natal; rotundifolia, 6 to 9 in., Brazil.
GREENHOUSE SPECIES CULTIVATED: A. Phillitidis, 1 ft., Cuba, Peru; tomentosa
(Syn. chelianthoides, deltoides and flexuosa), 1 to 2 ft., Mexico, etc.

Anemidictyon—See Anemia.

Anemone (Wind-flower)—Ord. Ranunculaceæ.   Hardy herbaceous and tuberous-
rooted perennials.
CULTURE OF HERBACEOUS SPECIES: Soil, good ordinary, well enriched with decayed
manure.   Position, sunny or partially shady borders.   Plant, autumn or spring.
CULTURE OF TUBEROUS-ROOTED SPECIES: Soil, moderately light, liberally mixed
with leaf-mould and decayed manure.   Position, partially shaded beds or borders.
Plant tubers 3 in. deep and 6 in. apart in Oct. or Nov.; or in Feb. and March.   Lift
tubers when foliage dies, and store away in cool place till planting time, or in well-
drained soils leave undisturbed until crowding indicates necessity for lifting, sepa-
rating and replanting.
PROPAGATION: Tuberous-rooted species by seeds sown in prepared beds of above
soil in Jan. or Feb. or in July.   Herbaceous species by seeds sown in sandy soil in
cold frame in spring; division of roots in Oct. or March; root cuttings in spring.
HERBACEOUS SPECIES CULTIVATED: A. alpina, white, May, 1 ft., Europe; angulosa
(Syn. Hepatica angulosa), blue, March, 1 ft., E. Europe; apennina, blue, rose, and
white, March, 6 in., Europe; baicalensis, white, pink exterior, May-July, 1 ft.,
Temperate Asia; baldensis, white, tinged reddish lilac, May-June, 6 in., Europe;

blanda, blue, Jan. to March, 6 in., Asia Minor; blanda scythinica, white and
blue, a choice variety from Kurdistan; canadensis (Syn. A. pensylvanica),
white, May to Aug., to 2 ft., N. America; dichotoma, white, May-June, 18 in.,
Siberia and N. America; Halleri, dusky violet, May-June, 9 in., Switzerland;
Hepatica, blue, Feb. and March, 6 in., N. Hemisphere, and its varieties alba (white),
cærulea (blue), cærulea plena (double blue), rubra (red), rubra plena (double red),
Barlowii (blue) and rosea (rose); japonica (Japanese Wind-flower), red, Sept., 2 ft.,
Japan, and numerous varieties described in trade lists; narcissiflora, white, May-
June, 1 ft., Europe and N. America; nemerosa (Wood Anemone), white, March,
6 in., Britain; nemerosa robinsoniana, blue; Pulsatilla (Pasque Flower), blue, April,
1 ft., Britain; palmata, white, May, 9 in., S. France; rivularis, white, May, 2 to 3 ft.,
Himalayas; sulphurea, lemon yellow, May-June, 1½ ft., Alps; sylvestris (Snowdrop
Anemone), white, April, 1 ft., Europe; vernalis, white and lilac, May-June, 4 in.,
Europe.
TUBEROUS-ROOTED SPECIES CULTIVATED : A. coronaria (Poppy Anemone), various
colours, spring, 1 ft., S. Europe; hortensis, various colours, spring, 1 ft., S. Europe;
hortensis fulgens (Scarlet Wind-flower), crimson, May, 1 ft., S. Europe; hortensis
pavonina or stellata (Peacock Anemone), double-flowered; ranunculoides (Yellow-
Wood Anemone), golden yellow, March, 1 ft., Britain, etc.

Anemonopsis (*Yerba Mansa*)—Ord. Ranunculaceæ.   **Hardy herbaceous**
perennial. First introduced 1869.
CULTURE : Soil, deep rich loam. Position, partially shaded border. Plant, Oct.,
Nov., March.
PROPAGATION : By division of roots in Oct. or March; seeds sown in heat in March,
planting seedlings out in May.
SPECIES CULTIVATED : A. macrophylla, lilac and purple, June and July, 2 to 3 ft.,
Japan.

Anethum.—See Peucedanum.

Angel's-Tears (*Narcissus triandrus albus*)—See Narcissus.

Angel's Trumpet (*Datura suaveolens*)—See Datura.

Angelica (Holy Ghost)—Ord. Umbelliferæ. Perennial herbaceous herb used
for flavouring confectionery and liquors.
CULTURE : Soil, deep, moist loam. Position, shady.
PROPAGATION : By seeds sown ½ in. deep in March where plants are to remain.
When seedlings are 3 in. high thin them to 6 in. apart.
SPECIES CULTIVATED : A. officinalis (Syn. Archangelica officinalis), green, July,
4 to 5 ft., Europe.

Angelica Tree (*Aralia spinosa*)—See Aralia.

Angelonia—Ord. Scrophulariaceæ. Stove and greenhouse herbaceous perennials. First introduced 1818.
CULTURE : Compost, equal parts of loam, peat, leaf-mould, and a little sand.
Position, pots in sunny parts of stove or greenhouse. Pot, March. Water freely
March to Oct., moderately afterwards. Temp., March to Oct. 65° to 75°, after-
wards 55° to 60° for stove species; March to Oct. 55° to 65°, Oct. to March 45°
to 55° for greenhouse kinds.
PROPAGATION : By division of roots in March; cuttings of young shoots inserted in
sand under bell-glass, in temp. 75° in April.
STOVE SPECIES CULTIVATED : A. salicariæfolia, blue, Aug., 2 ft., S. America.
GREENHOUSE SPECIES CULTIVATED : A. grandiflora, lilac, 1½ to 2 ft., S. America.

Angiopteris (Turnip-fern)—Ord. Filices. Stove tree fern. Evergreen.
CULTURE : Compost, equal parts peat, loam, leaf-mould, sand and charcoal. Pot,
Feb., March. Position, pots or tubs, standing in 3 in. of water in shade. Water
freely in spring and summer, moderately other times. Temp., March to Sept.
55 °to 60°; Sept. to March 45° to 50°.
PROPAGATION : By offsets only.
SPECIES CULTIVATED : A. evecta 10 to 15 ft., Tropics.

Angola Hemp—See Sanseviera.

Angræcum—Ord. Orchidaceæ. Stove epiphytal orchids. Flowers fragrant. First introduced 1815.

CULTURE : Compost, equal parts broken potsherds, charcoal, and sphagnum moss. Position, shady in suspended baskets or well-drained pots. Pot, March. Water freely March to Oct., moderately afterwards. Temp., Sept. to March 60° to 65° ; March to Sept. 70° to 80°. Resting period, winter. Flower spikes appear in axils of top leaves when growth is finished.

PROPAGATION : By division of plant in March.

SPECIES CULTIVATED : A. articulatum, white, May and June, 8 to 12 in., Madagascar ; caudatum, white, Aug., 12 to 15 in., Trop. Africa ; citratum, lemon-yellow, spring, 6 to 8 in., Madagascar ; eburneum, white, spring, 1 to 2 ft., Mascarene Islands ; Ellisii, white, May, 1 ft., Madagascar ; falcatum, white, spring, 4 to 6 in., Japan ; Humblotii, white, spring, 8 to 10 in., Comoro Islands ; fastuosum, white, spring, Madagascar ; scottianum, white, spring, 1 ft., Comoro Islands ; sanderianum, white, spring, 1 ft., Comoro Islands ; sesquipedale, white, Jan. to June, 1 ft., Madagascar.

Anguloa (Bull's Head ; Cradle Orchid)—Ord. Orchidaceæ. Warm greenhouse orchids. Flowers fragrant. First introduced 1842.

CULTURE : Compost, fibrous peat and charcoal. Position, pots, shady part of house. Pot when new growth begins. Water freely May to Sept., very little afterwards. Temp., April to Sept. 60° to 65° ; Sept. to March 55° to 60°. Resting period, winter. Flowers appear at base of new growth.

PROPAGATION : By division of pseudo-bulbs when repotting.

SPECIES CULTIVATED : A. Clowesii, yellow, May, 12 to 18 in., Colombia ; Ruckeri, yellow and crimson, May, 18 in., Colombia ; uniflora, cream, May, 2 to 3 ft., Colombia. Several varieties of each species will be found in trade lists.

Anhalonium—Ord. Cactaceæ. Greenhouse succulent-stemmed perennials. Grown for the beauty of globose stems. Allied to Mammilarias.

CULTURE : Compost, equal parts sandy loam, rough old mortar, and pounded bricks. Position, sunny, airy greenhouse or window. Pot, March or April, in well-drained pots just large enough to accommodate roots. Repot every third or fourth year only. Water moderately March to Sept., once a fortnight Sept. to Dec., none afterwards. Syringe on evenings of warm days, June to Sept. Apply soot water to healthy plants, June to Sept. Ventilate freely in summer. Temp., March to Sept. 60° to 70° ; Sept. to March 50° to 55°.

PROPAGATION : By seeds sown ⅛ in. deep in well-drained pans or pots of sandy soil in temp. 75° in March, keeping soil moderately moist ; by cuttings of the tops of the plants inserted in small pots of sandy, gritty compost in spring.

SPECIES CULTIVATED : A. Engelmanni, 4 to 6 in., Mexico ; prismaticum, 6 in., Mexico.

Anigozanthos—Ord. Hæmodoraceæ. Greenhouse herbaceous perennials. Nat. Australia. First introduced 1802.

CULTURE : Compost, one part loam, two parts peat, and one part silver sand. Pot in March. Position, pots in cool greenhouse fully exposed to light. Water freely in spring and summer, moderately in autumn and winter. Temp., 40° to 50° in winter ; no heat at other times.

PROPAGATION : By division of the roots in spring.

SPECIES CULTIVATED : A. flavida, scarlet, June ; Manglesii, green and red, July, 3 ft. ; pulcherrima, yellow and white, May, 2 ft. ; rufa, purple, June, 2 ft.

Animated Oat (*Avena sterilis*)—See Avena.

Anise—See Pimpinella.

Aniseed Tree (*Illicium floridanum*)—See Illicium.

Annatto (*Bixa orellana*)—See Bixa.

Anœctochilus (King-plant)—Ord. Orchidaceæ.   Stove terrestrial orchids.   Orn.
foliage.   Ht. 3 to 6 in.   Leaves, bronze, olive, golden, green.
CULTURE :   Compost, peat, sand, and sphagnum moss in equal parts.   Position,
shady, well-drained pans under a bell-glass not fixed down quite close.   Water
moderately at all times.   Pot, Feb. or March.   Temp., Sept. to Feb. 55° to 65° ;
March to Sept. 60° to 75°.
PROPAGATION : In Feb. by inserting portions of stems in same compost as advised
for plants, and under bell-glass.
SPECIES CULTIVATED :   A. argyroneurus, olive, veins silvery, Java ; concinnus,
olive, veins golden, Assam ; dawsonianus, velvety olive, veins copper, Malay
Archipelago ; Heriotii, reddish, veins golden, India ; hieroglyphicus, green, veins
silvery, Assam ; Lansbergiæ, velvety green, veins emerald-green, Malaya ; regalis,
velvety green, veins golden, Ceylon ; setaceus (King Plant), velvety green, veined
gold, Java ; Veitchii, velvety green, netted with gold.   Numerous other species
may be found in specialists' catalogues.

Anomatheca—See Lapeyrousia.

Anona (Alligator Apple ; Custard Apple ; Sweet Sop)—Ord. Anonaceæ.   Stove
evergreen shrubs.   First introduced 1690.   Leaves fragrant.   Fruit of A. muricata,
A. reticulata, and A. squamosa edible.
CULTURE :   Compost, two parts loam, one part peat, and a little silver sand.   Pot,
March or April.   Position, light and sunny.   Water freely March to Oct., mode-
rately afterwards.   Syringe daily April to Sept.   Shade from bright sunshine.
Temp., March to Oct. 70° to 80° ; Oct. to March 55° to 65°.
PROPAGATION : By seeds in spring, or by cuttings of firm shoots in moist sand under
bell-glass in temp. 75° in summer.
SPECIES CULTIVATED :   A. Cherimolia (Cherimoyer), brown, Aug., 12 to 18 ft., Peru ;
muricata (Sour Sop), yellow, summer, 10 ft., Trop. America ; palustris (Alligator
Apple), yellow, summer, 10 ft., Trop. America ; reticulata (Custard Apple), yellow
and brown, summer, 15 to 18 ft., Trop. America ; squamosa (Sweet Sop), white,
summer, 15 to 20 ft., W. Indies.

Anopterus (Tasmanian Laurel)—Ord. Saxifragaceæ.   Greenhouse flowering
shrub.   Evergreen.   First introduced 1823.
CULTURE :   Compost, two parts loam, one part peat and sand.   Pot and prune,
March.   Position, sunny greenhouse.   Temp., Sept. to March 45° to 50° ; March
to Sept. 55° to 65°.   Water moderately in winter, abundantly at other times.
PROPAGATION : By cuttings of firm shoots 3 in. long, in sandy peat under bell-glass
in temp. 65° in summer.
SPECIES CULTIVATED : A. glandulosus, white or pink, April, 2 to 3 ft., Tasmania.

Antarctic Beech—See Nothofagus.

Antennaria (Cat's-ear)—Ord. Compositæ.   Hardy herbaceous perennials.   Leaves,
silvery white ; useful for carpet bedding or edgings to borders, clothing dry spots.
CULTURE : Soil, ordinary.   Position, sunny borders or rockeries.   Plant, March or Oct.
PROPAGATION : By division of roots in March.
SPECIES CULTIVATED :   A. dioica, pink, June, 3 in., Britain ; dioica tomentosa, white,
summer, 1 in., Britain.   Last-named is a good carpet bedding plant.   A. margaritacea is now known as Anaphalis margaritacea, which see.

Anthemis (Chamomile)—Ord. Compositæ.   Hardy perennials.   Flowers of the
Common Chamomile (A. nobilis) used for making Chamomile Tea ; those of other
species for ordinary garden decoration.
CULTURE : Soil, ordinary.   Position, sunny borders for tall species ; rockeries for
dwarf ones.   Plant, Oct. or March.   Common Chamomile to be planted 2 ft. apart
in rows 30 in. asunder in April.   Gather flowers when fully expanded.
PROPAGATION : By division in March ; seeds sown outdoors in April.
SPECIES CULTIVATED :   A. biebersteiniana, white, summer, 1 to 2 ft., Orient ; mace-
donica, white, June, 6 to 8 in., Macedonia ; nobilis (Common Chamomile), white,
Aug., 1 ft., Europe ; tinctoria (Dyer's or Ox-eye Chamomile), yellow, Aug., 2 ft.,
Europe.

Anthericum (St. Bernard's Lily)—Ord. Liliaceæ. Hardy herbaceous perennials.
CULTURE : Soil, light, rich. Position, partially shaded borders. Plant, Oct., Nov.
PROPAGATION : By seeds sown ⅛ in. deep in light soil in cold frame in Sept. or
March ; division of roots in Oct.
SPECIES CULTIVATED : A. Liliago (St. Bernard's Lily), white, July and Aug., 12 to
18 in., S. Europe ; Liliago major, a superior form ; ramosum, white, June to Aug.,
2 ft., S. Europe. See the genera Paradisea and Chlorophytum for other species
formerly included in this genus.

Antholyza (African Corn-flag)—Ord. Iridaceæ. Hardy bulbous perennials.
First introduced 1756.
CULTURE : Soil, light, sandy. Position, sunny border, well drained ; pots in cool
greenhouse. Plant bulbs 6 in. deep, 6 in. apart in border, or six in a 6 in. pot, Oct.
Bulbs to be lifted in Aug., dried, and stored till Oct. in cool place.
PROPAGATION : By offsets at planting time ; seeds in slight heat in spring.
SPECIES CULTIVATED : A. æthiopica, red and yellow, June, 3 to 4 ft. ; crocosmioides,
a hybrid between A. paniculata and Crocosmia aurea ; paniculata, yellow and red,
July, 3 to 4 ft. Natives of S. Africa.

Anthony-nut (*Staphylea pinnata*)—See Staphylea.

Anthoxanthum (Sweet Vernal-grass)—Ord. Gramineæ. Hardy perennial
flowering grass. Inflorescence has the odour of newly mown hay, and is useful
for winter bouquets.
CULTURE : Soil, ordinary. Plant, Oct. or March. Position, open border.
PROPAGATION : By seeds sown ⅛ in. deep where plants are to grow in April; division
of roots, Oct. or March.
SPECIES CULTIVATED : A. odoratum, 1 ft., Europe.

Anthriscus (Chervil)—Ord. Umbelliferæ. Hardy annual herb used for garnish-
ing and flavouring. First introduced 1656.
CULTURE : Soil, ordinary. Position, shady in summer, south border in winter.
Sow seeds broadcast ½ in. deep, or similar depth in drills 6 in. apart in March or Oct.
SPECIES CULTIVATED : A. cerefolium (Chervil), 6 in., Europe, Asia, etc.

Anthurium (Flamingo-plant ; Tail-flower)—Ord. Aroideæ. Stove plants.
Flowering and orn. foliage. Flowering period, March to Aug. First introduced
1825.
CULTURE : Compost, equal parts rough peat, sphagnum moss. Position, pots,
well drained, shady. Pot, March. Water freely March to Nov., moderately
afterwards. Temp., Sept. to March 60° tp 65° ; March to Sept. 70° to 80°.
PROPAGATION : By division of roots in March ; seeds sown in a mixture of chopped
sphagnum moss, charcoal, and sand in temp. of 80° in spring.
SPECIES CULTIVATED, Flowering : A. andreanum, scarlet and white, Colombia ;
ornatum, white and purple, Venezuela ; scherzerianum, scarlet, Guatemala. Ornamental leaved : crystallinum, green, Peru ; magnificum, green and white, Colombia ;
Veitchii, green, Colombia ; and warocqueanum, green and white, Colombia. For
varieties, which are numerous, see trade lists.

Anthyllis (Kidney Vetch ; Lady's Fingers)—Ord. Leguminosæ. Hardy shrubs
and perennials.
CULTURE : Soil, ordinary. Position, open or partially shaded border. Plant, Oct.
PROPAGATION : Shrubby kinds by cuttings of young shoots under bell-glass in cold
frame in March ; herbaceous species by seeds sown ⅛ in. deep in warm border in
April or by division of root in Oct.
SHRUBBY SPECIES CULTIVATED : A. Barba-Jovis, pale yellow, March, 4 ft., Spain;
PERENNIAL SPECIES : A. montana, pink, June, 3 to 6 in., Alps ; Vulneraria (Wound-
wort or Lady's Fingers), yellow, June to Aug., 6 to 12 in., Britain.

Antigonon (Coral Vine ; Corallita)—Ord. Polygonaceæ. Tuberous-rooted
stove climbers. First introduced 1868.
CULTURE : Compost, equal parts loam, leaf-mould and sand. Position, borders;
shoots trained close to the glass in full sun. Plant, Nov. Water freely while

growth is active, little during winter months.   Temp. 60° to 65° Sept. to March, and 70° to 80° March to Sept.
PROPAGATION: By seeds sown ¼ in. deep in temp. 75° in March.
SPECIES CULTIVATED : A. leptopus, bright pink, summer, 10 to 15 ft., Mexico.

Antirrhinum (Snapdragon)—Ord. Scrophulariaceæ.   Hardy herbaceous perennials.
CULTURE : Soil, ordinary.   Position, warm, dry borders, rockeries, or walls. Plant, April.   For massed effects plant Tom Thumb, 6 in., Intermediates 1 ft. and tall varieties 1½ ft. apart.
PROPAGATION : By seeds sown in temp. 70° in March or outdoors in April, transplanting seedlings in May ; cuttings of young shoots in cold frame in Aug.   Best treated as annuals or biennials, fresh plants being raised every year.
SPECIES CULTIVATED : A. Asarina, yellow, summer, trailing, Italy ; glutinosum, cream and yellow, June, 4 to 6 in., spreading, Spain ; majus (Common Snapdragon), pink, July, 1 to 2 ft., Mediterranean Region, naturalised in Britain, and parent of the beautiful forms grown in gardens.

Aotus—Ord. Leguminosæ.   Greenhouse flowering shrub.   Evergreen.
CULTURE : Compost, equal parts loam, peat, sand, charcoal.   Pot in March. Position, pots, well drained, in light and sunny greenhouse.   Water moderately in winter, freely summer.   Prune shoots back after flowering.   Temp., Sept. to March 45° to 50° ; March to Sept. 55° to 60°.
PROPAGATION : By cuttings of firm shoots in pots of sandy soil under bell-glass, temp. 55°.
SPECIES CULTIVATED : A. gracillima, yellow and crimson, May, 3 ft., Australia. Other species of little merit.

Apennine Wind-flower (*Anemone apennina*)—See Anemone.

Aphelandra—Ord. Acanthaceæ.   Stove flowering shrubs.   Evergreen.   Flowers surrounded by lovely coloured bracts.   First introduced 1733.
CULTURE : Compost, equal parts peat, loam, leaf-mould, and sand.   Position, pots, moist temperature.   Water freely in summer, moderately in winter.   Prune shoots to within inch of base in Feb. and repot in March.   Temp., Sept. to March 60° to 65° ; March to Sept. 70° to 80°.
PROPAGATION : By cuttings of firm shoots inserted in sandy soil in bottom-heat (80°) March or April.
SPECIES CULTIVATED : A. aurantiaca, orange-scarlet, winter, 3 ft., Mexico ; aurantiaca Roezlii, scarlet, twisted leaves ; blanchetiana, golden yellow, Aug., Brazil ; chamissoniana, yellow, Nov., S. America ; fascinator, scarlet, Sept., 18 in., Colombia ; libanoniana, deep yellow and red, Brazil : macedoniana, leaves purple and green, Brazil ; Margaritæ, orange, leaves green and rose, Brazil ; nitens, vermilion scarlet, 2 to 3 ft., Colombia ; squarrosa, yellow and orange, Brazil ; tetragona (cristata), orange-scarlet, Aug.-Nov., 3 ft., W. Indies.

Aphelexis—See Helichrysum.

Apios (Ground Nut)—Ord. Leguminosæ.   Hardy tuberous-rooted climbing perennial.   Deciduous.   First introduced 1640.
CULTURE : Soil, ordinary.   Position, warm border against south wall or trellis. Plant tubers in March.
PROPAGATION : By division of tubers in March.
SPECIES CULTIVATED : A. tuberosa, brown and pink, Aug., 6 to 10 ft., N. America.

Apium (Celery ; Celeriac ; Turnip-rooted Celery)—Ord. Umbelliferæ.   Hardy esculent vegetable.   Biennial.   Blanched leaf-stalks used as salad ; leaves and roots for flavouring soups.
CULTURE OF CELERY : Soil, ordinary, well enriched with cow, pig, or horse manure. Position, moist, in trenches running north and south, 4 ft. apart, 15 in. wide, and 9 in. deep for single rows, or 18 in. wide for double rows.   Plant beginning of June for early crop ; end of June or July for main crop.   Distance apart for plants, 8 in. for single row ; 9 in. apart in row and 6 in. between rows for double rows.   Earth

up gradually from Sept. to Nov. in fine weather only. Sow seeds in light soil covering very thinly, in temp. 65° to 75° in Feb. for early crop; in March in similar temp. for main crop, or in cold frame in April. Seedlings in first two cases to be transplanted 2 in. apart in light soil in boxes, kept in temp. 55° to 65° for few weeks, then planted 6 in. apart in shady bed outdoors till required for planting in trenches. Water and feed liberally until earthed up to ensure crisp, solid hearts. Guano at rate of 1 oz. to gallon of water most suitable stimulant. Crop reaches maturity in 24 weeks from date seeds are sown.

CULTURE OF TURNIP-ROOTED CELERY OR CELERIAC : Soil, rich, light. Position, sunny level border. Plant in June 1 ft. apart in rows 18 in. asunder. Keep all side shoots removed. Draw little mould around base of each in Aug. Water freely in dry weather. Lift roots in Oct. and store in sand till required for use. Sow and treat seedlings as advised for ordinary celery.

SPECIES CULTIVATED : A. graveolens (Celery), Britain ; graveolens rapaceum (Celeriac).

Aponogeton (Cape Pond-weed ; Winter Hawthorn)—Ord. Aponogetonaceæ. Half-hardy floating aquatic. Nat. Cape of Good Hope. First introduced 1788.

CULTURE : Soil, ordinary. Position, shallow ponds or lakes, 1 ft. deep where there is a stream of water, or in a cold greenhouse tank or aquaria. Plant in pots, sinking the latter in the water during March. Not hardy in the north.

PROPAGATION : By offsets.

SPECIES CULTIVATED : A. distachyon, white, fragrant, summer.

Apple—See Pyrus.

Apple-bearing Rose (*Rosa pomifera*)—See Rosa.

Apple of Peru (*Nicandra physaloides*)—See Nicandra.

Apricot—See Prunus.

Aquilegia (Columbine)—Ord. Ranunculaceæ. Hardy perennials. Graceful plants for border or rockery culture and for yielding flowers for cutting.

CULTURE : Soil, sandy loam, enriched with leaf-mould. Position, well-drained, partially shady rockeries and borders. Plant, Oct. or March.

PROPAGATION : By seeds sown ⅛ in. deep in sandy soil in cold frame in Aug., or in open border in April ; division of the roots in Oct. or April.

SPECIES CULTIVATED : A. alpina, blue and white, May to July, 12 to 18 in., Alps ; canadensis, scarlet and yellow, April to June, 1 to 2 ft., N. America ; cærulea, blue and white, May, 12 to 18 in., N.W. America ; chrysantha, yellow, May to Aug., 3 ft., New Mexico ; flabellata, pale purple or white, summer, 1 to 1½ ft., Japan ; formosa (Syn. A. arctica), red and yellow, summer, 3 ft., N. America ; glandulosa, blue and white, April to June, 8 to 12 in., Siberia, and its variety jucunda ; pyrenaica, lilac blue, April to June, 9 to 12 in., Pyrenees ; sibirica, lilac and white, June and July, Siberia ; Skinneri, yellow and red, June to Aug., 2 to 3 ft ., Mexico ; Stuartii, blue and white, June, 9 in., hybrid ; vulgaris (Common Columbine), various colours, single and double, 3 ft., Britain. Hybrida, the most popular race of long spurred hybrids and selections from A. cærulea, californica, chrysantha, etc., embracing many delightful combinations of delicate colours. Several good strains are available through leading seedsmen.

Arabian Jasmine (*Jasminum Sambac*)—See Jasminum.

Arabis (Wall Cress ; Rock Cress)—Ord. Cruciferæ. Hardy annual and perennial Alpine trailing plants.

CULTURE : Soil, ordinary. Position, edgings to well-drained borders or massing on sunny rockeries ; carpeting beds of spring-flowering bulbs, etc. Plant, Oct. and Nov.

PROPAGATION : By seeds sown ¹⁄₁₆ in. deep outdoors in April ; cuttings inserted in shady border in Aug. ; division of roots in Oct.

SPECIES CULTIVATED : A. albida, white, spring, 6 to 9 in., Tauria, etc. ; albida flore-pleno, double-flowered ; albida variegata, leaves edged with white ; alpina, white,

March, 6 in., Europe ; alpina rosea, pretty pink var. ; androsacea, white, June, 3 in., Tauria ; bellidifolia (Syn. A. lucida), variegata, yellow-edged leaves, 6 in., Europe ; verna, purple, May, 4 in., S. Europe, an annual species.

Arachis (Monkey Nut ; Earth Nut ; Ground Nut)—Ord. Leguminosæ. Stove annual. Flowers, yellow ; May. After flowering the seed pod is gradually forced into the soil to ripen its seeds, which are edible.

CULTURE : Compost, loam, leaf-mould and sand. Sow seeds in temp. of 75° to 85° in spring ; plant seedlings in small pots and grow in a light position. Water moderately. Temp. 75° to 85°.

SPECIES CULTIVATED : A. hypogæa, 1 ft., West Indies.

Aralia (Angelica Tree)—Ord. Araliaceæ. Stove hardy plants and shrubs. Orn. foliage. Evergreen and deciduous. First introduced 1658.

CULTURE OF STOVE SPECIES : Compost, equal parts loam, peaty leaf-mould, charcoal, and sand. Pot, Feb. to March. Water freely March to Oct., moderately after-wards. Temp., March to Sept. 70° to 80° ; Sept. to March 60° to 70°.

CULTURE OF HARDY SPECIES : Soil, rich, well-drained loam. Position, shady borders for herbaceous species, margins of lakes or ponds, or moist, sheltered shrubberies for shrubby kinds. Plant, Sept. and Oct. or in March and April.

PROPAGATION : Hardy species by division in Oct. or March in case of herbaceous species ; suckers for shrubby species. Stove species by grafting in heat in spring ; inserting portions of roots in light soil in temp. 80° in April.

STOVE SPECIES CULTIVATED : A. elegantissima, Polynesia ; kerchoveana, Polynesian Islands ; Veitchii, New Caledonia ; Veitchii gracillima. See also Panax, Acantho-panax, Pseudo-panax, and Fatsia for other species formerly known as Aralias.

HARDY HERBACEOUS PERENNIALS CULTIVATED : A. cachemirica, white, summer, 6 ft., Himalayas ; cordata (Syn. edulis), white, summer, 4 to 6 ft., Japan ; nudicaulis, greenish, June, 3 to 4 ft., N. America ; racemosa, greenish white, June, N. America.

HARDY SHRUBBY SPECIES : A. chinensis (Syn. Dimorphanthus mandschuricus), 6 to 12 ft., elegant foliage, China ; chinensis folius aureo-variegata, variegated with yellow ; spinosa (Angelica Tree), white, autumn, 8 to 12 ft., N. America. See also Acanthopanax.

Araucaria (Monkey Puzzle ; Chilean Pine ; Moreton Bay Pine ; Norfolk Island Pine ; Bunya-Bunya Pine)—Ord. Coniferæ. Hardy and half-hardy trees. Ever-green. Orn. foliage. First introduced 1796.

OUTDOOR CULTURE : Soil, deep rich loam. Position, high, dry, and sheltered outdoors away from smoky districts. Plant, Sept. to Nov.

CULTURE OF GREENHOUSE SPECIES : Compost, two parts loam, one part leaf-mould, and one part silver sand. Position, pots or tubs well drained in sunny house. Repot in March. Water freely during spring and summer, moderately at other seasons. Avoid overcrowding ; give plenty of room. Temp., March to Oct. 55° to 65° ; Oct. to March 45° to 55°. Requires plenty of air in summer.

PROPAGATION : Greenhouse species by means of cuttings of ends of young shoots inserted in sandy loam in a warm greenhouse in autumn ; tall, overgrown plants by stem-rooting in spring. Hardy species by seeds sown 1 in. deep in light soil, temp. 65°, Feb., March, April.

HARDY SPECIES CULTIVATED : A. imbricata (Chile Pine), 50 to 100 ft., Chile ; imbri-cata aurea, golden-tinted foliage.

GREENHOUSE SPECIES CULTIVATED : A. Bidwillii (Bunya-Bunya Tree), 100 to 150 ft., Queensland ; Cookii, 150 to 200 ft., New Caledonia ; Cunninghamii (Moreton Bay Pine), 70 to 100 ft., Queensland ; excelsa (Norfolk Island Pine), 100 to 120 ft., Norfolk Island, and its varieties glauca, goldieana and robusta ; Rulei, 50 ft., New Caledonia.

Araujia—Ord. Asclepiadaceæ. Stove and half-hardy flowering evergreen climbers. Nat. Brazil. First introduced 1837.

CULTURE OF A. GRANDIFLORA : Compost, equal parts peat, loam and sand. Position, pots or beds ; shoots trained up roof or round wire trellis. Pot, Feb. or March. Water freely March to Sept., moderately afterwards. Syringe twice daily March to Aug. **Prune shoots moderately annually in Jan.** Apply liquid manure occasionally during May, June, and July. Temp., March to Oct. 65° to 75° ; Oct. to March 55° to 65°.

CULTURE OF A. SERICOFERA : On similar lines to above, except that the plant does not require stove heat. It will thrive in a cool conservatory, and in some sheltered districts survive against a warm wall outdoors.

PROPAGATION : By cuttings of young shoots 4 in. long inserted in sandy soil under propagating glass in temp. 75° to 80° in spring.

SPECIES CULTIVATED : A. grandiflora (Syn. A. graveolens and Schubertia grandiflora), white, fragrant, Oct. ; sericofera (Syn. Physianthus albens), white, Aug.

Arbor-vitæ (*Thuya occidentalis*)—See Thuya.

Arbutus (Strawberry-tree)—Ord. Ericaceæ. Hardy orn. foliage and fruit-bearing trees. Evergreen. Fruit, globular, scarlet, strawberry-like ; ripe in Oct., year after flowering.

CULTURE : Soil, sandy peat. Position, sunny, sheltered. Plant, Sept. to Dec.

PROPAGATION : By seeds sown 1 in. deep in well-drained pans of sandy peat in cold frame in March ; budding in July or Aug. ; or inarching in April.

SPECIES CULTIVATED : A. Andrachne, greenish white, April, 12 to 14 ft., Levant ; hybrida (Syn. A. andrachnoides), white, Sept., 8 to 10 ft., hybrid ; Menziesii, white, Sept., 10 ft., N. America ; Unedo, white, Sept., 10 to 20 ft., S. Europe, including Ireland. Kinds mentioned in catalogues under name of photinæfolia and quercifolia are varieties of A. hybrida.

Archangel (*Angelica officinalis*)—See Angelica.

Archangelica.—See Angelica.

Archontophœnix—Ord. Palmaceæ. Stove palms. First introduced 1870.

CULTURE : Compost, three parts good fibrous loam, one part old cow manure and a little coarse sand. Position, well-drained pots or tubs in sunny part of heated greenhouse. Pot, Feb. or March. Water moderately, Oct. to March ; freely March to Oct. Temp., March to Sept. 65° to 75° ; Sept. to March 55° to 65°.

PROPAGATION : By seeds sown 1 in. deep in light sandy soil under bell-glass or propagator in temp. 75°, March or April.

SPECIES CULTIVATED : A. Alexandræ, 20 to 80 ft., N. Australia ; cunninghamiana (Syn. Seaforthia elegans), 20 to 60 ft., Queensland and New South Wales.

Arctic Bramble (*Rubus arcticus*)—See Rubus.

Arctostaphylos (Bearberry)—Ord. Ericaceæ. Hardy deciduous and evergreen shrubs.

CULTURE : Soil, peat, leaf-mould, and loam. Position, moist, partially-shaded borders or rockeries. Plant in autumn.

PROPAGATION : By cuttings inserted in gritty soil in autumn.

SPECIES CULTIVATED : A. alpina, white, summer, succeeded by black berries, deciduous, 6 in. ; A. Uva-ursi, pink, spring, succeeded by red berries, evergreen, trailing. Both natives of Scotland.

Arctotis—Ord. Compositæ. Half-hardy herbaceous perennials.

OUTDOOR CULTURE : Soil, loamy, enriched with leaf-mould. Position, preferably sunny, but will do in shade. Plant in April or May. Protect by handlights or frames in winter. Best raised from seed or cuttings annually, and grown outside in summer only.

INDOOR CULTURE : Compost, equal parts of loam and leaf-mould with a little sand. Position, well-drained pots in sunny part of greenhouse. Water liberally from March to Oct., moderately at other seasons.

PROPAGATION : By seeds sown in a temp. of 55° to 65° in March. Avoid a too damp atmosphere. Also by cuttings of side shoots inserted in pots of sandy soil in a cold frame in early summer.

SPECIES CULTIVATED : A. breviscapa, orange, summer, 6 in., S. Africa ; scapigera, orange carmine, etc., summer, 6 in., S. Africa ; stœchadifolia (Syn. A. grandis), white, marguerite blossoms, lavender-blue reverse, summer, 2 ft., Africa.

Ardisia (Spear-flower)—Ord. Myrsinaceæ. Stove-flowering and berry-bearing plants. Evergreen. First introduced 1809.
CULTURE : Compost, equal parts loam, peat, leaf-mould, and sand. Pot, Feb. to March. Position, pots, in light, sunny part of stove. Water freely in summer, little in winter. Prune straggly shoots back closely in March. Temp., March to Sept. 70° to 80° ; Sept. to March 55° to 65°.
PROPAGATION : By seeds sown ¼ in. deep in above compost in temp. 75° in spring ; cuttings of side shoots in similar soil and temp., March.
SPECIES CULTIVATED : A. crenata, flowers white, borne in June, followed by pretty red berries, 3 to 4 ft., China ; crenata alba, a white-berried variety.

Areca (Betel-nut Palm)—Ord. Palmaceæ. Stove palms. Orn. foliage. First introduced 1690.
CULTURE : Compost, equal parts loam, peat, leaf-mould, and sand. Position, shady, moist. Water freely at all times. Pot, Feb., March. Temp., March to Sept. 70° to 85° ; Sept. to March 60° to 65°.
PROPAGATION : By seeds.
SPECIES CULTIVATED : A. Catechu (Betel-nut Palm), 20 to 30 ft., Trop. Asia. A. lutescens is now included in the genus Chrysalidocarpus, which see. See also Rhopalostylis.

Aregelia—Ord. Bromeliaceæ. Stove evergreen flowering and ornamental plants. Leaves in stiff rosettes, inner ones usually being brightly coloured.
CULTURE : Compost, equal parts fibrous loam, rough peat, leaf-mould and silver sand. Position, well-drained pots in light, moist part of stove. Pot, Feb. or March. Water moderately in winter ; freely at other times. Temp., March to Sept. 70° to 80° ; Sept. to March 65° to 70°.
PROPAGATION : By large-sized offshoots inserted singly in small pots of sandy peat in temp. 85°, Feb. to April.
SPECIES CULTIVATED : A. princeps (Syn. Karatas Meyendorfi), violet, 1 to 1½ ft., S. Brazil ; spectabilis, blood-red, white and pale blue, 1 ft., Brazil ; tristis, purple, April, 1 ft., Brazil. Some of these are occasionally wrongly listed as Nidularium.

Arenaria (Sand-wort)—Ord. Caryophyllaceæ. Hardy herbaceous perennials or rockery plants. First introduced 1731.
CULTURE : Soil, ordinary, moist. Position, partially shaded rockeries. Plant, Oct. to March.
PROPAGATION : By seeds sown ⅟₁₆ in. deep in sandy soil in boxes in cold frame, March ; cuttings under bell-glass in open, April ; division of plants in Oct. or March.
SPECIES CULTIVATED : A. balearica, white, 2 to 3 in., June, Balearic Isles ; gothica (Syn. A. ciliata), white, summer, 2 in., Orkney and Shetland Isles ; grandiflora, white, summer, 6 in., Europe ; laricifolia (Syn. Alsine laricifolia), white, June, 3 in., Europe ; ledebouriana, white, Levantine Alps ; montana, white, April, 3 in., Spain ; purpurascens, purple, summer, 6 in., Pyrenees ; tetraquetra, white, Aug., 4 in., South Europe ; verna, white, June, 2 in., Britain, etc. See also Sagina.

Argemone (Mexican Poppy ; Devil's Fig ; Prickly Poppy)—Ord. Papaveraceæ. Hardy annuals and perennials ; best grown as annuals. First introduced 1592.
CULTURE : Soil, sandy. Position, sunny borders, well drained. Plant in March.
PROPAGATION : By seeds sown ¼ in. deep in sandy soil outdoors in April or in heat in March, planting outdoors in May.
SPECIES CULTIVATED : A. grandiflora, white, summer, 2 to 3 ft., Mexico ; mexicana, yellow, June, 2 ft., annual, Mexico ; platyceras, white or purple, summer, 1 to 4 ft., N. and S. America.

Arisæma—Ord. Aroideæ. Stove, greenhouse, and hardy tuberous-rooted perennials. First introduced 1759. Flowers, arum-like in shape.
CULTURE OF STOVE AND GREENHOUSE SPECIES : Compost, equal parts peat, leaf-mould, loam and sand. Position, pots in stove or greenhouse. Pot, March. Water freely March to Oct., keep dry afterwards. Temp. 70° to 80° March to Oct.

and 60° to 65°, Oct. to March for stove species ; 40° to 50° Oct. to March and 55° to 60° March to Oct. for greenhouse species.

CULTURE OF HARDY SPECIES : Soil, ordinary. Position, sunny borders. Plant, Oct. or March. Top-dress with decayed manure after new growth begins. Apply liquid manure occasionally in summer.

PROPAGATION : By division of tubers.

STOVE SPECIES CULTIVATED : A. concinnum, white, June, 1 to 2 ft., Himalayas ; galeatum, white, July, 1 ft., Himalayas ; tortuosum, white, April, 4 ft., Himalayas.

GREENHOUSE SPECIES CULTIVATED : A. speciosum, white, March, 1 to 2 ft., Himalayas ; triphyllum (Syn. A. atrorubens), green and purple, June, 1 to 2 ft., N. America.

HARDY SPECIES CULTIVATED : A. Griffithii, brown, violet, and green, May, 12 to 18 in., Himalayas ; ringens, white and green, April, 2 ft., Japan.

Aristea—Ord. Iridiaceæ. Greenhouse evergreen flowering shrub. First introduced 1803.

CULTURE : Compost, two parts good peat, one part sandy loam and little sand. Position, well-drained pots in light, airy greenhouse. Pot, Feb. or March. Water copiously, April to Oct., moderately afterwards. Temp., Oct. to March 40° to 50° ; March to Oct. 50° to 60°. An abundance of air required in summer, moderate amount other times.

PROPAGATION : By seeds sown in sandy loam and peat in temp. 55° to 65° in spring ; by offsets removed from parent plant March or April.

SPECIES CULTIVATED : A. corymbosa (Syn. Witsenia corymbosa), purple, summer, 3 ft., S. Africa.

Aristolochia (Birth-wort ; Dutchman's Pipe)—Ord. Aristolochiaceæ. Stove and hardy climbing or herbaceous plants. Evergreen and deciduous. First introduced 1727.

CULTURE OF STOVE SPECIES : Compost, two-thirds fibrous loam, one-third leaf-mould and sharp sand. Position, pots or borders ; shoots trained close to roof of stove. Pot in March. Water freely in summer, little in winter. Temp., March to Sept. 70° to 80°, Sept. to March 60° to 65°. Prune straggly shoots only.

CULTURE OF HARDY SPECIES : Soil, good ordinary, well drained. Position, sunny borders for herbaceous species ; south, west or east walls, or pergolas, trellises, etc., for climbing kinds. Plant in autumn or spring.

PROPAGATION : Hardy species by cuttings of ripe shoots inserted in sandy soil in slight heat in summer. Stove and greenhouse species by seeds sown in light, rich soil in temp. 75° in March ; cuttings in similar soil and temp., Feb.

STOVE SPECIES CULTIVATED : A. braziliensis, purple, July, 15 to 20 ft., Brazil ; Duchartrei, yellow and brown, July, 2 ft., Brazil ; gigas, purple, June, 8 to 10 ft., Guatemala ; goldeiana, green and yellow, July, 10 ft., Old Calabar ; elegans, green, white, and red, 8 to 10 ft., Brazil.

HARDY HERBACEOUS SPECIES : A. Clematitis, yellow, June to Sept., 2 to 3 ft., Europe.

HARDY CLIMBING SPECIES : A. Sipho (Dutchman's Pipe), yellowish brown, May and June, 15 to 30 ft., N. America ; tomentosa, purple, July and Aug., 10 to 15 ft., N. America.

Armeria (Thrift ; Sea-pink ; Lady's Pincushion ; Cushion-pink)—Ord. Plumbaginaceæ. Hardy perennial.

CULTURE : Soil, sandy loam. Position, edgings to or massing on sunny borders or rockeries. Plant, Oct. or March.

PROPAGATION : By seeds sown $\frac{1}{16}$ in. deep in sandy soil in pans in cold frame, April ; division of plants in Oct. or March.

SPECIES CULTIVATED : A. cæspitosa, rose, June, 2 in., Spain and Portugal ; latifolia (Syn. A. Cephalotes), crimson, June, 6 to 12 in., Portugal ; maritima (Syn. A. vulgaris), pink, May and June, 4 in., Europe (Britain) ; maritima alba (white) ; maritima laucheana (crimson) ; plantaginea splendens, rose, June, 18 in., Europe.

Arnotto (*Bixa orellana*)—See Bixa.

Arnebia—Ord. Boraginaceæ. Hardy annuals and perennials.
CULTURE : Soil, ordinary. Position, sunny rockery, well drained. Sow seeds of annuals in light soil in gentle heat in March, and plant out seedlings in May. Plant perennial species in Oct. or March.
PROPAGATION : Perennial species by seeds or division in spring.
SPECIES : A. cornuta, yellow, spotted with purple, summer, 18 in. to 2 ft., Turkestan, annual ; echioides (Prophet Flower), yellow and purple, summer, to 1 ft., Armenia, perennial.

Arnica (Mountain Tobacco)—Ord. Compositæ. Hardy herbaceous perennials.
CULTURE : Soil, ordinary. Position, sunny border. Plant autumn or spring.
PROPAGATION : By division of roots in spring.
SPECIES CULTIVATED : A. Chamissonis, yellow, July-Sept., 2 ft. ; montana, yellow, May-July, 1 ft. ; sachalinensis, yellow, July-Sept., 1½ ft.

Arpophyllum—Ord. Orchidaceæ. Warm greenhouse terrestrial orchids. Evergreen. First introduced 1838.
CULTURE : Compost, good fibry peat and charcoal. Pot, Feb. or March. Position, well-drained pots in sunny part of house. Temp., Oct. to Feb. 45° to 55° ; other times 55° to 65°. Water moderately in winter, freely in summer. Resting period, winter. Flowers appear at base of new pseudo-bulb after resting.
PROPAGATION : By division of plants when repotting.
SPECIES CULTIVATED : A. cardinale, rose, summer, 1 ft., New Grenada ; giganteum, purplish rose, April, 2 ft., Mexico ; spicatum, purple, April, 1 ft., Mexico and Guatemala.

Arrow Arum (*Peltandra virginica*)—See Peltandra.

Arrow-head (*Sagittaria sagittifolia*)—See Sagittaria.

Arrow-root Plant (*Maranta arundinacea*)—See Maranta.

Arrow Wood (*Viburnum dentatum*)—See Viburnum.

Artemisia (Old Man ; Old Woman ; Lad's Love ; Wormwood ; Tarragon ; Southernwood)—Ord. Compositæ. Hardy shrubs, herbaceous perennials, with hoary and fragrant foliage. Evergreen and deciduous.
CULTURE OF SHRUBBY AND HERBACEOUS SPECIES : Soil, ordinary. Position, sunny borders or rockeries. Plant, Oct. or March.
CULTURE OF TARRAGON : Soil, light, dryish, ordinary. Position, sunny border. Plant roots 2 to 3 in. deep, 8 in. apart in rows 18 in. asunder, March or April. Replant annually. Cut foliage off in Sept., and dry it for use in winter. Place a few roots in ordinary soil in box or large pot, and put this in warm greenhouse in Oct. to supply young shoots during winter.
PROPAGATION : Tarragon by cuttings of shoots inserted in ordinary soil in temp. 55° in March or April, or under hand-light outdoors in July ; division of the roots in March or April. Shrubby and herbaceous species by cuttings inserted in open ground in summer ; division in Oct. or March for herbaceous species ; seeds sown outdoors in April for annual and other species.
SHRUBBY SPECIES : A. Abrotanum (Southernwood, Lad's Love, or Old Man), yellow, Aug., leaves fragrant, 2 to 4 ft., Europe ; tridentata, strongly fragrant, 6 to 8 ft., America.
HARDY PERENNIAL SPECIES CULTIVATED : A. Absinthium (Wormwood), yellow, Aug., 18 in., Europe ; alpina, yellow, summer, 6 in., Caucasus ; argentea, yellow, July, 18 in., Madeira ; cana, yellow, Aug., 2 to 3 ft., N. America ; dranunculus (Tarragon), 2 ft., S. Europe ; gnaphalioides, white, summer, 1 to 2 ft., N. America ; lactiflora, cream, Aug.-Oct., 5 ft., China ; pedemontana, silvery grey foliage, 4 to 6 in., Europe ; pontica, grey foliage, 2 ft., Austria ; stellariana (Syn. ludoviciana), yellow, summer, 1 to 2 ft., N.E. Asia and N. America.

Arthropodium—Ord. Liliaceæ. Greenhouse herbaceous perennials. First introduced 1800.
CULTURE : Compost, two parts sandy loam, one part peat, and a liberal quantity of

silver sand. Position, well-drained pots in sunny part of greenhouse. Pot, March or April. Water freely spring and summer, moderately autumn and winter. Temp., Oct. to March 40° to 45° ; March to Oct. 55° to 65°.

PROPAGATION : By seeds sown in a mixture of equal parts sandy loam, peat, leaf-mould and sand, in a temp. of 55° to 65° in spring ; also by off-sets or suckers removed in spring.

SPECIES CULTIVATED : A. cirrhatum, white, May, 3 ft., New Zealand ; neocaledonicum, white, May, 18 in., New Caledonia ; paniculatum, white, May, 3 ft., New South Wales.

Artichoke—See Cynara, Helianthus, and Stachys.

Artillery Plant (*Pilea muscosa*)—See Pilea.

Artocarpus (Bread-fruit or Jack-tree)—Ord. Urticaceæ. Stove evergreen trees. Orn. foliage. First introduced 1793. Leaves, large, crimson or green.

CULTURE : Compost, two parts loam, one part leaf-mould and sand. Pot, Feb., March. Position, shady and moist. Prune into shape, Feb. Water freely in summer, moderately in winter. Temp., March to Sept. 65° to 75° ; Sept. to March 55° to 60°.

PROPAGATION : By stem-rooting firm shoots in Feb., March ; suckers at any time.

SPECIES CULTIVATED : A. incisa (Bread Fruit Tree), 50 ft., Malaya ; integrifolia (Jack Tree), 50 ft., India and Malaya.

Arum (Cuckoo-pint ; Lords and Ladies ; Italian Arum)—Ord. Aroideæ. Hardy or half-hardy tuberous-rooted perennials. Grown more for their curiously formed flowers and showy red, poisonous berries than for their beauty.

CULTURE OF HARDY SPECIES : Soil, ordinary. Position, partially shady shrubbery borders or grassy spots. Plant, autumn or spring.

CULTURE OF HALF-HARDY SPECIES : Compost, two parts loam, one part decayed manure, and one part sand. Position, well-drained border at base of south wall, or pots in a cool greenhouse. Plant or pot in autumn. Water freely whilst growing in pots ; keep dry when foliage dies. Protect those outdoors with a covering of leaves in winter.

PROPAGATION : By off-sets in autumn.

HARDY SPECIES CULTIVATED : A. italicum (Italian Arum), creamy white, spring, 12 to 18 in., S. Europe ; italicum marmoratum, leaves marbled with yellow ; maculatum (Cuckoo-pint), yellowish green, spotted purple, 6 in., Britain.

HALF-HARDY SPECIES CULTIVATED : A. palæstinum (Syn. A. sanctum), yellow and purple, May, 2 ft., Syria. For other species formerly known as Arums see Arisæma, Helicodiceros, Dranunculus, and Richardia.

Arum Lily (*Richardia africana*)—See Richardia.

Arundinaria (Bamboo)—Ord. Gramineæ. Hardy Japanese shrubby plants with slender stems furnished with graceful grassy foliage.

CULTURE : Soil, loam, leaf-mould and sand. Position, sheltered, in isolated groups or masses on lawns or shrubberies ; not hardy N. of England. Plant, April.

PROPAGATION : By division of roots in April.

SPECIES CULTIVATED : A. anceps, 6 to 8 ft., Japan ; angustifolia, 2 to 4 ft., Japan ; chrysantha (Syn. Bambusa chrysantha), 3 to 4 ft., Japan ; falcata (Syn. Bambusa falcata), 7 to 10 ft., Himalayas ; Falconeri, 7 to 8 ft., Himalayas ; fastuosa, 20 ft., Japan, very hardy ; Fortunei, 2 to 4 ft., Japan, leaves striped with white ; graminea, 10 ft., Japan ; Hindsii (Syn. Bambusa erecta), 6 to 12 ft., Japan ; humilis, 2 to 5 ft., Japan ; japonica (Syn. Bambusa Metake), 10 to 15 ft., Japan ; marmorea, 3 to 5 ft., Japan, tender ; nitida, 6 to 12 ft., China ; palmata (Syn. Bambusa palmata), 6 to 10 ft., Japan ; pumila (Syn. Bambusa pumila), 12 to 18 in., Japan ; Simoni (Syn. Bambusa Simoni), 20 to 25 ft., China ; vagans, 18 in., creeping-stemmed, Japan ; Veitchii (Syn. Bambusa albo-marginata), 2 to 3 ft., Japan. See also Phyllostachys.

Arundo (Reed)—Ord. Gramineæ. Hardy perennial grasses. Flowering and orn. foliage.

CULTURE : Soil, well-drained sandy loam. Position, moist and sheltered in isolated

Ardisia crenata
(Spear-flower)

Argemone grandiflora
(Mexican Poppy)

Aristolochia gigas
(Birth-wort)

Artemisia Absinthium
(Wormwood)

Arundinaria japonica
(Bamboo)

Asclepias in Fruit
(Milkweed)

Asparagus plumosus nanus

Aspidistra lurida
(Parlour Palm)

Asplenium Filix-fœmina
(Lady Fern)

Aster Frikarti
(Michaelmas Daisy)

Aster Novi Belgii
(Michaelmas Daisy)

Astilbe japonica
(False Goat's-beard)

Aubrietia deltoidea
(Purple Rock-cress)

Babiana plicata
(Baboon-root)

Baptisia australis
(False-indigo)

Begonia Gloire de Lorraine

Begonia hydrocotylifolia

Begonia semperflorens

groups on lawns ; margins of water for A. Phragmites. **Plant, April. Protect** crowns with covering of tree leaves in winter.
PROPAGATION : By division of roots in spring.
SPECIES CULTIVATED : A. Donax, reddish white, Aug., 12 ft., S. Europe ; Donax versicolor or variegata, leaves striped with white, 3 ft. The species formerly known as A. conspicua is now placed in the genus Cortaderia, which see.

Asclepias (Swallow-wort ; Milkweed)—Ord. Asclepiadaceæ. Hardy herbaceous and stove perennials. First introduced 1690.
CULTURE : Soil, rich, light peat. Position, sunny and moist borders. Plant, Oct. or April. A. curassavica in pots in stove with winter temp. 60° to 65°.
PROPAGATION : By division of roots in Oct. or April ; also by seeds sown in temp. 50° to 75° in spring. All the hardy species require protection in severe weather.
SPECIES CULTIVATED : A. curassavica, red-purple, July-Sept., 2 to 3 ft., Trop. America ; incarnata, red, 2 ft., N. America ; obtusifolia (Syn. purpurascens), purple, July, 2 to 3 ft., Virginia ; speciosa (Syn. Douglasii), purple-lilac, fragrant, July, 2 to 3 ft., N.W. America ; syriaca (Syn. Cornuti), purple, fragrant, July, 3 to 5 ft., N. America ; tuberosa, orange, July to Sept., 1 to 2 ft., N. America.

Ash (*Fraxinus excelsior*)—See Fraxinus.

Ash-leaf Fern—See Marattia and Anemia.

Asparagus—Ord. Liliaceæ. Greenhouse climbers and hardy perennials, including the edible Asparagus. Foliage of the greenhouse species, fern-like, green, and extensively used as a substitute for fern fronds in floral decorations.
CULTURE OF GREENHOUSE SPECIES : Compost, two parts loam, one part of equal proportions of leaf-mould, peat and silver sand. Position, pots, tubs, or beds, for climbers, shoots trained up roof or back walls of greenhouse ; dwarf kinds in pots suspended from roof. Pot or plant in March. Water and syringe freely during the summer, moderately at other seasons. Apply weak liquid manure occasionally to establish plants. Temp., Sept. to March 50° to 55° ; March to Sept. 55° to 60°.
CULTURE OF EDIBLE ASPARAGUS : Soil, deep rich sandy loam. Position, open and sunny, or in partial shade. Size of beds, 3 ft. wide ; alleys 2 ft. wide. Preparation of soil : In Oct. or Nov., trench two spits deep and break up third spit with fork. Put a thick layer of manure over third spit and work in a liberal quantity of old mortar, decayed vegetable matter, and rotten manure among upper spits. In case of heavy wet soils put a thick layer of brick rubble under second spit. Plant in April. Spread out roots, plants to be 15 in. apart. Fill up trenches with soil and make level. " Crowns " or points of each plant to be 5 in. below surface. Three-year-old plants best for planting. Cutting : No shoots to be removed first year, moderate quantity second year, freely afterwards. Shoots should not be less than 6 in. long when cut. Cease cutting end of June. General treatment : Apply manure periodically. Keep beds free of weeds. Cut down stems early in Nov. Top-dress with decayed manure in Nov., previously lightly forking up surface. In March, rake off rough particles into alley, and leave smooth and neat. Manures : Decayed horse manure for heavy soils ; cow or pig manures for light soils ; seaweed mixed with above manures and applied as a top-dressing in Nov. ; common salt, 1 oz. to a square yard, occasionally ; Peruvian guano, 1 oz. to a square yard, applied once or twice between April and Sept.
FORCING IN FRAMES : Prepare hotbed of manure in usual way. Cover with 3 in. of light soil. Place roots on this and cover to depth of 5 in. Keep soil moist and frame closed until shoots appear, when admit a little air. Temp., 60° to 75°. Roots of no use after forcing.
PROPAGATION : Greenhouse species by seeds sown in temp. 70° in spring ; division of roots, March. Edible asparagus, by seeds sown in groups of three or four in holes 1 in. deep and 15 in. apart on prepared bed as above described ; or in drills 1 in. deep and 12 in. apart in ordinary soil—March or April. Thin seedlings raised by the first method to one in each group in May ; those by the second method to a foot apart when 3 in. high. Transplant latter into permanent beds when two or three years old. Seedlings ready to cut fourth year after sowing.

Seeds take 20 days to germinate. A quarter-pint of seed will sow a row of 50 ft. long.

GREENHOUSE SPECIES : A. acutifolius, flowers yellow, berries red, 5 to 6 ft., almost hardy, S. Europe ; æthiopicus, 10 ft., S. Africa ; medeolioides (Syn. Myrsiphyllum or Medeola asparagoides), commonly called " Smilax," 6 to 10 ft., S. Africa ; plumosus, 4 to 10 ft., S. Africa, and its varieties, nanus and tenuissimus ; scandens, S. Africa ; Sprengeri, 1 to 3 ft., Natal ; verticillatus, 10 ft., S. Africa.

HARDY SPECIES : A. officinalis (Edible Asparagus), Europe.

Asparagus Fern (*Asparagus plumosus*)—See Asparagus.

Aspen (*Populus tremula*)—See Populus.

Asperula (Woodruff ; Squinancy-wort)—Ord. Rubiaceæ. Hardy herbaceous perennials and annuals. Foliage fragrant when dry.

CULTURE : Soil, light, rich. Position under the shade of trees or rockeries or in open borders. Plant, Oct., Nov.

PROPAGATION : Perennial species by division of roots in March ; perennials and annuals by seeds sown ¼ in. deep in open border in April.

PERENNIAL SPECIES CULTIVATED : A. arcadiensis, pink, April, 3 in., Greece ; cyananchica (Squinancy-wort), white, June, 9 in., Europe (Britain) ; Gussoni, white, June to Sept., 6 in., Italy ; hexaphylla, white, June to Sept., 1 ft. ; hirta, white, changing to pink, July to Aug., 3 in., Pyrenees ; odorata (Sweet Woodruff), May, 6 in., Europe (Britain) ; suberosa (Syn. Athoa), pink, June to July, 3 in., Mt. Athos.

ANNUAL SPECIES CULTIVATED : A. azurea (Syns. Setosa-azurea and orientalis), blue, summer, fragrant, 6 to 10 in., Syria.

Asphodel (*Asphodelus ramosus*)—See Asphodelus.

Asphodeline (Leafless Asphodel)—Ord. Liliaceæ. Hardy herbaceous perennials. First introduced 1596.

CULTURE : Soil, ordinary, rich. Position, open or shady borders. Plant, Oct. or March.

PROPAGATION : By division of roots, Oct. or March.

SPECIES CULTIVATED : A. imperialis, pink, July and Aug., 6 to 8 in., Cilicia ; lutea (Syn. Asphodelus luteus), yellow, July and Aug., 3 to 4 ft., Mediterranean Region ; lutea flore-pleno, flowers double ; taurica (Syn. Asphodelus tauricus), white, July, 1 to 2 ft., Orient.

Asphodelus (Asphodel ; King's Spear ; Silver Rod)—Ord. Liliaceæ. Hardy herbaceous perennials. First introduced 1596.

CULTURE : Soil, ordinary. Position, shady or open borders. Plant in autumn or spring.

PROPAGATION : By division of roots Oct. or April ; seeds sown in a cold frame in March.

SPECIES CULTIVATED : A. acaulis, pink, May, 12 to 18 in., N. Africa ; albus, white, May, 2 ft., Europe ; ramosus, white, May, 4 to 5 ft., S. Europe. See Asphodeline.

Aspidistra (Parlour Palm)—Ord. Liliaceæ. Greenhouse or dwelling-room plants. Evergreen. Or. foliage. First introduced 1822. Leaves, large, green, or variegated with white.

CULTURE : Compost, two parts loam, one part leaf-mould and sand. Repot in March. Water freely in summer, moderately in winter. Room plants best watered by immersing pot for quarter of an hour in tepid water. Temp. min. 50°.

PROPAGATION : By division of roots in March.

SPECIES CULTIVATED : A. elatior, 2 ft., Japan, leaves green ; elatior variegata, leaves variegated ; lurida, leaves green, 1 to 2 ft., China ; lurida variegata, leaves striped yellow. Last two those generally grown.

Aspidium (Shield or Wood Fern)—Ord. Filices. Stove, greenhouse, and hardy ferns. Ht., 1 to 3 ft.

CULTURE OF STOVE AND GREENHOUSE SPECIES : Compost, two parts peat, one part loam, silver sand, and charcoal. Pot, March. Water freely in summer, moderately

in winter.   Shade from sun.   Temp. for stove species, Sept. to March 60° to 70°;
March to Sept. 70° to 80°; greenhouse, Sept. to March 50° to 55°, March to Sept.
55° to 65°.
CULTURE OF HARDY SPECIES : Compost, equal parts loam, peat, leaf-mould and
coarse silver sand.   Position, shady or partially shady spots.   Plant in Oct. or April.
Water freely in dry weather.
PROPAGATION : Hardy species by division of crowns in April, also by spores sown
on sterilised loam and kept close under glass cover.   Stove and greenhouse species
by spores sown in sandy peat at any time ; division in March.
STOVE SPECIES CULTIVATED : A. amabile, India and Japan ; mucronatum, Jamaica ;
trifoliatum, West Indies ; viviparum, West Indies.
GREENHOUSE SPECIES CULTIVATED : A. capense (Syn. A. coriaceum), Cape of Good
Hope, Tropical America, etc. ; falcatum (Syn. Cyrtomium falcatum), Japan, China,
etc. ; falcatum caryotideum, Japan ; falcatum Fortunei, Japan ; falcinellum,
Madeira ; frondosum, Madeira ; laserpitiifolium (Syn. Lastrea Standishii), Japan ;
lepidocaulon, Japan ; pungens, Cape Colony ; triangulum ilicifolium, N. India ;
vestitum, New Zealand, Chile, etc.
HARDY SPECIES CULTIVATED : A. acrostichoides (Syn. Polystichum acrostichoides),
N. America, and its varieties grandiceps and incisum ; aculeatum (Syn. Polystichum
aculeatum), the Prickly Shield Fern, Britain, etc., and its varieties, proliferum
angulare (Soft Shield Fern), lobatum, setosum, etc. ; Lonchitis (Syn. Polystichum
Lonchitis), the Holly Fern, Britain, etc. ; munitum (Syn. Polystichum munitum),
N. America.   See specialists' lists for names of varieties.   See also Nephrodium.
   Asplenium (Spleenwort ; Lady Fern ; Bird's-nest Fern ; Wall-rue Fern ; Scale
Fern, etc.)—Ord. Filices.   Stove greenhouse and hardy ferns.   Ht., 6 in. to 4 ft.
CULTURE OF STOVE AND GREENHOUSE SPECIES : Compost, equal parts peat, loam,
leaf-mould and sand.   Pot, March.   Water freely in summer, moderately in winter.
Temp., Stove species, Sept. to March 60° to 70°, March to Sept. 70° to 80° ; green-
house, Sept. to March 50° to 55° ; March to Sept. 55° to 65°.
CULTURE OF HARDY SPECIES : Compost, equal parts peat, loam, leaf-mould, sand
and old mortar rubbish.   Position, old walls for Scale, Wall-rue and Maidenhair
Spleenworts ; moist, shady borders for Lady Fern ; rockeries for other kinds.
Plant in April.
PROPAGATION : Hardy species by spores when ripe and division in April.   Stove
and greenhouse species by spores sown in sandy peat at any time.
STOVE SPECIES CULTIVATED : A. attenuatum, N.S. Wales, etc. ; Baptistii, South Sea
Islands ; Belangeri, Java, Borneo, etc. ; caudatum, India, Brazil, etc. ; formosum,
Trop. America ; longissimum, Java, etc. ; lunulatum, Tropics ; Nidus (Bird's-nest
Fern), Tropics, and its varieties, australasicum and musæfolium ; obtusilobum,
New Hebrides ; rutæfolium prolongatum, S. India ; viviparum, Mauritius.
GREENHOUSE SPECIES CULTIVATED : A. bulbiferum, New Zealand and Australia,
and its varieties Fabianum and laxum ; Colensoi, New Zealand ; dimorphum,
Norfolk Island ; ebeneum, Cape Colony ; flaccidum, Australia, etc. ; goringianum
pictum (Syn. Athyrium goringianum tricolor), Japan, hardy in warm districts ;
Hemionitis (Syn. A. palmatum), Madeira ; incisum, Japan ; obtusatum lucidum
(Syn. A. lucidum), New Zealand ; monanthemum, Temperate Zone ; præmorsum,
West Indies, etc. ; Sandersonii, Natal.
HARDY SPECIES CULTIVATED : A. Adiantum nigrum (Black Maiden-hair Spleenwort
or " French Fern " of the markets), Northern and Southern Temperate Zones,
including Britain ; Ceterach (Syn. Ceterach officinarum), the Scale Fern, a British
and European species ; Filix-fœmina (Syn. Athyrium Filix-fœmina), the Lady Fern,
Britain, and its numerous varieties as Frizelliæ, cristatum, plumosum, Victoriæ,
etc. ; fontanum (Rock Spleenwort), Britain, Europe ; germanicum (German
Spleenwort), Europe, Britain ; lanceolatum, Europe, Britain ; marinum (Sea Spleenwort), Europe, Britain ; Ruta-muraria (Wall-rue Fern), Britain ; septentrionale
(Forked Spleenwort), Britain ; Trichomanes (Maidenhair Spleenwort), Europe,
Britain ; thelypteroides (Syn. Athyrium thelypteroides, N. America ; viride (Green
Spleenwort), Europe, Britain.   Many varietal forms of the foregoing species will
be found in lists and works on British ferns.

Aster (Starwort; Michaelmas Daisy; Perennial Aster)—Ord. Compositæ. Hardy herbaceous perennials, flowering freely in autumn and yielding an abundance of flowers for cutting.

CULTURE: Soil, good ordinary. Position, sunny borders or wild gardens for tall species; rockeries for dwarf ones. Plant in Oct. or spring. Lift, divide, and replant every third year.

PROPAGATION: By seeds sown in heat or in a cold frame in spring; cuttings of young shoots in heat or cold frame in spring or summer; division of roots in autumn or spring. See Callistephus for China Aster.

SPECIES CULTIVATED: A. acris, lilac-purple, Aug., 3 ft., S. Europe, and its varieties dracunculoides (taller), nanus (dwarfer); alpinus, purple, July, 6 in., Europe; Amellus (Italian Starwort), purple, Aug., 2 ft., Europe, and many fine florists' varieties in shades of lavender, violet, and pink; Bellidiastrum, white, July, 1 ft., Europe; cordifolius, mauve, July, 2 ft., N. America; diffusus, white, Oct., 2 ft., N. America, and its variety horizontalis; diplostephioides, rich purple, June, 1 ft.; dumosus, mauve, Oct., 18 in., N. America; ericoides, white, Oct., 2 to 3 ft., N. America; Farreri, violet-blue, June to July, 1 ft., China; Frikarti, lavender-blue, Aug. to Oct., 2 to 3 ft., hybrid; grandiflorus, violet, Nov., 2 to 3 ft., Virginia; lævis, blue, Sept., 2 ft., N. America; Linosyris (Syn. Chrysocoma Linosyris), the Goldilocks, yellow, Aug., 1 ft., Europe; multiflorus, white, Sept. to Nov., 3 ft., N. America; Novæ-Angliæ, purple, Sept., 5 to 6 ft., N. America, and its numerous varieties; Novi-Belgii, blue, Sept., 4 ft., North America, and its numerous forms; paniculatus, pale lilac, Sept. to Oct., 3 ft., N. America; ptarmicoides, white, Aug., 18 in., N. America; puniceus, blue, Sept., 6 ft., N. America; Shortii, blush, 3 ft., Sept., United States; sub-cærulus, violet-blue, June, 9 in., Himalaya; Thompsoni, pale blue, July to Nov., 1 to 2 ft., Himalaya; Tradescanti, white, Oct., 4 ft. (True Michaelmas Daisy), N. America; turbinellus, mauve, Aug., 3 ft., N. America; versicolor, pink and white, Sept., 3 ft., N. America; vimineus, white, Sept., 3 ft., N. America; yunnanensis, lilac-blue, June to July, 9 to 12 in., Yunnan. Scores of varieties of many of the foregoing species will be found in trade lists. The plant listed in trade catalogues as Aster hybridus luteus is Solidago missouriensis, which see.

Astilbe (False Goat's-beard)—Ord. Saxifragaceæ. Hardy herbaceous and shrubby perennials. Used also for forcing for flowering early in greenhouses.

CULTURE OUTDOORS: Soil, loamy. Position, moist, shady borders, or margins of lakes or ponds. Plant in Oct. or spring. Require plenty of water in dry weather.

INDOOR CULTURE: Compost, two parts loam, one part of well-rotted manure or leaf-mould, and one of silver sand. Pot roots in Sept. or Oct. Place pots in cold frame and cover with cocoanut-fibre refuse till Dec., when introduce to a temp. of 45° for a week or so, then transfer to temp. of 55° to 60°. Water freely when growth begins. Apply weak liquid manure when flower spikes show. After flowering harden off in cold frame till May, then plant out in garden. Lift, divide, and replant following April, and lift and repot in autumn. Retarded roots will flower in six weeks from potting in cold house.

PROPAGATION: By division.

SPECIES CULTIVATED: A. Davidii, violet-red, Aug. to Sept., 4 to 5 ft., China; chinensis, white, July, 2 ft., China and Japan; japonica (Syn. Spiræa japonica), white, May, 2 ft., Japan; rivularis, white, July, Himalayas; Thunbergii, white, May, 1 to 2 ft., Japan, a shrubby species. Many choice hybrids will be found in trade lists. Those with A. Davidii as one parent are grouped under the heading A. Arendsi, while hybrids of Spiræa astilboides with astilbe are known as A. Lemoinei. See also Spiræa.

Astragalus (Milk Vetch)—Ord. Leguminosæ. Hardy perennial or shrubby herbs. Evergreen and deciduous. Siberia, Persia, N. America, Levant. Introduced 1570.

CULTURE: Soil, ordinary. Position, open border for tall, and rockery for dwarf soesies. Plant, Oct., Nov., March.

40

PROPAGATION : By seeds sown ¼ in. deep in light soil in cold frame in March, shrubby kinds by cuttings in a cold frame in summer.
SPECIES CULTIVATED : A. alopecuroides, yellow, June, 3 to 5 ft., Siberia ; danicus, blue, June, trailing, Europe ; danicus albus, white ; massiliensis (Syn. A. Tragacantha), violet, June, 2 to 3 ft., Mediterranean Region ; monspessulanus, rosy lilac and white, June, trailing, S. Europe ; Onobrychys, purple, July, 9 to 12 in., Persia.

Astrantia (Master Wort)—Ord. Umbelliferæ. Hardy herbaceous perennials. First introduced 1596.
CULTURE : Soil, ordinary. Position, shady borders or margins of woodland walks. Plant, Oct. or March.
PROPAGATION : By seeds sown in sandy loam in cold frame in April ; division of roots in Oct. or March.
SPECIES CULTIVATED : A. Biebersteinii, white, May, 2 ft., Caucasus ; carniolica, white, May, 1 ft., E. Europe ; helleborifolia, pink, July, 2 ft., Caucasus ; major, green and white, 2 ft., Europe ; minor, white, tinted green, June, 6 in., Europe.

Ataccia—See Tacca.

Atamasco Lily (*Zephyranthes Atamasco*)—See Zephyranthes.

Athanasia annua—See Lonas.

Athrotaxis—Ord. Coniferæ. Tender evergreen trees and shrubs. First introduced 1857.
CULTURE : Soil, good loam. Position, sheltered, in Cornwall and Ireland only. Plant, Sept. and Oct.
PROPAGATION : By seeds sown in pots in a cold frame.
SPECIES CULTIVATED : A. cupressoides, 20 to 45 ft., Tasmania ; laxifolia, 25 to 35 ft., Tasmania ; selaginoides, 40 ft., Tasmania.

Athyrium—See Asplenium.

Atragene—See Clematis.

Atriplex (Orache and Shrubby Goosefoot)—Ord. Chenopodiaceæ. Hardy annuals and shrubs. A. hortensis (Orache, or Mountain Spinach) occasionally grown as a substitute for Spinach. A. hortensis rubra (Red Orache) used for border decoration.
CULTURE OF ORACHE : Soil, ordinary. Sow seeds at intervals of a few weeks from March onwards in drills an inch deep and 2 ft. apart. When seedlings are 3 in. high, thin them to 18 in. apart. Gather youngest and most succulent leaves for cooking.
CULTURE OF RED ORACHE : Soil, ordinary. Position, sunny borders in wild garden. Sow seeds broadcast where required to grow in March or April. Usually reproduces itself freely from seeds.
CULTURE OF SHRUBBY SPECIES : Soil, ordinary. Position, near the sea. A. Halimus suitable for hedge culture. Plant in autumn. Trim into shape April.
PROPAGATION : By cuttings in summer.
SPECIES CULTIVATED : A. hortensis, green, summer, 3 to 5 ft., Tartary ; hortensis rubra, foliage red.
EVERGREEN SPECIES : A. canescens (Grey Sage Bush), leaves light grey, 5 to 6 ft., N.W. America ; Halimus (Tree Purslane), silvery-grey leaves, 4 to 5 ft., S. Europe ; portulacoides, grey leaves, 1 to 2 ft., native of Britain.

Aubergine (*Solanum melongena*)—See Solanum.

Aubrietia (Purple Rock-cress)—Ord. Cruciferæ. Hardy trailing perennial. Evergreen. First introduced 1710.
CULTURE : Soil, ordinary. Position, sunny rockery or border. Plant, Oct. or spring. This plant may be grown on old walls if seeds are sown in mossy chinks in March ; useful for edgings to borders and for spring bedding. Straggly plants best trimmed in closely after flowering.
PROPAGATION : By slips dibbled in shady border in June, transplanting them in Nov. ; seeds sown in shady border in April, or by division in autumn or spring.
SPECIES CULTIVATED : A. deltoidea, purple, spring, 2 to 3 in., S. Europe. There are many named varieties to be found in hardy plant catalogues.

Aucuba (Spotted Laurel ; Variegated Laurel)—Ord. Cornaceæ. Hardy evergreen shrub. Orn. foliage. First introduced 1783.
CULTURE : Soil, ordinary. Position, open or in shade ; grand town shrub. Plant, Oct., Nov., April. Female aucubas bear red berries freely in winter if a male plant be planted close to them, or if a branch of male blossom be placed on female plant when in bloom. Aucubas useful for pot culture in cool greenhouses or windows in winter.
PROPAGATION : By seeds sown ¼ in. deep in cold frame in Oct. ; cuttings inserted in sandy soil in sheltered border or cold frame in Sept., Oct., Nov.
SPECIES CULTIVATED : A. japonica, 6 to 10 ft., Japan, and its varieties, albo-variegata, aurea, fructo-alba, limbata, maculata, vera nana, viridis, etc.

Auricula (*Primula auricula*)—See Primula.

Australian Bean Flower (*Kennedya coccinea*)—See Kennedya.

Australian Blue-bell Creeper (*Sollya heterophylla*)—See Sollya.

Australian Currant (*Leucopogon Reichei*)—See Leucopogon.

Australian Daisy (*Erigeron mucronatus*)—See Erigeron.

Australian Everlasting—See Helipterum.

Australian Feather-palm (*Ptychosperma elegans*)—See Ptychosperma.

Australian Flea-bane (*Erigeron mucronatus*)—See Erigeron.

Australian Fuchsia—See Correa.

Australian Giant Lily (*Doryanthes excelsa*)—See Doryanthes.

Australian Heath—See Epacris.

Australian Honeysuckle—See Banksia.

Australian Hop (*Daviesia alata*)—See Daviesia.

Australian Ivy (*Muhlenbeckia adpressa*)—See Muhlenbeckia.

Australian Lilac—See Hardenbergia.

Australian Native Rose (*Boronia serrulata*)—See Boronia.

Australian Pitcher-plant (*Cephalotus follicularis*)—See Cephalotus.

Australian Sarsaparilla Tree—See Hardenbergia.

Australian Tree Fern (*Dicksonia antarctica*)—See Dicksonia.

Austrian Briar (*Rosa lutea*)—See Rosa.

Austrian Dragon's-head (*Dracocephalum austriacum*)—See Dracocephalum.

Austrian Leopard's Bane (*Doronicum austriacum*)—See Doronicum.

Austrian Pine (*Pinus Laricio nigricans*)—See Pinus.

Autumn Crocus (*Colchicum autumnale*)—See Colchicum.

Autumn-flowering Squill (*Scilla autumnalis*)—See Scilla.

Autumn Sneeze-wort (*Helenium autumnalis*)—See Helenium.

Avena (Animated Oat)—Ord. Gramineæ. Hardy orn. flowering grass. Awns susceptible to change of weather and animated.
CULTURE : Sow seeds outdoors in April in ordinary soil in borders. Gather when fully developed and dry for winter decoration.
SPECIES CULTIVATED : A. sterilis, 2 ft., Barbary.

Avens—See Geum.

Avocado Pear (*Persea gratissima*)—See Persea.

Ayrshire Rose (*Rosa arvenis*)—See Rosa.

Azalea—See Rhododendron and Loiseleuria.

Azara—Ord. Bixaceæ. Hardy evergreen shrubs. Orn. foliage. First introduced 1873. Flowers unattractive but very fragrant.
CULTURE : Soil, ordinary. Position, against south wall ; or in warm shrubberies in mild districts. Plant, Oct. or April.
PROPAGATION : By cuttings inserted in sandy soil in temp. 65° in March.
SPECIES CULTIVATED : A. dentata, yellow, June, 10 to 12 ft., Chile ; Gilliesii, yellow, May, 12 to 15 ft., Chile ; microphylla, greenish-white, May, 10 to 12 ft., berries orange-red, Chile.

Azolla—Ord. Salviniaceæ. Hardy floating aquatic perennials with delicate fern-like foliage.
CULTURE : Grow in shallow ponds or in indoor aquaria. Requires no soil, merely to float on surface of water.
PROPAGATION : By division.
SPECIES CULTIVATED : A. caroliniana, Carolina.

Azorean Forget-me-not (*Myosotis azorica*)—See Myosotis.

Azorean Thyme (*Thymus azoricus*)—See Thymus.

Babiana (Baboon-root)—Ord. Iridaceæ. Half-hardy bulbous plants. Nat. Cape of Good Hope. First introduced 1752. Flowers fragrant.
OUTDOOR CULTURE : Soil, light sandy. Position, sunny, well-drained border. Plant, Sept. to Jan., placing bulbs 4 in. deep and 2 in. apart. Lift and replant bulbs annually.
INDOOR CULTURE : Compost, two parts sandy soil and one part leaf-mould or decayed cow manure. Pots, 4½ in. in diameter, well drained. Place five bulbs 3 in. deep in each pot in Nov., and cover pots with cocoanut-fibre refuse until growth begins. Water moderately from time bulbs begin to grow until flowers fade, then gradually withhold it, keeping bulbs dry from Sept. to Jan. Temp., Sept. to Feb. 40° to 50° ; other times 50° to 60°.
PROPAGATION : By offsets.
SPECIES CULTIVATED : B. disticha, blue, June, 6 in.; plicata, blue, June, 6 in. ; ringens, scarlet, June, 6 to 8 in. ; stricta, white and blue, May, 6 to 8 in. There are also a number of pretty varieties mentioned in trade lists.

Baboon Root—See Babiana.

Baby Blue-eyes (*Nemophila insignis*)—See Nemophila.

Babylonian Centaury (*Centaurea babylonica*)—See Centaurea.

Baccharis (Tree Groundsel)—Ord. Compositæ. Hardy deciduous and evergreen shrubs. Flowers unisexual. First introduced 1683.
CULTURE : Soil, ordinary. Position, sea-coast gardens. Plant, autumn.
PROPAGATION : By cuttings of young shoots in summer.
SPECIES CULTIVATED : B. halimifolia, 6 to 12 ft., Eastern N. America ; patagonica (evergreen), 8 to 10 ft., Magellan Straits.

Bachelor's Buttons (*Ranunculus aconitifolius fl. pl.*)—See Ranunculus.

Bactris (Maharajah Palm ; Tobago Cane)—Ord. Palmaceæ. Stove palms. Orn. foliage. First introduced 1825. Ht., 20 to 50 ft.
CULTURE : Compost, equal parts loam, leaf-mould and sand. Pot, Feb., March. Water moderately Sept. to March, freely afterwards. Position, shady and moist in summer. Temp., Sept. to March 60° to 70° ; March to Sept. 70° to 80°.
PROPAGATION : By removing young plants from the base of old ones in March, and placing these in small pots ; also by seeds.
SPECIES CULTIVATED : B. caryotæfolia, Brazil ; Maraja, Brazil ; pallidispina, Guiana.

Bæria—Ord. Compositæ. Hardy annual. First introduced 1835.
CULTURE : Soil, ordinary. Position, sunny border.
PROPAGATION : By seeds sown ¼ in. deep in April where plants are to flower.
SPECIES CULTIVATED : B. chrysostoma, yellow, May, 8 to 12 in., California ; coronaria, yellow, summer, trailing, California.

Bahia (Woolly Bahia)—Ord. Compositæ. Hardy perennial herb. Leaves grey. CULTURE : Soil, ordinary. Position, sunny border. Plant, Oct. to April. PROPAGATION : By seeds sown ⅛ in. deep outdoors in April or division in March. SPECIES CULTIVATED : B. lanata, yellow, May to Aug., 12 to 18 in., N. America.

Bald Cypress (*Taxodium distichum*)—See Taxodium.

Baldmoney (*Meum athamanticum*)—See Meum.

Balearic Box Tree (*Buxus balearica*)—See Buxus.

Balloon Flower (*Platycodon grandiflorum*)—See Platycodon.

Balm (*Melissa officinalis*)—See Melissa.

Balm of Gilead (*Cedronella canariensis*)—See Cedronella.

Balm of Gilead Fir (*Abies balsamea*)—See Abies.

Balsam—See Impatiens.

Balsam Apple (*Momordica balsamina*)—See Momordica.

Balsam Fir (*Abies balsamea*)—See Abies.

Balsam Pear (*Momordica Charantia*)—See Momordica.

Balsam Poplar (*Populus balsamifera* and other species)—See Populus.

Balsam-scented Geranium (*Pelargonium radula*)—See Pelargonium.

Bamboo—See Bambusa, Arundinaria and Phyllostachys.

Bambusa (Bamboo)—Ord. Gramineæ. Hardy and half-hardy evergreen plants with graceful stems and elegant foliage. First introduced 1730. Grown in groups in the garden, also in pots or tubs for greenhouse decoration. OUTDOOR CULTURE : Soil, deep, rich loam. Position, warm sheltered nook or dell in garden. Plant May or June. Protect in winter with covering of leaves at base. Mulch with cow manure in spring. Water freely in dry weather. INDOOR CULTURE : Compost, equal parts loam, leaf-mould and sand. Position, large pots or tubs in cool greenhouse (winter temp. 40° to 45°). Water freely spring and summer, moderately other times. PROPAGATION : By seeds sown in sandy soil in heat in spring ; cuttings of rhizomes in heat in spring ; division in April or May. SPECIES CULTIVATED : B. arundinacea, 10 to 50 ft., India (this species is tender) ; disticha (Syn. B. nana) 2½ ft. ; quadrangularis, 6 to 12 ft., China and Japan ; vulgaris (Feathery Bamboo), 50 to 80 ft., Java, and its variety aureo-variegata (both are tender). See also Arundinaria and Phyllostachys for other species of Bamboo.

Banana (*Musa sapientum*)—See Musa.

Baneberry (*Actæa spicata*)—See Actæa.

Banksia (Australian Honeysuckle)—Ord. Protaceæ. Greenhouse shrubs or trees. Orn. foliage. Evergreen. Nat. Australia. First introduced 1788. CULTURE : Compost, equal parts peat, loam, and sand. Pot in March in well-drained pots. Water moderately in winter, freely in summer. Temp., Sept. to March 60° to 65° ; March to Sept. 55° to 65°. PROPAGATION : By cuttings of firm shoots in well-drained pots of sandy soil in July under bell-glass in temp. 55° to 65°. SPECIES CULTIVATED : B. collina, 6 ft. ; dryandroides, 6 ft. ; grandis, 30 to 40 ft. ; quercifolia, 5 ft., hardy in favoured situations, otherwise requiring cold greenhouse ; speciosa, 6 ft. ; serrata, to 20 ft. ; verticillata, 15 to 20 ft.

Banksian Rose (*Rosa Banksia*)—See Rosa.

Ban-Nut (*Juglans regia*)—See Juglans.

Banyan Tree (*Ficus benghalensis*)—See Ficus.

Baptisia (False-indigo)—Ord. Leguminosæ. Hardy herbaceous perennials. First introduced 1724. CULTURE : Soil, ordinary. Position, sunny, well-drained border. Plant, Oct. to April.

PROPAGATION : By seeds sown ¼ in. deep in sandy soil in shallow boxes in cold frame in April, or in sunny borders outdoors in May ; division in March.
SPECIES CULTIVATED : B. alba, white, June, 2 ft., N. America ; australis, blue, June, 3 to 4 ft., N. America ; leucantha, cream, July, 2 ft., N. America ; tinctoria, yellow, July, 2 ft., N. America.

Barbados Gooseberry (*Pereskia aculeata*)—See Pereskia.

Barbados Lily (*Hippeastrum equestre*)—See Hippeastrum.

Barbados Pride—See Adenanthera.

Barbarea (Winter or American Cress ; Double Yellow Rocket)—Ord. Cruciferæ. Hardy perennial herbs and salad vegetables.
CULTURE OF FLOWERING SPECIES : Soil, ordinary. Position, open garden ; edgings to beds or sunny rockeries for variegated kind.
CULTURE OF WINTER CRESS : Soil, ordinary. Position, moist, partially shaded border. Sow seeds in shallow drills 9 in. apart in Sept. for winter use ; in March and June for summer use. Gather tops or young leaves for salading.
PROPAGATION : By division of roots in March.
SPECIES CULTIVATED : B. verna (Winter or Land Cress), Syn. B. præcox, Britain ; B. vulgaris flore-pleno (Double Yellow Rocket), yellow, summer, 1 to 2 ft. ; vulgaris variegata, leaves yellow and green.

Barbary Fig—See Opuntia.

Barbe de Capucin (*Cichorium Intybus*)—See Cichorium.

Barberry—See Berberis.

Barberton Daisy (*Gerbera Jamesoni*)—See Gerbera.

Barkeria—See Epidendrum.

Barleria—Ord. Acanthaceæ. Stove flowering shrubs. Evergreen. First introduced 1759.
CULTURE : Compost, two parts peat and loam, one part decayed manure and sand. Plant in March in well-drained pots. Temp., Sept. to March 55° to 65° ; March to Sept. 70° to 85°. Water moderately in winter, freely in summer. Prune shoots back after flowering. Syringe daily during spring and summer.
PROPAGATION : By cuttings of young shoots inserted in sandy peat under bell-glass in temp. 85°, March to July.
SPECIES CULTIVATED : B. cristata, purple, white, July, 2 ft., India ; flava, yellow, winter, 18 in., Trop. Africa ; involucrata, blue, winter, 1 to 2 ft., Ceylon ; lupulina, yellow, Aug., 2 ft., Mauritius ; strigosa (Syn. cærulea), blue, July, 2 to 3 ft., India.

Barnardia—Now included in genus Scilla. See Scilla chinensis.

Barren Strawberry (*Waldsteinia fragarioides*)—See Waldsteinia.

Barren-wort—See Epimedium.

Bartonia—See Mentzelia.

Barton's Flower (*Mentzelia Lindleyi*)—See Mentzelia.

Basil—See Ocimum.

Basil Thyme (*Calamintha Acinos*)—See Calamintha.

Basket Fern (*Nephrodium Filix-mas*)—See Nephrodium.

Bass Wood (*Tilia americana*)—See Tilia.

Bastard Agrimony (*Ageratum mexicanum*)—See Ageratum.

Bastard Balm (*Melittis melissophyllum*)—See Melittis.

Bastard Cedar (*Cedrela sinensis*)—See Cedrela.

Bastard Cyperus (*Carex Pseudo-cyperus*)—See Carex.

Bastard Indigo—See Amorpha.

Bastard Jasmine—See Cestrum.

Batatas—See Ipomæa.

Batemannia—Ord. Orchidaceæ. Stove orchid. Evergreen. First introduced 1834.
CULTURE : Compost, equal parts fibry peat and sphagnum moss. Position, shallow basket or on blocks of wood. Repot, March. Water three times weekly April to Aug.; once a week other times. Temp., Sept. to March 55° to 65°; March to Sept. 75° to 85°.
PROPAGATION : By division of old plants at potting time.
SPECIES CULTIVATED : B. Colleyi, purple and green, Aug., 6 to 8 in., British Guiana.

Bat Willow (*Salix cærulea*)—See Salix.

Bauhinia—Ord. Leguminosæ. Stove flowering shrubs. Evergreen. Shy bloomers of no great value. First introduced 1690.
CULTURE : Compost, equal parts peat and loam, one-sixth sand. Pot firmly in March. Position, light, sunny, moist in summer. Water freely March to Sept., moderately other times. Temp., Sept. to March 60° to 70°; March to Sept. 70° to 80°.
PROPAGATION : By cuttings inserted in well-drained pots of sandy peat under bell-glass in temp. 75° in July.
SPECIES CULTIVATED : B. Galpini, white, July, 6 ft., S. Africa ; grandiflora, white, July, 6 ft., Peru ; natalensis, white, Sept., Natal ; purpurea, red and white, 10 to 15 ft., India ; tomentosa, yellow and red, 10 to 15 ft., India ; Vahlii, white, large climber, Himalaya ; variegata, rose, red and yellow, June, 6 to 20 ft., India.

Bayonet Plant (*Aciphylla squarrosa*)—See Aciphylla.

Bay-tree (*Laurus nobilis*)—See Laurus.

Bead-tree (*Melia Azedarach*)—See Melia.

Beam Tree (*Pyrus Aria*)—See Pyrus.

Bean Tree (*Ceratonia Siliqua*)—See Ceratonia.

Beard Tongue—See Pentstemon.

Bearberry (*Arctostaphylos alpina*)—See Arctostaphylos.

Bear Grass (*Camassia esculentea*)—See Camassia.

Bear's-breech (*Acanthus mollis*)—See Acanthus.

Bear's Ear (*Primula auricula*)—See Primula.

Bear's Ear Sanicle—See Cortusa.

Bear's Foot—See Acanthus.

Bear's-foot Fern (*Davallia Tyermanni*)—See Davallia.

Bear's Paw Fern (*Polypodium meyenianum*)—See Polypodium.

Beaucarnea—See Nolina.

Beaufortia (Beaufort Myrtle)—Ord. Myrtaceæ. Greenhouse flowering shrubs. Evergreen. First introduced 1803. Natives of Australia.
CULTURE : Compost, equal parts leaf-mould, loam, and peat, one-sixth sand. Pot and prune, March ; make soil quite firm and drain pots well. Water freely May to Aug., moderately at other times. Temp., Sept. to March 45° to 50° ; March to Sept. 55° to 65°.
PROPAGATION : By cuttings of firm shoots inserted in sandy soil in temp. 55° to 65° in summer.
SPECIES CULTIVATED : B. decussata, scarlet, May, 3 ft. ; carinata, scarlet, June, 3 ft. ; purpurea, purple, July, 2 to 3 ft. ; sparsa, red, June, 2 to 3 ft.

Beaumontia (Nepaul Trumpet-flower)—Ord. Apocynaceæ. Stove climber. Nat. E. Indies. First introduced 1820.
CULTURE : Compost, equal parts peat and loam, one-sixth sand. Position, large tub or border, well drained. Shoots to climb roof. Pot or plant, March. Water

abundantly May to Aug., moderately afterwards.   Temp., Sept. to March 60° to 70° ; March to Sept. 70° to 80°.
PROPAGATION : By cuttings inserted in sandy soil in temp. 75° in March.
SPECIES CULTIVATED : B. grandiflora, white, July to Aug., 15 to 20 ft.

Bee Balm (*Monarda didyma*)—See Monarda.

Beech—See Fagus.

Beech-fern (*Polypodium Phegopteris*)—See Polypodium.

Beech Wheat (*Fagopyrum esculentea*)—See Fagopyrum.

Beef-suet Tree (*Shepherdia argentea*)—See Shepherdia.

Bee Orchis (*Ophrys apifera*)—See Ophrys.

Beet—See Beta.

Bee-tree—See Tilia.

Begonia—Ord. Begoniaceæ.   Warm greenhouse fibrous and tuberous-rooted perennials.   Ornamental-leaved and flowering.   First introduced 1777.
CULTURE OF TUBEROUS-ROOTED TYPE : Compost, equal parts loam and leaf-mould and one part of equal proportions of dried cow manure and silver sand.   Start tubers to grow in Feb. or March by placing them in leaf-mould in shallow boxes in temp. 65° to 70°.   When rooted plant in small pots and afterwards transfer to large ones.   Water moderately at first, fully afterwards.   Feed with weak liquid manure when growth is active.   Shade from sun.   After flowering gradually withhold water and keep dry till Feb.   Store in pots on their sides in temp. 50° to 55° in winter.   For outdoor culture start tubers in March, and when rooting begins transplant into boxes, grow in heat till May, then plant out early in June in rich soil in partial shade.   Lift tubers in Sept., place in boxes to ripen off, then store as advised for pot tubers.
CULTURE OF FIBROUS-ROOTED SPECIES : Compost, same as advised for tuberous-rooted species.   Sow seeds in Jan. or Feb. in temp. of 65° to 75°, or insert cuttings in pots in a similar temp. in Feb. or March.   Grow the seedlings or rooted cuttings on first in small and then larger pots in temp. 55° to 65°.   Water moderately.   Syringe daily.   Shade from sun.   Keep moist during earlier stages of growth.   In autumn keep air drier and maintain temp. of 55°.   Feed occasionally with liquid manure.   After flowering gradually withhold water, and keep rather dry till March, when begin to give water and repot to grow and make larger plants.
CULTURE OF ORNAMENTAL-LEAVED KINDS : Compost as advised in previous case.   Pot in spring.   Grow in shady position.   Water freely in spring and summer, moderately in winter.   Winter temp. 45° to 55° ; summer temp. 55° to 65°.   Feed with weak liquid manure in summer.
PROPAGATION : Ornamental-leaved kinds by leaf cuttings in spring or summer.   Winter-flowering species by cuttings as described above or by seeds.   Fibrous-rooted species by seeds or cuttings.   Tuberous-rooted type by seeds sown on surface of fine sandy compost in temp. 65° to 75° in Feb., and grow seedlings on as advised for tubers ; also by cuttings of young shoots in the spring.
TUBEROUS-ROOTED SPECIES CULTIVATED : B. boliviensis, scarlet, summer, 2 ft., Bolivia ; Clarkei, rose, summer, Peru ; Davisii, red, summer, Peru ; Pearcei, red, summer, 1 ft., Bolivia ; rosæflora, rose, summer, Peru ; Veitchii, red, summer, Peru.   The foregoing were the original parents of the present race of single and double-flowered tuberous-rooted begonias grown in gardens.   For names of varieties see trade lists.
FIBROUS-ROOTED SPECIES CULTIVATED : B. albo-coccinea, scarlet and white, winter, 18 in., India ; acutifolia, white, spring, 3 to 4 ft., Jamaica ; angularis, white, white-veined foliage, 8 ft., Brazil ; ascotiensis, white, Aug., 2 ft., hybrid ; coccinea, scarlet, April, 3 to 4 ft., Brazil ; Dregei, white, July, 1 to 3 ft., South Africa ; evansiana, pink, Sept., China ; fuchsioides, scarlet, winter, 4 to 6 ft., Mexico ; Frœbellii incomparabilis, scarlet, winter, 2 ft., Ecuador ; foliosa, white and rose, summer, semi-pendulous, Colombia ; glaucophylla, rose-pink, winter, pendulous

or climbing, Brazil ; haageana, rose-pink, autumn, 4 ft., S. Brazil ; hydrocotylifolia, rose-pink, summer, 1 ft., Mexico ; incarnata, rose, winter, 2 to 3 ft., Mexico ; incana, white, winter, 1 to 2 ft., Brazil ; manicata, pink, winter, 9 to 12 in., Mexico ; nitida, pale pink or rose, Sept., 3 to 5 ft., Jamaica ; scharffiana, white, winter, 1 to 3 ft., Brazil ; semperflorens, rose, red or white, winter, 6 to 18 in., Brazil, and its varieties of which gigantea rosea is very distinct, bearing large, sterile flowers ; socotrana, rose-pink, Nov., 1 to 1½ ft., Isle of Socotra ; weltoniensis, Dec., 18 in., hybrid ; and numerous other hybrids and varieties such as Gloire de Lorraine, etc.

ORNAMENTAL-LEAVED SPECIES CULTIVATED : B. albo-picta, greenish-white, foliage glossy green spotted silver, 1 to 1½ ft., Brazil ; argenteo-guttata, white and pink, foliage speckled with white, 2 to 4 ft., hybrid ; heracleifolia, white or rose, foliage deeply lobed, 2 to 4 ft., hybrid ; imperialis, white, foliage deep velvety green and bright green, 6 to 12 in., Mexico ; laciniata (Syn. bowringiana), white, foliage purplish-black and green, 1½ to 2 ft., India, China ; maculata, rose or white, foliage green dotted white, 2 to 4 ft., Brazil ; metallica, blush-white, foliage green with metallic lustre, 3 to 4 ft., Brazil ; olbia, white, foliage bronzy-green dotted white, 1 ft., Brazil ; Rex, pale rose, foliage metallic green marked silver and purple, 2 ft., Assam ; ricinifolia, rose-pink, foliage lobed, bronzy-green, 2 to 4 ft., hybrid ; sanguinea, white, foliage rich green above, blood-red beneath, 4 ft., Brazil.

Belamcanda (Leopard-flower)—Ord. Iridaceæ. Half-hardy bulbous plant. First introduced 1823.

OUTDOOR CULTURE : Soil, light, rich, sandy. Position, sunny, well-drained border. Plant, Sept. to Jan., placing tubers 4 in. deep and 2 in. apart. Lift and replant tubers annually. Mulch surface of bed in March with cow manure.

POT CULTURE : Compost, two parts sandy loam, one part leaf-mould or decayed cow manure. Pots, 4½ in. in diameter, well drained. Place five tubers 3 in. deep in each pot in Nov., and cover with cocoanut-fibre refuse in cold frame or under cool greenhouse stage until growth begins. Water moderately from time growth begins until flowers fade, then gradually cease, keeping dry till Jan. Temp., Sept. to March 40° to 50° ; other times 50° to 60°.

PROPAGATION : By offsets treated as advised for tubers.

SPECIES CULTIVATED : B. chinensis, orange and red, June, 2 to 4 ft., China and Japan.

Belladonna Lily (*Amaryllis belladonna*)—See Amaryllis.

Bellflower—See Campanula and Wahlenbergia.

Bell Heather (*Erica tetralix*)—See Erica.

Bellidiastrum—See Aster.

Bellis (Daisy ; Hen and Chickens Daisy)—Ord. Compositæ. Hardy herbaceous perennials. Double-flowered varieties only cultivated. Neat and pretty spring-flowering plants.

CULTURE : Soil, ordinary. Position, sunny or shady. Plant, Oct. or March.

PROPAGATION : By division of old plant in June, inserting divisions 3 in. apart in shady border ; seeds sown ¼ in. deep in boxes of light soil in cold frame in March, transplanting seedlings in open border in July.

SPECIES CULTIVATED : B. perennis flore-pleno, and its numerous varieties, native of Britain, etc. ; rotundifolia cærulescens, white, tinged blue, June, 3 in., Algeria ; sylvestris, bright red, yellow disc, June, 4 to 6 in., Mediterranean.

Belleisle Cress (*Barbarea præcox*)—See Barbarea.

Bellium (False Daisy)—Ord. Compositæ. Hardy annuals and perennials. First introduced 1772.

CULTURE : Soil, sandy loam. Position, rockery or border sheltered from north-east winds. Plant, April.

PROPAGATION : By division of plants in March ; annuals by seeds sown similar to Bellis.

SPECIES CULTIVATED : B. bellidioides, white, July, 3 in., Mediterranean Region, annual ; minutum, white, Aug., 3 in., Greece, perennial.

Bellwort—See Uvularia and Codonopsis.

Beloperone—Ord. Acanthaceæ. Stove flowering shrubs. Evergreen. Nat. New Grenada, Brazil. First introduced 1832.
CULTURE : Compost, equal parts leaf-mould, loam and sand. Pot, March, moderately firm. Position, shady, moist. Temp., Sept. to March 60° to 70° ; March to Sept. 70° to 80°. Water freely May to Sept., moderately afterwards. Remove points of shoots occasionally in summer to induce dwarf growth.
PROPAGATION : By cuttings inserted singly in small pots of light sandy soil in temp. 75° in Feb., March, or April.
SPECIES CULTIVATED : B. atropurpurea, purple, Sept., 3 ft., Brazil ; oblongata, rosy purple, 3 ft., Aug., Brazil ; violacea, violet, Aug., 3 ft., Brazil.

Benjamin Bush (*Lindera Benzoin*)—See Lindera.

Benthamia—See Cornus.

Berberidopsis (Coral-berry)—Ord. Bixaceæ. Hardy climbing shrub in S. of England ; half-hardy only in Midlands and North. Evergreen. Flowering. Nat. Chile. First introduced 1862.
CULTURE : Soil, sandy loam. Position, against south or west wall ; protect in severe winter with straw or mats. Good wall shrub for cool greenhouse. Plant, Oct. or April. Prune straggly shoots only in April.
PROPAGATION : By seeds sown ⅛ in. deep in well-drained pots of sandy soil, in temp. 55° in March ; cuttings of young shoots in similar soil and temp. ; layering of shoots in the open in Sept., Oct., or Nov.
SPECIES CULTIVATED : B. corallina, crimson, summer, 5 to 10 ft., Chile.

Berberis (Barberry ; Jaundice-berry ; Jaundice-tree)—Ord. Berberidaceæ. Hardy flowering and ornamental-leaved shrubs. Evergreen and deciduous.
CULTURE : Compost, two parts loam, one part peat and sand for choice species ; ordinary soil for common ones. Position, sunny or shady. Plant, Sept., Oct., March, April. No pruning required.
PROPAGATION : By seeds sown 1 in. deep in sheltered border in Oct. or Nov. ; cuttings of firm shoots in sandy soil in cold frame in Sept. ; layering shoots in spring. Berries of Common Barberry (Berberis vulgaris) make excellent preserves, candy, or pickle. Inner bark forms a yellow dye for tanning leather.
DECIDUOUS SPECIES CULTIVATED : B. actinacantha, deep yellow, summer, berries blue-black, 3 ft., Chile ; ætnensis, yellow, May and June, berries red, 2 ft., Sicily ; aggregata, yellow, summer, berries red, 6 ft., China ; angulosa, orange-yellow, summer, berries scarlet and edible, 4 ft., N. India ; aristata, golden-yellow, summer, berries with bluish bloom, 10 ft., Himalaya ; brevipaniculata, pale yellow, summer, berries red, 4 to 6 ft., W. China ; canadensis, bright yellow, May, berries red, 3 to 5 ft., Virginia, N. Carolina ; concinna, deep yellow, summer, berries red, 3 ft., Himalaya ; dictyophylla, pale yellow, May, berries bright red, 4 to 6 ft., Yunnan ; heterophylla, orange-yellow, April, berries black with blue bloom, 3 to 4 ft., Chile and Patagonia ; heteropoda, orange-yellow, May, berries black with blue bloom, 6 to 8 ft., Turkestan ; Lycium (sometimes nearly evergreen), yellow, May to June, berries blue-purple, 6 to 8 ft., Himalaya ; polyantha, yellow, June to July, berries red, 6 to 10 ft., W. China ; Prattii, yellow, summer, berries salmon-red, 6 to 9 ft., W. China ; rubrostilla, yellow, summer, berries coral red, 4 to 8 ft., hybrid ; sibirica, yellow, May to June, berries dark red, 1½ to 2 ft., Siberia and Mongolia ; Sieboldii, pale yellow, summer, berries yellowish-red, 2 to 3 ft., Japan ; stapfiana (sometimes partially evergreen), pale yellow, summer, berries carmine-red, 5 to 6 ft., W. China ; sinensis, pale yellow, May to June, berries red, China and Corea ; Thunbergii, yellow and red, spring, berries red, 3 to 8 ft., China and Japan ; virescens, sulphur-yellow, summer, berries red, 6 to 9 ft., Sikkim ; vulgaris, yellow, May, berries red, 6 to 10 ft., Europe (Britain) and its varieties albo-spicata, asperma, dulcis, fructu-albo, purpurea and variegata ; Wilsonæ, pale yellow, summer, berries coral-red, 2 to 4 ft., W. China ; yunnanensis, pale yellow, summer, berries red, 3 to 6 ft., W. China.
EVERGREEN SPECIES CULTIVATED : B. aquifolium (Syn. Mahonia aquifolium),

yellow, April, berries black with violet bloom, 4 to 6 ft., Western N. America; asiatica, yellow, summer, red to purple, 5 to 6 ft., Himalaya; atrocarpa, yellow, May to June, berries red to black, 5 to 6 ft., W. China; buxifolia, yellow, March, berries dark purple, 6 to 10 ft., Chile; candidula, yellow, summer, berries purple, 1½ to 2 ft., China; Darwini, orange-yellow and red, April to May, berries plum coloured, 6 to 12 ft., Chile; empetrifolia, golden yellow, May, berries purplish-black, 12 to 18 in., Chile; Fortunei, yellow, Oct. to Nov., 5 to 6 ft., China; Fremontii, yellow, May to June, berries blue, 3 to 12 ft., South-western U.S.A. (requires protection); Gagnepainii, yellow, May to June, berries black with blue bloom, 4 to 6 ft., W. China; hakeoides, golden yellow, April to May, berries bluish-black, 6 to 12 ft., Chile; Hookeri, pale yellow, April to May, berries purplish-black, 3 to 5 ft., Himalaya; ilicifolia, orange-yellow, June, 4 to 8 ft., Chile; japonica, lemon-yellow, Feb. to March, berries purple, 8 to 12 ft., China, and its variety Bealei; nepalensis, yellow, March to April, berries black with bluish-white bloom, 7 to 20 ft., Himalaya; nervosa, yellow, summer, berries purplish-blue, 12 to 15 in., Western N. America; Neuberti, holly-like leaves, 4 to 6 ft., hybrid; pinnata, yellow, spring, 12 to 16 ft., Western N. America; pruinosa, citron yellow, summer, berries black with plum coloured bloom, 8 to 12 ft., Yunnan; sargentiana, pale yellow, spring, berries black, 4 to 6 ft., W. China; stenophylla, golden yellow, April to May, berries black with bluish-white bloom, 8 to 10 ft., hybrid, and numerous seedling forms; verruculosa, golden yellow, summer, berries black with blue bloom, 2 to 4 ft., W. China; wallichiana, yellow, spring, berries black, 8 to 10 ft., China.

Berchemia (Supple Jack)—Ord. Rhamnaceæ. Hardy climbing shrubs. Deciduous. First introduced 1714.
CULTURE OF HARDY SPECIES: Soil, sandy loam Position, against south wall, well-drained border. Plant, Oct. to Feb. Prune, Feb., cutting off soft points of strong shoots and removing weak shoots altogether.
PROPAGATION: Hardy species by cuttings of shoots 6 in. long inserted half their depth and 3 in. apart in sheltered border in Oct.; greenhouse species by cuttings at any time.
SPECIES CULTIVATED: B. flavescens, white, July, climbing, 6 to 10 ft., Himalaya and China; racemosa, greenish, Sept., 6 to 8 ft., Japan; volubilis, white, July, 10 to 12 ft., United States.

Bergamot (*Monarda didyma*)—See Monarda.

Bergamot Mint (*Mentha aquatica*)—See Mentha.

Berkheya (South African Thistle)—Ord. Compositæ. Thistle-like herbs with handsome foliage. First introduced 1812.
CULTURE: Porous, gritty soil, with lime rubble. Hot sunny situation.
PROPAGATION: By seeds sown in spring. Pot seedlings in young state, and plant in permanent quarters when well rooted.
SPECIES CULTIVATED: B. Adlami, yellow or lilac, 2½ ft., Aug., Transvaal; purpurea, bluish-purple, 3 ft., Aug. to Sept., S. Africa.

Bermuda Buttercup (*Oxalis cernua*)—See Oxalis.

Bermuda Lily (*Lilium longiflorum eximium*)—See Lilium.

Bermuda Satin-flower (*Sisyrinchium bermudianum*)—See Sisyrinchium.

Bertholletia (Brazil Nut, Para Nut)—Ord. Myrtaceæ. Tropical trees. B. excelsa is the species from which the Brazil nuts of commerce are obtained, but none of the genus are of any decorative value.

Bertolonia—Ord. Melastomaceæ. Stove trailing plants. Orn. foliage. First introduced 1850. Leaves, upper sides dark green, white, purple; under sides pink, purple.
CULTURE: Compost, equal parts peat, leaf-mould, and sand. Position, well-drained pans covered with bell-glass in shade. Pot, Feb. or March. Temp., Sept. to March 60° to 70°; March to Sept. 75° to 85°. Water daily April to Sept., once or twice a week at other times.

PROPAGATION : By cuttings inserted in light soil in pots or pans under bell-glass in temp. 75° in spring.

SPECIES CULTIVATED : B. houtteana, leaves green and carmine, 6 in. ; maculata, leaves pink and purple, 6 in. ; marmorata, leaves silvery white and purple, 6 in., natives of Brazil ; pubescens, leaves light green, with chocolate band, Ecuador.

Bessera (Coral Drops)—Ord. Liliaceæ. Half-hardy bulbous plant. First introduced 1850.

CULTURE : Compost, equal parts loam, leaf-mould, peat, and coarse silver sand. Position, well-drained pots in cold greenhouse. Pot, Oct. or Nov. Water freely during active growth. Keep more or less dry after foliage dies down until new growth begins. Requires plenty of sun. May be grown in well-drained border outdoors at foot of a south wall.

PROPAGATION : By offsets removed and treated as old bulbs at potting time.

SPECIES CULTIVATED : B. elegans, scarlet, summer, 18 in. to 2 ft., Mexico.

Beta (Beet-root ; Chard ; Spinach-beet)—Ord. Chenopodiaceæ. Esculent vegetables and orn. foliage plants. First introduced 1548. Leaves, crimson, green, or white.

CULTURE OF BEET-ROOT : Sow seeds 1½ in. deep in drills 15 in. apart in May. Thin seedlings in June to 8 in. apart in row. Sandy soil manured for previous crop best. Beet must not succeed spinach or root crops ; may follow cabbage tribe, potatoes, onions, beans, or peas. Lift roots in Nov. and store in cool shed. Suitable artificial manure for beet : Superphosphate, 5 parts ; sulphate of ammonia, 2 parts ; kainit, 3 parts. Apply 2 to 3 ozs. per square yard in March. Crop takes 18 weeks from time of sowing till ready for use. Seeds retain their vitality up to 10 years old. Two ounces of seed will sow a row of 50 ft. long.

CULTURE OF SPINACH-BEET : Sow seeds 1½ in. deep in rows 18 in. apart in April. Thin seedlings in May to 9 in. apart in row. Use leaves of this only, similar to spinach. Soil and manure as for beet-root.

CULTURE OF ORNAMENTAL BEET : Sow seeds ¼ in. deep in boxes of light soil in temp. 60° to 70° in March ; transfer seedlings to cold frame in April and plant in beds in flower garden in May.

SPECIES : B. Cicla (Silver Beet), large leaves with prominent mid-ribs, and its variety variegata (scarlet and green) ; B. vulgaris, parent of edible beetroots. Natives of S. Europe.

Betel-nut Palm (*Areca Catechu*)—See Areca.

Betle Pepper (Piper Betle)—See Piper.

Betonica (Betony)—Ord. Labiatæ. Hardy perennials. Related to the genus Stachys.

CULTURE : Soil, ordinary. Position, margins of sunny borders. Plant autumn or spring.

PROPAGATION : By division of the roots in March.

SPECIES CULTIVATED : B. formosa superba, rosy-purple, May to July, 1 ft. ; grandiflora robusta, rosy-purple, May to July, 18 in. ; spicata rosea, pale pink, May to July, 1 ft., Caucasus. The genus is by some authorities referred to Stachys.

Betony (*Betonica grandiflora*)—See Betonica.

Betula (Birch-tree ; Queen of the Woods)—Ord. Betulaceæ. Hardy ornamental trees and shrubs. Deciduous. Timber used for veneering purposes ; making fish casks, and bobbins. Bark used for tanning fish nets.

CULTURE : Soil, ordinary. Position, sheltered or exposed in valleys, hills, or mountain slopes ; good seaside and town trees. Plant, Oct. to March.

PROPAGATION : By seeds sown on the surface of sandy soil on sheltered borders in March ; seeds to be simply pressed in, not covered. Transplant seedlings when one year old. Dwarf birches propagated by layering shoots in Oct.

SPECIES CULTIVATED : B. lenta (Cherry Birch), 60 to 70 ft., N. America ; nana (Dwarf Birch), 2 to 3 ft., Northern Hemisphere ; nigra, 50 to 90 ft., U.S.A. ; papyrifera (Paper Birch), 60 to 70 ft., N. America ; populifolia (Grey Birch),

20 to 30 ft., N. America ; pubescens (White Birch), 50 to 70 ft., Europe and N. Asia, and its varieties aurea and urticifolia; verrucosa (Silver Birch), Syn. B. alba, 40 to 100 ft., Europe and N. Asia, and varieties dalecarlica (Swedish Birch), fastigiata (Erect Growing Birch), pendula Youngi (Young's Weeping Birch), and purpurea (Purple Birch).

Bhotan Pine Tree (*Pinus excelsa*)—See Pinus.

Bidens (Bur Marigold)—Ord. Compositæ. Hardy annual and perennial herbs.
CULTURE: Soil, ordinary. Position, sunny border. Plant perennials, Oct. or April.
PROPAGATION: Perennials by division of old plants in April; annuals by seed sown ⅛ in. deep in sandy soil in temp. 70° in March, transplanting seedlings outdoors in May.
SPECIES CULTIVATED : B. grandiflora, yellow, July, 3 ft., Mexico, annual ; humilis, yellow, July, 2 ft., Mexico, perennial.

Bigelowia (Rayless Golden Rod)—Ord. Compositæ. Evergreen subshrubby plant for sheltered recesses and warm sunny walls.
CULTURE : Well-drained soil, warmest position available (not hardy in exposed situations). Transplant from pots in spring, fasten growths to wall, spreading well.
PROPAGATION: By cuttings, young growth, in gentle bottom heat; pot singly, and harden off. Plunge in open for first summer, return to cool house for first winter, and plant out following spring.
SPECIES CULTIVATED : B. graveolens, yellow, Aug. to Sept., 6 to 8 ft., Western N. America.

Bignonia (Cross Vine ; Trumpet-flower)—Ord. Bignoniaceæ. Greenhouse and hardy climbing plants. Deciduous. First introduced 1710.
CULTURE : Compost, two parts loam, one part peat and silver sand. Pot, Feb. or March. Position, light sunny for greenhouse species ; south wall for hardy kind. Bed or border must not be more than 3 ft. square for one plant and 18 in. deep. Provide good drainage and make soil firm. Prune away one-third of strong shoots and two-thirds of weak shoots in Feb. Water freely April to Sept., very little at other times. Shade must not be given to greenhouse kinds. Temp. for greenhouse species, 45° to 55° Oct. to March ; 55° to 65° March to Oct.
PROPAGATION : By cuttings of young shoots 3 in. long, inserted in well-drained pots of sandy soil in temp. 65° to 70° in April.
HARDY SPECIES CULTIVATED : B. capreolata (Cross Vine), scarlet, summer, 12 to 15 ft., United States ; capreolata atrosanguinea, red and purple.
GREENHOUSE SPECIES CULTIVATED : B. speciosa, lavender, spring, 15 to 20 ft., S. Brazil, Argentina ; tweediana, yellow, summer, 15 to 20 ft., Buenos Aires; venusta, orange, autumn, 20 to 50 ft., S. America. See also Tecoma.

Bilberry (*Vaccinium myrtillus*)—See Vaccinium.

Billardiera (Blue Apple Berry)—Ord. Pittosporaceæ. Half-hardy evergreen climber. First introduced in 1810.
CULTURE : Soil, good ordinary, well-drained. Position, south or south-west wall in mild districts only. Plant, April. Prune away all weak or dead shoots in April.
PROPAGATION : By cuttings inserted in sandy soil in a temperature of 55° ; also by seeds sown in above temperature.
SPECIES CULTIVATED : B. longiflora, creamy-white to purple, summer, 10 to 15 ft., Tasmania. Succeeded by blue edible berries.

Billbergia—Ord. Bromeliaceæ. Stove flowering plants. Evergreen. First introduced 1826. Flowering season, spring.
CULTURE : Compost, equal parts fibrous loam, rough peat, leaf-mould and silver sand. Pot, March. Water freely always. Good drainage essential. Temp., Sept. to March 65° to 75° ; March to Sept. 70° to 80°.
PROPAGATION : By large-sized offshoots inserted singly in small pots of sandy peat in temp. 85° in April.

Begonia tuberosa hybrida

Bellis perennis flore pleno
(Daisy)

Berberis aquifolium
(Barberry)

Berberis nepalensis
(Barberry)

Berberis rubrostilla
(Barberry)

Berberis vulgaris
(Barberry)

Betula verrucosa
(Silver Birch)

Bocconia cordata
(Plume Poppy)

Boltonia asteroides
(False Chamomile)

Bougainvillea glabra

Bougainvillea glabra variegata

Bouvardia hybrida

Brachycome iberidifolia
(Swan River Daisy)

Brasso-Cattleya

Bruckenthalia spiculifolia

Buddleia alternifolia

Buddleia globosa
(Orange-ball-tree)

Buddleia variabilis

SPECIES CULTIVATED: B. iridifolia, scarlet, yellow, and crimson, 18 in., Brazil; liboniana, red, green and blue, 1 to 2 ft., Brazil; Lietzei, rosy-pink, 1 ft., Brazil; Moreli, blue, pink, and rose, 1 ft., Brazil; nutans, yellowish-green with blue margins, 1½ ft., Brazil; pallescens (Syn. B. Bakeri), green and violet, 18 in., Brazil; vittata, red and violet, 18 in. to 2 ft., Brazil; zebrina, 1 ft., Brazil.

Bindweed—See Calystegia.

Biota—See Thuya.

Birch—See Betula.

Bird Cherry (*Prunus padus*)—See Prunus.

Bird of Paradise Flower (*Strelitzia Reginæ*)—See Strelitzia.

Bird's Eye Maple (*Acer saccharinum*)—See Acer.

Bird's Eye Primrose (*Primula farinosa*)—See Primula.

Bird's-foot Stonecrop (*Sedum pulchellum*)—See Sedum.

Bird's-foot Trefoil (*Lotus corniculatus*)—See Lotus.

Bird's-foot Violet (*Viola pedata*)—See Viola.

Bird's-nest Fern (*Asplenium Nidus*)—See Asplenium.

Bird's Tongue Flower—See Strelitzia.

Birth-wort (*Aristolochia Sipho*)—See Aristolochia.

Bishop's Cap (*Mitella diphylla*)—See Mitella.

Bishop's Hat (*Epimedium alpinum*)—See Epimedium.

Bitter Almond Tree (*Prunus Amygdalus amara*)—See Prunus.

Bitter Nut (*Carya amara*)—See Carya.

Bitter Root (*Lewisia rediviva*)—See Lewisia.

Bitter Vetch (*Lathyrus vernus*)—See Lathyrus.

Bitter-wort—See Gentiana and Lewisia.

Bixa (Annatto, Arnotto)—Ord. Bixaceæ. Stove flowering tree. Evergreen. Nat. W. Indies.   First introduced 1690.
CULTURE : Compost, two parts loam, one part peat and silver sand.   Pot, March. Water freely March to Sept., moderately other times.   Temp., Sept. to March 60° to 70° ; March to Sept. 75° to 85°.
PROPAGATION : By cuttings of shoots six to twelve months old, inserted in small pots of sandy soil in temp. 85°, June to Aug.
SPECIES CULTIVATED : B. orellana, pink, summer, West Indies.

Blackberry—See Rubus.

Black Dahlia (*Dahlia Zimipani*)—See Dahlia.

Black-eyed Susan (*Thunbergia alata* or *Rudbeckia hirta*)—See Thunbergia and Rudbeckia.

Black Hellebore (*Helleborus niger*)—See Helleborus.

Blacking Plant (*Hibiscus rosa-sinensis*)—See Hibiscus.

Black Iris (*Ferraria undulata*)—See Ferraria.

Black Maidenhair Fern (*Adiantum capillus-veneris*)—See Adiantum.

Black Maple (*Acer saccharinum nigrum*)—See Acer.

Black Pepper (*Piper nigrum*)—See Piper.

Black Pine (*Pinus laricio nigricans*)—See Pinus.

Black Poplar (*Populus nigra*)—See Populus.

Black Spleenwort (*Asplenium adiantum-nigrum*)—See Asplenium.

Black Spruce (*Picea nigra*)—See Picea.

Black Thorn (*Prunus spinosa*)—See Prunus.

Blackwood Acacia (*Acacia melanoxylon*)—See Acacia.

Bladder Fern (*Cystopteris fragilis*)—See Cystopteris.

Bladder Herb (*Physalis Alkekengi*)—See Physalis.

Bladder Nut (*Staphylea pinnata*)—See Staphylea.

Bladder Senna (*Colutea arborescens*)—See Colutea.

Bladder Wort—See Utricularia.

Blaeberry (*Vaccinium Myrtillus*)—See Vaccinium.

Blandfordia (Christmas Bells)—Ord. Liliaceæ. Greenhouse fleshy rooted plants. Flowering. Evergreen. First introduced 1803.
CULTURE: Compost, equal parts peat, loam and silver or river sand. Pot, Oct. Good drainage, firm potting and moderate size pots essential. Water freely May to Aug., moderately Aug. to Oct. and Feb. to May, none at other times. Temp., Oct. to Feb. 40° to 50°; Feb. to April 50° to 55°; April to Oct. 55° to 65°.
PROPAGATION: By offsets or divisions of old plants at potting time.
SPECIES CULTIVATED: B. grandiflora (Syn. Cunninghamii), crimson, July, 2 ft., Australia; flammea, yellow, June, 18 in., Australia; marginata, crimson, summer, 2 ft., Australia; nobilis, orange, July, 2 ft., Australia.

Blanket Flower (*Gaillardia aristata*)—See Gaillardia.

Blazing Star—See Liatris.

Blechnum (Brazilian Tree Fern)—Ord. Filices. Stove and greenhouse ferns. Evergreen. First introduced 1691.
CULTURE: Compost, equal parts loam, peat, leaf-mould, and sand. Pot, Feb. or March. Position, shady. Water abundantly April to Sept., moderately afterwards. Temp., stove species, Sept. to March 60° to 70°, March to Sept. 70° to 80°; greenhouse, Sept. to March 50° to 55°, March to Sept. 55° to 65°.
PROPAGATION: By spores sown on fine sandy peat, in temp. 80°, at any time.
STOVE SPECIES CULTIVATED: B. longifolium, 1 to 2 ft., West Indies; occidentale, 1 to 2 ft., West Indies; unilaterale, 6 to 12 in., Trop. America.
GREENHOUSE SPECIES CULTIVATED: B. braziliense, 2 to 3 ft., Brazil and Peru; braziliense corcovadense; cartilagineum, 1 to 2 ft., Australia; hastatum, 1 to 2 ft., S. America; Lanceola, 6 to 12 in., Trop. America. See also Lomarea.

Bleeding Heart (*Dicentra spectabilis*)—See Dicentra.

Bleeding Nun (*Cyclamen europæum*)—See Cyclamen.

Blessed Thistle—See Carbenia and Silybum.

Bletia—Ord. Orchidaceæ. Stove, hardy, terrestrial, and epiphytal orchids. Deciduous. First introduced 1733.
CULTURE OF STOVE SPECIES: Compost, equal parts loam and leaf-mould. Pot, March. Position, pots with 2 in. of drainage in each. Water freely March to Aug., moderately Aug. to Oct., very little afterwards. Temp., March to Sept. 65° to 75°; Sept. to March 60° to 65°. Resting period, winter. Flowers appear at base of new pseudo-bulb.
CULTURE OF HARDY SPECIES: Compost, equal parts leaf-mould, loam, and sand. Position, sunny, sheltered rockery in S. of England only; in other parts in cool greenhouse (winter temp. 40° to 50°). Plant or pot, March. Water freely whilst growing. Keep dry when at rest.
PROPAGATION: By division of pseudo-bulbs after flowering.
STOVE SPECIES CULTIVATED: B. Shepherdii, red-purple and yellow, winter, 3 ft., Jamaica; verecunda, purple, March, West Indies.
HARDY SPECIES CULTIVATED: B. hyacinthina, rosy crimson, April, 1 ft., Japan.

Blighia (Akee)—Ord. Sapindaceæ. Tender tree cultivated in tropics for its edible fruits. First introduced 1793.
CULTURE : Soil, sandy loam and peat. Position, borders in warm greenhouse. Temp. March to Sept. 75° to 90° ; Sept. to March 65° to 75°.
PROPAGATION : By cuttings of half-ripened shoots rooted in sandy soil under hand-glass in temp. 75° to 85°.
SPECIES CULTIVATED : B. sapida, straw or magenta coloured fruits, 3 in. long, 30 to 40 ft., Guinea.

Blood Berry (*Rivina humilis*)—See Rivina.

Blood Elder (*Sambucus ebulus*)—See Sambucus.

Blood Flower (*Hæmanthus coccineus*)—See Hæmanthus.

Blood Root (*Sanguinaria canadensis*)—See Sanguinaria.

Bloomeria—Ord. Liliaceæ. Half-hardy bulbous plant. First introduced 1869.
CULTURE : Soil, light, sandy. Position, warm border or rockery. Plant bulbs 2 to 3 in. deep, and 3 in. apart, Sept. to Nov.
PROPAGATION : By offsets planted as directed for bulbs.
SPECIES CULTIVATED : B. aurea (Syn. Nothoscordum aureum), yellow, July, 1 ft. Clevelandii, yellow, July, 1 ft. Natives of California.

Blooming Sally (*Epilobium angustifolium*)—See Epilobium.

Blue African Lily (*Agapanthus umbellatus*)—See Agapanthus.

Blue Alpine Daisy (*Aster alpinus*)—See Aster.

Blue Amaryllis (*Griffinia hyacinthina*)—See Griffinia.

Blue Apple Berry (*Billardiera longiflora*)—See Billardiera.

Blue Beard (*Caryopteris mastacanthus*)—See Caryopteris.

Blue Bell (*Scilla nonscripta* and *Campanula rotundifolia*)—See Scilla and Campanula.

Blueberry (*Vaccinium corymbosum* and *V. pennsylvanicum*)—See Vaccinium.

Blue Cedar (*Cedrus atlantica glauca*)—See Cedrus.

Blue Cowslip (*Pulmonaria angustifolia*)—See Pulmonaria.

Blue Cupidone (*Catananche cærulea*)—See Catananche.

Blue-eyed Peacock Iris (*Iris pavonia*)—See Iris.

Blue-flowered Red-root (*Ceanothus azureus*)—See Ceanothus.

Blue Grass—See Carex.

Blue Gum-tree (*Eucalyptus globulus*)—See Eucalpytus.

Blue Lace Flower—See Trachymene.

Blue-leaved Wattle (*Acacia cyanophylla*)—See Acacia.

Blue Lotus of Egypt (*Nymphæa cærulea*)—See Nymphæa.

Blue Marguerite (*Agathæa cælestis*)—See Agathæa.

Blue Moonwort (*Soldanella alpina*)—See Soldanella.

Blue Rock Bindweed (*Convolvulus mauritanicus*)—See Convolvulus.

Blue Spider-wort (*Commelina cælestis*)—See Commelina.

Blue Spruce (*Picea pungens*)—See Picea.

Blue Throat-wort (*Trachelium cæruleum*)—See Trachelium.

Blue Willow (*Salix cærulea*)—See Salix.

Bluets (*Houstonia cærulea*)—See Houstonia.

Blumenbachia—Ord. Loasaceæ. Half-hardy annual, biennial and perennial twiners and trailers. First introduced 1826.
CULTURE : Soil, ordinary. Position, south bed, border, or wall. Plant perennials in April.

PROPAGATION : Annuals by seeds sown $\frac{1}{16}$ in. deep in shallow boxes of light soil in temp. 65° March, transplanting seedlings outdoors in June ; perennials by seed as advised for annuals, or division of roots in April.
SPECIES CULTIVATED : B. coronata, white, $1\frac{1}{2}$ ft., June, Chile, biennial ; insignis, white, July, trailing annual, Monte Video ;lateritia (Syn. Loasa lateritia), red, May, perennial, Tucuman ; multifida, red, July, annual, Buenos Aires.

Blush Wort—See Æschynanthus and Erythræa.

Bobartia (Bobart's Iris)—Ord. Iridaceæ. Half-hardy bulbous plants. Nat. Cape of Good Hope. First introduced 1810. Ht., 1 ft.
CULTURE : Position, south bed or border well drained, or on rockery. Plant bulbs 3 in. deep and 3 in. apart in Oct. Lift bulbs after flowering, dry and store away till planting time in cool place.
PROPAGATION : By offsets planted and treated as large bulbs.
SPECIES CULTIVATED : B. aphylla, white and purple, summer ; filiformis, purple, summer ; gladiata, yellow, summer ; spathacea, yellow, summer.

Bocconia (Plume Poppy ; Tree Celandine)—Ord. Papaveraceæ. Hardy herbaceous perennials. Orn. foliage. First introduced 1795.
CULTURE : Soil, rich loamy, well manured. Position, open, sunny, sheltered from cold winds. Plant, April. Cut down flower stems after blooming. Good plant for pot culture in cool greenhouse or window. Compost, two parts loam, one part leaf-mould and sand. Pot, March. Water freely spring and summer, moderately other times.
PROPAGATION : By cuttings of young shoots growing out of axils of leaves, inserted in small pots of sandy soil, temp. 55° under bell-glass, June to Aug. ; by suckers removed from root, placed in pots in cold frame in July.
SPECIES CULTIVATED : B. cordata, buff or whitish, July, 6 to 8 ft., China ; microcarpa, yellowish buff, June, 6 to 7 ft., N. China. The genus Bocconia is referred by some authorities to Macleaya.

Bog Arum (*Calla palustris*)—See Calla.

Bog Asphodel—See Narthecium.

Bog Bean (*Menyanthes trifoliata*)—See Menyanthes.

Bog Berry (*Vaccinium oxycoccus*)—See Vaccinium.

Bog Myrtle (*Myrica Gale*)—See Myrica.

Bog Pimpernel (*Anagallis tenella*)—See Anagallis.

Bog Trefoil (*Menyanthes trifoliata*)—See Menyanthes.

Bog Violet (*Pinguicula vulgaris*)—See Pinguicula.

Bollea.—See Zygopetalum.

Boltonia (False Chamomile)—Ord. Compositæ. Hardy herbaceous perennials. Nat. N. America. First introduced 1758.
CULTURE : Soil, ordinary moist loam. Position, sunny or shady borders. Plant, Oct. or April.
PROPAGATION : By division of roots in April.
SPECIES CULTIVATED : B. asteroides, white, July, 4 to 5 ft., N. America ; asteroides decurrens, blush pink, 4 ft. ; latisquama, blue-violet, 2 to 8 ft., N. America.

Bolton's Star-wort (*Boltonia asteroides*)—See Boltonia.

Bomarea—Ord. Amaryllidaceæ. Greenhouse climbing perennials. Flowering. First introduced 1806.
CULTURE : Compost, equal parts peat, leaf-mould, loam, and sand. Pot or plant, March. Position, large pots, tubs, or beds, well drained. Water freely April to Sept., moderately other times. Temp., Sept. to March 45° to 50° ; March to Sept. 55° to 65°.
PROPAGATION : By seeds sown $\frac{1}{4}$ in. deep in pots of light sandy soil in temp. 65° in March ; division of roots in March.

SPECIES CULTIVATED : B. acutifolia, red, yellow, and green, autumn, 5 to 6 ft., Mexico ; Carderi, rose, autumn, 6 to 8 ft., Colombia ; edulis, crimson, July, 5 to 6 ft., Trop. America ; patacocensis (Syn. B. conferta), carmine-rose, Aug. 6 to 8 ft., Colombia.

Bona-Nox (*Ipomæa Bona-nox*)—See Ipomæa.

Bonapartea Lystrix.—See Agave stricta.

Bonavist (*Dolichos Lablab*)—See Dolichos.

Bongardia—Ord. Berberidaceæ. Hardy tuberous-rooted perennial. **Flowering.** Nat. Persia, Syria. First introduced 1740.
CULTURE : Soil, light, sandy. Position, south bed or border, well drained. **Plant,** Oct. or April. Protect in severe weather by covering with handlight or litter.
PROPAGATION : By division of tubers Oct. or April, or by seeds sown in shallow boxes of light soil, temp. 55° to 65°, in March.
SPECIES CULTIVATED : B. Rauwolfii, yellow, spring, 6 to 12 in.

Borage—See Borago.

Borago (Borage)—Ord. Boraginaceæ. Hardy annual and perennial plants. Common species (B. officinalis) used for flavouring claret-cup and as a bee food.
CULTURE : Soil, ordinary. Position, sunny rockeries, dry banks. Sow seeds of common borage annually in March where required to grow, afterwards thinning seedlings to 8 in. apart.
PROPAGATION : Annuals by seed sown as above ; perennials by division of roots in April.
SPECIES CULTIVATED : B. laxiflora, blue, Aug., 1 ft., Corsica, perennial ; officinalis (Common Borage), blue, summer, 1 to 2 ft., Britain, annual.

Borecole—See Brassica.

Boronia (Australian Native Rose)—Ord. Rutaceæ. Greenhouse flowering shrubs. Evergreen. Nat. W. Australia. First introduced 1794. Flowers fragrant.
CULTURE : Compost, two parts fibrous peat, one part silver sand and pounded charcoal. Pot directly after flowering. Drain the pots well and make compost quite firm. Cut off points of young shoots when 3 in. long to promote bushy growth. Water freely April to Sept., moderately afterwards. Place plants in semi-shady position outdoors June to Aug. Temp., Sept. to March 45° to 50° ; March to Sept. 50° to 60°.
PROPAGATION : By cuttings of firm young shoots inserted in sandy soil, in temp. 55° June to Aug., under bell-glass.
SPECIES CULTIVATED : B. elatior, rosy carmine, May, 3 to 4 ft. ; heterophylla, rose, May, 2 to 3 ft. ; megastigma, maroon and yellow, April, 18 in. ; serrulata, rose, June, 2 to 3 ft.

Boss Fern (*Nephrodium molle*)—See Nephrodium.

Boston Ivy (*Vitis inconstans*)—Known as Ampelopsis Veitchii. See Vitis.

Botrychium (Moon Fern ; Moon Wort)—Ord. Filices. Hardy and half-hardy ferns. Deciduous.
CULTURE : Compost, equal parts sandy loam and peat. Position, moist, shady, rockery, or in grass. Half-hardy species in cool greenhouse. Plant, April. Water freely in dry weather during summer.
PROPAGATION : By division of roots in April.
SPECIES CULTIVATED : B. Lunaria (Common Moonwort), 4 to 5 in., Britain ; ternatum, 6 to 12 in., New Zealand, not hardy in Britain ; virginianum, 16 to 18 in., North Temperate Zone.

Bottle-brush Tree (*Callistemon speciosus*)—See Callistemon.

Bottle Gourd (*Lagenaria vulgaris*)—See Lagenaria.

Bougainvillea — Ord. Nyctaginaceæ. Stove climbing plants. **Flowering.** Deciduous. First introduced 1829. Coloured bracts chief floral attraction.

CULTURE : Compost, two-thirds turfy loam, one-third leaf-mould and sand. Pot or plant, Feb. Position : B. glabra in pots with shoots trained round wire trellis ; B. speciosa in bed 3 ft. wide and 18 in. deep, branches and shoots being trained up roof. Prune shoots of previous year's growth to within 1 in. of base annually in Feb. Water abundantly March to Sept., moderately Sept. to Nov., none afterwards. Temp., Feb. to May 55° to 60° ; May to Sept. 65° to 75° ; Sept. to Feb. 50° to 55°.

PROPAGATION : By cuttings of young shoots 3 in. long, removed with small portion of branch attached, inserted in 2 in. pots of sandy soil, under bell-glass in temp. 70° to 80°, March, April, or May.

SPECIES CULTIVATED : B. glabra, rose, summer, 5 to 8 ft., Brazil ; glabra sanderiana, rich rose ; spectabilis (Syn. B. speciosa), lilac-rose, summer, 15 ft., Brazil ; spectabilis superba, deep rose.

Bouncing Bet (*Saponaria officinalis flore pleno*)—See Saponaria.

Bourbon Lily (*Lilium candidum*)—See Lilium.

Bourbon Palm (*Livistona sinensis*)—See Livistona.

Bourbon Rose (*Rosa bourboniana*)—See Rosa.

Boursault Rose (*Rosa alpina*)—See Rosa.

Boussingaultia (Madeira Vine)—Ord. Chenopodiaceæ. Half-hardy tuberous-rooted climber. First introduced 1835. Flowers fragrant.

CULTURE : Soil, light, sandy. Position, back wall of greenhouse or south wall or fence outdoors during summer. Plant tubers in small pots in temp. 55° in March, for transplanting outdoors in June, or in bed in Feb. for greenhouse culture. Lift outdoor tubers in Oct. and store in sand during winter ; those in greenhouse bed leave undisturbed. Water freely in summer, none in winter.

PROPAGATION : By inserting tubercles removed from the stems in sandy soil in temp. 55° in spring or autumn.

SPECIES CULTIVATED : B. baselloides, white, autumn, 6 to 8 ft., Ecuador.

Bouvardia—Ord. Rubiaceæ. Greenhouse flowering shrubs. Evergreen. Flowers, fragrant. First introduced 1794.

CULTURE : Compost, equal parts fibrous loam, leaf-mould, peat, and silver sand. Pot, March. Prune, Feb., shortening shoots of previous year's growth to within 1 in. of their base. Water moderately Feb. to May and Aug. to Nov., freely May to Aug., little Nov. to Feb. Temp., Feb. to Sept. 55° to 75° ; Sept. to Feb. 55° to 60°. Place plants in cold frame from June to Sept.

PROPAGATION : By cuttings of young shoots 2 in. long, inserted in pots of sandy compost in March in temp. 65° ; cuttings of roots inserted in similar soil in spring ; division at potting time.

SPECIES CULTIVATED : B. angustifolia, red, Sept., 2 ft., Mexico ; flava, yellow, March, 18 in., Mexico; Humboldtii, white, winter, 2 to 3 ft.; Humboldtii corymbiflora, white ; jasminiflora, white, winter, 2 ft., S. America ; triphylla, scarlet, winter, 2 ft., Mexico ; and numerous hybrids as, Alfred Neuner, pink ; Hogarth flore-pleno, scarlet ; President Garfield, double pink ; and Vrielandii, white.

Bowman's Root (*Gillenia trifoliata*)—See Gillenia.

Bow-string Hemp—See Sanseviera.

Box Elder (*Acer Negundo*)—See Acer.

Box Holly (*Ruscus aculeatus*)—See Ruscus.

Box Thorn (*Lycium barbarum*)—See Lycium.

Box-tree (*Buxus sempervirens*)—See Buxus.

Boy's Love (*Artemisia abrotanum*)—See Artemisia.

Brachycome (Swan River Daisy)—Ord. Compositæ. Half-hardy annual. Flowering. Nat. W. Australia. First introduced 1843.

CULTURE : Soil, ordinary. Position, sunny bed or border.

58

PROPAGATION: By seeds sown ¼ in. deep in shallow boxes of light soil in temp. 55° in March, transplanting seedlings outdoors in May; or outdoors in April where plants are to flower.
SPECIES CULTIVATED: B. iberidifolia, blue or white, summer, 1 ft.

Brachypodium (False Brome Grass)—Ord. Gramineæ. Hardy annual flowering grass. Inflorescence, suitable for drying for winter decorations.
CULTURE: Soil, ordinary. Position, sunny borders. Sow seeds outdoors in April. Cut inflorescence when in full flower.
SPECIES CULTIVATED: B. distachyon, summer, 9 in., Europe.

Brachysema—Ord. Leguminosæ. Greenhouse climbing plants. Flowering. Evergreen. Nat. Australia. First introduced 1803.
CULTURE: Compost, equal parts loam, peat, leaf-mould, and silver sand. Pot, Feb. Position, well-drained pots or tubs, or beds 3 ft. wide and 18 in. deep; shoots to be trained round wire trellis or up the roof and fully exposed to sun. Water freely April to Aug., moderately other times. Temp., Sept. to March 45° to 50°; March to Sept. 55° to 65°.
PROPAGATION: By seeds sown 1/16 in. deep in sandy soil in temp. 55° in March; cuttings of shoots inserted in similar soil and temp. under bell-glass in June, July, or Aug.; layering shoots in Sept.
SPECIES CULTIVATED: B. latifolium, crimson and scarlet, April, 8 to 10 ft.; lanceolatum, scarlet, yellow and white, spring, 3 ft.; undulatum, violet, March, 3 to 6ft.

Bracken (*Pteris aquilina*)—See Pteris.

Brahea—Ord. Palmaceæ. Greenhouse palm. Orn. foliage. First introduced 1865.
CULTURE: Compost, equal parts peat, loam, and sand. Pot, Feb. Water freely in summer, moderately other times. Temp., Sept. to March 55° to 60°; March to Sept. 65° to 75°.
PROPAGATION: By seeds sown ½ in. deep in light soil in temp. 85° in March.
SPECIES CULTIVATED: B. dulcis, 3 ft., Mexico. See also Washingtonia.

Brake Fern (*Pteris aquilina*)—See Pteris.

Bramble (*Rubus fruticosus*)—See Rubus.

Bramble-leaved Rose (*Rosa rubrifolia*)—See Rosa.

Bramble Rose (*Rosa multiflora flore pleno*)—See Rosa.

Brasenia (Water Shield)—Ord. Nymphæaceæ. Hardy aquatic for pond or aquarium. First introduced 1798.
CULTURE: Soil, ordinary. Position, shallow ponds or lakes, 1 to 1½ ft. deep, or aquarium. Plant in pots or baskets sinking these in the water during April or May.
PROPAGATION: By offsets in May.
SPECIES CULTIVATED: B. Schreberi (Syn. peltata), purple, summer, N. America.

Brassavola—Ord. Orchidaceæ. Stove, epiphytal orchid. First introduced 1844. Flowers, fragrant.
CULTURE: Compost, sphagnum moss. Position, blocks of wood, suspended from roof. Water abundantly March to Sept., moderately other times. Temp., Oct. to Feb. 50° to 55°; Feb. to Oct. 60° to 70°. Resting period, winter. Flowers top of new growth after resting.
PROPAGATION: By division of plant at potting time.
SPECIES CULTIVATED: B. digbyana, creamy-white and purple, winter, 9 in., Honduras. This species has been much used in hybridisation with cattleyas and lælias giving rise to the races known as Brasso-cattleya and Brassocatlælia.

Brassia—Ord. Orchidaceæ. Stove epiphytal orchids. Evergreen. First introduced 1806.
CULTURE: Compost, rough fibrous peat and charcoal. Pot, Feb. Position, well. drained pots in partial shade. Water freely April to Aug., moderately other times

Temp., Oct. to Feb. 50° to 60° ; Feb. to Oct. 65° to 85°.   Resting period, none.
Flowers appear at base of last growth when completed.
PROPAGATION : By division of plants at potting time.
SPECIES CULTIVATED : B. antherotes, yellow, May and June, Colombia ; brachiata,
yellow, white and orange, July to Sept., Guatemala ; gireoudiana, yellow and red,
Aug., Costa Rica ; lanceana, yellow, brown and red, Jan. to Sept., Surinam ;
lawrenciana, yellow, cinnamon and green, spring, Brazil ; maculata, yellow, red
and brown, May, Trop. America ; verrucosa, white and purple, May and June,
Guatemala.

    Brassica (Borecole ; Broccoli ; Brussels Sprouts ; Cabbage ; Cauliflower ;
Colewort ; Couve Tronchuda ; Kale ; Kohl Rabi ; Mustard ; Rape ; Savoy ;
Turnip)—Ord. Cruciferæ. Hardy biennials with esculent roots or foliage. Nat.
Europe (Britain). Flowers, yellow ; May to Aug.
CULTURE OF BORECOLE OR KALE : Sow seeds ½ in. deep in drills 6 in. apart in April
or May. Transplant seedlings when third leaf forms 4 in. apart in nursery bed.
Plant out permanently **18 in. apart in rows 2 ft. asunder in June or July. Season**
of use, Nov. to April.
CULTURE OF BROCCOLI : For autumn use sow seeds ½ in. deep in shallow boxes of
light soil in temp. 65° in Feb. ; transplant seedlings 3 in. apart in cold frame, light
soil, in April or May ; plant out 2 ft. apart in rows 2 ft. asunder in June. For
winter use sow seeds ½ in. deep in drills 6 in. apart in open garden in April ; transplant seedlings 6 in. apart each way in June ; plant permanently 2 ft. apart all ways
in July. For spring use sow seeds end of April as for winter kinds ; plant out in
July. For summer use sow seeds end of May ; plant out in Aug.
CULTURE OF BRUSSELS SPROUTS : For early crop sow and treat as early broccoli.
Plant May, rows 3 ft., in rows 2 ft. apart. Sow for later batch outdoors early
in April. Transplant seedlings as advised for Broccoli, and plant out permanently
June or July. Season of use, Nov. to April. Cut, not break, off sprouts when
gathering. Do not remove heads till sprouts are finished.
CULTURE OF CABBAGE AND COLEWORT : For summer use sow and treat as early
broccoli ; plant out 12 in. apart in rows 18 in. asunder in April. For autumn use
sow seeds ½ in. deep in drills 6 in. apart in open position in March ; transplant
seedlings 6 in. apart in May ; plant out in June. For spring use sow in open garden
middle of July ; transplant seedlings 6 in. apart in Aug. ; plant out in Sept. Sow
Colewort in July and plant out 12 in. apart each way in Sept.
CULTURE OF CAULIFLOWER : For summer use sow seeds as advised for early broccoli.
For autumn use sow seeds in April in open ground ; transplant seedlings 6 in. apart in
May, and plant out 18 in. apart in rows 2 ft. asunder in June. For spring use sow,
as in last case, outdoors in Aug. ; transplant seedlings in cold frame for the winter,
and plant out in April. When hearts begin to form snap leaf over them to protect
tender flowers from sun and frost.
CULTURE OF KOHL-RABI : Sow seeds thinly outdoors in March. Thin seedlings
to 3 in. apart in May, and plant out permanently 2 ft. apart in rows 3 ft. asunder in
June. Gather swollen stems for use when the size of a turnip.
CULTURE OF SAVOY : Sow seeds outdoors in March for early crop and at the end of
April for maincrop. Treat seedlings as advised for cabbage. Plant dwarf varieties
12 in. apart in rows 15 in. asunder ; tall kinds 18 in. apart in rows 2 ft. asunder.
Gather for use after autumn frost.
CULTURE OF TURNIP : Sow seeds in Feb., March, April, May, June, and July to
furnish a continuous supply. Make drills ½ in. deep and 1 ft. apart. Dust seedlings
occasionally with lime or soot to keep off Turnip Flea. Thin when rough leaf
forms to 6 in. apart. Turnips may be easily forced on hotbed in Feb. or March.
Sow seeds broadcast and lightly cover with fine soil. Keep moist. Turnips ready
to gather eight weeks after sowing. Swede turnips should be sown in May, thinned
early, and brought to maturity for winter use.
CULTURE OF MUSTARD : Soil, ordinary. Position, open borders. Sow seeds on
surface of soil, water, and cover with mats or boards till they germinate ; or in
drills ½ in. deep, and 6 in. apart. Make first sowing end of March, follow with

successional sowings every five days until Sept., then cease.   Gather for salading
when 1 in. high.   Two crops sufficient off one piece of ground.
INDOOR CULTURE : Sow seed on surface of light soil in shallow boxes, moisten with
tepid water, cover with sheet of paper, slate or board, and place in warm position
in greenhouse or room.   Sow for succession every three days.   Two crops may be
grown in same soil.   Seeds may be sown on flannel kept moist in a warm room, at
any time of year.
CULTURE OF COUVE TRONCHUDA : Soil, ordinary, rich.   Position, sunny.   Sow
seeds thinly outdoors in April.   Transplant seedlings when 3 in. high, 6 in. apart
in a nursery bed.   Plant out finally 3 ft apart each way in June.   Gather outer leaves
first for their midribs, and hearts last of all.
SPECIES : B. alba (Syn. Sinapis alba), Mustard ; campestris napobrassica (Swede) ;
campestris napus (Rape) ; campestris Rapa (Turnip) ; oleracea (Cabbage) ; oleracea
acephala (Borecole or Kale) ; oleracea asparagoides (Broccoli) ; oleracea botrytis
(Cauliflower) ; oleracea bullata (Savoy) ; oleracea gemmifera (Brussels Sprouts) ;
oleracea rubra (Pickling Cabbage).

Brasso-Cattleya—A new race of orchids, the result of crossing species of
Brassavola with those of Cattleya.   Scientifically known as bi-generic hybrids.
Require similar culture and temperature to the Cattleyas, which see.

Brasso-Lælia—A new race of bi-generic hybrid orchids, the result of crossing
species of Brassavola with those of Lælia.   Culture and temperature as for Lælias,
which see.

Bravoa (Scarlet Twin-flower)—Ord. Amaryllidaceæ.   Half-hardy bulbous
plant.   Deciduous.   Nat. Mexico.   First introduced 1841.
OUTDOOR CULTURE : Soil, light, sandy.   Position, well-drained sunny border.
Plant bulbs 4 in. deep in Sept.   Protect in winter with a covering of cinder ashes.
GREENHOUSE CULTURE : Put four bulbs in a 5 in. pot, well drained, in Oct.   Cover
with ashes in cold frame until Jan., then remove to greenhouse.   Water moderately
until foliage turns yellow, then keep soil dry.
PROPAGATION : By offsets treated as advised for bulbs.
SPECIES CULTIVATED : B. geminiflora, orange red, July, 2 ft., Mexico.

Brazilian Spider-flower (*Tibouchina elegans*)—See Tibouchina.

Brazilian Tree Fern (*Blechnum braziliense*)—See Blechnum.

Brazil Nut Tree (*Bertholletia excelsa*)—See Bertholletia.

Bread-fruit Tree (*Artocarpus incisa*)—See Artocarpus.

Breeches Flower (*Dicentra Cucullaria*)—See Dicentra.

Brevoortia (Brodie's Lily ; Californian or Missouri Hyacinth ; Vegetable Fire-
cracker)—Ord. Liliaceæ.   Hardy bulbous-rooted plant.   First introduced 1870.
CULTURE : Same as for Brodiæas, which see.
SPECIES CULTIVATED : B. Ida-Maia (Syn. Brodiæa coccinea), red and green, June,
1 ft., California.

Breynia nivosa—See Phyllanthus nivosus.

Briar Rose (*Rosa canina*)—See Rosa.

Bridal Wreath (*Francoa ramosa*)—See Francoa.

Bridgesia—See Ercilla.

Brisbane Lily (*Eurycles Cunninghami*)—See Eurycles.

Bristle Fern (*Trichomanes radicans*)—See Trichomanes.

Brittle Bladder Fern (*Cystopteris fragilis*)—See Cystopteris.

Briza (Quaking Grass ; Pearl Grass)—Ord. Gramineæ.   Hardy ornamental
flowering grasses, the inflorescence of which is valuable for mixing with cut flowers,
or drying for winter decoration.
CULTURE : Soil, ordinary.   Position, sunny beds, borders, or banks.
PROPAGATION : By seeds sown ¼ in. deep in April where plants are required to flower.
Flowers should be cut and dried for winter decoration when fully developed.

SPECIES CULTIVATED: B. geniculata, 1 ft., S. Africa ; maxima (Pearl Grass), 1 ft., Mediterranean Region ; media (Quaking Grass), 1 ft., Britain ; minor or minima, 6 in., Europe ; rotundata, 1 ft., Mexico ; spicata, 9 in. Flowering in June and July.

Broad Bean (*Vicia faba*)—See Vicia.

Broad Buckler Fern (*Nephrodium dilatatum*)—See Nephrodium.

Broad-leaved Bell-flower (*Campanula latifolia*)—See Campanula.

Broad-leaved Holly (*Ilex latifolia*)—See Ilex.

Broad-leaved Spindle-tree (*Euonymus latifolius*)—See Euonymus.

Broad Prickly-toothed Fern (*Nephrodium dilatatum*)—See Nephrodium.

Broccoli—See Brassica.

Brodiæa (Missouri Hyacinth)—Ord. Liliaceæ. Hardy bulbous plants. Deciduous. Nat. California, N. America. First introduced 1806.

OUTDOOR CULTURE: Soil, rich, sandy loam. Position, warm, well-drained border. Plant bulbs Sept. and Oct., 4 in. deep and 3 in. apart. Lift and replant bulbs annually.

INDOOR CULTURE: Compost, two parts sandy loam and one part equal proportions of leaf-mould and sand. Grow in 4½ in. pots, placing bulbs 1 in. apart and just below surface of mould. Pot, Oct. Cover with ashes in cold frame till growth begins, then remove to a temp. 45° to 55°. Water freely whilst growing. Keep dry when foliage fades.

PROPAGATION: By seeds sown ⅛ in. deep in sandy soil in cold frame in March ; by offsets treated as advised for bulbs.

SPECIES CULTIVATED: B. Bridgesii, pale lilac, June, 1½ ft., California ; californica, rosy-purple, June, 1½ ft., California ; congesta, blue, June, 1 ft., N.W. America ; congesta alba, white ; capitata, blue, May, 2 ft., N.W. America ; capitata alba, white ; grandiflora, blue and purple, June, 1½ ft., N.W. America ; Hendersonii, salmon yellow with violet stripe, 6 to 8 in. ; ixioides, yellow, June, 9 in., California ; Howellii, blue, July, 2 ft., Oregon ; Howellii lilacina, lilac ; hyacinthina, white, July, 2 ft., California ; laxa, blue, June, 1½ ft., California ; uniflora (Syn. Tritelia uniflora), pale blue. Some of the above were formerly known as Milla. *White blue.*

Brodie's Lily (*Brevoortia Ida-Maia*)—See Brevoortia.

Brome Grass—See Bromus.

Bromelia—Ord. Bromeliaceæ. Stove herbaceous perennials. Flowering and ornamental leaved plants.

CULTURE: Compost, equal parts fibrous loam, rough peat, leaf-mould, and silver sand. Pot, March. Water freely always. Good drainage essential. Temp., Sept. to March 65° to 75° ; March to Sept. 70° to 80°.

PROPAGATION: By large-sized offshoots inserted singly in small pots of sandy peat in temp. 85° in April.

SPECIES CULTIVATED: B. fastuosa, purple, Aug., 4 ft., Brazil ; Pinguin, red, March, 3 ft., Trop. America.

Brompton Stock (*Matthiola incana*)—See Matthiola.

Bromus (Black Grass ; Brome Grass)—Ord. Gramineæ. Hardy ornamental grass. Biennial.

CULTURE: Soil, ordinary. Position, open borders. Flowers useful for drying for winter decoration ; cut them when fully developed.

PROPAGATION: By seeds sown ⅛ in. deep in Sept. or April where plants are to grow.

SPECIES CULTIVATED: B. brizæformis, 2 ft., Caucasus.

Broom—See Cytisus.

Broom Palm (*Thrinax argentea*)—See Thrinax.

Bugle Lily—See Watsonia.

Bulb-bearing Lily (*Lilium bulbiferum*)—See Lilium.

Bulbinella—Ord. Liliaceæ. Hardy herbaceous perennial. First introduced 1848.
CULTURE : Soil, rich, well drained, containing planty of leaf-mould. Position, partially shaded warm border. Plant in spring.
PROPAGATION : By division in spring.
SPECIES CULTIVATED : B. Hookeri (Syn. Chrysobactron Hookeri), white, summer, 2 to 3 ft., New Zealand.

Bulbocodium (Spring Meadow Saffron)—Ord. Liliaceæ. Hardy bulbous plant. First introduced 1649. Flowers appear in March, before leaves.
CULTURE : Soil, ordinary. Position, sunny or shady beds or borders. Plant bulbs 3 in. deep and 3 in. apart in Sept. Lift and replant bulbs every second year.
PROPAGATION : By offsets obtained when lifting the bulbs.
SPECIES CULTIVATED : B. vernum, purple, March, 6 in., Alps ; vernum versicolor, prettily tinted.

Bulbophyllum.—Ord. Orchidaceæ. Stove epiphytal orchids. Evergreen or deciduous. Chiefly of botanical interest.
CULTURE : Compost, equal parts peat and sphagnum moss. Position, well-drained pots or baskets suspended from the rafters. Water freely during growing season, little at other times. Temp., March to Sept. 70° to 80° ; Sept. to March 55° to 65°.
SPECIES CULTIVATED : B. barbigerum, purple, summer, 6 in., Tropical Africa ; comerum, whitish, Jan., 8 in., Burma ; Dearei, yellow and red, May to June, 6 in., Philippine Islands ; grandiflorum, yellow and white, Oct., 10 in., New Guinea ; lobbii, yellow and purple, May to June, 8 in., Java, Sumatra.

Bullace (*Prunus insititia*)—See Prunus.

Bullrush (*Typha latifolia*)—See Typha.

Bull's Head Orchid (*Anguloa Clowesi*)—See Anguloa.

Bunch Berry (*Cornus canadensis*)—See Cornus.

Bunya-Bunya Pine-tree (*Araucaria Bidwillii*)—See Araucaria.

Buphane—Ord. Amaryllidaceæ. Half-hardy or greenhouse bulbous-rooted plants. First introduced 1795.
CULTURE : Compost, equal parts peat, loam, and sand. Pot, Sept. Water only when new growth begins, then give moderate quantity ; cease to give any after leaves turn yellow. Temp., Sept. to Nov. 50° to 55° ; Nov. to March 55° to 65° ; March to Sept. 65° to 75°. Plants must have full exposure to sun.
PROPAGATION : By offsets inserted in small pots and grown similar to large bulbs.
SPECIES CULTIVATED : B. ciliaris, purple, summer, 1 ft. ; disticha, purple, summer, 1 ft., S. Africa.

Buphthalmum (Yellow Ox-eye)—Ord. Compositæ. Hardy herbaceous perennials. First introduced 1722.
CULTURE : Soil, ordinary. Position, open sunny border. Plant, Oct. or March.
PROPAGATION : By division of old plants in Oct. or March ; seeds sown outdoors in April.
SPECIES CULTIVATED : B. salicifolium, yellow, June, 18 in., S. Europe ; salicifolium grandiflorum, large-flowered variety ; speciosissimum (Syn. Telekia speciosissima), yellow, June, 2 ft., Europe ; speciosum (Syn. Telekia speciosa), yellow, June, 5 ft., Europe.

Bupleurum (Hare's-ear)—Ord. Umbelliferæ. Hardy evergreen shrub and perennials. First introduced 1596.
CULTURE OF SHRUBBY SPECIES : Soil, ordinary. Position, warm border. Plant, Oct. or April.
CULTURE OF PERENNIAL SPECIES : Soil, ordinary. Position, sunny borders or rockeries. Plant, Oct. or March.
PROPAGATION : Perennial species by seeds sown outdoors in April ; division in

March.   Shrubby species by cuttings inserted in sandy peat in cold frame in Oct. or March ; also by seeds.
SHRUBBY SPECIES CULTIVATED : B. fruticosum, yellow, July, 3 ft., Mediterranean.
PERENNIAL SPECIES CULTIVATED : B. aureum, yellow, 9 in., June to Aug., Europe ; Candollei, yellow, leaves glaucous, 1 ft., June to Aug., Europe ; petræum, yellow, June, 6 in., Europe ; stellatum, yellow, June, 9 in., S. Europe.

Burbidgea—Ord. Zingiberaceæ. Stove herbaceous flowering perennial. First introduced 1879.
CULTURE : Compost, equal parts peat, leaf-mould, and loam. Position, large pots, tubs, or beds. Plant, March. Water freely March to Aug., moderately other times.
PROPAGATION : By division of roots in April.
SPECIES CULTIVATED : B. nitida, orange red, summer, 3 ft., Borneo.

Burchellia (Bufflehorn-wood)—Ord. Rubiaceæ. Stove flowering shrub. Evergreen. Nat. Cape of Good Hope.
CULTURE : Compost, equal parts peat, loam, leaf-mould, and sand. Pot, March, Water freely April to Sept., moderately other times. Temp., Sept. to March 55° to 60° ; March to Sept. 65° to 75°.
PROPAGATION : By cuttings of young shoots inserted in sandy peat under bell-glass in temp. 75° in March, April, or May.
SPECIES CULTIVATED : B. capensis, scarlet, March to May, 3 ft.

Bur Marigold—See Bidens.

Burnet (*Poterium Sanguisorba*)—See Poterium.

Burnet Rose (*Rosa spinosissima*)—See Rosa.

Burning Bush (*Dictamnus albus*)—See Dictamnus.

Burr Oak (*Quercus macrocarpa*)—See Quercus.

Bush Basil (*Ocimum minimum*)—See Ocimum.

Bush Clover—See Lespedeza.

Bush Honeysuckle (*Diervilla rosea*)—See Diervilla.

Bush Mallow (*Lavatera Olbia*)—See Lavatera.

Bushman's Poison (*Acokanthera venenata*)—See Acokanthera.

Butcher's Broom (*Ruscus aculeatus*)—See Ruscus.

Butomus (Flowering Rush ; Lily Grass)—Ord. Alismaceæ. Hardy perennial. Pretty waterside plant.
CULTURE : Soil, ordinary. Position, in shallow water on margins of ponds, lakes, etc. Plant, Oct. or March.
PROPAGATION : By division of roots in March or April.
SPECIES CULTIVATED : B. umbellatus, rose, summer, 2 to 3 ft., Europe (Britain).

Butter and Eggs (*Narcissus incomparabilis plenus*)—See Narcissus.

Butter Bean (*Phaseolus vulgaris*)—See Phaseolus.

Buttercup—See Ranunculus.

Butterfly Flower—See Schizanthus.

Butterfly Iris—See Moræa.

Butterfly Orchid (*Oncidium Papilio*)—See Oncidium.

Butterfly Orchis (*Habenaria bifolia*)—See Habenaria.

Butterfly Pea—See Clitoria.

Butterfly Plant (*Phalænopsis amabilis*)—See Phalænopsis.

Butterfly Tulip—See Calochortus.

Butterfly-weed (*Asclepias tuberosa*)—See Asclepias.

Butter-nut (*Juglans cinerea*)—See Juglans.

Butterwort (*Pinguicula vulgaris*)—See Pinguicula.

Button Bush (*Cephalanthus occidentalis*)—See Cephalanthus.

Button Snake-root (*Liatris pycnostachya*)—See Liatris.

Buxus (Box-tree)—Ord. Buxaceæ. Hardy evergreen, ornamental-leaved shrubs. Nat. England, S. Europe. Leaves, green, golden, or silver variegated.
CULTURE : Soil, ordinary. Position, open or shady, shrubberies or banks ; choice kinds on lawns. Plant, March, April, Sept., Oct.
CULTURE FOR EDGINGS : Dwarf Box (B. suffruticosa) used for this purpose. Plant divisions with roots attached in shallow trench 6 in. deep in Oct., Nov., or March. Allow plants to nearly touch each other, and to have their tips about 2 in. above soil. Press soil firmly. Trim plants April or Aug. Nursery yard of box will make three yards of edging.
BOX HEDGES : Trench soil 3 ft. deep and 3 ft. wide, add decayed manure, and plant ordinary green box 12 in. high, 12 in. apart in Sept. or Oct. Trim annually in April or Aug.
PROPAGATION : By cuttings of young shoots 3 in. long inserted in shady border in Aug. or Sept. ; division of old plants in Oct. or March ; layering in Sept. or Oct.
SPECIES CULTIVATED : B. balearica, 8 ft., Balearic Islands ; japonica, 8 ft., Japan ; japonica aurea (golden-leaved) ; sempervirens, 8 ft., Europe (Britain), etc., and its numerous varieties, argentea (silver-leaved), aurea (golden-leaved), handsworthiensis, myrtifolia (myrtle-leaved), pyramidalis and suffruticosa (Dutch or edging box). See also Sarcococca.

Cabbage—See Brassica.

Cabbage Lettuce—See Lactuca.

Cabbage Palm (*Sabal Palmetto*)—See Sabal.

Cabbage Rose (*Rosa centifolia*)—See Rosa.

Cacalia—See Kleinia and Emilia.

Cactus—See under separate genera as Cereus, Echinopsis, Mammillaria, Phyllocactus, etc.

Cactus Dahlia (*Dahlia Juarezi*)—See Dahlia.

Cæsalpinia—Ord. Leguminosæ. Hardy deciduous and stove evergreen shrubs. First introduced 1739.
CULTURE OF HARDY SPECIES : Soil, ordinary. Position, warm, sheltered shrubberies. Plant, Oct. to Feb. Prune merely to keep in good shape.
CULTURE OF STOVE SPECIES : Compost, two parts peat or loam, one part leaf-mould, half a part silver sand. Position, pots in light part of stove or outdoors during July and Aug. Pot, Feb. or March. Water freely, March to Oct., moderately afterwards. Temp., March to Oct. 70° to 80° ; Oct. to March 55° to 65°.
PROPAGATION : Stove species by seeds sown in light sandy soil in temp. of 75° to 85° in spring ; cuttings of short young shoots inserted singly in small pots filled with pure sand under bell-glass in temp. 75° to 85° in summer. Hardy species by seeds sown in sandy soil in cold frame at any time.
HARDY SPECIES : C. japonica (Syn. C. sepiaria), yellow, spring, 6 to 8 ft., Japan ; Gilliesii (Syn. Poinciana Gilliesii), yellow, summer, 10 ft., S. America.
STOVE SPECIES : C. coriaria (Divi-Divi), 20 to 30 ft., reddish-brown pods used for dyeing and tanning, S. America ; pulcherrima (Syn. Poinciana pulcherrima), yellow and red, summer, 10 to 15 ft., Tropics.

Caffre Bread—See Encephalartos.

Caffre Butter Shrub—See Combretum.

Caffre Lily—See Schizostylis and Clivia.

Cakile (Sea Rocket)—Ord. Cruciferæ. Hardy annual. Nat. Europe, N. America.

CULTURE : Soil, sandy. Position, open borders.

PROPAGATION : By seeds sown $\frac{1}{16}$ in. deep where plants are to flower in March or April.

SPECIES CULTIVATED : C. maritima, lilac, June, 1 ft., Britain.

Caladium—Ord. Aroideæ. Stove deciduous perennials. Tuberous-rooted. Orn. foliage. First introduced 1773. Leaves, green, white, crimson, red, rose.

CULTURE : Compost, equal parts turfy loam, peat, leaf-mould, decayed manure, and silver sand. Position, well drained pots in shade. Pot moderately firm in pots just large enough to take tubers in Feb. or March ; transfer to larger pots in April or May. Water moderately Feb. to April and Sept. to Nov. ; freely April to Sept. ; keep quite dry Nov. to Feb. Temp., Feb. to Sept. 70° to 80° ; Sept. to Nov. 65° to 75° ; Nov. to Feb. 55° to 65°. C. Humboldtii used as an edging to subtropical beds in summer.

PROPAGATION : By dividing the tubers in Feb. or March.

SPECIES CULTIVATED : C. bicolor, 18 in., S. America, and its varieties Chantinii and pictum ; Humboldtii (Syn. C. argyrites), 9 in., Brazil ; marmoratum, 1 ft., Guayaquil ; Schomburgkii, 18 in., Brazil ; rutescens, Brazil ; venosum, Brazil. A host of beautiful varieties more generally grown than the species will be found in trade lists.

Calamintha (Calamint ; Basil Thyme)—Ord. Labiatæ. Hardy annuals and herbaceous perennials. Flowers, fragrant.

CULTURE : Soil, ordinary. Position, sunny rockeries and borders. Plant, Oct. to April.

PROPAGATION : By seeds sown $\frac{1}{16}$ in. deep outdoors in April ; cuttings of side shoots in cold frame in spring ; division of roots in Oct. or April.

ANNUAL SPECIES : C. Acinos (Basil Thyme), purple, July, 6 in., England.

PERENNIAL SPECIES : C. alpina, purple, June, 6 in., Europe ; grandiflora, purple, June, 1 ft., Europe.

Calamus (Rattan Palm)—Ord. Palmaceæ. Stove palms. Evergreen. Orn. foliage. First introduced 1819. Climbing or semi-climbing.

CULTURE : Compost, two parts turfy loam, one part leaf-mould and coarse sand. Position, well drained pots in shade. Pot firmly in March. Water moderately Sept. to March, freely afterwards. Temp., Sept. to March 60° to 65° ; March to Sept. 70° to 85°. Train shoots up trellis or rafters.

PROPAGATION : By seeds sown 1 in. deep in light soil, in temp. 80° in March ; by suckers growing from roots, inserted in small pots of light soil under bell-glass in temp. 80°.

SPECIES CULTIVATED : C. ciliaris, very slender, climber, Malaya ; Rotang, slender, climber, India.

Calandrinia (Rock-Purslane)—Ord. Portulaceæ. Hardy annuals, biennials, and perennials. First introduced 1826.

CULTURE : Soil, light, moderately rich. Position, sunny rockery for dwarf species ; borders for tall species. Plant perennials in April.

PROPAGATION : Annuals by seeds sown $\frac{1}{16}$ in. deep in shallow boxes of light soil in temp. 55° to 60° in March, transplant seedlings into small pots in April, and plant out in June, or sow seeds outdoors in April, where plants are to flower ; biennials by seeds sown as for annuals ; perennials by seeds or division of roots in April.

ANNUAL SPECIES : C. nitida, red, Aug., 6 in., Chile.

BIENNIAL SPECIES : C. umbellata, rose, all summer, 6 in., Peru.

PERENNIAL SPECIES : C. grandiflora, rosy-red, summer, 1 ft., Chile ; Menziesii, crimson, summer, 1 ft., California.

Caladium hybridum

Calandrinia grandiflora
(Rock-Purslane)

Calathea illustris
(Zebra-plant)

Calceolaria hybrida
(Slipper-flower)

Calendula officinalis
(Pot Marigold)

Callirrhœ pedata
(Poppy Mallow)

Calochortus venustus
(Butterfly Tulip)

Camassia esculenta
(Quamash)

Camellia japonica

Campanula carpatica
(Harebell)

Campanula latiloba
(Bellflower)

Campanula persicifolia
(Bellflower)

Campanula raddeana
(Harebell)

Canna hybrida
(Indian Shot-plant)

Cardamine **pratensis** flore pleno
(Cuckoo-flower)

Carpenteria californica
(Californian Mock Orange)

Catananche cærulea
(Blue Cupidone)

Cattleya intermedia

Calanthe—Ord. Orchidaceæ. Warm greenhouse terrestrial orchids. Deciduous and evergreen. First introduced 1819.
CULTURE : Compost, two parts loam, one part decayed manure, and leaf-mould. Position, shady or partially shady, pots with a third of drainage in each. Pot loosely in March. Cover drainage with layer of moss and allow compost to be well elevated above the rim of pot. Water deciduous kinds freely April to Sept., moderately Sept. to Jan. ; keep quite dry afterwards ; evergreen kinds water freely at all times. Temp., March to Sept. 65° to 85° ; Sept. to Jan. 60° to 70° ; Jan. to March 55° to 65°. Resting period, winter. Flowers appear in centre of new growth, or at base of pseudo-bulb, when growth is nearly completed.
PROPAGATION : By division of pseudo-bulbs in March.
SPECIES CULTIVATED : C. Masuca, violet, winter, 3 ft., India ; Regnieri, white and rose-pink, late winter, 2 to 3 ft., Cochin China ; Turneri, white and deep rose, late winter, 2 to 3 ft., Burma ; veratrifolia, white, May to July, 2 to 3 ft., evergreen, Ceylon, India and Australia, and its varieties luteo-oculata, oculata-gigantea and rubro-occulata ; vestita, white, winter, 2½ ft., India.
HYBRIDS : C. Bella, white, pink and carmine-crimson, winter, 1½ to 2½ ft. ; darblayana, pale rose, winter, 2 to 3 ft., and its varieties Bryan and Wm. Murray ; Dominii, lilac-purple, 2 ft., Feb. ; Harrisi, white, winter ; gigas (Syn. Baron Schrœder), white and rose, winter, 2 to 3 ft. ; porphyrea, crimson, spring, 2 ft. ; Sedeni, rose and purple, autumn and winter ; Veitchii (Syn. Limatodes rosea), rose, winter, 3 ft., and numerous other rare or little-grown forms.

Calathea (Zebra Plant)—Ord. Marantaceæ. Stove plants. Orn. foliage. Leaves, green, rose, yellow, white, and olive on upper sides ; rosy purple beneath.
CULTURE : Compost, equal parts coarse lumps of loam, peat, leaf-mould, and sand. Position, well drained pots in shade. Pot, March, moderately firm. Water freely April to Sept., moderately afterwards. Temp., March to Sept. 70° to 80° ; Sept. to March 65° to 70°.
PROPAGATION : By division of roots in March.
SPECIES CULTIVATED : C. angustifolia, 2 to 3 ft., Trop. America ; bachemiana, 9 in., Brazil ; Closoni, habitat unknown ; eximia, 2¼ ft., Trop. America ; grandiflora (Syn. C. flavescens), 18 in., Brazil ; illustris (Syn. C. roseopicta), 1 ft., Brazil ; insignis, 4 to 6 ft., Brazil ; Leitzei, 2 ft., Brazil ; leopardina, 2 ft., Brazil ; lindeniana, 1 ft., Peru ; luciana, 3 ft., Trop. America ; makoyana, 3 to 4 ft., Brazil ; ornata (Syn. C. sanderiana), 1 ft., Brazil ; picta, 3 to 4 ft., Brazil ; pulchella (Syn. C. tigrina), 1 ft., Brazil ; splendida, 1 to 1½ ft., Brazil ; Vandenheckei, 2 to 2½ ft., Brazil ; veitchiana, 3 ft., Bolivia ; zebrina, 2 to 3 ft., Brazil. Several of the above species were formerly known as Maranta.

Calathian Violet (*Gentiana pneumonanthe*)—See Gentiana.

Calceolaria (Slipper-flower ; Slipper-wort)—Ord. Scrophulariaceæ. Half-hardy or greenhouse shrubs and herbaceous perennials. First introduced 1733.
CULTURE OF HERBACEOUS KINDS : Sow seeds on surface of fine soil in well-drained pans or shallow boxes in July. Cover box or pan with sheet of glass, and stand them under bell-glass or in cold frame. Shade from sun, and keep moderately moist. Transplant seedlings 1 in. apart in fine soil in Aug., transfer them singly into 2 in. pots in Sept., into 5 in. in Oct., and 6 or 7 in. in March. Compost, two parts sandy loam, one part leaf-mould, decayed manure and sand. Water moderately until April, then apply freely. Apply liquid manure from April till plants are in flower. Temp., Aug. to March 45° to 50° ; March to May 50° to 55°. Discard plants after flowering.
CULTURE OF SHRUBBY KINDS : Compost, same as for herbaceous kinds. Position, pots in windows or greenhouses, or in sunny or shady beds outdoors in summer. Pot in March ; plant in May. Nip off points of shoots in March to make bushy plants.
CULTURE OF HARDY KINDS : Soil, ordinary, well enriched with leaf-mould. Position, rather moist and partially shaded places in the rock garden. Plant March or Sept. Water freely during hot, dry weather. Annual species should be sown in the open during March or April.

PROPAGATION : Shrubby kinds by cuttings 3 in. long inserted in sandy soil in cool shady frame in Sept. or Oct., or in pots or boxes in cool greenhouse or window in Sept. Cuttings to remain in frames, etc., till potting or planting time. Hardy kinds by division of roots in March or by seeds sown $\frac{1}{16}$ in. deep in pans or boxes in cold greenhouse or frame during Feb. or March.

HERBACEOUS SPECIES CULTIVATED : C. amplexicaulis, yellow, summer, 1 to 2 ft., Peru ; arachnoidea, purple, June to Sept., 1 ft., Chile ; Burbidgei, yellow and white, autumn and winter, 2 to 3 ft., hybrid ; corymbosa, yellow and purple, May to Oct., 1 to 1½ ft., Chile ; crenatiflora, yellow and orange-brown, summer, 1 to 2½ ft., Chile (this and the preceding species are parents of the greenhouse herbaceous calceolaria of which Clibrani and Albert Kent hybrids are well known forms) ; Fothergillii, yellow and red, May to Aug., 6 in., Falkland Islands ; Pavonii, yellow and brown, summer, 2 to 4 ft., Peru ; purpurea, reddish-violet, July to Sept., 1 ft., Chile.

SHRUBBY SPECIES CULTIVATED : C. alba, white, summer, 1 ft., Chile ; fuchsiæfolia, yellow, spring, 1 to 2 ft., Peru ; integrifolia (Syn. rugosa), yellow to red-brown, summer, 1 to 3 ft., Chile, parent of the bedding calceolaria ; thyrsiflora, yellow, June, 1 to 2 ft., Chile ; violacea, pale and dark violet, summer, 2 ft., Chile.

HARDY SPECIES CULTIVATED : C. biflora (Syn. plantaginea), yellow, June to July, 1 ft., Patagonia ; polyrrhiza, yellow, June, 6 in. ; scabiosæfolia, pale yellow, summer, 1 to 2 ft., Ecuador to Chile, annual.

Calendula (Pot Marigold)—Ord. Compositæ. Hardy annual.
CULTURE : Soil, ordinary. Position, sunny or shady beds or borders.
PROPAGATION : By seeds sown $\frac{1}{4}$ in. deep outdoors in March or April where plants are to flower. Reproduces itself freely from seed.
SPECIES CULTIVATED : C. officinalis, orange-yellow, summer, 12 in., S. Europe. Meteor and Orange King, Radio (with fluted petals), " The Ball," are superior varieties to the species. There are also lemon yellow varieties of good quality— see trade lists.

Calico Bush (*Kalmia latifolia*)—See Kalmia.

Californian Bluebell (*Nemophila insignis*)—See Nemophila.

Californian Buck-eye (*Æsculus californica*)—See Æsculus.

Californian Cedar (*Thuya plicata*)—See Thuya.

Californian Chain Fern (*Woodwardia radicans*)—See Woodwardia.

Californian Columbine (*Aquilegia formosa*)—See Aquilegia.

Californian Cone-flower (*Rudbeckia californica*)—See Rudbeckia.

Californian Fuchsia (*Zauschneria californica*)—See Zauschneria.

Californian Gum Plant (*Grindelia robusta*)—See Grindelia.

Californian Hyacinth (*Brevoortia Ida-Maia*)—See Brevoortia.

Californian Lace Fern (*Cheilanthes myriophylla*)—See Cheilanthes.

Californian Lilac (*Ceanothus integerrimus*)—See Ceanothus.

Californian May-bush (*Heteromeles arbutifolia*)—See Heteromeles.

Californian Mock Orange (*Carpenteria californica*)—See Carpenteria.

Californian Nutmeg (*Torreya californica*)—See Torreya.

Californian Pitcher-plant (*Darlingtonia californica*)—See Darlingtonia.

Californian Poppy (*Platystemon californicus* and *Eschscholtzia californica*)—See Platystemon and Eschscholtzia.

Californian Quamash—See Camassia.

Californian Redwood (*Sequoia sempervirens*)—See Sequoia.

Californian Silver Fir (*Abies concolor*)—See Abies.

Californian Tree Poppy (*Romneya Coulteri*)—See Romneya.

Californian Vine (*Vitis californica*)—See Vitis.

Calimeris—See Boltonia.

Calla (Bog Arum ; Water Dragon ; Marsh Calla)—Ord. Aroideæ. Hardy floating water perennial.
CULTURE : Soil, rich, boggy, or muddy. Position, moist bog or shallow pond. Plant, March or April.
PROPAGATION : By inserting portions of stems in boggy or muddy soil where plants are required to grow.
SPECIES CULTIVATED : C. palustris, white, summer, **6 in.**, N. Hemisphere. See also Richardia and Peltandra.

Calla Lily (*Richardia africana*)—See Richardia.

Callicarpa (French Mulberry ; Purple Mulberry)—Ord. Verbenaceæ. Stove, greenhouse, or hardy shrubs. Orn. fruit. First introduced 1822. Berries, deep violet, borne abundantly in axils of leaves ; Nov. to May.
CULTURE OF STOVE SPECIES : Compost, equal parts peat and loam, with little sand. Position, pots, sunny. Pot, March. Prune straggly shoots into shape before potting. Water moderately Sept. to March, freely afterwards. Temp., Sept. to March 55° to 65° ; March to Sept. 70° to 80°.
CULTURE OF HARDY SPECIES : Soil, ordinary, loamy. Position sheltered walls with southerly aspect in all but the mildest parts of the country. Plant Nov. Prune previous year's growth fairly severely in Feb.
PROPAGATION : Stove species by cuttings of young shoots inserted in 2 in. pots of sandy soil in March in temp. 80°. To ensure plenty of berries keep the points of shoots frequently pinched off and all flowers removed until the end of July. Hardy species by cuttings of half-ripened wood inserted in sandy soil under hand-glass during July or Aug.
STOVE SPECIES CULTIVATED : C. purpurea, 6 ft., China.
HARDY SPECIES CULTIVATED : C. americana, grey-blue, summer, berries violet-blue, 3 to 6 ft., Southern U.S.A., requires some protection in most districts ; japonica, pale pink, Aug., berries violet, 3 to 5 ft., Japan ; purpurea, deep lilac berries, 3 ft., China and Japan, best in cold greenhouse in most districts.

Callichroa—See Layia.

Calliopsis—See Coreopsis.

Calliphruria—Ord. Amaryllidaceæ. Greenhouse, bulbous-rooted perennial. First introduced 1843.
CULTURE : Compost, two parts sandy loam, one part leaf-mould, peat, and sand. Position, well-drained pots, sunny. Pot, March, placing one bulb 3 in. deep in a 5 in. pot. Water moderately March to Oct., very little afterwards. Temp., Sept. to March 50° to 55° ; March to Sept. 55° to 65°.
PROPAGATION : By offsets placed in small pots in March.
SPECIES CULTIVATED : C. hartwegiana, white, June, 1 ft., Bogota.

Callirrhoe (Poppy Mallow)—Ord. Malvaceæ. Hardy annuals and perennials. First introduced 1824.
CULTURE : Soil, ordinary. Position, open borders. Plant perennials Oct. or March.
PROPAGATION : Annual species by seeds sown ⅟₁₆ in. deep in pans of light soil in temp. 55° to 65° in March, transplanting seedlings outdoors in May, or where plants are to flower in April ; perennials by seeds sown ⅟₁₆ in. deep outdoors in April, or cuttings of young shoots inserted in sandy soil in cold frame in spring.
ANNUAL SPECIES : C. pedata, cherry-red, summer, 2 ft., Texas ; pedata compacta, crimson, white eye.
PERENNIAL SPECIES : C. involucrata, crimson, summer, 6 in., N. America ; lineariloba, striped, July, 6 in., N. America.

Callistemon (Bottle Brush Tree)—Ord. Myrtaceæ. Greenhouse evergreen flowering shrubs. First introduced 1788. Natives of Australia.
CULTURE : Compost, equal parts peat, loam, and silver sand. Position, in pots, or in well-drained beds at base of wall. Pot or plant March or April. Prune shoots

71

slightly after flowering. Water freely April to Sept., moderately afterwards. Temp., March to Sept. 55° to 65°; Sept. to March 40° to 50°.
PROPAGATION : By cuttings of firm shoots, 3 in. long, inserted in sandy peat under bell-glass, in temp. 55° to 65° during summer.
SPECIES CULTIVATED : C. lanceolatus, crimson, June, 8 to 10 ft. ; salignus, yellow, June, 6 ft. ; speciosus (Syn. Metrosideros speciosus), crimson, spring, 8 to 10 ft.

Callistephus (China Aster)—Ord. Compositæ. Hardy annuals. First introduced 1731.
CULTURE : Soil, rich, liberally manured. Position, open, sunny, well drained. Sow seeds ⅛ in. deep in light soil in temp. 55° to 65° in March, transplant seedlings in April 2 in. apart in shallow boxes or in bed of light soil in cold frame, plant out 6 to 12 in. apart in outdoor beds in May ; or sow seeds same depth and soil in cold frame, or in pots in window in April and plant outdoors in May. Apply weak liquid manure twice a week during July and Aug. To secure exhibition blooms pinch off all flower buds, except three or four on each plant directly they form.
POT CULTURE : Sow seeds as advised above. Transplant three seedlings into a 3 in. pot in April, into 5 in. in May, and 6 in. in June. Compost, equal parts loam, leaf-mould, decayed manure, and sand. Water freely, and apply liquid manure once a week when flower buds are formed. Thin out latter to three on each plant. Plants may be lifted from open ground in Aug. and placed in pots to flower if desired.
SPECIES CULTIVATED : C. chinensis, various colours, summer, 6 in. to 2 ft., China. Numerous types and refined strains are in commerce, such as Californian Giant, Chrysanthemum-flowered, Comet, Ostrich Plume, Pæony-flowered, Frilled, Victoria, and Single. These are all available in separate colours and named varieties.

Calluna (Ling ; Heather)—Ord. Ericaceæ. Hardy evergreen flowering shrubs.
CULTURE : Soil, bog, or peat. Position, moist, open beds, borders, or shrubbery margins. Plant, Sept., Oct., March, or April.
PROPAGATION : By division of plant in Oct. or April.
SPECIES CULTIVATED : C. vulgaris, purple, spring, 1 ft., Europe (Britain), and its varieties alba (white), Alporti (crimson), argentea (silvery-leaved), aurea (golden-leaved), flore pleno (double-flowered).

Calocephalus—Ord. Compositæ. Greenhouse sub-shrub with white cottony stems. Used mainly for carpet bedding.
CULTURE : Soil, ordinary. Position, sunny beds in summer only. Plant, May ; lift and winter in cool greenhouse in September.
PROPAGATION : By cuttings inserted in cold frame in August.
SPECIES CULTIVATED : C. Brownii (syn. Leucophyta Brownii), trailing.

Calochortus (Butterfly Tulip ; Star Tulip ; Mariposa Lily)—Ord. Liliaceæ. Half-hardy bulbous plants. Nat. California and N.W. America. First introduced 1826.
FRAME CULTURE : Prepare bed 12 in. deep with compost of equal parts loam, peat, leaf-mould, and sand. Plant bulbs 3 in. deep and 4 in. apart in Nov. Keep lights on in frosty weather ; off night and day in fair weather. Water in dry weather. Lift and replant every three years.
POT CULTURE : Use same compost as advised for frame culture. Place a dozen bulbs 2 in. deep in a 5 in. pot in Nov. Cover pots with ashes in cold frame, and give no water. Remove pots from ashes in Jan. and place in cool greenhouse near glass. Water moderately till after flowering, then gradually withhold it. Repot annually in Nov.
OUTDOOR CULTURE : Plant bulbs in similar soil and manner to that advised for frames. Bed must be dry in winter, sunny, at foot of south wall.
PROPAGATION : By seeds sown ⅛ in. deep in pans of sandy soil in temp. 45° to 55° in March, transplanting seedlings following year into small pots and treating similar to old bulbs ; by offsets planted like bulbs in Nov.
SPECIES CULTIVATED : C. albus (Syn. Cyclobothra alba), white, July, 1 ft. ; amabilis (Syn. C. pulchellus and Cyclobothra pulchellus), yellow, July, 1 ft. ; Benthami,

yellow, July, 8 in. ; cæruleus, lilac-blue, July, 6 in. ; clavatus, yellow, July, 2½ ft. ; elegans, white, June, 9 in. ; Gunnisonii, white, July, 2 ft. ; Howellii, white, July, 18 in. ; Kennedyi, orange-red, July, 2½ ft. ; lilacinus, lilac, July, 9 in. ; luteus, yellow, July, 1 ft. ; macrocarpus, pale lavender and green, July, 1½ ft., California ; maweanus, purple and white, June to July, 6 to 10 in., San Francisco ; Nuttallii (Syn. C. Leichtlinii), white, June, 6 in. ; Plummerae, soft lavender, July, 2 ft., California ; Purdyi, white, July, 1 ft. ; splendens, lilac, July, 1 ft. ; venustus, white, July, 18 in. A number of varieties will be found in specialists' lists.

Calodendron (Cape Chestnut)—Ord. Rutaceæ. Greenhouse flowering shrub. Evergreen. First introduced 1789.
CULTURE : Compost, two parts loam, one part peat and sand. Position, pots or tubs, sunny. Pot and prune, March. Water moderately Sept. to March, freely afterwards. Temp., Sept. to March 50° to 55° ; March to Sept. 55° to 65°.
PROPAGATION : By cuttings of shoots 3 in. long inserted in sandy soil under bell-glass in temp. 60° in June or July.
SPECIES CULTIVATED : C. capensis, pink, summer, 10 ft., S. Africa.

Calophaca—Ord. Leguminosæ. Hardy deciduous flowering shrub. First introduced 1786.
CULTURE : Soil, ordinary. Position, open shrubbery. Plant, Oct. to Feb.
PROPAGATION : By seeds sown ½ in. deep in Nov. or March ; by grafting on common laburnum in March.
SPECIES CULTIVATED : C. wolgarica, yellow, June, 3 ft., S. Russia.

Calopogon (Grass Pink Orchis)—Ord. Orchidaceæ. Hardy herbaceous orchid. First introduced 1791.
CULTURE : Soil, peaty. Position, moist, sheltered rockery. Plant, March or April. May also be grown in equal parts peat and loam in pots in cold frames or greenhouses.
PROPAGATION : By offsets treated as old plants.
SPECIES CULTIVATED : C. pulchellus, purple, July, 18 in., N. America.

Calostemma—Ord. Amaryllidaceæ. Greenhouse flowering bulbous perennials. First introduced 1819.
CULTURE : Compost, two parts loam, one part peat and sand. Pot, Aug. Position, sunny greenhouse. Water freely March to July, moderately July to Sept., very little afterwards. Temp., Sept. to March 45° to 50° ; March to Sept. 55° to 65°.
PROPAGATION : By offsets at potting time.
SPECIES CULTIVATED : C. album, white, May, 1 ft., N. Australia ; luteum, yellow, Nov., 1 ft., Australia ; purpureum, purple, Nov., 1 ft., Australia ; purpureum carneum, pale purple.

Caltha (Marsh Marigold ; Goldings ; Water Gowan ; Double Marsh Marigold) —Ord. Ranunculaceæ. Hardy herbaceous perennials.
CULTURE : Soil, rich. Position, damp borders, or banks of ponds, streams or lakes. Plant, Oct. or March.
PROPAGATION : By division of roots in March or July.
SPECIES CULTIVATED : C. leptosepala, yellow, May, 1 ft., N.W. America ; palustris (Marsh Marigold), yellow, April, 1 ft., Britain, and its varieties, alba (white), flore pleno (double yellow), monstrosa plena (yellow, double), and nana flore-pleno (dwarf) ; polypetala, yellow, 1½ ft., Asia Minor.

Calvary Clover (*Medicago echinus*)—See Medicago.

Calycanthus (Carolina Allspice)—Ord. Calycanthaceæ. Hardy deciduous flowering shrubs.
CULTURE : Compost, two parts peat, one part loam and leaf-mould. Position, south or west walls, or sheltered shrubbery South of England. Plant, Oct. to March.
PROPAGATION : By seeds sown ¼ in. deep in light soil in cold frame, March ; by layers of shoots in July and Aug.
SPECIES CULTIVATED : C. floridus, brownish purple, fragrant, June, 6 ft., S. United States ; fertilis (Syn. glaucus), brownish purple, May, 6 ft., United States ; occidentalis (Syn. C. macrophyllus), red, fragrant, Aug., 9 ft., California.

73

Calypso (*Calypso Orchis*)—Ord. Orchidaceæ. Hardy terrestrial orchid. First introduced 1820.

CULTURE : Compost, two parts leaf-mould, one part fibry peat and coarse sand. Position, shady margins of rockwork or bog. Plant, Oct. or March.

PROPAGATION : By offsets treated as old plants at planting time.

SPECIES CULTIVATED : C. borealis, rose, brown and yellow, Jan., 1 ft., N. Temperate Zone.

Calystegia (Bind-weed)—Ord. Convolvulaceæ. Hardy herbaceous trailing and climbing perennials.

CULTURE : Soil, ordinary. Position, sunny border where the fleshy roots can be confined and prevented from spreading over the garden. Plant, Oct. to March.

PROPAGATION : By seeds sown ¼ in. deep in pots of sandy soil in temp. 55° in March, or similar depth in April where plants are to flower; by division of roots in Oct. or March.

SPECIES CULTIVATED : C. hederacea (Syn. C. pubescens fl. pl.), Double Chinese Bindweed, rose, summer, 6 ft., China and Japan ; sepium, rose, July, 6 ft., Temp. Regions ; sepium dahurica, rosy purple, July, 6 ft., Siberia ; silvestris (Syn. C. sylvatica), white, July, 6 ft., Europe ; Soldanella (Syn. Convolvulus Soldanella), red, June, 3 ft., Temperate Zone.

Camassia (Bear Grass ; Wild Hyacinth ; Californian Quamash)—Ord. Liliaceæ. Hardy bulbous plants. First introduced 1837.

CULTURE : Compost, equal parts loam, leaf-mould, and coarse sand. Position, sheltered beds or borders. Plant bulbs 4 in. deep and 4 in. apart in Oct. or Feb. Top-dress annually with decayed manure. Lift and replant every four years.

PROPAGATION : By seeds sown ¼ in. deep in sunny position outdoors in March, or ¼ in. deep in boxes of light soil in temp. 55° in Nov. ; by offsets in Oct. or Feb.

SPECIES CULTIVATED : C. esculenta (Quamash), Syn. C. Fraseri, blue, July, 2 ft., N.W. America ; Cusickii, blue, July, 2½ ft., California.

Camellia (Tea-plant)—Ord. Ternstrœmiaceæ. Greenhouse and half-hardy flowering shrubs. Evergreen. First introduced 1739.

CULTURE : Compost, equal parts turfy loam, peat, and sand. Position, pots or tubs in greenhouse, against south wall, or in sheltered shrubberies outdoors in S. of England. Pot, March or April. Plant outdoors March or April. Water moderately Sept. to March, freely afterwards. Prune little, except to retain balance, and when this is essential, in March. Temp., Sept. to March 50° to 55° ; March to Sept. 55° to 65°. Place plants outdoors on bed of cinder ashes July to Sept. Apply stimulants once a week Aug. to March. Suitable stimulants : Solution of sheep droppings and soot, clear soot water, guano and water, or artificial manures. Cause of buds dropping, dry atmosphere and insufficient water at roots.

OUTDOOR CULTURE : Soil, well-decayed turfy loam and leaf-mould. Position, sunny, sheltered spots in the shrubbery, or against a south-west wall. Suitable only for mild districts. Protect in severe weather with garden mats. Plant in July. Prune back straggly shoots only after flowering.

PROPAGATION : By seeds sown ¼ in. deep in sandy peat in temp. 75° in March ; by cuttings of firm shoots inserted in well-drained pots of sandy peat in cool greenhouse in Aug., transferring pots in March to temp. 55° and putting cuttings in small pots following Sept. ; by layers of shoots in Sept. ; grafting in March.

SPECIES CULTIVATED : C. cuspidata, white, May, 6 ft., W. China ; japonica, parent of the numerous cultivated varieties, red, spring, 15 to 20 ft., Japan ; japonica anemonæflora, red ; reticulata, red, spring, 8 to 10 ft., China ; rosæflora, rose, spring, 3 ft., China ; Sasanqua, white, Feb., 6 ft., China ; Thea (China Tea Plant), Syn. C. theifera, white, May, 5 to 6 ft., China ; Thea assamica (Assam or Indian Tea Plant).

Campanula (Bellflower ; Harebell ; Canterbury Bell ; Garden Rampion)—Ord. Campanulaceæ. Hardy annuals, biennials, and perennials.

CULTURE OF PERENNIAL SPECIES : Soil, ordinary rich. Position, trailing species on sunny rockeries ; tall species beds and borders, sunny or shady. Plant, Oct. to April.

POT CULTURE : Compost, equal parts leaf-mould, loam, and sand. Trailing kinds grow in small pots in hanging baskets. Repot them in March. Water moderately in winter, freely other times. Tall kinds grow singly in 7 in. pots or three in a 10 in. pot. Sow seeds of these in cold frame in Aug. ; transplant seedlings singly in 3 in. pots in Oct., into 5 in. in April, 7 in. in May. Water moderately in winter, freely in summer.

CULTURE OF ANNUAL SPECIES : Sow seeds in gentle heat in March, transplant seedlings into boxes, harden off in cold frame in May and plant out in sunny borders early in June.

CULTURE OF CANTERBURY BELL : Sow seeds outdoors in April, May, or June. Transplant seedlings when 1 in. high, 6 in. apart in nursery bed, and plant out in borders in Oct. to flower following year.

CULTURE OF BIENNIAL SPECIES : Sow seeds in pans or boxes in cool greenhouse or frame in Feb. or March. Prick out into frame when large enough to handle and plant in flowering positions in May or June.

CULTURE OF RAMPION : Sow seeds in shallow drills 6 in. apart in shady border of rich soil in May. Thin seedlings to 4 in. apart. Lift and store roots in frost-proof place in Nov. Uses : Young roots and leaves for winter salads ; large roots cook and eat like parsnips.

PROPAGATION : Perennials by seeds sown $\frac{1}{16}$ in. deep in sandy soil in temp. 55° in March or Aug.; division of roots in Oct. or April.

ANNUAL SPECIES : C. drabæfolia, blue, July, 3 in., Greece ; kewensis (hybrid), rich blue, June and July, 3 in. ; Lœflingii, blue, July, 1 ft., Portugal ; macrostyla, blue, July, 18 in., Asia Minor ; ramosissima (Syn. Loreyi), purple-blue, June to July, 1 ft. to 1½ ft., Italy.

BIENNIAL SPECIES : C. kolenatiana, violet-blue, summer, 9 to 12 in., Southern Caucasus ; longestyla, blue-purple, summer, 1½ to 2½ ft., Caucasus ; medium (Canterbury Bell), blue, July, 3 ft., S. Europe, and several white, rose, and purple single and double varieties ; patula, pale violet, June, 2 to 3 ft., Europe (Britain) ; Rapunculus (Rampion), blue or white, July, 2 to 3 ft., Europe (Britain) ; speciosa, violet, summer, 1 to 1½ ft., S. Europe ; spicata, purple, summer, 1 ft., Alps ; thyrsoides, straw-yellow, July, 1 to 1½ ft., Alps.

PERENNIAL SPECIES : C. abietina, blue, July, 1 ft., Europe ; alliariæfolia, yellow, June, 18 in., Caucasus ; Allionii, blue, July, 3 in., France ; alpina, blue, July, 6 in., Europe ; arvatica, rich blue, trailing, Spain ; balchiniana, blue, July, 6 in., hybrid ; barbata, blue, June, 1 ft., Europe ; bellidifolia, violet-purple, summer, 3 in., Caucasus ; betonicæfolia, blue, May, 18 in., Mt. Olympus ; bononiensis, blue, July, 2½ ft., Europe ; cæspitosa, blue, summer, 6 in., Europe ; cæspitosa alba, white ; carpatica, blue, summer, 12 in., E. Europe ; carpatica alba, white ; carpatica turbinata, blue, 6 in. ; cenisia, blue, procumbent, May, Alps ; collina, blue, July, 1 ft., Caucasus ; Elatines, purple, summer, 3 in., Piedmont ; elatinoides, purple, summer, 3 in., Piedmont ; excisa, blue, May, 6 in., Alps ; fragilis (Syn. C. Barrelieri), lilac and purple, Aug., 6 in., Italy ; gargantica, blue, June, 6 in., Italy ; gargantica hirsuta, blue and white, hairy foliage, superior to type ; glomerata, blue, summer, 18 in., Europe (Britain), and its varieties dahurica (deep blue) and pusilla ; Halli, white, summer, 3 in., hybrid ; haylodgensis, bright blue, summer, 6 in., hybrid ; Hendersonii, mauve, July to Sept., 1 ft., hybrid ; isophylla, lilac-blue, July, 3 to 6 in., Italy, and its varieties alba (white) and Mayi (mauve) ; lactiflora (Syn. celtidifolia), white and blue, July, 3 ft., Caucasus ; lanata, pale yellow or pink, summer, 2 to 3 ft., S. Europe ; latifolia, blue, July, 4 to 6 ft., Britain, and its varieties alba (white), Burghaltii (lilac), and Van Houttei (violet-blue) ; latiloba (Syn. grandis), light blue, July to Sept., 3 ft., Bithynia ; mirabilis, pale blue, summer, 1 to 2 ft., Caucasus ; persicifolia, blue, June, 2 to 3 ft., Europe, and many varieties such as alba, Moerheimi, Telham Beauty, etc. ; phyctidocalyx (Syn. amabilis), purple, summer, 1 ft., S. Armenia ; pilosa, blue, summer, 6 in., N. Asia ; planiflora, powder-blue or white, July to Sept., 9 to 12 in., N. America ; portenschlagiana (Syn. muralis) blue, June, 6 in., S. Europe ; pulla, violet-blue, June, 3 in., Austria ; punctata (Syn. nobilis), creamy white spotted red, June to July, 1½ ft., Siberia, China and Japan ; pusilla (Syn. Bellardii), dark blue, July, 4 in., Alps, and its varieties alba (white) and pallida (pale blue) ; pyramidalis (Chimney Bellflower), blue, July, 4 to 6 ft., Dalmatia, and its variety alba (white); raddeana, violet, June to July, 9 to 12 in., Caucasus; Raineri, blue, June, 3 in., Alps; rapunculoides, bluish violet, June, 3 ft., Europe, Asia; rhomboidalis, purplish blue or white, June to July, 1 to 2 ft., Europe; rotundifolia (Harebell), blue, summer, 8 to 12 in., Britain, and its varieties alba (white) and Hostii (blue); sarmatica, pale blue, July to Aug., 1 to 2 ft., Caucasus; saxifraga, violet, summer, 2 to 3 in., Caucasus, Armenia; Stansfieldii, violet, June to July, 4 to 6 in., hybrid; Steveni, vinous lilac, May to June, 6 in., Europe and Asia; tommasiniana, pale blue, July to Aug., 9 in., Italy; Trachelium, blue, July, 3 ft., Europe, and its varieties alba (white), alba plena (double white) and flore pleno (double blue); tridentata, violet, summer, 3 in., Armenia. Cappadocia; Vidalii, white and yellow, summer, 1 to 2 ft., Azores (not hardy); waldsteiniana, violet, Aug., 6 in., Dalmatia; Warleyi, purple, July, 6 in., a hybrid; Wockii, pale blue, summer, 3 in., hybrid; Zoysii, pale blue, July to Sept., 2 to 3 in., S. Europe. See also Wahlenbergia and Legousia.

Camperdown Weeping Elm (*Ulmus montana Camperdowni*)—See Ulmus.

Campernelle (*Narcissus odorus*)—See Narcissus.

Campion—See Lychnis.

Canada Tea (*Gaultheria procumbens*)—See Gaultheria.

Canadian Columbine (*Aquilegia canadensis*)—See Aquilegia.

Canadian Golden Rod (*Solidago canadensis*)—See Solidago.

Canadian Lily (*Lilium canadense*)—See Lilium.

Canadian Rice (*Zizania aquatica*)—See Zizania.

Canadian Yew-tree (*Taxus canadensis*)—See Taxus.

Canarina (Canary Island Bellflower)—Ord. Campanulaceæ. **Greenhouse herbaceous perennial.** First introduced 1696.
CULTURE: Compost, equal parts loam, leaf-mould, decayed manure and silver sand. Position, pots. Pot, Feb.; good drainage very essential. Water liberally March to Aug., moderately Aug. to Nov., very little afterwards. Temp., Sept. to Feb. 45° to 55°; March to Sept. 55° to 65°.
PROPAGATION: By cuttings of young shoots inserted in sandy soil in temp. 65° in March or April; division of roots in Feb.
SPECIES CULTIVATED: C. campanulata, orange, Jan. to March, 4 ft., Canary Islands.

Canary Creeper (*Tropæolum aduncum*)—See Tropæolum.

Canary Grass (*Phalaris canariensis*)—See Phalaris.

Canary Island Bell-flower (*Canarina campanulata*)—See Canarina.

Candelabra-flower (*Brunsvigia Josephinæ*)—See Brunsvigia.

Candle-berry Myrtle (*Myrica Gale*)—See Myrica.

Candlemas Bells (*Galanthus nivalis*)—See Galanthus.

Candle Plant (*Kleinia articulata*)—See Kleinia.

Candy Mustard—See Æthionema.

Candytuft—See Iberis.

Canistrum—Ord. Bromeliaceæ. Stove evergreen flowering and ornamental plants. First introduced 1870. Flower spikes surrounded by red bracts. Brazilian.
CULTURE: Compost, equal parts of fibrous loam, rough peat, leaf-mould and silver sand. Position, well-drained pots in light, moist part of stove. Pot, Feb. or March. Water moderately in winter, freely at other times. Temp., March to Sept. 70° to 80°; Sept. to March 65° to 70°.
PROPAGATION: By large-sized offshoots inserted singly in small pots of sandy peat, in temp. of 85°, Feb. or April.
SPECIES CULTIVATED: C. amazonicum, greenish white, June, 1 to 1½ ft.; aurantiacum, orange-yellow, June to Sept., 2 ft.; roseum, rose, July, 18 in., Brazil. See also Æchmea. Some of the above are occasionally listed as Nidularium.

Ceanothus azureus
(Mountain Sweet)

Cedrus atlantica
(Mount Atlas Cedar)

Celastrus articulatus
(Staff-tree)

Celosia argentea cristata
(Cockscomb)

Celsia cretica
(Cretan Mullein)

Centaurea cyanus
(Cornflower)

Centaurea moschata
(Sweet Sultan)

Centranthus macrosiphon
(Red Valerian)

Cephalaria alpina

Cereus flagelliformis (Grafted
Plant) (Torch Thistle)

Chrysanthemum carinatum
(Annual Chrysanthemum)

Chrysanthemum coronarium
(Annual Chrysanthemum)

Chrysanthemum hybridum
(Border Chrysanthemum)

Chrysanthemum uliginosum
(Grand Ox-eye)

Chrysogonum virginianum
(Golden Knee)

Chysis aurea

Cimicifuga racemosa
(Snake-root)

Cistus purpureus
(Rock Rose)

Canna (Indian Shot-plant)—Ord. Cannaceæ. Stove herbaceous plants. First introduced 1570.
INDOOR CULTURE : Compost, equal parts loam, decayed manure, leaf-mould, and sand. Position, pots in sunny greenhouse. Pot, March. Water freely March to Oct., very little afterwards. Temp., Sept. to March 40° to 50° ; March to Sept. 65° to 85°. Apply weak liquid manure twice a week to plants in healthy growth.
OUTDOOR CULTURE : Place roots in pots in March in temp. 55° to 60°. Remove pots into temp. 55° end of April and plant outdoors early in June. Lift roots in Sept., place them in boxes filled with ordinary soil, keep latter nearly dry, and store in frost-proof position till potting time.
PROPAGATION : By seeds steeped for 24 hours in tepid water, then sown ½ in. deep in light soil in temp. 85° in Feb. ; division of roots at potting time. It will facilitate germination if a slight notch be filed in the seed before sowing.
SPECIES CULTIVATED : C. edulis, bright red, summer, 8 to 10 ft., W. Indies and S. America ; flaccida, yellow, summer, 4 to 5 ft., S. Carolina ; glauca, yellow, summer, 5 to 6 ft., Mexico, W. Indies, and S. America ; indica, yellow and red, summer, 6 ft., W. Indies ; iridiflora, rose, summer, 8 to 10 ft., Peru ; Warscewiczii, scarlet, tinged blue, summer, 3 to 5 ft., Costa Rica to S. America. With the exception of the first named which is cultivated for food these species are the parents of the numerous varieties grown in gardens. See trade lists for names.

Cannabis (Indian or Giant Hemp)—Ord. Urticaceæ. Hardy annuals. Orn. foliage.
CULTURE : Soil, ordinary. Position, sunny borders.
PROPAGATION : By seeds sown ½ in. deep outdoors, where plants are to grow, in April, or in temp. 55° in March, transplanting seedlings in June.
SPECIES CULTIVATED : C. sativa, green, June, 4 to 10 ft., India.

Cantaloup Melon (*Cucumis Melo*)—See Cucumis.

Canterbury Bells (*Campanula medium*)—See Campanula.

Cantua (Peruvian Magic-tree)—Ord. Polemoniaceæ. Greenhouse evergreen flowering shrubs. First introduced 1846.
CULTURE : Compost, two parts turfy loam, one part leaf-mould and sand. Position, pots, sunny greenhouse. Pot, March. Water moderately Sept. to March, freely March to Sept. Temp., Sept. to March 40° to 50° ; March to Sept. 50° to 60°.
PROPAGATION : By cuttings of shoots inserted in pure silver sand under bell-glasses in temp. 50° to 55°, May to Aug.
SPECIES CULTIVATED : C. bicolor, yellow and red, May, 4 ft., Bolivia ; buxifolia, rose, May, 5 ft., Peru.

Cape Aloe (*Aloe ferox*)—See Aloe.

Cape Aster (*Agathæa cœlestis*)—See Agathæa.

Cape Bladder Senna (*Sutherlandia frutescens*)—See Sutherlandia.

Cape Blue Water Lily (*Nymphæa capensis*)—See Nymphæa.

Cape Chestnut (*Calodendron capensis*)—See Calodendron.

Cape Cowslip (*Lachenalia tricolor*)—See Lachenalia.

Cape Crocus (*Gethyllis spiralis*)—See Gethyllis.

Cape Fig-wort (*Phygelius capensis*)—See Phygelius.

Cape Forget-me-not (*Anchusa capensis*)—See Anchusa.

Cape Gooseberry (*Physalis peruviana*)—See Physalis.

Cape Honey-flower (*Melianthus major*)—See Melianthus.

Cape Honeysuckle (*Tecoma capensis*)—See Tecoma.

Cape Ivy (*Senecio macroglossus*)—See Senecio.

Cape Jasmine (*Gardenia jasminoides*)—See Gardenia.

Cape Lead-wort (*Plumbago capensis*)—See Plumbago.

Cape Lily (*Crinum longifolium*)—See Crinum.

Cape Pond-weed (*Aponogeton distachyon*)—See Aponogeton.

Cape Primrose—See Streptocarpus.

Cape Silver-tree (*Leucadendron argenteum*)—See Leucadendron.

Cape Stock—See Heliophila.

Cape Treasure-flower (*Gazania pavonia*)—See Gazania.

Caper Bush (*Capparis spinosa*)—See Capparis.

Caper Spurge (*Euphorbia lathyris*)—See Euphorbia.

Capparis (Caper-bush)—Ord. Capparidaceæ. Half-hardy evergreen shrub. First introduced 1596.
CULTURE : Compost, two parts turfy loam, one part leaf-mould and sand. Position, pots in sunny greenhouse. Pot, March ; good drainage essential. Plant outdoors Sept. to Nov. Water moderately in pots Sept. to March, freely afterwards. Temp., Sept. to March 45° to 55° ; March to Sept. 55° to 65°. May be grown outdoors in sheltered position in S. of England.
PROPAGATION : By cuttings of firm shoots in sand under bell-glasses in temp. 65° to 75°, July or Aug.
SPECIES CULTIVATED : C. spinosa, white, June, 3 ft., S. Europe. This species yields the capers of commerce.

Capsicum (Cayenne Pepper ; Chilli ; Red Pepper)—Ord. Solanaceæ. Hothouse shrubby plant, usually grown as annual. First introduced 1548. Fruit, round, long, red and yellow.
CULTURE : Soil, light, rich. Position, pots in sunny greenhouse, against south wall outdoors in summer.
POT CULTURE : Sow seeds ⅛ in. deep in temp. 80° in Feb. Place seedlings singly in 3 in. pots in March and in 6 in. pots in May. Water freely and grow throughout in temp. 75° to 85°. Gather fruit when full red or yellow colour is attained.
OUTDOOR CULTURE : Sow seeds and grow seedlings in pots as advised in previous case. Plant out in June. Train shoots thinly to wall as they grow.
SPECIES CULTIVATED : C. frutescens (Syns. annuum and baccatum), white, summer, scarlet fruits, 1 to 6 ft., Tropics. There are numerous variations and forms of this, many with strangely shaped and very striking fruits. These are the Capsicums, Chillies, Red Peppers, Bird Peppers, Cayenne Peppers, Guinea Peppers, etc., of gardens.

Caragana (Siberian Pea-tree ; Chinese Pea-tree)—Ord. Leguminosæ. Hardy flowering trees and shrubs. Deciduous. First introduced 1752.
CULTURE : Soil, ordinary. Position, open shrubbery. Plant, Oct. to March.
PROPAGATION : By seeds sown 2 in. deep in ordinary soil outdoors in Nov. or March ; cuttings of roots inserted 3 in. deep outdoors in Oct. ; layers of strong shoots in Sept. ; grafting choice species on C. arborescens in March.
SPECIES CULTIVATED : C. arborescens, yellow, May, 15 ft., Siberia, and its varieties cuneifolia, Lorbergi, nana, pendula, and Redowski ; Chamlaga, reddish yellow, May to June, 3 to 4 ft., N. China ; frutescens, yellow, April, 3 ft., Russia and Japan ; gerardiana, pale yellow or white, 2 to 4 ft., N.W. Himalayas ; microphylla, yellow, May to June, 6 to 10 ft., N. Central Asia ; pygmæa, yellow, May to June, 3 to 4 ft. ; spinosa, yellow, May, 4 to 6 ft., Siberia.

Caraway (*Carum Carvi*)—See Carum.

Carbenia (Blessed Thistle)—Ord. Compositæ. Hardy biennial. Ornamental foliage.
CULTURE : Soil, ordinary. Position, sunny border. Sow seeds thinly in March, where plants are to grow, and afterwards thin out to a foot or so apart.
SPECIES CULTIVATED : C. benedicta, leaves green and blotched with white, 3 to 4 ft., Mediterranean Region. By some authorities this is now referred to Cnicus.

Cardamine (Cuckoo Flower; Tooth Flower; Lady's Smock; Coral Root); Ord. Cruciferæ. Hardy perennial herbs.
CULTURE: Soil, ordinary. Position, moist, shady border. Plant, Oct., Nov., March, or April.
PROPAGATION: By seeds sown ¼ in. deep outdoors in April; division of roots in Oct.
SPECIES CULTIVATED: C. asarifolia, white, May, 1 ft., Italy; macrophylla, pale purple, June, 1 ft., Eastern Asia; pratensis (Cuckoo Flower or Lady's Smock), pale purple, May, 18 in., Britain; pratensis flore pleno, double; trifolia, white, March to April, 3 to 4 in., S. Europe. See also Dentaria.

Cardinal Flower (*Lobelia cardinalis*)—See Lobelia.

Cardinal Monkey-flower (*Mimulus cardinalis*)—See Mimulus.

Cardoon—See Cynara.

Carex (Blue-grass; Sedge)—Ord. Cyperaceæ. Hardy herbaceous perennial grasses. Orn. foliage.
CULTURE: Soil, ordinary. Position, margins of ponds. Plant, March. The variegated kinds may be grown in pots in ordinary good soil in cool greenhouses or in rooms.
PROPAGATION: By seeds sown where plants are to grow in March; division of roots in March.
SPECIES CULTIVATED: C. acuta, 2 to 3 ft., Europe; baccans, purple fruits, 4 ft., Trop. Asia; depauperata, 1 ft., Europe; Pseudo-cyperus (Bastard Cyperus), 3 ft., Temperate Zone; paniculata (Sedge), pale brown inflorescence, summer, 3 to 4 ft., Britain; pendula, brown inflorescence, summer, 5 to 6 ft., Britain; tristachya (japonica of gardens), leaves striped with white, 1 ft., Japan; Vilmorinii (Syn. comans), 2 to 3 ft., New Zealand.

Carica (Papaya, Pawpaw)—Ord. Passifloraceæ. Stove evergreen tree. Grown in Tropics for its edible fruits. First introduced 1690.
CULTURE: Rich loam. Position, large pots or borders in warm greenhouse. Pot or plant March. Water freely during growing season; sparingly at other times. Temp., March to Oct. 65° to 85°; Oct. to March 55° to 65°.
PROPAGATION: By cuttings of ripened growths inserted with leaves in sandy soil under bell-glass in temp. 80°.
SPECIES CULTIVATED: C. Papaya, yellow, July, fruits yellow or orange, 3 to 20 in. long, 20 to 25 ft., Trop. America.

Carlina (Carline Thistle)—Ord. Compositæ. Hardy perennials. First introduced 1640.
CULTURE: Soil, ordinary. Position, open dryish border. Plant, March or April.
PROPAGATION: By seeds sown ⅛ in. deep in April where plants are required to grow.
SPECIES CULTIVATED: C. acaulis, white, June, 9 in., Europe; acanthifolia, white, June, 18 in., S. Europe.

Carline Thistle (*Carlina acanthifolia*)—See Carlina.

Carludovica—Ord. Cyclanthaceæ. Stove ornamental-leaved perennials. First introduced 1818. Leaves, green, divided, palm-like.
CULTURE: Compost, two parts peat, one part sandy loam. Position, moist, shady. Pot, March. Water moderately Nov. to March, freely afterwards. Temp., Sept. to March 55° to 65°; March to Sept. 65° to 75°.
PROPAGATION: By division of plant at potting time.
SPECIES CULTIVATED: C. atrovirens, 2 to 4 ft., Northern S. America; gracilis (Syn. C. Plumieri), 2 ft., W. Indies; insignis (Syn. C. palmata), 3 to 6 ft., Peru; Plumeri, 2 ft., W. Indies.

Carmichælia—Ord. Leguminosæ. Greenhouse or hardy shrubs. Deciduous. First introduced 1823.
CULTURE: Soil, ordinary with a little sand, leaf-mould, and peat. Position, sheltered borders or walls, or in borders in the cold greenhouse.

PROPAGATION : By cuttings of half-ripened side-growths inserted in sandy soil under a bell-glass in the cold greenhouse.
SPECIES CULTIVATED : C. australis, lilac, May to Aug., 2 to 4 ft., New Zealand ; flagelliformis, purplish lilac, June, 4 to 5 ft., New Zealand.

Carnation (*Dianthus caryophyllus*)—See Dianthus.

Carnation Poppy (*Papaver somniferum*)—See Papaver.

Carniola Lily (*Lilium carniolicum*)—See Lilium.

Carob Tree (*Ceratonia siliqua*)—See Ceratonia.

Carolina Allspice—See Calycanthus.

Carolina Pink (*Spigelia marilandica*)—See Spigelia.

Carolina Poplar (*Populus monilifera*)—See Populus.

Carolina Yellow Jasmine (*Gelsemium sempervirens*)—See Gelsemium.

Carpathian Bell-flower (*Campanula carpatica*)—See Campanula.

Carpenteria (Californian Mock Orange)—Ord. Saxifragaceæ. Hardy deciduous flowering shrub. First introduced 1880.
CULTURE : Soil, light loamy. Position, sheltered position in shrubbery or against south wall. Plant, Oct. or Nov. Prune away shoots that have flowered directly blossoms fade.
PROPAGATION : By cuttings of young shoots inserted in cold frame in April ; suckers removed from roots in autumn ; layering shoots in Sept.
SPECIES CULTIVATED : C. californica, white, fragrant, June, 4 ft., California.

Carpenter's-Leaf (*Galax aphylla*)—See Galax.

Carpet Plant (*Ionopsidium acaule*)—See Ionopsidium.

Carpinus (Hornbeam)—Ord. Cupuliferæ. Hardy deciduous trees. Orn. foliage.
CULTURE : Soil, ordinary ; not adapted for chalky soils. Position, open, exposed. Plant, Oct. to March. Native species (C. Betulus) makes good hedge. Plant three-year old seedlings 3 ft. apart for this purpose and prune shoots in closely every autumn.
PROPAGATION : By seeds sown 1 in. deep in autumn in ordinary soil outdoors. Transplant seedlings when a year old 2 ft. apart each way. Useful Data : Number of seeds in a pound, 40,000. Weight of a bushel of seeds, 40 lb. Quantity of seeds to sow an acre, 35 lb. Timber reaches maturity at 40 years.
SPECIES CULTIVATED : C. Betulus (Hornbeam), 50 to 80 ft., Europe (Britain), and its varieties asplenifolia, columnaris, incisa (cut-leaved), pendula (weeping), and variegata (variegated) ; caroliniana (Syn. C. americana), American Hornbeam, 20 ft., N. America ; japonica (Japanese Hornbeam), 40 to 50 ft., Japan ; orientalis, 10 ft., S. Europe ; polyneura, 20 to 30 ft., W. China.

Carrion Flower—See Stapelia.

Carrot—See Daucus.

Carthamus (Distaff Thistle ; Safflower)—Ord. Compositæ. Hardy annuals. First introduced 1551.
CULTURE : Soil, ordinary. Position, sunny border.
PROPAGATION : By seeds sown ½ in. deep in light soil in temp. 65° in March, transplanting seedlings where they are to flower in May.
SPECIES CULTIVATED : C. lanatus, yellow, July, 2 ft. ; Oxyacantha, yellow, July, 2 ft. ; tinctorius, orange, June, 3 ft. All natives of Europe.

Cartwheel Flower (*Heracleum villosum*)—See Heracleum.

Carum (Parsley ; Caraway)—Ord. Umbelliferæ. Hardy biennial culinary herbs and aromatic seed-bearing plants. Caraway seeds used for confectionary purposes ; Parsley for garnishing, etc. First introduced 1548.
CULTURE OF PARSLEY : Soil, ordinary, deep, rich, moist. Position, partially shady ;

as edgings to borders, or in rows. Sow in Feb., May, and July in drills $\frac{1}{2}$ in. deep and 12 in. apart. Thin seedlings when 1 in. high to 3 in. apart, and later on to 8 in. apart. Thinnings may be replanted to form a fresh bed if desired. When leaves become coarse cut them all off to induce fresh growth. Renew beds every second year. Seed retains its vegetative power three years. Quantity required for a row 50 ft. long, 1 oz.

SPECIES CULTIVATED : C. Petroselinum (Parsley), yellow, summer, 1 to 2 ft., Sardinia ; Carvi (Caraway), pinkish white, July, 30 in., Europe. An agricultural rather than horticultural crop ; grown for sheep forage and for the Caraway Seeds of commerce.

Carya (Hickory)—Ord. Juglandaceæ. Hardy deciduous trees. First introduced 1629. Full-grown trees bear edible nuts similar to walnuts.
CULTURE : Soil, ordinary. Position, shrubberies, woods, or as single specimens on lawns and in parks. Plant, Oct. to March. Prune, Nov., thinning out unsightly branches only.
PROPAGATION : By nuts. First place the nuts in a stout box between layers of soil ; place in shady spot outdoors, and keep soil well moistened. In March pot singly in 6 in. pots and place on gentle bottom heat. When seedlings appear harden off gradually and plant in permanent quarters before roots become pot-bound.
SPECIES CULTIVATED : C. alba (Shell-bark Hickory), 70 to 100 ft., N. America ; amara (Bitter Nut), 70 to 100 ft., N. America ; olivœformis (Pecan), 100 to 170 ft., Southern U.S.A., Texas, Mexico ; Porcina (Pig Nut), 80 to 90 ft., Eastern America ; tomentosa (Mocker Nut), 50 to 60 ft., Eastern America.

Caryopteris (Moustache plant)—Ord. Verbenaceæ. Half-hardy shrubby perennial. First introduced 1814.
CULTURE : Compost, two parts loam, one part leaf-mould and a little sand. Position, pots in cool greenhouse, or in border at foot of a warm, sheltered wall outdoors. Pot or plant, April. Water freely in spring and summer, moderately in winter.
PROPAGATION : By seeds sown in light soil in temp. 55° in spring ; cuttings of the young shoots or division of roots in March or April.
SPECIES CULTIVATED : C. Mastacanthus, blue, autumn, 4 to 8 ft., China and Japan.

Caryota (East Indian Wine Palm ; Toddy Palm)—Ord. Palmaceæ. Stove palms. Orn. foliage. First introduced 1788.
CULTURE : Compost, equal parts loam, leaf-mould, and coarse sand. Position, pots, moist, shady. Pot, March. Water freely March to Nov., moderately after-wards. Temp., Sept. to March 55° to 65° ; March to Sept. 65° to 85°.
PROPAGATION : By seeds sown 1 in. deep in light soil in temp. 85° in March ; suckers removed from roots, inserted in small pots, any time.
SPECIES CULTIVATED : C. mitis, 20 to 25 ft., Malaya ; urens, 30 to 40 ft., Trop. Asia.

Cashew Nut (*Anacardium occidentale*)—See Anacardium.

Cashmere Larkspur (*Delphinium cashmirianum*)—See Delphinium.

Cassandra—Ord. Ericaceæ. Hardy evergreen flowering shrubs. First intro-duced 1748.
OUTDOOR CULTURE : Soil, equal parts peat, leaf-mould, or silver sand. Position, open sheltered borders, rockeries, or bogs. Plant, Sept. to Nov., or March. Prune straggling shoots only moderately after flowering. Water freely in dry positions during summer.
POT CULTURE : Soil, equal parts peat, leaf-mould, and fine silver sand. Position, well-drained pots in cold greenhouse, Nov. to June ; in shady position outdoors, June to Nov. Pot, Oct. to Nov. Water moderately, Nov. to March, freely afterwards.
PROPAGATION : By seeds sown $\frac{1}{16}$ in. deep in sandy peat in cold frame, Nov. or March ; layering shoots in Sept. ; division of plants, Oct. or Nov.
SPECIES CULTIVATED : C. calyculata (Syn. Andromeda calyculata), white, spring, 3 ft., N. America.

Cassia (Senna plant)—Ord. Leguminosæ. Greenhouse evergreen shrubs and hardy perennials. First introduced 1723.
CULTURE OF GREENHOUSE SPECIES : Compost, two parts loam, one part peat and sand. Position, pots in greenhouse, or well-drained border against south wall. Pot, March. Plant outdoors April. Water moderately Nov. to Feb., freely afterwards. Prune straggling shoots to within 2 in. of base in Dec. or Jan. Temp., Sept. to March 50° to 55° ; March to Sept. 55° to 65°.
CULTURE OF HARDY SPECIES : Soil, ordinary well drained. Position, sunny borders. Plant, March or April. Protect in winter with covering of leaves or ashes.
PROPAGATION : By seeds sown ⅛ in. deep in light soil in temp. 75° in March ; cuttings of previous year's shoots inserted in sandy soil under bell-glass in temp. 80° in March ; herbaceous species by division in March.
GREENHOUSE SPECIES : C. acutifolia (Alexandrian Senna), shrubby, 3 to 4 ft., Upper Nile, produces the Senna leaves of medical service ; angustifolia (Indian Senna), an Arabian shrub of similar but stronger character as C. acutifolia and also of importance as a producer of Senna leaves ; corymbosa, yellow, summer, 6 to 10 ft., Buenos Ayres ; fistula (Pudding Pipe Tree), pale yellow, 20 to 30 ft., India, of economic interest only, it being the source of the Cassia pods of commerce.
HARDY SPECIES : C. marilandica, yellow, Sept., 3 ft., N. America. There are other species, but above are the only ones worth growing.

Cassia Bark Tree (*Cinnamomum Cassia*)—See Cinnamomum.

Cassie (*Acacia farnesiana*)—See Acacia.

Cassinia (Golden Bush)—Ord. Compositæ. Hardy evergreen flowering and ornamental-leaved shrub.
CULTURE : Soil, ordinary. Position, sunny, dryish borders. Plant in autumn.
PROPAGATION : By cuttings of young shoots inserted in sandy soil in cold frame in summer.
SPECIES CULTIVATED : C. fulvida, white, summer, 4 to 6 ft., leaves golden tinted, New Zealand (Syn. Diplopappus chrysophyllus) ; leptophylla, white, Aug. to Sept., 4 to 5 ft., New Zealand ; Vanvilliersi, white, 2 to 6 ft., New Zealand.

Cassiope—Ord. Ericaceæ. Hardy evergreen flowering shrubs. First introduced 1798.
CULTURE : Soil, sandy peat. Position, moist, shady beds or borders. Plant, Sept. to April.
PROPAGATION : By layering shoots in autumn.
SPECIES CULTIVATED : C. fastigiata, white, May, 6 to 12 in., Himalayas ; C. hypnoides white and red, June, 1 to 3 in., Arctic Regions. Formerly known under generic name of Andromeda.

Castanea (Sweet or Spanish Chestnut)—Ord. Corylaceæ. Hardy deciduous trees. Bears edible nuts, which should be separated from the husks when latter fall in autumn, then be thoroughly dried in the sun or warm oven, and stored in air-tight jars or boxes in a cool, dry place. Young trees much grown as coppice wood for game shelter. Probably introduced to Britain by Romans.
CULTURE : Soil, deep, rich, dry, and sandy. Position, open, sunny. Plant, Oct. to Feb. Transplant seedlings when a year old. Distance apart to plant, 25 ft. for avenues and 5 ft. apart for underwood. Useful Data : Timber most valuable in a young state ; brittle when old. One bushel of seed will yield 3,000 plants. Number of seeds in a pound, 115. Weight of bushel of seed, 58 lb. Quantity of seeds to sow an acre, 600 lb. Timber reaches maturity at 50 years. Average life, 500 years. Uses : Rafters in churches, cabinet work, post and rail fencing, rustic work.
PROPAGATION : By seeds sown as soon as ripe in the open ground ; choice varieties by grafting in spring on C. sativa.
SPECIES CULTIVATED : C. crenata, 20 to 30 ft., Japan ; dentata (Syn. C. americana), 50 to 100 ft., Eastern N. America ; pumila, 10 to 20 ft., Eastern N. America ; sativa, 50 to 60 ft., S. Europe, N. Africa, etc., and its varieties, aureo-marginata (golden-edged) and heterophylla (cut-leaved).

Castanopsis (Golden-leaved Chestnut)—Ord. Cupuliferæ. Hardy evergreen ornamental-leaved tree.
CULTURE : Soil, sandy or well-drained loam, peat and leaf-mould. Position, lawns or mixed shrubberies. Plant, Oct. to March.
PROPAGATION : As advised for Sweet Chestnut.
SPECIES CULTIVATED : C. chrysophylla (Syn. Castanea chrysophylla), 30 to 100 ft., Oregon and California.

Castilleja (Painted Cup)—Ord. Scrophulariaceæ. Half-hardy perennials. Plants with showy bracts.
CULTURE : Compost, two parts peat, one part of equal proportions of loam, leaf-mould, and sand. Position, sunny sheltered borders. Plant in April. Protect in winter.
PROPAGATION : By seeds sown in temp. 55° to 65° in March, hardening off seedlings in cold frame.
SPECIES CULTIVATED : C. acuminata (Indian Paint-brush), scarlet, N. America ; coccinea, yellow and scarlet, July, 1 ft. ; pallida, light purple, 1 ft., N. America.

Castor Oil Plant (*Ricinus communis*)—See Ricinus.

Catalpa (Indian Bean)—Ord. Bignoniaceæ. Hardy deciduous flowering and ornamental-leaved trees. First introduced 1726.
CULTURE : Soil, ordinary, good. Position, sunny, sheltered lawns. Plant, Oct. to April.
PROPAGATION : By cuttings of firm shoots inserted in sandy soil under bell-glass in temp. 55° to 65° in summer.
SPECIES CULTIVATED : C. bignonioides (Indian Bean), white, spotted purple and yellow, July, 25 to 50 ft., United States, and its variety aurea (golden-leaved) ; ovata (Syn. Kæmpferi), yellow, spotted red, July, 20 to 40 ft., Japan ; speciosa (Syn. Cordifolia), white, June, 30 to 100 ft., Southern Central United States.

Catananche (Blue Cupidone ; Blue Succory)—Ord. Compositæ. Hardy perennials and annuals. First introduced 1596. Flowers may be cut and dried for winter decoration. Gather when fully developed.
CULTURE : Soil, ordinary. Position, warm borders. Plant, April.
PROPAGATION : By seeds sown ⅛ in. deep in light soil in temp. 55° in March, transplanting seedlings outdoors in June.
SPECIES CULTIVATED : C. cærulea, blue, 2 ft., July and Aug., S. Europe ; cærulea bicolor, white and blue ; lutea, yellow, June, 1 ft., S. Europe. Last named is an annual.

Catasetum—Ord. Orchidaceæ. Stove deciduous orchids. First introduced 1822.
CULTURE : Compost, good fibry peat and sphagnum moss in equal parts, with pulverised brick and small charcoal. Position, pots or hanging baskets, well drained. Water freely from time new growth begins until leaves fall off, very little other times. Temp., March to Sept. 65° to 85° ; Sept. to March 60° to 70°. Resting period, winter. Flowers appear at base of new pseudo-bulb when growth is finishing.
PROPAGATION : By division of plant at potting time.
SPECIES CULTIVATED : C. Bungerothii, white, spring, Venezuela ; macrocarpum, bronzy yellow and purple, spring, Trop. America ; rodigasianum, green and purple-brown, summer, Brazil ; splendens, white and yellow, spring, Venezuela ; tabulare, green and white, Colombia. There are others, but above are the best.

Catch-fly—See Silene.

Catesbæa (Lily Thorn)—Ord. Rubiaceæ. Stove evergreen flowering shrub.
CULTURE : Compost, equal parts loam and peat, and a little sand. Position, well-drained pots and plenty of light. Pot in March. Water freely March to Sept., moderately afterwards. Temp., 55° to 65° Oct. to March, 75° to 85° afterwards.
PROPAGATION : By cuttings inserted in sand under bell-glass in a temp. of 75° in spring.
SPECIES CULTIVATED : S. spinosa, yellow, May, 10 ft., W. Indies.

83

Cathcartia (Cathcart's Poppy)—Ord. Papaveraceæ. Hardy herbaceous perennial. First introduced 1850.
CULTURE : Soil, ordinary, dryish. Position, sunny, well-drained rockery.
PROPAGATION : By seeds sown ⅛ in. deep in sandy soil in cold frame in July, transplanting seedlings into small pots in Aug., keeping them in frame till planting time.
SPECIES CULTIVATED : C. villosa, yellow, June, 1 ft., Himalayas.

Cat-Mint (*Nepeta Mussini*)—See Nepeta.

Cat-Thyme (*Teucrium marum*)—See Teucrium.

Cat's Ear (*Antennaria tomentosa*)—See Antennaria.

Cat's Valerian (*Valeriana officinalis*)—See Valeriana.

Cattleya—Ord. Orchidaceæ. Stove orchids. Evergreen. **First introduced 1815.**
CULTURE : Compost, coarse fibry peat, chopped living sphagnum moss, and Osmunda fibre in equal proportions with broken brick or potsherds, charcoal, and sand. Position, well-drained pots, hanging baskets, blocks. Pot, Feb. or March. Keep plants well above rim of pot. Water three times weekly March to Aug. ; once weekly Aug. to Nov. and Feb. to March ; once a month other times. Syringe freely in summer. Temp., March to Sept. 65° to 85° ; Sept. to March 60° to 70°. Resting period, winter. Flowers appear at top of new growth directly growth is completed.
PROPAGATION : By division of pseudo-bulbs at potting time.
SPECIES CULTIVATED : C. Aclandiæ, yellow, green and purple, June to July, 6 in., Brazil ; bicolor, green, copper, purple and rose, Sept., 2 ft., Brazil ; bowringiana, rosy purple, Oct., 12 in., British Honduras ; citrina, yellow, May to Aug., 4 in., Mexico ; dowiana, yellow and purple, Aug. to Nov., Costa Rica ; gaskelliana, white, rosy purple and yellow, late summer and autumn, Venezuela ; guttata, yellow and purple, Nov., 2 ft., Brazil ; intermedia, purple and rose, May and June, 1 ft., Brazil ; labiata, mauve, purple and yellow, autumn, 1 ft., Brazil—there are many fine forms, named varieties and hybrids of this species ; lawrenciana, rosy purple, March, 10 in., British Guiana ; Loddigesii, rosy lilac and yellow, Aug., 18 in., Brazil ; luddemanniana, amethyst purple and yellow or white, autumn or spring, Venezuela ; maxima, rose and purple, Nov., 1 ft., Peru ; Mendelli, rosy lilac and purple, April to May, Colombia ; Mossiæ, rose, crimson purple and yellow, May to July, Venezuela ; percivaliana, rosy lilac, amethyst purple and yellow, Jan. and Feb., Venezuela ; Rex, white, purple and gold, Aug., 1 ft.; schilleriana, yellow, rose and purple, May, 6 in., Bahia ; Schroderæ, rose, purple and orange, spring, Colombia ; Skinneri, rose, purple, and white, May, 10 in., Mexico ; superba, rose, purple, crimson, and yellow, July, 10 in., British Guiana ; Trianæ, rosy lilac, purple and orange, Jan. to May, New Grenada ; walkeriana, lilac, purple and white, Dec., Brazil ; Warscewiczii (Syn. Gigas), rosy mauve, purple and yellow, June to Nov., New Grenada ; Warneri, rose and crimson, summer, Brazil. Numerous hybrids.

Caucasian Comfrey (*Symphytum caucasicum*)—See Symphytum.

Caucasian Fir (*Abies nordmanniana*)—See Abies.

Caucasian Lily (*Lilium monadelphum*)—See Lilium.

Caucasian Scabious (*Scabiosa caucasica*)—See Scabiosa.

Caucasian Scarlet Poppy (*Papaver rhœas umbrosum*)—See Papaver.

Cauliflower—See Brassica.

Caulophyllum (Pappoose-root ; Squaw-root ; Blue Cohosh)—**Ord. Berberidaceæ.** Hardy tuberous-rooted perennial. First introduced 1755.
CULTURE : Soil, ordinary. Position, shady. Plant, Nov.
PROPAGATION : By division of roots March to Nov.
SPECIES CULTIVATED : C. thalictroides, yellow, April, succeeded by blue berries in autumn, 1 ft., N. America.

Cayenne Pepper (*Capsicum frutescens*)—See Capsicum.

Cayenne Pepper Plant (*Capsicum minimum*)—See Capsicum.

Ceanothus (Mountain Sweet; Californian Lilac; New Jersey Tea-plant)—Ord. Rhamnaceæ. Hardy and half-hardy evergreen and deciduous flowering shrubs. First introduced 1713.
CULTURE: Soil, light, ordinary. Position, against south or west walls or fences outdoors; in pots in cool greenhouse. Plant, Oct. to March. Pot, Oct. Prune weak shoots away entirely in March. Water moderately in pots in winter, freely in summer.
PROPAGATION: By cuttings 3 in. long inserted in pots of sandy soil in cold frame, cool greenhouse in Oct.; layering strong shoots in autumn or spring; seeds sown in heat in spring.
DECIDUOUS SPECIES CULTIVATED: C. americanus (New Jersey Tea), white, July, 5 ft., E. America; Arnouldi (Syn. C. delilianus), blue, July to Sept., 3 to 4 ft., hybrid; azureus, blue, July till autumn frosts, 8 to 10 ft., Mexico; Fendleri, bluish white, 4 to 6 ft., Rocky Mountains; integerrimus, white to pale blue, June, 9 to 12 ft., California; ovatus, white, June to Aug., 2 to 3 ft., U.S.A. Additional kinds of great merit are: Albert Petit, rose pink; Ceres, pink; Georges Simon, rosy lilac; Gloire de Plantieres, sky blue; Gloire de Versailles, lavender blue; Indigo, indigo blue; Lucie Moser, sky blue; Marie Simon, rose. All hybrids and flowering freely from July onwards.
EVERGREEN SPECIES CULTIVATED: C. dentatus, blue, May, 10 ft., California; papillosus, blue, June, 10 to 12 ft., California; rigidus, blue, April to June, 6 to 12 ft., California; thyrsiflorus (Californian lilac), blue, May to June, 15 to 30 ft., California; veitchianus, blue, June, 10 ft., California.

Cedar—See Cedrus.

Cedar of Lebanon (*Cedrus Libani*)—See Cedrus.

Cedrela (Bastard Cedar; Chinese Cedar)—Ord. Meliaceæ. Hardy deciduous ornamental-leaved tree. Handsome habit. First introduced 1862.
CULTURE: Soil, good ordinary, well drained. Position, sheltered on lawns or in shrubberies. Plant in autumn.
PROPAGATION: By root cuttings.
SPECIES CULTIVATED: C. sinensis (Syn. Ailanthus flavescens), white and pink, June, 30 to 70 ft., China.

Cedronella (Balm of Gilead)—Ord. Labiatæ. Half-hardy herbaceous perennials and shrubs. First introduced 1697. Leaves fragrant.
CULTURE: Compost, two parts sandy loam, one part leaf-mould and sand. Pot, March. Position, pots in sunny greenhouse. Temp., Sept. to March 50° to 55°; March to Sept. 55° to 65°. Water moderately in autumn and winter, freely other times. C. triphylla may be grown at base of south wall in dryish soil in S. of England.
PROPAGATION: Perennial species by division of roots in March; shrubby species by cuttings of young shoots inserted in pots of sandy soil in temp. 75° in March, April, or May.
PERENNIAL SPECIES: C. cana, crimson and blue, July, 3 ft., Mexico.
SHRUBBY SPECIES: C. canariensis (Balm of Gilead), purple, July, 3 ft., Canaries.

Cedrus (Mount Atlas and Silver Cedar; Cedar of Lebanon; Deodar; East Indian Cedar; Fountain-tree)—Ord. Coniferæ. Hardy evergreen trees. Orn. foliage. First introduced 1676. Wood of Cedar of Lebanon used in ancient times as incense. Oldest cedar in England at Brethby Park, Derbyshire; planted in 1676. Cones not produced by Cedrus Libani until tree is 40 to 100 years old.
CULTURE: Soil, rich, deep, sandy. Position, well drained, elevated. C. atlantica does well in seaside gardens; and all are suitable for chalky soils. Plant, Sept. to Nov., or March to May.
PROPAGATION: By seeds sown ½ in. deep in well-drained pans of light soil in cold frame in April, transplanting seedlings outdoors following spring.
SPECIES CULTIVATED: C. atlantica (Mout Atlas Cedar), 80 to 100 ft., N. Africa; atlantica argentea, foliage intense grey-blue; atlantica aurea, foliage golden; atlantica glauca, foliage bluish; deodara (Deodar Cedar), 200 to 250 ft., Himalayas,

and its varieties crassifolia, robusta and viridis ; Libani (Cedar of Lebanon), 80 ft., Mt. Lebanon and Asia Minor ; Libani glauca, glaucous leaved.

Ceiba pentandra—See Eriodendron anfractuosum.

Celandine (*Chelidonium majus*)—See Chelidonium.

Celandine Poppy (*Stylophorum diphyllum*)—See Stylophorum.

Celastrus (Staff-tree ; Climbing Bitter-sweet ; Staff-vine)—Ord. Celastraceæ. Hardy deciduous shrubs and climbers. First introduced 1722.
CULTURE OF HARDY SPECIES : Soil, ordinary. Position, walls, fences, and arbours. Plant, Oct. to March. Prune away weak shoots and tips of main shoots in Feb.
PROPAGATION : By layers of young shoots in autumn or spring.
HARDY SPECIES : C. articulatus, green, June, 15 ft., China and Japan ; hypoleucus, yellowish, capsules yellow and red when open, 20 to 30 ft., W. China ; latifolius, green, seed capsules orange and bright red when open, 10 ft., shrubby, China ; scandens, yellow, summer, capsules orange and scarlet when open, climbing, N. America.

Celeriac (*Apium graveolens rapaceum*)—See Apium.

Celery—See Apium.

Celosia (Cockscomb)—Ord. Amarantaceæ. Greenhouse annuals. First introduced 1570.
CULTURE OF CELOSIAS : Compost, two parts fibry loam, one part leaf-mould and well-decayed cow manure and sand. Position, warm greenhouse, exposed to light. Sow seeds ⅛ in. deep in well-drained pans of light soil in temp. 75° in March. Transplant seedlings 1 in. apart when 1 in. high in light soil in well-drained pots and keep in temp. 60° to 75°. When seedlings have formed four leaves place them singly in 3 in. pots, transferring them in June to 5 in. pots. Keep plants near the glass. Water roots moderately. Syringe foliage twice daily. Liquid manure, apply when flowers appear. Summer temp., 55° to 65°. May be used for summer bedding between May and Sept.
CULTURE OF COCKSCOMBS : Sow seeds as advised for Celosias. When seedlings appear place them close to glass and keep moderately moist. Transplant, when seedlings have formed three leaves, into 2 in. pots in above compost. Place pots on shelf near glass until " combs " show themselves. Select plants with finest " combs " and place them in 4 in. pots ; plunge these to rim on gentle hotbed (temp. 65° to 75°) and keep moderately moist at root. Syringe freely. Transfer plants when pots are full of roots into 5 in. pots and treat as before. Give liquid manure when " combs " are well advanced. Good specimen of " comb " should measure 9 to 12 in. long, 3 to 6 in. wide, and plant 6 to 9 in. high.
SPECIES CULTIVATED : C. argentea, white, summer, 2 ft., China ; argentea cristata (Cockscomb), red or crimson, summer, 2 ft., Tropics. Childsi, plumosa and Thompsoni are varieties commonly cultivated.

Celsia (Cretan Mullein)—Ord. Scrophulariaceæ. Half-hardy shrubs and biennials. First introduced 1752.
CULTURE : Compost, equal parts loam, leaf-mould, and sand. Position, pots in unheated greenhouse or in flower beds outdoors in summer. Pot or plant, March ; water moderately in winter, freely at other times.
PROPAGATION : Shrubby species by cuttings, 3 in. long, of young shoots, inserted in well-drained pots of sandy soil in cold frame or greenhouse in April, May, or June, or by seeds sown ¹⁄₁₆ in. deep in light sandy soil in similar position ; biennial species by seed sown ¹⁄₁₆ in. deep in sunny place outdoors in April or Aug.
SPECIES CULTIVATED : C. Arcturus, yellow, July, 3 to 4 ft., Crete, shrubby ; cretica, yellow, July, 4 ft., S. Europe, biennial

Celtis (Nettle Tree ; Hackberry)—Ord. Urticaceæ. Hardy deciduous ornamental-leaved trees. First introduced 1656.
CULTURE : Soil, ordinary. Position, sunny shrubberies. Plant, Oct. to Feb. Prune, Nov. to Feb.

PROPAGATION : By seeds sown outdoors in spring; layering shoots in autumn or spring; cuttings of firm shoots in Nov.
SPECIES CULTIVATED : C. australis, May, 50 to 70 ft., S. Europe ; davidiana, 15 to 25 ft., N. China ; occidentalis (Hackberry), spring, 40 to 130 ft., N. America ; sinensis, 15 to 25 ft., Japan and China.

Centaurea (Cornflower ; Sweet Sultan ; Centaury)—Ord. Compositæ. Hardy and tender perennials and annuals.
CULTURE OF ANNUAL SPECIES : Sow seeds outdoors in April where plants are required to flower. Thin seedlings when an inch or so high to 4 or 6 in. apart. Ordinary rich soil and a sunny position.
CULTURE OF PERENNIAL SPECIES : Soil, ordinary good. Position, sunny borders. Plant, autumn or spring. Lift, divide, and replant every third or fourth year.
PROPAGATION : By seeds sown outdoors in April, or in heat in spring, also by division of roots in autumn or spring.
CULTURE OF TENDER SPECIES : Rear plants from seeds sown in heat in spring or summer, and grow on in pots in greenhouse ; or from cuttings inserted in cold frame in July or Aug., lifting them when rooted and placing in pots in greenhouse. Plant out in beds end of May. Silvery foliage of these very striking for bedding.
ANNUAL SPECIES : C. americana, rose or purple, Aug., 2 to 5 ft., N. America ; cyanus (cornflower), blue, rose, white, etc., summer, 3 ft., Britain ; moschata (Purple Sweet Sultan), purple, summer, 2 ft., Orient ; moschata alba (White Sweet Sultan), white ; moschata flava (Yellow Sweet Sultan), yellow.
PERENNIAL SPECIES : C. babylonica, yellow, July, 5 to 7 ft., Levant ; dealbata, rose, summer, 18 in., Caucasus ; glastifolia, yellow, summer, 4 to 6 ft., Caucasus ; macrocephala, yellow, July, 3 to 5 ft., Caucasus ; montana, blue, July, 2 to 3 ft., Caucasus, Pyrenees ; montana alba, white ; montana rosea, rose ; orientalis, yellow, summer, 3 ft., Europe ; ruthenica, pale yellow, July to Aug., 3 to 4 ft., Caucasus and Siberia.
TENDER SPECIES : C. cineraria, 12 to 18 in., Italy ; Clementei, 2 to 3 ft., Spain ; gymnocarpa (Syn. argentea), 2 ft., S. Europe ; ragusina, 2 ft., S. Europe, all with elegant silvery foliage.

Centauridium Drummondii—See Xanthisma texanum.

Centaury (*Erythræa Centaurium*)—See Erythræa.

Centaury, Yellow (*Chlora perfoliata*)—See Chlora.

Centipede Plant (*Muehlenbeckia platyclados*)—See Muehlenbeckia.

Centradenia—Ord. Melastomaceæ. Stove flowering shrubs. Evergreen. First introduced 1840.
CULTURE : Compost, two parts peat, one part loam and sand. Position, sunny. Pot, Feb. Temp., Sept. to March 55° to 65° ; March to Sept. 65° to 75°. Water moderately Sept. to March, freely afterwards.
PROPAGATION : By cuttings of side-shoots 2 or 3 in. long inserted in pots of sandy peat under bell-glass in temp. 85° in Feb. and March.
SPECIES CULTIVATED : C. floribunda, red, July, 18 in., Mexico ; grandifolia, pink, Sept., 18 in., Mexico; inæquilateralis (Syn. C. rosea), rose, April, 1 ft., Mexico.

Centranthus (Red Valerian ; Spur Valerian ; German Lilac)—Ord. Valerianaceæ. Hardy herbaceous perennials and annuals. Sometimes spelled Kentranthus.
CULTURE : Soil, ordinary. Position, old walls, sunny rockeries, borders. Plant, March or April.
PROPAGATION : By seeds sown ⅛ in. deep in light soil in temp. 55° in March, transplanting seedlings outdoors in May ; or in sunny positions outdoors in April or June, transplanting seedlings in May or Aug.; perennials also by division in autumn or spring.
ANNUAL SPECIES : C. macrosiphon, red, July, 2 ft., Spain ; macrosiphon albus, white.
PERENNIAL SPECIES : C. ruber (Red Valerian), red, July, 18 in., Europe (Britain) ; ruber albus, white.

Centropogon—Ord. Campanulaceæ. Stove herbaceous perennial.
CULTURE : Compost, equal parts loam, peat, leaf-mould, and a little sand. Pot,

March. Position, stove Sept. to June ; June to Sept. sunny frame outdoors. Temp., Oct. to Feb. 50° to 55° ; Feb. to June 60° to 75°. Water moderately Sept. to Feb., freely afterwards. Prune shoots close to soil in Feb. when repotting. PROPAGATION : By cuttings of young shoots 3 in. long, removed with a portion of stem attached, and inserted in light sandy soil in well-drained pots under bell-glass in temp. 60° to 70°. SPECIES CULTIVATED : C. lucyanus, rose, autumn, 2 ft., a hybrid. Habitat of the genus : Trop. America.

Centrosema—Ord. Leguminosæ. Stove evergreen climber. CULTURE : Compost, equal parts peat, loam, leaf-mould, and silver sand. Position, pots on staging, shoots trained up rafters or round a trellis or sticks. Pot in March. Water freely in spring and summer ; moderately in winter. Temp., March to Sept. 75° to 85° ; Sept. to March 55° to 65°. PROPAGATION : By seeds in a temp. of 75° in March ; also by cuttings in sand in a temp. of 85° in summer. SPECIES CULTIVATED : C. Plumieri (Syn. Clitoria Plumieri), red and white, autumn, 6 ft., S. America.

Century Plant (*Agave americana*)—See Agave.

Cephalanthera (White Helleborine)—Ord. Orchidaceæ. Hardy terrestrial orchids. CULTURE : Soil, chalky loam. Position, open and well-drained border. Plant, Sept. and Oct. PROPAGATION : By division of roots in Sept. SPECIES CULTIVATED: C. ensifolia, white, June, 2 ft.; pallens (Syn. C. grandiflora), white and yellow, June, 18 in. ; rubra, purple and white, May, 18 in. Natives of Britain.

Cephalanthus (Button-bush)—Ord. Rubiaceæ. Hardy deciduous shrub. Orn. foliage. First introduced 1735. CULTURE : Soil, sandy peat. Position, open shrubberies. Plant, Oct. or Nov. PROPAGATION : By layers of shoots in Sept. or April. SPECIES CULTIVATED : C. occidentalis, white, Aug., 7 ft., N. America.

Cephalaria—Ord. Dipsaceæ. Hardy herbaceous perennials. First introduced 1759. CULTURE : Soil, ordinary. Position, borders or woods. Plant, March or April. PROPAGATION : By seeds sown ⅛ in. deep in sunny position outdoors in April, transplanting seedlings in May. SPECIES CULTIVATED : C. alpina (Syn. Scabiosa alpina), yellow, July, 5 ft., Europe ; tatarica, yellow, July, 5 ft., Siberia.

Cephalotaxus (Cluster-flowered Yew)—Ord. Coniferæ. Hardy conifers. Orn. foliage. Evergreen. First introduced 1837. Leaves similar to those of Yew. CULTURE : Soil, ordinary. Position, sheltered shrubberies or lawns. Plant, Sept. to Nov. or March to May. PROPAGATION : By seeds sown ¼ in. deep in light soil in cold frame in Sept or March, transplanting seedlings outdoors a year after ; cuttings of shoots 3 in. long inserted in sandy soil in shady cold frame, or under bell-glass or hand-light outdoors in Aug. or Sept. SPECIES CULTIVATED: C. drupacea, 10 to 30 ft., Japan; Fortunei, 10 to 20 ft., N. China ; pedunculata, 10 to 20 ft., Japan.

Cephalotus (Australian Pitcher-plant)—Ord. Saxifragaceæ. Greenhouse herbaceous perennial. First introduced 1822. Flowers, white. Pitchers, 1 to 3 in. long, dark green, purple, and pink. CULTURE : Compost, equal parts sphagnum moss, fibry peat, and silver sand. Position, pots or pans, well drained and covered with bell-glass ; shady cool greenhouse or window. Temp., Oct. to March 45° to 55°; March to Oct. 50° to 55°. Water moderately Sept. to April, freely afterwards. PROPAGATION : By division of roots in March. SPECIES CULTIVATED : C. follicularis, Australia ; 2 to 4 in.

Cerastium (Snow in Summer; Snow-plant)—Ord. Caryophyllaceæ. Hardy perennials. Evergreen and deciduous.
CULTURE : Soil, ordinary. Position, dryish borders, rockeries and edgings to flower beds. Plant, March or April.
PROPAGATION : By division of plants in March or April ; cuttings of shoots 3 in. long inserted in ordinary soil in shady position outdoors in June or July ; seeds sown ₁₆ in. deep in shady position outdoors in April, transplanting seedlings in June or July.
SPECIES CULTIVATED : C. alpinum, white, June, 3 to 4 in., Britain ; Biebersteinii, white, June, 6 in., leaves silvery, Asia Minor ; Boissieri, white, June, 8 to 9 in., leaves silvery ; grandiflorum, white, July, 6 in. ; tomentosum (Snow in Summer), white, May, 6 in., leaves silvery, Europe.

Cerasus (Cherry)—See Prunus.

Ceratonia (Carob-bean)—Ord. Leguminosæ. Tender evergreen tree. First introduced 1570. The fleshy pods are edible.
CULTURE : Position, against south walls ; suitable for S. and W. of England only ; or in conservatories or unheated greenhouses. Plant, Sept. to Nov. or March to May.
PROPAGATION : By seeds sown 1 in. deep in pots of sandy soil in temp. 85° in March, transplanting seedlings outdoors in June ; cuttings of firm shoots 4 in. long inserted in sandy soil under bell-glass in cold frame or greenhouse in Aug. or Sept.
SPECIES CULTIVATED : C. Siliqua, yellow and red, Sept., 40 to 50 ft., S. Europe.

Ceratopteris (Pod Fern)—Ord. Filices. Stove water floating fern. Annual.
CULTURE : Compost, equal parts loam and leaf-mould. Position, in pots or pans submerged to rim in tank of water. Temp., Sept. to March 55° or 60° ; March to Sept. 65° to 75°.
PROPAGATION : By spores sown in Feb. on surface of compost in pan in water as above ; pegging old fronds to surface of soil from which young plants will grow.
SPECIES CULTIVATED : C. thalictroides, Trop. America.

Ceratostigma (Lead-wort)—Ord. Plumbaginaceæ. Hardy perennial of dwarf, shrubby habit, and hardy shrubs.
CULTURE : Soil, sandy loam. Position, sunny rockery. Plant in autumn or spring.
PROPAGATION : By division in spring ; cuttings of nearly ripe growth in close frame in July or Aug.
SPECIES CULTIVATED : C. Griffithii, blue, 1 to 2 ft., Bhotan ; plumbaginoides (Syn. Plumbago Larpentæ), blue, autumn, 1 ft., China ; willmottianum, azure-blue, July to Oct., 3 to 10 ft., China.

Cercidiphyllum—Ord. Trochodendraceæ. Hardy, deciduous tree. First introduced 1881.
CULTURE : Soil, well-drained, peaty loam. Position sheltered from early frosts and cold winds.
PROPAGATION : By seeds sown in pans or boxes in cool greenhouse or frame in March, or by layering in spring.
SPECIES CULTIVATED : C. japonicum, 50 to 100 ft., Japan, China.

Cercis (Judas-tree ; Red-bud)—Ord. Leguminosæ. Hardy, deciduous flowering trees. First introduced 1596.
CULTURE : Soil, rich, deep, sandy. Position, warm sheltered shrubberies, or on lawns. N. of England against south wall. Plant, Oct. to March. Prune away old branches in Feb.
PROPAGATION : By seeds sown ¼ in. deep in light sandy soil in temp. 55° to 65° in March, transplanting seedlings outdoors in June, or by layers of strong shoots in autumn or spring.
SPECIES CULTIVATED : C. canadensis (Red-bud), pale rose, May to June, 15 to 40 ft., N. America ; chinensis, pink, May, 20 to 50 ft., China and Japan ; Siliquastrum (Judas-tree), purple or rose, April to May, 20 to 40 ft., S. Europe.

Cereus (Torch Thistle ; Night-flowering Cereus)—Ord. Cactaceæ. Greenhouse plants with fleshy, spiny stems, no leaves. First introduced 1690.

CULTURE : Compost, two parts fibry loam, one part coarse sand and pounded brick rubbish. Position, well-drained pots in sunny greenhouses or windows. Pot every three or four years, in March. Water once a month Sept. to April, once a week afterwards. Temp., Sept. to March 50° to 55° ; March to Sept. 55° to 65°.

PROPAGATION : By seeds sown ¼ in. deep in well-drained pans of sandy soil in temp. 75° in March, keeping soil moderately moist ; cuttings of stems inserted in small pots of sandy soil kept barely moist in summer ; grafting on common kind in April.

SPECIES CULTIVATED : C. aggregatus, scarlet, Sept., U. States ; Berlandieri, purple, Texas ; Blanckii, rose, summer, Mexico ; cærulescens, white, July, Mexico ; cæspitosus, rose, summer, U.S.A. ; enneacanthus, purple, July, Texas ; Fendleri, purple, June, Mexico, etc. ; flagelliformis, rosy red, March, Peru ; *fulgidus, orange-scarlet, July ; gemmatus, purple, summer, Mexico ; gigantus, white, California ; *grandiflorus, white, July, W. Indies ; leeanus, red, Mexico ; *Lemairii, yellow and white, June ; leptacanthus, purple-lilac and white, May ; *Macdonaldiæ, white and red, July, Honduras ; Mallisonii, red, summer, hybrid ; multiplex, scarlet, summer, Brazil ; *Napoleonis, yellow and white, autumn, Mexico ; *nycticalus, white, autumn, Mexico ; paucispinus, red and orange, summer, New Mexico ; pentalophus, rose, Mexico ; peruvianus, red, August, Peru ; polyacanthus, blood red, spring, Mexico ; procumbens, rosy purple, May, Mexico ; reductus, white and rose, summer, Mexico ; repandus, white, summer, W. Indies ; Royenii, rose, spring, New Grenada ; senilis (Old man cactus), columnar-shaped stem covered with white shaggy hairs, Mexico ; serpentinus, purple and white, Peru ; *speciosissimus, crimson, July, S. America ; *triangularis, white, Aug., W. Indies ; variabilis, green and red, July, S. America. Those indicated by an asterisk are night blooming.

Cerinthe (Honeywort ; Wax-plant)—Ord. Boraginaceæ. Hardy annuals and perennials. First introduced 1570.

CULTURE : Soil, ordinary. Position, sunny well-drained beds or borders. Plant perennial species Oct. or April.

PROPAGATION : Annuals by seeds sown ⅛ in. deep in April where plants are to flower, or in boxes of light sandy soil in temp. 55° to 65° in March, transplanting seedlings outdoors in May ; thin outdoor-sown seedlings to 2 in. apart ; perennials by seeds similar to annuals and by division of roots in April.

ANNUAL SPECIES : C. major, yellow and purple, July, 1 ft., Alps ; retorta, yellow and violet, July, 18 in., Greece.

PERENNIAL SPECIES : C. maculata, yellow, June, 18 in., S. Europe.

Ceropegia—Ord. Asclepiadaceæ. Greenhouse trailing plants. Ornamental-leaved.

CULTURE : Compost, equal parts peat, loam, leaf-mould, and silver sand. Position, baskets or pots suspended from roof of greenhouse, or in rockeries ; sunny. Pot, March. Water moderately between March and Sept., occasionally afterwards. Temp., March to Sept. 55° to 65°, afterwards 45° to 50°.

PROPAGATION : By cuttings of slender shoots inserted in silver sand, in well-drained pots, in a temp. of 65° in spring.

SPECIES CULTIVATED : C. elegans, white, brown, and purple, summer, 3 to 4 ft., India ; Sandersonii, green, autumn, 3 ft., Natal ; Woodii, white and purple, summer, 2 to 3 ft., S. Africa.

Cestrum (Bastard Jasmine)—Ord. Solanaceæ. Greenhouse flowering shrubs. Evergreen or semi-evergreen. First introduced 1787.

CULTURE : Compost, two parts loam, one part leaf-mould and sand. Position, pots or beds with shoots trained on wall, pillars, or roof of greenhouse. Pot, March. Prune into shape, Feb. Temp., Sept. to March 40° to 50° ; March to Sept. 55° to 60°. Water moderately in winter, freely other times.

PROPAGATION : By cuttings of side shoots 3 or 4 in. long, removed with portion

of old stem attached, inserted in well-drained pots of sandy soil in temp. 65° to 75° in July, Aug., or Sept.

SPECIES CULTIVATED : C. aurantiacum, orange-yellow, June, 5 ft., Guatemala; elegans, carmine, spring, 10 ft., Mexico ; Newellii, crimson, June, 10 ft. ; Parqui, greenish white or yellow, June to July, 7 ft., Western S. America. Formerly known under the generic name of Habrothamnus.

Ceterach—See Asplenium.

Chænostoma—Ord. Scrophulariaceæ. Half-hardy sub-shrub. First introduced 1816.

CULTURE : Soil, ordinary. Position, sunny beds or borders outdoors May to Oct., greenhouse or frame in winter. Plant outdoors in May.

PROPAGATION : By seeds sown ₁⁄₁₆ in. deep in light soil in temp. 65° to 70° in March ; cuttings inserted in well-drained pots of sandy soil in greenhouse or cold frame in Sept.

SPECIES CULTIVATED : C. hispidum, lilac, July, to 2 ft., S. Africa.

Chærophyllum (Bulbous-rooted Chervil)—Ord. Umbelliferæ. Hardy esculent vegetable. First introduced 1726. Roots carrot-like, yellowish white, sweet ; cooked and served as carrots.

CULTURE : Soil, ordinary. Position, sunny beds outdoors. Lift roots in Aug. and store them in dry, dark place until required for use.

PROPAGATION : By seeds sown 1 in. deep in drills 1 ft. apart in Aug., Sept., and Oct. Thin out seedlings to 8 in. apart in May.

SPECIES CULTIVATED : C. bulbosum, white, June, 2 to 3 ft., S. Europe. See also the genus Anthriscus.

Chain Fern (*Woodwardia radicans*)—See Woodwardia.

Chain Orchid—See Platyclinis.

Chalice Cup Narcissus (*Narcissus incomparabilis*)—See Narcissus.

Chalk Plant (*Gypsophila paniculata*)—See Gypsophila.

Chamæbatiaria Millefolium.—See Spiræa Millefolium.

Chamæcyparis—See Cupressus.

Chamædorea—Ord. Palmaceæ. Stove palms. Ornamental foliage. First introduced 1846.

CULTURE : Compost, two parts peat, one part loam and sand. Position, shady part of stove in pots or tubs. Pot, March. Water moderately Sept. to March, abundantly afterwards. Temp., Sept. to March 55° to 65° ; March to Sept. 65° to 75°.

PROPAGATION : By seeds sown 1 in. deep in above compost in pots, in temp. 85° in March.

SPECIES CULTIVATED : C. elatior, 20 to 30 ft., Mexico; elegans, 8 to 10 ft., Mexico.

Chamælirion (Wand Lily)—Ord. Liliaceæ. Hardy herbaceous perennial. Introduced 1759.

CULTURE : Soil, loam and leaf-mould. Position, cool, moist, and shady. Best grown in colonies. Plant in March.

PROPAGATION : By seeds sown soon as ripe in loam, peat, and leaf-mould in a cold frame. Division of the root-stock in March.

SPECIES CULTIVATED : C. luteum (Syn. C. carolinianum), yellow, June and July, 18 in., N. America.

Chamæpeuce—See Cnicus.

Chamærops (Fan Palm ; African Hair Palm ; European Palm)—Ord. Palmaceæ. Greenhouse and half-hardy palm. Orn. foliage. First introduced 1731. Leaves, fan-shaped, green.

CULTURE : Compost, two parts rich loam, one part decayed leaf-mould and sand. Position, well-drained pots in greenhouse or sheltered well-drained beds outdoors

in S. of England.   Pot, March.   Plant, April.   Temp., Sept. to March 40° to 50° ;
March to Sept. 50° to 60°.   Water moderately in winter, freely in summer.
PROPAGATION :   By seeds sown 1 in. deep in light soil in temp. of 80° in Feb. or
March ; suckers removed from parent plant in April or Aug.
SPECIES CULTIVATED :   C. humilis, 10 to 30 ft., S. Europe, N. Africa.   See also the
genus Trachycarpus.

Chamomile (*Anthemis nobilis*)—See Anthemis.

Chandelier Flower (*Brunsvigia Josephinæ*)—See Brunsvigia.

Chaplet Flower (*Stephanotis floribunda*)—See Stephanotis.

Chard—A variety of Leaf or Spinach Beet.   See Beta.

Charieis—Ord. Compositæ.   Hardy annual.   First introduced 1819.
CULTURE :   Soil, ordinary.   Position, sunny borders or rock gardens.   Sow seed in
March or April where plants are required, thinning out seedlings when large
enough to handle.
SPECIES CULTIVATED :   C. heterophylla, purplish blue, white or red, 6 to 12 in.,
S. Africa.

Chaste Tree (*Vitex Agnus-castus*)—See Vitex.

Chatham Island Forget-me-not (*Myosotidium nobile*)—See Myosotidium.

Cheddar Pink (*Dianthus cæsius*)—See Dianthus.

Cheilanthes (Californian Lace Fern ;   Lip Fern)—Ord. Filices.   Stove and
greenhouse ferns.   First introduced 1775.
CULTURE :   Compost, two parts peat, one part loam and silver sand.   Position, pots
in shade.   Pot, Feb. or March.   Water moderately Oct. to Feb., freely afterwards.
Temp., stove species, Sept. to March 55° to 65°, March to Sept. 65° to 75° ; green-
house, Sept. to March 45° to 50° ; March to Sept. 55° to 65°.
PROPAGATION :   By spores similar to Adiantum.
GREENHOUSE SPECIES :   C. argentea, 6 to 8 in., N. Asia, etc. ;   californica (Californian
Lip Fern), 6 in., California (also known as Hypolepis californica) ;   Clevelandii
(Cleveland's Lip Fern), 12 in., N. America ;   Eatonii, 6 in., N. America ;   fragrans,
2 to 4 ins., S. Europe ;   hirta, 4 to 8 in., Cape, Mexico, etc. ;   Lindheimeri, 3 to 6 in.,
Texas ;   microphylla (Plumier's Lip Fern), 6 to 8 in., N. America ;   pulchella, 9 in.,
Madeira ;   viscida (Sticky Lip Fern), 6 in., N. America.
STOVE SPECIES :   C. chlorophylla, 12 in., S. America ;   farinosa, 6 to 8 in., Abyssinia,
Java, etc. ;   myriophylla (Lace Fern), Syn. C. elegans, 4 to 8 in., Trop. America ;
radiata, 9 to 12 in., Trop. America ;   tenuis, 1 ft., Mexico.   See also Pellæa.

Cheiranthus (Gilliflower ;   Wallflower)—Ord. Cruciferæ.   Hardy perennials.
Of biennial duration only on heavy soils.   Flowers, single and double, fragrant.
CULTURE OF WALLFLOWERS :   Soil, ordinary well-drained, not too heavy ;   add lime
or old mortar.   Position, sunny borders, beds or old walls.   Sow either broadcast
or in drills 6 in. apart and ½ in. deep in May.   Transplant seedlings when third
leaf has formed, 6 in. apart each way, in a bed of firm soil limed as before, and plant
out finally a foot or so apart in Sept. or Oct.   Make soil firm around plants to
ensure sturdy firm growth.   Double-flowered varieties may be increased by
cuttings or slips of side shoots removed with a slight heel attached, and inserted in
cold frame or shady border in Aug.   Plant out in March.   To grow on old walls,
sow a pinch of seed in crevices, adding a little soil and cow manure to supply food
to young plants ;   or plant young seedlings in similar compost in spring.
CULTURE OF DWARF SPECIES :   C. alpinus, Marshallii, kewensis, and semperflorens
should be grown on sunny rockeries in good loamy soil and old mortar.   Plant in
spring.   Top-dress annually in March with well-rotted cow manure.
PROPAGATION :   As advised for Double Wallflowers.
POT CULTURE :   Plant seedlings in good ordinary mould in 6 in. pots in Sept. ;
keep in sunny cold frame till flower buds form, then transfer to greenhouse.   Water
moderately.   Feed with liquid manure when in flower.   Throw away after blooming.
SPECIES CULTIVATED :   C. alpinus, yellow, May, 6 in., Scandinavia, best grown on a
rockery ;   Cheiri (Wallflower), various colours, spring, 1 to 2 ft., Europe ;   Marshallii,

orange, 1 ft., hybrid ; kewensis, sulphur, orange, purple, **Nov. to May, 1 ft.,** hybrid ; semperflorens (Syn. C. mutabilis), purple, spring, 1 ft., Morocco. See also Erysimum. The plant known in gardens as Cheiranthus Allioni (Siberian Wallflower) is Erysimum asperum.

Chelidonium (Celandine ; Swallow-wort)—Ord. Papaveraceæ. Hardy perennial or biennial.

CULTURE : Soil, ordinary. Position, damp shady borders. Plant, March or April.

PROPAGATION : By seeds sown ⅛ in. deep in shade outdoors in April ; division of roots in April.

SPECIES CULTIVATED : C. majus, yellow, May, 2 ft., Britain ; majus flore pleno, double.

Chelone (Turtle Head ; Shell-flower)—Ord. Scrophulariaceæ. **Hardy her-**baceous perennials. First introduced 1752. See also Pentstemon.

CULTURE : Soil, rich, deep. Position, open borders. Plant, Oct. or March.

PROPAGATION : By seeds sown ₁₆ in. deep in light soil in temp. 55° to 65° in March, or similar depth in soil in cold frame in April, transplanting seedlings outdoors in May and June ; cuttings inserted in sandy soil in cold frame in June and July ; division of plants in Aug. and Sept.

SPECIES CULTIVATED : C. glabra, white, Aug., 2 to 3 ft., N. America ; Lyoni, purple, Aug., 2 to 3 ft., N. America ; obliqua, purple, Aug., 2 to 3 ft., N. America.

Chenopodium (Good King Henry ; Wild Spinach)—Ord. Chenopodiaceæ. Hardy perennials and annuals. C. Bonus-Henricus and C. Quinoa grown sometimes as a substitute for Spinach.

CULTURE OF GOOD KING HENRY : Soil, good, well trenched, and liberally manured. Position, dryish, sunny. Sow seeds 1 in. deep in drills 12 in. apart in April. Thin seedlings out to 9 in. apart in May. Cover bed in October with thin layer of manure. Gather young shoots in April as substitute for asparagus ; leaves in May and June in lieu of spinach. Renew beds every 3 or 4 years.

CULTURE OF ANNUAL SPECIES : Soil, ordinary. Position, sunny beds or borders. Sow seeds outdoors in April. Thin seedlings to 18 in. apart. Pinch out points of shoots to make bushy plants.

CULTURE OF C. QUINOA : Soil, ordinary. Position, open garden. Sow seeds in drills 1 in. deep and 2 ft. apart from March onwards at intervals of a few weeks. Gather leaves, cook, and eat like spinach.

PERENNIAL SPECIES : C. Bonus-Henricus (Good King Henry), 3 ft., Britain.

ANNUAL SPECIES : C. purpurascens (Syn. C. Atriplicis), reddish purple, Aug., 3 ft., leaves and shoots rosy violet, China ; Quinoa, 4 to 5 ft., Andes.

Chequer Berry (*Mitchella repens*)—See Mitchella.

Chequered Daffodil (*Fritillaria meleagris*)—See Fritillaria.

Cherimoyer (*Anona Cherimolia*)—See Anona.

Cherokee Rose (*Rosa lævigata*)—See Rosa.

Cherry—See Prunus.

Cherry Laurel (*Prunus Laurocerasus*)—See Prunus.

Cherry Pie (*Heliotropium peruvianum*)—See Heliotropium.

Cherry Plum-tree (*Prunus cerasifera*)—See Prunus.

Chervil—See Anthriscus.

Chervil, Bulbous-rooted—See Chærophyllum.

Chickweed Winter Green (*Trientalis europæa*)—See Trientalis.

Chicory—See Cichorium.

Chilian Arbor-vitæ (*Libocedrus chilensis*)—See Libocedrus.

Chilian Bell-flower—See Nolana.

Chilian Crocus (*Tecophilæa Cyanocrocus*)—See Tecophilæa.

Chilian Glory Flower (*Eccremocarpus scaber*)—See Eccremocarpus.

Chilian Gum Box (*Escallonia rubra*)—See Escallonia.

Chilian Pine-tree (*Araucaria imbricata*)—See Araucaria.

Chilian Pitcher-flower (*Sarmienta repens*)—See Sarmienta.

Chilian Rhubarb (*Gunnera manicata*)—See Gunnera.

Chili Jasmine (*Mandevilla suaveolens*)—See Mandevilla.

Chili Nettle (*Loasa lateritia*)—See Loasa.

Chili Pepper (*Capsicum annuum*)—See Capsicum.

Chili Strawberry (*Fragaria chiloensis*)—See Fragaria.

Chillies (*Capsicum frutescens*)—See Capsicum.

Chimaphila (Spotted Winter Green ; Ground Holly)—**Ord. Ericaceæ.** Hardy dwarf herbaceous perennials. First introduced 1752.
CULTURE : Compost, two parts leaf-mould, one part sand. Position, shady rockery outdoors. Plant, April.
PROPAGATION : By division of plants in April.
SPECIES CULTIVATED : C. maculata, pink and white, June, 6 in., N. America ; umbellata, white and pink, June, 6 in., N. America.

Chimney Bellflower (*Campanula pyramidalis*)—See Campanula.

Chimonanthus (Japan Allspice)—Ord. Calycanthaceæ. Hardy deciduous flowering shrub. First introduced 1766.
CULTURE : Soil, deep, rich, sandy. Position, against south or west walls. Plant, Feb. Prune in Feb., cutting away all shoots that have flowered to within 1 in. of base, except those required to furnish plants with branches.
PROPAGATION : By layering shoots in Sept. or Oct.
SPECIES CULTIVATED : C. fragrans, yellow and red, fragrant, Dec., 6 to 9 ft., China and Japan.

China Aster (*Callistephus hortense*)—See Callistephus.

China Creeper (*Ipomœa Quamoclit*)—See Ipomæa.

Chinaman's Breeches (*Dicentra spectabilis*)—See Dicentra.

China Rose (*Rosa indica*)—See Rosa.

Chincherinchee (*Ornithogalum lacteum*)—See Ornithogalum.

Chin Chin (*Ornithogalum lacteum*)—See Ornithogalum.

Chinese Apple (*Pyrus spectabilis*)—See Pyrus.

Chinese Arbor-vitæ (*Thuya orientalis*)—See Thuya.

Chinese Artichoke (*Stachys Sieboldii*)—See Stachys.

Chinese Bell-flower (*Platycodon grandiflorum*)—See Platycodon.

Chinese Cabbage (*Brassica campestris Chinensis*)—A vegetable with thick, fleshy midribs and crimped leaves. Leaves cooked like kale ; midribs like Seakale. Beet, or Portugal Cabbage. Sow in July and Aug. in shallow drills 1 ft. apart. Available for use in Oct. and Nov.

Chinese Crab (*Pyrus spectabilis*)—See Pyrus.

Chinese Hawthorn (*Photinia serrulata*)—See Photinia.

Chinese Ivy (*Trachelospermum jasminoides*)—See Trachelospermum.

Chinese Jasmine (*Trachelospermum jasminoides*)—See Trachelospermum.

Chinese Juniper (*Juniperus chinensis*)—See Juniperus.

Chinese Lantern (*Physalis Alkekengi*)—See Physalis.

Chinese Lilac (*Syringa chinensis*)—See Syringa.

Chinese Medlar (*Eriobotrya japonica*)—See Eriobotrya.

Chinese Pagoda-tree (*Sophora japonica*)—See Sophora.

Chinese Pea-tree (*Caragana frutescens*)—See Caragana.

Chinese Persimmon (*Diospyros Kaki*)—See Diosypros.

Chinese Pink (*Dianthus chinensis*)—See Dianthus.

Chinese Primrose (*Primula sinensis*)—See Primula.

Chinese Privet (*Ligustrum sinensis*)—See Ligustrum.

Chinese Rose Mallow (*Hibiscus rosa-sinensis*)—See Hibiscus.

Chinese Sacred Lily (*Narcissus Tazetta*)—See Narcissus.

Chinese Tree Pæony (*Pæonia Moutan*)—See Pæonia.

Chinese Water Lily (*Nelumbium speciosum*)—See Nelumbium.

Chinese Wax Privet (*Ligustrum lucidum*)—See Ligustrum.

Chinese Witch Hazel (*Hamamelis mollis*)—See Hamamelis.

Chinese Yam (*Dioscorea Batatas*)—See Dioscorea.

Chionanthus (Fringe Tree ; Virginian Snow-flower)—Ord. Oleaceæ. Hardy flowering trees and shrubs. Deciduous. First introduced 1796.
CULTURE : Soil, sandy loam. Position, moist sheltered shrubbery. Plant, Oct. to Feb. C. virginica suitable for pot culture for spring flowering in heated or cold greenhouses. Pot, Nov. Water moderately Nov. to April, freely afterwards. Plunge pot to rim outdoors from June to Feb.
PROPAGATION : By seeds sown in sandy soil in cold frame in April ; grafting on Ash in March ; budding on Ash in July.
SPECIES CULTIVATED : C. retusa, white, June to July, 8 to 30 ft., China and Japan ; virginica, white, June, 10 to 20 ft., Florida.

Chionodoxa (Glory of the Snow)—Ord. Liliaceæ. Hardy deciduous bulbous plants. First introduced 1877.
OUTDOOR CULTURE : Soil, sandy loam. Position, sunny rockeries, well drained. Plant bulbs 1 in. apart and 3 in. deep in Sept. Lift and replant every three years.
POT CULTURE : Compost, equal parts peat, loam, leaf-mould, and sand. Pot, Sept., planting 12 bulbs 1 in. deep in a 3 in. pot, well drained. Cover pot with ashes outdoors or in frame until Jan., then remove to window or greenhouse. Water moderately Jan. to April, freely April to June, none afterwards.
PROPAGATION : By seeds sown ¼ in. deep in boxes of light soil in cold frame in Aug. ; offsets as mature bulbs.
SPECIES CULTIVATED : C. cretica, blue and white, March, 6 in., Crete ; Luciliæ, blue and white, March, 6 in., Asia Minor, and its varieties gigantea (Syn. Allenii), grandiflora (violet), sardensis (blue), and Tmolusi (blue and white) ; nana, white and lilac, April, Crete.

Chionographis—Ord. Liliaceæ. Half-hardy herbaceous perennial. First introduced 1880.
CULTURE : Compost, equal parts loam, leaf-mould, peat, and sand. Position, warm, well-drained south border outdoors, or pot in cold frame. Plant, Oct. or Feb. Pot, Feb.
PROPAGATION : By seeds sown ⅛ in. deep in above compost in a pot, pan, or box in March, in cold frame ; division of roots in Sept.
SPECIES CULTIVATED : C. japonica, white, May, 1 ft., Japan.

Chirita—Ord. Gesneriaceæ. Stove herbaceous perennial and evergreen plants. First introduced 1840.
CULTURE : Compost, equal parts peat and leaf-mould, half a part fibry loam, and half a part of silver sand and charcoal. Pot, Feb. Shake away old soil from roots and put in small pots first, shifting into larger size when plants begin to grow. Water moderately at first, increasing supply when plants grow freely ; keep nearly dry Oct. to Feb. Position, on shelf near glass. Liquid or artificial manure may be

applied when flower buds appear.   Temp., Nov. to Feb. 55° to 65° ; Feb. to Nov. 70° to 85°.

PROPAGATION : By seeds sown in well-drained pots of above compost in March. Cover seeds with sprinkle of sand, place a square of glass over each pot and put latter in temp. 75° to 85°. Keep soil moderately moist. Transplant seedlings when three leaves are formed into small pots and treat as advised for old plants. Can be propagated also by large leaves, cutting their main ribs through and laying undersides on pans of sandy soil in temp. 65° to 75° in summer.

SPECIES CULTIVATED : C. depressa, violet, July, 6 to 8 in., China ; Horsefieldii, white and purple, Sept., 18 in., Java ; lilacina, white, blue, and yellow, summer, 18 in., Chiriqui ; Moonii, blue and purple, June, 2 ft., Ceylon ; sinensis, lilac, July, 6 in., China ; Walkeri, yellow, June, 18 in., Ceylon ; zeylanica, purple, June, 18 in., Ceylon.

Chives—See Allium.

Chlidanthus—Ord. Amaryllidaceæ. Half-hardy herbaceous plant. First introduced 1820.

OUTDOOR CULTURE : Compost, equal parts peat, leaf-mould, loam, and silver sand. Position, warm, well-drained bed or border outdoors. Plant bulbs 3 in. deep in April. Lift bulbs in Oct. and store them in sand in frost-proof place during winter. POT CULTURE : Plant bulbs 1 in. apart and 2 in. deep in above compost in 5 in. pots in April. Water moderately first, freely when in active growth. Grow in cold frame or cool greenhouse. Withhold water from roots after Sept., until repotting time.

PROPAGATION : By offsets in April.

SPECIES CULTIVATED : C. fragrans, yellow, fragrant, June, 10 in., Peru.

Chlora (Yellow Centaury ; Yellow-wort)—Ord. Gentianaceæ. Hardy biennials. Suitable for large gardens only.

CULTURE : Soil, heavy loam. Position, moist borders.

PROPAGATION : By seeds sown ⅛ in. deep in shady beds outdoors in July, transplanting seedlings into flowering positions in Oct.

SPECIES CULTIVATED : C. imperfoliata, yellow, June, 1 ft. ; perfoliata, yellow, June, 1 ft., Britain.

Chloris—Ord. Gramineæ. Hardy annual flowering grasses. Inflorescence suitable for winter decorations. Cut and dry when fully developed.

CULTURE : Soil, ordinary. Position, sunny borders. Sow seeds outdoors in April.

SPECIES CULTIVATED : C. barbata, 1 ft., E. Indies ; elegans, 1 ft., S. America.

Chlorogalum (Soap Plant). Ord. Liliaceæ. Hardy bulbous plant. First introduced 1819.

CULTURE : Soil, light. Position, south border, well drained. Plant bulbs 4 in. deep and 3 in. apart in Oct. or March. Replant every three years.

PROPAGATION : By offsets planted similarly to old bulbs ; by seeds sown ⅛ in. deep in well-drained pots of sandy soil in March.

SPECIES CULTIVATED : C. pomeridianum, white and purple, June, 2 ft., California.

Chlorophytum—Ord. Liliaceæ. Greenhouse plant. Orn. foliage. First introduced 1751.

CULTURE : Compost, equal parts loam, leaf-mould, peat, and sand. Position, variegated and tall kinds in pots ; drooping stemmed species in pots or baskets suspended in window or greenhouse. Pot, March. Temp., Oct. to March 45° to 50° ; March to Oct. 55° to 65°. Water moderately in winter, freely other times.

PROPAGATION : By seeds sown ⅛ in. deep in well-drained pots of light soil in temp. 65° in March ; by offshoots inserted singly in small pots under bell-glass in window or greenhouse in April ; by division of roots when repotting.

SPECIES CULTIVATED : C. elatum (Syn. Anthericum and Phalangium elatum), white, summer, 12 to 18 in., S. Africa ; elatum variegatum (Syn. Anthericum variegatum), leaves variegated with creamy white.

Chocolate-tree (*Theobroma cacoa*)—See Theobroma.

Choisya (Mexican Orange-flower)—Ord. Rutaceæ. Hardy evergreen flowering shrub. First introduced 1825.
OUTDOOR CULTURE: Soil, ordinary loam with peat or leaf-mould. Position, sheltered shrubberies S. and W. of England and Ireland, against south walls N. of England. Plant, Oct. or March. Prune after flowering, shortening straggling shoots only.
POT CULTURE: Compost, equal parts peat loam, leaf-mould and sand. Pot, Sept. or Oct. Water moderately Sept. to March, freely afterwards. Keep plants in cool greenhouse Nov. to May, remainder of time outdoors.
PROPAGATION: By cuttings of shoots 3 in. long inserted in well-drained pots of sandy soil under bell-glass in temp. 55° to 65°, March to June.
SPECIES CULTIVATED: C. ternata, white, summer, 6 ft., Mexico.

Chokeberry (*Pyrus arbutifolia*)—See Pyrus.

Choke Cherry (*Prunus virginiana*)—See Prunus.

Chorizema—Ord. Leguminosæ. Greenhouse flowering shrubs. Evergreen. First introduced 1803.
CULTURE: Compost, equal parts fibry peat and loam, one-fourth sand. Position, pots, or in well-drained beds in greenhouses. Pot, March or June; firm potting essential. Prune straggling shoots slightly after flowering. Water freely March to Sept., moderately afterwards. Temp., March to Sept. 55° to 65°; Sept. to March 45° to 50°. Stand plants outdoors from July to Sept. to mature flowering shoots for following year.
PROPAGATION: By seeds sown 1/18 in. deep in light sandy compost in temp. 65° to 70° in March; by cuttings in sandy peat under bell-glass in temp. 65° in summer.
SPECIES CULTIVATED: C. cordatum, red and yellow, April, 10 ft., Australia; diversifolium, orange-red, May, 2 ft., Australia; Henchmanni, scarlet, May, 2 ft., Australia; ilicifolium, yellow, May, 3 ft., Australia; varium (Syn. C. Chandlerii), yellow and red, May, 4 ft., Australia.

Chou de Russie—A variety of Borecole or Kale. See Brassica.

Christmas Bells—See Blandfordia.

Christmas Berry Tree (*Schinus terebinthifolius*)—See Schinus.

Christmas Pride (*Ruellia macrantha*)—See Ruellia.

Christmas Rose (*Helleborus niger*)—See Helleborus.

Christ's-Eye (*Inula Oculus-Christi*)—See Inula.

Christ's Thorn (*Paliurus australis*)—See Paliurus.

Chrysalidocarpus—Ord. Palmaceæ. Stove palm.
CULTURE AND PROPAGATION: Same as Areca.
SPECIES CULTIVATED: C. lutescens (Syn. Areca lutescens), 10 to 25 ft., Madagascar.

Chrysanthemum (Ox-eye Daisy; Marguerite; Pyrethrum; Corn Marigold; Shasta Daisy)—Ord. Compositæ. Greenhouse, hardy annual, herbaceous perennial and shrubby plants. First introduced 1764.
CULTURE OF ANNUAL SPECIES: Soil, ordinary, rich. Position, open, sunny. Plant seedlings out in May. Sow seeds ⅛ in. deep in boxes of light soil in temp. 65° to 70° in March, afterwards planting seedlings out; or similar depth where plants are to flower. Thin seedlings to 3 in. apart in June. Gather seed in Aug.
POT CULTURE OF ANNUAL SPECIES: Sow seed as above. Transplant seedlings when 2 in. high at rate of four in a 5 in. pot, or seven in a 6 in. pot. Compost, two parts good soil, one part leaf-mould or decayed manure and sand. Grow plants in cold frame or greenhouse. Water moderately. Thin flower buds if fine blooms are wanted. Give weak liquid manure when flower buds appear.
CULTURE OF MARGUERITES: Compost, equal parts loamy soil and leaf-mould, fourth part silver sand. Insert cuttings singly, or three in a 4 in. pot, in April. Cover pot with bell-glass or place in propagator. Pot cuttings when rooted in 3 in. pots, shifting them into 5 in. in August. Stand plants in full sun from July to Sept., place in cold frame from then to Nov., thence into greenhouse heated to temp. 50°

to 55°. Water moderately. Give liquid manure when pot is full of roots. Throw plants away when a year old, and raise fresh stock from cuttings.

CULTURE OF INDOOR CHRYSANTHEMUMS : Classes : Incurved, petals curving inwards ; Anemone-flowered, flowers with dense centres and petals fringing their base ; pompones, flowers small, petals reflexed, fringed or toothed ; singles, centres open, yellow, one or more rows of guard petals ; decoratives, easily grown and free flowering doubles of moderate size ; Japanese, flowers large, petals loosely arranged, variously shaped. Compost, three-parts fibry loam, one horse manure, one decayed tree leaves, one coarse silver sand, quarter part finely ground bones, same of dissolved bones, one part charcoal and wood ashes and little soot. Pot first time in 3 in. pots, March ; second, in 5 or 6 in., middle of April ; third, in 8 or 10 in., middle of June. Stop main stems 4 in. from base in March for ensuring bushy plants ; those to produce blooms for exhibition leave untouched. Cut down plants intended for dwarfs to within 6 in. of pot in May. Thin flower buds to one on each shoot when they are size of radish seed. Stand plants in full sun May to Sept., then remove to greenhouse. Water freely while outdoors, moderately in greenhouse. Apply liquid manure when flower buds form and continue till flowers open. Suitable liquid manures : two parts sulphate of ammonia, six parts superphosphate and one part sulphate of potash dissolved in water at the strength of $\frac{1}{3}$ oz. per gallon ; one part nitrate of potash and two parts superphosphate, $\frac{1}{2}$ oz. per gallon ; sheep and cow dung soaked in a sack in water till it is the colour of weak tea ; droppings from fowls or pigeons in weak solution. These mixtures should be alternated, and may be applied every four or five days.

CULTURE OF OUTDOOR CHRYSANTHEMUMS : Soil, good ordinary. Position, sunny beds or borders. Plant out 3 ft. apart in May. Stop shoots when 6 in. high, then allow plants to grow naturally. Do not disbud. Water freely in summer. Give liquid manure July to Sept.

CULTURE OF HARDY PERENNIAL SPECIES : Soil, ordinary rich. Position, sunny borders. Plant, autumn or spring. Lift, divide, and replant every third year.

PROPAGATION : Indoor and outdoor chrysanthemums by cuttings issuing from roots, inserting these singly in 2 in. pots in temp. 55° to 65° in Jan., Feb., or March, or in cold frames in Dec. ; by seeds sown $\frac{1}{8}$ in. deep in light soil in temp. 65° in March. After flowering cut stems down and place plants in cold frame to produce cuttings, after which plant out in garden or discard. Temp. for plants whilst in flower, 45° to 50°. Hardy perennial species may be increased by division in March, or by seeds sown in warm greenhouse in Feb. or March. Marguerites by cuttings as already described.

ANNUAL SPECIES : C. carinatum, white, yellow, and purple, summer, 2 ft., N. Africa ; coronarium, yellow and white, summer, 3 ft., S. Europe ; segetum (Corn Marigold), yellow, summer, 18 in., Europe (Britain) ; segetum grandiflorum, yellow.

HARDY PERENNIAL SPECIES : C. alpinum, white, summer, 3 to 6 in., Alps ; arcticum, white tinged lilac, June to July, 1 ft., Arctic Regions ; cinerariæfolium, white, July to Aug., 12 to 30 in., Dalmatia ; coccineum (Syn. Pyrethrum roseum), scarlet, summer, 2 to 3 ft., Caucasus, parent of the single and double race of pyrethrums (Coloured Marguerites) ; lacustre (Marsh Ox-eye), white, summer, 3 to 6 ft., S.W. Europe ; leucanthemum (Ox-eye Daisy), white, summer, 2 ft., Europe ; maximum (large Ox-eye or Shasta Daisy), white, summer, 1$\frac{1}{2}$ to 2 ft. ; nipponicum, white, 12 to 15 in., summer, Japan ; uliginosum (Grand Ox-eye), Syn. Pyrethrum uliginosum, white, autumn, 5 ft., E. Europe ; Parthenium (Feverfew), white, summer, 2 ft., Europe, and its variety aureum (Golden Feather).

TENDER SPECIES : C. indicum (Japanese Chrysanthemum), China and Japan ; frutescens (Marguerite or Paris Daisy), white or yellow, 3 ft., summer, Canary Islands ; sinense, yellow, China and Japan. The popular garden chrysanthemums have probably originated from C. indicum and C. sinense.

Chrysobactron—See Bulbinella.

Chrysocoma—Ord. Compositæ. Greenhouse evergreen flowering shrub. First introduced 1731.

CULTURE : Compost, equal parts peat, loam and silver sand. Position, well-drained pots in sunny part of greenhouse. Pot, March. Water freely in spring and summer, moderately other seasons. Temp., March to Oct. 55° to 65°; Oct. to March 45° to 50°.

PROPAGATION : By cuttings of firm shoots in silver sand under bell-glass in spring.

SPECIES CULTIVATED : C. Coma-aurea, yellow, July, 2 ft., S. Africa. See also the genus Aster.

Chrysogonum (Golden Knee)—Ord. Compositæ. Hardy herbaceous perennial.
CULTURE : Compost, equal parts loam, peat, and leaf-mould. Position, shady moist borders, Plant, Oct. or March.
PROPAGATION : By division of roots in March.
SPECIES CULTIVATED : C. virginianum, yellow, summer, 9 in., N. America.

Chrysophyllum—Ord. Sapotaceæ. Stove evergreen. First introduced 1737.
CULTURE : Equal parts fibrous loam, leaf-mould and sand. Position, borders in warm greenhouse. Temp., March to Oct. 75° to 90°; Oct. to March 65° to 75°. Water freely during the summer months, sparingly in winter.
PROPAGATION : By cuttings of well-ripened wood in close frame and temp. 80°. Seeds sown in heat in Feb. or March.
SPECIES CULTIVATED : C. Cainito (Star Apple), 30 to 50 ft., light green or purple fruits, 2 to 4 in. in diameter, with white pulp, Trop. America.

Chrysopsis (Golden Aster)—Ord. Compositæ. Hardy herbaceous perennial.
CULTURE : Soil, ordinary. Position, sunny borders.
PROPAGATION : By division of roots in March.
SPECIES CULTIVATED : C. villosa Rutteri, golden yellow, July to Sept., 9 in., N. America.

Chrysosplenium (Golden Saxifrage)—Ord. Saxifragaceæ. Hardy perennial herbs. Soil, boggy peat. Position, damp and shady water-courses or ditches. Plant, Oct. or March.
PROPAGATION : By division of plants in March.
SPECIES CULTIVATED : C. alternifolium, yellow, summer, 3 in., N. Hemisphere (Britain); oppositifolium, yellow, 3 in., Europe (Britain).

Chufa (*Cyperus esculentus*)—See Cyperus.

Chusan Palm (*Trachycarpus Fortunei*)—See Trachycarpus.

Chysis—Ord. Orchidaceæ. Stove deciduous epiphytal orchids. First introduced 1834.
CULTURE : Compost, equal parts fibry peat, moss, and potsherds. Position, well-drained pots or blocks of wood in partial shade. Pot, after flowering. Water freely March to Sept., moderately afterwards. Temp., Sept. to March 55° to 60°; March to Sept. 65° to 75°. Resting period, winter. Flowers appear on new growth directly after resting.
PROPAGATION : By division of pseudo-bulbs in Feb. or March.
SPECIES CULTIVATED : C. aurea, yellow, spring and summer, 1 ft., Colombia; bractescens, white and yellow, spring, 1 ft., Mexico; Chelsoni yellow and purple, spring, 1 ft., hybrid; langleyensis, white and rose, May, hybrid; Limmingheii, yellow and purple, spring, 1 ft., Mexico.

Cibotium—See Dicksonia.

Ciboul Onion (*Allium fistulosum*)—See Allium.

Cichorium (Chicory; Witloof; Endive)—Ord. Compositæ. Hardy esculent rooted and salad vegetables.
CULTURE OF CHICORY : Roots used when dry for mixing with coffee ; sleves, when forced, for salad. Soil, rich light. Position, open, away from trees. Sow seeds ¼ in. deep in drills 15 in. asunder first week in May. Thin seedlings when an inch high to 8 in. apart in row. No liquid or artificial manures required. Lift roots in Nov. and store them in dry soil or sand in outhouse. Force leaves for salad by placing roots close together in large pots or deep box, using ordinary soil. Put pots or boxes in temp. 55° to 65°, and keep quite dark. Gather blanched leaves when three to six inches long.

CULTURE OF ENDIVE : Leaves when blanched used for salads. Soil, light rich. Position, open garden or on south or west borders. Sow seeds ¼ in. deep in drills 4 in. apart in June for early crop, July for main crop, Aug. for late crop. Transplant seedlings when they have formed four leaves 12 in. apart each way. Water freely in dry weather. Blanch early crop in Aug., main crop in Sept., late crop in Oct. by covering each plant by slate, tile, board, or inverted pot with drainage hole plugged. Lift remaining plants in Nov. and store close together in cold frame, covering them with dry leaves to ensure blanching.

SPECIES CULTIVATED : C. Endivia (endive), blue, July, 2 ft., Orient ; Intybus (Chicory), blue, July, 2 ft., Britain. Introduced 1548.

Cimicifuga (Snake-root ; Bug-bane ; Bugwort)—Ord. Ranunculaceæ. Hardy herbaceous perennials. Introduced 1737.

CULTURE : Soil, ordinary. Position, moist shady borders. Plant, Oct., Nov., or March.

PROPAGATION : By seeds sown ⅟₁₆ in. deep in light soil in cold frame in Sept. ; division of roots in March.

SPECIES CULTIVATED : C. americana, white, Aug., 3 ft., N. America ; cordifolia, white, July, 3 ft., N. America ; davurica, white, July, 4 ft., China ; elata, white, July, 3 ft., N. America ; racemosa, white, Aug., 3 ft., N. America ; simplex, white, Aug. to Oct., 3 ft., Kamtschatka.

Cinchona (Quinine)—Ord. Rubiaceæ. Greenhouse evergreen tree.

CULTURE : Compost, equal parts turfy loam and fibrous peat with a little sand and charcoal. Position, large pots or borders in heated greenhouse. Pot or plant, Oct. Water freely during growing season. Temp., March to Oct. 60° to 75° ; Oct. to March 55° to 65°.

PROPAGATION : By cuttings of ripened wood under hand-light in temp. 75°.

SPECIES CULTIVATED : C. officinalis, rose, 20 to 40 ft., S. America, and its variety condaminea.

Cincinalis—See Nothochlæna.

Cineraria—See Senecio.

Cinnamomum (Cinnamon Tree ; Cassia Bark Tree ; Camphor Tree)—Ord. Lauraceæ. Stove evergreen trees and shrubs of interest on account of their economic value.

CULTURE : Compost, equal parts turfy loam and peat with a little sand. Position, large pots or borders in warm greenhouse. Water freely during growing season, and maintain a moist atmosphere. Temp., March to Oct. 70° to 80° ; Oct. to March 60° to 70°.

PROPAGATION : By cuttings of young shoots in April placed in close frame and temp. 80°.

SPECIES CULTIVATED : C. Camphora (Camphor Tree), yellow, 30 to 40 ft., China and Japan ; Cassia, flowers small in silky panicles, 20 to 30 ft., China ; zeylanicum, yellowish white, 20 to 30 ft., India, Malaya.

Cinnamon Fern (*Osmunda cinnamomea*)—See Osmunda.

Cinnamon Rose (*Rosa cinnamomea*)—See Rosa.

Cinnamon Tree—See Cinnamomum.

Cinque-foil—See Potentilla.

Cirrhopetalum—Ord. Orchidaceæ. Stove epiphytal evergreen orchids. First introduced 1839.

CULTURE : Compost, equal parts fibrous peat and sphagnum. Position, well-drained pots, baskets, or blocks of wood, in partial shade. Pot, March. Water freely when plants are growing, moderately other times. Temp., Oct. to March 55° to 65° ; March to Oct. 65° to 75°. Resting period, winter. Flowers appear at base of pseudo-bulb of previous year's growth after resting period.

PROPAGATION : By division of pseudo-bulbs in March.

SPECIES CULTIVATED : C. amesianum, yellow and purple, June, 6 in., Trop. Asia; Collettii, purple, yellow, April, 8 in., Burma; Cumingii, red and purple, autumn, 6 in., Philippines; ornatissimum, yellow and purple, Oct., 8 in., Himalayas; picturatum, green and red, 8 in., Malaya ; robustum, red, yellow, and purple, June, 1 ft., New Guinea.

Cirsium.—See Cnicus.

Cissus—Ord. Vitaceæ. Stove and greenhouse climbers. Evergreen.
CULTURE : Compost, turfy peat, loam, leaf-mould and sharp sand. Position, pots or borders in greenhouse. Temp. for C. discolor, March to Oct. 75° to 85° ; Oct. to March 65° to 75°. C. antarctica thrives in a cool greenhouse.
PROPAGATION : By cuttings of young growth 2 in. long with heel of old wood, inserted in sandy soil under hand-glass in temp. 80°.
SPECIES CULTIVATED : C. antarctica (Syn. Vitis antarctica), climbing shrub, Australia ; C. discolor, strong climber, Java. See also Vitis.

Cistus (Rock Rose ; Gum Cistus)—Ord. Cistaceæ. Hardy and half-hardy evergreen shrubs. First introduced 1548.
CULTURE : Soil, good, ordinary. Position, pots in frame or cold greenhouse, sunny rockeries or against south walls. Plant, March. Protect in severe weather.
PROPAGATION : By seeds sown $\frac{1}{8}$ in. deep in boxes of sandy soil in cold frame or unheated greenhouse in March, transplanting seedlings into small pots and planting outdoors in June ; by cuttings 4 in. long in pots of sandy soil in Sept. in cold frame or greenhouse.
SPECIES CULTIVATED : C. albidus, pale rosy lilac, 5 to 6 ft., S.W. Europe ; corbariensis, white, June, 3 to 4 ft., hybrid ; crispus, purple, 2 ft., S. Europe ; cyprius, white, 6 to 8 ft., Cyprus ; florentinus, white and yellow, 4 ft., natural hybrid ; ladaniferus, white and maroon, 4 ft., S.W. Europe ; ladaniferus albiflorus, white ; laurifolius, white, June to Aug., 6 to 8 ft., S.W. Europe ; Loretii, white and crimson, 3 to 4 ft., hybrid ; monspeliensis, white, 2 ft., S. Europe ; populifolius, white and yellow, 3 to 7 ft., S.W. Europe ; purpureus, purple, 2 ft., Levant ; salvifolius, white and yellow, summer, 2 ft., S. Europe ; villosus, purple or rose and yellow, summer, 3 to 4 ft., Mediterranean.

Citron (*Citrus medica*)—See Citrus.

Citron-scented Gardenia (*Mitriostigma axillaris*)—See Mitriostigma.

Citron-scented Geranium (*Pelargonium citriodorum*)—See Pelargonium.

Citron-scented Orchid (*Odontoglossum citrosmum*)—See Odontoglossum.

Citrullus (Water Melon)—Ord. Cucurbitaceæ. Tender climbing plant cultivated for its edible fruits.
CULTURE : As for ordinary melon (Cucumis melo) except that shoots should not be pinched.
SPECIES CULTIVATED : C. vulgaris, Trop. and S. Africa.

Citrus (Orange ; Lemon ; Shaddock ; Adam's Apple ; Lime ; Citron ; Forbidden Fruit)—Ord. Rutaceæ. Greenhouse evergreen shrubs. First introduced 1595. Flowers, white, fragrant ; May to July. Fruit : Sweet Orange, golden rind, globular ; Lemon, pale yellow, rind thin, oblong ; Citron, yellow, thick rind, long, egg-shaped, lump at tip ; Shaddock, greenish yellow, bitter rind, large, round ; Lime, greenish yellow, smooth rind, globular, with nipple at top ; Mandarin, reddish rind, dark red pulp, large; Tangerine, syn. with Mandarin ; St. Michael's, red rind, globular, large.
CULTURE : Compost, two parts good turfy loam, one part dry cow dung, charcoal, crushed bones, and ballast. Pot, Feb., March, or April. Position, pots, tubs, or beds, all to be well drained, in cool or slightly heated greenhouses. Water freely March to Oct., moderately afterwards. Apply liquid manure once a week to healthy plants from May to Oct. Syringe trees daily during summer. Stand trees in pots or tubs in sheltered position outdoors June to Sept. Repotting should not be done oftener than is actually necessary. Prune straggling shoots into

shape in March. Temp., Sept. to Feb. 45° to 50°; **Feb.** to Sept. 55° to 65°. Fruit formed one year will not ripen till next.

PROPAGATION : By seeds sown ⅛ in. deep in light soil in temp. 55° in March for producing stocks for grafting choice kinds on ; by cuttings inserted in small pots of sandy soil in July ; layering in Oct. , by budding in Aug. ; by grafting in March.

SPECIES CULTIVATED : C. aurantium (Sweet Orange), 12 to 15 ft., Trop. America ; aurantium bergamia (Bergamot Orange) ; aurantium bigaradia (Seville Orange) ; aurantium japonica (Kumquat) ; aurantium lusitanica (Portuguese Orange) ; aurantium melitensis (Blood Orange) ; aurantium myrtifolia (Myrtle-leaved Orange) ; aurantium variegata (Variegated Orange) ; decumana (Shaddock), 15 ft., Tropics ; medica (Citron), 10 ft., Trop. Asia ; medica limetta (Sweet Lime), 10 ft.; medica limonum (Lemon) ; nobilis major, 15 ft. (Mandarin Orange) ; nobilis tangerina (Tangerine Orange). See also Ægle.

Cladrastis (Yellow-wood Tree)—Ord. Leguminosæ. Hardy deciduous flowering shrubs. First introduced 1812.
CULTURE : Soil, ordinary. Position, open shrubberies, or singly on lawns. Plant, Oct. to Feb.
PROPAGATION : By seeds sown 1 in. deep in ordinary soil outdoors in March ; cuttings of root inserted outdoors in spring.
SPECIES CULTIVATED : C. sinensis, blush-white, July, 40 to 60 ft., China ; tinctoria, white, July, 15 ft., United States. See also Maackia.

Clarkia—Ord. Onagrariaceæ. Hardy annuals. First introduced 1826.
CULTURE : Soil, light, rich. Position, sunny borders or beds. Sow seeds ⅛ in. deep in April, May, or June in rows or masses where plants are required to flower. Thin seedlings to 8 in. apart when 3 in. high.
SPECIES CULTIVATED : C. elegans, rosy purple, July, 1 to 4 ft. ; pulchella, various colours, single and double, 1 to 1½ ft. Numerous superior varieties described in trade lists.

Clary (*Salvia Sclarea*)—See Salvia.

Claytonia—Ord. Portulacaceæ. Hardy annuals and perennials. First introduced 1768.
CULTURE : Soil, for annual species, ordinary ; for perennials, damp peat or bog. Position, rockery for annual species ; moist and shady border for perennials. Plant perennials in Oct. or March.
PROPAGATION : Annual species by seeds sown outdoors in April ; perennials by seeds similarly, or by offsets in Oct. or March.
ANNUAL SPECIES : C. perfoliata, white, June, 6 in., N. America ; sibirica, pink, March, 6 in., N. America.
PERENNIAL SPECIES : C. caroliniana, pink, May, 6 in., N. America ; virginica, white, April, 6 in., N. America.

Clematis (Virgin's Bower)—Ord. Ranunculaceæ. Greenhouse and hardy climbers and herbaceous perennials. Deciduous or evergreen. All very showy plants.
CULTURE OF HARDY CLIMBING SPECIES : Soil, rich, deep, well-drained loam containing plenty of old mortar and decayed manure. Position, sunny trellises, arches, old tree stumps, arbours, etc. ; also in beds with shoots trained over surface. Plant in autumn or spring. Prune in Feb. Pruning : Montana, alpina, flammula, Armandi, paniculata and tangutica should have sufficient old growth removed to keep them within bounds. The work should be done immediately the flowers fade. Varieties of the Azuræ, Floridæ and Lanuginosæ groups should be lightly thinned in Feb. Varieties of the Viticellæ and Jackmani groups should be pruned severely in Feb., either cutting the whole plant back to within a foot or so of the ground or else pruning each young growth to within one pair of buds of its base. Davidiana, integrifolia, necta, Pitcheri, Viorna, and crispa should have all growth that has been damaged by frost removed in Feb.
CULTURE IN POTS : Compost, two parts loam, one part of equal proportions of leaf-mould, decayed manure, and sand. Plant in pots or tubs in spring. Train

shoots up roof of cold or cool greenhouse, or around wire trellis fixed in pots. Water freely March to Sept. Apply weak liquid manure occasionally in summer. Keep soil nearly dry in winter. Prune shoots to 3 or 4 in. from base early in the year.

CULTURE OF GREENHOUSE SPECIES : Compost as for above. Grow in pots or in well-drained bed, planting in spring. Water freely during the summer, moderately in winter. Prune away weak growths and shorten rampant ones a little in Feb. Train shoots near the roof. Temp., Sept. to March 45° to 55°; March to Sept. 55° to 65°. Syringe freely daily in summer.

CULTURE OF HERBACEOUS SPECIES : Soil, ordinary rich. Position, sunny borders. Plant in autumn or spring. Top-dress annually with decayed manure in autumn. Prune shoots close to soil in autumn. Dwarf species best grown on sunny rockeries.

PROPAGATION : By seeds sown in sandy soil in cold frame in spring in case of hardy kinds, or in heat in spring in case of greenhouse species. Greenhouse species also by cuttings inserted in sandy soil in temp. of 75° in spring ; hardy climbers by grafting on roots of C. viticella or vitalba in heat in spring, also by layering shoots in summer ; herbaceous kinds by division in autumn or cuttings of young shoots in frame in summer.

GREENHOUSE SPECIES : C. indivisa, white, April, 15 to 20 ft., New Zealand, and its variety lobata.

HARDY CLIMBERS : C. æthusifolia, pale yellow, Aug. to Sept., 5 to 6 ft., N. China and Manchuria ; alpina, blue, April to May, 6 to 8 ft., N. Europe and N. Asia ; Armandi, white to rose, April, evergreen, 20 to 30 ft., Central and W. Africa ; aromatica, bluish violet, July to Sept., 4 to 6 ft., hybrid ; calycina (Syn. balearica), yellowish white and purple, Sept. to March, evergreen, 10 to 15 ft., Minorca, Corsica ; chrysocoma, white and pink, 6 to 8 ft., Yunnan ; cirrhosa, white or cream, evergreen, 6 to 8 ft., Spain, Algeria, etc.; coccinea, (Syn. texensis), scarlet, July, to 12 ft., Texas ; flammula, white, Aug. to Oct., 10 to 12 ft., France ; florida, white, 8 to 12 ft., summer, Japan ; Hendersoni, bluish purple, July to Sept., 6 to 8 ft., hybrid ; Jackmani, purple, summer, hybrid ; jouiniana (Syn. grata), yellowish white and lilac, Aug. to Oct., 10 ft., hybrid ; lanuginosa, white or pale lilac, June to Oct., 6 to 9 ft., China ; lasiandra, white or slaty purple, Oct., 8 to 12 ft., Japan and China ; montana, white, May, 15 to 25 ft., Himalayas, and its varieties rubens and Wilsoni ; orientalis (Syn. graveolens), yellow, Aug. to Sept., 10 to 20 ft., Caucasus, Himalayas, and Manchuria ; paniculata, white, Sept. to Oct., 25 to 30 ft., Japan ; patens (Syn. cærulea), white to violet-blue, 8 to 12 ft., summer, Japan ; Pitcheri (Syn. Simsii), greenish yellow and purplish, May to Sept., to 12 ft., Central U.S.A.; rehderiana, primrose-yellow, Aug. to Oct., 20 to 25 ft., W. China ; Viorna, reddish purple and greenish white, 8 to 12 ft., Eastern U.S.A. ; vitalba, white, July, 30 to 50 ft., Britain ; viticella, blue, July, 8 to 12 ft., Spain.

HERBACEOUS SPECIES : C. Fremonti, purple, summer, 1 ft., N. America ; heracleæfolia (Syn. tubulosa), purple, summer, 2 ft., China ; heracleæfolia davidiana, lavender-blue, fragrant, Aug. ; integrifolia, blue, Aug., 2 ft., S. Europe ; ochroleuca, yellow, summer, 2 ft., N. America ; recta, white, fragrant, Aug., 2 ft., S. Europe ; stans, white, Aug. to Sept., sometimes semi-climbing, Japan.

Cleome (Spider-flower) Ord. Capparidaceæ. Stove annual. First introduced 1817.

CULTURE : Compost, equal parts loam, leaf-mould, and sand. Position, pots in sunny stove. Water moderately at all times. Temp., 65° to 75°. Sow seeds ⅟₁₆ in. deep in light soil in temp. 70° in March, transplanting seedlings into pots when 1 in. high.

SPECIES CULTIVATED : C. spinosa (Syns. pungens and gigantea), rose-purple or white, summer, 3 to 4 ft., Trop. America.

Clerodendron (Glory-tree)—Ord. Verbenaceæ. Stove climbing and hardy flowering shrubs. First introduced 1790.

CULTURE : Compost, equal parts loam, peat, leaf-mould, decayed manure, and silver sand. Pot, Feb. Prune shoots after flowering to within 2 or 3 in. of their base. Water freely March to Sept., moderately Sept. to Nov., after which keep

dry. Temp., Oct. to Feb. 55° to 60°; Feb. to Oct. 65° to 85°. Plant hardy species in ordinary soil in sheltered, warm corners outdoors in Oct. or Nov.
PROPAGATION: By seeds sown ¼ in. deep in sandy soil in temp. 75° in March; cuttings of stems or shoots 3 in. long, inserted in sandy compost in temp. 70° to 75° in Jan., Feb., or March.
STOVE SPECIES: C. fallax, scarlet, Aug., 2 to 4 ft., Java; fragrans, white or blush, autumn, 6 ft., China; speciosum, dull red, summer, 10 ft., hybrid; splendens, scarlet, summer, 10 ft., Trop. Africa; Thomsonæ (Syn. C. Balfourii), crimson, summer, 6 ft., Trop. Africa.
HARDY SPECIES: C. Fargesi, white, Aug., 6 to 8 ft., W. China; fœtidum (C. Bungei), rose, Aug., 5 ft., China; trichotomum, white and red, summer, 10 to 12 ft., Japan.

Clethra (White Alder-bush; Pepper Bush)—Ord. Ericaceæ. Hardy evergreen and deciduous flowering shrubs. First introduced 1731.
CULTURE: Compost, two parts loam, one part peat and sand. Position, front of shrubberies. Plant, Nov. to Feb.
PROPAGATION: By seeds sown ¼ in. deep outdoors in March, or in boxes of light soil in temp. 55° in Feb.; cuttings inserted in sandy soil in gentle heat in Aug.; layering in Oct. C. alnifolia suitable for forcing to flower in winter.
SPECIES CULTIVATED: C. alnifolia (Sweet Pepper Bush), white, Aug., 8 to 9 ft., Florida; alnifolia paniculata, 4 ft.; acuminata (White Alder), white, Sept., 10 to 20 ft.; canescens (Syn. barbinervis), white, Aug., 8 to 9 ft., China; tomentosa, white, Sept., 6 to 8 ft., South-eastern U.S.A.

Clezera—Ord. Ternstroemiaceæ. Half-hardy evergreen shrub. First introduced about 1860. Leaves ovate, green, creamy white and yellow.
CULTURE: Compost, two parts loam, one part peat and sand. Position, pots in cool greenhouse or conservatory. Water moderately in winter, freely other times. May be grown against south wall outdoors in S. of England and Ireland.
PROPAGATION: By cuttings of young shoots under bell glass in temp. 60° to 65° in spring.
SPECIES CULTIVATED: C. Fortunei (Syn. Europa latifolia variegata), 5 to 6 ft., Japan. See also Eurya.

Clianthus (Glory Pea; Parrot's-bill; Sturt's Desert Pea)—Ord. Leguminosæ. Greenhouse climbing shrubs. First introduced 1832.
CULTURE: Compost, two parts loam, one part leaf-mould, and silver sand. Position, pots or beds in greenhouse. Pot or plant, March. Prune in April, shortening young shoots to within 2 in. of their base. Water freely March to Sept., moderately afterwards. Syringe foliage daily April to Aug. Temp., Oct. to March 45° to 50°; March to Oct. 55° to 65°. C. puniceus succeeds outdoors against warm walls in Devonshire.
PROPAGATION: By seeds sown ¼ in. deep in well-drained pot of light soil in temp. 75° in March; cuttings of shoots inserted in sandy soil in temp. 75° to 85° in March or April.
SPECIES CULTIVATED: C. Dampieri, scarlet, April, 3 ft., Australia; puniceus, crimson, May, 6 ft., New Zealand.

Cliff Brake Fern—See Pellæa.

Climbing Dahlia (*Hidalgoa Wercklei*)—See Hidalgoa.

Climbing Fern (*Lygodium scandens*)—See Lygodium.

Climbing Fumitory (*Adlumia cirrhosa*)—See Adlumia.

Climbing Groundsel (*Senecio mikanoides*)—See Senecio.

Climbing Hydrangea (*Schizophragma hydrangeoides*)—See Schizophragma.

Climbing Snake's-tongue Fern (*Lygodium scandens*)—See Lygodium.

Clintonia—Ord. Liliaceæ. Hardy herbaceous perennials. First introduced 1788.
CULTURE: Soil, sandy peat. Position, moist shady border. Plant, Oct. or March.
PROPAGATION: By division of roots in March or April.

SPECIES CULTIVATED : C. andrewsiana, rose, April, 2 ft., California ; borealis, yellow, May, 1 ft., N. America ; umbellata (Syn. Smilacina umbellata), white, May, 9 in., N. America.

Clintonia (Dough)—See Downingia.

Clitoria (Butterfly Pea)—Ord. Leguminosæ. Stove evergreen flowering climber. First introduced 1739.
CULTURE : Compost, equal parts peat, leaf-mould, loam, and silver sand. Position, pots, tubs, or beds in light plant stove. Pot or plant, March. Water freely April to Sept., moderately afterwards. Temp., Oct. to March 55° to 65° ; March to Oct. 70° to 80°.
PROPAGATION : By seeds sown ¼ in. deep in light soil in temp. 75° in March ; cuttings of side shoots inserted in sandy peat in temp. 80° at any time.
SPECIES CULTIVATED : C. ternatea, blue, July, 10 to 12 ft., E. Indies. See also Centrosema.

Clivia (Caffre Lily)—Ord. Amaryllidaceæ. Greenhouse evergreen flowering plants. Fleshy-rooted. Formerly known by the generic name of Imantophyllum. First introduced 1823.
CULTURE : Compost, two-thirds good loam, one-third decayed manure and sand. Position, sunny, close to glass in greenhouse. Pot, Feb. Water freely March to Sept., moderately other times. Temp. March to Sept. 60° to 65° ; Sept. to March 45° to 55°.
PROPAGATION : By seeds sown in light soil in temp. 75° in March ; division of roots at potting time.
SPECIES CULTIVATED : C. cyrtanthiflora, orange, winter and early spring, hybrid ; Gardeni, orange-yellow, Dec. to Feb., 18 in., S. Africa ; miniata, scarlet and yellow, spring and early summer, 1 to 1½ ft., Natal ; nobilis, red and yellow, May to July, 1 to 1½ ft., S. Africa. There are numerous varieties of C. miniata which are superior to the parent species.

Cloak Fern—See Nothloclæna.

Cloud Grass (*Agrostis nebulosa*)—See Agrostis.

Clove Gilliflower (*Dianthus caryophyllus*)—See Dianthus.

Clove-Pink (*Dianthus caryophyllus*)—See Dianthus.

Club Lily—See Kniphofia.

Club Moss (*Lycopodium clavatum*)—See Lycopodium.

Club Rush (*Scirpus nodosus*)—See Scirpus.

Clustered Bell-flower (*Campanula glomerata*)—See Campanula.

Clustered Wax-flower (*Stephanotis floribunda*)—See Stephanotis.

Cluster Flowered Yew—See Cephalotaxus.

Cluster Pine-tree (*Pinus pinaster*)—See Pinus.

Cnicus (Fishbone Thistle)—Ord. Compositæ. Hardy and half-hardy perennials. Orn. foliage.
CULTURE OF HARDY SPECIES : Soil, ordinary. Position, sunny borders. Plant, autumn or spring. Increased by seeds sown outdoors in April.
CULTURE OF HALF-HARDY SPECIES : Soil, ordinary. Position, pots in cool greenhouse, or ornamental beds outdoors in summer. Plant, May or June. Cut off flower heads directly they appear if handsome foliage be desired.
PROPAGATION : By seeds sown ⅛ in. deep in light soil in temp. of 60° to 70° in Feb., or in Sept. in similar temp., keeping seedlings in greenhouse during winter. All best grown as biennials.
HALF-HARDY SPECIES : C. benedictus, yellow, 1½ to 2 ft., Mediterranean Region and Caucasus ; Casabonæ (Syns. Chamæpeuce Casabonæ and Cirsium Casabonæ), purple, summer, leaves spiny, veined with white, 2 to 3 ft., S. Europe ; C. Diacantha

(Syns. Chamæpeuce Diacantha and Cirsium Diacantha), purple, summer, leaves green, veined white, ivory spines, 2 to 3 ft., Syria.

HARDY SPECIES : C. spinosissima (Syn. Cirsium spinosissimum), yellow, summer, 3 ft., Europe.

Cobæa (Cup and Saucer-plant ; Mexican Ivy)—Ord. Polemoniaceæ. Greenhouse and half-hardy cl̄imbing perennial, usually grown as an annual. First introduced 1792.

CULTURE : Compost, equal parts loam, leaf-mould, and silver sand. Position, pots or beds in greenhouse, or against south or south-west walls, arches, or trellises outdoors in summer. Pot, March. Plant outdoors in June. Temp., Sept. to March 50° to 55° ; March to Sept. 60° to 70°. Water freely in summer, moderately other times.

PROPAGATION : Ordinary species by seeds sown ⅛ in. deep in light soil in temp. 75° in March ; variegated species by cuttings of young side shoots inserted in sandy peat in temp. 75° in March or April.

SPECIES CULTIVATED : C. scandens, purple, summer, 10 to 30 ft., Mexico ; scandens aurea marginata, leaves variegated with yellow.

Cob-nut (*Corylus avellana*)—See Corylus.

Cobweb House Leek (*Sempervivum arachnoideum*)—See Sempervivum.

Cochineal Cactus—See Opuntia.

Cochlearia (Horse-radish)—Ord. Cruciferæ. Hardy esculent-rooted perennial.

CULTURE : Soil, ordinary, deep, rich. Position, open or shade. Plant, Jan. or Feb., 8 in. deep in rows 2 ft. apart. Sets (roots) to be 3 in. long, with ¼ in. of crown pared off. Replant every third year. Lift for use as wanted.

PROPAGATION : By seeds sown outdoors in July ; cuttings of roots at planting time.

SPECIES CULTIVATED : C. armoracia, white, May, 3 ft., England.

Cock's-Comb (*Celosia cristata*)—See Celosia.

Cock's-foot Grass (*Dactylis glomerata*)—See Dactylis.

Cocoanut Palm (*Cocos nucifera*)—See Cocos.

Cocoa Tree (*Theobroma cacao*)—See Theobroma.

Cocos (Cocoanut Palm)—Ord. Palmaceæ. Stove palms. Orn. foliage. First introduced 1690. Leaves, feather-shape (pinnate).

CULTURE : Compost, two parts loam, equal parts peat and sand. Position, pots in shady stove. Pot, March. Water freely March to Oct. ; moderately at other times. Temp. March to Sept. 70° to 85° ; Sept. to March 60° to 70°.

PROPAGATION : By seeds sown 1 in. deep in light soil in temp. 85° at any time.

SPECIES CULTIVATED : C. flexuosa, 20 to 50 ft., Brazil ; nucifera (Cocoa-nut Palm), 40 to 100 ft., Tropics ; plumosa, 40 to 50 ft., Brazil ; romanzoffiana, 30 to 40 ft., Brazil ; weddelliana, 2 to 4 ft., Brazil.

Codiæum (Croton or South Sea Laurel)—Ord. Euphorbiaceæ. Stove evergreen shrubs. Orn. foliage. First introduced 1804. Leaves beautifully variegated with various colours.

CULTURE : Compost, two parts rich loam, one part peat and sand. Position, pots in stove close to the glass. Pot, March. Water freely March to Sept., moderately afterwards. Temp., Oct. to March 55° to 65° ; March to Oct. 70° to 85°.

PROPAGATION : By cuttings of the ends of shoots inserted singly in 2 in. pots filled with sandy soil in temp. 75° at any time ; stem-rooting in March or April.

SPECIES CULTIVATED : C. variegatum, leaves yellow and green, 3 to 10 ft., Malaya.

PRINCIPAL HYBRIDS OR VARIETIES : C. aigburthiensis, leaves red and green : angustifolium, yellow and green ; Chelsoni, orange, red and crimson ; evansianum, green, yellow, crimson, and scarlet ; Hawkeri, creamy white and green ; illustris, green and yellow ; interruptum aureus, purple, green, and yellow ; Johannis, green and yellow ; Laingii, green, red, and salmon ; picturatum, green, yellow and red ; variegatum tricolor, green, golden yellow and cream ; Warrenii, green and orange, carmine ; Williamsii, green, crimson and magenta. Weismannii, green, crimson, and magenta.

Codlins and Cream—See Narcissus and Epilobium.

Codonopsis (Bellwort)—Ord. Campanulaceæ. Hardy perennial herbs.
CULTURE : Soil, ordinary good. Position, sunny borders. Plant, autumn or spring.
PROPAGATION : By seeds sown in cold frame in spring, planting out seedlings in June ; also by cuttings in autumn.
SPECIES CULTIVATED : C. clematidea (Syn. Glosocomia clematidea), white and blue, summer, 3 ft. ; ovata, blue, summer, 1 ft., Himalayas ; rotundifolia, blue and yellow, July to Aug., 1½ ft., Western Himalayas.

Cœlogyne—Ord. Orchidaceæ. Stove and intermediate house orchids. First introduced 1822.
CULTURE : Compost, equal parts fresh sphagnum moss and fibry peat. Position, pots or pans half-filled with potsherds, and placed close to glass. Pot, Feb. or March ; have base of plant well above rim of pot or pan. Temp. for C. dayana and C. pandurata, March to Sept. 75° to 85° ; Sept. to March 60° to 70° ; for other species, March to Sept. 65° to 75° ; Sept. to March 55° to 60°. Moist atmosphere essential for first two species. Water freely March to Aug., moderately Aug. to Nov., very little Nov. to March. Growing season, March to Aug. Resting period, Sept. to Feb.
PROPAGATION : By division of pseudo-bulbs at potting time.
SPECIES CULTIVATED : C. cristata, white and yellow, Feb. to April, 6 to 10 in., Himalayas ; cristata alba, white ; cristata lemoniana, yellow, white and lemon ; dayana, vellow, June, 6 in., Borneo ; fuscescens, red, brown, and green, Sept., 9 in., Himalayas ; massangeana, yellow and red, June, 1 ft., Assam ; pandurata, green, yellow, and black, Dec., 1½ to 2 ft., Borneo ; sanderiana, white and yellow, July, 1 ft., Sunda Islands ; speciosa, yellow and brown, autumn, 9 in., Malaya.

Coffea (Coffee Tree)—Ord. Rubiaceæ. Stove evergreen shrubs. First introduced 1696. Fruit, a small reddish, fleshy berry, containing two seeds enclosed in parchment-like shell. Bears the coffee berries of commerce.
CULTURE : Compost, two parts turfy loam, one part leaf-mould and sand. Position, pots in moist plant stove. Pot, March. Temp., March to Sept. 75° to 85° ; Sept. to March 60° to 70°. Water freely in summer, moderately other times.
PROPAGATION : By seeds sown ½ in. deep in light soil in temp. 85° in March ; cuttings of firm shoots inserted in sandy soil under bell-glass in temp. 85° in summer.
SPECIES CULTIVATED : C. arabica (Arabian Coffee), white, fragrant, Sept., 10 to 15 ft., Arabia.

Coffee Tree (*Coffea arabica*)—See Coffea.

Coix (Job's Tears)—Ord. Gramineæ. Half-hardy ornamental flowering annual grass. First introduced 1596.
CULTURE : Soil, light, rich. Position, sunny border outdoors.
PROPAGATION : By seeds sown ½ in. deep in light soil in temp. 65° to 75° in March, transplanting seedlings outdoors in May ; or similar depth outdoors in April where plants are to flower.
SPECIES CULTIVATED : C. Lachryma-Jobi, 2 to 3 ft., Trop. Asia. Grey pearly seeds chief attraction.

Colchican Bladder Nut (*Staphylea colchica*)—See Staphylea.

Colchican Laurel (*Prunus Laurocerasus colchica*)—See Prunus.

Colchicum (Autumn Crocus ; Meadow Saffron)—Ord. Liliaceæ. Hardy bulbous flowering plants.
CULTURE : Soil, light sandy loam, enriched with decayed manure or leaf-mould. Position, moist beds or rockeries, shrubbery borders, or lawns near shade of trees. Plant bulbs 3 in. deep and 3 in. apart in July or Aug. Foliage dies down in June and July, and does not reappear until after plant has flowered.
PROPAGATION : By seeds sown ⅛ in. deep in bed of fine soil outdoors in Aug. or Sept., or in pans or boxes of similar soil in cold frame at same time, transplanting

seedlings 3 in. apart when two years old; division of bulbs in. Aug. Seedling bulbs do not flower until four or five years old.

SPECIES CULTIVATED : C. agrippinum (Syn. tessalatum), rose-purple and white, autumn, 3 to 4 in., S. Europe ; autumnale, purple, Sept., 8 in., Europe (Britain) ; Bornmuelleri, rosy lilac, 8 to 12 in., Eastern Europe ; byzantinum, rose and purple, Sept., 6 in., Greece ; Decaisnei, pale rose, Oct. to Nov., Mt. Lebanon ; giganteum, soft rose and white, autumn, Asia Minor ; speciosum, lilac-purple, Sept., Caucasus ; variegatum, rose and purple, Sept., 6 in., E. Europe and Asia Minor. Also numerous varieties of C. autumnale.

Coleus (Flame Nettle ; Nettle Geranium)—Ord. Labiatæ. Stove perennials. Orn. foliage and flowering. First introduced 1764.

CULTURE : Compost, two parts turfy loam, one part well-decayed manure, leaf-mould, and little sand. Position, pots in stove in winter, greenhouse in summer. Pot, Feb. or March, pressing soil firmly in pots. Temp., Sept. to March 60° to 70° ; March to June 75° to 85° ; June to Sept. 65° to 75°. Water very moderately Sept. to March, freely afterwards. Ornamental-leaved kinds require to have points of their shoots pinched off in early stage of their growth to ensure dwarf or good shaped plants.

PROPAGATION : By seeds sown $\frac{1}{16}$ in. deep in light soil in temp. 75° in Feb., March or April ; cuttings of young shoots inserted in light soil of cocoanut-fibre refuse at any time ; grafting in spring.

SPECIES CULTIVATED : C. Blumei, white and purple, leaves bronze-red, Java, 2 to 3 ft., parent of the ornamental-leaved kinds, Verschaffelti being a well-known variety ; thrysoideus (Winter-flowering Coleus), blue, Jan. to April, 3 ft., Trop. Africa.

Cole-wort—See Brassica.

Colletia (Anchor-plant)—Ord. Rhamnaceæ. Half-hardy evergreen shrubs. First introduced 1823. Branches armed with formidable spines.

CULTURE : Soil, loamy. Position, sheltered, well-drained borders in S. of England. Plant in Oct.

PROPAGATION : By cuttings of firm shoots 6 in. long, inserted in well-drained pots of sandy soil in cold frame in Aug. or Sept.

SPECIES CULTIVATED : C. armata, white, Sept., bodkin-like spines, 10 ft., Chile ; cruciata, white, autumn, flattish, triangular spines, occasionally bodkin-like, 4 to 10 ft., Uruguay ; infausta (Syn. horrida), white, March, bodkin-like spines, 10 ft., Peru.

Collinsia (Collins's-flower)—Ord. Scrophulariaceæ. Hardy annuals. First introduced 1826.

CULTURE : Soil, ordinary. Position, open beds or borders.

PROPAGATION : By seeds sown ⅛ in. deep outdoors in Sept., March, or April where plants are required to flower. Thin seedlings to 6 in. apart when 2 in. high.

SPECIES CULTIVATED : C. bicolor, purple and white, summer, 1 ft., California ; bicolor alba, white ; grandiflora, purple and blue, June, 18 in., N.W. America ; verna, white and blue, May, 1 ft., N. America.

Collomia—Ord. Polemoniaceæ. Hardy annuals. First introduced 1826.

CULTURE : Soil, ordinary. Position, open beds or borders.

PROPAGATION : By seeds sown ⅛ in. deep outdoors in Sept., March or April where plants are required to flower. Thin seedlings to 3 in. apart when 2 in. high.

SPECIES CULTIVATED : C. coccinea, red, June, 18 in., Chile ; grandiflora, buff or salmon, summer, 18 in., California.

Colocasia (West Indian Kale ; Taro Root)—Ord. Aroideæ. Stove herbaceous plants with perennial tuberous roots. Orn. foliage. First introduced 1551. Leaves, shield-like, heart or egg-shaped, deep green.

CULTURE : Compost, equal parts turfy loam, peat, leaf-mould, and silver sand. Position, well-drained pots in shady plant stove. Pot moderately firm in pots just large enough to take tubers in Feb. or March ; transfer to larger pots in April or May. Water moderately Feb. to April and Sept. to Nov., freely April to Sept. ;

Clarkia elegans

Clematis lanuginosa
(Virgin's Bower)

Clethra alnifolia
(Sweet Pepper Bush)

Clianthus puniceus
(Parrot's-bill)

Clivia miniata hybrida
(Caffre Lily)

Cnicus diacantha
(Fishbone Thistle)

Cocos Weddelliana

Codiæum hybridum
(Croton)

Coleus hybridum
(Flame Nettle)

Colletia infausta
(Anchor-plant)

Collinsia bicolor alba
(Collin's Flower)

Colutea arborescens
(Bladder Senna)

Commelina cœlestis
(Blue Spider-wort)

Conandron ramondioides

Convolvulus tricolor

Coreopsis hybrida
(Tickseed)

Cornus Kousa

Coronilla glauca
(Crown Vetch)

keep quite dry Nov. to Feb.   Temp., Feb. to Sept. 70° to 80° ; Sept. to Nov. 65°
to 75° ; Nov. to Feb. 55° to 65°.
PROPAGATION : By dividing the tubers in Feb. or March.
SPECIES CULTIVATED : C. antiquorum, 2 to 4 ft., E. Indies, and its varieties illustris,.
Fontanesi and euchlora ; esculenta, 2 to 3 ft., Pacific Isles.   The tubers of the first-
named species are the Egyptian taro or culcas.   The tubers of C. esculenta are
similar but superior in quality, being the taro root of America.

Coloured Marguerite (*Chrysanthemum coccineum*)—See Chrysanthemum.

Colt's-foot—See Tussilago.

Columbine (*Aquilegia vulgaris*)—See Aquilegia.

Columnea—Ord. Gesneriaceæ.   Stove evergreen trailing shrubs.   First
introduced 1759.
CULTURE : Compost, equal parts fibrous peat, sphagnum moss and charcoal.
Position, hanging baskets.   Plant, March.   Water freely in summer, moderately
in winter.   Temp., Sept. to March 60° to 70° ; March to Sept. 70° to 80°.
PROPAGATION : By cuttings of firm shoots 3 in. long, inserted in pots of above
compost mixed with sand, in temp. 85°, Feb.
SPECIES CULTIVATED : C. gloriosa, scarlet and yellow, June, Costa Rica.

Colutea (Bladder Senna)—Ord. Leguminosæ.   Hardy deciduous flowering
shrubs.   First introduced 1568.
CULTURE : Soil, ordinary.   Position, open or shady shrubberies, banks, etc. Plant,
Oct. to Feb.   Prune, Nov., simply cutting away weak shoots and shortening
straggling ones.
PROPAGATION : By seeds sown 1 in. deep outdoors in Oct. or March ; cuttings of
firm shoots inserted in sandy soil outdoors in Oct.
SPECIES CULTIVATED : C. arborescens, yellow, Aug., 10 ft., S. Europe ; istria (Syn.
Pococki), coppery yellow, May to Aug., 3 to 4 ft., Asia Minor ; media, brownish
red, summer, 8 to 10 ft., hybrid ; orientalis, (Syn. cruenta), coppery red, June to
Sept., 4 to 6 ft., Orient.

Combretum (Caffre Butter-shrub)—Ord. Combretaceæ.   Stove evergreen
climbers.   First introduced 1820.
CULTURE : Compost, two parts loam, one part peat and sand.   Position, pots,.
tubs, or borders in plant stove, shoots trained to pillars or roof. Pot, March. Prune
side shoots to within 2 in. of base after flowering and cut away all weak ones. Water
freely March to Sept., moderately afterwards.   Syringe daily March to Aug.
Temp., March to Sept., 70° to 85° ; Sept. to March 55° to 65°.
PROPAGATION : By cuttings of side shoots 3 in. long, removed with slight portion of
stem attached, and inserted in well-drained pot of sandy soil in temp. 85° in summer.
SPECIES CULTIVATED : C. coccineum, scarlet, autumn, 20 ft., Madagascar ; grandiflorum, scarlet, 5 ft., Trop. Africa.

Comfrey—See Symphytum.

Commelina (Blue Spider-wort ; Day-flower)—Ord. Commelinaceæ.   Greenhouse and hardy herbaceous perennials.   First introduced 1759.
CULTURE OF GREENHOUSE SPECIES : Compost, equal parts peat, loam, leaf-mould, and
sand. Position, pots in sunny greenhouse. Pot, March. Water freely March to Sept.,.
very little afterwards.   Temp., March to Sept. 55° to 65° ; Sept. to March 45° to 50°.
CULTURE OF HARDY SPECIES : Soil, light, rich.   Position, warm, sheltered, well-
drained bed or border.   Plant fleshy roots in April.   Protect roots during winter
on light soils with thick layer of ashes or manure.   Lift roots in cold districts in
Sept. and store away similarly to dahlias in frost-proof place, replanting in April.
PROPAGATION : By seeds sown ⅛ in. deep in light soil in temp. 75° in March,.
transplanting seedlings outdoors in May to flower in Aug. ; division in April.
GREENHOUSE SPECIES : C. africana, yellow, May to Oct., 1 to 3 ft., S. Africa ;.
elliptica, white, July, 2 ft., Mexico.
HARDY SPECIES : C. cœlestis, blue, July, 18 in., Mexico ; cœlestis alba, white ;.
tuberosa, blue, June to July, 1 to 1½ ft., Mexico.

Comparettia—Ord. Orchidaceæ. Stove epiphytal orchids. First introduced 1836. CULTURE : Compost, sphagnum moss, fibry peat. Position, on blocks of wood suspended from roof in plant stove. Reblock, March or April. Water freely at all times. Temp., March to Sept. 65° to 85° ; Sept. to March 60° to 70°. Resting period, none.
PROPAGATION : By division of plant in March.
SPECIES CULTIVATED : C. coccinea, scarlet and orange, Aug., 1 ft., Brazil ; falcata, crimson-purple, May, 6 in., Mexico ; macroplectron, rose and purple, summer, New Grenada.

Compass Plant (*Silphium laciniatum*)—See Silphium.

Comptonia—Ord. Myricaceæ. Hardy deciduous shrub. First introduced 1714. CULTURE : Soil, peaty loam. Position, shady borders or shrubberies. Plant, Nov.
PROPAGATION : By layers in early spring.
SPECIES CULTIVATED : C. asplenifolia (Sweet Fern), (Syn. Myrica asplenifolia), elegant fern-like foliage, 2 to 4 ft., Eastern N. America.

Conandron—Ord. Gesneriaceæ. Hardy herbaceous perennial. First introduced 1879.
CULTURE : Soil, peat and loam. Position, fissures of moist, sheltered rockery. Plant, March or April. Protect in severe winters with covering of dry litter.
PROPAGATION : By seeds sown in well-drained pots of sandy peat and just covered with fine mould, in cold frame or greenhouse March or April ; division of plant in March.
SPECIES CULTIVATED : C. ramondioides, lilac and yellow, summer, 8 to 12 in., Japan.

Cone-flower—See Rudbeckia and Lepachys.

Cone-head—See Strobilanthes.

Constantinople Nut (*Corylus colurna*)—See Corylus.

Convallaria (Lily of the Valley ; May Lily)—Ord. Liliaceæ. Hardy herbaceous perennial.
OUTDOOR CULTURE : Compost, equal parts loam, leaf-mould, decayed manure, and sharp sand. Position, beds or borders under shade of trees, high walls, or fences for general culture ; south border for early flowering. Plant single crowns 2 or 3 in. apart, with points just below surface, in Sept. and Oct. Lift and replant every four years, always planting largest crowns by themselves, next size alone, and smallest similarly. Mulch bed annually in Feb. with decayed manure. Apply liquid manure once a week, May to Sept., to beds more than a year old.
POT CULTURE : Compost, equal parts good soil and leaf-mould. Plant one clump or a dozen single crowns in a 6 in. pot, well drained in Oct. or Nov. Place inverted pot over crowns and stand pots in cold frame or under greenhouse stage until Jan., then remove into heat, or allow to bloom naturally in greenhouse or window. Water only when soil needs moisture in winter, freely when growth begins.
FORCING : Place single crowns close together in shallow boxes, with cocoanut-fibre refuse between roots, and put boxes in temp. 80° to 85°. Cover points of crowns with inverted box or thick layer of moss until flowers appear, then remove it. After forcing, crowns of no value for flowering again, therefore discard them. Retarded roots flower quickly without much forcing.
PROPAGATION : By seeds sown ¼ in. deep in light soil outdoors in March ; division of crowns Sept. or Oct.
SPECIES CULTIVATED : C. majalis, white, spring, 6 in., Europe (Britain), etc. ; majalis flore pleno, double ; majalis prolificans, tall variety ; majalis rosea, rose tinted. Fortin's Giant is a large-flowered variety.

Convolvulus—Ord. Convolvulaceæ. Hardy annual and perennial plants. Mostly climbing or trailing.
CULTURE : Soil, ordinary rich. Position, dwarf kinds in open beds and borders ; tall kinds at base of arbours, trellises, walls, or trunks of trees. C. Cneorum and C. mauritanicus in sunny rock gardens. Plant perennials in March. Sow annual species in April where required to grow, and thin seedlings to 5 in. apart when 2 in. high.

PROPAGATION : By seeds sown ¼ in. deep outdoors in March where plants are to flower, or in nursery bed, afterwards transplanting seedlings to permanent position ; division of fleshy roots in March or April.

ANNUAL SPECIES : C. tricolor, various colours, summer, 1 ft., S. Europe.

PERENNIAL SPECIES : C. althæoides, rose-pink, June to Aug., 1 to 2 ft., Mediterranean Region ; aureus superbus (this is usually treated as an annual), golden-yellow, summer, 4 to 5 ft. ; cantabrica, pale rose, June to Aug., 1½ ft., Europe ; Cneorum, white tinged pink, summer, 2 to 3 ft., S. Europe ; mauritanicus, blue, July, trailing, S. Europe ; spithamæus (Syn. stans), white, June to Aug., 6 in., N. America. See also Calystegia and Ipomæa.

Cooperia (Evening Star)—Ord. Amaryllidaceæ. Half-hardy bulbous plants.

CULTURE : Compost, equal parts peat, loam, and leaf-mould. Position, pots in cool greenhouse or cold frame. Pot, Jan. or Feb. Water moderately until growth begins, then give freely ; discontinue watering after Sept. and keep soil dry during winter. Temp., Sept. to Feb. 40° to 45° ; Feb. to May 50° to 55° ; May to Sept. 55° to 65°.

PROPAGATION : By offsets in Feb.

SPECIES CULTIVATED : C. Drummondii, white, Aug., 9 in., Texas ; pedunculata, white, Aug., 8 in., Texas.

Copalm Balsam-tree (*Liquidambar styraciflua*)—See Liquidambar.

Copper-coloured Beech (*Fagus sylvatica* var. *cuprea*)—See Fagus.

Copper-leaf (*Acalypha musaica*)—See Acalypha.

Coprosma (Tasmanian Currant)—Ord. **Rubiaceæ.** Half-hardy evergreen shrubs. Orn. foliage.

CULTURE : Compost, two parts sandy loam, one part leaf-mould and sand. Position, pots in cool greenhouse. Repot, March. Prune straggling shoots into shape in March. Water moderately in winter, freely in summer. Temp., Sept. to March 40° to 45° ; March to Sept. 55° to 65°. Hardy in sheltered positions outdoors S. of England.

PROPAGATION : By cuttings removed in March, with small portion of old wood attached, and inserted in well-drained pots of sandy soil in temp. 85° under bell-glass.

SPECIES CULTIVATED : C. acerosa, almost prostrate, blue translucent berries ; Baueri, leaves green, 10 to 25 ft., New Zealand, Norfolk Islands ; Baueri variegata, leaves edged with yellow, 3 ft. ; Petriei, prostrate, purple berries, New Zealand.

Coptis (Gold Thread ; Mouth Root)—Ord. Raunculaceæ. Hardy evergreen bog plants. First introduced 1782.

CULTURE : Soil, boggy peat. Position, moist, shady. Plant, Oct. or March.

PROPAGATION : By seeds sown ⅟₁₆ in. deep in pans of fine sandy peat in shady cold frame in March ; division of roots in Oct. or March.

SPECIES CULTIVATED : C. asplenifolia, white, spring, 3 to 4 in., Japan ; quinquefolia, white, spring, 2 to 3 in. ; trifolia, white, April, 1 ft., N. Hemisphere.

Coral Berry (*Berberidopsis corallina*)—See Berberidopsis.

Coral Creeper (*Kennedya prostrata*)—See Kennedya.

Coral Drops (*Bessera elegans*)—See Bessera.

Coral-head-plant (*Abrus precatorius*)—See Abrus.

Corallita (*Antigonon leptopus*)—See Antigonon.

Coral Root—See Dentaria and Cardamine.

Coral Tree (*Erythrina Crista-galli*)—See Erythrina.

Coral Vine (*Antigonon leptopus*)—See Antigonon.

Cordyline—Ord. Liliaceæ. Greenhouse plants. Orn. foliage. Allied to and often called Dracænas. First introduced 1820.

CULTURE : Compost, two parts peat, one part loam and sand. Position, pots in greenhouse. Repot, March. Water moderately Oct. to March, freely afterwards. Temp., March to Sept. 55° to 65° ; Sept. to March 45° to 50°.

PROPAGATION : By seeds sown 1 in. deep in pots of light soil in temp. 85° in March ;

cuttings of main stems cut into lengths of 1 in. and partially inserted horizontally in pots of sandy soil in March ; cuttings of fleshy roots inserted 1 in. deep in pots of sandy soil, in March or April in temp. 75° to 80° ; stem rooting in March or April ; offsets inserted in 2 in. pots of sandy soil at any time.
SPECIES CULTIVATED : C. australis (Syn. C. Veitchii and Dracæna australis), leaves broad and green, 15 to 40 ft., New Zealand ; Banksii, ribbon-like leaves, 8 to 15 ft., New Zealand ; indivisa, green, narrow, New Zealand ; stricta (Syn. C. congesta), leaves green and narrow, 6 to 10 ft., Australia ; terminalis (Syn. Dracæna Baptistii), leaves broad and green, 3 to 10 ft., E. Himalayas, China and E. Indies.   There are many varieties with coloured or variegated leaves.   See also Dracæna.

Coreopsis (Tickseed)—Ord. Compositæ.   Hardy annual and perennial herbaceous plants.   First introduced 1699.
CULTURE : Soil, ordinary.   Position, sunny, well-drained beds or borders.   Plant perennials in Oct. or March, annuals in May or June.
PROPAGATION : Annuals by seed sown ⅛ in. deep in boxes of light soil in temp. 65° to 70° in March, or outdoors in April where plants are to flower ; perennials by seed sown outdoors in April, transplanting seedlings when large enough to handle to permanent position ; division of roots in Oct. or March.
ANNUAL SPECIES : C. atkinsoniana, yellow and purple, summer, 2 to 4 ft., Western U.S.A. ; cardaminefolia, yellow and brown-purple, summer, 6 to 24 in., Southern U.S.A. ; coronata, orange and purple, summer, 2 ft., Texas ; Drummondii, yellow and crimson, summer, 2 ft., Texas ; tinctoria (Syn. bicolor), yellow and purple, summer, 2 ft., N. America ; tinctoria atrosanguinea, purplish.
PERENNIAL SPECIES : C. grandiflora, yellow, Aug., 2 to 3 ft., Southern U.S.A. ; lanceolata, yellow, Aug., 2 to 3 ft., Eastern U.S.A. ; palmata, orange-yellow, July to Sept., 1½ to 3 ft., Central U.S.A. ; pubescens, yellow and purple, summer, 2 to 4 ft., Southern U.S.A., and its variety superba (large flowered) ; senifolia (Syn. major), deep yellow, July to Sept., 2 to 3 ft., South-eastern U.S.A. ; rosea, rose-pink, summer, 9 to 24 in., U.S.A. ; verticillata, yellow, Aug., 2 ft.   The plant listed in catalogues as C. auriculata is really C. pubescens.

Corfu Lily (*Funkia subcordata*)—See Funkia.

Coriander (*Coriandrum sativum*)—See Coriandrum.

Coriandrum (Coriander)—Ord. Umbelliferæ.   Hardy annual.   Leaves used for flavouring soups and salads.   Seed ripens in Aug. and is largely employed in confectionery.
CULTURE IN GARDENS : Soil, ordinary.   Position, south border.
PROPAGATION : By seeds sown ¼ in. deep in drills 12 in. apart, March or Sept.
SPECIES CULTIVATED : C. sativum, white, June, 18 in., S. Europe.

Coriaria—Ord. Coriariaceæ.   Half-hardy deciduous flowering shrubs.   Leaves and fruits poisonous.
CULTURE : Soil, ordinary.   Position, sunny, sheltered borders.   Plant in autumn.
PROPAGATION : By suckers or layers in autumn, or cuttings of half-ripened wood in sandy soil in frame or under hand-glass.
SPECIES CULTIVATED : C. myrtifolia, greenish, summer, 4 ft., S. France ; terminalis, greenish, succeeded in autumn by waxy, golden, currant-like berries, 4 ft., Sikkim. Last named the best species to grow.   The leaves of the former yield redoul which is used in curing leather and ink-making.

Coris (Montpelier Coris)—Ord. Primulaceæ.   Hardy biennial.   First introduced 1640.
CULTURE : Soil, sandy peat.   Position, well-drained beds on sunny rockery.   Plant, March or April.
PROPAGATION : By seeds sown 1/16 in. deep in Aug. or April where plants are to grow.
SPECIES CULTIVATED : C. monspeliensis, lilac, May, 1 ft., S. Europe.

Cork-barked Elm (*Ulmus nitens suberosa*)—See Ulmus.

Cork Oak (*Quercus suber*)—See Quercus.

Cornel (*Cornus sanguinea*)—See Cornus.

Cornelian Cherry (*Cornus mas*)—See Cornus.

Corn Flag (*Gladiolus communis*)—See Gladiolus.

Corn-flower (*Centaurea cyanus*)—See Centaurea.

Cornish Elm (*Ulmus stricta*)—See Ulmus.

Cornish Money-wort (*Sibthorpia europæa*)—See Sibthorpia.

Corn Marigold (*Chrysanthemum segetum*)—See Chrysanthemum.

Corn Salad (*Valerianella olitoria*)—See Valerianella.

Cornus (Bunch Berry ; Dwarf Cornel ; Cornelian Cherry ; Cornel-tree ; Dogwood ; Dogberry ; Skewerwood)—Ord. Cornaceæ. Hardy deciduous trees and shrubs and herbaceous perennials. Flowering and orn. foliage. Leaves, green, or variegated with white and crimson.
CULTURE OF SHRUBBY SPECIES : Soil, sandy peat for dwarf species, ordinary for others. Position, rocky for dwarf kinds ; open or shady shrubberies for tall species. Plant, Oct. to Feb. Prune, Nov. or Dec., simply cutting branches into shape.
HERBACEOUS SPECIES : Soil, bog or peat. Position, moist bed or rockery. Plant March.
PROPAGATION : Shrubby kinds by cuttings of firm shoots inserted in sandy soil outdoors in Nov. ; layering shoots in spring ; suckers, removed from plant in Nov. and replanted at once ; grafting variegated kinds in March ; seeds sown outdoors in March ; herbaceous species by division in March.
SHRUBBY SPECIES : C. alba, white, July, 8 to 10 ft., N. Asia ; alba sibirica variegata, variegated ; alba Spaethii, leaves bronze and gold ; capitata (Syn. Benthamia, fragifera), white, Aug., 10 ft., N. India, hardy S. of England only ; controversa (Syn. brachypoda), white, June to July, 30 to 50 ft., Japan ; florida (Flowering Dogwood), white, May, 10 to 15 ft., N. America ; Kousa, creamy white, May to June, 15 to 20 ft., Japan, Corea, and Central China ; macrophylla, yellowish white, July to Aug., 30 to 50 ft., Himalayas ; mas (Cornelian Cherry), yellow, Feb., 15 ft., Europe ; mas aurea elegantissima, leaves creamy white and red ; mas variegata, leaves edged creamy white ; Nuttallii, creamy white, May, 30 to 50 ft., Western N. America ; sanguinea (Dogwood), green, June, 8 ft., branches red.
HERBACEOUS SPECIES : C. canadensis (Dwarf Cornel), purplish white, May, 6 in., N. America.

Corokia—Ord. Cornaceæ. Half-hardy evergreen shrubs. First introduced 1835.
CULTURE : Soil, ordinary. Position, sheltered, south or west wall. Plant, Oct. to April.
PROPAGATION : By cuttings inserted in sand in well-drained pan under bell-glass ; layering shoots in Oct.
SPECIES CULTIVATED : C. buddleoides, yellow, summer, 10 ft., New Zealand ; Cotoneaster, yellow, 6 to 8 ft., New Zealand.

Coronilla (Crown Vetch ; Scorpion Senna)—Ord. Leguminosæ. Greenhouse and hardy shrubs and hardy perennials. First introduced 1596.
CULTURE OF GREENHOUSE SPECIES : Compost, two parts loam, one part peat and sand. Position, pots in light greenhouse. Repot, March. Prune off points of shoots in spring to induce bushy growth. Water moderately Oct. to March, freely afterwards. Temp., Sept. to March 40° to 45° ; March to Sept. 55° to 65°. Place plants outdoors in sunny position June to Sept.
CULTURE OF PERENNIALS : Soil, ordinary. Position, sunny rockeries or borders. Plant, Oct. or April.
PROPAGATION : Greenhouse species by seeds sown ½ in. deep in light soil in temp. 75° in March, or by cuttings inserted in well-drained pots of sandy soil under bell-glass in temp. 55° from March to May ; perennial species by seeds sown ½ in. deep outdoors in April, or division of roots in Oct. ; hardy shrubs by cuttings in cold frame in autumn.
CULTURE OF HARDY SHRUBS : Soil, ordinary. Position, sheltered, warm shrubberies, or south or west walls. Plant, Oct. Prune straggly shoots after flowering.

GREENHOUSE SPECIES : C. glauca, yellow, May, 10 to 12 ft., evergreen, France.
PERENNIAL SPECIES : C. cappadocica (Syn. iberica), yellow, July, 6 in., Iberia ; minima, yellow, June, 6 in., S. Europe ; varia, pink and white, summer and autumn, 1 to 2 ft., trailer, Europe.
HARDY SHRUBS : C. emeroides, yellow, May to Aug., 4 to 5 ft., deciduous, South-east Europe ; Emerus (Scorpion Senna), red and yellow, April, 7 to 9 ft., deciduous, Europe.

Correa (Australian Fuchsia)—Ord. Rutaceæ.   Greenhouse evergreen shrubs. First introduced 1793.
CULTURE : Compost, two parts peat, one part fibrous loam and sand. Position, pots, well drained, in light, airy greenhouse. Repot in July when new growth begins. Prune directly after flowering. Water moderately April to July and Oct. to April, freely July to Oct. Temp., Sept. to March 40° to 45° ; March to Sept. 55° to 65°. Place plants outdoors in sunny position July to Sept.
PROPAGATION : By cuttings inserted in well-drained pots of sandy peat under bell-glass in temp. 65° to 75° in April ; grafting on Correa alba or Eriostemon buxifolia in March.
SPECIES CULTIVATED : C. alba, white, June, 5 to 6 ft. ; cardinalis, scarlet, March, 3 ft. ; lawrenciana, green and white, April, 3 ft. ; speciosa, scarlet, June, 3 ft., and its varieties bicolor (crimson and white), Harrisii (crimson), pulchella (scarlet), and ventricosa (bright crimson and green).   All natives of Australia.

Corsican Pine-tree (*Pinus Laricio*)—See Pinus.

Cortaderia (Pampas Grass)—Ord. Gramineæ. Hardy herbaceous perennial grass. Flowering and orn. foliage. First introduced 1843. Inflorescence (male and female borne on different plants), white, purple, yellow ; Sept. to Nov.
CULTURE : Soil, rich, light, sandy. Position, sheltered shrubberies or lawns. Plant, Oct., March, or April. Water freely in dry weather. Gather plumes for winter decoration directly fully developed.
PROPAGATION : By seeds sown ⅛ in. deep in sandy soil in well-drained pots or pans under bell-glass in temp. 55° to 65° in Feb., March or April. Transplant seedlings outdoors in Aug. or Sept. Female plumes best and most durable for winter decoration.
SPECIES CULTIVATED : C. argentea (Pampas Grass), Syn. Gynerium argenteum, 5 to 10 ft., Brazil ; argentea argenteo-lineata, leaves green and golden ; conspicua (Syn. Arundo conspicua), New Zealand Silvery Reed Grass, 3 to 12 ft., New Zealand ; jubata, 4 to 6 ft., Ecuador.

Cortusa (Bear's-ear Sanicle)—Ord. Primulaceæ. Hardy perennial alpine plants. First introduced 1596.
CULTURE : Soil, sandy peat. Position, shady border or rockery. Plant, March or April.
PROPAGATION : By seeds sown ⅛ in. deep in sandy peat in cold frame in March or Aug ; division of plant in March.
SPECIES CULTIVATED : C. Matthioli, red, April, 1 ft., Europe ; Matthioli grandiflora, purple, April, 18 in. ; pubens, magenta-purple, May, 6 in., Transylvania.

Coryanthes (Helmet-orchid)—Ord. Orchidaceæ. Stove epiphytal orchids. First introduced 1829.
CULTURE : Compost, equal parts peat and sphagnum moss. Position, baskets suspended from roof of stove. Rebasket in March. Water freely April to Sept., very little afterwards. Temp., April to Aug. 65° to 85° ; Aug. to April 50° to 65°. Growing season, April to Aug. Resting period, Aug. to April. Flowers appear on new growth.
PROPAGATION : By division of plant in March.
SPECIES CULTIVATED : C. macrantha, green, purple, yellow and crimson, June, 1 ft., Venezuela ; maculata, yellow and purple, June, 1 ft., Trop. America.

Corydalis (Fumitory)—Ord. Fumariaceæ. Hardy annual and perennial herbs.
CULTURE : Soil, ordinary, good. Position, well-drained sunny borders, ledges of rockeries, fissures in old walls. Plant perennial and biennial species in March.

PROPAGATION : Annual species by seeds sown in April where plants are to flower ; perennials by seed similar to annuals, transplanting seedlings to permanent positions when large enough to handle ; also by division of the plants after flowering ; bulbous species by offsets in March.
PERENNIAL SPECIES : C. bulbosa (Syn. Solida), purple, April, 6 in., Europe ; cheilanthifolia, yellow, summer, 10 in., China ; lutea, yellow, spring and summer, 1 ft., Europe ; nobilis, yellow, May, 1 ft., Siberia ; ledebouriana, purple, summer, 1 ft., Altai Mountains ; thalictrifolia, yellow, summer, 1 ft., China.
ANNUAL SPECIES : C. glauca, scarlet, violet and orange, summer, 1 ft., Canada.

Corylopsis—Ord. Hamamelidaceæ. Hardy deciduous flowering shrubs. First introduced 1864.
CULTURE : Soil, sandy loam. Position, open, moist shrubbery in S. England ; south walls in other parts of country. Plant, Oct. to Feb.
PROPAGATION : By layering shoots in Oct.
SPECIES CULTIVATED : C. Griffithii (Syn. himalayana), yellow, March, 20 ft., Himalayas ; pauciflora, yellow, Feb., 3 to 4 ft., Japan ; platypetala, pale yellow, 4 to 6 ft., China ; sinensis, primrose-yellow, fragrant, April, 10 to 15 ft., China ; spicata, yellow, Feb., 6 ft., Japan ; veitchiana, yellow, fragrant, April, 5 to 6 ft., W. China ; Willmottiæ, greenish yellow, March to April, 6 to 12 ft., China ; Wilsoni, yellow, April, 5 to 6 ft., China.

Corylus (Hazel ; Cob-nut ; Filbert)—Ord. Corylaceæ. Hardy deciduous shrubs. Orn. foliage and nut-bearing. Flowers, male—grey, female—crimson ; March, April. Nuts ripe in Oct.
CULTURE : Soil, rich loam, well manured and deeply trenched. Position, open, sunny. Plant cob and hazel nuts 10 ft. apart each way, and filberts 15 ft. apart, in Oct. Prune end of March, cutting away shoots not less than two years old and shortening those of previous year's growth about one-third. Train each tree to have six main branches only. Gather nuts when husk becomes brown. Hang branches of hazel catkins (male flowers) in filbert bushes in Feb., if filbert catkins are scarce, to ensure fertilisation.
PROPAGATION : By seeds (nuts) 2 in. deep in Oct. in open garden, transplanting seedlings two years afterwards ; suckers, removed from base of old plants replanted in Oct. ; layering strong young shoots in Nov. ; grafting on seedlings of Constantinople Nut in March to form standards, half standards, and dwarf standards.
SPECIES : C. avellana (Common Hazel), Europe (Britain) ; avellana aurea, golden-leaved ; maxima (Filbert), S. Europe ; maxima atropurpurea, purple-leaved ; colurna (Constantinople Nut), S.E. Europe.
VARIETIES : Kentish Cob or Lambert's Filbert, nuts large, a good market kind ; Cosford, nuts round, shells thin, free bearer ; Webb's Prize Cob, large, good market sort ; Prolific Frizzled Filbert, free bearer, ripens early.

Corypha—See Livistona.

Cos Lettuce—See Lactuca.

Cosmidium—See Thelesperma.

Cosmos (Purple Mexican Aster)—Ord. Compositæ. Half-hardy annuals. First introduced 1799.
CULTURE : Soil, ordinary. Position, warm, dryish border.
PROPAGATION : By seeds sown in light soil in temp. of 65° to 70° in March, transplanting seedlings outdoors 2 to 3 ft. apart in May.
SPECIES CULTIVATED : C. bipinnatus, various colours, Aug., 3 ft., Mexico ; diversifolius, lilac, Sept., 3 ft., N. America ; diversifolius atrosanguineus, a superior variety ; sulphureus, pale yellow, July to Aug., 3 to 4 ft., Mexico. There are many fine hybrids in a variety of colours.

Costmary—See Tanacetum.

Cotoneaster (Rose Box)—Ord. Rosaceæ. Hardy evergreen and deciduous shrubs, bearing scarlet fruits in winter.
CULTURE : Soil, ordinary. Position, shrubberies, open, or in shade, trailing species

against walls or growing over tree roots and rocks, or bare ground under trees. Plant, Oct. to Feb.

PROPAGATION : By seeds sown 1 in. deep outdoors in March ; cuttings inserted in sandy soil outdoors in Oct.; layering shoots in spring; grafting on common species, quince, or hawthorn in March.

EVERGREEN SPECIES : C. amœna, white, April, 3 to 5 ft., berries red, Yunnan ; buxifolia, white, April, 10 to 12 ft., berries red, Himalayas ; congesta, pale pink, April, 1½ to 2½ ft., berries red, Himalayas ; Francheti, white and rose, May, 8 to 10 ft., berries orange-scarlet, Thibet and W. China ; harroviana, white, April, 5 to 6 ft., berries red, Yunnan ; henryana (Syn. rugosa henryana), white, June, 10 to 12 ft., berries brownish crimson, Central China ; humifusa (Syn. Dammeri), white, May, prostrate, berries coral red, Central China ; microphylla, white, April, 2 to 3 ft., berries dull red, Himalayas ; pannosa, white, April, 6 to 10 ft., berries dull red, Yunnan ; rotundifolia, white and pink, April, 4 to 8 ft., berries scarlet-red, Himalayas ; salicifolia, white, April, 12 to 20 ft., berries red, China, and its varieties floccosa and rugosa ; thymæfolia, white, April, 1 ft., berries red, Himalayas.

DECIDUOUS SPECIES : C. acuminata, pale pink, April, 10 to 14 ft., berries red, Himalayas ; acutifolia, white, April, 5 to 7 ft., berries black, China ; adpressa, white and rose, April, 1 to 1½ ft., berries red, China ; bacillaris, white, April, 12 to 16 ft., berries black, Himalayas ; dielsiana (Syn. applanata), white, April, 6 to 9 ft., berries scarlet, Central China ; divaricata, rose, April, 5 to 6 ft., berries red, W. Hupeh ; foveolata, pinkish white, April, 10 to 20 ft., berries black, China ; frigida, white, April, 15 to 30 ft., berries red, Himalayas ; horizontalis, white and pink, May, 2 ft., berries red, China ; multiflora (Syn. reflexa), white, May to June, 10 to 12 ft., berries red, North-western China ; racemiflora (Syn. nummularia), white, April, 6 to 8 ft., berries red, Europe ; integerrima (Syn. vulgaris), white and pink, May, 4 to 7 ft., berries red, Europe (Britain); Simonsi, white, April, 10 to 12 ft., berries scarlet, Himalayas ; Zabeli, rose, May to June, 6 to 9 ft., berries red, China.

Cotton Grass—See Eriophorum.

Cotton-plant (*Gossypium herbaceum*)—See Gossypium.

Cotton Thistle (*Onopordon Acanthium*)—See Onopordon.

Cotton-wood (*Populus balsamifera*)—See Populus.

Cotyledon—Ord. Crassulaceæ. Greenhouse and hardy evergreen succulent-leaved plants. Natives of Mexico, except when otherwise mentioned.

CULTURE OF GREENHOUSE SPECIES : Compost, two parts loam, one part sand and fine brick rubbish. Position, pots well drained, close to glass in window or greenhouse. Repot, March or April. Water freely March to Sept., very little afterwards. Temp., Sept. to March 50° to 55° ; March to Sept. 60° to 70°. Can also be grown outdoors in beds, June to Sept.

CULTURE OF HALF-HARDY SPECIES : Grow in ordinary soil on sunny rockeries, or as edgings to beds. Plant in May. Place in boxes in a cold frame in Oct.

CULTURE OF HARDY SPECIES : Soil, ordinary. Position, sunny beds or rock gardens. Plant, Oct. or March.

PROPAGATION : Greenhouse and half-hardy species by seeds sown on surface of above soil in well-drained pan or pot in temp. 55° to 65° in March ; cuttings of leaves with base inserted in well-drained pots of sandy soil in Aug., Sept., or Oct. in temp. 55° to 60°. Do not water leaves or cuttings until they begin to shrivel. Hardy species by division in March.

GREENHOUSE SPECIES : C. agavoides (Syn. Echeveria agavoides), orange, Sept., 1 ft. ; atropurpurea (Syn. Echeveria atropurpurea), red, Sept., 1 ft. ; californica (Syn. Echeveria californica), yellow, summer, 1 ft., California ; coccinea, scarlet and yellow, Oct., 2 ft. ; fulgens, (Syn. Echeveria fulgens), red and yellow, summer, 1 ft. ; gibbiflora (Syn. Echeveria gibbiflora), yellow and scarlet, autumn, 2 ft. ; gibbiflora metallica, leaves purplish glaucous ; glauca (Syn. Echeveria glauca), scarlet and yellow, autumn, 1 ft. ; retusa (Syn. Echeveria retusa), crimson and yellow, autumn, 1 ft.

Cortaderia argentea
(Pampas Grass)

Corylopsis Willmottiæ

Cosmos bipinnatus
(Mexican Aster)

Cotoneaster frigida

Cotyledon simplicifolia

Crassula falcata

Crinum Powelli album
(Cape Lily)

Crocus vernus hybridus

Crossandra infundibuliformis

Crucianella stylosa
(Cross-wort)

Cupressus Lawsoniana nana
(Cypress)

Cyclamen latifolium
(Sowbread)

Cymbidium hybridum

Cynoglossum amabile

Cyperus alternifolius
(Umbrella-plant)

Cypripedium spectabile
(Lady's Slipper)

Cytisus hybridum
(Broom)

Dahlia hybrida
(Collarette Dahlia)

HALF-HARDY SPECIES : C. secunda glauca (Syn. Echeveria secunda glauca), red and yellow, summer, 1 ft. ; secunda glauca major, large-leaved variety.
HARDY SPECIES : C. chrysantha, white or cream, June to Aug., 6 to 12 in., Asia Minor; simplicifolia, golden yellow, May to July, 4 to 6 in.; Umbilicus, greenish yellow, June to July, 8 to 12 in., Britain.

Couve Tronchuda—See Brassica.

Cow-berry (*Vaccinum Vitis-idæa*)—See Vaccinum.

Cow-horn Orchid (*Schomburgkia Tibicinis*)—See Schomburgkia.

Cow Parsnip (*Heracleum villosum*)—See Heracleum.

Cowslip-scented Orchid—See Vanda.

Crab's Claw (*Stratiotes aloides*)—See Stratiotes.

Crab's Eyes (*Abrus precatorius*)—See Abrus.

Crack Willow (*Salix fragilis*)—See Salix.

Cradle Orchid—See Anguloa.

Crake Berry—See Empetrum.

Crambe (Seakale)—Ord. Cruciferæ. Hardy herbaceous perennials and esculent vegetables.
CULTURE OF PERENNIAL SPECIES : Soil, ordinary, rich. Position, open borders. Plant roots 3 in. deep in groups of three or six in March.
CULTURE OF SEAKALE : Soil, deep, rich, sandy. Position, open, sunny. Trench soil 2 ft. deep in autumn, burying in abundance of manure. Plant roots 4 to 6 in. long, 2 in. deep, uprightly, 18 in. apart in rows 30 in. asunder in Feb. or March. Pare off crown buds before planting. Mulch beds with stable manure in April. Apply common salt at the rate of 1 lb. to a square rod, or 1 lb. of nitrate of soda to same area in June. Lift and replant every five years. Manure and dig between rows in Nov. Blanching : Cover roots in open ground with inverted pots, dry tree leaves, or cinder ashes in Nov.
FORCING OUTDOORS : Cover roots with inverted pots in Nov. and put thick layers of fresh manure and leaves on these in Jan.
FORCING INDOORS : Lift roots in Nov., Dec., or Jan. and place them close together in large pots or boxes, with ordinary soil between, in temp. 50° to 60°. Keep roots moist and dark. Roots of no value after forcing.
PROPAGATION : By seed sown 1 in. deep in rows 12 in. apart in March, thinning seedlings to 6 in. apart in June and transplanting them to permanent beds when a year old, or by cuttings of roots as advised for planting ; perennials by seeds sown ½ in. deep outdoors in March, transplanting seedlings in July ; cuttings of shoots or division of roots in March. Seeds germinate in 18 to 20 days. Crop arrives at maturity 2 years after sowing.
SPECIES CULTIVATED : C. maritima (Seakale), white, May and June, Europe (Britain) ; cordifolia (Flowering Seakale), white, May, 5 ft., Caucasus ; orientalis, white, fragrant, June, 4 ft., Orient. Last two hardy perennials.

Cranberry—See Oxycoccus.

Cranberry Gourd (*Abobra viridiflora*)—See Abobra.

Crane's-bill—See Geranium.

Crape Fern—See Todea.

Crape Myrtle (*Lagerstræmia indica*)—See Lagerstrœmia.

Crassula—Ord. Crassulaceæ. Greenhouse evergreen plants. First introduced 1711.
CULTURE : Compost, equal parts sandy loam, brick rubble, dried cow manure and river sand. Position, well-drained pots in light greenhouse, close to glass. Pot, March. Water freely April to Aug., moderately Aug. to Nov., very little afterwards. Temp., March to Sept. 55° to 65° ; Sept. to March 45° to 50°.
PROPAGATION : By seeds sown in well-drained pots or pans of sandy soil, just covering seeds with fine mould, in temp. 60° to 70° in March or April, seedlings to be kept close to glass and have little water ; cuttings of shoots 2 to 3 in. long,

exposed to sun for few days, then inserted in June, July, or Aug. in well-drained pots of sandy soil, placed on greenhouse shelf and given very little water.
SPECIES CULTIVATED: C. arborescens, pink, May, 2 ft., S. Africa; columnaris, white, summer, 6 in., S. Africa; falcata (Syn. Rochea falcata), yellow and red, summer, 6 in., S. Africa; lactea, white, autumn, 9 in., S. Africa. See also Rochea.

Cratægus (May; Hawthorn; Quick; Black Thorn; Cockspur Thorn; Glastonbury Thorn; Thorn)—Ord. Rosaceæ. Hardy deciduous trees and shrubs.
CULTURE: Soil, ordinary, rich. Position, trees and shrubs in woods, shrubberies, lawns, and pleasure grounds; evergreen species against east or north walls; common quick in hedges. Plant, Oct. to Feb. Prune in Nov., simply cutting tree or shrub into shape where necessary. Hedges: Soil, ordinary, trenched 2 ft. deep and 2 ft. wide. Plant, Nov. to March. Distance apart, 4 in. single row, 6 in., double row 6 in. asunder. Quantity of plants required per yard for single row, 9; double row, 12. Time to trim, July and Aug.
POT CULTURE: Double pink and white kinds adapted for pot culture in cool greenhouse, or for forcing. Pot, Oct. or Nov., in good soil. Water moderately Oct. to March, freely afterwards. Keep plants in cool structure till Jan., then place in temp. 55° to 65° to flower early or leave them in cool house to flower naturally. After flowering, place plants outdoors to make new growth.
PROPAGATION: By seeds (berries) sown 1 in. deep in open garden in Nov., transplanting largest seedlings following Oct., the remainder the next year; budding choice varieties on common hawthorn in July; grafting in March. Berries require to be stored in sand for a year before sowing.
DECIDUOUS SPECIES: C. Azarolus, white, fragrant, May, 15 ft., S. Europe; Carrierei, white, May, 12 to 15 ft., hybrid; coccinea (Scarlet Thorn), white, May, 20 ft., N. America; cordata, white, June, 15 ft., United States; Crus-galli (Cockspur Thorn), white, June, 20 ft., N. America, and its varieties arbutifolia, Downingii, lineraris, and pyracanthifolia; Douglasii, white, May, 15 ft., N.W. America; heterophylla, white, May to June, 20 ft., Armenia; Korolkowi, white, May to June, 25 ft., N. China; leeana, white, June, hybrid; macrantha, white, May to June, 15 ft., Eastern N. America; melanocarpa, white, May, 15 ft., Tauria; mollis, white and red, May, 20 ft., United States; monogyna (Hawthorn), white, May, 25 to 35 ft., Britain, and its varieties præcox (Glastonbury Thorn) and semperflorens; orientalis, white, May, 15 ft., Orient; Oxyacantha (Common Hawthorn), white, May, 15 ft., Europe, and its varieties alba plena (Double White Thorn), coccinea plena (Paul's Double Scarlet Thorn), and fructu luteo (fruits yellow); pinnatifida, white, May, 15 ft., Asia; punctata, white, June, 25 ft., Eastern N. America; tanacetifolia (Tansy-leaved Thorn), white, May, 15 ft., Levant; tomentosa, white, June, 15 ft., U.S.A. See also Pyracantha.

Cream Cups (*Platystemon californicus*)—See Platystemon.

Creeping Fig-tree (*Ficus pumila*)—See Ficus.

Creeping Forget-me-not (*Omphalodes verna*)—See Omphalodes.

Creeping Harebell (*Wahlenbergia hederacea*)—See Wahlenbergia.

Creeping Jenny (*Lysimachia nummularia*)—See Lysimachia.

Creeping Sailor (*Saxifraga sarmentosa*)—See Saxifraga.

Creeping Speedwell (*Veronica repens*)—See Veronica.

Creeping Willow (*Salix repens*)—See Salix.

Creeping Winter Green (*Gaultheria procumbens*)—See Gaultheria.

Crepis (Hawk's Beard)—Ord. Compositæ. Hardy herbaceous perennials and annuals.
CULTURE: Soil, ordinary, sandy. Position, sunny borders, banks, or rockeries. Plant perennial species in March or April.
PROPAGATION: Annual species by seeds sown ¼ in. deep in April where plants are required to flower; perennial species by seeds sown ¼ in. deep outdoors in April, transplanting seedlings in July, or by division of roots in March or April.

PERENNIAL SPECIES : C. aurea, orange, autumn, 12 in., Europe.
ANNUAL SPECIES : C. rubra, red, autumn, 1 ft., S. Europe. See also Tolpis.

Cress—See Lepidium.

Cretan Mullein—See Celsia.

Cretan Rock Rose (*Cistus creticus*)—See Cistus.

Cretan Spikenard (*Valeriana Phu*)—See Valeriana.

Crimean Iris—Popular name for dwarf bearded irises; I. pumila is the type.

Crimean Snowdrop (*Galanthus plicatus*)—See Galanthus.

Crimson Flag (*Schizostylis coccinea*)—See Schizostylis.

Crimson-flowered Flax (*Linum grandiflorum*)—See Linum.

Crimson Satin-flower (*Brevoortia Ida-Maia*)—See Brevoortia.

Crimson Stonecrop (*Sedum spurium*)—See Sedum.

Crinodendron—See Tricuspidaria.

Crinum (Cape Lily ; Cape Coast Lily)—Ord. Amaryllidaceæ. Stove, greenhouse and hardy deciduous bulbous plants. First introduced 1732.
CULTURE OF STOVE AND GREENHOUSE SPECIES : Compost, two parts turfy loam, one part peat and silver sand. Position, pots in light plant stove or greenhouse. Pot, March, in large pots or tubs well drained. Water freely March to Oct., very little afterwards. Store pots containing bulbs on their sides in stove or greenhouse during winter. Repot every 3 or 4 years. Apply liquid manure to established bulbs in summer. Temp., March to Sept. 75° to 85° for stove, 55° to 65° for greenhouse ; Sept. to March, 55° to 65° for stove, 45° to 50° for greenhouse.
CULTURE OF HARDY SPECIES : Soil, rich, deep. Position, south, well-drained border. Plant bulbs 6 in. deep in March.
PROPAGATION : By seeds sown in sandy soil in a temp. of 65° to 75° in spring ; also by offsets at potting on planting time. Seedling plants take several years to flower.
STOVE SPECIES : C. amabile, red, fragrant, summer, 3 ft., Sumatra ; erubescens, white, purplish red and pink, July, 2 to 3 ft., Trop. America ; Kirkii, white and red, Oct., 2 ft., Zanzibar ; sanderianum, white and red, 2 ft., Trop. Africa ; scabrum, white and crimson, May, 2 to 3 ft., Trop. Africa ; zeylanicum, white and red, July, 2 to 3 ft., Trop. Asia and Africa.
GREENHOUSE SPECIES : C. americanum, white, July, 1 to 2½ ft., Southern U.S.A., asiaticum, white, July, 2½ to 3½ ft., Trop. Asia ; Macowanii, white and purple, autumn, 3 ft., Natal ; Moorei, white and red, April to Oct., 2 ft., S. Africa ; Moorei album, white ; Moorei variegatum, leaves variegated.
HARDY SPECIES : C. longifolium (Syn. C. capense), pink, summer, 3 ft., S. Africa ; longifolium album, white ; Powelli, rose, summer, 3 ft., hybrid, and its varieties album (white) and rubrum (red).

Crithmum (Samphire)—Ord. Umbelliferæ. Hardy perennial herb. Leaves used for pickling.
CULTURE : Soil, sandy. Position, shady border. Sow seeds thinly in bed of ordinary sandy soil in March. Not an easy plant to grow away from the seashore.
SPECIES CULTIVATED : C. maritimum, white, summer, 1 ft., Seashores of Britain.

Crocosmia—Ord. Iridaceæ. Half-hardy bulbous-rooted flowering plant. First introduced 1846.
OUTDOOR CULTURE : Soil, light, rich, sandy. Position, well-drained south border. Plant bulbs, Sept. or Oct., 6 in. deep and 4 in. apart, surrounding each bulb with an inch of sand and protecting during winter with a covering of dry leaves or ashes. Lift and replant every three years.
POT CULTURE : Compost, equal parts turfy loam, peat, leaf-mould and silver sand. Position, cold frame or greenhouse. Pot, Oct., placing six bulbs 1 in. deep in a 5 in. pot, well drained, with an inch of decayed cow manure over drainage. Water when new growth commences, afterwards keep moderately moist until foliage dies down, then keep dry.

PROPAGATION : By seeds sown ⅛ in. deep in well-drained pans or boxes filled with sandy soil in cold greenhouse in Sept. or Oct. ; offsets in Oct.
SPECIES CULTIVATED : C. aurea, orange red, summer, 2 ft., S. Africa ; aurea imperialis, orange red, 4 ft.

Crocus—Ord. Iridaceæ.   Hardy bulbous flowering plants.
OUTDOOR CULTURE : Soil, light, rich. Position, margins of beds or borders or in grass plots and lawns, open or in shade, for common sorts ; sunny, well-drained beds, or on rockeries, for rare and choice kinds. Plant spring-flowering species and varieties in Oct., Nov., or Dec. ; autumn-flowering species in Aug. and Sept. Depth and distance : Common kinds, 3 in. ; choice and rare sorts, 2 in. Leave corms undisturbed for four or five years, unless their place is wanted for other plants. Lift when necessary in June or July, drying corms in sun and storing in cool room till planting time. Foliage should not be removed until it turns yellow.
CULTURE IN GRASS : Bore holes 3 in. deep and 2 in. apart, insert a corm in bottom of each, then fill up with ordinary soil ; or lift turf, fork up soil below, add a little bonemeal, place bulbs thereon and replace turf. Grass should not be cut till foliage turns yellow.
POT CULTURE : Compost, light, rich, sandy soil. Position, ten in 5 in. pot, or four in a 3 in. size, in Oct. or Nov. After potting, place pots in cold frame or under a wall and cover with cinder ashes till growth begins, then remove to greenhouse, etc. Water freely when growth begins ; give less as foliage fades. Corms of no use for flowering second time in pots, but may be planted out in garden. To force, place in temp. 55° to 65° in Dec. or Jan.
PROPAGATION : By seeds sown ⅛ in. deep and 1 in. apart in light sandy soil in cold frame in Sept., Oct., or Nov., transplanting seedlings in Aug. of second year ; offsets removed from old corms in July or Aug. and replanted 2 in. deep and 2 in. apart at same time. Seedling corms flower when three and four years old.
SPECIES CULTIVATED : C. aureus (Syn. C. mœsiacus), yellow, Feb., S.E. Europe ; alatavicus, white, Feb., Siberia ; asturicus, violet, autumn, Spain ; Balansæ, orange-yellow, March, Asia Minor ; banaticus, white and purple, March, Hungary ; biflorus (Scotch Crocus), lavender, Feb., Tuscany ; byzantinus (Syn. C. iridiflorus), purple and lilac, autumn, E. Europe ; cancellatus, yellow, white and purple, autumn, Asia Minor ; chrysanthus, orange-yellow, Jan. to March, S.E. Europe ; Clusii, white and purple, autumn, Spain ; dalmaticus, yellow and purple, Feb. to March, Dalmatia ; etruscus, lilac and yellow, March, Italy ; Fleischeri, yellow and purple, March, Asia Minor ; Imperati, lilac, Jan. to March, Italy ; Korolkowi, yellow, Feb. to March, Central Asia ; longiflorus, lilac, yellow, and purple, autumn, Italy ; Malyi, yellow, orange, and purple, March, Dalmatia ; medius, white and purple, autumn, Italy ; minimus, purple, March and April, Corsica ; nudiflorus, purple, autumn, Pyrenees ; ochroleucus, white and orange, autumn, Asia Minor ; pulchellus, lavender, blue, or yellow, autumn, Turkey ; reticulatus, white, lilac, and purple, March, E. Europe ; sativus (Saffron Crocus), white, lilac, and purple, autumn, Western Asia ; Sieberi, lilac and yellow, Feb. to March, Greece ; speciosus, lilac and purple, autumn, Central Europe ; suaveolens, orange, lilac, and purple, March, Italy ; susianus, orange and brown, Feb., Crimea ; tommasinianus, pale sapphire-lavender, spring, Dalmatia and Servia ; vernus, lilac, violet, and white, Feb. to April, Europe ; versicolor, white to purple, March, France and Italy ; zonatus, rosy lilac and yellow, autumn, S. Europe and Asia Minor. The numerous Dutch forms in cultivation were originally derived from C. vernus.

Crossandra—Ord. Acanthaceæ.   Stove evergreen flowering shrub.   First introduced 1800.
CULTURE : Compost, equal parts loam, peat and sand. Position, pots in moist plant stove. Pot, March. Water moderately during winter, freely other times. Temp., Oct. to March 55° to 65° ; March to Oct. 75° to 85°.
PROPAGATION : By cuttings of shoots 2 or 3 in. long, inserted in sand under bell-glass, in temp. of 85° at any time of year.
SPECIES CULTIVATED : C. guineensis, lilac, October, 6 in. ; infundibuliformis (Syn. undulæfolia), orange-scarlet, March, 12 to 18 in., India.

Cross of Jerusalem (*Lychnis chalcedonica*)—See Lychnis.

Cross Vine (*Bignonia capreolata*)—See Bignonia.

Cross-wort (*Crucianella stylosa* and *Gentiana cruciata*)—See Crucianella and Gentiana.

Croton—See Codiæum.

Crowberry—See Empetrum.

Crowfoot—See Ranunculus.

Crowea—Ord. Rutaceæ. Greenhouse evergreen shrubs. First introduced 1700.
CULTURE : Compost, two parts peat, one fibrous loam, and little sand. Position, pots in light airy greenhouse. Pot, March or April. Prune straggling shoots into shape in March. Water very little Oct. to March, moderately March to Oct. Temp., Sept. to March 40° to 45° ; March to Sept. 55° to 65°.
PROPAGATION : By cuttings inserted in sand under bell-glass in temp. of 65° to 75° in March or April ; grafting on Correa alba or Eriostemon buxifolia in March.
SPECIES CULTIVATED : C. angustifolia, red, summer, 1 to 3 ft., Australia ; saligna, pink, summer, 1 to 2 ft., Australia.

Crown Imperial Lily—See Fritillaria.

Crown-of-Thorns (*Medicago echinus*)—See Medicago.

Crown Vetch (*Coronilla varia*)—See Coronilla.

Crucianella (Cross-wort)—Ord. Rubiaceæ. Hardy herbaceous perennial. First introduced 1640.
CULTURE : Soil, sandy or chalky. Position, dry banks, rockeries, or borders. Plant, Oct. or March.
PROPAGATION : By seeds sown outdoors in March, transplanting seedlings to permanent positions in July or Aug.; division of roots in March, April, Oct. or Nov.
SPECIES CULTIVATED : C. stylosa, rose, summer, 9 to 12 in., Caucasus ; stylosa coccinea, scarlet ; stylosa purpurea, purple.

Cryptanthus—Ord. Bromeliaceæ. Stove and evergreen perennials ; flowering and orn. foliage. First introduced 1826.
CULTURE : Compost, equal parts fibrous loam, rough peat, leaf-mould and silver sand. Pot, March. Water freely always ; good drainage essential. Temp., Sept. to March 65° to 75° ; March to Sept. 75° to 85°.
PROPAGATION : By large-sized offsets inserted singly in small pots in temp. of 85° in April.
SPECIES CULTIVATED : C. Beuckeri, red and white, summer, 6 in., Brazil ; bivittatus, white, Aug., 8 to 10 in., Trop. America ; undulatus (Syn. C. acaulis), white, Aug., 3 to 6 in., Brazil ; zonatus (Syn. Tillandsia zonata), white, 6 in., Brazil. See also Tillandsia.

Cryptogramme (Parsley Fern ; Rock Brake)—Ord. Filices. Hardy deciduous fern with Parsley-like fronds.
CULTURE : Soil, equal parts loam and peat with a liberal supply of broken bricks or stone, quite free from lime. Position, cool, moist rockery. Does well in the moist fissures of rocks. Plant in spring.
PROPAGATION : By division in spring.
SPECIES CULTIVATED : C. crispa (Syn. Allosorus crispus), 3 to 6 in., Mountains of Wales, Scotland, etc. ; crispa acrostichoides, 6 to 8 in., N. America.

Cryptomeria (Japanese Cedar)—Ord. Coniferæ. Hardy evergreen coniferous tree. Orn. foliage. Nat. Japan. First introduced 1844. Foliage bright green in spring and summer ; bronzy crimson during winter.
CULTURE : Soil, deep, rich, moist loam. Position, sheltered on lawns. Plant, Oct. to April.
PROPAGATION : By seeds sown ⅛ in. deep in sandy loam in temp. of 55° in March or

outdoors in April ; cuttings of side shoots 2 or 3 in. long, inserted in sandy soil under hand-light, or in cold frame, in Sept. or Oct.
SPECIES CULTIVATED : C. japonica, 70 to 100 ft. Varieties : araucarioides, branchlets long and thin ; elegans, delicate glaucous green foliage changing to bronzy red in autumn ; elegans nana, 3 to 4 ft. ; Lobbii, branchlets stiffer and tufted ; spiralis, dwarf, dense habit.

Cuban Lily (*Scilla peruviana*)—See Scilla.

Cuckoo-Flower (*Cardamine pratensis*)—See Cardamine.

Cuckoo-pint (*Arum maculatum*)—See Arum.

Cucumber (*Cucumis sativus*)—See Cucumis.

Cucumber Tree (*Magnolia acuminata*)—See Magnolia.

Cucumis (Cucumber ; Melon ; Gherkin)—Ord. Cucurbitaceæ. Half-hardy trailing perennial fruiting plants.
CULTURE OF CUCUMBERS : Compost, two parts decayed turfy loam, one part horse droppings or decomposed manure. Position, pots or beds in heated or cold greenhouse and frames, or in sheltered corner outdoors in summer. Sow seed in Feb. or March for heated greenhouse or frame in summer, April for cold frames or outdoors, Sept. or Oct. for winter use. Plant, March, April, Sept., or Oct. in heat ; June in cold frames or outdoors. Train main shoot up roof of greenhouse, pinching out its point when 3 ft. high, also points of side (lateral) shoots at first beyond the young fruit ; or, when grown in frames, along surface of bed, removing point of main shoot when a foot long and points of side shoots at first joint beyond young fruit. Prune away old shoots that cease to bear and train young ones in their stead. Water moderately at first, freely afterwards. Syringe twice daily. Apply liquid manure to plants bearing heavy crops only. Ventilate when temp. reaches 90°, closing again when it falls below this. Temp., Feb. to Sept., for greenhouse and frame, 75° to 85° ; Sept. to Feb. 65° to 75°. Shade from hot sun. Fertilise first female blooms by divesting a male bloom of its petals and applying powdery parts to centre of former ; fertilisation not needful afterwards, unless seed is wanted. Fumigate occasionally to destroy insects.
CULTURE OF GHERKINS OR RIDGE CUCUMBERS : Dig a hole in May 2 ft. deep and 3 ft. wide in a sunny position, putting soil on north side. Fill hole with heated manure and cover with 3 in. of soil. Plant at once. Train as advised above. Water moderately at first, freely afterwards. Protect with hand-light until end of June. Sow seeds in light soil in temp. 55° in April. Japanese climbing cucumber requires to have its shoots trained up pea sticks.
CULTURE OF MELONS : Compost, three parts good turfy loam, one part decayed manure. Position, beds in greenhouses, pits, or frames, with shoots trained to roof or along surface of ground. Plant, March, April, or May. Sow seeds singly in 2 in. pots in temp. 75° in Feb. or March. Pinch out point of main shoot when 6 in. long, also of lateral shoots when 1 ft. long, and further shoots at the first joint beyond the young swelling fruit. Fertilise all the female blooms about 12 a.m. as directed for cucumbers. Allow one fruit to each shoot, removing any others gradually. Prune away any weak shoots not showing fruit. Water moderately at first, freely afterwards, less when fruit changes colour. Syringe twice daily until fruit begins to ripen, then cease. Shade from hot sun. Apply liquid manure when fruit begins to swell. Temp., March to time fruit is ripe, 75° to 85°. Ventilate when temp. reaches 85°, close when it falls below this.
SPECIES CULTIVATED : C. Melo (Melon), intro. 1570 ; sativus (Cucumber), intro. 1573. Natives of Tropics.

Cucurbita (Gourd ; Pumpkin ; Squash ; Vegetable Marrow)—Ord. Cucurbitaceæ. Half-hardy trailing annual edible or orn. fruited plants. First introduced 1570. Flowers, yellow, male and female distinct. Fruit globular, oval, or oblong.
CULTURE OF MARROWS AND PUMPKINS : Soil, ordinary, rich. Position, beds in frames, on heaps of decayed manure or refuse, or on banks, the shoots running down the slope, or in beds in open garden formed by digging out soil 15 in. deep, filling holes with heated manure and covering this with soil. Sow seeds in a temp.

of 55° in April, or where the plants are intended to grow in May. Plant, May, under hand-light, or in June without protection. Pinch out points of main shoots when 18 in. long ; no pinching required afterwards. Fertilise first female blooms ; not later ones. Water freely in dry weather. Apply liquid manure frequently after fruit is set. Fruit for preserving should be cut when yellow and then hung up in a dry room till wanted for use. Young shoots of marrows and gourds may be used as a substitute for spinach.

CULTURE OF GOURDS : Soil, rich, ordinary. Position, beds at base of low, sunny fences or walls, or on the summit of banks, shoots growing at will up and over the former or down the latter ; sunny. Plant, June. Water freely in dry weather. Apply liquid manure occasionally when plants are laden with fruit. Gather fruit when yellow, and hang it up till wanted for use in dry room. No pinching of shoots required.

PROPAGATION : By seeds sown ½ in. deep in light soil in temp. 55° to 65° in April, or where plants are to grow in May and June.

SPECIES CULTIVATED : C. maxima (Pumpkin), Trop. Asia ; Pepo (Gourd), Trop. Africa ; Pepo ovifera (Vegetable Marrow). Numerous varieties, for which see trade lists.

Cuminum (Cumin)—Ord. Umbelliferæ. Herb with aromatic fruits used as flavouring. Half-hardy annual.

CULTURE : Soil, ordinary. Position, sunny beds or borders. Sow seeds during May where plants are required. Gather seeds in July and Aug.

SPECIES CULTIVATED : C. Cyminum, white or rose, 6 in., Mediterranean Region.

Cunninghamia—Ord. Coniferæ. Hardy evergreen ornamental tree. First introduced 1804.

CULTURE : Soil, deep, well-drained loam. Position, sheltered from cold winds. Plant, November.

PROPAGATION : By seeds sown in sandy soil in warm greenhouse during Feb. or March.

SPECIES CULTIVATED : C. sinensis, 70 to 150 ft., China.

Cunonia (Red Alder)—Ord. Saxifragaceæ. Greenhouse evergreen flowering tree. Nat. Cape of Good Hope. First introduced 1816.

CULTURE : Compost, equal parts sandy loam and peat. Position, pots in light airy greenhouse. Pot, March. Prune into shape in March. Water moderately Oct. to March, freely afterwards. Temp., March to Sept. 55° to 65° ; Sept. to March 45° to 50°.

PROPAGATION : By cuttings of firm shoots inserted in sandy soil under bell-glass in temp. of 65° to 75° in summer.

SPECIES CULTIVATED : C. capensis, white, Aug., to 50 ft., S. Africa.

Cup and Saucer Flower (*Cobæa scandens*)—See Cobæa.

Cupania—Ord. Sapindaceæ. Stove orn. foliage evergreen trees. First introduced 1818.

CULTURE : Compost, equal parts loam and peat. Position, pots in moist plant stove. Pot, March. Water moderately in winter, freely other times. Prune occasionally to maintain a dwarf habit. Temp., Oct. to March 55° to 65° ; March to Sept. 75° to 85°.

PROPAGATION : By cuttings of firm shoots inserted in sand under bell-glass in temp. of 85° in summer.

SPECIES CULTIVATED : C. anacardioides, 20 to 30 ft., Australia ; elegantissima, 15 to 20 ft. ; grandidens, 20 to 30 ft., Zanzibar.

Cup-flower (*Nierembergia rivularis*)—See Nierembergia.

Cuphea (Mexican Cigar Flower)—Ord. Lythraceæ. Greenhouse evergreen flowering plants. First introduced 1845.

CULTURE : Compost, equal parts loam, leaf-mould, peat and sand. Position, 5 to 6 in. pots in greenhouse, or in beds outdoors in summer. Pot, March or April.

Plant outdoors in June. Water moderately Oct. to March, freely afterwards.
Temp., March to Sept. 60° to 70° ; Sept. to March 50° to 55°.
PROPAGATION : By seeds sown in light soil in temp. 65° to 75° in March ; cuttings of
young shoots inserted in sandy soil in temp. 65° to 75° in March, April, or Aug.
SPECIES CULTIVATED : C. æquipetala, purple, June, 2 ft., Mexico ; cyanea, yellow
and red, July, 2 ft., Peru ; hookeriana, vermilion and orange, July, 2 to 3 ft.,
Mexico ; ignea (Syn. C. platycentra), scarlet, black and white, July, 1 ft.. Mexico ;
ignea alba, white ; lanceolata, blue, July, 18 in., annual, Mexico ; micropetala,
scarlet, white and red, July, 1 ft., Mexico ; miniata (Syn. C. Llavea), bright red,
summer, 2 ft., Mexico.

   Cupidone (*Catananche cærulea*)—See Catananche.

   Cupid's-flower (*Ipomæa Quamoclit*)—See Ipomæa.

   Cup Plant (*Silphium perfoliatum*)—See Silphium.

   Cupressus (Cypress)—Ord. Coniferæ. Hardy evergreen trees. Orn. foliage.
Leaves, small dark green or glaucous, or variegated with white or yellow.
CULTURE : Soil, deep rich loam. Position, single specimens on lawns or pleasure
grounds, or in mixed shrubberies. Plant, Sept. to Nov. Distance apart for
planting in avenues, 20 ft.
HEDGE CULTURE : Trench soil 3 ft. wide and deep for site, adding little well-rooted
manure if poor. Plant shrubs 2 ft. high, 2 ft. apart in Sept. or Oct. Trim sides in
annually in April and Sept. Cupressus macrocarpa good for seaside gardens.
Cupressus lawsoniana and macrocarpa suitable for peaty or chalky soils.
PROPAGATION : By seeds sown ½ in. deep in pans of light soil in April, transplanting
seedlings singly into small pots following spring, and planting outdoors a year
afterwards ; by cuttings of branchlets 2 in. long, inserted in sandy soil in cold frame,
or under hand-light, in Sept.
SPECIES CULTIVATED : C. arizonica, 30 to 40 ft., Arizona ; funebris (Funereal Cypress),
weeping habit, 40 to 50 ft., China ; goveniana, compact habit, 20 to 30 ft., California ; lawsoniana (Lawson's Cypress), pyramidal habit, 100 to 150 ft., California,
and its varieties albo-spica, albo-variegata, Allumi, argentea, argenteo-variegata,
aureo-variegata, erecta viridis, filifera, gracilis pendula, lutea, nana, nana alba and
nana glauca ; lusitanica, 100 ft., Mexico ; macrocarpa (Monterey Cypress), spreading habit, 60 to 90 ft., California ; nootkatensis (Alaska Cypress), pyramidal habit,
100 to 120 ft., Western N. America, and its varieties argenteo-variegata, aureo-
variegata, compacta, glauca, lutea, pendula, and viridis ; obtusa (Syn. Retinospora
obtusa), spreading habit, 50 to 70 ft., Japan, and its varieties albo-picta, aurea,
compacta, filicoides, gracilisau rea, lycopodioides, nana, and tetragona ; pisifera
(Syn. Retinospora pisifera), slender, graceful habit, 70 to 100 ft., Japan, and its
varieties filifera, plumosa (Syn. Retinospora plumosa), plumosa argentea, plumosa
aurea, and squarrosa, all dwarfer than the type ; sempervirens, pyramidal habit,
40 to 60 ft., S. Europe, and its varieties horizontalis and stricta ; thyoides (Syn.
Retinospora ericoides), the White Cedar, 80 to 90 ft., United States, and its varieties
glauca (kewensis), variegata and leptoclada.

   Cups-and-Saucers (*Cobæa scandens*)—See Cobæa.

   Curculigo (Weevil-plant)—Ord. Amaryllidaceæ. Stove orn. evergreen foliage
plant. First introduced 1805. Leaves, strap-like, recurved.
CULTURE : Compost, equal parts lumpy peat and loam and little silver sand. Position, pots in moist plant stove. Pot, Feb. or March. Water moderately in winter,
freely other times. Temp., Sept. to March 55° to 65° ; March to Sept. 75° to 85°.
PROPAGATION : By suckers inserted in small pots of sandy soil in temp. 85° in March.
SPECIES CULTIVATED : C. recurvata, 3 to 4 ft., Trop. Asia ; recurvata variegata,
variegated foliage.

   Curcuma (Turmeric)—Ord. Zingiberaceæ Stove, fleshy rooted, perennials.
Some species yield arrowroot.
CULTURE : Compost, two parts peat, one part loam, and a little sand. Position,
pots in warm greenhouse. Well drained. Temp., March to Oct. 65° to 75° ; Oct.

to March 60°. Pot in Feb. Water freely during growing season. Dry off tubers after foliage dies down.

PROPAGATION : By offsets in spring treated same as tubers.

SPECIES CULTIVATED : C. Amada, yellow, 1 to 2 ft., Bengal ; ferruginea, yellow, 1 ft., Bengal ; latifolia, white and yellow, 12 ft., W. Indies ; longa, yellow, 2 ft., E. Indies.

Currant—See Ribes.

Cushion Fern (*Dicksonia Culcita*)—See Dicksonia.

Cushion Pink (*Silene acaulis* and *Armeria maritima*)—See Silene and Armeria.

Custard Apple (*Anona reticulata*)—See Anona.

Cut-leaved Elder (*Sambucus nigra laciniata*)—See Sambucus.

Cyananthus—Ord. Campanulaceæ. Hardy alpine herbaceous perennials. First introduced 1844.

CULTURE : Compost, equal parts sandy peat and leaf-mould. Position, sunny banks or crevices of rockeries. Plant, March or April. Protect in severe weather with ashes or leaves.

PROPAGATION : By cuttings of shoots 2 in. long inserted in sandy peat, in April, May, or June, and kept under bell-glass ; division of fleshy roots in March or April.

SPECIES CULTIVATED : C. incanus, azure-blue, Aug., 3 to 4 in., Sikkim ; lobatus, purplish blue, Aug., 4 in., Himalayas.

Cyanella—Ord. Hæmodoraceæ. Half-hardy bulbous plants. Nat. Cape of Good Hope. First introduced 1768. Flowers, fragrant.

CULTURE : Compost, two parts sandy soil, one part leaf-mould or decayed cow manure. Position, pots 4½ in. in diameter, well drained, in cold frame or greenhouse. Pot, Oct., placing five bulbs 2 in. deep in each pot, and covering pots with cocoanut-fibre refuse until growth begins. Water moderately when bulbs begin to grow ; keep bulbs dry Sept. to Jan.

PROPAGATION : By offsets in Nov.

SPECIES CULTIVATED : C. capensis, blue, July, 1 ft. ; lutea, yellow, July, 1 ft.

Cyanophyllum—See Miconia.

Cyathea (Tree Fern)—Ord. Filices. Stove and greenhouse evergreen tree ferns. First introduced 1793.

CULTURE : Compost, two-thirds peat and loam, and abundance of sand. Position, large pots or tubs, well drained, in shady stove, greenhouse, or conservatory. Repot, Feb. or March. Water moderately Oct. to March, freely afterwards. Syringe trunks daily March to Sept. Temp., Sept. to March 50° to 65° for stove, 45° to 55° for greenhouse ; March to Sept. 65° to 75° for stove, 55° to 65° for greenhouse. Shade in summer essential.

PROPAGATION : By spores sown at any time on surface of finely-sifted loam and peat in shallow well-drained pans ; cover with sheet of glass, and keep moist in shady position in temp. 75° to 85°.

STOVE SPECIES : C. Dregei, 10 to 12 ft., Trop. Africa ; insignis, 15 to 20 ft., Cuba and Mexico.

GREENHOUSE SPECIES : C. dealbata, 10 ft., New Zealand ; medullaris, 15 to 20 ft., New Zealand.

Cycas (Sago Palm)—Ord. Cycadaceæ. Stove ornamental-leaved plants. Leaves feather-shaped, dark green.

CULTURE : Compost, two parts turfy loam, one part silver sand. Position, well-drained pots in moist plant stove. Repot, Feb. and March. Water moderately Oct. to March, freely afterwards. Temp., March to Sept. 75° to 80° ; Sept. to March 55° to 65°. C. revoluta may be stood outdoors in sheltered position from June to Sept.

PROPAGATION : By seeds sown 1 in. deep in light soil in temp. 85° to 90° in March or April ; suckers obtained from base of plants inserted in small pots in temp. 80° to 85° at any time.

SPECIES CULTIVATED : C. circinalis, 8 ft., E. Indies ; revoluta, 6 to 8 ft., China.

Cyclamen (Sowbread)—Ord. Primulaceæ. Hardy and greenhouse perennial flowering plants. Tuberous-rooted. Deciduous. First introduced 1596.

CULTURE OF GREENHOUSE SPECIES : Compost, two parts loam, one part leaf-mould and sand. Position, pots in greenhouse Sept. to May ; cold frame other times. Repot, July or Aug. ; corm to be above surface of soil. Water moderately until new growth begins, then increase supply, decreasing it when plants have ceased to flower ; keeping roots nearly dry and cool May or July. Apply liquid manure when in flower. Temp., Sept. to April 50° to 55°. Corms should not be grown for more than two years. Best results obtained from seedling plants one year old. Shade from sun essential.

CULTURE OF HARDY SPECIES : Soil, rich, friable loam containing plenty of leaf-mould. Position, sheltered partially shady nooks of rockery or in turf under trees. Plant, Aug. or Sept., 2 or 3 in. apart and 1½ in. deep. Top-dress with cow manure and rich soil annually after leaves die down, first removing old soil as far as corms. May also be grown in pots or pans in cold greenhouse or frame.

PROPAGATION : Greenhouse kinds by seed sown ¼ in. deep and 1 in. apart in well-drained pans of light soil in temp. of 55° Aug. to Nov., or Jan. to March ; hardy species by seeds sown similarly in cold frame in Oct. or Nov., transplanting seedlings following spring. Cover surface of soil in seed pans with layer of moss to keep soil uniformly moist. Seeds take several weeks to germinate.

GREENHOUSE SPECIES : C. latifolium (Syn. C. persicum), red, white, etc., winter, 6 to 8 in., Asia Minor.

HARDY SPECIES : **C. africanum**, red and white, autumn, 6 in., N. Africa ; Coum, red, Feb. and March, 4 in., Greece and Asia Minor ; europæum, red, autumn, 4 in., Europe ; ibericum (Syn. C. vernum), red, Feb. and March, 3 in., Caucasus ; neapolitanum, red, autumn, 4 in., Europe ; neapolitanum album, white ; repandum, rosy red, March to May, 4 in., S. Europe. The plant grown as C. hederæfolium is usually C. repandum. C. Atkinsi is an attractive early spring flowering hybrid with purple and white blooms.

Cyclamen-flowered Daffodil (*Narcissus cyclamineus*)—See Narcissus.

Cyclobothra—See Calochortus.

Cycnoches (Swan's-neck Orchid)—Ord. Orchidaceæ. Stove deciduous orchids. First introduced 1830.

CULTURE : Compost, good fibry peat. Position, pots or hanging baskets, well drained. Water freely from time new growth begins until leaves fall off ; very little other times. Temp., March to Sept. 65° to 85° ; Sept. to March 60° to 70°. Growing period, Feb. to Aug. Resting period, Sept. to Feb. Flowers appear at base of new pseudo-bulb.

PROPAGATION : By division of plants at potting time.

SPECIES CULTIVATED : C. chlorochilon, yellow, June, Demerara ; pentadactylon, yellow and brown, various seasons, Brazil.

Cydonia (Quince)—Ord. Rosaceæ. Hardy ornamental trees and shrubs. Deciduous or semi-evergreen. First introduced 1796.

CULTURE : Soil, ordinary. Position, sunny shrubberies or walls. Plant, Nov.

CULTURE OF QUINCE : Soil, light, rich moist loam. Position, as standards in orchards or low-lying gardens, margins of water. May also be grown fan-trained against walls. Plant in autumn. Prune as advised for apples. Gather fruit in November. Store away from other fruits.

PROPAGATION : By seeds sown ¼ in. deep in sandy soil in pots as soon as ripe and exposed to frost during the winter ; selected varieties by layering in spring, cuttings outdoors in autumn, or suckers removed in Nov.

SPECIES CULTIVATED : C. cathayensis, white, 8 to 10 ft., large fragrant fruits, W. China ; japonica, scarlet to blood red, Feb. to June, 8 to 10 ft., China and Japan, and its varieties alba, aurora, Knapp Hill Scarlet, nivalis and Simoni ; Maulei, orange-red, scarlet or blood red, April to June, 2 to 4 ft., Japan, and its varieties alpina (Syn. Sargenti) and atrosanguinea ; sinensis, soft carmine, April to May, 15 to 20 ft., China ; vulgaris (Quince), pink or white, May, 15 to 20 ft., S. Europe.

Cymbidium—Ord. Orchidaceæ. Stove terrestrial orchids. First introduced 1789. Flowers, fragrant.

CULTURE : Compost, equal parts rough fibry peat, sphagnum moss, and sand. Position, pots, well drained. Repot, Feb. or March. Water freely in summer, moderately in winter. Temp., March to Sept. 65° to 85° ; Sept. to March 60° to 65°. Growing period, March to Aug. Resting period, Sept. to Feb. Flowers appear at base of pseudo-bulb last formed.

PROPAGATION : By division of plant at potting time.

SPECIES CULTIVATED : C. eburneo-lowianum, creamy white and crimson, spring, hybrid ; eburneum, white and yellow, Feb. and March, Khasya ; giganteum, yellow, purple and crimson, winter, Nepaul ; grandiflorum, yellow, crimson and purple, winter, Sikkim ; insigne, white, pink and red, Annam, and its varieties Sanderæ and splendens ; lowianum, yellow, cream and maroon, Feb. and March, Burma ; Lowii-eburneum, white, Feb., hybrid ; tigrinum, yellow, red and crimson-purple, spring, Burma ; traceyanum, yellow and crimson, winter, Burma. There are many fine hybrids.

Cymbopogon (Lemon Grass)—Orc. Grammæ. Stove ornamental flowering grass. First introduced 1786.

CULTURE : Compost, two parts loam, one part leaf-mould and sand. Position, pots in stove. Pot, March. Water freely March to Oct., moderately afterwards. Temp., March to Oct. 75° to 85° ; Oct. to March 55° to 65°.

PROPAGATION : By division in March.

SPECIES CULTIVATED : C. Martinii (Syn. Andropogon Schœnanthus), to 2 ft., foliage lemon scented, India.

Cynara (Cardoon ; Globe Artichoke)—Ord. Compositæ. Hardy herbaceous perennials. Immature flower heads of artichoke used as a vegetable ; blanched stalks and mid ribs of leaves of cardoon also edible.

CULTURE OF CARDOON : Soil, light, deep rich ordinary. Position, open and sunny. Prepare trenches 12 in. deep, 18 in. wide, and 4 ft. apart from centre to centre in Oct. Fork 6 in. of rotten manure into the soil in bottom of trench. The third week in April spread 2 to 3 in. of light vegetable mould along the trench. Sow the seeds in patches of three or four, 1 in. deep and 18 in. apart, along the centre of trench. Thin seedlings when 3 in. high to one in each patch. Place a stake to each plant when a foot high, and secure the leaves loosely to this. In Aug. draw the leaves tightly together, carefully wind a small hayband round each plant and cover with mould. Plants are sufficiently blanched for cooking eight weeks after earthing up. Seeds may be sown two in a 3 in. pot filled with ordinary soil, placed in temp. 55° to 65° in March, hardened off in April, and planted out in May.

CULTURE OF GLOBE ARTICHOKE : Soil, deep rich loam, liberally manured and trenched three spits deep. Position, open and sunny. Plant suckers, *i.e.* offshoots, 4 in. deep in triangular groups 9 in. from plant to plant, 2 ft. apart in rows 4 ft. asunder, early in April. Keep well watered first season. In Nov. surround each plant with dry litter and in severe weather cover with similar material, uncovering in mild weather. Fork surface over in March, and mulch with decayed manure. Apply liquid manure freely to established plants during summer. Gather flower heads for use when fully developed. Seaweed an excellent manure. Apply in spring. Replant bed every four years.

PROPAGATION : By offsets or suckers removed in April. Seeds do not ripen in England.

SPECIES CULTIVATED : C. cardunculus (Cardoon), purple, Aug., 4 to 6 ft., S. Europe ; scolymus (Globe Artichoke), Sept., 3 to 6 ft., Europe.

Cynoglossum—Ord. Boraginaceæ. Hardy perennials and alpines.

CULTURE : Soil, well-drained loam with sand and leaf-mould. Position, sunny beds and rock gardens.

PROPAGATION : C. Wallichi by division. C. amabile is best treated as a biennial, raising a fresh stock each year from seed sown in a cold frame in March or April.

SPECIES CULTIVATED : C. amabile, blue, June, 2 ft., S.W. China ; Wallichi, sky blue, summer, 8 in., Himalayas. See also Omphalodes.

Cynorchis—Ord. Orchidaceæ.   Stove terrestrial orchid.   First introduced 1835.
CULTURE : Compost, equal parts fibrous peat and sphagnum moss.   Position, well-drained pots in moist part of stove.   Pot in spring.   Water freely whilst growing; give little when at rest.
PROPAGATION : By division after flowering.
SPECIES CULTIVATED : C. lowiana, white, green, and lilac, winter, Madagascar.

Cypella—Ord. Irideæ.   Half-hardy bulbs.   Adapted for cool greenhouse and outdoor culture.   First introduced 1823.
OUTDOOR CULTURE : Soil, light rich sandy.   Position, sunny well-drained border. Plant, Sept. to Jan., placing bulbs 4 in. deep and 2 in. apart.   Lift and replant bulbs annually.   Mulch surface of bed in March with cow manure.
POT CULTURE : Compost, two parts sandy loam, one part leaf-mould or decayed cow manure.   Pots, 4½ in. in diameter, well drained.   Place five bulbs, 3 in. deep, in each pot in Nov., and cover with cocoanut-fibre refuse in cold frames or under cool greenhouse stage until growth begins.   Water moderately from time bulbs begin to grow until flowers fade, then gradually cease, keeping bulbs dry till Jan. Temp., Sept. to March 40° to 50° ; other times 50° to 60°.
PROPAGATION : By offsets treated as advised for bulbs.
SPECIES CULTIVATED : C. Herbertii (Syn. Tigridia Herbertii), yellow, summer, 1 ft., S. America ; peruviana, yellow and brown, summer, 1 ft., Peru.

Cyperus (Umbrella plant ; Galingale)—Ord. Cyperaceæ.   Greenhouse and hardy perennials.   Orn. foliage.   Foliage, grass-like, dark green, or variegated with white.
CULTURE OF GREENHOUSE SPECIES : Compost, two parts loam, one part leaf-mould and sand.   Position, pots in shady greenhouse.   Water moderately in winter, freely other times.   Repot, Feb. to March.   Temp., March to Sept. 55° to 65° ; Sept. to March 45° to 55°.
CULTURE OF HARDY SPECIES : Soil, heavy loam two parts, rotted cow manure one part.   Position, margins of lakes, ponds, etc.   Plant, Oct. to March.
PROPAGATION : By seeds sown in shallow boxes or pans of light soil in temp. 55° to 65° in March or April ; division of roots in March or April.
GREENHOUSE SPECIES : C. alternifolius, 2½ ft., leaves green, Africa ; alternifolius variegatus, leaves striped with white ; alternifolius gracilis, a dwarfer, more elegant form ; Papyrus (Syn. Papyrus Antiquorum), 8 to 10 ft., leaves green, Trop. Africa. HARDY SPECIES : C. esculentus (Chufa), producing underground edible tubers, 2 to 3 ft., N. America, Europe, and Asia ; longus (Galingale), 4 ft., Europe; vegetus, crowded heads of mahogany-coloured flowers, autumn and winter, Chile.

Cyphomandra (Tree Tomato)—Ord. Solanaceæ.   Greenhouse evergreen orn. foliage and fruiting shrub.   First introduced 1836.   Fruit, large, egg-shaped, red and edible ; ripe in Aug. and Sept.
CULTURE : Compost, two parts loam, one part leaf-mould and sand.   Position, pots in light sunny greenhouse.   Pot, March or April.   Water moderately Oct. to March, freely afterwards.   Temp., Oct. to March 45° to 55° ; March to Sept. 55° to 65°.   Prune plants into shape March or April.
PROPAGATION : By seeds sown ¼ in. deep in light soil in temp. 75° to 85° in March or April ; cuttings of side shoots 3 in. long inserted in sandy soil under bell-glass in temp. 75° to 80° in spring or early summer.
SPECIES CULTIVATED : C. betacea, purple and green, spring, 6 to 10 ft., S. America.

Cypress—See Cupressus.

Cypress Oak (*Quercus pedunculata fastigiata*)—See Quercus.

Cypress Spurge (*Euphorbia Cyparissias*)—See Euphorbia.

Cypress Vine (*Ipomæa Quamoclit*)—See Ipomæa.

Cypripedium (Lady's Slipper ; Mocassin-flower)—Ord. Orchidaceæ.   Stove, greenhouse, and hardy orchids.   First introduced 1731.
CULTURE OF STOVE SPECIES : Compost, two parts rough fibry peat, one part sphagnum moss and sand.   Position, pots or pans drained one-third of their depth.

Repot, April. Temp., March to Sept. 65° to 85° ; Sept. to March 60° to 65°. Water freely April to Aug., moderately afterwards.

CULTURE OF GREENHOUSE SPECIES : Compost and position, same as above. Repot, April. Water freely April to Aug., moderately other times. Temp., March to Sept. 60° to 65° ; Sept. to March 50° to 55°. Resting period, none. Flowers appear when growth is finished.

CULTURE OF HARDY SPECIES : Compost, equal parts loam, leaf-mould, road grit, and small stones. Position, partially shady sheltered nooks on rockery. Plant March or April. Water in dry weather.

PROPAGATION : All the species by division of the roots at potting or planting time.

SPOVE SPECIES : C. Argus, rose, white and purple, June, Philippines ; bellatulum, white and purple, May, Burma ; Boxallii, green and purple, Dec. to Feb., Burma ; callosum, white and purple, Dec. to Feb., Cochin China ; Charlesworthii, rose and white, autumn, Burma ; concolor, white, March to May, Burma ; dayanum, white and purple, Feb., Borneo ; lawrenceanum, white and purple, April, Borneo ; niveum, white and rose, spring, Malaya ; rothschildianum, yellow, purple and brown, March, Borneo ; superbiens, white and purple, Nov. ; venustum, green and red, Oct., Himalayas. There are also many fine hybrids.

GREENHOUSE SPECIES : C. insigne, white, purple and brown, Dec. to Feb., Khasia ; insigne Maulei, white and purple ; insigne Sanderæ, yellow ; insigne sanderianum, yellow ; spicerianum, white and purple, autumn, Assam ; villosum, brown and purple, winter, Moulmein. Numerous hybrids to be found in trade lists.

HARDY SPECIES : C. Calceolus (Lady's Slipper), yellow, summer, Europe (Britain) ; guttatum, white, rose and purple, N. America and Siberia ; macranthum, purple, June, Siberia ; japonicum, green, white and pink, summer, Japan ; parviflorum, yellow and red, June, N. America ; pubescens, yellow and purple, June, N. America ; spectabile, rose and white, May, N. America.

Cyrilla (Leatherwood)—Ord. Cyrillaceæ. Hardy evergreen flowering shrub. Flowers, borne in tufts on the ends of old wood. First introduced 1765.

CULTURE : Soil, loam and peat. Position, warm, sheltered nooks. Plant, Sept. or April.

PROPAGATION : By cuttings in silver sand under bell-glass in temp. 55° to 65°.

SPECIES CULTIVATED : C. racemiflora, white, summer, 6 ft., S.U. States.

Cyrtanthus—Ord. Amaryllidaceæ. Greenhouse bulbous plants. First introduced 1774. Flowers, fragrant.

CULTURE : Compost, two parts loam, one part sand and peat. Position, well-drained pots on shelf in light greenhouse. Pot bulbs in Oct. or Nov., 2 in. deep. Water freely March to Oct., very little other times. Temp., Nov. to April 50° to 55° ; April to Nov. 60° to 65°.

PROPAGATION : By offsets in Nov.

SPECIES CULTIVATED : C. carneus, red, summer, 1 ft., S. Africa ; collinus, red, Aug., 1 ft., S. Africa ; Mackenii, white, Dec. to March, 1 ft., Natal ; sanguineus, red, summer, 1 ft., S. Africa.

Cyrtochilum—See Oncidium.

Cyrtomium—See Aspidium.

Cyrtopodium—Ord. Orchidaceæ. Stove epiphytal orchids. First introduced 1804.

CULTURE : Compost, two parts rich fibrous loam and decayed manure. Position, large pots or pans, well drained, in plant stove. Pot, March or April. Water freely April to Aug., moderately Aug. to Nov., afterwards keep nearly dry. Temp., March to Sept. 70° to 80° ; Sept. to March 60° to 70°. Growing period, March to Aug. Resting period, Aug. to March. Flowers appear with new growth.

PROPAGATION : By division of pseudo-bulbs at potting time.

SPECIES CULTIVATED : C. Aliceæ, yellow and brown, autumn, Brazil ; Andersoni, yellow and green, spring, West Indies ; punctatum, yellow, red, and purple, April and May, West Indies.

Cystopteris (Bladder Fern)—Ord. Filices. Hardy deciduous ferns.

CULTURE : Soil, rich, deep, sandy loam, freely mixed with pieces of limestone or dried mortar. Position, well-drained shady sheltered rockery. Plant, March or April. Water moderately in dry weather.

POT CULTURE : Compost, two parts good loam, one part leaf-soil mixed with old mortar or sand. Position, well drained in cold frame or cold greenhouse in shade. Repot, March or April. Water freely April to Sept., moderately Sept. to Nov., keeping nearly dry afterwards.

PROPAGATION : By spores sown on surface of fine sandy soil in shallow boxes or pans, cover with sheet of glass, and place in cold frame at any time ; division of plant in March or April.

SPECIES CULTIVATED : C. bulbifera, 6 to 12 in., N. America ; fragilis, 6 to 8 in., and its varieties angustata and dickieana, Europe (Britain), etc. ; montana, 6 to 8 in., Europe and N. America.

Cytisus (Broom)—Ord. Leguminosæ. **Greenhouse and hardy deciduous** evergreen flowering shrubs.

CULTURE OF GREENHOUSE SPECIES : Compost, two parts turfy loam, one part lumpy peat and sharp sand. Position, pots in greenhouse. Pot, May or June. Prune shoots to within 2 in. of base directly after flowering, and place plants in temp. 50° to 55° to make new growth before potting. Place plants in sunny position outdoors from end of July to Oct. to ripen growth. Water freely March to May, moderately during May and June, freely June to Nov., moderately afterwards. Apply weak liquid or artificial manure to plants during time they are in flower. Temp., Nov. to Feb. 45° to 50° ; Feb. to May 50° to 55° ; May to June 55° to 60°.

CULTURE OF HARDY SPECIES : Soil, ordinary. Position, sunny rockery for C. Ardoini kewensis, etc ; shrubbery borders for C. albus, C. purpureus, præcox, scoparius andreanus, and choice kinds ; rough banks, woodlands, etc. for C. scoparius. Plant, Oct. to Dec. Prune directly after flowering, shortening old shoots to base of promising young ones. Transplant best when young. C. præcox, C. purpureus, and C. andreanus make excellent pot plants for flowering early in cold greenhouse.

PROPAGATION : Greenhouse species by cuttings of young shoots 3 in. long, with small portions of branches attached, inserted in sandy soil in well-drained pots under bell-glass in temp. 75° to 80° in March, April, or May ; seeds sown ¼ in. deep in well-drained pots of light soil in temp. 65° to 70° in March ; hardy species by seeds sown ¼ in. deep outdoors in March or April ; Aug. cuttings in sandy soil ; grafting in March or April. Seeds of Common Broom may be scattered broadcast on banks or in woodlands.

GREENHOUSE SPECIES : C. canariensis (Syn. Genista canariensis), yellow, fragrant, spring and summer, to 6 ft., Canaries, and its variety ramosissimus (small leaved) ; filipes, white, March, 4 to 6 ft., Canaries ; fragrans (Syn. C. racemosus), yellow, summer, 2 to 3 ft., Canaries ; fragrans elegans, yellow, 4 ft. ; fragrans everestianus, rich yellow.

HARDY SPECIES : C. albus (White Spanish Broom), white, May, 6 to 10 ft., Spain ; Ardoini, yellow, spring, 4 to 6 in., Maritime Alps ; Beani, deep yellow, May, 6 to 18 in., hybrid ; Dallimorei, rosy pink and crimson, May, 8 to 9 ft., hybrid ; decumbens, yellow, May to June, 4 to 6 in., S. Europe ; Heuffeli, yellow, 2 to 4 ft., Hungary ; hirsutus, yellow, 1 to 2 ft., S. Europe ; kewensis, creamy white, May, prostrate, hybrid ; leucanthus (Syn. C. schipkænsis), yellowish white, June to Oct., 4 to 10 in., S.E. Europe ; monspessulanus (Syn. Genista candicans), yellow, May, 5 to 7 ft., S. Europe ; nigricans, yellow, June, 4 to 6 ft., Europe ; præcox, creamy yellow, May, 4 to 6 ft., hybrid ; purgans, deep yellow, April to May, 3 to 4 ft., France and Spain ; purpureus, purple, May, 1 to 1½ ft., E. Europe ; ratisbonensis, (Syn. C. biflorus), yellow, May, 4 to 6 ft., Europe ; scoparius (Common Broom), yellow, April to July, 5 to 10 ft., Europe (Britain) ; scoparius sulphureus, sulphur yellow ; scoparius andreanus (Syn. Genista andreanus), yellow and crimson, hybrid ; sessilifolius, yellow, June, 5 to 6 ft., S. Europe and N. Africa ; supranubius, milky white tinged rose, May, 8 to 10 ft., Canaries ; versicolor, yellowish purple, May, 2 to 3 ft., hybrid. There are many more fine hybrids of C. scoparius such as Dorothy Walpole, Firefly, and Daisy Hill.

Daböecia (Irish Heath : St. Dabeoc's Heath)—Ord. Ericaceæ. Evergreen flowering shrub.
CULTURE : Compost, sandy peat and loam. Position, sunny banks or rockeries. Plant, Sept., Oct., March, or April.
PROPAGATION : By cuttings inserted in sandy soil in summer under hand-light ; layers of shoots in autumn.
SPECIES CULTIVATED : D. polifolia (Syn. Menziesia polifolia), purple, July, 2 ft., Europe (Ireland) ; polifolia alba, white.

Dacrydium—Ord. Taxaceæ. Half-hardy ornamental evergreen trees. First introduced 1825.
CULTURE : Soil, sandy peat. Position, as specimens in open places or upon lawns in mildest districts only. Plant, Sept. to Oct. and April to May.
PROPAGATION : By cuttings of ripened wood in cold frame in Aug. or Sept. ; seeds sown in sandy peat in pans in cool greenhouse during Feb. or March.
SPECIES CULTIVATED : D. cupressinum, 80 to 100 ft., New Zealand ; Franklini (Huon Pine), 80 to 100 ft., Tasmania.

Dactylis (Cock's-foot Grass)—Ord. Gramineæ. Hardy orn. grass. Leaves, variegated with white.
CULTURE : Soil, ordinary. Position, margins of flower beds or borders in sun or shade, or mixed with bedding plants. Plant, Oct. or April, 3 to 6 in. apart.
PROPAGATION : By division of plants in Oct. or April.
SPECIES CULTIVATED : D. glomerata variegata, leaves silvery, 6 to 8 in., Britain.

Dædalacanthus—See Eranthemum.

Dæmonorops—Ord. Palmaceæ. Stove ornamental-leaved climbing palms. Useful for table decoration.
CULTURE : Compost, equal parts loam, peat, leaf-mould and sand. Position, pots in a young state ; in beds or tubs with shoots trained up pillars when large. Pot or plant in March. Water freely in summer, moderately in winter. Syringe daily ; moist atmosphere essential. Temp., March to Oct. 75° to 85° ; Oct. to March 60° to 65°.
PROPAGATION : By seeds sown in above compost in spring.
SPECIES CULTIVATED : D. Draco, Malaya ; grandis, Malaya ; jenkinsianus, India ; lewisianus, Penang ; palembanicus, Sumatra.

Daffodil—See Narcissus.

Daffodil Garlic (*Allium neapolitanum*)—See Allium.

Daffodil Lily (*Amaryllis belladonna*)—See Amaryllis.

Dahlia—Ord. Compositæ. Half-hardy herbaceous tuberous-rooted perennials. Nat. Central America and Mexico. First introduced 1789. Many varieties.
TYPES—Show : Flower, large, circular ; florets, quilled ; colour, all one tint. Fancy : Flower, large, circular ; florets, quilled ; colour, florets tipped, striped or flaked different tint to ground colour. Cactus : Flower, high in centre, circular ; florets, long, narrow, pointed, not quilled or fluted, reflexed at edges. Pompon : Flower, small, circular, florets and colours like those of show and fancy types. Single : Flower, circular ; florets, broad, flat, eight in number, overlapping each other, rounded, recurving at tips. Collarette : Flowers, single, with "collar" of very shortened florets ; outer florets broad and flattened. Pæony-flowered : Flower, semi-double ; outer florets, broad ; inner ones, short and narrow. Charm and Miniature Pæony-flowered : Flower, semi-double ; florets, broad and more or less flattened ; plants bushy and branching ; colours very varied. Decorative : Flower, semi-double ; florets, flat. Anemone-flowered : Flowers, double ; outer florets, broad and flattened ; inner florets, short and densely packed. Star : Flowers, semi-double ; florets, long, narrow, pointed, reflexed at edges and incurving towards centre. Orchid : Flowers, single ; florets, broad, flattened and twisted. Dwarf Bedding : Flowers, single or semi-double ; florets, broad and more or less flattened ; habit, dwarf and branching, very free flowering.
OUTDOOR CULTURE : Soil, ordinary, well enriched with manure. Position, open

sunny beds or borders. Plant tubers 3 in. deep in April, or start them to grow in pots in temp. 55° in March, planting outdoors in May or June. Thin shoots to three on each plant in July; flower buds to one on each shoot in Aug. Apply liquid manure occasionally in July, Aug., and Sept. Lift and store tubers in frost-proof place in Oct., just covering them with soil or cocoanut-fibre refuse. Cut down stems to within 6 in. of tubers before lifting.

CULTURE IN POTS: Compost, two parts turfy loam, one part decayed manure. Place tubers in well-drained 6 in. pots in March, in temp. 55°. Water moderately and keep close to glass. Transfer to 8 in. pots in May. Stand plants outdoors in June. Apply liquid manure in July. Thin shoots to three on each plant; flower buds to one on each shoot in Aug. Withhold water after flowering and store away in frost-proof place.

PROPAGATION: By seeds sown ⅛ in. deep in light soil in temp. 65° to 75° in March; cuttings of shoots 3 in. long issuing from tubers, inserted in 2 in. pots of sandy soil, in temp. 65° to 70° in Feb., March, or April; division of tubers in spring.

SPECIES CULTIVATED: D. coccinea, scarlet, autumn, 4 ft. (parent of Single Dahlia); excelsa, purplish pink, summer, 15 to 20 ft.; gracilis, orange-scarlet, autumn, 5 ft.; imperialis, white, lilac and red, Oct., 10 to 12 ft.; Juarezi (parent of Cactus Dahlias), scarlet, autumn, 3 ft.; Mercki, lilac and yellow, Oct., 3 ft.; variabilis (Syn. pinnata), (parent of Show, Fancy, and Pompon Dahlias), scarlet, autumn, 4 ft.; Zimapani (Black Dahlia), Syn. Bidens atrosanguinea, black and crimson, July, 3 ft., Mexico.

Dahurian Bell-flower (*Campanula dahurica*)—See Campanula.

Daisy (*Bellis perennis*)—See Bellis.

Daisy-bush (*Olearia Haastii*)—See Olearia.

Daisy-flowered Bramble (*Rubus ulmifolius*)—See Rubus.

Dalechampia—Ord. Euphorbiaceæ. Stove flowering evergreen shrubs. Firs; introduced 1867. Flowers, insignificant. Bracts, rich carmine-rose, summer.

CULTURE: Compost, equal parts loam, peat, leaf-mould, and sand. Position, shady part of plant stove. Pot, March. Water moderately Sept. to April, freely afterwards. Temp., Sept. to March 55° to 65°; March to Sept. 70° to 80°.

PROPAGATION: By cuttings inserted in sandy peat under bell-glass in March, April, or May, in temp. 85°.

SPECIES CULTIVATED: D. roezliana, 12 in., Mexico.

Dalmatian Crocus (*Crocus dalmaticus*)—See Crocus.

Damask Rose (*Rosa damascena*)—See Rosa.

Dame's Rocket (*Hesperis matronalis*)—See Hesperis.

Dame's Violet (*Hesperis matronalis*)—See Hesperis.

Dame Wort (*Sambucus Ebulus*)—See Sambucus.

Damson—See Prunus.

Danæ (Alexandrian Laurel)—Ord. Liliaceæ. Hardy evergreen berry-bearing shrub. Introduced 1707.

CULTURE: Soil, ordinary, medium, or light, moist. Position, under shade of trees; good carpeting shrub. Plant in autumn.

PROPAGATION: By seeds sown outdoors in autumn; by division in spring.

SPECIES CULTIVATED: D. racemosa (Syns. D. Laurus and Ruscus racemosus), greenish-white flowers, succeeded by red berries, 2 to 3 ft., S. Europe.

Dandelion (*Taraxacum officinale*)—See Taraxacum.

Danebrog Poppy (*Papaver somniferum*)—See Papaver.

Dane's-blood (*Sambucus ebulus*)—See Sambucus.

Daphne (Garland flower; Spurge Laurel; Mezereon)—Ord. Thymelæaceæ. Greenhouse and hardy deciduous evergreen flowering shrubs. Flowers, fragrant.

CULTURE OF GREENHOUSE SPECIES: Compost, two parts loam, one part peat and sand. Position, airy greenhouse from Sept. to June, outdoors June to Sept. Pot,

Dahlia, Orchid Flowered

Daphne Cneorum
(Garland Flower)

Datura Stramonium
(Thorn Apple)

Delphinium elatum hybridum
(Larkspur)

Dendrobium Phalænopsis

Dendromecon rigidum

Desmodium tillæfolium

Deutzia Lemoinei
(Japanese Snow-flower)

Dianthus sinensis laciniatus
(Indian Pink)

Dianthus sinensis
(Indian Pink)

Dianthus Sweet Wivelsfield

Dicentra spectabilis
(Bleeding Heart)

Diervilla hybrida
(Bush Honeysuckle)

Digitalis hybrida
(Foxglove)

Disa grandiflora
(Table Mountain Orchid)

Doronicum plantagineum
(Leopard's-bane)

Draba imbricata
(Whitlow Grass)

Echinops Ritro
(Globe Thistle)

Feb. Pinch out points of young shoots in June. Water moderately Sept. to April, freely afterwards. Temp., Sept. to March 40° to 50° ; March to Sept. 55° to 65°.
PROPAGATION : Greenhouse species by cuttings of side shoots inserted, in Oct. or Nov., in well-drained pots or pans of sandy peat under bell-glass in temp. 50° to 55° ; layers in March or April ; grafting on D. laureola and D. pontica in spring ; hardy species by layering shoots in autumn and seed sown as soon as ripe.
CULTURE OF HARDY SPECIES : Soil, sandy peat. Position, drooping over front of rockeries for trailing species ; summit of rockery or open border for erect species. Plant, Oct., Nov., March, or April.
GREENHOUSE SPECIES : D. odora (Syn. D. indica), purple, March, 2 to 3 ft., Japan.
HARDY EVERGREEN SPECIES CULTIVATED : D. blagayana, white, March to April, fragrant, 9 to 12 in., E. Europe ; Cneorum (Garland Flower), pink, May, fragrant, 10 to 12 in., Central and South Europe ; collina, purplish rose, March to June, fragrant, 2 to 3 ft., Italy and Asia Minor ; Dauphini (Syn. hybrida) reddish purple, spring and autumn, fragrant, 3 to 4 ft., hybrid ; Laureola, yellowish green, Feb. to March, fragrant, S. and W. Europe (Britain) ; neapolitana (Syn. Fioniana), rosy purple, March to May, fragrant, 2 to 3 ft., hybrid ; oleoides, purplish rose to white, 2 to 3 ft., S. Europe ; petræa (Syn. rupestris), bright pink, June, fragrant, 3 to 5 in., Southern Tyrol ; pontica, yellowish green, April, fragrant, 2 to 3 ft., Asia Minor ; retusa (Syn. tangutica), rosy purple and white, May, fragrant, 1 to 2 ft., W. China.
HARDY DECIDUOUS SPECIES CULTIVATED : D. alpina, white, May to June, fragrant, 6 to 18 in., Alps ; caucasica, white, May to June, fragrant, 3 to 4 ft., Caucasus ; Mezereum, purplish red or white, Feb. to March, fragrant, 3 to 5 ft., Europe and Siberia.

Daphniphyllum—Ord. Euphorbiaceæ. Hardy evergreen shrubs. First introduced 1879.
CULTURE : Soil, ordinary rich. Position, moist shady borders or shrubberies. Plant, Nov.
PROPAGATION : By cuttings of nearly ripe wood in close frame in July.
SPECIES CULTIVATED : D. humile, blue-black fruits, 1½ to 2 ft., Japan ; macropodum, blue-black fruits, 8 to 12 ft., Japan.

Darling River Pea (*Swainsona coronilliflora*)—See Swainsona.

Darlingtonia (Californian Pitcher-plant)—Ord. Sarraceniaceæ. Hardy herbaceous orn. foliage plant. Insectivorous. First introduced 1861. Pitchers, borne on summit of leaves, hood-like, bright green, mottled with white and pink.
GREENHOUSE CULTURE : Compost, equal parts peat, chopped sphagnum, sharp sand, and small pieces of limestone. Position, under hand-light in shady greenhouse. Pot, Feb. or March. Water freely at all times. Syringe daily March to Sept. Ventilate hand-light daily.
OUTDOOR CULTURE : Compost, spongy fibrous peat and chopped sphagnum moss. Position, damp, by side of stream, or in bog exposed to sun, but sheltered from cold winds. Plant, March or April.
PROPAGATION : By seeds sown on surface of mixture of fibrous peat, charcoal, sphagnum and sand in a pan stood partly in water and covered with a bell-glass in cool greenhouse in April or May ; division of side shoots inserted in small pots at any time of year.
SPECIES CULTIVATED : D. californica, white, April, 12 in., California.

Darwinia—Ord. Myrtaceæ. Greenhouse evergreen shrubs. First introduced 1820.
CULTURE : Compost, equal parts loam, peat, and sand. Position, well-drained pots in airy greenhouse. Pot firmly in Feb. or March. Water moderately Sept. to March, freely March to Sept. Prune, Feb. or March. Temp., Sept. to March 40° to 50° ; March to Sept. 50° to 60°.
PROPAGATION : By cuttings of young shoots 2 or 3 in. long inserted in sandy peat under bell-glass in temp. 40° to 50° in April or May.
SPECIES CULTIVATED : D. fimbriata, rose, June, 5 ft., Australia ; macrostegia (Syn. Genetyllis tulipifera), crimson, May, 3 ft., Australia.

Darwin's Barberry (*Berberis Darwini*)—See Berberis.

Dasylirion—Ord. Liliaceæ.   Greenhouse evergreen plants.   Orn. foliage.' First introduced 1835.   Leaves, glaucous green, with spiny margins.
CULTURE : Compost, two parts loam and peat, one sand.   Position, pots or tubs in airy greenhouse, dwelling-rooms, or outdoors in beds May to Sept.   Pot firmly Feb. or March.   Water very little Oct. to March, freely afterwards.   Temp., Sept. to March 40° to 50° ; March to Sept. 50° to 60°.
PROPAGATION : By seeds sown in sandy peat in well-drained pans or pots under bell-glass in temp. 50° to 60° in March, April, or May.
SPECIES CULTIVATED : D. acrotrichum, 6 to 8 ft., Mexico ; glaucophyllum, 10 ft., Mexico ; Hookeri, 3 ft., Mexico.

Date Palm (*Phœnix dactylifera*)—See Phœnix.

Date Plum (*Diospyrus Lotus*)—See Diospyros.

Datisca (False Hemp)—Ord. Datisoaceæ.   Hardy herbaceous perennial.   Orn. foliage.   First introduced 1739.   Male and female flowers borne on separate plants. Leaves, pinnate, green.
CULTURE : Soil, deep rich, ordinary.   Position, open and sunny border.   Plant, Oct., Nov., March, and April.   Female plant most effective.
PROPAGATION : By seeds sown $\frac{1}{16}$ in. deep in fine soil outdoors in March, April, or May, transplanting seedlings to permanent positions any time.
SPECIES CULTIVATED : D. cannabina, greenish white, summer, 3 to 6 ft., W. Asia.

Datura (Thorn Apple ; Trumpet Flower)—Ord. Solanaceæ.   Half-hardy and greenhouse annuals, shrubs, and trees.
CULTURE OF ANNUAL SPECIES : Soil, light sandy.   Position, sunny borders outdoors. Plant, May.
CULTURE OF SHRUBBY SPECIES : Compost, equal parts loam, fibrous peat, well decomposed manure, and silver sand.   Position, pots, tubs, or borders well drained in sunny greenhouse.   Pot or plant, March.   Prune freely Sept. or Oct.   Water very little Oct. to March, freely afterwards.   Temp., Sept. to March 45° to 55°, March to Sept. 55° to 65°.   Place plants outdoors in sunny position June to Sept. Apply liquid manure occasionally whilst plants are in flower.
PROPAGATION : Annuals by seed sown $\frac{1}{4}$ in. deep in light sandy soil in well-drained pots in temp. 55° to 65° in March or April, and transfer the seedlings to small pots until planting time ; shrubby species by cuttings of shoots 6 in. long inserted in sandy soil under bell-glass in temp. 65° to 75° in spring or autumn.
ANNUAL SPECIES : D. ceratocaula, white, July, 3 ft., Trop. America ; fastuosa (Syn. D. Metel), blue and white, summer, 2 ft., Tropics ; fastuosa flore-pleno, double white ; fastuosa rubra, red ; Stramonium (Thorn Apple), white, July, 2 ft., Britain, etc.
SHRUBBY SPECIES : D. arborea, white, Aug., 7 to 10 ft., Peru ; cornigera (Horn of Plenty), creamy white, summer, 10 ft., Organ Mountains ; meteloides (Syn. D. Wrightii), bluish violet, summer, 2 ft., California ; sanguinea (Syn. Brugmansia sanguinea), orange yellow, summer, 4 to 6 ft., Peru ; suaveolens, white, fragrant, Aug., 8 to 10 ft., Mexico.

Daucus (Carrot)—Ord. Umbelliferæ.   Hardy biennial.   A well-known edible rooted vegetable.   Reputed to be first introduced into England by the Flemings in time of Queen Bess.   Types—Short-horn : Roots, short, conical.   Stump-rooted : Roots, medium, blunt at ends.   Intermediate : Root, spindle-shaped, midway in length between a Short-horn and Long-rooted carrot.   Long-rooted : Roots, long and tapering.
CULTURE : Soil, deep, rich, and sandy, well manured for previous crop.   Position, open spot for main crops, south border for early ones.   Time to sow Short-horn varieties, Feb. and Aug. ; others in March or April.   Thin seedlings to 6 in. and 9 in. apart when 2 in. high.   Lift and store roots in frost-proof place in Oct. and Nov.   Artificial manures : Kainit, 2$\frac{1}{2}$ lb., sulphate of ammonia, 1 lb., guano, 2$\frac{1}{2}$ lb. ; apply this quantity to each square rod at time of sowing.   Seeds germinate in 12 to

18 days ; retain germinating powers for 4 years.   Crop matures in 20 to 24 weeks from date of sowing.

FORCING ON HOTBEDS : Sow seeds thinly on bed of light rich soil over a hotbed of manure covered by a frame in Jan. or Feb.   Water moderately, ventilate by day when temp. reaches 75°.   Thin seedlings to 3 in. apart when an inch high.   Short-horn varieties best for this purpose.

SPECIES CULTIVATED : D. carota sativa, white, summer, Europe (Britain).

Davallia (Hare's-foot Fern ; Bear's-foot Fern ; Squirrel's-foot Fern)—Ord. Filices. Stove and greenhouse evergreen ferns. The rhizomes of D. bullata are extensively used for training round various fancy objects, as boats, monkeys, etc., also balls of peat and moss.   First introduced 1699.

CULTURE OF STOVE SPECIES : Compost, two parts loam, one part leaf-mould, peat, pounded charcoal, and sand. Pot, Feb., March, or April. Position, pots or hanging baskets in light part of plant stove.   Water moderately Oct. to Feb., freely afterwards.   Temp., Sept. to March 55° to 60° ; March to Sept. 65° to 75°.

CULTURE OF GREENHOUSE SPECIES : Compost, same as for stove species. Pot, March or April. Position, pots or baskets in partial shade. Water moderately Sept. to March, freely afterwards.   Temp., Sept. to March 40° to 50° ; March • Sept. 50° to 60°.

PROPAGATION : By spores sown on surface of sandy peat in pans under bell-glass in temp. 55° to 75° at any time ; division of rhizomes in Feb. or March.

STOVE SPECIES : D. aculeata, habit climbing, 6 ft., W. Indies ; affinis, habit creeping, 9 to 12 in., Ceylon, Java, etc. ; alpina, habit trailing, dwarf, 6 in., Java, Borneo, etc. ; dissecta, habit dwarf, Java ; divaricata, habit robust, creeping, N. India ; elegans, habit very vigorous, Ceylon, Java, etc. ; fijiensis, habit free, evergreen, Fiji ; heterophylla, habit dwarf, creeping, Malay Peninsula ; hirta cristata (Syn. Microlepia hirta cristata), habit spreading, South Sea Islands ; pallida, habit robust (Syn. D. mooreana), Borneo ; tenuifolia veitchiana, habit drooping, Malaya.

GREENHOUSE SPECIES : D. bullata (Squirrel's-foot Fern), habit, dwarf and creeping, Japan ; canariensis (Hare's-foot Fern), habit robust, Canaries ; Mariesii, habit dwarf, deciduous, Japan ; Novæ-Zelandiæ (Syn. Acrophorus hispida), habit slender creeping, New Zealand ; Tyermanni (Bear's-foot Fern), habit creeping, West Africa.

Davidia—Ord. Cornaceæ. Hardy ornamental tree. Deciduous. First introduced 1897.

CULTURE : Soil, ordinary. Position, as specimens on lawns or at back of shrub borders. Plant, Nov.

PROPAGATION : By seed sown in pans in cold frame in Feb., or cuttings of ripened wood in Oct.

SPECIES CULTIVATED : D. involucrata, large creamy-white bracts, May, 40 to 65 ft., Central and West China.

David's Clematis (*Clematis davidiana*)—See Clematis.

David's Harp (*Polygonatum multiflorum*)—See Polygonatum.

David's-root (*Celastrus scandens*)—See Celastrus.

Daviesia (Australian Hop)—Ord. Leguminosæ. Greenhouse evergreen flowering shrubs.   First introduced 1805.

CULTURE : Compost, equal parts loam, peat, and silver sand. Position, well-drained pots in airy greenhouse. Pot firmly March or April. Water very little Oct. to March, moderately other times. Temp., Sept. to March 40° to 50° ; March to Sept. 50° to 60°.

PROPAGATION : By cuttings of firm young shoots inserted in sand under bell-glass in temp. 50° to 55° in spring ; seeds sown 1/8 in. deep in sandy peat in temp. 55° in March.

SPECIES CULTIVATED : D. alata, yellow, summer, 3 ft., Australia ; cordata, yellow, summer, 3 ft., Australia ; ulicina, yellow, summer, 2 ft., Australia.

Day-flower (*Commelina cælestis*)—See Commelina.

Day-lily—See Hemerocallis.

Dead-Nettle (*Lamium maculatum*)—See Lamium.

Decaisnea—Ord. Berberidaceæ. Hardy deciduous ornamental shrub. First introduced 1897.
CULTURE : Soil, rich loamy. Position, sunny shrubberies sheltered from north and east winds. Plant, Nov.
PROPAGATION : By seeds sown in pans of sandy soil in Feb. or March.
SPECIES CULTIVATED : D. Fargesi, yellowish green, large dull blue fruits, 7 to 10 ft., W. China.

Deciduous Cypress (*Taxodium distichum*)—See Taxodium.

Decumaria—Ord. Saxifragaceæ. Hardy deciduous flowering twiner. First introduced 1785. Flowers, fragrant.
CULTURE : Soil, light rich. Position, against south or west walls, arbours or trellis work. Plant, Oct., Nov., or Dec. Prune away weak and head shoots in Feb.
PROPAGATION : By cuttings of shoots inserted in ordinary soil under hand-light in shady position outdoors in summer.
SPECIES CULTIVATED : D. barbara, white, June, 10 to 20 ft., United States.

Deer Berry (*Mitchella repens*)—See Mitchella.

Deer Fern (*Lomaria Spicant*)—See Lomaria.

Deer Grass (*Rhexia virginica*)—See Rhexia.

Deil's Spoons (*Alisma Plantago*)—See Alisma.

Delphinium (Larkspur)—Ord. Ranunculaceæ. Hardy annuals and herbaceous perennials. Showy plants for border culture.
CULTURE OF ANNUAL SPECIES : Soil, ordinary, rich. Position, open beds or borders. Sow seeds ⅛ in. deep where plants are to flower in April, or in light soil in shallow boxes in temp. 55° in March, transplanting, pricking out seedlings when large enough to handle and outdoors in May.
CULTURE OF PERENNIAL SPECIES : Soil, deep, rich. Position, sunny beds or borders. Plant 3 ft. apart in Oct., Nov., March, or April. Cut down flower stems in Aug. or Sept. Feed liberally with liquid manures in summer, and mulch with decayed manure in early spring. Lift and replant every three years in Oct. or March.
PROPAGATION : By seeds sown ⅛ in. deep outdoors in April, or in pans or boxes of light soil in temp. 55° in March; cuttings of young shoots, 3 in. long, inserted in 2 in. pots of sandy soil in cold frame in Sept. or March; division of roots in Oct. or March.
ANNUAL SPECIES : D. Ajacis (Rocket Larkspur), blue, summer, 12 to 18 in., Europe ; consolida, blue, summer, 2 ft., Europe ; cardinale, scarlet, Aug., 3 ft., California. Many beautiful strains of annual kinds to be found in trade lists.
PERENNIAL SPECIES : D. brunonianum, light purple, 12 to 18 in., Thibet ; cardinale, scarlet, summer, 3 to 6 ft., California ; cashmirianum, blue, July, 18 in., Kashmir ; cheilanthum, dark blue, summer, 2 to 3 ft., Dahuria ; elatum, blue, June, 2 to 3 ft., Alps ; formosum, azure blue, summer, 2 to 4 ft., Armenia ; grandiflorum (Syn. sinense), blue or white, June to Sept., 1 to 3 ft., Siberia ; nudicaule, red, Aug., 12 to 18 in., California ; ochroleucum, soft yellow, summer, 3 to 4 ft., Levant and Caucasus, and its variety sulphureum ; Pylzowi, violet blue, summer, 6 to 10 in., China ; tatsiense, azure blue, summer, 12 to 18 in., China ; trolliifolium, bright blue, April to May, 1½ to 3 ft., N.W. America ; Zalil, yellow, summer, 6 ft., Syria. Latter best grown as a biennial. See trade lists for varieties. The popular garden delphiniums are hybrids between several species such as D. elatum, D. cheilanthum and D. formosum.

Dendrobium—Ord. Orchidaceæ. Stove epiphytal evergreen and deciduous orchids. First introduced 1801.
CULTURE : Compost, equal parts peat, living sphagnum moss, and charcoal. Position, erect species in well-drained pots ; drooping species in baskets and on blocks or rafts of wood. Place in pots, etc. Feb. or March. Water freely April to Sept., very little afterwards. Apply weak liquid manure occasionally during growing season. Temp., March to Sept. 75° to 85° ; Sept. to Feb. 60° to 65° ;

Feb. to March 65° to 75°. Growing period, March to Aug. Resting period, Oct,
to Feb. Flowers appear before or after resting on old or new pseudo-bulbs.
PROPAGATION : By offsets or cuttings of pseudo-bulbs inserted in well-drained pots
of peat and sphagnum moss under bell-glass, in temp. 85° to 95° at any time.
SPECIES CULTIVATED : D. atro-violaceum, creamy white and purple, spring, New
Guinea ; aureum, yellow and crimson, fragrant, spring, 18 in., India ; barbatulum,
white, March, 1 ft., India ; Bensonæ, creamy white, orange and purple, May, 2 ft.,
Moulmein ; bigibbum, purple, autumn, 18 in., N. Australia ; brymerianum, yellow
and orange, fragrant, spring, 18 in., Burma ; chrysanthum, yellow and purple,
winter, 4 to 6 ft., Nepaul ; chrysotoxum, yellow and orange, March, 1 ft., Moulmein ; crassinode, magenta-purple and white, Jan. and Feb., 2 ft., Siam ; Dearei,
white, summer, 3 ft., Philippines ; densiflorum, yellow and orange, spring, 18 in.,
India ; devonianum, cream, purple and orange, spring, 3 ft., India ; Falconeri,
white, purple and orange, May and June, 3 ft., N. India ; Farmeri, white, pink and
yellow, April and May, 18 in., India ; fimbriatum oculatum, orange-yellow and red,
March and April, 4 ft., India ; findlayanum, white, pink and yellow, Jan. and Feb.,
18 in., Moulmein ; formosum giganteum, white and yellow, May, 18 in., Moulmein ;
infundibulum, white and yellow, summer, 2 ft., Moulmein ; jamesianum, white
and red, May, 18 in., Moulmein ; nobile, white, rosy purple and crimson, winter,
2 ft., India ; Phalænopsis, autumn, 12 to 18 in., N. Australia ; Pierardii, blush,
white and purple, winter, 18 in., India ; primulinum, rosy lilac and yellow, winter,
12 to 18 in., Burma ; pulchellum (Syn. D. dalhousianum), yellow, rose and crimson,
spring, 4 to 5 ft., Burma ; speciosum, creamy yellow and purple, spring, 12 in.,
Australia ; superbiens, magenta-rose and purple, spring, 3 to 4 ft., Philippines ;
thyrsiflorum, white, pink and orange, spring, 2 ft., Burma ; wardianum, white,
purple and yellow, winter, 2 ft., Assam.
HYBRIDS CULTIVATED : D. Ainsworthii, white and crimson-purple, spring ; Curtisii,
white, purple and yellow, fragrant, May ; dominianum, rosy purple and white,
spring ; nobile-wardianum, white, rose, purple and yellow, winter, and many others.

Dendrochilum—See Platyclinis.

Dendromecon—Ord. Papavaraceæ. Half-hardy, semi-woody shrub. Deciduous. First introduced about 1854.
CULTURE : Soil, good loam with sand and mortar rubble. Position, borders at the
foot of south walls. Plant, Nov.
PROPAGATION : By cuttings of well-ripened growth placed singly in sandy soil in
small pots during July and Aug. They should be stood in a propagator with a
little bottom heat till rooted.
SPECIES CULTIVATED : D. rigidum, yellow, summer, 2 to 10 ft., California.

Dentaria—Ord. Cruciferæ. Hardy perennials and alpines.
CULTURE : Soil, peaty loam with leaf-mould and sand. Position, moist shady
banks and margins of woodland. Plant, Oct. or March.
PROPAGATION : By division in spring.
SPECIES CULTIVATED : D. bulbifera (Syn. Cardamine bulbifera), pale purple, April,
1 to 2 ft., Britain ; enneaphylla, creamy white, April to May, 9 to 12 in., Alps ;
digitata, lavender-rose, April, 1 to 2 ft., Central Europe.

Deodar (*Cedrus Deodara*)—See Cedrus.

Desert Rod (*Eremostachys laciniata*)—See Eremostachys.

Desfontainea—Ord. Loganiaceæ. Hardy evergreen flowering shrub. **First**
introduced 1853. Leaves, oval, dark shiny green, with spiny margins.
OUTDOOR CULTURE : Compost, equal parts peat and loam. Position, sheltered
borders outdoors, or against south wall. Plant, Oct., Nov., or April.
GREENHOUSE CULTURE : Compost, equal parts peat, loam, charcoal, and sand.
Position, well-drained pots, tubs, or borders. Pot or plant, March or April.
Water moderately Oct. to March, freely afterwards.
PROPAGATION : By cuttings inserted in sandy peat and loam in well-drained pots
under bell-glass or hand-light in temp. 55° to 65° in spring.
SPECIES CULTIVATED : D. spinosa, scarlet and yellow, Aug., 2 to 4 ft., Chile.

Desmodium (Tick Trefoil ; Telegraph Plant)—Ord. Leguminosæ. Hardy and stove flowering shrubs and perennials. Leaves of stove species (D. gyrans) pinnate ; leaflets move rapidly up and down, especially during sunshine.

CULTURE OF STOVE SPECIES : Compost, equal parts peat, loam, and silver sand. Position, pots in plant stove. Pot, Feb., or March. Water moderately Oct. to Feb., freely afterwards. Temp., Sept. to March 55° to 65° ; March to Sept. 65° to 75°.

CULTURE OF HARDY SPECIES : Soil, ordinary. Position, open sunny borders. Plant, March.

CULTURE OF SHRUBBY SPECIES : Soil, light, well drained. Position, sunny borders. Plant, Nov.

PROPAGATION : Stove species by seeds sown in light sandy soil in temp. 75° to 80° in Feb. or March, or by cuttings inserted in sandy peat under bell-glass in temp. 75° to 80° in March or April ; hardy perennial species by division in March ; hardy shrubby species by division in spring.

STOVE SPECIES : D. gyrans (Telegraph Plant), violet, July, 2 to 3 ft., India.

HARDY PERENNIAL SPECIES : D. canadense (Tick Trefoil), purple, July, 3 ft., N. America.

HARDY SHRUB : D. tillæfolium, pale lilac to deep pink, Aug. to Oct., 2 to 4 ft., Himalayas. See also Lespedeza.

Deutzia (Japanese Snow-flower)—Ord. Saxifrageæ. Hardy deciduous flowering shrubs.

OUTDOOR CULTURE : Soil, ordinary. Position, sunny well-drained border. Plant, Oct. to Feb. Prune, June, shortening shoots that have flowered only.

POT CULTURE OF D. GRACILIS : Compost, two parts loam, one part decayed manure and sand. Pot, Oct. or Nov. Position, cold frame Nov. to Feb. ; greenhouse Feb. to May ; outdoors afterwards. Water very little Oct. to Feb., moderately Feb. to April, freely April to Oct. Temp., Feb. to May 55° to 65°. Plants will flower in cold greenhouse without heat if desired. Plant out deutzias that have flowered in heat in open garden for a year, then lift and repot.

PROPAGATION : By cuttings of young shoots, 3 in. long, inserted in sandy soil under bell-glass in cold frame in June or July, also of firm shoots, 10 to 12 in. long, inserted in ordinary soil outdoors in Nov., Dec., or Jan.

SPECIES CULTIVATED : D. corymbosa, white, June, 9 ft., Himalayas ; gracilis, white, April, 2 ft., Japan ; gracilis folius aureis, leaves variegated with yellow ; Lemoinei, white, May, 2 ft., hybrid ; longifolia, purplish rose, June, 4 to 6 ft., W. China ; purpurascens, white and purple, June, 6 to 7 ft., Yunnan ; scabra (Syn. crenata), white, June, 6 ft., Japan, and its varieties flore-pleno (double) and Watereri (rosy); setchuensis, white, May to June, 6 ft., China ; sieboldiana, white, June, 3 to 4 ft., Japan ; Vilmorinæ, white, 8 ft., W. China ; Wilsoni, white, May to June, 4 to 6 ft., Western and Central China.

Devil-in-a-Bush (*Nigella damascena*)—See Nigella.

Devil's Apple (*Mandragora officinarum*)—See Mandragora.

Devil's Fig—See Argemone.

Dew Berry (*Rubus cæsius*)—See Rubus.

Dianella (Flax Lily ; Paroo Lily)—Ord. Liliaceæ. Half-hardy fibrous-rooted perennials. Orn. foliage and fruiting plants. First introduced 1731.

OUTDOOR CULTURE : Compost, equal parts loam and peat. Position, sheltered borders ; S. of England only. Plant, Oct., March, or April.

GREENHOUSE CULTURE : Compost, equal parts peat, loam, leaf-mould, and sand. Position, well-drained pots in unheated greenhouse. Pot, Feb., March, or April. Water moderately Sept. to March, freely afterwards.

PROPAGATION : By seeds sown $\frac{1}{16}$ in. deep in light soil in temp. 55° to 65° in spring ; division of fibrous roots Oct. or March.

SPECIES CULTIVATED : D. cærulea, blue, May, 2 ft., Australia ; lævis, blue, spring, 2 ft., Australia.

Dianthus (Carnation; Pink; Picotee; Sweet William; Tree, Perpetual, American Carnation; Malmaison Carnation; Indian and Chinese Pink)—Ord. Caryophyllaceæ. Hardy perennials and biennials.

TYPES—Florists' Carnation : Flowers perfectly round. Bizarres : Ground colour one shade, marked or striped with another colour. Flakes : Ground colour of one shade, flaked with other colours. Selfs : One shade of colour only. Picotee : Ground colour of one tint, edged or margined with another. Border Carnation : Self-coloured, striped or flaked, laced or fringed, free flowering, some clove-scented, and robust growers. Margaret or Marguerite Carnation : A race of hybrid carnations with fringed, fragrant flowers of all shades of colour. Jacks : A race of coarse-growing, mostly single-flowered kinds, grown largely for sale, by costers. Pinks : Show or Laced, petals finely fringed, broad ends white with a velvet eye, or a velvet eye with laced velvet edges, and a white centre. Sweet Williams : Show type, smooth edged petals with dark centres ; Auricula-eyed, smooth edged petals, white eye, surrounded with crimson or other tints. Tree, Perpetual, or American Carnation : Habit, tall ; flowers, self, striped, or flaked, appearing all the year round. Malmaison : Habit, sturdy ; flowers, large, self-coloured.

CULTURE OF CARNATIONS AND PICOTEES : Soil, three parts decayed turfy loam, one part of equal proportions of well-decayed cow manure and river sand for exhibition kinds ; good, well drained, rich, ordinary soil for border kinds. Position, sunny beds or borders. Plant 12 in. apart in Oct. or March. Top-dress with decayed manure in April. Thin flower buds to one on each shoot in June, and place india-rubber band round calyx of flower to prevent bursting early in July. Stake flower stems in May. Apply liquid manure once a week when buds form. Suitable artificial manure : Sulphate of ammonia, ½ oz. , and kainit, ¼ oz. to 2 gallons of water. Shade exhibition blooms from hot sun.

POT CULTURE : Compost, as advised for exhibition culture. Position, cold frame, Oct. to Feb., cold greenhouse afterwards. Plant singly in 3 in. pots in Oct. ; two in an 8 in. pot in Feb. Water moderately Oct. to March, freely afterwards. Apply liquid manure once a week April to July. Thin buds to three on each shoot in May. Give plenty of air.

CULTURE OF TREE OR PERPETUAL CARNATIONS : Insert cuttings, *i.e.* points of shoots, 3 in. long, pulled out, and with few lower leaves removed, in well-drained pots of pure sand between Nov. and March. Place in a box or propagator, keep moist, and shaded from sun till rooted. Temp. 50° and slight bottom heat. When rooted, plant cuttings singly in small pots in compost of two parts sandy loam and one part equal proportions of leaf-mould and sand. Stand potted plants in temp. 45° to 55° till pots are filled with roots, then repot into larger pots in compost of two-thirds loam and one part equal proportions old manure, wood ashes, and sand, and handful of bone-meal to each peck of soil. Stop or pinch shoots at the third or fourth joint after first potting ; again at intervals when shoots are a few inches long, ceasing to do so in Sept. Feed with liquid manures when well rooted. Stand outdoors May to Sept., then house. Winter temp., 45° to 55°. Ventilate freely in fine weather. Syringe daily during spring and summer. May also be grown outdoors like border carnations.

CULTURE OF MALMAISON CARNATIONS : Propagate by layering shoots in July. Plant rooted layers in small pots in Aug. or Sept. Place in cold frame or green-house, and transfer to 5 or 6 in. pot in Oct. Water moderately during winter. Temp., 36° to 46°. Feed with liquid manure when buds form. Shade in spring from sun. Admit air freely on fine days.

CULTURE OF PINKS : Soil, ordinary, rich. Position, sunny borders. Plant 9 in. apart in autumn or spring. Thin shoots to four on each plant to ensure fine blooms. Feed with liquid manure in May and June.

CULTURE OF SWEET WILLIAMS : Soil, ordinary, rich. Position, sunny beds or borders. Plant 12 in. apart each way in autumn.

CULTURE OF BIENNIAL SPECIES : Sow seeds in gentle heat in spring, harden off seedlings in cold frame, and plant out in beds and borders in May to flower same season ; or, sow in open border in April, plant out in July to flower following year.

CULTURE OF PERENNIAL SPECIES : Soil, sandy loam. Position, sunny rockeries. Plant, Oct. or March.
PROPAGATION : Carnations, pinks, and picotees by seeds sown in sandy soil in heat or in cold frames in spring ; pinks by cuttings or pipings in cold frames in summer ; carnations and picotees by layering in July or Aug. Sweet Williams by seeds sown outdoors in April or July ; cuttings in cold frames in summer ; perennial species by cuttings in July or seeds in spring in cold frame.
BIENNIAL SPECIES : D. sinensis (Chinese or Indian Pink), various colours, 6 to 12 in., Central Asia.
PERENNIAL SPECIES : D. alpestris, pink, summer, 6 in., Alps ; alpinus, rose, crimson, summer, 3 to 4 in., Alps ; anatolicus, pale pink and yellow, summer, 1 to 3 ft., Asia Minor ; arenarius, white, purple, summer, 6 in., N. Europe ; atrorubens, red, summer, 1 ft., S. Europe ; barbatus (Sweet William), various colours, 1 to 2 ft., S. Europe ; cæsius (Cheddar Pink), rose, fragrant, July, 3 to 6 in., Britain, and its varieties arvernensis and suavis ; callizonus, pale pink and maroon, 2 to 4 in., Alps ; Carthusianorum, crimson, 1 to 2 ft., Europe ; Caryophyllus (Carnation, Clove), various, 18 to 24 in., Europe; cruentus, scarlet, summer, 18 in., E. Europe; deltoides (Maiden Pink), rose and white, summer, 6 to 9 in., Britain; fragrans, white, summer, 6 in., Caucasus; fimbriatus, rose, summer, 12 to 16 in., Europe and Asia; glacialis (Glacier Pink), purple, summer, 4 in., S. Europe, and its variety Freynii (cushion); graniticus, pink, June to Sept., trailing, Europe; Knappii, yellow, May to July, 6 in., Europe ; microlepis, pink or white, summer, cushion, Transylvania ; monspessulanus, pink, June to July, 9 to 12 in., S. Europe ; neglectus, rose, summer, 2 in., Pyrenees ; petræus, rose, summer, 6 in., E. Europe ; plumarius (Pink), various, 12 in., E. Europe ; Seguieri, rosy purple, June to July, 9 to 12 in., S. Europe ; squarrosus, white or pink, summer, 9 to 12 in., Crimea ; Sternbergii, rose, summer, 6 in., S. Europe ; superbus (Fringed Pink), rose, summer, 9 to 18 in., Europe ; sylvestris, rose-pink, May to July, 9 to 12 in., Alps. There are numerous hybrid forms and races in cultivation.

Diapensia—Ord. Diapensiaceæ. Hardy dwarf evergreen alpine shrubs. First introduced 1801.
CULTURE : Soil, deep sandy peat mixed with stones. Position, exposed on sunny rockery. Water freely June, July and Aug. Plant, March or April.
PROPAGATION : By division of plants in March or April.
SPECIES CULTIVATED : D. lapponica, white, July, 3 in., Northern Regions.

Diascia—Ord. Scrophulariaceæ. Half-hardy annual. First introduced 1871.
INDOOR CULTURE : Compost, two parts sandy loam and one part leaf-mould and sand. Sow seeds in a temp. of 60° in March or April. Transplant seedlings when the third leaf forms, four or five in a 4½ in. pot. Grow on shelf near the glass. Water freely when flower buds form. Give weak liquid manure occasionally. Shoots may require to be supported by twiggy sticks.
OUTDOOR CULTURE : Sow seeds in temp. of 60° in March or April. Transplant in pots or boxes when large enough to handle. Gradually harden off in cold frame, and plant out in good ordinary soil in sunny position at the end of May.
SPECIES CULTIVATED : D. Barberæ, rosy pink, summer, 1 ft., S. Africa.

Dicentra (Bleeding Heart ; Lyre Flower ; Dutchman's Breeches)—Ord. Fumariaceæ. Hardy herbaceous tuberous and fibrous-rooted perennials. First introduced 1731.
CULTURE : Soil, deep light rich sandy. Position, warm sheltered borders ; dwarf species on rockeries. Plant, Oct., Nov., March, or April. Protect during winter by covering with layers of ashes or manure. Top-dress with decayed manure in March.
POT CULTURE OF D. SPECTABILIS : Compost, equal parts loam, leaf-mould and sand. Pot, Oct. or Nov. Position, cold frame Oct. to Feb. ; greenhouse Feb. to May ; afterwards planting out in borders. Water moderately when new growth begins, freely when in full growth. Apply liquid manure once or twice weekly when flower buds appear.
FORCING D. SPECTABILIS : Pot, Oct. Place in cold frame till Jan. Transfer to

remp. 55°, to 65° in Jan. After forcing, plant out in open border. Plants should only be forced in pots one year.
PROPAGATION : By dividing the crowns in Feb., March, or April ; cuttings of fleshy roots 2 in. long inserted in sandy soil in temp. 55° in March or April.
SPECIES CULTIVATED : D. canadensis, white, May, 6 in., N. America ; Cucullaria (Dutchman's Breeches), white and yellow, spring, 6 in., United States ; eximia, reddish purple, April to Sept., 12 in., N. Carolina ; formosa, red, May, 6 in., N. America ; spectabilis (Syn. Dielytra spectabilis), the Chinaman's Breeches or Bleeding Heart, rosy crimson, spring and summer, 2 ft., Siberia and Japan.

Dichæa—Ord. Orchidaceæ. Stove epiphytal orchid. First introduced 1870.
CULTURE : Compost, fresh sphagnum moss. Position, blocks of wood suspended from roof of stove. Water daily. Temp., March to Aug. 65° to 85° ; Aug. to March 50° to 60°.
PROPAGATION : By division of plants in Feb. or March.
SPECIES CULTIVATED : D. picta, green and purple, winter, Trinidad.

Dichorisandra—Ord. Commelinaceæ. Stove ornamental-leaved and flowering perennials.
CULTURE : Compost, one-third each of peat, loam, and leaf-mould and a little silver sand. Position, pots in shady part of stove. Pot in March. Water freely March to Oct., moderately afterwards. Syringe daily in spring and summer. Temp., March to Oct. 75° to 85° ; Oct. to March 55° to 65°.
PROPAGATION : By seeds in spring ; division in March.
SPECIES CULTIVATED : D. mosaica, leaves green marked with white, 2 ft., Peru ; pubescens tæniensis, leaves striped with white, 2 ft., Brazil ; thyrsiflora, blue, autumn, 5 to 10 ft., Brazil.

Dicksonia (Tasmanian Tree Fern ; New Zealand Tree Fern)—Ord. Filices. Stove and greenhouse tree ferns. First introduced 1786.
CULTURE : Compost, two-thirds peat and loam, and abundance of sand. Position, large pots or tubs well drained in shady stove, greenhouse or conservatory. Repot, Feb., March. Water moderately Oct. to March, freely afterwards. Syringe trunks daily March to Sept. Temp., Sept. to March 55° to 65° for stove, 45° to 55° for greenhouse ; March to Sept. 65° to 75° for stove, 55° to 65° for greenhouse. Shade in summer essential.
PROPAGATION : By spores sown at any time on surface of finely sifted loam and peat in well-drained pots covered with a sheet of glass, and kept moist.
STOVE SPECIES : D. Lathami, 10 to 15 ft., hybrid ; Schiedei, 10 to 15 ft., Guatemala and Mexico.
GREENHOUSE SPECIES : D. antarctica (Tasmanian Tree Fern), 18 to 20 ft., Tasmania ; Barometz, 18 to 20 ft., China and Malay ; Culcita (Cushion Fern), dwarf, Madeira ; squarrosa (New Zealand Tree Fern), 15 to 20 ft., New Zealand.

Dictamnus (Burning Bush ; Dittany ; Fraxinella ; Gas plant)—Ord. Rutaceæ. Hardy herbaceous perennial. First introduced 1596. Foliage, fragrant.
CULTURE : Soil, ordinary, dryish. Position, sunny or partially shady borders. Plant, Oct., Nov., March, or April.
PROPAGATION : By seeds sown ¼ in. deep in light soil outdoors in Aug. or Sept. ; cuttings of fleshy roots inserted 2 in. deep in frame in March or April ; division of roots in Oct., Nov. or March.
SPECIES CULTIVATED : D. albus (Syn. D. Fraxinella), white, May, 3 ft., Europe ; albus purpureus, purplish, May, 3 ft.

Dictyosperma—Ord. Palmaceæ. Stove palms. Orn. foliage. First introduced 1842. Leaves pinnate.
CULTURE : Compost, equal parts loam, leaf-mould, and sand. Position, pots in shady moist plant stove. Pot, Feb. or March. Water freely at all times. Temp., March to Sept. 70° to 85° ; Sept. to March 60° to 65°.
PROPAGATION : By seeds sown 1 in. deep in pots of sandy peat in temp. 85° in Feb., March, or April.
SPECIES CULTIVATED : D. album, 15 to 20 ft., Mauritius ; aureum, 10 ft., Mauritius ; tibrosum, 5 ft., Madagascar.

F   141

Didiscus—See Trachymene.

Didymocarpus—Ord. Gesneraceæ. Stove perennial herbs. First introduced 1845.

CULTURE : Compost, equal parts peat and loam, one-fourth part cow dung and sand. Position, well-drained pots in moist plant stove. Pot, Feb., March, or April. Water moderately Oct. to Feb., freely afterwards. Temp., Sept. to March 55° to 65° ; March to Sept. 65° to 75°.

PROPAGATION : By cuttings of young side shoots inserted in sandy soil under bell-glass in temp. 80° to 85° in March or April.

SPECIES CULTIVATED : D. humboldtiana, lilac, autumn, 3 to 4 in., Ceylon ; malayana, yellow, summer, 4 to 6 in., Malaya.

Didymochlæna—Ord. Filices. Stove fern. First introduced 1838.

CULTURE : Compost, two parts loam, one peat, pounded charcoal and sand. Pot, Feb. or March. Position, well-drained pots in shady part of greenhouse. Water moderately Oct. to Feb., freely afterwards. Temp., Sept. to March 60° to 70° ; March to Sept. 70° to 80°.

PROPAGATION : By spores sown on surface of sandy peat under bell-glass in temp. 70° to 80° at any time.

SPECIES CULTIVATED : D. lunulata, tree-like habit, Tropics.

Dieffenbachia (Dumb Cane)—Ord. Aroideæ. Stove evergreen perennials. Orn. foliage. First introduced 1863. Leaves, broad, deep green, variegated with white or yellow.

CULTURE : Compost, equal parts peat and loam, one-fourth part decayed manure and silver sand. Position, well-drained pots in moist plant stove. Pot, Feb. or March. Water moderately Sept. to Feb., freely afterwards. Syringe daily June, July, and Aug. Shade in summer essential. Temp., Sept. to Feb. 55° to 65° ; Feb. to Sept. 65° to 85°.

PROPAGATION : By cuttings of stems 1 to 2 in. long inserted in sandy soil under bell-glass in temp. 75° to 85° in spring.

SPECIES CULTIVATED : D. Bausei, leaves yellowish green, blotched dark green and spotted white, hybrid ; Carderi, leaves variegated, Colombia ; Chelsoni, leaves green and yellow, Colombia ; Jenmani, pea-green leaves with elongated blotches, British Guiana ; magnifica, leaves green and white, Venezuela ; picta (Syn. Shuttle-worthi), leaves dull green and white or yellow, S. America ; Regina, leaves white and green, S. America ; Rex, leaves white and green, S. America ; Sequine (Syns. Leopoldii and nobilis), leaves green and white, Brazil.

Dielytra—See Dicentra.

Dierama (Wandflower)—Ord. Iridaceæ. Hardy bulbous-rooted plant with sword-shaped leaves and long graceful flower stems.

CULTURE : Soil, light or sandy. Position, well-drained border at base of a south wall. Plant bulbs 3 in. deep and 3 in. apart in Nov. Lift and replant every third year.

PROPAGATION : By offsets from old bulbs.

SPECIES CULTIVATED : D. pulcherrima (Syn. Sparaxis pulcherrima), blood red, Sept., 3 to 4 ft. ; D. pendula, lilac, Sept., 4 ft., S. Africa.

Diervilla (Bush Honeysuckle)—Ord. Caprifoliaceæ. Hardy deciduous shrubs. First introduced 1739. Formerly known by the generic name of Weigela.

CULTURE : Soil, ordinary. Position, moist shady shrubberies, or against south, east, or west walls or fences. Plant, Oct. to Feb. Prune directly after flowering, shortening shoots that have borne flowers. No winter pruning required.

PROPAGATION : By cuttings of young shoots inserted in pots of sandy soil under bell-glass in cool greenhouse in spring ; cuttings of firm shoots 6 in. long inserted 3 in. deep and 2 in. apart in north border under hand-light in Oct. or Nov.

SPECIES CULTIVATED : D. floribunda, purple, June, 3 ft., Japan ; florida (Syn. Weigela rosea), rose and white, May, 6 to 8 ft., China ; grandiflora, pink, June, 6 to 8 ft., Japan ; japonica, pale rose, summer, 4 ft., Japan, and its white variety hortensis ; middendorfiana, yellow, summer, 4 ft., Siberia ; sessilifolia, sulphur yellow, July to Aug., 2 to 3 ft., South-eastern U.S.A.   Abel Carrière, Eva Rathke, Van Houttei, and variegata are popular varieties or hybrids.

Digitalis (Foxglove)—Ord. Scrophulariaceæ.   Hardy biennial and perenial herbs.

CULTURE OF PERENNIAL SPECIES : Soil, rich ordinary. Position, open shady border, or naturalised in woodlands and wild gardens.   Plant, Oct. or April.
CULTURE OF BIENNIAL SPECIES : Sow seeds ⅛ in. deep in shady border outdoors in April.   Transplant seedlings 3 in. apart in shady bed in June.   Transfer seedlings to flowering position in Oct. or Nov.
PROPAGATION : Perennials by seeds sown as directed for biennials ; division of plants in March.
PERENNIAL SPECIES : D. ambigua (Syn. D. grandiflora and ochroleuca), yellow, July and Aug., 3 ft., Europe ; Thapsi, rosy purple, June to Aug., 2 to 4 ft., Western Europe.
BIENNIAL SPECIES : D. gloxinioides, rose-pink and purple, summer, 4 to 6 ft. ; lanata, grey and white or purple, summer, 2 to 3 ft., S.E. Europe ; purpurea (Foxglove), purple, July to Sept., 3 to 5 ft., Europe (Britain).   There are numerous varieties and hybrid strains to be found in trade lists.

Dill—See Peucedanum.

Dillwynia—Ord. Leguminosæ.   Greenhouse evergreen flowering shrubs.   First introduced 1794.
CULTURE : Compost, equal parts fibry peat and loam, one-fourth part sand.   Position, pots in sunny greenhouse.   Pot, March or June ; firm potting essential.   Prune straggling shoots little after flowering.   Water freely March to Sept., moderately afterwards.   Temp., March to Sept. 60° to 65° ; Sept. to March 45° to 50°.   Place plants outdoors July to Sept. to mature growth.
PROPAGATION : By seeds sown ⅛ in. deep in light sandy compost in temp. 65° to 70° in March ; cuttings inserted in pots of sandy peat under bell-glass in temp. 65° in summer.
SPECIES CULTIVATED : D. ericifolia, yellow and red, spring, 2 ft., Australia ; floribunda, yellow and red, spring, 18 in., Australia ; hispida, orange and red, spring, 1 ft., Australia.

Dimorphanthus mandschuricus—See Aralia chinensis.

Dimorphotheca—Ord. Compositæ.   Half-hardy annuals and perennials.   Usually grown as annuals.   First introduced 1774.
INDOOR CULTURE : Compost, two parts sandy loam, one part leaf-mould and a liberal addition of silver sand.   Pot, March or April.   Grow in cool sunny greenhouse.   Water freely during spring and summer, moderately in autumn and winter.   Temp., Oct. to March 40° to 50°.
OUTDOOR CULTURE : Soil, ordinary, sandy.   Position, sunny, warm border.   Plant, May and June.
PROPAGATION : By seeds sown in a temp. of 55° to 65° in sandy soil in early spring.
SPECIES CULTIVATED : D. aurantiaca, white, red, yellow, or orange, summer, 2 ft. ; Ecklonis, white and purple, summer, 2 ft. ; pluvialis, white and purple, summer, 18 in. ; pluvialis flore-pleno, double.   Native of S. Africa.   There are hybrid forms in cultivation.

Dionæa (Venus' Fly-trap)—Ord. Droseraceæ.   Greenhouse herbaceous perennial.   Insectivorous.   Leaves, two-lobed, margined with teeth and sensitive.
CULTURE : Compost, equal parts peat and living sphagnum.   Position, pots or pans well drained and partly immersed in pans of water, and placed under glass in cool greenhouse.   Pot, March or April.   Water freely always.   Temp., Oct. to March 40° to 45° ; March to Sept. 45° to 55°.
PROPAGATION : By seeds sown in mixture of sphagnum moss and peat, kept moist under bell-glass in March or April ; division of plants in March.
SPECIES CULTIVATED : D. muscipula, white, July and Aug., 6 in., Carolina.

Dioscorea (Yam)—Ord. Dioscoreaceæ.   Hardy tuberous-rooted climbing perennials.   Tubers, large, milky, edible, cooked like potatoes.
CULTURE : Soil, ordinary.   Position, sunny, open.   Plant small tubers 3 in. deep and 12 in. apart in March.   Fix stakes or branches for shoots to climb on.   Lift and store tubers in frost-proof place in Oct.
PROPAGATION : By cuttings of stems 1 in. long with leaf attached, inserted ¼ in. deep in sandy soil under bell-glass in temp. 55° in summer.
SPECIES CULTIVATED : D. Batatas (Chinese Yam), white, summer, 12 ft., Philippines.

Diosma (African Steel-bush)—Ord. Rutaceæ.   Greenhouse evergreen flowering shrub.   Leaves, fragrant.
CULTURE : Compost, two parts fibrous peat, one part loam, and silver sand.   Pot, May, June.   Pinch off points of vigorous shoots in July and Aug.   Water very little Oct. to March, moderately afterwards.   Temp., Sept. to March 40° to 45°; March to Sept. 50° to 55°.
PROPAGATION : By cuttings inserted in sandy peat under bell-glass in temp. 55° to 65° in March, April, or May.
SPECIES CULTIVATED : D. ericoides, white, spring, 2 to 3 ft., S. Africa.

Diospyros (Date Plum ; Persimmon)—Ord. Ebenaceæ.   Hardy deciduous or semi-evergreen trees.   First introduced 1596.   Fruit yellow, plum-shaped, sweet flavour.
CULTURE : Soil, ordinary.   Position, shrubberies for D. armata, D. Lotus and D. virginiana ; south wall for D. Kaki, except in extreme S. of England.   Plant, Oct. to Feb.   Prune similarly to apple trees.
PROPAGATION : By seeds sown 1 in. deep outdoors in Sept. or Oct.
SPECIES CULTIVATED : D. armata, yellow fruits, 20 ft., Central China ; Kaki (Chinese Persimmon), white and green, spring, yellow fruits, 12 to 20 ft., China ; Lotus (Common Date Plum), reddish white, July, purple or yellow fruits, 20 to 30 ft., S. Europe ; virginiana (Persimmon), yellow, July, pale yellow and red fruits, 20 to 30 ft., N. America.

Dipelta—Ord. Caprifoliaceæ.   Hardy deciduous shrub.   Introduced 1902.
CULTURE : Soil, moist loam.   Position, sunny sheltered shrubberies.   Plant, autumn.   Prune away dead wood only.
PROPAGATION : By cuttings inserted in cold frame in autumn.
SPECIES CULTIVATED : D. floribunda, pink and yellow, fragrant, May and June, 10 to 15 ft., W. China ; ventricosa, deep rose and orange, May, 6 to 15 ft., W. China.

Diphylleia (Umbrella-leaf)—Ord. Berberidaceæ.   Hardy herbaceous perennial First introduced 1812.
CULTURE : Soil, peaty.   Position, moist shady borders.   Plant, Oct. to March.
PROPAGATION : By division of plants in March or April.
SPECIES CULTIVATED : D. cymosa, white, May, 1 ft., N. America.

Diplacus—See Mimulus.

Dipladenia—Ord. Apocynaceæ.   Stove flowering climbers.   Evergreen.   First introduced 1841.
CULTURE : Compost, rough fibry peat and one-fourth silver sand.   Position, well-drained pots, with shoots trained to roof of stove or to wire trellis.   Pot, Feb. or March.   Prune, Oct., cutting away shoots that have flowered only.   Water very little Oct. to Feb., moderately Feb. to April, freely afterwards.   Temp., Oct. to Feb. 55° to 60° ; Feb. to Oct. 65° to 75°.
PROPAGATION : By cuttings of young side shoots 3 in. long inserted in pots of sandy peat under bell-glass in temp. 80° in Feb., March, or April.
SPECIES CULTIVATED : D. atropurpurea, purple, summer, 10 ft., Brazil ; boliviensis, white and yellow, summer, 8 to 10 ft., Bolivia ; Sanderi, rose, summer, 10 ft., Brazil ; splendens, white, rose and purple, summer, 8 to 12 ft., Brazil, and its varieties amabilis (rosy crimson), brearleyana (crimson), hybrida (crimson-red), and profusa (carmine).   See also Odontodenia.

Diplopappus—See Cassinia.

Disa (Flower of the Gods; Table Mountain Orchid)—Ord. Orchidaceæ. Greenhouse terrestrial orchids. First introduced 1825.
CULTURE: Compost, equal parts peat and living sphagnum moss. Position, pots or pans, well drained, in shady cold greenhouse Sept. to June; shady corner outdoors June to Sept. Pot, Feb., keeping roots well above rim. Water moderately Sept. to March, freely afterwards. Atmosphere airy, but not draughty. Resting period, autumn. Growing period, Dec. to June. Flowers appear in centre of new growth.
PROPAGATION: By seeds sown on living sphagnum moss under bell-glass in cold greenhouse in spring.
SPECIES CULTIVATED: D. grandiflora, crimson, July, 1 ft., S. Africa; racemosa, rosy purple, summer, 18 in., S. Africa; tripetaloides, creamy white, pale pink and crimson, South Africa. Several hybrids are cultivated such as kewensis, Luma and Veitchii. These have flowers in all shades of pink and rosy purple and are summer blooming.

Distaff Thistle—See Carthamus.

Dittany (*Dictamnus albus*)—See Dictamnus.

Dittany of Crete (*Origanum dictamnus*)—See Origanum.

Divi-Divi (*Cæsalpinia coriaria*)—See Cæsalpinia.

Dodecatheon (American Cowslip)—Ord. Primulaceæ. Hardy herbaceous perennials. First introduced 1744.
OUTDOOR CULTURE: Soil, light loam enriched with plenty of leaf-mould. Position, sheltered beds on rockeries, or in borders under shade of trees. Plant, Jan. or Feb. Top-dress in Feb. with well-decayed manure.
POT CULTURE: Compost, equal parts loam, leaf-mould, and sand. Position, 6 in. pots, well drained, in cold frame Nov. to March, then in unheated greenhouse till after flowering, when stand outdoors. Pot, Nov. Water moderately when new growth appears, freely when in full growth.
PROPAGATION: By seeds sown in pots of light sandy soil in cold frame in Sept. or March; division of crowns in Oct. or March.
SPECIES CULTIVATED: D. Clevelandii, violet blue, May, 1 ft., California; Hendersoni, crimson and yellow, March, 6 in., Oregon; Jeffreyi, purple-rose, spring, 6 in., California; Lemoinei, shades of amaranth and purple, May to July, 1½ to 2 ft, hybrid; Meadia, rosy purple, white and lilac, April, 12 in., N. America; Meadia album, white; Meadia lilacinum, lilac.

Dog-berry (*Cornus sanguinea*)—See Cornus.

Dog Rose (*Rosa canina*)—See Rosa.

Dog-wood—See Cornus.

Dog's-Tooth Violet (*Erythronium Dens-canis*)—See Erythronium.

Dog Violet (*Viola canina*)—See Viola.

Dolichos (Hyacinth Bean)—Ord. Leguminosæ. Greenhouse evergreen twiner. First introduced 1776.
CULTURE: Compost, equal parts loam and peat, little sand. Position, well-drained pots, shoots twining round trellis, posts or pillars. Pot, Feb. Water moderately in winter, freely in summer. Temp., Sept. to March 50° to 55°; March to Sept. 55° to 65°.
PROPAGATION: By seeds sown in light soil in temp. 65° in March; cuttings inserted in sandy soil under bell-glass in temp. 65° in April.
SPECIES CULTIVATED: D. Lablab, rosy purple, July, 1 to 2 ft., Tropics.

Dombeya—Ord. Sterculiaceæ. Stove ornamental evergreen trees. First introduced 1820.
CULTURE: Compost, equal parts sandy loam and fibrous peat. Position, large pots or borders in warm greenhouse. Temp., March to Oct. 75° to 90°; Oct. to March 65° to 75°. Water freely during growing season.

PROPAGATION : By cuttings of nearly ripe wood in sandy soil under hand-light in April. Temp. 80°.
SPECIES CULTIVATED : D. natalensis, white, fragrant, Natal ; spectabilis, white, 20 to 30 ft., East Trop. Africa ; Wallichi, scarlet, 20 to 30 ft., Madagascar.

Dondia epipactis—See Hacquetia epipactis.

Doodia—Ord. Filices. Greenhouse evergreen ferns. Nat. Australia. First introduced 1808.
CULTURE : Compost, two parts loam, one part leaf-mould, charcoal and sand. Pot, Feb., March or April. Position, pots in shady part of greenhouse. Water moderately Sept. to March, freely afterwards. Temp., Sept. to March 40° to 50 ° ; March to Sept. 50° to 60°.
PROPAGATION : By spores sown on surface of sandy peat in pans under bell-glass in temp. 65° to 75° at any time.
SPECIES CULTIVATED : D. aspera, 6 to 8 in., Australia, and its varieties corymbifera and multifida ; caudata, 6 to 12 in., Australia ; media, 12 to 18 in., Australia and New Zealand.

Doronicum (Leopard's-bane)—Ord. Compositæ. Hardy herbaceous perennials.
CULTURE : Soil, ordinary, rich. Position, open borders, banks, or under shade of trees. Plant, Oct., Nov., March, or April. This genus also does well in pots for early flowering in cold greenhouse.
PROPAGATION : By division of roots in Oct. or March.
SPECIES CULTIVATED : D. austriacum, yellow, March, 18 in., Europe ; caucasicum, yellow, April, 1 ft., Europe ; pardalianches, yellow, May, 2 ft., Europe (Britain) ; plantagineum, yellow, March, 3 ft., Europe (Britain) ; plantagineum excelsum, an improved form.

Doryanthes (Australian Giant Lily ; Spear Lily)—Ord. Amaryllidaceæ. Greenhouse flowering plants. Orn. foliage. First introduced 1800.
CULTURE : Equal parts loam and leaf-mould, little sand. Position, well-drained pots in light airy greenhouse. Pot, Feb., March, or April. Water very little Sept. to April, moderately afterwards. Temp., Sept. to March 50° to 55° ; March to Sept. 65° to 70°.
PROPAGATION : By suckers removed from old plants and placed in small pots in temp. 55° to 65° at any time.
SPECIES CULTIVATED : D. excelsa, scarlet, summer, 8 to 12 ft., N.S. Wales ; Guilfoylei, crimson, summer, 12 to 15 ft., Queensland ; Palmeri, red, summer, 12 ft., Queensland.

Double Bindweed (*Calystegia hederacea*)—See Calystegia.

Double Cherry (*Prunus Cerasus Rhexii*)—See Prunus.

Double Chinese Cherry (*Prunus japonica fl.-pl.*)—See Prunus.

Double Dropwort (*Filipendula hexapetala flore-pleno*)—See Filipendula.

Double Furze (*Ulex europæus plenus*)—See Ulex.

Double Marsh Marigold (*Caltha palustris fl.-pl.*)—See Caltha.

Double Mayweed (*Matricaria inodora fl.-pl.*)—See Matricaria.

Double Peach (*Prunus Persica flore-pleno*)—See Prunus.

Double Persian Ranunculus (*Ranunculus asiaticus fl.-pl.*)—See Ranunculus.

Double Red Campion (*Lychnis dioica fl.-pl.*)—See Lychnis.

Double Red Daisy (*Bellis perennis rubra plena*)—See Bellis.

Double Rose Campion (*Lychnis coronaria fl.-pl.*)—See Lychnis.

Double Scarlet Avens (*Geum coccineum fl.-pl.*)—See Geum.

Douglasia—Ord. Primulaceæ. Hardy evergreen alpine plants. First introduced 1827.
CULTURE : Compost, equal parts peat and loam. Position, sunny rockery. Plant, Oct., Nov., March, or April.
PROPAGATION : By seeds sown ⅛ in. deep in sandy peat in cold frame, or under hand-light in March or April ; division of plants in autumn.
SPECIES CULTIVATED : D. lævigata, rosy pink, March to Sept., 1 in., Oregon Mountains ; nivalis, pink, April, 1 in., Rocky Mountains ; Vitaliana (Syn. Androsace Vitaliana), yellow, May to July, 2 in., Alps.

Dovaston Yew Tree (*Taxus baccata* var. *Dovastoni*)—See Taxus.

Dovedale Moss (*Saxifraga hypnoides*)—See Saxifraga.

Dove Orchid (*Peristeria elata*)—See Peristeria.

Downingia—Ord. Campanulaceæ. Hardy annuals. First introduced 1827.
CULTURE : Soil, ordinary, rich. Position, sunny beds or borders. Sow seeds where plants are to flower in April. Thin seedlings to 6 in. apart in May or June.
POT CULTURE : Compost, equal parts loam, leaf-mould and sand. Sow seeds ⅛ in. deep in 5 or 6 in. pots placed in temp. 55°, or in cold frame in April or May. Water moderately. Apply weak liquid manure when plants are in flower. Place plants when in flower in cool greenhouse or window.
SPECIES CULTIVATED : D. elegans (Syn. Clintonia elegans), blue and white, summer, 6 in., N.W. America ; pulchella (Syn. Clintonia pulchella), blue, white, and yellow, summer, 6 in., W. America.

Down Thistle (*Onopordon Acanthium*)—See Onopordon.

Draba (Whitlow Grass)—Ord. Cruciferæ. Hardy perennials. Pretty rockery plants.
CULTURE : Soil, ordinary. Position, crevices in sunny rockeries, or on old walls. Plant, March or April.
PROPAGATION : By seeds sown where plants are to grow or in pans of sandy soil in April ; division of roots in March.
SPECIES CULTIVATED : D. aizoides, yellow, March, 3 in., Europe (Britain) ; Aizoon, yellow, April, 3 in., W. Europe ; alpina, yellow, April, 3 in., N. Europe ; bruniæfolia, yellow, June, 3 in., Caucasus ; dedeana, white, May, 3 in., Spain ; imbricata, yellow, spring, 1 in., Caucasus ; Mawii, white, spring, 3 in., Spain ; olympica, golden yellow, 3 in., Asia Minor ; pyrenaica, lilac-purple, fragrant, April, 3 in., S. Europe.

Dracæna (Dragon-plant ; Dragon Tree)—Ord. Liliaceæ. Stove evergreen plants. Orn. foliage. First introduced 1640. Leaves, variegated with various colours.
CULTURE : Compost, two parts peat, one part loam and sand. Position, well-drained pots in light part of stove. Pot, Feb. to March. Water moderately Oct. to March, freely afterwards. Temp., March to Sept. 75° to 85° ; Sept. to March 55° to 65°.
PROPAGATION : By seeds sown 1 in. deep in pots of light sandy soil in temp. 85° in March ; cuttings of main stems cut into lengths of 1 in. and partially buried horizontally in pots of sandy soil in March ; cuttings of fleshy roots inserted 1 in. deep in pots of sandy soil in temp. 75° to 80° in March or April ; stem-rooting March or April ; offsets inserted 2 in. deep at any time.
SPECIES CULTIVATED : D. concinna, leaves green, margined with red, 4 to 6 ft., Madagascar ; deremensis (Syn. Pleomele deremensis), leaves long and pointed, 10 to 15 ft., Upper Guinea ; Draco (Dragon Tree), leaves glaucous, hardy in Cornwall and Scilly Isles, 40 to 50 ft., Canary Islands ; fragrans (Syn. Pleomele fragrans), leaves green, 15 to 20 ft., Trop. Africa ; fragrans Lindenii, leaves yellow and green ; fragrans massangeana, leaves white and green ; godseffiana (Syn. Pleomele godseffiana), leaves white and green, 3 ft., Trop. Africa ; goldieana (Syn. Pleomele

goldieana), leaves green and white, 4 to 6 ft., Trop. Africa ; sanderiana (Syn. Pleomele sanderiana), leaves white and green, 5 ft., Trop. Africa. See also Cordy-line. Many varieties are offered in trade lists.

Dracocephalum (Dragon's-head ; Moldavian Balm)—Ord. Labiatæ. Hardy annual and perennial herbs. First introduced 1596.

CULTURE : Soil, light ordinary. Position, cool, partially shady borders. Plant, Oct., Nov., March, or April.

PROPAGATION : Annual and perennial species by seeds sown ⅛ in. deep in light sandy soil outdoors in April ; cuttings of young shoots inserted in light sandy soil under hand-light or in cold frame in April or May ; division of roots in Oct., Nov., or March.

ANNUAL SPECIES : D. Moldavica (Moldavian Balm), blue, July and Aug., 12 to 18 in., E. Sibeïia.

PERENNIAL SPECIES : D. austriacum, blue, summer, 12 to 18 in., Europe ; grandi-florum, blue, summer, 6 to 9 in., Siberia ; ruyschiana, purplish blue, June, 12 to 18 in., Alps ; speciosum, lilac, June, 18 in., Himalayas. See also Physostegia.

Dracunculus (Dragon ; Snake-plant)—Ord. Aroideæ. Hardy tuberous-rooted perennial. First introduced 1548. Leaves, flesh colour mottled with black, resembling skin of snake.

CULTURE : Soil, sandy. Position, well-drained sunny border. Plant tubers 3 in. deep in Oct. or Nov.

PROPAGATION : By division of tubers in Oct. or March.

SPECIES CULTIVATED : D. vulgaris (Syn. Arum dracunculus), chocolate brown, July, 3 ft., S. Europe.

Dragon Arum—See Dracunculus.

Dragon Plant—See Dracæna.

Dragon Tree (*Dracæna draco*)—See Dracæna.

Dragon's-head (*Dracocephalum grandiflorum*)—See Dracocephalum.

Dragon's-mouth—See Helicodiceros.

Dragon's-mouth Orchid—See Epidendrum.

Drimis—Ord. Magnoliaceæ. Hardy ornamental tree. Deciduous. First introduced 1827.

CULTURE : Soil, good loamy. Position, warm, sheltered borders. Plant, Oct.

PROPAGATION : By cuttings of ripened wood inserted in a cold frame in autumn, or by layering in spring.

SPECIES CULTIVATED : D. Winteri, ivory white, aromatic, April to May, 12 to 40 ft., S. America.

Drooping Urn Flower (*Urceolina pendula*)—See Urceolina.

Dropwort (*Filipendula hexapetala*)—See Filipendula.

Drosera (Sundew ; Youth-wort)—Ord. Droseraceæ. Greenhouse and hardy perennial insectivorous plants.

CULTURE : Compost, equal parts living sphagnum moss, peat, potsherds. Position, well-drained pots partly immersed in pan of water and covered with bell-glass in cool greenhouse. Water daily.

PROPAGATION : By seeds sown on surface of living sphagnum moss and peat in well-drained pots under bell-glass in temp. 55° to 65° at any time ; division of the crowns in March or April ; cuttings of roots ½ to 1 in. long embedded in pan of moss and peat under bell-glass in temp. 65° to 75°.

SPECIES CULTIVATED : D. binata, white, June to Sept., 3 to 4 in., Australia ; capensis, purple, June to July, 3 to 4 in., Cape of Good Hope ; longifolia (Syns. D. anglica and D. intermedia), white, July, 3 in., Europe (Britain) ; rotundifolia, white, July, 4 in., Europe (Britain).

Drosophyllum (Portuguese Sundew)—Ord. Droseraceæ. Greenhouse shrubby insectivorous plants. First introduced 1869.

CULTURE : Soil, light sandy loam. Position, well-drained pots close to glass in

Elæagnus pungens
(Oleaster)

Epacris hybrida
(Australian Heath)

Epidendrum Wallisii
(Dragon's-mouth Orchid)

Epilobium angustifolium
(Rose Bay Willow Herb)

Eragrostis japonica
(Feather Grass)

Eranthis hyemalis
(Winter Aconite)

Eremurus robustus

Erica carnea
(Heath)

Erigeron speciosus
Flea-bane)

Erinus alpinus

Eriogonum umbellatum

Erodium Sibthorpianum
(Heron's Bill)

Eryngium planum
(Sea Holly)

Erysimum asperum
(Siberian Wallflower)

Erysimum linifolium
(Alpine Wallflower)

Erythronium Dens-canis
(Dog's-tooth Violet)

Escallonia langleyensis
(Chilian Gum Box)

Eucalyptus Gunnii
(Australian Gum)

light airy greenhouse. Water moderately summer, little winter. Temp., Sept. to March 40° to 50° ; March to Sept. 50° to 60°.
PROPAGATION : By seeds sown on the surface of sandy loam in well-drained pots in spring.
SPECIES CULTIVATED : D. lusitanicum, yellow, May, 1 ft., Portugal.

Drumhead Cabbage—See Brassica.

Dryas (Mountain Avens)—Ord. Rosaceæ. Hardy evergreen trailing plants.
CULTURE : Soil, moist peat. Position, sunny rockery or borders. Plant, Oct., Nov. or March.
PROPAGATION : By seeds sown ⅛ in. deep in sandy peat in shallow pans or boxes in cold frame April or May ; cuttings of shoots 2 in. long inserted in sandy soil in cold frame in autumn ; division of plants in Oct., Nov., or March.
SPECIES CULTIVATED : D. Drummondii, yellow, June, 3 in., N. America ; octopetala, white, June, 3 in., trailing, Europe; Sundermani, white, June, 3 to 4 in., hybrid.

Drymis—See Drimis.

Drynaria—See Polypodium.

Drypis—Ord. Caryophyllaceæ. Hardy herbaceous perennial. First introduced 1775.
CULTURE : Soil, ordinary. Position, sunny rockeries or borders. Plant, Oct., Nov., March, April.
PROPAGATION : By seeds sown in light soil in cold frame or under hand-light in March or April ; cuttings inserted in sandy soil under hand-light or in cold frame in Sept. or Oct.
SPECIES CULTIVATED : D. spinosa, blue, summer, 9 in., Mediterranean Region.

Duck's-foot (*Podophyllum peltatum*)—See Podophyllum.

Duke of Argyll's Tea-plant (*Lycium barbarum*)—See Lycium.

Dumb Cane—See Dieffenbachia.

Dusty Miller (*Primula auricula* and *Senecio cineraria*)—See Primula and Senecio.

Dutch Agrimony (*Eupatorium cannabinum*)—See Eupatorium.

Dutch Honeysuckle (*Lonicera Periclymenum belgica*)—See Lonicera.

Dutchman's Breeches (*Dicentra Cucullaria*)—See Dicentra.

Dutchman's Pipe (*Aristolochia Sipho*)—See Aristolochia.

Dutch Myrtle (*Myrica Gale*)—See Myrica.

Dwarf Sunflower—See Actinella.

Dyckia—Ord. Bromeliaceæ. Greenhouse succulent orn. foliage plants. First introduced 1839.
CULTURE : Compost, two parts loam, one part leaf-mould and little sand. Position, pots in light airy greenhouse ; outside June to Sept. Water moderately April to Aug., little afterwards. Repot every five or six years ; good drainage essential Temp., Sept. to March 50° to 55° ; March to Sept. 55° to 65°.
PROPAGATION ; By offsets or suckers inserted in small pots in greenhouse at any time.
SPECIES CULTIVATED : D. altissima, yellow, autumn, 2 ft., Brazil ; brevifolia, yellow, Aug., 1 ft., Brazil.

Dyer's Chamomile (*Anthemis tinctoria*)—See Anthemis.

Dyer's Greenweed (*Genista tinctoria*)—See Genista.

Dyer's Tick-Seed (*Coreopsis tinctoria*)—See Coreopsis.

Ear Drops—See Fuchsia.
Earth Nut (*Arachis hypogæa*)—See Arachis.

Easter Flower (*Euphorbia pulcherrima*)—See Euphorbia.

Eastern Valerian (*Patrinia scabiosæfolia*)—See Patrinia.

East Indian Cedar (*Cedrus deodara*)—See Cedrus.

East Indian Flax (*Reinwardtia trigyna*)—See Reinwardtia.

East Indian Periwinkle (*Vinca rosea*)—See Vinca.

East Indian Pitcher-plant—See Nepenthes.

East Indian Rose-bay (*Tabernæmontana coronaria*)—See Tabernæmontana.

East Indian Wine Palm—See Caryota.

Eccremocarpus (Chilian Glory-flower)—Ord. Bignoniaceæ. Half-hardy climbing plant. Stems herbaceous in the open. First introduced 1825.
CULTURE : Soil, light rich. Position, against south or south-west walls. Plant, June. Protect roots in Oct. by layer of cinder ashes on surface of soil; base of plant in severe weather by mats.
PROPAGATION : By seeds sown $\frac{1}{16}$ in. deep in well-drained pots of light sandy soil in temp. 65° to 75° in March or April.
SPECIES CULTIVATED : E. scaber, scarlet and yellow, summer, 15 to 20 ft., Chile.

Eccremocarpus Vine (*Eccremocarpus scaber*)—See Eccremocarpus.

Echeveria—See Cotyledon.

Echinacea (Purple Cone-flower)—Ord. Compositæ. Hardy herbaceous perennials. First introduced 1799.
CULTURE : Soil, deep, rich, light loam. Position, well-drained sunny borders. Plant, Oct., Nov., or March.
PROPAGATION : By seeds sown $\frac{1}{8}$ in. deep in boxes of light soil in temp. 50° to 55° in March, or outdoors in sunny position in April ; division in Oct., March, or April.
SPECIES CULTIVATED : E. angustifolia, purplish red, summer, 1 to 2 ft., N. America ; purpurea, purplish red, Aug., 3 ft., N. America.

Echinocactus (Hedge-hog Cactus)—Ord. Cactaceæ. Greenhouse succulent plants. First introduced 1796.
CULTURE : Compost, two parts fibrous sandy loam, one part brick rubble, old mortar and sand. Position, well-drained pots in sunny greenhouse or window. Repot every three or four years in March. Water once a month Sept. to April, once a week afterwards. Temp., Sept. to March 50° to 55° ; March to Sept. 65° to 75°.
PROPAGATION : By seeds sown $\frac{1}{8}$ in. deep in well-drained pans of sandy soil in temp. 75° in March, keeping soil moderately moist ; cuttings of stems inserted in small pots of sandy soil kept barely moist in summer ; grafting on common kinds in April.
SPECIES CULTIVATED : E. brevihamatus, pink and rose, summer, 4 to 6 in., New Mexico ; centeterius, yellow, summer, 6 in., Mexico ; cinnabarinus, red, summer, 4 in., Bolivia ; concinnus, yellow, summer, 4 in., Mexico ; coptonogonus, white and purple, May, 4 in., Mexico ; cornigerus, purple, summer, Mexico ; corynodes, yellow, summer, 4 in., Argentina ; crispatus, purple, summer, 8 in. ; Cummingii, yellow, summer, Bolivia ; cylindraceus, yellow, summer, 4 ft., Colorado ; Emoryi, yellow and red, autumn, Colorado ; gibbosus, white, June, 4 in., Mexico ; Grusonii, red and yellow, summer, 6 in., Mexico ; leeanus, white and rose, May, Argentina ; multiflorus, white, summer, 5 in., Mexico ; scopa, yellow, spring, 12 to 18 in., Brazil ; scopa crista, stem fasciated ; Simpsoni, purple, summer, 4 in., Mexico, a very hardy species. The last named may be grown outdoors in S. of England.

Echinocystis—Ord. Cucurbitaceæ. Hardy annual climber, bearing small prickly cucumber-like fruits. United States.
CULTURE : Sow seeds in heat in spring, and plant out in moist rich soil in May against a sunny trellis, fence, or arch.
SPECIES CULTIVATED : E. lobata (Wild Balsam Apple), greenish white, summer, 8 to 10 ft.

Echinops (Globe Thistle)—Ord. Compositæ.   Hardy biennials and perennials. First introduced 1570.
CULTURE : Soil, ordinary.   Position, well-drained sunny borders.   Plant, Oct., Nov. or March.
PROPAGATION : By seeds sown ⅛ in. deep in sunny position outdoors in April ; division of roots in Oct., Nov., or March.
PERENNIAL SPECIES : E. bannaticus (Syn. E. ruthenicus), violet blue, summer, 2 to 3 ft., Hungary ; Ritro, blue, summer, 3 ft., S. Europe ; sphærocephalus, pale blue, summer, 3 to 4 ft., Europe.

Echinopsis (Hedge-hog Cactus)—Ord. Cactaceæ.   Greenhouse succulent plants.   First introduced 1835.
CULTURE : Compost, two parts fibrous sandy loam, one part brick rubble, old mortar and sand.   Position, well-drained pots in sunny greenhouse or window. Repot every three or four years in March.   Water once a month Sept. to April, once a week afterwards.   Temp., Sept. to March 50° to 55° ; March to Sept. 65° to 75°.
PROPAGATION : By seeds sown ⅛ in. deep in well-drained pans of sandy soil in temp. 75° in March, keeping soil moderately moist ; cuttings of stems inserted in small pots of sandy soil, kept barely moist in summer ; grafting on common kinds in April.
SPECIES CULTIVATED : E. campylacantha, rose, summer, 1 ft., Chile ; cristata, creamy white, summer, 1 ft., Bolivia ; decaisneana, white and yellow, July, 1 ft. ; Eyriesii, white, fragrant, July, 4 to 6 in., Mexico ; Eyriesii flore-pleno, double ; oxygona, rose, summer, 6 in., Brazil ; Pentlandii, white and red, July, 6 in., Mexico ; tubiflora, white, summer, 4 in., Mexico.

Echites—Ord. Apocynaceæ.   Stove evergreen flowering and climbing shrub. First introduced 1867.
CULTURE : Compost, rough fibry peat and one-fourth silver sand.   Position, well-drained pots, with shoots trained to roof of stove or to wire trellis.   Pot, Feb. or March.   Prune, Oct., cutting away shoots that have flowered only.   Water very little Oct. to Feb., moderately Feb. to April, freely afterwards.   Temp., Oct. to Feb. 55° to 60° ; Feb. to Oct. 65° to 75°.
PROPAGATION : By cuttings of young side shoots 3 in. long inserted in pots of sandy peat under bell-glass in temp. 80° in Feb., March, or April.
SPECIES CULTIVATED : E. rubrovenosa, emerald green leaves, speckled red or yellow, Brazil.

Echium (Viper's Bugloss)—Ord. Boraginaceæ.   Hardy annuals, biennials and perennials.
CULTURE : Soil, ordinary.   Position, sunny well-drained borders or wild garden. Plant, Aug. or April.
PROPAGATION : By seeds sown ⅛ in. deep in sunny position outdoors in April or Aug.
BIENNIAL SPECIES : E. plantagineum, bluish purple, summer, 2 to 3 ft., S. Europe (Britain) ; vulgare, purple or blue, summer, 3 to 4 ft., Britain.
ANNUAL SPECIES : E. creticum, violet, July, 12 to 18 in., S. Europe.
PERENNIAL SPECIES : E. albicans, rose or violet, summer, 1 ft., Spain.

Edraianthus—See Wahlenbergia.

Edelweiss (*Leontopodium alpinum*)—See Leontopodium.

Edwardsia—See Sophora.

Eel-Grass (*Vallisneria spiralis*)—See Vallisneria.

Egg-plant (*Solanum melongena*)—See Solanum.

Eggs-and-Bacon Daffodil (*Narcissus incomparabilis fl.-pl.* var.)—See Narcissus.

Eglantine (*Rosa rubiginosa*)—See Rosa.

Egyptian Bean (*Nelumbium speciosum*)—See Nelumbium.

Egyptian Kidney Bean (*Dolichos Lab-lab*)—See Dolichos.

Egyptian Lily (*Richardia africana*)—See Richardia.

Egyptian Lotus (*Nymphæa lotus*)—See Nymphæa.

Egyptian Onion (*Allium Cepa proliferum*)—See Allium.

Egyptian Rose (*Scabiosa atropurpurea*)—See Scabiosa.

Egyptian Water Lily (*Nymphæa lotus*)—See Nymphæa.

Egyptian Yarrow (*Achillea ægyptica*)—See Achillea.

Eichhornea (Water Hyacinth)—Ord. Pontederiaceæ. Tender floating aquatic perennials. First introduced 1879.
CULTURE : Plant in tanks or aquariums. Temperature of water March to Oct. 60° to 75° ; Oct. to March 55° to 60°. Plant, May.
PROPAGATION : By division in May.
SPECIES CULTIVATED : E. azurea, lavender blue and purple, July, Brazil ; crassipes, violet blue and yellow, summer, Trop. and Sub-Trop. America, and its variety major.

Elæagnus (Oleaster)—Ord. Elæagnaceæ. Hardy deciduous and evergreen shrubs. Orn. foliage. First introduced 1633. Leaves, green or variegated with white.
CULTURE : Soil, ordinary. Position, open sheltered dryish borders, or against south or west walls. Plant deciduous species in Oct., Nov., or Dec. ; evergreen in April or Sept.
PROPAGATION : By seeds sown ½ in. deep in boxes of light soil in temp. 55° in March ; cuttings inserted in sandy soil in cold frame in Sept. ; layering in spring.
EVERGREEN SPECIES : E. glabra, white, Aug., 4 to 6 ft., China and Japan ; macrophylla, yellow, Sept., 6 ft., Japan ; pungens, yellow, autumn, 6 ft., China and Japan ; pungens aureo-maculata, golden-leaved ; pungens variegata, silver-leaved.
DECIDUOUS SPECIES : E. angustifolius, silvery white and yellow, June, 15 to 20 ft., S. Europe and W. Asia ; argentea (wrongly known as Shepherdia argentea), yellow, July, 8 ft., N. America ; multiflora, creamy, April to May, 6 to 10 ft., Japan.

Elder (*Sambucus nigra*)—See Sambucus.

Elderberry (*Sambucus nigra*)—See Sambucus.

Elder-scented Orchis (*Orchis sambucina*)—See Orchis.

Elecampane (*Inula Helenium*)—See Inula.

Elephant's Ear (*Begonia Rex*)—See Begonia.

Elephant's Ear Fern (*Acrostichum crinitum*)—See Acrostichum.

Elephant's Foot (*Testudinaria elephantipes*)—See Testudinaria.

Elephant's-tooth Cactus (*Mammillaria elephantidens*)—See Mammillaria.

Elephant's Trunk (*Martynia proboscidea*)—See Martynia.

Eleven o'Clock Lady (*Ornithogalum umbellatum*)—See Ornithogalum.

Elisena—Ord. Amaryllidaceæ. Warm greenhouse bulbous plant. First introduced 1837.
CULTURE : Compost, two parts light sandy loam, one part leaf-mould and one part of coarse sand. Position, well-drained pots in warm, sunny greenhouse. Pot, autumn. Water freely during growing period. Keep nearly dry when at rest. Temp., Sept. to March 55° to 65° ; March to Sept. 65° to 75°.
PROPAGATION : By offsets removed and treated as parent bulbs at potting time.
SPECIES CULTIVATED : E. longipetala, white, spring, 3 ft., Peru.

Elk's-horn Fern (*Platycerium alcicorne*)—See Platycerium.

Elk Tree (*Oxydendrum arboreum*)—See Oxydendrum.

Elm (*Ulmus campestris*)—See Ulmus.

Elsholtzia—Ord. Labiatæ. Semi-woody hardy plant. **First introduced** 1909.
CULTURE : Soil, rich loam. Position, beds or shrubberies in full sunshine. Plant, Nov.
PROPAGATION : By cuttings of young growth inserted under a hand-glass in sandy
soil during June or July.
SPECIES CULTIVATED : E. Stauntoni, purplish pink, autumn, 3 to 5 ft., China.

Elwes's Snowdrop (*Galanthus Elwesi*)—See Galanthus.

Embothrium—Ord. Proteaceæ. Half-hardy evergreen shrub. **First introduced**
1851.
OUTDOOR CULTURE : Soil, sandy peat. Position, against south walls outdoors S.
of England, pots in cold greenhouse N. of England. Protect with mats in severe
weather. Plant, March or April.
GREENHOUSE CULTURE : Compost, two parts peat, one part loam, and one part sand.
Pot, March. **Prune,** March. Water moderately Oct. to April, freely in summer.
Place plants in sunny position outdoors May to Oct.
PROPAGATION : By cuttings inserted in sandy peat under bell-glass in temp. 55° in
spring ; also by cuttings of roots inserted in sandy peat in temp. 75° in spring ; by
grafting young shoots on portions of its own roots in spring ; also by sowing
imported or home-saved seeds in sandy peat, in temp. 75°, in spring.
SPECIES CULTIVATED : E. coccineum, scarlet, May to July, 10 to 15 ft., Chile.

Emilia (Tassel-flower)—Ord. Compositæ. Half-hardy annual.
CULTURE : Soil, rich loam. Position, sunny beds and borders. Sow seed in boxes
or pans in warm greenhouse in Feb. or March, pricking out seedlings into boxes as
soon as large enough to handle, and hardening off for planting out in May.
SPECIES CULTIVATED: E. flammea (Syn. Cacalia coccinea), scarlet, summer, 1 to 2 ft.,
Trop. America.

Empetrum (Black-berried Heath ; Crake-berry ; Crow-berry)—**Ord.** Empe-
traceæ. Hardy evergreen fruiting shrub. Berries, black, edible ; ripe in Sept.
CULTURE : Soil, boggy. Position, damp, moist, shady. Plant, March or April.
PROPAGATION : By cuttings inserted in June, July or Aug. in sandy peat under
bell-glass in shady position.
SPECIES CULTIVATED : E. nigrum, pink, May, 8 to 10 in., N. Hemisphere. Nigrum
scoticum and rubrum are varieties.

Encephalartos (Caffre Bread)—**Ord.** Cycadaceæ. Greenhouse evergreen plants.
First introduced 1835. Leaves, feather-shaped, bluish green.
CULTURE : Compost, two parts good loam, one part sand. Position, well-drained
pots in light part of greenhouse. Repot, March. Water liberally April to Aug.,
very little afterwards. Growth occasionally stationary for a few years. Temp.,
Sept. to April 55° to 60° ; April to Sept. 65° to 75°.
PROPAGATION : By seeds sown ½ in. deep in light soil in temp. 85° to 95° in March
or April.
SPECIES CULTIVATED : E. Altensteinii, 8 ft., S. Africa ; caffra, 8 to 10 ft., S. Africa.

Endive—See Cichorium.

Endres's Crane's-bill (*Geranium Endresi*)—See Geranium.

English Elm (*Ulmus campestris*)—See Ulmus.

English Iris (*Iris xiphiodes*)—See Iris.

English Maiden-hair Fern (*Asplenium trichomanes*)—See Asplenium.

English Stonecrop (*Sedum anglicum*)—See Sedum.

English Sundew (*Drosera longifolia*)—See Drosera.

Enkianthus—Ord. Ericaceæ. Hardy deciduous shrubs.
CULTURE: Soil, ordinary, moist, with a little peat and leaf-mould. Position, warm,
sheltered shrubberies or beds. Plant, Sept. or April.
PROPAGATION : By cuttings of firm shoots in sandy soil in heat in spring.
SPECIES CULTIVATED : E. campanulatus, red, summer, 6 ft., Japan ; japonicus, white,
Feb., 5 to 6 ft., Japan.

Eomecon—Ord. Papaveraceæ. Hardy perennial. First introduced 1889.
CULTURE : Soil, sandy peat and leaf-mould. Position, sunny, well-drained border.
Plant, Oct. to March. Water freely in very dry weather.
PROPAGATION : By division of the roots in March or early April.
SPECIES CULTIVATED : E. chionantha, white, summer, 1 to 2 ft., China.

Epacris (Australian Heath ; Tasmanian Heath)—Ord. Epacrideæ. Greenhouse
evergreen flowering shrubs. First introduced 1803.
CULTURE : Compost, three-fourths fibry peat, one-fourth silver sand. Position,
light airy greenhouse Sept. to July, sunny place outdoors July to Sept. Repot,
April, May, or June ; good drainage essential. Prune shoots of erect kinds to
within 1 in. of base directly after flowering ; pendulous kinds about half-way.
Water moderately at all times. Syringe plants daily March to July. Temp., Sept.
to March 45° to 50° ; March to July, 55° to 60°. Stimulants not essential.
PROPAGATION : By seeds sown immediately they ripen on surface of sandy peat
under bell-glass in temp. 55° ; cuttings of ends of shoots inserted in pots of sandy
peat covered with bell-glass placed in cool greenhouse in Aug. or April.
SPECIES CULTIVATED : E. hyacinthiflora, white to red, March, 2 to 3 ft., Australia ;
hyacinthiflora candidissima, white ; hyacinthiflora carminata, carmine ; hyacinthiflora
fulgens, pink ; longiflora, crimson and white, May and June, 2 to 4 ft., Australia ;
longiflora splendens, red, tipped white ; purpurascens, white and red, winter, 2 to
3 ft., Australia. Numerous varieties and hybrids will be found in trade lists.

Ephedra (Shrubby Horsetail)—Ord. Gnetaceæ. Hardy evergreen, ornamental-
leaved shrubs with slender, cylindrical, rush-like branchlets.
CULTURE : Soil, a well-drained loam. Position, sunny banks where the branches
can sprawl about. Plant in autumn.
PROPAGATION : By layering the branches in summer.
SPECIES CULTIVATED : E. distachya, branchlets rigid, 3 to 4 ft., S. Europe ; gerardiana, branchlets slender and spreading, 2 ft., Himalayas, etc. ; nebrodensis,
branchlets prostrate, 3 ft., N. Africa.

Epi-Cattleya—Ord. Orchidaceæ. Bigeneric orchids, the result of hybridising two
distinct genera—Epidendrum and Cattleya. Habit, intermediate between the two
parents. Flowers borne in terminal spikes. Require similar culture to Epidendrums.
HYBRIDS CULTIVATED : E. matutina (C. bowringiana × E. radicans), yellow and
vermilion ; radiato-bowringiana (E. radiatum × C. bowringiana), rosy purple.

Epidendrum (Dragon's-mouth Orchid)—Ord. Orchidaceæ. Stove and
greenhouse epiphytal orchids. Flowers fragrant. First introduced 1835.
CULTURE : Compost, two parts fibry peat, one part chopped living sphagnum moss,
charcoal and sand. Position, well-drained pots, hanging baskets, or on blocks of
wood. Repot or block, Feb. or March ; pots must be well drained. Water three
times weekly March to Aug. ; once a week Aug. to Nov. and Feb. to March ; once
a month Nov. to Feb. Temp. for stove species, 65° to 75° March to Sept., 60° to 65°
Sept. to March ; for greenhouse species, 45° to 55° Nov. to April, 55° to 65° April
to Nov. Resting period, March to Nov. Growing period, Nov. to March.
PROPAGATION : By division of plants, or by offsets when new growth begins.
STOVE SPECIES : E. atropurpureum, brown, white, and purple, spring, 3 ft., Trop.
America ; prismatocarpum, creamy yellow, purple, and rose, summer, 3 ft., Central
America ; Wallisii, yellow, crimson, and white, winter, 3 ft., Colombia.
GREENHOUSE SPECIES : E. vitellinum, orange, scarlet, and yellow, autumn, 1 ft.,
Guatemala ; vitellinum majus (a superior variety) ; Medusæ (Syn. Nanodes Medusæ),
purple, summer, 4 to 6 ins., Ecuador.
HYBRIDS : Clarissa, red and purple, April ; Endresio-Wallisii, yellow, white, and
purple, spring ; o'brienianum, yellow and carmine, July. Require stove treatment.

Epigæa (American Ground Laurel ; New England May-flower)—Ord. Eri-
caceæ. Hardy evergreen creeping shrub. First introduced 1736.
CULTURE : Soil, sandy peat. Position, shady borders or rockeries. Plant, Sept.,
Oct. or April.

PROPAGATION : By division of plant in Oct. or April.
SPECIES CULTIVATED : E. repens, white, fragrant, May, trailing, N. America.

Epi-Lælia—Ord. Orchidaceæ. Bigeneric orchids, the result of hybridising species of Epidendrum with those of Lælia. Habit, like that of an Epidendrum. Flowers borne in erect scapes. Culture, same as required by Epidendrums.
HYBRIDS CULTIVATED : E. hardyana (L. anceps × Epidendrum ciliare), white, rose, and crimson-purple ; radico-purpurata (L. purpurata × E. radicans), orange-scarlet, reddish purple, and lemon-yellow.

Epilobium (Willow Herb ; Rose Bay Willow Herb)—Ord. Onagraceæ. Hardy perennial herbs. Showy plants for wild or town gardens.
CULTURE : Soil, ordinary. Position, shady or sunny borders, or side of water-courses. Dwarf species in sunny rock gardens. Plant, Oct. or March.
PROPAGATION : By seeds sown $\frac{1}{8}$ in. deep in shady position outdoors in March, April, or Aug. ; division of roots in Oct. or March.
SPECIES CULTIVATED : E. angustifolium (Rose Bay or French Willow), crimson, July, 4 to 8 ft., Europe (Britain) ; angustifolium album, white ; Dodonæi (Syn. E. Fleischeri), rosy purple, Aug., 9 to 12 in., Europe ; Hectori, pale pink, summer, 4 to 6 in., New Zealand ; hirsutum (Codlins and Cream), pink or white, July, 4 ft., Britain ; luteum, yellow, summer, 6 in., N. America ; macropus, creamy white, summer, creeping, New Zealand ; obcordatum, rosy purple, summer, 6 in., California ; rosmarinifolium, red, July, 2 ft., Europe.

Epimedium (Barren-wort ; Bishop's Hat)—Ord. Berberidaceæ. Hardy herbaceous perennials. First introduced 1830. Leaves, green, margined with coppery bronze.
CULTURE : Soil, sandy loam and peat. Position, cool shady border or rockery ; will do well under trees. Plant, Oct., Nov., March, or April.
PROPAGATION : By division of roots in autumn.
SPECIES CULTIVATED : E. alpinum, crimson and yellow, May, 9 in., Europe, and its variety rubrum ; concinnum, purple, March, 8 in., Japan ; macranthum, white and blue, May, 10 in., Japan ; pinnatum, yellow, May, 12 in., Persia, and its varieties colchicum and elegans.

Epipactis (Helleborine)—Ord. Orchidaceæ. Hardy terrestrial orchids.
CULTURE : Soil, peat and chalk. Position, moist shady borders or near ponds or rivulets. Plant in early autumn. Collect wild specimens directly after flowering.
PROPAGATION : By division of plant in March or April.
SPECIES CULTIVATED : E. latifolia, purple, July, 1 ft., Europe (Britain) ; palustris, purple, July, 1 ft., Europe (Britain).

Epiphronitis—Ord. Orchidaceæ. A bigeneric hybrid orchid obtained by crossing Sophronitis grandiflora with Epidendrum radicans. Habit, similar to latter parent but dwarfer. Flowers, large. Culture, similar to that required by Epidendrums.
HYBRID CULTIVATED : E. Veitchii, crimson and yellow.

Epiphyllum (Leaf-flowering Cactus)—Ord. Cactaceæ. Succulent greenhouse trailing plants. First introduced 1810.
CULTURE : Compost, equal parts turfy loam, peat and leaf-mould, one-fourth silver sand. Position, light warm greenhouse Sept. to June, sunny place outdoors or cold frame June to Sept. Water moderately Sept. to April, little more freely other times. Temp., Nov. to March 50° to 60° ; March to June 55° to 65° ; Sept. to Nov. 40° to 45°.
PROPAGATION : By cuttings inserted singly in 2 in. pots filled with sandy soil and brick dust in March or April ; grafting on Pereskia aculeata or P. Bleo in temp. 65° to 75° in Feb., March, or April.
SPECIES CULTIVATED : E. russellianum, rose, May, Brazil ; truncatum, rosy red, winter, Brazil.
HYBRIDS AND VARIETIES : E. bicolor, purple and white ; coccineum, scarlet ; Gærtneri (hybrid), scarlet and violet ; salmoneum, salmon ; violaceum, carmine, white and purple.

Epistephium—Ord. Orchidaceæ. Stove terrestrial orchid. First introduced 1864.
CULTURE : Compost, two parts fibrous loam, one part sand. Pot, Feb. ; good drainage essential ; keep soil below rim of pot. Water three times weekly March to Aug. ; once weekly Aug. to Nov. and Feb. to March ; once a month other times. Syringe freely in summer. Temp., March to Sept. 65° to 85° ; Sept. to March 60° to 70°.
PROPAGATION : By division of pseudo-bulbs at potting time.
SPECIES CULTIVATED : E. Williamsii, mauve, rose, white, and yellow, summer, 12 in., Bahia.

Equisetum (Horsetail ; Fox-tailed Asparagus)—Ord. Equisetaceæ. Hardy deciduous herbaceous perennials. Orn. foliage. Leaves, green, narrow, rush-like, elegant.
CULTURE : Soil, ordinary. Position, bogs, margins of ponds, moist shady corners, or in pots in a cool shady greenhouse. Plant or pot, April. Water plants in pots freely whilst growing, moderately at other times.
PROPAGATION : By division of rootstocks in March or April.
SPECIES CULTIVATED : E. robustum (Syn. E. præaltum), to 11 ft., N. America, Asia ; maximum (Syn. E. Telmateia), 3 to 6 ft., Britain.

Eragrostis (Feather Grass ; Love Grass)—Ord. Gramineæ. Hardy annual flowering grasses. Nat. Temperate Regions. Inflorescence, light, feathery and graceful.
CULTURE : Soil, ordinary. Position, open sunny beds or borders.
PROPAGATION : By seeds sown ⅛ in. deep where plants are to grow in April. Gather inflorescence in July and dry for winter use.
SPECIES CULTIVATED : E. abyssinica, 2 to 3 ft., N. Africa ; japonica (Syn. E. elegans), 2 to 3 ft., Japan ; maxima, 2 to 3 ft., Madagascar ; pilosa, 1 to 1½ ft., Europe ; suaveolens, 2 to 3 ft., W. Asia.

Eranthemum—Ord. Acanthaceæ. Stove flowering plants. Orn. foliage. First introduced 1796.
CULTURE : Compost, equal parts peat, leaf-mould, loam and sand. Position, well-drained pots in light stove Sept. to June, sunny frame June to Sept. Pot, March or April. Water moderately in winter, freely other times. Temp., Sept. to March 55° to 65° ; March to June, 65° to 75°. Prune shoots to within 1 in. of base after flowering. Apply liquid or artificial manure occasionally to plants in flower.
PROPAGATION : By cuttings of young shoots inserted in sandy peat under bell-glass in temp. 75° March to July.
SPECIES CULTIVATED : E. albiflorum, white, summer, 2 ft., Brazil ; Andersonii, white and purple, autumn, 1 ft., Malaya ; cinnabarinum, scarlet, winter, 3 ft., Burma ; Cooperi, white and purple, June, 2 ft., New Caledonia ; igneum (Syn. Stenandrium igneum), yellow, Peru ; pulchellum (Syn. Dædalacanthus nervosus), blue, April, to 4 ft., India.

Eranthis (Winter Aconite)—Ord. Ranunculaceæ. Hardy tuberous-rooted perennial. First introduced 1596.
CULTURE : Soil, ordinary. Position, shady borders, beds, lawns, under trees or on rockeries. Plant 2 in. deep and 2 in. apart in Oct., Nov., or Dec. Tubers should not be lifted, but left permanently in the soil.
POT CULTURE : Compost, equal parts leaf-mould, loam and sand. Position, 3 in. pots or large pans in cool greenhouse or window. Plant tubers ½ in. deep and close together in pots or pans in Oct. or Nov. Water moderately. After flowering, plant tubers out in borders.
PROPAGATION : By division of tubers in Oct. or Nov.
SPECIES CULTIVATED : E. cilicica, yellow, Jan. to March, 4 to 6 in., Asia Minor ; hyemalis, yellow, Jan. to March, 3 to 4 in., Europe (Britain) ; sibirica, yellow, Jan. to March, 2 to 3 in., Siberia.

Ercilla—Ord. Phytolaccaceæ. Hardy evergreen creeper. First introduced 1840.
CULTURE : Soil, sandy loam. Position, south walls or old tree trunks ; sunny

Plant, Sept. or April. Prune after flowering, cutting away weak and shortening strong shoots one fourth. Shoots cling to the wall like those of ivy.

PROPAGATION : By cuttings or layers in autumn.

SPECIES CULTIVATED : E. volubilis (Syn. Bridgesia spicata), purple, spring, 10 to 15 ft., Chile.

Eremostachys (Desert Rod)—Ord. Labiatæ. Hardy perennial. First introduced 1731.

CULTURE : Soil, light rich. Position, sunny well-drained borders. Plant, Oct. or April. Cut off spikes after flowering.

PROPAGATION : By seeds sown $\frac{1}{16}$ in. deep in light soil in sunny position outdoors in April ; division of roots in Oct. or April.

SPECIES CULTIVATED : E. laciniata, yellow, summer, 2¼ ft., Asia Minor.

Eremurus—Ord. Liliaceæ. Hardy herbaceous perennials. First introduced 1800.

CULTURE : Soil, light deep rich sandy, well-manured loam. Position, sunny well-drained beds or borders. Plant, Sept. or Oct. Transplanting must not be done oftener than is really necessary. Mulch freely with well-decayed manure in autumn. Water copiously in hot weather. Protect in winter by a covering of bracken or dry litter.

PROPAGATION : By division of roots in Oct. or March ; seeds sown in heat in spring, growing seedlings on in cold frame for first three years. Seeds sometimes take a long time to germinate.

SPECIES CULTIVATED : E. Bungei, yellow, June and July, 1 to 3 ft., Persia ; himalaicus, white, May and June, 8 ft., Himalayas ; Kaufmannii, yellow, June, 4 ft., Turkestan ; Olgæ, lilac-purple, fragrant, 2 to 4 ft., Turkestan ; robustus, pink, May and June, 6 to 10 ft., Turkestan, and its variety elwesianus ; spectabilis, yellow and orange, June, 2 to 4 ft., Siberia. A number of fine hybrids are offered in trade lists.

Eria—Ord. Orchidaceæ. Stove epiphytal orchids. First introduced 1837.

CULTURE : Compost, equal parts peat and sphagnum, with broken crocks and charcoal. Position, teak baskets suspended from roof or well-drained pans. Plant, spring. Water freely March to Sept. ; moderately, Sept. to Nov. ; keep almost dry remainder of year. Temp., May to Sept. 70° to 85° ; Sept. to May 60° to 70°. Growing period, spring and summer. Resting period, winter.

PROPAGATION : By division of pseudo-bulbs in spring.

SPECIES CULTIVATED : E. barbata, yellow and maroon, autumn, N. India ; convallarioides, white and yellow, early summer, N. India ; excavata, white, yellow and purple, Himalayas ; flava, yellow and purple, spring, Himalayas ; stellata, yellowish red, spring, Java.

Erianthus (Woolly Beard Grass ; Ravenna Grass)—Ord. Gramineæ. Hardy orn. foliage perennial grass. Inflorescence similar to pampas plumes. Leaves, narrow, green.

CULTURE : Soil, deep loam. Position, sunny well-drained lawns or borders. Plant, March or April.

PROPAGATION : By division of roots in March or April.

SPECIES CULTIVATED : E. Ravennæ, 6 to 12 ft., S. Europe to India.

Erica (Heath)—Ord. Ericaceæ. Hardy and greenhouse evergreen flowering shrubs.

CULTURE OF HARDY SPECIES : Soil, sandy peat. Position, sunny rockeries or margins of borders, or massed on banks or in the wild garden. Plant, Oct. or March. Prune straggly shoots in April.

CULTURE OF GREENHOUSE SPECIES : Compost, two-thirds fibrous peat, one-third silver sand. Position, well-drained pots in light airy greenhouse Oct. to July, sunny place outdoors July to Oct. Repot autumn- and winter-flowering kinds in March, summer-flowering sorts in Sept. Press the compost firmly in pots. Water carefully always, giving sufficient to keep soil uniformly moist ; rain, not spring water, essential. Prune shoots to within 1 or 2 in. of base immediately after flowering. Temp., Oct. to March 40° to 45° ; March to July 45° to 55°. Sootwater best stimulant.

PROPAGATION : Greenhouse species by cuttings of shoots 1 in. long inserted in well-drained pot of sandy peat under bell-glass in temp. 60° to 70° in spring ; hardy species by cuttings inserted in sandy peat under bell-glass or hand-light in gentle bottom heat during July and August; division of plants in Oct. ;. layering shoots in spring.

HARDY SPECIES : E. arborea, white, May, 10 to 20 ft., Mediterranean Region, hardy only in S. of England ; australis, purplish red, spring, 3 to 4 ft., Spain and Portugal ; carnea (Syn. E. herbacea), pink, Jan. to April, 6 in., Europe ; carnea alba, white ; ciliaris (Dorset Heath), red, summer, 8 to 12 in., Britain ; cinerea (Scotch Heather), crimson-purple, July to Sept., 6 to 12 in., Britain and Ireland, and its varieties alba (white), atropurpurea (purple), coccinea (scarlet), purpurea rosea (purplish rose) ; darleyensis, red, Nov. to May, 2 ft., hybrid ; lusitanica (Syn. E. codonodes), pinkish white, Jan. to April, 2 to 6 ft., Spain ; Mackayi, red, July to Oct., 1 to 2 ft., hybrid ; mediterranea, pink, April and May, 4 to 5 ft., France, Spain, etc., and its variety hibernica (glauca) ; stricta, rosy purple, June to Sept., 8 to 9 ft., S.W. Europe ; tetralix (Cross-leaved Heath or Bell Heather), rosy red, July to Sept., 6 to 12 in., Britain and Ireland ; tetralix alba, white ; tetralix rubra, red ; vagans (Cornish Heath), pink, July to Sept., 6 in. to 2 ft., England, France, and Ireland ; vagans alba, white ; vagans rubra, red ; Veitchii, white, March, 3 to 4 ft., hybrid.

GREENHOUSE SPECIES : E. aitoniana, white and purple, Aug., 18 in., S. Africa ; caffra, white, May, 18 in., S. Africa ; cavendishiana, yellow, May, 4 ft., hybrid ; coccinea, scarlet, June, 1 ft., S. Africa ; cupressina (Syn. E. bergiana), red, May to June, 1 to 3 ft., S. Africa ; elegans, rose and green, Aug., 6 in., S. Africa ; gracilis, reddish purple, 1 ft., S. Africa ; hyemalis, pink, Dec. to March, hybrid ; jasmini-flora, pink, Aug., 2 ft., S. Africa ; macnabiana, pink and white, June, 18 in., hybrid ; mammosa, reddish purple, July to Oct., 2 ft., S. Africa ; marnockiana, purple, crimson and white, July and Aug., 18 in., hybrid ; melanthera, rosy, winter, 2 to 3 ft., S. Africa ; persoluta, purple, April, 16 in., S. Africa ; perspicua, reddish purple, April to June, S. Africa ; regerminans, pale red, May to Aug., 1½ to 2 ft., S. Africa ; spenceriana, purplish lilac, spring and summer, hybrid ; ventricosa, pink, June, 1 ft., S. Africa, and its varieties alba (white), carnea (flesh), and coccinea (scarlet) ; vestita, white, June, 3 ft., S. Africa, and its varieties alba (white), carnea (flesh), coccinea (scarlet), incarnata (pink), lutea (yellow), purpurea (purple), and rosea (rose) ; willmoreana, red, June, 12 in., a hybrid.

Erigeron (Flea-bane)—Ord. Compositæ. Hardy herbaceous perennials. First introduced 1628.

CULTURE : Soil, ordinary. Position, sunny moist rockeries or borders. Plant, Oct. or March. Cut down stems after flowering.

PROPAGATION : By seeds sown ¼ in. deep in light soil in shady position outdoors in April, May, or June ; division of roots in Oct. or March.

SPECIES CULTIVATED : E. alpinus (Syn. Roylei), purple and yellow, Aug., 12 in., Northern Regions ; aurantiacus (Orange Daisy), orange, summer, 12 in., Turkestan ; macranthus, violet blue, June to Sept., 1 ft., N.W. America ; mucronatus, white, pink, and yellow, summer, 12 in., Mexico ; philadelphicus, lilac-pink, summer, 1 to 2 ft., N. America ; speciosus, violet blue, summer, 1½ to 2 ft., N. America.

Erinacea (Hedgehog Broom)—Ord. Leguminosæ. Dwarf evergreen spring-flowering shrub. Introduced 1759.

CULTURE : Soil, loam and peat. Position, sunny rockeries, or borders at base of a south wall. Plant, May or Sept.

PROPAGATION : By cuttings in sandy loam and peat in a cold frame in autumn.

SPECIES CULTIVATED : E. pungens, pale blue, spring, 1 ft., Spain.

Erinus—Ord. Scrophulariaceæ. Hardy herbaceous perennial. First introduced 1739.

CULTURE : Soil, decayed vegetable mould and old mortar. Position, crevices of old sunny walls or dryish rockeries. Plant, March or April.

PROPAGATION : By seeds sown where plants are to grow in April ; division of plants in April.

SPECIES CULTIVATED : E. alpinus, violet purple, spring, 6 in., Pyrenees. Albus (white) and Dr. Hanele (carmine) are fine varieties.

Eriobotrya (Loquat ; Chinese Medlar)—Ord. Rosaceæ. Half-hardy evergreen flowering shrub. Fruit bearing. Fruit of loquat about the size of green walnut, pale orange-red, downy, borne in bunches.
OUTDOOR CULTURE : Soil, light deep loam. Position, against south walls S. and S.W. of England and Ireland only. Plant, Sept. to Nov., April or May. Prune, April. Protect in severe weather with mats or straw hurdles.
INDOOR CULTURE : Soil, two parts sandy loam, one part leaf-mould. Position, beds against back wall of cold or slightly heated sunny greenhouse. Plant, Oct. or April. Water moderately Sept. to April, freely afterwards. Syringe daily May to Sept. Prune straggling shoots in April.
PROPAGATION : By seeds sown ½ in. deep in pots of light soil in cold greenhouse or frame, spring or autumn ; cuttings of firm shoots inserted in sandy soil in cold frame or greenhouse, Aug.
SPECIES CULTIVATED : E. japonica, white, summer, 10 to 30 ft., China and Japan. Known also as Photinia japonica.

Eriodendron—Ord. Malvaceæ. Stove deciduous tree. Yields the kapok of commerce. First introduced 1739.
CULTURE : Compost, three parts loam, one part each leaf-mould, decayed manure, and sand. Position, large pots or borders in warm greenhouse. Pot or plant, Nov. or March.
PROPAGATION : By seeds sown in Feb. in sandy soil and temp. 80° to 85°.
SPECIES CULTIVATED : E. anfractuosum (Syn. Ceiba pentandra), white or rose, seeds with cotton-like fibre, to 120 ft., Tropics.

Eriogonum—Ord. Polygonaceæ. Hardy herbaceous perennial.
CULTURE : Soil, ordinary. Position, open borders. Plant, Oct. or March.
PROPAGATION : By seeds sown ½ in. deep in light soil outdoors in April ; division of roots in March.
SPECIES CULTIVATED : E. umbellatum, golden yellow, summer, 12 in., N.W. Africa.

Eriogyna pectinata—See Spiræa pectinata.

Eriophorum (Cotton Grass)—Ord. Cyperaceæ. Hardy aquatic perennials. Inflorescence borne in spikelets, with cottony tufts on their extremities.
CULTURE : Soil, ordinary. Position, margins of ponds. Plant, March.
PROPAGATION : By seeds sown where plants are to grow ; division of plants in March.
SPECIES CULTIVATED : E. alpinum, 1 ft., N. Hemisphere ; polystachion, 1 ft., Britain ; vaginatum, 1 ft., Britain.

Eriopsis—Ord. Orchidaceæ. Stove evergreen epiphytal orchid. First introduced 1845.
CULTURE : Compost, fibrous peat, little sphagnum moss. Repot, March or April. Position, light sunny part of stove. Water three times weekly March to Aug. ; once weekly Aug. to Nov. and Feb. to March ; once a month other times. Syringe freely in summer. Temp., March to Sept. 65° to 85° ; Sept. to March 60° to 70°.
PROPAGATION : By division of pseudo-bulbs at potting time.
SPECIES CULTIVATED : E. Helenæ, orange, summer ; rutidobulbon, brown and yellow, summer, 2 ft., Colombia.

Eriostemon—Ord. Rutaceæ. Greenhouse evergreen shrubs. First introduced 1822.
CULTURE : Compost, equal parts sandy loam and peat. Position, well-drained pots in light airy greenhouse. Repot, March, pressing soil down firmly. Water moderately Sept. to April, freely afterwards. Prune straggly growths in Feb. Temp., Sept. to April 45° to 50° ; April to Sept. 50° to 60°. Ventilate greenhouse freely in summer.
PROPAGATION : By cuttings 2 in. long inserted in sandy peat under bell-glass in temp. 60° in March ; grafting on Correa alba in March.
SPECIES CULTIVATED : E. buxifolius, pink, May or June, 3 to 4 ft., Australia ; pulchellus, pink, May, 2 to 3 ft., hybrid ; salicifolius, red, spring, 2 ft., Australia.

Eritrichium (Fairy Borage ; Fairy Forget-me-not)—Ord. Boraginaceæ. Hardy perennial alpine plant. Nat. Alps. First introduced 1869.
CULTURE : Compost, equal parts broken limestone, sandstone, fibry loam, peat and sand. Position, sheltered crannies of open rockeries, where foliage can be protected from excessive moisture in winter. Plant, April. Protect by panes of glass in rainy weather.
PROPAGATION : By division of plants in April ; seeds sown in gentle heat in spring.
SPECIES CULTIVATED : E. nanum, sky blue and yellow, summer, 2 to 3 in., N. Temperate Regions.

Erodium (Heron's-bill)—Ord. Geraniaceæ. Hardy perennial herbs. First introduced 1640.
CULTURE : Soil, sandy. Position, dry sunny borders or rockeries. Plant, March or April. Transplant very seldom.
PROPAGATION : By seeds sown ¼ in. deep in pots of sandy soil in temp. 55° in March or April, transplanting seedlings outdoors in June or July ; division of roots in April.
SPECIES CULTIVATED : E. chamædryoides (Syn. E. Reichardi), white and pink, April to Sept., 2 to 3 in., Balearic Islands ; chrysanthum, pale yellow, summer, 6 in., Greece ; corsicum, pink, summer, trailing, Corsica and Sardinia ; guttatum, pink, summer, 6 in., Mediterranean Region ; macradenum, violet, flesh and purple, summer, 6 in., Pyrenees ; Manescavi, purplish red, summer, 1 to 2 ft., Pyrenees ; sibthorpianum, rosy lilac, summer, 6 in., Bithynia ; trichomanefolium, violet-veined rose, summer, 4 to 6 in., Syria.

Erpetion reniforme—See Viola hederacea.

Eryngium (Sea Holly)—Ord. Umbelliferæ. Hardy perennial herbs. Orn. foliage. Flower heads surrounded by spiny coloured bracts.
CULTURE : Soil, light sandy. Position, dryish sunny borders. Plant, Oct., Nov., March, or April.
PROPAGATION : By seeds sown ¹⁄₁₆ in. deep in boxes of sandy soil in cold frame in April or May ; division of plants in Oct. or April.
SPECIES CULTIVATED : E. alpinum, blue and white, summer, 1 to 2 ft., Europe ; amethystinum, purple, July and Aug., 12 to 18 in., Europe ; Bourgati, blue, June to Aug., 1 to 2 ft., Spain ; giganteum, blue with ivory-white involucrum, summer, 3 to 4 ft., Armenia, usually treated as a biennial ; maritimum, bluish white, July to Oct., 1 to 2 ft., Britain ; oliverianum, blue, summer, 2 to 4 ft., Orient ; pandanifolium, purplish, summer, 10 to 15 ft., Monte Video ; planum, blue, summer, 1 to 2 ft., Europe ; Zabelli, amethyst blue, summer, 1½ ft., hybrid.

Eryngo (*Eryngium amethystinum*)—See Eryngium.

Erysimum (Alpine Wallflower)—Ord. Cruciferæ. Hardy annuals, biennials, and perennials. First introduced 1823.
CULTURE : Soil, ordinary. Position, dryish sunny beds or rockeries. Plant, March or April.
PROPAGATION : Annual species, by seeds sown where plants are required to grow in April ; biennials, by seeds sown in sunny place outdoors in June, transplanting seedlings to flowering positions in Aug. ; perennials, by seeds sown as advised for biennials, also by cuttings inserted in sandy soil under hand-light or cold frame in Aug. ; division of plants in March or April.
ANNUAL SPECIES : E. perofskianum, reddish orange, spring to autumn, 1 ft., Caucasus.
BIENNIAL SPECIES : E. murale, golden yellow, May to July, 1 to 1½ ft., Europe. May be grown as an annual.
PERENNIAL SPECIES : E. asperum, orange or yellow, spring and early summer, 1 to 2 ft., N. America, the plant commonly grown in gardens as Cheiranthus Allioni ; linifolium (Syn. Cheiranthus linifolius), rosy lilac, summer, 1 to 1½ ft., Spain ; ochroleucum, sulphur yellow, fragrant, April to July, Europe ; pumilum, sulphur yellow, spring and early summer, 6 in., Europe ; purpureum, purple, spring and

The Gardens
St Lawrence

Dear Mr Gregory,

Hilda found
the name of the plant
in the "Garden
Dictionary" in the
Library. It gives its
as "Dutchman's Breeches"
proper name "Dicentra
Cucullaria" 5 in high.
But my books give
Dicentra Cucullaria
as white with
D. exima purple flowers
D. formosa red "
D. thalictrofolia yellow .
D. spectabilis red or
                        white
So take your choice.
Yours sincerely E. Durham

VENTNOR
7 15 PM
5 MAY
1959
ISLE OF WIGHT

POST CARD

THE ADDRESS TO BE WRITTEN ON THIS SIDE

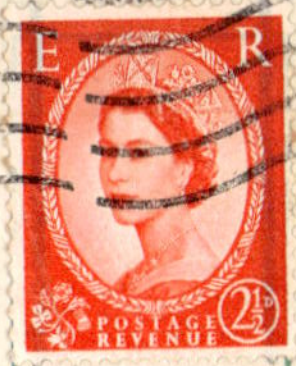

H. Gregory, Esq. M.B.E.
Lemon Villa
Ventnor
I.O.W.

summer, 6 in., Asia Minor ; rupestre (Syn. E. pulchellum), sulphur yellow, fragrant, spring, 1 ft., Asia Minor ; suffrutescens, pale yellow, spring and early summer, 1½ to 2 ft., California.

Erythræa (Blush-wort ; Centaury)—Ord. Gentianaceæ. Hardy annual or perennial alpine plants.
CULTURE : Soil, sandy loam. Position, sunny rockeries. Plant, March or April.
PROPAGATION : By seeds sown ₁₆ in. deep in light soil in cold frame in April ; perennial species by division of plants in March or April.
ANNUAL SPECIES : E. centaurium, pink, June to Sept., 6 to 15 in., Britain.
PERENNIAL SPECIES : E. Massoni, rose, summer, 4 to 6 in., Azores.

Erythrina (Coral-tree)—Ord. Leguminosæ. Half-hardy herbaceous perennials and greenhouse deciduous shrubs. Flowering and orn. foliage. First introduced 1690.
CULTURE OF SHRUBBY SPECIES : Compost, equal parts loam, peat, well-decayed manure and sand. Position, pot in warm greenhouse, or at base of south wall S. of England. Pot or plant, March. Prune shoots away close to old wood in Oct. Water freely April to Sept. ; keep almost dry remainder of time. Temp., Sept. to March 45° to 50° ; March to Sept. 55° to 65°. Store plants in pots on their sides in greenhouse during winter. Place in light part of structure March to June, then stand in sunny position outdoors. Protect outdoor plants with covering of ashes.
CULTURE OF HERBACEOUS SPECIES : Compost, same as above. Position, pot in warm sunny greenhouse. Pot, March. Cut down flowering stems in autumn. Water freely April to Sept. ; keep nearly dry afterwards. Temp., Sept. to March 45° to 55° ; March to Sept. 60° to 70°.
PROPAGATION : Shrubby species by cuttings of young shoots removed in spring with portion of old wood attached and inserted singly in well-drained pots of sandy peat in temp. 75° ; herbaceous species by division in spring.
SHRUBBY SPECIES : E. Crista-galli (Coral-tree), scarlet, June to Aug., 6 to 8 ft., Brazil.
HERBACEOUS SPECIES : E. herbacea, scarlet, June to Sept., 3 to 4 ft., W. Indies.

Erythronium (Dog's-tooth Violet ; Yellow Adder's-tongue)—Ord. Liliaceæ. Hardy bulbous perennials. First introduced 1596.
CULTURE : Compost, equal parts loam, peat and leaf-mould. Position, sheltered rockeries, beds, borders, or under shade of trees. Plant bulbs 3 in. deep and 2 in. apart in Aug. Transplant very seldom. Top-dress annually with decayed manure.
POT CULTURE : Compost, same as above. Plant bulbs 1 in. deep and ½ in. apart in well-drained pots in Aug. Store pots in cold frame during winter. Water very little until Feb., then give a moderate supply. Place plants in greenhouse or window to flower in March.
PROPAGATION : By offsets in Aug.
SPECIES CULTIVATED : E. albidum, white and yellow, April, 6 in., N. America ; americanum (Yellow Adder's-tongue), golden yellow and purple, May, 6 in., N. America ; californicum, creamy white, spring, 9 to 12 in., California ; citrinum, yellow, orange, and pink, spring, 6 in., Oregon ; Dens-canis (Dog's-tooth Violet), rose, spring, 6 in., Europe, and its varieties album (white), purpureum (purple), roseum (rose), violaceum (violet) ; grandiflorum, yellow, spring, N.W. America ; Hartwegi, creamy white, May, 6 in., N.W. America ; Hendersoni, purple-rose, March, 6 in., Oregon ; Howelli, yellow and orange, spring, 6 in., Oregon ; purpurascens, yellow, purple, and orange, spring, California ; purpurascens multiflorum, lilac ; revolutum, rose pink, spring, 8 to 12 in., California, and its varieties albiflorum (Syn. Watsoni), white and maroon, and Johnsonii, rosy pink.

Escallonia (Chilian Gum Box)—Ord. Saxifragaceæ. Half-hardy evergreen or deciduous shrubs. First introduced 1827.
CULTURE : Soil, ordinary rich, well drained. Position, against south walls in Midlands and in open garden S. of England. May also be planted against back walls of cold greenhouses. Suitable for hedges in mild districts. Plant, Oct.,

Nov., March, or April. Prune straggly shoots only in April. Thrives successfully in seaside gardens as a shrub or a hedge.
PROPAGATION : By seeds sown ⅟₁₆ in. deep ; cuttings inserted in sandy soil under bell-glass Aug. or Sept. ; layering shoots in Oct. ; suckers removed and replanted in April.
EVERGREEN SPECIES CULTIVATED : E. exoniensis, white or rose-tinted, June to Oct., 15 to 20 ft., hybrid ; floribunda, white, late summer and autumn, 10 ft., S. America ; illinita, white, Aug., 10 to 12 ft., Chile ; langleyensis, rosy purple, June, 8 ft., hybrid ; macrantha, crimson-red, June, 6 to 10 ft., Chile ; montevidensis (Syn. floribunda), white, July, 10 ft., Monte Video ; organensis, rosy red, Sept. 4 to 6 ft., Brazil ; pterocladon, white, June to Aug., 4 to 8 ft., Patagonia ; pulverulenta, white, July to Sept., 10 to 12 ft., Chile ; punctata, red, July, 6 to 10 ft., Chile ; revoluta, white, June to Aug., 15 to 20 ft., Chile ; rubra, red, July to Sept., 6 ft., Chile ; viscosa, white, June to Aug., 10 ft., Chile.
DECIDUOUS SPECIES CULTIVATED : E. philippiana, white, June to Aug., Valdivia.

Eschscholtzia (Californian Poppy)—Ord. Papaveraceæ. Hardy annuals. First introduced 1790.
CULTURE : Soil, ordinary. Position, sunny well-drained beds or borders.
PROPAGATION : By seeds sown ⅟₁₆ in. deep in Aug. or April where plants are to flower. Thin seedlings out to 2 in. apart when 1 in. high.
SPECIES CULTIVATED : E. californica, orange-yellow, summer, 1 to 2 ft., California ; californica crocea, orange. Numerous varieties will be found in trade lists.

Eucalyptus (Australian Gum ; Blue Gum)—Ord. Myrtaceæ. Greenhouse and half-hardy evergreen trees. Orn. foliage. First introduced 1810. Leaves mostly ovate-lanceolate, fragrant.
CULTURE : Compost, two parts fibry loam, one part leaf-mould, charcoal and sand. Position, pots in greenhouse heated to temp. 45° to 50° in winter, 55° to 60° other times ; dwelling rooms, sunny beds outdoors in summer ; sheltered places outdoors all the year S. of England. Pot, March or April. Plant outdoors June ; lift, Oct. Water plants in pots moderately Oct. to April, freely afterwards. Pruning not required.
PROPAGATION : By seeds sown ⅛ in. deep in pots of sandy soil in temp. 65° in Feb., March or April ; young plants should be raised annually for pot culture.
SPECIES CULTIVATED : E. citriodora (Citron-scented Gum), 15 to 20 ft., Australia, suitable for pot culture ; globulus (Blue Gum), 15 to 20 ft., Australia, pots or outdoors ; Gunnii, 15 to 20 ft., suitable for outdoor culture ; resinifera, 30 to 60 ft.

Eucharidium—Ord. Onagraceæ. Hardy annuals. First introduced 1787.
CULTURE : Soil, ordinary rich. Position, sunny well-drained beds or borders.
PROPAGATION : By seeds sown ⅟₁₆ in. deep where plants are to grow in Aug. or Sept. for early summer flowering, in March or April for mid-summer flowering, and June for autumn flowering. Thin seedlings to 2 in. apart when 1 in. high.
SPECIES CULTIVATED : E. Breweri, white, lilac, and purple, summer, 8 in., California ; concinnum, purple, summer, 1 ft., California.

Eucharis (Amazon Lily)—Ord. Amaryllidaceæ. Stove bulbous flowering plants. Evergreen. First introduced 1851.
CULTURE : Compost, two parts fibrous loam, one part peat, decomposed sheep manure and sand. Position, well-drained pots on a bed or stage heated beneath to temp. 85° in plant stove. Pot in June or July, placing six bulbs in a 10 in. pot. Press down compost firmly. Repotting not needful oftener than once every three or four years. Water moderately Oct. to April, freely afterwards. Syringe freely in summer. Liquid manure, apply twice a week after flower stems appear. Top-dress established plants annually in March with rich compost. Temp., March to Sept. 70° to 80° ; Sept. to Dec. 55° to 65° ; Dec. to March 65° to 75°.
PROPAGATION : By seeds sown ½ in. deep in sandy soil in temp. 85° in Feb. or March ; offsets removed from old bulbs and placed singly in 3 in. pots in June or July.
SPECIES CULTIVATED : E. candida, white, autumn, 1 ft., Colombia ; grandiflora (Syn. E. amazonica), white, March to Dec., 1 to 2 ft., Colombia, and its variety

Moorei ; Lowi, white, spring, 1 to 2 ft., hybrid ; Mastersii, white, spring, 12 to 18 in., Colombia ; Sanderi, white and yellow, spring, 12 to 18 in., Colombia ; Stevensii, white and yellow, spring, 1 ft., hybrid.

Eucomis (Pine-apple Flower ; King's Flower)—Ord. Liliaceæ. Half-hardy bulbous flowering plants. Nat. Cape of Good Hope. First introduced 1760.
POT CULTURE : Compost, two parts sandy loam, one part well-decayed manure and sand. Position, well-drained pots in light, warm greenhouse. Pot, Oct. or March, placing one bulb in a 5 in. pot. Water very little Sept. to March, moderately March to May, freely afterwards. Temp., Sept. to March 45° to 50° ; March to Sept. 55° to 65°. Apply liquid manure occasionally when flower spike shows.
OUTDOOR CULTURE : Soil, ordinary light rich. Position, sunny well-drained border. Plant, Sept., Oct., or March, placing bulbs 6 in. below surface and 6 in. apart. Protect in winter by covering of ashes, cocoanut-fibre refuse or manure.
PROPAGATION : By offsets removed and transplanted in Sept. or Oct.
SPECIES CULTIVATED : E. bicolor, greenish yellow, Aug., 1 to 2 ft., Natal ; punctata, green and brown, Aug., 18 in. to 2 ft. ; regia, green and purple, spring, 2 ft.

Eucryphia—Ord. Rosaceæ. Half-hardy evergreen or partially deciduous flowering shrub.
CULTURE : Soil, good ordinary. Position, warm shrubberies ; against S. or S.W. walls ; or in cold greenhouse. Plant in autumn.
PROPAGATION : By layers in autumn.
SPECIES CULTIVATED : E. cordifolia, white, July to Aug., 15 to 20 ft., Chile ; pinnatifolia, white, Aug., 10 to 20 ft., Chile.

Eugenia (Fruiting Myrtle)—Ord. Myrtaceæ. Stove and greenhouse flowering shrubs. Evergreen. First introduced 1768. Fruit, black, rose ; globular, fragrant, edible ; autumn.
CULTURE : Compost, two parts sandy loam, one leaf-mould or sand. Pot, Feb. or March. Position, pots in stove or greenhouse. Water moderately Oct. to April, freely afterwards. Syringe April to Aug. Prune straggly shoots in March. Temp. for stove species, 55° to 65° Sept. to March ; 65° to 75° March to Sept. ; for greenhouse species, 40° to 50° Oct. to March, 55° to 65° March to Oct.
PROPAGATION : By cuttings of firm shoots inserted in sandy soil under bell-glass in temp. 55° to 75° in summer.
STOVE SPECIES : E. caryophyllata, white, summer, 15 to 20 ft., Moluccas ; Jambos (Rose Apple), white, summer, 20 ft., Trop. Asia ; malaccensis (Malay Apple), scarlet, summer, 15 to 20 ft., Malaya. See also the genus Myrtus.
GREENHOUSE SPECIES : E. myriophylla, leaves narrow and elegant, 6 ft., Brazil.

Eulalia—See Miscanthus.

Euonymus (Spindle-tree ; Japanese Spindle-tree)—Ord. Celastraceæ. Hardy and half-hardy deciduous and evergreen shrubs. Orn. foliage. Leaves mostly oval-shaped, green, or variegated with white and yellow.
CULTURE : Soil, ordinary. Position, deciduous species in shrubberies ; evergreen species against south or west walls, edgings to beds, window boxes, hedges and front of shrubberies. Plant deciduous species in Sept., Oct. or Nov. ; evergreen in Sept., Oct., March, or April. Prune, Oct. or April. Good seaside shrubs.
POT CULTURE OF EVERGREEN SPECIES : Compost, two parts loam, one part leaf-mould and sand. Position, well-drained pots in cool greenhouse, corridors, balconies, windows. Pot, Sept., Oct., or March. Water moderately in winter, freely other times. Syringe foliage frequently in summer.
PROPAGATION : By cuttings of shoots of current year's growth, well ripened, inserted in sandy soil in cool greenhouse, window or frame, in Sept. or Oct. ; E. radicans by division at planting time.
DECIDUOUS SPECIES : E. alatus, 6 to 8 ft., China and Japan ; americanus, 2 ft., United States ; atropurpureus, 10 ft., N. America ; europæus, 10 to 15 ft., Europe (Britain) and Siberia ; latifolius, 8 ft., Europe and Asia.
EVERGREEN SPECIES : E. japonicus, leaves green, 4 to 6 ft., China and Japan, and

its varieties albo-marginata (leaves margined with white), aureus (leaves yellow), latifolius albo-variegatus (leaves broad and variegated with white), ovatus aureus (leaves golden) ; radicans, 1 ft., Japan, and its silvery- and golden-leaved forms.

Eupatorium (Hemp Agrimony)—Ord. Compositæ. Hardy herbaceous and greenhouse shrubby plants.
CULTURE OF HARDY SPECIES : Soil, ordinary. Position, open borders, shrubberies. Plant, Oct., Nov., March, or April.
CULTURE OF SHRUBBY GREENHOUSE SPECIES : Compost, equal parts loam and dried cow manure with a little sand. Position, pots in light greenhouse Sept. to June ; cold frame June to Sept. Pot, March to April. Prune immediately after flowering. Water moderately Sept. to March, freely afterwards. Temp., Sept. to March 45° to 50° ; March to June 55° to 60°. Apply liquid manure frequently to plants in flower. Both species may be planted out in the open garden in June, have their shoots frequently pinched, and then be lifted and placed in pots for flowering in greenhouse.
PROPAGATION : Hardy species by division in Oct. or March ; greenhouse species by cuttings of young shoots inserted in sandy soil in temp. 55° to 65° in March or April.
HARDY SPECIES : E. cannabinum (Hemp Agrimony), reddish purple, July, 2 to 4 ft., Britain ; purpureum (Trumpet Weed), purplish, autumn, 3 to 6 ft., N. America ; urticæfolium (Syn. E. ageratoides), white, summer, 2 to 4 ft., N. America.
GREENHOUSE SPECIES : E. atrorubens (Syn. Hebeclinium atrorubens), red, Jan. to March, 12 to 18 in., Mexico ; ianthinum (Syn. Hebeclinium ianthinum), purple, winter, 2 ft., Mexico ; riparium, white, spring, 2 to 3 ft., Mexico ; weinmannianum (Syn. E. odoratum), white, autumn, 2 to 3 ft., Mexico.

Euphorbia (Spurge ; Caper Spurge ; Poinsettia)—Ord. Euphorbiaceæ. Stove and hardy flowering shrubs or herbs.
CULTURE OF WARM HOUSE SPECIES : Compost, equal parts fibrous loam and peat with liberal amount of sand. Position, sunny dry part of stove, with shoots trained up roof, wall, or on trellis. Pot, March or June. Water moderately Sept. to Jan. ; keep almost dry Jan. to May ; freely afterwards. Temp., Jan. to May 50° to 55° ; May to Sept. 65° to 75° ; Sept. to Jan. 55° to 65°. Prune E. fulgens in June, cutting shoots back to within 1 in. of base.
CULTURE OF POINSETTIA : Flowers, insignificant. Bracts, scarlet, white ; winter. Foliage, green or variegated with creamy white. Compost, four parts fibrous loam, one part decayed cow manure, and half a part silver sand. Position, pots or beds with shoots trained to back wall of stove. YOUNG PLANTS : Place old plants in temp. 65° to 75° in May. Remove young shoots when 2 to 3 in. long, insert singly in 2 in. pots filled with sandy loam and peat, and plunge to the rims in bottom heat of 85°, under a bell-glass or in propagator. When rooted, place singly in 4 in. pots, plunge again in bottom heat for a few days, then remove to shelf near glass. As soon as well rooted transfer to 6 or 8 in. pots, keep near glass for week or so, then gradually harden. Place in cold sunny frame until Sept., when remove to temp. 55°. Shade from mid-day sun when in cold frame. Water freely. Syringe twice daily. Ventilate freely on fine days. Transfer plants into temp. 60° to 65° end of Sept. Water moderately. Apply stimulants into a temp. After flowering remove to a temp. of 40° to 45°, keep roots quite dry and store pots on their side under staging. OLD PLANTS : Prune shoots, unless required for producing cuttings, to second latent bud or eye from their base, end of April. When new shoots form 1 in. long, turn plants out of their pots, remove old soil from roots, cut off the straggling ends of latter, and repot in pots just large enough to take roots and little compost. Place in temp. 65° to 75° from pruning time. Repot into larger size when small pots are filled with roots. Place in cold sunny frame or pits during July and Aug. Water and syringe freely. Remove to temp. 55° to 60°, Sept. ; 60° to 70°, Oct. onwards. Apply stimulants twice a week Oct., until bracts are fully developed, then cease. After flowering treat as advised for young plants. Beds : Compost, as above. Plant, July. Train the shoots thinly to wall. Water freely while growing ; after flowering keep quite dry. Prune shoots to within one latent bud of their base, end of Sept. Temp., April to Sept.

Eucomis punctata
(Pine-apple flower)

Eucryphia cordifolia flore-pleno

Eupatorium ianthinum

Fabiana imbricata
(False Heath)

Fagus pendula
(Weeping Beech)

Fatsia japonica
(Japanese Aralia)

Ficus elastica
(India-rubber plant)

Filipendula hexapetala flore-
pleno (Dropwort)

Fittonia variegata

Forsythia intermedia spectabilis
(Japanese Golden Bell-tree)

Francoa ramosa
(Bridal Wreath)

Fraxinus Ornus
(Manna Ash)

Freesia refracta hybrida

Fremontia californica

Fritillaria Imperialis
(Crown Imperial)

Fritillaria Meleagris
(Snake's-head)

Fuchsia hybrida
(Lady's Ear Drops)

Fuchsia procumbens
(In Fruit)

65° to 75°; Sept. to April 55° to 60°.   Average height of a well-grown young plant 12 to 18 in.   Average diameter of a well-grown head of bracts 10 to 15 in.
CULTURE OF HARDY SPECIES : Soil, ordinary.   Position, dry borders, banks, sunny rockeries.   Plant, March or April.
PROPAGATION : Stove species by cuttings of young shoots 3 in. long inserted in well-drained pots of sandy compost in temp. 70° in May, June, or July ; hardy species by cuttings inserted in sandy soil in cold frame in summer, seeds sown in dryish positions outdoors in April, division of plants in Oct. or April.
STOVE SPECIES : E. fulgens (Syn. E. jacquinæflora), scarlet, autumn and winter, 2 to 3 ft., Mexico ; pulcherrima (Syn. Poinsettia pulcherrima), scarlet, autumn, 3 to 6 ft., Mexico ; punicea, scarlet, April, 6 ft., Jamaica ; splendens, red, summer, 4 ft., Madagascar.
HARDY SPECIES : E. amygdaloides, yellow, late summer, Europe and Orient ; Cyparissias (Cypress Spurge), yellow, June, 2 ft., Europe ; epithymoides, soft yellow, early spring, 9 in., Europe ; Lathyris (Caper Spurge), yellow, June and July, 3 to 4 ft., biennial, Europe ; Myrsinites, yellow, summer, trailing, S. Europe ; pilosa major, yellow, spring, 1 to 1½ ft., Europe, N. Asia ; polychroma, yellow, spring and summer, 1 to 1½ ft., Europe ; Wulfeni, yellow, summer, 3 ft., Europe.

European Cyclamen (*Cyclamen europæum*)—See Cyclamen.

European Palm (*Chamærops humilis*)—See Chamærops.

Eurya—Ord. Ternströmiaceæ.   Half-hardy evergreen shrubs.
CULTURE : Compost, two parts loam, one part peat and sand.   Position, pots in cool greenhouses, dwelling-rooms or windows.   Pot, March or April.   Water moderately in winter, freely other times.   E. japonica may be grown outdoors in S. of England and Ireland.   Requires protection when young.
PROPAGATION : By cuttings of young shoots inserted in sandy soil in temp. 60° to 65° in spring.
SPECIES CULTIVATED : E. japonica, 5 ft., India, China, and Japan ; japonica variegata, leaves green and creamy white ; ornacea (Syn. Clezera ornacea), China. See also Clezera.

Eurycles (Brisbane Lily)—Ord. Amaryllidaceæ.   Stove bulbous plants.   First introduced 1759.
CULTURE : Compost, three parts sandy loam, one part leaf-mould and sand.   Position, well-drained pots in light part of stove.   Pot, Feb.   Water freely March to Sept., keep nearly dry remainder of time.   Temp. for stove species, Sept. to March 50° to 55° ; March to Sept. 65° to 75°.
PROPAGATION : By offsets removed and placed singly in small pots in Feb.
SPECIES CULTIVATED : E. Cunninghami, white, July, 1 ft., Australia ; sylvestris, white, spring, 1 to 1½ ft., Malaya and Australia.

Euterpe—Ord. Palmaceæ.   Stove ornamental-leaved palms.   First introduced 1656.
CULTURE : Compost, equal parts loam, peat, leaf-mould, and sand.   Pot, Feb. to March.   Position, pots in shady part of stove.   Water freely always.   Shade from sun.   Temp., March to Sept. 70° to 85° ; Sept. to March 60° to 65°.
PROPAGATION : By seeds sown 1 in. deep in above compost, in temp. 85° in spring.
SPECIES CULTIVATED : E. edulis, 10 to 20 ft., Trop. America ; oleracea, 10 to 20 ft., Brazil.

Eutoca—See Phacelia.

Evening Flower—See Hesperantha.

Evening Primrose (*Œnothera biennis*)—See Œnothera.

Evening Star (*Cooperia Drummondi*)—See Cooperia.

Evergreen Alkanet (*Anchusa sempervirens*)—See Anchusa.

Evergreen Candytuft (*Iberis sempervirens*)—See Iberis.

Evergreen Fire-thorn (*Pyracantha coccinea*)—See Pyracantha.

Evergreen Maple (*Acer creticum*)—See Acer.

Evergreen Oak (*Quercus Ilex*)—See Quercus.

Evergreen Orpine (*Sedum Anacampseros*)—See Sedum.

Evergreen Rose (*Rosa sempervirens*)—See Rosa.

Everlasting Flowers—See Helipterum, Helichrysum, Waitzia and Xeranthemum.

Everlasting Pea (*Lathyrus latifolius*)—See Lathyrus.

Everlasting Sand-flower (*Ammobium alatum*)—See Ammobium.

Eve's-cushion (*Saxifraga hypnoides*)—See Saxifraga.

Ewer's Stonecrop (*Sedum Ewersi*)—See Sedum.

Exacum—Ord. Gentianaceæ. Stove annuals and perennials. First introduced 1848.
CULTURE : Compost, equal parts peat, loam, and sand. Position, pots in light part of plant stove. Water freely. Temp., 65° to 75°.
PROPAGATION : By seeds sown on surface of fine compost in temp. 75° to 80° in April, transplanting seedlings when large enough to handle into small pots and thence into a larger size later on ; perennial species also by cuttings.
PERENNIAL SPECIES : E. affine, bluish lilac, fragrant, June to Oct., 6 in., Socotra.
ANNUAL SPECIES : E. zeylanicum macranthum, violet purple, autumn, 2 ft., Ceylon.

Exeter Elm (*Ulmus montana* var. *fastigiata*)—See Ulmus.

Exochorda (Pearl Bush)—Ord. Rosaceæ. Hardy deciduous flowering shrubs. First introduced 1854.
CULTURE : Soil, ordinary. Position, shrubberies. Plant, Oct. to Feb. Prune after flowering.
PROPAGATION : By seeds sown in sandy soil in cold frame in spring or autumn ; cuttings of young shoots inserted in sandy soil under bell-glass in summer ; grafting on portions of its own roots in temp. 60° in spring.
SPECIES CULTIVATED : E. Giraldi, white, May, 10 ft., N. and W. China ; Korolkowi (Syn. E. Alberti), white, May, to 12 ft., Turkestan ; racemosa (Syns. E. grandiflora and Spiræa grandiflora), white, May, 6 ft., China.

Fabiana (False Heath)—Ord. Solanaceæ. Hardy flowering shrub. Evergreen. First introduced 1838.
CULTURE : Soil, ordinary. Position, protected by south or west walls ; cool greenhouses N. of England. Plant, Oct. or April. Water plants in pots moderately in winter, freely in summer. Repot, March or April.
PROPAGATION : By cuttings of firm young shoots inserted in sandy soil under bell-glass in cold greenhouse, or in cold frame in March or April.
SPECIES CULTIVATED : F. imbricata, white, May, 3 ft., Chile.

Fagopyrum (Buckwheat)—Ord. Polygonaceæ. Hardy annual. Grown for yielding seed for pheasant and poultry feeding ; also for ploughing or digging in as a green manure. Good bee plant also.
CULTURE : Soil, light, sandy, or brashy ; clay unsuitable. Sow in May in shallow drills 6 in. to 8 in. apart. Harvest when greatest amount of seed has matured, as seeds do not ripen all at once. Cut early in morning when moist with dew. Dig in as green manure when flowering begins.
SPECIES CULTIVATED : F. esculentum (Syn. F. sagitattum), pink and white, summer, 3 ft., Central Asia.

Fagus (Beech)—Ord. Cupuliferæ. Hardy deciduous and evergreen orn. foliage trees. Leaves, oblong, light green, silver-striped, golden-striped, copper, purple.
CULTURE : Soil, sandy or chalky, and gravelly loam. Position, open dryish

shrubberies, lawns, copses ; also good seaside tree. Plant deciduous species and varieties Oct. to Feb. ; evergreen, Sept. or April. Common species (F. sylvatica) good hedge shrub. Plant 9 in. apart and keep sides closely trimmed. Timber used for making joiners' tools, gun stocks, saddle trees, and wheel felloes.

PROPAGATION : By seeds sown ¾ in. deep in rows 15 in. apart in March or April, transplanting seedlings when two years old ; variegated kinds by grafting in March on common species.

SPECIES CULTIVATED : F. sylvatica (Common Beech), 70 to 80 ft., deciduous, Europe (Britain), and its varieties cuprea (Copper Beech), heterophylla, incisa and querci-folia (Cut-leaved Beeches), pendula (Weeping Beech), purpurea (Purple Beech) and argenteo-variegatis (Silver-leaved Beech).

Fair Maids of February (*Galanthus nivalis*)—See Galanthus.

Fair Maids of France (*Ranunculus aconitifolius* and *Saxifraga granulata*)—See Ranunculus and Saxifraga.

Fair Maids of Kent (*Ranunculus aconitifolius*)—See Ranunculus.

Fairy Borage (*Eritrichium nanum*)—See Eritrichium.

Fairy Fingers (*Digitalis purpurea*)—See Digitalis.

Fairy Floating Moss (*Azolla caroliniana*)—See Azolla.

Fairy Forget-me-not (*Eritrichium nanum*)—See Eritrichium.

Fairy Heron's-bill (*Erodium chamædryoides*)—See Erodium.

Fairy Rose (*Rosa indica minima*)—See Rosa.

Fairy Wallflower (*Erysimum pumilum*)—See Erysimum.

False Acacia—See Robinia.

False Brome Grass (*Brachypodium distachyon*)—See Brachypodium.

False Chamomile (*Boltonia asteroides*)—See Boltonia.

False Daisy—See Bellium.

False Dragon's Head (*Physostegia virginiana*)—See Physostegia.

False Goat's-beard (*Astilbe japonica*)—See Astilbe.

False Grape (*Vitis quinquefolia*)—See Vitis.

False Heath—See Fabiana.

False Hellebore (*Veratrum nigrum*)—See Veratrum.

False Hemp (*Datisca cannabina*)—See Datisca.

False Honeysuckle (*Rhododendron ponticum*)—See Rhododendron.

False Indigo (*Baptisia australis*)—See Baptisia.

False Mallow—See Malvastrum.

False Mitre-wort (*Tiarella cordifolia*)—See Tiarella.

False Plantain—See Heliconia.

False Spikenard (*Smilacina racemosa*)—See Smilacina.

False Starwort (*Boltonia asteroides*)—See Boltonia.

Fan Palm (*Chamærops humilis*)—See Chamærops.

Farfugium—See Senecio.

Fatsia (Japanese Aralia ; Rice-paper Plant ; Fig-leaf Palm)—Ord. Araliaceæ. Hardy and half-hardy evergreen shrubs. First introduced 1838.

GREENHOUSE CULTURE : Compost, two parts sandy loam, one part leaf-mould, decayed manure and sand. Position, well-drained pots in cool greenhouse, or dwelling-room. Pot or plant, Feb., March, or April. Water moderately Sept. to April, freely afterwards. Temp., Sept. to April 40° to 50°; April to Sept. 55° to 65°.

OUTDOOR CULTURE : Soil, ordinary, well drained. Position, sheltered, partially shaded shrubberies. Requires protection in severe weather. Plant, May.

PROPAGATION : By cuttings of roots inserted in light soil in temp. 80° in March or April ; variegated kinds by grafting on common species in temp. 75° in March or April ; tall plants by stem rooting in spring.
SPECIES CULTIVATED : F. japonica (Syn. Aralia Sieboldii), the Japanese Aralia or Fig-leaf Palm, leaves green, palmate, 6 to 15 ft., Japan, a popular room and green-house plant, but hardy around London ; papyrifera (Chinese Rice-paper Plant), Syns. Aralia papyrifera and Tetrapanax papyriferum, 6 to 8 ft., China. There are silver and golden variegated forms of F. japonica.

Feather-few (*Chrysanthemum Parthenium*)—See Chrysanthemum.

Feather-foil (*Hottonia palustris*)—See Hottonia.

Feather Grass (*Stipa pennata* and *Eragrostis japonica*)—See Stipa and Eragrostis.

Feather Hyacinth (*Muscari comosum monstrosum*)—See Muscari.

Fedia (Horn of Plenty)—Ord. Valerianaceæ. Hardy annual. First introduced 1796.
CULTURE : Soil, ordinary. Position, open beds, rockeries, or borders.
PROPAGATION : By seeds sown in boxes or pots of light soil in temp. 55° in March, transplanting into borders in May ; or outdoors in April where plants are to grow.
SPECIES CULTIVATED : F. Cornucopiæ, red, lilac, rose, and carmine, July, 6 to 12 in., S. Europe.

Feea—See Trichomanes.

Feijoa—Ord. Myrtaceæ. Half-hardy evergreen flowering tree. First introduced 1898.
CULTURE : Compost, equal parts sandy loam and leaf-mould with a liberal addition of well-decayed manure. Position, well-drained pots in cool greenhouse or sheltered shrubberies in mild districts. Water freely during growing season.
PROPAGATION : By seeds sown in sandy soil during Feb. or March in temp. 55° to 60° ; cuttings of young growth during June or July under bell-glass in gentle bottom heat.
SPECIES CULTIVATED : F. sellowiana, white and purplish, autumn, to 18 ft., S. America.

Felicia—Ord. Compositæ. Half-hardy annuals, biennials and sub-shrubs. Best treated as annuals. Natives of S. Africa.
CULTURE : Soil, ordinary. Position, sunny beds or borders. Sow seeds thinly in well-drained pans during Feb. or March in temp. 60° to 65°. Prick off when large enough to handle and harden off for planting out in May.
SPECIES CULTIVATED : F. bergeriana, blue, dwarf, summer; petiolata, rose to blue, summer, prostrate; tenella (Syn. F. fragilis), pale blue, summer, 12 to 14 in. See also Agathæa.

Felt-wort (*Verbascum Thapsus*)—See Verbascum.

Fendlera—Ord. Saxifragaceæ. Hardy flowering shrub. Deciduous. First introduced 1879.
CULTURE : Soil, sandy loam. Position, sunny rockeries or against S. or S.W. walls. Plant, Nov. to Feb.
PROPAGATION : By cuttings of young growth during June or July under bell-glass in gentle bottom heat.
SPECIES CULTIVATED : F. rupicola, white or rose-tinted, May to June, 3 to 6 ft., S.W. United States.

Fennel (*Fœniculum vulgare*)—See Fœniculum.

Fennel Flower (*Nigella damascena*)—See Nigella.

Fennel-leaved Pæony (*Pæonia tenuifolia*)—See Pæonia.

Fen Rue (*Thalictrum flavum*)—See Thalictrum.

Fenugreek (*Trigonella fœnum-græcum*)—See Trigonella.

Fenzlia—See Gilia.

Fern-leaved Beech (*Fagus sylvatica heterophylla*)—See Fagus.

Fern-leaved Chestnut (*Castanea sativa heterophylla*)—See Castanea.

Fern-leaved Oak (*Quercus pedunculata filicifolia*)—See Quercus.

Fern-leaved Sumach (*Rhus glabra laciniata*)—See Rhus.

Fern Palm (*Cycas revoluta*)—See Cycas.

Ferraria (Black Iris)—Ord. Iridaceæ. Half-hardy bulbous plant. Deciduous. First introduced 1755.
CULTURE : Compost, two parts sandy loam, one peat. Position, cool greenhouse. Pot, Nov. Place bulbs with point just below surface and 1 to 2 in. apart. Water occasionally Nov. to Feb. ; moderately Feb. to June ; keep quite dry July to Nov. Temp., Nov. to Feb. 40° to 45° ; Feb. to June, 50° to 60°.
SPECIES CULTIVATED : F. undulata, brown and purple, March and April, 6 to 8 in., S. Africa.

Ferula (Giant Fennel)—Ord. Umbelliferæ. Hardy herbaceous plants. Orn. foliage. First introduced 1596. Foliage, elegant, fern-like, deep green.
CULTURE : Soil, ordinary. Position, open, margins of shrubberies, borders, ponds, isolated on lawns and summits of rockeries or banks. Plant, Nov. to March.
PROPAGATION : By seeds sown in Sept., Oct., or Nov. in light soil outdoors, transplanting seedlings following summer ; division of roots in Oct. or Nov.
SPECIES CULTIVATED : F. communis (Giant Fennel), yellow, June, 8 to 12 ft., Mediterranean Region ; glauca, yellow, June, 6 to 8 ft., S. Europe ; tingitana, yellow, June, 6 to 8 ft., N. Africa.

Fescue Grass (*Festuca ovina*)—See Festuca.

Festuca (Fescue Grass)—Ord. Gramineæ. Hardy perennial grass.
OUTDOOR CULTURE : Soil, ordinary. Position, edgings of flower beds or borders. Plant, Sept., Oct., March, or April.
POT CULTURE : Compost, two parts good soil, one part leaf-mould and sand. Position, cold or warm greenhouses and windows. Pot, March or April. Water moderately in winter, freely other times.
PROPAGATION : By seeds sown outdoors in April ; division in March or April.
SPECIES CULTIVATED : F. ovina glauca, leaves bristly, glaucous green, 6 in., Britain.

Feverfew (*Chrysanthemum Parthenium*)—See Chrysanthemum.

Fever Tree (*Eucalyptus globulus*)—See Eucalyptus.

Ficus (Fig-tree ; India Rubber-plant)—Ord. Urticaceæ. Stove, greenhouse and hardy deciduous and evergreen trees and shrubs. Orn. foliage and fruit bearing. Flowers unisexual, borne inside the fruit.
CULTURE OF TENDER SPECIES : Compost, three parts loam, one part peat and sand. Position, erect species (F. elastica, etc.) in pots in stove, greenhouse, or dwelling-rooms ; creeping species (F. pumila) in beds with shoots clinging to walls, rockeries, etc. Pot or plant, Feb., March, or April. Water moderately Oct. to March, freely afterwards. Syringe stove species daily Feb. to Aug. Temp. for stove species, 55° to 65° Oct. to Feb., 75° to 85° Feb. to Oct. ; for greenhouse species, 50° to 55° Sept. to March, 60° to 70° March to Sept.
CULTURE OF INDIA-RUBBER PLANT IN ROOMS : Compost, see above. Position, light, near window, away from draughts. Pot, March or April. Water once a week Nov. to March, twice and three times weekly other times. Temp., Sept. to April 40° to 50° ; April to Sept. 55° to 60°. Sponge leaves weekly.
OUTDOOR CULTURE IN SUMMER : Plunge pots to rim in sunny beds middle of June. Lift and place in greenhouse again in Sept. Water freely daily.
OUTDOOR CULTURE OF FIG : Compost, two parts fibry loam, one part brick rubbish and old mortar. Position, against south or south-west walls. Plant, April, in border 2 ft. deep and 3 ft. wide, enclosed with brick or concrete wall. Mode of bearing : Entire length of previous year's shoots ; only one crop borne outdoors in England. Prune, April or July, simply removing deformed, dead, or very weak

branches. Pinch point off vigorous young shoots in July. Apply liquid manure once in Aug. to trees bearing heavily. Figlets size of filberts remove in Sept. or Oct. Protect branches in Dec. with straw or mats, removing both in April.
CULTURE OF FIG UNDER GLASS : Compost, position, border, time of planting as above. Branches trained up roof or against wall. Mode of bearing : On shoots of previous year's growth for first crop ; those of current year for second crop. Prune and pinch as above. Disbud young shoots when too many are forming. Water and syringe freely in summer. Apply liquid manure occasionally in summer. Temp. for forcing, 50° to 65°.
POT CULTURE OF FIG : Compost, turfy loam, little bonemeal. Position, ordinary greenhouse, vinery or forcing house. Pot, Nov. to April. Size of pots, 10 or 12 in. Water freely when growing, very little when not. Apply liquid manure twice weekly to trees bearing fruit. Syringe daily when in growth. Pinch points off young shoots when latter are 9 in. long. Protect pots with covering of straw Nov. to Jan. and partially expose branches to the air.
PROPAGATION : Tender species by cuttings of shoots inserted in sandy peat in a temp. of 75° in spring or summer ; cuttings of stem 1 in. long, and with one leaf attached, slightly burying stem portion in soil and supporting leaf with a stake, and placing in above temp. ; stem rooting in case of tall india-rubber plants in spring. Expose cuttings to air for a short time to allow base to dry before inserting in soil. Fig by seeds sown in light soil in a temp. of 65° to 70° in Jan., afterwards growing seedlings on in pots until they bear fruit and it can be seen if they are worth growing ; cuttings of previous year's shoots 6 in. long and having a heel of older wood attached at base, inserted in a warm border outdoors or in pots in gentle heat between Oct. and March ; cuttings of young shoots, 3 or 4 in. long, removed with a heel of older wood, and inserted in pots of light sandy soil in a propagating frame (temp. 70°) in June ; layering shoots in summer ; grafting by approach just after tree comes into leaf ; budding in July ; suckers in autumn.
TENDER SPECIES : F. enghalensis (Banyan Tree), fruits round, red, 30 to 40 ft., India ; elastica (India-rubber Plant), leaves green, India ; elastica variegata, leaves variegated ; Parcelli, leaves green and white, Polynesia ; pumila (Syn. F. repens), leaves green, shoots creeping (a good plant for covering walls), Japan ; pumila minima, a smaller variety ; radicans variegata, leaves variegated with silver ; rubiginosa (Syn. F. australis), leaves with a rusty appearance beneath, Australia, and its variety variegata.
HARDY SPECIES : F. Carica (Fig), Mediterranean Region ; introduced in 1548.

Fig-leaf Palm (*Fatsia japonica*)—See Fatsia.

Fig Marigold (*Mesembryanthemum crystallinum*)—See Mesembryanthemum.

Fig Tree (*Ficus carica*)—See Ficus.

Filbert (*Corylus maxima*)—See Corylus.

Filipendula (Dropwort : Queen of the Meadow)—Ord. Rosaceæ. Hardy herbaceous perennials.
CULTURE : Soil ordinary, well manured for F. Ulmaria. Position, open sunny borders and wild gardens. Plant Oct. to Nov. or March to April.
PROPAGATION : By division in spring.
SPECIES CULTIVATED : F. hexapetala flore-pleno (Syn. Spiræa filipendula fl.-pl.), creamy-white, June, 2 to 3 ft., Europe (Britain) ; Ulmaria (Syn. Spiræa Ulmaria), white, June, to 6 ft., Europe and Asia. See also Spiræa.

Filmy Ferns—See Hymenophyllum, Todea, and Trichomanes.

Finger Fern (*Asplenium ceterach*)—See Asplenium.

Finger Flower (*Digitalis purpurea*)—See Digitalis.

Finocchio (*Fœniculum dulce*)—See Fœniculum.

Fir—See Abies, Picea, and Pinus.

Fir Club Moss (*Lycopodium Selago*)—See Lycopodium.

Fire Bush (*Pyracantha coccinea*)—See Pyracantha.

Fire Cracker (*Brevoortia Ida-Maia* and *Cuphea ignea*)—See Brevoortia and Cuphea.

Fire Pink (*Silene virginica*)—See Silene.

Fire Thorn (*Pyracantha coccinea*)—See Pyracantha.

Fish-bone Thistle (*Cnicus Casabonæ*)—See Cnicus.

Fittonia—Ord. Acanthaceæ. Warm greenhouse evergreen perennial trailing plants. Orn. foliage. First introduced 1869. Leaves, dark green or bright green, with red or pure white veins.

CULTURE : Compost, equal parts peat, loam, and sand. Position, shallow pans, pots, or surface of beds in shady part of plant stove ; also in Wardian cases. Water moderately Nov. to Feb., freely afterwards. Temp., Oct. to March 55° to 60° ; March to Oct. 65° to 75°.

PROPAGATION : By cuttings of firm shoots inserted in sandy soil in temp. 75° to 85° under bell-glass in Feb., March, or April ; division of plants in Feb. or March.

SPECIES CULTIVATED : F. argyroneura, leaves green, veined with white, 6 in., Peru ; gigantea, leaves green, veined with red, 12 to 15 in., Peru ; Verschaffeltii, leaves green, veined with red, 8 in., Peru, and its variety Pearcei, leaves glaucous below.

Five-leaved Indian Cress (*Tropæolum pentaphyllum*)—See Tropæolum.

Flag (*Iris germanica*)—See Iris.

Flame Flower (*Tropæolum speciosum*)—See Tropæolum.

Flamingo Plant—See Anthurium.

Flannel Flower (*Actinotus Helianthi*)—See Actinotus.

Flannel Plant (*Verbascum Thapsus*)—See Verbascum.

Flat Pea—See Platylobium.

Flax—See Linum.

Flax Lily—See Dianella.

Fleabane—See Inula and Erigeron.

Fleur-de-Lis (*Iris Pseudacorus*)—See Iris.

Florence Fennel (*Fœniculum dulce*)—See Fœniculum.

Florentine Iris (*Iris florentina*)—See Iris.

Florida Water Lily (*Nymphæa flava*)—See Nymphæa.

Floss-flower (*Ageratum mexicanum*)—See Ageratum.

Flower-de-Luce (*Iris Pseudacorus*)—See Iris.

Flower Fern—See Anemia.

Flowering Ash (*Fraxinus Ornus*)—See Fraxinus.

Flowering Currant (*Ribes sanguinea*)—See Ribes.

Flowering Dogwood (*Cornus florida*)—See Cornus.

Flowering Fern (*Osmunda regalis*)—See Osmunda.

Flowering Grass (*Lapeyrousia cruenta*)—See Lapeyrousia.

Flowering Nutmeg-tree (*Leycesteria formosa*)—See Leycesteria.

Flowering Rush (*Butomus umbellatus*)—See Butomus.

Flowering Seakale (*Crambe cordifolia*)—See Crambe.

Flower-of-a-day (*Tradescantia virginica*)—See Tradescantia.

Flower-of-an-hour (*Hibiscus Trionum*)—See Hibiscus.

Flower-of-the-Dead (*Oncidium tigrinum*)—See Oncidium.

Flower of the Gods (*Disa grandiflora*)—See Disa.

Flower of the West Wind—See Zephyranthes.

Fly Honeysuckle (*Lonicera xylosteum*)—See Lonicera.

Fly Orchis (*Ophrys muscifera*)—See Ophrys.

Fly-trap (*Dionæa muscipula*)—See Dionæa.

Foam Flower (*Tiarella cordifolia*)—See Tiarella.

Fœniculum (Fennel)—Ord. Umbelliferæ. Hardy perennial and annual herbs. Leaves used for sauces and garnishing.
CULTURE : Soil, ordinary. Position, sunny border. Plant F. vulgare, March or April, 12 in. apart in rows 15 in. asunder. Sow seeds of F. dulce in drills 18 in. apart where plants are required, thinning out seedlings to 6 in. asunder. Remove flower stems as soon as seen, unless seed is wanted.
PROPAGATION : F. vulgare by seeds sown ¼ in. deep in drills 6 in. apart in March ; division of roots in March.
SPECIES CULTIVATED : F. vulgare (Fennel), yellow, autumn, 2 ft., Europe (Britain) ; dulce (Florence Fennel), 2½ ft., annual, Italy.

Fontanesia—Ord. Oleaceæ. Hardy deciduous ornamental shrubs. First introduced 1787.
CULTURE : Soil, ordinary. Position, sunny shrubberies, or as hedge plants. Plant, Nov. to Feb.
PROPAGATION : By cuttings inserted in sandy soil in cold frame during late summer.
SPECIES CULTIVATED : F. Fortunei, greenish white, summer, 10 to 15 ft., China ; phillyreoides, greenish white, June, 6 to 10 ft., Orient.

Forbidden Fruit (*Citrus decumana*)—See Citrus.

Forestiera (Syn. Adelia)—Ord. Oleaceæ. Hardy deciduous shrub. First introduced 1812.
CULTURE : Soil, ordinary. Position, sunny shrubberies. Plant, Nov. to Feb.
PROPAGATION : By cuttings in late summer.
SPECIES CULTIVATED : F. acuminata, greenish yellow, 10 to 30 ft., S.E. United States.

Forget-me-not—See Myosotis.

Forked Spleenwort (*Asplenium septentrionale*)—See Asplenium.

Forsythia (Japanese Golden Bell-tree)—Ord. Oleaceæ. Hardy flowering shrubs. Deciduous. First introduced 1845.
OUTDOOR CULTURE : Soil, ordinary. Position, against south or west walls, or in sheltered parts of shrubbery. Plant, Oct. to Feb. Prune after flowering.
POT CULTURE : Compost, two parts loam, one leaf-mould and sand. Position, well-drained pots in cool or warm greenhouse Dec. to May, outdoors remainder of year. Pot, Oct. to Dec. Water very little till March, then apply freely.
PROPAGATION : By cuttings inserted in sandy soil under bell-glass, July and Aug. ; or in cold frame, Oct. or Nov. ; layering in Oct. or Nov.
SPECIES CULTIVATED : F. europæa, yellow, March, 3 to 6 ft., Albania ; intermedia, yellow, Feb. and March, 8 ft., hybrid, and its variety spectabilis ; suspensa, yellow, March, 8 ft., China, and its varieties atrocaulis, Fortunei and Sieboldi ; viridissima, yellow, March, 10 ft., China and Japan.

Fothergilla (American Wych Hazel)—Ord. Hamamelidaceæ. Hardy flowering shrubs. Deciduous. First introduced 1765.
CULTURE : Compost, well-drained soil, sandy peat. Position, borders. Plant, Oct. to March. Prune after flowering.
PROPAGATION : By seeds sown ₁/₁₆ in. deep in pans of moist sandy peat in temp. of 45° to 55° in March or April ; layering shoots in Oct. or Nov.
SPECIES CULTIVATED : F. Gardeni (Syn. F. alnifolia), white, fragrant, May, 3 to 6 ft., United States ; major, pinkish white and yellow, May, 6 to 8 ft., Virginia and S. Carolina.

Fountain Plant (*Amaranthus tricolor salicifolius*)—See Amaranthus.

Fountain Tree (*Cedrus deodara*)—See Cedrus.

Fox Chop (*Mesembryanthemum vulpinum*)—See Mesembryanthemum.

Foxglove (*Digitalis purpurea*)—See Digitalis.

Fox Rose (*Rosa spinosissima*)—See Rosa.

Fox-tailed Asparagus—See Equisetum.

Fragaria (Strawberry)—Ord. Rosaceæ. Hardy and half-hardy perennial fruit-bearing and orn. trailing plants. Virginian Strawberry first introduced 1629.

CULTURE OF ORNAMENTAL SPECIES (F. indica) : Compost, two parts loam, one part leaf-mould and sand. Position, pots in hanging baskets in cool greenhouse or window, or on sunny well-drained rockery. Pot or plant, March. Water moderately. Apply liquid manure occasionally in summer.

CULTURE OF STRAWBERRY : Soil, deep rich sandy loam ; clay unsuitable. Position, open plots or borders, trenched 2 ft. deep ; alpine kind under shade of trees or on banks. Plant, Aug., Sept., or March 18 in. apart in rows 2½ ft. asunder ; alpines 6 in. apart. Mulch annually with manure in March, and a thin layer of straw in May. Suitable artificial manure, one part sulphate of potash and two parts superphosphate applied in autumn at the rate of 1 oz. per square yard, and 1 oz. of nitrate of soda per square yard, applied when fruit has set. Remove runners when they appear. No digging between rows necessary. Renew beds every three or four years.

POT CULTURE : Compost, two-thirds calcareous loam, one-third decayed manure, little bone dust. Position, on bed of cinder ashes outdoors Aug. to Oct. ; frames Oct. to Jan ; greenhouses or vineries after Jan. Pot singly in 6 in. pots in Aug. Water moderately till Oct., very little till Jan., freely afterwards. Fertilise blossoms by means of camel-hair brush. Thin fruit when set to a few on each plant. Feed with liquid manure after fruit has set until it begins to ripen. Plant out in garden after fruiting. Temp. for forcing : Jan. to March 45° to 55° ; March to ripening period, 65° to 75°.

PROPAGATION : By seeds sown $\frac{1}{16}$ in. deep in light soil outdoors, or in boxes in greenhouse in March or April; by runners on plants that fruit freely. Peg runners on surface of soil in 3 in. pots in June or July, or into open ground around plants. Runners rooted into pots best for pot culture.

SPECIES CULTIVATED : F. chiloensis (Chile Strawberry), white, May, 1 ft., fruit crimson, Chile, ornamental, and its variety grandiflora (Pine Strawberry) with pine-apple-flavoured fruits ; elatior (Hautbois Strawberry), (Syn. F. moschata), white, summer, 6 in., fruit red, aroma musky, edible, Europe (Britain); indica (Indian Strawberry), yellow, June, trailing, India, an ornamental species suited for rockeries or hanging baskets; vesca (Alpine Strawberry), white, May, 6 to 12 in., fruit scarlet, edible, Europe, and its varieties variegata and semperflorens ; viridis (Green Pine Strawberry), (Syn. F. collina), white, May, 6 ins., fruit green, pineapple flavoured, edible, Europe ; virginiana (Scarlet Strawberry), white, May, fruit scarlet, edible, United States, parent of the many forms of garden strawberries.

Fragrant Garland Flower (*Hedychium coronarium*)—See Hedychium.

Fragrant Hellebore (*Helleborus odorus*)—See Helleborus.

Fragrant Olive—See Osmanthus.

Fragrant Wood Fern (*Nephrodium fragrans*)—See Nephrodium.

Franciscea—See Brunfelsia.

Francoa (Maiden's Wreath ; Bridal Wreath)—Ord. Saxifragaceæ. Hardy and half-hardy perennial plants. First introduced 1830.

OUTDOOR CULTURE : Soil, light rich loam. Position, sunny sheltered borders, banks, or rockeries. Plant, March or April.

POT CULTURE : Compost, two parts loam, one part leaf-mould and sand. Position, well-drained pots in cool greenhouse, frame, or window. Pot, March or April. Water moderately Oct. to April, freely afterwards. Apply little liquid manure to plants in flower. Temp., Oct. to April 40° to 50° ; April to Sept. 55° to 65°.

PROPAGATION : By seeds sown on the surface of a well-drained pan of sandy peat under bell-glass in temp. of 50° to 55° in Feb., March, or April ; division of plants at potting time.

SPECIES CULTIVATED : F. appendiculata, red, July, 1 to 2 ft., Chile ; ramosa, white. July and Aug., 2 ft., Chile ; sonchifolia, pink, summer, 2 ft., Chile.

Frankenia (Sea Heath)—Ord. Frankeniaceæ. Hardy flowering plant. Evergreen. Habit, creeping.
CULTURE : Soil, light sandy. Position, sunny dry rockeries or borders. Plant, Oct. or April.
PROPAGATION : By division of plants in Oct. or April ; seeds in cold frame in April.
SPECIES CULTIVATED : F. lævis, rose, July and Aug., Europe (Britain).

Frangipanni-plant (*Plumiera acutifolia*)—See Plumiera.

Frankincense (*Mohria caffrorum*)—See Mohria.

Fraser's Balsam (*Abies Fraseri*)—See Abies.

Fraxinella (*Dictamnus albus*)—See Dictamnus.

Fraxinus (Ash ; Flowering Ash ; Manna Ash)—Ord. Oleaceæ. Hardy deciduous trees. Orn. foliage and flowering. Flowers, white, green, yellow ; March to May.
CULTURE : Soil, ordinary. Position, dryish, sheltered. Suitable for seaside gardens, towns, chalky or gravelly situations. Plant, Oct. to Feb. Prune, Oct. to March. Timber used for tool handles, wooden rakes, ploughs, hoops, dairy utensils, and agricultural implements ; also by cabinet makers for furniture making. Average life, 300 years. Timber reaches maturity at 70 years.
PROPAGATION : By seeds, buried in dry sand for a year, then sown 1 in. deep in light soil outdoors in Feb., transplanting seedlings when a year old ; grafting on common species in March.
SPECIES CULTIVATED : F. americana (White Ash), to 120 ft., Canada ; angustifolia, 60 to 70 ft., S. Europe and N. Africa ; excelsior (Common Ash), 100 to 140 ft., Europe (Britain), and its varieties crispa (Curl-leaved Ash), aurea (Golden Ash), pendula (Weeping Ash) ; floribunda, white, to 120 ft., Himalayas, slightly tender ; lanceolata, to 60 ft., U.S.A. ; Ornus (Flowering or Manna Ash), 50 to 65 ft., S. Europe ; pennsylvanica, 40 to 60 ft., Eastern N. America ; spæthiana, 30 to 50 ft., Japan.

Freesia—Ord. Iridaceæ. Greenhouse bulbous plants. Deciduous. Nat. Cape of Good Hope. Flowers, fragrant.
INDOOR CULTURE : Compost, equal parts decayed manure, loam, leaf-mould and sand. Position, pots in cool greenhouse, frame, or window. Pot, Aug. to flower in Jan., Oct. for Feb., Nov. for March, Dec. for April. Plant bulbs 1 in. deep and 2 in. apart. Suitable sized pot, 4½ in. diameter. Stand pots in cool position and give very little water until growth commences. Water freely when growth well advanced and until plants have flowered, then gradually decrease supply, keeping soil quite dry till July. Temp., not lower than 40°. Apply weak liquid or artificial manure to plants showing flower. Repot, annually.
OUTDOOR CULTURE : Soil, light, rich, sandy. Position, sunny well-drained borders S. of England only. Plant bulbs 2 in. deep and 2 in. apart in Aug. or Sept. Protect in winter.
PROPAGATION : By seeds sown ⅛ in. deep in pots or pans of light sandy soil in cool greenhouse or frame as soon as ripe, or in March or April ; by offsets at potting time. Do not transplant seedlings first year.
SPECIES CULTIVATED : F. refracta, white and orange, May to Aug., 1 ft., and its varieties Leichtlinii (yellow, cream, and orange), alba (white), odorata (yellow and very fragrant), and a number of other fine colour forms to be found in trade lists.

Fremontia—Ord. Sterculiaceæ. Half-hardy deciduous flowering shrubs. First introduced 1851.
CULTURE : Soil, sandy loam. Position, against west or north walls or fences, or in shrubberies S. of England. Plant, Oct. to March. Prune after flowering.
PROPAGATION : By seeds sown ⅛ in. deep in well-drained pots of sandy soil under bell-glass or frame in March or April.
SPECIES CULTIVATED : F. californica, yellow, June, 6 to 10 ft., California ; mexicana, deep yellow, to 10 ft., S. California.

French Bean (*Phaseolus vulgaris*)—See Phaseolus.

French Fern (*Asplenium adiantum-nigrum*)—See Asplenium.

French Honeysuckle (*Hedysarum coronarium*)—See Hedysarum.

French Marigold (*Tagetes patula*)—See Tagetes.

French Mulberry (*Callicarpa americana*)—See Callicarpa.

French Rose (*Rosa gallica*)—See Rosa.

French Sorrel—See Oxalis.

French Willow (*Epilobium angustifolium*)—See Epilobium.

Fresh-water Soldier (*Stratiotes aloides*)—See Stratiotes.

Fringed Buck-bean (*Limnanthemum peltatum*)—See Limnanthemum.

Fringed Pink (*Dianthus superbus*)—See Dianthus.

Fringed Water Lily (*Limnanthemum peltatum*)—See Limnanthemum.

Fringe Flower—See Schizanthus.

Fringe Tree (*Chionanthus virginica*)—See Chionanthus.

Fritillaria (Fritillary, Crown Imperial ; Chequered Daffodil ; Snake's-head Fritillary ; Persian Lily)—Ord. Liliaceæ. Hardy bulbous plants. Deciduous.
OUTDOOR CULTURE : Soil, ordinary deep rich. Position, shady borders for Crown Imperial ; Snake's-head Fritillary, borders, or naturalised in turf ; well-drained open borders for other species. Plant, 4 to 6 in. deep and 6 to 8 in. apart, Sept. to Nov. Top-dress annually with decayed manure. Do not transplant bulbs oftener than once in four years.
POT CULTURE : Compost, equal parts loam, peat, leaf-mould, decayed manure and sand. Position, well-drained pots in cold frame or cold greenhouse. Pot, Sept. or Oct., placing one bulb in centre of 5, 6, or 8 in. pot. Water very little till growth begins, then give moderate supply. Apply liquid manure when plants show flower. After flowering gradually withhold water, keeping soil quite dry after foliage has died.
PROPAGATION : By seeds sown ⅛ in. deep in pots or pans of sandy soil in cold frame or greenhouse as soon as ripe, or in spring ; by offsets at planting time. Do not transplant seedlings first year. Seedlings do not flower until four to six years old.
SPECIES CULTIVATED : F. armena, yellow, April, 6 in., Asia Minor ; askabadensis, chrome yellow and green, March, 3 to 4 ft., Central Asia ; aurea, yellow and brown, 6 in., May, Asia Minor ; citrina, green and yellow, 8 in., May, Asia Minor ; coccinea, red, May, 8 in. ; Elwesii, green and brown, May, 1 ft. ; Imperialis (Crown Imperial), yellow, May, 2 to 3 ft., Orient, and its varieties aurora (orange), lutea (yellow), rubra (red), and aureo-marginata (leaves edged yellow) ; latifolia, red, etc., May, 1 ft., Caucasus ; Meleagris (Snake's-head), purple, yellow, and white, May, 12 to 18 in., Europe (Britain) ; Meleagris alba, white ; pallidiflora, yellow, rose, and purple, May, 9 in., Siberia ; persica, violet blue, May, 2 ft., Asia Minor ; pudica, golden yellow, April, 6 in., N.W. America ; pyrenaica, plum, olive, and maroon, summer, 1½ ft., Pyrenees ; recurva, orange-scarlet, May, 2 ft., California ; ruthenica, black, May, 1 ft., Caucasus.

Fritillary (*Fritillaria meleagris*)—See Fritillaria.

Frog-bit (*Hydrocharis Morsus-ranæ*)—See Hydrocharis.

Fruiting Duck Weed (*Nertera depressa*)—See Nertera.

Fruiting Myrtle—See Eugenia.

Fuchsia (Ear Drops ; Lady's Ear Drops)—Ord. Onagraceæ. Greenhouse and hardy flowering shrubs. Deciduous. First introduced 1788.
CULTURE OF GREENHOUSE SPECIES : Compost, two parts good fibrous loam, one part well-decayed manure and leaf-mould, with liberal quantity of silver or river sand. Position, shady part of greenhouse or window March to July ; sunny place outdoors July to Oct. ; cool dry part of greenhouse or room remainder of year. Pot old plants in Feb. or March, young ones when needed. Prune old plants in

Feb.   Water moderately March to May, freely May to Oct., very little at other times.   Temp., Oct. to Feb. 40° to 45° ; Feb. to Oct. 55° to 65°.   Apply liquid or artificial manure to healthy plants showing flower.   Pinch out points of shoots frequently in spring and early summer to induce bushy growth.   When repotting old plants, remove soil from roots and place in small pots till growth begins, then shift into larger size.   Syringe foliage Feb. to May.
SUMMER CULTURE IN BEDS : Plant out in June.   Lift, pot and store plants in greenhouse in Sept.
CULTURE OF HARDY SPECIES : Soil, ordinary deep rich.   Position, well-drained borders, base of south or west walls, or in sheltered position in the open S. of England.   Plant, Oct. or April.   Prune shoots off close to base in Nov.   Protect in winter with layer of dry litter or leaves.
PROPAGATION : By seeds sown $\frac{1}{16}$ in. deep in well-drained pots of light sandy soil in temp. 55° in March or April ; cuttings of young shoots inserted singly in small pots of sandy soil in temp. 70° to 80° in Jan., Feb., or March, or in cool greenhouse or window in April, May, or June.
GREENHOUSE SPECIES : F. corymbiflora, deep red, summer, 6 ft., Peru ; fulgens, scarlet, July, 3 to 4 ft., Mexico ; procumbens, yellow and blue, summer, magenta-crimson berries, habit trailing, New Zealand ; splendens, scarlet, summer, 6 ft., Mexico ; triphylla, cinnabar red, summer, 1 to 1½ ft., Mexico. Numerous varieties.
HARDY SPECIES : F. macrostemma, scarlet and purple, July, 10 to 20 ft., Chile, and its varieties conica (scarlet), corallina (crimson and plum), globosa (purplish red), gracilis (scarlet and purple), pumila (scarlet), and Riccartoni (scarlet).

Fuchsia-flowered Currant (*Ribes speciosum*)—See Ribes.

Fulham Oak (*Quercus luccombeana fulhamensis*)—See Quercus.

Fulham Yew (*Taxus erecta*)—See Taxus.

Fuller's Herb (*Saponaria officinalis*)—See Saponaria.

Fumaria (Fumitory)—Ord. Fumariaceæ. Hardy annual climber.
CULTURE : Soil, ordinary.   Position, against S.E. or W. walls, in open borders with shoots running up sticks, or against arbours and trellis-work.
PROPAGATION : By seeds sown $\frac{1}{16}$ in. deep in April where plants are to flower.
SPECIES CULTIVATED : F. capreolata, white and purple, summer, 3 to 4 ft., Europe (Britain).

Fume-wort (*Corydalis lutea*)—See Corydalis.

Fumitory—See Corydalis and Fumaria.

Funereal Cypress (*Cupressus funebris*)—See Cupressus.

Funkia (Plantain Lily ; Japanese Day Lily ; Corfu Lily)—Ord. Liliaceæ. Hardy orn.-foliaged and herbaceous flowering plants. Deciduous.   First introduced 1790. Flowers, fragrant. Leaves, large, deep green or variegated with white and yellow.
CULTURE : Soil, ordinary, well enriched with decayed manure.   Position, open sunny well-drained borders. Plant, Oct. or March.   Top-dress annually with decayed manure.
POT CULTURE : Compost, two parts loam, one part well-decayed manure and river sand.   Position, pots in cold frame Oct. to March, greenhouse or window March to Oct.   Pot, March or April.   Water moderately Oct. to March, freely March to Oct. Apply liquid manure to healthy plants in flower.
PROPAGATION : By division of crowns in Oct., March, or April.
SPECIES CULTIVATED : F. Fortunei, lilac, July, 18 in., Japan ; lancifolia, lilac, Aug., 9 in., Japan, and its varieties alba (white), albo-marginata (leaves edged silvery white), undulata (leaves waved), and variegata (leaves blotched with white) ; ovata (Syn. F. cærulea), bluish lilac, May to July, 1 ft., Japan, and its varieties aurea (golden-leaved), and marginata (leaves edged creamy white) ; sieboldiana (Syn. F. cordata), white and lilac, summer, 1 ft. ; subcordata (Corfu Lily), Syn. F. grandi-flora, white, Aug., 1 ft., Japan.   The genus is also known as Hosta.

Furcræa (Giant Mexican Lily)—Ord. Amaryllidaceæ. Greenhouse succulent plants. Orn. foliage. First introduced 1690. Leaves, long, fleshy, spined.

CULTURE : Compost, two parts loam, one part old mortar and river sand. Position, pots or tubs in greenhouses ; may be stood outside June to Sept. Water moderately April to Aug., little afterwards. Pot every five or six years ; good drainage essential. Temp., winter 50° to 55° ; summer 55° to 65°.
PROPAGATION : By offsets inserted in small pots at any time.
SPECIES CULTIVATED : F. Bedinghausii, green, May to Nov., to 15 ft., Mexico ; elegans, green, May to Nov., 10 to 15 ft., Mexico ; gigantea, greenish, to 25 ft., Trop. America ; longæva, greenish, 30 to 40 ft., Mexico ; Selloana, greenish, 15 to 20 ft., Mexico, Guatemala.

Furze (*Ulex europæus*)—See Ulex.

Gagea (Yellow Star of Bethlehem)—Ord. Liliaceæ. Hardy deciduous bulbous plants.
CULTURE : Soil, sandy. Position, sunny borders, or in turf. Plant 3 in. deep and 3 in. apart, Aug. to Nov. Lift only when bulbs unhealthy.
PROPAGATION : By offsets, treated as advised for bulbs.
SPECIES CULTIVATED : G. lutea, yellow, March to May, 6 in., Europe (Britain).

Gaillardia (Blanket-flower)—Ord. Compositæ. Hardy annual and perennial herbacous plants. First introduced 1787.
CULTURE : Soil, moderately light rich. Position, sunny well-drained beds or borders. Plant, March or April. Apply weak liquid manure to plants in flower. Mulch beds with decayed manure in summer.
PROPAGATION : Annual and perennial species by seeds sown $\frac{1}{16}$ in. deep in shallow boxes of light mould in temp. 55° to 65° in April, transplanting seedlings outdoors in June ; perennials by cuttings of shoots issuing from roots, inserted in sandy soil under hand-light or in cold frame, Aug. to Oct., division of plants Oct. or March, cuttings of roots laid in shallow boxes of sandy soil, Feb. or March.
ANNUAL SPECIES : G. amblyodon, red, autumn, 2 to 3 ft., Texas ; pulchella, crimson and yellow, 2 to 3 ft., summer, N. America ; pulchella picta lorenziana, orange, red, and yellow, double 1 ft.
PERENNIAL SPECIES : G. aristata, yellow, autumn, 18 in., N. America. Grandiflora and maxima are superior forms of the latter species, and there are many named forms to be found in trade lists.

Galanthus (Snowdrop ; Fair Maids of February)—Ord. Amaryllidaceæ. Hardy bulbous flowering plants.
OUTDOOR CULTURE : Soil, ordinary rich. Position, margins of beds ; groups in open or shady borders ; banks, rockeries, or in turf. Plant bulbs 2 in. deep and 1 in. apart, Sept. to Dec. Bulbs must only be lifted when they show signs of deterioration.
POT CULTURE : Compost, two parts ordinary soil, one part leaf-mould and sand. Position, cold or warm greenhouse, frame, or window. Pot, Sept. to Nov., placing bulbs 1 in. deep and 1 in. apart in 4 or 5 in. pots or shallow pans. Place pots, etc. in cold frame or outdoors and cover with cinder ashes until growth begins. Water moderately till after flowering, then gradually cease. Plant bulbs outdoors following autumn.
PROPAGATION : By seeds sown as soon as ripe $\frac{1}{4}$ in. deep and 2 in. apart in shallow boxes filled with light sandy soil and placed at base of north wall outdoors ; by offsets treated as bulbs. Seedlings flower when three years old.
SPECIES CULTIVATED : G. Alleni, white, Feb. and March, 6 to 9 in., Asia Minor ; byzantinus, green and white, Feb., 9 to 12 in., S.E. Europe ; caucasicus, white and green, March, 6 in., Caucasus ; Elwesii, white, Feb., 9 to 12 in., Asia Minor, and its varieties robustus, unguiculatus and Whittallii ; Fosteri, white, Feb., 6 in., Asia Minor ; Ikariæ, white, Feb., 8 in., Nikaria ; latifolius, white and green, Feb. and March, 6 in., Caucasus ; nivalis (Common Snowdrop), white, Jan. to March, 6 in., Europe, and its varieties Imperati, Atkinsii and Melvillei ; plicatus (Crimean Snowdrop), white, Jan. to Feb., 10 to 12 in.

Galax (Wand-plant ; Carpenter's Leaf)—Ord. Diapensiaceæ. Hardy herbaceous perennial. First introduced 1756.
CULTURE : Compost, equal parts peat, leaf-mould, and silver sand. Position, ledges of moist rockery or margin of rhododendron beds. Plant, Oct. to March.
PROPAGATION : By division of plants Oct. to March ; seeds sown in peaty soil in cold frame in spring.
SPECIES CULTIVATED : G. aphylla, white, July, 3 to 6 in., N. America.

Galaxia—Ord. Iridaceæ. Greenhouse bulbous plants. Deciduous. Nat. Cape of Good Hope. First introduced 1795.
CULTURE : Compost, two parts sandy peat, one part light loam. Position, well-drained pots in cold frame or greenhouse. Pot, Aug. to Nov., placing bulbs with apex just below surface, one in a 5 in. or three in a 6 in. pot. Cover pots with ashes till growth begins. Water moderately when growth commences, freely afterwards, cease after flowering. Repot annually.
PROPAGATION : By seeds sown ⅛ in. deep in well-drained pans or shallow boxes of sandy peat in cool greenhouse or frame Aug. or Sept. ; by offsets treated as bulbs Aug. to Nov.
SPECIES CULTIVATED : G. graminea, yellow, July, 6 in. ; ovata, yellow, autumn, 6 in.

Gale (*Myrica Gale*)—See Myrica.

Galega (Goat's Rue)—Ord. Leguminosæ. Hardy perennial herbs. First introduced 1568. Flowers useful for cutting.
CULTURE : Soil, ordinary. Position, open borders or shrubberies. Plant, Oct. to March. Cut down flower stems in Oct. Replant every two or three years.
PROPAGATION : By seeds sown ¼ in. deep in April in ordinary soil in sunny position ; division of roots Oct. to March.
SPECIES CULTIVATED : G. officinalis, blue, summer, 3 to 5 ft., S. Europe, and its varieties alba (white), Duchess of Bedford, and Hartlandii (blue) ; orientalis, blue, summer, 2 to 3 ft., Caucasus.

Galingale (*Cyperus longus*)—See Cyperus.

Galium—Ord. Rubiaceæ. Hardy herbaceous perennials.
CULTURE : Soil, ordinary. Position, sunny borders or rock gardens. Plant, Oct. or March.
PROPAGATION : By division when planting or by seeds sown outdoors in April.
SPECIES CULTIVATED : G. olympicum, white, summer, 2 to 3 in., Mediterranean Region ; purpureum, brownish red, summer, 9 to 12 in., S. Europe ; mollugo, white, summer, 3 ft., Europe.

Galligaskins (*Primula veris*)—See Primula.

Galtonia (Spire Lily)—Ord. Liliaceæ. Hardy bulbous flowering plant. Deciduous. Nat. S. Africa.
OUTDOOR CULTURE : Soil, ordinary rich, well drained. Position, open sunny borders. Plant, Oct. to March, placing bulbs 6 in. deep and 6 in. apart. Lift and replant only when the bulbs show signs of deterioration.
POT CULTURE : Compost, two parts loam, one part decayed manure and silver sand. Position, cold or warm greenhouse. Pot, Oct. to Dec. to flower in spring ; Feb. to April to flower in autumn. Place one bulb with apex just showing through surface of soil in a well-drained 6-in. pot. Cover with ashes in cold frame until growth begins. Water moderately when leaves appear ; freely when in full growth ; keep nearly dry after flowering. Apply weak liquid manure occasionally to plants in flower. Bulbs not adapted for flowering second time in pots.
PROPAGATION : By seeds sown ¼ in. deep in shallow boxes of sandy soil in cold frame Oct. or March ; offsets treated as bulbs in autumn. Seedlings flower when four or five years old.
SPECIES CULTIVATED : G. candicans, white, fragrant, summer, 2 to 3 ft.

Gamboge-tree (*Garcinia Cambogia*)—See Garcinia.

Ganymede's Cup (*Narcissus triandrus*)—See Narcissus.

Garcinia (Mangosteen-tree ; Gamboge-tree)—Ord. Guttiferæ. Stove evergreen fruit-bearing tree. Orn. foliage. First introduced 1789. Fruit, size of an orange ; chestnut-brown colour ; edible.
CULTURE : Compost, two parts peat, one part loam and sand. Position, pots or boxes in light part of plant stove. Pot and prune, Feb. to March. Temp., March to Oct. 65° to 85° ; Oct. to March 55° to 65°. Water moderately Sept. to April, freely other times.
PROPAGATION : By cuttings of firm shoots 2 to 3 in. long inserted in silver sand under bell-glass in temp. 75° to 85° in spring or summer.
SPECIES CULTIVATED : G. Cambogia (Gamboge-tree), yellow, Nov., 40 ft., East Indies ; Mangostana, red, June, 6 to 10 ft., Molucca Islands.

Gardener's Garters (*Phalaris arundinacea variegata*)—See Phalaris.

Gardenia (Cape Jasmine)—Ord. Rubiaceæ. Stove evergreen flowering shrubs. First introduced 1754.
CULTURE : Compost, one part loam, one part peat, one part well-decayed manure and charcoal. Position, well-drained pots, or beds in plant stove. Pot or plant, Feb. or March. Prune into shape, Feb. or March. Temp., March to Sept. 65° to 85° ; Sept. to March 55° to 65°. Water moderately Oct. to Feb., freely afterwards. Syringe daily (except when in bloom) March to Sept. Apply liquid manure occasionally to healthy plants in flower. Plants one to two years old produce the best blooms.
PROPAGATION : By cuttings of firm young side shoots 2 to 3 in. long, inserted in well-drained pots of sandy peat under bell-glass in temp. 75° to 85°, Jan. to April.
SPECIES CULTIVATED : G. grandiflora, white, fragrant, 20 ft. or more, Cochin-China ; jasminoides (Cape Jasmine), Syn. G. florida, white, fragrant, summer, China and Japan ; jasminoides flore-pleno, double white ; jasminoides radicans, white, fragrant ; Thunbergia, white, fragrant, Jan. to March, to 10 ft., S. Africa. See also Mitriostigma. There are several named hybrids.

Gardenia Flowered Narcissus (*Narcissus poeticus alba plena odorata*)—See Narcissus.

Garland Flower (*Daphne Cneorum*)—See Daphne.

Garlic—See Allium.

Garrya—Ord. Cornaceæ. Hardy evergreen shrubs. Orn. foliage and flowering. First introduced 1818. Flowers (pendulous catkins), male and female borne on separate trees.
CULTURE : Soil, ordinary, well drained. Position, against south or west walls outdoors ; sheltered shrubberies S. of England. Plant, Oct. to Nov. or March to May. Male plant only cultivated ; female plant very rare in gardens.
PROPAGATION : By seeds sown ⅛ in. deep in well-drained pans of sandy soil in cold frame Sept. or Oct. ; cuttings of firm shoots 3 to 4 in. long inserted in sandy soil under hand-light or cold frame Aug. to Sept. ; layering shoots in Sept.
SPECIES CULTIVATED : G. elliptica, greenish white, March to June, 5 to 10 ft., California ; Thuretti, greenish white, Feb., to 8 ft., hybrid.

Gas Plant (*Dictamnus albus*)—See Dictamnus.

Gasteria—Ord. Liliaceæ. Greenhouse evergreen succulent plants. Orn. foliage. Nat. Cape of Good Hope. First introduced 1731. Leaves, thick, fleshy, prickly ; green, spotted with white, or purple.
CULTURE : Compost, two parts loam, one part peat, old mortar and river sand. Position, well-drained pots in sunny greenhouse or window. Pot, March or April. Water moderately April to Sept. Temp., March to Sept. 55° to 65° ; Sept. to March 50° to 55°.
PROPAGATION : By seeds sown ₁₆ in. deep in well-drained pots or pans of sandy soil, temp. of 65°, March to Aug.
SPECIES CULTIVATED : G. brevifolia, red, July ; Croucheri, rose, Aug. ; lingua (Syn. disticha), scarlet, July ; verrucosa, red, July, 3 to 4 in.

Gaultheria (Canada Tea ; Creeping Winter-green ; Partridge Berry ; Shallon)—
Ord. Ericaceæ. Hardy evergreen shrubs. First introduced 1762. Berries, red,
purple, or blue ; edible.
CULTURE : Soil, peaty. Position, moist rockeries or margins of open or shady
shrubberies and beds. Plant, Sept. to Nov. or March to May.
PROPAGATION : By seeds sown ¼ in. deep in bed of peaty soil outdoors in autumn.
SPECIES CULTIVATED : G. cuneata, white, June, 9 in., W. China ; nummularioides,
white and pink, summer, trailing, Himalayas ; procumbens (Canada Tea or Partridge Berry), white, July, creeping, N. America ; Shallon (Shallon), white and red,
May, 4 ft., N.W. America ; trichophylla, pink, May, 3 to 6 in., Himalayas ; veitchiana, white, early summer, 1 to 3 ft., W. China.

Gaura—Ord. Onagraceæ. Hardy perennial, but usually grown as an annual.
First introduced 1850.
CULTURE : Position, sunny well-drained beds or borders. Plant, March or April.
PROPAGATION : By seeds sown ¹⁄₁₆ in. deep in light soil outdoors April, transplanting
seedlings when 1 in. high to flowering position.
SPECIES CULTIVATED : G. Lindheimeri, white and rose, July to Oct., 3 to 4 ft.,
Texas.

Gaya—See Plagianthus.

Gaylussacia (Huckleberry)—Ord. Vacciniaceæ. Evergreen or deciduous berry-
bearing shrubs. First introduced 1772.
CULTURE AND PROPAGATION : As for Vaccinium.
SPECIES CULTIVATED : G. brachycera, white or pink, berries blue, 6 to 12 in., Eastern
U.S.A. ; dumosa, white to red, berries black, 1 to 2 ft., Eastern N. America ;
frondosa, greenish purple, berries blue, 3 to 6 ft., Eastern U.S.A. ; resinosa (Syn.
baccata), reddish, fruits black, 1 to 3 ft., Eastern N. America.

Gazania (Treasure-flower)—Ord. Compositæ. Half-hardy perennials. Nat.
Cape of Good Hope. First introduced 1755.
INDOOR CULTURE : Compost, two parts loam and one of peat and sand. Position,
well-drained pots in sunny part of greenhouse. Pot, March or April. Water very
little Oct. to March, moderately other times. Prune into shape, March. Temp.,
March to Sept. 55° to 75° ; Sept. to March 45° to 55°.
OUTDOOR CULTURE : Soil, ordinary. Position, sunny ; edgings to beds, or trailing
over ledges of rockery. Plant, June. Lift in Oct. and place in pots in heated
greenhouse for the winter.
PROPAGATION : By cuttings of side shoots removed from base of plant and inserted
in boxes of sandy soil or in a bed in cold frame July to Sept. ; cuttings may remain
in cold frame if protected from frost.
SPECIES CULTIVATED : G. montana, yellow and black, summer, 6 to 8 in. ; Pavonia,
yellow, brown, and white, summer, 12 in.; rigens, yellow and black, June, 1 ft. ;
splendens, orange, black, and white, summer, 1 ft., hybrid.

Gean (*Prunus avium*)—See Prunus.

Gelsemium (Carolina Yellow Jessamine)—Ord. Loganiaceæ. Half-hardy evergreen climber.
CULTURE : Soil, well-drained sandy loam. Position, south walls in mild districts
or borders in cool greenhouse. Plant Oct. or April.
PROPAGATION : By cuttings of half-ripened shoots during July or Aug. under bell-
glass in gentle bottom heat.
SPECIES CULTIVATED : G. sempervirens (Syn. G. nitidum), bright yellow, all summer,
climbing, Southern N. America.

Genetyllis—See Darwinia.

Genista (Needle Furze ; Petty Whin)—Ord. Leguminosæ. Hardy deciduous
flowering shrubs.
CULTURE : Soil, ordinary. Position, shrubbery for tall species ; rockery for
dwarf kinds. Plant, Oct. to March. Prune after flowering.
PROPAGATION : By seeds sown ¼ in. deep outdoors in March or April ; by layering

Funkia subcordata
(Corfu Lily)

Galanthus Elwesii
(Snowdrop)

Galega officinalis
(Goat's Rue)

Garcinia Mangostana
(Mangosteen-tree)

Gaultheria species

Gaura Lindheimeri

Gentiana sino-ornata
(Gentian)

Geranium grandiflorum
(Crane's-bill)

Gerbera Jamesoni hybrida
(Barberton Daisy)

Gesnera hybrida

Geum coccineum hybridum
(Avens)

Gillenia trifoliata
(Indian Physic)

Gladiolus Colvillei
(The Bride)

Gladiolus hybridus
(Sword Lily)

Gladiolus primulinus
(Maid of the Mist)

Gleichenia rupestris
(Umbrella Fern)

Gossypium barbadense
(Cotton-plant)

Grevillea robusta
(Silk-bark Oak)

in Oct. or Nov.; grafting on laburnum in March; budding on similar stocks in July.

SPECIES CULTIVATED: G. ætnensis, yellow, June to Aug., 6 to 12 ft., Sicily; anglica (Petty Whin), yellow, May and June, 1 to 2 ft., Britain; anxantica (Neapolitan Broom), yellow, summer, deciduous, 1 ft., Italy; dalmatica, golden yellow, June and July, 6 to 12 in., Dalmatia; hispanica (Spanish Gorse), yellow, May to July, fragrant, 6 to 12 in., N.W. Europe; hispanica flore-pleno, double; pilosa, yellow, May to June, 1 to 1½ ft., Europe (Britain); radiata, yellow, summer, 2 to 4 ft., S. Europe; tinctoria (Dyer's Greenweed), yellow, July to Sept., 1 to 2 ft., Britain; tinctoria flore-pleno, double; virgata, yellow, June to July, 6 to 12 ft., Madeira. See also the genus Cytisus.

Gentian—See Gentiana.

Gentiana (Gentian; Gentianella)—Ord. Gentianaceæ. Hardy perennials.

CULTURE: Compost, two parts good loam, one part peat and one part grit or broken limestone and coarse sand. Position, sunny borders for G. acaulis and tall kinds, sunny rockeries for dwarf kinds; all to be fairly dry in winter and moist in summer. Plant, Sept., Oct., March, or April. Top-dress in March with little well rotted leaf mould. Water freely on dry soils in summer.

PROPAGATION: By seeds sown ⅟₁₆ in. deep in well-drained pots or pans of sandy loam in cold frame, March; division of plants, March. Seeds sometimes take one to two years to germinate, and soil must be kept moderately moist.

SPECIES CULTIVATED: G. acaulis (Gentianella), blue, March to May, 3 in., Europe; Andrewsii, blue, Aug., 1 to 2 ft., N. America; asclepiadea (Swallow-wort), purple blue, July, 6 to 18 in., S. Europe, and its variety alba (white); bavarica, blue, June to July, 2 in., Europe; cruciata (Cross-wort), blue, June, 1 ft., Europe; Farreri, silvery blue with a white throat, Aug. to Nov., 3 in., China; freyniana, bright blue, July and Aug., 4 in.; Kurroo, azure blue, Aug. to Sept., 6 in., Himalayas; lutea (Bitter-wort), yellow, July, 2 to 3 ft., Europe; Pneumonanthe (Windflower), blue, Aug. and Sept., 1 to 2 ft., Britain; pyrenaica, bright violet, May and June, 3 in.; septemfida, blue, July, 1 ft., Caucasus, and its dwarf form lagodechiana; sino-ornata, rich blue, Sept., 3 in., China; straminea, pale yellow, July and Aug., 9 in.; verna, blue, April and May, 3 in., Europe (Britain and Ireland).

Gentianella (*Gentiana acaulis*)—See Gentiana.

Gentian Gromwell (*Lithospermum prostratum*)—See Lithospermum.

Gentian Speedwell (*Veronica gentianoides*)—See Veronica.

Geonoma—Ord. Palmaceæ. Stove palm. Orn. foliage. First introduced 1820. Leaves, feather-shaped; pale green.

CULTURE: Compost, two parts peat, one part loam, sand and charcoal. Position, pots in moist shady part of plant stove. Pot, Feb. or March. Water freely Oct. to Feb., abundantly other times. Syringe daily. Temp., Sept. to March 55° to 65°; March to Sept. 65° to 70°.

PROPAGATION: By seeds sown 1 in. deep in above compost in pots in temp. 85°, March; offshoots from base of plants in small pots in temp. 80° to 85°, any time.

SPECIES CULTIVATED: G. gracilis, 6 ft., Costa Rica.

Georgian Fleabane (*Inula glandulosa*)—See Inula.

Geranium (Crane's-bill)—Ord. Geraniaceæ. Hardy herbaceous perennials.

CULTURE: Soil, ordinary rich. Position, tall kinds in sunny well-drained borders, dwarf kinds on sunny rockeries. Plant, Oct., Nov., March, or April. Apply weak liquid manure occasionally to established plants in flower.

PROPAGATION: By seeds sown ¼ in. deep in ordinary soil in sunny position outdoors, March or April, or in shallow boxes of sandy soil in cold frame or greenhouse, March; division of roots, Oct., Nov., March, or April.

SPECIES CULTIVATED: G. argenteum, rose, summer, 1 ft., Alps; armenum, purple, June and July, 2 ft., Orient; cinereum, red, summer, 6 in., Pyrenees; cinereum album, white; Endressi, rose, summer, 1 ft., Pyrenees; grandiflorum, bluish mauve, June to Sept., 6 in., Himalayas ; ibericum, blue, summer, 1 ft., Caucasus ; macrorrhizum, red or purple, May to July, 1 ft., E. Europe ; phæum, purplish brown, May to July, 1 ft., Europe ; pratense, blue, summer, 2 to 3 ft., Britain, and its double blue and double white varieties ; pylzowianum, pale pink, summer, 6 to 9 in., Thibet ; sanguineum, crimson, summer, 2 ft., and its varieties lancastriense (flesh), album (white), Britain ; sylvaticum, blue, summer, 2 to 3 ft., Britain ; tuberosum, purple, June, 9 in., S. Europe. For greenhouse "Geraniums" see the genus Pelargonium.

Geranium-scented Polypody (*Dryopteris robertianum*)—See Dryopteris.

Gerbera (Barberton or Transvaal Daisy)—Ord. Compositæ. Greenhouse perennial herbs. First introduced 1888.

CULTURE : Grow in a compost of sandy loam and peat in a temperature of 45° to 50° from Nov. to May ; without artificial heat afterwards. Water sparingly from Nov. to April ; freely afterwards. Repot annually in spring. No shade required. G. Jamesoni may be grown outdoors in warm nooks in mild districts.

PROPAGATION : By seeds sown in sandy peat in March in temperature of 55° ; by cuttings of side shoots in spring.

SPECIES CULTIVATED : G. asplenifolia, purple, summer, 1 ft. ; Jamesoni (Barberton Daisy), orange-scarlet, June to Oct., 18 in.

German Catchfly (*Lychnis viscaria*)—See Lychnis.

Germander (*Teucrium Scorodonia*)—See Teucrium.

German Iris (*Iris germanica*)—See Iris.

German Ivy (*Mikania scandens* and *Senecio mikanioides*)—See Mikania and Senecio.

German Lilac (*Centranthus ruber*)—See Centranthus.

German Spleenwort (*Asplenium germanicum*)—See Asplenium.

German Tamarisk (*Myricaria germanica*)—See Myricaria.

Gesnera—Ord. Gesneriaceæ. Stove tuberous-rooted herbaceous perennials. Flowering and orn. foliage. First introduced 1752.

CULTURE : Compost, two parts fibrous peat, one part loam, one part leaf-mould, with a little decayed manure and silver sand. Position, well-drained pots or pans in shady part of plant stove. Pot, March to flower in summer ; May to flower in autumn ; June to flower in winter. Place tubers 1 in. deep singly in 5 in. pots, or 1 to 2 in. apart in larger sizes. Water moderately from time growth begins until plants are 3 or 4 in. high, then freely. After flowering gradually withhold water till foliage dies down, then keep dry till potting time. Apply weak liquid manure once or twice a week when flower buds show. Syringing not required. Temp., March to Sept. 65° + 85° ; Sept. to March 55° to 65°. Store when foliage has died down on their side ler stage till potting time in temp. of 50° to 55°.

PROPAGATION : By s sown on surface of well-drained pots of sandy peat, in temp. 75°, March o ril ; cuttings of young shoots inserted in pots of sandy peat in temp. 75° to 85' spring ; fully matured leaves pegged on surface of pots in sandy peat in temp. 75° to 85° ; stalk ends of leaves inserted vertically in pans of sandy peat in temp. 75° to 85°.

SPECIES CULTIVATED : G. cardinalis, crimson and white, autumn, 12 to 18 in. ; Donklarii, red and yellow, 2 ft., summer, Colombia ; Douglassii, red and yellow, autumn, 18 in., Brazil ; exoniensis, orange, scarlet, and yellow, winter, 1 ft., hybrid ; Leopoldii, scarlet, summer, 1 ft., Brazil ; Lindleyi, yellow and scarlet, July, 1 ft., Brazil ; nægelioides, rosy pink, autumn, 18 in. ; refulgens, violet and white, summer, 18 in., hybrid. See also Isoloma and Næglia.

Gethyllis (Cape Crocus)—Ord. Amaryllidaceæ. Greenhouse bulbous plants. Deciduous. First introduced 1780.

CULTURE : Compost, equal parts peat, loam and sand. Position, well-drained pots in cold greenhouse or frame. Pot, Aug. to Nov., placing bulbs singly in 5 in. pots, with points just below surface. Cover with ashes in cold frame or greenhouse

till growth begins. Water moderately from time growth begins till flowers fade; keep quite dry after foliage has died down until potting time. Repot annually.
PROPAGATION : By seeds sown ⅛ in. deep in well-drained pots of sandy soil in cold frame or greenhouse, March or April; offsets treated as bulbs at potting time.
SPECIES CULTIVATED : G. afra, red and white, summer, 6 ft., S. Africa; ciliaris, white, summer, 6 in., S. Africa; spiralis, white, autumn, 9 ft., S. Africa.

Geum (Avens)—Ord. Rosaceæ. Hardy perennial flowering herbs.
CULTURE : Soil, ordinary rich. Position, tall species in sunny borders, dwarf species on sunny rockeries. Plant, Oct. to April. Cut down flower stems in Sept.
PROPAGATION : By seeds sown 1⁄16 in. deep in shallow boxes or well-drained pots of light soil in cold frame, March or April, or in sunny positions (similar depth and soil) outdoors, April or July; division of plants, Oct. to April.
SPECIES CULTIVATED : G. Borisi (of gardens), orange, summer and autumn, 9 to 12 in.; chiloense, scarlet, summer, 2 ft., Chile, and its varieties grandiflorum plenum (double-flowered) and miniatum (orange); coccineum, scarlet, summer, 1 ft., Asia Minor; Heldreichii, orange-red, July, 1 ft.; montanum, yellow, May, 2 ft., Europe; reptans, yellow, summer, trailing, Europe; rivale (Guildford variety), old rose, summer, 9 to 12 in., Britain. There are numerous named forms of G. coccineum such as Mrs. Bradshaw, scarlet; Lady Stratheadon, yellow; and Fire Opal, orange.

Ghent Azalea (*Rhododendron ponticum*)—See Rhododendron.

Gherkin—See Cucumis.

Giant Cow-parsnip (*Heracleum giganteum*)—See Heracleum.

Giant Fennel—See Ferula.

Giant Fern Palm (*Macrozamia peroffskyana*)—See Macrozamia.

Giant Hemp (*Cannabis sativa*)—See Cannabis.

Giant Ivy (*Hedera Helix rægneriana*)—See Hedera.

Giant Knot-weed (*Polygonum cuspidatum*)—See Polygonum.

Giant Lily (*Lilium giganteum*)—See Lilium.

Giant Scabious (*Cephalaria tartarica*)—See Cephalaria.

Giant White Californian Poppy (*Romneya Coulteri*)—See Romneya.

Gibraltar Mint (*Mentha pulegium gibraltarica*)—See Mentha.

Gilia—Ord. Polemoniaceæ. Annuals, biennials, and sub-shrubs. Some hardy. First introduced 1826.
CULTURE OF HARDY ANNUALS : Soil, ordinary. Position, sunny beds or borders. Sow seeds 1⁄16 in. deep in April where plants are to flower, thinning seedlings in May to 3 in. apart.
CULTURE OF HALF-HARDY BIENNIALS : Soil, ordinary. Position, sunny beds or borders. Sow in pans or boxes in January in temp. 60° to 65°, pricking off seedlings as soon as large enough to handle and hardening off for planting out in May.
CULTURE OF HALF-HARDY SUB-SHRUBS : Compost, equal parts fibrous loam, leafmould and sand. Sow in pans or boxes in late summer or early autumn in temp. 60° to 65°. Prick off seedlings when large enough and grow on in same temp., either hardening off plants in spring for planting outdoors or else potting them singly for flowering in the greenhouse.
HARDY ANNUALS CULTIVATED : G. achilleæfolia, purplish blue, Aug., 1 ft., California; androsacea (Syn. Leptosiphon parviflorus), lilac, pink, and white, Aug., 1 ft., California; densiflora (Syn. Leptosiphon densiflorus), lilac, June, 6 in.; densiflora alba, white; dianthoides (Syn. Fenzlia dianthiflora), lilac and yellow, July, 4 in., California; liniflora, white, summer, 1 ft., California; micrantha (Syn. Leptosiphon roseus), rose, summer, 9 in., California; tricolor, orange and purple, June, 1 ft., California, and its varieties alba, atroviolacea, rosea, and splendens.
HALF-HARDY BIENNIAL CULTIVATED : G. coronopifolia, scarlet, summer, 9 to 18 in., California.
HALF-HARDY SUB-SHRUB : G. californica, pink, July, 3 ft., California.

183

Gillenia (Indian Physic)—Ord. Rosaceæ. Hardy perennials. First introduced 1713.

CULTURE : Soil, peaty. Position, moist shady bed or border. Plant, Oct. to Dec., or March. Cut down flowering stems in Sept.

PROPAGATION : By division of roots in March or April.

SPECIES CULTIVATED : G. stipulata, white, June, 1 to 2 ft., N. America ; trifoliata, red or white, July, 1 to 2 ft., N. America.

Gillyflower (*Dianthus caryophyllus* and *Cheiranthus Cheiri*)—See Dianthus and Cheiranthus.

Ginger-plant (*Zingiber officinale*)—See Zingiber.

Ginkgo (Ginkgo-tree ; Maidenhair-tree)—Ord. Coniferæ. Hardy deciduous coniferous tree. Orn. foliage. First introduced 1754. Flowers, male and female borne on separate trees ; spring. Fruit, small, globular ; edible. Leaves, fan-shaped ; green and variegated.

CULTURE : Soil, ordinary, well drained. Position, sheltered shrubberies or lawns S. of England, against south or west walls other parts. Plant, Oct. to Feb.

PROPAGATION : By seeds sown 1 in. deep in pans of light sandy soil in cold frame, Oct. or March.

SPECIES CULTIVATED : G. biloba (Syn. Salisburia adiantifolia), 60 to 80 ft., China and Japan.

Ginseng (*Panax quinquefolium*)—See Panax.

Glacier Pink (*Dianthus glacialis*)—See Dianthus.

Gladiolus (Corn Flag ; Sword Lily)—Ord. Iridaceæ. Half-hardy bulbous flowering plants. Deciduous. First introduced 1596.

TYPES—Large flowered : Habit vigorous ; colours various ; height, 2 to 4 ft. ; individual flowers open, 4 to 8 in. in diameter. Primulinus : Habit less vigorous but free flowering ; colours various, embracing many art shades ; height, 1½ to 3 ft. ; individual flowers hooded, 1 to 2 in. in diameter. There are now many hybrids intermediate between these two classes. Colvillei : Flowers small, widely open, early, usually grown under glass.

OUTDOOR CULTURE : Soil, deep rich, liberally manured. Position, sunny well-drained beds or borders. Plant in late March or April. Place corms 4 in. deep and 6 in. apart. Lift corms in Nov., dry off in a frost-proof shed or glasshouse, remove old shrivelled corms, which are useless, from the base of the new corms and store latter in shallow trays in an airy place secure from frost. Apply liquid manure when flower buds form. Fix sticks to spikes when 2 or 3 in. high.

POT CULTURE : Compost, two parts loam, one part well-decayed manure and river sand. Position, pots in cold frame, cool greenhouse or window. Pot Colvillei varieties Oct. or Nov., placing five corms 1 in. deep in a 6 in. pot ; late kinds March or April, one 1 in. deep in a 6 in. pot or three 1 in. deep in an 8 in. pot. Place pots in cold frame till flower spikes show, then remove to greenhouse or window. Water moderately at first, freely afterwards. Apply liquid manure when flower spikes show. After flowering gradually withhold water till foliage dies, then clean off corms and store in trays as with those grown outdoors. Forcing : Pot early kinds Oct. to Dec. Temp., 55° to 65°.

PROPAGATION : By seeds sown ¼ in. deep in pans of light rich soil in Feb., in temp. 55° to 65° ; by bulbils (spawn) growing at base of corms, planted 2 in. deep and 6 in. apart in sunny border outdoors, March. Seedlings flower when three years old ; bulbils when two years old.

SPECIES CULTIVATED : G. blandus, white, red, and yellow, June, 18 in., S. Africa ; byzantinus, red and purple, June, 2 ft., Asia Minor ; cardinalis, scarlet, July and Aug., 3 to 4 ft., S. Africa ; communis, rose, June to Aug., 1 to 2 ft., S. Europe ; cruentus, scarlet and white, Sept., 12 to 18 in. Natal ; primulinus (Maid of the Mist), golden yellow, fragrant, Aug., 3 to 4 ft., Trop. Africa ; psittacinus, scarlet and yellow, summer, 3 ft., S. Africa ; purpureo-auratus, yellow and purple, Aug., 3 to 4 ft., S. Africa ; Saundersii, crimson, pink and white, autumn, 2 to 3 ft., S.

Africa; tristis, red and yellow, July, 1 ft., Natal. Colvillei, crimson and white, summer, 2 ft., and its variety The Bride (white) are pretty hybrids of G. tristis and G. cardinalis. There are many other races of hybrids which were formerly distinguished by such names as hemoinei, nanceianus, Childsii, Froebelli, princeps, etc., but are now included together as large flowered florist varieties. G. primulinas has also given rise to fine races of hybrids. See also Watsonia.

Gladwyn (*Iris fœtidissima*)—See Iris.

Gland Bellflower—See Adenophora.

Glastonbury Thorn (*Cratægus monogyna præcox*)—See Cratægus.

Glaucium (Horn Poppy; Sea Poppy)—Ord. Papaveraceæ. Hardy biennials. CULTURE: Soil, ordinary rich. Position, sunny well-drained beds or borders. PROPAGATION: By seeds sown $\frac{1}{16}$ in. deep in beds of light soil outdoors in May, transplanting seedlings into flowering position in July or Aug. SPECIES CULTIVATED: G. corniculatum, crimson and black, summer, 9 in., Mediterranean Region, and its red variety rubrum; flavum (Syn. G. luteum), yellow, summer, 1 to 2 ft., Europe (Britain), etc.

Gleditschia (Honey Locust; Water Locust)—Ord. Leguminosæ. Hardy, ornamental deciduous trees. First introduced 1700. Leaves, feather-shaped, green. Shoots, spiny. CULTURE: Soil, ordinary. Position, sheltered borders or shrubberies. Plant, Oct. to Feb. PROPAGATION: By seeds sown 1 in. deep in light soil outdoors, March, transplanting seedlings when two years old. SPECIES CULTIVATED: G. aquatica (Syns. G. monosperma and inermis), the Water Locust, green, July, 20 to 30 ft., United States; caspica, green, 20 to 30 ft., N. Persia; triacanthos (Honey Locust), green, summer, 30 to 50 ft., United States.

Glechoma hederacea—See Nepeta Glechoma.

Gleichenia (Umbrella Fern; Net Fern)—Ord. Filices. Orn. evergreen stove and greenhouse ferns. First introduced 1823. Fronds, feather-shaped. Stems, creeping. CULTURE: Compost, two parts fibrous peat, one part fibrous loam, charcoal and sand. Position, well-drained pans in shady stove or greenhouse. Pot, Feb. or Mar. Water moderately in winter, freely at other times. Syringing unnecessary. Temp., stove species, Sept. to March 55° to 65°, March to Sept. 65° to 75°; greenhouse species, Sept. to March 45° to 50°, March to Sept. 55° to 65°. PROPAGATION: By spores sown on surface of sandy peat in well-drained pots under bell-glass at any time of year; division of creeping stems, Feb. or March. STOVE SPECIES: G. dichotoma, 6 ft., Tropics. GREENHOUSE SPECIES: G. circinata, 6 ft., Australia, New Zealand, and Malaya, and its varieties Mendelii and semi-vestita; dicarpa, 6 ft., Australia and New Zealand, and its varieties alpina, glauca and longipinnata; flabellata, 5 ft., Australia and New Zealand; rupestris, 5 ft., Australia.

Globe Amaranth (*Gomphrena globosa*)—See Gomphrena.

Globe Artichoke (*Cynara scolymus*)—See Cynara.

Globe Daisy—See Globularia.

Globe Flower (*Trollius europæus*)—See Trollius.

Globe Thistle (*Echinops Ritro*)—See Echinops.

Globularia (Globe Daisy)—Ord. Selaginaceæ. Hardy sub-shrubs and perennial herbs. First introduced 1629. CULTURE: Soil, ordinary moist. Position, sunny rockeries or margins of borders. Plant, Oct., Nov., March, or April. G. Alypum may be grown in a greenhouse. PROPAGATION: By seeds sown on surface in boxes of light sandy soil in cold frame in March or April; division of plants, Oct. or April.

SPECIES CULTIVATED: G. Alypum, blue, Aug., 2 ft., shrubby, S. Europe; cordifolia, blue, June, 6 in., shrubby, S. Europe; nudicaulis, blue, summer, 6 in., herbaceous, Europe; trichosantha, blue, summer, 6 to 8 in., herbaceous, Asia Minor; vulgaris. blue, summer, 6 to 12 in., herbaceous, S. Europe.

Gloneria—See Psychotria.

Gloriosa (Malabar Glory Lily; Mozambique Lily)—Ord. Liliaceæ. Stove flowering climbers. Deciduous and tuberous-rooted. First introduced 1690.

CULTURE : Compost, equal parts loam, peat, leaf-mould, decayed manure and silver sand. Position, well-drained pots, with shoots trained to roof or trellis. Pot, Feb., placing tubers 2 in. deep, one in a 6 in. pot or several in an 8 or 12 in. pot. Water moderately till growth is well advanced, then freely. After flowering gradually withhold water and keep soil quite dry till potting time. Temp., Feb. to Sept. 70° to 85°; Sept. to Feb. 55° to 65°.

PROPAGATION : By seeds inserted singly ¼ in. deep in 3 in. pots filled with light soil in temp. 75° in Feb. or March; offsets removed from large tubers at potting time.

SPECIES CULTIVATED : G. superba, orange and red, summer, 6 to 10 ft., Tropics; rothschildiana, ruby red and yellow, summer, Uganda; virescens, yellow and red, summer, 5 ft., Trop. Africa, and its varieties Planti and grandiflora.

Glory Flower (*Eccremocarpus scaber*)—See Eccremocarpus.

Glory Lily (*Gloriosa superba*)—See Gloriosa.

Glory-of-the-Snow (*Chionodoxa Luciliæ*)—See Chionodoxa.

Glory-of-the-Sun (*Leucocoryne ixioides*)—See Leucocoryne.

Glory Pea of New Zealand (*Clianthus Dampieri*)—See Clianthus.

Glory Tree (*Clerodendron fragrans*)—See Clerodendron.

Glosocomia clematidea—See Codonopsis clematidea.

Gloxinia—See Sinningia.

Glycyrrhiza (Liquorice-plant)—Ord. Leguminosæ. Hardy herbaceous perennial. Orn. foliage and flowering. Edible rooted. Nat. Europe. First introduced 1562. Ht. 3 to 5 ft.

CULTURE : Soil, deep rich sandy. Position, open sunny. Plant, Feb. or March, 18 in. apart and 3 in. deep in rows 3 ft. asunder. Cut down foliage and remove creeping stems close to root in Nov. Roots ready for use third year.

PROPAGATION : By division of creeping stems, Feb. or March.

SPECIES CULTIVATED : G. glabra (Spanish Liquorice), blue, May to Sept., Mediterranean Region.

Gnaphalium—See Anaphalis and Leontopodium.

Gnidia—Ord. Thymelaceæ. Greenhouse evergreen flowering shrubs. Nat. Cape of Good Hope. First introduced 1768.

CULTURE : Compost, two parts fibrous peat, one part loam and silver sand. Position, well-drained pots near glass in airy greenhouse during autumn, winter and spring, cold frame June to Sept. Pot, March. Press compost firmly in pots. Prune straggling shoots into shape directly after flowering. Water carefully always, giving sufficient to keep soil uniformly moist; rain, not spring water, essential. Temp., Oct. to March 40° to 45°; March to July 45° to 55°.

PROPAGATION : By cuttings of young shoots 2 in. long inserted in sandy peat in well-drained pots under bell-glass in temp. 45° to 55° in March, April, or May.

SPECIES CULTIVATED : G. denudata, yellow, summer, 18 in.; pinifolia, white, fragrant, spring, 2 ft.

Goat-root (*Ononis Natrix*)—See Ononis.

Goat's Beard (*Spiræa Aruncus*)—See Spiræa.

Goat's Rue (*Galega officinalis*)—See Galega.

Goat Willow (*Salix caprea*)—See Salix.

Godetia—See Œnothera.

Gœthea—Ord. Malvaceæ. Stove evergreen shrubs. First introduced 1852.
CULTURE : Compost, two parts loam, one part peat and sand. Pot, March. Shady
position desirable. Water freely from March to Sept. ; moderately in winter.
Syringe freely during summer months. Temp., March to Sept. 65° to 75°; Sept.
to March 55° to 65°.
PROPAGATION : By cuttings in sandy soil under bell-glass in steady bottom heat.
SPECIES CULTIVATED : G. makoyana, crimson, 2 ft., Brazil ; strictiflora, yellowish,
tinged red, Aug., 1½ ft., Brazil. See also Pavonia.

Gold Basket (*Alyssum saxatile*)—See Alyssum.

Gold Dust-plant (*Alyssum saxatile*)—See Alyssum.

Golden Ash (*Fraxinus excelsior aurea*)—See Fraxinus.

Golden Aster (*Chrysopsis villosa Rutteri*)—See Chrysopsis.

Golden Bell-tree (*Forsythia suspensa*)—See Forsythia.

Golden Bush (*Cassinia fulvida*)—See Cassinia.

Golden Chain (*Laburnum vulgare*)—See Laburnum.

Golden Club (*Orontium aquaticum*)—See Orontium.

Golden Creeping Jenny (*Lysimachia nummularia aurea*)—See Lysimachia.

Golden Cretan Spikenard (*Valeriana Phu aurea*)—See Valeriana.

Golden Dead Nettle (*Lamium maculatum aureum*)—See Lamium.

Golden Drop (*Onosma echioides*)—See Onosma.

Golden Elder (*Sambucus nigra foliis aureis*)—See Sambucus.

Golden Elm (*Ulmus campestris* Louis van Houtte)—See Ulmus.

Golden Feather (*Chrysanthemum Parthenium aureum*)—See Chrysanthemum.

Golden-flowered Currant (*Ribes aureum*)—See Ribes.

Golden-flowered Garlic (*Allium Moly*)—See Allium.

Golden Hair (*Chrysocoma Coma-aurea*)—See Chrysocoma.

Golden Iris (*Iris Monnieri*)—See Iris.

Golden Knee (*Chrysogonum virginianum*)—See Chrysogonum.

Golden-leaved Chestnut (*Castanea chrysophylla*)—See Castanea.

Golden-leaved Spindle-tree (*Euonymus japonicus aureo-variegatus*)—See Euonymus.

Golden Lily (*Lycoris aurea*)—See Lycoris.

Golden Lime-tree (*Tilia platyphyllos aurea*)—See Tilia.

Golden Maiden-hair Fern (*Nothochlæna flavens* and *Adiantum æthiopicum
sulphureum*)—See Nothochlæna and Adiantum.

Golden Oak (*Quercus pedunculata Concordia*)—See Quercus.

Golden Osier (*Salix vitellina*)—See Salix.

Golden Polypody (*Polypodium aureum*)—See Polypodium.

Golden Privet (*Ligustrum ovalifolium aureum*)—See Ligustrum.

Golden Rain (*Laburnum vulgare*)—See Laburnum.

Golden Rod (*Solidago virgaurea*)—See Solidago.

Golden Saxifrage—See Chrysosplenium.

Golden Thistle (*Scolymus hispanicus*)—See Scolymus.

Golden Urn-flower (*Urceolina pendula*)—See Urceolina.

Golden Vine (*Stigmaphyllon ciliatum*)—See Stigmaphyllon.

Golden Wand (*Bulbinella Hookeri*)—See Bulbinella.

Golden Wattle (*Acacia pycnantha*)—See Acacia.

Golden Yew (*Taxus baccata aurea*)—See Taxus.

Gold Fern (*Gymnogramme chrysophylla*)—See Gymnogramme.

Goldings (*Caltha palustris*)—See Caltha.

Goldfussia—See Strobilanthes.

Goldilocks (*Aster Linosyris*)—See Aster.

Gold-netted Honeysuckle (*Lonicera japonica aureo-reticulata*)—See Lonicera.

Gold Thread (*Coptis trifolia*)—See Coptis.

Gombo (*Hibiscus esculentus*)—See Hibiscus.

Gomphia (South American Button-flower)—Ord. Ochnaceæ. Stove evergreen shrub. Orn. foliage and flowering.
CULTURE : Compost, two parts fibrous loam, one part peat, little silver sand. Position, pots in light part of plant stove. Pot, Feb. or March. Press compost down firmly in pot. Prune into shape Feb. or March. Water moderately Oct. to March, freely afterwards. Syringe daily in summer. Temp., March to Oct. 65° to 75° ; Oct. to March 50° to 60°.
PROPAGATION : By cuttings of firm young shoots, 2 to 3 in. long, inserted in pots of silver sand under bell-glass in temp. 75° in spring.
SPECIES CULTIVATED : G. decora, yellow, spring, 10 to 15 ft., Brazil.

Gompholobium—Ord. Leguminosæ. Greenhouse evergreen flowering shrubs. Trailing and erect. Nat. Australia. First introduced 1803.
CULTURE : Compost, two parts rough peat, one part rough loam, charcoal and sand. Position, well-drained pots in light part of greenhouse. Pot, Feb. or March. Prune into shape after flowering. Water carefully at all times. Temp., Sept. to April 45° to 50° ; April to Sept. 50° to 60°. Ventilate greenhouse freely in summer.
PROPAGATION : By cuttings of young shoots 2 in. long inserted in well-drained pots of sandy peat under bell-glass in temp. 45° to 55° in March or April.
SPECIES CULTIVATED : G. grandiflorum, yellow, June, 2 ft. ; polymorphum, yellow, scarlet and purple, spring, 2 ft. ; venustum, purple, spring, 3 ft.

Gomphrena (Globe Amaranth ; Globe Everlasting)—Ord. Amaranthaceæ. Greenhouse flowering annual. Nat. India. First introduced 1714.
CULTURE : Compost, two parts fibrous loam, one part leaf-mould, well-decayed cow manure and sand. Position, warm greenhouse, exposed to light. Sow seeds ⅛ in. deep in well-drained pots of light soil in temp. 75° in March. Transplant seedlings 1 in. apart when 1 in. high in light soil in well-drained pots and keep in temp. of 60° to 75°. When seedlings have formed four leaves place singly in 4 in. pots. Transfer them in June to 5 in. pots and keep near the glass. Water moderately. Syringe foliage twice daily. Apply liquid manure when flowers appear. Summer temp., 55° to 65°. Cut flowers immediately they are fully developed for drying for winter decoration.
SPECIES CULTIVATED : G. globosa, white, red or purple, summer, 12 to 18 in., and its varieties aurea superba (yellow), carnea (flesh), purpurea (purple), and nana (dwarf).

Gongora—Ord. Orchidaceæ. Stove evergreen epiphytal orchids. First introduced 1824.
CULTURE : Compost, equal parts rough peat, sphagnum moss and lumps of charcoal. Position, hanging baskets in sunny part of stove. Rebasket, Feb. or March. Water abundantly March to Sept., very little other times. Temp., May to Sept. 70° to 85° ; Sept. to May 60° to 70°. Growing period, spring and summer.
PROPAGATION : By division of pseudo-bulbs in Feb.
SPECIES CULTIVATED : G. atropurpurea, purplish brown, summer, Brit. Guiana ; bufonia, yellow and purple, summer, Brazil ; quinquenervis (Syn. maculata), yellow and reddish brown, spring, Trinidad.

Goniophlebium—See Polypodium.

Good King Henry (*Chenopodium Bonus-Henricus*)—See Chenopodium.

Goodyera (Rattlesnake Plantain ; Adder's Violet)—Ord. Orchidaceæ. Stove, greenhouse, and hardy terrestrial orchids. Flowering and orn. foliage. Leaves, bronze, chocolate, olive green, purplish green, reddish crimson, variegated with white or yellow.

CULTURE OF STOVE AND GREENHOUSE SPECIES : Compost, two parts fibrous peat, one part loam and sand. Position, well-drained pots or shallow pans in shady part of stove or greenhouse. Pot, Feb. or March. Water freely March to Sept., moderately other times. Temp., stove species, March to Sept. 65° to 75°, Sept. to March 55° to 65° ; greenhouse species, March to Sept. 55° to 65°, Sept. to March 45° to 55°.

CULTURE OF HARDY SPECIES : Compost, two parts peat, leaf-mould and sand. Position, rockery or border, well drained. Plant, March or April. Water freely in dry weather.

PROPAGATION : By cuttings of shoots removed with roots attached, inserted singly in small pots of peaty compost under bell-glass in temp. 45° to 65° in spring.

STOVE SPECIES : G. Domini, leaves velvety bronze and greenish white, hybrid ; Veitchii, leaves red, brown, and white, hybrid.

GREENHOUSE SPECIES : G. macrantha, rosy pink and white, June, Japan .

HARDY SPECIES : G. pubescens, white, July, N. America ; repens, white, summer, Europe.

Gooseberry (*Ribes grossularia*)—See Ribes.

Gordonia—Ord. Ternstrœmiaceæ. Half-hardy deciduous and evergreen flowering shrubs. First introduced 1774.

CULTURE : Soil, peat, and leaf-mould. Position, warm, sheltered borders, or against a south wall. Plant evergreen species, April. Deciduous species, Nov.

PROPAGATION : By layering the shoots in spring.

DECIDUOUS SPECIES CULTIVATED : G. pubescens, white, large camellia-like, fragrant, summer, 4 to 6 ft., N. America.

EVERGREEN SPECIES CULTIVATED : G. anomala (Syn. G. axillaris), white, summer, 15 ft., S. China. Good for cool greenhouse or conservatory.

Gorse (*Ulex europæus*)—See Ulex.

Gossypium (Cotton-plant)—Ord. Malvaceæ. Stove perennial herbs. First introduced 1594. Fruit (capsule) furnishes cotton of commerce.

CULTURE : Compost, equal parts loam, leaf-mould, and little sand. Position, well-drained pots in sunny part of stove. Pot, March or April. Water moderately Sept. to April, freely afterwards. Temp., March to Oct. 65° to 75° ; Oct. to March 55° to 65°.

PROPAGATION : By seeds sown $\frac{1}{16}$ in. deep in light soil in temp. 65° to 75°, March or April. Transplant seedlings when 1 in. high singly into 2 in. pots.

SPECIES CULTIVATED : G. barbadense, yellow and purple, Sept., 5 ft., Barbados ; herbaceum, yellow and purple, summer, 3 to 4 ft., East Indies.

Gourd (*Cucurbita Pepo*)—See Cucurbita.

Gout Ivy—See Ajuga.

Grammanthes—Ord. Crassulaceæ. Half-hardy annual. First introduced 1774.

CULTURE : Soil, light sandy. Position, sunny rockeries.

PROPAGATION : By seeds sown on surface of sandy soil in well-drained pans in temp. 60° to 65° in March. Transplant seedlings outdoors in May.

SPECIES CULTIVATED : G. chloræflora, orange-yellow and red, summer, 3 to 4 in., S. Africa.

Grammatocarpus (Cup Flower)—Ord. Loasaceæ. Half-hardy annual climber.

CULTURE : Sow seeds in gentle heat in March, harden seedlings off later on, and plant in June. Ordinary soil. Suitable for low sunny trellises, vases, etc.

SPECIES CULTIVATED : G. volubilis (Syn. Scyphanthus elegans), yellow and red, summer, 3 ft., Chile.

Grammatophyllum (Queen of the Orchids)—Ord. Orchidaceæ. Stove epiphytal orchids. First introduced 1837.
CULTURE : Compost, equal parts peat, fibrous loam, and leaf-mould. Position, large pots in light part of stove. Pot, Feb. or March. Water very freely Feb. to Oct. ; little at other seasons. Plenty of atmospheric moisture essential. Temp., Feb. to Oct. 75° to 90° ; Oct. to Feb. 65° to 75°. Growing period, Feb. to Nov. Resting period, Nov. to Feb.
PROPAGATION : By division of pseudo-bulbs at potting time.
SPECIES CULTIVATED : G. rumphianum (Syn. fenzlianum), yellow and brown, summer, 4 ft., Amboyna ; speciosum, yellow and purple, winter, 5 to 8 ft., Malaya.

Granadilla (*Passiflora quadrangularis*)—See Passiflora.

Grape Fern (*Botrychium lunaria*)—See Botrychium.

Grape Flower Vine—See Wistaria.

Grape Fruit (*Citrus decumana*)—See Citrus.

Grape Hyacinth—See Muscari.

Grape Pear (*Amelanchier vulgaris*)—See Amelanchier.

Grape Vine (*Vitis vinifera*)—See Vitis.

Grass of Parnassus (*Parnassia palustris*)—See Parnassia.

Gravia paradoxa—See Monstera acuminata.

Great Oriental Bellflower (*Ostrowskia magnifica*)—See Ostrowskia.

Greek Love Plant (*Catananche bicolor*)—See Catananche.

Greek Valerian (*Polemonium cæruleum*)—See Polemonium.

Green Hellebore (*Helleborus viridis*)—See Helleborus.

Green Man Orchis (*Aceras anthropophora*)—See Aceras.

Green Spleen-wort (*Asplenium viride*)—See Asplenium.

Green Wattle (*Acacia decurrens*)—See Acacia.

Green-winged Orchis (*Orchis morio*)—See Orchis.

Greig's Tulip (*Tulipa Greigi*)—See Tulipa.

Grevillea (Silk-bark Oak)—Ord. Proteaceæ. Greenhouse hardy evergreen shrubs. Flowering and orn. foliage. First introduced 1790.
CULTURE OF GREENHOUSE SPECIES : Compost, equal parts fibrous peat, turfy loam, and silver sand. Position, well-drained pots in airy greenhouse, window, or dwelling-room. Pot, March or April. Water moderately Sept. to April, freely afterwards. Prune off points of shoots occasionally to induce bushy growth. Temp., March to Oct. 55° to 65° ; Oct. to March 45° to 55°.
CULTURE OF HARDY SPECIES : Soil, peaty. Position, sheltered shrubberies S. of England ; against south walls other parts. Plant, Oct. or April. Prune, April. Protect in severe weather.
PROPAGATION : Greenhouse species by seeds sown ¼ in. deep in well-drained pots of light soil in temp. 65° to 70° in March ; cuttings of young shoots 3 in. long, with small heels of old wood attached, inserted in sandy soil in well-drained pots under bell-glass in temp. 75° to 80° in March, April, or May ; hardy species by seeds sown ¼ in. deep outdoors in March or April; layers in Oct. or Nov.; grafting in March.
GREENHOUSE SPECIES : G. robusta, orange, summer, 10 to 20 ft., Australia ; rosmarinifolia, red, summer, 6 ft., Australia. The last may be grown outdoors in south.
HARDY SPECIES : G. sulphurea, yellow, summer, 10 ft., Australia.

Grey Birch (*Betula populifolia*)—See Betula.

Grey Poplar (*Populus canescens*)—See Populus.

Grey Sage Bush (*Atriplex canescens*)—See Atriplex.

Griffinia (Blue Amaryllis)—Ord. Amaryllidaceæ. Stove bulbous flowering plants. Evergreen. First introduced 1815.
CULTURE : Compost, two parts fibrous loam, one part peat, decomposed sheep

manure and sand. Position, well-drained pots on a bed or stage heated beneath to temp. 85° in plant stove. Pot, June or July. Press compost down firmly. Re-potting not needful oftener than once every three or four years. Water moderately Oct. to April, freely afterwards. Syringe freely in summer. Top-dress established plants annually in March with rich compost. Temp., March to Sept. 70° to 80° ; Sept. to Dec. 55° to 65° ; December to March 65° to 75°.
PROPAGATION : By seeds sown ½ in. deep in sandy soil in temp. 85° in Feb. or March ; offsets removed from old bulbs and placed singly in 3 in. pots at potting time.
SPECIES CULTIVATED : G. Blumenavia, pink, summer, 1 ft., Brazil ; hyacinthina (Blue Amaryllis), blue, summer, 18 in., Brazil.

Grim-the-Collier (*Hieracium aurantiacum*)—See Hieracium.

Grindelia (Californian Gum Plant)—Ord. Compositæ. Hardy perennial plants.
CULTURE : Soil, ordinary. Position, sunny beds or borders. Plant 6 ft. apart in March or April.
PROPAGATION : By seeds sown in warm greenhouse in Feb. or March ; division at planting time.
SPECIES CULTIVATED : G. integrifolia, yellow, summer, to 3 ft., N. America ; inuloides, yellow, summer, 18 in., Mexico ; robusta, yellow, summer, to 2ft., California.

Griselinia (New Zealand Broad-leaf)—Ord. Cornaceæ. Hardy evergreen shrubs. Orn. foliage. Nat. New Zealand. First introduced 1872.
CULTURE : Soil, rich loam. Position, shady sheltered borders. Plant, Oct., Nov., March, and April. Prune into shape, April.
PROPAGATION : By cuttings inserted in sandy soil in sheltered border or cold frame Sept., Oct., or Nov. ; layering shoots in Oct. or Nov.
SPECIES CULTIVATED : G. littoralis, green, spring, 20 to 30 ft. ; lucida, green, spring, 10 to 12 ft., and its variety macrophylla.

Gromwell (*Lithospermum prostratum*)—See Lithospermum.

Ground Cistus (*Rhodothamnus chamæcistus*)—See Rhodothamnus.

Ground Holly—See Chimaphila.

Ground Ivy (*Nepeta Glechoma*)—See Nepeta.

Ground Nut (*Apios tuberosa* and *Arachis hypogæa*)—See Apios and Arachis.

Ground Rattan Cane—See Rhapis.

Grove Fern—See Alsophila.

Guava-tree (*Psidium Guava*)—See Psidium.

Guelder Rose (*Viburnum Opulus*)—See Virburnum.

Guernsey Elm (*Ulmus Wheatleyi*)—See Ulmus.

Guernsey Lily (*Nerine sarniensis*)—See Nerine.

Guernsey Orchis (*Orchis laxiflora*)—See Orchis.

Guevina—Ord. Proteaceæ. Half-hardy evergreen shrub or small tree.
CULTURE : Soil, peaty loam. Position, sheltered shady borders or shrubberies in southern gardens or borders in unheated greenhouse.
PROPAGATION : By cuttings of half-ripened wood in July in slight bottom heat.
SPECIES CULTIVATED : G. Avellana, white, June, Chile.

Guinea Pepper (*Capsicum annuum*)—See Capsicum.

Gumbo (*Hibiscus esculentus*)—See Hibiscus.

Gum Box (*Escallonia macrantha*)—See Escallonia.

Gum Cistus (*Cistus ladaniferus*)—See Cistus.

Gum Tree—See Acacia and Eucalyptus.

Gunnera (Prickly Rhubarb)—Ord. Haloraginaceæ. Hardy herbaceous peren-nials. Orn. foliage. First introduced 1849. Leaves, large, 4 to 6 ft. in diameter.
CULTURE : Soil, ordinary rich. Position, damp, sunny sheltered margins of ponds or bogs. Plant, March or April. Protect with leaves in winter. Water abundantly in dry weather.

PROPAGATION : By seeds sown $\frac{1}{16}$ in. deep in pans of light soil in temp. 55° to 65° in March, transplanting seedlings outdoors in June ; division of plants in spring.
SPECIES CULTIVATED : G. chilensis (Syn. G. scabra), leaves 4 to 6 ft. in diameter, 6 to 10 ft., Chile ; manicata, leaves 4 to 6 ft. in diameter, 4 to 6 ft., Brazil ; magellanica, very dwarf, 3 in., S. Chile.

Guzmania—Ord. Bromeliaceæ. Stove herbaceous perennials. Flowering and orn. foliage. First introduced 1820. Bracts, yellow, green, purple, scarlet. Leaves, sword-shaped ; bright green.
CULTURE : Compost, equal parts fibrous loam, rough peat and leaf-mould. Pot, March. Water freely always. Good drainage essential. Temp., Sept. to March 60° to 70° ; March to Sept. 70° to 80°.
PROPAGATION : By offshoots inserted in small pots at any time.
SPECIES CULTIVATED : G. lingulata, yellowish white, summer, 1 ft., bracts purplish red, Trop. America ; musaica (Syn. Tillandsia musaica), yellowish, stemless, bracts yellow and rose, Colombia. See also Tillandsia.

Gymnocladus (Kentucky Coffee Tree ; Soap Tree)—Ord. Leguminosæ. Hardy and half-hardy deciduous trees. Orn. foliage and flowering. First introduced 1748. Leaves, feather-shaped, bluish green, 3 ft. long and 2 ft. wide.
CULTURE : Soil, ordinary, well drained. Position, shady shrubberies or lawns for G. canadensis. G. chinensis is only hardy in the mildest parts of the country. Elsewhere it should be grown in borders or large tubs in the unheated glasshouse. Plant, Oct. to Feb. Prune young trees, Jan.
PROPAGATION : By seeds sown 1 in. deep in light soil in shady cool greenhouse in Oct., Nov., April, or March ; cuttings of roots inserted 2 in. deep in similar position in Oct. or March.
SPECIES CULTIVATED : G. canadensis (Kentucky Coffee Tree), white, May to July, to 110 ft., N. America ; chinensis (Soap Tree), white, June, to 40 ft., China.

Gymnogramme (Gold Fern ; Silver Fern)—Ord. Filices. Stove and greenhouse evergreen ferns. First introduced 1790. Fronds finely divided, upper sides green, under sides in most cases covered with white or yellow powder.
CULTURE : Compost, one part fibrous peat, one part leaf-mould and loam, one part silver sand, charcoal, and coarsely ground bones. Position, erect species in well-drained pots ; drooping species in hanging baskets. Pot, Feb. or March. Water moderately Oct. to Feb., freely afterwards. Syringing or shading not necessary. Temp., stove species, Sept. to March 55° to 65°, March to Sept. 65° to 75° ; greenhouse species, Sept. to March 45° to 50°, March to Sept. 55° to 65°.
PROPAGATION : By spores sown on surface of fine sandy peat under bell-glass in temp. 75° to 85° any time ; division of plants at potting time ; fronds furnished with plantlets pegged on to surface of sandy peat under bell-glass in temp. 70° to 80° at all times.
STOVE SPECIES : G. calomelanos, fronds dull green above, creamy white below, W. Indies, and the following varieties—chrysophylla (Gold Fern), fronds golden yellow, and peruviana argyrophylla (Silver Fern), fronds silvery ; decomposita, fronds yellow, hybrid ; schizophylla, fronds silvery, pretty for baskets, Jamaica ; sulphurea, fronds golden, West Indies ; tartarea (Syn. G. dealbata), fronds silvery, Trop. America.
GREENHOUSE SPECIES : G. japonica, fronds not powdered, Japan.

Gymnolomia—Ord. Compositæ. Hardy annual. Useful plant for cutting.
CULTURE : Soil, ordinary. Position, sunny borders. Sow seeds in patches outdoors during April. Thin out seedlings later on to a few inches apart.
SPECIES CULTIVATED : G. multiflora, yellow, Aug., 18 in., Mexico.

Gymnothrix—See Pennisetum.

Gynerium—See Cortaderia.

Gynura—Ord. Compositæ. Stove perennials with ornamental foliage. Leaves purple-tinted.
CULTURE : Compost, equal parts peat, loam, leaf-mould, and sand. Position, pots

in partial shade. Pot in March. Water freely March to Oct., moderately after-wards. Temp., March to Oct. 70° to 80° ; Oct. to March 55° to 65°.
PROPAGATION : By cuttings in spring.
SPECIES CULTIVATED : G. aurantiaca, 2 ft., Java ; bicolor, 3 ft., Moluccas ; sarmen-tosa, 6 to 8 ft., Malaya.

Gypsophila (Chalk-plant)—Ord. Caryophyllaceæ. Hardy perennial and annual herbs. First introduced 1759. Flowers valuable for cutting for floral decoration.
CULTURE : Soil, ordinary, freely mixed with old mortar or brick rubbish. Position, dryish well-drained borders for erect species ; sunny rockeries and margins of borders for dwarf species. Plant, Oct., Nov., March, or April. Cut down flower stems in Oct.
PROPAGATION : Annual species by seeds sown in April on surface of soil where plants are to flower, thinning seedlings out to 3 to 6 in. apart when 1 in. high ; perennial species by seeds sown in sunny position outdoors in April, transplanting seedlings to permanent position in June, July, or Aug. ; G. paniculata by cuttings of secondary laterals, 2 in. long, in silver sand under bell-glass in gentle bottom heat during June and July ; trailing species by division in spring and cuttings.
ANNUAL SPECIES : G. elegans, white, June to Oct., 12 to 18 in., Caucasus ; viscosa, rose, fragrant, summer, 12 to 18 in., Asia Minor.
PERENNIAL SPECIES : G. acutifolia, white or rosy, autumn, 4 ft., Caucasus ; cerastioi-des, white, veined red, May to Sept., 2 in., Himalayas ; glauca, white, summer, 18 in., Caucasus ; paniculata, white, summer, 2 to 3 ft., Europe ; paniculata flore-pleno, double white ; repens, white, summer, 6 in., Alps, and its varieties rosea and monstrosa ; Steveni, white, summer, 2 ft., Caucasus.

Habenaria (Butterfly Orchis ; Rein Orchis)—Ord. Orchidaceæ. Hardy and stove terrestrial orchids. Deciduous. Flowers, fragrant.
CULTURE OF HARDY SPECIES : Compost, equal parts leaf-mould, peat and sand. Position, moist, partially shaded borders. Plant, Oct. or April. Mulch surface of bed in June with leaf-mould, cocoanut-fibre refuse, or short grass. Water freely in summer in dryish positions. Replanting necessary only when plants show signs of deterioration.
CULTURE OF STOVE SPECIES : Compost, one-half of equal proportions of fibrous peat, loam and fresh-chopped sphagnum moss and another half of fine crocks and coarse silver sand. Pot when growth commences. Position, shady. Water moderately till growth is well advanced, then freely ; very little when at rest. Resting period, directly after flowering.
PROPAGATION : By division at potting time.
HARDY SPECIES : H. bifolia (Butterfly Orchid), white, June, 1 ft., Britain, and its variety chlorantha ; blephariglottis, white, summer, 1 ft., N. America ; ciliaris, orange, Aug., 18 in., N. America ; conopsea, red or white, summer, 18 in., Europe (Britain) ; fimbriata, purple, June, 1 ft., N. America.
STOVE SPECIES : H. carnea, pink and white, summer, Penang, and its white variety nivosa ; pusilla (Syn. militaris), green and scarlet, summer, 1 ft., Cochin China ; rhodocheila, rosy red and vermilion, summer, China. See also Platanthera.

Haberlea—Ord. Gesneraceæ. Hardy herbaceous perennial. First introduced 1880.
CULTURE : Soil, fibrous sandy peat. Position, vertical fissures of rockery in shade. Plant, Oct., March, or April. Water freely in dry weather.
PROPAGATION : By seeds sown ⅟₁₆ in. deep in well-drained pots or pans of sandy peat in cold frame in March or April ; by division of plants in March or April.
SPECIES CULTIVATED : H. rhodopensis, lilac, May, 6 in., Greece, and its white variety virginalis.

Hablitzia—Ord. Chenopodiaceæ. Hardy herbaceous climber. First intro-duced 1828.
CULTURE : Soil, ordinary. Position, base of naked trunks of trees, south or west

trellises, arbours, walls, or fences. Plant, Oct. ot March. Cut down stems to the ground in Oct.
PROPAGATION : By seeds sown ⅟₁₆ in. deep in sunny place outdoors in March or April, or similar depth in boxes of light soil in greenhouse or cold frame in March, transplanting seedlings outdoors in May or June ; by division of roots Oct. or April.
SPECIES CULTIVATED : H. tamnoides, green, summer, 8 to 10 ft., Caucasus.

Habranthus—See Zephyranthes and Hippeastrum.

Habrothamnus—See Cestrum.

Hackberry (*Celtis occidentalis*)—See Celtis.

Hacquetia—Ord. Umbelliferæ. Hardy herbaceous perennial.
CULTURE : Soil, ordinary. Position, sunny rockery or margin of border. Plant in March.
PROPAGATION : By division of the roots in March.
SPECIES CULTIVATED : H. epipactis (Syn. Dondia epipactis), yellow, spring, 3 to 6 in., Europe.

Hæmanthus (Blood-flower ; Blood Lily ; Red Cape Tulip)—Ord. Amaryllidaceæ. Stove and greenhouse bulbous plants. Deciduous. Nat. S. Africa. First introduced 1722.
CULTURE : Compost, two parts sandy loam, one part peat, well-decayed manure and sand. Position, well-drained pots exposed to full sun in stove or greenhouse whilst growing ; under staging whilst at rest. Pot early-flowering species Aug. to Nov. ; late-flowering species March or April. Place bulbs half their depth in compost. Water very little till growth begins, then moderately ; gradually withhold it when flowers fade, and keep soil quite dry from time foliage turns yellow till repotting time. Apply weak liquid manure once or twice weekly to plants in flower. Temp., greenhouse species, Sept. to March 45° to 55°, March to Sept. 55° to 65° ; stove species, Sept. to March 55° to 65°, March to Sept. 65° to 75°. Bulbs flower best when only repotted every three or four years.
PROPAGATION : By offsets removed at potting time and placed in small pots.
STOVE SPECIES : H. cinnabarinus, red, April, 1 ft. ; coccineus, scarlet, autumn, 1 ft. ; multiflorus (Syn. Kalbreyeri), scarlet, April, 1 ft.
GREENHOUSE SPECIES : H. Katharinæ, red, spring, 1 ft. ; natalensis, green, purple and yellow, Feb., 1 ft. ; puniceus, orange-scarlet, summer, 1 ft.

Hair Grass (*Aira capillaris pulchella*)—See Aira.

Hakea—Ord. Proteaceæ. Tender evergreen shrubs. First introduced 1790.
CULTURE : Compost, equal parts fibrous loam, leaf-mould and sharp sand. Position, well-drained large pots, tubs or borders in unheated glasshouse, or sheltered borders in the open in the mildest parts of the country.
PROPAGATION : By cuttings of half-ripened wood in July under hand-light in slight bottom heat.
SPECIES CULTIVATED : H. saligna, white, spring, 6 to 8 ft., Australia ; suaveolens, white, fragrant, summer, 10 ft., W. Australia.

Halesia (Silver-bell ; Snowdrop-tree)—Ord. Styracaceæ. Hardy flowering trees. Deciduous. First introduced 1756.
CULTURE : Soil, deep sandy loam. Position, sheltered borders, shrubberies, or lawns. Plant, Oct. to Feb. Prune into shape after flowering.
PROPAGATION : By cuttings of roots inserted in sandy soil outdoors in March or Oct. ; by layering shoots in Oct. or Nov.
SPECIES CULTIVATED : H. carolina (Snowdrop Tree), Syn. tetraptera, white, May, 15 to 20 ft., N. America ; diptera, white, May, to 30 ft., N. America.

Halimodendron (Salt-tree)—Ord. Leguminosæ. Hardy flowering and orn. foliage shrub. Deciduous. First introduced 1779. Leaves, feather-shaped, whitish and downy.
CULTURE : Soil, deep sandy. Position, shrubberies and open borders. Plant, Oct. to Feb. Prune into shape, Nov.
PROPAGATION : By seeds sown ½ in. deep in sandy soil outdoors in March or April;

cuttings of firm shoots 4 to 6 in. long inserted in sandy soil outdoors in Oct. and Nov. ; layering in Oct., and by grafting on Carragana arborescens in March.
SPECIES CULTIVATED : H. argenteum, purplish, May to July, 4 to 6 ft., Russia.

Hamamelis (Witch Hazel)—Ord. Hamamelidaceæ. Hardy flowering shrubs. Deciduous. First introduced 1736.
CULTURE : Soil, deep rich loam. Position, damp borders or shrubberies and margins of lakes. Plant, Oct. to Feb. Prune into shape, Feb.
PROPAGATION : By layering branches in Oct. or Nov. ; grafting rare species on common kind in March.
SPECIES CULTIVATED : H. japonica, lemon yellow, Dec. to Feb., 12 ft., Japan, and its varieties arborea and zuccariniana ; mollis, yellow, Jan. and Feb., 10 ft., China ; virginiana, yellow, Dec. to Feb., N. America.

Hamburgh Parsley (*Carum Petroselinum*)—See Carum.

Haplocarpha—Ord. Compositæ. Half-hardy perennial. First introduced 1883.
CULTURE : Soil, sandy loam. Position, sunny, dry, and well-drained border. Plant, April.
PROPAGATION : By seeds sown in temp. 55° in spring ; also by cuttings inserted in temp. 55° in spring ; or in cold frame during summer.
SPECIES CULTIVATED : H. Leitchlinii, yellow and purple, summer, 1 ft., S. Africa.

Hardenbergia (Australian Sarsaparilla-tree ; Australian I ilac)—Ord. Leguminosæ. Greenhouse flowering twining plants. Evergreen. Nat. S. Australia. First introduced 1790.
CULTURE : Compost, equal parts loam and peat, little silver sand. Position, pots, with shoots trained to trellis, or planted out in beds, and shoots trained up rafters. Pot or plant, Feb. or May. Water freely March to Sept., moderately at other times. Prune straggling plants into shape in Feb. Apply weak stimulants occasionally to healthy plants in flower. Temp., March to Sept. 55° to 65° ; Sept. to March 40° to 50°.
PROPAGATION : By seeds sown ⅛ in. deep in well-drained pots of light sandy soil in temp of 55° to 65° in March or April ; cuttings of firm young shoots, 2 to 3 in. long, inserted in well-drained pots of sandy peat under bell-glass in temp. 55° to 65°, March to July.
SPECIES CULTIVATED : H. comptoniana, purple, March, 10 ft. ; monophylla, purple, April, 8 to 10 ft.

Hard Fern (*Lomaria Spicant*)—See Lomaria.

Hare-bell (*Campanula rotundifolia*)—See Campanula.

Hare's-ear—See Bupleurum.

Hare's-foot Fern (*Davallia canariensis*)—See Davallia.

Hare's-tail Grass (*Lagurus ovatus*)—See Lagurus.

Haricot Bean (*Phaseolus vulgaris*)—See Phaseolus.

Harlequin Flower (*Sparaxis grandiflora*)—See Sparaxis.

Harpalium—See Helianthus.

Harrison's Musk (*Mimulus moschatus Harrisoni*)—See Mimulus.

Hart's-tongue Fern (*Scolopendrium vulgare*)—See Scolopendrium.

Hatchet Cactus (*Pelecyphora asseliformis*)—See Pelecyphora.

Hautbois Strawberry (*Fragaria elatior*)—See Fragaria.

Hawk's Beard (*Crepis aurea*)—See Crepis.

Hawk Weed (*Hieracium aurantiacum*)—See Hieracium.

Haworthia—Ord. Liliaceæ. Greenhouse succulent-leaved plants. Orn. foliage. Nat. S. Africa. First introduced 1720. Flowers, greenish. Leaves, fleshy, transparent, warty and variegated.
CULTURE : Compost, equal parts light loam, broken bricks, mortar rubbish and river

sand. Position, well-drained pots in light greenhouse shaded from sun. Pot, March or April. Water moderately April to Sept., occasionally other times. Repotting necessary only when plants show signs of ill-health. Temp., March to Sept. 60° to 65° ; Sept. to March 50° to 55°.

PROPAGATION : By seeds sown ₁₆ in. deep in well-drained pots or pans in above compost in temp. 65°, March to Aug. ; by suckers placed in small pots and treated as advised for plants.

SPECIES CULTIVATED : H. albicans, 3 to 4 in. ; arachnoides, 3 in. ; atrovirens, 1 in. ; attenuata, 3 in. ; margaritifera, 3 in. ; Reinwardtii, 2 in. ; tortuosa, 2 in. ; viscosa, 2 in.

Hawthorn (*Cratægus monogyna* and *C. Oxyacantha*)—See Cratægus.

Hay-scented Fern (*Nephrodium æmulum*)—See Nephrodium.

Hazel (*Corylus Avellana*)—See Corylus.

Heart-flowered Orchis (*Serapias cordigera*)—See Serapias.

Heart-leaved Saxifrage (*Saxifraga cordifolia*)—See Saxifraga.

Heart's Ease (*Viola tricolor*)—See Viola.

Heath—See Erica.

Heath Gentian (*Gentiana Pneumonanthe*)—See Gentian.

Heather (*Calluna vulgaris*)—See Calluna.

Heath-leaved St. John's-wort (*Hypericum coris*)—See Hypericum.

Heath-leaved Starwort (*Aster ericoides*)—See Aster.

Heavenly Bamboo (*Nandina domestica*)—See Nandina.

Hebeclinium—See Eupatorium.

Hebenstretia—Ord. Selaginaceæ. Half-hardy perennial treated as an annual.
CULTURE : Soil, good ordinary. Position, sunny borders. Sow seeds in heat in March, harden seedlings off early in May, and plant out late in May 12 to 18 in. apart in groups. Seeds may also be sown thinly where required to flower about the middle of April.
SPECIES CULTIVATED : H. comosa, white and scarlet, summer, 2 to 4 ft., S. Africa.

Hedera (Ivy)—Ord. Araliaceæ. Hardy evergreen climbing shrubs. Orn. foliage. Flowers, green ; Oct. to Nov. Leaves, green, purplish, or variegated with yellow and white. Berries, purplish black, reddish orange, golden ; winter.
OUTDOOR CULTURE : Soil, ordinary rich. Position, green-leaved kinds against walls of all aspects, railings, tree stumps, arbours, trellises, on banks and under shade of trees ; variegated kinds against south or west walls or fences. Plant, Sept., Oct., Nov., Feb., March, or April. Peg shoots to surface of soil when first planted in any position. Prune April, cutting off old leaves and straggling shoots. Water freely in dry weather. Apply stimulants if vigorous growth is desired.
POT CULTURE : Compost, two parts loam, one part leaf-mould or decayed manure and sand. Position, well-drained pots in unheated greenhouses, balconies or windows. Pot, Oct. or March. Water moderately Oct. to March, freely after-wards. Prune into shape, April. Apply stimulants to established plants in summer only.
HANGING BASKETS : Compost, same as above. Plant, Oct. or March. Position, unheated greenhouses, balconies or windows. Water moderately Sept. to April, freely afterwards.
PROPAGATION : By cuttings of firm shoots 6 to 8 in. long inserted in ordinary soil at base of north wall or fence, Sept. to Nov., in well-drained pots in cold frame in Oct., or in temp. 55° to 65°, Sept. to Nov. ; tree and variegated kinds by cleft grafting on common species in temp. 55° in Feb.
SPECIES CULTIVATED : H. Helix (ivy), green, Europe, N. Africa and N. Asia.
VARIETIES CULTIVATED : H. Helix algeriensis, green ; arborescens (Tree Ivy), green and variegated forms ; canariensis (Irish Ivy), green ; chrysocarpa, green ; con-

Gypsophila elegans
(Chalk-plant)

Hamamelis mollis
(Witch Hazel)

Hebenstretia comosa

Hedera Helix rægneriana
(Giant Ivy)

Hedychium Gardnerianum
(Fragrant Garland-flower)

Helenium hybridum
(Helen-flower)

Helianthus debilis
(Sunflower)

Helichrysum bracteatum
(Everlasting Flower)

Heliopsis scabra zinniæflora
(North American Ox-eye)

Heliotropium peruvianum
(Heliotrope)

Helleborus guttatus

Hemerocallis hydrida
(Day Lily)

Hemerocallis minor
(Day Lily)

Hesperis matronalis
(Sweet Rocket)

Heuchera brizoides gracillima
(Alum-root)

Hippeastrum hybridum
(Barbados Lily)

Hippeastrum pratense
(Barbados Lily)

Hyacinthus orientalis
(Hyacinth)

glomerata, green ; cuspidata minor, purplish green ; deltoidea, purple bronze ;
digitata, dark green ; donerailense, purplish brown ; gracilis, purplish bronze ;
lobata major, deep green ; lucida, green and yellow ; marginata, white and reddish
pink ; marginata rubra, green and rosy red ; marmorata, creamy white ; palmata,
green ; purpurea, purplish ; rægneriana (Giant Ivy), deep green, large ; rhombea,
green and white ; sagittæfolia, green and bronze ; variegata, green and white.

Hedgehog Broom (*Erinacea pungens*)—See Erinacea.

Hedgehog Cactus—See Echinocactus and Echinopsis.

Hedgehog Holly (*Ilex aquifolium ferox*)—See Ilex.

Hedge Pink (*Saponaria officinalis*)—See Saponaria.

Hedychium (Fragrant Garland-flower)—Ord. Zingiberaceæ.   Stove and greenhouse herbaceous perennials.   First introduced 1791.   Flowers, fragrant.
CULTURE : Compost, two parts peat, one of loam and one of sand.   Position, well-
drained pots, tubs or boxes, or planted in beds in stove or warm greenhouse.   Pot
plants may be stood outdoors July to Aug.   Pot, March or April.   Water freely
April to Nov., occasionally other times.   Apply liquid manure twice a week to
plants in flower.   Temp., stove species, March to Nov. 65° to 75°, Nov. to March
50° to 55° ; greenhouse species, March to Nov. 55° to 65°, Nov. to March 45° to
50°.   Cut down flower stems immediately after flowering.   H. gardnerianum
adapted for outdoor culture in summer.   Plant, May, in rich soil.   Water freely
in dry weather.   Apply liquid manure when in flower.   Lift roots in Oct. and store
in frost-proof place till planting time.
PROPAGATION : By division of rhizomes (creeping stems) in March or April.
STOVE SPECIES : H. coronarium, white, summer, 5 ft., India.
GREENHOUSE SPECIES : H. flavum, yellow and orange, July, 5 ft., Himalayas ;
gardnerianum, lemon yellow, summer, 4 ft., Himalayas ; Greeni, red, summer, 6 ft.,
Himalayas.

Hedysarum (French Honeysuckle)—Ord. Leguminosæ.   Hardy perennial herbs
and shrubs.   First introduced 1596.
CULTURE : Soil, ordinary.   Position, sunny rockeries, banks, or slopes for dwarf
species ; sunny well-drained borders for tall species.   Plant, Oct., March, or April.
Cut down flower stems in Oct.
PROPAGATION : By seeds sown ½ in. deep outdoors in April, transplanting seedlings
in June to final position ; perennial species by division of roots, Oct. or April ;
shrubby species by layering in spring or by cuttings in Aug.
PERENNIAL SPECIES : H. coronarium (French Honeysuckle), red, summer, 3 to 4 ft.,
S. Europe ; coronarium album, white ; hedysaroides (Syn. obscurum), crimson,
summer, 6 to 12 in., Europe ; microcalyx, crimson-violet, June to July, 2 to 3 ft.
Himalayas ; neglectum, rosy purple, June to Aug., 9 to 15 in., Siberia.
SHRUBBY SPECIES : H. multijugum, red, June, 4 ft., Mongolia.

Hedyscepe (Umbrella Palm)—Ord. Palmaceæ.   Stove palm.   Orn. foliage.
A good room plant.   Leaves, feather-shaped, green.
CULTURE : Compost, equal parts loam and peat, little silver sand.   Position, well-
drained pots in shady plant stove.   Pot, Feb., March, or April.   Water freely
March to Oct., moderately afterwards.   Springe twice daily March or Sept.   Temp.,
March to Sept. 70° to 85° ; Sept. to March 60° to 65°.
PROPAGATION : By seeds sown 1 in. deep in light soil, in temp. 70° to 80°, in Feb.
or March.
SPECIES CULTIVATED : H. canterburyana (Syn. Kentia canterburyana), Lord Howe's
Island.

Helen-flower (*Helenium autumnale*)—See Helenium.

Helenium (Helen-flower ; Sneeze-wort ; Sneeze-weed)—Ord. Compositæ.
Hardy herbaceous perennials and annuals.   First introduced 1729.
CULTURE OF PERENNIAL SPECIES : Soil, ordinary rich.   Position, sunny well-drained
borders.   Plant, Oct., Nov., March, or April.   Cut down flower stems in Oct.

PROPAGATION : By seeds sown ½ in. deep outdoors in April, transplanting seedlings in June or July ; division of roots in Oct. or March.

CULTURE OF ANNUAL SPECIES : Soil, ordinary. Position, sunny borders. Sow seeds in patches in borders in March or April.

PERENNIAL SPECIES : H. autumnale, yellow, July to Oct., 3 to 5 ft., N. America ; autumnale pumilum, 1 ft. ; autumnale striatum, yellow and brown, 4 ft. ; Bigelovii, yellow and brown, Aug. to Oct., 4 ft., California ; Bolanderi, yellow and brown, summer, 18 in., California ; Hoopesii, yellow, summer, 2 ft., N. America. There are several named varieties such as Wyndley, Madame Canivet and Crimson Beauty.

ANNUAL SPECIES : H. tenuifolium, yellow, summer, 1½ to 2 ft., N. America.

Helianthemum (Sun Rose)—Ord. Cistaceæ. Hardy flowering shrubs. Evergreen.

CULTURE : Soil, light sandy. Position, sunny banks or rockeries. Plant, Oct., March, or April. Prune into shape, March.

PROPAGATION : By seeds sown ⅟₁₆ in. deep in bed of light soil outdoors in April ; cuttings of shoots, 1 to 2 in. long, inserted in well-drained pots of sandy soil in cold frame in Aug. or Sept. ; division of plants in Oct. or April.

SPECIES CULTIVATED : H. alyssoides, yellow, May to July, 2 ft., Spain and Portugal ; formosum, yellow, June, 3 to 4 ft., Portugal ; halimifolium, yellow, May to June, 2 to 3 ft., S. Europe ; ocymoides, yellow and black, June, 2 ft., S. Europe ; Tuberaria, yellow, summer, trailing, S. Europe ; umbellatum, white and yellow, May to June, 1 to 1½ ft., Mediterranean Region ; vulgare, yellow, June, trailing, and its numerous double and single varieties, of which cupreum, rhodanthe carneum and venustum are typical.

Helianthi (*Helianthus doronicoides*)—See Helianthus below.

Helianthus (Sunflower ; Jerusalem Artichoke)—Ord. Compositæ. Hardy annual or perennial herbs ; tubers of Jerusalem Artichoke edible.

CULTURE OF ANNUAL SPECIES : Soil, ordinary. Position, sunny borders. Sow seeds ¼ in. deep in April where plants are to flower, or in pots in temp. 55° to 65° in April, transplanting seedlings outdoors in June. Apply stimulants occasionally when flower buds form.

CULTURE OF PERENNIAL SPECIES : Soil, ordinary rich. Position, sunny well-drained borders. Plant, Oct., Nov., or April. Cut down flower stems in Oct. Water in dry weather. Apply stimulants occasionally when plants show flower buds. Replant every third year.

CULTURE OF JERUSALEM ARTICHOKE : Soil, ordinary rich. Position, open or shady. Plant, Feb. or March, placing tubers 6 in. deep and 12 in. apart in rows 3 ft. asunder. Earth-up when stems are 6 in. high. Lift tubers in Nov. and store in sand or dry soil in outhouse, or leave in ground and dig as required.

PROPAGATION : Annual and perennial species by seeds sown ¼ in. deep in sunny place outdoors in March or April ; perennials by division of roots, Oct., March, or April ; Jerusalem Artichoke, by tubers treated as above.

ANNUAL SPECIES : H. annuus (Common Sunflower), yellow, summer, 6 to 10 ft., N. America ; argophyllus, yellow, 6 ft., N. America ; debilis (Syn. cucumerifolius), yellow, 3 to 4 ft.

PERENNIAL SPECIES : H. decapetalus, sulphur yellow, summer, 4 to 6 ft., Canada ; doronicoides, yellow, summer, 7 ft., roots tuberous, N. America ; lætiflorus, yellow, autumn, 5 to 7 ft., N. America ; multiflorus, yellow, July, 4 ft., N. America ; multiflorus maximus, large-flowered ; multiflorus flore-pleno, double-flowered ; orgyalis, yellow, Aug., 6 ft., N. America ; rigidus (Syn. Harpalium rigidum), yellow, Aug., 5 ft., N. America ; sparsifolius, yellow, Aug. to Sept., 5 to 6 ft., N. America ; tuberosus (Jerusalem Artichoke), yellow, 6 ft., N. America. There are several named varieties such as Miss Mellish and Soleil d'Or to be found in trade lists.

Helichrysum (Everlasting-flower ; Immortelle-flower)—Ord. Compositæ. Half-hardy annuals, hardy perennials, and greenhouse shrubs.

CULTURE OF ANNUAL SPECIES : Soil, ordinary. Position, sunny. **Sow seeds in** gentle heat in March and plant out in May ; or sow outdoors in April.   Gather flowers for winter decoration directly they are fully expanded.

CULTURE OF PERENNIAL SPECIES : Soil, rich loam.   Position, sunny well-drained borders and rock gardens.   Plant, March or April.

CULTURE OF HARDY SHRUBBY SPECIES : Soil, rich loam.   Position, sunny well-drained borders or sheltered shrubberies.   Plant, Sept. or Oct.   Protect in very severe weather.

CULTURE OF GREENHOUSE SPECIES : Compost, two parts peat and one part of equal proportions of leaf-mould, charcoal, and sand.   Position, sunny greenhouse. Pot firmly in Feb. or March.   Water freely in summer, moderately other seasons. Temp., 45° to 50° in winter ; 55° to 60° other seasons.

PROPAGATION : Hardy species by seeds sown outdoors in April or cuttings in cold frame in spring ; greenhouse species by cuttings in fine sand under bell-glass in spring.

ANNUAL SPECIES : H. bracteatum (Everlasting Flower), colours various, summer, 3 to 4 ft., Australia.

PERENNIAL SPECIES : H. angustifolium, white, summer, to 1 ft., Mediterranean Region ; arenarium (Yellow Everlasting), yellow, summer, 6 to 12 in., Europe ; bellidioides, silvery white, summer, 3 to 4 in., New Zealand ; lanatum, yellow, summer, to 15 ins., S. Africa.

HARDY SHRUBBY SPECIES : H. rosmarinifolium (Syn. Ozothamnus rosmarinifolium), white, summer, 6 to 9 ft., Tasmania.

GREENHOUSE SHRUBBY SPECIES : H. humile (Syn. Aphelexis humilis), pink, summer, 3 ft., S. Africa.

Helicodiceros (Dragon's Mouth)—Ord. Aroideæ.   Hardy tuberous-rooted perennial.   Flowers, arum-like.

CULTURE : Soil, ordinary, well drained.   Position, sunny borders.   Plant in autumn or early spring.

PROPAGATION : By offsets in autumn.

SPECIES CULTIVATED : H. crinitus (Syn. Arum crinitum), spathe, purplish brown, summer, 2 ft., S. Europe.

Heliconia (False Plantain)—Ord. Musaceæ.   Stove herbaceous perennials. Orn. foliage.   First introduced 1786.   Leaves, green ; stem striped with black, green, and yellow.

CULTURE : Compost, two parts fibrous loam, one part leaf-mould, peat, and sand. Position, pots in shady part of plant stove.   Pot, Feb. or March.   Water freely March to Sept., moderately Sept. to Nov., none Nov. to March.   Syringe daily March to Sept.   Temp., Feb. to Sept. 65° to 75° ; Sept. to Nov. 60° to 70° ; Nov. to Feb. 55° to 65°.

PROPAGATION : By division of roots in Feb. or March.

SPECIES CULTIVATED : H. aureo-striata, green and yellow leaves, 3 ft., New Britain ; illustris, green and red leaves, 3 ft., South Sea Islands ; Sanderi, variegated, 2 ft., New Guinea.

Heliophila (Cape Stock ; Sun Cress)—Ord. Cruciferæ.   Hardy annuals.   Nat. S. Africa.   First introduced 1774.

CULTURE : Soil, ordinary.   Position, sunny well-drained borders.   Water in dry weather.

PROPAGATION : By seeds sown $\frac{1}{16}$ in. deep in pans or boxes of light soil in temp. of 55° in March, transplanting seedlings outdoors end of May, or similar depth in April where plants are to flower.

SPECIES CULTIVATED : H. amplexicaulis, white and purple, summer, 9 in. ; coronopifolia, bluish white, summer, 2 ft. ; pilosa, blue, summer, 6 to 12 in.

Heliopsis (North American Ox-eye)—Ord. Compositæ.   Hardy herbaceous perennials.   First introduced 1714.

CULTURE : Soil, ordinary rich.   Position, sunny well-drained borders.   Plant, Oct., Nov., March, or April.   Cut down flower stems in Oct.   Water in dry weather.   Apply stimulants occasionally when plants show flower buds.

PROPAGATION : By division of plants, Oct., March, or April.
SPECIES CULTIVATED : H. lævis, yellow, autumn, 5 ft., N. America, perennial, and its variety pitcheriana ; scabra, yellow, July to Sept., 4 ft., U.S.A., and its varieties major and zinniæflora (double-flowered).

Heliotrope (*Heliotropium peruvianum*)—See Heliotropium.

Heliotropium (Heliotrope ; Cherry Pie ; Turnsole)—Ord. Boraginaceæ. Greenhouse flowering shrub. First introduced 1757. Flowers, fragrant.
CULTURE : Compost, equal parts light loam, leaf-mould, and sand. Position, pots or beds, with shoots growing loosely or trained to trellis, walls, pillars, or rafters in greenhouse ; in sunny beds outdoors June to Sept., or in pots in windows. Pot, Feb. to May. Plant outdoors, June. Lift and repot, Sept. Water freely March to Oct., moderately afterwards. Apply liquid or artificial manure to healthy plants in flower. Prune old plants in closely in Feb. Training : Nip off points of main, also lateral shoots when 3 in. long to form dwarf plants ; points of main shoots when 12 in. long, and side shoots when 3 to 6 in. long, to form pyramids ; points of main shoots when 2 ft. long, and of lateral shoots at apex when 3 to 6 in. long— all side shoots to within 4 in. of apex to be removed altogether—to form standards. Temp., Feb. to Oct. 60° to 70° ; Oct. to Feb. 50° to 55°. Pot plants do best in cold frame or sunny position outdoors July and Aug.
PROPAGATION : By seeds sown $\frac{1}{16}$ in. deep in well-drained pots or pans of light soil in temp. 65° to 75° in March ; by cuttings of shoots 2 to 3 in. long inserted in pots of sandy soil under bell-glass, or in propagator in temp. 65° to 75° in March, April, Aug., or Sept.
SPECIES CULTIVATED : H. peruvianum, blue and white, spring to winter, 1 to 6 ft., Peru ; numerous varieties.

Helipterum (Australian Everlasting ; Immortelle-flower)—Ord. Compositæ. Hardy annuals. Nat. W. Australia. First introduced 1863.
CULTURE OF H. HUMBOLDTIANUM : Soil, light rich. Position, sunny well-drained borders.
PROPAGATION : By seeds sown $\frac{1}{8}$ in. deep in well-drained pots of light soil, in temp. 55° in March, transplanting seedlings outdoors end of May or early in June.
CULTURE OF H. MANGLESII AND ROSEUM : Soil, ordinary. Position, sunny beds or borders. Sow seeds $\frac{1}{8}$ in. deep in light sandy soil in temp. 55° to 65° in March or April, harden off in May, and plant out in June. Gather blooms when fully grown and dry thoroughly in summer for winter decorations.
POT CULTURE : Compost, equal parts sandy peat, leaf-mould, loam, and decayed cow manure. Sow seeds thinly in shallow pan or box in temp. 55° to 65° in Sept. for spring flowering, and in March for summer blooming. Transplant when three leaves have formed, several 1 in. apart in a 5 in. pot. Grow on shelf near glass. Water moderately at first ; freely later on. Apply weak stimulants once a week when seedlings are 6 in. high. Support with neat stakes when 3 to 6 in. high. No shade required. Winter temp., 45° to 55°.
SPECIES CULTIVATED : H. humboldtianum (Syn. H. Sandfordii), yellow, summer, 1 ft., Australia ; Manglesii (Syn. Rhodanthe Manglesii), rosy pink and yellow, summer, 12 to 18 in., Australia ; roseum (Syn. Acroclinium roseum), rose, summer, 2 ft., Australia ; roseum album, white.

Hellebore (*Helleborus niger*)—See Helleborus.

Helleborine (*Cephalanthera pallens* and *Epipactis latifolia*)—See Cephalanthera and Epipactis.

Helleborus (Hellebore ; Christmas Rose ; Lenten Rose)—Ord. Ranunculaceæ. Hardy perennials. Evergreen and deciduous.
OUTDOOR CULTURE : Soil, rich loamy. Position, shady well-drained east border. Plant, Oct., Nov., and March, 12 in. apart. Mulch with well-decayed manure in April. Water freely in dry weather. Apply liquid manure occasionally May to Sept. Disturb roots as little as possible. Protect with hand-lights, cloches, or

frames, or cover surface of bed with moss when in bloom. Manure soil freely prior to planting.

POT CULTURE : Compost, two parts fibry loam, one part decayed manure. Position, cold frame, or greenhouse heated to temp. 40° to 50°. Pot, Oct. Lift fresh plants annually for pot culture, replanting old ones outdoors in April or May. Water moderately. Size of pot for single plants, 6 to 8 in.

PROPAGATION : By seeds sown ⅛ in. deep in shallow boxes of sandy soil in cold frame Oct. or March, transplanting seedlings outdoors when a year old ; by division of roots in March.

SPECIES CULTIVATED : H. abchasicus, purplish green, Jan. to March, 1 ft., Caucasus ; antiquorum, rose pink, Feb. to April, 1½ ft., Caucasian Region ; atrorubens, purple, March and April, 18 in., S. Europe (Caucasus) ; caucasicus, pale green, Feb. to April, 2 ft., Caucasus ; colchicus, deep purple, Jan. to March, 18 in., Asia Minor ; corsicus (Syns. argutifolius and lividus), green, March, 2 ft., Corsica ; fœtidus (Stinking Hellebore), green and purple, Feb., 2 to 3 ft., Britain ; guttatus, white and crimson, Jan. to April, 1½ ft., Caucasus, and its variety subpunctatus ; niger (Christmas Rose), white, winter, 6 to 15 in., Europe, and its varieties altifolius or maximus (white and purple), angustifolius (white), and major (white) ; odorus (Fragrant Hellebore), green, March, 18 in., Hungary ; olympicus, purple, Feb. to April, 1 to 2 ft., Greece ; orientalis (Lenten Rose), rose, Feb. to May, 1 to 2 ft., Greece, and its variety roseus ; viridis (Green Hellebore), green, March, 18 in., Europe. Many varieties will be found in trade lists.

Helmet-flower—See Aconitum and Scutellaria.

Helmet Orchid—See Coryanthes.

Helonias (Stud-flower)—Ord. Liliaceæ. Hardy herbaceous perennial. Nat. N. America. First introduced 1758.

CULTURE : Soil, sandy loam and peat. Position, moist, shady borders or margins of lakes or ponds. Plant, Oct., March, or April.

PROPAGATION : By seeds sown 1/16 in. deep in a well-drained pan of sandy peat in cold shady frame in March or April ; division of roots, Oct. or March.

SPECIES CULTIVATED : H. bullata, purplish rose, summer, 18 in. See also Zygadenus.

Helxine—Ord. Urticaceæ. Hardy perennial, with creeping or trailing shoots.

CULTURE : Soil, ordinary, mixed with a little leaf-mould and sand. Position, in pots suspended in windows or as edgings to beds, or carpeting small beds on rockery in sun or shade. Pot in spring, or plant out in May. Water moderately those grown in pots.

PROPAGATION : By division in spring.

SPECIES CULTIVATED : H. Solierolii, 2 to 3 in., Corsica. Has tiny neat green foliage.

Hemerocallis (Day Lily)—Ord. Liliaceæ. Hardy herbaceous perennials. First introduced 1596.

CULTURE : Soil, ordinary deep rich. Position, moist borders, open or slightly shady. Plant, Oct., Nov., March, or April ; singly or in groups. Lift and replant only when they become unhealthy. Mulch established clumps with decayed manure in April or May.

PROPAGATION : By division of roots, Oct., Nov., or March.

SPECIES CULTIVATED : H. aurantiaca major (Japanese Day Lily), apricot, summer, 3 ft., Japan ; Dumortieri, orange-yellow, July, 2 ft., Japan ; flava, orange-yellow, fragrant, July, 2 to 3 ft., S. Europe ; fulva, yellow, June, 2 to 3 ft., Europe and Japan ; fulva crocea, yellow ; fulva disticha, yellow and red ; fulva kwanso, double flowered ; Middendorffii, golden yellow, summer, 2 ft., Siberia and Japan ; minor (Syn. H. graminea), yellow, fragrant, 8 in., Siberia and Japan ; Thunbergii, yellow, July, fragrant, 2 ft., Japan. There are also many fine hybrids.

Hemionitis (Ivy-leaved Fern)—Ord. Filices. Warm greenhouse evergreen ferns. First introduced 1793. Fronds, heart- or hand-shaped.

CULTURE : Compost, two parts peat and one of sand. Position, small well-drained pots in shade. Pot, Feb. or March. Water moderately March to Sept., occasionally

other times.   Syringing not required.   Temp., March to Sept. 60° to 70° ; Sept.
to March 55° to 60°.
PROPAGATION : By spores sown on surface of pans of sandy peat under bell-glass in
temp. 65° to 75° at any time.
SPECIES CULTIVATED : H. cordata, 6 in., Ceylon, etc. ; palmata, 8 in., West
Indies.

Hemitelia (Smith's Tree Fern)—Ord. Filices.   Stove and greenhouse evergreen
tree ferns.   First introduced 1824.   Fronds, feather-shaped.
CULTURE : Compost, equal parts peat, loam, and sand.   Position, well-drained pots
or tubs in shade.   Pot, March.   Water freely March to Sept., moderately after-
wards.   Syringe trunks daily March to Sept.   Temp., Sept. to March 55° to 65°,
March to Sept. 65° to 75° for stove species ; Sept. to March 45° to 55°, March to
Sept. 55° to 65° for greenhouse species.
PROPAGATION : By spores sown at any time on surface of finely sifted loam and peat
in shallow well-drained pans under bell-glass in moist, shady position in temp.
75° to 85°.
STOVE SPECIES : H. horrida, 6 to 10 ft., W. Indies.
GREENHOUSE SPECIES : H. capensis, 6 to 10 ft., S. Africa ; Smithii, 10 to 12 ft., New
Zealand ; Walkeræ, 4 to 6 ft., Ceylon.

Hemlock Spruce—See Tsuga.

Hemp Agrimony—See Eupatorium.

Hemp-seed (*Cannabis sativa*)—See Cannabis.

Hen and Chickens Daisy (*Bellis perennis prolifera*)—**See Bellis.**

Hepatica—See Anemone.

Heracleum (Giant Cow Parsnip ; Cartwheel Flower)—Ord. Umbelliferæ.
Hardy perennial herbs.   Orn. foliage.   Leaves, large, feather-shaped, green.
CULTURE : Soil, ordinary.   Position, open or sheltered shrubberies, borders,
margins of ponds, lakes, etc.   Plant, Oct. or Nov.   Remove flower stems immediately they appear early in June if fine, healthy foliage is desired.
PROPAGATION : By seeds sown ¼ in. deep in ordinary soil outdoors, March or April ;
division of roots, Oct. or March.
SPECIES CULTIVATED : H. mantegazzianum, white, summer, very large foliage, 7 to
9 ft., Caucasus ; villosum (Syn. H. giganteum), white and yellow, summer, 10 to
12 ft., Caucasus.

Herb Christopher (*Actæa spicata*)—See Actæa.

Herb-Lily—See Alstromeria.

Herb-Louisa (*Lippia citriodora*)—See Lippia.

Herb-of-Grace (*Ruta graveolens*)—See Ruta.

Herb-of-Repentance (*Ruta graveolens*)—See Ruta.

Herb Paris (*Paris quadrifolia*)—See Paris.

Herb Patience (*Rumex Patientia*)—See Rumex.

Herb-Twopence (*Lysimachia nummularia*)—See Lysimachia.

Herminium (*Musk Orchis*)—Ord. Orchidaceæ.   Hardy terrestrial orchid with
musk-scented flowers.
CULTURE : Soil, light turfy loam with plenty of chalk or old mortar and leaf-mould
added.   Position, sunny rockeries ; or in pots in cold frame.   Plant wild roots
directly flowers have faded ; pot grown roots in early spring.
PROPAGATION : By division in spring.
SPECIES CULTIVATED : H. monorchis, green and yellow, July, 6 in., Britain.

Hermodactylus tuberosus.—See Iris tuberosus.

Herniaria (Rupture-wort)—Ord. Illicebraceæ. Hardy perennial trailing herbs. Ornamental-leaved.

CULTURE : Soil, ordinary. Position, sunny or shady rockeries, or as edgings to carpet-beds, or for carpeting surface of beds containing choice bulbs. Plant, Oct., Nov., March to June.

PROPAGATION : By seeds sown $\frac{1}{16}$ in. deep in light sandy soil outdoors, March or April ; division of plants, Oct., Nov., March, April or May.

SPECIES CULTIVATED : H. glabra, leaves dark green, 1 in., Europe (Britain) ; glabra aurea, leaves golden ; hirsuta, leaves hairy, prostrate, Europe.

Heron's-bill—See Erodium.

Herring-bone Fern (*Lomaria Spicant*)—See Lomaria.

Herring-bone Thistle (*Cnicus Casabonæ*)—See Cnicus.

Hesperantha (Evening-flower)—Ord. Iridaceæ. Greenhouse bulbous flowering plants. Deciduous. Nat. S. Africa. First introduced 1787. Flowers, fragrant, opening in the evening.

CULTURE : Compost, two parts fibrous loam, one part leaf-mould or decayed cow manure, and little sand. Position, well-drained pots in cold frame, cool greenhouse or window till growth begins, then remove to temp. 45° to 55°. Pot, Nov., placing five bulbs 3 in. deep in a 5 in. pot. Cover pots with cocoanut-fibre refuse or cinder ashes till growth begins. Water moderately from time growth commences till flowers fade, then gradually withhold, keeping bulbs quite dry from Sept. to Jan.

PROPAGATION : By offsets treated as advised for bulbs.

SPECIES CULTIVATED : H. cinnamomea, white, April and May, 6 in. ; falcata, brown and white, May, 10 in ; pilosa, white and red, April, 6 in. ; radiata, white and red, May, 6 in.

Hesperis (Sweet Rocket ; Dame's Violet ; Dame's Rocket ; Double Rocket)— Ord. Cruciferæ. Hardy perennial and biennial herbs. First introduced 1597. Flowers, fragrant.

CULTURE OF PERENNIAL SPECIES : Soil, ordinary rich moist. Position, sunny beds or borders. Plant, Oct., Nov., March or April. Mulch with decayed manure in May. Apply liquid manure occasionally in summer to double varieties. Cut down flower stems in Oct. Lift and replant double kinds every second year.

PROPAGATION : Single kinds by seeds sown $\frac{1}{4}$ in. deep in sunny position outdoors in April, transplanting seedlings in June or July ; double kinds by cuttings of young shoots 3 in. long inserted in sandy soil in shady position outdoors, July to Sept., or under hand-light or in cold frame, Sept. or Oct., transplanting in March ; also by division of roots, Oct. or March.

CULTURE OF BIENNIAL SPECIES : Soil, ordinary. Position, well-drained borders or old walls. Sow seeds where plants are to flower, in July thinning seedlings to from 6 to 12 in.

PERENNIAL SPECIES : H. matronalis (Sweet Rocket), white or lilac, May to July, 2 to 3 ft., S. Europe, and its double white and purple flowered varieties.

BIENNIAL SPECIES : H. tristis, white, cream or purplish, summer, 1 to 2 ft., S. Europe ; violacea, violet, summer, 6 to 12 in., Asia Minor.

Hessea—Ord. Amaryllidaceæ. Greenhouse bulbous flowering plants. Deciduous. Nat. Cape of Good Hope. First introduced 1774.

CULTURE : Compost, two parts sandy soil, one part leaf-mould or decayed cow manure, and little sand. Position, well-drained pots in cold frame, cool greenhouse, or window till growth begins, then remove to temp. 45° to 55°. Pot, Nov., placing five bulbs 3 in. deep in a 5 in. pot. Cover pots with cocoanut-fibre refuse or cinder ashes till growth begins. Water moderately from time growth commences till flowers fade, then gradually withhold, keeping bulbs quite dry till potting time. Repot annually. May be grown outdoors in sunny borders in the mildest parts of the country.

PROPAGATION : By offsets treated as bulbs.

SPECIES CULTIVATED : H. crispa, pink, summer, 3 in. ; gemmata, yellow, Aug., 10 in.

Heteromeles (Tollon)—Ord. Rosaceæ. Half-hardy evergreen tree. First introduced 1796.

CULTURE: Soil, well-drained open loam. Position, sheltered shrubberies or walls in mild districts. Large well-drained pots in cool greenhouse elsewhere.

PROPAGATION: By seeds sown in sandy soil in pans during Feb. in temp. 60° to 65°; cuttings of partially ripened shoots during July under bell-glass in gentle bottom heat.

SPECIES CULTIVATED: H. arbutifolia (Syn. Photinia arbutifolia), white, Aug., 15 ft., California.

Heuchera (Alum-root; American Sanicle)—Ord. Saxifrageæ. Hardy perennial herbs. Flowering and orn. foliage. First introduced 1656.

CULTURE: Soil, ordinary light rich or peaty; not suited for clay soils. Position, open sunny well-drained borders. Plant, Oct., Nov., March, or April.

PROPAGATION: By division of roots or crowns, March to May; also by seeds sown in light soil in cold frames in spring, transplanting seedlings into small pots and planting out following spring.

SPECIES CULTIVATED: H. americana, red, summer, 18 in., N. America; brizoides, pink, summer, 1 ft., hybrid; micrantha (Syn. erubescens), yellowish white, summer, 2 ft., N. America; pubescens, pale red and yellow, summer, brown mottled foliage, 2 to 3 ft., N. America; sanguinea, red, summer, 12 to 18 in., Mexico; tiarelloides, pink, summer, 6 in., hybrid between H. sanguinea and Tiarella cordifolia. There are several pretty varieties to be found in trade lists.

Hexacentris—See Thunbergia.

Hibbertia—Ord. Dilleniaceæ. Greenhouse evergreen flowering climbers. Nat. Australia. First introduced 1816.

CULTURE: Compost, equal parts loam and peat and little sand. Position, pots, tubs, or beds; shoots trained up rafters. Pot or plant, Feb. or March. Prune straggling shoots, Feb. Water abundantly March to Sept., moderately afterwards. Temp., March to Oct. 55° to 75°; Oct. to March 45° to 55°.

PROPAGATION: By cuttings of moderately firm shoots to 3 in. long inserted in well-drained pots of sandy peat under bell-glass in temp. 55° to 65°, April to Aug.

SPECIES CULTIVATED: H. dentata, yellow, summer, trailing or twining; volubilis, yellow, summer, strong climber.

Hibiscus (Hemp Mallow; Musk Mallow; Rose Mallow; Malabar Rose; Blacking Plant; Rose of Sharon; Shrubby Althæa)—Ord. Malvaceæ. Stove evergreen and hardy deciduous shrubs, hardy annuals and perennials. Flowering and orn. foliage. First introduced 1596.

CULTURE OF STOVE SPECIES: Compost, equal parts fibry peat and loam, with charcoal and sand. Position, well-drained pots or beds, with shoots trained to wall. Pot or plant, Feb. or March. Prune into shape, Feb. Water abundantly March to Oct., moderately afterwards. Temp., March to Oct. 65° to 75°; Oct. to March 55° to 65°.

CULTURE OF PERENNIAL SPECIES: Soil, ordinary. Position, well-drained sunny border. Plant, Oct. or March. Cut down stems in Oct.

CULTURE OF ANNUAL SPECIES: Soil, ordinary. Position, sunny beds or borders. Sow seeds of H. Trionum ⅛ in. deep in April where plants are to flower. Seed of H. esculentus should be sown in well-drained pans during Feb. in temp. 60° to 65° and grown on in pots in the greenhouse or planted outdoors in June.

CULTURE OF HARDY SHRUBBY SPECIES: Soil, rich light loam. Position, sheltered, sunny well-drained border. Plant, Oct. Prune after flowering, thinning out weak and dead wood only.

PROPAGATION: Stove species by seeds sown ⅛ in. deep in well-drained pots of sandy peat under bell-glass in temp. 75° in March, by cuttings of firm shoots inserted in sandy peat under bell-glass in temp. 75° in spring or summer, by grafting in March; perennial species by seeds sown outdoors in April or division of roots in March; annual species by seeds sown as directed above; shrubby species by cuttings inserted in sandy peat in cold frame in summer or grafting in March.

STOVE SPECIES: H. Cameroni, rose, July, 4 to 5 ft., Madagascar; coccineus, scarlet, summer, 10 ft., America; marmoratus, white and rose, spring, 3 ft., Mexico; rosasinensis (Blacking Plant), crimson, summer, to 30 ft., Tropics; schizopetalus, orange-red, 10 ft., East Trop. Africa.

HARDY ANNUAL SPECIES: H. Trionum, yellow and purple, summer, 2 ft., Africa; esculentus (Okra or Gumbo), yellow and reddish, summer, to 6 ft., fruits to 1 ft. in length are edible when immature, Tropics of the Old World.

HARDY PERENNIAL SPECIES: H. militaris, rose, summer, 3 to 4 ft., U. States; Moscheutos, white and rose, summer, 3 to 5 ft., N. America; rosea, rose and purple, summer, 4 to 6 ft., N. America.

HARDY SHRUBBY SPECIES: H. syriacus (Rose of Sharon or Shrubby Althæa), Syn. Althæa frutex, various colours, late summer, 6 to 8 ft., deciduous, Syria. There are several varieties of this species.

HALF-HARDY SPECIES: H. Manihot, yellow and purple, summer, 6 to 8 ft., Tropics. Rear from seed in heat in spring and plant out in June in sunny borders.

Hickory (*Carya alba*)—See Carya.

Hidalgoa (Climbing Dahlia)—Ord. Compositæ. Half-hardy climbing perennial. First introduced 1898.

OUTDOOR CULTURE: Raise plants from seed or cuttings in heat in spring and plant out against a sunny trellis or arch late in May. Water freely, and feed with liquid manure when plants begin to bloom. Cut down shoots in Sept., lift roots, and place them in pots in a heated house to furnish cuttings in spring.

GREENHOUSE CULTURE: Grow in equal parts loam and leaf-mould, with plenty of sand. Water freely in spring and summer; little at other seasons. Train shoots up roof.

PROPAGATION: By cuttings of young shoots in spring.

SPECIES CULTIVATED: H. Wercklei, scarlet and yellow, summer, 12 to 15 ft., Costa Rica.

Hieracium (Mouse-ear; Hawk-weed)—Ord. Compositæ. Hardy perennial herbs.

CULTURE: Soil, ordinary. Position, sunny banks or elevated borders. Plant, Oct. or March.

PROPAGATION: By seeds sown $\frac{1}{8}$ in. deep outdoors in March or April; division of roots any time in spring.

SPECIES CULTIVATED: H. aurantiacum, orange-red, summer, 12 to 18 in., N. Europe; Pilosella, pale yellow, summer, 6 to 12 in., Europe (Britain); villosum, yellow, May to July, 1 ft., Europe.

Hierochloë (Holy Grass)—Ord. Gramineæ. Hardy orn. perennial grasses. Inflorescence, chestnut-coloured, fragrant, borne in panicles; May to July.

CULTURE: Soil, ordinary. Position, damp, shady borders or margins of ponds. Plant, March or April.

PROPAGATION: By seeds sown in damp positions outdoors in spring; division of plants in March.

SPECIES CULTIVATED: H. borealis, 1 to 2 ft., Europe (Britain).

Himalayan Honeysuckle (*Leycesteria formosa*)—See Leycesteria.

Himalayan Hound's-tongue (*Lindelofia spectabilis*)—See Lindelofia.

Himalayan Lung-wort (*Lindelofia spectabilis*)—See Lindelofia.

Himalayan May Apple (*Podophyllum Emodi*)—See Podophyllum.

Himalayan Poppy—See Meconopsis.

Himalayan Primrose (*Primula sikkimensis*)—See Primula.

Hindsia—Ord. Rubiaceæ. Stove evergreen flowering shrubs. First introduced 1844.

CULTURE: Compost, equal parts rough fibrous peat, light loam, silver sand and charcoal. Position, well-drained pots in light stove. Pot, Feb. or March. Water

H   205

freely April to Sept., moderately afterwards. Prune into shape, Feb. Temp., Feb. to Aug. 65° to 75°; Aug. to Nov. 60° to 70°; Nov. to Feb. 55° to 65°.
PROPAGATION : By cuttings of firm shoots inserted in well-drained pots of pure silver sand under bell-glass in temp. 65° to 75° from March to June.
SPECIES CULTIVATED : H. longiflora, blue, summer, 2 to 3 ft., Brazil, and its variety alba, white ; violacea, violet blue, May, 3 ft., Brazil.

Hippeastrum (Barbados Lily ; Knight's Star Lily)—Ord. Amaryllidaceæ. Stove bulbous plants, popularly known as Amaryllises. Deciduous. First introduced 1677.
CULTURE : Compost, two parts turfy loam, one part river sand and a few crushed bones. Position, well-drained pots in light part of stove. Pot, Jan., burying bulb about two-thirds of its depth. Water freely from time growth begins (about Feb.) until July, when keep quite dry. Apply liquid manure when flower spike shows. Top-dress large bulbs annually and repot every three or four years only. Temp., Feb. to Sept. 65° to 75°; Sept. to Feb. 50° to 55°.
PROPAGATION : By seeds sown $\frac{1}{16}$ in. deep in well-drained pots of sandy loam in temp. 65° to 70° in March, placing seedlings singly in 2 in. pots and keeping them moderately moist all the year round for three years ; by offsets treated as old bulbs. Seedlings are three years or so before they flower.
SPECIES CULTIVATED : H. aulicum, crimson and orange, winter, 2 ft., Brazil ; equestre, red, summer, 18 in., Trop. America ; Leopoldii, crimson and white, spring, 1 ft., Peru ; pardinum, green, yellow and scarlet, spring, 2 ft., Peru ; pratense, scarlet, spring and early summer, Chile ; psittacinum, orange and scarlet, summer, 2 ft., Brazil ; Reginæ, red and white, spring, 2 ft., S. America ; reticulatum, rose or scarlet, spring, 1 ft., Brazil ; rutilum, bright crimson and green, spring, 1 ft., S. Brazil ; vittatum, crimson and white, spring, 2 ft., Peru. Numerous hybrids, more beautiful than the species, will be found in trade lists.

Hippocrepis (Horse-shoe Vetch)—Ord. Leguminosæ. Hardy evergreen trailing herb.
CULTURE : Soil, ordinary. Position, sunny rockeries or elevated borders. Plant, March or April.
PROPAGATION : By seeds sown $\frac{1}{16}$ in. deep in fine soil in sunny position outdoors in March or April ; division of roots in March.
SPECIES CULTIVATED : H. comosa, yellow, May to Aug., Europe, Africa, etc.

Hippophæ (Sea Buckthorn ; Sallow-thorn)—Ord. Elæagnaceæ. Hardy deciduous berry-bearing shrub. Male and female flowers borne on separate plants. Both must be grown to ensure a crop of berries. Berries, orange.
CULTURE : Soil, ordinary. Position, open or shady shrubberies and inland or seaside gardens. Plant, Oct. to Feb.
PROPAGATION : By seeds sown $\frac{1}{2}$ in. deep outdoors in Nov. or Dec. ; by cuttings of roots inserted in Feb. or March in ordinary soil outdoors ; layering shoots in autumn.
SPECIES CULTIVATED : H. rhamnoides, yellow, May, 8 to 12 ft., Europe.

Hippuris (Mare's-tail)—Ord. Haloragaceæ. Hardy aquatic perennial. Orn. foliage. Leaves, narrow, strap-shaped ; in circles round the stem.
CULTURE : Soil, mud. Position, bogs, ponds, or damp places. Plant, March to June.
PROPAGATION : By division of roots, March.
SPECIES CULTIVATED : H. vulgaris, 8 to 12 in., Europe (Britain).

Hoffmannia—Ord. Rubiaceæ. Warm greenhouse herbaceous perennials and shrubs. First introduced 1850.
CULTURE : Compost, equal parts fibrous loam and leaf-mould, with liberal addition of sharp sand. Position, large well-drained pots in sunny greenhouse. Water freely during growing season. Sparingly at other times. Temp., March to Sept. 60° to 70°; Sept. to March 55° to 60°.

PROPAGATION : By cuttings of young growth inserted in sandy soil in propagating frame with brisk bottom heat.
SPECIES CULTIVATED : H. discolor, red, foliage shining green above, purple beneath, 6 in., Mexico ; Ghiesbreghtii, red and yellow, foliage velvety green above, purple beneath, 4 ft., Mexico, and its variety variegata ; regalis, yellow, foliage deep green above, purplish red beneath, 1 ft., Mexico.

Hog Plum (*Spondias lutea*)—See Spondias.

Hoheria—Ord. Malvaceæ.   Half-hardy flowering evergreen shrub.
CULTURE : Soil, rich loam.   Position, sheltered borders or shrubberies in Cornwall and similar mild districts.   Large pots in unheated glasshouse elsewhere.   Water freely during summer months.
PROPAGATION : By cuttings of half-ripened shoots in July inserted in sandy soil under hand-light in gentle bottom heat.
SPECIES CULTIVATED : H. populnea, white, July, 10 to 30 ft., New Zealand, and its varieties angustifolia and lanceolata (Syn. H. sexstylosa).

Holbœllia—Ord. Berberidaceæ.   Cool greenhouse flowering climber.   Evergreen.   First introduced 1846.
CULTURE : Compost, two parts loam, one part of equal proportions of leaf-mould and silver sand.   Position, large pots or tubs, shoots trained up roof.   Prune away weak shoots in autumn.   Water freely during spring and summer, moderately in winter.   Syringe freely when not in flower.   Temp. Sept. to March 40° to 50° ; March to Sept. 50° to 60°.
PROPAGATION : By cuttings inserted in sandy soil in gentle heat in spring.
SPECIES CULTIVATED : H. latifolia (Syn. Stauntonia latifolia), white, fragrant, spring, 10 to 20 ft., Himalayas.

Holcus (Variegated Soft Grass).—Ord. Gramineæ.   Hardy orn. perennial grass.   Leaves, soft, woolly, green, variegated with silvery white.
CULTURE : Soil, ordinary.   Position, edgings to beds or borders, or in clumps in borders.   Plant, Oct., March, or April.
PROPAGATION : By division of plants in Oct., March, or April.
SPECIES CULTIVATED : H. lanatus albo-variegatus, 6 to 12 in., Britain.

Hollow-leaved Violet (*Viola cucullata*)—See Viola.

Holly (*Ilex aquifolium*)—See Ilex.

Holly Fern (*Aspidium Lonchitis*)—See Aspidium.

Hollyhock (*Althæa rosea*)—See Althæa.

Holly-leaved Barberry (*Berberis aquifolium*)—See Berberis.

Holly-leaved Olive (*Osmanthus aquifolium*)—See Osmanthus.

Holly Oak (*Quercus Ilex*)—See Quercus.

Holm Oak (*Quercus Ilex*)—See Quercus.

Holy Ghost (*Angelica officinalis*)—See Angelica.

Holy Ghost-flower (*Peristeria elata*)—See Peristeria.

Holy Grass (*Hierochloë borealis*)—See Hierochloë.

Holy Rose (*Andromeda polifolia*)—See Andromeda.

Holy Thistle—See Carbenia and Silybum.

Homeria—Ord. Iridaceæ.   Handsome greenhouse bulbous plants.   First introduced 1793.   Natives of S. Africa.
POT CULTURE : Compost, loam, leaf-mould, and sand in equal parts.   Place bulbs 1 in. apart and 1 in. deep in 5 in. pots during Sept. and Oct.   Stand in a cold frame and cover with a few inches of cocoanut-fibre refuse till growth begins, then remove to greenhouse.   Plant in pots near the glass.   Water freely during active growth.   Keep nearly dry after flowers fade to ripen bulbs.   Repot annually in autumn.
OUTDOOR CULTURE : Plant bulbs 3 to 4 in. deep in light, rich, well-drained soil in a south border between Oct. and Jan.   Protect with bracken litter in winter.
PROPAGATION : By offsets removed at planting time.

SPECIES CULTIVATED : H. collina (Syn. Moræa collina), red and yellow, spring, 1 ft. ; collina aurantiaca, orange, red and yellow, spring, 1 ft. ; elegans, yellow, brown and orange, summer, 1 ft. ; lineata, red and yellow, spring, 1 ft. ; miniata, red, spring, 6 to 8 in.

Honesty (*Lunaria biennis*)—See Lunaria.

Honey Balm (*Melitis Melisophyllum*)—See Melitis.

Honey Locust (*Gleditschia triacanthos*)—See Gleditschia.

Honey-plant (*Hoya carnosa*)—See Hoya.

Honeysuckle—See Lonicera.

Honey-wort—See Cerinthe.

Hoodia—Ord. Asclepiadaceæ. Greenhouse succulent plants. Flowering and orn. foliage. First introduced 1874. Stems, cylindrical, prickly, leafless.
CULTURE : Compost, equal parts sandy loam, old mortar, broken bricks and dry cow manure. Position, well-drained pots, fully exposed to sun in warm green-house. Repot every three or four years in Feb. or March. Water moderately March to Oct., keep quite dry Oct. to March. Temp., April to Sept. 65° to 75° ; Sept. to April 45° to 55°.
PROPAGATION : By portions of fleshy stems 3 in. long cut clean at base and laid on sunny shelf to dry for several days ; then insert in small well-drained pots of sandy soil in temp. of 55° to 65°, April to Aug.
SPECIES CULTIVATED : H. Bainii, yellow, Aug., 1 ft., S. Africa ; Gordoni, yellow and purple, July, 18 in., S. Africa.

Hoop Petticoat Daffodil (*Narcissus Bulbocodium*)—See Narcissus.

Hop (*Humulus lupulus*)—See Humulus.

Hop Hornbeam (*Ostrya carpinifolia*)—See Ostrya.

Hop-tree (*Ptelea trifoliata*)—See Ptelea.

Hordeum (Squirrel-tail Grass)—Ord. Gramineæ. Hardy annual flowering grass. Nat. N. America. First introduced 1782. Inflorescence, barley-like, borne in spikes ; June to Sept. ; very useful for cutting.
CULTURE : Soil, ordinary. Position, open dryish borders.
PROPAGATION : By seeds sown ½ in. deep in March or April in borders where plants are required to flower.
SPECIES CULTIVATED : H. jubatum, 2 ft.

Horehound—See Marrubium.

Horminum (Pyrenean Dead-nettle)—Ord. Labiatæ. Hardy herbaceous peren-nial. First introduced 1820.
CULTURE : Soil, ordinary. Position, open well-drained borders. Plant, Oct., Nov., March and April.
PROPAGATION : By seeds sown ⅟₁₆ in. deep outdoors in March or April ; by division of roots, Oct. to March.
SPECIES CULTIVATED : H. pyrenaicum, blue, summer, 1 ft., Pyrenees.

Horminum Clary (*Salvia Horminum*)—See Salvia.

Hornbeam (*Carpinus betulus*)—See Carpinus.

Horned Poppy (*Glaucium luteum*)—See Glaucium.

Horned Rampion (*Phyteuma orbiculare*)—See Phyteuma.

Horned Violet (*Viola cornuta*)—See Viola.

Horn of Plenty (*Fedia Cornucopiæa* and *Datura cornigera*)—See Fedia and Datura.

Horse Chestnut (*Æsculus hippocastanum*)—See Æsculus.

Horse Radish (*Cochlearia armoracia*)—See Cochlearia.

Horseshoe Vetch (*Hippocrepis comosa*)—See Hippocrepis.

Horse-tail—See Equisetum.

Hose-in-Hose Polyanthus (*Primula elatior* var.)—See Primula.

Hosta—See Funkia.

Hottentot Fig (*Mesembryanthemum edule*)—See Mesembryanthemum.

Hottentot's Bread (*Testudinaria elephantipes*)—See Testudinaria.

Hottonia (Water Violet)—Ord. Primulaceæ. Hardy aquatic perennial herb.
CULTURE : Soil, ordinary. Position, margins of ponds and rivulets or in bogs.
Plant, March or April.
PROPAGATION : By seeds sown in muddy soil in shallow water in March or April ;
division of plants, March or April.
SPECIES CULTIVATED : H. palustris, lilac and yellow, June, 1 ft., Europe (Britain).

Houlletia—Ord. Orchidaceæ. Stove epiphytal orchids. Evergreen. First
introduced 1841. Flowers, fragrant.
CULTURE : Compost, two parts fibrous peat, one part sphagnum. Position, baskets
suspended from roof of stove. Rebasket, Feb. or March. Water abundantly
March to Sept., moderately Sept. to March. Temp., May to Aug. 65° to 85° ;
Aug. to Nov. and March to May 60° to 70° ; Nov. to May 55° to 65°.
PROPAGATION : By division of pseudo-bulbs when growth commences.
SPECIES CULTIVATED : H. brocklehurstiana, brown and yellow, summer, 2 ft.,
Brazil ; chrysantha, yellow, chocolate and crimson, summer, 2 ft., Colombia ;
lowiana, yellow and white, summer, 1 ft., Colombia ; odoratissima, red, summer,
2 ft., Colombia.

House Leek (*Sempervivum tectorum*)—See Sempervivum.

Houstonia (Bluets)—Ord. Rubiaceæ. Hardy herbaceous perennials. First
introduced 1785.
CULTURE : Soil, leaf-mould and sand. Position, partially shaded crevices, nooks,
and crannies of moist rockeries. Plant, March or April.
PROPAGATION : By seeds sown $\frac{1}{16}$ in. deep in pans of leaf-mould and sand in cold
frame in spring or autumn ; division of roots in Sept. or Oct.
SPECIES CULTIVATED : H. cærulea (Bluets), blue, May to July, 4 to 6 in., Virginia ;
cærulea alba, white ; purpurea, white to pink, summer, 6 to 12 in., N. America ;
serpyllifolia, white, summer, 3 in., N. America.

Hovea—Ord. Leguminosæ. Greenhouse flowering shrubs. Evergreen. Nat.
Australia. First introduced 1818.
CULTURE : Compost, three parts peat, one part loam and little silver sand. Position,
well-drained pots in light airy greenhouse. Pot, Feb. or March. Nip off points of
young shoots in spring to induce bushy growth. Water freely April to Sept.,
moderately Sept. to April. Temp., March to July 55° to 65°, Sept. to March
45° to 50°. Stand plants outdoors from July to Sept. to mature flowering shoots
for following year.
PROPAGATION : By seeds sown $\frac{1}{16}$ in. deep in well-drained pots of sandy peat in
temp. of 55° to 65° in March or April ; cuttings inserted in sandy soil under bell-
glass in temp. 55°, April to July.
SPECIES CULTIVATED : H. Celsi, blue, spring, 3 ft., Australia ; longifolia, purple,
spring, 5 ft., Australia.

Howea—Ord. Palmaceæ. Greenhouse palms. Elegant plant for house decoration. Nat. Lord Howe's Island. Leaves, feather-shaped, graceful.
CULTURE : Compost, equal parts loam and peat, little silver sand. Position, well-
drained pots in greenhouse, or in dwelling rooms during summer. Pot, Feb. or
March. Temp., Sept. to March 45° to 55° ; March to Sept. 55° to 65°. Water
moderately Oct. to Feb. ; freely afterwards. Apply weak liquid manure to healthy
plants once a week May to Sept. Syringe plants daily. Sponge leaves of those
grown in dwelling rooms once weekly.
PROPAGATION : By seeds sown 1 in. deep in light soil in temp. 80°, Feb. or March.
SPECIES CULTIVATED : H. belmoreana (Syn. Kentia belmoreana), 6 to 10 ft. ;
forsteriana (Syn. Kentia forsteriana), 6 to 15 ft.

Hoya (Honey-plant, Wax-flower)—Ord. Asclepiadaceæ. Stove and greenhouse climbing flowering plants. Evergreen. First introduced 1802.
CULTURE : Compost, equal parts peat and loam, little charcoal and sand. Position, well-drained pots, beds, or hanging baskets, with shoots trained round trellises, up rafters, or against walls, and fully exposed to the light. Pot or plant, Feb. or March. Water freely March to Sept., moderately Sept. to March. Temp., stove species, 65° to 75° March to Oct., 55° to 65° Oct. to March ; greenhouse species, 55° to 65° March to Sept., 45° to 55° Sept. to March. Prune into shape, Feb. Foot stalks of flowers should not be removed after blooming, as these will produce a second crop of flowers.
PROPAGATION : By cuttings of shoots of preceding year's growth inserted in well-drained pots of sandy peat under bell-glass in temp. of 75° to 85° in March, April, or May ; layering shoots in pots of sandy peat in spring or summer.
STOVE SPECIES : H. bella, white and crimson, summer, 3 ft., Burma.
GREENHOUSE SPECIES : H. carnosa, pink and white, summer, 10 to 12 ft., China and Australia.

Huckle-berry—See Gaylussacia.

Hudsonia (American False Heath)—Ord. Cistaceæ. Hardy evergreen flowering shrubs. First introduced 1805.
CULTURE : Compost, two parts peat and one of sea sand. Position, well-drained rock gardens, full sun, sheltered from winds, or in pots for unheated greenhouse. A difficult plant to establish, but sometimes succeeds in a slightly saline soil.
PROPAGATION : By cuttings of firm shoots 1 to 2 in. long inserted in well-drained pots of silver sand under bell-glass in greenhouse, April to Aug.; layering in Sept. and Oct.
SPECIES CULTIVATED : H. ericoides, yellow, May to July, 6 to 8 in., U. States ; tomentosa, yellow, June, 1 ft., N. America.

Humble-plant (*Mimosa pudica*)—See Mimosa.

Humea (Amaranth Feathers)—Ord. Compositæ. Half-hardy biennial. First introduced 1800.
GREENHOUSE CULTURE : Compost, two parts sandy loam, half a part decayed manure, half a part charcoal and silver sand. Position, well-drained pots in cold frame during summer ; airy greenhouse in winter and when in flower. Pot, March. Water freely March to Oct., very little afterwards. Syringing unnecessary. Temp., Oct. to April 45° to 55° ; April to Oct. 55° to 65°. Discard plants after flowering. Fine plants can be obtained in 10 in. pots.
OUTDOOR CULTURE : Soil, ordinary rich. Position, sunny well-drained beds or borders. Plant, June. Water freely in dry weather.
PROPAGATION : By seeds sown on surface of fine mould in well-drained pots or pans, covering seeds slightly with fine soil, in July, in cold frame or greenhouse, potting seedlings singly in 2 in. pots when large enough to handle.
SPECIES CULTIVATED : H. elegans, red, pink, and crimson, in feathery panicles, June to Oct., 3 to 10 ft., Australia.

Humulus (Common Hop ; Japanese Hop)—Ord. Urticaceæ. Hardy annual and perennial twining climbers. Male blooms borne in axillary panicles, and female blooms in cones in clusters on separate plants ; the latter form the hop of commerce and are the most ornamental.
CULTURE OF ANNUAL SPECIES : Soil, ordinary rich. Position, sunny or shady walls, fences, arbours, trellises, or tree stumps. Plant, May or June. Water freely in dry weather. This species is an excellent plant for covering unsightly objects rapidly in summer.
CULTURE OF PERENNIAL SPECIES : Soil, deep, rich and well-manured loam. Position, sunny walls, fences, arbours, trellises, tree stumps, or in open ground with shoots trained round poles. Plant in groups of three, or 6 or 12 in. apart in rows 4 to 5 ft. asunder, Feb. or March. Top-dress annually with decayed manure in Feb. or

March.   Water freely in dry weather.   Gather female flowers (hops) in Sept. for drying.   Cut down plants in Oct.
PROPAGATION :   Annual species by seeds sown ⅛ in. deep in pots of ordinary soil in cool or heated greenhouse in April, or where plants are required to grow in May ; perennial species by seeds sown ⅛ in. deep in ordinary soil outdoors in March or April ; division of roots in March.
ANNUAL SPECIES :   H. japonicus variegatus (Japanese Hop), 8 to 10 ft., green and white variegated foliage, Japan.
PERENNIAL SPECIES :   H. lupulus (Hop), 10 to 15 ft., Europe.   The golden-leaved form is superior for garden cultivation.

Hungarian Lilac (*Syringa Josikæa*)—See Syringa.

Hunnemannia—Ord. Papaveraceæ.   Half-hardy herbaceous perennial.   First introduced 1827.
CULTURE :   Soil, ordinary rich.   Position, sunny well-drained border at base of south wall.   Plant, March.   Protect with dry litter in winter.
PROPAGATION :   By seeds sown as soon as ripe in a cold frame, planting out seedlings following June.
SPECIES CULTIVATED :   H. fumariæfolia, yellow, Aug., 2 ft., Mexico.

Huntingdon Elm (*Ulmus vegeta*)—See Ulmus.

Huntingdon Willow (*Salix alba*)—See Salix.

Huntsman's Cup (*Sarracenia purpurea*)—See Sarracenia.

Huntsman's Horn (*Sarracenia flava*)—See Sarracenia.

Huon Pine-tree (*Dacrydium Franklini*)—See Dacrydium.

Hutchinsia—Ord. Cruciferæ.   Hardy annuals and perennials.
CULTURE :   Soil, sandy.   Position, open sunny rockeries or margins of borders. Plant, March or April.
PROPAGATION :   Annual species by seeds sown and slightly covered with fine soil where plants are required to grow in March or April ; perennial species by seeds sown similarly, or by division of plants in March or April.
ANNUAL SPECIES :   H. petræa, white, spring, 3 in., Britain.
PERENNIAL SPECIES :   H. alpina, white, spring, 1 in., Alps.

Hyacinth (*Hyacinthus orientalis*)—See Hyacinthus.

Hyacinth Bean (*Dolichos Lablab*)—See Dolichos.

Hyacinthus (Hyacinth)—Ord. Liliaceæ.   Hardy bulbous flowering plants. First introduced 1596.
CULTURE OF COMMON HYACINTHS IN POTS :   Compost, fibrous loam, leaf-mould, and sharp sand.   Position, first plunge under cinder ashes in cold frame or outdoors, afterwards in window or greenhouse.   Pot, Sept. to early Nov., placing one bulb half its depth in a 6 in. pot or three in an 8 in. pot.   Water only when growth begins, and with increasing liberality afterwards.   Apply liquid manure occasionally when flower spikes form.   After flowering plant bulbs outdoors.
CULTURE IN GLASSES :   Place bulbs in glasses so that base just touches water.   Time, Sept. to Oct.   Water, soft or rain, and little charcoal ; add fresh as required.   Put in dark position until roots form, then remove to light.   No stimulant needful.
CULTURE IN BEDS :   Soil, ordinary, enriched with manure previous autumn.   Position, open, sunny.   Plant bulbs 3 to 4 in. deep and 8 in. apart, Sept. to Oct.   Protect surface of bed by covering of cocoanut-fibre refuse.   Apply liquid manure once or twice when flower spikes appear.   Lift and dry bulbs in June, storing in cool place till planting time.
CULTURE OF ROMAN HYACINTH :   Compost, as advised above.   Position, pots under ashes in cold frame or outdoors till rooted, then in heated greenhouse or window. Pot, Aug., Sept., and Oct., placing three in a 5 in. pot.   Depth for planting, 1 in. Water only when removed from the ashes, and regularly afterwards.   Temp. when in greenhouse or window, 55° to 65°.

CULTURE OF SPANISH HYACINTH : Soil, light rich. Position, well-drained sunny borders. Plant, Sept. or Oct. Top-dress annually with decayed cow manure in Feb. Lift and replant only when bulbs show signs of deterioration.
PROPAGATION : By seeds sown ½ in. deep in light sandy soil in boxes in cold frame or outdoors in Sept. ; by offsets removed from old bulbs when lifted and planted 6 in. apart each way outdoors in Oct. Seedling bulbs flower when three years old, and attain full size when seven years old.
SPECIES CULTIVATED : H. amethystinus (Spanish Hyacinth), blue, spring, 1 ft., Pyrenees ; amethystinus albus, white ; azureus, sky blue, 6 in., Asia Minor ; orientalis (Common Hyacinth), various colours, spring, Mediterranean Region ; orientalis albulus (Roman Hyacinth), white.

Hydrangea—Ord. Saxifragaceæ. Greenhouse and hardy flowering shrubby plants. Deciduous. First introduced 1736.
CULTURE OF H. HORTENSIS AND VARIETIES : Compost, two parts rich loam, one part well-decayed manure and sharp sand. Position, cool greenhouse, frame, or room, Oct. to March ; greenhouse, window or warm terrace, March to Oct. Pot, Feb. to March. Water abundantly March to Oct., moderately Oct. to March. Prune, Aug. or Sept., cutting out all weak shoots and such as have flowered. Flowers borne on vigorous shoots of previous year's growth. Best blooms obtained on plants propagated by cuttings annually in Aug. Apply liquid or artificial manure frequently to plants showing flower. Temp. for early flowering (Jan. to May), 55° to 65°. Blue flowers may be obtained by planting in a compost of five parts loam and one part iron filings, or by applying one of the following solutions : Dissolve a tablespoonful of alum in a gallon of soft water and use 12 hours afterwards ; one tablespoonful of saltpetre and half a tablespoonful of oxide of iron in three gallons of water and use 24 hours afterwards. Apply both twice a week.
OUTDOOR CULTURE : Soil, ordinary rich. Position, sunny, well-drained borders. Plant, Oct., Nov., March, or April. Prune straggling or dead shoots in March. Top-dress annually with decayed cow manure. Apply liquid manure when in flower. A good plant for seaside gardens in S. and W. of England.
CULTURE OF H. PANICULATA IN POTS : Compost, as above. Position, cold frames, unheated greenhouses, or windows. Pot, Feb. or March. Prune previous year's shoots to within 1 in. of base in Jan. or Feb. Water freely March to Oct., keep nearly dry Oct. to March. Apply liquid manure frequently when showing flower. After flowering place in sunny position outdoors until Nov.
OUTDOOR CULTURE OF H. PANICULATA : Soil, ordinary. Position, open well-drained bed or border. Plant, Oct., Nov., or March. Top-dress annually with decayed manure in Feb. or March. Water freely in dry weather. Apply liquid manure when flower buds appear. Prune as advised for pot culture in March.
CULTURE OF OTHER SPECIES : Plant H. petiolaris against a west wall in well-drained border ; it will grow like ivy. Other species may be grown in rich loamy soil and open or partially shaded position. Plant Nov. to March. Young growth of H. sargentiana is liable to be injured by early spring pests. H. arborescens should be pruned annually as instructed for H. paniculata.
PROPAGATION : By cuttings of young shoots inserted singly in 2 in. pots of light sandy soil under bell-glass in temp. 55° to 65° in March or April ; cuttings of points of firm shoots 2 to 3 in. long inserted in well-drained pots of sandy soil in cold frame in Aug. ; suckers separated from the parent plant in Nov. or March ; H. quercifolia by layering in spring.
SPECIES CULTIVATED : H. arborescens, white, fragrant, summer, 4 to 6 ft., U. States ; aspera, white, summer, 4 ft., China ; Bretschneideri, white to pink, June to July, 8 to 10 ft., China ; Hortensis, white or blue, spring and summer, 3 to 4 ft., and its varieties acuminata (blue or pink), Lindleyi (japonica), white or blue, Mariesi (mauve-pink), nigra (bright rose), otaksa (flesh), stellata (pink), rose, or pale blue, and many other named garden forms to be found in trade lists ; involucrata, rosy lilac or pink, summer, 1½ to 2 ft., Japan ; paniculata, white, summer, 4 to 6 ft., Japan, and its variety grandiflora (large-flowered) ; petiolaris, white, June, climbing, Japan ; quercifolia, white, July, 4 to 6 ft., Florida ; sargentiana, pinkish white, July

Hydrangea Sargentiana

Hymenanthera crassifolia
(In Fruit)

Hymenocallis ovata

Iberis coronaria
(Rocket Candytuft)

Iberis sempervirens
(Evergreen Candytuft)

Impatiens Balsamina
(Balsam)

Impatiens Sultani
(Balsam)

Incarvillea Delavayi

Indigofera Gerardiana
(Indigo)

Inula grandiflora
(Flea-bane)

Iris pallida hybrida
(Bearded Iris)

Iris Xiphium
(Spanish Iris)

Iris unguicularis

Ixia hybrida
(African Corn Lily)

Ixiolirion montanum tataricum
(Ixia Lily)

Jacobinia magnifica carnea

Jasminum nudiflorum
(Jasmine)

Kalanchoe flammea

to Aug., 6 to 8 ft., China ; sinensis, white, summer, 2 to 6 ft., China ; Thunbergii, rose or blue, summer, 3 ft., Japan ; vestita, white, July to Aug., 10 to 15 ft., Himalayas and China.

Hydrocharis (Frog-bit)—Ord. Hydrocharitaceæ.   Hardy aquatic perennial. Stems floating.

CULTURE : Soil, muddy. Position, shallow ponds, lakes, or rivulets. Plant, March or April.

PROPAGATION : By creeping shoots detached from plant and inserted in mud under water in March or April.

SPECIES CULTIVATED : H. Morsus-ranæ, green and white, summer, Europe (Britain).

Hydrocleis—Ord. Alismaceæ. Half-hardy aquatic perennial. First introduced 1831.

CULTURE : Soil, two parts loam and one part leaf-mould. Position, sunny, shallow ponds or tubs sunk in ground. Plant 6 in. below surface of water in March. In cold districts plants best wintered in frost-proof greenhouse.

PROPAGATION : By seeds in pots of rich soil sunk in water or division of roots in spring.

SPECIES CULTIVATED : H. Commersonii (Syn. Limnocharis Humboldtii), yellow, July to Sept., Buenos Ayres.

Hymenanthera—Ord. Violaceæ.   Hardy semi-evergreen berry-bearing shrub. Introduced 1875.

CULTURE : Soil, loam, peat, and leaf-mould. Position, margin of a rhododendron or azalea bed, or on a sunny rockery. Plant, May or September. Prune to remove dead wood only.

PROPAGATION : By cuttings of ripened shoots in sandy peat in a cold frame in autumn.

SPECIES CULTIVATED : H. crassifolia, yellow, pansy-like flowers, succeeded by pearly-white berries in autumn, 3 to 4 ft., New Zealand.

Hymenocallis—Ord. Amaryllidaceæ.   Stove and greenhouse bulbous plants. Evergreen and deciduous. First introduced 1758. Flowers, fragrant.

CULTURE : Compost, two parts sandy loam, one part decayed manure and half a part silver sand. Position, well-drained pots in sunny part of stove and greenhouse. Pot, March. Repotting necessary every three or four years only. Water abundantly April to Sept., moderately Sept. to Dec., keep quite dry Dec. to March. Apply liquid manure once or twice a week May to Sept. Temp. for stove species, 70° to 80° March to Sept., 55° to 65° Sept. to March ; greenhouse species, 55° to 65° April to Sept., 45° to 50° Sept. to April.

PROPAGATION : By offsets removed from old bulbs in March and treated as above.

STOVE SPECIES : H. macrostephana, white, spring, 2 ft., hybrid ; ovata, white, autumn, 1 ft., W. Indies ; speciosa, white, spring, 1 ft., W. Indies.

GREENHOUSE SPECIES : H. calathina, white, spring, 1 ft., Peru.

Hymenophyllum (Tunbridge Fern ; Filmy Fern)—Ord. Filices. Stove, greenhouse, half-hardy ferns. Fronds, feathery, delicate, membranous.

CULTURE OF STOVE AND GREENHOUSE SPECIES : Compost, equal parts peat, loam, leaf-mould, charcoal, sandstone, and silver sand. Position, moist, shady, in damp recesses of rockeries, under bell-glasses or in cases. Plant, March. Water freely March to Oct., moderately Oct. to March. Syringing unsuitable. Shade most essential. Temp. for stove species, 65° to 75° March to Oct., 55° to 65° Oct. to March ; greenhouse species, 55° to 60° March to Sept., 45° to 55° Sept. to March.

CULTURE OF HARDY SPECIES : Compost, as above. Position, deep, moist, shady frames, pits, caverns, or tubs ; away from direct light and sunshine. Plant, March. Water freely in summer, moderately other times. No syringing required. Protect in severe weather.

CULTURE IN CASES IN ROOMS : Compost, as above. Position, shady window, not exposed to sun. Plant, March. Top-dress with fresh compost annually in March. Water freely April to Sept., moderately afterwards. Ventilate case few minutes daily.

PROPAGATION : By spores sown on surface of sandy peat in shallow pan covered with bell-glass in temp. 65° to 75° at any time ; by division of plant at potting time.
STOVE SPECIES : H. caudiculatum, Chile ; chiloense, dwarf, Chile and Chiloe ; dichotomum, Chile ; fosterianum, Brazil.
GREENHOUSE SPECIES : H. demissum, New Zealand and Malaya ; flabellatum, Australia.
HARDY SPECIES : H. tunbridgense, Britain.

Hyophorbe—Ord. Palmaceæ. Stove palm. Orn. foliage. First introduced 1866. Leaves, feather-shaped, deep green.
CULTURE : Compost, equal parts peat, loam, leaf-mould, and sand. Position, shady, moist. Pot, Feb. or March. Water abundantly March to Oct., moderately afterwards. Temp., March to Sept. 70° to 85° ; Sept. to March 60° to 65°.
PROPAGATION : By seeds sown 1 in. deep in pots of light soil in temp. 85° in March.
SPECIES CULTIVATED : H. Verschaffeltii, 5 to 10 ft., Mascarene Islands.

Hypericum (Aaron's Beard ; Rose of Sharon ; St. John's-wort ; Tutsan)—Ord. Hypericaceæ. Hardy and half-hardy shrubs and herbaceous perennials. Evergreen and deciduous.
CULTURE OF SHRUBBY SPECIES : Soil, ordinary. Position (H. calycinum) on banks and under shade of trees ; others in sunny borders. Plant, Oct., Nov., Feb., March. Prune into shape, Feb.
CULTURE OF PERENNIAL SPECIES : Soil, ordinary, sandy. Position, sunny borders or rockeries. Plant, Oct. or April. Cut down stems in Oct. Top-dress with decayed manure in April.
PROPAGATION : Perennial species by seeds sown $\frac{1}{8}$ in. deep in sandy soil in sunny position outdoors in March, by division of roots in April or Oct. ; shrubby species by cuttings of firm shoots 3 in. long inserted in sandy soil outdoors, Aug. or Sept.
SHRUBBY SPECIES : H. ægypticum, yellow, summer, 6 to 18 in., Levant ; Androsæmum (Sweet Amber or Tutsan), yellow, summer, 2 ft., Europe ; aureum, orangeyellow, summer and autumn, 4 ft., Georgia ; calycinum (St. John's-wort or Rose of Sharon), yellow, summer, 1 ft., Orient and Britain ; elatum, yellow, July, 5 ft., Canary Islands ; empetrifolium, yellow, summer, 6 to 12 in., Greece ; hircinum (Goat-scented St. John's-wort), yellow, summer, 4 ft., Europe ; hookerianum, yellow, summer, 2 ft., Himalayas and Assam ; moserianum, yellow, summer, 18 to 30 in., hybrid ; moserianum tricolor, leaves white and rosy carmine ; patulum, yellow, summer, 6 ft., Japan, and its varieties Henryi and Forestii ; uralum, yellow, summer, 2 ft., Nepaul.
PERENNIAL SPECIES : H. coris, yellow, summer, 6 to 9 in., S. Europe ; fragile, golden yellow, summer, 5 in., Europe ; nummularium, yellow, summer, 3 to 6 in., Pyrenees ; olympicum, golden yellow, June to Sept., 1 ft., Asia Minor ; orientale, yellow, summer, 6 to 12 in., Levant ; polyphyllum, pale yellow, June to Aug., 6 in., Asia Minor ; repens, bright yellow, June to Aug., 6 to 8 in., Asia Minor ; reptans, golden yellow, trailing, June to Aug., Sikkim.

Hypolepis—Ord. Filices. Stove and greenhouse ferns. Evergreen. First introduced 1824. Fronds, feather-shaped.
CULTURE OF STOVE SPECIES : Compost, equal parts loam, leaf-mould, and sand. Position, well-drained pots or hanging baskets in shady part of stove. Pot, March. Water freely March to Sept., moderately afterwards. Syringing undesirable. Temp., March to Sept. 65° to 75° ; Sept. to March 55° to 65°.
CULTURE OF GREENHOUSE SPECIES : Compost, as above. Position, well-drained pans or beds in shade. Pot, March. Water freely March to Sept., moderately afterwards. Temp., March to Sept. 55° to 65° ; Sept. to March 45° to 55°.
PROPAGATION : By spores sown on surface of well-drained pans of sandy peat and leaf-mould under bell-glass in temp. 65° to 75° at any time ; division of creeping rhizomes in March.
STOVE SPECIES : H. repens, creeping rhizomes, Trop. America.
GREENHOUSE SPECIES : H. bergiana, creeping rhizomes, S. Africa.

Hypoxis (American Star Grass)—Ord. Amaryllidaceæ. Greenhouse bulbous-rooted plants. Nat. S. Africa. First introduced 1752.
CULTURE : Compost, two parts peat, one of leaf-mould and sand. Position, well-drained pots, or beds in cold frame. Pot, Aug. to Nov., covering pots with cinder ashes in cold frame or greenhouse till growth begins. Water moderately from time bulbs begin to grow until flowers fade, then gradually withhold it, keeping bulbs dry until growth recommences. Temp., Sept. to Feb. 40° to 50° ; 50° to 60° afterwards.
PROPAGATION : By offsets, removed at potting time and treated as old bulbs.
SPECIES CULTIVATED : H. elegans, yellow and black, summer, 6 in. ; hemerocallidea, yellow, spring, 8 in. ; stellata, white and black, spring, 6 in. ; villosa, yellow, spring, 6 in.

Hyssop (*Hyssopus officinalis*)—See Hyssopus.

Hyssopus (Hyssop)—Ord. Labiatæ. Hardy evergreen shrub. First introduced 1548. Leaves, narrow, aromatic. Shoots and flowers, infused in water, are largely used as an expectorant ; also for distilling for yielding oils for perfumery and flavouring liquors.
CULTURE : Soil, ordinary, light. Position, dry, warm borders. Plant, March to May, 12 in. apart each way. Prune into shape, April. Gather shoots for medicinal purposes at any season ; when flowers open for distilling.
PROPAGATION : By seeds sown $\frac{1}{16}$ in. deep outdoors in April—transplant June or July ; cuttings of shoots inserted in shady position in April or May ; division of roots in Feb., March, Sept. or Oct.
SPECIES CULTIVATED : H. officinalis, blue, June to Sept., 1 to 2 ft., S. Europe.

Iberian Crane's-bill (*Geranium ibericum*)—See Geranium.

Iberian Cyclamen (*Cyclamen ibericum*)—See Cyclamen.

Iberian Iris (*Iris iberica*)—See Iris.

Iberis (Candytuft)—Ord. Cruciferæ. Hardy annuals and evergreen perennials. Flowers, fragrant.
CULTURE OF ANNUAL SPECIES : Soil, ordinary. Position, sunny beds or borders. Sow seeds $\frac{1}{8}$ in. deep in patches or lines in March, April, or May for flowering in summer, Aug. or Sept. for spring flowering. Thin out seedlings to 2 in. apart in June.
POT CULTURE : Compost, two parts good soil, one part decayed manure, leaf-mould, and sand. Size of pots, 5 in. in diameter. Sow seeds $\frac{1}{8}$ in. deep in April or May. Place pots in cold frame till June, then stand outdoors. Thin seedlings to an inch apart in June. Water moderately. Apply weak liquid manure occasionally when flowers show.
CULTURE OF PERENNIAL SPECIES : Soil, light sandy loam. Position, fissures or ledges of sunny rockeries or margins of well-drained sunny borders. Plant, Oct., March, or April.
PROPAGATION : Annual species by seeds sown as above ; perennial species by seeds sown $\frac{1}{16}$ in. deep in shallow boxes of sandy soil in cold frame in April ; cuttings of partially ripened shoots, from 1 to 2 in. long, inserted in well-drained pots in cold frame or in beds under hand-light outdoors, July to Oct. ; division of roots, Oct. or March.
ANNUAL SPECIES : I. coronaria (Rocket Candytuft), white, summer, 1 ft. ; umbellata (Common Candytuft), purple, summer, 1 ft., S. Europe ; several varieties.
SHRUBBY SPECIES : I. corræfolia, white, May and June, 1 ft., hybrid ; gibraltarica, white or pink, May, 1 to 2 ft., Spain ; Pruitii, white, May, 6 in., Sicily ; saxatilis (Rock Candytuft), white, spring, 3 to 6 in., S. Europe ; semperflorens, white, spring, 1 to 2 ft., S. Europe ; sempervirens (Evergreen Candytuft), white, spring, 9 to 12 in., S. Europe ; tenoreana, white or rose, spring and autumn, 6 to 8 ins., Spain and Italy.

Iceland Poppy (*Papaver nudicaule*)—See Papaver.

Ice Plant (*Mesembryanthemum crystallinum*)—See Mesembryanthemum.

Idesia—Ord. Bixaceæ. Hardy flowering and orn. foliage tree. Deciduous, Flowers in panicles ; male and female borne on separate trees ; male flowers orange, female green. Berries, small, purplish black. Leaves, heart-shaped.
CULTURE : Soil, ordinary, sandy. Position, well-drained shrubberies. Plant, Oct. to Feb. Prune into shape after flowering.
PROPAGATION : By seeds sown ⅛ in. deep in sandy soil in temp. 65° to 75° in March ; cuttings of firm shoots, 3 to 4 in. long, inserted in well-drained pots of sandy soil under bell-glass in temp. 65° to 75° in March or Sept.
SPECIES CULTIVATED : I. polycarpa, 10 to 15 ft., Japan.

Ilex (Holly ; Paraguay Tea)—Ord. Aquifoliaceæ. Hardy and greenhouse evergreen shrubs. Orn. foliage. Flowers, greenish ; May and June ; male and female flowers usually borne on separate trees. Berries, red ; autumn and winter. Leaves, dark green or variegated with white or yellow. Timber, white, used for cabinet making and turnery purposes. Bark used for making bird lime. Wood sometimes dyed black and used as a substitute for ebony. Average weight of wood per cubic foot, 47½ lb. One bushel of seeds will yield about 17,000 plants.
CULTURE OF HARDY SPECIES : Soil, ordinary. Position, well-drained shrubberies, banks, exposed slopes, etc., or near the sea. Plant, May or Sept. Prune, Sept. to April.
HEDGE CULTURE : Soil, ordinary, trenched two spits deep and 3 ft. wide. Plant hollies (8 in. high), 18 in. apart, May or Sept. Trim into shape, April and Sept. One holly and six thorns or one Berberis Darwinii and two hollies per lineal yard make splendid evergreen hedges.
POT CULTURE : Soil, ordinary. Position, window boxes, cold corridors, balconies, and greenhouses. Pot, Sept. Water freely March to Oct., moderately afterwards. Heat unnecessary.
CULTURE OF GREENHOUSE SPECIES : Soil, two parts loam, one part peat and sand. Position, well-drained pots exposed to full light. Pot, March. Prune, Feb. Water freely in summer, occasionally other times. Temp., March to Oct. 55° to 65° ; Oct. to March 45° to 50°.
PROPAGATION : Common species by seed (berries) gathered in Nov., buried in sand until following Oct., then sown 1 in. deep and 1 in. apart in ordinary soil outdoors, transplanting seedlings when two years old ; variegated kinds by budding on common species in Aug. ; grafting in March ; cuttings of half ripened side shoots with heel of older wood inserted in sandy soil under bell-glass in slight bottom heat.
GREENHOUSE SPECIES : I. cassine, red berries, S. U. States ; insignis, 15 to 20 ft., Malaya ; paraguayensis (Paraguay Tea), 10 to 15 ft., Paraguay.
HARDY SPECIES : I. aquifolium (Common Holly), 10 to 30 ft., berries red, Europe (Britain) ; cornuta, berries red, 20 to 30 ft., China ; crenata, 5 to 9 ft., Japan ; dipyrena, berries large, red, 20 to 40 ft., Himalayas ; glabra (Ink-berry), 2 to 3 ft., U. States ; latifolia, large-leaved, 20 ft., Japan.; opaca, 20 to 40 ft., U. States ; Perneyi, berries red, 15 to 30 ft., Central and W. China ; verticillata, deciduous, red fruits, 6 to 10 ft., Eastern N. America.
GOLDEN-LEAVED HOLLIES : Aurea marginata, aurea medio-picta, aurea pendula, aurea regina (Golden Queen), ferox aurea, flavescens (Moonlight Holly), lawsoniana, scotica aurea.
SILVER-LEAVED HOLLIES : Argentea regina (Silver Queen), argentea marginata, argentea medio-picta (Silver Milkmaid), ferox argentea, handsworthensis (Handsworth New Silver) ; argentea marginata pendula (Perry's Weeping).
GREEN-LEAVED HOLLIES : Altaclerensis, angustifolia, balearica, crassifolia, donningtonensis, ferox (Hedgehog Holly), Foxii, Hendersonii, heretophylla, maderensis, Mundyi, myrtifolia, nobilis pendula (Weeping), recurva (Syn. tortuosa), scotica, Shepherdii, wateriana, and Wilsoni.

Illicium (Aniseed-tree)—Ord. Magnoliaceæ. Half-hardy evergreen shrubs. Flowering and orn. foliage. First introduced 1771. Flowers, fragrant. Leaves, oblong ; emitting odour of aniseed.
CULTURE : Compost, equal parts sandy loam and peat. Position, sheltered shrubberies or against south walls, S. of England ; in pots in cold greenhouses or conservatories, N. of England. Plant outdoors, April, Sept., or Oct. Pot, Oct. Water plants in pots freely in summer, moderately in winter. Prune into shape, April or May.
PROPAGATION : By layers of firm young shoots 2 to 3 in. long, inserted in well-drained pots of sandy soil under bell-glass in temp. of 55° to 65°, May to Aug.
SPECIES CULTIVATED : I. anisatum (Syn. I. religiosum), yellowish white, summer, 4 ft., China and Japan ; floridanum, purple-red, summer, 8 ft., Florida.

Imantophyllum—See Clivia.

Immortelle-flower—See Helichrysum, Xeranthemum, Waitzia, and Helipterum.

Impatiens (Balsam)—Ord. Geraniaceæ. Stove, greenhouse, and hardy annuals and perennials.
CULTURE OF STOVE SPECIES : Compost, equal parts peat, loam, leaf-mould, and sand. Position, well-drained pots in light part of stove Sept. to May, greenhouse June to Sept. Pot, Feb. or March. Water moderately March to Sept., occasionally afterwards. Temp., Oct. to March 55° to 65° ; March to June 65° to 75°. Prune into shape, Feb. May be grown in the flower garden during the summer.
CULTURE OF BALSAM (I. Balsamina) : Sow seeds ⅛ in. deep in light soil in temp. 65° to 75° in March or April. Transplant seedlings singly into 2 in. pots when 1 in. high. Compost, equal parts loam, leaf-mould, and sand. Position, near glass in greenhouse, not shaded. Transfer from 2 in. into 5 in., and then into 6 and 8 in. pots. Apply liquid manure daily to plants showing flower. Water freely. Temp., March to June, 55° to 65°. May be grown in flower garden during the summer. Plant, June. Soil, ordinary. Position, sunny borders.
CULTURE OF HARDY SPECIES : Sow seeds ⅛ in. deep in April where plants are to grow. Soil, ordinary. Position, sunny borders. Thin seedlings to 6 in. apart when 1 in. high.
PROPAGATION : Stove species by seeds sown ₁/₁₆ in. deep in light rich soil in temp. 65° in March ; by cuttings of side shoots inserted in small pots of light sandy soil in temp. 75° March to Aug.
STOVE SPECIES : I. auricoma, yellow, summer, 2 ft., Comoro Isles ; Hawkeri, carmine, summer, 2 ft., Sunda Islands ; Holstii, brick red, summer, 3 ft., E. Trop. Africa ; Sultani, scarlet, summer, 1 ft., Zanzibar. All perennials.
GREENHOUSE SPECIES : I. Balsamina (Balsam), rose, scarlet, and white, summer, 2 ft., Trop. Asia. Annual.
HARDY SPECIES : I. amphorata, purple, Aug., 5 ft., Himalayas ; Roylei (Syn. glandulifera), purple, summer, 6 ft., Himalayas.

Imperati's Crocus (*Crocus Imperati*)—See Crocus.

Incarvillea—Ord. Bignoniaceæ. Hardy herbaceous perennials. May be grown in pots in cool greenhouses as well as outdoors. First introduced 1880.
OUTDOOR CULTURE : Soil, light, rich, and well-drained. Position, sunny and sheltered borders. Plant in March or April. Protect crowns of the plant in winter by a covering of dry litter. Apply weak liquid manure occasionally in summer.
INDOOR CULTURE : Compost, two parts loam, one part of equal proportions of leaf-mould, decayed manure, and silver sand. Position, fairly large pots, well drained, in cool or cold greenhouse. Pot in Oct. or March. Water freely in spring and summer ; keep nearly dry in autumn and winter ; give weak liquid manure occasionally in summer.
PROPAGATION : By seeds sown in a temp. of 55° in March, or in cold frame in April, and transplant seedlings outdoors in June. Sow also in Sept. in cold frame and plant out seedlings following April. Divide large plants in autumn.
217

SPECIES CULTIVATED : I. Delavayi, rose, summer, 2½ ft., China ; grandiflora, rose, summer, 1½ to 2 ft., China, and its variety brevipes (crimson) ; Olgæ, purple, summer, 3 to 4 ft., Turkestan ; variabilis, rose-purple, Aug., 18 in., Western China.

Incense Cedar (*Libocedrus decurrens*)—See Libocedrus.

Incense Juniper (*Juniperus thurifera*)—See Juniperus.

Indian Arrowroot (*Maranta arundinacea*)—See Maranta.

Indian Azalea (*Rhododendron indicum*)—See Rhododendron.

Indian Butterfly Plant—See Phalænopsis.

Indian Bean (*Catalpa bignonioides*)—See Catalpa.

Indian Corn (*Zea Mays*)—See Zea.

Indian Cress—See Tropæolum.

Indian Cup (*Sarracenia purpurea*)—See Sarracenia.

Indian Daphne (*Daphne indica*)—See Daphne.

Indian Date (*Tamarindus indica*)—See Tamarindus.

Indian Fig (*Opuntia ficus indica*)—See Opuntia.

Indian Forget-me-not (*Ipomæa Quamoclit*)—See Ipomæa.

Indian Grass (*Molinia cærulea*)—See Molinia.

Indian Hawthorn (*Raphiolepis indica*)—See Raphiolepis.

Indian Hemp (*Cannabis sativa*)—See Cannabis.

Indian Ivy (*Monstera deliciosa*)—See Monstera.

Indian Lilac (*Lagerstræmia indica*)—See Lagerstrœmia.

Indian Mallow—See Abutilon.

Indian Physic (*Gillenia trifoliata*)—See Gillenia.

Indian Pink (*Dianthus sinensis*)—See Dianthus.

Indian Poke (*Phytolacca decandra*)—See Phytolacca.

Indian Reed (*Canna indica*)—See Canna.

Indian Rice (*Zizania aquatica*)—See Zizania.

Indian Shell-flower (*Alpinia speciosa*)—See Alpinia.

Indian Shot (*Canna indica*)—See Canna.

Indian Strawberry (*Fragaria indica*)—See Fragaria.

India-rubber Plant (*Ficus elastica*)—See Ficus.

Indigo (*Indigofera tinctoria*)—See Indigofera.

Indigofera (Indigo)—Ord. Leguminosæ. Stove, greenhouse, and hardy flowering shrubs. Evergreen and deciduous. First introduced 1731.
CULTURE OF STOVE SPECIES : Compost, equal parts turfy loam, leaf-mould, and sand. Position, well-drained pots or beds. Pot or plant, Feb. or March. Prune into shape, Feb. or March. Water freely March to Oct., moderately Oct. to March. Temp., March to Oct. 65° to 75° ; Oct. to March 55° to 65°.
CULTURE OF GREENHOUSE SPECIES : Compost, as above. Position, large well-drained pots, or in beds, with shoots trained up pillars or against walls. Pot or plant, March. Prune into shape, March or April. Water freely March to Oct., moderately afterwards. Temp., March to Oct. 55° to 65° ; Oct. to March 45° to 55°. Stand plants in sunny place outdoors June to Sept.
CULTURE OF HARDY SPECIES : Compost, equal parts loam, leaf-mould, and peat. Position, well-drained bed or border. Shoots may be trained against S. wall. Plant,

Oct. to Feb. **Prune** moderately after flowering, removing those shoots only that have flowered.

PROPAGATION : By seeds sown ⅛ in. deep in well-drained pots of sandy soil in temp. 75° to 85° for stove species, 65° to 70° for greenhouse and hardy species, in Feb. or March ; cuttings of firm young shoots 2 to 3 in. long inserted in pots of sandy peat under bell-glass in temp. 70° to 75° for stove species, 60° to 65° for greenhouse and hardy species, during July and Aug.

STOVE SPECIES : I. tinctoria (Indigo), red, summer, 4 to 6 ft., Tropics.

GREENHOUSE SPECIES : I. australis, rose, spring, 4 ft., Australia.

HARDY SPECIES : I. decora, deciduous, white, crimson, and pink, July to Aug., 1 to 2 ft., China ; gerardiana, red, summer, 6 ft., Himalayas.

Ink-berry (*Ilex glabra*)—See Ilex.

Intermediate Stock (*Matthiola annua*)—See Matthiola.

Inula (Flea-bane ; Elecampane)—Ord. Compositæ. Hardy herbaceous perennials.

CULTURE : Soil, ordinary rich. Position, moist sunny beds or borders. Plant, Oct., Nov., March, or April. Cut down flower stems in Oct. Top-dress with well-decayed manure in April.

PROPAGATION : By seeds sown 1/16 in. deep in partially shady border outdoors in April ; division of roots, Oct. or March.

SPECIES CULTIVATED : I. acaulis, yellow, spring and early summer, 2 in., Cilicia ; ensifolia, yellow, Aug., 10 in., S. Europe ; glandulosa, yellow, Aug., 2 ft., Caucasus ; grandiflora, yellow, July to Sept., 2 ft., Himalayas ; Helenium (Elecampane), yellow, July to Sept., 6 to 8 ft., Europe ; Hookeri, yellow, Aug. and Sept., 2 ft., Himalayas ; Oculus-Christi (Christ's Eye), yellow, summer, 18 in., Europe ; royleana, deep golden yellow, Aug. to Sept., 2 ft., Himalayas.

Ionopsidium (Carpet-plant ; Violet-flowered Cress)—Ord. Cruciferæ. Hardy annual. First introduced 1845.

OUTDOOR CULTURE : Soil, ordinary. Position, ledges of rockeries or as edgings to flower beds. Sow seeds where plants are to grow in April, just covering with fine mould.

POT CULTURE : Compost, equal parts loam, leaf-mould, and sand. Position, shady window, cold frame, or greenhouse. Sow seeds 1/16 in. deep in 5 in. pot well drained and filled with above compost, in April or Sept. Thin seedlings to 1 in. apart. Water moderately. Apply liquid manure occasionally when flower buds show.

SPECIES CULTIVATED : I. acaule, lilac, white, and violet, summer, 3 in., Portugal.

Ionopsis—Ord. Orchidaceæ. Warm house epiphytal orchid. First introduced 1865.

CULTURE : Compost, peat and sphagnum moss in equal parts. Position, attached to blocks of wood suspended from roof ; or in shallow pans. Reblock, Feb. or March. Water freely March to Sept., moderately other times. Syringe twice daily Feb. to Oct. Temp., Oct. to Feb. 50° to 55° ; Feb. to Oct. 60° to 70°.

PROPAGATION : By division of plants at reblocking time.

SPECIES CULTIVATED : I. paniculata, white, purple, and yellow, winter, 6 in., Brazil.

Ipomæa (American Bell-bind ; Moon Creeper ; Morning Glory)—Ord. Convolvulaceæ. Stove, greenhouse, hardy perennial and half-hardy annual climbers. First introduced 1597.

CULTURE OF STOVE SPECIES : Compost, equal parts fibrous loam, leaf-mould, decayed manure, and silver sand. Position, pots, beds, or borders in stove ; shoots trained up roof, or on trellises. Pot or plant, Feb., March, or April. Temp., March to Sept. 65° to 75° ; Sept. to March 55° to 65°. Water freely April to Sept., moderately afterwards. Prune straggly growths of perennials into shape, Feb. Sow three seeds of the annual species ¼ in. deep in a 2½ in. pot in temp. 65° in March. Transfer seedlings when 2 in. high into 5 in. pots. Train shoots to trellis or sticks

CULTURE OF HALF-HARDY ANNUALS : Soil, light rich. Sow seeds ⅛ in. deep in pots in temp. 65° in March. Transfer seedlings to cold frame in May. Plant, June. Position, sunny walls or borders ; shoots trained to trellis or to sticks.
CULTURE OF HARDY PERENNIAL SPECIES : Soil, ordinary. Position, sunny walls, fences, or arbours. Plant, Oct. or Nov.
CULTURE OF SWEET POTATO : Compost, two parts loam and one part decayed manure. Plant tubers singly in 6 in. pots in Feb., in temp. 65°, or 6 in. deep and 8 in. apart in prepared border in greenhouse. Water moderately Feb. to May ; freely May to Sept., then give none, keeping tubers dry. Tubers are edible.
PROPAGATION : Annual species by seeds as above ; perennials by cuttings of side shoots inserted in sandy peat under bell-glass in temp. 75° to 85°, March to Aug., or grafting in March ; sweet potato by division of tubers in Feb. ; I. pandurata by cuttings of young shoots in April.
STOVE SPECIES : I. Bona-Nox, white, summer, 10 ft., Trop. America ; Horsfalliæ, rose, winter, 10 to 15 ft., W. Indies ; Learii, blue, summer, 10 ft., Trop. America ; Quamoclit, red, summer, 6 ft., Tropics, annual ; ternata (Syn. Thomsonii), white, summer, 10 ft., W. Indies ; rubro-cærulea, red, Mexico.
GREENHOUSE SPECIES : I. batatas (Sweet Potato), white, summer, tubers edible, 2 to 4 ft., Tropics.
HALF-HARDY ANNUAL SPECIES : I. hederacea, blue or pale purple, summer, twining, Tropical America ; purpurea (Syn. Convolvulus major), purple, summer, twining, Tropical America ; versicolor (Syn. Mina lobata), rosy crimson and yellow, summer, 6 to 8 ft., Trop. America. There are numerous varieties of I. hederacea and I. purpurea.
PERENNIAL SPECIES : I. pandurata (Syn. Convolvulus pandurata), white and purple, summer, climber, N. America.

Ipsea—Ord. Orchidaceæ. Stove terrestrial orchid. Flowers, fragrant. First introduced 1840.
CULTURE : Compost, equal parts leaf-mould, peat, sphagnum moss, and small crocks. Position, light part of stove. Pot, Feb. or March, in well-drained pots. Water freely March to Aug., moderately Aug. to Oct., very little afterwards. Temp., March to Sept. 60° to 65° ; Sept. to March 50° to 55°.
PROPAGATION : By division of pseudo-bulbs after flowering.
SPECIES CULTIVATED : I. speciosa, yellow, spring, 1 ft., Ceylon.

Iresine (Blood-leaf)—Ord. Amarantaceæ. Stove and half-hardy orn. foliaged plants. First introduced 1864. Leaves, heart- and lance-shaped; deep blood red, carmine, green, golden, crimson.
POT CULTURE : Compost, equal parts peat, loam, leaf-mould, and sand. Position, sunny part of stove. Pot, Feb. or March. Water freely March to Sept., moderately other times. Temp., March to Oct. 65° to 75° ; Oct. to March 55° to 65°.
OUTDOOR CULTURE : Soil, ordinary. Position, edgings to sunny beds or borders. Plant, June. Lift, repot, and remove to stove in Sept. Pinch off points of shoots frequently to induce bushy growth.
PROPAGATION : By cuttings of young shoots inserted in pots or pans of light sandy soil in temp. of 65° to 75°, Feb., March, April, Sept., or Oct.
SPECIES CULTIVATED : I. Herbstii, leaves maroon and crimson, 1 ft., Brazil ; Herbstii aurea reticulata, leaves green, gold, and red ; Lindeni, leaves blood red, 1 ft.

Iris (Flag ; Orrice Root ; Fleur de Luce)—Ord. Iridaceæ. Hardy evergreen rhizomatous and bulbous-rooted perennials. Sections : Tall Bearded, Dwarf Bearded, Beardless, Cushion, Japanese and Bulbous-rooted.
CULTURE OF TALL BEARDED SECTION : Soil, ordinary, well-drained, and with plenty of lime or old mortar rubble. Position, sunny borders. Plant in Oct. or March, keeping rhizomes near surface. Top-dress with superphosphate of lime in April at the rate of 1 to 2 oz. per sq. yd. Lift and replant every fourth year.
CULTURE OF DWARF BEARDED SECTION : Soil as above. Position, sunny well-drained borders. Plant and treat as advised for foregoing section.
CULTURE OF BEARDLESS SECTION : Moist soil and margins of ponds or streams for

I. versicolor, sibirica, ochroleuca and pseudacorus. Plant, Oct. or March. Cool, deep soil well supplied with humus and a partially shady position for I. gracilipes. Plant, March or April. Ordinary rich soil and sunny borders or rockeries for other species. Plant in Oct. or March.

CULTURE OF JAPANESE SECTION : Rich loamy soil on the margins of ponds, or in a half cask filled with loam and sunk in garden in sunny spot. Plant in Oct. or March. Apply liquid manure in growing season.

CULTURE OF CUSHION SECTION : Soil, light, rich loam with a liberal addition of old mortar rubble. Position, raised bed against a south wall. Plant in Oct. Protect by a cold frame or hand-light in winter. Lift rhizomes in July and store in dry sand in sunny shed or greenhouse until Oct.

CULTURE OF BULBOUS-ROOTED SECTION : Plant choice kinds in a compost of equal parts fibrous loam, leaf-mould, and sharp sand. Place bulbs 3 in. deep and 3 in. apart. Plant in Aug. or Sept. Spanish and English kinds to be planted in ordinary soil in sunny beds or borders in Sept. or Oct., placing bulbs 3 in. deep and 6 in. apart. Lift and replant every third year.

POT CULTURE OF BULBOUS SPECIES : Compost, equal parts loam, leaf-mould, and silver sand. Place in cold frame till growth begins, when remove to cold green-house or leave in frame to flower. Pot in Oct., placing five bulbs of the Spanish or English kinds, and I. tingitana in a 5 in. pot. Three bulbs of I. reticulata may be place in a 3 in. pot. Give water only when growth has begun. Withhold water after leaves begin to decay. Spanish and English iris must not be placed in artificial heat. I. tingitana can be gently forced to flower from January onwards.

PROPAGATION : All the species by seeds in sandy soil in cold frame as soon as ripe ; division of rhizomes in autumn or spring ; offsets in autumn.

TALL BEARDED IRISES : I. albicans, white, 2 to 3 ft., Spain ; Bilioti, purple, white, and yellow, May to June, 3 ft., Asia Minor ; Cengialti, violet and orange, May, 18 in., Tyrol ; germanica (Flag Iris), purple and lilac, fragrant, May, 2 to 2½ ft., S. Europe, and its variety florentina (Orrice Root) ; kashmiriana, creamy white, lavender, or purple, May to June, 2 ft., Kashmir ; pallida, lilac, purple, and white, May, fragrant, 3 ft., Southern Tyrol, and its variety plicata ; squalens, lilac purple and yellow, May, 3 ft., Europe, natural hybrid ; trojana, purple and violet, 3 ft., Asia Minor ; variegata, yellow and chestnut, May, 18 in., E. Europe. In trade lists a large number of lovely forms will be found described.

DWARF BEARDED IRISES : I. aphylla, purple, May, 9 to 15 in., E. Europe, a plant with many synonyms such as biflora, bifurca, bohemica, breviscapa, extrafoliacea, falcata, Fieberi, furcata, hungarica, nudicaulis, reflexa, rigida, Schmidti, and sub-triflora ; Chamæiris, yellow or purple, April, 4 to 6 in., S. Europe ; pumila (Crimean Iris), lilac purple, April, 4 in., S. Europe, and its many varieties, which range in colour from white to purple.

BEARDLESS IRISES : I. aurea, golden yellow, June to July, 4 ft., Kashmir ; chryso-graphes, violet purple, veined gold, 1½ to 2 ft., South-western China ; cristata, lilac, white, and orange, May, 6 to 12 in., S.E. United States ; ensata, slaty blue or white, sometimes with a creamy ground, 18 in., Temperate Asia ; fœtidissima (Gladwin Iris), purple, June, 18 to 24 in., Britain ; foliosa, blue, lavender, and greenish white, June, 1 ft., S.E. United States ; Forrestii, clear yellow, June, 18 in., N.W. Yunnan ; fulva, coppery maroon, June to July, 18 to 24 in., banks of Mississippi near New Orleans ; gracilipes, lilac pink, May, 9 to 12 in., Japan ; graminea, blue and purple, June, 4 to 10 in., S. Europe ; Grant Duffii, sulphur yellow, May, 6 in., Holy Land ; japonica (Syn. I. fimbriata), amethyst blue and gold, April, 18 in., Japan and China ; longipetala, violet and white, June, 2 ft., California ; Milesii, reddish purple with darker mottlings, June to July, 24 to 36 in., Himalayas ; Monnieri, lemon yellow, fragrant, June, 3 ft., Crete ; monspur, lilac blue, June, 4 ft., hybrid ; ochroleuca, white and yellow, June to July, 4 to 5 ft., Western Asia Minor ; orientalis, blue-purple, May to June, 1½ to 2 ft., Manchuria and Japan ; pseudacorus (Yellow Water Flag), yellow, May and June, 3 ft., Britain ; setosa, purplish blue, May, 8 to 24 in., Northern Siberia, Japan, Alaska, and Labrador ; sibirica, blue and white, May and June, 3 ft., Central Europe and Russia ; spuria, blue to reddish purple, June, 3 ft., Europe ; tectorum (Japanese Roof Iris), lilac or blue-purple, 1 ft.,

Central and South-western China ; unguicularis (Syn. stylosa), lavender blue, Jan. and Feb., 1 ft., Algeria ; verna, lilac blue, fragrant, April to May, 3 in., N. America ; versicolor, purple, May to June, 2 ft., Eastern Canada and Eastern U.S.A. ; Wilsoni, yellow, June, 2 ft., China. Here also numerous varieties exist which may be found in trade lists.

CUSHION IRISES : I. bismarckiana, purple, yellow, blue, and white, May, 12 to 15 in., Mt. Lebanon ; Barnumæ, vinous red, May, 2 to 6 in., N.E. Asia Minor ; Gatesii, grey, purple, and white, May, 12 to 18 in., Kurdistan ; hoogiana, grey-blue or blue-purple, May, 18 to 24 in., Turkestan ; iberica, lilac, white, and purple, May, 6 in., Caucasus ; Korolkowi, creamy white and olive green, May, 1 ft., Turkestan ; Lortetii, crimson and cream, May, 1 ft., S. Lebanon ; paradoxa, blue-purple, white, and purplish black, May, 4 to 6 in., Persia ; susiana (Mourning Iris), brown, black, and lilac, May, 1 ft., habitat uncertain.

JAPANESE IRISES : I. Kaempferi, reddish purple and yellow, June to July, 18 to 30 in., Manchuria, Corea, and Japan ; lævigata, blue-purple, June, 15 to 18 in., E. Siberia, Manchuria, and Corea.

BULBOUS-ROOTED IRISES : I. alata, lilac purple and yellow, Oct., 1 ft., S. Europe ; bakeriana, white, violet, and blue, fragrant, Jan., 6 to 12 in., Armeria ; bracteata, yellow and purple, May, 4 to 6 in., Oregon ; bucharica, white and yellow, April, 12 to 18 in., Bokhara ; filifolia, red-purple, blue, and orange, June, 10 to 15 in., S. Spain and N. Africa ; Histrio, bright blue and yellow, Dec. and Jan., 1 ft., Asia Minor ; histrioides, blue-purple, white, and yellow, Jan., 1 ft., N. Asia Minor ; orchioides, yellow, April, 9 in., Turkestan ; persica, white, greenish blue, purple, and orange, Feb., 1 to 2 in., Persia ; reticulata, violet, purple, and yellow, violet scented, Feb., 6 in., Caucasus, and its varieties Krelagei and cyanea ; sindjarensis, azure blue and pale yellow, Feb. and March, 9 to 12 in., Mesopotamia ; tingitana, lilac blue, deep blue, and yellow, March, 2 ft., Tangier ; tuberosa (Syn. Hermodactylus tuberosus), violet, black, and green, March, 9 to 12 in., Mediterranean ; Vartani, slate grey or white, Dec. and Jan., 6 to 12 in, Nazareth ; xiphioides (English Iris), various colours, 1 to 2 ft., Pyrenees ; Xiphium (Spanish Iris), various colours, June, 1 to 2 ft., S. Europe and N. Africa. The plant known in gardens as Iris pavonia is actually Moræa glaucopis or M. pavonia, *q.v.*

Irish **Gorse** (*Ulex europæus strictus*)—See Ulex.

Irish **Heath** (*Daboëcia polifolia*)—See Daboëcia.

Irish **Ivy** (*Hedera helix canariensis*)—See Hedera.

Irish **Juniper** (*Juniperus communis fastigiata*)—See **Juniperus.**

Irish **Yew** (*Taxus baccata fastigiata*)—See Taxus.

Iron-weed—See Vernonia.

Ismene—See Hymenocallis.

Isolepis—See Scirpus.

Isoloma—Ord. Gesneraceæ. Stove flowering tuberous rooted plants. The plants known as Tydæas are now merged in this genus.

CULTURE : Compost, two parts fibrous peat, one part loam, one part leaf-mould, with a little decayed manure and silver sand. Position, well-drained pots or pans in shady part of plant stove. Pot, March to flower in summer ; May to flower in autumn ; June to flower in winter. Place tubers 1 in. deep singly in 5 in. pots, or 1 to 2 in. apart in larger sizes. Water moderately from time growth begins until plants are 3 or 4 in. high, then freely. After flowering gradually withhold water till foliage dies down, then keep dry till potting time. Apply weak liquid manure once or twice a week when flower buds show. Syringing not required. Temp., March to Sept. 65° to 85° ; Sept. to March 55° to 65°. Store when foliage has died down on their sides under stage till potting time in temp. of 50° to 55°.

PROPAGATION : By seeds sown on surface of well-drained pots of sandy peat, in temp. 75°, March or April ; cuttings of young shoots inserted in pots of sandy peat in temp. 75° to 85° in spring ; fully matured leaves pegged on surface of pots of sandy peat in temp. 75° to 85°.

SPECIES CULTIVATED : I. amabile, rose and purple, 1 to 2 ft., Colombia ; digitaliflorum, rose, purple, and white, winter, 1 ft. ; hondense (Syn. Gesnera hondense), yellow and red, winter, 1 ft., New Grenada ; Lindeni (Syn. Tydæa Lindeni), white and violet, winter, 1 ft., Ecuador.

Isopyrum—Ord. Ranunculaceæ. Hardy herbaceous perennial. Orn. foliage. First introduced 1759. Foliage finely divided like that of maidenhair fern.

CULTURE : Soil, ordinary. Position, sunny or shady rockery, bed or border. Plant, Oct. or March.

PROPAGATION : By seeds sown $\frac{1}{16}$ in. deep outdoors in April or May ; division of roots in Oct. or Nov.

SPECIES CULTIVATED : I. thalictroides, white, spring, 8 in., Europe.

Italian **Alkanet** (*Anchusa italica*)—See Anchusa.

Italian **Arum** (*Arum italicum*)—See Arum.

Italian **Corn Salad** (*Valerianella eriocarpa*)—See Valerianella.

Italian **Cypress** (*Cupressus sempervirens*)—See Cupressus.

Italian **Pimpernel** (*Anagallis Monelli*)—See Anagallis.

Italian **Starwort** (*Aster Amellus*)—See Aster.

Italian **Stone Pine-tree** (*Pinus Pinea*)—See Pinus.

Italian **Yellow Jasmine** (*Jasminum humile*)—See Jasminum.

Itea (Virginian Willow)—Ord. Saxifragaceæ. Hardy evergreen and deciduous shrubs. Orn. foliage and flowering. First introduced 1744.

CULTURE : Soil, peaty. Position, moist sheltered shrubberies. Plant, Oct. to Feb. Prune moderately after flowering.

PROPAGATION : By seeds sown $\frac{1}{4}$ in. deep in sandy soil outdoors in April ; suckers removed in Oct. or Nov. ; layering shoots in July or Aug.

SPECIES CULTIVATED : I. ilicifolia, greenish white, Aug., 8 to 15 ft., evergreen, W. China ; virginica, white, July, 4 to 6 ft., deciduous, N. America.

Ivy (*Hedera helix*)—See Hedera.

Ivy-leaved **Campanula** (*Wahlenbergia hederacea*)—See Wahlenbergia.

Ivy-leaved **Cypress-vine** (*Ipomœa hederacea*)—See Ipomæa.

Ivy-leaved **Fern** (*Hemionites cordata*)—See Hemionites.

Ivy-leaved **Groundsel** (*Senecio macroglossus*)—See Senecio.

Ivy-leaved **Harebell** (*Wahlenbergia hederacea*)—See Wahlenbergia.

Ivy-leaved **Pelargonium** (*Pelargonium peltatum*)—See Pelargonium.

Ivy-leaved **Toad-flax** (*Linaria cymbalaria*)—See Linaria.

Ixia (African Corn Lily)—Ord. Iridaceæ. Half-hardy bulbous plants. Nat. S. Africa. First introduced 1744. Flowers, fragrant.

OUTDOOR CULTURE : Soil, light, rich, sandy. Position, sunny well-drained border. Plant, Sept. to Jan., placing bulbs 4 in. deep and 2 in. apart. Lift and replant bulbs annually. Mulch surface of bed in March with cow manure.

POT CULTURE : Compost, two parts sandy loam, one part leaf-mould or decayed cow manure. Pots, 4½ in. in diameter, well drained. Place five bulbs, 3 in. deep, in each pot in Nov., and cover with cocoanut-fibre refuse in cold frame or under cool greenhouse stage until growth begins. Water moderately from time bulbs begin to grow until flowers fade, then gradually cease, keeping bulbs dry till Jan. Temp., Sept. to March 40° to 50° ; other times 50° to 60°.

PROPAGATION : By offsets, treated as advised for bulbs.

SPECIES CULTIVATED : I. flexuosa, pink, spring, 1 ft. ; maculata, orange yellow, spring, 1 ft. ; patens, pink, spring, 1 ft. ; speciosa (Syn. crateroides), purple and crimson, summer, 1 ft. ; viridiflora, green, spring, 1 ft. Numerous varieties.

Ixia Lily (*Ixiolirion montanum tataricum*)—See Ixiolirion.

Ixiolirion (Ixia Lily)—Ord. Amaryllidaceæ. Half-hardy bulbous plant. **First** introduced 1844.

CULTURE : Soil, light sandy loam. Position, well-drained sunny border at foot of S. wall. Plant bulbs 3 in. deep and 4 in. apart in March. Mulch surface of bed with cow manure in April. After flowering cover with bell-glass or hand-light to ensure thorough ripening of bulbs. Lift bulbs in Sept. and store in dry sand in cool, frost-proof place till planting time.

PROPAGATION : By offsets removed at any time, planted and treated as advised for normal bulbs. May also be grown in pots as advised for Ixias.

SPECIES CULTIVATED : I. montanum, blue, June, 1 ft., W. Asia, and its variety tataricum (Syn. Pallasi).

Ixora (West Indian Jasmine)—Ord. Rubiaceæ. Stove flowering shrubs. Evergreen. First introduced 1690. Flowers, fragrant.

CULTURE : Compost, two parts good fibrous peat, one part fibrous loam and silver sand. Position, shady part of stove whilst growing, light situation when at rest. Pot, Feb. or March ; good drainage indispensable. Prune into shape in Feb. Water freely March to Sept., moderately afterwards. Syringe twice daily March to Aug. Apply liquid manure once or twice a week to healthy plants in flower. Temp., March to Sept. 75° to 85° ; Sept. to March 55° to 65°.

PROPAGATION : By cuttings of firm young shoots 2 to 3 in. long, inserted singly in small pots in sandy peat under bell-glass in temp. 75° to 85°, March to May.

SPECIES CULTIVATED : I. coccinea, orange-scarlet, summer, 3 to 4 ft., India ; macrothyrsa (Syn. I. Duffi), deep red tinged crimson, summer, 10 to 12 ft., Sumatra ; stricta, light orange, summer, 2 to 3 ft., China. Numerous varieties and hybrids.

Jaborosa—Ord. Solanaceæ. Half-hardy herbaceous perennial. First introduced 1831.

CULTURE : Soil, rich loamy. Position, well-drained border at base of S. wall. Plant, Oct. to March. Protect in winter with covering of ashes or litter.

PROPAGATION : By seeds sown $\frac{1}{16}$ in. deep in light sandy soil in well-drained pots in temp. 55° to 65° in March or April ; cuttings of young shoots inserted in sandy soil under bell-glass, hand-light, or in cold frame, July to Sept. ; division of creeping stems in March or April.

SPECIES CULTIVATED : J. integrifolia, white, summer, 9 in., Buenos Ayres.

Jacaranda (Mimosa-leaved Ebony-tree ; Green Ebony-tree)—Ord. Bignoniaceæ. Stove evergreen tree. Flowering and orn. foliage. First introduced 1818. Leaves, fern-like, downy, very elegant.

CULTURE : Compost, equal parts peat, fibry loam and silver sand. Position, well-drained pots in light part of plant stove Sept. to April, sunny place outdoors July to Sept. Pot, Feb. to March. Prune into shape, Feb. Water freely March to Oct., moderately Oct. to March. Temp., Sept. to March 55° to 65° ; March to July 70° to 80°. Plants form decorative specimens when 1 to 3 ft. high ; flowering specimens when grown as standards, 10 to 15 ft. high.

PROPAGATION : By seeds sown $\frac{1}{4}$ in. deep in light sandy peat in well-drained pots under bell-glass in temp. of 75° to 85°, Feb. to June ; cuttings of firm shoots inserted in sandy peat under bell-glass in temp. of 75°, June to Sept.

SPECIES CULTIVATED : J. ovalifolia (Syns. J. acutifolia and J. mimosifolia), blue, to 50 ft., Brazil.

Jack-go-to-bed-at-noon (*Ornithogalum umbellatum*)—See Ornithogalum.

Jack-in-prison (*Nigella damascena*)—See Nigella.

Jack-in-the-green (*Primula vulgaris* var.)—See Primula.

Jack-tree (*Artocarpus integrifolia*)—See Artocarpus.

Jacobæa (*Senecio elegans*)—See Senecio.

Jacobean Lily (*Sprekelia formosissima*)—See Sprekelia.

Jacobinia—Ord. Acanthaceæ. Stove flowering plants. First introduced 1770.
CULTURE : Compost, equal parts peat, loam, leaf-mould and sand. Position, well-drained pots in light stove Sept. to June, sunny frame June to Sept. Pot, March to April. Water moderately Sept. to March, freely other times. Temp., Sept. to March 55° to 65° ; March to June 65° to 75°. Prune shoots to 1 in. of base after flowering. Nip off points of young shoots occasionally, May to Aug., to induce bushy growth. Apply liquid or artificial manure twice a week to plants in flower.
PROPAGATION : By cuttings of young shoots inserted singly in small pots or sandy soil under bell-glass in temp. 75°, March to July.
SPECIES CULTIVATED : J. chrysostephana, yellow, winter, 3 ft., Mexico ; ghiesbreghtiana (Syn. Sericographis ghiesbreghtiana), scarlet, Dec., 2 ft., Mexico ; magnifica carnea (Syn. Justicia carnea), rose, summer, 3 to 4 ft., Brazil ; pauciflora (Syn. Libonia pauciflora), scarlet and yellow, winter, 2 ft., Brazil ; penrhoziensis (Syn. Libonia penrhoziensis), carmine and yellow, winter, 2 ft., hybrid.

Jacob's-ladder (*Polemonium cæruleum*)—See Polemonium.

Jacob's-rod (*Asphodelus luteus*)—See Asphodelus.

Jalap-plant (*Mirabilis jalapa*)—See Mirabilis.

Jamaica Allspice (*Pimenta officinalis*)—See Pimenta.

Jamaica Mountain Sage—See Lantana.

Jamaica Sago-tree (*Zamia furfuracea*)—See Zamia.

Jamesia—Ord. Saxifragaceæ. Hardy deciduous flowering shrub. First introduced 1820.
CULTURE : Soil, ordinary. Position, sunny rockeries or borders. Plant, Oct. to Feb. Prune directly after flowering.
PROPAGATION : By cuttings inserted under hand-light or in cold frame in autumn.
SPECIES CULTIVATED : J. americana, white, spring, 6 to 8 ft., Rocky Mountains.

Japan Allspice (*Chimonanthus fragrans*)—See Chimonanthus.

Japan Clover (*Lespedeza bicolor*)—See Lespedeza.

Japanese Aralia (*Fatsia japonica*)—See Fatsia.

Japanese Arbor-vitæ (*Thuya occidentalis*)—See Thuya.

Japanese Barberry (*Berberis japonica*)—See Berberis.

Japanese Cedar (*Cryptomeria japonica*)—See Cryptomeria.

Japanese Climbing Fern (*Lygodium scandens*)—See Lygodium.

Japanese Clover (*Lespedeza bicolor*)—See Lespedeza.

Japanese Day Lily (*Hemerocallis aurantiaca major*)—See Hemerocallis.

Japanese Foam Flower (*Tanakea radicans*)—See Tanakea.

Japanese Golden Bell Tree (*Forsythia suspensa*)—See Forsythia.

Japanese Groundsel (*Senecio japonicus*)—See Senecio.

Japanese Hare's-foot Fern (*Davallia Mariesi*)—See Davallia.

Japanese Hop (*Humulus japonicus*)—See Humulus.

Japanese Lady's-slipper (*Cypripedium japonicum*)—See Cypripedium.

Japanese Larch (*Larix leptolepis*)—See Larix.

Japanese Lilac (*Syringa japonica*)—See Syringa.

Japanese Maple (*Acer palmatum*)—See Acer.

Japanese Monk's-hood (*Aconitum japonicum*)—See Aconitum.

Japanese Pepper (*Piper Futokadsura*)—See Piper.

Japanese Primrose (*Primula japonica*)—See Primula.

Japanese Privet (*Ligustrum japonicum*)—See Ligustrum.

Japanese Quince (*Pyrus japonica*)—See Pyrus.

225

Japanese **Red Pine** (*Pinus densiflora*)—See Pinus.

Japanese **Roof Iris** (*Iris tectorum*)—See Iris.

Japanese **Rose** (*Rosa rugosa*)—See Rosa.

Japanese **Snow-flower** (*Deutzia gracilis*)—See Deutzia.

Japanese **Spindle-tree** (*Euonymus japonicus*)—See Euonymus.

Japanese **Spruce** (*Tsuga Sieboldii*)—See Tsuga.

Japanese **Toad Lily** (*Tricyrtis hirta*)—See Tricyrtis.

Japanese **Vine** (*Vitis Coignetiæ*)—See Vitis.

Japanese **Wind-flower** (*Anemone japonica*)—See Anemone.

Japanese **Wineberry** (*Rubus phœnicolasius*)—See Rubus.

Japanese **Yew** (*Taxus cuspidata*)—See Taxus.

Japan **Honeysuckle** (*Lonicera japonica*)—See Lonicera.

Japan **Laurel** (*Aucuba japonica*)—See Aucuba.

Japan **Lily** (*Lilium speciosum*)—See Lilium.

Japonica—A common name loosely applied to Pyrus japonica.

Jasione (Sheep's-bit Scabious)—Ord. Campanulaceæ. Hardy annuals and herbaceous perennials.
CULTURE OF ANNUAL SPECIES : Soil, ordinary. Position, well-drained sunny beds or borders. Sow seeds $\frac{1}{16}$ in. deep in April or Sept. where plants are to grow.
CULTURE OF PERENNIAL SPECIES : Soil, good light loam. Position, sunny well-drained borders. Plant, Oct. or March. Cut down flower stems, Oct.
PROPAGATION : By seeds sown $\frac{1}{16}$ in. deep in light soil outdoors, April to Sept. ; division of roots, Oct. or March.
ANNUAL SPECIES : J. montana, lilac blue, summer, 1 ft., Europe (Britain).
PERENNIAL SPECIES : J. humilis, blue, July to Aug., 6 in., Pyrenees ; Jankæ, blue, July to Sept., 9 to 12 in., E. Europe ; perennis, blue, June, 18 in., W. Europe.

Jasmine (*Jasminum officinale*)—See Jasminum.

Jasmine Box (*Phillyrea angustifolia*)—See Phillyrea.

Jasmine Nightshade (*Solanum jasminoides*)—See Solanum.

Jasminum (Jasmine ; Jessamine)—Ord. Oleaceæ. Stove, greenhouse and hardy climbing and trailing flowering plants. Evergreen and deciduous. First introduced 1548.
CULTURE OF STOVE SPECIES : Compost, equal parts loam, peat and leaf-mould, with little sand. Position, well-drained pots, with shoots trained to trellis or up rafters, or in beds or borders, with shoots trained up walls or rafters. Pot or plant, Feb. or March. Prune moderately, Feb. Water freely March to Oct., moderately Oct. to March. Temp., March to Sept. 65° to 75° ; Sept. to March 55° to 65°. Syringe daily from March to Aug.
CULTURE OF GREENHOUSE SPECIES : Compost, as above. Position, beds or borders, with shoots trained up rafters or walls, or well-drained pots in light part of greenhouse Sept. to June, sunny place outdoors June to Sept. Pot or plant, Feb. to March. Prune slightly, Feb. Water freely March to Sept., moderately afterwards. Temp., Sept. to March 45° to 55° ; March to June 55° to 65°.
CULTURE OF HARDY SPECIES : Soil, ordinary rich. Position, well-drained borders at base of S. or S.W. walls. Plant, Oct., Nov., Feb., or March. Prune moderately after flowering, removing shoots that have flowered only.
PROPAGATION : Stove and greenhouse species by cuttings of firm shoots, inserted in well-drained pots of sandy peat under bell-glass in temp. of 65° to 75°, March to Sept. ; hardy species by cuttings of shoots 3 to 6 in. long inserted in well-drained pots of sandy soil in cold frame or in sheltered borders outdoors Sept. to Dec. ; layering shoots near base of plants spring or summer ; variegated kinds by budding on common species July or Aug.

STOVE SPECIES : J. gracillimum, white, winter, 4 ft., Borneo ; Sambac, white, autumn, 6 ft., Trop. Asia.
GREENHOUSE SPECIES : J. grandiflorum, white, autumn, 10 ft., Malaya ; primulinum, white, winter, 6 to 10 ft., China.
HARDY SPECIES : J. beesianum, rose, June to July, 3 ft., W. China ; humile, yellow, summer, 3 ft., Trop. Asia ; floridum, yellow, summer, 10 ft., China ; fruticans, yellow, summer, 10 ft., Orient ; nudiflorum, yellow, winter, 10 ft., China ; officinale (Jasmine), white, summer, 15 to 20 ft., Persia ; officinale foliis-aureis, variegated ; revolutum, yellow, June to Aug., 9 to 12 ft., nearly evergreen, Afghanistan.

Jaundice-berry (*Berberis vulgaris*)—See Berberis.

Jeffersonia (Twin-leaf)—Ord. Berberidaceæ. Hardy perennial herb. First introduced 1792.
CULTURE : Soil, peaty. Position, shady edges of rockery or borders. Plant, Oct., March or April.
PROPAGATION : By seeds sown $\frac{1}{16}$ in. deep in sandy soil in cold frame, July to Sept. ; division of roots, Oct. or March.
SPECIES CULTIVATED : J. diphylla (Syn. binata), white, spring, 6 in., N. America.

Jersey Elm (*Ulmus stricta Wheatleyi*)—See Ulmus.

Jerusalem Artichoke (*Helianthus tuberosus*)—See Helianthus.

Jerusalem Cherry (*Solanum Pseudo-capsicum*)—See Solanum.

Jerusalem Cowslip (*Pulmonaria officinalis*)—See Pulmonaria.

Jerusalem Cross (*Lychnis chalcedonica*)—See Lychnis.

Jerusalem Pine (*Pinus halepensis*)—See Pinus.

Jerusalem Sage (*Phlomis fruticosa*)—See Phlomis.

Jessamine (*Jasminum officinale*)—See Jasminum.

Jesuit's Nut (*Trapa natans*)—See Trapa.

Jew-bush (*Pedilanthus tithymaloides*)—See Pedilanthus.

Jew's Mallow (*Kerria japonica*)—See Kerria.

Job's Tears (*Coix Lachryma-Jobi*)—See Coix.

Jonquil (*Narcissus jonquilla*)—See Narcissus.

Joy Weed—See Telanthera.

Judas-tree (*Cercis siliquastrum*)—See Cercis.

Juglans (Walnut-tree ; Butter-nut)—Ord. Juglandaceæ. Hardy deciduous nut-bearing and orn. foliage trees. Walnut introduced in 1592.
CULTURE OF WALNUT : Soil, sandy and calcareous, or stiff loams on gravelly subsoil. Position, S. or S.W., open, not shaded by trees or buildings. Plant, Oct. or Nov., placing roots 3 to 4 in. below surface of ground previously deeply trenched. Pruning unnecessary. Gather nuts for pickling before shell gets too hard. Ripe nuts place in thin layers in dry position till husks fall off, then pack in alternate layers with sand in barrels, casks, or jars sprinkled with salt. Grafted or budded trees bear earlier than seedlings. Culture of other species, same as above.
USEFUL DATA : Juglans regia and nigra good for town gardens. Timber used for making gun stocks, furniture and veneering. One bushel of nuts will yield about 5,000 seedlings. Average life of a walnut tree, 300 years. Average weight of timber per cubic foot, 47 lb.
PROPAGATION : By seed (nuts) sown 2 in. deep in light soil outdoors in Nov., transplanting seedlings following Oct. ; budding in Aug. ; grafting in March.
SPECIES CULTIVATED : J. cinerea (Butter-nut), 50 to 60 ft., N. America ; nigra (Black Walnut), 80 to 100 ft., N. America ; regia (Walnut), 50 to 60 ft., Caucasus to Himalayas.

Jujube (*Zizyphus sativa*)—See Zizyphus.

June-berry (*Amelanchier canadensis*)—See Amelanchier.

Juniper (*Junipirus communis*)—See Juniperus.

Juniperus (Juniper ; Savin)—Ord. Coniferæ. Hardy evergreen coniferous trees. Habit, pyramidal or bushy. Leaves, needle-shaped, narrow, scale-like. CULTURE : Soil, good ordinary. Position, open, well-drained shrubberies or lawns for erect species, rockeries or banks for dwarf species. Plant, Sept., Oct., or April. PROPAGATION : By seeds sown ½ in. deep in beds of light soil in cold frame in April, transplanting seedlings singly into small pots when 2 in. high and planting outdoors a year afterwards ; cuttings of young branches inserted in sandy soil in cold frame or under hand-light in Sept. or Oct.
SPECIES CULTIVATED : J. chinensis, to 60 ft., China and Japan, and its varieties aurea (leaves golden) and japonica (dwarf); communis (Common Juniper), 30 to 40 ft., Europe, and its varieties fastigiata (Irish Juniper) and compressa (very dwarf); excelsa, 6 to 12 ft., Asia Minor ; excelsa stricta (upright growing) ; sabina (Savin), 5 to 10 ft., Europe and N. America, and its variety tamariscifolia (spreading habit) ; squamata, 2 ft., Himalayas and China ; thurifera (Incense Juniper), 30 to 40 ft., S.W. Europe and N. Africa ; virginiana (Red Cedar), 40 to 50 ft., N. America, and its varieties bedfordiana (columnar), aureo variegata (golden variegated), glauca (blue foliage), and pendula (branches drooping).

Jupiter's-flower (*Lychnis Flos-Jovis*)—See Lychnis.

Justicia—Ord. Acanthaceæ. Stove flowering and orn. foliage plant. First introduced 1824.
CULTURE : Compost, equal parts peat, loam, leaf-mould and sand. Position, well-drained pots in light stove Sept. to June, sunny frame June to Sept. Pot, March or April. Water moderately Sept. to March, freely other times. Temp., Sept. to March 55° to 65° ; March to June, 65° to 75°. Prune shoots to 1 in. of base after flowering. Nip off points of young shoots occasionally May to Aug. to induce bushy growth. Apply liquid or artificial manure twice a week to plants in flower. PROPAGATION : By cuttings of young shoots inserted singly in small pots of sandy soil under bell-glass in temp. 75°, March to July.
SPECIES CULTIVATED : J. calycotricha (Syn. flavicoma), yellow, winter, 2 ft., Brazil. See also the genus Jacobinia.

Kadsura—Ord. Magnoliaceæ. Half-hardy climbing, flowering shrub. Evergreen. First introduced 1860. Flowers succeeded by scarlet berries.
CULTURE : Soil, peaty. Position, well-drained borders against S. or W. walls. Plant, Sept., Oct., or April. Prune straggling shoots moderately in April.
PROPAGATION : By cuttings of firm shoots 2 to 3 in. long, inserted in silver sand under bell-glass in cold greenhouse or frame, July to Oct.
SPECIES CULTIVATED : K. japonica, yellowish white, June to Sept., climbing, Japan and Corea, and its variety variegata (leaves variegated creamy white).

Kæmpferia—Ord. Zingiberaceæ. Stove herbaceous perennials. Orn. foliage. First introduced 1728. Flowers, fragrant. Leaves, egg or lance-shaped, green bordered or flaked with white above and purple benwath.
CULTURE : Compost, equal parts fibrous loam and peat with little silver sand and charcoal. Position, well-drained pots in light part of stove during growing period ; on their sides under staging in dry part of house during resting period. Pot, Feb. or March. Water freely March to Sept., keep almost dry afterwards. Temp., March to Sept. 65° to 75° ; Sept. to March 55° to 60°. Growing period, Feb. to Oct. Resting period, Oct. to Feb.
PROPAGATION : By division of root stocks in Feb.
SPECIES CULTIVATED : K. Gilbertii, leaves variegated white and green, 1 ft., Burma ; Kirkii, rosy purple, Aug., 6 in., Zanzibar ; rotunda, white and violet, Aug., 1 ft., India.

Kæmpfer's Iris (*Iris Kæmpferi*)—See Iris.

Kafir Lily—See Clivia and Schizostylis.

Kalmia angustifolia
(Sheep Laurel)

Kerria japonica flore-pleno
(Jew's Mallow)

Kniphofia aloides
(Red-hot Poker)

Lachenalia tricolor
(Cape Cowslip)

Lælia hybrida

Lælio Cattleya hybrida

Lagurus ovatus
(Hare's-tail Grass)

Lapageria rosea

Lapageria rosea albiflora

Lathyrus grandiflorus

Lathyrus latifolius
(Everlasting Pea)

Lavatera Olbia
(Tree Mallow)

Leontopodium alpinum
(Edelweiss)

Leptospermum scoparium
(South Sea Myrtle)

Leucocoryne ixioides
(Glory of the Sun)

Leucojum æstivum
(Summer Snowflake)

Lewisia Howellii
(Bitter-wort)

Liatris pycnostachya
(Button Snake-root)

Kalanchoe—Ord. Crassulaceæ. Greenhouse perennial flowering plants. First introduced 1781. Flowers, fragrant.
CULTURE : Compost, equal parts sandy loam, brick rubble, dried cow manure and river sand. Position, well-drained pots in light greenhouse, close to glass. Pot, March. Water freely April to Aug., moderately Aug. to Nov., very little after-wards. Prune old plants after flowering, shortening shoots to 1 in., and repot when new shoots are 1 in. long. Temp., March to Sept. 55° to 65° ; Sept. to March 45° to 50°.
PROPAGATION : By seeds sown in well-drained pots or pans of sandy soil, just covered with fine mould, in temp. 60° to 70° in March or April, seedlings to be kept close to glass and have little water ; cuttings of shoots 2 to 3 in. long exposed to sun for few days, then inserted in June, July, or Aug. in well-drained pots of sandy soil, placed on greenhouse shelf, and given very little water.
SPECIES CULTIVATED : K. carnea, flesh, summer, 18 in., S. Africa ; flammea, orange-scarlet, summer, 2 ft., Somaliland ; marmorata (Syn. grandiflora), white, summer, 2 ft., Abyssinia.

Kale (Borecole)—See Brassica.

Kalmia (Calico Bush ; American Laurel ; Swamp Laurel ; Mountain Laurel ; Sheep Laurel)—Ord. Ericaceæ. Hardy evergreen or deciduous flowering shrubs. First introduced 1734.
CULTURE : Soil, sandy peat and leaf-mould free from lime or chalk. Position, moist and cool, partially shaded. Plant, Sept., Oct., April, or May. Pruning unnecessary. Foliage of K. latifolia poisonous to cattle.
POT CULTURE : Compost, two parts sandy peat, one part leaf-mould and sand. Position, well-drained pots in greenhouse (temp. 45° to 55°) from Nov. to May ; sunny place outdoors afterwards. Water moderately in winter, freely other times.
PROPAGATION : By seed sown in April or Oct., $\frac{1}{16}$ in. deep, in well-drained shallow pans of sandy peat in cold frame ; cuttings of young shoots inserted in pots of sandy peat under bell-glass in shady cold frame April to Aug. ; layers in spring.
SPECIES CULTIVATED : K. angustifolia (Sheep Laurel), crimson, June, 3 ft., ever-green, N. America, and its varieties nana (dwarf), rosea (pink) and rubra (red) ; cuneata, white, June to July, 3 to 4 ft., deciduous or partially evergreen, South-eastern U.S.A. ; glauca, lilac purple, May, 2 ft., N. America ; latifolia (Calico Bush), rose, summer, 6 to 10 ft., N. America, and its varieties myrtifolia and polypetala.

Kalosanthes—See Crassula and Rochea.

Kangaroo Thorn (*Acacia armata*)—See Acacia.

Kangaroo Vine (*Cissus antarctica*)—See Cissus.

Karatas—Ord. Bromeliaceæ. Stove flowering and orn. foliaged plant. Ever-green. First introduced 1739. Bracts, green, red, or crimson. Leaves, strap-shaped, green above, purplish or whitish beneath, spiny.
CULTURE : Compost, equal parts fibrous loam, rough peat, leaf-mould, and silver sand. Position, well-drained pots in light, moist part of stove. Pot, Feb. or March. Water moderately in winter, freely at other times. Temp., March to Sept. 70° to 80° ; Sept. to March 65° to 75°.
PROPAGATION : By large-sized offshoots inserted singly in small pots of sandy peat, in temp. of 85°, Feb. or April.
SPECIES CULTIVATED : K. Plumieri, purple, summer, 18 in., Tropical America. See also Aregelia, Canistrum and Nidularium, as many species formerly accredited to Karatas are now placed in these genera.

Kaulfussia—See Charieis.

Kenilworth Ivy (*Linaria cymbalaria*)—See Linaria.

Kennedya (Coral Creeper ; Australian Bean Flower)—Ord. Leguminosæ. Greenhouse flowering and twining plants. Evergreen. Nat. Australia. First introduced 1788.
CULTURE : Compost, equal parts peat and loam, little silver sand. Position, pots, with shoots trained to trellis, or planted out in beds, and shoots trained up rafters.

Pot or plant, Feb. or May.   Water freely March to Sept., moderately at other times. Prune straggling plants into shape in Feb.   Apply weak stimulants occasionally to healthy plants in flower.   Temp., March to Sept. 55° to 65°; Sept. to March 40° to 50°.

PROPAGATION :   By seeds sown ¼ in. deep in well-drained pots of light sandy soil in temp. of 55° to 65° in March or April ; cuttings of firm young shoots, 2 to 3 in. long, inserted in well-drained pots of sandy peat under bell-glass in temp. 55° to 65°, March to July.

SPECIES CULTIVATED :   K. coccinea, scarlet, summer, 10 to 15 ft., Australia ; nigricans, purple-black and green, large climber, Australia ; prostrata, scarlet, spring, prostrate, Australia.   See also the genus Hardenbergia.

Kentia—Ord. Palmaceæ.   Stove palm.   Leaves, feather-shaped, graceful.

CULTURE :   Compost, equal parts loam and peat, little silver sand.   Position, well-drained pots in stove.   Pot, Feb. or March.   Temp., 70° to 85° March to Sept. ; 60° to 65° Sept. to March.   Water moderately Oct. to Feb., freely afterwards. Apply weak liquid manure to healthy plants once a week, May to Sept.   Syringe plants daily.

PROPAGATION :   By seeds sown 1 in. deep in light soil in temp. 80°, Feb. or March.

SPECIES CULTIVATED :   K. australis, 6 to 10 ft., Lord Howe's Island.   See also the genera Howea Hedyscepe and Rhopalostylis.

Kentranthus—See Centranthus.

Kentucky Coffee-tree (*Gymnocladus canadensis*)—See Gymnocladus.

Kermes Oak (*Quercus coccifera*)—See Quercus.

Kerria (Jew's Mallow)—Ord. Rosaceæ.   Hardy deciduous flowering shrub. Nat. Japan.   First introduced 1700.

CULTURE :   Soil, good ordinary.   Position, against S. or W. walls or fences, or in mixed shrubberies.   Plant, Oct. to March.   Prune in May or June, cutting off old or weak shoots only.

POT CULTURE :   Compost, two parts loam, one part leaf-mould and sand.   Pot, Oct. Place in cold greenhouse and water moderately.   After flowering place plants in sunny position outdoors till Oct.   Forcing : place plants in temp. 55° to 65° in Jan.   Water moderately.   Transfer plants to sunny position outdoors after flowering.

PROPAGATION :   By cuttings of young shoots 2 to 3 in. long, inserted in sandy soil under bell-glass or hand-light or in cold frame in summer ; layering shoots in spring.

SPECIES CULTIVATED :   K. japonica, yellow, May, 6 to 10 ft., China, and its varieties flore-pleno (double), variegata (silver variegated) and variegata aurea (golden variegated).   See also Rhodotypos.

Kidney Bean (*Phaseolus vulgaris*)—See Phaseolus.

Kidney-bean-tree (*Wistaria sinensis*)—See Wistaria.

Kidney Fern (*Trichomanes reniforme*)—See Trichomanes.

Kidney Vetch—See Anthyllis.

Killarney Fern (*Trichomanes radicans*)—See Trichomanes

Kilmarnock Willow (*Salix Caprea pendula*)—See Salix.

King Fern (*Osmunda regalis*)—See Osmunda.

King-plant—See Anæctochilus.

King's Flower (*Eucomis regia*)—See Eucomis.

King's Spear—See Asphodelus.

Kitaibelia—Ord. Malvaceæ.   Hardy perennial herb.   Flowering and orn. foliage. First introduced 1801.   Foliage, vine-like.

CULTURE :   Soil, ordinary.   Position, open, large border or shrubbery.   Plant, Oct. or April.

PROPAGATION : By division of roots in Oct. or April ; seeds sown outdoors in April.

SPECIES CULTIVATED : K. vitifolia, white and rose, summer, 6 to 8 ft., E. Europe.

Kleinia (Candle Plant)—Ord. Compositæ. Greenhouse perennials with fleshy cylindrical bluish-grey leaves. K. articulata (Candle Plant) a curious and interesting plant for culture in windows. K. repens used for carpet bedding in summer. First introduced 1759.

CULTURE : Compost, equal parts loam, peat, leaf-mould, broken crocks, and silver sand. Pot in spring. Position, sunny part of greenhouse or near windows in rooms. Temp., Oct. to March 45° to 50° ; March to Oct. 55° to 60°. Water sparingly Oct. to March, freely in summer. For outdoor culture, plant out late in May and lift again in Oct.

PROPAGATION : By cuttings of shoots dried for a few hours before insertion and then inserted in gritty compost any time during summer.

SPECIES CULTIVATED : K. articulata (Syn. Cacalia articulata), Candle Plant, yellow, 18 in., summer, S. Africa ; ficoides, white, summer, creeping, S. Africa ; fulgens, orange and red, May, 2 ft., S. Africa ; Galpini, orange, autumn, 1 ft., S. Africa ; neriifolia, yellow, winter, 4 ft., Canaries ; pendula, vermilion and orange, autumn, Somaliland ; repens, white, June, creeping, S. Africa.

Knee Holly (*Ruscus aculeatus*)—See Ruscus.

Knight's Star Lily (*Hippeastrum equestre*)—See Hippeastrum.

Kniphofia (Red-hot Poker Plant ; Torch Lily ; Club Lily)—Ord. Liliaceæ. Hardy herbaceous perennials. Plants of noble aspect and with showy flowers borne in spikes on tall stems. Formerly known under the generic name of Tritoma.

CULTURE : Soil, sandy, well enriched with manure. Position, sunny well-drained borders. Plant, Nov. or April. Top-dress annually in April with well-decayed manure. Water freely in dry weather during spring and summer. Apply liquid manure once a week to established plants in summer. Protect in severe weather by covering of dry leaves or straw. Dwarf species suitable for the rock garden.

PROPAGATION : By seeds sown ⅛ in. deep in sandy soil in shallow boxes in cold frame in March or April ; transplanting seedlings outdoors when large enough to handle ; division of roots in Nov. or April.

SPECIES CULTIVATED : K. aloides (Syn. Tritoma uvaria), red and yellow, autumn, 4 ft., S. Africa, and its varieties nobilis (large), grandis (broad, short flower spike), grandiflora (good form), and many named varieties and hybrids to be found in trade lists ; Burchellii, scarlet, yellow and green, autumn, 3 ft., S. Africa ; caulescens, reddish salmon, July, 4 to 5 ft., S. Africa ; comosa, apricot yellow, Sept., 2 ft., Abyssinia ; corallina, scarlet, autumn, 3 ft., hybrid ; erecta, coral scarlet, Aug. to Sept., 4 to 5 ft., origin unknown ; Leitchlinii, red and yellow, Aug., 4 ft., Abyssinia ; Macowani, orange-red, Aug., 2 ft., S. Africa ; Nelsoni, orange-scarlet and yellow, Aug. 18 to 24 in., Orange River Colony ; Northiæ, yellow and red, July, 4 to 5 ft., S. Africa ; pauciflora, canary yellow, Aug., 1½ to 3 ft., Natal ; præcox, red and yellow, May to June, 3 to 4 ft., S. Africa ; pumila, orange-red, Aug., 18 in., S. Africa ; Rooperi, orange-red, summer, 2 ft., Kaffraria ; rufa, red and yellow, Aug., 2 ft., Orange River Colony ; Tuckii, yellow and red, June, 4 ft., Cape Colony ; Tysoni, rosy scarlet and yellow, Aug., 3 to 4 ft., S. Africa.

Knotted Marjoram (*Origanum Marjorana*)—See Origanum.

Knotweed—See Polygonum.

Kochia (Summer or Mock Cypress)—Ord. Chenopodiaceæ. Hardy orn.-leaved annual. Flowers, uninteresting. Leaves, narrow and green, changing to a brilliant crimson-purple tint in early autumn.

CULTURE : Soil, ordinary. Position, sunny borders. Sow seeds in light soil in a temp. of 55° in March ; transplant seedlings into pots or boxes, harden off in a cold frame, and plant out 2 ft. apart each way in June.

SPECIES CULTIVATED : K. scoparia trichophylla, 2 to 3 ft., Europe.

Kœlreuteria—Ord. Sapindaceæ. Hardy deciduous flowering tree. Nat. N. China. First introduced 1763. A graceful tree for lawn or shrubbery. CULTURE : Soil, ordinary. Position, open but sheltered. Plant, Oct. to March. Pruning unnecessary. PROPAGATION : By cuttings of young shoots inserted in sandy soil under hand-light or in cold frame in April or May ; layering branches in spring. SPECIES CULTIVATED : K. paniculata, yellow, July, 30 to 60 ft., China.

Kœniga—See Alyssum maritimum.

Kohl-Rabi—See Brassica.

Kolpakowsky's Tulip (*Tulipa kolpakowskyana*)—See Tulipa.

Korolkow's Tulip (*Tulipa Korolkowi*)—See Tulipa.

Kramer's Lily (*Lilium Krameri*)—See Lilium.

Kum-quat (*Citrus aurantium japonica*)—See Citrus.

Labichea—Ord. Leguminosæ. Greenhouse flowering shrub. Evergreen. Nat. Australia. First introduced 1840. CULTURE : Compost, equal parts peat, loam, and sand. Position, well-drained pots in light, sunny greenhouse. Pot, March. Prune into shape, Feb. Water moderately Oct. to April ; freely afterwards. Temp., March to Sept. 55° to 65° ; Sept. to March 45° to 55°. Requires plenty of air April to Oct. PROPAGATION : By cuttings of firm shoots inserted in sand under bell-glass in cool greenhouse, June to Aug. SPECIES CULTIVATED : L. lanceolata, yellow, spring, 4 to 6 ft.

Labrador Tea-plant (*Ledum latifolium*)—See Ledum.

Laburnum (Golden Chain)—Ord. Leguminosæ. Hardy deciduous flowering trees. First introduced 1596. CULTURE : Soil, ordinary. Position, sunny shrubberies. Plant, Oct. to March. Prune directly after flowering. May also be trained over pergolas, arches, etc. Seeds are poisonous. PROPAGATION : By seeds sown ¼ in. deep outdoors in March or April ; by layers, Oct. or Nov. ; varieties by grafting in March ; or budding in July on common species. SPECIES CULTIVATED : L. Adami (Purple Laburnum), yellow or purple, spring, 15 to 20 ft., a graft hybrid between Cytisus purpureus and Laburnum vulgare, often has its racemes of flowers half yellow and half purple ; alpinum (Scotch Laburnum), yellow, June, 15 to 20 ft., Europe ; vulgare (Common Laburnum or Golden Chain), yellow, spring, 20 to 30 ft., Europe, and its varieties foliis-aureis or aureum (golden-leaved), quercifolium (Oak-leaved), Carlieri (long racemes), and pendulum (weeping). L. Parksi, L. Vossi and L. Watereri are fine yellow-flowered hybrids between L. alpinum and L. vulgare.

Lace-bark Pine (*Pinus bungeana*)—See Pinus.

Lace Fern (*Cheilanthes myriophylla*)—See Cheilanthes.

Lace-leaf Plant (*Ouvirandra fenestralis*)—See Ouvirandra.

Lachenalia (Cape Cowslip ; Leopard Lily)—Ord. Liliaceæ. Greenhouse bulbous flowering plants. Deciduous. Nat. S. Africa. First introduced 1752. CULTURE : Compost, two parts fibrous sandy loam, half part leaf-mould, half part decayed cow manure, and one part river or coarse silver sand. Position, well-drained pots, pans, or baskets ; light. Pot, Aug., placing six bulbs ½ in. deep in a 5 in. pot or 1 to 2 in. apart in pans or baskets. After potting water and place pots in cold frame until Nov., then remove to airy shelf in greenhouse. Temp., 45° to 55°. Water moderately when growth begins ; freely when well advanced. Apply weak stimulants occasionally when flower spikes form ; discontinue when in bloom. After flowering gradually withhold water, place pots in sunny position outdoors, and keep quite dry to ripen bulbs. Growing period, Sept. to June ; resting period, June to Sept. Forcing (L. tricolor) : Pot and treat as above until Nov., then remove into temp. of 55° to 65°.

PROPAGATION : By offsets, removed and placed in separate pots at potting time.

SPECIES CULTIVATED : L. Nelsoni, yellow, April to May, 9 to 12 in., hybrid ; pendula, yellow, red, and purple, April to May, 8 to 12 in. ; tricolor (Syns. L. aurea and L. luteola), red and yellow, spring, 1 ft., and its variety quadricolor (yellow, green, and reddish purple). Many fine named hybrids are to be found in trade lists.

Lactuca (Flowering and Edible Lettuce)—Ord. Compositæ. Hardy border perennials and salad vegetables. Edible lettuce introduced 1562.

CULTURE OF FLOWERING LETTUCE : Soil, sandy loam. Position, open, sunny, dryish border. Plant, Oct. or March.

PROPAGATION : Flowering lettuce by seeds sown ⅛ in. deep outdoors in April ; division of roots in March.

CULTURE OF EDIBLE LETTUCE : Soil, light, rich, deeply dug, well manured. Position, south borders for spring and winter crops ; open, sunny for summer crops. Sow seeds ⅛ in. deep in light soil in temp. 65° in Jan., Feb., or March, for planting outdoors in March, April, and May ; in bed of rich soil in sunny spot outdoors in March, April, May, and June, for planting out in April, May, June, and July ; outdoors in Aug. and Sept., for planting out in Sept. and Oct. ; in cold frames in Oct., for planting out in March. Plant, 10 in. apart in rows 12 in. asunder. Blanch cos varieties by tying bast round outside a week before required for use. Surround each newly planted seedling with a cordon of soot or lime. Water freely when first planted, if weather dry. Cabbage varieties best for poor dry soil ; cos for heavy and rich soil. Suitable artificial manures : Superphosphate of lime applied before planting at the rate of 1½ lb. per square rod ; nitrate of soda when plants begin to grow freely, at rate of 1 lb. to square rod, giving two applications at intervals of a fortnight. For producing seed, plant in poor soil in April or May. Seed retains vegetative powers for about four years. Crop reaches maturity in 10 or 12 weeks.

SPECIES CULTIVATED : L. alpina (Syn. Mulgedium alpinum), blue, Aug., 3 ft., N. Europe ; gigantea, pale blue and pink, July to Sept., 5 ft., garden variety ; Plumieri (Syn. Mulgedium Plumieri), purple, summer, 8 ft., Pyrenees ; sativa, yellow, summer, 3 to 4 ft., the cultivated lettuce of gardens and probably an evolutionary form of L. Scariola, a European (British) species, and its varieties angustana (asparagus lettuce), capitata (cabbage lettuce), crispa (curled lettuce) and longifolia (cos lettuce).

Ladder Fern (*Nephrolepis exaltata*)—See Nephrolepis.

Lad's-love (*Artemisia Abrotanum*)—See Artemisia.

Lady Fern (*Asplenium Filix-fœmina*)—See Asplenium.

Lady Grass (*Phalaris arundinacea variegata*)—See Phalaris.

Lady-in-the-Bower (*Nigella damascena*)—See Nigella.

Lady Orchis (*Orchis purpurea*)—See Orchis.

Lady's Bower (*Clematis vitalba*)—See Clematis.

Lady's Fingers (*Anthyllis Vulneraria*)—See Anthyllis.

Lady's Garters (*Phalaris arundinacea variegata*)—See Phalaris.

Lady's Hair (*Briza media*)—See Briza.

Lady's Mantle—See Alchemilla.

Lady's Pincushion (*Armeria maritima*)—See Armeria.

Lady's Seal (*Polygonatum multiflorum*)—See Polygonatum.

Lady's Slipper (*Cypripedium Calceolus*)—See Cypripedium.

Lælia—Ord. Orchidaceæ. Stove orchids. Evergreen. First introduced 1831.

CULTURE : Compost, fibrous peat, osmunda fibre and chopped sphagnum moss equal parts with a liberal addition of sand and finely broken crocks. Position, pots, pans, or hanging baskets, or on blocks with moss only. Pot or reblock, Feb. or

March. Fill pots two-thirds with broken crocks and keep plants well above rim. Secure plants and moss to blocks by means of copper wire. Water pot and basket plants frequently, March to Aug. ; moderately, Aug. to Nov. and Feb. to March ; little other times. Plants on blocks daily March to Aug. ; and twice a week Aug. to Nov. and Feb. and March ; once a week other times. Syringe freely in summer. Temp., March to Sept. 75° to 85° ; Sept. to March 60° to 70°. Growing period, spring to winter. Resting period, winter. Mexican species require a longer resting period in temp. 50° to 55° and plenty of sun during the summer months. Flowers appear top of new pseudo-bulb.

PROPAGATION : By division of pseudo-bulbs at potting time.

SPECIES CULTIVATED : L. albida, white and rose, fragrant, winter, Mexico ; anceps, rose, crimson, purple, and yellow, winter, Mexico, and its varieties alba (white), amesiana (white and purple), sanderiana (white and crimson), Schroderæ (deep purple), and Stella (white) ; autumnalis, rose, purple, white and yellow, fragrant, autumn, Mexico ; cinnabarina, red, spring, Brazil ; crispa, white and purple, autumn, Brazil ; flava, orange yellow, May to June, Brazil ; gouldiana, rosy lilac, purple and white, Nov., Mexico ; harpophylla, orange, April and May, Brazil ; jongheana, rose-purple and yellow, Feb. to April, Brazil ; monophylla, orange-scarlet and purple, autumn, Jamaica ; Perrinii, rosy purple, magenta and yellow, autumn, Brazil ; pumila, rosy purple, Sept. and Oct., Brazil, and its varieties dayana (purple) and præstans (deep purple) ; purpurata, white, yellow and rosy purple, spring, Brazil ; speciosa (Syn. L. majalis), rose-violet, April to May, Mexico ; superbiens, rose, lilac, purple and yellow, winter, Guatemala ; tenebrosa, coppery bronze and purple, spring, Bahia. Numerous hybrids. See trade lists for other species and hybrids.

Lælio-Cattleya—A race of orchids obtained by the inter-crossing of species of the genus Cattleya with those of the genus Lælia. This new race of bigeneric hybrids require the same cultural conditions as Cattleyas, which see. Upwards of 300 to 400 hybrids have been obtained, and their names will be found in trade lists.

Lagenaria (Bottle Gourd ; Trumpet Gourd)—Ord. Cucurbitaceæ. Hardy orn. fruiting annual. Nat. Trop. Asia and Africa. First introduced 1597. Fruit, not edible, oblong, bottle-like, 1 to 6 ft. long.

CULTURE : Soil, rich ordinary. Position, beds at foot of low sunny walls, fences, or arbours, or on the summit of sunny banks, shoots growing at will. Plant, June. Water freely and apply stimulants when fruit has formed. No pinching of shoots required. May also be grown in pots in sunny greenhouses, training shoots up roof.

PROPAGATION : By seeds sown ½ in. deep in light soil in temp. 55° to 65° in April.

SPECIES CULTIVATED : L. vulgaris, white, summer, 10 ft.

Lagerstrœmia (Indian Lilac ; Queen's Flower)—Ord. Lythraceæ. Stove and greenhouse evergreen flowering shrubs. First introduced 1792.

CULTURE : Compost, equal parts loam and peat, little sand. Position, well-drained pots in light part of greenhouse or stove. Pot, Feb. or March. Prune, slightly in Oct. or Nov. Water freely March to Oct. ; very little Oct. to March. Syringe twice daily March to Sept. Temp., stove species, 55° to 60° Oct. to March ; 65° to 75° March to Oct. ; greenhouse species, Oct. to March 45° to 55° ; March to Oct. 60° to 70°.

PROPAGATION : By cuttings of firm shoots inserted in sandy peat under bell-glass , in temp. of 70° to 80° in March, April, Aug., or Sept.

STOVE SPECIES : L. Flos-Reginæ (Queen's Flower), rosy purple, summer, 50 to 60 ft., Trop. Asia.

GREENHOUSE SPECIES : L. indica (Indian Lilac), pink, summer, 6 to 10 ft., Trop. Asia ; indica alba, white.

Lagurus (Hare's-tail Grass)—Ord. Gramineæ. Hardy orn. annual grass. Inflorescence borne in egg-shaped heads, white, downy ; June to Sept. Very useful in dried state for winter decorations.

CULTURE : Soil, ordinary. Position, open dryish borders. Gather inflorescence for drying in Aug.

PROPAGATION : By seeds sown ¼ in. deep outdoors in April where plants are required to grow, or in well-drained pans of light soil in cold frame in Oct., planting outdoors in April.

SPECIES CULTIVATED : L. ovatus, 1 ft., S. Europe (Britain).

Lamarckia—Ord. Gramineæ. Hardy orn. annual grass. First introduced 1770. Inflorescence plume-like, silky and golden ; June to Sept. Useful in a dried state for winter decorations.

CULTURE : Soil, ordinary. Position, patches in open sunny borders. Gather inflorescence for winter use in Aug.

PROPAGATION : By seeds sown ¼ in. deep outdoors in April where plants are required to grow, or in well-drained pans of light soil in cold frame in Oct., planting outdoors in April.

SPECIES CULTIVATED : L. aurea, 8 in., S. Europe.

Lamb Mint (*Mentha viridis*)—See Mentha.

Lamb's Ear (*Stachys lanata*)—See Stachys.

Lamb's Lettuce (*Valerianella olitoria*)—See Valerianella.

Lamb's Tongue (*Stachys lanata*)—See Stachys.

Lamb's Skin—See Arnica.

Lamium (Dead-Nettle)—Ord. Labiatæ. Hardy perennial herb. Flowering and orn. foliage. Leaves, egg- or heart-shaped, with serrated margins.

CULTURE : Soil, ordinary. Position, dryish, sunny borders. Very effective dwarf edging plant for borders in summer. Plant, Oct. or April.

PROPAGATION : By division of roots, Oct. or March.

SPECIES CULTIVATED : L. maculatum aureum, leaves variegated with golden yellow, 1 ft., Europe (Britain).

Land Cress (*Barbarea præcox*)—See Barbarea.

Lantana (Jamaica Mountain Sage ; Surinam Tea-plant)—Ord. Verbenaceæ. Greenhouse and half-hardy evergreen flowering shrubs. First introduced 1690.

POT CULTURE : Compost, two parts loam, one part peat, leaf-mould, or decayed manure, little sand, and charcoal. Position, well-drained pots in light greenhouse. Pot, firmly, March. Water freely April to Oct. ; moderately Oct. to April. Prune into shape, Feb. Temp., Oct. to March 45° to 55° ; March to Oct. 55° to 65°. Apply weak stimulants once or twice weekly, May to Sept.

OUTDOOR CULTURE : Soil, rich sandy. Position, sunny, dryish beds or borders. Plant, June. Lift in Sept. ; repot and replace in greenhouse for winter.

PROPAGATION : By seeds sown ⅟₁₆ in. deep in well-drained pots or pans of sandy peat and leaf-mould, in temp. of 70° to 80°, in Feb., March or April ; by cuttings of firm shoots, 2 to 3 in. long, inserted in small pots of sandy peat under bell-glass in temp. of 55° to 65° in Aug. or Sept. ; or by cuttings of young side shoots 2 in. long inserted as above in temp. 60° to 70°, March or April.

SPECIES CULTIVATED : L. Camara, violet, summer, 4 ft., Trop. America ; nivea, white, summer, 2 to 3 ft., Trop. America ; sellowiana, rosy lilac, summer, 3 ft., S. America. Numerous varieties superior to species in trade lists.

Lantern-flower (*Abutilon Darwinii*)—See Abutilon.

Lapageria—Ord. Liliaceæ. Greenhouse and half-hardy flowering climber. Evergreen. Nat. Chile. First introduced 1847.

INDOOR CULTURE : Compost, three parts fibrous peat, one part loam, one part equal proportions of sand and charcoal. Position, shady in large well-drained pots, tubs, beds, or borders, with shoots trained to trellises or up walls or rafters of greenhouse. Pot or plant, Feb. or March. Good drainage very essential. Water freely April to Sept. ; moderately afterwards. Syringe daily from March until flowers develop. Prune away dead or sickly shoots only in March. Ventilate freely April to Oct. Temp., Oct. to March 40° to 50° ; March to Oct. 55° to 65°. Foliage must be kept free from insects.

OUTDOOR CULTURE : Soil, equal parts peat and loam. Position, west walls, sheltered, in S. of England only. Plant, Oct. or March, in well-drained bed. Protect in severe weather. Water freely in dry weather.

PROPAGATION : By seeds sown ⅛ in. deep in well-drained pots or pans of sandy peat and leaf-mould in temp. of 55° to 65° in March or April ; by layering strong shoots in sandy peat in spring or autumn.

SPECIES CULTIVATED : L. rosea, rose, summer, 15 to 20 ft., and its varieties albiflora, (white), and superba (crimson).

Lapeyrousia—Ord. Iridaceæ. Hardy and half-hardy bulbous flowering plants. Nat. Cape of Good Hope. First introduced 1791.

OUTDOOR CULTURE : Soil, sandy loam and leaf-mould. Position, sunny well-drained borders or rockeries. Plant bulbs 4 in. deep and 3 in. apart, Sept. to Oct.

POT CULTURE : Compost, equal parts sandy loam, leaf-mould, and sand. Position, cold frame Sept. to Feb. ; cool or cold greenhouse afterwards. Pot, Sept., placing six bulbs in a 6 in. pot, and cover with cinder ashes till growth begins. Water moderately when new growth commences ; keep dry after flowering till potting time.

PROPAGATION : By offshoots removed at planting or potting time and treated as old bulbs.

SPECIES CULTIVATED : L. cruenta (Syn. Anomatheca cruenta), crimson, summer, 1 ft., hardy ; grandiflora, red and yellow, summer, 1 ft., tender, best grown in pots.

Larch (*Larix europæa*)—See Larix.

Lardizabala—Ord. Berberidaceæ. Half-hardy evergreen flowering climber. Orn. foliage. Nat. Chile. First introduced 1844.

CULTURE : Soil, equal parts sandy loam and peat. Position, well-drained border at base of S. or W. walls in mild districts. Plant, Sept., Oct., March, or April. Prune away dead or straggly shoots only in April. Suitable also for growing against walls in cold greenhouses or conservatories.

PROPAGATION : By cuttings of firm shoots, 1 to 2 in. long, inserted in sandy loam and peat in well-drained pots under bell-glass in temp. 45° to 55°, July or August.

SPECIES CULTIVATED : L. biternata, purple, autumn, 15 to 20 ft.

Larix (Larch)—Ord. Coniferæ. Hardy deciduous trees. Grown largely for timber purposes. First introduced 1629.

CULTURE : Soil, gravelly, stony, or any except heavy clay. Position, hill slopes or banks, sheltered from north ; low, damp situations not suitable. Plant in autumn. Distance for planting, 3 to 4 ft. each way. Also make fine specimen trees planted singly on lawns or in open places. Best age to plant, two years old. Land best trenched a good spit deep before planting. Number of trees required to plant an imperial acre at 3 ft., 4,840 ; at 4 ft., 2,722. Thinning should commence at five years old. Each imperial acre should contain about 1,200 trees at tenth year ; 900 at fifteenth year ; 600 at twentieth year ; 450 at twenty-fifth year ; and 300 in thirtieth year ; latter number to be permanent crop. Trees attain maturity when 30 to 70 years old. Bears seed when 30 to 40 years old. Number of seeds in a pound, 5,000. Weight of a bushel of seed, 14 lb. Weight of timber per cubic foot, 38 lb. Timber used for fencing, pit wood, scaffold poles, and boat building. Quantity of seeds to sow 100 ft. square of bed, 8 oz.

PROPAGATION : By seeds sown 1 in. deep in March. Transplant seedlings when two years old.

SPECIES CULTIVATED : L. americana (Tamarack) ; dahurica, 50 to 80 ft., Siberia ; europæa (Common Larch), 60 to 120 ft., Europe, and its varieties pendula and sibirica (Siberian Larch) ; Griffithii (Sikkim Larch), 40 to 60 ft., Himalayas ; lepto-lepis (Japanese Larch), also known as japonica, 80 to 100 ft., Japan ; occidentalis (American Larch), 100 to 200 ft., N. America. L. pendula is a hybrid between L. americana and L. europæa.

Larkspur—See Delphinium.

Lasiandra—See Tibouchina.

Libertia ixioides

Ligustrum ovalifolium aureum
(Golden Privet)

Lilium auratum

Lilium giganteum
(Giant Lily)

Lilium Martagon
(Turk's Cap Lily)

Lilium pardalinum
(Panther Lily)

Lilium philippinense
formosanum

Limnanthes Douglasii

Linum grandiflorum rubrum
(Flax)

Linum narbonense
(Flax)

Lithospermum rosmarinifolium
(Gromwell)

Lobelia tenuior

Lonicera japonica
(Honeysuckle)

Lunaria annua
(Common Honesty)

Lupinus polyphyllus
(Lupin)

Lycaste Skinneri

Lychnis Cœli rosa
(Rose of Heaven)

Lychnis viscaria
(German Catchfly)

Lasthenia—Ord. Compositæ. Hardy annuals. First introduced 1834.
CULTURE : Soil, ordinary. Position, warm, sheltered rockeries, beds, or borders.
PROPAGATION : By seeds sown ½ in. deep in April where plants are required to grow
for summer flowering ; in Sept. or Oct. similarly for spring flowering.
SPECIES CULTIVATED : L. glabrata (Syn. californica), yellow, summer, 1 ft., Cali-
fornia ; glabrata glaberrima, yellow, June, 1 ft.

Lastrea—See Nephrodium and Aspidium.

Latania—Ord. Palmaceæ. Stove palms. Orn. foliage. Leaves, fan-shaped, bright
green.
CULTURE : Compost, two parts loam, one part peat and a little charcoal and sand.
Position, well-drained pots in shady part of stove. Pot, Feb. or March. Water
freely March to Sept. ; moderately afterwards. Syringe once daily in winter ;.
twice other times. Temp., March to Sept. 65° to 75° ; Sept. to March 55° to 65°.
PROPAGATION : By seeds sown ½ in. deep in rich light soil in temp. of 80° to 90°,.
Feb., March, or April.
SPECIES CULTIVATED : L. Commersonii, 7 ft., Mauritius and Bourbon ; Verschaffeltii
(Syn. L. aurea), 7 ft., Mauritius. See also Livistona borbonica, which is frequently
erroneously named Latania borbonica.

Lathyrus (Everlasting Pea ; Sweet Pea)—Ord. Leguminosæ. Hardy annuals
and herbaceous perennial climbers. Sweet Pea introduced 1700.
CULTURE OF SWEET PEA : Soil, rich ordinary, well manured. Position, groups in
sunny borders, shoots supported by tree branches or bamboo canes ; against sunny
walls or fences ; in sunny window boxes ; in rows in open garden. Sow seeds
three or four in a 3 in. pot in light soil in temp. 55° to 60° in Feb., transplanting
seedlings outdoors in April ; or 2 in. deep and 3 to 6 in. apart in Oct. or March
where plants are to grow. Water liberally in dry weather. Apply liquid manure
once or twice weekly to plants in flower. Remove seed pods as they form, to ensure
plenty of flowers. Grow other annual species thus.
POT CULTURE : Sow four seeds 1 in. deep in 3 in. pots in temp. 55° to 60° in Jan. or
Feb. Compost, two parts loam, one part leaf-mould and sand. Transfer four
seedlings, when 2 in. high, to a 5 in. pot. Support shoots with small tree branches.
or bamboo canes. Water liberally. Apply liquid manure when flowers show.
Grow in cool greenhouse, conservatory, or window when in flower.
EXHIBITION OR SPECIAL CULTURE : Grow in rows 10 ft. apart. Remove trenches.
18 in. wide and 2 ft. deep. Fork into subsoil 2 in. of rotten manure, then fill up
trench to within 2 in. of top with ordinary soil and good loam. Add a handful each
of superphosphate and kainit to each lineal yard of trench and fork in. Sow seeds
1 in. deep and 3 in. apart in Oct., or five seeds in a 3 in. pot of good soil in cold
frames in Oct., and plant out seedlings 4 to 6 in. apart in April. Stake early, using
bamboo canes at least seven feet high. Feed with half-ounce of sulphate of
ammonia to gallon of water. Give 3 gallons to each group or lineal yard of row
once a week. Remove all side growths, keeping each plant to a single stem. Nip
off points of shoots when top of sticks is reached, or, alternatively, untie each plant,
loop the old growth around the bottom of its stake, and allow the growing point
to climb to the top once more. Remove spent blooms daily.
CULTURE OF PERENNIAL SPECIES : Soil, ordinary deep rich. Position, against sunny
walls, fences, arbours, or tree stumps or banks. Plant, Oct., Nov., March, or April.
Apply liquid manure occasionally in summer. Water freely in dry weather. Prune
away stems close to ground in Oct. Top-dress with decayed manure in March.
PROPAGATION : Perennial species by seeds sown in light soil in temp. 55° to 65° in
March, transplanting seedlings outdoors in May ; or outdoors in April ; by division
of roots in March or April.
ANNUAL SPECIES : L. odoratus (Sweet Pea), various, 6 to 10 ft., Italy ; sativus
azureus, blue, summer, 2 ft., S. Europe ; tingitanus (Tangier Pea), purple and red,
summer, 4 to 6 ft., Tangier.
PERENNIAL SPECIES : L. grandiflorus, rosy crimson, summer, 5 ft., S. Europe ;
latifolius (Everlasting Pea), red, crimson, and violet, 8 to 10 ft., Europe ; latifolius
albus, white ; magellanicus (Lord Anson's Pea), purple, June to Sept., 6 to 8 ft.,.

I

Straits of Magellan ; pubescens, pale blue, July to Sept., 3 to 5 ft., Chile ; rotundi-folius, rosy pink, summer, 6 ft., Asia Minor ; splendens, carmine red, summer, California, rather tender ; undulatus (Syn. Sibthorpii), rosy purple, May and June, 2 to 3 ft., Dardanelles ; vernus (Syn. Orobus vernus), purple and blue, spring, 1 ft., Europe.

Lattice-leaf Plant (*Ouvirandra fenestralis*)—See Ouvirandra.

Laurel (*Prunus Laurocerasus*)—See Prunus.

Laurus (Bay Tree ; Sweet Bay ; Victor's Laurel ; Poet's Laurel)—Ord. Laur-aceæ. Hardy evergreen tree. Orn. foliage. First introduced 1562. Flowers, male and female borne on separate trees, yellow, insignificant. Berries, dark purple ; ripe, Oct. Leaves, lance-shaped, dark green, aromatic ; used for flavouring.
CULTURE : Soil, ordinary. Position, open sunny lawns, sheltered shrubberies or borders. Plant, Sept., March, or April. Prune in April.
CULTURE IN TUBS : Compost, two parts loam, one part leaf-mould and sand. Posi-tion, well-drained in summer. Plant, Sept., Oct., March, or April. Place outdoors, Oct. to May. Water very little Oct. to April ; freely afterwards.
PROPAGATION : By cuttings of shoots, 3 to 4 in. long, inserted in sandy soil under hand-lights in shady place outdoors, Aug., Sept., or Oct. ; layering shoots in Sept. or Oct.
SPECIES CULTIVATED : L. nobilis, 20 to 40 ft., S. Europe.

Laurustinus (*Viburnum Tinus*)—See Viburnum.

Lavandula (Lavender)—Ord. Labiatæ. Hardy flowering shrubs. Evergreen. First introduced 1568. Flowers highly esteemed for their fragrance in a dried state, and for distilling for perfumery purposes.
CULTURE : Soil, ordinary light. Position, warm, dry, and sunny. Plant, March or Sept., a foot apart in rows 2 ft. asunder. Water occasionally in dry weather. Prune straggly plants into shape, March or April. Gather blossoms for drying or distilling when they assume a brown colour. Dry slowly in shade and store in dry place. Leaves of all species fragrant.
PROPAGATION : By cuttings of ripened wood with a heel and inserted in ordinary soil in sunny position outdoors in Sept. ; also by seeds sown outdoors in April.
SPECIES CULTIVATED : L. Spica, grey-blue, July to Aug., 3 to 4 ft., Mediterranean Region ; vera, lavender, fragrant, July and Aug., 3 ft., S. Europe. There are several named varieties including Munstead (dwarf) and Grappenhall (giant).

Lavatera (Tree Mallow)—Ord. Malvaceæ. Hardy shrubs and annuals. Flower-ing and orn. foliage. Leaves, hand-shaped, green, or variegated with white.
CULTURE OF SHRUBBY SPECIES : Soil, ordinary. Position, warm, dryish borders. Plant, June.
CULTURE OF ANNUAL SPECIES : Soil, ordinary light rich. Position, sunny beds or borders. Sow seeds ⅛ in. deep where plants are required to grow, in Sept. or April.
PROPAGATION : Shrubby species by seeds sown in pots or boxes of light soil in temp. of 55° to 60° in Feb. or March ; or in sunny position outdoors, April or May ; variegated species by cuttings of young shoots inserted in sandy soil under bell-glass in gentle bottom heat during June or July.
SHRUBBY SPECIES : L. assurgentiflora, purple, summer, 6 to 10 ft., S. California ; arborea (Tree Mallow), purple, autumn, 8 to 10 ft., Europe (Britain), and its variety variegata (leaves variegated with white) ; Olbia, rosy pink, summer and autumn, 6 ft., S. Europe.
ANNUAL SPECIES : L. trimestris, rose, summer, 4 to 6 ft., S. Europe ; trimestris alba, white.

Lavender—See Lavandula.

Lavender Cotton (*Santolina Chamæcyparissus*)—See Santolina.

Lavender Grass (*Molinia cærulea*)—See Molinia.

Lawn Pearl-wort (*Sagina glabra pilifera*)—See Sagina.

Lawn Spurrey—See Sagina.

Lawson's Cypress (*Cupressus lawsoniana*)—See Cupressus.

Lawyer Vine (*Rubus australis*)—See Rubus.

Layia (Tidy-tips Flower)—Ord. Compositæ. Hardy annuals. First introduced 1834.

CULTURE : Soil, ordinary. Position, sunny beds or borders.

PROPAGATION : By seeds sown ⅛ in. deep in light mould in temp. 55° to 65° in April, transplanting seedlings outdoors end of May ; or outdoors in April where plants are required to grow.

SPECIES CULTIVATED : L. calliglossa, yellow, summer, 1 ft., California ; chrysanthemoides (Syn. Oxyura chrysanthemoides), yellow and white, summer, 1 ft., California ; elegans, yellow and white, summer, 1 ft., California ; glandulosa, white, summer, 6 to 18 in., N. America ; platyglossa (Syn. Callichroa platyglossa), yellow, summer, 1 ft., California.

Lead Plant (*Amorpha canescens*)—See Amorpha.

Lead-wort—See Plumbago and Ceratostigma.

Leaf-flowering Cactus (*Epiphyllum truncatum*)—See Epiphyllum.

Leafless Asphodel—See Asphodeline.

Leather-wood (*Cyrilla racemiflora*)—See Cyrilla.

Lebanon Candytuft (*Æthionema coridifolium*)—See Æthionema.

Lebanon Cedar (*Cedrus Libani*)—See Cedrus.

Ledum (Labrador Tea ; Marsh Rosemary)—Ord. Ericaceæ. Hardy flowering shrubs. Evergreen. First introduced 1762.

CULTURE : Soil, equal parts peat, leaf-mould, and sand. Position, open, well-drained beds or borders in company with azaleas, kalmias, etc. Plant, Oct., Nov., or March, disturbing roots as little as possible.

PROPAGATION : By seeds sown ⅛ in. deep in a well-drained pan of sandy peat in a cold frame in March ; by layering in Sept. ; division of roots in Sept. or Oct.

SPECIES CULTIVATED : L. glandulosum, white, spring, 3 to 6 ft., Western N. America ; latifolium (Labrador Tea), white, April, 3 ft., N. America ; palustre (Marsh Rosemary), white, May, 2 ft., N. Europe. See also Leiophyllum.

Leea—Ord. Ampelidaceæ. Stove shrub. Orn. foliage. First introduced 1880. Leaves, feather-shaped, bronzy green, striped with white above and dark red below.

CULTURE : Compost, two parts loam, one part well-decayed manure or leaf-mould and one part sharp silver sand. Position, well-drained pots in shade. Pot, Feb. or March. Temp., March to Sept., 65° to 75° ; Sept. to March, 55° to 65°. Water freely March to Sept., moderately afterwards. Syringe daily April to Aug.

PROPAGATION : By cuttings of side shoots inserted in sandy soil under bell-glass in temp. 75° to 85° in spring.

SPECIES CULTIVATED : L. amabilis, 3 ft., Borneo ; amabilis splendens, superior form.

Leek—See Allium.

Legousia (Venus's Looking Glass)—Ord. Campanulaceæ. Hardy annuals.

CULTURE : Soil, ordinary. Position, sunny beds or borders. Sow seeds in April thinly ⅛ in. deep in patches or lines where required to grow. Thin seedlings when 1 or 2 in. high to 3 to 6 in. apart. Support plants with small twigs when 3 to 6 in. high.

SPECIES CULTIVATED : S. hybrida (Syn. Campanula hybrida), the Corn Violet, blue and lilac, July, 1 ft., Europe ; pentagonia (Syn. Campanula pentagonia), blue, summer, 1 ft., Asia Minor ; perfoliata, blue, June, 12 to 18 in., N. America ; speculum-veneris (Syn. Campanula Speculum), Venus's Looking Glass, purple, summer, 1 ft., Europe. This genus was formerly known as Specularia.

Leiophyllum (Sand Myrtle)—Ord. Ericaceæ. Hardy flowering shrubs. Evergreen. First introduced 1736.

CULTURE : Soil, equal parts peat, leaf-mould, and sand. Position, open margins of well-drained beds or borders. Plant, Oct., Nov., or March.

PROPAGATION : By seeds sown ⅛ in. deep in well-drained pan of sandy peat in a cold frame in March ; by layering in Sept.

SPECIES CULTIVATED : L. buxifolium (Syn. Ledum thymifolium), white, May, 1 ft., Carolina ; buxifolium prostratum (Syn. Lyonii), prostrate growing.

Lemon Grass (*Cymbopogon Martinii*)—See Andropogon.

Lemon Oil-plant (*Citrus medica limonum*)—See Citrus.

Lemon-scented Geranium (*Pelargonium crispum*)—See Pelargonium.

Lemon-scented Gum-tree (*Eucalyptus citriodora*)—See Eucalyptus.

Lemon-scented Thyme (*Thymus citriodorus*)—See Thymus.

Lemon-scented Verbena (*Lippia citriodora*)—See Lippia.

Lemon-tree (*Citrus medica limonum*)—See Citrus.

Lens (Lentils)—Ord. Leguminosæ. Hardy annual. First introduced 1548. Leaves, feather-shaped. Pods, about ¾ in. long, ½ in. broad, containing two seeds. Seeds, edible, used chiefly in soups, etc.
CULTURE : Soil, light c iinary. Position, sunny borders. Sow seeds 2 in. deep and 2 in. apart in drills 18 in. asunder early in April. Allow the plants to grow till quite yellow, then pull up, dry thoroughly in the sun, gather pods and store in a dry place till required for use.
SPECIES CULTIVATED : L. esculenta (Syn. L. culinaris), blue, June to Aug., 1 ft., Orient.

Lenten Rose (*Helleborus orientalis*)—See Helleborus.

Lentils (*Lens esculenta*)—See Lens.

Lent Lily (*Narcissus pseudo-narcissus*)—See Narcissus.

Leonotis (Lion's Ear)—Ord. Labiatæ. Greenhouse and half-hardy flowering shrub. Evergreen. First introduced 1712.
INDOOR CULTURE : Compost, two parts rich loam, one part equal proportions of leaf-mould, charcoal, and silver sand. Position, well-drained pots in light, airy part of greenhouse, Sept. to June ; sunny place outdoors, June to Sept. Pot, March or April. Prune into shape after flowering. Water moderately April to Sept., very sparingly afterwards. Temp., Sept. to April 40° to 50° ; April to June 55° to 65°.
OUTDOOR CULTURE : Soil, sandy loam. Position, warm, sheltered border in mild southern districts only. Plant May. Protect in winter with bracken or straw.
PROPAGATION : By cuttings of shoots inserted in light sandy soil in temp. 55° to 65° in March or April. Young plants require tops of shoots to be removed occasionally.
SPECIES CULTIVATED : L. Leonurus, orange-scarlet, summer, 3 to 5 ft., S. Africa.

Leontice (Lion's Leaf ; Lion's Turnip)—Ord. Berberidaceæ. Hardy tuberous-rooted perennials. First introduced 1597.
CULTURE : Soil, equal parts sandy loam, leaf-mould, and sand. Position, sheltered, sunny rockery. Plant tubers in Sept. or Oct. ; base only of tuber to be buried in the soil, leaving the upper part exposed. Mulch with cocoanut-fibre refuse or decayed leaves in summer and protect tubers with covering of ashes in winter.
PROPAGATION : By offsets, removed and planted in Sept. or Oct.
SPECIES CULTIVATED : L. Alberti (Lion's Turnip), brown and yellow, spring, 6 to 8 in., Turkestan ; Leontopetalum (Lion's Leaf), yellow, spring, 1 ft., Caucasus.

Leontopodium (Edelweiss)—Ord. Compositæ. Hardy perennial herb. First introduced 1776.
CULTURE : Soil, well-drained, sandy. Position, exposed sunny rockeries. Plant, March or April. Protect from heavy rains in autumn and winter by placing a square of glass, supported by sticks at each corner, a few inches above the plants. Gather flowers in Aug. and dry for preserving. Best results are obtained by raising fresh plants from seed annually, or by dividing old plants in spring.
PROPAGATION : By seeds sown in March in a well-drained pan of fine loam, leaf-mould, and granite chips, placed under a hand-light, or in a cold frame in a cool shady spot, transplanting seedlings outdoors in Aug. or Sept. ; by division in April.
SPECIES CULTIVATED : L. alpinum (Edelweiss), yellow, May to July, surrounded by star-shaped, white, cottony involucre, 6 in., Alps.

Leopard-flower (*Belamcanda chinensis*)—See Belamcanda.

Leopard Lily (*Lachenalia tricolor*)—See Lachenalia.

Leopard's-bane (*Doronicum Pardalianches*)—See Doronicum.

Leopard's-bane Groundsel (*Senecio Doronicum*)—See Senecio.

Lepachys (Coneflower)—Ord. Compositæ. Hardy perennials. First introduced 1803.
CULTURE: Soil, ordinary. Position, sunny beds or borders. Plant, Oct. to Nov. or March to April. Sometimes grown as an annual.
PROPAGATION: By seeds sown in well-drained boxes in cool greenhouse or frame during March or April.
SPECIES CULTIVATED: L. columnaris, yellow and brown, late summer, 2 to 2½ ft., N.W. America; pinnata, yellow and brown, late summer, 3 to 5 ft., N. America.

Lepidium (Cress)—Ord. Cruciferæ. Hardy annual. First introduced 1548. Leaves, finely divided, agreeably flavoured and largely used in conjunction with mustard for salads.
OUTDOOR CULTURE: Soil, ordinary. Position, open borders. Sow seeds on surface of soil, water, and cover with mats or boards until they germinate; or in drills ½ in. deep and 6 in. apart. Make first sowing end of March, follow with successional sowings every 10 days until Sept., then cease. Gather for salading when 1 in. high. Two crops sufficient off one piece of ground.
INDOOR CULTURE: Sow seed on surface of light soil in shallow boxes, moisten with tepid water, cover with sheet of paper, slate, or board, and place in warm position in greenhouse or room. Sow for succession every 7 days. Two crops may be grown in same soil. Seeds may be sown on flannel kept moist in a warm room, at any time of year.
SPECIES CULTIVATED: L. sativum (Common Cress), white, 3 to 6 in., Persia. Two varieties—plain and curled.

Leptosiphon—See Gilia.

Leptospermum (South Sea Myrtle)—Ord. Myrtaceæ. Half-hardy evergreen flowering shrub. First introduced 1876.
CULTURE: Soil, equal parts of peat, loam, and sand. Position, sheltered gardens near the seaside or against a south wall in cold districts. Plant in April or May. Prune slightly in April when required.
PROPAGATION: By cuttings in sandy peat, in pots, in a cold frame in autumn.
SPECIES CULTIVATED: L. scoparium, white, hawthorn-like, fragrant, spring and early summer, 6 to 8 ft., New Zealand, and its variety Nicholli (carmine red).

Leptosyne—Ord. Compositæ. Hardy annuals and perennials.
CULTURE: Soil, ordinary. Position, sunny well-drained beds or borders. Plant, perennial species in Oct. or March; annual species, May or June.
PROPAGATION: All species by seeds sown ⅛ in. deep in light soil in temp. 65° to 75° in March; transplant seedlings when 1 in. high, 2 in. apart in boxes of light soil, and keep in cool greenhouse till May or June, then plant outdoors.
ANNUAL SPECIES CULTIVATED: L. calliopsidea, yellow, Sept., 18 in., California; Douglasii, yellow, autumn, 1 ft., California; Stillmanii, yellow, autumn, 1 ft., California.
PERENNIAL SPECIES CULTIVATED: L. maritima, yellow, autumn, 1 ft., California.

Leptotes—Ord. Orchidaceæ. Stove epiphytal orchid. First introduced 1831.
CULTURE: Compost, equal parts fibrous peat, sphagnum moss, and charcoal. Position, light, fastened by copper wire to small blocks of teak, and roots covered with sphagnum moss; or in small well-drained pots or teak baskets. Place on blocks, or in pots or baskets in March. Temp., Nov. to Feb. 45° to 55°; March to May 50° to 60°; May to Nov. 55° to 65°. Water once a week Nov. to Feb.; twice Feb. to April; daily April to Nov.
PROPAGATION: By division of plants in March.
SPECIES CULTIVATED: L. bicolor (Syn. Tetramicra bicolor), white and purple, winter, 2 in., Brazil.

Leschenaultia—Ord. Goodenovieæ. Greenhouse flowering shrubs. Evergreen. First introduced 1824.
CULTURE : Compost, two parts fibrous peat and one part silver sand. Pot, March or April. Position, well-drained pots in light, sunny greenhouse. Temp., Sept. to March 40° to 50°; March to Sept. 55° to 65°. Water sparingly Oct. to April, moderately afterwards; use soft water only. Manures or stimulants not required. After flowering nip off the points of the shoots. Repotting only necessary every second year. Firm potting essential. Ventilate freely in fine weather.
PROPAGATION : By cuttings of young growth inserted in sandy peat under bell-glass in temp. 50° to 55° from April to July.
SPECIES CULTIVATED : L. biloba, blue, summer, 1 ft., Australia; biloba major, large-flowered; formosa, scarlet, summer, 1 ft., Australia.

Lespedeza (Bush Clover; Japanese Clover)—Ord. Leguminosæ. Hardy flowering shrubs. Deciduous. First introduced 1789.
CULTURE : Soil, sandy loam. Position, sheltered, sunny borders. Plant, Oct. or Nov., Feb. or March. Prune slightly after flowering.
PROPAGATION : By seeds sown ½ in. deep in light soil in a sheltered position outdoors in Feb. or March; cuttings inserted in heat in spring; layering in spring.
SPECIES CULTIVATED : L. bicolor, rosy purple, Sept., 3 ft., China and Japan; bicolor alba, white; juncea, white and blue, Sept., 2 to 3 ft., Himalayas, China and Siberia; Sieboldii, purple, autumn, 5 ft., China and Japan.

Letter-leaf (*Grammatophyllum speciosum*)—See Grammatophyllum.

Lettuce—See Lactuca.

Leucadendron (Cape Silver Tree)—Ord. Proteaceæ. Greenhouse evergreen tree with silvery silky leaves. In Cape Colony the leaves are utilised for ornamental purposes, especially for painting local scenes thereon. First introduced 1693.
CULTURE : Compost, equal parts sandy loam and peat, with some charcoal and sand. Position, light, airy greenhouse, free from damp in winter. Pot in March. Water moderately in summer; very little in winter. Temp., March to Oct. 60° to 65°; Sept. to March 40° to 50°.
PROPAGATION : By seeds sown in sandy peat in a temp. of 55° to 65° directly they are imported; by cuttings of firm shoots in sand in a temp. of 55° in summer.
SPECIES CULTIVATED : L. argenteum, yellow, Aug., 15 ft., S. Africa.

Leucocoryne (Glory of the Sun)—Ord. Liliaceæ. Half-hardy bulbous-rooted perennial. First introduced 1826.
OUTDOOR CULTURE : Soil, light rich sand. Position, sunny well-drained border. Plant, Sept. to Jan., placing bulbs 4 in. deep and 2 in. apart. Lift and replant annually.
POT CULTURE : Compost, two parts sandy loam and one part leaf-mould. Place five bulbs 3 in. deep in pot 4½ in. in diameter. Plunge pots in cocoanut fibre in cold frame or under staging in cool greenhouse in sunny part of greenhouse or frame. Water moderately from time bulbs commence to grow until flowers fade, then gradually cease, keeping pots dry till growth recommences. Temp., Sept. to March 40° to 50°; March to Sept. 50° to 60°. Pot, Sept. to Oct.
PROPAGATION : By seeds sown in Feb. or March in sandy soil in temp. 55° to 60°; by offsets detached when bulbs are lifted and grown on in same way.
SPECIES CULTIVATED : L. ixioides, pale blue and white, fragrant, March to June, 1½ to 2 ft., Chile.

Leucojum (Snowflake; Summer Snowdrop)—Ord. Amaryllidaceæ. Hardy bulbous plants.
CULTURE : Soil, ordinary rich. Position, Summer Snowflake (L. æstivum) in sunny or shady borders or woodlands; Spring Snowflake (L. vernum) in shady borders or on rockeries. Both may also be naturalised in grass. Plant bulbs 4 in. deep and 3 in. apart, Aug. to Nov. Bulbs do not usually flower first year after planting, and only require to be lifted and replanted every five to eight years.
PROPAGATION : By offsets, removed and replanted in Sept. or Oct.

SPECIES CULTIVATED : L. æstivum (Summer Snowflake), white and green, May, 1 ft., Europe (Britain) ; autumnale (Acis autumnalis), white and pink, autumn, 4 in., Mediterranean Region ; hyemale (Syn. Acis hyemale), white and green, April, 9 in., Italy and S. France ; pulchellum (Syn. L. Hernandezi), white and green, May, 1 ft., Balearic Isles ; roseum, rosy red, Sept. to Oct., 4 in., Corsica ; vernum (Spring Snowflake), white and green, March, 1 ft., Europe ; vernum carpaticum, white and yellow.

Leucophyta—See Calocephalus.

Leucopogon (Australian Currant)—Ord. Epacridaceæ. Greenhouse flowering shrubs. Evergreen. Nat. Australia. First introduced 1815.
CULTURE : Compost, three-fourths fibry peat, one-fourth silver sand. Position, light, airy greenhouse Sept. to July, sunny place outdoors July to Sept. Repot, April, May, or June ; good drainage essential. Water moderately at all times. Syringe plants daily March to July. Temp., Sept. to March 40° to 50° ; March to July 55° to 60°. Stimulants not essential.
PROPAGATION : By seeds sown immediately they ripen on surface of sandy peat under bell-glass in temp. 55° ; cuttings of ends of shoots inserted in pots of sandy peat covered with bell-glass placed in cool greenhouse in Aug. or April.
SPECIES CULTIVATED : L. lanceolatus, white, May, 8 to 10 ft. ; Reichei, white, May, 4 to 6 ft.

Leucothoe—Ord. Ericaceæ. Hardy flowering shrubs. Evergreen. First introduced 1765.
CULTURE : Soil, equal parts peat, leaf-mould, and sand. Position, open, sheltered borders. Plant, Sept., Oct., March, or April. Pruning not necessary.
PROPAGATION : By seeds sown $\frac{1}{8}$ in. deep in sandy peat in cold frame, Feb. or March ; layering shoots in Sept. ; division, Oct. or Nov.
SPECIES CULTIVATED : L. axillaris (Syn. Andromeda axillaris), white, May, 3 ft., S.E. United States ; Catesbæi (Syn. Andromeda Catesbæi), white, May, 3 to 6 ft., Georgia ; Davisiæ, white, July, 1 to 3 ft., California ; racemosa (Syn. Andromeda and Lyonia racemosa), white, May, 6 to 12 ft., N. America.

Lewisia (Bitter-wort ; Spatlum)—Ord. Portulacaceæ. Hardy herbaceous perennials. First introduced 1826.
CULTURE : Soil, equal parts sandy loam, peat, and sand. Position, crevices of moist sunny rockeries. Plant, Sept., Oct., March, or April. Water occasionally in dry weather. Leaves wither at the time of flowering, or may not be produced at all. Growing period above ground, about six weeks.
PROPAGATION : By seeds sown in well-drained pans of sandy loam and peat in a cool shady frame in March or April ; division of the roots in March or April.
SPECIES CULTIVATED : L. Howellii, apricot and rose, June, 3 to 4 in., Oregon ; rediviva, rose, summer, 2 to 3 in., California ; Tweedyi, pink, summer, 4 in., California.

Leycesteria (Himalayan Honeysuckle ; Flowering Nutmeg)—Ord. Caprifoliaceæ. Hardy flowering shrub. Deciduous. First introduced 1824.
CULTURE : Soil, ordinary. Position, sunny, sheltered borders. Plant, Oct., Nov., Feb., or March. Prune into shape in Feb.
PROPAGATION : By seeds sown $\frac{1}{16}$ in. deep in light soil in temp. 45° to 55° in March or April ; cuttings of side shoots inserted in light soil and similar temp. in April, also of firm shoots inserted in sandy soil under hand-light in Sept. or Oct.
SPECIES CULTIVATED : L. formosa, white and purple, May to Aug., succeeded by purple berries, 4 to 6 ft., Himalayas ; formosa variegata, leaves variegated.

Liatris (Button Snake-root)—Ord. Compositæ. Hardy perennial herbs. First introduced 1732.
CULTURE : Soil, light, rich, ordinary. Position, open, sunny beds or borders. Plant, Sept., Oct., March, or April. Cut off decayed stems in Oct. Mulch with decayed manure in April. Water freely in dry weather.
PROPAGATION : By seeds sown $\frac{1}{8}$ in. deep in light sandy soil outdoors in Aug. or

Sept., transplanting seedlings the following May; division of plants in March or April.

SPECIES CULTIVATED : L. elegans, white, July to Sept., 3 to 4 ft., N. America; graminifolia, rosy mauve, July to Sept., 2 to 3 ft., N. America, and its variety dubia (taller) ; ligulistylis, purple, summer, 1 to 1½ ft., Colorado ; pycnostachya, purple, Aug., 3 to 4 ft., N. America ; scariosa, purple, Aug., 2 to 3 ft., N. America ; spicata, purple, Aug., 4 to 5 ft., N. America.

Libertia—Ord. Iridaceæ. Hardy evergreen perennials. Flowering and orn. foliage. First introduced 1823. Leaves, sword-shaped or grass-like, graceful, dark green.

CULTURE : Soil, equal parts sandy loam, peat, and leaf-mould. Position, well-drained sunny borders or, preferably, rockeries. Plant, Sept., Oct., March, or April. Protect, Nov. to April, by covering with dry fern, tree leaves, or strawy manure.

PROPAGATION : By seeds sown ⅛ in. deep in sandy soil in cold frame or greenhouse, Aug. to Nov. ; division of creeping rhizomes, March or April.

SPECIES CULTIVATED : L. formosa, white, June, 2 to 3 ft., Chile ; grandiflora, white, June, 2 to 3 ft., New Zealand ; ixioides, white, June, 2 ft., New Zealand.

Libocedrus (Incense Cedar)—Ord. Coniferæ. Half-hardy evergreen trees. Ornamental foliage. First introduced 1847. Leaves, scale-like, flat, glossy, or milk-green. Habit, pyramidal or column-like. Cones, small, oblong.

CULTURE : Soil, rich loam ; subsoil, gravelly. Position, warm, sheltered ; as single specimens on lawns in mild districts in S. of England only. L. doniana only suitable for conservatory and winter garden cultivation. Plant, Sept. to Nov.

PROPAGATION : By seeds sown ⅛ in. deep in pans of sandy soil in cold frame or greenhouse, Oct. to April ; cuttings of firm shoots or branchlets inserted in sandy soil in cold frame or under hand-light in Aug. or Sept.

SPECIES CULTIVATED : L. chilensis, 60 to 80 ft., Chile ; decurrens (Incense Cedar), 100 to 150 ft., California ; doniana (Syn. L. plumosa), 70 to 100 ft., New Zealand.

Libonia—See Jacobinia.

Licuala—Ord. Palmaceæ. Stove palms. Orn. foliage. First introduced 1802. Leaves, fan-shaped, green.

CULTURE : Compost, two parts peat and one of loam and sand. Position, well-drained pots in light part of stove. Pot, Feb. to April. Water moderately Oct. to March ; freely afterwards. Syringe twice daily March to Sept. ; once daily Sept. to March. Temp., March to Sept. 65° to 75° ; Sept. to March 55° to 65°.

PROPAGATION : By seeds sown ½ in. deep in light rich soil in temp. 80° to 90°, Feb., March, or April.

SPECIES CULTIVATED : L. grandis (Syn. Pritchardia grandis), 10 ft., New Britain ; spinosa (Syn. L. horrida), 10 to 15 ft., Malaya, sometimes erroneously cultivated as L. peltata.

Ligularia—See Senecio.

Ligurian Bell-flower (*Campanula isophylla*)—See Campanula.

Ligustrum (Privet)—Ord. Oleaceæ. Hardy deciduous and evergreen shrubs. Orn. foliage and flowering. Flowers, white, borne in terminal panicles, fragrant. Berries, round, shining, black or yellow. Leaves, oblong, oval, and pointed, green or variegated with white or yellow.

CULTURE : Soil, loam or good ordinary. Position, common species in shrubberies, under shade of trees, in open or as hedges ; others in open shrubberies. Plant, deciduous kinds, Oct. to Feb. ; evergreen kinds, Oct. to April. Prune deciduous kinds in autumn, evergreens in April.

HEDGE CULTURE : Soil, ordinary, trenched two spits deep and 3 ft. wide. Plant privet (1 to 3 ft. high) 6 to 9 in. apart, Oct. to April. Trim into shape, June and July. Privet and hawthorn planted alternately makes a splendid hedge. Varieties suitable, Common Privet (L. vulgare), Oval-leaved Privet (L. ovalifolium), and

Golden Privet (Ovalifolium aureum). Also suitable shrubs for growing in town gardens.
PROPAGATION : By seeds (berries) sown 1 in. deep in open ground in Nov., transplanting largest seedlings the following Oct. ; the remainder next year; cuttings of young shoots, 2 to 4 in. long, inserted in a shady position outdoors or under a handlight in summer ; also cuttings of firm shoots, 8 to 12 in. long, inserted in shady position in ordinary soil outdoors, Sept. to Nov. ; layering shoots in Sept. or Oct.
SPECIES CULTIVATED : L. delavayanum (Syn. L. Prattii), 5 to 6 ft., evergreen, W. Szechuan ; Henryi, 4 to 6 ft., evergreen, Central China ; Ibota (Syn. amurensis), 8 to 10 ft., deciduous, Japan ; japonicum, 6 to 8 ft., evergreen, Japan ; japonicum coriaceum, 3 to 4 ft., evergreen, Japan ; lucidum, 10 to 18 ft., evergreen, China ; lucidum tricolor, variegated ; ovalifolium (Oval-leaved Privet), 6 to 8 ft., semi-evergreen, Japan ; ovalifolium variegatum, leaves blotched with yellow or white ; ovalifolium aureum (Golden Privet), golden-leaved, much used for window boxes and hedges ; Quihoni, 6 to 10 ft., deciduous, China ; sinense, 10 to 20 ft., evergreen, China ; vulgare (Common Privet), 6 to 10 ft., deciduous, Britain.

Lilac (*Syringa vulgaris*)—See Syringa.

Lilium (Lily)—Ord. Lilaceæ. Hardy and half-hardy bulbous flowering plants. First introduced 1596.
CLASSIFICATION OF LILIUMS : Erect, cup-shaped flowers (Isolirion group).—L. bulbiferum, L. concolor and vars., L. dauricum and vars., L. philadelphicum, L. elegans and vars. Trumpet-shaped flowers (Eulirion group).—L. Browni, L. candidum and vars., L. cordifolium, L. giganteum, L. Krameri, L. longiflorum and vars., L. Parryi and L. washingtonianum. Recurved flowers (Martagon group).—L. canadense, L. carolineum, L. chalcedonicum, L. Hansoni, L. Henryi, L. Humboldtii, L. Leichtlinii, L. Martagon and vars., L. monadelphum and var., L. pomponium, L. pyrenaicum, L. superbum and vars., L. tenuifolium, L. testaceum. Flowers drooping (Archelirion group).—L. auratum and vars., L. speciosum and vars., L. trigrinum and vars., and L. roseum.
OUTDOOR CULTURE : Soil, ordinary, with well-decayed leaf-mould and a little sand for Liliums Batemanniæ, bulbiferum, candidum, chalcedonicum, columbianum, croceum, dauricum, elegans, Henryi, longiflorum, martagon, pomponium, pyrenaicum, regale, tigrinum, testaceum, and umbellatum. Lime-free loam, fibrous peat, leaf-mould and sand for Liliums auratum, Browni, concolor, Davidi, Hansoni, Humboldtii, rubellum, speciosum, sulphureum, and tenuifolium. Soil, peaty loam, leaf-mould, and sand, well drained yet with abundant moisture during the summer months, and shady position for Liliums canadense, giganteum, Grayi, Krameri, pardalinum, Parryi, philadelphicum, Roezli, superbum, and washingtonianum. Plant L. candidum in Aug. or Sept. ; others from Oct. to Feb. Lilies should only be transplanted when overcrowded or unhealthy. Plant stem-rooting lilies such as auratum, Batemanniæ, Browni, concolor, croceum, Davidi, elegans, Hansoni, Henryi, Krameri, longiflorum, ochraceum, philadelphicum, philippinense, regale, rubellum, speciosum, sulphureum, tenuifolium, tigrinum, umbellatum, and Willmottiæ 6 in. deep and 6 in. apart and draw soil around the stems as growth progresses. L. giganteum and L. candidum should only be just covered with soil. Other lilies plant 4 in. deep and 6 in. apart. Place a handful of silver sand under each bulb and a little around it. Mulch all lilies with leaf-mould in April. Protect choice kinds during winter with covering of strawy manure. Cut down flower stems when leaves turn yellow. Water in very dry weather. Apply liquid manure once or twice weekly when plants are in flower.
TREATMENT OF IMPORTED BULBS : Remove injured scales and surround bulbs with thin layer of cocoanut-fibre refuse in shallow box in cool position until latter become plump, then plant out.
POT CULTURE : Compost, equal parts loam, leaf-mould, decayed manure, and sand. Pot, Sept. to March, placing one bulb in a 5 or 6 in. pot or three in an 8 or 10 in. pot. For stem-rooting kinds put ¼ drainage, then half fill with compost, place bulbs thereon, and cover with ½ in. of compost. Top-dress with similar compost as growth progresses. Other kinds may be potted about 3 in. deep in the ordinary

I 2

way. After potting place pots in cold frame, greenhouse, or shed and cover with 2 in. of cinder ashes or cocoanut-fibre refuse. Allow them to remain thus till growth begins, then remove to light, airy part of greenhouse or to a window or cool room till they flower, or until June, then stand outdoors. Water moderately when growth begins ; freely when in full growth. Suitable stimulants : Soot-water, guano-water ($\frac{1}{2}$ oz. to a gallon), liquid cow or horse manure. Temp. for forcing L. Harrisii, L. neilgherrense, and L. philippinense, 55° to 65°. Repot L. Harrisii annually in Sept. ; others in Oct. or Nov., and treat as advised for first potting. After flowering place plants in sunny position outdoors, gradually withhold water, and keep quite dry from Oct. to Feb. L. Harrisii should, however, never be kept quite dry—only moderately for six weeks, then watered as before. Species most suitable for indoor culture are Liliums longiflorum, neilgherrense, ochraceum, sulphureum, speciosum and philippinense.

PROPAGATION : By seeds sown $\frac{1}{16}$ in. deep in well-drained pans or boxes of sandy soil in cold frame in autumn or spring, transplanting seedlings when large enough to handle into similar soil in boxes, and in specially prepared bed outdoors when two years old ; offsets or bulbils, planted 1 inch deep and 2 or 3 inches apart in boxes of sandy soil, or in similar soil in sunny cold frame in autumn. Seedlings flower when six to seven years old ; offsets or bulbils when three to five years old.

TENDER SPECIES : Those best grown under glass are : L. longiflorum Harrisii or eximium (Bermuda Lily), white, winter to summer, 3 ft., Japan ; neilgherrense, sulphur yellow, autumn, 3 ft., S. India ; ochraceum (Syn. L. nepalense), yellow and purple, autumn, 3 to 4 ft., Upper Burma ; sulphureum (Syn. L. wallichianum superbum), sulphur yellow and brown, summer, 6 ft., Burma ; philippinense, white, Aug., 2 ft., Philippines ; philippinense formosanum, white and reddish brown, Aug., 2 to 3 ft., Formosa.

HARDY SPECIES : L. auratum, white, yellow and purple, summer, 4 to 5 ft., Japan, and its numerous varieties platyphyllum, virginale, Wittei, etc. ; Batemanniæ, reddish apricot, Aug. to Sept., 3 ft., Japan ; Bolanderi, purple and red, summer, 3 ft., California ; Brownii, white and brown, summer, 3 to 4 ft., China and Japan, and its variety Colchesteri (very fragrant) ; bulbiferum, red, summer, 3 ft., Europe ; canadense, yellow and red, summer, 3 ft., N. America ; candidum (Madonna or Bourbon Lily), white, summer, 4 to 5 ft., S. Europe ; carniolicum, red, summer, 3 ft., Carniola ; centifolium, white, yellow and brown, July to Aug., 5 to 8 ft., China ; chalcedonicum (Turk's Cap Lily), scarlet, summer, 3 ft., Greece ; columbianum, golden yellow and red, July to Aug., 2 to 3 ft., N. America ; concolor, red, summer, 1 to 2 ft., Central China ; cordifolium, white, Aug., 3 ft., Japan ; croceum (Orange Lily), orange, June, 3 ft., S. Europe ; dauricum (Syn. L. davuricum), yellow, red and black, June, 2 to 3 ft., Siberia ; Davidi (Syn. L. pseudo-tigrinum), orange-red and maroon, July to Aug., 4 to 5 ft., Western China ; elegans (Syn. L. thunbergianum), scarlet, July, 1 to 2 ft., Japan, and its numerous varieties ; giganteum (Giant Lily), white, July, 10 to 12 ft., Himalayas ; Grayi, crimson-purple and yellow, July, 2 to 4 ft., Virginia and N. Carolina ; Hansoni, yellow, June, 3 to 4 ft., Corea ; Henryi, orange yellow, July, 6 to 10 ft., China ; Humboldtii, yellow and purple, July, 5 ft., California ; japonicum (Syn. L. Krameri), rose, summer, 2$\frac{1}{2}$ ft., Japan ; Kelloggii, mauve, purple and yellow, July, 2 to 5 ft., California ; longiflorum, white, June, 3 ft., Japan, and its varieties giganteum, formosum and Wilsoni (eximium) ; Leichtlinii, yellow and purple, July, 3 ft., Japan ; Lowii, white and violet, summer, 3 ft., Burma ; Martagon (Turk's Cap Lily), purple, summer, 3 ft., Europe ; Martagon album, white ; monadelphum szovitzianum, yellow, June, 4 ft., Caucasus ; pardalinum (Panther Lily), orange-crimson, July, 4 to 6 ft., California ; Parryi, yellow and brown, summer, 3 ft., California ; parvum, orange yellow and brown, July, 4 ft., California ; philadelphicum, orange and maroon, June to July, 1$\frac{1}{2}$ to 2$\frac{1}{2}$ ft., N. America ; pomponium (Scarlet Pompone Lily), red, May to June, 3 ft., Lombardy ; pyrenaicum, yellow, summer, 3 ft., Pyrenees ; regale, white, gold and rosy purple, July, 3 to 6 ft., Western China ; Roezli, orange and maroon, June, 2 to 5 ft., California ; roseum (Syn. L. thomsonianum), lilac, spring, 1$\frac{1}{2}$ to 3 ft., Himalayas ; rubellum, pink, May, 1 to 2 ft., Japan ; speciosum (Syn. L. lancifolium), white and red, summer, 4 ft., Japan, and its varieties album Kraetzeri,

CULTURE OF ANNUAL SPECIES : Soil, ordinary sandy. Position, sunny borders or rockeries. Sow seeds in well-drained pots filled with sandy loam, cover slightly with fine soil, place in temp. 55° to 65°, Feb. or March. Transplant when large enough to handle ; harden off and plant outdoors in May.

PROPAGATION : By seeds sown in pans of sandy soil in temp. 55° to 60° in Feb. or March ; cuttings of roots inserted in similar soil and cold frame in Feb. or March.

GREENHOUSE SPECIES CULTIVATED : L. profusum, blue, summer, 2 to 3 ft., hybrid ; fruticans, blue, summer, Canaries ; imbricatum, blue, summer, 1½ ft., Teneriffe ; macrophyllum (Syn. L. Halfordii), blue, June, 1 to 2 ft., Canaries.

PERENNIAL SPECIES CULTIVATED : L. bellidifolium (Syn. L. caspium), lavender, summer, 6 in., Europe ; eximium, rosy lilac, summer, 1 ft., Central Asia ; Gmelini, blue and rose, summer, 1 to 2 ft., Caucasus ; incanum, pink and white, summer, 6 to 9 in., Siberia ; latifolium, blue, 2 to 3 ft., Bulgaria, and its variety grandiflorum ; sinense, yellow, summer, 1 ft., China ; tataricum, red and white, summer, 1 ft., Caucasus ; vulgare (Common Sea Lavender), Syn. Statice Limonium, purple, summer, 1 ft., Europe (Britain).

ANNUAL SPECIES CULTIVATED : L. Bonduelli, yellow, summer, 1 to 2 ft., Algeria ; sinuata, blue and cream, summer, 1 to 2 ft., Mediterranean Region, and several colour forms, really a perennial but always grown as an annual ; Suworowi, lilac and pink, summer, 18 in., Central Asia. The genus was formerly known as Statice.

Linaria (Toad-flax)—Ord. Scrophulariaceæ. Hardy perennial sub-shrubs, herbs, and annuals.

CULTURE OF PERENNIAL SPECIES : Soil, ordinary, mixed with grit or old mortar. Position, moist rockeries or margin of borders for L. æquitriloba, L. alpina, L. hepaticæfolia, L. saxatilis, and L. originifolia ; sunny or shady walls for L. cymbalaria and L. pallida ; open, sunny borders for L. dalmatica, L. purpurea, L. vulgaris, and L. triornithophora. Plant, Oct., Nov., March, or April.

CULTURE OF ANNUAL SPECIES : Soil, ordinary. Position, sunny beds or borders. Sow seeds $\frac{1}{16}$ in. deep in patches in April for flowering in summer ; in Aug. for flowering in spring. L. tristis, a pretty dwarf annual for beds or rockeries.

POT CULTURE OF L. CYMBALARIA : Compost, two parts loam, one part of equal proportions of dried cow manure, old mortar, and sand. Sow seeds $\frac{1}{16}$ in. deep in 3 or 5 in. pots in March or April. Place pots in shady window or greenhouse until seedlings appear, then remove to light and suspend in a basket. Water moderately at first, freely afterwards ; keep nearly dry during winter.

PROPAGATION : Perennial species by seeds sown in ordinary soil in sunny position outdoors in Sept., March, or April ; division in Oct. or April.

ANNUAL SPECIES : L. bipartita, red, violet, purple, rose, and white, summer, 1 ft., Algeria ; heterophylla (Syn. L. aparinoides), blue and yellow, summer, 1 to 3 ft., Morocco ; maroccana, red-purple, June, 9 to 12 in., Morocco ; Brousonetti (Syn. L. multipunctata), yellow and brown, summer, 6 in., Algiers ; reticulata, purple and yellow, summer, 2 to 4 ft., Portugal ; tristis, yellow and brown, July, 12 in., Spain.

PERENNIAL SPECIES : L. æquitriloba, pale violet, summer, trailing, Corsica ; alpina, blue, violet, and yellow, summer, 6 in., Alps ; Cymbalaria (Ivy-leaved Toad-flax, Kenilworth Ivy, or Mother o' Millions), lilac, summer, trailing, Britain ; dalmatica, yellow, summer, 3 to 5 ft., Dalmatia ; hepaticæfolia, lilac, summer, trailing, Corsica ; originifolia, violet and orange, summer, 6 to 9 in., S. Europe ; pallida, blue, summer, 3 in., Italy ; purpurea, maroon-purple, summer, 2 to 3 ft., Europe ; saxatilis, yellow and brown, summer, trailing, Spain ; triornithophora, purple and yellow, summer, 1 ft., Portugal ; vulgaris (Common Toad-flax), yellow, summer, 2 ft., Britain.

Lindelofia (Himalayan Lung-wort)—Ord. Boraginaceæ. Hardy perennial herb. First introduced 1839.

CULTURE : Soil, ordinary. Position, sunny well-drained borders. Plant, Oct., Nov., March or April. Cut off flower stems, Sept. Apply weak liquid manure occasionally during flowering period, or dig decayed manure into surface of soil round base of plants in March or April.

PROPAGATION : By seeds sown $\frac{1}{18}$ in. deep in sandy soil in sunny position outdoors in April or May, transplanting seedlings following Aug. or Sept. for flowering the next year ; division of roots in March.
SPECIES CULTIVATED : L. spectabilis, purple, July, 18 in., Himalayas.

Linden Tree (*Tilia europæa*)—See Tilia.

Lindera (Benjamin Bush ; Spice Bush)—Ord. Lauraceæ. Hardy flowering trees. Deciduous and evergreen. First introduced 1683.
CULTURE : Soil, ordinary. Position, open, sunny shrubberies or borders. Plant, Oct. to Feb. Prune into shape when necessary after flowering.
PROPAGATION : By cuttings of shoots, 6 to 8 in. long, inserted in sandy soil in shady, sheltered position outdoors, Oct. to Nov. ; layering in spring.
SPECIES CULTIVATED : L. Benzoin, deciduous, yellow, spring, 15 to 20 ft. ; mega-phylla, evergreen, black fruits, 15 to 20 ft., Central China ; obtusiloba, deciduous, yellow, black fruits, March to April, 20 to 25 ft., Japan and Corea.

Lindsaya—Ord. Filices. Greenhouse evergreen ferns. Fronds, feather-, kidney- or arrow-shaped. First introduced 1813.
CULTURE : Compost, two parts turfy loam, one part lumpy peat, and one part equal proportions of broken crocks, charcoal, and sand. Position, moist, shady part of stove, in wardian case, or under bell-glasses. Pot very firmly in well-drained pots, Feb. or March. Water abundantly March to Oct., moderately afterwards. Temp., March to Sept. 55° to 65° ; Sept. to March 50° to 55°.
PROPAGATION : By spores sown on fine sandy peat, in well-drained pans under bell-glass, in temp. 55° to 65° at any time.
SPECIES CULTIVATED : L. linearis, 6 in., New Zealand ; trichomanoides, 6 in., New Zealand.

Ling (*Calluna vulgaris*)—See Calluna.

Linnæa (Twin-flower)—Ord. Caprifoliaceæ. Hardy trailing flowering shrub. Evergreen.
CULTURE : Soil, sandy peat. Position, moist rockeries or banks, or as edgings to beds of N. American shrubs. Plant, Oct. to March. Water freely in dry weather.
POT CULTURE : Compost, two parts peat and one part leaf-mould and little silver sand. Position, well-drained pots, with shoots trained to trellises or stakes, or suspended in baskets in cool or unheated greenhouse or frame. Pot, Feb. or March. Water freely March to Oct., moderately afterwards.
PROPAGATION : By division of plants in Oct. or March.
SPECIES CULTIVATED : L. borealis, white and pink, fragrant, May to July, N. Europe.

Linseed Oil Plant (*Linum usitatissimum*)—See Linum.

Linum (Flax ; Linseed Oil Plant)—Ord. Linaceæ. Hardy annuals, perennials, and shrubs.
CULTURE OF ANNUAL SPECIES : Soil, ordinary. Position, sunny beds or borders. Sow seeds $\frac{1}{8}$ in. deep in April, in lines or masses where plants are required to flower.
CULTURE OF PERENNIAL SPECIES : Soil, good ordinary. Position, sunny rockeries, borders, or banks. Plant, Oct. to Nov. or Feb. to April.
CULTURE OF HARDY SHRUBBY SPECIES : Soil, sandy loam, leaf-mould, peat, and sand. Position, warm, sheltered rockeries or dry walls. Plant, Oct. or Nov. Prune straggly shoots into shape, March or April.
CULTURE OF L. GRANDIFLORUM IN POTS : Soil, two parts good mould, one part decayed manure and sand. Sow seeds $\frac{1}{16}$ in. deep in April in 6 in. pots filled with above compost to within $\frac{1}{2}$ in. of rim. Place pots in cold frame or shady window till seedlings appear, then remove to full light. Water moderately at first, freely after-wards. Apply weak stimulants when in flower. Support shoots by inserting small twiggy branches between them. Sow again in July, plunging pots to rim in garden soil, and keep well supplied with water to flower in autumn.
PROPAGATION : Perennial species by seeds sown $\frac{1}{2}$ in. deep outdoors in April, also by division in March or April ; shrubby species by cuttings of young shoots inserted in sandy soil under bell-glass in brisk bottom heat during June or July.

ANNUAL SPECIES : L. grandiflorum, rose, summer, 1 ft., Algeria, and its varieties, coccineum (scarlet), splendens (rose), and rubrum (red) ; usitatissimum (Common Flax), blue, June, 18 in., Europe.
PERENNIAL SPECIES : L. alpinum, blue, summer, 6 in., Europe ; campanulatum, yellow, summer, 1 ft., Europe ; capitatum, yellow, June to July, 6 to 9 in., Europe ; flavum, yellow, summer, 18 in., Austria ; monogynum, white, June to Oct., 1 to 2 ft., New Zealand ; narbonense, blue, May to July, 2 ft., S. Europe ; perenne, blue or white, summer, 18 in., Britain ; salsoloides, white, tinged pink, June to July, 9 in., S.W. Europe. See also Reinwardtia.
SHRUBBY SPECIES : L. arboreum, yellow, June, 1 ft., Crete.

Lion's-ear (*Leonotis Leonurus*)—See Leonotis.

Lion's-foot (*Leontopodium alpinum*)—See Leontopodium.

Lion's-leaf (*Leontice Leontopetalum*)—See Leontice.

Lion's-tail (*Leonotis Leonurus*)—See Leonotis.

Lion's-turnip (*Leontice Albertii*)—See Leontice.

Lip Fern (*Cheilanthes californica*)—See Cheilanthes.

Lippia (Sweet-scented Verbena ; Herb Louisa)—Ord. Verbenaceæ. Greenhouse deciduous shrub and dwarf perennial. First introduced 1781.
CULTURE OF SHRUBBY SPECIES : Compost, two parts loam, one leaf-mould and sand. Position, pots in windows or greenhouses ; beds outdoors against south walls S. England and Ireland. Pot or plant, March. Water freely March to Sept., little afterwards. Prune shoots Feb. to within an inch of base. Temp., 45° to 50° in winter ; 50° to 55° other times.
CULTURE OF PERENNIAL SPECIES : Soil, light, sandy. Position, warm, sunny banks in rock garden. Plant, Nov. or March to April.
PROPAGATION : Shrubby species by cuttings pulled off stem when 4 in. long and inserted in sandy soil under bell-glass, in temp. 65°, March ; perennial species by division in March or April.
SHRUBBY SPECIES CULTIVATED : L. citriodora (Syn. Aloysia citriodora), lilac, Aug., 10 to 15 ft., foliage fragrant, S. America.
PERENNIAL SPECIES CULTIVATED : L. nodiflora, rose pink, summer, 3 in., S. America.

Liquidambar (Sweet Gum-tree)—Ord. Hamamelidaceæ. Hardy deciduous trees. Orn. foliage. First introduced 1681. Flowers greenish yellow, inconspicuous ; spring. Leaves, hand-shaped, downy, very fragrant.
CULTURE : Soil, deep, moist loam. Position, sheltered in shrubberies or on lawns. Plant, Oct. to Dec. Prune into shape when necessary in Nov.
PROPAGATION : By seeds sown ⅛ in. deep in sandy soil outdoors, Oct., Nov., March, or April, transplanting seedlings two to three years afterwards ; layering shoots, in spring.
SPECIES CULTIVATED : L. formosana (Syn. acerifolia), 60 to 80 ft., China ; orientalis, 80 to 100 ft., Asia Minor ; styraciflua (Sweet Gum), 100 to 150 ft., U. States. In this country these trees do not usually attain more than half the heights stated.

Liquorice-plant (*Glycyrrhiza glabra*)—See Glycyrrhiza.

Liriodendron (Tulip-tree)—Ord. Magnoliaceæ. Hardy deciduous tree. Flowering and orn. foliage. First introduced 1668. Flowers, very fragrant. Leaves, saddle-shaped, bright green.
CULTURE : Soil, deep, rich loam. Position, sunny, sheltered shrubberies or as specimen on lawns. Plant, Oct. to Feb. Prune straggling shoots only into shape, Nov. or Dec.
PROPAGATION : By seeds sown ⅛ in. deep, in moist, sandy loam in sheltered position outdoors, Sept. to Nov. ; layering in spring.
SPECIES CULTIVATED : L. tulipifera, yellow, June to Aug., 100 to 200 ft., N. America.

Liriope—Ord. Hœmodoraceæ. Hardy evergreen perennials. Grass-like foliage in tufts. First introduced 1821.

CULTURE : Soil, sandy loam. Position, as an edging to beds in the open or as a small pot plant in cool greenhouse or conservatory. Plant or pot, March to April.

PROPAGATION : By division at planting time.

SPECIES CULTIVATED : L. spicata, lilac, autumn, 1 to 1½ ft., Japan and China.

Lissochilus—Ord. Orchidaceæ. Stove terrestrial orchids. First introduced 1818.

CULTURE : Compost, equal parts fibrous loam, leaf-mould, and silver sand. Position, shallow pans or well-drained pots in warm, moist part of stove during the growing period and cool part when at rest. Pot, Feb. or March. Water freely March to Sept., moderately Sept. to Nov., keeping quite dry Nov. to March. Apply weak liquid manure every ten days during growth. Temp., March to Oct. 65° to 75°; Oct. to March 60° to 65°. Growing period, March to Oct.; resting period, Oct. to March.

PROPAGATION : By division of pseudo-bulbs, March.

SPECIES CULTIVATED : L. giganteus, pink, yellow, and purple, autumn, 10 to 16 ft., River Congo; Krebsii, brown, purple, and yellow, May to Oct., 3 ft., Natal; speciosus, yellow, June, 3 ft., Cape of Good Hope.

Lithospermum (Gromwell)—Ord. Boraginaceæ. Hardy dwarf trailing evergreen flowering shrubs and perennials.

CULTURE : Soil, sandy or loamy. Position, margins of sunny borders or on ledges of sunny rockeries. Plant, Oct., Nov., March, or April. L. prostratum an excellent plant for draping stones on rockeries.

PROPAGATION : By seeds sown ⅟₁₆ in. deep in well-drained pots of sandy soil in cold frame in March or April, transplanting seedlings when an inch high singly in 2 in. pots and growing in frame until following spring, then planting out; cuttings of ripened shoots, 2 to 3 in. long, inserted in well-drained pots of sandy soil in cold frame in Aug., Sept., or Oct.; layering shoots in Sept.

SPECIES CULTIVATED : L. canescens, yellow, July, 1 ft., N. America; Frœbelli, deep blue, early summer, 6 in., hybrid; Gastoni, blue, summer, 1 ft., Pyrenees; graminifolium, blue, June to Aug., 1 ft., Italy; intermedium, deep blue, May to June, 8 in., hybrid; petræum (Syn. Moltkia petræa), pale blue and purple, summer, 6 to 9 in., Greece; prostratum (Gromwell), blue, summer, trailing, S. Europe; purpureo-cæruleum, bluish purple, June and July, 1 ft., Europe; rosmarinifolium, azure blue, winter, 1 to 2 ft., Italy.

Lithy-tree (*Viburnum lantana*)—See Viburnum.

Littonia—Ord. Liliaceæ. Greenhouse herbaceous perennial climber. First introduced 1853.

CULTURE : Compost, two parts loam, one part each of leaf-mould, peat, and silver sand. Position, well-drained pots or bed in warm greenhouse. Pot or plant, March. Train shoots up roof or wall. Water freely during spring and summer, moderately autumn and winter. Syringe morning and evening during early period of growth. Plant likes plenty of sunshine. Temp., March to Sept. 65° to 75°; Sept. to March 50° to 60°.

PROPAGATION : By division of the plant at potting time.

SPECIES CULTIVATED : L. modesta, orange, April, 3 to 4 ft., S. Africa.

Live-long (*Sedum telephium*)—See Sedum.

Liver Leaf (*Anemone Hepatica*)—See Anemone.

Livistona—Ord. Palmaceæ. Warm greenhouse palms. Orn. foliage. First introduced 1816.

CULTURE : Compost, two parts loam, one part peat, little sand. Position, well-drained pots in warm greenhouse, Sept. to June; outdoors or in cool greenhouse in summer. Pot, Feb. or March. Water freely March to Sept., moderately afterwards. Syringe twice daily March to Oct.; once Oct. to March. Temp., March to Sept. 60° to 70°; Sept. to March 55° to 60°.

PROPAGATION : By seeds sown ½ in. deep in rich light soil in temp. 80° to 90° in Feb. or March.
SPECIES CULTIVATED : L. humilis, 6 to 15 ft., Australia ; rotundifolia, to 80 ft , Java ; sinensis (Syn. Latania borbonica), 20 to 30 ft., leaves large, fan-shaped, China and Japan.

Lizard Orchis (*Orchis hircina*)—See Orchis.

Lizard's Tail—See Saururus.

Llavea—Ord. Filices. Stove evergreen fern. First introduced 1853. Fronds, large, three times divided ; upper portion contracted, fertile ; lower portion broad, barren.
CULTURE : Compost, equal parts loam, peat, sand. Position, well-drained pots in shady part of stove. Pot, March or April. Water freely March to Sept., moderately Sept. to March. Temp., March to Sept. 70° to 80° ; Sept. to March 60° to 70°.
PROPAGATION : By spores sown on fine sandy peat in well-drained pans under bell-glass in temp. 70° to 80° at any time.
SPECIES CULTIVATED : L. cordifolia, 2 to 3 ft., Mexico.

Lloydia (Mountain Spider-wort)—Ord. Liliaceæ. Hardy bulbous flowering plant.
CULTURE : Soil, sandy loam. Position, sunny, dryish borders or rockeries. Plant, Sept. or Oct. Depth for bulbs, 3 to 4 in. Lift and replant when unhealthy only.
PROPAGATION : By offsets, removed and planted in Sept. or Oct.
SPECIES CULTIVATED : L. serotina, white and green, June, 6 in., Britain (Snowdon).

Loasa (Chile Nettle)—Ord. Loasaceæ. Greenhouse and half-hardy annual climbing and twining plants. First introduced 1822.
OUTDOOR CULTURE : Sow seeds 1/16 in. deep in light mould in temp. 65° in Feb. or March. Transplant seedlings singly in 3 in. pots when 1 in. high and grow in temp. 55° till June, then plant outdoors. Position, against sunny walls or fences. Soil, ordinary.
INDOOR CULTURE : Sow seeds as above. Transplant seedlings singly into 3 in. pots, and when 6 in. high into 5 in. size, or place three in an 8 in. size. Compost, two parts sandy loam, one part leaf-mould and sand. Train shoots round wire trellis or stakes inserted in the soil. Water moderately at first, freely afterwards. Apply stimulants occasionally to plants in bloom. Temp., 55° to 65°. All the species are furnished with stinging hairs and hence should not be touched by naked hands.
SPECIES CULTIVATED : L. lateritia, coral red, Aug., 10 to 20 ft., Chile ; vulcanica, white, yellow, and red, summer, 2 to 3 ft., Ecuador. See also Blumenbachia.

Lobelia (Cardinal Flower)—Ord. Campanulaceæ. Hardy and half-hardy herbaceous perennials. First introduced 1629.
OUTDOOR CULTURE OF HARDY SPECIES : Soil, ordinary rich. Position, sunny, moist borders. Cool rock garden for L. linnæoides. Plant, Oct., March, or April. On cold, damp soils all the species (except L. syphilitica and linnæoides) best lifted in Oct., placed in pots, stored in cold frame till March, then replanted.
POT CULTURE : Compost, two parts sandy loam, one part leaf-mould and sand. Pot, Oct. or March. Position, cold frame, Oct. to March ; cool greenhouse, March till past flowering, then outdoors. Water very little Oct. to March, freely afterwards. Apply stimulants, May to Aug.
CULTURE OF HALF-HARDY SPECIES : Soil, ordinary. Position, pots in greenhouse heated to temp. 55°, Oct. to June ; as edgings to beds, etc., outdoors, June to Oct. Plant, June, 3 to 6 in. apart. Lift plants in Sept., place in small pots, and store in greenhouse to furnish cuttings in spring. Cut off flower stems a fortnight before lifting.
POT CULTURE : Compost, equal parts good soil, leaf-mould, and sand. Position, dwarf kinds in 4 or 5 in. pots and trailing kinds in pots or baskets, in shady or sunny greenhouse or window. Pot, March to July. Water freely in summer, moderately other times. Apply stimulants to plants in flower.
PROPAGATION : Hardy perennial species by seeds sown 1/16 in. deep in sandy loam and leaf-mould in cold frame in Sept. or Oct., or in temp. 55° in March ; cuttings

of shoots inserted in small pots in temp. 55° in spring ; division in March. Half-hardy species by seeds sown in heat in Feb., transplanting seedlings 2 in. apart in boxes, hardening off in cold frame, and planting out in May ; cuttings of young shoots inserted in sandy soil in temp. 65° to 75° in spring ; division in March or April.

HARDY PERENNIAL SPECIES : L. cardinalis (Cardinal Flower), scarlet, summer, 3 ft., N. America ; fulgens, scarlet, May, 1 to 3 ft., Mexico ; Gerardii, violet, July, 3 to 4 ft., hybrid ; laxiflora, red and yellow, summer, 4 to 5 ft., Mexico ; splendens, scarlet, 2 to 3 ft., N. America ; syphilitica, blue, July, 2 to 3 ft., N. America ; Tupa, red, Aug. to Sept., 4 to 6 ft., Chile. See also genus Pratia.

HALF-HARDY PERENNIAL SPECIES : L. Cavanillesii, red, July, 2 to 3 ft., Chile ; Erinus, blue, blue and white, summer, 6 in., parent of bedding varieties, S. Africa ; tenuior, bright blue, Sept., 12 to 18 in., W. Australia. There are several named varieties of L. Erinus, of which Mrs. Clibrans is one.

Lobster-flower (*Euphorbia pulcherrima*)—See Euphorbia.

Locks and Keys (*Dicentra spectabilis*)—See Dicentra.

Locust Tree (*Robinia pseudacacia*)—See Robinia.

Loganberry—See Rubus.

Loiseleuria (Alpine Azalea ; Trailing Azalea)—Ord. Ericaceæ. Hardy trailing flowering shrub. Evergreen.

CULTURE : Soil, deep, sandy peat. Position, open, moist rockeries. Plant, Sept. to Nov.

PROPAGATION : By layering shoots, Sept. to Nov.

SPECIES CULTIVATED : L. procumbens (Syn. Azalea procumbens), rose to white, May, Subarctic Regions.

Lomaria (Deer Fern)—Ord. Filices. Tree and dwarf evergreen ferns. Stove, greenhouse, and hardy.

CULTURE OF STOVE SPECIES : Compost, equal parts loam, leaf-mould, peat, and sand. Position, pots, beds, or rockeries in shady part of stove. Pot or plant, Feb. or March. Water abundantly April to Sept., moderately afterwards. Temp., March to Sept. 70° to 80° ; Sept. to March 60° to 70°. Syringe tree species twice daily Feb. to Sept.

CULTURE OF GREENHOUSE SPECIES : Compost, as above. Pot, March or April. Position, pots, beds, or rockery in shady part of house. Water freely March to Oct., moderately Oct. to March. Syringe as advised for stove species. Temp., March to Sept. 55° to 65° ; Sept. to March 50° to 55°.

CULTURE OF HARDY SPECIES : Soil, two parts sandy peat, one part loam and pounded limestone. Position, shady rockeries. Plant, Oct. to April. Water freely in dry weather. Protect L. alpina in very severe weather.

PROPAGATION : By spores sown on fine sandy peat in well-drained pans in temp. 80° any time ; dwarf species by division of plants, Oct. or April.

STOVE SPECIES : L. attenuata, Tropics ; gibba, New Caledonia, and its varieties Platyptera and rosea ; L'Herminieri, Tropical America.

GREENHOUSE SPECIES : L. boryana, West Indies ; discolor, Australia, and its varieties bipinnatifida and nuda ; lanceolata, New Zealand ; pumila, New Zealand.

HARDY SPECIES : L. alpina, New Zealand, etc. ; Spicant (Hard Fern), Syn. Blechnum Spicant, Britain ; Spicant trinervis.

Lomatia—Ord. Proteaceæ. Greenhouse evergreen shrubs. Orn. foliage. First introduced 1792. Leaves, feather- or egg-shaped, green or glaucous.

CULTURE : Compost, equal parts peat, loam, and sand. Position, well-drained pots in sunny, airy greenhouse, or sheltered borders in Cornwall and similar mild districts. Pot, Feb. to April. Prune into shape when necessary, Feb. Water moderately Sept. to April, freely afterwards. Ventilate freely April to Sept., moderately afterwards. Temp., March to Oct. 55° to 65°; Oct. to March 45° to 55°.

PROPAGATION : By cuttings of firm shoots, 2 to 3 in. long, inserted in sandy peat under bell-glass in temp. 60° to 70°, June to Sept.
SPECIES CULTIVATED : L. ferruginea (Syn. pinnatifolia), rosy red and white, 10 to 12 ft., Chile ; longifolia, 8 to 10 ft., N.S. Wales ; obliqua, white, to 20 ft., Chile ; silaifolia, white, May to June, 3 ft., Australia ; tinctoria, 2 to 3 ft., Australia.

Lombardy Poplar (*Populus nigra italica*)—See Populus.

Lonas—Ord. Compositæ. Hardy annual. Introduced 1686.
CULTURE : Soil, ordinary. Position, sunny borders.
PROPAGATION : By seeds sown outdoors in April where plants are required to grow.
SPECIES CULTIVATED : L. inodora, yellow, June to Aug., 1 ft., Barbary.

London Plane (*Platanus acerifolia*)—See Platanus.

London Pride (*Saxifraga umbrosa*)—See Saxifraga.

Lonicera (Honeysuckle)—Ord. Caprifoliaceæ. Hardy and half-hardy, erect and twining, deciduous and evergreen shrubs. Flowering and orn. foliage. Flowers fragrant.
CULTURE OF TWINING SPECIES : Soil, rich ordinary. Position, S. or W. walls or fences for evergreen kinds ; fences, walls, or arbours in any aspect for deciduous kinds. Plant, Oct. to April. Top-dress with well-decayed manure in March or April. Prune L. fragrantissima slightly after flowering ; other kinds in Feb., shortening shoots of previous year's growth to within 1 to 3 in. of base. Water freely in dry weather. Apply weak liquid manure occasionally in summer.
POT CULTURE : Compost, two parts sandy loam, one part leaf-mould or well-decayed manure and sand. Pot, Oct. to Dec. Position, cold frame or greenhouse, Nov. to Feb. ; warm greenhouse, Feb. to June ; sunny place outdoors, June to Nov. Water freely Feb. to Oct., moderately afterwards. Apply stimulants occasionally when in flower. Prune previous year's shoots to within 1 or 2 in. of base in June.
CULTURE OF L. SEMPERVIRENS IN GREENHOUSE : Compost, same as for pot culture. Plant, Oct. to March. Position, small well-drained bed, or tub with shoots trained up rafter or trellis. Prune slightly after flowering. Water freely March to Sept., moderately afterwards. Temp., March to Sept. 55° to 65° ; Sept. to March 40° to 50°.
CULTURE OF SHRUBBY SPECIES : Soil, ordinary. Position, open or shady shrubberies. Plant, Oct. to March. Prune away weak growths only, Dec. to Feb. Mulch with decayed manure, Feb. or March. L. nitida suitable for hedge-making. Plant 1 to 1½ ft. apart and clip fairly closely in June and July.
PROPAGATION : By cuttings of firm shoots, 8 in. long, inserted in sandy soil under hand-light in Sept. or Oct. ; firm young shoots in close frame and gentle bottom heat in July or Aug. ; layering shoots, Aug. to Nov. ; seeds sown in well-drained pans in temp. 55° to 60° in Feb. or March.
TWINING SPECIES : L. Caprifolium (Goat-leaf Honeysuckle), yellow, June to July, 10 to 15 ft., Europe (Britain) ; ciliosa, yellow or orange-scarlet, Western N. America ; dioica, yellow and purple, June to July, Eastern N. America ; etrusca, purple and yellow, May, 8 to 10 ft., Mediterranean Region ; flava, yellow, June, 10 ft., N. America ; Giraldii, purplish red, June, evergreen, Szechuan ; glaucescens, yellow, June to July, N. America ; Heckrottii, orange yellow and pink, June to Sept., hybrid ; italica, yellow and reddish purple, June to Aug., natural hybrid ; japonica, red and white, July to Sept., 8 to 10 ft., evergreen, Japan ; japonica aureo-reticulata, leaves netted with yellow ; japonica flexuosa, pale red and white ; japonica halliana, white to yellow ; Periclymenum (Common Honeysuckle), red and yellow, June to Sept., 10 to 20 ft., Britain, and its varieties belgica (Early Dutch) and serotina (Late Dutch) ; sempervirens (Evergreen Honeysuckle), scarlet and yellow, May to Aug., 10 to 15 ft., N. America (hardy only in S. of England) ; tragophylla, orange yellow, June to Sept., 10 to 20 ft., W. China.
SHRUBBY SPECIES : L. alpigena, yellow, tinged red, April to May, 6 ft., Europe ; angustifolia, pinkish white, April to May, 8 to 10 ft., Himalayas ; bella, rosy yellow, April to May, 4 to 6 ft., hybrid ; cærulea, yellowish white, April, 2 to 4 ft., Northern

Hemisphere ; chætocarpa, primrose yellow, June, 3 to 5 ft., Central China ; chrys-antha, yellowish white, April, to 12 ft., N.E. Asia to Japan ; fragrantissima, creamy white, Dec. to March, 6 to 8 ft., partially evergreen, China ; hispida, yellow, May to June, 3 to 5 ft., Turkestan ; Ledebourii, orange yellow and red, June, 8 to 9 ft., California ; Maacki, white or yellow, May to June, to 10 ft., Manchuria and China ; Morrowi, white to yellow, May to June, 6 to 8 ft., China and Japan ; nitida, evergreen with neat foliage, 4 to 6 ft., W. China ; pyrenaica, rose and white, May to June, 2 to 3 ft., Pyrenees ; Standishii, creamy white, Nov. to March, 6 to 8 ft., partially evergreen, China ; syringantha, lilac, May to June, to 8 ft., China and Thibet ; tatarica, pink or white, May, 8 to 10 ft., Siberia, etc. ; quinquelocularis, creamy white, June, 12 to 15 ft., Himalayas and China ; xylosteum (Fly Honeysuckle), yellow, May, 4 to 6 ft., Europe.

Loofah Gourd (*Luffa ægyptica*)—See Luffa.

Loosestrife—See Lysimachia and Lythrum.

Lopezia—Ord. Onagraceæ.   Half-hardy annual and perennial.   First introduced 1804.
CULTURE : Soil, ordinary.   Position, sunny borders.
PROPAGATION : By seeds sown 1/16 in. deep in light soil in temp. 55° to 65° in March, transplanting outdoors in May.
SPECIES CULTIVATED : L. coronata, red, Aug., 1 ft., annual, Mexico ; albiflora, pinkish white, late summer and autumn, 2 ft., Mexico, perennial.   This may be grown in pots for flowering in the greenhouse.

Lophospermum—See Maurandya and Rhodochiton.

Loquat (*Eriobotrya japonica*)—See Eriobotrya.

Lord Anson's Pea (*Lathyrus magellanicus*)—See Lathyrus.

Lord Harrington's Yew (*Cephalotaxus pedunculata*)—See Cephalotaxus.

Lords and Ladies (*Arum maculatum*)—See Arum.

Loropetalum—Ord. Hamamelidaceæ.   Hardy evergreen flowering shrubs, adapted for outdoor and cold greenhouse culture.
OUTDOOR CULTURE : Soil, ordinary light rich.   Position, warm, sheltered borders.   Plant, Oct. to Feb.   Prune to maintain good shape after flowering.
GREENHOUSE CULTURE : Compost, two parts sandy loam, one part leaf-mould, and a liberal amount of sand.   Position, pots in cold, sunny greenhouse ; must not be forced.   Water freely between March and Oct., moderately afterwards.   Pot in Oct. ; stand outdoors in full sun from June to Oct. to ripen wood.
PROPAGATION : By cuttings in sandy soil in a cold frame in summer or autumn ; by seeds in similar soil in a cold frame at any time.
SPECIES CULTIVATED : L. sinense, white, autumn to winter, 5 to 6 ft., China.

Lotus (Bird's-foot Trefoil)—Ord. Leguminosæ.   Greenhouse and hardy perennials.
CULTURE OF GREENHOUSE SPECIES : Compost, two parts sandy loam, one part leaf-mould, half part each pounded charcoal and sand.   Pot, Feb. or March.   Position, pots in light, airy part of sunny greenhouse.   Water moderately March to Sept., very little afterwards.   Apply weak stimulants to healthy plants in flower.   Temp., March to Sept. 55° to 65° ; Sept. to March 45° to 55°.
CULTURE OF HARDY SPECIES : Soil, ordinary rich.   Position, sunny rockeries or elevated beds.   Plant, March or April.   This species makes a very pretty rock plant.
PROPAGATION : Greenhouse species by seeds sown 1/16 in. deep in sandy soil in well-drained pot or pan in temp. 55° to 65° in March or April ; cuttings of shoots inserted in well-drained pots of sandy soil under bell-glass in temp. 55° to 65° in summer.   Hardy species by seeds sown 1/16 in. deep in April where plants are required to grow ; division of plants in March or April.
GREENHOUSE SPECIES : L. Bertheloti (Syn. peliorhynchus), scarlet, summer, 2 ft., Canaries.
HARDY SPECIES : L. corniculatus (Bird's-foot Trefoil), yellow, summer, creeping, Britain.

Lotus (*Nymphæa lotus*)—See Nymphæa.

Lotus-tree (*Diospyros lotus*)—See Diospyros.

Love-apple (*Lycopersicum esculentum*)—See Lycopersicum.

Love Grass (*Eragrostis japonica*)—See Eragrostis.

Love-in-a-Mist (*Nigella damascena*)—See Nigella.

Love-lies-bleeding (*Amaranthus caudatus*)—See Amaranthus.

Love Pea (*Abrus precatorius*)—See Abrus.

Love-tree (*Cercis siliquastrum*)—See Cercis.

Low's Silver Fir (*Abies lowiana*)—See Abies.

Luculia—Ord. Rubiaceæ. Greenhouse evergreen shrubs. Flowering and orn. foliage. First introduced 1823.
CULTURE : Compost, equal parts fibrous loam, peat, charcoal, and sand. Position, in large well-drained pots, or preferably in beds 2 to 3 ft. wide and 18 in. deep. Put 6 in. of drainage into latter. Pot or plant, Feb., March, or April. Prune young shoots moderately after flowering to a length of 2 or 3 ins. Water freely April to Nov., withhold entirely afterwards. Syringe foliage twice daily April to Sept. Temp., April to Sept. 60° to 70° ; Sept. to Dec. 55° to 65°; Dec. to April 45° to 55°. PROPAGATION : By seeds sown ⅛ in. deep in well-drained pans of light, sandy soil in temp. of 60° to 70° in Feb., March, or April ; cuttings of young shoots inserted in sandy soil under bell-glass in temp. 70° to 80° in June or July. Seedlings flower when three to five years old.
SPECIES CULTIVATED : L. gratissima, rose, autumn, 8 to 10 ft., Himalayas ; pinceana, rose, autumn, 10 ft., Himalayas.

Luffa (Loofah)—Ord. Cucurbitaceæ. Stove climbing annual bearing curious gourd-like fruits.
CULTURE : Sow seeds in a compost of equal parts leaf-mould and loam in a temp. of 75° in Feb. Transfer seedlings when third leaf forms singly into 3 in. pots, and later on to 8 or 10 in. pots, using three parts of loam to one of leaf-mould. Train shoots up roof. Water freely. Syringe daily. Feed with weak liquid manure when fruit has formed.
SPECIES CULTIVATED : L. ægyptica, yellow, spring, fruits club-shaped, Tropics.

Lunaria (Common Honesty ; Money Flower ; Satin Flower)—Ord. Cruciferæ. Biennial and perennial flowering and orn. fruiting plants. First introduced 1595. Seed pods flat, oval, containing a satiny partition ; very useful for drying for winter decorations.
CULTURE OF BIENNIAL SPECIES : Soil, ordinary. Position, partially shaded borders or margins of shrubberies. Plant, Aug. to Nov., singly or in groups of three or six. Discard plants after flowering.
CULTURE OF PERENNIAL SPECIES : Soil, light rich ordinary. Position, partially shaded borders. Plant, Oct., Nov., March, or April.
PROPAGATION : Biennial species by seeds sown in shallow drills or patches outdoors in sunny position in April, transplanting seedlings when third leaf is formed 6 in. apart each way ; perennial species by seeds similarly, or by division of roots in March or April.
ANNUAL SPECIES : L. annua (Common Honesty), Syn. L. biennis, lilac, white, or purple, May and June, 2 to 3 ft., Europe.
PERENNIAL SPECIES : L. rediviva, purple, fragrant, June, 2 to 3 ft., Europe.

Lung-wort (*Pulmonaria officinalis*)—See Pulmonaria.

Lupine (*Lupinus polyphyllus*)—See Lupinus.

Lupinus (Lupine or Lupin)—Ord. Leguminosæ. Hardy shrubby and herbaceous perennials and annuals. Flowering and orn. foliage. First introduced 1596.
CULTURE OF SHRUBBY PERENNIALS : Soil, sandy loam. Position, sunny shrubberies or open, sheltered borders. Plant, Oct. or April. Prune into shape after flowering.

CULTURE OF HERBACEOUS PERENNIALS : Soil, ordinary rich. Position, open sunny or partially shaded borders. Plant, Oct., Nov., March, or April. Mulch with decayed manure in April. Cut down flower stems in Oct.

CULTURE OF ANNUAL SPECIES : Sow seeds ⅛ in. deep and 1 in. apart in April in patches where required to flower. Thin seedlings in May to 6 to 12 in. apart. Remove seed pods directly they form to ensure continuous display of flowers. Apply stimulants when in flower. Water freely in dry weather.

PROPAGATION : Perennial species by seeds sown ¼ in. deep outdoors in April, transplanting seedlings into flowering positions June to Aug. ; cuttings of young growth taken in March before they have become hollow and rooted in sandy soil in unheated frame.

SHRUBBY SPECIES : L. arboreus (Tree Lupine), yellow, fragrant, summer, 6 to 9 ft. ; arboreus albus, white ; Paynei, blue, pink, or white with yellow blotch, spring, to 8 ft., California.

HERBACEOUS SPECIES : L. nootkatensis, blue, purple, and yellow, summer, 1 ft., N. America ; polyphyllus (Perennial Lupin), blue, summer, 3 to 6 ft., California ; polyphyllus albus, white ; polyphyllus roseus, pink. There are also many named varieties to be found in trade lists.

ANNUAL SPECIES : L. densiflorus (Syn. Menziesii), yellow, fragrant, Aug., 2 ft., California ; Hartwegii, blue, white, and rose, Aug. to Sept., 2 to 3 ft., Mexico ; hirsutissimus, reddish purple, July, 9 in., California ; hirsutus, blue and white, July to Aug., 1½ to 2½ ft., Mediterranean Region ; luteus, yellow, June to Aug., 1 to 2 ft., S. Europe ; mutabilis, white, blue, and yellow, fragrant, summer, 3 to 4 ft., Colombia, and its variety Cruckshanksii, violet and purple ; nanus, lilac and blue, summer, 1 ft., California ; pubescens, violet blue and white, July to Sept., 1½ to 3 ft., Mexico and Guatemala, and its varieties albococcineus, atrococcineus, Dunnettii, elegans, speciosus, superbus, tricolor, etc. ; subcarnosus, blue and yellow, summer, 1 ft., Texas.

Lycaste—Ord. Orchidaceæ. Warm greenhouse, evergreen, and deciduous orchids. First introduced 1790.

CULTURE : Compost, equal parts fibry peat and chopped sphagnum moss, with little sand and charcoal. Position, well-drained pots, pans, or baskets, in light part of greenhouse. Pot when new growth commences. Water freely from time new growth begins until Nov., then occasionally. Syringe once or twice daily whilst making growth. Ventilate freely May to Sept. Temp., April to Oct. 55° to 65° ; Oct. to April 45° to 55°. Growing period, Feb. to Oct. ; resting period, Oct. to Feb. Plants may be grown in sitting-room or cool conservatory when in flower. Flowers appear at base of new pseudo-bulb when latter begins to form.

PROPAGATION : By division of pseudo-bulbs immediately after flowering.

SPECIES CULTIVATED : L. aromatica, yellow and orange, June, 1 ft., Mexico ; Deppei, green, purple, yellow, and crimson, March to July, 1 ft., Mexico ; lasioglossa, golden yellow and purple, spring, Guatemala ; macrobulbon, orange yellow and brown, winter, S. America ; macrophylla, white and rose, winter, Bolivia ; macrophylla measuresiana, brown, green, white, and purple, winter ; Skinneri, white, rose, and crimson, Oct. to March, 1 ft., Guatemala ; Skinneri alba, white ; tetragona, green, white, purple, and crimson, fragrant, summer, 1 ft., Brazil.

Lychnis (Campion ; German Catchfly ; Rose Campion)—Ord. Caryophyllaceæ. Hardy annuals and perennials.

CULTURE OF PERENNIAL SPECIES : Soil, light rich loam for L. alpina and L. Lagascæ ; open, dryish beds, borders, or banks for other species. Plant, Oct. to Dec. and Feb. to May. Cut down flower stems of L. chalcedonica and L. vespertina in Oct. or Nov. Top-dress border species with well-decayed manure in March or April. Apply weak liquid manure occasionally to border species when in flower. Lift and replant border species every other year.

CULTURE OF ANNUAL SPECIES : Soil, ordinary. Position, sunny beds or edgings to or masses in borders. Sow in March or April for summer blooming ; Sept. for spring flowering.

PROPAGATION : By seeds sown ¼ in. deep in light soil in sunny position outdoors in

March or April, transplanting seedlings into flowering position Aug. to Nov. ; division of plants, Sept. to Dec. and Feb. to April.

PERENNIAL SPECIES : L. alba (White Campion), Syn. L. vespertina, white, May to Aug., 3 ft., Britain ; alpina, rosy pink, summer, 6 in., Europe (Britain) ; Arkwrightii, scarlet, summer, 1½ ft., hybrid ; chalcedonica (Scarlet Lychnis or Jerusalem Cross), scarlet, summer, 3 ft., Russia, and its varieties alba (white) and flore-pleno (double) ; coronaria (Syn. Agrostemma coronaria), crimson, July and Aug., 2 to 3 ft., S. Europe, and its varieties atrosanguinea (crimson red), alba (white), and flore-pleno (red) ; dioica (Red Campion), purple, rose, summer, 3 ft., Britain ; Flos-cuculi (Ragged Robin), rose, May and June, 1 to 2 ft., Britain, and its double variety flore-pleno ; Flos-Jovis, bright pink, summer, 1½ to 2 ft., Europe ; fulgens, vermilion, May to Sept., 6 to 12 in., Siberia ; grandiflora, salmon, scarlet, summer, 18 in., Japan ; haageana, scarlet, summer, 9 to 12 in., hybrid ; Lagascæ, rose and white, summer, 3 in., Pyrenees ; viscaria (German Catchfly), reddish purple, summer, 1 ft., Europe (Britain) ; viscaria splendens, red ; viscaria alba, white ; viscaria flore-pleno, rose, double.

ANNUAL SPECIES : L. Cœli-rosa (Syn. Agrostemma Cœli-rosa), Rose of Heaven, rose and purple, summer, 1 ft., Levant, and its varieties alba (white), kermesina (red), and oculata (purple-eyed).

Lycium (Box-thorn ; African Tea-tree ; Duke of Argyll's Tea-tree)—Ord. Solanaceæ. Hardy erect and climbing flowering shrubs. Deciduous. First introduced 1696. Branches more or less spiny.

CULTURE : Soil, ordinary. Position, well-drained borders with shoots trained to fences, arbours, porches, pergolas, verandas, trellises, or walls in any aspect ; also suitable for hedges. Plant, Oct. to Feb. Prune, Oct. to Feb., removing weak shoots entirely and shortening vigorous ones a little.

HEDGE CULTURE : Trench ground two spits deep and 3 ft. wide. Plant 12 in. apart in single rows, Oct. to Feb. Trim into shape, June and July. L. europæum an excellent climber for positions near the sea.

PROPAGATION : By cuttings of firm shoots, 6 to 8 in. long, inserted in ordinary soil in shady position in Sept. or Oct. ; layering shoots, spring ; by removing suckers with roots attached, Oct. to Feb.

SPECIES CULTIVATED : L. afrum, crimson and violet, June and July, 6 to 8 ft., S. Africa ; halimifolium, lilac purple, May to July, 8 to 9 ft., S.E. Europe and West Asia ; pallidum, green and purple, June to July, 5 to 6 ft., South-eastern U.S.A. ; sinense (Syn. L. barbarum), the Common Box-thorn or Duke of Argyll's Tea-tree, purple and yellow, summer, 10 to 12 ft., succeeded by scarlet berries, China.

Lycopersicum (Love-apple ; Tomato)—Ord. Solanaceæ. Tender annual. First introduced 1596. Fruit, variously shaped, red or yellow ; edible.

POT CULTURE : Compost, two parts decayed turfy loam, one part well-decomposed manure. Position, warm, light greenhouse, June ; cold, sunny greenhouse, June to Oct. Sow seeds in Jan. in temp. 75° for warm greenhouse ; in March in temp. 65° for cold greenhouse. Depth for sowing seeds, ⅛ in. Ordinary light mould suitable for sowing seeds in. Transfer seedlings when three leaves have formed singly into 2 in. pots, or 2 in. apart in larger pots or boxes ; into 6 in. pots when 6 in. high ; into 8 or 10 in. pots when 12 in. high. Drain pots well and pot firmly. Fill pots two-thirds full only with compost. Train plants with one stem only. Rub off all side shoots. Water sparingly till fruit forms. Fertilise flowers at mid-day by tapping with a stick. Apply liquid or artificial manures when fruit has set. Top-dress when bearing freely with compost of two parts loam and one part decayed manure, adding tablespoonful of superphosphate to every bushel. Ventilate freely when in flower. Dry atmosphere essential to ensure good set. Temp. for warm greenhouse, Feb. to June, 55° to 65°.

CULTURE IN BOXES : Size of boxes for single plants 10 in. square ; for two plants 12 in. wide, 18 in. long, 9 in. deep ; for four plants 18 in. wide, 2 ft. long, 9 in. deep ; for eight plants 18 in. wide, 36 in. long, 12 in. deep. Half fill with compost only until fruit sets, then top-dress. Cultural details same as for pots.

CULTURE IN BEDS : Compost, decayed turfy soil only ; no manure. Place compost

in ridge 18 in. wide and 12 in. high in centre on staging near front of house, or in beds on floor 2 ft. wide and 18 in. deep, enclosed with dry sticks or turves. Alternatively, the borders in the greenhouse may be dug and enriched with a little well-rotted manure and the plants set out in these. Plant 12 in. apart. Remove all side shoots. Water very little till fruit has set, then freely. Apply stimulants only when fruit has formed. Fertilise as for pot plants. Ventilate freely during fine weather. Top-dress when several bunches of fruit have formed with similar compost to that advised for pot plants. Temp., Feb. to June, 55° to 65°.
CULTURE IN FRAMES : Compost, as above. Plant in heated frame in Feb., March, or April ; in cold frame, June. Allow three plants to each light and train to single stems, these resting on trellis or branches near glass. Water moderately until fruit forms, then freely. Ventilate freely during middle of day. Shade not required. Stimulants, top-dressing, and training as above. Temp. for heated frame, 55° to 65°.
WINTER CULTURE : Compost, as above. Position, pots preferably or beds. Sow seed in June. Plant or pot, Aug. or Sept. Water sparingly. Apply stimulants only to plants bearing freely. Train as already described. Dry atmosphere necessary to ensure flowers setting. Temp., 55° to 65°.
OUTDOOR CULTURE : Soil, ordinary, not recently manured. Position, against S. or W. walls or fences, or in open. Plant, June, 12 in. apart against walls and 2 ft. apart each way in open. Train to one stem, removing all side shoots. Place stout stakes to plants in open. Apply stimulants when fruit has set. Remove growing point after fourth truss has set. Fruits which have not ripened at the end of Sept. should be gathered and stood in a sunny window or greenhouse to colour.
SUITABLE MANURES FOR TOMATOES : 1. One part nitrate of potash, one part nitrate of soda, two parts superphosphate of lime. Use ½ oz. to a gallon of water, or apply dry at rate of 1 oz. to six pots. 2. One part nitrate of soda, one part dried blood, one part kainit, and two parts superphosphate of lime. Apply to plants in beds at rate of 1 oz. per square yard when fruit has set. Apply above quantities every three or four days.
USEFUL DATA : Seeds germinate in ten to twelve days. One ounce of seed will yield approximately 2,000 plants. Seeds will retain their germinating powers for about six years.
SPECIES CULTIVATED : L. esculenteum (Tomato), yellow, fruits red or yellow, 6 ft. and over, Western S. America, and its varieties cerasiforme (Cherry Tomato) and pyriforme (Pear-shaped Tomato) ; pimpinellifolium (Currant Tomato), Syn. L. racemiforme, yellow, fruits small, red, weakly climber, Peru. There are many named varieties and colour forms of the common tomato.

Lycopodium (Fir Club Moss ; Stag's-horn Moss)—Ord. Lycopodiaceæ. Stove and hardy perennial mosses. Orn. foliage. Habit, creeping or erect. Stems clothed with scale-like, dark green leaves.
CULTURE OF STOVE SPECIES : Compost, equal parts loam, peat, limestone, and silver sand. Position, well-drained shallow pans under bell-glass or in beds in wardian cases. Pot or plant, Feb. to April. Water freely March to Sept., moderately afterwards. Syringe once or twice daily April to Sept. Shade from direct rays of sun. Temp., March to Sept. 65° to 75° ; Sept. to March 55° to 65°.
CULTURE OF HARDY SPECIES : Soil, deep, moist, sandy peat. Position, low bed on open, sunny rockery. Plant, March or April. Water freely in dry weather.
CULTURE OF HARDY SPECIES IN WARDIAN CASES : Compost, two parts peat, one part leaf-mould, one part charcoal, and liberal quantity of limestone chips or tufa. Bed to be well drained. Plant, Feb. to April. Water once or twice a week April to Sept., once a fortnight Sept. to Dec., once a month Dec. to April. Syringe or dew over daily April to Oct. Shade from sun. Ventilate a little daily.
PROPAGATION : By division, Feb. to April.
STOVE SPECIES : L. squarrosum, 2 ft. or more, India ; taxifolium, W. Indies ; verticillatum, Tropics.
HARDY SPECIES : L. clavatum (Club or Stag's-horn Moss), creeping, Britain ; Selago (Fir Club Moss), 3 in., Britain. See also the genus Selaginella.

Lycoris (Golden Lily)—Ord. Amaryllidaceæ. Greenhouse flowering bulbs. Deciduous. First introduced 1758.
CULTURE : Compost, two parts sandy loam, one part equal proportions of leaf-mould and cow manure. Pot dry bulbs Sept. to Dec., afterwards repotting annually immediately after flowering. Bury bulbs about two-thirds of their depth. Water moderately from time flowers show till leaves appear, then freely ; keep quite dry after leaves fade. Temp., Sept. to April, 55° to 65°. Place pots from April to Sept. in light, sunny, cool position.
PROPAGATION : By offsets, treated as bulbs, Sept. to Dec.
SPECIES CULTIVATED : L. aurea (Syn. Amaryllis aurea), yellow, Aug., 1 to 2 ft., China ; radiata (Syn. Nerine japonica and Amaryllis radiata), scarlet, June, 18 in., China and Japan, and its varieties alba (white) and variegata (crimson and white) ; squamigera, rosy lilac, fragrant, summer, 2 ft., Japan.

Lygodium (Climbing Fern)—Ord. Filices. Stove and greenhouse climbing ferns. Deciduous and evergreen. First introduced 1793. Fronds, slender, twining ; divisions, tongue- or hand-shaped.
CULTURE : Compost, equal parts peat, loam, sand, and charcoal. Position, well-drained pots or beds in shade with fronds twined round sticks, pillars, string, or trellis. Plant or pot, Feb. to April. Water freely Feb. to Oct., moderately after-wards. Temp : Stove species, Sept. to March 55° to 65°; March to Sept. 65° to 75°: Greenhouse species, Sept. to March 45° to 50° ; March to Sept. 55° to 65°.
PROPAGATION : By spores sown on surface of fine sandy peat under bell-glass in temp. 75° to 85° any time ; division of plants at potting time.
STOVE SPECIES : L. dichotomum, Trop. Asia ; reticulatum, Polynesia ; scandens, Tropics of the Old World.
GREENHOUSE SPECIES : L. japonicum, Japan, etc., ; palmatum, U. States.

Lyonia—Ord. Ericaceæ. Hardy flowering shrubs. Evergreen. First introduced 1748.
CULTURE : Soil, peaty. Position, moist, shady borders. Plant, Sept. to Nov. and Feb. to April. Pruning unnecessary.
PROPAGATION : By seeds sown on surface of sandy peat under bell-glass in shade in cold frame or greenhouse in Oct. or April ; layering shoots, Sept. or Oct.
SPECIES CULTIVATED : L. ligustrina (Syn. L. paniculata), white, June, 4 to 8 ft., N. America. See also Leucothoe.

Lyon's Shell-flower (*Chelone Lyoni*)—See Chelone.

Lyre Flower (*Dicentra spectabilis*)—See Dicentra.

Lyre-tree (*Liriodendron tulipifera*)—See Liriodendron.

Lysimachia (Yellow Loose-strife ; Creeping Jenny ; Yellow Pimpernel)— Ord. Primulaceæ. Hardy erect or creeping herbaceous perennials.
CULTURE OF HERBACEOUS SPECIES : Soil, ordinary rich. Position, moist, shady borders, margins of ponds or streams. Plant, Oct. to April. Cut down flower stems, Nov.
OUTDOOR CULTURE OF CREEPING JENNY : Soil, ordinary. Position, moist, shady rockeries or margins of beds, ponds, or streams. Plant, March to June.
INDOOR CULTURE : Compost, two parts good ordinary soil or loam, one part leaf-mould, decayed manure, or cocoanut-fibre refuse and one part sand. Position, well-drained pots or baskets suspended in shady window or cool greenhouse. Pot, March to May. Water freely April to Sept., moderately Sept. to Dec., keep nearly dry Dec. to April. Apply stimulants once or twice a week May to Aug.
PROPAGATION : By division of plants, autumn or spring.
HERBACEOUS SPECIES : L. atropurpurea, purple, summer, 2 ft., Greece ; clethroides, white, July to Sept., 3 ft., Japan ; ephemerum, white, summer, 3 ft., S. Europe ; Fortunei, white, summer, 1½ ft., China and Japan ; punctata (Syn. verticillata), yellow, summer, 2 to 3 ft., Europe ; thyrsiflora, yellow, June and July, 3 ft., N. Europe ; vulgaris (Yellow Loose-strife), yellow, July and Aug., 3 ft. Britain.

CREEPING SPECIES : L. nemorum (Yellow Pimpernel), yellow, May to July, Britain ; L. nummularia (Creeping Jenny), yellow, June to Sept., Britain ; nummularia aurea (Golden Creeping Jenny), golden-leaved.

Lythrum (Purple Loose-strife)—Ord. Lythraceæ.   Hardy herbaceous and shrubby perennials.

CULTURE : Soil, ordinary. Position, moist shady borders or margins of ponds or streams. Plant, Oct. to Dec. or Feb. to April. Cut down flower stems in Nov. Water freely in dry weather. Top-dress with well-decayed manure, March or April. Lift, divide, and replant every third year.

PROPAGATION : By division of plants, Oct. or April.

SPECIES CULTIVATED : L. alatum, purple, July to Oct., 2 to 4 ft., N. America ; Salicaria (Common Loose-strife), reddish purple, July, 3 to 4 ft., Britain, and its varieties roseum and superbum ; virgatum, purple, summer, 3 ft., Europe.

Maackia—Ord. Leguminosæ.   Hardy deciduous flowering tree.   First introduced 1864.

CULTURE : Soil, loamy.   Position, sunny shrubberies.   Plant, Nov. to Feb.

PROPAGATION : By seeds sown in well-drained pans in temp. 55° to 60° during Feb. or March ; cuttings of roots placed in pans in similar temp. and at same season.

SPECIES CULTIVATED : M. amurensis (Cladrastis amurensis), white, July to Aug., 15 to 40 ft., Manchuria and Japan.

Macartney Rose (*Rosa bracteata*)—See Rosa.

Mace Reed (*Typha latifolia*)—See Typha.

Mackaya—Ord. Acanthaceæ.   Greenhouse flowering shrub.   Deciduous.   First introduced 1869.

CULTURE : Compost, two parts decayed fibrous loam, one part dried cow manure, half a part sharp silver sand. Position, light, airy greenhouse. Pot, March. Prune after flowering, shortening shoots to 2 or 3 in. Water freely March to Sept., moderately Sept. to Nov., keep quite dry Nov. to March. Temp., April to Oct. 55° to 65° ; Oct. to April 45° to 55°.

PROPAGATION : By cuttings inserted singly in 2 in. pots filled with sandy soil, June to Aug. Transfer to 5 in. pots when rooted ; prune closely in April and shift into 8 and 10 in. pots. Plants flower when two or three years old.

SPECIES CULTIVATED : M. bella, lilac and purple, April to June, 4 to 6 ft., Natal.

Macleania—Ord. Vacciniaceæ.   Greenhouse trailing flowering shrubs.   Evergreen.   First introduced 1848.

CULTURE : Compost, equal parts turfy loam, peat, and sand. Position, well-drained pots with shoots drooping over front of staging, or in suspended baskets. Pot, March or April. Water freely March to Sept., moderately afterwards. Prune straggling shoots into shape, March. Temp., March to Sept. 55° to 65° ; Sept. to March 45° to 55°.

PROPAGATION : By cuttings inserted in fine sand in temp. 55° to 65° in summer.

SPECIES CULTIVATED : M. pulchra, yellow and scarlet, spring, 8 to 10 ft., Colombia ; speciosissima, yellow and scarlet, spring, trailing, Colombia.

Macleaya—See Bocconia.

Maclura (Osage Orange)—Ord. Urticaceæ. Hardy deciduous tree. Orn. foliage. First introduced 1818. Flowers, yellowish green, inconspicuous. Fruit, round, golden yellow, 3 to 5 in. in diameter ; rarely borne in this country. Leaves, egg-shaped, bright green.

CULTURE : Soil, ordinary. Position, in open, sheltered shrubberies or hedges. Plant, Oct. to Feb. Prune into shape when necessary, Nov. to Feb.

HEDGE CULTURE : Plant 12 in. apart in single row. Soil to be trenched two spits deep and 3 ft. wide. Trim into shape, July and Nov.

PROPAGATION : By cuttings, 6 to 8 in. long, inserted in ordinary soil in shady position, Oct. to March.

SPECIES CULTIVATED : M. aurantiaca, 20 to 40 ft., N. America.

Macrotomia—See Arnebia.

Macrozamia (Swan River Fern Palm; Giant Fern Palm)—Ord. Cycadaceæ. Greenhouse evergreen perennials. Orn. foliage. First introduced 1846. Leaves, feather-shaped, green; very graceful.

CULTURE : Compost, equal parts peat, loam, and sand. Position, well-drained pots, in light greenhouse, shaded from sun. Pot, Feb. or March. Water freely April to Oct., moderately afterwards. Syringe daily April to Sept. Temp., March to Sept. 60° to 70°; Sept. to March 55° to 60°.

PROPAGATION : By seeds sown in sandy peat in temp. 75° in March; division of plants in March; offsets in Feb. or March.

SPECIES CULTIVATED : M. Fraseri, W. Australia; Hopei, Australia; peroffskyana, Australia; tenuifolia, Australia.

Madagascar Chaplet Flower (*Stephanotis floribunda*)—See Stephanotis.

Madagascar Jasmine (*Stephanotis floribunda*)—See Stephanotis.

Madagascar Periwinkle (*Vinca rosea*)—See Vinca.

Madeira Orchis (*Orchis foliosa*)—See Orchis.

Madeira Vine (*Boussingaultia basselloides*)—See Boussingaultia.

Madia (Madia Oil Plant)—Ord. Compositæ. Hardy annuals. First introduced 1794.

CULTURE : Soil, ordinary. Position, shady borders.

PROPAGATION : By seeds sown ⅛ in. deep in April in patches where required to flower, thinning out seedlings when 2 in. high, to 3 in. apart.

SPECIES CULTIVATED : M. elegans, yellow, Aug., 1 ft., N.W. America; sativa, yellow, Aug., 1 ft., N. America.

Madonna Lily (*Lilium candidum*)—See Lilium.

Mad-wort (*Alyssum saxatile*)—See Alyssum.

Magnolia (Cucumber Tree; Yulan)—Ord. Magnoliaceæ. Hardy deciduous and evergreen trees and shrubs. Flowering and orn. foliage. First introduced 1688.

GREENHOUSE CULTURE : Compost, two parts sandy loam, one part peat or leaf-mould and sand. Position, well-drained pots or tubs, or against walls in sunny greenhouse. Pot or plant, March. Water freely in summer, moderately other times. Syringe daily March to Sept. Temp. for forcing, 55° to 65°. Prune straggling shoots only into shape, March or April. M. Campbellii, Lennei and stellata good kinds for greenhouse culture.

OUTDOOR CULTURE : Soil, rich, deep sandy loam. Position, sheltered parts of lawn or pleasure garden, or against S. or S.W. walls; against S. or W. walls for evergreen species. Plant, March or April. When necessary, prune evergreen species in spring; deciduous species after flowering. Protect evergreen species in very severe weather.

PROPAGATION : By seeds sown ⅛ in. deep in spring or autumn in well-drained pots of sandy soil in a cold frame or greenhouse; layering in summer or autumn; grafting in heat in July or Aug.

DECIDUOUS SPECIES : M. conspicua (Yulan), white, spring, 30 to 45 ft., China; acuminata (Cucumber Tree), green and yellow, May to July, 60 to 90 ft., N. America; Campbellii, rosy crimson, fragrant, Feb. to April, to 150 ft., Himalayas, does best in greenhouse; cordata, canary yellow, May to June, 15 to 20 ft., S. United States; Fraseri, creamy yellow, fragrant, May, 30 to 40 ft., S. United States; hypoleuca, creamy white, fragrant, spring, 50 to 80 ft., Japan; Kobus, creamy white, April, 70 to 80 ft., Japan; Lennei, rosy purple, April and May, 10 to 15 ft., hybrid; macrophylla, white and purple, fragrant, June, 30 to 50 ft., N. America; obovata, white and purple, fragrant, May, 12 ft., Japan; obovata purpurea, deeper coloured; parviflora, white and rosy crimson, May, 7 to 15 ft., Japan; salicifolia, white, April, 15 to 20 ft., Japan; soulangeana, white and purple, May, 20 ft., hybrid; stellata, white, fragrant, March to May, 10 to 15 ft., Japan; Thompsoniana, creamy white, hybrid; tripetala (Syn. M. Umbrella), the Umbrella Tree, white, fragrant, April

and May, 20 to 30 ft., S. United States; Watsoni, creamy white and crimson, June, to 20 ft., Japan.
EVERGREEN SPECIES : M. Delavayi, creamy white, June, 20 to 30 ft., requires wall protection, W. China ; grandiflora, white, fragrant, July and Aug., 15 to 20 ft., S. United States; glauca (Swamp Bay), creamy white, fragrant, June, 20 to 60 ft., semi-evergreen, E. United States.

Mahaleb Cherry (*Prunus Mahaleb*)—See Prunus.

Maharajah Palm—See Bactris.

Mahogany Tree (*Swietenia Mahagoni*)—See Swietenia.

Mahonia—See Berberis aquifolium.

Maianthemum (Twin-leaved Lily-of-the-Valley)—Ord. Liliaceæ. Hardy herbaceous perennial. Leaves and habit similar to the Lily-of-the-Valley.
CULTURE : Soil, ordinary rich. Position, shady borders in the open or under shrubs. Plant, Sept. and Oct. Water freely in dry weather.
PROPAGATION : By division of creeping root stocks in Sept. or April.
SPECIES CULTIVATED : M. convallaria (Syn. Smilacina bifolia), white, May, 6 in., N. Europe.

Maiden-hair Fern (*Adiantum capillus-veneris* and *A. cuneatum*)—See Adiantum.

Maiden-hair Grass (*Briza media*)—See Briza.

Maiden-hair Meadow Rue (*Thalictrum adiantifolium*)—See Thalictrum.

Maiden-hair Spleen-wort (*Asplenium Trichomanes*)—See Asplenium.

Maiden-hair Tree (*Gingko biloba*)—See Gingko.

Maiden Pink (*Dianthus deltoides*)—See Dianthus.

Maiden's Wreath—See Francoa.

Maid-of-the-Mist (*Gladiolus primulinus*)—See Gladiolus.

Maid's Love (*Artemisia Abrotanum*)—See Artemisia.

Maize (*Zea Mays*)—See Zea.

Malabar Glory Lily (*Gloriosa superba*)—See Gloriosa.

Malay Apple (*Eugenia malaccensis*)—See Eugenia.

Malcomia (Virginian Stock)—Ord. Cruciferæ. Hardy annual. First introduced 1713.
CULTURE : Soil, ordinary. Position, edging to sunny beds, masses on sunny borders, or on banks or rockeries. Sow seeds for summer flowering ⅟₁₆ in. deep in March, April, May, or June where plants are required to grow, and similar depth in Sept. for flowering in spring.
POT CULTURE : Compost, two parts good ordinary soil, one part leaf-mould, cocoanut-fibre refuse, decayed manure, and sand. Position, in 5 in. pots, well drained, in cold, sunny greenhouse or window. Sow seeds ⅟₁₆ in. deep in above pots in March, April, or May. Water moderately when first sown, freely when in full growth. Thin seedlings to ¼ in. apart when 1 in. high. Apply weak stimulants when flower buds show.
SPECIES CULTIVATED : M. maritima (Virginian Stock), various colours, summer, 6 in., S. Europe.

Male Dog-wood (*Cornus Mas*)—See Cornus.

Male Fern (*Nephrodium Filix-mas*)—See Nephrodium.

Mallow—See Malva.

Malmaison Carnation—See Dianthus.

Malope (Large-flowered Mallow-wort)—Ord. Malvaceæ. Hardy annuals. First introduced 1710.
CULTURE : Soil, rich ordinary. Position, sunny beds, or in masses in borders. Water freely in dry weather. Apply stimulants occasionally when plants show flower.

PROPAGATION : By seeds sown ⅛ in. deep in pots or boxes of light soil in temp. 55° in March, transplanting into flowering positions in May or June : or by seeds sown ⅛ in. deep and 4 to 6 in. apart where required to grow, in April or May.
SPECIES CULTIVATED : M. malacoides, rosy pink and purple, summer, 1 ft., S. Europe ; trifida, purple, summer, 2 to 3 ft., Spain ; trifida alba, white ; trifida grandiflora, crimson.

Maltese Clover (*Hedysarum coronarium*)—See Hedysarum.

Malva (Musk Mallow)—Ord. Malvaceæ. Hardy annual and perennial flowering plants.
CULTURE OF PERENNIAL SPECIES : Soil, ordinary. Position, sunny or partially shaded beds or borders. Plant, Oct. or March. Mulch with manure in autumn.
CULTURE OF ANNUAL SPECIES : Soil, ordinary. Position, sunny. Plant, May or June.
PROPAGATION : Annual species by seeds sown ⅛ in. deep in light, sandy soil in temp. 55° in March or April ; perennial species by seeds sown similarly, or by cuttings inserted in cold frame in July or Aug.
ANNUAL SPECIES : M. crispa, white and purple, summer, 3 to 6 ft., Europe ; sylvestris, purple-rose, summer, 2 to 3 ft., Europe, biennial usually grown as annual ; sylvestris mauritiana, purple, summer, 3 to 4 ft.
PERENNIAL SPECIES : M. Alcea, rosy purple, summer, 4 ft., Europe, best grown as an annual ; moschata (Musk Mallow), rose, summer, 3 ft., Britain ; moschata alba, white. See also Malvastrum.

Malvastrum (False Mallow)—Ord. Malvaceæ. Hardy perennials. First introduced 1811.
CULTURE : Soil, ordinary. Position, sunny rockeries for dwarf species ; sunny well-drained borders for tall species. Plant, Oct. or March. Protect in severe winters with a layer of cinder ashes, manure, or leaf-mould.
PROPAGATION : By seeds sown ⅛ in. deep in light, sandy soil in temp. 55° in March or April ; cuttings inserted in cold frame in July or Aug.
SPECIES CULTIVATED : M. coccineum, scarlet, July to Sept., 6 in., U. States ; Gilliesii (Syn. Modiola geranoides), red, summer, 6 in., S. America ; lateritium (Syn. Malva lateritia), salmon pink, summer, 1 ft., Uruguay.

Mammillaria (Nipple Cactus ; Elephant's Tooth Cactus)—Ord. Cactaceæ. Greenhouse succulent perennials. First introduced 1690. Flowers generally expanding about 11 a.m. and closing at 1 p.m. ; somewhat fugitive. Stems leafless, cylindrical, or globular, bearing at even distance over their surface small tubercles or teats crowned with rosettes or stars of spines.
CULTURE : Compost, equal parts sandy loam, rough old mortar, and pounded bricks. Position, sunny, airy greenhouse or window. Pot, March or April, in well-drained pots just large enough to accommodate roots. Repot every third or fourth year only. Water moderately March to Sept., once a fortnight, Sept. to Dec., none afterwards. Syringe on evenings of warm days June to Sept. Apply soot-water to healthy plants June to Sept. Ventilate freely in summer. Temp., March to Sept. 60° to 70° ; Sept. to March 50° to 55°.
PROPAGATION : By seeds sown ⅛ in. deep in well-drained pans or pots of sandy soil in temp. 75° in March, keeping soil moderately moist ; by cuttings of the tops of the plants inserted in small pots of sandy, gritty compost in spring ; by grafting on Cereus speciosissimus at any time.
SPECIES CULTIVATED : M. bicolor, purple, June, 6 to 12 in., Mexico ; chlorantha, greenish yellow, summer, 6 in., Mexico ; cirrhifera, rose, summer, 4 in., Mexico ; clava, green, red, and yellow, June 1 ft., Mexico ; compressa (Syn. augularis), rosy purple, summer, 4 to 8 in., Mexico ; dasyacantha (Thimble Cactus), red, summer, 3 in., Mexico ; discolor, rosy red, 2 in., Mexico ; dolichocentra, pale purple, summer, 6 to 8 in., Mexico ; echinata, rose, summer, 6 in., Mexico ; echinus, yellow, June, 2 to 3 in., Mexico ; elegans, 2 in., Mexico, grown for its stem only ; elephantidens, violet-rose, autumn, 6 in., Paraguay ; elongata, yellow, summer, 3 in., Mexico ; floribunda, rose, summer, 5 in., Chile ; gracilis, yellow or white, summer, 2 in., Mexico ; Grahami, rose, July, 3 in., Colorado ; haageana, carmine rose, June, 4 in.,

Mexico; longimamma, citron yellow, June, 4 in., Mexico; macromeris, carmine, Aug., 4 in., Mexico; microthele, yellow, June, Mexico; micromeris, white or pink, Aug., 4 in., Mexico; multiceps, yellow and red, summer, 1 ft., Mexico; neumanniana, rose, summer, 6 in., Mexico; Ottonis, white, May, 3 in., Mexico; phellosperma, 5 ft., Mexico; pulchra, rose, June, 4 in., Mexico; pusilla, yellowish white and red, May, 2 in., Mexico; pycnacantha, yellow, July, 6 in., Mexico; sanguinea, crimson, June, 6 in., Mexico; Scheerii, yellow and cream, summer, 7 in., Mexico; Schelhasii, white and rose, summer, 4 in., Mexico; schiedeana, white, summer, 3 in., Mexico; sempervivi, 3 in., Mexico; senilis, scarlet, summer, 6 in., Mexico; stella-aurata, white, summer, 2 in., Mexico; subpolyhedra, yellow and red, summer, 8 in., Mexico; sulcolanata, yellow, summer, 4 in., Mexico; tetracantha, rose, July, 9 in., Mexico; tuberculosa, pale purple, May, 6 in., Mexico; turbinata, yellow, June, Mexico; uncinata, purple, May and June, 4 in., Mexico; vetula, yellow, May and June, 3 in., Mexico; villifera, rose and purple, May, 3 in., Mexico; viridis, yellow, May and June, 4 in., Mexico; vivipara, purple, May and June, 2 in., N. America; wildiana, rose, summer, 3 to 4 in., Mexico; Wrightii, purple, May, Mexico; zuccariniana, purple, May and June, 3 in., Mexico.

Mammoth Tree of California (*Sequoia gigantea*)—See Sequoia.

Mandarin Orange-tree (*Citrus nobilis major*)—See Citrus.

Mandevilla (Chile Jasmine)—Ord. Apocynaceæ. Greenhouse flowering climber. Deciduous. First introduced 1837.
CULTURE : Compost, equal parts peat and loam, half part each of sand and pounded charcoal. Position, well-drained beds or borders ; shoots trained up trellis, pillars, or roof of sunny greenhouse. Plant, Feb. Water freely Feb. to Sept., moderately Sept. to Dec., none afterwards. Syringe twice daily Feb. to July. Temp., Feb. to Sept. 55° to 65° ; Sept. to Dec. 45° to 55° ; Dec. to Feb. 40° to 50°. Prune shoots to within two buds of their base immediately after flowering.
PROPAGATION : By seeds sown in pans or bed of sandy peat slightly covered with fine soil in a temp. of 65° to 75°, Feb. to April ; cuttings of firm side shoots, 2 to 3 in. long, inserted in sand under bell-glass in temp. of 70° to 85° in summer.
SPECIES CULTIVATED : M. suaveolens, white, fragrant, summer, 15 to 30 ft., Buenos Ayres.

Mandragora (Mandrake)—Ord. Solanaceæ. Hardy perennial herbs. First introduced 1548.
CULTURE : Soil, deep rich. Position, well-drained sunny borders. Plant, Oct. or March.
PROPAGATION : By seeds sown in pans or boxes in cool greenhouse in March ; careful division in March.
SPECIES CULTIVATED : M. autumnalis, violet, Sept., 6 to 12 in., S. Europe ; officinarum (Devil's Apple), greenish yellow, May, 1 ft., S. Europe.

Manetti Stock—See Rosa Manetti.

Manettia—Ord. Rubiaceæ. Greenhouse evergreen climber. First introduced 1832.
CULTURE : Compost, equal parts loam, peat with a liberal admixture of pounded charcoal, and silver sand. Position, well-drained pots or beds ; shoots trained to trellises, round pillars, or up rafters. Plant, Feb. to March. Prune slightly after flowering. Water freely March to Sept., moderately afterwards. Syringe daily March to Sept. Temp., Feb. to Oct. 55° to 65° ; Oct. to Feb. 45° to 55°.
PROPAGATION : By seeds sown in shallow pans of sandy soil, slightly covered with fine mould, and placed in temp. 55° to 65°, Feb. or March ; cuttings of young shoots, 2 to 3 in. long, inserted in small pots of sandy soil in temp. 65° to 75° in summer.
SPECIES CULTIVATED : M. luteo-rubra (Syn. bicolor), scarlet and orange, March to Dec., 10 to 15 ft., S. America.

Mangosteen-tree (*Garcinia Mangostana*)—See Garcinia.

Manila Hemp (*Musa textilis*)—See Musa.

Manna Ash (*Fraxinus Ornus*)—See Fraxinus.

Manna-plant (*Tamarix anglica*)—See Tamarix.

Man Orchis (*Aceras anthropophora*)—See Aceras.

Maple (*Acer campestre*)—See Acer.

Maple-leaved Plane-tree (*Platanus acerifolia*)—See Platanus.

Maple Vine (*Menispermum canadense*)—See Menispermum.

Marajah Palm (*Bactris caryotæfolia*)—See Bactris.

Maranta (Arrowroot Plant)—Ord. Marantaceæ. Stove herbaceous perennials. Orn. foliage. First introduced 1732. Leaves, egg-, lance- or heart-shaped, roundish or oblong ; greyish, purplish, or rose below, upper sides green, blotched or streaked with white, yellow, brown, purple, or rose.
CULTURE : Compost, two parts fibrous peat, one part rich loam, one part sand. Position, well-drained pots in shady part of stove. Pot, Feb. or March. Water abundantly March to Sept., moderately Sept. to Dec., keep nearly dry afterwards. Syringe daily March to Sept. Apply weak stimulants occasionally during summer. Temp., Feb. to Oct. 65° to 75° ; Oct. to Feb. 55° to 65°. Repot annually.
PROPAGATION : By division of tubers or rhizomes in Feb. or March.
SPECIES CULTIVATED : M. arundinacea variegata (Indian Arrowroot), Syn. Phyrnium variegatum, leaves green and white, 2 to 6 ft., S. America ; bicolor, leaves olive green, 1 ft., Brazil ; Chantrieri, leaves grey and dark green, 1 ft. ; leuconeura, leaves light green, white, and purple, 1 ft., Brazil, and its varieties kerchoveana (leaves spotted with red) and massangeana (leaves purple beneath). See also Calathea.

Marattia (Ash-leaf Fern)—Ord. Filices. Greenhouse evergreen ferns. Ht., 3 to 5 ft. Fronds, 5 to 12 ft. long, feather-shaped ; leaflets twice or three times divided. First introduced 1793.
CULTURE : Compost, two parts peat, equal parts loam, leaf-mould, and sand. Position, large well-drained pots or moist beds. Pot or plant, Feb. or March. Shade from sun essential. Water freely March to Oct., moderately afterwards. Syringing not required. Temp., Feb. to Oct. 60° to 70° ; Oct. to Feb. 50° to 60°.
PROPAGATION : By spores sown on surface of sandy peat in shallow, well-drained pans placed under bell-glass in temp. 65° to 75° any time.
SPECIES CULTIVATED : M. alata, Central America ; attenuata (Syn. Cooperi), New Caledonia ; fraxinea, Tropics.

Mare's-tail (*Hippuris vulgaris*)—See Hippuris.

Marguerite (*Chrysanthemum frutescens*)—See Chrysanthemum.

Margyricarpus (Pearl Berry ; Pearl Fruit)—Ord. Rosaceæ. Hardy evergreen trailing shrub. Orn. fruiting. First introduced 1829.
CULTURE : Soil, equal parts leaf-mould, loam, and sand. Position, sunny rockery, with shoots trailing over stones. Plant, Feb. to May.
PROPAGATION : By seeds sown ¹⁄₁₆ in. deep in shallow boxes of light, sandy soil in cold frame in autumn or spring ; cuttings of young shoots, 1 to 2 in. long, inserted in sandy peat under bell-glass in cold frame in summer ; layering branches in Sept. or Oct.
SPECIES CULTIVATED : M. setosus, green, summer, berries white, prostrate, Chile.

Marica (Toad-cup Lily)—Ord. Iridaceæ. Stove herbaceous perennials. First introduced 1789.
CULTURE : Compost, equal parts peat, leaf-mould, and sand. Position, well-drained pots in light part of stove. Pot, Feb. or March. Water freely March to Oct., keep dry Nov. to Feb. Apply weak stimulants occasionally when in flower. Temp., 65° to 75° March to Sept. ; Sept. to March 55° to 65°.
PROPAGATION : By division of rhizomatous roots, Feb. or March.
SPECIES CULTIVATED : M. brachypus, yellow and red, summer, 18 in., Trinidad ; cærulea, blue, yellow, brown, and orange, summer, 2 ft., Trop. America ; northiana, white, yellow, and red, summer, 3 to 4 ft., Trop. America.

Marigold (*Calendula officinalis*)—See Calendula.

Mariposa-lily—See Calochortus.

Marjoram (*Origanum vulgare*)—See Origanum.

Marmalade Plum (*Achras sapota*)—See Achras.

Marrubium (Horehound)—Ord. Labiatæ.   Hardy perennial medicinal herb. Leaves and young shoots used as a popular remedy for coughs.
CULTURE: Soil, ordinary.   Position, sunny, dry borders.   Plant, March or April.
PROPAGATION : By seeds sown ⅓ in. deep in shady position outdoors, March to May ; cuttings inserted in shady border in April ;   division of roots in March.
SPECIES CULTIVATED : M. vulgare, white, June to Sept., 1 ft., Britain.

Marsh Cistus (*Ledum palustre*)—See Ledum.

Marsh Elder (*Viburnum opulus*)—See Viburnum.

Marsh Fel-wort (*Swertia perennis*)—See Swertia.

Marsh Fern (*Nephrodium Thelypteris*)—See Nephrodium.

Marsh-flower—See Limnanthemum.

Marsh Gentian (*Gentiana pneumonanthe*)—See Gentiana.

Marsh Helleborine (*Epipactis palustris*)—See Epipactis.

Marsh Mallow (*Althæa officinalis*)—See Althæa.

Marsh Marigold (*Caltha palustris*)—See Caltha.

Marsh Orchis (*Orchis latifolia*)—See Orchis.

Marsh Ox-eye Daisy (*Chrysanthemum lacustre*)—See Chrysanthemum.

Marsh Rosemary (*Ledum palustre* and *Andromeda polifolia*)—See **Ledum and** Andromeda.

Marsh Trefoil (*Menyanthes trifoliata*)—See Menyanthes.

Marsh Violet (*Viola palustris*)—See Viola.

Martagon Lily (*Lilium Martagon*)—See Lilium.

Martynia (Elephant's Trunk ;   Unicorn Plant)—Ord. Pedalineæ.   Half-hardy annuals.   First introduced 1731.   Fruit edible and used for making pickles.
POT CULTURE : Compost, equal parts loam, leaf-mould, decayed manure, and sand. Sow seeds 1 in. deep singly in 2 in. pots and place in temp. of 60° to 70°, Feb. or March.   Transfer to 5 in. pots in April or May ;   to 6 or 7 in. pots in June.   Pot firmly.   Position, light, sunny greenhouse or window.   Water moderately at first, freely when in full growth.   Apply weak stimulants occasionally to healthy plants in flower.   Temp., Feb. to May 60° to 70° ;   afterwards 55° to 65°.
OUTDOOR CULTURE : Soil, ordinary rich.   Position, sunny, well-drained, sheltered beds or borders.   Sow seeds 1 in. deep singly in 3 in. pots, or 3 in. apart in shallow boxes of light soil in temp. of 60° to 70° in Feb. or March, transplanting seedlings 8 to 12 in. apart early in June.   Mulch with cocoanut-fibre refuse or decayed manure after planting.   Water in dry weather.
SPECIES CUTIVATED : M. fragrans (Unicorn Plant), crimson-purple, summer, 2 ft., Mexico ;   proboscidea, light violet or purple, summer, 1 to 3 ft., N. Mexico.

Marvel of Peru (*Mirabilis Jalapa*)—See Mirabilis.

Maryland Pink Root (*Spigelia marilandica*)—See Spigelia.

Masdevallia (Spectral-flowered Orchid)—Ord. Orchidaceæ.   Greenhouse epiphytal orchids.   Evergreen.   First introduced 1842.
CULTURE : Compost—for robust species (M. coccinea, etc.), two parts fibrous peat, one part sphagnum moss and sand ;   for other species (M. Chimæra, etc,), equal parts peat, moss, and lumps of charcoal and a little sand.   Pot annually in Feb. or March.   Position, well-drained pots for M. coccinea ;   teak-wood baskets, lined

with moss, for M. Chimæra. Shade from sun essential. Water freely April to Sept., moderately afterwards, and keep atmosphere moist all the year round. Syringe staging, floors, and pots daily in summer. Temp., Nov. to March 45° to 55°; March to Nov. 55° to 65°. Ventilate freely in summer. Resting period, none. Flowers appear at base of last-made leaves.

PROPAGATION : By division of plants in Feb.

SPECIES CULTIVATED : M. amabilis, rose, crimson, orange, and yellow, summer, 6 in., Colombia ; bella, yellow, crimson, and white, spring, 6 in., Colombia ; caudata, buff, yellow, and rose, summer, 4 in., Colombia ; Chestertoni, yellow, purple, and pink, spring, 6 in., Colombia ; Chimæra, yellow and purple, spring, 8 in., Colombia ; coccinea, scarlet and rose, spring, 6 to 8 in., Colombia ; coccinea harryana, a variety ; Davisii, yellow and orange, Aug., 8 in., Peru ; ignea, red, orange, and purple, spring, 6 in., Colombia ; rosea, crimson, purple, and rosy lilac, summer, 6 in., Peru ; tovarensis, white, winter, 6 in., Venezuela ; veitchiana, vermilion and purple, spring, 1 ft., Peru. There are also numerous hybrids.

Mask-flower (*Alonsoa incisifolia*)—See Alonsoa.

Mastic Tree (*Pistacia Lentiscus*)—See Pistacia.

Master Wort—See Astrantia.

Matricaria (Double May Weed)—Ord. Compositæ. Hardy perennial herb.

CULTURE : Soil, ordinary. Position, open, sunny beds or borders. Plant, Oct., Nov., March, or April.

PROPAGATION : By cuttings inserted in ordinary soil in shady position outdoors in spring ; division of roots in Oct. or March.

SPECIES CULTIVATED : M. inodora plenissima (Double Mayweed), white, double, summer, 1 ft., Britain.

Matthiola (Ten-week, Brompton, German, Night-scented, Intermediate, Cape Giant, and Wallflower-leaved Stock)—Ord. Cruciferæ. Half-hardy annuals and biennials. First introduced 1731. Also spelt Mathiola.

CULTURE OF TEN-WEEK STOCK OUTDOORS : Soil, deep, rich, well manured. Position, open, sunny beds or borders. Sow seeds 1/16 in. deep in light soil in temp. 55° to 65° in March, transplanting seedlings outdoors end of May ; or in cold frame or out-doors in April, transplanting seedlings in June. Plant, dwarf kinds 9 in. and tall kinds 12 to 15 in. apart each way. Mulch surface of soil after planting with decayed manure. Remove seed pods as they form.

POT CULTURE OF TEN-WEEK STOCKS : Sow seeds as above advised. Transplant three seedlings 1 in. high into a 3 in. pot, and when 3 to 4 in. high into a 5 in. pot. Compost, two parts good soil, one part decayed manure and sand. Position, cold frame during May ; afterwards outdoors. Water freely.

CULTURE OF WALLFLOWER-LEAVED STOCK : Same as for Brompton.

CULTURE OF NIGHT-SCENTED STOCK : Soil, ordinary. Position, sunny beds or borders. Sow seeds 1/2 in. deep in April where required to flower.

CULTURE OF INTERMEDIATE STOCK : Sow seeds 1/8 in. deep in light soil in well-drained pots or boxes in cold frame in June or July. Transplant seedlings when 1 in. high singly in a 2 in. pot or four in a 4 in. pot, or in sheltered border out of doors. Compost, equal parts loam, leaf-mould, and old mortar. Plunge pots to rim in cinder ashes in sunny, cold frame. Water sparingly. Ventilate freely in fine weather. Plant out in rich soil in March, or transfer single plants to a 5 in. or three plants to a 6 in. pot. Water moderately. Apply stimulants when flowers show. For autumn flowering, sow seeds in March or April and plant out in June.

CULTURE OF BROMPTON AND QUEEN STOCKS : Sow seeds 1/8 in. deep in light soil in cold frame in June or July. Transplant seedlings when 1 in. high 8 to 12 in. apart where required to flower following year ; or place singly in 2 in. pots, keep in cold frame, and plant out in March. Seed saving : Largest percentage of double flowers obtained from plants grown in poor soil and of the dwarfest habit.

SPECIES CULTIVATED : M. annua (or incana annua), parent of the Ten-week and Intermediate Stocks, annual, S. Europe ; bicornis (Night-scented Stock), purplish red, spring, fragrant at night, 1 ft., annual, Greece ; fenestralis, scarlet or purple,

Lygodium scandens
(Climbing Fern)

Lysimachia thyrsiflora
(Yellow Loose-strife)

Lythrum Salicaria
(Common Loose-strife)

Magnolia stellata
(Yulan)

Malope grandiflora
(Mallow-wort)

Malva moschata
(Musk Mallow)

Martynia fragrans
(Unicorn Plant)

Masdevallia hybrida
(Spectral-flowered Orchid)

Matricaria inodora plenissima
(Double Mayweed)

Matthiola annua
(Stock)

Maurandia Barclayana

Meconopsis sinuata latifolia
(Himalayan Poppy)

Melissa officinalis
(Common Balm)

Mesembryanthemum echinatum

Miltonia Warscewiczii

Mimulus hybridus
(Monkey-flower)

Mirabilis Jalapa
(Marvel of Peru)

Monarda didyma
(Sweet Bergamot)

summer, 1 ft., biennial, Crete ; incana (Brompton, Queen, and Wallflower-leaved Stock), purple or violet, summer, 1 to 2 ft., biennial, Levant ; tricuspidata, lilac, summer, 1 ft., annual, S. Europe.

Maurandia—Ord. Scrophulariaceæ. Half-hardy climbing perennials. First introduced 1796.

INDOOR CULTURE : Compost, equal parts loam and leaf-mould and little sand. Pot, March to May. Position, well-drained pots with shoots draping over front of stage, or trained up trellises, walls, or rafters, or suspended in baskets in sunny greenhouse. Water freely March to Sept., moderately Sept. to Nov., keep nearly dry afterwards. Apply stimulants to healthy plants in flower only. Temp., March to Sept. 55° to 65° ; Sept. to March 45° to 55°.

OUTDOOR CULTURE : Soil, ordinary rich. Position, against S. walls or in sunny vases or window boxes. Plant, June. Lift, repot, and place in greenhouse in Sept. Water freely in dry weather.

PROPAGATION : By seeds sown ⅟₁₆ in. deep in ordinary light soil in temp. of 60° to 70° in March, transplanting seedlings when 1 in. high singly into 2 or 3 in. pots ; cuttings of young shoots inserted in samdy soil under bell-glass in temp. 55° to 65°, March to Aug.

SPECIES CULTIVATED : M. barclayana, violet purple, summer, Mexico ; erubescens (Syn. Lophospermum erubescens), rose and white, summer, Mexico ; scandens (Syn. Lophospermum scandens), purple and violet, summer, Mexico.

Maxillaria—Ord. Orchidaceæ. Warm greenhouse terrestrial orchids. Deci-duous and evergreen. First introduced 1832.

CULTURE : Compost, equal parts fibry peat and chopped sphagnum moss with little sand and charcoal. Position, well-drained pots, pans, or baskets in light part of greenhouse. M. houtteana and M. tenuifolia on teak raft suspended from the roof or against the stem of a tree fern. Pot when new growth commences. Water deciduous species freely from time new growth begins until Nov., then occasionally ; evergreen species freely from March to Nov., moderately Nov. to March. Syringe once or twice daily whilst making growth. Ventilate freely May to Sept. Temp., April to Oct. 55° to 65° ; Oct. to April 45° to 55°. Growing period, Feb. to March ; resting period, Oct. to Feb. Plants may be grown in sitting room or cool conserva-tory when in flower. Flowers appear at base of new pseudo-bulb.

PROPAGATION : By division of pseudo-bulbs immediately after flowering.

SPECIES CULTIVATED : M. grandiflora, white and yellow, fragrant, autumn, Peru ; houtteana, green and crimson-brown, spring, Trop. America ; luteo-alba, yellow, white, and purple, fragrant, various seasons, Colombia ; picta, yellow, purple, and white, winter, Colombia ; sanderiana, white and crimson, spring, Peru ; tenuifolia, yellow and crimson, spring, Mexico ; venusta, white and yellow, winter, Colombia.

Max Leichtlin's Lily (*Lilium Leichtlini*)—See Lilium.

May (*Cratægus Oxyacantha*)—See Cratægus.

May Apple (*Podophyllum peltatum*)—See Podophyllum.

May Flower (*Epigæa repens*)—See Epigæa.

May Lily (*Convallaria majalis*)—See Convallaria.

Mazus—Ord. Scrophulariaceæ. Hardy dwarf perennial herbs, suitable for rockery culture. First introduced 1780.

CULTURE : Soil, moist, sandy loam. Position, sunny rockery. Plant in spring.

PROPAGATION : By seeds sown in sandy soil in April in a cold frame, the seedlings being grown on until the following spring before planting out ; by division of the tufts in spring.

SPECIES CULTIVATED : M. pumilio, purplish blue, May to Oct., 2 in., New Zealand ; reptans, rosy lavender, white and brown, May to Oct., 1 in., Himalayas ; rugosus, lilac blue, summer, Asia.

Meadow Beauty (*Rhexia virginica*)—See Rhexia.

Meadow Crocus (*Colchicum autumnale*)—See Colchicum.

Meadow **Geranium** (*Geranium pratense*)—See Geranium.

Meadow **Grass**—See Poa.

Meadow **Pink** (*Dianthus deltoides*)—See Dianthus.

Meadow **Rue**—See Thalictrum.

Meadow **Saffron** (*Colchicum autumnale*)—See Colchicum.

Meadow **Sage** (*Salvia pratensis*)—See Salvia.

Meadow **Saxifrage** (*Saxifraga granulata*)—See Saxifraga.

Meadow-**sweet** (*Filipendula Ulmaria*)—See Filipendula.

Meconopsis (Welsh Poppy; Himalayan Poppy; Prickly Poppy; Nepaul Poppy)—Ord. Papaveraceæ. Hardy monocarpic and perennial herbs.
CULTURE OF MONOCARPIC SPECIES : Sow seeds $\frac{1}{16}$ in. deep in light, sandy soil in temp. 60° to 70° in March or April. Transplant seedlings when large enough to handle into a cold frame and plant out in permanent positions as soon as they have formed tufts of seven or eight leaves each. Soil, deep loam with sand, leaf-mould, and peat. Position, well-drained sunny rockery. Water freely in summer ; keep dry as possible in winter. Monocarpic species flower when two to four years old and afterwards die.
CULTURE OF PERENNIAL SPECIES : Soil, deep rich loam mixed freely with decayed manure and leaf-mould. Position, sunny, sheltered borders or rockeries. Plant, March or April. Water, as above advised.
PROPAGATION : Perennial species by seeds sown $\frac{1}{16}$ in. deep in light, sandy soil in temp. 55° to 60° as soon as ripe or in Feb. or March, transplanting as advised above for monocarpic species.
MONOCARPIC SPECIES ; M. aculeata, pale blue and violet, 12 to 16 in., N.W. Himalayas ; cambrica (Welsh Poppy), yellow, summer, 1 ft., Europe (Britain) ; cambrica flore-pleno, double-flowered ; Delavayi, violet, 6 to 8 in., W. China ; horridula, blue, 8 in., Central and Eastern Asia ; integrifolia, primrose yellow, May to Aug., 18 in., W. China ; lancifolia, violet, 3 to 6 in., Central Asia ; nepalensis, purplish blue, 3 to 5 ft., Himalayas ; paniculata, yellow, July to Aug., 5 to 6 ft., W. China ; punicea, crimson, late autumn, 1 to 1½ ft., Thibet ; Prattii, blue or purple, June to July, 15 to 18 in., China ; pseudo-integrifolia, sulphur yellow, 6 to 8 in., W. China ; racemosa, lavender blue or violet, 18 in., W. China and Thibet ; rigidiuscula, blue, 2 to 2½ ft., Eastern Asia ; rudis, blue, 18 in., W. China ; simplicifolia, sky blue, summer, 2 ft., Himalayas ; sinuata, pale blue, May to June, 1 to 1½ ft., Eastern Himalayas, and its variety latifolia.
PERENNIAL SPECIES : M. Baileyi (Syn. betonicifolia), azure blue, June to July, 3 to 4 ft., Himalayas ; grandis, violet blue or slaty blue, June, 3 ft., Sikkim ; quintuplinervia, lavender blue, May, 12 to 18 in., Thibet ; Wallichii (Satin Poppy), blue, summer, 4 to 6 ft., Himalayas.

Medeola—See Asparagus.

Medicago (Calvary Clover; Crown of Thorns)—Ord. Leguminosæ. Hardy annual. Flowers succeeded by curiously twisted legumes. First introduced 1818.
CULTURE : Sow seeds $\frac{1}{8}$ in. deep in ordinary soil in sunny position outdoors, April or May. Thin seedlings when 1 in. high to 6 in. apart. Water freely in dry weather.
POT CULTURE : Compost, two parts good soil, one part leaf-mould, half a part each of old mortar and sand. Sow seeds thinly in 5 in. pots filled with above compost. When seedlings are 1 in. high, thin to 3 in each pot. Water moderately. Position, sunny window or greenhouse.
SPECIES CULTIVATED : M. echinus (Calvary Clover), yellow, summer, 6 in., S. Europe.

Medinilla—Ord. Melastomaceæ. Stove evergreen flowering shrubs. First introduced 1845.
CULTURE : Compost, two parts fibrous peat, one part loam, half part sand, half part well-decayed manure. Position, sunny, moist part of stove Feb. to Sept. ; light and moderately dry part afterwards. Pot, Feb. Temp., Feb. to Sept. 75° to 85° ;

Sept. to Nov. 70° to 80°; Nov. to Feb. 65° to 75°. Water freely March to Sept., moderately afterwards. Syringe twice daily March to Sept. Moist atmosphere very essential. Apply stimulants when plants commence flowering. Prune straggly shoots into shape, Jan. or Feb.

PROPAGATION : By cuttings of firm young side shoots, 3 to 4 in. long, inserted in sandy peat and leaf-mould under bell-glass in temp. 85° in spring or summer.

SPECIES CULTIVATED : M. amabilis (Syn. Teysmannii), rosy pink, spring, 4 ft., Java; Curtisii, white, Sumatra ; magnifica, rosy pink, May, 4 ft., Philippines.

Mediterranean Heath (*Erica mediterranea*)—See Erica.

Mediterranean Lily (*Pancratium maritimum*)—See Pancratium.

Medlar (*Mespilus germanica*)—See Mespilus.

Medusa's Head Orchid (*Epidendrum Medusæ*)—See Epidendrum.

Megasea—See Saxifraga.

Melaleuca—Ord. Myrtaceæ. Greenhouse flowering shrubs. First introduced 1788. Natives of Australia.

CULTURE : Compost, equal parts peat, loam, and silver sand. Position, pots in greenhouse or well-drained borders in the open at base of S. wall in the mildest counties. Pot or plant, March or April. Prune shoots a little after flowering. Water freely April to Sept., moderately afterwards. Temp., March to Sept. 55° to 65° ; Sept. to March 40° to 50°.

PROPAGATION : By cuttings of nearly ripened shoots inserted in sandy peat under hand-light in temp. 55° to 65° during July or Aug.

SPECIES CULTIVATED : M. armillaris, white, June, 10 to 30 ft. ; decussata, lilac, August, 15 to 20 ft. ; ericifolia, yellowish white, July to Sept., 15 to 20 ft. ; hypericifolia, rich red, July to Aug., 10 to 20 ft. ; Leucadendra (Cajuput-tree), creamy white, 20 ft. or more ; linariifolia, white, 15 to 20 ft.

Melancholy Gentleman (*Hesperis tristis*)—See Hesperis.

Melia (Bead-tree ; Indian Lilac)—Ord. Meliaceæ. Half-hardy deciduous tree. Flowering and orn. foliage. First introduced 1656. Leaves, graceful, feather-shaped, green.

CULTURE : Soil, sandy loam. Position, large well-drained pots in cool greenhouse or conservatory, or sheltered shrubberies outdoors S. of England. Pot or plant, Oct. to Feb. Water freely (in pots) March to Oct. ; little afterwards.

PROPAGATION : By cuttings inserted in sand under bell-glass in temp. 55° to 65°, summer or autumn.

SPECIES CULTIVATED : M. Azedarach, lilac, summer, leaves fragrant, to 40 ft., India and China, and its variety umbraculiformis (Texas Umbrella Tree).

Melianthus (Great Cape Honey-flower)—Ord. Sapindaceæ. Half-hardy ever-green shrubs. Orn. foliage. First introduced 1688. Leaves, graceful, feather-shaped, green. Natives of S. Africa.

POT CULTURE : Compost, two parts loam, one part leaf-mould and sand. Position, well-drained pots in sunny greenhouse. Pot, Feb. or April. Water freely March to Oct., moderately afterwards. Temp., March to Sept. 55° to 65°; Sept. to March 40° to 50°.

OUTDOOR CULTURE : Soil, ordinary rich. Position, sunny beds or borders. Plant, May or June. Cover roots and base of plant with dry litter in late Sept. as protec-tion from frost or else lift, pot, and winter in cool greenhouse or conservatory. May be grown entirely outdoors in warm, sheltered parts of England.

PROPAGATION : By seeds sown $\frac{1}{16}$ in. deep in light, sandy soil in temp. 65° to 75° in Jan., Feb., or March, or in similar soil in temp. 55° to 65° in Aug. or Sept.; by cuttings inserted in light, sandy soil under bell-glass in temp. 55° to 65° in spring or summer.

SPECIES CULTIVATED : M. comosus, orange-red and green, autumn, 3 to 5 ft.; major, brown, summer, 4 to 6 ft. ; minor, dark brown, Aug., 5 ft. ; pectinatus, scarlet, winter, 6 to 10 ft.

Meliosma—Ord. Sabiaceæ. Deciduous trees and shrubs. Hardy, or nearly so. First introduced 1879.
CULTURE: Soil, good loamy. Position, sheltered shrubberies, or as specimen plants on lawns. M. myriantha requires protection when young in all but the mildest parts of the country.
PROPAGATION: By cuttings of half-ripened shoots inserted in sandy soil and slight bottom heat during July.
SPECIES CULTIVATED: M. cuneifolia, yellowish white, fragrant, summer, to 20 ft., W. China; myriantha, yellowish white, fragrant, June to July, 20 ft., Japan, etc.; veitchiorum, white, purplish-black berries, 30 to 40 ft., W. China.

Melissa (Common Balm)—Ord. Labiatæ. Hardy herbaceous perennials. Aromatic foliage. Leaves, egg-shaped, dark green, or variegated with yellow; fragrant.
CULTURE: Soil, ordinary light. Position, warm, sunny beds or borders. Plant, Oct. or March in groups or 12 in. apart in rows. Gather stems when flowers open for drying for winter use. Cut stems off close to ground after flowering.
PROPAGATION: By seeds sown ¼ in. deep outdoors in March; division of roots in Oct. or March.
SPECIES CULTIVATED: M. officinalis (Balm), white or yellow, summer, 3 ft., Europe (Britain); officinalis variegata, leaves golden.

Melittis (Bastard Balm)—Ord. Labiatæ. Hardy perennial.
CULTURE: Soil, ordinary rich. Position, partially shaded beds or borders. Plant, Oct., Nov., March, or April.
PROPAGATION: By division of roots directly after flowering.
SPECIES CULTIVATED: M. melissophyllum, creamy white and pink, May, 18 in., Europe (Britain).

Melocactus (Melon Cactus; Melon Thistle; Turk's Cap Cactus; Pope's Head) —Ord. Cactaceæ. Greenhouse succulent perennial. First introduced 1788. Stems globular, ribbed, spiny, surmounted by a cylindrical cap.
CULTURE: Compost, two parts fibrous sandy loam, one part brick rubble, old mortar, and sand. Position, well-drained pots in sunny greenhouse or window. Repot every three or four years in March. Water once a month Sept. or April; once a week afterwards. Temp., Sept. to March 50° to 55°; March to Sept. 65° to 75°.
PROPAGATION: By seeds sown ⅛ in. deep in well-drained pans of sandy soil in temp. 75° in March, keeping soil moderately moist; cuttings of stems inserted in small pots of sandy soil kept barely moist in summer; grafting on common kinds in April.
SPECIES CULTIVATED: M. communis (Turk's Head or Melon Cactus), rosy red, summer, 12 to 18 in., W. Indies.

Melon (*Cucumis melo*)—See Cucumis.

Melon-cactus (*Melocactus communis*)—See Melocactus.

Melon Thistle (*Melocactus communis*)—See Melocactus.

Meniscium—Ord. Filices. Stove evergreen rhizomatous ferns. First introduced 1793. Fronds entire or once divided.
CULTURE: Compost, equal parts loam, leaf-mould, peat, and sand. Position, well-drained pots or ledges of rockery in shady part of stove. Pot or plant, Feb. or March. Water freely April to Sept. moderately afterwards. Temp., March to Sept. 65° to 75°; Sept. to March 55° to 65°.
PROPAGATION: By spores sown on surface of pans of fine sandy peat in temp. 75° to 80° any time; division of plants at potting time.
SPECIES CULTIVATED: M. reticulatum and its variety macrophyllum, W. Indies; serratum, W. Indies; simplex, Tropical Asia.

Menispermum (Moon Seed; Moon Creeper)—Ord. Menispermaceæ. Hardy deciduous flowering climber. First introduced 1691.
CULTURE: Soil, ordinary rich. Position, moist, shady borders with shoots twined up walls, arbours, pergolas, or trellises. Plant, Oct. or March. Prune away weak or unhealthy shoots, Nov. to Feb.

PROPAGATION : By cuttings of young shoots inserted in sandy soil in shady position outdoors, or under hand-light in spring ; division of roots, Oct. to March.
SPECIES CULTIVATED : M. canadense, yellow, summer, 10 to 15 ft., N. America.

Mentha (Mint ; Pennyroyal)—Ord. Labiatæ. Hardy perennials. Aromatic foliage.
CULTURE OF SPEARMINT : Soil, rich, moist, ordinary. Position, sunny or partially shady border. Plant roots 2 in. deep in rows 9 in. apart in Feb. or March. Mulch with layer of decayed manure in March. Water freely in dry weather. Cut off stems close to ground in Sept. and cover bed with 2 in. of soil. Lift and replant every three years. Gather shoots for drying when flowers first open. Forcing : Place roots close together (with ordinary soil between) in large pot or box and put in a temp. of 55° to 65°, Oct. to March. Keep soil moist.
CULTURE OF PEPPERMINT : Same as advised for Spearmint. Gather when in flower for distillation.
CULTURE OF PENNYROYAL : Soil, moist loamy. Position, partially shaded border. Plant, Sept., March, or April, 6 in. apart in rows 12 in. asunder. Water freely in dry weather. Mulch with decayed manure in April.
CULTURE OF OTHER SPECIES : Soil, light rich. Position, partially shaded borders. Plant, March or April. M. Requienii an excellent creeping plant for covering surface of soil in moist places. M. Pulegium gibraltarica should be wintered in a cold frame and planted out in April or May.
PROPAGATION : Spearmint and Peppermint by division of roots in Feb. or March ; also cuttings of young shoots, 3i n. long, inserted in shady position outdoors in summer ; Pennyroyal by offshoots or divisions in Oct. or March ; ordinary species by division in Oct. or Feb.
SPECIES CULTIVATED : M. aquatica (Bergamot Mint), purple, summer, 1 ft., Europe ; piperita (Peppermint), purple, autumn, 1 ft., Europe ; Pulegium (Pennyroyal), purple, Aug., 4 to 6 in., Europe ; Pulegium gibraltarica (Gibraltar Mint), 2 in., used for carpet bedding ; Requienii, purple, summer, creeping, Corsica ; viridis (Spearmint or Lamb Mint), purple, Aug., 2 ft., Europe.

Mentzelia—Ord. Loasaceæ. Hardy annuals. First introduced 1811.
CULTURE : Sow seeds ⅛ in. deep in light, sandy soil in temp. 55° to 65° till May ; place in cold frame and plant outdoors in June ; or sow outdoors in sunny borders in April or May. Soil, ordinary. Position, sunny well-drained borders.
SPECIES CULTIVATED : M. bartonioides, yellow, summer, 1 ft., U. States ; Lindleyi (Syn. Bartonia aurea), golden yellow, summer, 1 ft., California ; ornata, white, fragrant, Aug., 1 ft., N. America.

Menyanthes (Buck Bean ; Bog Bean ; Bog Trefoil ; Marsh Trefoil ; Water Trefoil)—Ord. Gentianaceæ. Hardy perennial aquatic.
CULTURE : Soil, ordinary mud or bog. Position, shallow streams, pools, or ponds, marshes and bogs. Plant, Sept. to Nov. and March or April.
PROPAGATION : By inserting pieces of creeping stems in the mud, March to Oct.
SPECIES CULTIVATED : M. trifoliata, white, red, and purple, fragrant, March to June, Europe (Britain).

Menziesia—Ord. Ericaceæ. Deciduous flowering shrub. Hardy. First introduced 1806.
CULTURE : Soil, peaty loam. Position, sunny or partially shady shrubberies, borders, or rock gardens. Plant, Nov. to Feb.
PROPAGATION : By seed sown in sandy peat in well-drained pans during Feb. in temp. 55° to 60° ; cuttings of current year's growth during July in sandy soil and gentle bottom heat.
SPECIES CULTIVATED : M. pilosa (Syn. M. globularis), yellowish white, May to June, 3 to 6 ft., Eastern N. America. See also Daboëcia and Phyllodoce.

Menzies' Spruce (*Picea pungens*)—See Picea.

Mercury (*Chenopodium Bonus-Henricus*)—See Chenopodium.

Merendera (Pyrenean Meadow Saffron)—Nat. Ord. **Liliaceæ.** Hardy bulbous perennials. First introduced 1820. Flowers fragrant.
CULTURE : Soil, light, sandy loam enriched with decayed manure or leaf-mould. Position, moist beds or rockeries, shrubbery borders, or lawns near shade of trees. Plant bulbs 3 in. deep and 3 in. apart in July or Aug. Foliage dies down in June and July and does not reappear until after plant has flowered.
PROPAGATION : By seeds sown ⅛ in. deep in bed of fine soil outdoors in Aug. or Sept., or in pans or boxes of similar soil in cold frame at same time, transplanting seedlings 3 in. apart when two years old ; division of bulbs in Aug. Seedling bulbs do not flower until four or five years old.
SPECIES CULTIVATED : M. bulbocodium, rosy lilac, autumn, 3 in., Spain ; caucasica, rosy purple, spring, 3 in., Caucasus ; persica, lilac, Nov., 3 in., Persia.

Mertensia (Virginian Cowslip)—Ord. Boraginaceæ. Hardy perennial herbs.
CULTURE : Soil, sandy peat and loam. Position, partially shady rockeries or borders. Plant, Oct. and Nov., March and April. Lift and replant in fresh soil every four or five years. M. sibirica will thrive in ordinary soil in partial shade.
PROPAGATION : By seeds sown 1/16 in. deep in sandy peat in cold frame in autumn ; division of roots in Oct. or March.
SPECIES CULTIVATED : M. alpina, blue, May to July, 6 in., Rocky Mountains ; ciliata, pink and blue, all summer, 18 to 24 in., Rocky Mountains ; echioides, deep blue, summer, 6 to 9 in., Himalayas ; primuloides, brilliant blue, summer, 3 in., Himalayas ; virginica (Syn. M. pulmonarioides), the Virginian Cowslip, purple and blue, May to June, 12 to 18 in., N. America ; sibirica, purple and blue, May to Sept., 18 in.

Mesembryanthemum (Fig Marigold ; Ice Plant)—Ord. Ficoidaceæ. Greenhouse and hardy annuals and herbaceous and shrubby perennials. Mostly evergreen and trailing. First introduced 1690. This genus is under considerable revision by botanists, many species being referred to new genera such as Lamphanthus, Cryophytum, Erepsia, Glottiphyllum and Conophytum.
CULTURE OF GREENHOUSE SHRUBBY AND SUCCULENT-LEAVED SPECIES : Compost, equal parts old mortar, pounded crocks, sandy loam, well-decayed manure or leaf-mould and sand. Position, well-drained pots in sunny greenhouse or window. Pot, March to May. Water freely April to Sept., moderately March and Sept., keep nearly dry during the remainder of year. Temp., March to Oct. 55° to 65° ; Oct. to March 40° to 50°. These species may be planted in sunny beds or on rockeries in June ; lifted, repotted, and placed in greenhouse in Sept.
CULTURE OF ANNUAL SPECIES IN POTS : Sow seeds 1/16 in. deep in April in 4 or 5 in. pots filled with above compost in temp. 55° to 65°. Thin seedlings to ½ in. apart. Treat otherwise as advised for shrubby species.
CULTURE OF ANNUAL SPECIES OUTDOORS : Soil, ordinary, with liberal addition of old mortar. Sow seeds 1/16 in. deep in April where plants are required to grow. Thin to 1 in. apart. Position, sunny well-drained rockery.
CULTURE OF M. CORDIFOLIUM VARIEGATUM : Propagate by cuttings inserted in sandy soil in March, April, or Sept., in temp. 60° to 70°. Grow in temp. 50° to 60° Oct. to May, in cold frame until June, then plant outdoors.
CULTURE OF ICE PLANT : Soil, ordinary. Position, sunny bed, border, or rockery. Sow seeds ⅛ in. deep in sandy soil in temp. 55° to 65° in March, transplanting seedlings outdoors in June.
CULTURE OF HARDY SPECIES : Soil, ordinary. Position, sunny well-drained borders in S. of England. Plant, May.
PROPAGATION : Annual species by seeds sown 1/16 in. deep in spring in similar compost to that advised for plants ; shrubby and herbaceous species by seeds ; also by cuttings inserted in old mortar, loam, and sand in temp. 55° to 65°, March to Sept.
GREENHOUSE SHRUBBY SPECIES : M. aurantiacum, bright orange, summer, 1 to 2 ft., S. Africa ; aureum, yellow, June, 1 ft., S. Africa ; blandum, white, June, 18 in. ; Bolusii, yellow and red, July, 1 ft. ; Brownii, orange-red, summer, 1 ft. ; coccineum, scarlet, July, 18 in. ; Cooperi, rosy purple, summer, 1 ft. ; cruciatum, yellow, 6 in., summer ; deltoides, pink, May, 18 in. ; echinatum, yellow, Aug., 1 ft. ; Haworthi,

purple, summer, 1½ ft., S. Africa; inclaudens, purplish pink, June, 1½ ft., S. Africa; multiflorum, white, Aug., 3 ft.; polyanthon, pink, Aug., 1 to 1½ ft., S. Africa; roseum, pale rose, July, 1½ to 2 ft., S. Africa; tigrinum, yellow, autumn, 6 in.; violaceum, purple, July, 1 ft.

GREENHOUSE SUCCULENT-LEAVED SPECIES: M. cordifolium, purple, summer, 1 to 2 ft., S. Africa, and its variety variegatum (leaves golden yellow); densum, pink, June, trailing; floribundum, pink, July, 6 in.; spectabile, red, May, 1 ft.

ANNUAL SPECIES: M. crystallinum (Ice Plant), white, July; pomeridianum, yellow, July, 1 ft.; pyropæum (Syn. M. tricolor), rose and white, June, 6 in.

HARDY SPECIES: M. acinaciforme, reddish, Aug., trailing, S. Africa; edule (Hottentot Fig), yellow, July; uncinatum, red, summer.

Mespilus (Medlar)—Ord. Rosaceæ. Hardy deciduous tree. Cultivated for its edible fruits.

CULTURE: Soil, ordinary. Position, sunny shrubberies, or as specimens on lawns. Plant, Nov. to Feb.

PROPAGATION: By seeds sown in the open during March or April; grafting in April on pear, quince, or hawthorn; budding on same stocks in July.

SPECIES CULTIVATED: M. germanica, white, May to June, fruits brown, to 20 ft., Europe and Asia Minor.

Metake Bamboo (*Arundinaria japonica*)—See Arundinaria.

Metrosideros—Ord. Myrtaceæ. Greenhouse evergreen flowering trees. First introduced 1840.

CULTURE: Compost, peaty loam and sand. Position, large well-drained pots or borders in cool greenhouse. Plant or pot, Oct. or April. Water freely during summer months. Temp., March to Sept. 55° to 65°: Sept. to March 40° to 50°.

PROPAGATION: By cuttings of young growth during May. inserted in sandy soil under hand-light in gentle bottom heat.

SPECIES CULTIVATED: M. lucida, bright red, to 60 ft., New Zealand; robusta, dark red, May, to 100 ft., New Zealand; tomentosa, dark red, July, to 70 ft., New Zealand.

Meum (Baldmoney; Spignel)—Ord. Umbelliferæ. Hardy perennial aromatic herb.

CULTURE: Soil, ordinary. Position, sunny beds, borders, banks, or rockeries. Plant, Oct., Nov., March, or April. Cut down flower stems, Sept. Water freely in dry weather.

PROPAGATION: By division of the roots, Oct., Nov., March, or April.

SPECIES CULTIVATED: M. athamanticum, white, May, 1 ft., Europe (Britain).

Mexican Blue Sage (*Salvia azurea grandiflora*)—See Salvia.

Mexican Cigar-flower—See Cuphea.

Mexican Ivy (*Cobæa scandens*)—See Cobæa.

Mexican Lily—See Furcræa.

Mexican Marigold (*Tagetes mexicana*)—See Tagetes.

Mexican Orange-flower (*Choisya ternata*)—See Choisya.

Mexican Poppy (*Argemone mexicana*)—See Argemone.

Mexican Soap-plant—See Agave.

Mexican Sunflower (*Tithonia speciosa*)—See Tithonia.

Mexican Tiger Flower (*Tigridia Pavonia*)—See Tigridia.

Meyenia—See Thunbergia.

Mezereon (*Daphne mezereum*)—See Daphne.

Michaelmas Daisy—See Aster.

Michauxia (Michaux's Bell-flower)—Ord. Campanulaceæ. Hardy perennials. First introduced 1787.

CULTURE: Soil, moist, sandy loam. Position, warm, sheltered, sunny borders. Best grown as biennials.

PROPAGATION : By seeds sown ⅛ in. deep in sunny position outdoors in April, transplanting seedlings into flowering position following July or Aug. ; or by sowing seeds in April where plants are required to grow.
SPECIES CULTIVATED : M. Tchihatcheffi, white, July to Sept., 5 to 7 ft., Asia Minor ; campanuloides, white, July, 4 to 6 ft., Asia Minor.

Michaux's Bell-flower (*Michauxia campanuloides*)—See Michauxia.

Michelia—Ord. Magnoliaceæ. Evergreen flowering tree. Closely allied to Magnolia. First introduced 1894.
CULTURE : Soil, rich, deep, sandy loam. Position, border against S. or W. wall. Plant, March or April.
PROPAGATION : By seeds sown singly in small pots during Feb., in temp. 55° to 60°.
SPECIES CULTIVATED : M. compressa, pale yellow, fragrant, to 40 ft., Japan.

Miconia—Ord. Melastomaceæ. Stove evergreen orn. foliage plants. First introduced 1858. Leaves, broad, upper surface velvety green, under side reddish purple.
CULTURE : Compost, equal parts fibrous peat and leaf-mould, fourth part silver sand. Position, pots in moist, shady plant stove. Pot, Feb. or March. Water moderately in winter, freely other times. Syringe foliage March to Sept. Temp., March to Sept. 75° to 85° ; Sept. to March 60° to 70°.
PROPAGATION : By seeds sown in fine light compost in temp. 85° in March or April ; cuttings of shoots of stems inserted in light soil in temp. 80° to 90° in spring.
SPECIES CULTIVATED : M. flammea, leaves green, 1 to 2 ft., Brazil ; hookeriana, leaves green and white, 1 to 2 ft. ; magnifica, leaves bronzy green, 2 to 3 ft., Mexico.

Microglossa (Shrubby Star-wort)—Ord. Compositæ. Hardy shrubby perennial. First introduced 1883.
CULTURE : Soil, ordinary. Position, sunny borders. Plant, Oct., Nov., March, or April.
PROPAGATION : By seeds sown ⅛ in. deep in sunny position outdoors, March or April, or in sandy soil in cold frame, April ; division of roots, Oct. or March.
SPECIES CULTIVATED : M. albescens, lilac blue or bluish white, autumn, 2 to 3 ft., Himalayas.

Microlepia—See Davallia.

Micromeria—Ord. Labiatæ. Half-hardy shrubby perennials.
CULTURE : Soil, ordinary. Position, sunny rockeries. Plant, Oct., Nov., March, or April. Protect in winter with hand-lights.
PROPAGATION : By cuttings inserted in ordinary sandy soil under hand-light in cold frame, Sept. to Nov.
SPECIES CULTIVATED : M. Piperella, purplish white, July to Oct., 3 in., S. Europe ; croatica, pale rose, spring, 6 in., Croatia.

Microstylis—Ord. Orchidaceæ. Stove terrestrial orchids. Orn. foliage. First introduced 1830.
CULTURE : Equal parts peat, sand, and finely chopped sphagnum moss. Position, well-drained pans in shady part of the intermediate house. Abundant moisture essential during season of growth. Water moderately at other times. Pot, Feb. or March. Temp., Sept. to Feb. 55° to 65° ; Feb. to Sept. 65° to 75°.
PROPAGATION : In Feb. by inserting portions of stem in same compost as advised for plants, under bell-glass.
SPECIES CULTIVATED : M. calophylla, greenish-bronze and greyish-green foliage, 4 to 6 in., Malaya ; metallica, glossy purple and rose foliage, Borneo ; Scottii, bronze, yellow, green, and purple foliage, Penang.

Mignonette (*Reseda odorata*)—See Reseda.

Mikania (German Ivy ; Parlour Ivy)—Ord. Compositæ. Half-hardy perennial flowering climber. First introduced 1823.
OUTDOOR CULTURE : Soil, good ordinary. Position, against S. or W. walls, sunny arbours, or trellises. Plant, May. Lift in Oct. and store in pots in frost-proof greenhouse or frame.

Morina longifolia
(Whorl-flower)

Muscari comosum monstrosum
(Feather Hyacinth)

Myrtus communis
(Common Myrtle)

Narcissus Barri

Narcissus cyclamineus
(Cyclamen Flowered Daffodil)

Narcissus Leedsi
(Chalice Cup Daffodil)

Narcissus poeticus
(Pheasant's Eye)

Narcissus poeticus plenus
(Gardenia Flowered Narcissus)

Narcissus Primrose Phœnix
(Double Narcissus)

Narcissus pseudo-narcissus
(Trumpet Daffodil)

Narcissus Tazetta
(Polyanthus Narcissus)

Narcissus triandrus albus
(Angel's Tears)

Nelumbium speciosum
(Sacred Bean)

Nemesia strumosa hybrida

Nepenthes Wittei
(Pitcher-plant)

Nepeta Glechoma variegata
(Ground Ivy)

Nerine flexuosa hybrida
(Guernsey Lily)

Nerium Oleander
(Oleander)

INDOOR CULTURE : Compost, two parts loam, one part leaf-mould or well-decayed manure, and little sand. Position, well-drained pots with shoots trained round trellises, or up rafters or in suspended baskets with shoots hanging down, in sunny greenhouse or window. Pot, Feb. or March. Water freely March to Oct., moderately afterwards. Apply stimulants occasionally May to Sept. Temp., March to Oct. 55° to 65° ; Oct. to March 40° to 50°.
PROPAGATION : By cuttings of shoots inserted in sandy soil in temp. 55° to 65° in spring.
SPECIES CULTIVATED : M. scandens, yellow and white, summer, 6 to 8 ft., Trop. America.

Milanji Cypress (*Widdringtonia Whytei*)—See Widdringtonia.

Milfoil—See Achillea.

Military Orchis (*Orchis militaris*)—See Orchis.

Milk Thistle (*Silybum Marianum*)—See Silybum.

Milk Vetch—See Astragalus.

Milk-weed—See Asclepias.

Milk-weed Gentian (*Gentiana asclepiadea*)—See Gentiana.

Milk-wort—See Polygala.

Milla—See Brodiæa.

Miltonia—Ord. Orchidaceæ. Stove epiphytal orchids. First introduced 1830.
CULTURE : Compost, three parts osmunda fibre, polypodium fibre, or good quality peat, one part finely chopped sphagnum moss and beech or oak leaves. Position, well-drained pots or pans in shady part of stove. Pot, Feb. or March. Water freely March to Sept., moderately afterwards. Shade from sun and moist atmosphere essential. Temp., March to Oct. 65° to 75° ; Oct. to March 60° to 65°. Growing period, Feb. to Sept. ; resting period, Sept. to Feb. Flowers appear at base of last-made pseudo-bulb.
PROPAGATION : By division of pseudo-bulbs at potting time.
SPECIES CULTIVATED : M. candida, red, brown, yellow, and white, autumn, 12 to 18 in., Brazil ; Clowesii, yellow, brown, white, and purple, Sept. and Oct., 2 ft., Brazil ; cuneata, brown, yellow, white, and rose, Feb., 12 to 18 in., Brazil ; flavescens, yellowish, spring and summer, 1 ft., Brazil ; Phalænopsis, white and purple, May, 1 ft., Colombia ; Regnelli, rose, purple, and white, autumn, 1 ft., Brazil ; Roezlii, white, purple, and green, autumn, 1 ft., Colombia ; schroederiana, yellow, brown, purple, and white, fragrant, 1 ft., Sept., Costa Rica ; spectabilis, cream, rose, and purple, summer, 8 to 10 in., Brazil ; spectabilis moreliana, purple, Nov., 1 ft. ; vexillaria, white, rose, yellow, and orange, spring, 18 in., Colombia, and its many forms ; Warscewiczii, brown, purple, white, and lilac, spring, 1 ft., Colombia.

Mimosa (Sensitive Plant ; Humble Plant)—Ord. Leguminosæ. Stove perennials. Orn. foliage. First introduced 1638. Leaves, feather-shaped, green, sensitive.
CULTURE : Compost, equal parts peat, loam, and sand. Position—For sensitive plants (M. pudica and M. sensitiva), well-drained pots in light part of stove ; for M. marginata, similar, but with shoots trained up roof. Pot, Feb. or March. Water freely March to Sept., moderately afterwards. Temp., March to Oct. 65° to 75°.
PROPAGATION : By seeds sown ⅛ in. deep in light soil in temp. 65° to 75°, Feb. or March ; cuttings of young shoots inserted in sandy soil in temp. 65° to 75° at any time. M. pudica and M. sensitiva, though strictly perennials, are generally treated as annuals.
SPECIES CULTIVATED : M. marginata, pink, summer, 5 to 10 ft., Mexico ; pudica (Sensitive or Humble Plant), rose, summer, 12 to 18 in., Brazil ; sensitiva, purple, summer, 3 to 6 ft., Brazil.

K 2   277

Mimosa (*Acacia dealbata*)—See Acacia.

Mimosa-leaved Ebony Tree (*Jacaranda ovalifolia*)—See Jacaranda.

Mimulus (Cardinal Monkey-flower; Monkey-flower; Musk; Harrison's Musk)—Ord. Scrophulariaceæ. Greenhouse and hardy annual and perennial herbs. First introduced 1826.

POT CULTURE OF MUSK : Compost, two parts loam, one part each of leaf-mould and decayed cow manure and sand. Pot, Feb. to April. Position, shady window or greenhouse. Water freely March to Oct., moderately Oct. to Dec., keep nearly dry afterwards. Apply stimulants two or three times weekly May to Sept. Suitable stimulants : Soot-water, liquid guano, nitrate of soda, cow and horse manure. Temp., March to Oct. 50° to 65° ; Oct. to March 40° to 50°.

OUTDOOR CULTURE OF MUSK : Soil, ordinary rich. Position, moist, shady border. Plant, April or May.

CULTURE OF ANNUAL SPECIES : Sow seeds on surface of light soil ; slightly cover with fine mould and place in temp. 55° to 65°, Feb., March, or April. Transplant seedlings when three leaves have formed 1 in. apart in shallow boxes of light mould. Place in temp. 55° until May, then transfer to cold frame. Plant, outdoors, 4 in. apart, in June. Position, shady bed or border. Soil, light, moist, well enriched with decayed manure. Mulch with cocoanut-fibre refuse or decayed manure. Apply stimulants occasionally July to Sept.

CULTURE OF PERENNIAL SPECIES (M. cardinalis, etc.) : Soil, ordinary rich. Position, moist, shady border. Plant, March to June. Apply stimulants occasionally June to Oct. May be grown in pots similar to common musk.

CULTURE OF SHRUBBY SPECIES : Compost, two parts loam, one leaf-mould, decayed cow manure, and sand. Position, well-drained pots in light, airy greenhouse ; shoots trained on sticks or trellis. Pot, March. Prune, Feb. Water moderately Oct. to March, freely afterwards. Temp., Oct. to March 40° to 50° ; March to Oct. 50° to 60°.

PROPAGATION : By seeds sown, Feb. to May on surface of light soil and covered with a little sand or fine mould, in temp. 55° to 60° ; cuttings of young shoots inserted in light sandy soil in temp. 55° to 65° at any time ; division of roots, Feb. to May ; by cuttings of shoots, 2 in. long, inserted in sandy soil under bell-glass in temp. 55° to 65° in March, or in cool greenhouse or window in summer.

ANNUAL SPECIES : M. brevipes, yellow, summer, 1½ to 2 ft., California ; cupreus, copper colour, summer, 6 to 8 in., Chile ; Fremonti, crimson, summer, 6 to 8 in., California.

PERENNIAL SPECIES : M. cardinalis (Cardinal Monkey-flower), scarlet, summer, 1 to 2 ft., N. America ; guttatus (Syn. M. Langsdorfi), yellow, spotted red, summer, 1 to 1½ ft., N. America ; Lewisii, rose, July to Oct., 1 ft., N.W. America ; luteus, yellow, spotted red, summer, 9 to 12 in., Chile ; luteus alpinus, red, 6 in. ; moschatus, pale yellow and brown, summer, 6 in., N. America, and its variety Harrisoni ; ringeus, violet, summer, 2 to 4 ft., N. America. See also Mazus.

SHRUBBY SPECIES : M. glutinosus (Syns. Diplacus glutinosus and M. aurantiacus, deep yellow, all the year, 4 ft., California ; glutinosus puniceus, orange-red.

Mina lobata—See Ipomæa versicolor.

Miniature Sun-flower (*Heliopsis lævis*)—See Heliopsis.

Minorca Box Tree (*Buxus balearica*)—See Buxus.

Minorca Holly (*Ilex aquifolium balearica*)—See Ilex.

Mint (*Mentha viridis*)—See Mentha.

Mirabilis (Marvel of Peru)—Ord. Nyctaginaceæ. **Half-hardy perennials.** Tuberous rooted. First introduced 1596.

CULTURE : Soil, good ordinary. Position, sunny beds or borders. Plant tuberous roots in April ; seedlings in June. Apply stimulants occasionally when plants are flowering. Lift tubers in Oct. and store in sand, cocoanut-fibre refuse, or cinder ashes in frost-proof place until April.

PROPAGATION : By seeds sown ¼ in. deep in light soil in temp. 65° to 75°, Feb. or

March, transferring seedlings to cold frame in May and planting out in June; division of tubers at planting time.   Marvel of Peru may be treated as an annual.
SPECIES CULTIVATED : M. hybrida, various colours, summer, 2 ft., hybrid ; Jalapa (Marvel of Peru), various colours, summer, fragrant, 2 to 3 ft., Trop. America ; longiflora, various colours, summer, fragrant, 3 ft., Mexico ; multiflora, purple, summer, 2 to 3 ft., N.W. America.

Miscanthus (Zebra-striped Rush)—Ord. Gramineæ. Hardy orn. foliaged grass. Nat. Japan.   Leaves, narrow, deep green, creamy, yellow.
CULTURE : Soil, ordinary.   Position, pots in cold or heated greenhouse ; in groups on lawns, or sunny borders.   Pot or plant, March or April.   Water plants in pots moderately in winter, freely in summer.   Variegated kinds best adapted for pot culture.
PROPAGATION : By division of plants in March or April.
SPECIES CULTIVATED : M. saccharifer (Syn. Eulalia saccharifer), leaves with prominent white mid-rib, 6 ft., Japan ; sinensis (Syn. Eulalia japonica), green with white mid-rib, 6 to 10 ft., China and Japan, and its varieties gracillimus (dwarf and narrow-leaved), univittatus (leaves with longitudinal yellow stripe), variegatus (leaves striped yellow or white), and zebrinus (leaves cross-banded yellow).

Missouri Currant (*Ribes aureum*)—See Ribes.

Missouri Hyacinth—See Brevoortia and Brodiæa.

Mistletoe (*Viscum album*)—See Viscum.

Mistletoe Cactus—See Rhipsalis.

Mitchella (Chequer-berry ; Deer-berry ; Partridge-berry)—Ord. Rubiaceæ. Hardy evergreen trailing herb.   First introduced 1761.   Flowers succeeded by small scarlet berries.
CULTURE : Soil, equal parts peat and leaf-mould.   Position, shady borders or rockeries.   Plant, Oct., Nov., March, or April.
PROPAGATION : By division of roots in Oct. or March.
SPECIES CULTIVATED : M. repens, white and purple, fragrant, summer, 3 in., N. America.

Mitella (Mitre-wort ; Bishop's Cap)—Ord. Saxifragaceæ.   Hardy perennial herb.   First introduced 1731.
CULTURE : Soil, sandy peat.   Position, partially shaded rockeries.   Plant, March.
PROPAGATION : By division of the roots, March or April.
SPECIES CULTIVATED : M. diphylla (Mitre-wort), white, spring, 6 in., N. America.

Mitraria (Mitre Flower ; Scarlet Mitre-pod)—Ord. Gesneraceæ.   Half-hardy evergreen flowering shrub.   First introduced 1848.
CULTURE : Soil, two parts fibrous peat, one part sand.   Position, moist, sheltered, shady borders or walls.   Plant, Sept. or April.
POT CULTURE : Compost, two parts sandy peat, one part leaf-mould and sand. Pot, Sept. or Oct.   Position, well-drained pots in shady, cold greenhouse or fernery. Water freely March to Oct., moderately afterwards.
PROPAGATION : By cuttings of shoots inserted in light soil under bell-glass in cold, shady frame or greenhouse, April to Sept. ; division of roots in April.
SPECIES CULTIVATED : M. coccinea, scarlet, May to Aug., climbing, Chile.

Mitre-pod (*Mitraria coccinea*) —See Mitraria.

Mitre-wort (*Mitella diphylla*)—See Mitella.

Mitriostigma (Citron-scented Gardenia)—Ord. Rubiaceæ.   Stove evergreen flowering shrub.   First introduced 1856.
CULTURE : Compost, one part loam, one part peat, one part well-decayed manure and charcoal.   Position, well-drained pots, or beds in plant stove.   Pot or plant, Feb. or March.   Prune into shape, Feb. or March.   Temp., March to Sept. 65° to 85° ; Sept. to March 55° to 65°.   Water moderately Oct. to Feb., freely afterwards.

Syringe daily (except when in bloom) March to Sept. Apply liquid manure occasionally to healthy plants in flower.
PROPAGATION : By cuttings of firm young side shoots, 2 to 3 in. long, inserted in well-drained pots of sandy peat under bell-glass in temp. 75° to 85°, Jan. to April.
SPECIES CULTIVATED : M. axillaris (Syn. Gardenia citriodora), white, fragrant, spring, 3 to 5 ft., S. Africa.

Mocassin Flower (*Cypripedium spectabile*)—See Cypripedium.

Mock Cypress (*Kochia scoparia*)—See Kochia.

Mocker Nut (*Carya tomentosa*)—See Carya.

Mock Orange (*Philadelphus coronarius*)—See Philadelphus.

Mock Plane (*Acer pseudo-platanus*)—See Acer.

Mock Privet (*Phillyrea angustifolia*)—See Phillyrea.

Modiola—See Malvastrum.

Mohria (Frankincense Fern)—Ord. Filices. Greenhouse evergreen fern. First introduced 1842. Fronds, feather-shaped, green, fragrant.
CULTURE : Compost, two parts peat, one part small lumps of sandstone, one part silver sand. Position, well-drained pots in shady part of greenhouse, or in beds in wardian cases in dwelling room. Pot or plant, Feb. or March. Water moderately Oct. to Feb., freely afterwards. Temp., March to Sept. 55° to 65° ; Sept. to March 45° to 55°.
PROPAGATION : By spores sown on surface of fine sandy peat in pans and placed in temp. 75° to 85° any time.
SPECIES CULTIVATED : M. caffrorum, S. Africa.

Moldavian Balm (*Dracocephalum Moldavica*)—See Dracocephalum.

Molinia (Indian Grass ; Lavender Grass)—Ord. Gramineæ. Hardy perennial grass. Leaves, smooth, rigid, variegated with white.
CULTURE : Soil, ordinary. Position, open or shady, as edgings to beds or borders. Plant, Oct. or March to June.
PROPAGATION : By division of roots, autumn or spring.
SPECIES CULTIVATED : M. cærulea variegata, 2 to 3 ft., Britain.

Molopospermum—Ord. Umbelliferæ. Hardy perennial. Orn. foliage. Leaves, fern-like and graceful. First introduced 1596.
CULTURE : Soil, deep rich. Position, sunny, fully exposed borders, or naturalising in wild garden. Plant in March.
PROPAGATION : By seeds sown outdoors when ripe, or in cold frame in March ; also by division of roots in April.
SPECIES CULTIVATED : M. cicutarium, yellow and white, May, 3 to 4 ft., Central Europe.

Moltkia—See Lithospermum.

Molucella (Molucca Balm)—Ord. Labiatæ. Half-hardy annuals or biennials. First introduced 1570.
CULTURE : Soil, sandy loam. Position, sunny beds or borders. Sow seeds in pans or boxes during Feb. or March in temp. 60° to 65°. Prick out when large enough to handle and gradually harden off for planting outdoors in May.
SPECIES CULTIVATED : M. laevis (Shell-flower), white, Aug., 2 to 3 ft., W. Asia; spinosa, white, summer, 6 to 8 ft., S. Europe and Syria.

Momordica (Balsam Apple)—Ord. Cucurbitaceæ. Half-hardy annuals, climbers. Orn. foliage. First introduced 1568. Fruit, round, oblong, or cylindrical, reddish orange ; Sept.
INDOOR CULTURE : Compost, two parts decayed turfy soil, one part horse droppings or decomposed manure. Position, pots or beds with shoots trained up roof of sunny greenhouse. Pot or plant, April or May. Size of pots, 8 or 10 in. Water

freely. Syringe twice daily. Moist atmosphere essential. Apply stimulants occasionally when fruit forms. Nip off point of shoot at first joint beyond fruit. Shade from hot sun. Temp., 65° to 75°.
OUTDOOR CULTURE : Soil, ordinary rich. Position, against sunny walls, trellises, arbours, or trailing over banks. Plant, June. Water freely in dry weather. Apply stimulants occasionally when fruit forms. Pruning of shoots not required.
PROPAGATION : By seeds sown singly in 2 in. pots filled with light soil in temp. 65° to 75° in Feb. or March.
SPECIES CULTIVATED : M. Balsamina (Balsam Apple), yellow, June, 4 ft., Tropics ; Charantia (Balsam Pear), yellow, June, 4 to 6 ft., Tropics.

Monarch of the East (*Sauromatum guttatum*)—See Sauromatum.

Monarda (Sweet Bergamot; Wild Bergamot; Bee Balm; Oswego Tea)—Ord. Labiatæ. Hardy herbaceous perennials. First introduced 1656. Leaves, mint-, balm- or sage-scented.
CULTURE : Soil, ordinary. Position, singly, or in masses in open or partially shaded borders. Plant, Oct., Nov., March, or April. Top-dress with decayed manure in autumn or spring.
PROPAGATION : By seeds sown $\frac{1}{16}$ in. deep in light soil in partially shaded position outdoors, March or April, or in boxes of light soil in cold frame or greenhouse in March ; division of roots in Oct. or Nov.
SPECIES CULTIVATED : M. didyma (Oswego Tea or Sweet Bergamot), scarlet, summer, 1 to 2 ft., N. America ; fistulosa (Wild Bergamot), purple, summer, 3 to 4 ft., N. America.

Monardella—Ord. Labiatæ. Hardy annual and perennial herbs. First introduced 1853. Leaves, fragrant.
CULTURE : Soil, ordinary. Position, open or partially shaded borders. Plant, Oct., Nov., March, or April. Sow annual species outdoors where required to grow, in March or April. Top-dress with decayed manure in autumn or spring.
PROPAGATION : By seed sown $\frac{1}{16}$ in. deep in light soil in partially shaded position outdoors, March or April, or in boxes of light soil in cold frame or greenhouse in March ; division of roots, Oct. or March.
ANNUAL SPECIES : M. candicans, white, summer, 1 ft., N. America.
PERENNIAL SPECIES : M. macrantha, scarlet, autumn, fragrant, 6 in., N. America.

Money-flower (*Lunaria biennis*)—See Lunaria.

Money-in-both-Pockets (*Lunaria biennis*)—See Lunaria.

Money-wort (*Lysimachia nummularia*)—See Lysimachia.

Monkey-flower—See Mimulus.

Monkey Nut (*Arachis hypogæa*)—See Arachis.

Monkey-puzzle (*Araucaria imbricata*)—See Araucaria.

Monkshood (*Aconitum Napellus*)—See Aconitum.

Monochætum—Ord. Melastomaceæ. Greenhouse evergreen flowering shrubs
CULTURE : Compost, two parts fibrous peat, one part light loam, one part leaf-mould, and little sand. Position, well-drained pots in light greenhouse, Sept. to June ; cold, sunny frames, June to Sept. Pot, March. Prune shoots moderately close immediately after flowering. Water moderately Oct. to March, freely after-wards. Syringe twice daily March to June. Apply stimulants occasionally June to Oct. Temp., Sept. to March 45° to 55°; March to June 55° to 65°.
PROPAGATION : By cuttings of shoots, 2 to 3 in. long, inserted in well-drained pots of sandy peat under bell-glass in temp. 65° to 75°, March or April. Nip off points of shoots of young plants occasionally, April to Aug., to induce bushy growth.
SPECIES CULTIVATED : M. alpestre, red, winter, 2 ft., Mexico ; hartwegianum, rose, winter, 2 ft., Peru ; humboldtianum, red and purple, winter, 2 ft., Caracas ; lemoineanum, rose and violet, winter, 2 ft. ; sericeum multiflorum, mauve, spring, 2 ft., New Grenada.

Monstera (Shingle Plant)—Ord. Aroideæ. Stove evergreen climbers. Orn. foliage and fruiting. Leaves, large, handsome, perforated, dark green. Stems, creeping, furnished with aerial roots. Fruit, cylindrical, fragrant, pineapple-flavoured ; ripe in autumn.

CULTURE : Compost, equal parts peat, leaf-mould, and loam, little sand. Position, well-drained border against damp wall of stove or warm fernery. Plant, Feb. to April. Water freely March to Oct., moderately afterwards. Syringe twice daily March to Sept., once daily afterwards. Temp., March to Sept. 65° to 75° ; Sept. to March 55° to 65°.

PROPAGATION : By cuttings of the stems inserted in light soil in temp. 70° to 80° any time.

SPECIES CULTIVATED : M. acuminata (Syn. M. tenuis and Gravia paradoxa), the Shingle Plant, yellow, summer, Trop. America ; deliciosa, yellow, summer, fruit delicious, Mexico.

Montbretia—See Tritonia.

Monterey Cypress (*Cupressus macrocarpa*)—See Cupressus.

Monterey Pine-tree (*Pinus insignis*)—See Pinus.

Monthly Rose (*Rosa indica*)—See Rosa.

Moon Creeper—See Menispermum and Ipomæa.

Moon Daisy (*Chrysanthemum leucanthemum*)—See Chrysanthemum.

Moon Fern (*Botrychium lunaria*)—See Botrychium.

Moon-seed (*Menispermum canadense*)—See Menispermum.

Moon-wort (*Botrychium lunaria*)—See Botrychium.

Moræa (Butterfly Iris ; Wedding Flower)—Ord. Iridaceæ. Half-hardy bulbous plants. First introduced 1597.

CULTURE : Soil, light, rich, sandy. Position, sunny well-drained border. Plant Sept. to Jan., placing bulbs 4 in. deep and 2 in. apart. Lift and replant bulbs annually. Mulch surface of bed in March with cow manure.

POT CULTURE : Compost, two parts sandy loam, one part leaf-mould or decayed cow manure. Pots, 4½ in. in diameter, well drained. Place five bulbs 3 in. deep in each pot in Nov. and cover with cocoanut-fibre refuse in cold frame or under cool greenhouse stage until growth begins. Water moderately from time bulbs begin to grow until flowers fade, then gradually cease, keeping bulbs dry till Jan. Temp., Sept. to March 40° to 50° ; other times 50° to 60°.

PROPAGATION : By offsets, treated as advised for bulbs.

SPECIES CULTIVATED : M. bicolor, yellow and brown, summer, 2 ft., S. Africa ; glaucopis, white and blue-black, 1 to 2 ft., S. Africa ; iridioides, white and yellow, 1 to 2 ft., S. Africa ; pavonia (Syn. Iris pavonia), Peacock Iris, red and blue-black, 1 to 2 ft., S. Africa ; robinsoniana (Syn. Iris robinsoniana), the Wedding Flower, white, summer, 4 to 6 ft., Lord Howe's Islands ; spathacea, yellow and purple, 1 to 2 ft., S. Africa ; unguiculata (Syn. Vieussexia unguicularis), white and red, summer, 1 ft. See also genus Homeria.

Moreton Bay Lily (*Eurycles Cunninghami*)—See Eurycles.

Moreton Bay Pine-tree (*Araucaria Cunninghami*)—See Araucaria.

Moreton Bay Trumpet Jasmine (*Tecoma jasminoides*)—See Tecoma.

Morina (Whorl-flower)—Ord. Dipsaceæ. Hardy perennial herbs. First introduced 1839.

CULTURE : Soil, deep, moist, sandy loam. Position, partially shaded, sheltered borders. Plant, Sept. to Nov., March, or April. Protect, Nov. to March, by covering of litter.

PROPAGATION : By seeds sown $\frac{1}{16}$ in. deep in sandy peat and leaf-mould in cold frame in Sept. or Oct., March or April ; division of roots, Sept.

SPECIES CULTIVATED : M. coulteriana, yellow, June, 18 in., Himalayas ; longifolia, white to crimson, July, 2 to 3 ft., Himalayas ; persica, red and white, 1 to 2 ft., Himalayas.

Morisia—Ord. Cruciferæ. Hardy dwarf alpine perennial. Introduced 1890.
CULTURE : Soil, sandy, gritty loam. Position, in the moraine or in a moist bed of stone chippings and sand. Requires full exposure to the sun. Plant in spring.
PROPAGATION : By seeds sown in sandy soil in a cold frame or by root cuttings laid in sand in spring.
SPECIES CULTIVATED : M. monanthos (Syn. hypogæa), bright golden yellow, early spring, prostrate, N. Corsica and Sardinia.

Mormodes—Ord. Orchidaceæ. Stove deciduous epiphytal orchids. First introduced 1837. Flowers, fragrant.
CULTURE : Compost, equal parts fibrous peat and sphagnum moss with a liberal addition of finely broken crocks, charcoal, and sand. Position, pots or hanging baskets, well drained. Water freely from time new growth begins until leaves fall off ; very little other times. Temp., March to Sept. 65° to 85° ; Sept. to March 60° to 70°. Resting period, winter. Flowers appear at base of new pseudobulb.
PROPAGATION : By division of plant at potting time.
SPECIES CULTIVATED : M. luxata, lemon yellow and brown, July, Mexico ; luxata eburnea, creamy white ; pardina, yellow and crimson, July and Aug., Mexico.

Morning Glory (*Ipomæa purpurea*)—See Ipomæa.

Morus (Mulberry)—Ord. Urticaceæ. Hardy deciduous trees. Orn. foliage and fruit-bearing. First introduced 1548. One of the oldest of cultivated fruits. Flowers, greenish white ; May to July. Fruit, oblong, white, red, or black berries ; ripe, Sept. and Oct.
CULTURE OF MULBERRY (M. nigra) : Soil, light, deep, moist loam. Position, sunny, sheltered from north winds, in England ; against south walls in Scotland. Plant, Nov. to March. Depth of roots below surface, 6 in. Prune in Feb., simply thinning overcrowded branches and shortening straggling ones. Shorten young shoots growing out of front of branches of trees grown against walls to 6 in. in July. Top-dress surface of soil equal to spread of branches with well-decayed manure in Oct. or Nov. Suitable artificial manure : two parts nitrate of soda, one part superphosphate, one part kainit. Apply in Feb. or March at the rate of 4 oz. per square yard. Gather fruit when ready to drop. Spread layer of straw or lawn mowings for fruit to fall upon.
CULTURE OF OTHER SPECIES : Soil, ordinary. Position, sunny, sheltered shrubberies or singly on lawns. Plant, Oct. to March. Prune as advised for mulberry.
PROPAGATION : By seeds sown ¼ in. deep in light, sandy soil in temp. 55° to 65° in March, transplanting seedlings outdoors in June or July, or in similar soil and depth outdoors in May ; cuttings 6 to 8 in. long, partly of current and partly of two-year-old shoots removed from upper part of tree and inserted half their depth in light soil in sheltered position outdoors, Sept., Oct., or March ; layering shoots in Nov. or Feb. ; grafting in March.
SPECIES CULTIVATED : M. alba (White Mulberry), 30 to 45 ft., Asia, and its varieties fegyvernekiana (pygmy), heterophylla, laciniata, latifolia, macrophylla, and pendula (Weeping Mulberry) ; nigra (Black or Common Mulberry), 20 to 30 ft., East ; rubra (Red Mulberry), 50 to 60 ft., N. America.

Moschosma—Ord. Labiatæ. Greenhouse perennial flowering plant with nettle-like foliage.
CULTURE : Compost, equal parts loam and decayed manure, little sand. Position—Greenhouse, Sept. to June ; cold frame, June to Sept. Pot, March. Water freely March to Oct., moderately afterwards. Apply stimulants occasionally a month after repotting until flowers expand, then cease. Temp., Sept. to March 45° to 55° ; March to June 55° to 65°. Cut down shoots to within 3 in. of their base after flowering. Young plants : Insert cuttings 3 in. long of young shoots in light, sandy soil in temp. 65° in Feb. or March. When rooted, place singly in 3½ in. pots. Nip off point of main shoots, also of succeeding shoots when 3 in. long. Shift into 5 or 6 in.

pots when former pots are filled with roots. Water freely. Apply stimulants occasionally. Place in cold frame, June to Sept.
PROPAGATION : By cuttings inserted in sandy soil in temp. 65° in spring.
SPECIES CULTIVATED : M. riparium, white and purple, winter, 2 to 3 ft., S. Africa.

Moss—See Selaginella.

Moss Campion (*Silene acaulis*)—See Silene.

Moss Pink (*Phlox subulata* and *Silene acaulis*)—See Phlox and Silene.

Moss Rose (*Rosa centifolia muscosa*)—See Rosa.

Mossy Phlox (*Phlox subulata*)—See Phlox.

Mossy Saxifrage—A section of the genus Saxifraga, of which S. hypnoides is the type.

Mother o' Millions (*Linaria Cymbalaria*)—See Linaria.

Mother-of-Thousands (*Linaria Cymbalaria* and *Saxifraga sarmentosa*)—See Linaria and Saxifraga.

Moth Orchid (*Phalænopsis schilleriana*)—See Phalænopsis.

Mound Lily—See Yucca.

Mountain Ash (*Pyrus aucuparia*)—See Pyrus.

Mountain Avens (*Dryas octopetala*)—See Dryas.

Mountain Bladder Fern (*Cystopteris montana*)—See Cystopteris.

Mountain Buckler Fern (*Nephrodium montanum*)—See Nephrodium.

Mountain Centaury (*Centaurea montana*)—See Centaurea.

Mountain Clematis (*Clematis montana*)—See Clematis.

Mountain Elm (*Ulmus montana*)—See Ulmus.

Mountain Fringe (*Adlumia cirrhosa*)—See Adlumia.

Mountain Kidney Vetch (*Anthyllis montana*)—See Anthyllis.

Mountain Laurel (*Kalmia latifolia*)—See Kalmia.

Mountain Mad-wort (*Alyssum montanum*)—See Alyssum.

Mountain Mint (*Monarda didyma*)—See Monarda.

Mountain Parsley Fern (*Cryptogramme crispa*)—See Cryptogramme.

Mountain Pine (*Pinus montana pumilio*)—See Pinus.

Mountain Sage—See Lantana.

Mountain Sandwort (*Arenaria montana*)—See Arenaria.

Mountain Snow (*Arabis albida*)—See Arabis.

Mountain Spider-wort (*Lloydia alpina*)—See Lloydia.

Mountain Spinach (*Atriplex hortensis*)—See Atriplex.

Mountain Sweet (*Ceanothus americanus*)—See Ceanothus.

Mountain Tea-plant (*Gaultheria procumbens*)—See Gaultheria.

Mountain Tobacco (*Arnica montana*)—See Arnica.

Mount Atlas Cedar (*Cedrus atlantica*)—See Cedrus.

Mournful Widow (*Scabiosa atro-purpurea*)—See Scabiosa.

Mourning Iris (*Iris Susiana*)—See Iris.

Mouse Ear—See Hieracium.

Moustache Plant (*Caryopteris Mastacanthus*)—See Caryopteris.

Mozambique Lily (*Gloriosa virescens*)—See Gloriosa.

Muehlenbeckia (Native Ivy of Australia)—Ord. Polygonaceæ. Hardy and greenhouse trailing and climbing plants. Deciduous. First introduced 1822.
CULTURE : Soil, sandy loam. Position, sunny rockery for M. axillaris ; sheltered walls for M. complexa. Large well-drained pots in cool greenhouse for tender species. Plant, Oct., Nov., March, or April. Protect, Nov. to April, by covering of dry litter or fern.
PROPAGATION : By cuttings inserted in sandy soil in shady position outdoors, June to Sept.
GREENHOUSE SPECIES CULTIVATED : M. adpressa, large rambling shrub, Australia ; platyclados (Centipede Plant), grown as curiosity, to 10 ft., Solomon Islands.
HARDY SPECIES CULTIVATED : M. axillaris, 1 to 2 in., Australasia ; complexa, climber with interlaced wiry stems, New Zealand.

Mulberry—See Morus.

Mule Fern (*Hemionitis palmata*)—See Hemionitis.

Mule Pink—Hybrid varieties of Dianthus.

Mulgedium—See Lactuca.

Mullein (*Verbascum Thapsus*)—See Verbascum.

Mummy Pea (*Pisum sativum* var.)—See Pisum.

Munby's Violet (*Viola munbyana*)—See Viola.

Musa (Banana ; Plantain)—Ord. Musaceæ. Stove herbaceous perennials. Orn. foliage and edible fruiting. First introduced 1690. Inflorescence, yellow, scarlet, green ; Jan. to April ; succeeded by oblong pods borne in huge clusters. Leaves, very large, oblong, green.
CULTURE : Compost, two parts good loam, one part well-decayed manure and one part sand. Position, pots, tubs, or beds in lofty sunny stove. Pot or plant, Jan. to April. Water copiously Feb. to Oct. ; about once fortnightly afterwards. Syringe twice daily Feb. to Sept. ; once daily Sept. to Feb. Moist atmosphere essential. Apply stimulants twice or three times weekly March to Oct. Temp., March to Oct. 70° to 85° ; Oct. to March 60° to 70°.
OUTDOOR CULTURE OF M. ENSETE : Position, sunny, sheltered borders or nooks. Place in position first or second week in June, plunging pot or tub to its rim in the ground. Water copiously. Apply stimulants once a week. Lift and replace in stove in Sept. May also be planted in ordinary rich soil in June, freely watered, lifted in Sept., and roots stored close together in temp. 45° to 55° until following June.
PROPAGATION : By suckers removed from parent plant and placed in pots in temp. 75° to 85° any time of year.
SPECIES CULTIVATED : M. Cavendishii, 5 to 10 ft., China ; Ensete, 20 to 40 ft., Abyssinia, kind used for garden decoration in summer ; paradisiaca (Plantain), to 30 ft., Trop. Asia, and its variety sapientum (Banana) ; textilis (Manila Hemp), to 20 ft., Philippine Islands.

Muscari (Grape Hyacinth)—Ord. Liliaceæ. Hardy bulbous flowering plants.
OUTDOOR CULTURE : Soil, deep, sandy loam. Position, sunny beds, borders, or rockeries. Plant, Aug. to Nov., in lines or masses. Depth for planting : Small bulbs 2 in. deep and 1 in. apart ; large bulbs 4 in. deep and 3 to 4 in. apart. Mulch with decayed manure, Nov. Lift, divide, and replant every third year.
POT CULTURE : Compost, two parts sandy loam, one part leaf-mould or well-decayed cow manure, and one part river sand. Pot, Aug. to Nov., placing 18 to 20 small bulbs, 1 in. apart, in a 5 in. pot ; or 3 to 5 large-sized bulbs 1 in. deep in similar pots. Position, under layer of cinder ashes from time of potting till growth commences, then in cold frame, cool greenhouse, or window till past flowering, afterwards in sunny spot outdoors. Water moderately from time growth commences till foliage fades, then keep dry. Repot annually. Apply weak stimulants once or twice during flowering period.

PROPAGATION : By seeds sown ⅛ in. deep in light, sandy soil in boxes or cold frames, or outdoors in Sept. ; offsets from old bulbs removed when lifting and planted as advised for full-sized bulbs. Seedlings flower when three to four years old.

SPECIES CULTIVATED : M. botryoides, blue, spring, 6 in., Europe ; botryoides album, white ; comosum (Tassel Hyacinth), blue, April, 8 in., Europe ; comosum monstrosum (Feather Hyacinth), blue, April, 8 in. ; conicum (Heavenly Blue variety), blue, April, 8 in., Trebizond ; Heldreichii, blue, May, 8 in., Greece ; moschatum (Musk Hyacinth), yellow and violet, April, 8 in., Asia Minor ; racemosum (Starch Hyacinth), blue, April, 6 in., Europe.

Mushroom—See Agaricus.

Musk (*Mimulus moschatus*)—See Mimulus.

Musk Daffodil (*Narcissus moschatus*)—See Narcissus.

Musk Grape Hyacinth (*Muscari moschatum*)—See Muscari.

Musk Mallow (*Malva moschata*)—See Malva.

Musk Orchis (*Herminium monorchis*)—See Herminium.

Musk-scented Rose (*Rosa moschata*)—See Rosa.

Mussænda—Ord. Rubiaceæ. Stove evergreen flowering shrubs. First introduced 1805.

CULTURE : Compost, equal parts peat, loam, leaf-mould, and silver sand. Position, well-drained pots in light, moist stove. Pot, Feb. to April. Prune moderately after flowering. Temp., Feb. to Oct. 65° to 85° ; Oct. to Feb. 55° to 65°. Water freely April to Sept., moderately Sept. to Nov. and Feb. to April, keep somewhat dry Nov. to Feb. Syringe daily Feb. to Oct.

PROPAGATION : By cuttings of young shoots in sandy soil under bell-glass in temp. 70° to 80°, May to July.

SPECIES CULTIVATED : M. erythrophylla, yellow, bracts crimson, winter, 1 ft., Trop. Africa ; frondosa, yellow, Aug., 2 to 3 ft., India ; luteola, bright yellow, autumn and winter, 5 to 6 ft., Trop. Africa ; macrophylla, orange, May, 4 to 6 ft., Nepaul.

Mustard (Salading)—See Brassica.

Mutisia—Ord. Compositæ. Greenhouse or hardy climbing flowering shrubs. First introduced 1823.

CULTURE OF GREENHOUSE SPECIES : Compost, two parts loam, one part leaf-mould, half-part sand. Position, pots or beds ; shoots trained up rafters or round trellises. Pot or plant, Feb. or March. Prune slightly after flowering. Water freely March to Sept., moderately afterwards. Apply stimulants occasionally May to Sept. Temp., March to Sept. 55° to 65° ; Sept. to March 40° to 50°.

CULTURE OF HARDY SPECIES : Soil, ordinary rich. Position, well-drained border against sheltered, partially shaded wall. Plant, Oct., March, or April. Water freely in dry weather. Protect from slugs by placing layer of fine coke or cinders round base of stems.

PROPAGATION : Greenhouse species by cuttings of half-ripened shoots inserted in sand under bell-glass in temp. 55° to 65°, May or June ; hardy species by cuttings of similar shoots inserted in sand in shady, cold frame or greenhouse, April or May.

GREENHOUSE SPECIES : M. Clematis, scarlet, summer, 20 to 30 ft., Peru.

HARDY SPECIES : M. decurrens, orange, summer, 6 to 10 ft., Chile.

Myosotidium (Chatham Islands Forget-me-not)—Ord. Boraginaceæ. Hardy herbaceous perennial. First introduced 1858.

CULTURE : Soil, ordinary. Position, cool, damp, sheltered border. Plant, Oct. or March. Water freely in dry weather.

PROPAGATION : By seeds sown ⅛ in. deep in April where plants are required to grow. This plant should be disturbed as little as possible.

SPECIES CULTIVATED : M. nobile, blue and white, spring, 12 to 18 in., Chatham Islands.

Myosotis (Forget-me-not; Scorpion Grass)—Ord. Boraginaceæ. Hardy perennials.

CULTURE OF M. ALPESTRIS : Soil, moist, gritty loam. Position, partially shady rockery, surrounded by small pieces of sandstone. Plant, March or April.

CULTURE OF OTHER SPECIES : Soil, ordinary. Position, as edgings to or in masses in partially shady beds or borders. Plant, Oct., Nov., or March, 4 to 6 in. apart. These are best treated as biennials—namely, raised from seed sown outdoors in April, May, or June and transplanted into the beds or borders in Oct. to flower following year.

PROPAGATION : By seeds sown 1/16 in. deep outdoors in spring or summer; cuttings inserted in sandy soil under hand-light in June or July ; division of roots in March or Oct.

SPECIES CULTIVATED : M. alpestris (Syn. M. pyrenaica), blue and white, fragrant, June and July, 6 to 8 in., Europe, and its many selected forms ; azorica, blue, summer, 6 to 10 in., Azores ; azorica Imperatrice Elisabeth, bluish purple ; cæspitosa, blue and yellow, June to July, 3 to 6 in., Europe ; dissitiflora, sky blue, March to July, 8 to 10 in., Alps ; dissitiflora alba, white ; palustris, sky blue, May to July, 6 to 12 in., Britain ; palustris semperflorens, long flowering ; rupicola, sky blue, May to June, 2 to 3 in., Europe ; sylvatica, blue and yellow, summer, 1 to 2 ft., Britain.

Myrica (Candle-berry Myrtle)—Ord. Myricaceæ. Hardy deciduous and evergreen shrubs. Leaves, lance-shaped, green, highly fragrant.

CULTURE : Soil, moist, sandy peat. Position, open, sheltered borders. Plant, Oct. to March. Prune deciduous species, Nov. to Feb. ; evergreen species, April.

PROPAGATION : By seeds sown ¼ in. deep in ordinary soil in sheltered position outdoors in autumn ; cuttings inserted in sandy soil in sheltered position outdoors, Sept. or Oct. ; layering shoots in Sept. or Oct. ; division of plants, Oct. to March.

SPECIES CULTIVATED : M. cerifera (Candle-berry or Wax Myrtle), brown, May, 20 to 40 ft., America ; Gale (Sweet Gale), brown, May, 4 ft., N. Europe (Britain). See also Comptonia.

Myricaria (German Tamarisk)—Ord. Tamaricaceæ. Hardy deciduous flowering shrub. First introduced 1582.

CULTURE : Soil, ordinary sandy. Position, open, sunny borders or banks. Plant, Oct. to March. Prune into shape, Nov. to Feb.

PROPAGATION : By seeds sown 1/16 in. deep in sandy soil in open, sunny position outdoors in March or April ; cuttings of firm young shoots inserted in sandy soil outdoors, Aug. to Nov.

SPECIES CULTIVATED : M. germanica (Syn. Tamarix germanica), pink, July, 6 to 8 ft., Europe.

Myrobalan Plum (*Prunus cerasifera*)—See Prunus.

Myrrhis (Sweet Cicely)—Ord. Umbelliferæ. Hardy perennial aromatic herb. Orn. foliage. Leaves finely divided, fern-like, fragrant.

CULTURE : Soil, ordinary. Position, open, sunny borders. Plant, Oct. or March.

PROPAGATION : By seeds sown ⅓ in. deep in ordinary soil outdoors, Sept. or April ; division of roots, Oct. or March.

SPECIES CULTIVATED : M. odorata, white, May, 3 ft., Europe (Britain).

Myrsiphyllum—See Asparagus.

Myrtle (*Myrtus communis*)—See Myrtus.

Myrtle Grass (*Acorus calamus*)—See Acorus.

Myrtus (Myrtle)—Ord. Myrtaceæ. Greenhouse and half-hardy evergreen shrubs. Flowering and orn. foliage. First introduced 1597. Flowers, white, fragrant; May to July. Fruit, oblong or round, purplish-black berries; fragrant and edible. Leaves, egg- or lance-shaped, green, fragrant.

CULTURE IN GREENHOUSES : Compost, two parts sandy loam, one part leaf-mould, half a part sand. Position, well-drained pots or tubs, or in beds with shoots trained to walls, in light, sunny, airy greenhouses. Place pot plants in sunny position outdoors, June to Sept. Pot, Feb. or March. Prune into shape, Feb. Water copiously March to Oct., moderately afterwards. Syringe daily March to Oct. Apply stimulants once a week, May to Sept., to healthy plants only. Temp., March to Sept. 55° to 65°; Sept. to March 45° to 50°. May be grown in dwelling rooms or windows under similar treatment.

OUTDOOR CULTURE: Soil, ordinary sandy. Position, well-drained borders against sheltered S. walls in S. or S.W. of England only. Plant, Oct. or March. Protect, Oct. to March, in severe winters, with mats or straw. M. bullata, communis, communis tarentina, communis variegata, Luma, and Ugni are all suitable for outdoor culture.

PROPAGATION: By seeds sown ⅛ in. deep in sandy soil in temp. 60° to 70° in autumn or spring; cuttings of young shoots, 2 in. long, inserted in sandy soil under bell-glass in temp. 65° to 75°, spring and summer; cuttings of firm shoots, 2 to 3 in. long, inserted in sandy soil in cool greenhouse or window, June or July.

SPECIES CULTIVATED: M. bullata, 15 to 25 ft., New Zealand; communis (Common Myrtle), 6 to 10 ft., S. Europe; communis tarentina, leaves small; communis variegata, variegated; Luma (Syn. Eugenia Luma), 15 to 20 ft., Chile; Ugni (Syn. Eugenia Ugni), 4 to 6 ft., Chile.

Nægelia—Ord. Gesneriaceæ. Stove tuberous-rooted herbaceous perennials. Flowering and orn. foliage. First introduced 1840. Leaves, heart-shaped, green or crimson, velvety.

CULTURE: Compost, two parts fibrous peat, one part loam, one part leaf-mould, with a little decayed manure and silver sand. Position, well-drained pots or pans in shady part of plant stove. Pot, March to flower in summer; May to flower in autumn; June to flower in winter. Place tubers 1 in. deep singly in 5 in. pots, or 1 to 2 in. apart in larger sizes. Water moderately from time growth begins until plants are 3 or 4 in. high, then freely. After flowering gradually withhold water till foliage dies down, then keep dry till potting time. Apply weak liquid manure once or twice a week when flower buds show. Syringing not required. Temp., March to Sept. 65° to 85°; Sept. to March 55° to 75°. Store when foliage has decayed on their sides under stage till potting time in temp. of 50° to 55°.

PROPAGATION: By seeds sown on surface of well-drained pots of sandy peat, in temp. 75°, March or April; cuttings of young shoots inserted in pots of sandy peat in temp. 75° to 85° in spring; division of rhizomes at potting time.

SPECIES CULTIVATED: N. cinnabarina (Syn. Gesneria cinnabarina), scarlet, summer, 2 ft., Mexico; multiflora (Syn. Achimenes amabilis), white, Aug., 1½ ft., Mexico; zebrina, yellow and scarlet, Oct., 2 ft., Mexico.

Nail-wort—See Paronychia.

Naked-flowered Azalea (*Rhododendron nudiflorum*)—See Rhododendron.

Nandina (Heavenly Bamboo)—Ord. Berberidaceæ. Half-hardy evergreen flowering shrubs. First introduced 1804.

CULTURE: Soil, peat and loam. Position, sheltered beds or borders in mild districts only. Plant in May or Sept.

PROPAGATION: By cuttings inserted in sandy peat in a warm greenhouse in spring or summer.

SPECIES CULTIVATED: N. domestica, white, summer, 6 to 8 ft., leaves assume reddish tint in autumn, Japan.

Nankeen Lily (*Lilium testaceum*)—See Lilium.

Nanodes—See Epidendrum.

Narbonne Flax (*Linum narbonense*)—See Linum.

Narcissus (Daffodil; Jonquil; Chinese Sacred Lily; Chalice Flower; Lent Lily)—Ord. Amaryllidaceæ. Hardy bulbous perennials.

CLASSIFICATION: Narcissi are divided into the following main sections or groups, viz.: I. Trumpet Daffodils: Examples—King Alfred, Emperor, and Golden Spur.

II. Incomparabilis : Examples—Sir Watkin, Will Scarlet, and Bernardino. III. Barri : Examples—Barri conspicuous, Bath's Flame, and Firetail. IV. Leedsi : Examples—White Lady, Mrs. Langtry, and Lord Kitchener. V. Triandrus Hybrids : Examples—Queen of Spain, Silver Fleece, and Princess Ena. VI. Cyclamineus Hybrids : Examples—Orange Glory, February Gold, and Flycap. VII. Jonquilla Hybrids : Examples—Buttercup, odorus, and odorus Campanelle. VIII. Tazetta Hybrids : Examples—Elvira, Paper White, and Grand Monarque. IX. Poeticus : Examples—Horace, Glory of Lise, and Red Rim. X. Doubles : Examples—Codlins and Cream, Primrose Phœnix, and Inglescombe. XI. Various : Examples—Narcissus bulbocodium, N. cyclamineus, N. juncifolius, etc.

OUTDOOR CULTURE : Soil, ordinary for common kinds ; sandy loam for N. bulbocodium and vars. ; peaty soil for N. cyclamineus. No manure must be applied. Position, partially or quite shady beds or borders facing N. or N.E. for robust kinds ; rockeries sheltered from N. or N.E. winds for choice or dwarf kinds. Plant, Aug. to Nov. Depth for planting robust kinds. 3 to 4 in. on heavy soils ; 6 in. on light soils. Distance apart, 4 to 6 in. Rock garden narcissus, 2 to 3 in. deep and the same apart. Lift N. bulbocodium in July and replant in Oct. ; other kinds every three or four years in July. Do not remove foliage until quite dead. Manures : 4 oz. of basic slag or 4 oz. of bonemeal for heavy soils ; ¼ oz. of sulphate of potash for sandy soils. Apply above quantities per square yard before planting.

CULTURE IN TURF : Make holes 2 to 3 in. wide, 3 in. deep. Place one bulb in each and cover with soil and turf. Plant, Aug. to Oct. Grass must not be cut until leaves turn yellow.

INDOOR CULTURE : Compost, two parts fibrous loam, one part well-decayed manure or leaf-mould, one part sand. Pot, Aug. to Nov., placing 3 large, 6 medium-sized, or 12 small bulbs in a 5 in. pot. Depth for planting : Allow apex to just appear above surface of soil. Position, under cinder ashes outdoors or in frame until growth begins, then remove to greenhouse or window. Water only when growth commences, moderately afterwards. Apply weak stimulants when flowers appear. Temp. for forcing, 55° to 65°. After flowering plant bulbs, except those of N. bulbocodium and N. cyclamineus, outdoors. Keep soil out of the latter dry after flowering.

CULTURE OF CHINESE SACRED LILY : Half fill a Japanese bowl with shingle or gravel and add sufficient water to just cover this. Place bulb on the shingle and surround with pebbles. Put bowl in dark cupboard until growth begins, then remove to light. Change water once a week ; use tepid water only. Bulbs usually flower five to six weeks after being placed in bowls ; useless after flowering.

PROPAGATION : By seeds sown ⅛ in. deep in pans of sandy loam in cold frame in autumn, transplanting seedlings following year 1 in. apart in bed of sandy soil in shady position outdoors ; by offsets, removed from old bulbs in July or Aug. and replanted at once as advised for parent bulbs. Seedling bulbs flower when three to six years old.

SPECIES CULTIVATED : N. biflorus, white and yellow, May, 1 ft., Europe ; Broussonetii, pure white, 1½ to 2 ft., Morocco ; bulbocodium (Hoop-petticoat Daffodil), yellow, April, 6 in., S. Europe, and its varieties citrinus (sulphur yellow), conspicuus (yellow), Graellsii (sulphur yellow), and monophyllus (white) ; cernuus, white, spring, 1 ft., Pyrenees ; cyclamineus (Cyclamen-flowered Daffodil), lemon and yellow, spring, 1 ft., Portugal ; gracilis, yellow, April, 1 ft., France ; incomparabilis (Chalice-cup Daffodil), yellow, April, 1 ft., Europe ; intermedius, lemon and orange yellow, 1½ ft., natural hybrid Pyrenees ; Johnstonii, pale sulphur, 1 ft., Portugal ; jonquilla (Jonquil), yellow, April, 9 in., S. Europe and Algeria ; juncifolius (Rush-leaved Daffodil), yellow, spring, 6 to 8 in., S. Europe ; Macleayi, cream and yellow, March, 6 in., Pyrenees ; major, yellow, March, 1 ft., Europe ; maximus, yellow, April, 1 ft., Europe ; minor, yellow, March, 6 in., Europe ; minor minimus (Pigmy Daffodil), sulphur yellow, 4 in. ; moschatus (Musk Daffodil), white, April, 1 ft., Pyrenees ; muticus, sulphur yellow, March, 12 in., Pyrenees ; odorus (Campernelle), yellow, May, 1 ft., France and Spain ; poeticus (Poet's Daffodil and Pheasant's Eye Narcissus), white, May, 1 ft., Mediterranean Region, and its varieties ornatus (early) and recurvus (late) ; pseudo-narcissus (Common Daffodil, Ajax Daffodil, Trumpet

Daffodil, or Lent Lily), yellow, March, 1 ft., Europe (Britain) ; pseudo-narcissus bicolor, white and yellow ; serotinus, white and yellow, Sept., 1 ft., S. Europe ; Tazetta (Polyanthus Narcissus), white and yellow, March, 1 ft., Mediterranean Region, and its variety orientalis (Chinese Sacred Lily) ; triandrus (Cyclamen-flowered Daffodil or Gannymedes Cup), white, April, 6 to 9 in., Spain ; triandrus albus (Angel's Tears), white ; triandrus calathinus, sulphur yellow.

PRINCIPAL HYBRIDS : N. Backhousei, sulphur and yellow ; Barrii, sulphur and orange ; Burbidgei, white, yellow, and red ; Humei, sulphur and lemon yellow ; Leedsii, white and sulphur ; Poetaz, various combinations of white, yellow, and orange. Numerous varieties of each of above.

PRINCIPAL DOUBLE-FLOWERED DAFFODILS : Capax plenus, lemon ; cernuus plenus, white ; jonquilla flore-pleno, yellow ; lobularis plenus, yellow ; minor plenus, yellow ; Telamonius plenus, yellow ; incomparabilis (Butter and Eggs), yellow and orange ; incomparabilis (Eggs and Bacon), white and orange ; incomparabilis (Codlins and Cream), white and sulphur ; Primrose Phœnix, yellow ; poeticus albus plenus odoratus (Gardenia Flowered Narcissus, Double White), white ; Queen Anne's Jonquil (N. odorus plenus), yellow.

Nard (*Valeriana celtica*)—See Valeriana.

Narthecium (Common Bog Asphodel)—Ord. Liliaceæ. Hardy herbaceous perennial.
CULTURE : Soil, ordinary. Position, moist beds, borders, or margins of ponds. Soil, ordinary, or boggy peat. Plant, Oct. or March.
PROPAGATION : By seeds sown in March or April where plants are required to grow ; division of roots in Oct. or March.
SPECIES CULTIVATED : N. ossifragum, yellow, July, 6 in., Europe (Britain).

Nasturtium—A term commonly but erroneously applied to Tropæolum majus.

Nasturtium (Water Cress)—Ord. Cruciferæ. Hardy perennial herb. Aquatic. Leaves, green or brown ; largely used for salads.
CULTURE IN BEDS IN WATER : Soil, ordinary. Position, open. Dimensions of beds, 3 to 4 ft. wide ; 3 to 6 in. deep ; no limit as to length. Depth of soil, 1½ to 3 in. Depth of water, 1½ in. when first planted ; 3 in. when growing freely : 6 in. in winter. Water must flow through beds, but not be stagnant. Plant, May and June for gathering in Aug. to Feb. ; Sept. to Nov. for gathering in Feb. to May. Replant beds twice annually. Distance for planting, 6 in. apart in rows, 2 ft. between rows. Soil must be removed each planting. Gather the tops once a week ; cut, not break, them off.
CULTURE IN PANS : Soil, ordinary. Position, tubs or tanks of water in open air or under glass. Sow seeds ⅟₁₆ in. deep in March or Sept. and partly immerse pan in water ; wholly when seedlings appear. Insert cuttings 2 to 3 in. apart in spring or autumn ; partly immerse at first, wholly after.
CULTURE IN TRENCHES : Soil, ordinary. Position, sunny. Dig trench 2 ft. wide, 1 ft. deep. Put 6 in. decayed manure in, and 3 in. of soil on this. Sow seeds thinly ⅛ in. deep in April and Aug. Keep well watered. Cress sown in April gather June to Sept. ; in Aug., Nov. to May.
PROPAGATION : For beds by seeds sown on a shady border in April, and kept moist ; by division of the plants in May or Aug.
SPECIES CULTIVATED : N. officinale, white, June, Britain. See Tropæolum for garden nasturtiums.

Natal Lily (*Clivia miniata*)—See Clivia.

Native Ivy of Australia (*Muelenbeckia adpressa*)—See Muehlenbeckia.

Navel-wort (*Cotyledon umbilicus*)—See Cotyledon.

Neapolitan Broom (*Genista anxantica*)—See Genista.

Neapolitan Cyclamen (*Cyclamen neapolitanum*)—See Cyclamen.

Neapolitan Violet (*Viola odorata pallida plena*)—See Viola.

Necklace Poplar (*Populus monilifera*)—See Populus.

Nectarine—See Prunus.

Needle Furze—See Genista.

Neilgherry Lily (*Lilium neilgherrense*)—See Lilium.

Neillia (Nine Bark)—Ord. Rosaceæ. Hardy deciduous shrubs. Flowering and orn. foliage. First introduced 1690.
CULTURE : Soil, ordinary. Position, open, sunny shrubberies or banks. Plant, Oct. to March. Prune flowering species moderately after blooming; variegated variety in Feb.
PROPAGATION : By seeds sown ⅛ in. deep in sandy soil in sheltered position outdoors, autumn or spring ; cuttings of half-ripened shoots, 2 to 3 in. long, inserted in sand under bell-glass during July and Aug.
SPECIES CULTIVATED : N. amurensis (Syn. Spiræa amurensis), white, summer, 6 to 8 ft., Manchuria ; opulifolia (Syn. Spiræa opulifolia), white, tinged rose, June, 6 to 10 ft., N. America ; opulifolia lutea, leaves golden ; sinensis, white or pinkish, May to June, 5 to 6 ft., Central China ; thyrsiflora, white, Aug. to Sept., 4 ft., Sikkim.

Nelson's Phlox (*Phlox Nelsoni*)—See Phlox.

Nelumbium (Sacred Bean ; Egyptian Bean ; Chinese Water Lily)—Ord. Nymphaceæ. Greenhouse aquatic rhizomatous-rooted perennials. Orn. foliage and flowering. First introduced 1787. Flowers, fragrant. Leaves, shield-shaped, 1 to 2 ft. in diameter, bluish green.
CULTURE : Compost, two parts loam, one part well-decayed manure. Position, in tanks or tubs of water heated to a temp. of 60° to 65°. Plant rhizomes 3 to 4 in. below surface of water in Feb. or March. Temp., March to Oct. 55° to 65° ; Oct. to March 45° to 55°. Draw off water from tank in Oct. and keep rhizomes dry till Feb. N. speciosum may be grown in tank in sunny position outdoors, June to Sept.
PROPAGATION : By seeds sown in sandy soil, 2 to 3 in. below surface of water, heated to temp. of 60° to 70° any time of year ; division of rhizomes in Feb.
SPECIES CULTIVATED : N. luteum, yellow, July, S. United States ; speciosum, white and rose, July, Trop. Asia. Numerous varieties of N. speciosum are to be found in trade lists.

Nemastylis—Ord. Iridaceæ. Half-hardy flowering bulbs. Deciduous. First introduced 1875.
OUTDOOR CULTURE : Soil, light, rich, sandy. Position, sunny well-drained border. Plant, Jan., placing bulbs 4 in. deep and 2 in. apart. Lift and replant bulbs annually. Mulch surface of bed in March with cow manure.
POT CULTURE : Compost, two parts sandy loam, one part leaf-mould or decayed cow manure. Pots, 4½ in. in diameter, well drained. Place five bulbs, 3 in. deep, in each pot in Nov. and cover with cocoanut-fibre refuse in cold frame or under cool greenhouse stage until growth commences. Water moderately from time bulbs begin to grow until flowers fade, then gradually cease, keeping bulbs dry till Jan. Temp., Sept. to Mar. 40° to 50° ; other times 50° to 60°.
PROPAGATION : By offsets, treated as advised for bulbs.
SPECIES CULTIVATED : N. cœlestina, blue, May to June, 2 ft., California ; geminiflora, purplish blue, May to June, 2 ft., California.

Nemesia—Ord. Scrophulariaceæ. Half-hardy annuals. Nat. S. Africa. First introduced 1774. Flowers, fragrant.
CULTURE : Soil, ordinary. Position, sunny beds or rockeries.
PROPAGATION : By seeds sown in March ฑ in. deep in well-drained pots or pans filled with light fibrous loam and little wood ashes. Place in temp. 55° to 65°, transplanting seedlings when they have formed three leaves 1 in. apart in well-drained pots, placing in temp. of 55°, and planting into flowering position outdoors in June, or repot into 6 in. pots for flowering in the greenhouse ; also seeds sown in May ฑ in. deep in patches outdoors where plants are required to flower, afterwards thinning seedlings to 2 or 3 in. apart.
SPECIES CULTIVATED : N. strumosa, various colours, summer, 1 ft., and its variety Suttoni (dwarf) ; versicolor, many colours, summer, 8 to 12 in. There are several fine hybrid races to be found in trade lists.

Nemophila (Californian Blue-bell)—Ord. Hydrophyllaceæ. Hardy trailing annuals. First introduced 1822.

OUTDOOR CULTURE : Soil, ordinary. Position, in masses or in lines as edgings to sunny beds or borders. Sow seeds $\frac{1}{16}$ in. deep in March or April for flowering in summer ; in Aug. or Sept. for flowering in spring. Thin seedlings to 1 or 2 in. apart when $\frac{1}{2}$ in. high.

POT CULTURE : Compost, two parts good ordinary soil, one part leaf-mould or well-decayed manure. Size of pots, $4\frac{1}{2}$ in. diameter. Place 1 in. of drainage in pots, cover with moss, and fill up to within $\frac{1}{4}$ in. of rim with above compost pressed firmly. Sow seeds thinly, slightly covering with fine mould, and place pots in cool, shady frame or window. Water moderately at first, freely when seedlings appear. Apply weak stimulants once or twice weekly when plants begin to flower. Position when in flower, cold, sunny greenhouse, window, or frame.

SPECIES CULTIVATED : N. aurita, purple and violet, summer, 1 ft., California ; insignis, blue or white, summer, trailing, California ; maculata, white and purple, summer, 6 in., California ; Menziesi (Syn. N. atomaria), white or blue, summer, trailing, California.

Nepaul Laburnum (*Piptanthus nepalensis*) —See Piptanthus.

Nepaul Poppy (*Meconopsis nepalensis*)—See Meconopsis.

Nepaul Trumpet-flower (*Beaumontia grandiflora*)—See Beaumontia.

Nepenthes (Pitcher-plant)—Ord. Nepenthaceæ. Stove evergreen sub-shrubby perennials. Orn. foliage. First introduced 1789. Flowers, greenish, diœcious, insignificant. Leaves, oblong or lance-shaped, terminating in a pitcher-like appendage ; green, variously mottled with red, brown, and crimson.

CULTURE : Compost, two parts good brown fibrous peat, one part sphagnum moss. Position, in baskets suspended from roof in shady part of stove. Plant or rebasket, Feb. or March. Temp., March to Sept. 70° to 85° ; Sept. to March 65° to 75°. Water copiously March to Sept., moderately afterwards. Syringe twice daily all the year round. Moist atmosphere very essential. Shade from sun.

PROPAGATION : By seeds sown on surface of mixture of fibrous peat and sphagnum moss in well-drained pan covered with bell-glass and placed in a moist frame heated to temp. of 80° to 85° ; cuttings of one-year-old shoots inserted singly in small pots plunged in bottom heat of 85° any time.

SPECIES CULTIVATED : N. ampullaria, green, Malaya ; bicalcarata, green, Borneo ; Curtisii, green, crimson, and purple, Borneo ; hookeriana, pale green and red Borneo ; northiana, green and purple, Borneo ; phyllamphora, bright green and red, S. China and E. Indies ; rafflesiana, green, red, and brown, India ; sanguinea, blood red, Malaya ; Veitchii, green, Borneo ; ventricosa, green, brown, and crimson, Philippines. Numerous pretty hybrids such as amesiana (green and red), atrosanguinea (pale green and reddish purple), dicksoniana (light green and reddish crimson), dominiana (deep green and purple), henryana (brownish red and pale green), intermedia (green and purple), mastersiana (deep green, purple, and crimson), Sedeni (light green and brownish crimson), and Wittei (green and dark red).

Nepeta (Cat-mint ; Ground Ivy)—Ord. Labiatæ. Hardy herbaceous perennials. Leaves, heart-shaped, dark green or variegated with white.

CULTURE : Soil, ordinary. Position, sunny beds, borders, or rockeries. Plant, Oct. to March. N. Glechoma variegata also makes a pretty basket plant for a cool greenhouse or window ; or for draping staging in greenhouse.

PROPAGATION : By seeds sown $\frac{1}{16}$ in. deep where plants are required to grow, March to May ; division of roots, Oct. to March.

SPECIES CULTIVATED : N. Glechoma variegata (Variegated Ground Ivy), Syn. Glechoma hederacea, leaves silvery, trailing, Europe (Britain) ; macrantha, lavender blue, July to Sept., 2 to 3 ft., Siberia ; Mussinii, blue, summer, 1 to 2 ft., Caucasus.

Nephrodium (Buckler Fern)—Ord. Filices. Stove, greenhouse, and hardy ferns. CULTURE OF GREENHOUSE SPECIES : Compost, equal parts loam, leaf-mould, peat, and sand. Position, well-drained pots, borders, or rockeries, in shade. Pot or

Nicandra physaloides
(Apple of Peru)

Nicotiana alata grandiflora
(Sweet-scented Tobacco)

Odontioda Bradshawiæ

Odontioda Vuylstekeæ

Odontoglossum crispum

Odontoglossum hybridum

Odontoglossum hybridum

Œnothera amœna
(Godetia)

Olearia nitida
(New Zealand Daisy Bush)

Oncidium Forbesii
(Butterfly Orchid)

Ononis Natrix
(Goat Root)

Onosma tauricum
(Golden Drop)

Opuntia leucotricha

Orchis foliosa
(Madeira Orchis)

Ornithogalum narbonense
(Onion Plant)

Osmanthus Delavayi
(Fragrant Olive)

Ostrowskia magnifica
(Great Oriental Bell-flower)

Ourisia coccinea

plant, Feb., March, or April. Water moderately Oct. to Feb., freely afterwards. Temp., Oct. to March 40° to 50° ; March to Oct. 55° to 65°.
CULTURE OF STOVE SPECIES : Compost, equal parts loam, leaf-mould, peat, and sand Position, well-drained pots in shady part of stove. Pot, March. Water moderately Oct. to March, freely afterwards. Temp., Sept. to March 55° to 60° ; March to Sept. 65° to 75°.
CULTURE OF HARDY SPECIES : Soil, ordinary light rich. Position, shady borders or rockeries. Plant, April. Water freely in dry weather, May to Sept. Top-dress annually with leaf-mould or well-decayed manure. Protect in severe weather with bracken or litter. Do not remove dead fronds until April.
PROPAGATION : Stove and greenhouse species by spores sown on surface of fine sandy peat, under bell-glass, in temp. 75° to 85° any time ; division of plants at potting or planting time ; hardy species by spores sown on surface of sandy soil in shady, cold frame ; division in April.
STOVE SPECIES : N. albo-punctatum, Mascarene Islands ; dissectum, Tropics.
GREENHOUSE SPECIES : N. cuspidatum, Ceylon ; decompositum (Syn. Lastrea decomposita), Australia, etc. ; erythrosorum (Syn. Lastrea erythrosa), Japan ; hispidum, New Zealand ; lepidum, Polynesia ; molle and its varieties corymbiferum and grandiceps, Tropics and Subtropics ; Otaria (Syn. Lastrea aristata), Japan ; patens (Spreading Wood Fern), Tropics and Subtropics ; prolificum, Japan, almost hardy ; Richardsii multifidum, New Caledonia ; Sieboldii (Syn. Lastrea Sieboldii) and its variegated form, Japan.
HARDY SPECIES : N. æmulum (Syn. Lastrea recurva), Hay-scented Buckler Fern, Britain ; cristatum (Syns. Aspidum cristatum and Lastrea cristata), Crested Buckler Fern, Britain and N. America ; dilatatum, Britain ; Filix-mas (Syn. Lastrea Filixmas), Male Fern, and its numerous varieties, Britain and the Temperate Zone ; fragrans (Fragrant Wood Fern), N. America ; goldieanum, N. America ; hirtipes (Syn. Lastrea atrata), Trop. Asia ; montanum (Syn. Lastrea Oreopteris), Mountain Buckler Fern, and its varieties, Europe (Britain) and N. America ; rigidum (Syn. Lastrea rigidum), N. Temperate Zone ; spinulosum (Syn. Lastrea dilatata), Prickly Buckler Fern, N. Temperate Zone (Britain) ; Thelypteris (Syn. Lastrea Thelypteris), Female Buckler Fern, N. Temperate Zone (Britain).

Nephrolepis (Ladder Fern)—Ord. Filices. Stove evergreen ferns. First introduced 1793. Fronds, linear, narrow, once divided, plain or crested.
CULTURE : Compost, equal parts loam, leaf-mould, and sand, two parts lumpy peat. Position, in baskets suspended from roof, or in well-drained pots or beds in shady part of stove. Pot or plant, Feb. or March. Water moderately Oct. to March, freely afterwards. Temp., Sept. to March 55° to 60° ; March to Sept. 65° to 75°.
PROPAGATION : By spores sown on surface of pans of sandy peat under bell-glass and placed in temp. 75° to 85° any time ; division of plants, Feb., March, or April ; pegging down creeping stems bearing young plants and removing when rooted.
SPECIES CULTIVATED : N. acuta, 2 to 4 ft., Cuba, Polynesia, Hong Kong, etc. ; Bausei, 12 to 18 in., garden origin ; cordifolia, 1 to 2 ft., Tropics and Subtropics (will thrive in warm greenhouse), and its varieties compacta and pectinata ; davallioides, 2 to 3 ft., Java, and its variety furcans ; Duffii, 1 ft., Australia ; exaltata (Ladder Fern), 2 to 3 ft., Tropics ; philippinensis, Philippine Islands ; Pluma, 3 to 4 ft., Madagascar ; rufescens, 2 to 3 ft., Tropics ; tripinnatifida, 2 to 3 ft., Solomon Islands. Several varieties.

Nerine (Guernsey Lily ; Scarlet Guernsey Lily)—Ord. Amaryllidaceæ. Greenhouse bulbous plants. Deciduous. First introduced 1680. All are natives of S. Africa and flower from June well on into the autumn.
CULTURE : Compost, two parts sandy loam, one part well-decayed cow manure or leaf-mould, one part coarse sand. Pot, Aug. to Nov., placing one bulb half its depth in a 4½ in. pot or three in a 6 in. pot ; good drainage essential. Position, light, cool greenhouse, Sept. to May ; cold frame or sunny spot outdoors, May to Sept. Water moderately Sept. to May, or as soon as flower spikes show ; keep quite dry May to Sept. Apply stimulants occasionally during growth. Top-dress

annually with equal parts sandy loam, decayed cow manure, and sand in Aug. Repotting only necessary every three or four years. Season of growth, Sept. to May ; season of rest, May to Sept.

CULTURE OUTDOORS : Soil, light sandy, enriched with decayed cow manure. Position, sunny well-drained borders at base of S. wall. Plant, Aug. to Nov., 2 to 3 in. deep. Protect, Nov. to April, with covering of dry litter. Top-dress annually in Aug. with leaf-mould or decayed cow manure. Lift and replant every four or five years.

PROPAGATION : By offsets, removed when repotting and treated as old bulbs.

SPECIES CULTIVATED : N. appendiculata, pink, 1 ft. ; Bowdenii, pink, 1½ ft. ; curvifolia, scarlet, 1 ft. ; curvifolia Fothergillii, deep scarlet ; filifolia, red, 1 ft. ; flexuosa, pink, 2 ft. ; flexuosa angustifolia, pink, 2 ft. ; flexuosa pulchella, pink and red, 2 ft. ; sarniensis (Guernsey Lily), salmon, 2 ft. ; sarniensis corusca, orange-scarlet, 1 ft. ; sarniensis Plantii, crimson ; sarniensis rosea, rose ; sarniensis venusta, scarlet ; pudica, white and pink, 18 in. ; Moorei, scarlet, 1 ft. ; undulata, pink, 1 ft. Numerous hybrids. See also Lycoris.

Nerium (Oleander ; Rose Bay)—Ord. Apocynaceæ. Greenhouse evergreen flowering shrubs. First introduced 1596. Flowers, fragrant.

CULTURE : Compost, two parts sandy loam, one part well-decomposed manure, one part leaf-mould, and one part sand. Position, pots, tubs, or well-drained beds in light, sunny greenhouse or window ; place pot or tub plants outdoors, June to Sept. Pot or plant, Feb. or March. Prune immediately after flowering, or in Oct. shortening shoots of previous year's growth to within 3 or 4 in. of their base. Temp., Sept. to March 45° to 55° ; March to June 55° to 65°. Water copiously March to Sept., moderately Sept. to Nov., keep nearly dry Nov. to March. Apply stimulants once or twice weekly May to Sept. Remove young shoots that issue from base of flower trusses as soon as they appear. No shade required. Syringe twice daily March to June.

PROPAGATION : By cuttings of firm young shoots, 3 to 6 in. long, inserted singly in 2 in. pots in a compost of equal parts peat, loam, leaf-mould, and sand, placed under bell-glass in temp. 60° to 70°, spring or summer.

SPECIES CULTIVATED : N. Oleander (Oleander or Rose Bay), white, red, or purple, summer, to 20 ft., Orient, and its varieties album plenum (double white), Henri Mares (double rosy pink), Madonna grandiflorum (double cream), splendens (double red), and variegatum (leaves variegated) ; odorum (Syn. N. indicum), rosy pink or white, June to Aug., 6 to 8 ft., Persia and Japan. There are several varieties of the last, including a double.

Nertera (Fruiting Duckweed)—Ord. Rubiaceæ. Greenhouse and half-hardy creeping perennial herb. Orn. fruiting. First introduced 1868. Berries round, bright orange-red or crimson.

INDOOR CULTURE : Compost, two parts sandy loam, one part leaf-mould and sand. Position, small well-drained pots or pans in shady part of greenhouse. Pot, Feb. or March. Water freely March to Sept., moderately afterwards. Temp., March to Oct. 50° to 60° ; Oct. to March 40° to 50°.

OUTDOOR CULTURE : Soil, ordinary light rich. Position, moist, sheltered ledges of shady rockery. Plant, March or April. Water in dry weather. Protect in severe weather with bell- or hand-glass.

PROPAGATION : By seeds sown ⅟₁₆ in. deep in light, sandy soil in temp. 55° to 65°, March or April ; division of plants in March or April.

SPECIES CULTIVATED : N. depressa, 1 in., flowers green, Australasia.

Net Fern—See Gleichenia.

Nettle Geranium—See Coleus.

Nettle-leaved Bell-flower (*Campanula Trachelium*)—See Campanula.

Nettle Tree (*Celtis australis*)—See Celtis.

Nevada Lily (*Lilium washingtonianum*)—See Lilium.

Neviusia (Alabama Snow Wreath)—Ord. Rosaceæ. Hardy deciduous flowering shrub. First introduced 1879.

CULTURE : Soil, good ordinary. **Position, sunny, sheltered shrubbery. Plant in autumn.**

PROPAGATION : By cuttings of half-ripened shoots inserted in sandy soil in cold frame in summer ; also by layering in autumn.

SPECIES CULTIVATED : N. alabamensis, white, May, 6 ft., Alabama.

New Caledonia Pine-tree (*Araucaria Cookii* and *A. Ruleii*)—See Araucaria.

New England Mayflower (*Epigæa repens*)—See Epigæa.

New England Star-wort (*Aster Novæ-Angliæ*)—See Aster.

New Jersey Tea-plant (*Ceanothus americanus*)—See Ceanothus.

Newman's Cone-flower (*Rudbeckia speciosa*)—See Rudbeckia.

New Zealand Broad-leaf (*Griselinia lucida macrophylla*)—See Griselinia.

New Zealand Broom (*Notospartium Carmichaeliæ*)—See Notospartium.

New Zealand Bur (*Acæna Novæ-Zelandiæ*)—See Acæna.

New Zealand Clematis (*Clematis indivisa lobata*)—See Clematis.

New Zealand Crow-foot (*Ranunculus Lyallii*)—See Ranunculus.

New Zealand Daisy Bush (*Olearia Haastii*)—See Olearia.

New Zealand Dragon-plant (*Cordyline australis*)—See Cordyline.

New Zealand Flax—See Phormium.

New Zealand Glory Pea (*Clianthus puniceus*)—See Clianthus.

New Zealand Holly (*Osmanthus ilicifolius*)—See Osmanthus.

New Zealand Laburnum-tree (*Sophora tetraptera*)—See Sophora.

New Zealand Palm (*Rhopalostylis sapida*)—See Rhopalostylis.

New Zealand Reed (*Cortaderia conspicua*)—See Cortaderia.

New Zealand Spinach (*Tetragonia expansa*)—See Tetragonia.

New Zealand Tree-fern (*Dicksonia squarrosa*)—See Dicksonia.

New Zealand Water Lily (*Ranunculus Lyallii*)—See Ranunculus.

Nicandra (Apple of Peru)—Ord. Solanaceæ. Hardy annual. First introduced 1759.

CULTURE : Soil, ordinary. Position, sunny, open borders.

PROPAGATION : By seeds sown ¼ in. deep in pots or boxes of light soil in temp. 55° to 65° in March, transplanting seedlings 3 ft. apart outdoors in May ; or by sowing seed in sunny position outdoors in April, transplanting seedlings in June.

SPECIES CULTIVATED : N. physaloides, blue and white, summer, 18 in. to 2 ft., Peru.

Nicotiana (Tobacco Plant)—Ord. Solanaceæ. Half-hardy annuals. Flowering and orn. foliage. N. tabacum is the tobacco of commerce. First introduced 1570.

POT CULTURE : Compost, two parts loam, one part leaf-mould or decayed manure, and one part sand. Position, sunny or shady greenhouse or window. Water freely when in full growth, moderately at other times. Apply stimulants once or twice a week when in flower. Temp., March to Sept. 55° to 65° ; Sept. to March 40° to 50°.

OUTDOOR CULTURE : Soil, ordinary. Position, sunny beds or borders. Plant in June in groups of three or six. Protect N. alba in winter with covering of cinder ashes, tan, or decayed manure. Will only survive winter in well-drained soils.

CULTURE OF TOBACCO PLANT : Soil, ordinary. Position, sunny beds or borders. Plant, June. Gather leaves of N. tabacum in Sept. for drying. Water freely in dry weather.

PROPAGATION : By seeds sown on the surface of fine light mould in a shallow box or pan in shade, in a temp. of 65° to 75°, in March or April ; also by cuttings of the roots inserted in sandy soil in temp. 55° to 65° in autumn or spring.

SPECIES CULTIVATED : N. alata grandiflora (Syn. Affinis), the Sweet-scented Tobacco, white, fragrant, summer, 3 to 5 ft., strictly a perennial, Brazil; sylvestris, white, summer, 3 to 4 ft., Argentina; tabacum (Tobacco Plant), rose, summer, 4 ft., S. America; tabacum macrophyllum, red, rose, or purple, summer; tomentosa (Syn. N. colossea), pale green and yellow, tinged red, 10 to 20 ft., S. America; suaveolens, white, summer, 2 ft., S. America; Sanderæ, red, pink, carmine, etc., summer, 2 to 3 ft., hybrid.

Nidularium—Ord. Bromeliaceæ. Stove flowering and orn. foliaged plants. Bracts green, red, or crimson. Leaves in dense basal rosettes. First introduced 1830.
CULTURE : Compost, equal parts fibrous loam, rough peat, leaf-mould, and silver sand. Position, well-drained pots in light, moist part of stove. Pot, Feb. or March. Water moderately in winter, freely at other times. Temp., March to Sept. 70° to 80°; Sept. to March 65° to 75°.
PROPAGATION : By largish offshoots inserted singly in small pots of sandy peat in temp. of 85°, Feb. or April.
SPECIES CULTIVATED : N. fulgens, white and violet, leaves spotted dark green, 9 to 12 in., Brazil; Innocentii, white, leaves tinted brown or red, Brazil; purpureum, red, leaves flushed purple-brown, Brazil. Chantrieri is a fine hybrid. See also Canistrum and Aregelia.

Nierembergia (Tall Cup-flower; Trailing Cup-flower)—Ord. Solanaceæ. Hardy and half-hardy creeping perennial herbs. First introduced 1831.
CULTURE OF HARDY SPECIES : Soil, equal parts sandy loam and leaf-mould. Position, sunny or moist border or ledges of rockery. Plant, Oct., March, or April. Water freely in dry weather. Top-dress annually in March with decayed cow manure. Protect in very severe weather with covering of litter.
CULTURE OF HALF-HARDY SPECIES : Compost, two parts sandy loam, one part well-decomposed cow manure, and one part sand. Position, well-drained pots or pans in shady part of greenhouse or cold frame all the year round, or outdoors in shady spot, May to Oct. Pot, Feb. or March. Water freely March to Sept., moderately afterwards.
PROPAGATION : By seeds sown in light, sandy soil in temp. 55° to 65° Nov. to April; cuttings inserted in sandy soil under bell-glass in shady part of cool greenhouse in Aug., transferring when well rooted singly into 2 in. pots and placing in light, airy position in greenhouse or window.
HARDY SPECIES : N. rivularis (Cup-flower), white, summer, 6 in., S. America.
HALF-HARDY SPECIES : N. frutescens, blue, summer, white and yellow, tinged blue, 1 to 3 ft., Chile, and its variety atroviolacea (dark violet); gracilis (Syns. N. calycina and N. filicaulis), white and yellow, tinged purple, summer, 6 to 9 in., S. America.

Nigella (Fennel-flower; Devil-in-a-bush; Love-in-a-mist; Love-in-a-puzzle) —Ord. Ranunculaceæ. Hardy annuals. First introduced 1548. Flowers surrounded by a green mossy involucre. Foliage, green, graceful, feathery.
CULTURE : Soil, ordinary. Position, sunny, open beds or borders.
PROPAGATION : By seeds sown ¼ in. deep in lines, bands, or masses in March or April; thin seedlings out 6 in. apart each way, May or June.
SPECIES CULTIVATED : N. damascena, blue, summer, 1 to 2 ft., S. Europe; damascena flore-pleno, double, blue; damascena alba, white; N. hispanica, blue, summer, 1 to 2 ft., Spain; sativa, pale blue, summer, 1½ ft., Mediterranean Region (cultivated for seeds, which are used in seasoning and known as black cummin).

Night-blooming Cactus (*Cereus grandiflorus*)—See Cereus.

Night-scented Stock (*Matthiola tristis*)—See Matthiola.

Nine Bark—See Neillia.

Niphobolus—See Polypodium.

Nipple Cactus (*Mammillaria bicolor*)—See Mammillaria.

Noble Silver Fir (*Abies nobilis*)—See Abies.

Noisette Rose (*Rosa noisettiana*)—See Rosa.

Nolana (Chilian Bell-flower)—Ord. Convolvulaceæ. Hardy annuals. First introduced 1761.
CULTURE : Soil, ordinary. Position, open, sunny beds, borders, or rockeries.
PROPAGATION : By seeds sown $\frac{1}{16}$ in. deep in patches in March or April where plants are required to grow, thinning seedlings to 2 or 3 in. apart in May or June.
SPECIES CULTIVATED : N. atriplicifolia (Syn. N. grandiflora), blue and white, summer, trailing, Peru ; lanceolata, blue, white, and green, summer, 6 in., Peru ; paradoxa, white, summer, 12 to 18 in., Peru ; tenella, pale blue, trailing, summer, Peru.

Nolina—Ord. Liliaceæ. Greenhouse orn.-leaved plants. First introduced 1845. Leaves, long, narrow, green.
CULTURE : Compost, two parts fibrous loam, one part silver sand. Pot, March, in well-drained pots. Water freely March to Sept., moderately other times. Temp., Sept. to March 45° to 50° ; March to Sept. 55° to 65°.
PROPAGATION : By seeds sown in sandy loam in temp. 65° in Feb. or March.
SPECIES CULTIVATED : N. glauca, leaves glaucous or milky white, 3 to 5 ft. ; glauca latifolia, leaves broader than those of the species ; recurvata, leaves recurved. Natives of Mexico. This genus was formerly known as Beaucarnea.

None-so-Pretty (*Saxifraga umbrosa*)—See Saxifraga.

Nootka Fir (*Pseudotsuga Douglasii*)—See Pseudotsuga.

Nootka Sound Arbor-vitæ (*Thuya plicata*)—See Thuya.

Nootka Sound Cypress (*Cupressus nootkatensis*)—See Cupressus.

Norfolk Island Palm (*Rhopalostyle Baueri*)—See Rhopalostyle.

Norfolk Island Pine-tree (*Araucaria excelsa*)—See Araucaria.

Norfolk Island Tree-fern (*Alsophila excelsa*)—See Alsophila.

North American Crab (*Pyrus coronaria*)—See Pyrus.

North American Ox-eye (*Heliopsis lævis*)—See Heliopsis.

North American Pitcher Plant—See Sarracenia.

North American Sunflower (*Actinomeris squarrosa*)—See Actinomeris.

Northern Fox Grape (*Vitis Labrusca*)—See Vitis.

Norway Maple (*Acer platanoides*)—See Acer.

Norway Spruce (*Picea excelsa*)—See Picea.

Nothochlæna (Cloak Fern ; Gold and Silver Maiden-hair Ferns)—Ord. Filices. Stove and greenhouse ferns. First introduced 1778. Fronds, once or thrice divided, upper surface green, underneath covered with white powder or scales. Ht., 3 to 18 in.
CULTURE : Compost, equal parts loam, leaf-mould, peat, and sand, with little charcoal and sandstone broken small. Position, pots in shady part of house. Pot, Feb. or March. Water moderately Oct. to Feb., freely other times. Syringing not required. Temp., stove species, Sept. to March 55° to 65° ; March to Sept. 65° to 75° ; greenhouse species, Sept. to March 45° to 50° ; March to Sept. 55° to 65°.
PROPAGATION : By spores sown on surface of fine sandy peat in pans under bell-glass in temp. 75° to 85° any time ; division at potting time.
STOVE SPECIES : N. flavens (Syn. Chrysophylla), Central America ; nivea (Silver Maiden-hair Fern), Mexico and Peru ; sinuata, Trop. America ; trichomanoides, Jamaica and Cuba.
GREENHOUSE SPECIES : N. dealbata (Syn. Cincinalis dealbata), N. America ; Hookeri (Syn. Cincinalis Hookeri), N. America ; lanuginosa, S. Europe and Australia ; Marantæ, S. Europe, N. Africa, etc. ; Newberryii, California.

Nothofagus (Southern Beech)—Ord. Fagaceæ. Evergreen or deciduous orn. trees. Half-hardy. First introduced 1830.
CULTURE: Soil, moist loam. Position, specimens on lawns or in open spaces in milder counties such as Devon and Cornwall. Plant deciduous species Nov. to Feb., evergreen species Sept. or April.
PROPAGATION: By layering in spring.
DECIDUOUS SPECIES CULTIVATED: N. antarctica (Antarctic Beech), 40 to 60 ft., S. America; obliqua, 50 to 100 ft., Chile.
EVERGREEN SPECIES CULTIVATED: N. betuloides, 40 to 60 ft., S. America; cliffortioides, 30 to 50 ft., New Zealand; Cunninghamii, 40 to 60 ft., Tasmania; fusca, 50 to 100 ft., New Zealand; Menziesi, 40 to 60 ft., New Zealand.

Notholæna—See Nothochlæna.

Nothoscordum—See Bloomeria.

Notospartium (New Zealand Broom)—Ord. Leguminosæ. Half-hardy evergreen flowering shrub. First introduced 1883.
CULTURE: Soil, light, well-drained loam. Position, sunny, sheltered border. Plant, April or May. Prune in April, thinning out weak wood only.
PROPAGATION: By seeds sown in sandy soil in a cold frame in spring; cuttings in a cold frame in autumn.
SPECIES CULTIVATED: N. Carmichaeliæ, pink, Aug., 4 to 10 ft., New Zealand.

Nuphar (Yellow Water Lily)—Ord. Nymphaceæ. Hardy aquatic perennials.
CULTURE: Soil, two parts strong rich loam, one part well-decayed manure. Position, sunny, shallow streams, ponds, or lakes. Depth of water, 6 to 12 in. Plant, March or Oct. Methods of planting: (1) Fill a shallow wicker basket with compost, place the plant in it and a few stones on the surface, then lower into the water. (2) Place some compost round the roots, then add a few stones, and surround with canvas or matting and lower into the water.
PROPAGATION: By seeds sown ¼ in. deep in rich soil in a shallow basket immersed in water, Oct. to April; division of the plant in March.
SPECIES CULTIVATED: N. advena, yellow, July, N. America; luteum (Brandy Bottle or Yellow Water Lily), yellow, June, N. Europe (Britain); minimum, yellow, July, Europe.

Nutmeg-scented Geranium (*Pelargonium fragrans*)—See Pelargonium.

Nuts—See Corylus.

Nuttallia (Oso-berry-tree)—Ord. Rosaceæ. Hardy deciduous flowering shrub. First introduced 1848. Flowers succeeded by purplish plum-like fruit.
CULTURE: Soil, ordinary. Position, shady or sunny shrubberies. Plant, Oct. to Feb. Prune when necessary immediately after flowering.
PROPAGATION: By seeds sown ⅛ in. deep in ordinary soil in shady position outdoors in spring or autumn; suckers removed from parent plant and planted Oct. or Nov.; cuttings of ripened shoots in cold frame in autumn; layering in autumn.
SPECIES CULTIVATED: N. cerasiformis, white, March, 6 to 10 ft., California.

Nycterinia—See Zaluzianskia.

Nymphæa (Water Lily)—Ord. Nymphaceæ. Stove and hardy aquatic tuberous-rooted perennials. Evergreen and deciduous. First introduced 1786.
CULTURE OF STOVE SPECIES: Two parts rich turfy loam and one part well-decayed manure. Position, large pots or tubs immersed 8 to 12 in. below surface of water in tanks fully exposed to light. Plant, Feb. to April. Temp. of atmosphere, 65° to 75° March to Sept.; 50° to 60° Sept. to March. Temp. of water, 65° to 75° March to Sept.; 55° to 65° Sept. to March. Repot annually in Feb. or March.
CULTURE OF HARDY SPECIES: Compost, two parts strong rich loam, one part well-decayed manure. Position, open, sunny ponds or lakes. Depth of water, 2 to 3 ft. for large growing species; 1 to 1½ ft. for weaker growing species such as Nymphæas camdida, Laydeckeri, odorata, and pygmæa. Plant, March to Oct. Methods of planting: (1) Place plant in small wicker basket containing above compost and lower to the bottom of pond or lake. (2) Inclose roots with soil and large stone in

piece of canvas or matting, tie securely, and immerse as above. (3) Place large hillock or mound of compost at bottom of pond when dry, plant tubers in centre, afterwards submerging with water.

PROPAGATION : Stove species by seeds sown $\frac{1}{8}$ in. deep in pots of rich soil immersed in water heated to a temp. of 65° to 75°, March or April. Hardy species by seeds sown $\frac{1}{4}$ in. deep in rich soil in shallow basket and immersed in ponds or lakes in spring ; division of tubers or rhizomes, March or April.

STOVE SPECIES : N. ampla, white, July, W. Indies ; blanda, white, July, S. America ; cærulea (Blue Lotus of Egypt), blue, N. and Central Africa ; capensis (Cape Blue Water Lily), blue, S. Africa, and its variety zanzibariensis ; daubenyana, pale blue, hybrid ; flava (Syn. N. mexicana), yellow, Mexico ; gigantea, blue, summer, Australia ; gracilis (Syn. N. flavovirens), white, summer, Mexico ; Lotus (Egyptian Lotus), white, summer, Egypt, and its variety dentata ; rubra, purplish red, India ; stellata, blue, summer, India ; stellata zanzibariensis, blue.

HARDY SPECIES : N. alba (Common White Water Lily), white, summer, Europe (Britain) ; alba candidissima, white ; alba rosea, rose ; candida, white, Bohemia ; odorata, white and red, summer, N. America ; odorata rosea, pink ; odorata sulphurea, yellow ; tetragona (Syn. pygmæa), white, June, Himalayas ; tetragona helvola, yellow ; tuberosa, white, July, N. America ; tuberosa Richardsoni, double.

HARDY HYBRID WATER LILIES : Marliacea albida, white ; M. carnea, pink or white ; M. chromatella, primrose and rose ; M. flammea, rose and carmine ; M. ignea, rose and orange-red ; M. rosea, rosy pink ; Laydeckeri lilacea, pink and crimson ; L. fulgens, crimson-magenta ; L. lucida, vermilion ; L. purpurata, rosy crimson ; and L. rosea, carmine, and many named varieties to be found in trade lists.

Nyssa (Tupelo Tree)—Ord. Cornaceæ. Hardy deciduous trees. Grown for the beauty of their rich scarlet tinted foliage in August.

CULTURE : Soil, ordinary. Position, margins of streams, lakes, etc. Plant in autumn.
PROPAGATION : By layering in autumn.
SPECIES CULTIVATED : N. aquatica, white, May, 40 to 50 ft., U. States ; sylvatica, white, 30 to 100 ft., June, N. America.

Oak (*Quercus robur*)—See Quercus.

Oakesia—See Uvularia.

Oak Fern (*Polypodium Dryopteris*)—See Polypodium.

Oak-leaved Geranium (*Pelargonium quercifolium*)—See Pelargonium.

Ochna—Ord. Ochnaceæ. Stove evergreen flowering shrubs. First introduced 1816. Flowers succeeded by black and crimson globular fruits.

CULTURE : Compost, equal parts fibrous loam, peat, and sand. Position, well-drained pots in sunny, light part of stove. Pot, Feb. or March. Prune into shape, Feb. Water freely March to Oct., moderately afterwards. Syringe daily Feb. to Oct. Temp., March to Sept. 70° to 75° ; Sept. to March 60° to 65°.

PROPAGATION : By cuttings of firm shoots, 2 to 3 in. long, inserted in sandy peat under bell-glass in temp. 65° to 75°, summer.

SPECIES CULTIVATED : O. atropurpurea, yellow and purple, spring, 4 ft., S. Africa ; multiflora, yellow, spring, 6 ft., Trop. Africa.

Ocimum (Sweet Basil ; Bush Basil)—Ord. Labiatæ. Half-hardy annual aromatic herbs. First introduced 1548. Leaves, egg-shaped, aromatic ; used for flavouring stews, soups, and salads.

CULTURE : Soil, ordinary light rich. Position, sunny well-drained border. Plant, 6 in. apart in rows 9 to 12 in. asunder in May. Shade from sun first few days after planting. Water freely in dry weather. Gather leaves and tops when coming into flower, dry and reduce to powder for winter use.

PROPAGATION : By seeds sown $\frac{1}{16}$ in. deep in light soil in shallow box in temp. 55° to 65° in March, transplanting seedlings when three leaves are formed an inch apart in similar soil and gradually hardening off in cold frame.

SPECIES CULTIVATED : O. Basilicum (Sweet Basil), white, summer, 1 ft., Trop. Asia ; minimum (Bush Basil), white, summer, 6 in., Trop. Asia.

Odontadenia—Ord. Apocynaceæ.   Stove flowering climber.   First introduced 1854.

CULTURE : Compost, rough turfy loam, peat, sharp sand, and a little broken charcoal. Position, well-drained pots, with shoots trained to roof of stove or to wire trellis. Pot, Feb. or March.   Prune, Oct., cutting away shoots that have flowered only. Water very little Oct. to Feb., moderately Feb. to April, freely afterwards.   Temp., Oct. to Feb. 55° to 60° ; Feb. to Oct. 65° to 75°.

PROPAGATION : By cuttings of young side shoots, 3 in. long, inserted in pots of sandy peat under bell-glass in temp. 80° in Feb., March, or April.

SPECIES CULTIVATED : O. speciosa (Syn. Dipladenia Harrisi), yellow and orange, fragrant, summer, climbing, Trinidad.

Odontioda—By-generic hybrid orchids, the result of crossing species of Cochlioda with those of Odontoglossum.   Suitable for cool house culture.   Flower in winter and spring.

CULTURE : Compost, equal parts osmunda fibre and fresh sphagnum moss with a small quantity of decayed oak leaves.   Repot every second year after flowering. Pots to be filled two-thirds with crocks and base of plant elevated just level with rim of pot.   Water freely daily in summer ; every other day in spring and autumn ; every fourth day in winter.   Shade from direct sun.   Temp., spring 55° to 65° ; summer 60° to 70° ; autumn 55° to 65° ; winter 45° to 55°.

PROPAGATION : By division at potting time.

PRINCIPAL HYBRIDS : O. Bradshawiæ, scarlet and orange ; Charlesworthii, ruby red and yellow ; Chelsiensis, rose, carmine, and pink ; Cooksoniæ, orange-scarlet, vermilion, and yellow ; Heatonensis, white, pink, violet, and yellow ; Vuylstekeæ, cream, red, scarlet, and yellow ; Zephyr, scarlet, yellow, and orange.

Odontoglossum (Almond-scented Orchid ;   Violet-scented Orchid)—Ord. Orchidaceæ.   Greenhouse epiphytal and terrestrial orchids.   Evergreen.   First introduced 1835.   Flower spikes produced from base of pseudo-bulbs.

CULTURE : Compost, equal parts fibrous peat and sphagnum moss with a little broken charcoal.   Position, teak-wood baskets or pans suspended from roof, blocks of wood, well-drained pots ; partial shade in summer, exposed to full light at other times.   Pot, Feb., March, or April.   Fill pots or pans two-thirds of their depth with potsherds and charcoal.   Place layer of moss on drainage and fill remainder of space with compost to 1 in. above rim.   Secure plant on this by means of fine copper wire and top-dress with layer of sphagnum moss and secure firmly with copper wire.   Water freely during summer, moderately Sept. to Nov. and Feb. to April, keep almost dry during remainder of year.   Syringe lightly daily in summer.   Keep atmosphere uniformly moist in summer by damping stages, floor, etc., several times daily.   Ventilate freely in summer, moderately other times. Temp., May to Sept. 55° to 65° ; Sept. to Feb. 45° to 55° ; Feb. to May 50° to 60°. Growing period, March to Nov. ; resting period, Dec. to Feb.

PROPAGATION : By division of the pseudo-bulbs at potting time.

SPECIES CULTIVATED : O. bictoniense, green, brown, and rose, 2 ft., autumn, Mexico and Guatemala ; Cervantesii, white and brown, spring, 6 in., Mexico ; cirrhosum, white and purple, spring, 1 to 2 ft., Ecuador ; citrosmum, white, rose, and yellow, fragrant, May, 6 to 8 in., Mexico ; crispum (Syn. Alexandræ), white, rose, crimson, etc., spring, 12 to 18 in., Colombia, and many beautiful varieties ; Edwardii, purple and yellow, fragrant, spring, 2 to 3 ft., Ecuador ; gloriosum, yellow and brown, fragrant, 2 ft., Colombia ; grande, yellow and red, autumn, 1 ft., Guatemala ; Hallii, yellow and red, spring, 2 to 3 ft., Peru and Ecuador ; harryanum, yellow, white, purple, and brown, spring, 1 to 2 ft., Colombia ; hastilabium, greenish yellow and purple, summer, New Grenada ; Kegeljani (Syn. O. polyxanthum), yellow and light brown, April to May, Ecuador ; luteo-purpureum, yellow, white, and red, spring, 1 to 2 ft., Colombia ; maculatum, yellow, brown, and white, winter, 1 to 2 ft., Mexico ; madrense, white and reddish purple, summer, fragrant, Mexico ; nobile (Syn. Pescatorei), white, purple, yellow, and red, spring, 1 to 2 ft., Colombia ; pulchellum, white, fragrant, winter, 1 ft., Guatemala ; Rossii, white and brown, winter, 6 in., Mexico ; triumphans, yellow, brown, and white, spring, 1 to 2 ft., Colombia ; Uroskinneri, yellow, brown, and rose, winter, 1 to 2 ft., Guatemala. Numerous hybrids.

Odontonema Schomburgkianum—See Thyrsacanthus rutilans.

Œnothera (Evening Primrose ; Sun-drops ; Tree Primrose)—Ord. Onagraceæ. Hardy annuals, biennials, herbaceous and shrubby perennials. First introduced 1629.

CULTURE OF ANNUAL SPECIES : Soil, ordinary. Position, sunny where plants are to flower, or in boxes of light soil in temp. 55° to 65° in April, transplanting seedlings outdoors in May. Thin seedlings sown outdoors to 6 in. apart in June.

POT CULTURE : Compost, two parts good soil, one part leaf-mould, well-decayed manure, and sand. Position, well-drained 6 in. pots in cold frame, greenhouse, or window. Thin seedlings when 1 in. high to six or eight in each pot. Water moderately at first, freely when in full growth. Apply liquid manure twice a week when plants show flower.

CULTURE OF BIENNIAL SPECIES : Soil, ordinary. Position, sunny beds or borders. Sow seeds $\frac{1}{18}$ in. deep in shady position outdoors in April, transplanting seedlings when 1 in. high, 3 in. apart each way, in sunny border, again transplanting into flowering position following Sept. or March.

CULTURE OF PERENNIAL SPECIES : Soil, light, sandy loam. Position, sunny well-drained borders, beds, or rockeries. Plant, Oct., March, or April. Water freely in dry weather. Mulch annually with decayed cow manure. Lift and replant every three or four years. Prune away straggling shoots of shrubby species after flowering.

PROPAGATION : Perennial species by seeds sown in light soil in shallow box or well-drained pans in cold frame or under hand-light in March or April, transplanting outdoors end of May or June ; cuttings of young shoots inserted in sandy soil under hand-light in shade in spring or summer ; suckers removed with roots attached, spring or autumn ; division of roots, March or April.

ANNUAL SPECIES : Œ. amœna (Syn. Godetia rubicunda), rose and crimson, summer, 1 to 2 ft., California ; amœna rubicunda, lilac purple ; bistorta, yellow and red, summer, 1 ft., California ; Drummondi, yellow, June to Oct., 1 to 2 ft., Texas ; odorata, yellow, summer, 1 to 2 ft., Chile ; tenella, purple, June, 6 in., Chile ; Whitneyi (Syn. Godetia Whitneyi), red, crimson, or white, summer, 6 to 12 in., California, parent of the annuals known as Godetia Lady Albemarle, Duke of York, Bridesmaid, etc. ; tetraptera, white, summer, 1 ft., Mexico, and its variety rosea (pink), sometimes erroneously named Œ. mexicana rosea.

BIENNIAL SPECIES : Œ. biennis (Evening Primrose), yellow, fragrant, June to Oct., 4 to 5 ft., N. America, and its varieties grandiflora and Lamarckiana ; Clutei, soft yellow, summer, 3 to 4 ft., Arizona.

PERENNIAL SPECIES : Œ. acaulis (Syn. Œ. taraxacifolia), white or blush, summer, prostrate, Chile, sometimes a biennial ; cæspitosa (Syns. eximia and marginata), white, fragrant, July, 4 to 9 in., California ; fruticosa (Sun-drops), golden yellow, summer, 1 to 2 ft., U. States, and its varieties major and Youngii ; glauca, yellow, summer, 2 to 3 ft., Southern U. States, and its variety Fraseri ; linearis, yellow, summer, 12 to 18 in., U. States ; missouriensis (Syn. Œ. macrocarpa), yellow, summer, trailing, N. America ; Nuttalli, white or pink, summer, 6 to 9 in., California ; pumila (Syn. Œ. riparia), yellow, summer, 9 to 18 in., N. America ; rosea, rose, summer, 1 to 2 ft., Texas and New Mexico; ovata, golden yellow, May, 6 in., U. States ; speciosa, white or pink, summer, 1 to 2 ft., U.S.A.

Okra (*Hibiscus esculentus*)—See Hibiscus.

Old Man (*Artemisia Abrotanum*)—See Artemisia.

Old Man Cactus (*Cereus senilis*)—See Cereus.

Old Man's Beard (*Clematis vitalba* and *Tillandsia usneoides*)—See Clematis and Tillandsia.

Old Woman (*Artemisia argentea*)—See Artemisia.

Olea (Olive)—**Ord. Oleaceæ.** Half-hardy evergreen flowering shrub. First introduced 1570.
CULTURE : Soil, sandy loam. Position, sheltered, sunny borders, or against S. or W. walls S. of England only. Plant, Sept., Oct., or April. Prune when necessary, April. Protect in very severe weather with litter or mats.
POT CULTURE : Compost, two parts sandy loam, one part leaf-mould, and sand. Position, cool greenhouse, Sept. to May ; outdoors, June to Sept. Temp., Sept. to May 40° to 50°. Water moderately in winter, freely in summer. Syringe daily April to Sept.
PROPAGATION : By seeds sown 1/16 in. deep in sandy peat in greenhouse in spring or autumn ; cuttings inserted in sandy soil under bell-glass in shade in greenhouse in summer.
SPECIES CULTIVATED : O. europæa (Wild Olive), white, fragrant, summer, 20 to 40 ft., Asia Minor and Syria. See also Osmanthus.

Oleander (*Nerium Oleander*)—See Nerium.

Oleander Fern (*Oleandra articulata*)—See Oleandra.

Oleandra (Oleander Fern)—Ord. Filices. Stove evergreen ferns. Stems rhizomatous and scandent. Fronds, strap-shaped, green. First introduced 1837.
CULTURE : Compost, two parts peat and one of loam, leaf-mould, and sand. Position, hanging baskets, or against pillars and walls covered with layer of peaty soil secured by wire netting. Plant, Feb. or March. Water copiously March to Sept., moderately afterwards. Syringe plants or pillars and walls daily March to Oct. Temp., March to Sept. 65° to 75° ; Sept. to March 55° to 65°.
PROPAGATION : By spores sown in surface of fine sandy peat under bell-glass in temp. 75° to 85° any time ; division of creeping rhizomes at potting time.
SPECIES CULTIVATED : O. articulata, Trop. Africa ; nodosa, W. Indies.

Olearia (New Zealand Daisy Bush ; Victorian Snow Bush)—Ord. Compositæ. Hardy and half-hardy evergreen flowering shrubs. First introduced 1793.
OUTDOOR CULTURE : Soil, sandy loam. Position, sunny borders for O. Haastii, S. or W. walls for O. dentata, O. gunniana, O. Forsteri, etc., in cold districts ; borders or shrubberies elsewhere. Plant, Sept. to Nov. or April. Protect those grown against walls during very severe weather by covering of mats or straw. Pruning not required except to remove dead or unhealthy shoots in April. Not adapted for outdoor culture in N. of England.
POT CULTURE : Compost, two parts sandy loam, one part leaf-mould or peat, one part sand. Position, well-drained pots, or in beds with shoots trained up pillars or against walls in cold greenhouses or conservatories. Pot or plant, Sept. to April. Water freely March to Sept., moderately afterwards. Syringe freely in summer except when in bloom. Place pot plants in sunny position outdoors until they flower. Plunge pots to rim in cinder ashes.
PROPAGATION : By cuttings of firm young shoots, 2 to 3 in. long, inserted in well-drained pots of sandy soil under bell-glass in cold, shady frame in summer.
SPECIES CULTIVATED : O. argophylla, white, July to Sept., to 25 ft., Australia ; Forsteri, white, Sept., 10 to 25 ft., New Zealand ; gunniana (Syn. O. stellulata), white, summer, 5 ft., Australia ; Haastii (New Zealand Daisy Bush), white, Aug., 4 to 9 ft., New Zealand ; ilicifolia, white, summer, 5 to 10 ft., New Zealand ; insignis, white, summer, 3 to 5 ft., New Zealand ; macrodonta, white, summer, to 20 ft., New Zealand, and its variety minor ; moschata, white, July to Sept., 2 to 3 ft., New Zealand ; myrsinoides, white, May to June, 3 to 4 ft., Australia ; nitida, white, summer, 10 to 15 ft., New Zealand ; nummularifolia, white, June, 2 to 3 ft., New Zealand ; Solandri, white, summer, 3 to 5 ft., New Zealand ; Traversii, white, summer, 10 to 20 ft., New Zealand.

Oleaster—See Eleagnus.

Olive-tree (*Olea europæa*)—See Olea.

Olympian Mullein (*Verbascum olympicum*)—See Verbascum.

Omphalodes (Venus's Navel-wort ; Rock Forget-me-not ; Creeping Forget-me-not)—Ord. Boraginaceæ. Hardy annual and perennial herbs. First introduced 1633.

CULTURE OF ANNUAL SPECIES : Soil, ordinary. Position, partially shaded borders. Sow seeds in masses where required to grow—in April to flower in June, June to flower in Sept., and Sept. to flower in spring.

CULTURE OF PERENNIAL SPECIES : Soil, ordinary rich, moist. Position, partially shaded, well-drained borders or rockeries, or in rhododendron beds. Plant, Oct., Nov., March, or April. Water copiously in dry weather. Mulch with decayed cow manure annually in spring.

PROPAGATION : By seeds sown ⅛ in. deep in light, rich soil in semi-shaded position in April, transplanting seedlings when 1 in. high ; division of roots, March or April.

ANNUAL SPECIES : O. linifolia (Venus's Navel-wort), white, June, 6 to 9 in., S. Europe.

PERENNIAL SPECIES : O. cappadocica, blue, early summer and autumn, 6 to 9 in., S. Europe ; Luciliæ (Rock Navel-wort), blue, summer, 6 in., Asia Minor ; verna (Creeping Forget-me-not or Blue-eyed Mary), blue, spring, 6 in., Europe ; verna alba, white.

Oncidium (Butterfly Orchid)—Ord. Orchidaceæ. Stove and greenhouse epiphytal orchids. Flowers appear at base of new pseudo-bulb directly latter is fully grown. First introduced 1791.

CULTURE : Compost, equal parts fibrous peat and sphagnum moss with a little broken charcoal. Position, pots, wood or earthenware baskets, rafts or blocks. Pot, Feb. or March. Fill pots or pans two-thirds of their depth with potsherds. Place layer of moss on this, then fill remainder of space with compost to 1 in. above rim. Put plants on this, cover roots with compost and layer of moss, and secure firmly with copper wire. Baskets : Line interior with moss, then fill with compost and place plant on top, securing it firmly with copper wire. Blocks : Place roots next wood, cover with peat and sphagnum moss, and secure firmly with copper wire. Water freely during summer, moderately from Sept. to Nov. and from Feb. to April, little in winter. Syringe lightly daily in summer. Moist atmosphere highly essential. Shade from bright sunshine only. Ventilate freely in summer. Temp. for stove species, Nov. to April 60° to 70° ; April to Nov. 70° to 85° ; for greenhouse species, May to Oct. 65° to 75° ; Oct. to May 55° to 65°. Growing period, March to Sept. ; resting period, Oct. to Feb.

PROPAGATION : By division of pseudo-bulbs at potting time.

STOVE SPECIES : O. ampliatum, yellow, red, and brown, March to May, 12 to 16 in., Central America ; cavendishianum, yellow and brown, winter, Guatemala ; jonesianum, white, brown, and red, Oct. to Feb., 1 ft., Paraguay ; kramerianum, red, brown, and yellow, March to Oct., 8 to 10 in., Ecuador ; lanceanum, yellow, rose, purple, and brown, summer, 18 in., Guiana ; Papilio (Butterfly Orchid), red, crimson, and yellow, March to Oct., 8 to 10 in., W. Indies ; splendidum, yellow and brown, winter, 1 ft., Guatemala.

GREENHOUSE SPECIES : O. bracteatum, greenish yellow and purple, summer, Central America ; concolor, yellow, May, 6 in., Brazil : crispum, red, brown, and yellow, June to Feb., 1 ft., Brazil ; flexuosum, reddish brown and yellow, summer, Brazil ; Forbesii, brown and yellow, autumn, 2 to 3 ft., Brazil ; Gardneri, brown and yellow, summer, 8 in., Brazil ; incurvum, white and rosy pink, fragrant, autumn, 1 ft., Mexico ; leucochilum, yellowish green and brown, Jan. to May, Mexico ; macranthum, yellow, brown, white, and purple, spring, 18 in., Trop. America ; marshallianum, yellow and brown, summer, 1 ft., Brazil ; olivaceum (Syn. O. cucullatum), rose and reddish purple, spring, New Granada ; ornithorhynchum, rose, lilac, and yellow, 1 ft., Mexico ; Phalænopsis, white, purple, and violet, spring, 1 to 2 ft., Ecuador ; pubes, reddish brown and yellow, spring, Brazil ; sarcodes, yellow and brown, spring, 1 ft., Brazil ; sphacelatum, brown and yellow, spring, 2 ft., Mexico ; splendidum, yellow and brown, winter, 1 ft., Guatemala ; superbiens, yellow, brown, and purple, spring, 1 ft., Colombia ; tigrinum, yellow and brown, violet-scented, autumn and winter, 1 ft., Mexico ; varicosum, yellow and brown, winter, 1 ft., Brazil ; varicosum Rogersii, superior variety.

Onion—See Allium.

Onion-plant (*Ornithogalum longibracteatum*)—See Ornithogalum.

Onoclea (Sensitive Fern ; Ostrich Fern)—Ord. Filices. Hardy deciduous ferns. First introduced 1799. Fronds, barren ones, broad, once divided, green ; fertile ones, narrow, contracted, once divided, brown.
OUTDOOR CULTURE : Soil, two parts good loam, one part leaf-mould. Position, semi-shaded, cool, moist border or margin of ponds. Plant, April.
POT CULTURE : Compost, two parts fibrous loam, one part leaf-mould, one part sand. Position, well-drained pots in shady, cold frame or greenhouse. Pot, March or April. Water copiously April to Sept., moderately Sept. to Nov., keep nearly dry Nov. to March. Repot annually.
PROPAGATION : By spores gathered just before the cases burst and sown on surface of well-drained pan of sandy peat and leaf-mould with square of glass, and kept moderately moist in shady position in cold frame or greenhouse ; division of plants, March or April.
SPECIES CULTIVATED : O. germanica (Syn. Struthiopteris germanica), the Ostrich Fern, 2 to 3 ft., N. Temperate Zone ; sensibilis (Sensitive Fern), 2 to 3 ft., N. America and N. Asia.

Ononis (Rest-harrow)—Ord. Leguminosæ. Hardy herbaceous perennials and deciduous shrubs. First introduced 1570.
CULTURE OF PERENNIAL SPECIES : Soil, ordinary. Position, sunny borders, banks, or rockeries. Plant, Oct., Nov., March, or April. Cut down flower stems, Oct. Mulch with manure, March. Lift and replant in fresh soil every four or five years.
CULTURE OF SHRUBBY SPECIES : Soil, ordinary. Position, sunny borders or banks. Plant, Oct. to Feb. Prune into shape, Jan. to Feb.
PROPAGATION : By seeds sown $\frac{1}{16}$ in. deep in ordinary soil in semi-shady position outdoors, March or April ; or in shallow boxes or pans in cold frame or greenhouse in March ; perennials by division of roots, Oct. to March.
PERENNIAL SPECIES : O. arvensis (Rest-harrow), rose and white, summer, 6 in., Europe (Britain) ; Natrix (Goat Root), yellow and red, summer, 1 to 2 ft., S. Europe.
SHRUBBY SPECIES : O. fruticosa, purple, summer, 2 ft., Europe ; rotundifolia, rose pink, May to Aug., 1¼ ft., Europe.

Onopordon (Cotton Thistle ; Scotch Thistle)—Ord. Compositæ. Hardy biennial and perennial herbs. Orn. foliage.
CULTURE OF BIENNIAL SPECIES : Sow seeds ¼ in. deep in ordinary soil in sunny position outdoors, March or April. Transplant seedlings following Sept. to where required to flower.
CULTURE OF PERENNIAL SPECIES : Soil, ordinary rich. Position, well-drained sunny borders. Plant, Oct. or March, singly in groups of three.
PROPAGATION : By seeds sown ¼ in. deep in ordinary soil in sunny position outdoors March or April, transplanting seedlings to flowering position Sept. or Oct.
BIENNIAL SPECIES : O. arabicum, 8 to 10 ft., S. Europe ; illyricum, 6 ft., S. Europe.
PERENNIAL SPECIES : O. Acanthium (Scotch Thistle), 5 ft., Europe (Britain).

Onosma (Golden Drop)—Ord. Boraginaceæ. Hardy perennial herbs. First introduced 1683.
CULTURE : Soil, two parts sandy loam, one part grit or small stones. Position, sunny rockery where roots can descend close to cool, moist stones and shoots trail over edge. Plant, March or April. Place a few small stones on surface of soil around plant. Water occasionally in dry weather. Mulch annually with decayed cow manure in March or April.
PROPAGATION : By seeds sown $\frac{1}{16}$ in. deep in sandy loam and grit in shallow pans in shady, cold frame of cool greenhouse in March, planting outdoors in May ; cuttings of shoots inserted in sandy soil in close, shady frame or under hand-light in July or Aug.
SPECIES CULTIVATED : O. albo-roseum, white and rose, summer, 6 in., Asia Minor ; Bourgæi, white, summer, 6 in., Armenia ; cassium, yellow, summer, 18 in., Northern

Syria; helveticum, pale yellow, summer, 1 ft., Europe; stellulatum, yellow and white, May, 6 in., Europe; tauricum (Golden Drop), Syn. O. echioides, yellow, May, 1 ft., Europe.

Onychium—Ord. Filices. Stove and greenhouse evergreen ferns. Fronds, four times divided, light and graceful, green.

CULTURE : Compost, two parts peat and loam, leaf-mould and sand in equal parts. Position, well-drained pots, beds, or rockeries in shade. Pot or plant, Feb. or March. Water copiously March to Sept., moderately afterwards. Moist atmosphere essential. Temp. for stove species, March to Sept. 65° to 75°; Sept. to March 55° to 65°; for greenhouse species, March to Sept. 55° to 65°; Sept. to March 40° to 50°.

PROPAGATION : By spores sown on surface of fine sandy peat in well-drained pans in shade and temp. 70° to 80° any time; division of plants at potting time.

STOVE SPECIES : O. auratum, 1 ft., Malaya.

GREENHOUSE SPECIES : O. japonicum, 1 ft., Japan and Himalayas.

Ophioglossum (Adder's Tongue Fern; Adder's Spear)—Ord. Filices. Hardy deciduous fern. Fronds, barren, egg-shaped, pale green; fertile, contracted, spike-like.

OUTDOOR CULTURE : Soil, moist, loamy. Position, in tufts of grass on partially shaded rockery. Plant, April to Aug. Lift plants growing wild with large sod attached and plant in same. Water freely in dry weather.

POT CULTURE : Compost, sandy loam and leaf-mould in equal parts. Position, shallow pans, well drained, in cold, shady frame. Plant, April to Aug. Water freely March to Sept., keep just moist afterwards.

PROPAGATION : By spores gathered when ripe in July and sown on surface of pans of above soil, covered with a sheet of glass, and placed in a cool, moist frame or greenhouse; division of plants in April.

SPECIES CULTIVATED : O. vulgatum, 4 to 6 in., Britain, in moist meadows.

Ophiopogon (Snake's-beard)—Ord. Hæmodoraceæ. Hardy perennial herbs. Flowering and orn. foliage. First introduced 1784. Leaves, long, narrow, green, and variegated with yellow or creamy white.

OUTDOOR CULTURE : Soil, sandy loam. Position, edgings to or groups in sunny borders. Plant, Oct. or March. Lift, divide, and replant every four or five years.

POT CULTURE : Compost, two parts sandy loam, one part leaf-mould or decayed manure, and one part sand. Position, well-drained pots or in small beds in cold or heated greenhouses, conservatories, ferneries, or windows. Adapted for sun or shade. Pot or plant, Feb. or March. Water copiously March to Oct., moderately afterwards. Apply stimulants once or twice weekly April to Sept.

PROPAGATION : By division of plants in Feb. or March.

SPECIES CULTIVATED : O. intermedius argenteo-marginatus, lilac, summer, 1 ft., leaves margined with white, Himalayas; Jaburan variegatus, white, July, 1 ft., leaves striped with green and white, Japan; japonicus variegatus, white, summer, 1 ft., leaves striped with creamy white, Japan. See also Liriope spicata.

Ophrys (Bee Orchis; Fly Orchis; Spider Orchis)—Ord. Orchidaceæ. Hardy terrestrial orchids. Deciduous.

OUTDOOR CULTURE : Soil, sandy loam mixed with pieces of chalk or broken lime-stone. Position, dry, sunny rockeries. Plant, Aug. to Nov. Cover surface of soil between plants with pieces of chalk or limestone, or mulch with layer of cocoanut-fibre refuse.

POT CULTURE : Compost, two parts sandy loam, one part pieces of broken limestone or chalk. Position, small well-drained pots or pans in cold, sunny frame or green-house. Pot, Aug. to Nov., placing tubers 1 in. below surface and pressing soil firmly. Place five tubers in 6 in. pot. Plunge pots to rims in cocoanut-fibre refuse or ashes during growing period. Water freely from time growth begins till foliage dies down, then keep nearly dry. Repot every two or three years.

PROPAGATION : By division of tuberous roots in March or April.

SPECIES CULTIVATED : O. apifera (Bee Orchis), purple, orange, and yellow, April to

June, 1 ft., Europe (Britain); arachnites, green and brown, May, 6 in., Europe (Britain); aranifera (Spider Orchis), brown and yellow, April to June, 6 in., Europe (Britain); Bertoloni, pink and purple, April, Italy; bombylifera, green and chocolate, April, S. Europe; lutea, yellow and purplish black, April, 7 in., S. Europe; muscifera (Fly Orchis), brown, blue, and yellow, May, 6 in., Europe (Britain); speculum, green, gold, and purple, April, 4 to 12 ins., S. Europe; tenthredinifera (Sawfly Orchis), green, brown, and yellow, May and June, 1 ft., Europe.

Opium Poppy (*Papaver somniferum*)—See Papaver.

Oplismenus (Variegated Panicum)—Ord. Gramineæ. Greenhouse perennial, trailing grass. Orn. foliage. First introduced 1867. Flowers insignificant. Stems, small, wiry, trailing. Leaves, green, variegated with white and pink.

CULTURE: Compost, equal parts peat, loam, leaf-mould, and sand. Position, small pots with shoots draping front of staging, or in baskets suspended from roof; sun or shade. Pot, March. Water freely March to Oct., moderately afterwards. Apply stimulants occasionally in summer. Temp., March to Sept. 60° to 75°; Sept. to March 55° to 65°.

PROPAGATION: By cuttings of young shoots inserted in light, sandy soil in small pots under bell-glass or hand-light in temp. 65° to 75° at any time.

SPECIES CULTIVATED: O. Burmannii variegatus (Syn. Panicum variegatum), trailing, Tropics.

Opuntia (Indian Fig; Prickly Pear; Cochineal Cactus; Barbary Fig)—Ord. Cactaceæ. Greenhouse and hardy succulent plants. First introduced 1596. Stems, fleshy, flat, bristly. Leaves, small, unimportant, fugacious.

CULTURE OF GREENHOUSE SPECIES: Compost, two parts sandy loam, one part powdered brick rubbish and old mortar. Position, sunny, airy greenhouse or window. Pot, March or April in pots filled ⅛ of depth with potsherds and just large enough to accommodate roots. Repot every three or four years only. Water moderately March to Sept., once a fortnight Sept. to Nov., none afterwards. Apply stimulants to healthy plants June to Sept. Ventilate freely in summer. Temp., March to Sept. 60° to 70°; Sept. to March 50° to 55°.

CULTURE OF HARDY SPECIES: Soil, sandy loam freely interspersed with powdered brick or old mortar. Position, sunny well-drained rockeries. Plant, March or April. Cover surface of soil between plants with small pieces of stone. Sprinkle soot freely between plants occasionally to keep away slugs. Apply weak liquid manure occasionally during summer to healthy plants only.

PROPAGATION: By seeds sown ⅛ in. deep in well-drained pots or pans of sandy soil in temp. 75° in March. Keep soil moderately moist; cuttings of portions of stems exposed for a few days, then inserted in small well-drained pots of lime and brick dust in temp. 65° to 75°, summer; delicate species by grafting on robust kinds in April.

GREENHOUSE SPECIES: O. arborescens, purple, June, 5 to 30 ft., Southern U. States; Bigelovii, flowers not known, 10 ft., California; brasiliensis, yellow, June, 10 to 30 ft., Brazil; cylindrica, scarlet, summer, 4 to 6 ft., Peru, and its crested variety cristata; decumana, orange, summer, 10 to 15 ft., S. America; echinocarpa, green, summer, 18 in., U. States; Emoryi, yellow and purple, Aug. and Sept., 18 in., Mexico; ficus-indica (Indian Fig), yellow, May, 2 ft., Trop. America; filipendula, purple, May and June, 2 ft., Texas; leucotricha, yellow, June, Mexico; monacantha variegata, variegated, 1 ft., S. America; rosea, rose, June, Mexico; tuna, reddish orange, July, 10 to 20 ft., S. America; Whipplei, red, June, U. States.

HARDY SPECIES: O. Engelmanni, yellow, May and June, 6 in., Southern U. States; mesacantha (Syn. vulgaris), the Prickly Pear, yellow, June, 2 ft., U. States; missouriensis, yellow, May and June, 6 in., N. America; Rafinesqui, yellow and red, June, 1 ft., N. America; rhodantha, carmine, June, Colorado; xanthostema, carmine red, summer, Colorado.

Orache—See Atriplex.

Orange (*Citrus aurantium*)—See Citrus.

Orange-ball Tree (*Buddleia globosa*)—See Buddleia.

Orange Daisy (*Erigeron aurantiacus*)—See Erigeron.

Orange Lily (*Lilium croceum*)—See Lilium.

Orange Monkey-flower (*Mimulus glutinosus*)—See Mimulus.

Orange Stone-crop (*Sedum kamtschaticum*)—See Sedum.

Orchis—Ord. Orchidaceæ.　Hardy terrestrial orchids.　Deciduous.
OUTDOOR CULTURE : Soil, rich loam.　Position, sunny, deep, well-drained borders or rockeries.　Plant, Aug. to Nov., placing tubers 2 in. below surface.　Water freely during growing period.　Mulch with decayed manure annually in March or April. Lift and replant when unhealthy only.　Apply weak stimulants during summer.
POT CULTURE : Compost, equal parts good loam, sandy peat, leaf-mould, charcoal, broken chalk, and silver sand.　Position, well-drained pots in cold, shady frame. Pot, Aug. to Nov., placing tubers 1 in. below surface and three to five in a 6 in. pot. Make compost firm.　Plunge pots to rims in cinder ashes or cocoanut-fibre refuse. Water copiously from time growth begins till foliage fades ; then keep nearly dry. Apply weak stimulants from April till flowers fade.　Remove flower spikes when blooms fade.　Repot every two or three years.　Protect from Dec. to Feb. by covering of cocoanut-fibre refuse or cinder ashes.
PROPAGATION : By division of tubers, Aug. to Nov.
SPECIES CULTIVATED : O. foliosa (Madeira Orchis), purple, May, 2 ft., Madeira ; hircina (Lizard Orchis), greenish white, June and July, 1 to 5 ft., Europe (Britain) ; latifolia (Marsh Orchis), purple, June, 1 ft., Europe (Britain) ; laxiflora (Guernsey Orchis), purple, May and June, 1 ft., Europe (Channel Islands) ; longicornu, purple and lilac, May, 1 to 1½ ft., N. America ; maculata (Spotted Orchis), purple and white, June, 1 ft., Europe (Britain) ; mascula (Purple Orchis), purple, spring, 4 to 8 in., Britain ; militaris, lilac and purple, spring, 1 to 2 ft., Southern England ; pyramidalis (Pyramidal Orchis), rosy purple, summer, 1 ft., Britain ; purpurea (Lady Orchis), Syn. O. fusca, purple and rose, May, 1 ft., Europe (Britain) ; sambucina, straw yellow, April, 9 in., Europe, and its variety purpurea (purple) ; spectabilis (North American Orchis), purple and white, May, 6 in., N. America.

Oregon Cypress (*Cupressus lawsoniana*)—See Cupressus.

Oregon White Cedar (*Cupressus lawsoniana*)—See Cupressus.

Oreodaphne—See Umbellularia.

Oriental Goat's Rue (*Galega orientalis*)—See Galega.

Oriental Hellebore (*Helleborus orientalis*)—See Helleborus.

Oriental Plane-tree (*Platanus orientalis*)—See Platanus.

Oriental Poppy (*Papaver orientale*)—See Papaver.

Oriental Strawberry-tree (*Arbutus Andrachne*)—See Arbutus.

Origanum (Sweet Marjoram ; Pot Marjoram ; Dittany of Crete)—Ord. Labiatæ. Hardy herbaceous shrubby plants and aromatic herbs.　First introduced 1551.
CULTURE OF COMMON POT AND WINTER MARJORAM : Soil, ordinary rich.　Position, sunny borders.　Plant, Feb. or March, 10 in. apart in rows 15 in. asunder.　Top-dress annually in March with decayed manure.　Lift, divide, and replant every three or four years.
CULTURE OF SWEET MARJORAM : Soil, ordinary rich.　Position, sunny borders. Sow seeds ⅛ in. deep in light soil in shallow boxes in temp. 55° to 65° in March, transplanting seedlings when 2 in. high 6 in. apart in rows 9 in. asunder in April outdoors, thinning seedlings to one in each group when 1 to 2 in. high.　Gather shoots when coming into flower, dry in shade, and store away for winter use.
CULTURE OF DITTANY OF CRETE : Compost, two parts sandy loam, one part leaf-mould and sand.　Position, well-drained pots in sunny window or greenhouse. Pot, Feb. or March.　Water freely March to Sept., moderately afterwards.　Suitable for suspending in pots or baskets.　Apply stimulant occasionally during summer.
PROPAGATION : Common pot or winter marjoram by seeds sown ⅛ in. deep in ordinary soil in sunny position outdoors in March or April ; division of roots, March or April ; shrubby species by cuttings of young shoots inserted in sandy soil under bell-glass in greenhouse or window in summer.

SPECIES CULTIVATED: O. Dictamnus (Dittany of Crete), pink, summer, 1 ft., Crete; Marjorana (Sweet Marjoram), purple or white, summer, 2 ft., N. Africa ; Onites (Pot Marjoram), white, summer, 1 ft., S. Europe ; pulchrum, purple, summer, 6 to 9 in., Greece.

Ornithogalum (Star of Bethlehem ; Onion Plant)—Ord. Liliaceæ. Hardy and greenhouse bulbous plants.
OUTDOOR CULTURE: Soil, rich ordinary, sandy. Position, sunny borders, rockeries, or turf. Plant, Aug. to Nov., placing small bulbs 3 in. and large bulbs 4 to 6 in. below surface and 2 to 3 in. apart. Mulch annually in March with decayed manure. Apply weak stimulants occasionally in summer.
INDOOR CULTURE: Compost, two parts sandy loam, one part equal proportions leaf-mould, peat, and sand. Position, pots in sunny greenhouse or window. Pot, Sept. to Feb., placing several small or one large bulb in a 5 or 6 in. pot. Good drainage essential. Water moderately when growth begins, freely when in full growth, gradually withholding when foliage turns yellow and keeping dry till new growth begins. Apply stimulants occasionally whilst in full growth. Repot annually. Temp., March to Sept. 55° to 65° ; Sept. to March 40° to 50°.
CULTURE OF ONION PLANT: Compost, two parts sandy loam, one part leaf-mould and well decayed manure, and little sand. Position, sunny window or outdoors June to Sept. Pot, Feb. or March. Good drainage and firm potting essential. Water moderately Feb. to May, freely May to Sept., moderately Sept. to Nov., keep quite dry Nov. to Feb. Apply stimulants once a week May to Sept.
PROPAGATION: By offsets, removed from old bulbs and repotted, Sept. to Feb.
GREENHOUSE SPECIES: O. arabicum, white, fragrant, summer, 2 ft., S. Europe (hardy in sheltered borders with slight winter protection) ; biflorum, white, April, 1 ft., Chile and Peru ; lacteum (Chincherinchee), white, summer, 1½ ft., S. Africa ; longibracteatum (Onion Plant), white, May, 1 to 2 ft., S. Africa, and its variety variegatum.
HARDY SPECIES: O. nutans, silvery grey and pale green, spring, 1 ft., Europe (Britain) ; nutans boucheanum, a superior form ; narbonense, white, early summer, 2 ft., Mediterranean Region, and its variety pyramidale ; pyrenaicum, yellowish green, June, 2 ft., S. Europe ; umbellatum (Star of Bethlehem), white, May, 1 ft., Europe, and its varieties Leichtlinii and splendens.

Orobus—See Lathyrus and Vicia.

Orontium (Golden Club)—Ord. Aroideæ. Hardy aquatic perennial. First introduced 1775.
CULTURE: Soil, boggy. Position, margins of shallow ponds or rivulets. Plant, Oct. to March, placing roots 6 to 12 in. below surface of water.
PROPAGATION: By division of root stock in Oct. or March.
SPECIES CULTIVATED: O. aquaticum, green, May, 1 to 1½ ft., N. America.

Orpine (*Sedum telephium*)—See Sedum.

Orrice Root (*Iris florentina*)—See Iris.

Ortgiesia—See Æchmea.

Osage Orange (*Maclura aurantiaca*)—See Maclura.

Osier—See Salix.

Osier Willow (*Salix viminalis*)—See Salix.

Osmanthus (Fragrant Olive ; Holly-leaved Olive)—Ord. Oleaceæ, hardy and half-hardy evergreen flowering shrubs. First introduced 1771.
CULTURE: Soil, loamy. Position, sheltered, sunny borders, or against S. or W. walls, O. fragrans in sunny, unheated greenhouse. Plant, Sept., Oct., or April. Prune when necessary, April.
POT CULTURE: Compost, two parts sandy loam, one part leaf-mould and sand. Position, unheated, sunny greenhouse, Sept. to June; outdoors, June to Sept. Pot, Sept. or Oct. Water freely April to Oct., moderately other times. Temp., Sept. to May 40° to 50°.

Oxalis enneaphylla
(Wood Sorrel)

Oxytropis montana
(Oxytrope)

Pæonia Moutan
(Tree Pæony)

Pæonia officinalis
(Pæony)

Pandanus candelabrum
variegatus (Screw Pine)

Papaver nudicaule
(Iceland Poppy)

Papaver Rhœas flore-pleno
(Shirley Poppy)

Papaver somniferum
Opium Poppy)

Passiflora cærulea
(Passion-flower)

Patrinia palmata
(Eastern Valerian)

Pelargonium zonale hybridum
(Double Geranium)

Pellæa hastata
(Cliff Brake-fern)

Pentstemon cæruleus
(Beard-Tongue)

Pentstemon hybridum
(Beard's Tongue)

Pernettya mucronata
(Prickly Heath)

Perowskia atriplicifolia

Phaius Wallichii

Philadelphus coronarius
(Mock Orange)

PROPAGATION : By seeds sown $\frac{1}{16}$ in. deep in sandy peat in cold frame in spring or autumn ; by cuttings of firm young shoots inserted in sandy soil under hand-light outdoors or in frame in summer.
SPECIES CULTIVATED : O. Aquifolium (Syn. Olea ilicifolia), white, Sept. to Oct., 10 to 20 ft., Japan, and its varieties variegatus (variegated), purpureus (purple-leaved), myrtifolius (myrtle-leaved), and rotundifolius (dwarf); armatus, creamy white, autumn, 8 to 15 ft., W. China ; Delavayi, white, fragrant, April, 5 to 10 ft., Yunnan ; Fortunei, white, fragrant, autumn, hybrid, 6 ft. ; fragrans (Syn. Olea fragrans), white, fragrant, June to Aug., 6 to 10 ft., China and Japan.

Osmunda (Royal Fern ; Flowering Fern)—Ord. Filices. Greenhouse and hardy evergreen and deciduous ferns. Fronds, feather-shaped, plain or crested ; fertile portions contracted.
CULTURE OF GREENHOUSE SPECIES : Compost, equal parts turfy loam and peat, little sand. Position, pots or beds in moist, shady part of greenhouse or fernery. Pot or plant, March or April. Water copiously April to Oct., moderately afterwards. Temp., 55° to 65° April to Sept., 45° to 55° Sept. to April.
CULTURE OF HARDY SPECIES : Soil, one part each loam, leaf-mould, and sand, two parts peat. Position, bases of sheltered, moist rockeries or margins of ponds in shade or partial shade. Plant, April. Top-dress annually in April with compost of peat, leaf-mould, and loam. Remove dead fronds in March. Water plants growing otherwise than on the margins of ponds copiously in dry weather.
PROPAGATION : By spores sown on surface of sandy peat and leaf-mould in well-drained pans covered with sheet of glass or hand-light in shady part of cool greenhouse at any time ; offsets from established plants in April.
GREENHOUSE SPECIES : O. bipinnata, 2 ft., Hong Kong ; javanica, 2 to 4 ft., Java.
HARDY SPECIES : O. cinnamomea, 2 to 4 ft., N. America, West Indies, etc. ; Clay-toniana, 2 to 3 ft., N. America and Himalayas ; regalis (Royal Fern), 3 to 6 ft., Britain, etc., and its varieties corymbifera, cristata, japonica, and palustris.

Oso-berry-tree (*Nuttallia cerasiformis*)—See Nuttallia.

Osteomeles—Ord. Rosaceæ. Half-hardy evergreen shrubs. First introduced 1892.
CULTURE : Soil, loamy. Position, well-drained borders against sheltered wall or large pots in sunny, unheated greenhouse. Plant or pot, Sept. to Oct. or April to May.
PROPAGATION : By cuttings of half-ripened shoots during June and July, inserted in sandy soil under bell-glass in gentle bottom heat.
SPECIES CULTIVATED : O. anthyllidifolia, white, June, 4 to 6 ft., Hawaii ; Schwerinæ, white, June, 6 to 8 ft., W. China ; subrotunda, white, June, 3 to 5 ft., China.

Ostrich Fern (*Onoclea germanica*)—See Onoclea.

Ostrowskia (Great Oriental Bell-flower)—Ord. Campanulaceæ. Hardy perennial flowering herb. Introduced in 1887.
CULTURE : Soil, deep, sandy loam. Position, warm, well-sheltered border. Cover with hand-light after foliage has died down. Carrot-like roots penetrate the soil to a depth of 2 ft. Plant in March.
PROPAGATION : By seeds sown in light soil in a cold frame in spring. Seedlings take several years to flower.
SPECIES CULTIVATED : O. magnifica, mauve-lilac or white, summer, 4 to 5 ft., Eastern Bokhara.

Ostrya (Hop Hornbeam)—Ord. Betulaceæ. Hardy deciduous trees. Flowers, greenish white, hop-like ; May. First introduced 1622.
CULTURE : Soil, ordinary moist. Position, by the side of streams, lakes, or in shrubberies in damp situations. Plant, Oct. to Feb.
PROPAGATION : By seeds placed in a heap outdoors till spring, then sown in sandy soil outdoors ; by cuttings inserted outdoors in autumn ; by layering in summer ; by grafting on the Hornbeam (Carpinus betulus) in March.
SPECIES CULTIVATED : O. carpinifolia (Hop Hornbeam), 50 to 60 ft., S. Europe ; virginiana (Ironwood), 30 to 50 ft., N. America.

L 2

Oswego Tea-plant (*Monarda didyma*)—See Monarda.

Otaheite Apple (*Spondias dulcis*)—See Spondias.

Otaheite Gooseberry (*Phyllanthus distichus*)—See Phyllanthus.

Othonna (African Rag-wort)—Ord. Compositæ. Greenhouse trailing herb. First introduced 1870.
CULTURE : Compost, two parts sandy loam, one part leaf-mould, and one part sand. Position, small well-drained pots or baskets suspended from roof. Pot, March or April. Water freely April to Oct., moderately afterwards. Apply stimulants to healthy plants occasionally during summer. Full exposure to light and sun essential.
PROPAGATION : By cuttings of shoots inserted in sandy soil in cool greenhouse or frame in summer ; division of plants in April.
SPECIES CULTIVATED : O. crassifolia, yellow, summer, trailing, S. Africa.

Othonnopsis—Ord. Compositæ. Half-hardy rock plant. First introduced 1752.
CULTURE : Soil, sandy loam. Position, warm, sunny rock gardens. Protect in severe weather.
PROPAGATION : By division in March or April or cuttings of young growth when three or four inches in length in sandy soil under bell-glass.
SPECIES CULTIVATED : O. cheirifolia, yellow, spring and summer, 1 ft., N. Africa.

Ourisia—Ord. Scrophulariaceæ. Hardy perennial creeping herb. First introduced 1862.
CULTURE : Soil, moist, loamy. Position, partially shaded rockery, with its roots placed close to a lump of soft, porous stone. Plant, March or April. Water freely in dry weather. Must not be exposed to sunshine.
PROPAGATION : By division of roots in March or April.
SPECIES CULTIVATED : O. coccinea, scarlet, summer, 8 in., Chile.

Our Lady's Thistle (*Silybum Marianum*)—See Silybum.

Ouvirandra (Lattice or Lace-leaf Plant)—Ord. Aponogetonaceæ. Stove aquatic perennial. Orn. foliage. First introduced 1855. Leaves, broad, oblong, lace-like.
CULTURE : Compost, equal parts loam and leaf-mould. Position, in small pot immersed in tub or tank of water 12 to 18 in. deep. Pot, Feb. or March. Temp. of water, 65° to 75°. Change water occasionally. Temp., March to Sept. 65° to 75° ; Sept. to March 55° to 65°.
PROPAGATION : By seed sown ⅛ in. deep in above compost in small pot immersed in water heated to temp. 75° any time ; division of roots, Feb. to March.
SPECIES CULTIVATED : O. fenestralis, white, Aug., Madagascar.

Oxalis (Wood Sorrel ; French Sorrel)—Ord. Geraniaceæ. Greenhouse and hardy annuals, herbaceous perennials, and bulbous rooted plants.
CULTURE OF GREENHOUSE SPECIES : Compost, sandy loam. Position, well-drained pots in sunny greenhouse or window. Pot autumn-flowering kinds in Aug. ; winter-flowering kinds in Sept. or Oct. ; spring-flowering kinds, Jan. or Feb., and summer-flowering kinds, March or April. Put bulbs ½ in. deep and ½ in. apart in 5 in. pots. Put potting place in warm part of greenhouse or window. Water moderately till leaves appear, then freely. Apply stimulants occasionally when flowers form. Gradually withhold water when flowers fade, and keep quite dry and cool till growth begins. Repot annually.
CULTURE OF HARDY SPECIES : Soil, sandy loam. Position, edgings to sunny borders or on rockeries. Cool, deep soil and partial shade for O. enneaphylla. Plant O. adenophylla and O. enneaphylla Aug. to Nov. ; other species in March or April. Lift O. floribunda, purpurata, Deppei, and lasiandra in Sept. or Oct. Store in sand in cool, frost-proof place till March, then plant out.
PROPAGATION : By seeds sown ¹⁄₁₆ in. deep in light, sandy soil in temp. 55° to 65° in spring ; division of roots or offsets at potting or planting time.
GREENHOUSE SPECIES : O. carnosa, yellow, autumn, 6 in., Chile ; cernua (Bermuda Butter-cup), yellow, spring, 6 in., S. Africa ; cernua flore-pleno, double ; hirta, red, summer, 3 in., S. Africa ; pentaphylla, lilac and yellow, summer, 6 in., S. Africa ; rosea, rose, spring, 6 to 8 in., Chile ; tetraphylla, red, summer, 6 in., Mexico ;

variabilis, red, white, or crimson, autumn, 3 in., S. Africa. The following are
bulbous rooted : cernua, floribunda, Deppei, and tetraphylla.
HARDY SPECIES : O. Acetosella (Wood Sorrel), white, spring, 2 to 3 in., Britain ;
adenophylla, lilac pink, May to June, 3 in., Chile ; corniculata rubra, yellow,
summer, 6 in., leaves purple, Britain ; Deppei, red, March, 4 to 6 in., S. America ;
enneaphylla, blush white, June, 4 in., Falkland Isles ; floribunda, rose, March,
8 to 12 in., Brazil ; lasiandra, rosy crimson, summer, 9 in., Mexico ; lobata, yellow,
Sept., 2 to 3 in., Chile ; magellanica, pearly white, summer, 1 in., S. America ;
purpurata (Syn. Bowiei), rosy purple, Oct., 3 in., S. Africa ; valdiviensis, yellow
and brown, summer, 3 to 8 in., Chile (usually grown as an annual).

Oxeye—See Bupthalmum and Adonis.

Oxeye Chamomile (*Anthemis tinctoria*)—See Anthemis.

Oxeye Daisy (*Chrysanthemum leucanthemum*)—See Chrysanthemum.

Oxlip (*Primula elatior*)—See Primula.

Oxycoccus (Common Cranberry ; American Cranberry)—Ord. Vacciniaceæ.
Hardy evergreen trailing shrubs. Edible fruiting. Berries, globular, deep red.
CULTURE : Soil, peat, sand, and a little loam. Position, open, moist beds near ponds
or streamlets. Excavate soil to depth of 6 in. below surrounding surface and place
9 in. of soil and loose stones in, and allow water to percolate to within 3 in. of
surface. Plant, Sept. or March, 2 ft. apart each way.
PROPAGATION : By cuttings of shoots inserted in sandy, moist peat under hand-light in
shade in summer ; layering shoots in autumn ; division of plants in Sept. or March.
SPECIES CULTIVATED : O. macrocarpus (American Cranberry), pink, spring, creeping,
N. America ; palustris (Common Cranberry), pink, May, creeping, Britain.

Oxydendrum—Ord. Ericaceæ. Hardy deciduous orn. tree. First introduced
1752.
CULTURE : Soil, lime-free loam, peat, and sand. Position, as specimens on lawns or
in open places. Plant, Nov. to Feb.
PROPAGATION : By seeds sown during Feb. or March in well-drained pans in
compost of sandy peat. Cover very lightly and place in greenhouse or frame.
SPECIES CULTIVATED : O. arboreum, white, June to July, 10 to 50 ft., Eastern
N. America.

Oxypetalum—Ord. Asclepiadeæ. Stove and warm greenhouse evergreen
climbers. First introduced 1823.
CULTURE : Compost, equal parts fibrous peat, loam, and sand. Position, well-
drained pots ; shoots trained up roof. Pot, March or April. Water freely in
summer, moderately autumn and winter. Syringe morning and evening in spring-
time. Prune into shape, Feb. Repot, March. Temp., March to Sept. 65° to 75° ;
Sept. to March 55° to 65°.
PROPAGATION : By seeds sown in sandy peat in a temp. of 75° in spring, or by
cuttings placed in sand under a bell-glass over bottom heat in spring.
SPECIES CULTIVATED : O. cæruleum (Syn. Tweedia cærulea), blue, summer, fragrant,
3 ft., Argentina ; solanoides, blue, rose, orange, and purple, fragrant, summer,
6 ft., Brazil.

Oxytropis (Oxytrope)—Ord. Leguminosæ. Hardy perennial herbs.
CULTURE : Soil, dry, gravelly, or sandy loam. Position, open, sunny rockeries.
Plant, March or April. Lift and replant only when unhealthy.
PROPAGATION : By seeds sown ¼ in. deep in April or May where required to grow ;
division of roots in March.
SPECIES CULTIVATED : O. campestris, pale yellow and purple, July, 3 to 6 in.,
Northern and Arctic Regions (Scotland) ; cyanea, purple and blue, summer, 6 in.,
Caucasus ; Lambertii, white, blue, and purple, summer, 1 ft., N. America ; mon-
tana, reddish purple, July, 6 in., Alps ; pyrenaica, purple and lilac, summer, 6 in.,
Pyrenees ; uralensis (Syn. O. Halleri), purple, summer, 4 in., Europe (Scotland).

Oxyura—See Layia.

Ozothamnus rosmarinifolius—See Helichrysum rosmarinifolium.

Pachysandra—Ord. Euphorbiaceæ. Hardy subshrubs. Evergreen or deciduous. First introduced 1800.
CULTURE : Soil, moist loam. Position, shady borders or rock gardens. Plant, Nov. to Feb.
PROPAGATION : By cuttings of nearly ripened growths in sandy soil under bell-glass during July or Aug.
SPECIES CULTIVATED : P. procumbens, nearly deciduous, greenish white, March, 6 in., S.E. United States ; terminalis variegata, evergreen, leaves bordered with white, 6 to 9 in., Japan.

Pachystoma—See Ancistrochilus.

Pæonia (Pæony ; Peony ; Piony)—Ord. Ranunculaceæ. Hardy herbaceous and shrubby perennials. First introduced 1548.
CULTURE OF TREE PÆONIES OUTDOORS : Soil, two parts loam, one part decomposed cow manure. Position, sheltered nooks and sunny shrubberies or borders. Plant, Sept., Oct., or March, in beds of above compost, 18 in. deep and 2 ft. wide, well drained. Bury point of union between stock and scion 3 in. below surface. Mulch in spring with thick layer of cow manure. Protect in severe weather with covering of litter. Plants flower three years after planting.
CULTURE IN POTS : Compost, two parts loam, one part decayed cow manure and sand. Pot, Oct. or Nov. Place in cold frame till March, then remove to greenhouse. Stand in sunny position outdoors, June to Oct. Water freely March to Sept., moderately in winter. Apply weak manure water occasionally March to Sept. Plants flower once in three years only. Temp for forcing, 55° to 65°.
CULTURE OF HERBACEOUS SPECIES : Soil, moist loam well enriched with cow manure and trenched 3 ft. deep. Position, sunny or shady borders. Plant, Oct. to April, 4 ft. apart each way. Top-dress annually with well-decayed manure lightly forked into surface in Oct. or Nov. Mulch on dry soils in April. Apply liquid or artificial manures occasionally April to Aug. Water copiously in dry weather. Shade blooms required for exhibition from sun.
PROPAGATION : Herbaceous species by seeds sown ¼ in. deep in boxes, pots, or pans of sandy soil in cold frame in Sept. ; also by division of roots in March or April. Tree species by grafting on the fleshy roots of P. albiflora and P. officinalis in Aug.; layering in Sept. or Oct. ; offsets, March or April.
SPECIES CULTIVATED : P. albiflora, white or pink, May, 3 ft., Siberia, China, and Japan ; anomala, bright crimson, May, 2 to 3 ft., N. Europe and Asia, and its variety insignis ; arietina (Syn. P. Breweri), dark red, May, 2 to 3 ft., Orient ; Browni, dull red, May, 1½ ft., California ; Corallina, crimson, May, 3 ft., Europe (Britain) ; decora, rosy crimson, May, 2 to 3 ft., E. Europe and Levant ; humilis, crimson, May, 1½ ft., S. Europe ; lutea, yellow, June, 3 ft., Yunnan ; Moutan (Tree Pæony), rose, May, 3 to 6 ft., China ; officinalis (Common Herbaceous Pæony), crimson, May, 2 to 3 ft., Europe, and its varieties anemonæflora, lobata, and rosea ; peregrina, crimson, May, 1½ to 2 ft., S. Europe ; tenuifolia, crimson, May, 1 to 1½ ft., Europe ; wittmanniana, yellow, May, 2 ft., Orient. Many garden varieties.

Pæony (*Pæonia officinalis*)—See Pæonia.

Pæony Poppy (*Papaver somniferum*)—See Papaver.

Painted Cup—See Castilleja.

Pale Maidens (*Sisyrinchium filifolium*)—See Sisyrinchium.

Paliurus—Ord. Rhamnaceæ. Hardy deciduous flowering shrub. First introduced 1596. Branches, spiny. Fruit, ornamental.
CULTURE : Soil, ordinary. Position, shrubberies or walls. Plant, Oct. to Feb.
PROPAGATION : By seeds sown ¼ in. deep in ordinary soil outdoors, Oct. to Nov. ; cuttings of roots planted 3 in. deep and 6 in. apart, Oct. to Feb. ; layering shoots, Sept. to Nov. ; removing suckers with roots attached, Sept. to Dec.
SPECIES CULTIVATED : P. australis (Syn. P. aculeatus), greenish yellow, June, 15 to 20 ft., S. Europe.

Palma Christi (*Ricinus communis*)—See Ricinus.

Palm Lily (*Cordyline indivisa*)—See Cordyline.

Pampas Grass (*Cortaderia argentea*)—See Cortaderia.

Panax—Ord. Araliaceæ. Stove evergreen shrubs. Orn. foliage. First introduced 1740. Leaves, coarsely and finely divided, green and variegated with white. CULTURE : Compost, equal parts loam, peaty leaf-mould, charcoal, and sand. Pot, Feb. to March. Water freely March to Oct., moderately afterwards. Temp., March to Sept. 70° to 80° ; Sept. to March 60° to 70°. PROPAGATION : By grafting in heat in spring ; inserting portions of roots in light soil in temp. 80° in April. SPECIES CULTIVATED : P. Balfouri, leaves green and creamy white, New Caledonia ; fruticosum, handsome pinnate foliage, 4 to 6 ft., Trop. Asia, and its varieties Guilfoylei, multifidum, and Victoriæ. P. quinquefolium (Ginseng), Syn. Aralia quinquefolia, is a hardy herbaceous species of no special merit.

Pancratium (Mediterranean Lily ; Sea Daffodil)—Ord. Amaryllidaceæ. Stove and hardy evergreen and deciduous bulbous plants. First introduced 1596. CULTURE OF STOVE SPECIES : Compost, two parts sandy loam, one part decayed manure, and half a part silver sand. Position, well-drained pots in sunny part of stove. Pot, March. Repotting necessary every three or four years only. Water abundantly April to Sept., moderately Sept. to Dec., keep quite dry Dec. to March. Apply liquid manure once a week May to Sept. Temp., 70° to 80° March to Sept., 55° to 65° Sept. to March. CULTURE OF HARDY SPECIES : Soil, three parts sandy loam, one part leaf-mould. Position, warm, exposed, well-drained borders. Plant bulbs 3 to 4 in. deep, Oct., Nov., or March. Protect in winter by layer of decayed manure, cocoanut-fibre refuse, or cinder ashes. Mulch after growth commences with decayed cow manure. Apply weak stimulants occasionally during summer. Lift, divide, and transplant every three years. PROPAGATION : Greenhouse and stove species by offsets removed from old bulbs in March ; hardy kinds similarly when replanting. STOVE SPECIES : P. canariense, white, Oct. and Nov., 18 in., fragrant, Canary Isles. HARDY SPECIES : P. illyricum, white, summer, 1 to 2 ft., S. Europe ; maritimum (Mediterranean Lily or Sea Daffodil), white, June, 2 to 2½ ft., Mediterranean Region.

Pandanus (Screw Pine)—Ord. Pandanaceæ. Stove evergreen shrubs. Orn. foliage. First introduced 1771. Leaves, narrow, strap-like, serrated. CULTURE : Compost, two parts sandy loam, one part equal proportions leaf-mould, charcoal, and sand. Pot, Jan. to April. Position, sunny, moist part of stove. Water moderately Oct. to Feb., freely afterwards. Syringe twice daily March to Sept. Temp., March to Sept. 65° to 85° ; Sept. to March 55° to 65°. PROPAGATION : By suckers, Feb. to April. SPECIES CULTIVATED : P. Baptistii, leaves yellow and green, 4 to 6 ft., New Caledonia ; candelabrum, leaves green, 15 to 30 ft., Trop. Africa ; candelabrum variegatus (Syn. P. javanicus variegatus), leaves green and white, 2 to 3 ft. ; Sanderi, leaves green and yellow, 3 ft. ; utilis, leaves glaucous green with reddish spines, 30 to 60 ft., Madagascar ; Veitchii, leaves green and white, 3 ft., Polynesia.

Panicum (Panick Grass)—Ord. Gramineæ. Hardy and half-hardy annual and perennial grasses. Inflorescence, light, feathery, graceful. Leaves, green. CULTURE OF STOVE SPECIES : Compost, equal parts peat, loam, leaf-mould, and sand. Position, well-drained pots in sunny or shady greenhouse. Water freely March to Oct. ; moderately at other times. Temp., March to Sept. 70° to 80° ; Sept. to March 60° to 65°. CULTURE OF HARDY ANNUALS : Soil, ordinary. Position, sunny borders. Sow seeds ¼ in. deep in patches where required to flower, in March or April. Thin seedlings when 1 in. high to 2 in. apart. Gather inflorescence in July or Aug. and dry for winter use. CULTURE OF HARDY PERENNIALS : Soil, good ordinary. Position, sunny borders. Plant, Oct. or April. Lift, divide, and replant every two or three years.

313

PROPAGATION : Stove species by division ; hardy kinds by seeds sown outdoors in April or May, and by division of roots in Oct. or March.
ANNUAL SPECIES : P. capillare, 2 ft., W. Hemisphere.
PERENNIAL SPECIES : P. bulbosum, 5ft., Mexico ; virgatum, 3 to 4 ft., N. America.
STOVE SPECIES CULTIVATED : P. plicatum niveo-vittatum, leaves striped white, 3 ft., Tropics. See also the genus Oplismenus.

Pansy (*Viola tricolor*)—See Viola.

Pantaloons Polyanthus—See Primula.

Panther Lily (*Lilium pardalinum*)—See Lilium.

Papaver (*Poppy*)—Ord. Papaveraceæ. Hardy annual and perennial herbs.
CULTURE OF ANNUAL SPECIES : Soil, good ordinary. Position, sunny beds or borders. Sow seeds 1/16 in. deep in patches where required to grow—in April for flowering in summer ; Sept. for flowering in spring. Thin seedlings to 1 or 2 in. apart when ½ in. high.
CULTURE OF PERENNIAL SPECIES : Soil, deep, sandy loam. Position, sunny borders for tall species ; rockeries for P. alpinum. Plant, Oct., March, or April. Top-dress with decayed manure in March or April.
PROPAGATION : Annual species by seeds as above ; perennial species by seeds sown in sunny place outdoors in March or April ; division of roots in March or April.
ANNUAL SPECIES : P. glaucum (Tulip Poppy), crimson, summer, 18 in., Syria ; lævigatum, scarlet, black, and white, summer, 2 ft., Greece ; pavoninum (Peacock Poppy), scarlet and black, 18 in., Afghanistan ; Rhæs (Corn or Shirley Poppy), various colours, 18 in., Britain, and its variety umbrosum (red and black) ; somniferum (Opium Poppy), various colours, summer, 3 ft., Europe and Asia ; umbrosum, crimson and black, summer, 1½ ft., Caucasus.
PERENNIAL SPECIES : P. nudicaule (Iceland Poppy), yellow, orange, and white, summer, 1 ft., Arctic Regions ; alpinum (Alpine Poppy), yellow, orange, salmon, and white, summer, 6 in., Europe ; californicum, orange, June, 1 ft., California ; orientale (Oriental Poppy), orange-scarlet, June, 3 ft., Asia Minor ; pilosum, orange, summer, 2 ft., Greece ; rupifragum (Spanish Poppy), terra-cotta, summer, 2 ft., Spain, and its variety atlanticum. Alpinum and nudicaule best grown as annuals or biennials.

Papaya (*Carica Papaya*)—See Carica.

Paper Birch (*Betula papyrifera*)—See Betula.

Paper Mulberry (*Broussonetia papyrifera*)—See Broussonetia.

Paphiopedilum—See Selenepedium.

Pappoose-root (*Caulophyllum thalictroides*)—See Caulophyllum.

Papyrus Antiquorum—See Cyperus Papyrus.

Paradisea (St. Bruno's Lily)—Ord. Liliaceæ. Hardy herbaceous perennials. First introduced 1629.
CULTURE : Soil, ordinary, well enriched with leaf-mould and decayed manure. Position, partially shady borders. Plant, Oct. or March.
PROPAGATION : By division of roots in Oct. or March ; seeds sown in cold frame or greenhouse in spring.
SPECIES CULTIVATED : P. Liliastrum, white, fragrant, May and June, 1 to 2 ft., Alps ; Liliastrum major, 4 to 5 ft., larger flowers than the parent. Formerly known as Anthericum Liliastrum.

Paradise Apple (*Pyrus malus paradisiaca*)—See Pyrus.

Paraguay Tea (*Ilex paraguayensis*)—See Ilex.

Para Nut—See Bertholletia.

Parasol Fir-tree (*Sciadopitys verticillata*)—See Sciadopitys.

Parchment Bark (*Pittosporum crassifolium*)—See Pittosporum.

Pardanthus—See Belamcanda.

Paris (Herb Paris)—Ord. Liliaceæ. Hardy perennial herb.
CULTURE : Soil, sandy loam. Position, shady borders, woods, or shrubberies.
Plant, Oct. to March.
PROPAGATION : By seeds sown in moist position outdoors in autumn ; division of
roots, Oct. or March.
SPECIES CULTIVATED : P. quadrifolia (Herb Paris), green, summer, 6 in., Britain.

Paris Daisy (*Chrysanthemum frutescens*)—See Chrysanthemum.

Parlour Ivy (*Mikania scandens*)—See Mikania.

Parlour Palm (*Aspidistra lurida*)—See Aspidistra.

Parnassia (Grass of Parnassus)—Ord. Saxifragaceæ. Hardy perennial herbs.
CULTURE : Soil, peaty or boggy. Position, moist, shady borders, bogs, or margins
of streams or ponds. Plant, Oct., Nov., March, or April.
PROPAGATION : By seeds sown in moist, boggy peat in shady position outdoors in
autumn or spring ; division of roots in March or April.
SPECIES CULTIVATED : P. caroliniana, white, summer, 6 in., N. America ; palustris
(Grass of Parnassus), white and green, summer, 6 in., Britain.

Parochetus (Blue-flowered Shamrock ; Shamrock Pea)—Ord. Leguminosæ.
Hardy trailing herbaceous perennial. First introduced 1820.
CULTURE : Soil, ordinary. Position, moist, partially shady banks or rock gardens.
Plant, Oct., March, or April.
PROPAGATION : By seeds sown 1/16 in. deep in light, sandy soil in cold frame in March ;
division of plants in March.
SPECIES CULTIVATED : P. communis, blue, March to June, trailing, Himalayas.

Paronychia (Nail-wort ; Whitlow-wort)—Ord. Illecebraceæ. Dwarf-creeping
perennial herbs. First introduced 1879. Flowers, white, surrounded by silvery
bracts produced in June.
CULTURE : Soil, ordinary. Position, dry, sunny banks or rockeries, or for carpeting
surfaces of beds. Plant, March to June.
PROPAGATION : By seeds sown in sunny spot outdoors in March or April ; division
of plants, Oct. or March.
SPECIES CULTIVATED : P. argentea, trailing, S. Europe ; capitata (Syn. P. chionæa),
trailing, E. Europe ; serpyllifolia, trailing, S. Europe.

Paroo Lily (*Dianella cærulea*)—See Dianella.

Parrotia (Persian Iron-wood)—Ord. Hamamelidaceæ. Hardy deciduous trees
and shrubs. Orn. foliage. First introduced 1848. Leaves, ovate, green in summer,
rich crimson with shades of orange and yellow in autumn.
CULTURE : Soil, good ordinary. Position, open shrubberies or, in the case of
P. persica, as specimen tree on lawn. Plant, Oct. to Feb. Prune shoots of trees
grown against walls to within an inch of base annually in Feb.
PROPAGATION : By seeds sown 1/8 in. deep in well-drained pots of sandy soil in cold
frame in autumn or spring ; layering shoots in autumn.
SPECIES CULTIVATED : P. jacquemontiana, yellow, April to July, 15 to 20 ft., Himalayas ; persica, reddish, March, 30 to 40 ft., Persia.

Parrot-beak-plant (*Clianthus puniceus*)—See Clianthus.

Parrot Tulip (*Tulipa gesneriana* var.)—See Tulipa.

Parrot's-bill of New Zealand (*Clianthus puniceus*)—See Clianthus.

Parry's Lily (*Lilium Parryi*)—See Lilium.

Parsley (*Carum Petroselinum*)—See Carum.

Parsley Fern (*Cryptogramme crispa*)—See Cryptogramme.

Parsley-leaved Elder (*Sambucus nigra laciniata*)—See Sambucus.

Parsnip (*Peucedanum sativum*)—See Peucedanum.

Parthenocissus Thompsoni—See Vitis Thompsoni.

Partridge-berry—See Gaultheria and Mitchellia.

Partridge-breast Aloe (*Aloe variegata*)—See Aloe.

Pasque-flower (*Anemone pulsatilla*)—See Anemone.

Passiflora (Passion-flower)—Ord. Passifloraceæ. Stove greenhouse and half-hardy climbing plants. First introduced 1629.

CULTURE OF STOVE SPECIES : Compost, equal parts fibrous loam and peat, one-fourth silver sand. Pot, Feb. or March. Prune, Feb., thinning out weak shoots and shortening strong ones one-third. Position, well-drained tubs or pots, or beds 18 in. deep and 2 ft. wide ; shoots trained up rafters or walls ; sunny. Water copiously March to Sept., moderately afterwards. Syringe twice daily April to Sept. Apply stimulants occasionally to healthy plants when in flower only. Temp., March to Oct. 65° to 75° ; Oct. to March 55° to 65°.

CULTURE OF GREENHOUSE SPECIES : Compost, as for stove species. Position, grown in pots, tubs, or beds and shoots trained up rafters. Prune, pot, and water as advised for stove species. Temp., March to Oct. 55° to 65° ; Oct. to March 45° to 50°.

CULTURE OF HALF-HARDY SPECIES : Soil, good ordinary mixed with a little decayed manure. Position, south or south-west walls. Plant, Oct. or March. Prune in Feb., shortening small shoots to 3 and 6 in. and strong ones to 2 and 3 ft. Water freely in dry weather. Apply liquid manure to healthy plants once a month in summer. Protect base of plant with straw or dry bracken during severe weather.

PROPAGATION : Stove and greenhouse species by seeds sown ¼ in. deep in pots of sandy soil in temp. 65° to 75° at any time ; by cuttings of young shoots 4 to 6 in. long inserted in sandy soil under bell-glass in temp. 65°, April to Sept. Hardy species by similar cuttings inserted in cold frame in summer ; layering young shoots in summer.

STOVE SPECIES : P. alata, crimson, white, and purple, summer, 15 to 20 ft., Peru ; edulis (Purple Granadilla), white and purple, summer, 20 ft., Brazil ; quadrangularis (Giant Granadilla), red, violet, and white, fragrant, summer, 20 ft., Trop. America ; racemosa (Syn. P. princeps), red, white, and purple, summer, 20 ft., Brazil.

GREENHOUSE SPECIES : P. Belottii, rose and blue, hybrid ; incarnata, white and purple or pink, summer, 20 to 30 ft., S. United States and Texas.

HALF-HARDY SPECIES : P. cærulea, white, blue, and purple, summer, 20 to 25 ft., Brazil, and its white variety Constance Elliot.

Passion-flower—See Passiflora and Tacsonia.

Pastinacea—See Peucedanum.

Paternoster Pea (*Abrus precatorius*)—See Abrus.

Patrinia (Eastern Valerian)—Ord. Valerianaceæ. Hardy perennials. Natives of Central and Eastern Asia. Plants with graceful foliage and attractive flowers. First introduced 1751.

CULTURE : Soil, light, rich, ordinary. Position, sunny borders. Plant in Oct., March, or April. Grow in groups of three or six.

PROPAGATION : By seeds sown outdoors in April ; division of the plants in autumn or spring.

SPECIES CULTIVATED : P. intermedia (Syn. P. rupestris), yellow, fragrant, May, 1 ft., Siberia ; palmata, June and July, 9 in., Japan ; scabiosæfolia, yellow, June and July, 2 ft., Siberia.

Paullinia—Ord. Sapindaceæ. Stove evergreen twining plant. First cultivated 1816. Leaves, finely divided, green, downy.

CULTURE : Compost, two parts loam, two parts leaf-mould and sand. Position, well-drained pots, with shoots trained round wire trellis or up rafters of roof. Pot, March. Prune slightly in Jan. and Feb. Water moderately Oct. to Feb., freely afterwards. Syringe twice daily March to Sept.

PROPAGATION : By cuttings of firm shoots, 2 to 3 in. long, inserted in small pots of sandy soil under bell-glass in temp. 75° to 85° any time.

SPECIES CULTIVATED : P. thalictrifolia, pink, Sept., 10 to 15 ft., S. America.

Paulownia—Ord. Scrophulariaceæ. Hardy deciduous tree. Orn. foliage and flowering. First introduced 1840. Leaves, large, soft, and downy.
CULTURE: Soil, rich, well-drained loam. Position, sunny, sheltered shrubberies or lawns. Plant, Oct. to Feb. Prune shoots annually in Feb. to within two or three inches of their base if only foliage is desired ; leave unpruned for flowering.
PROPAGATION : By seeds sown ⅛ in. deep in sandy loam in cold frame in spring or autumn ; by cuttings of roots inserted in sandy soil in frame in Feb.
SPECIES CULTIVATED : P. imperialis, violet, June, 30 to 50 ft., China.

Pavetta—Ord. Rubiaceæ. Stove and greenhouse evergreen shrubs. Orn. foliage. First introduced 1791.
CULTURE : Compost, two parts good fibrous peat, one part fibrous loam and silver sand. Position, shady part of warm greenhouse whilst growing, light situation when at rest. Pot, Feb. or March ; good drainage indispensable. Prune into shape in Feb. Water freely from March to Sept. ; moderately afterwards. Syringe twice daily March to Aug. Apply liquid manure once or twice a week to healthy plants in flower. Temp. for P. borbonica, March to Sept. 75° to 85° ; Sept. to March 55° to 65° ; for P. caffra, March to Sept. 60° to 70° ; Sept. to March 50° to 55°.
PROPAGATION : By cuttings of firm young shoots, 2 to 3 in. long, inserted singly in small pots in sandy peat under bell-glass in temp. 75° to 85°, March to May.
SPECIES CULTIVATED : P. borbonica, 3 to 4 ft., Bourbon ; caffra, white, June to Aug., 3 to 4 ft., Cape of Good Hope.

Pavia—See Æsculus.

Pavonia—Ord. Malvaceæ. Stove evergreen plants. First introduced 1778.
CULTURE : Compost, two parts loam, one part peat and sand. Pot, March. Position, pots in shade. Water freely March to Sept., moderately afterwards. Syringe daily in summer. Temp., March to Sept. 65° to 75° ; Sept. to March 55° to 65°.
PROPAGATION : By cuttings in fine sand under bell-glass in temp. 75° at any time.
SPECIES CULTIVATED : P. intermedia (Syn. Gœthea intermedia), white, hybrid ; kermesina (Syn. G. kermesina), white, dwarf, hybrid ; multiflora (Syns. P. Wioti and G. multiflora), purple, autumn, 1 to 2 ft., Brazil ; spinifex, yellow, 10 to 20 ft., Trop. America. See also Gœthea.

Pawpaw (*Carica Papaya*)—See Carica.

Pea (*Pisum sativum*)—See Pisum.

Peach (*Prunus persica*)—See Prunus.

Peach-leaved Bell-flower (*Campanula persicifolia*)—See Campanula.

Peach Trumpet-flower (*Solandra grandiflora*)—See Solandra.

Peacock Anemone (*Anemone hortensis pavonina*)—See Anemone.

Peacock-flower (*Cæsalpinia pulcherrima*)—See Cæsalpinia.

Peacock Iris (*Moræa pavonia*)—See Moræa.

Peacock Poppy (*Papaver pavoninum*)—See Papaver.

Peacock Treasure-flower (*Gazania pavonia*)—See Gazania.

Pear (*Pyrus communis*)—See Pyrus.

Pearl-berry (*Margyricarpus setosus*)—See Margyricarpus.

Pearl-bush (*Exochorda grandiflora*)—See Exochorda.

Pearl Cud-weed (*Anaphalis margaritacea*)—See Anaphalis.

Pearl-grass (*Briza maxima*)—See Briza.

Pearl-wort (*Sagina glabra*)—See Sagina.

Pearly Everlasting (*Anaphalis margaritacea*)—See Anaphalis.

Pecan (*Carya olivæformis*)—See Carya.

Pedilanthus (Slipper Spurge ; Jew-bush)—Ord. Euphorbiaceæ. Stove succulent shrub. First introduced 1874.

CULTURE : Compost, two parts sandy loam, one part brick rubbish, half a part decayed cow manure and silver sand. Pot, March or April. Position, dry, sunny part of stove. Temp., Sept. to March 60° to 70° ; March to Sept. 60° to 80°. Water once in three weeks from Sept. to March ; once a week afterwards. No syringing or stimulants required.

PROPAGATION : By cuttings of shoots, 2 to 3 in. long, exposed to sun for one or two days, then inserted singly in sand in 2 in. pots, and placed on a shelf near the glass, any time during summer.

SPECIES CULTIVATED : P. tithymaloides, bright red or purple, 6 ft., Trop. America.

Peerless Daffodil (*Narcissus incomparabilis*)—See Narcissus.

Pelargonium—Ord. Geraniaceæ. Greenhouse and hardy herbaceous, evergreen, shrubby, and tuberous-rooted perennials. Flowering and orn. foliage. Popularly known as " Geraniums." P. grandiflorum first introduced 1794 ; P. peltatum, 1701 ; P. zonale, 1710.

CLASSIFICATION OF TYPES : (1) Zonal: Leaves roundish, cordate, lobed, pubescent, green, with or without horse-shoe mark near margin of upper surface. Subclasses : Bicolor—Leaves green edged with white or white edged with green. Tricolor—Leaves green, white, yellow, and crimson. Bronze—Yellow, with bronze zone. (2) Show : Leaves palmately lobed, toothed margins, wrinkled, green ; flowers large, with smooth or wrinkled edges. Subclass : Regal—Flowers semi-double. (3) Fancy : Leaves similar to show kinds ; flowers smaller, spotted, or blotched. (4) Ivy-leaved : Leaves ivy-shaped, fleshy, five-angled, green, or variegated ; stems trailing or climbing. (5) Scented-leaved : Leaves variously shaped, scented.

CULTURE OF HARDY HERBACEOUS SPECIES : Soil, sandy loam. Position, sunny well-drained rockery or border. Plant, March or April. Protect in winter with covering of cocoanut-fibre refuse.

CULTURE OF ZONAL PELARGONIUMS : For summer flowering : Insert cuttings in Aug. or Sept. singly in 2 in. pots. Place in temp. 45° till March, then transfer to 4 in. size. Nip off points of main shoot in Feb. or March, also of side shoots when 2 in. long. Transfer to 6 in. pots when roots reach side of 5 in. sizes. Pot firmly. Compost for first potting, two parts yellow fibrous loam, half a part well-decayed manure, half a part leaf-mould, one part coarse sand, and tablespoonful of superphosphate or a quarter of a pint of bonemeal to each bushel ; for final potting, same proportion of loam, manure, and leaf-mould, quarter part each of coarse sand and charcoal, tablespoonful of superphosphate or pint of bonemeal to each bushel. Remove flower buds until fortnight after final potting. Water moderately first ten days after potting, freely afterwards. Apply stimulants month after final potting. Shade from sun when in bloom. Temp., Aug. to March 40° to 50° ; March to May 55° to 60° ; ordinary cool greenhouse or window afterwards. After flowering shorten shoots and keep soil just moist, repotting following spring to make large plants. For winter flowering : Insert cuttings singly in 2 in. pots in Feb. or March in temp. 55° to 65°. Transfer when well rooted into 4 in. and again into 6 in. pots in June. Nip off points of main shoot in April and of side shoots in May or June. Pinch off flower buds appearing before Sept. Stand in sunny, cold frame or plunge to rim of pots in cinder ashes in open position, June to Sept. Remove into greenhouse in Sept. Water freely outdoors, moderately indoors. Apply stimulants twice a week June to Sept., once a week afterwards. Compost, as above. Temp., Sept. to March 50° to 55°. Dry atmosphere essential to prevent damping of blooms. After flowering shorten shoots, keep moderately moist, and repot. Zonals, Bicolors, and Tricolors for bedding : Insert cuttings in Aug. or Sept., several in 5 in. pots, or 2 in. apart in shallow boxes. Keep thus until Feb., then transfer singly to 3 in. pots, place in temp. 55° until April, then remove to cold frame, and plant outdoors in June. Lift plants in Sept., placing bicolors, tricolors, and bronzes singly in 3 in. pots ; zonals singly in similiar pots, three in a 4 or 5 in. pot, or a few inches apart in shallow boxes, and storing in temp. 40° to 45°, in greenhouse, room, or cellar. Specimen Zonals : Insert cuttings in

Aug. or Sept., grow in 2 in. pots until March, then transfer to 4 in. sizes. Compost, as above : Nip off points of main shoot in March, also of side shoots when 3 in. long. Tie these firmly to wire fixed to rim of pot and allow young shoots to form in centre. Remove all blooms first year. Transfer to 6 in. pot in May or June. Grow in greenhouse near glass. Water freely during summer, moderately in winter. Apply stimulants June to Sept. Shorten shoots two-thirds in Jan. When new shoots form repot. Nip off points of shoots where necessary to ensure good shape. Compost, as above. Stimulants for Zonals : Liquid horse, cow, sheep, or deer dung diluted with two-thirds water and applied twice a week in summer, once a week in winter ; nitrate of soda, ¼ oz. to a gallon of water, applied once a week, when soil is moist only, for three or four weeks, then cease ; sulphate of ammonia, same as nitrate of soda : soot-water (one peck each of sheep and cow dung and ½ peck of soot to 36 gall. of water), diluted with half water, applied twice a week.

CULTURE OF SHOW AND FANCY PELARGONIUMS : Insert cuttings of firm shoots, 2 to 3 in. long, in July or Aug., singly in 2 in. pots in cold frame or greenhouse. Sandy soil. When rooted transfer to 4 in. pots, and place on a shelf close to glass in temp. 45° to 50°. Nip off points of main shoot just before potting. When new shoots are 3 in. long nip off points. Transfer to 5 in. pots in Jan. Keep near glass. When flowers show apply liquid manure twice a week. Water moderately until March, then freely until June, when give less. Temp., Sept. to March 45° to 50° ; March to May 50° to 55°. After flowering stand in sunny place outdoors. Prune shoots to within 1 in. of base in July. When new shoots form turn plants out of pots, remove loose soil, and repot in 4 or 5 in. pots. Replace in greenhouse in Sept. Transfer to 6 or 8 in. pots in Dec. or Jan. Compost, three parts good fibrous loam, one part decayed horse or cow dung, half a part coarse sand, and a tablespoonful of superphosphate to each bushel. Good drainage and firm potting essential. Stimulants as above.

CULTURE OF IVY-LEAVED PELARGONIUMS : Insert cuttings singly in 2 in. pots, or three or four in a 4 in. pot, in Aug. or Sept. Grow in greenhouse near glass until Feb. or March, then transfer to 4 in. pots. Nip off points of main shoots in Feb. or March. Repot in 5 in. pots in April or May. Train shoots to stakes or place plants in suspended baskets, and let them droop over sides. Water moderately Sept. to April, freely April to Sept. Apply stimulants May to Sept. Temp., Sept. to March 40° to 50° ; March to Sept. 50° to 60°. Plant outdoors June. Prune old plants Feb. or March. Compost and stimulants same as for zonals.

CULTURE OF FRAGRANT-LEAVED PELARGONIUMS : Compost, two parts loam, half a part each of decayed manure and leaf-mould, quarter part sand. Pot and treat as advised for zonals.

PROPAGATION : By seeds sown 1/16 in. deep in a well-drained pot or pan filled with light, sandy soil in temp. 55° to 65°, Feb. to April ; cuttings inserted as above directed in each section ; grafting on common kinds in close frame or under bell-glass in temp. 55° to 65° in spring ; tuberous-rooted kinds by division in spring.

HARDY HERBACEOUS SPECIES : P. endlicherianum, rose, July to Oct., 2 ft., Orient.

FRAGRANT-LEAVED SPECIES : P. capitatum (Rose-scented), rose and purple, summer, 2 to 3 ft., S. Africa ; citriodorum (Citron-scented), white, summer, 2 to 3 ft., S. Africa ; crispum (Lemon-scented), rose, Sept., 2 to 3 ft., S. Africa ; denticulatum (Fern-leaved), Syn. P. filicifolium, purple, summer, 1 ft., S. Africa ; fragrans (Nutmeg-scented), white and pink, summer, 2 ro 3 ft., S. Africa ; graveolens, rose and purple, 2 to 3 ft., S. Africa ; odoratissimum, white, 1½ ft., S. Africa ; quercifolium (Oak-leaved), pink and purple, May, 3 ft., S. Africa ; radula (Balsam-scented), and purple, summer, 2 to 3 ft., S. Africa ; tomentosum (Peppermint-scented), white, summer, 3 ft., S. Africa.

OTHER SPECIES : P. inquinans, scarlet, rose, or white, summer, 2 ft., S. Africa ; peltatum (Syn. hederæfolium), parent of the Ivy-leaved Geraniums, white and red, summer, S. Africa ; grandiflorum, white and red, summer, 2 ft., S. Africa ; zonale (Horseshoe or Zonal Geranium), parent of the zonal, bicolor and tricolor geraniums, various colours, summer, 2 ft., S. Africa. The bedding and zonal pelargoniums of gardens are hybrids between P. inquinans and P. zonale.

Pelecyphora (Hatchet Cactus)—Ord. Cactaceæ. Greenhouse succulent perennial. First introduced 1843.
CULTURE : Compost, equal parts sandy loam, rough old mortar, and pounded bricks. Position, sunny, airy greenhouse or windows. Pot, March or April in well-drained pots just large enough to accommodate roots. Repot every third or fourth year only. Water moderately March to Sept., once a fortnight Sept. to Dec., none afterwards. Syringe on evenings of warm days June to Sept. Apply soot-water to healthy plants June to Sept. Ventilate freely in summer. Temp., March to Sept. 60° to 70° ; Sept. to March 50° to 55°.
PROPAGATION : By seeds sown ⅛ in. deep in well-drained pans or pots of sandy soil in temp. 75° in March, keeping soil moderately moist ; by cuttings of the tops of the plants inserted in small pots of sandy, gritty compost in spring.
SPECIES CULTIVATED : P. aselliformis, white and rose, June, 4 in., Mexico.

Pellæa (Cliff Brake-fern)—Ord. Filices. Greenhouse evergreen and deciduous ferns. First introduced 1770. Fronds, hand-shaped or once or twice divided ; green.
CULTURE : Compost, equal parts loam, leaf-mould, peat, and sand, with a little charcoal and sandstone. Pot or plant, March. Position, well-drained pots in shady part of greenhouse or in beds or rockeries in shade. Water moderately Oct. to Feb., freely afterwards. Temp., Sept. to March 45° to 55° ; March to Sept. 60° to 65°. P. atropurpurea is sufficiently hardy to grow outdoors in sheltered rockeries if protected with litter or hand-light in winter.
PROPAGATION : By spores sown on surface of sandy peat in shallow pan in temp. 70° or 80° any time ; division of plants in Feb. to April.
SPECIES CULTIVATED : P. adiantoides (Syn. Platyloma adiantoides), W. Indies ; alabamensis (Syn. Cheilanthes alabamensis), N. America ; atropurpurea, N. America ; Breweri, N. America ; calomelanos, Cape Colony ; cordata, Mexico ; cordata flexuosa (Syn. Platyloma flexuosa), Western S. America ; falcata, Tropics, Australia, and New Zealand ; hastata (Syn. Pteris hastata), S. Africa ; mucronata, California ; ternifolia, Trop. America.

Pellionia—Ord. Urticaceæ. Stove creeping herbs. Orn. foliage. First introduced 1880. Leaves roundish, oval, or heart-shaped ; olive-green with violet and white markings.
CULTURE : Compost, two parts sandy loam, one part leaf-mould and sand. Pot or plant, March or April. Position, shallow pans, or on surface of beds or rockeries or under staging. Water moderately Oct. to Feb., freely afterwards. Temp., Sept. to April 55° to 65° ; April to Sept. 65° to 75°.
PROPAGATION : By cuttings of creeping shoots inserted in sandy soil in small pots under bell-glass in temp. 75° to 85° in spring ; division of plants in March or April.
SPECIES CULTIVATED : P. daveauana, Cochin China ; pulchra, Cochin China.

Peltandra (Arrow Arum)—Ord. Aroideæ. Hardy perennial herb. Orn. foliage First introduced 1759. Leaves spearhead-shaped, broad, deep green.
CULTURE : Soil, rich, boggy, or muddy. Position, moist bog or shallow pond. Plant, March or April, enclosing roots and small quantity of soil in piece of canvas or sacking and dropping the whole into the water.
PROPAGATION : By inserting portions of creeping stems in muddy soil in ponds where required to grow.
SPECIES CULTIVATED : P. virginica, white, June, 1 ft., N. America.

Peltaria—Ord. Cruciferæ. Hardy herbaceous perennial herb. First introduced 1601. Plant, garlic-scented.
CULTURE : Soil, ordinary. Position, sunny borders, beds, or rockeries. Plant, Oct., March, or April.
PROPAGATION : By seeds sown ⅛ in. deep outdoors, March or April, where plants are required to grow ; division of plants in March or April.
SPECIES CULTIVATED : P. alliacea, white, summer, 1 ft., E. Europe.

Pendulous Bell-flower—See Symphandra.

Pennisetum—Ord. Gramineæ. Hardy perennial grasses. Flowering and orn. foliage. Inflorescence very graceful and useful for cutting and drying for winter decoration.

CULTURE OF P. LATIFOLIUM : Soil, sandy loam. Position, sheltered, well-drained borders in warm parts of the kindgom only. Plant, April. Protect in severe weather with covering of mats, or lift in Nov., place in large pots or tubs, and remove to greenhouse, replanting outdoors in April or May.

CULTURE OF P. LONGISTYLUM : Soil, ordinary. Position, sunny borders. Sow seeds $\frac{1}{16}$ in. deep in patches a foot or more in diameter, in March or April, where plants are to flower. Gather inflorescence for winter use, end of July. This species is best treated as an annual.

PROPAGATION : P. latifolium by seed sown $\frac{1}{16}$ in. deep in sandy soil in shallow boxes or pans in temp. 60° to 65°, March or April, transplanting seedlings outdoors in May or June ; division of root in April.

SPECIES CULTIVATED : P. latifolium (Syn. Gymnothrix latifolia), 5 to 8 ft., Argentina ; longistylum, 12 to 18 in., Abyssinia.

Pennyroyal (*Mentha pulegium*)—See Mentha.

Pentas—Ord. Rubiaceæ. Stove evergreen flowering shrubs. First introduced 1842.

CULTURE : Compost, equal parts fibrous peat and leaf-mould, half part each light loam and sand. Pot, Feb. to April. Position, well-drained pots in light part of stove. Water moderately Sept. to April, freely at other times. Syringe daily April to Sept. Prune plants into shape immediately after flowering. Nip off points of young shoots occasionally during May, June, and July to induce bushy habit of growth. Temp., Sept. to April 50° to 60° ; April to Sept. 60° to 75°.

PROPAGATION : By cuttings of young shoots, 2 to 3 in. long, inserted singly in 2 in. pots filled with sandy compost and placed under bell-glass in temp. of 75°, spring or summer.

SPECIES CULTIVATED : P. carnea, pink, winter, 18 in., Trop. Africa ; carnea kermesina, rose and violet ; carnea quartiniana, pink.

Pentstemon (Beard Tongue)—Ord. Scrophulariaceæ. Hardy perennials. First introduced 1794.

CULTURE : Soil, two parts rich loam, one part decayed manure or leaf-mould. Plant, March or April. Position, sunny beds or borders, well drained. Apply stimulants once or twice a week in summer. Suitable stimulants : Liquid cow or horse manure ; $\frac{1}{4}$ oz. each superphosphate, kainit, and sulphate of ammonia to 2 galls. of water, applied twice a week ; Peruvian guano $\frac{1}{2}$ oz. to gall. of water twice a week.

PROPAGATION : By seeds sown $\frac{1}{16}$ in. deep in a well-drained pot or pan of light soil in temp. 55° to 65° in Feb. or March, transplanting seedlings outdoors in May ; cuttings of young shoots, 3 in. long, inserted in sandy soil in boxes or a bed under hand-light, or in cold frame in Aug., allowing them to remain there until April ; division in April.

SPECIES CULTIVATED : P. antirrhinoides, lemon yellow, July, 1 to 3 ft., S. California ; azureus, blue, Aug., 1 ft., N. America ; barbatus (Syn. Chelone barbata), scarlet, summer, 3 ft., U.S.A. ; Bridgesi, scarlet, July to Sept., 1 to 2 ft., N. America ; cæruleus (Syn. P. angustifolia), mauve or soft blue, July, 8 to 12 in., Western U.S.A. ; campanulatus, rosy purple, violet, or white, June, 1 to 2 ft., Mexico and Guatemala ; centranthifolius, scarlet, summer, 1 to 3 ft., California and W. Arizona ; Cobæa, purple or white, Aug., 1 to 2 ft., U.S.A. ; confertus cæruleo-purpureus, purple and blue, 1 ft., summer, Rocky Mountains ; cordifolius, scarlet, summer, partially climbing, S. California ; diffusus, blue or purple, summer, 1 to 2 ft., Western N. America ; glaber (Syn. P. Gordoni), purple, summer, 1 to 2 ft., U. States, and its varieties alpinus and cyananthus ; glaucus, purple violet, July, 8 to 15 in., Rocky Mountains ; Hartwegii, scarlet, summer, 2 ft., Mexico ; heterophyllus, pinkish to sky blue, July, 1 to 3 ft., California ; lævigatus digitalis, white or pink, 2 to 3 ft., U.S.A. ; Menziesii, purple, June, 6 in., N.W. America ; ovatus, blue to purple, Aug. to Oct., 2 to 3 ft., U.S.A. ; pubescens, purple or violet, July, 1 to 3 ft., U.S.A. ; Richardsoni, violet, summer, 1$\frac{1}{2}$ to 2 ft., U.S.A. ; rupicola (Syn. P.

Davidsoni), ruby red, May, 2 to 3 in., N.W. America ; Scouleri, lilac, May to June, 1 to 2 ft., U.S.A. ; spectabilis, rose-purple or lilac, summer, 2 to 4 ft., Mexico and S, California. The kinds grown so largely in gardens were originally derived from hybrids between P. Cobæa and P. Hartwegii.

Peony (*Pæonia officinalis*)—See Pæonia.

Peperomia (Pepper Elder)—Ord. Piperaceæ. Stove herbaceous perennials ; creeping and erect ; orn. foliage. First introduced 1815. Leaves roundish or egg-shaped ; green variegated with white.
CULTURE : Compost, equal parts fibrous loam and peat with half a part sand. Pot, March or April. Position, small well-drained pots for erect species, shallow pans or beds for creeping species. Shade from sun. Water moderately in winter, freely in summer. Syringe daily April to Sept. Temp., April to Sept. 60° to 75°, Sept. to April 55° to 65°.
PROPAGATION : By cuttings of shoots or single joints with leaf attached inserted in sandy peat and plunged in bottom heat in temp. 65° to 75° in spring.
SPECIES CULTIVATED : P. marmorata, leaves green and white, Brazil ; metallica, leaves green, Peru ; nummulariæfolia, round, green leaves, Trop. America ; Sandersii, leaves green and white, Brazil, and its variety argyreia, which has light-coloured patches between the veins.

Pepper Elder—See Peperomia.

Pepper Tree (*Schinus molle*)—See Schinus.

Peppermint (*Mentha piperita*)—See Mentha.

Peppermint-scented Geranium (*Pelargonium tomentosum*)—See Pelargonium.

Pepper-plant—See Piper and Capsicum.

Perennial Candytuft—See Iberis.

Perennial Flax (*Linum perenne*)—See Linum.

Perennial Honesty (*Lunaria rediviva*)—See Lunaria.

Perennial Lupin (*Lupinus polyphyllus*)—See Lupinus.

Perennial Sun-flower (*Helianthus multiflorus*)—See Helianthus.

Pereskia (Barbados Gooseberry)—Ord. Cactaceæ. Stove succulent perennials. First introduced 1696.
CULTURE : Compost, equal parts loam, peat, and leaf-mould, one-fourth sand. Pot, March. Position, small well-drained pots in light, dry part of stove, or in beds with shoots trained to dry wall. Water moderately Sept. to April, freely afterwards. Temp., Sept. to March 50° to 60° ; March to Sept. 65° to 75°. P. aculeata and P. Bleo grown chiefly for stocks for grafting epiphyllums on.
PROPAGATION : By cuttings of stem inserted in 2 in. pots filled with sandy soil and placed on a light, dry shelf in temp. 65° to 75° in spring. Allow one shoot only to grow for forming a stock, and train this to a stake fixed in soil until high enough, then graft.
SPECIES CULTIVATED : P. aculeata, 10 to 30 ft., W. Indies ; Bleo, 10 to 15 ft., Mexico.

Perilla—Ord. Labiatæ. Half-hardy orn.-foliaged annual. First introduced 1770. Leaves egg-shaped, pointed, green or dark bronzy purple, with fimbriated edges.
CULTURE : Sow seeds ¼ in. deep in shallow boxes or pans filled with ordinary light soil placed in temp. 65° to 75° in Feb. or March. Transplant seedlings when three leaves have formed singly into 2 in. pots, or 2 in. apart in shallow boxes. Keep in temp. 55° to 65° till May, then transfer to cold frame ; gradually harden off and plant outdoors in June. Adapted for masses in borders or for lines in, or edgings to, beds.
SPECIES CULTIVATED : P. frutescens crispa (Syn. P. nankinensis), leaves bronzy purple, 1 to 3 ft., China, Japan, and Himalayas.

Periploca (Silk-vine)—Ord. Asclepiadaceæ. Hardy deciduous twiner. First introduced 1597.
CULTURE: Soil, ordinary. Position, walls, arbours, summer-houses, or trellises in any aspect. Plant, Oct., Nov., Feb., or March. Prune away very weak or old distorted shoots only in March. Apply liquid manure occasionally during the flowering season.
PROPAGATION: By cuttings inserted under bell-glass or hand-light outdoors, July to Oct.; layering shoots, Sept. or Oct.
SPECIES CULTIVATED: P. græca, green and brown, July to Aug., 20 to 30 ft., S.E. Europe.

Peristeria (Dove Flower; Dove Orchid)—Ord. Orchidaceæ. Stove evergreen orchid. First introduced 1826.
CULTURE: Compost, equal parts loam, leaf-mould, and fine crocks. Pot, March, or when new growth begins. Position, well-drained pots or teak baskets. Water freely April to Sept., keep nearly dry afterwards. Temp., Oct. to April 60° to 65°; April to Oct. 65° to 75°. Apply weak stimulants occasionally when plants are growing freely. Growing period, March to Oct.; resting period, Oct. to March. Flowers appear at base of new pseudo-bulb after resting.
PROPAGATION: By division of pseudo-bulbs, March.
SPECIES CULTIVATED: P. elata (Dove Orchid), white and purple, fragrant, summer, Central America.

Periwinkle—See Vinca.

Pernettya (Prickly Heath)—Ord. Ericaceæ. Hardy evergreen berry-bearing shrub. First introduced 1828. Berries, crimson, blue, black, rose, cream; autumn.
OUTDOOR CULTURE: Soil, peaty. Position, moist rockeries or margins of open or shady shrubberies and beds. Plant, Sept. to Nov. or March to May.
POT CULTURE: Compost, two parts peat, one part leaf-mould and sand. Position, cold or cool greenhouses or dwelling-rooms. Pot, Oct. or Nov. Water moderately. When berries shrivel or fall off, plants no further use for pot culture; plant outdoors.
WINDOW BOXES: Soil, ordinary. Position, sunny or shady. Plant, Sept. to Jan. Remove when berries shrivel.
PROPAGATION: By seeds sown ¼ in. deep in bed of peaty soil outdoors in autumn; layering shoots in March or April.
SPECIES CULTIVATED: P. mucronata, white, spring, 2 to 5 ft., Magellan Islands.

Perowskia—Ord. Labiatæ. Hardy, deciduous, semi-woody shrub.
CULTURE: Soil, good, well-drained loam. Position, sunny borders or shrubberies. Plant, Nov. to Feb. in groups of three or four. Cut away dead growth in early spring.
PROPAGATION: By cuttings of nearly ripened growth in July, inserted in sandy soil under bell-glass.
SPECIES CULTIVATED: P. atriplicifolia, violet blue, Aug. to Sept., 3 to 5 ft., Himalayas and Afghanistan.

Persea (Avocado or Alligator Pear)—Ord. Laurineæ. Stove evergreen shrub. Fruit, pear-shaped, purplish when ripe, and edible. First introduced 1739.
CULTURE: Compost, equal parts loam and peat and a little sand. Position, moist stove in pots. Pot in March. Water freely in summer, little in winter. Syringe daily in spring and summer. Temp., March to Sept. 75° to 85°; Sept. to March 55° to 65°.
PROPAGATION: By seeds sown in above compost in a temp. of 85°; by cuttings in sand under bell-glass in a similar temperature in spring.
SPECIES CULTIVATED: P. gratissima, green, summer, to 60 ft., W. Indies.

Persian Cyclamen (*Cyclamen persicum*)—See Cyclamen.

Persian Iron-wood (*Parrotia persica*)—See Parrotia.

Persian Lilac (*Syringa persica*)—See Syringa.

Persian Lily (*Fritillaria persica*)—See Fritillaria.

Persimmon (*Diospyros virginiana*)—See Diospyros.

Peruvian Majic Tree—See Cantua.

Peruvian Mastic Tree (*Schinus molle*)—See Schinus.

Peruvian Nasturtium (*Tropæolum tuberosum*)—See Tropæolum.

Peruvian Swamp Lily (*Zephyranthes candida*)—See Zephyranthes.

Peruvian Trumpet-flower (*Datura suaveolens*)—See Datura.

Pescatorea cerina—See Zygopetalum cerinum.

Petasites (Winter Heliotrope)—Ord. Compositæ. Hardy perennial herb, Flowering and orn. foliage. Leaves, kidney- or heart-shaped, large, downy beneath. green. First introduced 1806.
CULTURE : Soil, ordinary. Position, shrubberies or woodland, partially shaded borders. Plant, Oct. or Nov.
PROPAGATION : By division, Oct. or Nov.
SPECIES CULTIVATED : P. fragrans, pale lilac, fragrant, Feb., 6 in., Mediterranean Region.

Petrea (Purple Wreath)—Ord. Verbenaceæ. Stove-flowering shrubs and climbers ; deciduous. First introduced 1733.
CULTURE : Compost, equal parts loam, leaf-mould, peat, and sand ; little charcoal. Position, well-drained pot, bed, or border, with shoots of climbing species trained up rafters or trellises in shady part of stove. Pot or plant, Feb. or March. Prune slightly Feb. Water freely March to Sept., moderately afterwards. Syringe daily March to Sept. Temp., March to Sept. 65° to 75° ; Sept. to March 55° to 60°.
PROPAGATION : By cuttings of firm young shoots inserted in sandy soil in well-drained pot under bell-glass in temp. 65° to 75°, spring and summer.
SPECIES CULTIVATED : P. arborea, violet blue, summer, 12 ft., shrub, Colombia ; volubilis (Purple Wreath), purple, summer, climber, to 15 ft., Trop. America.

Petroselinum crispum—See Carum petroselinum.

Petty Whin (*Genista anglica*)—See Genista.

Petunia—Ord. Solanaceæ. Half-hardy herbaceous perennials. First introduced 1823.
INDOOR CULTURE : Compost, two parts decayed turfy loam, one part well-rotted manure, quarter part silver sand. Position, sunny greenhouse or window. Shade only from bright sun. Pot, Feb. to June, moderately firm. Size of pots, 3, 5, and 6 in. Pinch out point of young shoots occasionally in spring to induce bushy growth. Prune shoots of old plants moderately close in Feb. or March. Water moderately Sept. to April, freely afterwards. No syringing required. Apply stimulants to established plants when flower buds form. Train shoots to stakes. Suitable liquid manures : ¼ oz. nitrate of soda or sulphate of ammonia to 1 gallon of water, applied three or four successive times only ; ¼ oz. guano to a gallon of water, applied twice a week ; weak, liquid, natural manure, applied as advised for guano. Temp., March to Oct. 55° to 65° ; Oct. to March 40° to 50°.
OUTDOOR CULTURE : Soil, ordinary rich. Position, sunny beds, borders, vases, or trellises. Plant, June. Lift, Sept., and store in pots in greenhouse to furnish cuttings in spring. Water freely in dry weather. Place in cold frame in May to harden before planting out. Apply stimulants as above.
PROPAGATION : By seeds sown on surface of a compost of equal parts good soil, leaf-mould, and sand in a well-drained pot or pan, in temp. 65° to 75°, in Feb., March, or April ; by cuttings of young shoots inserted in light, sandy soil in pots, pans, or boxes in temp. 55° to 65° any time in spring.

Philadelphus Lemoinei Virginal
(Mock Orange)

Phlomis fruticosa
(Jerusalem Sage)

Phlox Drummondii

Phlox hybrida

Phormium tenax
(New Zealand Flax)

Phyllocactus Ackermanni

Phyllocactus hybridum

Physalis Alkekengi
(Winter Cherry)

Physostegia virginiana
(False Dragon-head)

Phyteuma orbiculare
(Horned Rampion)

Picea excelsa
(Common Spruce)

Pieris floribunda

Pinus parviflora pentaphylla
(Japanese Stunted Pine)

Plagianthus Lyalli

Platycodon grandiflorum Mariesii (Chinese Bell-flower)

Platystemon californicus
(Cream Cups)

Polemonium humile

Polianthes tuberosa flore-pleno
(Tuberose)

species cultivated: P. nyctaginiflora, white, Aug., 2 ft., Argentina ; violacea, purple, summer, 6 to 10 in., Argentina. The garden varieties are hybrids between these two species.

Peucedanum (Parsnip ; Dill)—Ord. Umbelliferæ. Hardy biennial esculent-rooted vegetable and annual or biennial herb.

culture : Soil, rich ordinary previously trenched three spits deep, and not recently manured. Position, open and sunny. First method : Draw drills 1 in. deep and 15 in. apart. Sow seeds in groups of three or four 12 in. apart, March or April. Thin seedlings when 2 in. high to one in each group. Second method : Dig out a trench 30 in. wide, 18 in. deep. Put ¾ lb. decayed manure in bottom, then 6 in. of soil mixed with a little manure, and fill up with fine friable soil. Sow two or three seeds in groups 1 foot apart down centre of the trench. Reduce the seedlings when 2 in. high to one in each group. Third method : Make holes 3 ft. deep, 8 in. in diameter at top and 15 in. apart each way. Fill the lower six inches of the hole with a compost of fine soil, decayed manure, and a pinch of superphosphate. The remaining space fill with similar material, but with the addition of soot and a pinch of salt. Sow the seeds in groups of three or four, and thin to one plant when 2 in. high. Suitable artificial manures : 2¾ lb. kainit, 1 lb. sulphate of ammonia, 2½ lb. guano per square rod, to be applied half before sowing and remainder after crop is thinned. Lift and store roots only in event of bad weather ; they retain their flavour better lifted as wanted from the ground. Seed retains its vegetative powers for one year only. Quantity required for a row 50 ft. long, ½ oz. Crop reaches maturity in 24 to 27 weeks. Seed take 15 to 20 days to germinate.

culture of dill : Soil, ordinary. Sow seeds 1 in. deep in drills 9 in. apart in March. Thin seedlings to 8 in. apart. Gather leaves as required for use.

species cultivated : P. graveolens (Dill), Syn. Anethum graveolens, yellow, July, 3 ft., India ; sativum (Parsnip), Syn. Pastinacea sativa, yellow, July and Aug., 4 ft., Europe.

Phacelia—Ord. Hydrophyllaceæ. Hardy annuals. Good bee flowers. First introduced 1826.

culture : Soil, ordinary rich. Position, sunny or partially shaded beds or borders. Sow seeds in patches or lines where required to grow in April. Thin seedlings 2 to 3 in. apart in June.

species cultivated : P. campanularia, blue, summer, 8 in., California ; congesta, blue or lavender, June, 2 to 3 ft., Texas and New Mexico ; Parryi, violet, summer, 1 ft., California ; tanacetifolia, blue or lilac, July, 2 to 3 ft., California ; viscida (Syn. Eutoca viscida), blue and white, summer, 1½ to 2 ft., S. California ; Whitlavia (Syn. Whitlavia grandiflora), blue, Sept., 1 ft., California.

Phædranassa (Queen Lily)—Ord. Amaryllidaceæ. Greenhouse flowering bulbous plants. First introduced 1800.

culture : Compost, two parts sandy loam, one part leaf-mould, and half a part sand. Position, well-drained pots near the glass March to Oct. ; in dry place under stage Oct. to March. Pot, Feb. or March. Water moderately March to May, freely May to Oct. keep nearly dry Oct. to March. Apply stimulants May to Aug. only. Temp., March to Sept. 55° to 65° ; Sept. to March 40° to 50°. Repot annually, removing old soil away from bulbs. Place in small pots first ; shift into larger sizes later on. No shade required.

propagation : By seeds sown ¼ in. deep in well-drained pots or pans of sandy soil in temp. of 60° to 65° in spring ; offsets removed and treated as old bulbs at potting time.

species cultivated : P. Carmioli, red and green, summer, 2 ft., Costa Rica ; chloracea, scarlet and green, summer, 18 in., Ecuador ; Lehmanni, scarlet, summer, 2 ft., Colombia.

Phænocoma—Ord. Compositæ. Greenhouse evergreen flowering shrub. First introduced 1789.

culture : Compost, two parts good brown fibrous peat, one part silver sand, and little charcoal. Position, well-drained pots in light part of greenhouse ; no shade. Pot, March or April. Firm potting most essential. Prune straggling shoots only, moderately in Feb. or March. Water moderately Sept. to April, freely afterwards No syringing required. Admit air freely in summer. Shoots can be trained round stakes or trellis.

PROPAGATION : By cuttings of firm young shoots inserted in well-drained pots of sandy peat under bell-glass in temp. of 55° to 65°, summer.

SPECIES CULTIVATED : P. prolifera, crimson, rose, and purple, May to Sept., 3 to 4 ft., S. Africa ; prolifera Barnesii, superior form.

Phaius—Ord. Orchidaceæ. Stove terrestrial orchids. First introduced 1778. Spikes of bloom are from 2 to 4 ft. high.

CULTURE : Compost, equal parts leaf-mould, loam, and decayed cow manure. Pot, March or April. Position, well-drained pots in warm, moist part of stove during growing period ; cool and dry part during resting period. Cover drainage with layer of moss and do not allow compost to be higher than half-an-inch below rim. Water freely April to Sept., moderately Sept. to Jan., keep nearly dry Jan. to March. Temp., March to Sept. 65° to 85° ; Sept. to Jan. 60° to 70° ; Jan. to March 55° to 65°. Growing period, March to Oct ; resting period, Oct. to March. Flowers appear at base of new bulb soon after growth is completed.

PROPAGATION : By division of pseudo-bulbs, March or April.

SPECIES CULTIVATED : P. bicolor, red, white, rose, and yellow, summer, Ceylon ; Blumei, brown, white, crimson, and yellow, spring, Java ; grandifolius, yellow, brown, rose, and purple, spring, Trop. Asia and Australia ; Humbloti, rose, purple, brown, white, crimson, and yellow, summer, Madagascar ; maculatus, yellow and brown, spring, N. India ; simulans, white, rose, purple, yellow, and crimson, winter, Madagascar ; tuberculosus, yellow and purple, winter, Madagascar ; Wallichii, white, orange, purple, and yellow, winter, India.

Phalænopsis (Moth Orchid ; Indian Butterfly-plant)—Ord. Orchidaceæ. Stove evergreen epiphytal orchids. First introduced 1836.

CULTURE : Compost, sphagnum moss, charcoal, and clean potsherds. Position, shallow pans, small teak baskets, or fixed to blocks of wood suspended from roof of stove. Plant in pans or baskets or fix to blocks, Feb. to March. In fastening plants to blocks, first place layer of moss, then roots of plant, then another layer of moss, and secure firmly with copper wire. Pans to be well drained. Water daily March to Sept. ; baskets or blocks by dipping in tepid water once or twice a week Oct. to March. Moist atmosphere very essential in summer. Shade from sun. Temp., March to Oct. 75° to 85° ; Oct. to March 60° to 70°. Growing period, March to Oct. ; resting period, Oct. to March. Flowers appear in axil of leaf. Admit moderate amount of air in summer.

PROPAGATION : By division or by offsets removed from flowering stems when well rooted.

SPECIES CULTIVATED : P. amabilis, white and yellow, March to Oct., Malaya ; Aphrodite, white, yellow, and purple, summer, Philippines ; Esmeralda, rosy purple, summer, 6 in., Cochin China ; gloriosa, white and purple, summer, Sulu Archipelago ; Lowii, white and purple, summer, 4 in., Moulmein ; lueddemanniana, white and purple, various periods, 8 in., Philippines ; rosea, white, rosy purple, and brown, summer, Philippines ; sanderiana, rose, purple, white, and yellow, winter, 8 in., Philippines ; schilleriana, mauve, white, yellow, and red, spring, 1 ft., Philippines ; speciosa, purple, orange, and white, winter, 8 in., Andamans ; stuartiana, white, purple, and yellow, winter, 2 to 3 ft., Philippines ; violacea, violet, rose, and purple, summer, 8 in., Malaya. Numerous hybrids.

Phalangium elatum—See Chlorophytum.

Phalaris (Gardener's Garters ; Lady's Garters ; Ribbon Grass ; Silver Grass)— Ord. Gramineæ. Hardy annual and perennial flowering and orn. grasses. Flowers, white, green, purple, borne in panicles ; July. Leaves, green or variegated with white.

CULTURE OF ANNUAL SPECIES : Sow seeds ½ in. deep in April where required to grow. Soil, ordinary. Position, sunny.

CULTURE OF PERENNIAL SPECIES : Soil, ordinary. Position, sunny or shady borders. Plant, Oct. to April. Lift, divide, and replant every two or three years.
PROPAGATION : Perennials by seeds sown outdoors in April, transplanting seedlings following Oct. ; division of plants, Oct. to April.
ANNUAL SPECIES : P. canariensis (Canary Grass), 18 in., S. Europe.
PERENNIAL SPECIES : P. arundinacea variegata, leaves striped with silvery white, 3 to 6 ft., N. Regions.

Phaseolus (Kidney Bean ; Scarlet Runner ; Haricot Bean ; French Bean)— Ord. Leguminosæ. Stove and hardy perennials and annuals. Kidney or French Bean first introduced 1509 ; Runner Bean 1663.
CULTURE OF SNAIL FLOWER : Compost, equal parts loam and peat ; little sand. Position, well-drained pots, shoots twining round trellises, posts, or pillars. Pot, Feb. Water moderately in winter, freely in summer. Temp., Sept. to March 50° to 55° ; March to Sept. 55° to 65°.
PROPAGATION : By seeds sown in light soil in temp. 65° in March ; cuttings inserted in sandy soil under bell-glass in temp. 65° in April.
CULTURE OF KIDNEY OR FRENCH BEAN : Soil, light, rich, well manured and dryish. Position, open, sunny. Draw drills 3 in. deep and 18 in. apart. Sow seeds 4 in. apart end of April, middle of May, beginning of June, and end of July. Thin seedlings when three leaves appear to 12 in. apart, replanting thinnings to form another row or rows. Water the drills thoroughly if soil be dry before sowing the seeds. Mulch with manure when seedlings appear. Water freely in dry weather. Apply stimulants when pods form. Plants bear earlier if sown along centre of early celery ridges than if sown in open garden.
POT CULTURE : Compost, two parts good soil, one part decayed manure. Size of pots, 8 in. Put 1 in. of crocks in bottom, next a layer of half-decayed tree leaves or fresh horse droppings, then enough compost to half fill the pot. Dibble seeds ½ in. deep, 2 in. apart. Moisten with tepid water. Water moderately when seeds sprout, freely when 1 in. high. Top-dress with equal parts soil and manure when plants reach rim of pot. Apply stimulants after top-dressing has been done a fortnight. Temp., 55° to 65°. Support shoots with small twigs. No shade required. Keep close to glass.
CULTURE OF RUNNER BEANS : Soil, light, deep, well manured. Position, sunny or partially shady garden, arbour, trellis, or fences ; former best. Sow seeds first week in May 4 in. apart and 3 in. deep in drills 6 ft. asunder ; in double rows 9 in. apart and 8 ft. asunder ; in trenches 9 in. wide, 12 in. deep containing 3 in. manure and 6 in. soil, seeds being dibbled 2 in. deep, 4 in. apart in two rows 6 in. asunder. Support plants with long stakes or trellises or strands of twine when 6 in. high, or nip off point of main shoot when 2 ft. high and subsequent shoots when 6 in. long to ensure dwarf habit. Mould up those sown in drills. Mulch with manure. Water freely in dry weather, otherwise flowers will fall off. Apply stimulants freely when pods form. Suitable artificial manures : 2 lb. kainit ; 5 lb. nitrate of soda ; 9 lb. superphosphate ; 1 lb. sulphate of iron per square rod, to be applied when the plants are 3 in. high. Liquid manures : ¼ oz. nitrate of soda to a gallon ; 1 oz. guano to a gallon ; one-third horse or cow manure diluted with two-thirds water, to be applied when pods form. Quantity of seed required for a row 50 ft. long : ¼ pint of kidney beans ; 1 pint of runner beans. Seeds retain their vegetative powers for three years and germinate in ten to twelve days. French beans reach maturity fourteen weeks after sowing and runner beans sixteen weeks afterwards.
ORNAMENTAL SPECIES : P. Caracalla (Snail Flower), lilac, summer, climbing perennial, India.
CULINARY SPECIES : P. multiflorus (Scarlet Runner Bean), scarlet and white, summer, 8 to 12 ft., perennial, Mexico ; vulgaris (Kidney, French, and Haricot Bean), white and lilac, summer, 2 to 3 ft., annual, S. America.

Pheasant's-eye (*Adonis autumnalis*)—See Adonis.

Pheasant's-eye Narcissus (*Narcissus poeticus*)—See Narcissus.

Phegopteris—See Polypodium.

Phellodendron—Ord. Rutaceæ.   Hardy deciduous trees.   Handsome foliage. First introduced about 1870.
CULTURE : Soil, deep, rich loam.   Position, as specimens on lawns and in other open places.   Plant, Nov. to Feb.
PROPAGATION : By seed sown in pans in greenhouse or frame during Feb. or March or by cuttings of nearly ripe wood inserted under bell-glass in sandy soil during July.
SPECIES CULTIVATED : P. amurense, 20 to 40 ft., Amurland, Manchuria, etc. ; japonicum, 20 to 35 ft., China and Japan ; sachalinense, 30 to 50 ft., Japan, Corea, and China.

Philadelphus (Syringa ; Mock Orange)—Ord. Saxifragaceæ.   Hardy deciduous flowering shrubs.   First introduced 1596.
CULTURE : Soil, ordinary good.   Position, sunny borders or forecourts.   Plant, Oct. to Feb.   Prune immediately after flowering, thinning out shoots that have bloomed only.   Apply soap suds or liquid manure occasionally to old-established shrubs in summer.
POT CULTURE : Compost, two parts sandy loam, one part leaf-mould, and sand. Repot annually after flowering.   Position, cold greenhouse, Dec. to May, or warm greenhouse, Dec. to April ; outdoors afterwards in sunny spot ; pots plunged to rim in coal ashes or soil.   Water moderately indoors, freely outside.
PROPAGATION : By cuttings of young shoots inserted in sandy soil in temp. 55° and gentle bottom heat in April, or in close cold frame outdoors in May ; suckers or layers in spring.
SPECIES CULTIVATED : P. brachybotrys, white, June, 6 to 8 ft., China ; coronarius (Mock Orange), white, June, 10 ft., S. Europe, and its varieties foliis-aureis (golden-leaved), flore-pleno (double), and nanus (dwarf) ; Delavayi, pure white, fragrant, June, 6 to 10 ft., W. China ; Falconeri, white, June, 10 to 12 ft., hybrid ; grandi-florus, white, June, 10 to 15 ft., U. States ; gordonianus, white, June, 10 ft., N.W. America ; incanus, white, July, 5 to 7 ft., W. China ; inodorus, white, 4 to 6 ft., South-eastern U.S.A. ; insignis (Syn. P. Souv. de Billiard), white, June, 10 to 12 ft., hybrid ; Lemoinei, white, June, 5 to 7 ft., hybrid, and its variety Virginal ; Lewisi, white, June, 10 to 12 ft., Western N. America ; Magdalenæ, white, July, 5 to 6 ft., W. China ; mexicanus, yellowish white, June to July, 5 to 6 ft., Mexico, requires wall shelter ; microphyllus, white, June, 3 to 4 ft., Colorado, Arizona, etc. ; purpureo-maculatus, white and rose, June, 4 to 5 ft., hybrid ; Satsumi (Syn. P. acuminata), white, July, 6 to 8 ft., Japan ; tomentosus, creamy white, May to June, 6 to 8 ft., Himalayas ; Wilsoni, deciduous, white, borne in long bunches, June, 6 ft., China ; Zeyheri, white, June, 10 to 12 ft., Western N. America.

Philesia—Ord. Liliaceæ.   Half-hardy evergreen flowering shrub.   First intro-duced 1853.
CULTURE : Compost, equal parts peat, loam, and coarse silver sand.   Position, against walls or in pots in cold or cool greenhouse ; against walls or in sheltered nooks outdoors, S.W. of England or Ireland.   Pot or plant, Feb. to April.   Water freely March to Oct., moderately afterwards.   Syringe foliage daily in greenhouse March to Oct.   Prune directly after blooming.   Apply weak stimulants once a week May to Sept.
PROPAGATION : By cuttings inserted in sandy peat under bell-glass in greenhouse in summer ; suckers in spring.
SPECIES CULTIVATED : P. buxifolia, rosy crimson, June, 3 ft., S. Chile.

Phillyrea (Jasmine Box ; Mock Privet)—Ord. Oleaceæ.   Hardy evergreen shrubs.   Flowering and orn. foliage.   First introduced 1597.   Leaves, lance- or egg-shaped, dark green.
CULTURE : Soil, ordinary.   Position, sunny borders ; sheltered corners N. England. Plant, Sept. to April.   Prune straggly shoots only in April.
PROPAGATION : By cuttings of firm shoots inserted in sandy soil in cold frame in Sept. ; grafting on common privet in March.
SPECIES CULTIVATED : P. angustifolia, white, May, 8 to 10 ft., Mediterranean Region ;

angustifolia rosmarinifolia, rosemary-leaved ; decora, white, May, 8 to 10 ft., Lazistan ; latifolia, white, May, 20 ft., Mediterranean Region ; latifolia ilicifolia, holly-leaved ; media, white, May, 10 to 20 ft., Mediterranean Region ; media buxifolia, box-leaved.

Philodendron—Ord. Aroideæ. Stove evergreen dwarf or climbing plants. Orn. foliage. First introduced 1759. Leaves, heart-, egg- or arrow-shaped, oblong. CULTURE : Compost, equal parts peat, leaf-mould, loam, and silver sand. Pot or plant, Jan. to April. Position, dwarf kinds in pots ; tall ones in beds or borders, with shoots trained up walls or pillars. Water freely all the year round. Syringe daily. Temp., March to Sept. 70° to 80° ; Sept. to March 65° to 70°. PROPAGATION : By cuttings of stems inserted in light soil in temp. 75° at any time. SPECIES CULTIVATED : P. andreanum, climber, spathe black, purple, and creamy white, Colombia ; Devansayeanum, leaves deep red, climbing, Peru ; gloriosum, leaves green, white, and pink, climbing, Colombia ; giganteum, broadly heart-shaped leaves, climbing, W. Indies ; verrucosum (Syn. Lindenii), dwarf, Colombia. Many other species of little interest.

Phlebodium—See Polypodium aureum.

Phlomis (Jerusalem Sage)—Ord. Labiatæ. Hardy perennials and evergreen shrubs. First introduced 1596. CULTURE OF PERENNIAL SPECIES : Soil, ordinary. Position, sunny beds, borders, rockeries, or banks. Plant, Oct. to April. Lift, divide, and replant every three years. CULTURE OF SHRUBBY SPECIES : Soil, good ordinary or sandy loam. Position, sunny well-drained borders or rockeries. Plant, Oct. to April. Mulch with decayed manure in March. PROPAGATION : By seeds sown in light soil in warm greenhouse in March or sunny spot outdoors in April ; herbaceous kinds also by division, Oct. or March ; shrubs by cuttings inserted in cold frame in Aug. PERENNIAL SPECIES : P. cashmeriana, lilac, July, 2 ft., Himalayas ; Herba-venti, purple and violet, summer, 12 to 18 in., S. Europe ; Samia, yellow and orange, May to Aug., 2 to 3 ft., N. Africa ; tuberosa, rose-purple, June, 3 to 5 ft., S. Europe and Asia Minor ; viscosa (Syn. P. russelliana), golden yellow, June, 2 to 3 ft., Syria. SHRUBBY SPECIES : P. fruticosa (Jerusalem Sage), yellow, June, 3 to 4 ft., S. Europe.

Phlox—Ord. Polemoniaceæ. Hardy and half-hardy annual and perennial herbs. First introduced 1725. Phloxes for garden cultivation are divided into four classes, viz., Alpines, Early-flowering or Tall, Late-flowering (tall), and Annual. CULTURE OF ALPINE SPECIES : Soil, deep, rich, sandy loam containing a little leaf-mould or peat. Position, masses on, or as edgings to, sunny borders, or on ledges of rockeries. Plant, March to May. Lift and divide only when grown too large for the position they occupy ; March. POT CULTURE OF ALPINES : Compost, two parts sandy loam, one part leaf-mould, and half a part sand. Pot, March. Position, cold frame or greenhouse. Water moderately Oct. to April, freely other times. Admit air freely always. CULTURE OF EARLY- AND LATE-FLOWERING KINDS : Soil, deep, rich, moderately heavy loam ; light soils not suitable. Position, sunny or partially shaded borders ; former preferable. Plant, Oct., Nov., Feb., or March. Mulch liberally with decayed manure in March or April. Apply liquid manure frequently May to Sept. Water freely in dry weather. Cut down stems in Oct. Lift, divide, and replant in fresh rich soil triennially. POT CULTURE : Compost, two parts turfy loam, one part leaf-mould or rotten cow manure, and one part coarse sand. Position, cold, partially shaded greenhouse in summer ; cold frame in winter. Pot, March. Water freely April to Oct., very little afterwards. Apply stimulants once a week May to Sept. CULTURE OF ANNUAL SPECIES : Sow seeds $\frac{1}{16}$ in. deep in light soil in box, pan, or pot in temp. 55° to 65°, March. Transplant seedlings 2 in. apart in boxes or pots, gradually harden off and plant outdoors, 6 in. apart, in rich soil, in sunny position, in June. Nip off point of main shoot after planting to induce bushy growth. Water freely in dry weather. Mulch with manure or cocoanut-fibre refuse.

POT CULTURE : Compost, two parts loam, one part decayed manure or leaf-mould, and little sand. Plant four seedlings in 5 in. pot in April. Keep in temp. 55° until June, then place in cold frame or on outside window sill. Water freely. Apply stimulants when 3 in. high. Nip off points of shoots when 3 in. high. No repotting required.

PROPAGATION : Early and late kinds by seeds sown $\frac{1}{16}$ in. deep in sandy soil in temp. 55° in autumn or spring ; by cuttings of shoots obtained from base of old plants inserted in sandy soil in temp. 55° in March ; by division of plants in Oct. or March ; by cuttings of shoots covered $\frac{1}{4}$ in. of soil in temp. 55° in March or April. Alpines by cuttings of shoots inserted in sandy soil in cold frame in July ; division in March or April.

ALPINE SPECIES : P. amœna, rose, May to June, 6 in., N. America ; divaricata (Syn. P. canadensis), lavender blue, May, 1 ft., N. America, and its varieties alba (white) and Laphami (blue violet) ; Douglasii, lilac, May to June, 2 to 4 in., Rocky Mountains ; ovata, rose, 1 ft., May to Aug., N. America ; pilosa, purplish rose, May to Aug., 1 to 1½ ft., N. America ; procumbens, lilac blue, June, 6 in., hybrid ; Stellaria, pale blue, June, 6 in., Illinois ; stolonifera (Syn. P. reptans), purple, May to June, 8 to 12 in., N. America ; subulata (Moss Pink), purple or white, May, 6 in., U. States. Frondosa (pink), Nelsonii (white), and setacea (rosy pink) are varieties of the last species.

TALL PERENNIAL SPECIES : P. glaberrima, red, May to June, 1 to 2 ft., N. America, and its variety suffruticosa, rose, spring, 1 to 2 ft., U. States, parent of the early-flowering phloxes ; maculata (Wild Sweet William), purple, July, fragrant, 2 ft., N. America, one of the parents of the late flowering phloxes ; paniculata (Syn. P. decussata), purple and white, Aug., fragrant, 3 to 4 ft., U. States, another parent of late-flowering phloxes. Phlox Arendsii is a hybrid between P. divaricata and P. paniculata, the plants being from 1 to 2 ft. in height and bearing flowers in various shades of mauve and violet from June till Aug.

ANNUAL SPECIES : P. Drummondii, various colours, summer, 1 ft., Texas, and its varieties cuspidata (pointed petals), grandiflora (large-flowered), and nana (dwarf).

Phœnix (Date Palm)—Ord. Palmaceæ. Stove palms. Orn. foliage. First introduced 1597. Leaves, feather-shaped, green.

CULTURE : Compost, three parts good fibrous loam, one part old cow manure, and a little coarse sand. Position, well-drained pots or tubs in sunny part of stove. Pot, Feb. or March. Water moderately Oct. to March, copiously March to Oct. Syringe foliage morning and evening daily April to Sept., morning only Sept. to April. Apply weak stimulants occasionally May to Sept. Place a lump of sulphate of iron on surface of soil occasionally to keep foliage of a rich, healthy green hue. Temp., March to Sept. 65° to 75° ; Sept. to March 55° to 65°.

PROPAGATION : By seeds sown 1 in. deep in light, sandy soil under bell-glass or in propagator in temp. 75°, March or April.

SPECIES CULTIVATED : P. acaulis, 8 to 12 ft., India ; canariensis, 30 to 40 ft., Canary Isles ; dactylifera (Date Palm), 80 to 100 ft., N. Africa ; humilis, 3 to 6 ft., India ; reclinata, 25 to 35 ft., S. Africa ; Rœbeleni, 4 to 6 ft., S.E. Asia ; rupicola, 15 to 20 ft., Himalayas ; sylvestris, 30 to 40 ft., India.

Phormium (Common Flax Lily ; New Zealand Flax)—Ord. Liliaceæ. Half-hardy perennial herbs. First introduced 1798.

INDOOR CULTURE : Compost, two parts turfy loam, one part each of leaf-mould and sand. Position, pots, tubs, or beds in cold or warm greenhouse, conservatory, balcony, or dwelling-room. Pot, Feb. to April. Water copiously April to Oct., moderately afterwards. May be stood outdoors in sunny position June to Sept.

OUTDOOR CULTURE : Soil, light, deep loam. Position, margins of ponds or streams, isolated specimens on lawns, or in beds or borders S. and S.W. of England and Ireland only. In other districts plants must be put out in May, lifted in Oct., and stored in greenhouse until following May. Plant permanently in April or May. Water freely in dry weather. Protect those left outdoors all winter with straw or dried fern.

PROPAGATION : By seeds sown ⅛ in. deep in pots of sandy soil in greenhouse or frame in March ; by division of roots in April.

SPECIES CULTIVATED : P. cookianum (Syn. P. Colensoi), yellow and green, summer, 4 to 6 ft., New Zealand ; Hookeri, green, summer, 5 ft., New Zealand ; tenax, yellow, summer, 10 to 15 ft., New Zealand, and its varieties purpureum (leaves purple), variegatum (leaves yellow, green, and white), and Veitchii (leaves creamy white).

Photinia (Chinese Hawthorn)—Ord. Rosaceæ. Half-hardy evergreen and deciduous flowering shrubs. First introduced 1796.

INDOOR CULTURE : Soil, two parts sandy loam, one part leaf-mould. Position, beds against back wall of cold or slightly heated sunny greenhouse. Plant, Oct. or April. Water moderately Sept. to April, freely afterwards. Syringe daily May to Sept. Prune straggling shoots in April.

OUTDOOR CULTURE : Soil, light, deep loam. Position, against south walls S. and S.W. of England and Ireland only. Plant, Sept. to Nov., April, or May. Prune, April. Protect in severe weather with mats or straw hurdles.

PROPAGATION : By seeds sown ⅛ in. deep in pots of light soil in cold greenhouse or frame, spring or autumn ; cuttings of firm shoots inserted in sandy soil in cold frame or greenhouse, Aug. ; layering in Oct. ; grafting on common quince in March ; budding on hawthorn in July.

SPECIES CULTIVATED : P. Davidsonæ, white, 20 to 45 ft., evergreen, W. China ; serrulata (Chinese Hawthorn), white, spring, 15 ft., evergreen, China ; villosa (Syn. P. variabilis), white, May, 10 to 15 ft., deciduous, Japan, China, and Corea. See also Eriobotrya and Heteromeles.

Phrynium variegatum—See Maranta arundinacea variegata.

Phuopsis stylosa—See Crucianella stylosa.

Phygelius (Cape Fig-wort)—Ord. Scrophulariaceæ. Half-hardy herbaceous perennial. First introduced 1855.

CULTURE : Soil, light, rich, ordinary. Position, sunny well-drained border at base of south wall S. and W. of England and Ireland only. Plant, March or April. Protect in winter by covering of ashes or dry fern fronds placed around base of stem. Lift, divide, and replant every three or four years.

PROPAGATION : By seeds sown 1/16 in. deep in shallow pans or boxes filled with light, rich soil and placed in a temp. of 55° to 65°, Feb. or March, transplanting seedlings outdoors May or June ; by cuttings of ripened shoots inserted in pots in propagator in greenhouse or cold frame in July or Aug. ; division of roots, March or April.

SPECIES CULTIVATED : P. capensis, orange-scarlet, summer, 3 ft., S. Africa.

Phyllagathis—Ord. Melastomaceæ. Stove flowering subshrub.

CULTURE : Compost, equal parts peat and sand with a little leaf-mould. Position, well-drained pots in heated greenhouse. Water abundantly during growing season. Moderately at other times. Moist atmosphere essential during summer months. Temp., March to Sept. 75° to 85° ; Sept. to March 65° to 70°.

PROPAGATION : By leaf cuttings inserted in sandy compost in temp. 85° and brisk bottom heat.

SPECIES CULTIVATED : P. rotundifolia, pink flowers surrounded by deep purple bracts, July, leaves large, glossy green tinged metallic blue and purple, red beneath, 1 to 2 ft., Sumatra.

Phyllanthus—Ord. Euphorbiaceæ. Stove orn.-foliaged plants. First introduced 1699. Leaves, oval or oblong, small, variegated with purple, white, yellow.

CULTURE : Compost, equal parts sandy loam and fibry peat, one part equal proportions of charcoal, dried cow manure, powdered brick, and coarse silver sand. Position, well-drained pots in shady part of stove. Pot, Feb. or March. Water moderately Oct. to March, freely afterwards. Syringe morning and evening, April to Sept. Prune into shape, Jan. Temp., Sept. to March 60° to 65° ; March to Sept. 70° to 80°.

PROPAGATION : By cuttings of firm shoots, 2 to 3 in. long, inserted singly in small pots of sandy soil under propagator or bell-glass in temp. 75°, spring or summer.

SPECIES CULTIVATED : P. angustifolius, reddish, July, 8 to 10 ft., Jamaica ;

atropurpureus, leaves purplish, 6 to 8 ft., Commoro Isles ; distichus (Otaheite Gooseberry), yellow, 15 to 20 ft., Trop. Asia ; Emblica (Syn. P. mimosæfolius), yellow,
mimosa-like foliage, 20 to 30 ft., Trop. Asia ; nivosus (Syn. Breynia nivosa).
greenish, leaves green and white, 6 to 10 ft., South Sea Islands ; pulcher (Syn.
Reidia glaucescens), yellow, summer, leaves green, 3 to 4 ft., Malaya, a pretty table
plant ; speciosus, white, Sept., 15 to 20 ft., Jamaica.

Phyllocactus—Ord. Cactaceæ.   Greenhouse fleshy-stemmed plants with no
leaves.   First introduced 1710.
CULTURE : Compost, two parts light fibrous loam, one part of equal proportions
of dried cow dung, leaf-mould, brick rubble, and silver sand.   Position, well-
drained pots close to glass in warm greenhouse or sunny window, Sept. to July ;
outdoors fully exposed to the sun, July to Sept.   Pot, April.   Repot every three
years only.   Firm potting and good drainage essential.   Water freely May to Oct.,
keep nearly dry Oct. to May .   Apply weak stimulants to plants that have been potted
a year, once a week, May to Sept.   Syringe plants daily May to Sept.   Shade from
sun for a few weeks after repotting, also for a short time after removal to open air.
Temp., Oct. to April 50° to 55° ; April to Oct. 60° to 75°.
PROPAGATION : By seeds sown ⅛ in. deep in light soil in pan or shallow box placed
in temp. 65° to 75° in spring ; by cuttings of stems dried in the sun for a day or
two, then inserted singly in 2 in. pots filled with light, sandy soil, and placed on
sunny shelf in greenhouse, April to Sept.
SPECIES CULTIVATED : P. Ackermanni, crimson, summer, 3 to 4 ft., Mexico ;
anguliger, yellow, fragrant, autumn, 1 to 2 ft., Mexico ; crenatus, white, fragrant,
summer, Honduras ; grandis, white, fragrant, 2 to 3 ft., Honduras ; Hookeri,
white, fragrant, summer, 2 to 3 ft., Brazil ; latifrons, creamy white, summer, 6 to
8 ft., Mexico ; phyllanthoides, rose and white, summer, 1 to 2 ft., Mexico.   Also
numerous hybrids and seedlings.

Phyllodoce—Ord. Ericaceæ.   Dwarf hardy evergreen shrubs.
CULTURE : Soil, sandy peat.   Position, cool, well-watered spots in the rock garden,
Plant, Sept. to Oct. and April to May.
PROPAGATION : By seeds, cuttings of nearly ripened shoots in July and Aug., or by
layers in spring.
SPECIES CULTIVATED : P. Breweri, purplish rose, May, 6 to 12 in., California ;
cærulea, bluish purple, June to July, 6 to 9 in., Europe, Asia, and N. America ;
empetriformis, reddish purple, April, 6 to 9 in., Western N. America ; nipponica
(Syn. P. amabilis), white and pink, May, 4 to 8 in., Japan.   Some of these were
formerly known as Menziesia.

Phyllostachys (Whangee Cane)—Ord. Gramineæ.   Half-hardy orn.-foliaged
grasses.   Nat. China and Japan.   Ht., 4 to 12 ft.   Inflorescence borne in panicles ;
summer.   Foliage, narrow, lance-shaped, green.   Habit of growth, graceful.
CULTURE : Soil, rich, deep, sandy loam.   Position, moist, sheltered borders S. and W.
of England and Ireland only.   Protect in winter with thick covering of dry fern
fronds or litter in autumn.   Plant, April or May.
PROPAGATION : By division of plants in March or April.
SPECIES CULTIVATED : P. aurea (Syn. Bambusa aurea), stems yellow, leaves green,
10 to 15 ft. ; Castillonis (Syn. Bambusa Castillonis), stems yellow, leaves green and
creamy, 8 to 10 ft. ; flexuosa, leaves dark green, 6 to 8 ft. ; Henonis (Syn. P.
puberula), leaves dark green, 12 to 14 ft. ; mitis (Syn. Bambusa mitis), leaves green,
15 to 20 ft. ; nigra (Syn. Bambusa nigra), leaves green, stems black, 10 to 20 ft. ;
Quilioi, leaves bright green, 10 to 18 ft., and its variety marliacea (Syn. Bambusa
marliacea) ; ruscifolia (Syn. P. Kumasaca), leaves dark green, 1 to 2 ft. ; viridi-
glaucescens (Syn. Bambusa viridi-glaucescens), leaves green, stems yellowish,
14 to 18 ft.

Phyllotænium—See Xanthosoma.

Phymatodes—See Polypodium.

Physalis (Ground or Winter Cherry ; Red Winter Cherry ; Cape Gooseberry ;
Peruvian Cape Gooseberry)—Ord. Solanaceæ.   Greenhouse and hardy perennial

Polygonatum officinale
(Solomon's Seal)

Polygonum sachalinense
(Knot Weed)

Polypodium aureum
(Polypody)

Portulaca grandiflora
(Sun Plant)

Potentilla nepalensis
(Cinquefoil)

Poterium canadense
(Burnet)

Primula denticulata

Primula malacoides

Primula Parryi

Primula sinensis

Prostanthera lasianthos

Prunella grandiflora
(Selfheal)

Prunus spinosa purpurea

Prunus subhirtella autumnalis

Prunus triloba flore-pleno

Pyracantha Lalandei
(Fire Thorn)

Pyrus Scheideckeri

Quercus Mirbeckii
(Oak)

herbs. Fruit of Cape Gooseberry edible—a berry enclosed in an inflated calyx.
CULTURE OF HARDY SPECIES : Soil, rich. Position, sunny well-drained border. Plant, March or April. Lift, divide, and replant in fresh soil every third year. Gather stems bearing fruits in Sept. and dry for winter decorations.
CULTURE OF GREENHOUSE SPECIES : Soil, two parts loam, one part well-decayed manure or leaf-mould, and little sand. Position, singly in 5 or 6 in. pots, with shoots trained to sticks and placed close to front of sunny greenhouse, or planted in small beds and shoots trained up back wall. Pot or plant, Feb. or March. Water freely April to Sept., moderately afterwards. Apply weak stimulants once or twice a week May to Sept. Gather fruit when ripe and fully coloured.
PROPAGATION : Hardy species by seeds sown in sunny spot outdoors in April ; by division of roots in March or April. Greenhouse species by seeds sown $\frac{1}{16}$ in. deep in shallow pots or pans of light soil and placed in temp. 65° to 75°, Feb. or March ; cuttings inserted singly in pots of light, sandy soil placed in propagator or under bell-glass in temp. 65° to 75°, Jan. to April.
HARDY SPECIES : P. Alkekengi (Bladder Herb or Winter Cherry), white, summer, fruit scarlet, 1 to 2 ft., Europe ; Franchetti, white, summer, fruit red, 1½ to 2½ ft., Japan. P. Bunyardi is a fine hybrid growing to a height of 3 ft.
GREENHOUSE SPECIES : P. peruviana (Cape Gooseberry), Syn. P. edulis, white, summer, fruit purplish, 3 ft., Tropics.

Physianthus—See Araujia sericofera.

Physostegia (False Dragon-head)—Ord. Labiatæ. Hardy herbaceous perennials. First introduced 1683.
CULTURE : Soil, light ordinary. Position, cool, partially shaded borders. Plant, Oct., Nov., March, or April.
PROPAGATION : By seeds sown ⅛ in. deep in light, sandy soil outdoors in April ; cuttings of young shoots inserted in light, sandy soil under hand-light or in cold frame, April or May ; division of roots, Oct., Nov., or May.
SPECIES CULTIVATED : P. virginiana (Syn. Dracocephalum virginianum), rosy pink, June to Sept., 1 to 4 ft., N. America.

Phyteuma (Horned Rampion)—Ord. Campanulaceæ. Hardy perennial herbs.
CULTURE : Soil, deep, rich loam mixed with limestone grit and old mortar and leaf-mould or peat. Position, sunny rockeries for dwarf species ; sunny borders for tall kinds. Plant, March or April. Lift, divide, and replant only when overgrown. Top-dress dwarf species with a mixture of peat, leaf-mould, lime, and a little old mortar annually in Feb. or March. Water freely in dry weather.
PROPAGATION : By seeds sown in light, sandy soil in shallow boxes in cold frame, Sept. or Oct. ; transplanting seedlings in permanent positions, April or May ; division of plants in March or April.
SPECIES CULTIVATED : P. comosum, amethyst blue, July, 3 to 4 in., S. Europe ; Halleri, violet, May to July, 6 to 12 in., Europe ; hemisphæricum, blue, June to July, 3 to 4 in., Alps ; orbiculare (Horned Rampion), blue, July, 6 to 12 in., Europe (Britain) ; Michelii, blue, summer, 1 to 2 ft., Europe ; Scheuchzeri, blue, summer, 1 ft., Europe ; serratum, blue, summer, 2 to 3 in., Corsica ; Sieberi, blue, summer, 6 to 8 in., Europe ; spicatum, cream, summer, 3 to 4 ft., Europe.

Phytolacca (Virginian Poke ; Red-ink Plant ; Pigeon-berry)—Ord: Phytolaccaceæ. Hardy herbaceous perennials. First introduced 1768. Flowers succeeded by deep purple berries in autumn. Leaves, broad, ovate, dark green, changing to rich purple in autumn.
CULTURE : Soil, good ordinary. Position, sunny or shady borders in woodlands, banks, or ferneries. Plant, Oct., Nov., March, or April.
PROPAGATION : By seed sown ⅛ in. deep in sandy soil outdoors in spring or autumn ; division of plants in Oct. or March.
SPECIES CULTIVATED : P. acinosa (Indian Poke), white, summer, 5 ft., Himalayas ; decandra (Virginian Poke), white, summer, 5 ft , N. America.

M   333

Picea (Norway Spruce; Black Spruce)—Ord. Coniferæ. Hardy evergreen trees. First introduced 1700. Orn. foliage. Leaves, needle-shaped, spirally scattered. Cones, erect, cylindrical, thin-scaled. Timber, white, soft, fine-grained; used for sleepers, pit wood, headings for barrels, packing cases, etc.
CULTURE : Soil, deep, rich, sandy loam. Position, high, dry, open lawns or shrubberies away from sea coast; Norway Spruce as a shelter hedge for fruit plantations, or as nurses to larch and forest trees. Plant, Oct. to April. No pruning required.
PROPAGATION : By seeds sown ⅛ in. deep in sandy loam in temp. of 55° in March or outdoors in April; cuttings inserted in sandy soil in cold frame or in pots under bell-glass or hand-light outdoors, Aug. or Sept.; layering shoots or branches in autumn; inarching or grafting in March. Quantity of seeds to sow bed 100 ft. square, 3½ oz.
SPECIES CULTIVATED : P. ajanensis, 70 to 80 ft., Japan; alba (Syn. Abies canadensis), 60 to 100 ft., N.E. America; alcockiana, 40 to 80 ft., Japan; breweriana, 70 to 100 ft., California; Engelmannii, 80 to 100 ft., Western N. America; excelsa (Syns. Abies Picea and Pinus Abies), Common Spruce, 100 to 120 ft., N. Europe, and its varieties clanbrassiliana (very dwarf), Cranstoni (snake-like branches), dumosa (dwarf), eremita (stiff habit), gregoryana (dwarf, rounded habit), inverta (pendulous), and stricta (erect, spire-like); hondœnsis, 60 to 80 ft., Japan; morinda (Syn. P. smithiana), 80 to 100 ft., Himalayas; morindoides, 150 to 200 ft., Himalayas; nigra (Black Spruce), 20 to 50 ft., N.E. America; Omorika, 70 to 100 ft., Servia and Bosnia; orientalis, 70 to 100 ft., Caucasus; polita (Tiger Tail Spruce), 40 to 80 ft., Japan; pungens (Syns. P. parryana and P. commutata), 80 to 100 ft., Colorado, New Mexico, etc., and its varieties glauca (Blue Spruce) and kosteriana (Syn. pendula), branchlets drooping; sitchensis, 100 to 150 ft., Western N. America.

Pickerel-weed (*Pontederia cordata*)—See Pontederia.

Picotee (*Dianthus caryophyllus* var.)—See Dianthus.

Pieris—Ord. Ericaceæ. Hardy evergreen flowering shrubs. First introduced 1736.
OUTDOOR CULTURE : Soil, equal parts peat, leaf-mould, and silver sand. Position, open, sheltered borders, rockeries, or bogs. Plant, Sept. to Nov., or March. Prune straggling shoots only moderately after flowering. Water freely in dry positions during summer.
POT CULTURE : Soil, equal parts peat, leaf-mould, and fine silver sand. Position, well-drained pots in cold greenhouse, Nov. to June; in shady position outdoors, June to Nov. Pot, Oct. or Nov. Water moderately Nov. to March, freely afterwards.
PROPAGATION : By seeds sown 1/16 in. deep in sandy peat in cold frame, Nov. or March; layering shoots in Sept.; division of plants, Oct. or Nov.
SPECIES CULTIVATED : P. floribunda, white, spring, 4 to 6 ft., Virginia; formosa, white, spring, 8 to 12 ft., Himalayas; japonica, white, spring, 9 to 10 ft., Japan; japonica variegata, variegated; mariana, white and red, June, 3 to 4 ft., Eastern U.S.A.; nitida, white and red, June to July, 5 to 7 ft., South-east U.S.A. The species above mentioned formerly belonged to the genera Andromeda and Zenobia.

Pigeon-berry (*Phytolacca decandra*)—See Phytolacca.

Pigmy Daffodil (*Narcissus minimus*)—See Narcissus.

Pigmy Sun-flower (*Actinella grandiflora*)—See Actinella.

Pigmy Water Lily (*Nymphæa pygmæa*)—See Nymphæa.

Pig Nut (*Carya Porcina*)—See Carya.

Pilea (Artillery or Pistol Plant; Stingless Nettle)—Ord. Urticaceæ. Stove perennial herbs. Orn. foliage. First introduced 1793. Flowers, insignificant; unexpanded buds burst when in contact with moisture and discharge pollen.
CULTURE : Compost, equal parts loam, leaf-mould, and silver sand. Position, small pots in partially shaded part of stove. Pot, Feb. to April. Water freely April to Sept., moderately afterwards. Temp., Sept. to March 55° to 65°; March to Sept. 70° to 80°.

PROPAGATION : By seeds sown on surface of light, sandy soil slightly covered with fine mould and placed in temp. 65° to 75° in spring ; cuttings inserted singly in small well-drained pots of sandy soil in temp. 65° to 75°, Jan. to May ; division of plants, Feb. or March.

SPECIES CULTIVATED : P. muscosa (Syn. P. microphylla), 3 to 15 in., W. Indies.

Pilocereus—See Cereus.

Pilumna—See Trichopilia.

Pimelea (Rice-flower)—Ord. Thymeæaceæ. Greenhouse evergreen flowering shrubs. First introduced 1793.

CULTURE : Compost, three parts fibrous peat, one part turfy loam, half a part silver sand. Position, well-drained pots in light, airy greenhouse. Prune moderately close immediately after flowering. Pot soon as new growth commences. Firm potting essential. Nip off points of shoots of young plants occasionally to induce bushy growth. Water freely April to Oct., moderately afterwards. Grow in a moist atmosphere for a few weeks after potting, then gradually harden off and place in an airy greenhouse. Temp., Sept. to March 40° to 50°; March to Sept. 55° to 65°.

PROPAGATION : By seeds sown 1/16 in. deep in light, sandy soil under bell-glass in temp. 55° to 65°, Feb. to May ; cuttings of young shoots, 2 in. long, inserted in compost of one part peat, two parts silver sand, under bell-glass, in temp. 55° to 65°, March or April.

SPECIES CULTIVATED : P. ferruginea (Syn. P. decussata), rose, May, 2 ft., Australia ; ligustrina (Syn. hypericina), white, May, 5 to 6 ft., Australia ; spectabilis, white and pink, May, 4 ft., Australia.

Pimenta (Allspice ; Wild Clove ; Pimento Bush)—Ord. Myrtaceæ. Stove evergreen flowering trees. First introduced 1759. Leaves and berries aromatic.

CULTURE : Compost, two parts sandy loam, one part leaf-mould, and one part sand. Position, well-drained pots or beds with branches trained to wall. Pot, Feb. or March. Water moderately Oct. to April, freely afterwards. Syringe April to Aug. Prune straggling shoots moderately in March. Temp., Sept. to March 60° to 65° ; March to Sept. 65° to 75°.

PROPAGATION : By cuttings of firm shoots inserted in sandy soil under bell-glass in temp. 65° to 75° in summer.

SPECIES CULTIVATED : P. acris (Wild Clove), white and pink, May, 20 to 30 ft., W. Indies ; officinalis (Allspice), white, summer, 20 to 40 ft., W. Indies.

Pimento Bush (*Pimenta officinalis*)—See Pimenta.

Pimpernel—See Anagallis.

Pimpinella (Anise)—Ord. Umbelliferæ. Hardy annual herb. Seeds used as a condiment.

CULTURE : Soil, well-drained, ordinary. Position, warm beds or borders. Sow seeds thinly in April where plants are to remain.

SPECIES CULTIVATED : P. Anisum, to 2 ft., Greece to Egypt.

Pinanga—Ord. Palmaceæ. Stove palms. Orn. foliage. First introduced 1848. Leaves, feather-shaped, green.

CULTURE : Compost, one part loam, two parts peat, half a part silver sand. Position, well-drained pots in shady, lofty stove. Pot, Feb. or March. Water copiously March to Oct., moderately afterwards. Syringe twice daily March to Sept., once daily afterwards. Place few crystals of sulphate of iron on surface of soil occasionally to insure deep green foliage. Temp., March to Oct. 75° to 85° ; Oct. to March 55° to 65°.

PROPAGATION : By seeds sown ½ in. deep singly in 2 in. pots of sandy loam and peat under bell-glass in temp. 75° to 85° in spring.

SPECIES CULTIVATED : P. disticha, 6 ft., Malaya ; maculata, 10 to 12 ft., Philippines.

Pincushion-flower (*Scabiosa atropurpurea*)—See Scabiosa.

Pine-apple (*Ananas sativa*)—See Ananas.

Pine-apple Flower (*Eucomis punctata*)—See Eucomis.

Pine-apple-scented Sage (*Salvia rutilans*)—See Salvia.

Pine Barren Beauty (*Pyxidanthera barbulata*)—See Pyxidanthera.

Pine Strawberry (*Fragaria chilænsis*)—See Fragaria.

Pine-tree—See Pinus.

Pinguicula (Butter-wort ; Bog Violet)—Ord. Lentibulariaceæ. Greenhouse and hardy perennial herbs. Plants belonging to the insectivorous class.

CULTURE OF GREENHOUSE SPECIES : Compost, equal parts fibrous peat, sphagnum moss, and clean crocks. Position, well-drained pots or shallow pans placed on inverted pots in saucer of water under bell-glass or hand-light in shade. Pot, March or April. Water freely April to Sept., moderately afterwards. Admit air for a few minutes daily every morning by tilting bell-glass or hand-light. Temp., March to Oct. 55° to 65° ; Oct. to March 45° to 55°.

CULTURE OF HARDY SPECIES : Soil, rich loam for P. grandiflora ; peat and rough gravel for P. alpina ; moist peat or peaty loam for P. vulgaris. Plant, March or April. Water freely in dry positions in summer. Mulch with thick layer of cocoanut-fibre refuse in May.

PROPAGATION : By seeds sown on surface of shallow pans filled with equal parts of sphagnum moss, peat, and sand, placed under bell-glass, and kept moist in temp. of 55° to 65°, Feb., March, or April ; division of plants at potting or planting time.

GREENHOUSE SPECIES : P. caudata, carmine, autumn, 6 in., Mexico.

HARDY SPECIES : P. alpina, white and yellow, May, 4 in., Europe (Britain) ; grandiflora, blue and violet, summer, 4 in., Europe (Britain) ; vulgaris (Bog Violet), violet, summer, 4 to 6 in., Britain.

Pink (*Dianthus plumarius*)—See Dianthus.

Pin Oak (*Quercus palustris*)—See Quercus.

Pinus (Fir ; Deal ; Pine Tree)—Ord. Coniferæ. Hardy orn.-leaved trees. Evergreen. Habit, free and picturesque. Leaves, needle-like, two to five in a whorl. Cones, conical and erect.

CULTURE : Soil and position, P. austriaca, Laricio, montana, and Pinaster suitable for seaside gardens and ordinary soil : P. austriaca a good town tree ; P. austriaca, cembra, excelsa, Laricio, Pinaster, strobus, and sylvestris suitable for chalky soils ; P. austriaca, halepensis, Laricio, Pinaster, pumilo, and sylvestris adapted for gravelly or sandy soils ; others in good ordinary soil. P. austriaca good shelter tree. P. sylvestris will grow in the poorest soils and on rocky slopes. Plant, Sept. to Nov. For shelter purposes plant 10 to 15 ft. apart.

PROPAGATION : By seeds sown ½ in. deep in pots filled with sandy loam, placed in cold greenhouse or frame in April, and transplanting seedlings outdoors following spring ; or ¼ in. deep outdoors in April in bed of moist, sandy soil, transplanting seedlings the next year ; grafting on common species in April.

USEFUL FACTS : Average age, 150 years. Timber reaches maturity at 80 years. Weight per cubic ft., 30 lb. Timber, close-grained and resinous ; used in young state for props, staves, etc. ; when matured for deal flooring, etc. Seeds ripe in Nov. One pound of seed will yield about 8000 plants.

SPECIES CULTIVATED : P. Armandi, 50 to 60 ft., W. China ; Ayacahuite, 60 to 100 ft., Mexico ; balfouriana, 20 to 50 ft., California ; bungeana (Lace Bark Pine), 70 ft., N. China ; cembra (Stone Pine), 60 to 100 ft., Central Europe ; Coulteri, 50 to 70 ft., California ; densiflora (Japanese Red Pine), 100 to 120 ft., Japan ; edulis, 20 to 30 ft., Rocky Mountains, seeds edible ; excelsa (Bhotan Pine), 100 to 150 ft., Himalayas ; flexilis, 40 to 80 ft., N.W. America ; halepensis (Jerusalem Pine), 50 ft., Mediterranean Region ; lambertiana, 70 to 200 ft., N.W. America ; Laricio (Corsican Pine), 100 to 150 ft., S. Europe ; Laricio nigricans (Syn. P. austriaca), (Black Pine), 70 to 100 ft., N. Europe ; montana pumilio (Mountain Pine), 5 to 10 ft., Europe, and its variety Mughus ; montana uncinata, 60 to 80 ft., France and Spain ; Montezumæ, 50 to 70 ft., Mexico, only hardy in Cornwall and similar mild districts ; muricata, 50 to 90 ft., California ; parviflora, 30 to 40 ft., Japan, and its variety pentaphylla ; Peuke, 50 to 100 ft., Macedonia ; Pinaster (Cluster Pine), 100 to 120 ft., Mediterranean Region ; pinea (The Umbrella Pine), 40 to 100 ft., Mediterranean Region ; ponderosa, 100 to 150 ft., N.W. America ; radiata (Monterey Pine), Syn. P. insignis, 100 to 120 ft., California ; strobus (Weymouth Pine), 60 to 100 ft., N.E. America ; sylvestris (Scotch Fir), 50 to 100 ft., N. Europe (Britain), and its dwarf varieties beuvronensis and globosa ; Thunbergi (Black Pine), 80 to 100 ft., Japan, frequently erroneously named P. massoniana.

Pinxter-flower (*Rhododendron nudiflorum*)—See Rhododendron.

Piper (Pepper Plant)—Piperaceæ. Stove and greenhouse evergreen shrubs. Orn. foliage. First introduced 1748. Leaves, large, green, or purple, marbled or blotched with white or bronze.
CULTURE OF STOVE SPECIES : Compost, two parts loam, one part leaf-mould, half a part sand. Position, well-drained pots in shade. Pot, Feb. to April. Prune slightly into shape, Feb. Water freely April to Oct., moderately afterwards. Syringe twice daily April to Sept., once daily afterwards. Temp., March to Oct. 75° to 85° ; Oct. to March 55° to 65°.
CULTURE OF GREENHOUSE SPECIES : Compost, as for stove species. Position, well-drained pots in partial shade. Pot, March or April. Water moderately Oct. to April, freely afterwards. Temp., March to Oct. 55° to 65° ; Oct. to March 50° to 55°.
PROPAGATION : By cuttings of half-ripened shoots inserted in small pots of sandy soil under bell-glass in temp. of 65° to 75°, March to July.
STOVE SPECIES : P. Betle (Betle Pepper), green, climber, India ; nigrum (Black Pepper), green, 4 to 6 ft., India.
GREENHOUSE SPECIES : P. excelsum aureo-pictum, leaves green and creamy white, 4 to 6 ft., Australia ; Futokadsura (Japanese Pepper), greenish, 4 to 6 ft., Japan.

Pipe-tree (*Syringa vulgaris*)—See Syringa.

Pipe Vine (*Aristolochia Sipho*)—See Aristolochia.

Piptanthus (Nepaul Laburnum)—Ord. Leguminosæ. Hardy evergreen flowering shrub. First introduced 1821.
CULTURE : Soil, rich, sandy loam. Position, warm, sheltered shrubberies S. and S.W. of England ; against S. walls, N. of London. Plant, Sept., Oct., April, or May. Prune straggling shoots moderately after flowering.
PROPAGATION : By seeds sown in sandy soil in cool greenhouse or cold frame in spring ; cuttings of ripened shoots inserted in small pots of sandy soil under bell-glass or hand-light outdoors, Aug. or Sept. ; layering shoots, Sept. or Oct.
SPECIES CULTIVATED : P. nepalensis, yellow, May, 8 to 12 ft., Himalayas.

Piqueria—Ord. Compositæ. Greenhouse flowering perennial. First introduced 1798.
CULTURE : Compost, loam, leaf-mould, and sand. Position, pots in greenhouse or bedded out during the summer months. Pot, March or April. Plant in open, May or June. Lift and repot in early Oct.
PROPAGATION : By cuttings in spring in gentle bottom heat ; by division at potting time ; by seeds sown in temp. 60° in Feb.
SPECIES CULTIVATED : P. trinervia, white, various seasons, 1 to 1½ ft., Mexico, etc., and its variety variegata (leaves marked with white). This plant is frequently listed in catalogues as Stevia serrata.

Pistachio-nut (*Pistacia vera*)—See Pistacia.

Pistacia (Pistachio-nut Tree ; Mastic Tree)—Ord. Anacardiaceæ. Hardy evergreen and deciduous trees. Flowering and orn. foliage. First introduced 1656. Leaves, unequally feather-shaped, green ; reddish in young state.
CULTURE : Soil, deep, rich, sandy loam. Position, sheltered shrubberies S. and S.W. England ; against S. walls N. of London. Plant evergreen species, Sept., Oct., April, or May ; deciduous species, Nov. to Feb. Prune evergreen species, April ; deciduous species, Nov. to Feb.
PROPAGATION : By cuttings inserted in sandy soil in cold frame or under hand-light, Sept. or Oct. ; layering in Sept.
SPECIES CULTIVATED : P. atlantica, leaves pinnate, deciduous, 40 ft., Canary Isles ; chinensis, deciduous, to 80 ft., China ; Lentiscus (Mastic Tree), leaves pinnate,

evergreen, 20 ft., S. Europe ; Terebinthus (Turpentine Tree), yellow, June, 30 ft., deciduous, Asia Minor and Mediterranean Region ; vera (Pistachio-nut Tree), brown, deciduous, April, 20 ft., Syria.

Pistia (Tropical Duck Weed ; Water Lettuce)—Ord. Aroideæ. Stove aquatic perennial. First introduced 1843. Flowers, green, borne on spadix at base of leaves. Leaves, wedge-shaped, notched, pale green, hairy.

CULTURE : Plant in shallow tub or tank in stove. This plant is a floating aquatic and does not require any soil. Place 2 in. layer of soil on bottom of tub or tank and plant on surface of water. Replenish with tepid water occasionally. Add fresh soil annually. Temp., March to Oct. 70° to 85° ; Oct. to March 60° to 70°.

PROPAGATION : By offsets.

SPECIES CULTIVATED : P. Stratiotes, 1 to 3 in., Jamaica.

Pisum (Garden Pea ; Sugar Pea ; Crown or Mummy Pea)—Ord. Leguminosæ. Hardy annuals. Edible seeded and podded vegetables.

CULTURE OF GARDEN PEAS : Soil, deep, rich calcareous loam, previously trenched three spits deep and containing a liberal dressing of manure incorporated with second spit. Position, open, sunny, protected from N. and N.E. and E. winds. Suitable manures : Solid—Horse dung or peat-moss litter for heavy soils ; cow or pig dung for light or sandy soils. Chemical—(1) Kainit 2 lb., nitrate of soda 5 lb., super-phosphate of lime 9 lb.—half of each to a square rod before sowing, remainder when plants are 6 in. high ; (2) native guano 6 lb. to a square rod applied before sowing, and 6 lb. when plants are 3 in. high ; (3) Peruvian guano 1 lb. for square rod before sowing, also 1 lb. when plants are 3 in. high ; weak liquid natural manure applied twice weekly; nitrate of soda ¼ oz. to gallon—all to be applied when ground is moist only and when pods have just formed. Direction of rows : E. to W. or S.E. to N.W. for early sorts ; N. to S. for main crops. Depth of drills, 2½ to 3 in. ; width, 6 to 9 in. Distance apart for sowing the seeds : 1 in. each way for dwarf sorts ; 2 in. for medium kinds ; 3 in. for tall varieties, arranged in two rows, thus : ·.·.·.· Distance between rows : 18 in. for varieties not exceeding 2 ft. in height ; 3 ft. for those not more than 4 ft. high ; 6 to 8 ft. for those growing 5 to 6 ft. high. Sow earliest sorts on south border, Nov. and Jan., or in 4½ in. pots in temp. 55° in Jan., hardening plants off when 3 in. high in cold frame and planting outdoors in Feb. or March ; second early sorts in open garden in Feb. and March ; main crop, April and May ; late crops, June and July. Draw mould up to each side of row when plants are 6 in. high and place supports to them. Mulch to width of 15 in. on each side of row with manure. Water copiously in dry weather. Nip off points of shoots of tall kinds when 4 ft. high, and again when 5 ft. high. Early peas, seeds round ; late ditto, wrinkled (marrowfats). Quantity of seed required for a row 50 ft. long, 1 pint. Seeds retain their vegetative powers for 3 to 4 years and seeds germinate in 10 to 20 days. Crop reaches maturity in 18 to 24 weeks. Round-seeded sorts germinate more quickly than wrinkled kinds. Protect seeds from mice and birds by soaking them in paraffin oil for four hours before sowing.

CULTURE OF SUGAR PEAS : Soil, same as for garden peas. Sow in March or April, 2½ in. deep in drills 6 in. wide and 6 ft. apart, and earth up and stake in the usual way. Gather pods when fully developed and cook like French beans. Rotation : Peas may follow potatoes, carrots, parsnips, turnips, broccoli, or cabbage and be succeeded by cabbage, turnips, spinach, or celery.

CULTURE OF MUMMY PEA : Soil, ordinary. Position, open, sunny borders. Sow seeds ½ in. deep, three or four in a 3 in. pot filled with light soil and placed in warm window or greenhouse in March, transplanting seedlings outdoors in May ; or 2½ in. deep in open ground in April. Support with stakes when 6 in. high. Water copiously in dry weather. Apply stimulants occasionally when flowers appear.

SPECIES CULTIVATED : P. sativum (Garden Pea), white or red, summer, Europe, etc. ; arvense (Field Pea), pinkish, summer, climber, Europe ; elatius, blush, summer, 4 to 6 ft., Mediterranean Region. These species (and in particular P. sativum) are the progenitors of garden races such as round peas, marrowfats, sugar peas, dwarf peas, crown peas, mummy peas, edible podded peas, etc.

Pitcairnia—Ord. Bromeliaceæ. Stove perennial herbs. First introduced 1777. Leaves, narrow or sword-shaped ; margins prickly.
CULTURE : Compost, equal parts fibrous loam, rough peat, and leaf-mould. Pot, March. Water freely always. Good drainage essential. Temp., Sept. to March 60° to 70° ; March to Sept. 70° to 80°.
PROPAGATION : By offshoots, inserted in small pots at any time.
SPECIES CULTIVATED : P. andreana, yellow and red, summer, 1 ft., Venezuela and Colombia ; aphelandræflora, red, summer, 1 ft., Brazil ; beycalena (Syn. P. muscosa), red, winter, 1 ft., Brazil ; violacea, violet, summer, 1 ft., Brazil. There are forty or more other species of little merit.

Pitcher-plants (*Sarracenias* and *Nepenthes*), which see.

Pittosporum (Parchment-bark)—Ord. Pittosporiaceæ. Half-hardy flowering shrubs. First introduced 1783.
CULTURE IN GREENHOUSE : Compost, two parts fibrous loam, one part fibrous peat, half a part silver sand. Position, pots or tubs in light, airy, sunny greenhouse. Pot, March or April. Prune straggling shoots moderately immediately after flowering. Water moderately Sept. to April, freely afterwards. Syringe occasionally, except when in flower, during summer. Temp., Oct. to April 40° to 50° : April to Oct. 60° to 70°.
CULTURE OUTDOORS : Soil, deep, sandy loam. Position, well-drained border against S. walls S. and S.W. England ; pots in cold greenhouse, Oct. to May ; sunny border outdoors, May to Oct., N. of London. Plant, March or April.
PROPAGATION : By cuttings of moderately firm shoots, 2 to 3 in. long, inserted singly in small pots of sandy soil under bell-glass in shade in temp. 55° to 65° in summer.
HALF-HARDY SPECIES : P. crassifolium (Parchment-bark), purple, spring, 15 to 20 ft., New Zealand ; eugenioides, greenish yellow, 20 to 30 ft., New Zealand ; Ralphi, dark purple, spring, 15 ft., New Zealand ; tenuifolium (Syn. P. Mayi), chocolate-purple, May, fragrant, 20 to 30 ft., New Zealand ; Tobira, white, fragrant, summer, 10 to 20 ft., Japan and China ; undulatum, creamy white, May to July, 30 to 40 ft., Australia ; viridiflorum, greenish yellow, June, to 25 ft., S. Africa.

Placea—Ord. Amaryllidaceæ. Greenhouse bulbs. Deciduous. First introduced 1840.
CULTURE : Compost, two parts sandy loam, one part well-decayed cow manure or leaf-mould, and one part coarse sand. Plant in borders in greenhouse during Aug. or Sept., placing point of bulb just below surface of soil. These plants do not thrive well when confined to pots. Repot annually in Aug. Season of growth, Jan. to Aug. ; season of rest, Aug. to Jan. Temp., Dec. to April 50° to 55° ; April to Aug. 60° to 70° ; Aug. to Dec. 35° to 40°.
PROPAGATION : By offsets in Aug.
SPECIES CULTIVATED : P. Arzæ, yellow and purple, summer, 1 ft. ; grandiflora, white and crimson, summer, 1 ft. ; ornata, white and red, 1 ft. All natives of Chile.

Plagianthus—Ord. Malvaceæ. Half-hardy deciduous and evergreen flowering trees and shrubs. Introduced 1870.
CULTURE : Soil, sandy loam and leaf-mould. Position, sheltered border or against a south wall for P. Lyalli. Plant : evergreen species, Sept. or April ; deciduous species, Nov. to Feb. Prune away shoots that have flowered directly after blooming.
PROPAGATION : By cuttings in sandy soil in a cold frame in autumn or by layers in spring.
SPECIES CULTIVATED : P. betulinus, yellowish white, unisexual, summer, 30 to 40 ft., deciduous, New Zealand ; Lampeni, white, 10 to 20 ft., evergreen, Tasmania ; Lyalli (Syn. Gaya Lyalli), pure white, summer, 20 to 30 ft., deciduous, New Zealand.

Planera Richardi—See Zelkowa crenata.

Plane-tree—See Platanus.

Plantain (*Musa sapientum paradisiaca*)—See Musa.

Plantain Lily—See Funkia.

Plantain-tree (*Musa sapientum paradisiaca*)—See Musa.

Platanus (Plane-tree)—Ord. Platanaceæ. Hardy deciduous trees. Orn. foliage. First introduced 1548. Leaves more or less deeply lobed.

CULTURE : Soil, deep, rich, moist loam. Position, parks, avenues, etc. for Oriental Plane ; streets, squares in towns, or in open gardens or shrubberies in country for London Plane. Plant, Oct. to March. Prune into shape when desirable, Oct. to Feb. Plenty of moisture at roots essential ; dry soil not suitable.

PROPAGATION : By seeds simply pressed into surface of soil in moist position out-doors in autumn ; cuttings of shoots, 6 to 8 in. long, inserted in moist soil in sheltered position in Nov. ; layering shoots in autumn or spring.

SPECIES CULTIVATED : P. acerifolia (London Plane), 70 to 100 ft., habitat uncertain ; orientalis (Oriental Plane), 80 to 100 ft., Orient.

Platycerium (Elk's-horn Fern ; Stag's-horn Fern)—Ord. Filices. Stove and greenhouse evergreen ferns. First introduced 1808. Fronds more or less broad, divided ; resembles stag's horn.

CULTURE : Compost, equal parts fibrous peat and sphagnum moss. Position, blocks of wood suspended from roof or sides of greenhouse or stove. Place plant on block of wood, cover roots with layer of moss and peat, and secure in position by means of copper wire. Top-dress annually with fresh peat and moss in Feb. or March. Water copiously April to Sept., moderately Sept. to March. Shade from sun. Temp.: for stove species, 55° to 65°, Oct. to March ; 70° to 80°, March to Oct. ; greenhouse species, 45° to 55°, Oct. to March ; 60° to 70°, March to Oct.

PROPAGATION : By offsets in Feb. or March ; also by spores sown in sandy peat in temp. 75° to 85°.

STOVE SPECIES : P. æthiopicum, Trop. Africa ; grande, Trop. Asia ; Wallichii, Malaya ; Willinckii, Java.

GREENHOUSE SPECIES : P. alcicorne (Common Elk's-horn Fern), Australia, and its varieties Hillii (fronds much forked), Queensland, and majus (very large), Polynesia.

Platyclinis (Chain Orchid)—Ord. Orchidaceæ. Stove epiphytal orchids. First introduced 1836.

CULTURE : Compost, equal parts fibrous peat and sphagnum. Position, well-drained pots in plant stove. Water moderately Sept. to April, freely afterwards. Temp., Oct. to March 60° to 65° ; March to Oct. 70° to 85°. Flowers appear in centre of new growth. Resting period, winter.

PROPAGATION : By dividing pseudo-bulbs and plants when beginning to grow.

SPECIES CULTIVATED : P. filiformis (Syn. Dendrochilum filiformis), yellow, fragrant, June to Aug., Philippines ; glumacea (Syn. Dendrochilum glumaceum), greenish white, fragrant, spring, Philippines.

Platycodon (Chinese Bell-flower)—Ord. Campanulaceæ. Hardy herbaceous perennial. First introduced 1782.

CULTURE : Soil, ordinary rich. Position, sunny well-drained borders or rockeries. Plant, Oct. to April.

PROPAGATION : By seeds sown $\frac{1}{16}$ in. deep in sandy soil in temp. 55°, March or Aug. ; cuttings, 3 in. long, of young shoots inserted singly in small pots of light, sandy soil in temp. 55° in March or April ; division of plants in April.

SPECIES CULTIVATED : P. grandiflorum, blue, July to Sept., 1 ft., China and Japan, and its varieties album (white) and Mariesii (white and dwarf).

Platylobium (Flat Pea)—Ord. Leguminosæ. Greenhouse flowering shrub. Evergreen. Nat. Australia. First introduced 1832.

CULTURE : Compost, three parts peat, one part loam, and little silver sand. Position, well-drained pots in light, airy greenhouse. Pot, Feb. or March. Nip off points of young shoots in spring to induce bushy growth. Water freely April to Sept., moderately Sept. to April. Temp., March to Sept. 55° to 65° ; Sept. to March 45° to 50°. Stand plants outdoors from July to Sept. to mature flowering shoots for following year.

PROPAGATION : By seeds sown ₁₆ in. deep in well-drained pots of sandy peat in temp. of 55° to 65° in March or April ; cuttings inserted in sandy soil under bell-glass in temp. 55°, April to July.
SPECIES CULTIVATED : P. obtusangulum, yellow and red, May, 1 ft.

Platyloma—See Pellæa.

Platystemon (Californian Poppy ; Cream Cups)—Ord. Papaveraceæ. Hardy annual. First introduced 1833.
CULTURE : Soil, good ordinary. Position, sunny beds, borders, or rockeries. Sow seed ⅛ in. deep in patches where required to grow in April. Thin seedlings 1 to 2 in. apart when ½ in. high. Water freely in dry weather. Mulch with decayed manure or cocoanut-fibre refuse in June.
SPECIES CULTIVATED : P. californicus, yellow, July, 1 ft., California.

Platytheca—Ord. Tremandreæ. Greenhouse evergreen flowering shrub. First introduced 1845.
CULTURE : Compost, two parts fibrous peat, one part turfy loam, one part equal proportions charcoal, broken pots, and silver sand. Position, well-drained pots in light, airy greenhouse. Pot, Feb. or March. Water moderately at all seasons ; rain water only to be used. Shade from sun June to Sept. Temp., Oct. to April 40° to 50° ; April to Oct. 50° to 65°.
PROPAGATION : By cuttings of side shoots inserted in sand under bell-glass in shade in temp. of 55° to 65° in summer.
SPECIES CULTIVATED : P. galioides (Syn. Tremandra verticillata), blue, June, 1 ft., S.W. Australia.

Pleione—Ord. Orchidaceæ. Greenhouse epiphytal orchids. Deciduous. First introduced 1837.
CULTURE : Compost, sphagnum moss with peat, loam, and sand in equal parts added. Position, well-drained pans with deep layer of sphagnum moss over crocks. Pot in early spring as soon as flowers fade. Place pans near glass after potting and water sparingly. When growing freely water should be given in abundance. Decrease supply as leaves fade and give little during the dormant season. Temp., March to Sept. 55° to 60° ; Sept. to March 45° to 55°.
PROPAGATION : By offsets at potting time.
SPECIES CULTIVATED : P. hookeriana, rosy purple, brown, and yellow, winter, Sikkim ; humilis, blush white and blue-purple, winter, N. India ; lagenaria, rosy lilac, white, crimson, and yellow, Jan. to Feb., India ; maculata, white and yellow, autumn, N. India ; præcox, rosy purple, yellow, and white, Nov. to Dec., N. India.

Pleomele—See Dracæna.

Pleroma—See Tibouchina.

Pleurisy-root (Asclepias tuberosa)—See Asclepias.

Pleurothallis—Ord. Orchidaceæ. Greenhouse epiphytal orchids. First introduced 1826.
CULTURE : Compost, sphagnum moss only. Position, small blocks of wood suspended from roof. Place layer of moss on block, then roots of plant, then another layer of moss, and secure with copper wire. Water abundantly March to Oct., moderately afterwards. Shade from sun. Syringe blocks two or three times daily in summer ; once daily in winter and autumn. Temp., Nov. to March 45° to 55° ; March to Nov. 55° to 60°.
PROPAGATION : By division, Feb. to March.
SPECIES CULTIVATED : P. barberiana, yellow, purple, and white, spring, 4 to 6 ft., S. America ; ornata, yellow, purple, and white, April, Trop. America ; punctulata, yellow, purple, and brown, spring, Colombia ; Roezlii, blood purple, spring, 2 ft., Colombia.

Plum—See Prunus.

Plumbago (Leadwort; Cape Leadwort)—Ord. Plumbaginaceæ. Stove and greenhouse evergreen flowering shrubs. First introduced 1777.

CULTURE OF STOVE SPECIES: Compost, equal parts fibrous peat and leaf-mould, half a part each loam and sand. Position, pots, shoots trained to stakes or balloon trellis; or in borders, shoots trained to wall in light part of stove. Pot, Feb. to April. Prune shoots moderately in Jan. Water freely April to Oct., moderately afterwards. Syringe daily March to Sept. Shade from sun. Temp., March to Oct. 75° to 85°; Oct. to March 55° to 65°.

CULTURE OF GREENHOUSE SPECIES: Compost, two parts fibrous loam, half a part of silver sand. Position, pots, shoots trained to stakes or trellis; borders, with shoots trained up rafters, pillars, or walls in light part of house. Pot or plant, Feb. or March. Prune shoots to within 1 in. of base immediately after flowering; flowers borne on points of shoots of current year's growth. Water copiously March to Sept., moderately Sept. to Nov., very little afterwards. Syringe daily until flowering begins. Apply weak stimulants twice a week during flowering period. Shade only from very bright sun. Temp., March to Oct. 55° to 65°; Oct. to March 45° to 55°.

PROPAGATION: By seeds sown on surface of sandy peat and slightly covered with fine sandy soil in temp. 65° to 75° in Feb. or March; cuttings of side shoots, 2 to 3 in. long, inserted singly in 2 in. pots of sandy peat in temp. 60° to 70°, Feb. to Aug.

STOCK SPECIES: P. rosea, purplish red, winter, 2 ft., India, and its variety coccinea (scarlet).

GREENHOUSE SPECIES: P. capensis, blue, summer, 10 to 15 ft., S. Africa; capensis alba, white.

HARDY SPECIES: See Ceratostigma.

Plume Poppy (*Bocconia cordata*)—See Bocconia.

Plumeria (Frangipanni Plant)—Ord. Apocynaceæ. Stove evergreen flowering shrubs. First introduced 1690. Frequently spelt Plumeria.

CULTURE: Compost, two parts sandy loam, one part fibry peat, half a part silver sand. Position, well-drained pots in light stove. Pot, Feb. to April. Prune straggling shoots moderately close immediately after flowering. Water freely March to Oct., moderately afterwards. Syringe daily March and until flowers appear. Temp., March to Sept. 70° to 80°; Sept. to March 65° to 75°.

PROPAGATION: By cuttings of ripe shoots, 2 to 3 in. long, inserted in small pots filled with sand under bell-glass in temp. 65° to 75° in Feb.

SPECIES CULTIVATED: P. acutifolia, white and yellow, fragrant, July, 15 to 20 ft., Mexico; bicolor, white and yellow, July, 10 to 15 ft., S. America; rubra (Frangipanni Plant), red, July, 10 to 15 ft., Trop. America.

Plum Fir (*Prumnopitys elegans*)—See Prumnopitys.

Plumy Bleeding Heart (*Dicentra eximia*)—See Dicentra.

Poa (Variegated Meadow Grass)—Ord. Gramineæ. Hardy perennial flowering and orn.-foliaged grass.

CULTURE: Soil, ordinary. Position, edgings to sunny beds or borders, or in clumps in borders. Plant, Oct., Nov., March, or April.

POT CULTURE: Compost, two parts good ordinary soil, one part leaf-mould, half a part sand. Position, in 4 or 5 in. pots in cold or cool greenhouse or window. Pot, March or April. Water moderately Oct. to March, freely afterwards. Repot and divide annually.

PROPAGATION: By division of plants, March or April.

SPECIES CULTIVATED: P. trivialis albo-vittata, leaves edged with white, 6 in., Europe (Britain).

Pod Fern (*Ceratopteris thalictroides*)—See Ceratopteris.

Podocarpus (Totara Pine)—Ord. Taxaceæ. Hardy and half-hardy evergreen trees. Orn. foliage. First introduced 1774.

CULTURE: Soil, good deep loam, well-drained. Position, sunny, sheltered lawns or shrubberies. Half-hardy species only suitable for southern gardens or sheltered districts. Plant, Oct., Nov., March, or April.

PROPAGATION : By cuttings of firm young shoots inserted in small pots of sandy loam under bell-glass in temp. 60° to 70°, summer.
HARDY SPECIES : P. alpina, 3 to 4 ft., Tasmania.
HALF-HARDY SPECIES : P. chilina (Syn. P. andina), 40 to 60 ft., Chilean Andes; macrophylla, 25 to 50 ft., China and Japan ; nubigena, 20 to 30 ft., Chile ; spicata, 60 to 80 ft., New Zealand.

Podolopis—Ord. Compositæ. Hardy annuals. Nat. Australia. First introduced 1803.
OUTDOOR CULTURE OF ANNUAL SPECIES : Soil, ordinary. Position, sunny well-drained beds or borders or rockeries. Sow seeds ⅟₁₆ in. deep in well-drained pots of light soil in temp. of 55° to 65° in March, transplanting seedlings outdoors in flowering position, end of May ; or sow outdoors in sunny position end of April where required to grow and flower, thinning seedlings to 3 in. apart when ½ in. high.
ANNUAL SPECIES : P. acuminata, yellow, summer, 1 ft. ; aristata, yellow and pink, summer, 1 ft.

Podophyllum (Duck Foot ; May Apple)—Ord. Berberidaceæ. Hardy herbaceous perennials. Orn. foliage. First introduced 1664. Leaves, large, shield-shaped, divided, ornamental.
CULTURE : Soil, moist peat. Position, partially shaded borders, woods, marshes, or bog gardens. Plant, March or April.
PROPAGATION : By division of roots in March or April.
SPECIES CULTIVATED : P. Emodi (Himalayan May Apple), white, May, 1 ft., coral-red fruits, Himalayas ; peltatum (May Apple), white, May, 12 to 15 in., yellow fruits, N. America.

Poet's Daffodil (*Narcissus poeticus*)—See Narcissus.

Poet's Laurel (*Laurus nobilis*)—See Laurus.

Poet's Narcissus (*Narcissus poeticus*)—See Narcissus.

Poinciana—Ord. Leguminosæ. Stove evergreen tree. Flowering and orn. foliage. First introduced 1828. Leaves, fern-like, green, graceful.
CULTURE : Compost, two parts peat or loam, one part leaf-mould, half a part silver sand. Position, pots in light part of stove or outdoors during July and Aug. Pot, Feb. or March. Water freely March to Oct., moderately afterwards. Temp., March to Oct. 70° to 85° ; Oct. to March 55° to 65°.
PROPAGATION : By seeds sown in light, sandy soil in temp. of 75° to 85° in spring ; cuttings of short young shoots inserted singly in small pots filled with pure sand under bell-glass in temp. 75° to 85° in summer.
SPECIES CULTIVATED : P. regia, crimson, summer, 20 to 30 ft., Madagascar. See also Caesalpinia.

Poinsettia—See Euphorbia.
Poison Ash (*Chionanthus virginica*)—See Chionanthus.
Poison Bay Tree (*Illicium floridanum*)—See Illicium.
Poison-dart—See Aglaonema.
Poison Ivy (*Rhus toxicodendron*)—See Rhus.
Poivrea—See Combretum.
Poke (*Phytolacca decandra*)—See Phytolacca.
Polar Plant (*Silphium laciniatum*)—See Silphium.

Polemonium (Jacob's Ladder ; Greek Valerian)—Ord. Polemoniaceæ. Hardy herbaceous perennials.
CULTURE : Soil, good ordinary or deep, rich, well-drained loam. Position, open, sunny borders for P. cæruleum and vars. ; sunny well-drained rockeries for other species. Plant, Oct., Nov., March, or April. Cut off flower stems immediately after flowering. Top-dress annually in spring with well-decayed manure or leaf-soil.

PROPAGATION : P. cæruleum by division of plants in Oct. or Nov. ; other species by division in March or April.

SPECIES CULTIVATED : P. cæruleum (Jacob's Ladder or Greek Valerian), blue, June, 2 ft., Europe (Britain) ; cæruleum album, white ; carneum, cream to rose, summer, 12 to 18 in., N.W. America ; confertum, blue, summer, 6 to 8 in., N.W. America ; flavum, yellow, summer, 3 ft., New Mexico ; humile (Syn. P. Richardsoni), blue, July, 6 in., N. America ; reptans, blue, spring, 6 in., N. America.

Polianthes (The Tuberose)—Ord. Amaryllidaceæ. Half-hardy bulbous plant. Flowers fragrant. First introduced 1629.

CULTURE : Compost, two parts fibrous loam, one part of equal proportions of leaf-mould, decayed manure, and coarse silver sand. Pot, African kinds in Oct., Nov., and Dec., to flower following autumn ; American or Pearl varieties in Jan., Feb., March, and April, to flower following winter and spring. Plant bulbs about two-thirds of their depth singly in a 5 in. pot, or three in a 6 in. size. Pot firmly. After treatment : (*a*) Plunge pots to their rims in bottom heat, 75° to 85°, and give one application of water only until growth begins, then remove to a shelf near the glass in temp. 55° to 65°, and remove to temp. 50° to 55° when in bloom. (*b*) Place pots on bed of coal ashes in cold frame, cover with 4 in. cocoanut-fibre refuse, and give no water until growth begins. After this remove the fibre refuse, water moderately, and transfer most forward plants to the greenhouse. (*c*) Pot bulbs in April, plunge pots just above rim in a sunny spot in garden, keep moderately moist, lift pots in Sept. or Oct., and place in greenhouse to flower. Water freely when in full growth. Syringe foliage frequently. Apply stimulants (½ oz. guano or Clay's fertiliser) once a week when growing freely. After flowering bulbs of no further use.

OUTDOOR CULTURE : Soil, ordinary rich. Position, warm, sunny border. Plant bulbs 3 in. deep and 6 in. apart, March to April, to flower in Aug. and Sept. Plant fresh bulbs annually.

PROPAGATION : By offsets.

SPECIES CULTIVATED : P. tuberosa (Tuberose), white, fragrant, autumn and winter, 3 ft., Mexico, and its variety flore-pleno (double-flowered).

VARIETIES : Double African, American, Italian, and The Pearl.

Polyantha Rose (*Rosa multiflora*)—See Rosa.

Polyanthus (*Primula variabilis*)—See Primula.

Polyanthus Narcissus (*Narcissus tazetta*)—See Narcissus.

Polybotrya—See Acrostichum.

Polygala (Milk-wort)—Ord. Polygaleæ. Hardy herbaceous perennials, greenhouse and hardy evergreen flowering shrubs. First introduced 1658.

CULTURE OF HARDY SPECIES : Soil, sandy peat. Position, sunny border or rockery. Plant, Oct., Nov., or April. No pruning required.

CULTURE OF GREENHOUSE SPECIES : Compost, two parts fibrous peat, one part silver sand. Position, well-drained pots in cool, airy greenhouse. Pot, Feb. or March. Prune straggly shoots only into shape, Feb. Water freely April to Sept., moderately afterwards. No stimulants required. Shade unnecessary. Temp., March to Sept. 55° to 65° ; Sept. to March 40° to 50°.

PROPAGATION : Hardy species by cuttings inserted in sandy peat under hand-light or in cold frame in autumn, or by suckers removed in Sept. ; greenhouse species by cuttings of young shoots inserted in small pots of sandy peat under bell-glass in temp. 55° to 65° in spring.

GREENHOUSE SPECIES : P. dalmaisiana, purplish red, flowers continuously, 4 to 6 ft., hybrid, will grow in the open against a south wall ; myrtifolia grandiflora, purple, spring, 4 to 6 ft., S. Africa.

HARDY SPECIES : P. Chamæbuxus, cream and yellow, summer, 6 to 12 in., Alps.

Polygonatum (Solomon's Seal)—Ord. Liliaceæ. Hardy herbaceous perennials.

CULTURE : Soil, ordinary light mould. Position, partially shaded beds, borders, or woodlands. Plant, Oct., Nov., or March. Top-dress annually with decayed manure in March. Apply stimulants occasionally in summer.

POT CULTURE OF P. MULTIFLORUM : Pot roots in ordinary light soil in 6 or 8 in. pots in Nov. Cover with cocoanut-fibre refuse outdoors or in frame until growth begins, then remove to heated or cold greenhouse to flower. Water freely.
PROPAGATION : By division of roots in Oct., Nov., or March.
SPECIES CULTIVATED : P. biflorum, green and white, May, 1 to 3 ft., N. America ; latifolium, white, July, 2 to 3 ft., Europe ; multiflorum (David's Harp), white, June, 3 ft., Europe ; officinale (Common Solomon's Seal), white, May, 1 ft., Europe (Britain) ; oppositifolium, white and green, April, 3 ft., Himalayas. There are double-flowered forms of P. multiflorum and officinale.

Polygonum (Knot Weed)—Ord. Polygonaceæ. Hardy annuals, herbaceous perennials, and shrubby climbers.
CULTURE OF ANNUAL SPECIES : Soil, ordinary. Position, sunny well-drained borders. Sow seeds $\frac{1}{8}$ in. deep in light soil in temp. 65° in March, planting seedlings outdoors in June ; or sow in open border in April. Water freely in dry weather. Apply stimulants during flowering period.
CULTURE OF PERENNIAL SPECIES : Soil, good, rich, ordinary. Position of large species, in sunny or shady, moist borders, as isolated specimens on lawns, or on margins of ponds ; climbing species for covering arbours, pergolas, or tree trunks ; dwarf species in ordinary sunny borders or on rockeries. Plant, Oct., Nov., March, or April. Mulch with decayed manure annually in March. Apply stimulants occasionally during July and Aug. Water copiously in dry weather. Prune away the dead points of shoots of P. baldschuanicum in early spring.
PROPAGATION : Perennials by seeds, as advised for annuals, or by division of roots in Oct. or March ; greenhouse species by cuttings inserted in sandy peat under bell-glass in temp. 65° to 75° in spring.
ANNUAL SPECIES : P. orientale, rosy purple, Aug., 4 to 6 ft., Tropics. There are some dwarfer races to be found in trade lists.
PERENNIAL SPECIES : P. affine (Syn. P. Brunonis), rose, autumn, 6 to 9 in., Himalayas ; alpinum, white, Aug., 2 to 3 ft., S. Europe ; amplexicaule, rose red, autumn, 3 ft., Himalayas ; Auberti, pinkish, autumn, 20 to 30 ft., climbing, W. China ; baldschuanicum, white, autumn, 20 to 30 ft., climbing, Bokhara ; bistorta superba, deep carmine, summer, 1$\frac{1}{2}$ ft., Britain ; campanulatum, blush white, late summer, 2 to 3 ft., Himalayas ; compactum, white, autumn, 2 ft., Japan ; cuspidatum (Syn. P. Sieboldi), white, July and Aug., 6 to 8 ft., Japan ; sachalinense, white, summer, 8 to 10 ft., Sachalin Isles ; vaccinifolium, rose, autumn, 6 in., Himalayas ; viviparum, white, May to June, 3 in., Arctic Regions.

Polypodium (Common Polypody ; Oak Fern ; Beech Fern)—Ord. Filices. Stove, greenhouse, and hardy ferns. Evergreen and deciduous.
CULTURE OF STOVE AND GREENHOUSE SPECIES : Compost, equal parts loam, peat, leaf-mould, and silver sand. Pot, Feb. to April. Position, pots, baskets, or rock beds. Shade from sun essential. Moist atmosphere Feb. to Sept., moderately moist afterwards. No syringing required. Water freely March to Sept., moderately Sept. to March. No stimulants. Temp. : for greenhouse species, March to Oct. 55° to 65° ; Oct. to March 40° to 50° ; stove species, March to Oct. 65° to 75° ; Oct. to March 55° to 65°.
CULTURE OF HARDY SPECIES : Soil, equal parts fibry peat, decayed turfy loam, leaf-mould, and coarse silver sand for P. vulgare and vars. ; equal parts peat, loam, coarse sand, and small lumps of sandstone for P. dryopteris (Oak Fern) and P. phegopteris (Beech Fern) ; two-thirds sandy, fibry loam, one-third pounded limestone for P. dryopteris robertianum. Position, shady fernery, bank, or rockery for P. vulgare ; partially shaded dryish rockery for P. dryopteris and P. phegopteris ; dry, partially shady rockery for Robertianum ; other species anywhere in shade in ordinary soil. Plant, April. Water in dry weather. Top-dress annually in April with the special soils described above.
POT CULTURE OF HARDY SPECIES : Composts, as above. Pot, March. Position, shady, airy, cold greenhouse, pit, or frame. Water evergreen kinds freely in summer, moderately at other times ; deciduous kinds freely whilst growing ; occasionally after foliage dies down. Repot annually.

PROPAGATION : By spores sown on surface of shallow pan or box filled with fine sandy peat, covered with pane of glass, and placed in temp. 65° to 75° ; division of roots in March or April.

STOVE SPECIES : P. albo-squamatum (Syn. Phymatodes albo-squamatum), Malaya ; chnoodes (Syn. Goniophlebium chnoodes), W. Indies ; conjugatum, Trop. Asia ; Heracleum (Syn. Drynaria Heracleum), Java ; irioides, Old World Tropics ; Lingua (Syn. Nipholobus Lingua), Manchuria ; loriceum latipes (Syn. P. Catherinæ), W. Indies ; meyenianum (Bear's Paw Fern), Philippines ; musæfolium, Malaya ; pectinatum, W. Indies ; persicæfolium, Malaya ; refractrum, Brazil ; sub-auriculatum, Malaya ; verrucosum, Philippines.

GREENHOUSE SPECIES : P. aureum (Syn. Phlebodium aureum), W. Indies ; Billardieri (Syn. Phymatodes Billardieri), Australia ; drepanum (Syn. Phegopteris drepanum), Madeira ; pustulatum (Syn. Phymatodes pustulata), Scented Polypody, Australia and New Zealand ; P. Schneiderii, a hybrid.

HARDY SPECIES : P. alpestre (Alpine Polypody), Europe (Britain) ; Dryopteris (Oak Fern), Britain, etc. ; Dryopteris robertianum (Geranium-scented Polypody) ; Phegopteris (Beech Fern), Britain, etc. ; Phegopteris multifidum, fronds finely cut ; vulgare (Common Polopody), Britain, etc. ; vulgare cambricum (Welsh Polypody), and several other varieties as cristatum, multifido-cristatum, etc.

Polypody (*Polypodium vulgare*)—See Polypodium.

Polyscias paniculata—See Terminatia elegans.

Polystichum—See Aspidium.

Pomegranate-tree (*Punica Granatum*)—See Punica.

Pontederia (Pickerel Weed)—Ord. Pontederiaceæ.   Hardy aquatic perennials. First introduced 1579.
CULTURE : Soil, rich loam.   Position, shallow ponds or tanks containing water 6 to 12 in. in depth.   Plant, Oct., Nov., March, or April.
PROPAGATION : By division of roots any time in spring.
SPECIES CULTIVATED : P. cordata, blue, white, and green, summer, 2 ft., N. America, and its variety angustifolia (Syn. lanceolata), bright blue.

Pontic Daphne (*Daphne pontica*)—See Daphne.

Pope's-head (*Melocactus communis*)—See Melocactus.

Popinac (*Acacia farnesiana*)—See Acacia.

Poplar—See Populus.

Poppy—See Papaver.

Poppy Anemone (*Anemone coronaria*)—See Anemone.

Poppy Mallow—See Callirhoë.

Populus (Aspen-tree ; Abele-tree ; Poplar)—Ord. Salicaceæ.   Hardy decidous trees.   Orn. foliage.   Flowers, catkin-shaped ;   March and April.   Leaves, roundish, lobed, toothed, green, whitish beneath.   Wood, soft, yellow, or white ; used for toy-making, spade handles, etc.   Weight of timber per cubic foot, 30 lb.
CULTURE : Soil, ordinary moist.   Position, margins of ponds, lakes, rivers, moist shrubberies or woods.   P. deltoidea and N. nigra pyramidalis good trees for forming screens in town or suburban gardens.   Plant, Oct. to Feb.   For screens, plant 4 to 6 ft. apart.   Prune, Nov. to Feb.   Dry soils not suitable.
PROPAGATION : By seeds sown ⅛ in. deep in ordinary soil in moist border in autumn ; cuttings of firm shoots, 8 in. long, inserted in ordinary soil outdoors in Oct. or Nov. ; layering shoots in Oct. ; suckers, Oct. to Feb. ; weeping kinds by grafting on common poplars in March.
SPECIES CULTIVATED : P. alba (White Poplar or Abele), 50 to 90 ft., Europe (Britain), N. Asia, etc. ; angulata, 60 to 80 ft., habitat uncertain ; balsamifera (Balsam Poplar), 60 to 70 ft., N. America, and its variety candicans; canescena (Grey Poplar), 70 to 80 ft., Britain ; lasiocarpa, 40 to 60 ft., Central China ; monilifera, to 100 ft., N. America ;

nigra (Black Poplar), 50 to 80 ft., Europe ; nigra italica (Lombardy Poplar), Syns. P. nigra pyramidalis and P. nigra fastigiata, 60 to 80 ft., Europe and Asia ; nigra betulifolia, young growth downy, to 90 ft., Europe and Asia ; serotina, 80 to 100 ft., hybrid, and its variety aurea (young foliage yellow) ; szechuanica, large green leaves, rosy salmon beneath, W. China ; tremula (Aspen), 50 to 80 ft., Europe (Britain) and N. Asia, and its variety pendula.

Porcupine Rush (*Scirpus facustris*)—See Scirpus.

Portlandia—Ord. Rubiaceæ.   Stove evergreen flowering shrubs.   First introduced 1775.
CULTURE : Compost, equal parts fibrous loam and leaf-mould and half a part silver sand. Pot, Feb. or March. Position, well-drained pots in partially shaded part of stove. Prune into shape immediately after flowering. Water copiously April to Sept., moderately afterwards. Syringe twice daily March to Oct., once afterwards. Temp., March to Sept. 70° to 85° ; Sept. to March 60° to 70°.
PROPAGATION : By cuttings of firm shoots, 2 to 3 in. long, inserted in sand under bell-glass in temp. 75° to 85° in summer.
SPECIES CULTIVATED : P. grandiflora, white, June, fragrant, 8 to 10 ft., W. Indies ; platantha, white, summer, 1½ to 3 ft., habitat uncertain.

Portugal Broom (*Cytisus albus*)—See Cytisus.

Portugal Laurel (*Prunus lusitanica*)—See Prunus.

Portuguese Sundew (*Drosophyllum lusitanicum*)—See Drosophyllum.

Portulaca (Purslane ; Sun Plant)—Ord. Portulacaceæ. Hardy and half-hardy annual flowering and edible-leaved plants. Leaves of purslane form an excellent summer salading. First introduced 1582.
CULTURE OF HALF-HARDY ANNUAL SPECIES : Soil, good ordinary. Position, sunny rockeries, raised beds or borders. Sow seeds thinly on surface of light, sandy soil in well-drained pot, box, or pan, lightly cover with fine soil, and place in temp. 65° in March. Transplant seedlings when three leaves formed singly into 2 in. pots, gradually harden off, and plant outdoors end of May. Water in dry weather. Plant 3 in. apart each way.
POT CULTURE : Compost, equal parts loam, leaf-mould, and coarse silver sand. Raise plants from seeds as advised above. Transplant seedlings 1 in. apart in 5 in. pots, well-drained and filled with above compost. Grow near glass in temp. 55° to 65°. Water freely. Apply weak stimulants when in flower.
CULTURE OF PURSLANE : Soil, light, rich ordinary. Position, sunny well-drained borders. Sow seeds thinly broadcast, middle of April, lightly rake in and keep well watered. To insure a succession, sow at intervals of a month up to Aug. Gather shoots when 2 to 3 in. long, cutting them off close to the ground.
SPECIES CULTIVATED : P. grandiflora (Sun Plant), red, yellow, rose, or white, 6 in., Brazil, and its varieties compacta (various colours), Thellusoni (orange-scarlet), Thornburni (yellow), and many others ; oleracea (Purslane), June, 6 in., Tropics.

Posoqueria—Ord. Rubiaceæ. Stove evergreen flowering shrubs. First introduced 1815.
CULTURE : Compost, one part loam, one part peat, one part well-decayed manure and charcoal. Position, well-drained pots, or beds in plant stove. Pot or plant, Feb. or March. Prune into shape, Feb. or March. Temp., March to Sept. 65° to 85° ; Sept. to March 55° to 65°. Water moderately Oct. to Feb., freely afterwards. Syringe daily (except when in bloom) March to Sept. Apply liquid manure occasionally to healthy plants in flower. Plants one to two years old produce the best blooms.
PROPAGATION : By cuttings of firm young side shoots, 2 to 3 in. long, inserted in well-drained pots of sandy peat under bell-glass in temp. 75° to 85°, Jan. to April.
SPECIES CULTIVATED : P. formosa, white, fragrant, summer, 15 to 20 ft., Venezuela ; fragrantissima, white, fragrant, summer, 8 to 10 ft., Brazil ; latifolia, white, Oct., 6 ft., Trop. America.

Potato (*Solanum tuberosum*)—See Solanum.

Potato Onion (*Allium cepa aggregatum*)—See Allium.

Potato-tree (*Solanum crispum*)—See Solanum.

Potato Vine (*Ipomœa pandurata*)—See Ipomœa.

Potentilla (Cinquefoil)—Ord. Rosaceæ. Hardy herbaceous perennials. **The** hybrid garden potentillas are the result of crosses between P. argyrophylla and P. nepalensis.

CULTURE OF HERBACEOUS SPECIES : Soil, ordinary deep, rich, sandy. Position, sunny rockeries for dwarf species ; sunny borders for tall kinds. Plant, Oct., Nov., March, or April. Mulch tall kinds with decayed manure annually in March. Water copiously in dry weather. Apply stimulants occasionally during flowering period. Lift, divide, and replant border kinds in fresh soil every three or four years.
CULTURE OF SHRUBBY SPECIES : Soil, deep loam. Position, sunny shrubberies or borders. Plant, Nov. to Feb. Plants require abundant moisture. Mulch with strawy manure in May.
PROPAGATION : Herbaceous species by seeds sown $\frac{1}{18}$ in. deep in shallow pans or boxes of light, sandy soil in temp. 55° to 65°, March, transplanting seedlings outdoors in May or June, or similar depth in partially shaded border outdoors in April ; division of roots, Oct., Nov., March, or April ; shrubby species by seeds treated as herbaceous kinds, or by cuttings of well-ripened wood during Aug. or Sept. in sandy soil in unheated frame.
HERBACEOUS SPECIES CULTIVATED : P. alba, white, spring, 6 in., Europe ; alchemilloides, white, summer, 6 to 12 in., Pyrenees ; ambigua, yellow, summer, 6 in., Himalayas ; argyrophylla, yellow, summer, 2 to 3 ft., Himalayas ; argyrophylla atrosanguinea, crimson ; clusiana, milk white, June to July, 4 to 6 in., Europe ; Crantzi (Syn. P. alpestris), yellow, May to June, 6 to 9 in., Europe, and its variety pyrenaica ; fragiformis, yellow, May to June, 6 to 9 in., N.W. America ; grandiflora, yellow, summer, 6 to 12 in., Alps ; hopwoodiana, yellow and rose, summer, 18 in., hybrid ; nepalensis, rosy red, summer, 18 in., Himalayas, and its variety Willmottiæ, 9 in. ; nitida, rose, summer, 3 to 4 in., Europe ; nitida alba, white ; nitida grandiflora, pink ; rupestris, white, May to July, 1 to 1½ ft., Europe ; Tonguei, terra-cotta, summer, 3 in., hybrid. Many beautiful hybrids, for which see trade lists.
SHRUBBY SPECIES CULTIVATED : P. davurica, white, May to Sept., 1 to 1½ ft., China and Siberia ; Friedrichseni, pale yellow, June to Sept., to 6 ft., hybrid ; fruticosa, yellow, May to Sept., 2 to 4 ft., Northern Hemisphere (England), and its varieties grandiflora (large-flowered), tenuifolia (narrow leaflets), Veitchii (white), and vilmoriniana (creamy white) ; Salesoviana, white, tinted rose, June to July, 3 to 4 ft., Siberia.

Poterium (Burnet)—Ord. Rosaceæ. Hardy perennial herbs.
CULTURE : Soil, ordinary. Position, sunny or shady borders, or by water-side. Plants appreciate abundant moisture during the growing season. Plant, Oct. to Nov. or March to April.
PROPAGATION : By seed sown in pans in sandy soil during Feb. or March ; by division of the roots in March or April.
SPECIES CULTIVATED : P. canadense, July to Sept., 4 ft., N. America ; obtusum, pink, July to Sept., 2 to 3 ft., Japan ; sitchense, crimson, July to Sept., 3 ft., N. America.

Pothos—Ord. Aroideæ. Stove evergreen climbing shrubs. Orn. foliage. First introduced 1821. Leaves, roundish or lance-shaped, green, or variegated with creamy yellow.
CULTURE : Compost, equal parts rough peat, sphagnum moss, charcoal, and coarse sand. Position, pots, with shoots trained to old tree stems, trunks of tree ferns, or walls. Pot, Feb. or March. Water copiously March to Oct., moderately afterwards. Syringe freely all the year round. Temp., Sept. to March 60° to 65° ; March to Sept. 80° to 85°. Shade from sun essential.

PROPAGATION : By division of roots, Feb. or March.
SPECIES CULTIVATED : P. argenteus, leaves silvery grey, Borneo ; celatocaulis, stems clinging, Borneo ; scandens, stems climbing, India. The plant formerly known as P. aureus is now Scindapsus aureus, *q.v.*

Pot Marigold (*Calendula officinalis*)—See Calendula.

Pot Marjoram (*Origanum Onites*)—See Origanum.

Prairie Rose (*Rosa setigera*)—See Rosa.

Prairie Sun-flower (*Helianthus rigidus*)—See Helianthus.

Pratia—Ord. Campanulaceæ. Hardy herbaceous perennial trailing plants. First introduced 1827.
OUTDOOR CULTURE : Soil, two parts peat, one part leaf-mould, and little sand. Position, sunny well-drained rockeries. Plant, March or April. Water freely in dry weather.
POT CULTURE : Compost, two parts sandy loam, half a part each leaf-mould and silver sand. Pot, March. Position, cool or cold greenhouse, frame, or window. Water freely April to Sept., moderately afterwards. Apply weak stimulants occasionally when flowering. Shade from midday sun.
PROPAGATION : By seeds sown $\frac{1}{16}$ in. deep in equal parts loam, leaf-mould, and sand in temp. 85°, March ; cuttings of young shoots inserted in well-drained pots, July to Sept., and stored in cold frame or greenhouse until March, then planted outdoors.
SPECIES CULTIVATED : P. angulata (Syn. Lobelia littoralis), white, summer, 1 in., New Zealand ; begonifolia (Syn. Lobelia begonifolia), blue, summer, Himalayas.

Prickly Ash (*Zanthoxylum americanum*)—See Zanthoxylum.

Prickly Buckler Fern (*Nephrodium spinulosum*)—See Nephrodium.

Prickly Cedar (*Juniperus oxycedrus*)—See Juniperus.

Prickly Date Palm—See Acanthophœnix.

Prickly Heath—See Pernettya.

Prickly Ivy (*Smilax aspera*)—See Smilax.

Prickly Pear—See Opuntia.

Prickly Poppy (*Argemone mexicana* and some species of *Meconopsis*)—See Argemone and Meconopsis.

Prickly Rhubarb (*Gunnera chilensis*)—See Gunnera.

Prickly-seeded Spinach (*Spinacia oleracea spinosa*)—See Spinacia.

Prickly Shield Fern (*Aspidium aculeatum*)—See Aspidium.

Prickly Thrift (*Acantholimon glumaceum*)—See Acantholimon.

Pride-of-Barbados (*Cæsalpinia pulcherrima*)—See Cæsalpinia.

Primrose (*Primula vulgaris*)—See Primula.

Primula (Auricula ; Oxlip ; Primrose ; Polyanthus)—Ord. Primulaceæ. Greenhouse and hardy perennial herbs. First introduced 1596.
CULTURE OF AURICULA : Alpine type have blooms one colour, white or yellow eye, stems smooth and free from powder. Florists' type, stems and blooms covered with mealy powder ; blooms with more than one colour and white-, grey- or green-edged petals. Properties of florists' auricula : Stem erect, elastic, carrying truss well above foliage ; stalk proportionately long to size of petals ; pips (blooms) seven to each truss, round ; anthers, bold ; eye, white, smooth and round ; colours, well defined, rich ; edges, distinct. Compost, two parts turfy loam, one part cow manure and leaf-mould, half a part silver sand. Position, choice kinds in 3 in. pots in airy frame or cool greenhouse ; others in rich soil in shady borders. Pot and plant, Feb. or March. Water those in pots moderately in winter, freely other times.

Top-dress with rich soil in March plants that were not repotted. Apply liquid manure in a weak state to plants in flower.

PROPAGATION : By seeds sown in pans of light, rich soil, just covered with fine soil, in March, in cold frame or greenhouse ; by offsets in Feb.

CULTURE OF CHINESE PRIMULA : First introduced 1820. Compost, one part fibrous loam, half a part each of leaf-mould and decayed cow manure, half a part silver sand. Sow seeds in May on surface of a compost of two parts leaf-mould and one part loam, half a part sand, pressed moderately firm in a shallow pan or 6 in. pot half filled with drainage. Cover seeds thinly with similar soil. Place pane of glass over pot or pan and put in temp. 55° to 65°. Shade from sun. Keep soil just moist. Transplant seedlings when three leaves form 1 in. apart in 3 in. pots, well drained and filled with compost for advised seeds. Still keep in temp. 55° to 65°. When leaves of seedlings meet each other place singly in 2 in. pots, keep in same temp. for a week, then transfer to cold frame. Shade from sun. Admit air freely. Sprinkle foliage in evening. Transfer to 5 in. pots when well rooted. Replace in frame, shade from sun, water moderately, and sprinkle foliage as before. Apply liquid soot and cow or sheep manure—1 bushel of latter and 1 peck of former to 36 gallons of water—diluted with two-thirds water twice a week when well rooted. Water freely. Remove to temp. 50° to 55° in Sept. Admit air freely on fine days. Nip off first truss of bloom if not required to flower before Nov. Temp. for flowering, 50° to 55°. When potting allow base of leaves to just touch the compost. Pot moderately firm. Suitable artificial manures : ¼ oz. each sulphate of ammonia and kainit to 2 gall. of water. To be applied twice a week to plants established in flowering pots. Single-flowered kinds best raised from seed annually, rejecting old plants after flowering. Sow in June for spring flowering. Double varieties require to be propagated annually by cuttings inserted singly in small pots filled with equal parts leaf-mould, loam, and sand, placed in temp. 65° to 70°, after flowering ; or by division of plants in April. Culture same as advised for seedlings. Temp. for flowering, 55° to 60°. Semi-double varieties raised from seed as advised for singles.

CULTURE OF P. OBCONICA : Compost and mode of raising from seed and general treatment same as advised for P. sinensis. Temp. for flowering, 45° to 55°. Top-dress old plants with decayed cow manure in Feb. to promote spring flowering. Repot old plants in March to flower in summer. Old plants may also be divided in March.

CULTURE OF PRIMROSE, COWSLIP, AND OXLIP. Hardy herbaceous perennial. Soil, ordinary rich, moist. Position, partially or wholly shaded beds and borders. Plant, Oct., Nov., Feb., and March. Mulch surface of beds containing choice sorts with decayed manure in Feb. Lift those grown in flower beds directly after flowering, divide and replant 6 in. apart each way in shady border until Oct., then replant in beds. Pot culture, as advised for Polyanthus.

CULTURE OF POLYANTHUS : Hardy herbaceous perennial. Supposed to be a hybrid between the primrose and cowslip. Flowers, various ; spring. CLASSIFICATION : Gold-laced, having centre and edges of bloom golden ; Fancy, blooms of various hues ; Hose-in-Hose, semi-double, one bloom growing out of another ; Jack-in-the-Green, bloom surrounded by a collar-like calyx ; Pantaloons, small, curiously coloured blooms. Properties of Gold-laced Polyanthus : Pip (bloom) perfectly flat and round, slightly scalloped on edge, and divided into five or six lobes or segments ; tube or throat, thrum-eyed—that is, not showing the pistil ; edging and centre of lobes or florets to be even in width and of same shade of sulphur, lemon, or yellow as the eyes and one shade of yellow only in centre ; ground or body colour, black or red ; flower stem, stiff, strong, erect. OUTDOOR CULTURE : Same as for Primrose. POT CULTURE : Compost, two parts good yellow fibrous loam, one part of equal proportions of thoroughly decayed manure, leaf-mould, and silver sand. Pot in Aug. Place in shady, cold frame in a north aspect after potting until Oct., then transfer to frame in south aspect. Give just enough water to keep soil moist between Aug. and March, afterwards water freely. Admit air freely always, except in severe weather. Top-dress in Feb. with compost of equal parts loam and decayed cow manure. Apply weak stimulants once a week March to

July.   Transfer to cold frame or greenhouse with north aspect when in flower. Repot annually.

CULTURE OF ROCK GARDEN PRIMULAS FOR COOL POSITIONS : Soil, open, sandy loam containing plenty of peat and leaf-mould. Position, cool, shady banks and glades in the rock garden. All require abundant moisture during the growing season and should be freely watered in dry weather. Plant, Sept. to Oct. and March to April.

CULTURE OF ROCK GARDEN PRIMULAS FOR OPEN POSITIONS : Soil, light, well-drained peaty loam with plenty of sand and stone chippings. Position, open, sunny banks in the rock garden or deep crevices between boulders. Plant, Sept. to Oct. and March to April.

CULTURE OF BOG PRIMULAS : Soil, peaty loam. Position, bogs, or by the side of ponds and streams. Sun or shade. Plant, Sept. to Oct. and March to April.

PROPAGATION : Miscellaneous species by seeds sown on surface of equal parts peat, leaf-mould, and loam in shallow pans or boxes in shady, cold frame in March or April or by division in spring ; P. verticillata and P. floribunda by seeds sown as advised for P. sinensis, also by division after flowering ; Primrose and Polyanthus by seeds sown on surface of light, sandy soil slightly covered in cold frame in March or April ; or outdoors in shady position in April, likewise by division after flowering.

GREENHOUSE SPECIES : P. floribunda, yellow, winter and spring, 6 in., Himalayas ; Forbesi, rosy lilac, winter and spring, 12 to 15 in., China ; kewensis, yellow, winter and spring, 6 to 12 in., hybrid ; malacoides, rosy lilac, winter and spring, 12 to 18 in., China, and its several colour variations ; obconica, lilac, winter and spring, 8 to 12 in., China, and its many forms with white, pink, red, or purplish flowers ; sinensis (Chinese Primrose), various colours, winter and spring, 6 to 9 in., China ; verticillata, yellow, spring, 12 to 18 in., Arabia.

BORDER SPECIES CULTIVATED : P. auricula (Auricula), various colours, 6 in., Europe ; elatior (Oxlip), yellow, 6 to 9 in., Britain ; officinalis (Cowslip), yellow, 4 to 8 in., Britain ; variabilis (Polyanthus), various, 6 to 9 in., hybrid ; vulgaris (Syn. acaulis), Primrose, various, 4 to 6 in., Britain.

SPECIES FOR COOL POSITIONS : P. capitata, purple, July, 9 in., Himalayas, and its variety Mooreana ; carniolica, rosy lilac and white, July, 6 in., Carniola ; cockburniana, orange-scarlet, June, 1 ft., W. China ; cortusoides, bright rose, April to May, 9 in., Japan, Siberia, etc. ; denticulata, soft lavender, April to May, 1 ft., Himalayas, and its varieties alba and cashmiriana ; Juliæ, deep rose, March to April, 2 to 3 in., Caucasus ; juliana, various shades of rosy red and claret, hybrids ; littoniana, purplish violet, June to Aug., 2 ft., Yunnan ; luteola, yellow, July to Aug., 9 to 12 in., Caucasus ; pulverulenta, crimson-purple, June, 2 ft., W. China, and the Bartley strain, pink with deeper eye ; Parryi, rose-purple, 12 to 18 in., N.W. America ; Sieboldi, white, rose, or purple, spring, 6 to 9 in., Japan ; Veitchii, deep rose, June, 12 in., W. China.

SPECIES FOR OPEN POSITIONS : P. Allionii, rosy mauve and white, March to April, 4 in., Maritime Alps ; chionantha, creamy white, May, 12 in., W. China ; clusiana, carmine and white, May, 3 to 4 in., Austrian Alps ; cottia, rose, June, 4 in., Cottian Alps ; giraldiana, purple, May to June, 8 to 12 in., W. China ; glaucescens (calycina), rosy lilac, May, 4 in., Lombardy ; glutinosa, violet blue, May, 4 in., Europe ; hirsuta, pink or mauve, spring and autumn, 2 to 4 in., Europe, and its varieties alba and ciliata ; integrifolia, purplish lilac, 3 to 4 in., Alps ; marginata, lilac, April, 4 in., Alps ; minima, rosy pink, May, 1 to 2 in., Europe ; œnensis, purplish crimson, spring, 2 to 3 in., S. Tyrol and Italian Alps ; pedemontana, rose pink and white, 6 in., Piedmont ; pubescens, various, 3 to 6 in., May to June, hybrids (the white form is sometimes erroneously offered as P. nivalis) ; spectabilis, pink and white, May to June, 3 in., Tyrol ; Winteri, lavender blue, winter and spring, 4 in., Himalayas ; wulfeniana, rosy mauve, April to May, 2 in., Carinthia, etc.

BOG PRIMULAS : P. beesiana, crimson-purple, June to July, 18 in., Yunnan ; bulleyana, apricot yellow, June, 1 ft., W. China ; farinosa, rosy lilac, May, 6 in., N Regions ; anisodora, dark crimson, summer, 2 ft., Yunnan ; grandis, yellow, summer, 12 to 18 in., Caucasus ; glycosma, yellow, May to June, 3 ft., Yunnan ;

involucrata, white, May, 1 ft., Himalayas ; japonica, crimson, May to June, 2 to 3 ft., Japan ; Florindæ, yellow, 3 to 4 ft., W. China ; microdonta alpicola, sulphur yellow, summer, 1½ to 2 ft., W. China ; Poissoni, purple, June to July, 2 ft., China ; rosea, rosy carmine, May, 6 in., Himalayas ; sikkimensis, yellow, June, 1½ to 2 ft., Himalayas ; secundiflora, purplish crimson, May to June, 12 in., W. China ; Wardii, lilac pink and white, spring and autumn, 9 to 12 in., W. China.

Prince's-Feather (*Amaranthus hypochondriacus*)—See Amaranthus.

Prince of Wales' Feather Fern (*Todea superba*)—See Todea.

Prinsepia—Ord. Rosaceæ. Hardy deciduous flowering shrub. First introduced 1908.
CULTURE : Soil, ordinary loamy. Position, open shrubberies or borders. Plant, Nov. to Feb.
PROPAGATION : By seeds sown in boxes in autumn and allowed to become frozen in winter soil and seeds subsequently being re-sown in March or April in drills in the open ; cuttings of young wood in gentle bottom heat ; layering in spring.
SPECIES CULTIVATED : P. sinensis, yellow, Feb. to March, 3 to 6 ft., Manchuria.

Pritchardia—Ord. Palmaceæ. Warm greenhouse palms. Orn. foliage. First introduced 1870. Leaves more or less fan-shaped, green.
CULTURE : Compost, two parts peat and one part of loam and sand. Position, well-drained pots in light part of stove. Pot, Feb. to April. Water moderately Oct. to March, freely afterwards. Syringe twice daily March to Sept., once daily Sept. to March. Temp., March to Sept. 65° to 75° ; Sept. to March 55° to 65°
PROPAGATION : By seeds sown ⅛ in. deep in light, rich soil in temp. 80° to 90°, Feb., March, or April.
SPECIES CULTIVATED : P. Martii, 4 to 10 ft., Sandwich Islands ; pacifica, 20 to 30 ft., Fiji ; Thurstoni, 4 to 10 ft., Fiji ; Vuylstekiana, 4 to 10 ft., Potomos Islands. See also Licuala and Washingtonia.

Privet (*Ligustrum vulgare*)—See Ligustrum.

Promenæa—See Zygopetalum.

Prophet's-flower (*Arnebia echioides*)—See Arnebia.

Prostanthera—Ord. Labiatæ. Greenhouse flowering shrubs. Evergreen. First introduced 1808. Natives of Australia.
CULTURE : Compost, peaty loam and sand. Position, large well-drained pots in unheated greenhouse. Water freely during summer, moderately in spring and autumn, little in winter. Pot, Sept. to Oct. or April to May.
PROPAGATION : By cuttings of young growth in sandy soil under bell-glass with gentle bottom heat.
SPECIES CULTIVATED : P. lasianthos, white, tinged red, June, 3 to 6 ft. ; rotundifolia, purple, May to June, 3 ft. Both may be grown in mild districts outdoors against a south wall.

Protea—Ord. Proteaceæ. Greenhouse evergreen flowering shrubs. First introduced 1774.
CULTURE : Compost, two parts light, well-decayed turfy loam, one part equal proportions silver sand, charcoal, broken pots, freestone, and peat. Position, light, airy greenhouse fully exposed to sunshine. Pot, March. Drain pots one-third of depth with broken potsherds. Pot firmly. Water moderately March to Sept., occasionally afterwards, keeping soil just moist. No syringing or stimulants required. Stand plants in sunny position outdoors during June, July, and Aug. Temp., Sept. to March 40° to 50° ; March to June 55° to 65°.
PROPAGATION : By cuttings of firm shoots cut off close to a joint, pared quite smooth, inserted thinly in small pots half filled with drainage, and remainder with pure sand, placed under bell-glass in cool part of greenhouse in summer.
SPECIES CULTIVATED : P. cordata, purple, spring, 18 in., S. Africa ; grandiflora, white, May, 6 to 8 ft., S. Africa.

Provence Rose (*Rosa centifolia provincialis*)—See Rosa.

Prumnopitys—Ord. Taxaceæ. Hardy evergreen tree. **Orn. foliage. First** introduced 1863.

CULTURE OF HARDY SPECIES : Soil, good, deep loam, well drained. Position, sunny, sheltered lawns. Plant, Oct., Nov., March, or April.

PROPAGATION : By cuttings of firm young shoots inserted in small pots of sandy loam under bell-glass in temp. 60° to 70°, summer.

SPECIES CULTIVATED : P. elegans (Plum Fir), Syn. Podocarpus andina, 40 to 50 ft., Chile.

Prunella (Selfheal)—Ord. Labiatæ. Hardy herbaceous perennials.

CULTURE : Soil, ordinary light, rich. Position, moist shady, border or rockery. Plant, Oct., Nov., March, or April. Lift, divide, and replant ever two or three years. Water in dry weather. Mulch with decayed manure in March.

PROPAGATION : By division of roots, Oct., Nov., or March.

SPECIES CULTIVATED : P. grandiflora, purple, July and Aug., 6 in., Europe, and its varieties alba (white) and rubra (red) ; vulgaris laciniata, purple, July, leaves finely cut, 1 ft., Britain ; webbiana, purple, summer, 6 in., botanical position uncertain.

Prunus (Plum ; Damson ; Myrobalan Plum ; Double Chinese Plum)—Ord. Rosaceæ. Hardy deciduous and evergreen trees and shrubs. Edible fruit-bearing, flowering and orn. foliage. First introduced : Peach and Nectarine, 1562 ; Almond, 1548 ; Apricot, 1548 ; Common Laurel, 1629 ; Portugal Laurel, 1648.

CULTURE OF PEACH AND NECTARINE : Soil, deep but not over-rich sandy loam, well drained, and free from manure. Position, south or south-west walls fully exposed to sun. Height of wall, 12 to 14 ft. Plant, Oct. to Feb. Distances for planting : Cordons, 18 in. ; dwarf fan-trained, 15 ft. ; standard fan-trained, 15 ft. Depth of soil above roots, 4 to 6 in. Prune, Jan. or Feb. Fruit borne on old spurs and shoots of previous years' growth. Do not shorten the latter unless very strong. Always cut back if possible to a triple bud. Train previous year's shoots 2 to 3 in. apart all over tree. Remove a small proportion of shoots that have borne fruit annually to make room for new ones. Fruit buds, conical, downy. Wood buds, pointed, narrow. Disbud, *i.e.* rub off young shoots, April, May, and June, removing those growing out of front of branches, leaving one at base and one at tip of each growth formed the previous year, and reducing those issuing from the sides of previous year's shoots to 6 in. apart each side. Train young shoots when 3 to 6 in. long to the wall. Protect blossoms from frost by covering of tiffany or fish-netting in Feb. and March. Thin fruit when size of a hazel nut to 3 or 4 in. apart ; again when size of a walnut to 10 and 12 in. apart. Average number of fruit for a full-grown tree to carry, about 240. Mulch with decayed manure in March or April. Apply stimulants occasionally April to Aug. Suitable artificial manures : (1) 1 part (by weight) crude magnesium sulphate, 6 parts muriate of potash, 18 parts superphosphate forked into the soil at the rate of 3 oz. per sq. yard, after pruning ; (2) ½ lb. kainit, ¾ lb. each of superphosphate and nitrate of soda, applied as advised for No. 2. Liquid manure : Nitrate of soda and super-phosphate of lime, ¼ oz. each per gall. ; guano 1 oz. to gallon ; horse and cow manure diluted one-third—all applied in spring and summer. UNDER GLASS : Soil, planting, pruning, manuring, same as for outdoors. Temp. for forcing : Jan. 40° to 50° ; Feb. 45° to 55° ; March and onwards 55° to 65°. Disbud when shoots are an inch or so long. Syringe twice daily until blossoms open, then cease ; commencing again when fruit forms, and discontinuing when it begins to ripen. Ventilate freely in summer. Thin the fruit when the size of a hazel nut to 3 or 4 in. apart, and again when as large as a walnut to a foot apart. Water border thoroughly in Jan. or Feb., again in March, May, July, and Sept. Apply stimulants March, May, July, and Sept. TREES IN POTS : Compost, two parts decayed turfy loam, one part well-decayed manure, a quarter part crushed bones, and a tablespoonful of superphosphate to each bushel. Pot, Nov. Stand the trees in a sheltered corner till Jan., when remove to greenhouse. Water moderately at first, freely in spring and summer, none in winter. Pruning, manuring, etc., as advised above.

CULTURE OF CHERRY : Soil, rich, sandy ; stiff or gravelly unsuitable. Position, standards, pyramids, and bushes open and sunny ; May Duke and early kinds on S. and W. walls or fences ; Bigarreau and Morello on E. or N. walls. Plant standards 25 ft. apart ; pyramids, 15 ft. ; horizontal or fan-trained, 15 ft. ; bush-trained, 5 to 8 ft. ; cordons, 18 in. Time to plant, Oct. to Feb. Depth for roots, 6 in. Stocks for standard trees, seedling Duke or Morello ; for dwarf trees, Mahaleb Cherry. Mode of bearing : Morello bears fruit along full length of shoot of previous year's growth ; other kinds at base of shoots only, called " spurs." Pruning : Standards, simply remove branches when too thick ; pyramids and bushes, summer prune lateral shoots to four leaves, leaders to six leaves in July ; cordons, cut all shoots except leading one similarly ; horizontal and fan-trained, shorten laterals to fourth leaf, leaders to six leaves in July. Morello, remove old or weak shoots only in Dec. Winter pruning consists of removal of dead or overcrowded shoots and cutting back those omitted in summer. Protect early cherries by nets or tiffany. POT CULTURE : Plant in 10 or 12 in. pots in Oct. Compost, two parts turfy loam, one part decayed manure. Place trees in sheltered position outdoors till Jan., then remove them to greenhouse or vinery. Temp., Jan. to March 45° to 60° ; March to June 55° to 65°. Water moderately. Ventilate moderately before and after flowering, freely when in flower.

CULTURE OF PLUM : Soil, shallow, moderately moist, sandy loam, or good ordinary, intermixed freely with old mortar. Subsoil, gravelly or chalky. Position, open, sunny, sheltered gardens, orchards, walls, or fences. Plant, Nov. to Feb. Distance for planting : Standards, 21 to 24 ft. each way ; pyramids, 9 to 10 ft. ; fan-trained, 15 ft. ; bush-trained, 6 to 9 ft. ; cordons, 18 in. Distance from paths : Pyramids, 5 ft. ; bush-treained, 2 ft. 6 in. Mode of bearing : On spurs formed at base of shoots of previous years' growth and on older branches. Prune, summer, July and Aug. ; winter, Dec. to Feb. Simply thin out branches of standards and keep centres open. Shorten leading shoots of pyramids and bushes at sixth leaf from base in July ; remainder to the forth leaf a week or so later. Shorten leading shoots of fan-trained trees in Dec. ; also side or front shoots not required to forward new branches to within 4 in. of base, July or Aug. Leading shoots of cordons to grow unpruned until full height is attained ; side shoots to be shortened to the fourth leaf in July. Thin fruit of greengages to 3 in. apart ; large kinds to 4 or 6 in. apart, when size of hazel nut. Mulch newly-planted trees with thick layer of cow manure. Root prune vigorous and unfruitful trees in Nov. Shake out, root prune, and repot pot-grown pyramids, bush, and cordon trees every third year. Chemical manures : Kainit (sulphate of potash), 5 parts ; magnesium sulphate, 2 parts ; super-phosphate, 2 parts, all by weight. Apply at rate of 3 oz. per sq. yd., immediately after pruning to area of soil equal to circumference of branches, and 1 oz. more in March, forking it in.

CULTURE OF DAMSON : Soil, moderately rich, deep loam. Position, south aspect, well-drained site. Shape of trees, standard, pyramidal, or bush. Plant bush-trained trees 5 ft. apart ; pyramidal, 15 ft. ; standards, 24 ft., in Nov., Dec., or Jan. Depth for roots, 6 in. Prune in Dec., simply cutting away old branches or weak shoots and moderately shortening strong ones. Manures, same as for plums.

CULTURE OF APRICOT : Soil, light, well-drained loam containing plenty of old mortar rubbish. Position, S. walls in Midlands and North ; E. and W. walls in the South. May be grown as bushes or standards in sheltered gardens in S. of England. Plant, Sept. to Nov., 2 ft. apart for cordons and 18 ft. for fan-trained trees. Fruit borne on spurs, and upon young wood of the previous year's growth. Prune in Jan., shortening shoots not required to form new branches to within an inch of their base and cutting out old wood that is overcrowding the tree. Young shoots are trained back in their place. Disbud from June onwards, rubbing off all young shoots save one at the base and one at the tip of each growth made the previous season. These basal shoots will take the place of the two-year-old wood when the latter is cut out in winter. Protect when in flower with tiffany or fish-netting. Mulch roots with decayed manure in hot, dry seasons. Water copiously in summer. Feed with manures advised for peaches. Thin fruit out early to 1 ft. apart. Por CULTURE : Same as for Peaches.

CULTURE OF MYROBALAN PLUM : Used chiefly for hedges ; occasionally as a stock for plums. Soil, ordinary. Position, sunny. Plant, Oct. to Feb. Distance apart to plant, 6 in. Size of plants, two-year-old. Trim into shape, June or July. Makes an impenetrable hedge.
CULTURE OF PORTUGAL AND CHERRY LAURELS : Soil, good ordinary. Position, mixed shrubberies or hedges for Cherry Laurel ; lawns or shrubberies for Portugal Laurel. Plant, Sept. to Oct. or in May. Prune in April, merely shortening straggly growths. HEDGE CULTURE OF CHERRY LAUREL : Trench side 3 ft. wide and 2 ft. deep, mixing plenty of rotten manure with soil. Plant, 12 in. to 24 in. apart. Prune in April.
CULTURE OF FLOWERING SPECIES : Soil, ordinary. Position, well-drained sunny borders or shrubberies ; Almond good town tree. Plant, Oct. to Feb. Prune only to cut away dead wood, or to shorten straggly growths after flowering. POT CULTURE OF P. TRILOBA : Compost, two parts sandy loam, one part leaf-mould, half a part silver sand. Position, cold greenhouse, Jan. to June ; outdoors, pots plunged to rim in garden soil, June to Nov. ; sheltered corner or pit, Nov. to Jan. Pot, Nov. Repot annually. Water freely March to Oct., moderately afterwards. Apply stimulants occasionally April to Sept. Temp. for forcing, 55° to 65°.
PROPAGATION : Peach and Nectarine by budding in July or Aug. on seedling Almonds or Plums ; Cherry by budding in July or Aug. on the Mahaleb Cherry for dwarfs, or seedling Cherry for standards ; Plums by budding in July or Aug. on the Brussel, Pershore, Common Plum, Myrobalan, St. Julien, Brompton and Common Mussel Damsons by seed ; Almonds by budding on seedling Plums ; other species by budding on the Myrobalan Plum ; Laurels and Myrobalan Plum by cuttings inserted in sheltered border or cold frame in autumn ; Flowering species by cuttings of half-ripened wood taken with a heel in July and Aug. and struck in sandy soil under bell-glass in gentle bottom heat ; all kinds by seeds to produce new varieties.
FRUIT-BEARING SPECIES : P. Persica (Peach), rose, April, 15 to 25 ft., China ; Persica lævis (Nectarine) ; communis (Plum), white, spring, 20 ft., native habitat unknown ; Cerasus (Cherry), white, April, 15 to 20 ft., Europe (Britain), etc. ; Armeniaca (Apricot), blush, Feb. and March, 15 to 25 ft., N. China ; insititia (Bullace), white, April, 10 to 20 ft., Europe (Britain) ; insititia var. (Damson), white, spring, 20 ft., Britain ; spinosa (Sloe), white, March, 10 to 15 ft., Europe (Britain).
FLOWERING SPECIES : P. acida, white, May, 8 to 10 ft., E. Europe, and its varieties dumosa (dwarf) and semperflorens ; americana (Wild Red Plum), white, April, 12 to 30 ft., U.S.A. ; Amygdalus (Almond), rose, March and April, 20 to 30 ft., S. Europe ; Amygdalus amara (Bitter Almond) ; Amygdalus dulcis (Sweet Almond) ; Avium (Gean), white, April to May, 40 to 60 ft., Europe (Britain), and its varieties decumara, flore-pleno, and pendula ; cerasifera (Cherry or Myrobalan Plum), white, March, 20 to 30 ft., Caucasus, and its varieties Pissardi (foliage purple), blireiana (semi-double pink), and Moseri (semi-double pink) ; Cerasus Rhexi (Double Cherry), Syn. P. Cerasus flore-pleno, white, double, April, 15 to 20 ft., Europe ; Conradinæ, flesh pink, March to April, 20 to 25 ft., China ; davidiana, white, Jan. to March, 20 to 30 ft., China ; incisa, pink, spring, 8 to 12 ft., Japan ; japonica, blush white, April, 3 ft., Japan, and its varieties flore-pleno (double white) and flore roseo pleno (double pink) ; Mahaleb (Mahaleb Cherry), white, April to May, 30 to 40 ft., Europe, and its varieties Bommi and pendula ; Mume (Japanese Apricot), pale rose, March, 10 to 30 ft., Corea, and its varieties alba, alba-pleno, flore-pleno, and pendula ; nana (Dwarf Almond), pink or blush, March, 3 to 5 ft., S. Russia ; Padus (Bird Cherry), white, May, 30 to 50 ft., Europe (Britain), and its varieties flore-pleno (double) and Watereri ; Persica flore roseo pleno (Double Peach), rose, double, March, 10 to 20 ft. ; Persica flore alba pleno, white, double ; Persica foliis rubris, leaves purple ; Persica Clara Meyer, deep rose ; pilosiuscula, pink, Feb., 15 to 20 ft., W. China ; pumila, white, May, 2 to 8 ft., North-eastern U.S.A. ; serotina, white, May, 30 to 80 ft., N. America ; serrulata, white or pink, April to May, 15 to 25 ft., China and Japan, and its many varieties such as vietchiana, Hizakura, Shiro-fugen, Benifugen, and pendula (weeping) ; Sieboldii (Syn. P. pseudo-cerasus Watereri), double blush or rose, April to May, 15 to 25 ft., Japan ; subhirtella, shell pink, April, 20 to 30 ft., Japan, and its varieties ascendens (vigorous and

upright), autumnalis (winter-flowering), and pendula (Syn. P. sinensis pendula
rosea), weeping ; spinosa flore-pleno, double white, March, 10 to 15 ft., Europe
(Britain) ; spinosa purpurea, pink, March, 10 to 15 ft., leaves red when young,
becoming coppery purple ; tomentosa, white, tinged rose, March to April, 4 to 8 ft.,
China ; triloba flore-pleno, silvery rose, double, March to April, 12 to 15 ft., China ;
virginiana (Virginian Bird Cherry), white, May, 10 to 15 ft., N. America.
EVERGREEN SPECIES : P. Laurocerasus (Common or Cherry Laurel), white, spring,
8 to 20 ft., E. Europe, Orient, etc., and its varieties caucasica, colchica, latifolia,
etc. ; ilicifolia, white, March to May, 3 to 5 ft., California, rather tender, requires
wall shelter ; lusitanica (Portugal Laurel), white, June, 10 to 15 ft., Portugal.

Pseudolarix (Golden Larch)—Ord. Coniferæ. Hardy deciduous orn. tree.
First introduced 1853.
CULTURE : Soil, gravelly or stony. Position, as specimens in open places or upon
lawns. Plant in autumn.
PROPAGATION : By seeds sown 1 in. deep in beds in the open during March, trans-
planting seedlings when two years old.
SPECIES CULTIVATED : P. Fortunei (Syns. P. Kæmpferi and Larix Kæmpferi), 100 to
130 ft., foliage turns rich yellow in autumn, China.

Pseudopanax—Ord. Araliaceæ. Greenhouse evergreen shrub. Orn. foliage.
First introduced 1846. Leaves, hand-shaped, shining.
CULTURE : Compost, equal parts loam, peaty leaf-mould, charcoal, and sand. Pot,
Feb. to March. Water freely March to Oct., moderately afterwards. Temp.,
March to Sept. 55° to 60° ; Sept. to March 45° to 55°.
PROPAGATION : By grafting in heat in spring ; inserting portions of roots in light
soil in temp. 80° in April.
SPECIES CULTIVATED : P. crassifolium, 5 to 10 ft., New Zealand.

Pseudotsuga (Douglas Fir)—Ord. Coniferæ. Hardy evergreen orn. tree.
First introduced 1827.
CULTURE : Good deep loam. Position, as specimens in open places or upon lawns.
Thrives in districts where there is an abundant rainfall.
PROPAGATION : By seeds sown 1 in. deep in beds in the open during March, trans-
planting seedlings when two years old.
SPECIES CULTIVATED: P. Douglasii (Syns. P. taxifolia and Abies Douglasii), 200 to
250 ft., Western N. America, and its varieties glauca (leaves glaucous), pendula
(branches pendulous), taxifolia (leaves long and narrow), and Fretsi (leaves short
and broad).

Psidium (Guava Tree)—Ord. Myrtaceæ. Stove evergreen shrubs. Flowering
and edible fruit-bearing. First introduced 1692. Fruit (berries), yellow or claret-
coloured, round or pear-shaped, aromatic, edible.
CULTURE : Compost, two parts fibrous sandy loam, one part equal proportions dry
cow manure and silver sand. Position, well-drained pots, tubs, or beds, with shoots
trained to back walls of stove, warm greenhouse, or vinery. Pot or plant, Feb. or
March. Prune into shape annually, Feb. Water freely April to Oct., moderately
afterwards. Syringe freely, March, until fruit begins to ripen, then keep foliage
dry. Apply weak stimulants occasionally after berries form until fruit ripens.
Temp., March to Oct. 65° to 75° ; Oct. to March 55° to 60°.
PROPAGATION : By cuttings of firm young shoots, 2 to 3 in. long, inserted in sand
under bell-glass in temp. 75° to 80°, spring or summer.
SPECIES CULTIVATED : P. cattleianum (Strawberry Guava), white, June, 15 to 25 ft.,
fruits purplish red, obovate to globose, Brazil ; Guava (Common Guava), white,
summer, 20 to 30 ft., fruits, yellow, globose, pyriform, or ovoid.

Psoralea (Scurvy Pea)—Ord. Leguminosæ. Greenhouse evergreen flowering
shrubs. First introduced 1690.
CULTURE : Compost, equal parts fibrous loam, peat, and silver sand. Position, pots
in sunny, airy greenhouse. Pot, Feb. or March. Prune into shape, Feb. Water
freely April to Sept., moderately afterwards. Good drainage essential. No

stimulants or shade required.   Temp., March to Sept. 55° to 65° ; Sept. to March 40° to 50°.

PROPAGATION : By cuttings of firm shoots, 2 to 3 in. long, inserted in pots half filled with drainage, remainder layer of moss and pure sand, placed under bell-glass in shady part of greenhouse, May or June.

SPECIES CULTIVATED : P. aculeata, blue and white, summer, 3 ft., S. Africa ; glandulosa, white and blue, May to Sept., 4 ft., Chile ; pinnata, blue, summer, 3 to 6 ft., S. Africa.

Psychotria—Ord. Rubiaceæ.   Stove evergreen flowering shrub.   Of similar habit to the Ixora.   First introduced 1860.

CULTURE : Compost, two parts fibrous peat, one part fibrous loam, one part silver sand.   Position, shady part of stove whilst growing ; light one when at rest. Pot, Feb. or March.   Prune into shape, Feb.   Water freely March to Sept., moderately afterwards.   Syringe morning and evening in spring and summer.   Apply weak liquid manure once a week to healthy plants in flower.   Temp., March to Sept. 75° to 85° ; Sept. to March 55° to 65°.

PROPAGATION : By cuttings in sandy peat under bell-glass in temperature of 75° to 85° in spring.

SPECIES CULTIVATED : P. jasminiflora (Syn. Gloneria jasminiflora), snow-white, summer, 3 ft., Brazil.

Ptelea (Hop Tree)—Ord. Rutaceæ.   Hardy deciduous tree.   Flowering and orn. foliage.   First introduced 1704.   Leaves, trifoliate, green, or variegated with yellow.

CULTURE : Soil, ordinary well drained.   Position, open shrubberies, plantations, or woods.   Plant, Nov. to Feb.   Prune into shape, Dec. to Feb.

PROPAGATION : By seeds sown ¼ in. deep in sunny position outdoors in March or April ; layering shoots in spring.

SPECIES CULTIVATED : P. trifoliata (Swamp Dogwood), green, June to July, 15 to 20 ft., N. America ; trifoliata aurea, young leaves golden.

Pteris (Bracken ; Brake-fern ; Spider Fern)—Ord. Filices.   Stove, greenhouse, and hardy ferns.   Evergreen and deciduous.   Young shoots of bracken, gathered when 6 in. long, may be cooked and eaten like Asparagus.

CULTURE OF HARDY SPECIES : Soil, ordinary.   Position, shady borders or woods. Plant, April.

CULTURE OF STOVE SPECIES : Compost, equal parts loam, leaf-mould, peat, and sand.   Position, pots, beds, or rockeries in shady part of stove.   Pot or plant, Feb. or March.   Water abundantly April to Sept., moderately afterwards.   Temp., March to Sept. 70° to 80° ; Sept. to March 60° to 70°.

CULTURE OF GREENHOUSE SPECIES : Compost, as above.   Pot, March or April. Position, pots, beds, or rockery in shady part of house.   Water freely March to Oct., moderately Oct. to March.   Temp., March to Sept. 55° to 65° ; Sept. to March 50° to 55°.

PROPAGATION : By spores sown on fine sandy peat in well-drained pans in temp. 80° any time ; dwarf species by division of plants, Oct. or April.

HARDY SPECIES : P. aquilina (Brake- or Bracken-fern), 2 to 4 ft., Britain, etc. Several varieties.

STOVE SPECIES : P. aspericaulis, 6 to 8 in., India ; aspericaulis tricolor, fronds green, white, and red ; palmata nobilis, 1 ft., Brazil ; quadriaurita argyrea, fronds with white centres, 1 ft., Tropics.

GREENHOUSE SPECIES : P. Bausei, hybrid ; cretica, and its varieties albo-lineata, Mayi, major, and Wimsettii, Tropics and Subtropics ; ensiformis, and its varieties cristata, Reginæ, and Victoriæ, Tropics ; longifolia, Tropics and Subtropics, and its variety Mariesii, Japan ; scaberula, New Zealand ; serrulata (Spider Fern), and its variety cristata, China, Japan, etc. ; tremula (Trembling Fern), and its varieties Smithieana, elegans, and variegata, Australia.   See also Pellæa.

Pterocarya (Wing Nut)—Ord. Juglandaceæ.   Hardy deciduous orn. trees. First introduced 1800.   Handsome pinnate foliage.

CULTURE : Soil, deep loam.   Position, as specimens in open places or on lawns.

All require abundant moisture. Plant, Nov. to Feb. Young plants liable to damage by late spring frosts.

PROPAGATION : By seeds sown 1 in. deep in the open in light soil during March ; suckers in autumn ; layers in spring ; cuttings of ripened wood in Sept. or Oct.

SPECIES CULTIVATED : P. caucasica (Syn. P. fraxinifolia), 50 to 100 ft., Caucasus ; hupehensis, 60 to 80 ft., W. China ; rehderiana, 40 ft., hybrid ; stenoptera, 50 to 60 ft., China.

Ptychosperma (Australian Feather Palm)—Ord. Palmaceæ. Stove palms. Orn. foliage. Leaves, feather-shaped, green, very graceful. First introduced 1868.

CULTURE : Compost, equal parts loam and leaf-mould, half a part silver sand. Position, shady part of stove, warm greenhouse, or conservatory ; pots or tubs. Pot, Feb. or March. Water copiously March to Sept., moderately afterwards. Syringe freely daily March to Oct. Shade from sun. Top-dress large plants occasionally with layer of cow manure. Apply stimulants occasionally April to Sept. Temp., March to Oct. 60° to 75° ; Oct. to March 55° to 60°.

PROPAGATION : By seeds sown ⅛ in. deep in light, rich soil in temp. 80° to 90°, Feb., March, or April.

SPECIES CULTIVATED : P. elegans, 10 to 20 ft., Australia ; sanderiana, 10 to 20 ft.

Pulmonaria (Lung-wort ; Blue Cowslip ; Sage of Bethlehem)—Ord. Boraginaceæ. Hardy herbaceous herbs. Orn. foliage. Leaves, lance-shaped, green, spotted with white.

CULTURE : Soil, ordinary. Position, partially shaded rockeries or borders. Plant, Oct., Nov., March, or April. Lift and replant in fresh soil every four or five years.

PROPAGATION : By seeds sown ¹⁄₁₆ in. deep in ordinary soil in shady position outdoors, March or April ; division of roots, Oct. or March.

SPECIES CULTIVATED : P. angustifolia (Blue Cowslip), blue and pink, spring, 1 ft., Europe, and its varieties arvernensis (purple-blue) and azurea (blue) ; officinalis (Sage of Bethlehem or Lung-wort), red and violet, spring, 1 ft., Europe (Britain) ; rubra, brick red, spring, 9 to 12 in., Transylvania ; saccharata, pink, April to July, 1 ft., Europe.

Pultenæa—Ord. Leguminosæ. Greenhouse evergreen flowering shrubs. First introduced 1792.

CULTURE : Compost, two parts fibrous peat, one part equal proportions silver sand and pounded charcoal. Position, light, airy greenhouse. Pot, Feb. or March. Well-drained pots and firm potting essential. Water freely April to Sept., moderately other times. Use soft water only. No stimulants required. Shade unnecessary. Stand plants in sunny position outdoors during July and Aug. Temp., Sept. to March 40° to 50° ; March to July 55° to 65°.

PROPAGATION : By seeds sown on surface of shallow, well-drained pans filled with sandy peat, slightly covered with fine peat, placed under bell-glass in temp. 55° to 65°, March or April ; cuttings of firm shoots, 2 to 3 in. long, inserted in sandy peat under bell-glass in shade in temp. 55° to 65° in summer.

SPECIES CULTIVATED : P. obcordata, yellow, April, 3 ft. ; rosea, pink, spring, 1 ft. ; stricta, yellow, spring, 3 ft. ; villosa, yellow, spring, 3 ft. All natives of Australia.

Pumpkin (*Cucurbita maxima*)—See Cucurbita.

Punica (Pomegranate)—Ord. Lythraceæ. Hardy deciduous fruit-bearing trees. Fruits, roundish, golden red. First introduced 1548.

CULTURE : Compost, two parts rich fibrous loam, one part thoroughly decayed cow manure. Position, well-drained borders against S. and S.W. walls, S. and S.W. England ; in tubs, pots, or borders, with shoots trained against back wall of cool or cold houses or conservatories, in other parts of the country. Plant, Oct. to Feb. Train branches thinly to walls. Prune weak shoots only. Blossom and fruit borne on extremities of shoots of previous years' growth. Water outdoor trees copiously in dry weather ; indoor trees frequently in summer ; moderately in autumn and spring ; give none in winter. Mulch surface of soil annually with cow manure in March or April.

PROPAGATION : By seeds sown ¼ in. deep in well-drained pots of sandy soil in temp. 55° to 65° in spring, transplanting seedlings singly into small pots and keeping in greenhouse until following spring, then plant outdoors or continue to grow in pots. Double-flowered sorts by cuttings of firm shoots, 6 to 8 in. long, inserted in well-drained pots of sandy soil in cold frame or greenhouse any time ; layering shoots, Oct. or Nov. ; grafting on single-flowered species in March.
SPECIES CULTIVATED : P. Granatum, red, June to Sept., 15 to 20 ft., Persia, and its varieties albescens (white or yellowish) and flore-pleno (double **red**) ; Granatum flore-pleno, double ; Granatum nana, dwarf.

Purple Beech (*Fagus sylvatica purpurea*)—See Fagus.

Purple Birch (*Betula verrucosa purpurea*)—See Betula.

Purple Clover (*Trifolium repens purpureum*)—See Trifolium.

Purple Cone-flower (*Echinacea purpurea*)—See Echinacea.

Purple-leaved Filbert (*Corylus Avellana purpurea*)—See Corylus.

Purple Mexican Aster (*Cosmos bipinnatus*)—See Cosmos.

Purple Milk Vetch (*Astragalus Monspessulanus*)—See Astragalus.

Purple Mulberry (*Callicarpa purpurea*)—See Callicarpa.

Purple Orchis (*Orchis mascula*)—See Orchis.

Purple Osier (*Salix purpurea*)—See Salix.

Purple Rock-cress (*Aubrietia deltoidea*)—See Aubrietia.

Purple Sand Verbena (*Abronia umbellata*)—See Abronia.

Purple Snowdrop (*Sisyrinchium grandiflorum*)—See Sisyrinchium.

Purple Sow Thistle (*Lactuca Plumeri*)—See Lactuca.

Purple Tassels (*Muscari comosum*)—See Muscari.

Purple Toad-flax (*Linaria purpurea*)—See Linaria.

Purple Willow (*Salix purpurea*)—See Salix.

Purple Wreath (*Petrea volubilis*)—See Petrea.

Purslane (*Portulaca oleracea*)—See Portulaca.

Puschkinia (Striped Squill)—Ord. Liliaceæ. Hardy bulbous flowering plants. First introduced 1819.
CULTURE : Soil, ordinary light, sandy. Position, sunny well-drained border or rockery. Plant bulbs 4 in. deep, 1 in. apart, Oct. or Nov. Protect immediately after planting with covering 1 in. deep of cocoanut-fibre refuse or decayed manure. After flowering remove protective material, fully exposing surface to sun to ripen bulbs. Lift and replant every two or three years.
PROPAGATION : By seeds sown ⅛ in. deep in shallow, well-drained pans filled with light, sandy soil in Aug. or Sept., placed in cold frame ; offsets, removed and planted as advised for old bulbs, Oct. or Nov.
SPECIES CULTIVATED : P. scilloides (Syn. libanotica), white, striped with blue, spring, 4 in., Asia Minor ; scilloides compacta, dwarf.

Pycnostachys—Ord. Labiatæ. Greenhouse perennial.
CULTURE : Soil, loam, leaf-mould, and sand. Position, well-drained pots in sunny greenhouse. Water freely during the growing season, sparingly other times. Temp., Sept. to March 45° to 55° ; March to Sept. 60° to 65°.
PROPAGATION : By division ; seeds in a temp. of 65° in spring
SPECIES CULTIVATED : P. Dawei, blue, winter, 4 to 6 ft., Uganda.

Pyracantha (Firethorn)—Ord. Rosaceæ. Evergreen flowering and berried orn. shrubs. Hardy or half-hardy. First introduced 1629.
CULTURE : Soil, ordinary loamy. Position, sunny, sheltered shrubberies or trained as wall climbers. Plant, Sept. to Oct. and April to May. Prune into shape in Feb.
PROPAGATION : By seeds sown in boxes of sandy soil in cool greenhouse or frame

during Feb. or March ; cuttings of nearly ripened young growth in sandy soil in frame during Aug. or Sept.

SPECIES CULTIVATED : P. angustifolia, white, May to June, 10 to 12 ft., orange yellow berries, W. China, requires south wall ; coccinea, white, June, 10 to 15 ft., coral red berries, S. Europe and Asia Minor, and its variety Lalandei (orange berries) ; crenulata, white, May to June, 10 to 15 ft., berries orange yellow, Himalayas, requires south wall ; Gibbsii, white, May to June, 10 to 15 ft., berries scarlet, China ; rogersiana, white, May to June, 10 to 15 ft., berries yellow, China.

Pyramidal Orchis (*Orchis pyramidalis*)—See Orchis.

Pyrenean Dead-nettle (*Horminum pyrenaicum*)—See Horminum.

Pyrenean Lily (*Lilium pyrenaicum*)—See Lilium.

Pyrenean Meadow Saffron (*Merendera bulbocodium*)—See Merendera.

Pyrenean Violet (*Viola cornuta*)—See Viola.

Pyrethrum—See Chrysanthemum.

Pyrola (Winter Green)—Ord. Ericaceæ. Hardy perennial herbs.

CULTURE : Soil, equal parts peat, leaf-mould, and sandy loam. Position, moist, partially shady borders or rockeries. Plant, March or April. Water freely in dry weather. Lift, divide, and replant only when overgrown.

PROPAGATION : By seeds sown thinly and slightly covered with very fine sandy peat in position where intended to grow, March or April ; division of roots, April.

SPECIES CULTIVATED : P. elliptica, white, fragrant, summer, 6 in., N. America ; media, white and red, summer, 4 in., Britain ; minor, white and red, summer, 8 in., Europe (Britain) ; rotundifolia, white, fragrant, summer, 6 in., Britain.

Pyrus (Apple ; Pear ; Crab ; Medlar ; Quince ; Mountain Ash ; Rowan Tree ; White Beam Tree)—Ord. Rosaceæ. Hardy deciduous fruit-bearing and flowering trees and shrubs.

CULTURE OF APPLE : Soil, deep loam. Position, open, sheltered gardens, N.W. or E. walls. Plant, Nov. to Feb. Distance for planting : Cordons, 18 in. ; bush-trained trees, 12 ft. ; pyramids, 12 ft. ; fan-trained trees, 15 ft. ; espaliers, 18 ft. ; standards, 21 to 24 ft. Distance from paths : Pyramids, 5 ft. ; bush-trained, 2 ft. 6 in. Mode of bearing : On spurs formed on older branches and base of shoots of previous year's growth. Fruit buds may be distinguished from growth buds by their plumpness and roundness. Summer pruning : Shorten all side shoots on cordon trees to 4 to 6 in. during July and August ; leave the leader unpruned. Remove the points of the strongest young shoots on pyramids and bushes in July ; leave the weak ones untouched. Secure to the wall suitably placed young shoots of fan-trained trees to form future branches and shorten remaining ones as advised for Cordons. Allow the extremity of each espalier branch to grow unchecked and shorten side growths to four leaves in July. Standards require no summer pruning. Winter pruning : Shorten side shoots of cordons to within 1 to 2 in. of their base in Nov., and leader by one-third. Shorten all shoots, except leading ones, of bushes and pyramids to within 2 to 4 in. of their base, and leading shoots to 6 or 8 in., in Nov. Prune to within 2 to 4 in. of base, according to strength, all side shoots on fan-trained trees ; leading shoots, intended to form new branches, to 6, 9, or 12 in., in Nov. Espalier side shoots shorten to 1 to 2 in., and leaders at end of branches to 6, 9, or 12 in., in Nov. Simply thin out branches of standards, keep centre quite open, and shorten any extra vigorous shoots. Mulch newly-planted trees with thick layer of manure. Root prune vigorous unfruitful trees in Oct. or Nov. Gather fruit when, on lifting it by the hand from a vertical to a horizontal position, it readily parts from the tree. Store in dark, cool, frost-proof room (temp. 40° to 45°). Chemical manures : (1) Superphosphate of lime, 12 parts (by weight) ; nitrate of potash, 10 parts ; common salt, 4 parts ; sulphate of magnesia, 2 parts ; sulphate of iron, 1 part ; sulphate of lime, 8 parts. To be applied at the rate of ¼ lb. per square yard in March or April. (2) Equal parts (by weight) kainit, sulphate of soda, and superphosphate of lime. To be applied at the rate of 6 lb. per tree after pruning. Natural manures : (3) Decayed cow manure spread on surface of soil over roots in Nov. or Dec. (4) Poultry dung applied in a similar manner. (5) Liquid horse or cow manure and urine applied at any time. Stocks used for budding or grafting : Crab and seedling apple ; Paradise stocks, of which Malling Type I (English Broad-leaved Paradise) is vigorous, Type II (English Paradise or Doucin) is moderately vigorous, Type IX (Jaune de Metz) is dwarfing, and Types XIII and XVI are very vigorous.

CULTURE OF PEARS : Soil, deep, rich loam ; clay soil unsuitable. Position, S., W., or E. walls, fences, or arches for cordons, fan- or espalier-trained trees ; open, sheltered garden for pyramids or bushes ; N. walls for early sorts. Plant, Nov. to Feb. Cultural details, except chemical manures and stocks, as advised for the apple. Chemical manures : Kainit, 4 parts (by weight) ; superphosphate, 1 part. Apply at rate of 4 lb. per tree in Feb. or March. Apply also nitrate of soda at the rate of ¼ oz. per gallon of water in liberal quantities once a week, July to Sept. Stocks : Common pear for standards ; quince for pyramids, bushes, and cordons.

CULTURE OF ORNAMENTAL SPECIES : Hardy deciduous trees and shrubs. Flowering, orn. foliaged, berry-bearing, and fruit-bearing. Soil, ordinary. Position, sunny borders or shrubberies, or as specimens in open places. Plant, Nov. to Feb.

PROPAGATION : Apples and pears for new sorts by seeds sown 3 in. deep outdoors in March ; established varieties by grafting in March or budding in July and Aug. ; flowering species by seeds sown 3 in. deep in sandy soil in sunny position outdoors in Oct. ; cuttings of shoots, 8 to 12 in. long, inserted in ordinary soil outdoors in autumn ; layering in autumn.

FRUIT-BEARING SPECIES : P. communis (Pear), white, April to May, 40 ft., Europe (Britain) and Asia ; Malus (Apple ; Crab), pink, white, May, 20 to 30 ft., Europe (Britain), and its variety paradisiaca (Paradise Stock). The Medlar, formerly classed under Pyrus, is now to be found under Mespilus, *q.v.* The Quince, formerly Pyrus vulgaris, is now Cydonia vulgaris, *q.v.*

ORNAMENTAL SPECIES : P. alnifolia, white, May, fruits bright red, 40 to 50 ft., Japan and Corea ; arbutifolia (Chokeberry), white or rosy, May, fruits red, 5 to 10 ft., Eastern N. America ; Aria (Whitebeam Tree), white, May to June, 30 to 45 ft., fruits red, handsome foliage, N. Temperate Zone (Britain), and its varieties flabellifolia (leaves snow-white beneath), majestica (large leaves and fruits), rupicola (small growing), and sinensis (variable in habit) ; aucuparia (Mountain Ash, Rowan Tree), creamy white, May, 30 to 60 ft., fruits scarlet, leaves finely cut, N. Hemisphere, and its varieties fructu-luteo (fruits yellow), laciniata (leaves deeply lobed), and moravica (dulcis), fruits large ; arnoldiana, pink, May, 20 to 30 ft., fruits yellow and red, hybrid ; chamæmespilus (Bastard Medlar), rosy, May and June, 6 ft., fruits scarlet, Europe ; communis flore-pleno (Double-flowered Pear), white, double, May, 20 to 40 ft. ; Conradinæ, white, May, foliage assumes fine autumn colour, China ; coronaria (Sweet-scented Crab), rose, May, 20 ft., fruits yellowish green, U. States ; coronaria flore-pleno, double ; floribunda, rose, April to May, 20 to 30 ft., fruits yellow, Japan, and its variety atrosanguinea (rich rose) ; halliana (frequently erroneously named P. floribunda flore-pleno), deep rose, May, 12 to 18 ft., fruits purple, W. China ; intermedia, white, May, 20 to 40 ft., fruits red, Europe (Britain) ; iœnsis, white or rosy, May, 20 to 30 ft., fruits yellowish, U. States and its variety flore-pleno (double-flowered), frequently erroneously named P. angustifolia flore-pleno and P. coronaria flore-pleno ; latifolia (Syn. P. rotundifolia), white, May, 30 to 45 ft., fruits brownish red, Europe ; Malus aldenhamensis, wine red, April to May, 20 to 30 ft., reddish-purple foliage and fruits ; Malus niedzwetzkyana, carmine, April to May, purplish-red foliage and fruits ; melanocarpa, white, May, 3 to 5 ft., fruits black, Eastern N. America ; munda sub-arachnoidea, white fruits, China ; nivalis (Snow Tree), white, May, 6 ft., Levant ; pinnatifida, white, May, 20 to 50 ft., fruits red, Europe ; pohuashanensis, creamy white, May, 30 to 40 ft., fruits red, China ; prunifolia, white, April to May, 15 to 20 ft., fruits red, Siberia, and its varieties lutea (yellow fruits) and Rinki (Syn. P. Ringo), flowers pink, fruits bright yellow ; salicifolia, white, April, 15 to 25 ft., pear-like fruits, Levant ; Sargenti, white, May, 3 to 5 ft., fruits dark red, Japan ; Scheideckeri, pale rose, May, 20 to 25 ft., fruits yellow, hybrid ; sinensis (Snow or Sand Pear), white, April, 30 to 40 ft., China ; Sorbus (Service Tree), creamy white, May, 30 to 60 ft., fruits green, tinged red, Europe; spectabilis, red, April and May, 20 to 30 ft., fruits yellow, China and Japan, and its variety flore-pleno (double); Toringo (Syn. P. Sieboldi), white, May, 10 to 30 ft., fruits red, Japan; toringoides, white, May, 20 to 25 ft., fruits yellow and red, W. China; Vilmorinii, white, June, 10 to 20 ft., fruits rosy red, becoming white, W. China; vestita, white, May to June, 30 to 40 ft., Himalayas; Zumi, pink and white, May, 10 to 20 ft., fruits red, Japan. Cheals Crimson, John Downie, Dartmouth Crab, and Veitch's Scarlet are varieties of P. Malus with highly-coloured fruits.

Pyxidanthera (Pine Barren Beauty)—Ord. Diapensiaceæ. Hardy evergreen creeping shrub. First introduced 1851.
CULTURE : Soil, equal parts sandy peat and leaf-mould. Position, sunny rockeries. Plant, Sept., Oct., March, or April.
PROPAGATION : By seeds sown where required to grow, lightly covering with fine sandy peat, Sept., Oct., or March; division of plants, Oct. or March.
SPECIES CULTIVATED : P. barbulata, white, rose, summer, 2 in., N. America.

      Quaking Grass (*Briza media*)—See Briza.
      Quamash (*Camassia esculenta*)—See Camassia.
      Quamoclit (*Ipomæa Quamoclit*)—See Ipomæa.
      Queen Lily—See Phædranassa.
      Queen of the Meadows (*Filipendula Ulmaria*)—See Filipendula.
      Queen of the Orchids—See Grammatophyllum.
      Queen of the Prairie (*Spiræa lobata*)—See Spiræa.
      Queen of the Woods (*Betula alba*)—See Betula.
      Queen's Cushion (*Saxifraga hypnoides*)—See Saxifraga.
      Queen's-flower (*Lagerstræmia Flos-reginæ*)—See Lagerstrœmia.
      Queen's Gilliflower (*Hesperis matronalis*)—See Hesperis.
      Queensland Elk's-horn Fern (*Platycerium grande*)—See Platycerium.
      Queensland Spear Lily (*Doryanthes Palmeri*)—See Doryanthes.
      Queen's Stock (*Matthiola incana*)—See Matthiola.
      Queen Victoria's Water Lily (*Victoria regia*)—See Victoria.

      Quercus (Oak)—Ord. Cupuliferæ. Hardy deciduous and evergreen trees and shrubs. Orn. foliage. Flowers, greenish; male and female organs borne in different flowers on the same plant; April. Male blooms in long pendulous catkins; females, short, solitary, or clustered. Fruit or seeds (acorns) more or less bullet-shaped. Autumn.
CULTURE : Soil, good deep loam, preferably rather moist. Position, open well-drained shrubberies, fields, and woods. Q. Ilex and Q. Cerris well adapted for planting near the sea. Plant: evergreen kinds, Sept. to Nov., or April; deciduous ones, Oct. to Feb. Depth for planting in heavy soils, 6 in.; light soils, 9 in. Distance apart for deciduous oaks, 20 to 25 ft.; evergreen oaks (used for shelter), 6 to 10 ft.; for hedges, 4 to 6 ft. Prune deciduous oaks in Dec.; evergreen kinds in April.
PROPAGATION : By acorns gathered in autumn, stored in sand until March, then sown 2 in. deep and 3 in. apart each way. Transplant when one year old 12 in. apart each way and plant in permanent position when three or four years old. Also choice kinds by grafting in March on common oak.
USEFUL DATA : Average extreme age of oak tree, 1000 to 1500 years. Average spread of branches of largest trees, 180 ft. Supposed oldest oak in England, the Cowthorpe; its assumed age, 1800 years. Timber used for building, cabinet work, cartwheel spokes, fencing, barge building, etc.; very durable. Weight of oak per cubic ft., 53 lb. One bushel of acorns will yield about 7000 trees.
EVERGREEN SPECIES : Q. acuta, 15 to 40 ft., Japan; coccifera, 10 to 12 ft., Medi-

terranean Region ; Ilex (Evergreen Holm or Holly Oak), 60 ft., Mediterranean Region ; Suber (Cork Oak), 50 to 60 ft., the source of the cork of commerce, S. Europe.

DECIDUOUS SPECIES : Q. castaneæfolia, 60 to 100 ft., Caucasus and Persia ; Cerris (Turkey Oak), to 120 ft., S. Europe, and its varieties laciniata and variegata ; coccinea (Scarlet Oak), 50 to 70 ft., N. America ; conferta, 60 to 100 ft., S.E. Europe ; dentata, 50 to 70 ft., Japan and Corea ; lucombeana (Lucombe Oak), semi-evergreen, 60 to 100 ft., hybrid, and its varieties crispa, diversifolia, and fulhamensis ; macrocarpa (Burr Oak), 50 to 170 ft., N. America ; Mirbeckii, 50 to 120 ft., Spain and N. Africa ; palustris (Pin Oak), 70 to 100 ft., Eastern U.S.A. ; pedunculata (Syn. Q. Robur), the Common Oak, 100 to 120 ft., Europe (Britain) and Asia, and its varieties fastigiata (Cypress Oak), filicifolia (Fern-leaved Oak), purpurascens (leaves and young shoots purple), Concordia (Golden Oak), and pendula (Weeping Oak) ; rubra (Red Oak), 60 to 100 ft., Eastern U.S.A. ; sessiliflora, 100 to 120 ft., Europe (Britain) and Asia.

Quick (*Cratægus monogyna* and *C. oxyacantha*)—See Cratægus.

Quick-set Thorn (*Cratægus monogyna* and *C. oxyacantha*)—See Cratægus.

Quince-tree (*Cydonia vulgaris*)—See Cydonia.

Quinine (*Chinchona officinalis*)—See Chinchona.

Quinoa—See Chenopodium.

Quisqualis (Rangoon Creeper)—Ord. Combretaceæ. Stove climbing flowering shrub. Deciduous. First introduced 1815.

CULTURE : Compost, two parts loam, one part peat, and a little sand. Position, well-drained pot or tub, or in a bed with shoots trained up rafters. Pot, Feb. Prune shoots moderately close after flowering. Water freely April to Oct., keep nearly dry remainder of year. Syringe daily April to Sept. Shade from mid-day sun only.

PROPAGATION : By cuttings of young shoots taken off with a small portion of old stem attached and inserted in sandy soil in small pots under a bell-glass in a temp. of 75° to 85° in spring.

SPECIES CULTIVATED : Q. indica, white, changing to red, fragrant, summer, 10 to 15 ft., India.

Rabbit-berry (*Shepherdia argentea*)—See Shepherdia.

Radish (*Raphanus sativus*)—See Raphanus.

Ragged Robin (*Lychnis Flos-cuculi*)—See Lychnis.

Ragwort—See Senecio.

Ramondia (Rosette Mullein)—Ord. Gesneraceæ. Hardy herbaceous perennial. Flowering. First introduced 1731.

OUTDOOR CULTURE : Two parts sandy peat, one part leaf-mould. Position, fissures or recesses of moist, well-drained, shady rockeries, or in partially shady peaty beds or borders. Plant, March or April. Water occasionally in dry weather. Should not be disturbed oftener than is absolutely necessary.

POT CULTURE : Compost, two parts peat, one part equal proportions of leaf-mould and silver sand. Position, shady, well-ventilated frames. Pot, March or April, in 3 or 4½ in. pots. Water moderately April to Sept., moderately afterwards. Repot annually. No stimulants required.

PROPAGATION : By seeds sown on the surface of sandy peat in well-drained pots or pans under bell-glass in cold, shady frame or greenhouse, March to May ; division of plants, March or April.

SPECIES CULTIVATED : R. Heldreichii, violet, summer, 3 in., Thessaly ; pyrenaica, (Rosette Mullein), violet, May to June, 4 to 6 in., Pyrenees ; serbica Nathaliæ, lavender blue, May to June, 4 to 6 in., Serbia.

Rampion (*Campanula rapunculus*)—See Campanula.

Ram's-head Orchid (*Cypripedium arietinum*)—See Cypripedium.

Randia—Ord. Rubiaceæ. Stove evergreen flowering shrubs. Climbing. **First** introduced 1733.

CULTURE : Compost, one part loam, one part peat, one part well-decayed manure **and** charcoal. Position, well-drained pots, or beds in plant stove. Pot or plant, Feb. or March. Prune into shape, Feb. or March. Temp., March to Sept. 65° to 85° ; Sept. to March 55° to 65°. Water moderately Oct. to Feb., freely afterwards. Syringe daily (except when in bloom) March to Sept. Apply liquid manure occasionally to healthy plants in flower. Plants one to two years old produce the best blooms.

PROPAGATION : By cuttings of firm young side shoots, 2 to 3 in. long, inserted in well-drained pots of sandy peat under bell-glass in temp. 75° to 85°, Jan. to April.

SPECIES CULTIVATED : R. macrantha, yellow, summer, 20 to 30 ft., Trop. Africa.

Rangoon Creeper (*Quisqualis indica*)—See Quisqualis.

Ranunculus (Crow-foot ; Fair Maids of France ; Fair Maids of Kent ; Buttercup)—Ord. Ranunculaceæ. Hardy and half-hardy annuals ; herbaceous, tuberous-rooted, and aquatic perennials.

CULTURE OF TUBEROUS-ROOTED SPECIES (Turban, Persian, Dutch, and Scotch Ranunculus) : Soil, two parts good sandy loam and one part decayed cow manure for fine blooms ; good ordinary soil enriched with rotten manure and leaf-mould for general culture. Position, open, sunny beds or borders. Plant Turban, Scotch, and Dutch varieties in Oct. or Nov., in warm, sheltered districts ; end of Feb. otherwise ; Persian kinds, end of Feb. Place tubers claw-side downwards 2 in. deep and 3 in. apart if to be grown in beds ; 2 in. deep and 4 in. apart in rows 5 in. asunder if to be grown in lines in border. Press tubers firmly in soil and cover with fine soil. Protect autumn-planted tubers with mulch of manure or leaves. Mulch in April with rotten manure or cocoanut-fibre refuse. Water copiously in dry weather. Sprinkle Peruvian guano on the bed at the rate of 1 oz. per square yard when leaves appear. Apply liquid manures—¼ oz. each of nitrate of soda, superphosphate, and sulphate of iron to 2 gall. of water—once a week from time leaves appear until flower buds open. Lift tubers when flowers fade and leaves turn yellow—generally early in July—dry them in the sun, and store away in sand in cool place till planting time.

CULTURE OF HARDY SPECIES : Soil, ordinary. Position, shady or partially shady border. Plant, Oct., Nov., March, or April. Lift, divide, and replant in fresh soil triennially. Mulch annually in March with decayed manure.

CULTURE OF TENDER SPECIES : Soil, sandy peat. Position, shady border at base of wall or fence ; or in pots standing in shallow pans of water in cool frame or greenhouse. Pot, Feb. or March. Plant in March. Water freely outdoors in dry weather ; also at all times when grown in pots. Repot annually.

PROPAGATION : By seeds sown as soon as ripe in autumn 1/16 in. deep in boxes or pans filled with equal parts loam, leaf-mould, and sand and placed in a cold frame or cool greenhouse ; herbaceous kinds by division in Oct. or March.

TENDER SPECIES : R. cortusæfolius, yellow, spring, 2 ft., Canaries.

TUBEROUS-ROOTED SPECIES : R. asiaticus (Turban, Persian, French, Dutch, and Scotch Ranunculus), various colours, summer, 6 to 12 in., Orient.

HARDY SPECIES : R. aconitifolius, white, May, 1½ to 2 ft., Europe ; aconitifolius flore-pleno (Fair Maids of France), double ; acris flore-pleno (Double Buttercup or Bachelor's Buttons), yellow, spring, 1 to 2 ft., Europe (Britain) ; alpestris, white, summer, 4 in., Europe, and its variety Traunfellneri ; amplexicaulis, white, May, 6 to 12 in., S. Europe ; bulbosus flore-pleno, yellow, double, spring, 1 ft., Europe (Britain) ; bullatus, orange yellow, May, 1 ft., rather tender, Mediterranean Region ; carpaticus, yellow, May to June, 4 to 6 in., Carpathians ; crenatus, white, April to July, Transylvania ; geranifolius (Syn. R. montanus), yellow, May to June, 3 to 4 in., Europe ; glacialis, white and rose, summer, 6 in., Arctic Regions ; gramineus, yellow, spring, 6 to 8 in., Europe ; lingua (Spearwort), yellow, summer, 3 to 4 ft., Europe (Britain) ; Lyallii (Rockwood Lily), white, spring, 2 to 3 ft., New Zealand ;

Ramondia serbica Nathaliæ
(Rosette Mullein)

Ranunculus acris flore-pleno
(Double Buttercup)

Ranunculus asiaticus

Rehmannia angulata

Reseda odorata
(Mignonette)

Rhododendron hybridum

Rhododendron Keysii

Rhododendron racemosum

Rhus Cotinus
(Smoke Tree)

Ribes sanguineum Brocklebanki
(Golden-leafed Currant)

Richardia africana
(Arum Lily)

Robinia hispida
(Rose Acacia)

Rodgersia pinnata
(Rodgers' Bronze-leaf)

Romneya Coulteri
(Californian Tree Poppy)

Rosa multiflora hybrida
(Polyantha rose)

Roscœa cautleoides

Rudbeckia laciniata
Golden Glow (Cone-flower)

Rudbeckia speciosa
(Cone-flower)

monspeliacus, yellow, spring, 1 ft., Mediterranean Region ; parnassifolius, white, June, 6 in., Europe ; pyrenæus, white, summer, 6 in., S. Europe ; Seguieri, white or rose-tinted, May to July, 4 in., Europe ; Thora, yellow, May to July, 6 in., S. Europe ; rutæfolius (Syn. Callianthemum coriandrifolium), white, 3 in., Europe and Siberia.

Raoulia—Ord. Compositæ. Dwarf perennials of creeping habit, suitable for carpeting the surface of the soil on rockeries.
CULTURE : Soil, sandy or gritty loam. Position, ledges of sunny rockeries or the surface of a moraine. Plant in spring.
PROPAGATION : By division of the plants in March.
SPECIES CULTIVATED : R. australis, silvery foliage, New Zealand ; glabra, emerald green foliage, New Zealand ; subsericea (Syn. R. australis minor), silvery foliage, very minute, New Zealand.

Rape (*Brassica napus*)—See Brassica.

Raphanus (Radish)—Ord. Cruciferæ. Hardy annual. Used extensively for salads. First introduced 1548. Flowers, white and purple ; May. Roots, long, round, or oval, crimson and white shades.
OUTDOOR CULTURE OF COMMON RADISH : Soil, light ordinary. Position, warm south border for first and last sowing ; cool, partially shady ones for intermediate crops. Sow for first crop in Feb., either broadcast or in drills 1 in. deep and 6 in. apart ; successional crops in similar manner at intervals of a month until Oct. Long-rooted kinds best for spring sowing ; round and oval ones for summer. Thin when three leaves form to 1 in. apart. Water copiously in dry weather. Seed required, ¼ oz. for square yard or ½ oz. for a 10w 50 ft. long. Manures : (1) ½ oz. kainit, 1 oz. sulphate of ammonia, 2 oz. superphosphate, ½ oz. iron sulphate to 4 gall. of water—to be applied twice a week from time seedlings are 1 in. high. (2) ½ oz. Peruvian guano to 1 gall. of water applied as No. 1. (3) ¼ oz. nitrate of soda to 1 gall. of water applied as No. 1. (4) ½ lb. of native guano per square yard, forked in before sowing. Forcing : Make a hotbed of manure, cover with 4 in. of fine mould, and place a frame over it. Sow seeds thinly, lightly cover with mould, moisten with tepid water, and keep close until seedlings appear, then admit air daily. Thin early to insure good roots. First sowing should be made in Dec., second in Jan., third in Feb., and fourth in March. Apply stimulants as advised for outdoor kinds. Long-rooted varieties best for forcing. Seeds germinate in three to five days. Crop reaches maturity in five to six weeks.
CULTURE OF SPANISH RADISH : Sow seeds in drills 1 in. deep and 6 in. apart in July or Aug. Thin seedlings when 1 in. high to 6 in. apart. Water freely in dry weather and apply stimulants as directed for ordinary kinds. Lift roots in Nov. and store in sand in a cool shed to use as required.
CULTURE OF RAT-TAILED RADISH (R. caudatus) : Nat. Java. Introduced 1815. Sow seeds in drills 1 in. deep and 6 in. apart in April, May, or June. Thin to 6 in. apart when 1 in. high. Gather seed pods when grown for pickling, mixing with salads, or cooking and eating, like asparagus.
SPECIES CULTIVATED : R. sativus (Common Radish), Europe ; caudatus (Rat-tail Radish), Java.

Raphiolepis (Indian Hawthorn)—Ord. Rosaceæ. Half-hardy and hardy ever-green flowering shrubs. First introduced 1806.
CULTURE : Soil, equal parts peat, loam, and silver sand. Position, S. and S.W. walls or well-drained borders for half-hardy species ; sunny rockeries or sheltered borders for hardy species. Plant, Sept., Oct., or April. Prune straggling shoots into shape, April. Protect half-hardy species in severe weather with mats or straw hurdles.
POT CULTURE OF HALF-HARDY SPECIES : Compost, as above. Position, well-drained pots in cold greenhouse or pit, Sept. to May ; sunny place outdoors, May to Sept. Pot, Feb. or March. Water copiously April to Oct., moderately afterwards.
PROPAGATION : By cuttings of firm shoots, 2 to 3 in. long, inserted in compost of equal parts sand, peat, and loam under bell-glass or hand-light in cold frame, Aug. to Nov.

N   365

HARDY SPECIES : R. Delacourei, pink, May, 5 ft., hybrid ; japonica, white, fragrant, June, 10 ft., Japan.
HALF-HARDY SPECIES : R. indica (Indian Hawthorn), white, tinged pink, summer, 4 to 8 ft., China.

Raspberry (*Rubus idæus*)—See Rubus.

Raspberry Blackberry—See Rubus.

Rat's-tail Cactus (*Cereus flagelliformis*)—See Cereus.

Rat-tailed Radish (*Raphanus caudatus*)—See Raphanus.

Rattan Palm—See Calamus.

Rattle-root (*Cimicifuga racemosa*)—See Cimicifuga.

Rattle-snake Fern (*Botrychium virginianum*)—See Botrychium.

Rattle-snake Plantain (*Goodyera pubescens*)—See Goodyera.

Ravenala (Traveller's Tree)—Ord. Musaceæ. Stove evergreen perennial. Orn. foliage. Leaves, very large, green.
CULTURE : Compost, two parts good loam, one part well-decayed manure, and one part sand. Position, pots, tubs, or beds in lofty sunny stove. Pot or plant, Jan. to April. Water copiously Feb. to Oct., about once fortnightly afterwards. Syringe twice daily Feb. to Sept., once daily Sept. to Feb. Moist atmosphere essential. Apply stimulants twice or three times weekly March to Oct. Temp., March to Oct. 70° to 85° ; Oct. to March 60° to 70°.
PROPAGATION : By suckers removed from parent plant and placed in pots in temp. 75° to 85° any time of year.
SPECIES CULTIVATED : R. madagascariensis (Traveller's Tree), 15 to 30 ft., Madagascar.

Ravenea—Ord. Palmaceæ. Stove palm. Orn. foliage. Leaves, feather-shaped, green. First introduced 1878.
CULTURE : Compost, equal parts peat, loam, leaf-mould, and sand. Position, shady, moist. Pot, Feb. or March. Water abundantly March to Oct., moderately afterwards. Temp., March to Sept. 70° to 85° ; Sept. to March 60° to 65°.
PROPAGATION : By seeds sown 1 in. deep in pots of light soil in temp. 85° in March.
SPECIES CULTIVATED : R. Hildebrandtii, 5 to 10 ft., Comoro Islands.

Ravenna Grass (*Erianthus Ravennæ*)—See Erianthus.

Rayless Golden Rod (*Bigelowia graveolens*)—See Bigelowia.

Red Alder (*Cunonia capensis*)—See Cunonia.

Red Buckeye (*Æsculus Pavia*)—See Æsculus.

Red-bud (*Cercis canadensis*)—See Cercis.

Red Californian Cedar (*Libocedrus decurrens*)—See Libocedrus.

Red Campion (*Lychnis dioica*)—See Lychnis.

Red Cape Tulip—See Hæmanthus.

Red Cedar (*Juniperus virginiana*)—See Juniperus.

Red Currant—See Ribes.

Red Fir (*Abies magnifica*)—See Abies.

Red Helleborine (*Cephalanthera rubra*)—See Cephalanthera.

Red-hot-poker-plant (*Kniphofia aloides*)—See Kniphofia.

Red-ink-plant (*Phytolacca decandra*)—See Phytolacca.

Red Maple (*Acer rubrum*)—See Acer.

Red Oak (*Quercus rubra*)—See Quercus.

Red-root (*Ceanothus americanus*)—See Ceanothus.

Red Star Lily (*Lilium concolor*)—See Lilium.

Red Valerian (*Centranthus ruber*)—See Centranthus.

Red-veined Rhubarb (*Rheum Emodi*)—See Rheum.

Reed—See Arundo and Cortaderia.

Reed Mace (*Typha latifolia*)—See Typha.

Rehmannia—Ord. Scrophulariaceæ. Half-hardy perennial herb. First introduced 1835.
OUTDOOR CULTURE: Soil, moist, sandy peat. Position, partially shady borders, or at base of walls running E. and W. Plant, March or April. Water freely in dry weather. Mulch liberally with cocoanut-fibre refuse or decayed manure in April. In cold districts it is best to lift plants in Oct., place in pots and store in cold frame or pit until following March, then plant out.
POT CULTURE: Compost, two parts sandy peat, one part leaf-mould. Position, well-drained pots in cold frame, pit, or greenhouse. Pot, Feb. or March. Water liberally April to Oct., moderately afterwards. Apply weak stimulants once a week during flowering period. Shade from bright sun essential.
PROPAGATION: By seeds sown in well-drained pans in warm greenhouse during Feb.
SPECIES CULTIVATED: R. angulata, red and orange, 1 to 3 ft., China; elata (often wrongly called R. angulata), rosy purple and yellow, summer, 2 to 3 ft., China, and its variety Pink Perfection; sinensis, purple, April, 1 to 2 ft., China and Japan.

Reidia—See Phyllanthus.

Reineckea—Ord. Liliaceæ. Hardy herbaceous perennial. Flowering and orn. foliage. First introduced 1792. Leaves, green or striped with creamy yellow.
CULTURE: Soil, ordinary good. Position, sunny rockeries or borders; variegated variety as edgings to borders. Plant, March or April. Lift, divide, and replant every three or four years. Water copiously in dry weather.
PROPAGATION: By division of creeping rhizomes in March or April.
SPECIES CULTIVATED: R. carnea, pink, fragrant, April, 6 in. China and Japan; carnea variegata, variegated.

Rein Orchis (*Habenaria ciliaris*)—See Habenaria.

Reinwardtia (East Indian Flax; Winter Flax)—Ord. Linaceæ. Greenhouse evergreen flowering shrubs. First introduced 1799.
CULTURE: Compost, equal parts loam and peat, little sand. Pot, March or April. Prune previous year's shoots to within 1 in. of their base in Feb. or March. Position, warm greenhouse Sept. to June; cold, sunny frame June to Sept. Water moderately Oct. to March, freely other times. Syringe twice daily Feb. to Sept. Apply weak stimulants occasionally when in flower. Temp., Sept. to Feb. 55° to 65°; Feb. to June 65° to 70°. Nip off points of young shoots in June to induce bushy growth.
PROPAGATION: By cuttings of shoots, 2 to 3 in. long, inserted in sandy soil under bell-glass in temp. 65° to 75° in April or May.
SPECIES CULTIVATED: R. tetragyna, yellow, winter, 3 ft.; trigyna (Syn. Linum trigynum), yellow, autumn, 2 to 4 ft. Both natives of India.

Renanthera—Ord. Orchidaceæ. Stove epiphytal orchids. A shy blooming plant. First introduced 1816.
CULTURE: Fix plant to blocks of wood or stems of dead tree ferns by means of copper wire. Syringe roots twice daily March to Oct., about once a week afterwards. Shade from mid-day sun; expose fully to light other times. Growing period, March to Oct.; resting period, Oct. to March. Temp., March to Sept. 65° to 85°; Sept. to March 60° to 70°.
PROPAGATION: By division of pseudo-bulbs at potting time.
SPECIES CULTIVATED: R. coccinea, orange, red, and crimson, summer, 4 to 8 ft., Burma; imschootiana, vermilion, summer, 12 to 18 in., Burma (this should be treated in the same way as a stove Vanda).

Reseda (Mignonette)—Ord. Resedaceæ. A perennial, but usually grown as an annual. First introduced 1752.
OUTDOOR CULTURE: Soil, ordinary, containing old mortar or slaked lime. Position, sunny beds, borders, or rockeries. Sow seeds ⅛ in. deep in masses or rows in

March or April. Thin seedlings when 1 in. high to 2 or 3 in. apart. Water freely in summer. Apply stimulants occasionally when in flower. In warm, dry positions plants will survive the winter outdoors for several years.

INDOOR CULTURE : Compost, equal parts loam, leaf-mould, dried manure, old mortar, and silver sand. Sow March or April for summer flowering, July or Aug. for winter and spring. Fill 3 in. pots to within ¼ in. of rim, sow five or six seeds in each, cover with ⅟₁₆ in. of soil, and place in temp. 55° to 65°. When seedlings are 1 to 2 in. high transfer bodily to flowering pots (5 in.). Pot firmly and disturb roots as little as possible. Water moderately at first, freely afterwards. Pinch off points of main shoots when 3 in. high if abundance of bloom is required. Apply stimulants—¼ oz. ammonia to 1 gall. of water—once a week from time flower spike forms till blooms expand.

TREE MIGNONETTE : Insert cuttings singly in 2 in. pots in spring in temp. 55° to 65°. Transfer to larger pots when well rooted. Nip off all shoots and allow main stem to grow one or more feet high, then remove point, and let side shoots form at apex. Shorten these from time to time until bushy head is obtained, then allow blooms to form. Water freely in summer, moderately in winter. Apply stimulants when in bloom. Repot annually.

SPECIES CULTIVATED : R. odorata (Mignonette), yellow and white, summer, 1 to 2 ft., N. Africa and Egypt.

Rest Harrow—See Ononis.

Restrepia—Ord. Orchidaceæ. Cool greenhouse epiphytal orchids. First introduced 1837.

CULTURE : Compost, equal parts peat and sphagnum with a little broken charcoal. Position, well-drained pans in shady part of the house. Water abundantly March to Oct., moderately afterwards. Shade from sun. Syringe freely in summer. Temp., Nov. to March 45° to 55° ; March to Nov. 55° to 60°.

PROPAGATION : By division, Feb. to March.

SPECIES CULTIVATED : R. antennifera, yellow and red, Colombia ; elegans, white, purple, and yellow, Jan., Venezuela ; maculata, yellow, purple, and crimson, Nov. to Feb., Colombia ; pandurata, white and crimson, winter, Colombia ; striata, yellow and maroon, Colombia.

Resurrection Plant (*Anastatica Hierochuntica* and *Selaginella lepidophylla*)—See Anastatica and Selaginella.

Retinospora—See Cupressus.

Rhamnus (Buckthorn)—Ord. Rhamnaceæ. Hardy evergreen and deciduous trees and shrubs.

CULTURE : Soil, ordinary. Position, sunny or shady shrubberies ; good seaside shrubs. Plant, Oct. to March. Prune, Feb.

PROPAGATION : By seeds sown outdoors in autumn ; cuttings inserted outdoors in ordinary soil in Sept. ; by layering in Sept. or March.

SPECIES CULTIVATED : R. Alaternus, 10 to 20 ft., evergreen, S.W. Europe, and its varieties angustifolia and variegata (leaves margined with creamy white) ; californica, 10 to 15 ft., evergreen, Western N. America ; cathartica (Buckthorn), 5 to 10 ft., deciduous, Europe (Britain) ; Frangula, 15 to 20 ft., deciduous, Europe (Britain) ; imeretina (sometimes wrongly called R. libanotica), 10 ft., deciduous, fine autumn colour, Western Caucasus ; libanotica, 4 to 6 ft., deciduous, Asia Minor ; pumila, 6 in., deciduous, Alps.

Rhapis (Ground Rattan Cane)—Ord. Palmaceæ. Greenhouse palms. Orn. foliage. First introduced 1774. Leaves, fan-shaped, green ; variety, green striped with white.

CULTURE : Compost, two parts rich loam, one part decayed leaf-mould and sand. Position, well-drained pots in greenhouse or dwelling-room during summer. Pot, Feb. or March. Water copiously April to Oct., moderately afterwards. Apply weak stimulants occasionally during summer. Place small lumps of sulphate of iron on surface of soil to insure deep healthy green foliage. Shade from sun

essential. Syringe twice daily in summer, once other times. Temp., March to Sept. 55° to 65° ; Sept. to March 45° to 55°.
PROPAGATION : By seeds sown 1 in. deep in light soil in temp. of 80° in Feb. or March ; suckers removed in April or Aug.
SPECIES CULTIVATED : R. flabelliformis, 3 to 4 ft., China and Japan ; humilis, 3 ft., China.

Rhazya—Ord. Apocynaceæ. Hardy subshrub. First introduced 1889.
CULTURE : Soil, sandy loam. Position, sunny well-drained slopes or rock gardens. Plant, March to April.
PROPAGATION : By seeds sown in pans in warm greenhouse during Feb. or March.
SPECIES CULTIVATED : R. orientalis, blue, late summer, 9 to 12 in., Levant.

Rheum (Rhubarb)—Ord. Polygonaceæ. Hardy herbaceous perennials. Edible stalked and orn. foliage plants. Leaves, large, hand-shaped, green. Roots, large, fleshy. First introduced 1573.
CULTURE OF EDIBLE RHUBARB : Soil, light, deep, rich. Position, sunny, open. Plant single roots with crowns 2 in. below surface, 3 ft. apart in rows 3 ft. asunder, in Nov., Feb., or March. Top-dress with manure in Nov. or Feb., forking it into surface of soil. Lift, divide, and replant every four years. No stalks should be gathered the first year. Remove flower stems directly they appear. FORCING : Cover two or more year old crowns with pots or headless casks or tubs, and place fresh manure and tree leaves over these in Jan. or Feb., or lift strong roots and place them close together in deep boxes underneath staging in warm greenhouse, or in corners of dark cellars, in the mushroom houses, with a little soil between. Keep moist and dark. Temp., 55° to 75°. Forcing season, Nov. to Feb. Roots, two to five years old best for forcing. Reject roots after forcing. Chemical manures : 2 oz. kainit, 2 oz. superphosphate, ¼ oz. iron sulphate to 4 gall. of water applied at intervals of a week during growth.
PROPAGATION : By seeds sown ⅛ in. deep in ordinary soil outdoors in March or April ; by division of roots with crowns or buds attached, Nov. to Feb.
CULTURE OF ORNAMENTAL-LEAVED SPECIES : Soil, deep, rich, ordinary. Position, isolated specimens on lawns, wild gardens, islands ; sunny. Plant, Nov. to Feb. Water copiously in dry seasons. Apply stimulants occasionally in summer.
SPECIES CULTIVATED : R. acuminatum, 8 to 10 ft., Himalayas ; collinianum, 6 ft., China ; Emodi, 6 to 8 ft., Himalayas ; officinale (Medicinal Rhubarb), 8 to 10 ft., Thibet ; palmatum, 5 to 6 ft., China, and its variety tanghuticum ; rhaponticum (Garden or Edible Rhubarb), 4 ft., Siberia ; Ribes, 4 ft., Persia.

Rheumatism-root (*Jeffersonia diphylla*)—See Jeffersonia.

Rhexia (Deer Grass ; Meadow Beauty)—Ord. Melastomaceæ. Hardy perennial herb. First introduced 1759.
CULTURE : Soil, sandy peat or bog earth. Position, open, sunny bog, swamp, or moist border. Plant, Oct., Nov., March, or April.
PROPAGATION : By division of roots in March or April.
SPECIES CULTIVATED : R. virginica, purple, summer, 6 to 12 in., N. America.

Rhipsalis (Mistletoe Cactus)—Ord. Cactaceæ. Greenhouse succulent shrubs. First introduced 1758.
CULTURE : Compost, equal parts sandy loam, leaf-mould, brick rubbish, and coarse silver sand. Position, well-drained pots in light greenhouse. Pot, April or May ; pots to be drained one-sixth depth for large plants, one-third for small plants. Press compost in firmly. Water moderately April to Aug., keep almost dry Aug. to April. Shade from bright sunshine. Temp., March to Sept. 55° to 65° ; Sept. to March 50° to 55°.
PROPAGATION : By seeds sown ⅛ in. deep in well-drained sandy soil and placed in temp. 75°, March ; keep soil moderately moist. By cuttings of stems inserted in small pots of sandy soil in summer ; grafting on Cereus speciosissimus.
SPECIES CULTIVATED : R. Cassytha, yellow, Sept., 1 ft., W. Indies ; crispata, white, Dec., 1 ft. ; funalis (Syn. R. grandiflora), white, Feb., 3 ft., S. America ; Houlletii, yellow, winter, Brazil ; mesembryanthoides, white, spring, 6 in., S.

America ; pachyptera, white, Feb., Trop. America ; Saglionis, yellow, March, 1 ft. Buenos Ayres ; sarmentacea, white, spring, Argentina ; swartziana, white, June, W. Indies.

Rhodanthe—See Helipterum.

Rhodochiton—Ord. Scrophulariaceæ. Greenhouse climbing herb. Nat. Mexico. First introduced 1833.

CULTURE : Compost, equal parts loam and leaf-mould and half a part silver sand. Position, well-drained pots, boxes, beds, or borders, with shoots trained up trellis, walls, or rafters of sunny greenhouse. Pot, March to May. Water freely March to Sept., moderately Sept. to March. Apply stimulants during flowering period. Shade from bright sun. Thin out and shorten shoots moderately in Feb. Temp., March to Sept. 55° to 65° ; Sept. to March 45° to 55°.

PROPAGATION : By seeds sown $\frac{1}{16}$ in. deep in ordinary light soil in temp. 50° to 60°, March, transplanting seedlings when an inch high singly in 2 or 3 in. pots ; cuttings of shoots inserted in sandy soil under bell-glass in temp. 45°, March to Aug.

SPECIES CULTIVATED : R. volubile (Syn. Lophospermum atrosanguineum), reddish purple, summer, 10 to 15 ft., Mexico.

Rhododendron—Ord. Ericaceæ. Greenhouse and hardy evergreen and deciduous flowering shrubs. The genus Azalea is now included with the Rhododendron. R. ponticum, parent of hardy kinds, first occurred 1763 ; R. indica (Indian Azalea), 1808.

HARDY HYBRID RHODODENDRONS : In the main the hybrid garden races of evergreen rhododendrons have sprung from such species as catawbiense, ponticum, caucasicum, and arboreum. A lesser part has been played by maximum, griffithianum, Fortunei, Thomsoni, and discolor. The deciduous hybrid " azaleas " have been obtained from Rhododendrons flavum, calendulaceum, nudiflorum, viscosum, occidentale, molle, sinense, and others. The Ghent azaleas (R. gandavense) are in the main derived from flavum, viscosum, nudiflorum, and calendulaceum. R. Kosterianum is the result of crossing R. molle with R. sinense. The dwarf Japanese azaleas such as Hinodigeri and malvatica are closely allied to R. amœnum and R. obtusum, those known as " Kurume azaleas " being forms raised over a period of many years by Japanese horticulturists around the city of Kurume in the southern island of Kyushu, Japan. A newer race of hardy azaleas has been obtained by crossing forms of R. amœnum and R. obtusum with R. Kæmpferi. The greenhouse azaleas are, in the main, hybrids of R. indicum and R. ledifolium.

CULTURE OF GREENHOUSE RHODODENDRONS : Compost, two parts turfy peat, one part silver sand. Position, well-drained pots or tubs indoors all the year round for stove kinds ; pots indoors from Sept. to June ; outdoors on bed of cinder ashes in sunny position ; June to Sept. for greenhouse kinds. Pot, April or May, directly after flowering. Water freely April to Oct., moderately afterwards. Rain water preferable ; water containing lime injurious. Apply a little artificial manure to surface of soil when buds show. Repotting only necessary every three or four years. Temp.: for stove species, 55° to 65° Sept. to March ; 70° to 80° March to Sept. ; for greenhouse species, 45° to 55° Sept. to March ; 55° to 65° March to Sept.

CULTURE OF HARDY RHODODENDRONS : Soil, peat or loam free from lime or ordinary. soil mixed with peat. Position, open, sunny borders and shrubberies for tall kinds ; sunny rockeries for dwarf kinds like R. hirsutum, R. chamæcistus, R. ferrugineum, etc. Plant, Sept. to Feb or April, 3 to 6 ft. apart. Prune, April. Remove seed pods directly flowers fade. Water copiously in dry weather. Mulch choice kinds with 2 to 3 in. of decayed manure in May. To insure flowers annually thin out flower buds freely in April. Apply liquid cow manure occasionally during summer.

CULTURE OF THE INDIAN AZALEA : Compost, three parts peat, one part loam, and one part of equal proportions of leaf-mould and silver sand. Position, well-drained pots in sunny greenhouses from Oct. to June ; in partial shade outdoors June to Sept. Repot directly after flowering. Firm potting essential. Prune only to shorten straggly growths. Syringe daily after flowering till plants are

370

stood outdoors. Water moderately Oct. to March, afterwards freely, never allowing roots to get dry. Apply weak liquid manure when flower buds form. Temp., Oct. to March 45° to 55°; March to June 65°. Remove seed pods directly they form.

CULTURE OF AZALEA PONTICA, ETC. : Soil, sandy peat and leaf-mould. Position, beds on lawn ; or in groups in front of shrubberies. Plant in autumn. No pruning required. Remove seed pods directly they form. Mulch annually in winter with decayed manure. Supply freely with water in dry weather. May also be grown in pots in cool greenhouses, or forced into flower early in temp. 65° to 75° in winter. Plants grown in pots should be kept under glass till July, then be stood outdoors till Nov., when remove to cold house or frame. Syringe foliage after flowering till placed outdoors. Repot every second year directly after flowering.

PROPAGATION OF RHODODENDRONS, ETC. : Propagate rhododendrons by seeds sown on surface of sandy peat, slightly covered with fine sand, placed under bell-glass in temp. 55° to 65° if stove or greenhouse kinds ; in cold frame if hardy. Cover with bell-glass and keep moderately moist. Also by cuttings of firm shoots, 3 in. long, with a heel, taken towards the end of July, inserted in sandy peat under bell-glass in temp. 45° to 55° at first, then 10° higher. Steady bottom heat aids rooting. By layering in Sept. or March. By grafting on common species in a close frame or propagator in March. Indian azaleas by seeds as advised for rhododendrons ; cuttings of half-ripened shoots with a heel inserted in pots of sandy peat under bell-glass in temp. 65° to 75° in spring ; also by grafting. Hardy deciduous azaleas by seeds sown as advised for rhododendrons ; cuttings of half-ripened shoots inserted in sandy peat in a cold frame in Aug. ; layering shoots in spring ; grafting in spring.

EVERGREEN SPECIES CULTIVATED : True rhododendrons : R. ambiguum, pale yellow, April to May, 5 to 6 ft., W. China ; arboreum, blood red, Feb. to March, 30 to 40 ft., Himalayas, and its varieties album, Campbelliæ, cinnamomeum, and wellsianum ; argyrophyllum, white and pink, May, 6 to 20 ft., W. China and Thibet ; Augustini, white, pink, or blue, May, 4 to 10 ft., Central China ; auriculatum, white or pink, Aug., 10 to 30 ft., Central China ; azaleoides (Syns. R. odoratum and R. fragrans), white, fragrant, June to July, 4 to 6 ft., hybrid ; barbatum, blood red, March, 20 to 30 ft., W. Sikkim ; Broughtoni aureum, primrose yellow and reddish brown, 2 to 3 ft., hybrid ; campanulatum, rosy purple, April to May, 6 to 12 ft., Himalayas ; campylocarpum, pale yellow, May, 4 to 8 ft., Sikkim ; calophytum, white or rosy, fragrant, 30 to 45 ft., W. China and Thibet ; catawbiense, lilac purple, June, 6 to 10 ft., South-eastern United States, and its varieties everestianum and fastuosum ; caucasicum, yellowish white or pale lilac, April to May, 2 ft., Caucasus ; ciliatum, rosy red to white, March to April, 3 to 9 ft., Sikkim (only hardy in mild districts) ; cinnabarinum, cinnabar red, May to June, 6 to 10 ft., Sikkim ; decorum, white or pale rose, fragrant, April to May, 6 to 12 ft., Yunnan ; discolor, white or blush, June to July, 10 to 18 ft., W. China ; ferrugineum, rosy scarlet, June, 3 to 4 ft., Alps ; fastigiatum, lavender blue, May, 9 to 12 in., Yunnan ; fictolacteum, white and crimson, 20 to 30 ft., Yunnan ; flavidum, primrose yellow, April, 2 ft., W. China ; Fortunei, blush to white, fragrant, May, to 12 ft., China ; fulgens, blood red, Feb. to March, 6 to 12 ft., Nepal and Sikkim ; glaucum, rosy red, May, 3 ft., Sikkim and Bhutan ; hirsutum, rosy pink, June, 2 to 3 ft., Alps ; kewense, white and rose, May, hybrid ; impeditum, pale purple, May, 6 to 18 in., W. China ; intricatum, lavender blue, April, 1 to 2 ft., W. China ; kamtschaticum, rosy crimson, 4 to 10 in., N.E. Asia ; Keysii, brick red, May, 6 ft., Bhutan ; lutescens, pale yellow, April, 3 to 7 ft., W. China and Thibet ; Loderi, white, May, hybrid ; Luscombei, deep pink, April to May, hybrid ; Manglesi, white, spotted red, May, hybrid ; maximum, purplish pink, June to July, 30 ft., U.S.A. ; Metternichii (Syn. R. japonicum), rose, May, 6 to 8 ft., Japan, and its variety pentamerum ; micranthum, white, June, 4 to 6 ft., China ; moupinense, white and purple, March, 2 to 3 ft., Thibet and W. China ; mucronulatum, rose-purple, Feb. to April, 7 to 8 ft., Manchuria and Corea ; multiflorum, white and pink, 3 to 4 ft., hybrid ; myrtifolium, rose, June, 4 to 5 ft., hybrid ; neriiflorum, deep crimson, April to May, 4 to 8 ft., Yunnan ; niveum, purplish lilac, May, 6 to 8 ft., Sikkim ; nobleanum, bright rose, Jan. to March, 10 to 15 ft., hybrid ; orbiculare (Syn. R. rotundifolium), rosy red,

6 to 9 ft., W. China ; pachytrichum, white or pale rose, April to May, 20 ft., W. China ; parvifolium, rosy purple, Jan. to March, 2 to 3 ft., Siberia, China, etc. ; polylepis, pale purple and yellow, May, 5 to 6 ft., China ; ponticum, purple and pink, June, 8 to 15 ft., Spain, Portugal, and Asia Minor ; præcox, rosy lilac, Feb. to March, 4 to 6 ft., hybrid ; punctatum, pale pink or rose, May to June, 2 to 4 ft., Eastern N. America ; racemosum, soft pink, April to May, 5 to 6 ft., W. China ; rubiginosum, rosy lilac and maroon, April to May, 6 to 10 ft., S.W. China ; sinogrande, white and crimson, 20 to 30 ft., Yunnan ; Smirnowi, purplish rose, May, 4 to 6 ft., Caucasus ; Souliei, white or pale rose, May, 3 to 8 ft., W. China ; spinuliferum, pale pink to red, March to April, 3 to 8 ft., China ; strigillosum, rich red, Feb. to March, 15 to 20 ft., China ; sutchuenense, rosy lilac and purple, March, 10 ft., China ; Thomsoni, blood red, April, 10 to 12 ft., Nepal and Sikkim ; yunnanense, pink and brownish crimson, May, 8 to 12 ft., Yunnan.

EVERGREEN GREENHOUSE SPECIES CULTIVATED : R. albescens, white, fragrant, hybrid ; balsaminæflorum, various colours, winter, 4 ft., hybrid ; ciliicalyx, white or pink, China ; Dalhousiæ, white, tinged rose, spring, 6 ft., Himalayas ; Edgeworthii, white and yellow, fragrant, June, 6 ft., Himalayas ; exoniense, creamy white, tinged rose, hybrid ; Falconeri, creamy white and purple, spring, 20 to 30 ft., Himalayas ; formosum (Syn. R. Gibsoni), white and rose, fragrant, spring, 6 to 8 ft., Himalayas ; fragrantissimum, white, tinged pink, very fragrant, hybrid ; grande, rosy to white, spring, to 40 ft., Himalayas ; griffithianum (Syn. R. Aucklandi), white and pink, fragrant, May, 10 to 15 ft., Sikkim and Bhutan ; jasminiflorum, white and pink, May, 3 ft., Java ; javanicum, orange and red, all seasons, 4 ft., Java ; Maddeni, white and blush, summer, 6 to 10 ft., Himalayas, and many named hybrids ; Nuttalli, white, yellow, and pink, May, 12 to 30 ft., Himalayas ; veitchianum, white, spring, 6 ft., Burma ; Wightii, yellow and red, June, 10 to 14 ft., Himalayas. There are numerous fine hybrids between R. jasminiflorum and R. javanicum.

HARDY SPECIES CULTIVATED : Section azalea (most of these were formerly classed as azaleas) : R. amœnum, rosy purple, May, 2 to 4 ft., evergreen, Japan ; arborescens, white, tinged pink, June to July, to 20 ft., deciduous, Eastern N. America ; calendulaceum, red, orange, and yellow, May, 10 ft., deciduous, Eastern N. America ; Daviesii, white, May, 4 to 6 ft., deciduous, hybrid ; indicum, red to pink, May to June, 4 to 6 ft., evergreen, China and Japan (hardy only in mild districts), and its variety balsaminæflorum (Syn. rosæflorum), dwarf, with double salmon flowers ; Kæmpferi, rose to scarlet, May, 6 to 10 ft., evergreen, Japan ; ledifolium (Syn. R. rosmarinifolium), white, fragrant, May, 5 to 6 ft., evergreen, China and Japan, and its variety narcissiflorum ; linearifolium, rosy lilac, May, 2 to 4 ft., evergreen, Japan ; luteum (Syns. R. flavum and Azalea pontica), yellow, May, 8 to 10 ft., deciduous, Asia Minor ; molle, rose to orange red, April to May, 4 to 8 ft., deciduous, Japan ; nudiflorum, pink, May, 7 to 9 ft., deciduous, Eastern N. America ; obtusum (Syn. R. indicum obtusum), scarlet, May, 3 ft., evergreen, Japan, and its variety album ; occidentale, white and yellow, fragrant, June, 8 ft., deciduous, Western N. America ; Rhodora (Syns. R. canadense and Rhodora canadense), rosy purple, April, 3 to 4 ft., deciduous, Eastern N. America ; rhombicum, purple, April, 4 to 5 ft., deciduous, Japan ; sinense, yellow, April to May, 4 to 8 ft., deciduous, China ; Schlippenbachii, soft rose, May, 3 to 5 ft., deciduous, Manchuria and Japan ; Vaseyi, pale pink, April to May, 12 to 15 ft., deciduous, Carolina ; viscosum (Swamp Honeysuckle), white or pink, June to July, 6 to 8 ft., Eastern N. America ; yedœnse (Syn. R. Yodogawa), double, lavender pink, May, 4 to 6 ft., evergreen, Japan. See also Rhodothamnus.

Rhodothamnus (Ground Cistus)—Ord. Ericaceæ. Hardy evergreen flowering shrub. First introduced 1786.
CULTURE : Soil, equal parts peat, loam, and sand. Position, fissures between pieces of limestone on rockeries. Plant, March or April. Water freely in dry weather.
PROPAGATION : By means of division at planting time, pulling off pieces with a few roots attached, as advised for rhododendron.
SPECIES CULTIVATED : R. chamæcistus (Syn. Rhododendron chamæcistus), pink, spring, 6 to 12 in., Austrian Alps.

Ruellia macrantha
(Christmas Pride)

Ruscus aculeatus
(Butcher's Broom)

Saintpaulia ionantha
(African Violet)

Salix babylonica
(Weeping Willow)

Salpiglossis sinuata hybrida
(Scalloped Tube-tongue)

Salvia patens

Sambucus canadensis
(Elder)

Sanguinaria canadensis
(Blood-root)

Saponaria ocymoides
(Rock Soap-wort)

Sarracenia hybrida
(Huntsman's Horn)

Saxifraga Burseriana Gloria
(Rockfoil)

Scabiosa atropurpurea
(Sweet Scabious)

Schizanthus Wisetonensis
(Butterfly Flower)

Schizopetalon Walkeri

Schizostylis coccinea
(Caffre Lily)

Scilla campanulata
(Blue Bell)

Scolopendrium vulgare
(Hart's-tongue Fern)

Scutellaria baicalensis
(Helmet Flower)

Rhodotypos (White Kerria)—Ord. Rosaceæ. Hardy deciduous flowering shrub. First introduced 1866.
CULTURE : Soil, good ordinary. Position, against S. or W. walls or fences. Plant, Oct. to March. Prune in May or June, cutting off old or weak shoots only.
POT CULTURE : Compost, two parts loam, one part leaf-mould and sand. Pot, Oct. Place in cold greenhouse and water moderately. After flowering place plants in sunny position outdoors till Oct. FORCING : Place plants in temp. 55° to 65° in Jan. Water moderately. Transfer plants to sunny position outdoors after flowering.
PROPAGATION : By cuttings of half-ripened shoots in sandy soil under bell-glass in brisk bottom heat.
SPECIES CULTIVATED : R. kerrioides, white, May to July, 10 to 15 ft., Japan. This shrub is frequently erroneously called Kerria japonica alba.

Rhœo—Ord. Commelinaceæ. Greenhouse herbaceous perennial. First introduced 1868.
CULTURE : Compost, equal parts loam, leaf-mould, and sand. Position, pots, or baskets suspended from roof. Pot, Jan. to April. Water freely March to Oct., moderately afterwards. Shade from strong sunshine. Temp., Oct. to April 40° to 50° ; April to Oct. 55° to 65°.
PROPAGATION : By cuttings of young shoots inserted in light soil under a bell-glass in above temp., March to Oct.
SPECIES CULTIVATED : R. discolor (Syn. Tradescantia discolor), white, summer, creeping, Mexico, and its variety vittata (Syn. Tradescantia variegata), leaves striped with pale yellow.

Rhopalostylis—Ord. Palmaceæ. Stove palms. Orn. foliage. Leaves, feather-shaped, green. First introduced 1832.
CULTURE : Compost, equal parts loam, peat, leaf-mould, and sand. Position, pots or tubs in moist, shady greenhouse or conservatory. Pot, Feb. or March. Water copiously April to Oct., moderately afterwards. Apply stimulants occasionally May to Sept. Keep piece of sulphate of iron on surface of soil to insure deep green foliage. Syringe twice daily April to Sept., once daily afterwards. Temp., March to Sept. 70° to 85° ; Sept. to March 55° to 65°.
PROPAGATION : By seeds sown 1 in. deep in light, sandy soil in well-drained pot in temp. 75° under bell-glass or in propagator, March or April.
SPECIES CULTIVATED : R. Baueri (Syn. Areca Baueri), 10 to 20 ft., Norfolk Island ; sapida (Syn. Areca or Kentia sapida), 10 to 20 ft., New Zealand.

Rhubarb (*Rheum rhaponticum*)—See Rheum.

Rhus (Sumach ; Smoke Tree ; Wig Tree ; Stag's-horn Sumach)—Ord. Anacardiaceæ. Hardy deciduous trees and climbers. Flowering and orn. foliage. Foliage nicely tinted in autumn. First introduced 1629. Leaves, entire or once divided, green.
CULTURE : Soil, ordinary. Position, sunny borders or shrubberies. Walls or old tree trunks for R. Toxicodendron radicans. Plant, Oct. to Feb. Prune flowering species moderately after blooming ; others in Nov. or Dec.
PROPAGATION : By cuttings of firm shoots, 6 to 8 in. long, inserted in ordinary soil in cold frame or under hand-light, Oct. to Nov. ; cuttings of roots, 2 to 3 in. long, planted 3 in. deep in sandy soil, Oct. or Nov. ; layering shoots in autumn.
SPECIES CULTIVATED : R. canadensis, yellow, April, 3 to 5 ft., N. America ; copallina, yellowish, July to Aug., 3 to 5 ft., red fruits, Eastern N. America ; cotinoides (American Smoke Tree), 6 to 8 ft., barren flower stalks, covered with fine hairs, have a smoke-like appearance, leaves assume rich tints in autumn, Southern U.S.A. ; Cotinus (Smoke Tree, or Wig Tree, or Venetian Sumach), 8 to 12 ft., hair-covered, barren flower stalks as in R. cotinoides, inflorescence and foliage richly tinted in autumn, Europe ; cotinus atropurpurea, foliage purplish ; glabra (Smooth Sumach), 4 to 10 ft., close, erect panicle of small fruits densely covered with crimson hairs, U.S.A. ; glabra laciniata, leaves finely cut, scarlet tinted in autumn ; Toxicodendron (Poison Ivy), foliage taking red tints in autumn, 8 to 9 ft., Eastern U.S.A., and its variety radicans (climbing) ; typhina (Stag's-horn Sumach), 15 to 25 ft., crimson panicle of small fruits as in R. glabra, U.S.A.

N 2   373

Rhyncospermum—See Trachelospermum.

Ribbon-fern (*Pteris serrulata*)—See Pteris.

Ribbon-grass (*Phalaris arundinacea variegata*)—See Phalaris.

Ribes (White, Red, and Black Currant; Gooseberry)—Ord. Saxifragaceæ. Hardy deciduous fruit-bearing and flowering shrubs. Berries, black, red, white. CULTURE OF BLACK CURRANT (R. nigrum): Soil, good ordinary. Position, sunny. Plant, 5 ft. apart each way, Nov. to Feb. Prune, Nov. to Feb., thinning out old shoots only. Fruit borne on shoots of previous year's growth and on older ones. CULTURE OF RED AND WHITE CURRANT (R. rubrum and R. r. album): Soil, good ordinary. Position, sunny for early crops; against N. walls or fences for late ones. Plant, Nov. to Feb., 5 to 6 ft. apart each way. Pruning: Allow as many current year's shoots as are required to form branches to remain and shorten remainder to within four leaves of their base in June or July. Shorten the selected shoots to 4, 6, or 8 in., according to shape of tree, between Nov. and Feb. Cut out old or distorted branches at same time. Keep centres of trees well open. Fruit borne on base of previous year's and older shoots only. CULTURE OF GOOSEBERRY (R. grossularia): Soil, good ordinary. Position, sunny for early crops; against N. or E. walls for late crops. Plant, Nov. to Feb., 5 to 6 ft. apart each way. Pruning: Shorten all weak shoots of current year's growth to within four leaves of base in June or July. Thin out remaining shoots in winter, shortening those left to 4 or 6 in. Shorten side shoots of trees grown against walls to 1 in. in July. MANURES FOR CURRANTS AND GOOSEBERRIES: (1) Decayed cow, horse, or pig dung applied liberally in autumn and forked lightly into surface of ground. (2) 1½ oz. each of superphosphate of lime and kainit per square yard applied in autumn and 1 oz. of nitrate of soda per square yard applied in spring. (3) 1 oz. nitrate of soda, ⅛ oz. each of sulphate of iron and superphosphate to 4 gall. of water applied occasionally during summer. CULTURE OF FLOWERING CURRANTS: Soil, ordinary. Position, sunny. Plant, Oct. to Feb. Prune directly after flowering only. Top-dress with decayed manure in autumn. PROPAGATION: By seeds sown ¼ in. deep in ordinary fine soil outdoors in Sept. or Oct.; by cuttings, 6 to 8 in. long, inserted in ordinary soil outdoors, Oct. to Feb.; by layering in autumn; suckers, Nov. to Feb. FRUITING SPECIES: R. grossularia (Gooseberry), N. Hemisphere; nigrum (Black Currant), N. Europe; vulgare (Red Currant), N. Hemisphere; vulgare album (White Currant). FLOWERING SPECIES: R. alpinum (Alpine Currant), red fruits, 6 ft., suitable for shady places, N. Hemisphere; americanum (American Black Currant), black fruits, crimson and yellow foliage in autumn, 3 to 4 ft., N. America; aureum (Buffalo Currant), yellow, April, 6 to 8 ft., N. America; gordonianum, yellow and red, April and May, 6 to 8 ft., hybrid; sanguineum (Flowering Currant), rose, May, 6 to 8 ft., California, and its varieties album (white), atrorubens (red), atrosanguineum (dark red), carneum (rose), and splendens (blood red); speciosum (Fuchsia-flowered Currant), rich red flowers, April and May, 6 to 9 ft., California.

Riccarton's Fuchsia (*Fuchsia Riccartoni*)—See Fuchsia.

Rice-flower—See Pimelea.

Rice-paper Plant (*Fatsia papyrifera*)—See Fatsia.

Rice's Acacia (*Acacia riceana*)—See Acacia.

Richardia (Arum or Calla Lily; Lily of the Nile)—Ord. Aroideæ. Greenhouse herbaceous perennials. First introduced 1731. CULTURE OF R. AFRICANA (Arum Lily): Compost, equal parts loam, cow manure, and coarse silver sand. Position, greenhouse or dwelling-room Oct. to May; outdoors remainder of year. Repot annually in Aug. or Sept. Water moderately Sept. to March, freely March to May. Apply stimulants once a week during flowering period. Plant 15 in. apart in ordinary rich soil in sunny position outdoors in May, lift and repot in Aug. or Sept., singly in 5 or 6 in. pots. Supply freely with water in dry weather when outdoors. Suitable stimulants: ½ oz. of Peruvian guano; 1 teaspoonful of Albert's or Clay's manures; or ¼ oz. nitrate of soda or sulphate of ammonia to 1 gall. of water. Temp., Sept. to March 40° to 55°; March to May 50° to 60°.

CULTURE OF OTHER SPECIES : Compost, same as for R. africana. Position, greenhouse Oct. to June; cold frame remainder of year. Repot annually in Feb. Water moderately Feb. to April and Aug. to Oct., freely April to Aug., keep nearly dry Oct. to Feb. Apply stimulants during flowering period. Temp., Oct. to March 55° to 65°; March to Oct. 65° to 75°.

PROPAGATION : By seeds sown ⅛ in. deep in loam, leaf-mould, and sand in temp. 65° to 75° in spring; division of plants when planting outdoors or repotting; suckers removed at potting time.

SPECIES CULTIVATED : R. africana (Syn. Calla æthiopica), white, winter and spring, 3 to 4 ft., S. Africa; africana nana compacta, dwarf; albo-maculata, yellow or milk white, summer, 2 ft., leaves spotted white, S. Africa; elliotiana, yellow, Aug., 3 ft., S. Africa; melanoleuca, yellow and purple, summer, 18 in., S. Africa; Pentlandii, rich yellow and purple, summer, 2 ft., S. Africa; Rehmannii, rosy purple, summer, 2 ft., Natal.

Ricinus (Castor Oil Plant)—Ord. Euphorbiaceæ. Half-hardy annual herb; in the Tropics a tree to 40 ft. high. Orn. foliage. First introduced 1548. Flowers, insignificant. Leaves, hand-shaped, large, green, purplish.

INDOOR CULTURE : Sow seeds, previously steeped for a few hours in tepid water, ½ in. deep in pots of light, sandy soil in temp. of 70° to 75° in March, transplanting seedlings when three leaves form singly into 2 in. pots, and keep in similar temp. until well rooted, then transfer to 5 or 6 in. pots, after which remove to cool greenhouse or dwelling-room. Water moderately. Shade from sun.

OUTDOOR CULTURE : Sow seeds and transplant into small pots as above. Transfer to cold frame or pit in May to harden. Plant out, June. Position, sunny beds or borders.

SPECIES CULTIVATED : R. communis, 3 to 6 ft., Trop. Africa, and its several varieties borboniensis arboreus, cambodgensis, sanguineus, Gibsonii, zanzibarensis, etc.

Rigid Shield Fern (*Nephrodium rigidum*)—See Nephrodium.

River-side Windflower (*Anemone rivularis*)—See Anemone.

Rivina (Blood Berry; Rouge Berry; Rouge Plant)—Ord. Phytolaccaceæ. Greenhouse evergreen berry-bearing plant. Pretty for table decoration. First introduced 1699. Flowers succeeded by scarlet berries.

CULTURE : Compost, equal parts leaf-mould and sandy loam, half a part silver sand. Position, small well-drained pots in light part of warm greenhouse (temp. 50° to 60°), Sept. to June; cold, sunny frames, June to Sept. Pot, Feb. or March. Water freely April to Oct., moderately afterwards. Apply weak stimulants occasionally Oct. to Feb. Shade from sun. Best results obtained by raising plants from seed or cuttings annually.

PROPAGATION : By seeds sown ⅟₁₆ in. deep in well-drained pots or shallow pans of good light soil placed in temp. 55° to 65°, spring; cuttings of young shoots inserted in Feb., March, or April in small pots of light, sandy soil in temp. of 65° to 75°, spring.

SPECIES CULTIVATED : R. humilis, white, June, 1 to 3 ft., Caribbean Islands.

Roast-beef-plant (*Iris fœtidissima*)—See Iris.

Robinia (False Acacia; Locust Tree)—Ord. Leguminosæ. Hardy deciduous flowering trees and shrubs. First introduced 1640.

CULTURE : Soil, ordinary. Position, sunny well-drained borders and shrubberies. Plant, Oct. to Feb. Prune, Nov. to Feb. Rose Acacia (R. hispida) may be grown against S. or W. walls, side shoots being pruned annually to 1 in. of base, Nov. Dec.

PROPAGATION : Choice varieties by grafting on common species (R. pseudacacia) in March; other kinds by seeds sown ½ in. deep in ordinary soil outdoors, Nov. or

March ; cuttings of shoots, 6 to 8 in. long, inserted in ordinary soil in sheltered position outdoors in autumn ; suckers removed from parent tree and planted Oct. or Nov. ; layering, Sept. or Nov.

SPECIES CULTIVATED : R. hispida (Rose Acacia), rose, May, 6 to 8 ft., Southern U.S.A.; hispida macrophylla, without prickles ; Kelseyi (Kelsey's False Acacia), rose, June, 8 to 12 ft., Eastern U.S.A. ; Pseudacacia (Locust Tree; False Acacia), white, June, 70 to 80 ft., Eastern U.S.A., and its varieties aurea (golden-leaved) and bessoniana latifolia (larger but fewer leaflets), decaisneana (pink-flowered), inermis (mop-headed), monophylla (one to three leaflets), and semperflorens (flowering through-out the summer) ; viscosa, pale rose and yellow, June, 30 to 40 ft., Carolina.

Robinson's Iris (*Moræa robinsoniana*)—See Moræa.

Rocambole—See Allium.

Rochea—Ord. Crassulaceæ. Greenhouse succulent plants. First introduced 1710.
CULTURE : Compost, equal parts sandy loam, brick rubble, dried cow manure, and river sand. Position, well-drained pots in light greenhouse, close to glass. Pot, March. Water freely April to Aug., moderately Aug. to Nov., very little after-wards. Prune old plants after flowering, shortening shoots to 1 in., and repot when new shoots are 1 in. long. Temp., March to Sept. 55° to 65° ; Sept. to March 45° to 50°.

PROPAGATION : By seeds sown in well-drained pots or pans of sandy soil, just covering seeds with fine mould, in temp. 60° to 70° in March or April ; seedlings to be kept close to glass and have little water ; cuttings of shoots, 2 to 3 in. long, exposed to sun for few days, then inserted in June, July, or Aug. in well-drained pots of sandy soil, placed on greenhouse shelf, and given very little water.

SPECIES CULTIVATED : R. coccinea, scarlet, July, 1 ft., S. Africa ; jasminea, white, spring, 6 to 9 in., S. Africa ; versicolor, white and red, spring, 2 ft., S. Africa. See also the genus Crassula.

Rock Brake-fern (*Cryptogramme crispa*)—See Cryptogramme.

Rock Broom (*Genista tinctoria*)—See Genista.

Rock Candytuft (*Iberis saxatilis*)—See Iberis.

Rocket Candytuft (*Iberis coronaria*)—See Iberis.

Rock Cress (*Arabis albida* and *Aubrietia deltoidea*)—See Arabis and Aubrietia.

Rock Daphne (*Daphne rupestris*)—See Daphne.

Rocket Larkspur (*Delphinium Ajacis*)—See Delphinium.

Rockfoil—See Saxifraga.

Rock Forget-me-not (*Omphalodes Luciliæ*)—See Omphalodes.

Rock Gromwell (*Lithospermum petræum*)—See Lithospermum.

Rock Jasmine—See Androsace.

Rock Knot-weed (*Polygonum vaccinifolium*)—See Polygonum.

Rock Lychnis (*Lychnis Lagascæ*)—See Lychnis.

Rock Mad-wort (*Alyssum saxatile*)—See Alyssum.

Rock Navel-wort (*Omphalodes Luciliæ*)—See Omphalodes.

Rock Pink (*Dianthus petræus*)—See Dianthus.

Rock Purslane (*Calandrinia umbellata*)—See Calandrinia.

Rock Rose—See Cistus.

Rock Soap-wort (*Saponaria ocymoides*)—See Saponaria.

Rock Speedwell (*Veronica saxatilis* and *V. Teucrium dubia*)—See Veronica.

Rock Spleenwort (*Asplenium fontanum*)—See Asplenium.

Rock Stonecrop (*Sedum rupestre*)—See Sedum.

Rock Wallflower (*Erysimum pulchellum*)—See Erysimum.

Rock Wood Lily (*Ranunculus Lyalli*)—See Ranunculus.

Rock Yarrow (*Achillea rupestris*)—See Achillea.

Rocky Mountain Columbine (*Aquilegia cærulea*)—See Aquilegia.

Rodgers' Bronze-leaf (*Rodgersia podophylla*)—See Rodgersia.

Rodgersia (Rodgers' Bronze-leaf)—Ord. Saxifragaceæ. Hardy herbaceous perennials. Orn. foliage. First introduced 1880. Leaves, very large, bronzy green.
CULTURE : Compost, two parts peat, one part loam. Position, partially shaded border. Plant, March or April. Water freely in dry weather. Protect in severe weather with covering of fern fronds or litter.
PROPAGATION : By division, March or April.
SPECIES CULTIVATED : R. æsculifolia, rosy white, summer, 2 to 3 ft., bronze foliage, China ; pinnata, rosy crimson, summer, 2 to 3 ft., China ; podophylla, creamy white, summer, 3 ft., Japan ; tabularis, creamy white, summer, 3 ft., bright green foliage, N. China.

Rodriguezia—Ord. Orchidaceæ. Stove epiphytal orchids. First introduced 1820.
CULTURE : Compost, equal parts fibrous peat and sphagnum moss. Position, baskets suspended from roof. Place in baskets, Feb. or March. Water freely March to Sept., moderately other times. Shade from sun. Moist atmosphere very essential in summer. Temp., Oct. to Feb. 50° to 60° ; Feb. to Oct. 60° to 70°.
PROPAGATION : By division of pseudo-bulbs at potting time.
SPECIES CULTIVATED : R. decora, rose, red, and white, May and June, 1 ft., Brazil ; fragrans, white and yellow, April and May, fragrant, Brazil ; pubescens, white and yellow, Brazil ; secunda, rosy pink, Brazil.

Roella (South African Harebell)—Ord. Campanulaceæ. Greenhouse evergreen shrub. First introduced 1774.
CULTURE : Compost, equal parts of peat and loam and a fair quantity of sand. Position, pots in light and dry part of greenhouse. Pot, March. Water very carefully during spring and summer and give very little in autumn and winter. Syringing or wetting the foliage must be avoided at all seasons. Ventilate freely in summer and moderately at other times. Dry atmosphere essential in autumn and winter. Remove flowers directly they fade ; also all blooms that form in autumn and winter. Temp., Sept. to April 40° to 45° ; April to Sept. 50° to 60°.
PROPAGATION : By cuttings of strong shoots, 2 in. long, inserted in moist sand in temp. 58° in spring. Shade from sun.
SPECIES CULTIVATED : R. ciliata, white and purple, summer, 1 ft., S. Africa.

Roman Hyacinth (*Hyacinthus orientalis albulus*)—See Hyacinthus.

Romanzoffia (Sitcha Water-leaf)—Ord. Hydrophyllaceæ. Hardy perennial herb. First introduced 1873.
CULTURE : Soil, ordinary. Position, sunny ledges of sunny rockery. Plant, March or April.
PROPAGATION : By division, March or April.
SPECIES CULTIVATED : R. sitchensis, white, spring, 3 to 4 in., N.W. America ; unalaschkensis, white, 3 in., Aleutian Islands.

Romneya (Californian Tree Poppy)—Ord. Papaveraceæ. Half-hardy perennials. First introduced 1875.
OUTDOOR CULTURE : Soil, sandy loam with peat and leaf-mould. Position, well-drained border at base of S. wall or sheltered sunny rockery. Plant, April or May. Protect in severe weather with covering of fern or litter.
PROPAGATION : By seeds sown in sandy soil in well-drained pans during Feb. or March in temp. 55°. Root cuttings in sandy compost during Feb. in temp. 55°, placing cuttings singly in small pots.
SPECIES CULTIVATED : R. Coulteri, white, fragrant, late summer and autumn, 4 to 6 ft., California ; trichocalyx, white, fragrant, Aug. to Oct., 5 ft., California.

Romulea—Ord. Iridaceæ. Hardy and half-hardy bulbous plants. First introduced 1739.

CULTURE : Soil, light, rich, sandy. Position, sunny well-drained border. Plant, Sept. to Jan., placing tubers 4 in. deep and 2 in. apart. Lift and replant tubers annually. Mulch surface of bed in March with cow manure.

PROPAGATION : By offsets, treated as advised for tubers.

SPECIES CULTIVATED : R. Bulbocodium, yellow and violet, March to April, 4 to 6 in., Europe ; clusiana, lavender and orange, spring, 9 in., Spain and Portugal ; parviflora (Syn. R. Columnæ), lilac, May, 6 in., Europe ; ramiflora, yellow and lilac, May, 6 to 8 in., Mediterranean Region ; Requieni, violet, spring, 4 in., Corsica ; rosea speciosa, carmine, March to May, 6 in., S. Africa.

Rondeletia—Ord. Rubiaceæ. Stove evergreen flowering shrubs. First introduced 1752.

CULTURE : Compost, equal parts rough fibrous peat and loam, one part equal proportions charcoal lumps and coarse silver sand. Position, well-drained pots in light part of stove with shoots trained to sticks or trellis. Pot, Feb. or March. Prune moderately after flowering. Water freely April to Oct., moderately afterwards. Syringe daily March to Sept. Shade from bright sunshine. Temp., March to Sept. 70° to 80° ; Sept. to March 55° to 60°.

PROPAGATION : By cuttings of firm shoots inserted in pure sand under bell-glass in temp. 75° to 85°, spring or summer.

SPECIES CULTIVATED : R. amœna, pink, summer, 3 to 4 ft., Mexico ; Backhousei, pink, summer, 3 ft., Trop. America ; cordata, pink or dull red, summer, 3 to 7 ft., Guatemala ; gratissima, pink, fragrant, summer, 3 to 4 ft., Mexico ; odorata (Syns. R. splendens and speciosa), orange-red and yellow, fragrant, summer, 4 to 6 ft., Cuba and Panama.

Rosa (Rose)—Ord. Rosaceæ. Hardy and half-hardy evergreen and deciduous shrubs.

CLASSIFICATION—Summer blooming types : Provence, Pompon, Moss, Damask, Hybrid China, Hybrid Bourbon, Hybrid Noisette, Alba, Austrian Briar, Scotch, Sweet Briar, Ayrshire, Boursault, Banksian, Evergreen, Polyantha, Multiflora, and Wichuraiana ramblers. Summer and autumn blooming: Hybrid Perpetual, Hybrid Tea, Tea, Noisette, China, Bourbon, Perpetual, Hybrid Musks, Hybrid Bracteata, Dwarf Polyantha, Pernetiana, Polyantha Pompom, Perpetual Moss, and Perpetual Scotch.

CULTURE OF DWARF ROSES : Soil, deep, rich loam well enriched with decayed manure. If light, add clay and cow dung. If heavy, road grit, leaf-mould, burnt refuse, horse dung, and lime. Position, sunny beds or borders. Plant, Nov., or Feb. to March. Distance apart to plant, 18 in. Depth of soil over roots, 4 to 6 in. on heavy and 7 to 8 in. on light soils. Pruning : Time, end of March and early in April. Hybrid Perpetuals : Remove damaged and weak shoots and shorten others to dormant bud nine to eighteen inches from base, according to strength. Hybrid Teas, Teas, and Pernetianas : Remove damaged and weak shoots and shorten others to dormant bud three to nine inches from base, according to strength. Noisettes : Thin out all weak and worn-out wood and shorten others a little according to strength, leaving the best of the previous year's growth full length. Bourbons : Remove old and weakly growth but leave the best lateral bearing wood unpruned. Provence, Damask, Moss, Chinas, and Pompons : Thin out the oldest and weakliest wood so as to make room for healthy new growth, which should be retained full length. Austrian and Scotch Briars : Thin out weak or dead growths only. Hybrid Sweet Briars : Thin out older shoots only after flowering. Protect Tea, China, and tender roses in winter by drawing soil to a height of six inches around the base of each plant and put bracken or dry litter among the shoots.

CULTURE OF STANDARD ROSES : Soil, position, and planting, as for dwarfs. Distance apart to plant, 3 ft. Pruning—Hybrid Perpetuals, Hybrid Teas, Teas, and Bourbons : Thin out weak shoots in centre of tree and shorten remaining shoots to three to nine inches, according to vigour. Noisettes : Thin out weak shoots freely and shorten remaining ones to a foot or so, according to strength.

CULTURE OF CLIMBING ROSES : Soil, as advised for dwarfs. Position, against walls, fences, arbours, pergolas, arches, tree trunks, trellises, pillars, etc. Distance apart to plant, 5 to 6 ft. Plant in Oct. or Nov. or in March. Pruning—Rambler type : Cut away old flowering shoots after blooming and thin out dead or weakly growths in April ; no further pruning required. Banksian type : Thin out the strong young shoots not required to add to size of plant directly after flowering. Do not remove older or small shoots. Teas, Noisettes, Hybrid Teas, Singles, etc., grown as climbers, to have old flowering shoots thinned out after blooming, dead or weak growths removed in April, and the soft, unripened tips of shoots cut off at same time. Ayrshire, Boursault, and Evergreen types only require to have weak growths thinned out in March.

CULTURE OF WEEPING ROSES : Soil and planting, as advised for dwarfs. Distance to plant, 10 ft. Pruning : Thin out weak and old growths in March, and remove soft, unripened ends of shoots only.

MANURES FOR ROSES : Cow or pig dung for light soils ; horse manure for heavy ones. Top-dress with above directly after pruning and lightly fork in. Suitable artificial manures : (1) Superphosphate of lime, 48 lb. ; sulphate of potash, 20 lb. ; sulphate of ammonia, 25 lb. ; sulphate of iron, 4 lb. Mix thoroughly together and apply at the rate of 3 oz. per square yard directly after pruning. One dose per annum sufficient. (2) Dissolve ⅜ oz. superphosphate of lime, ¼ oz. sulphate of ammonia, and ¼ oz. sulphate of iron in 2 gall. of water. Apply above quantity to each tree once a week from time buds form till flowers develop. Liquid soot-water, cow and sheep dung also good for roses outdoors or in pots.

STOCKS FOR ROSES : For standards, the wild dog rose of the hedgerow and the Rugosa ; for dwarfs and climbers, the seedling and cutting wild dog rose, the Manetti, de la Grifferaie, the Rugosa, the Laxa, the Multiflora, and the Polyantha rose.

CULTURE OF ROSES IN POTS : Classes of roses suitable for pot culture—Hybrid Perpetual, Hybrid Tea, Tea-scented, Polyantha, and Lawrenciana. Compost, two parts turfy loam, two parts decomposed cow or hotbed manure, one part sand. Pot, Oct. Repot annually in Aug. or Sept. Prune newly lifted and potted plants in Nov., shortening shoots to 3, 2, and 1 " eyes " of the base, according to size ; established plants of hybrid perpetuals and hybrid teas to 6, 3, and 2 " eyes " ; also tea-scented, Chinese, fairy, and polyantha kinds to 8, 6, and 4 " eyes " in Nov. for early flowering ; Dec. or Jan. for late flowering. Position, sheltered corner outdoors, with pots protected from frost by straw, or in cold frame, Oct. to Jan. ; greenhouse, Jan. to May ; sunny place outdoors afterwards. Water moderately Jan. to April, freely April to Oct., keep nearly dry Oct. to Jan. Apply stimulants once or twice a week during flowering period. Syringe freely in greenhouse. Temp. for forcing : Jan., 40° by night and 45° by day ; Feb., 45° by night and 55° by day ; March and onwards, 55° by night and 60° to 65° by day. Plants for forcing require to be established in pots one year.

CULTURE OF CLIMBERS IN GREENHOUSE : Compost, same as for pots. Beds or tubs for each plant, 18 in. deep and 2 ft. wide. Each bed or tub to be provided with 3 in. of drainage. Plant, Sept. to Nov., or March. Prune each shoot first year to within 8 in. of its base at time of planting ; second and future years thin out old wood and shorten young growth by a third or a half, according to their strength, immediately after flowering. Water freely March to Nov., keep nearly dry after-wards. Apply stimulants weekly April to Sept. to established plants. Syringe daily in spring. Admit air freely in summer and autumn to ripen shoots.

PROPAGATION : By seeds sown ⅛ in. deep in light, sandy soil in cold frame in March or April, or ⅛ in. deep in ordinary soil outdoors in April, transplanting seedlings when a year old ; cuttings, 6 to 8 in. long, inserted in pots of sandy soil in cold frame in Oct., or in sheltered position outdoors, Sept. to Nov. ; or by small side shoots of tea-scented and other kinds removed with a little of old stem attached and inserted in small pots of light, sandy soil in summer under a bell-glass or in a propagator ; by budding in July ; grafting in Feb. or March in temp. 55° to 65° ; layering in Sept. or Oct.

SPECIES CULTIVATED : R. acicularis, rosy pink, May, 6 ft., Siberia ; alba, white, June, 6 ft., Europe ; alpina (Syn. R. pendulina), pink, June, 8 ft., Europe, one of

the parents of the Boursault Rose), Banksiæ (Banksian Rose), white, June, 15 to
20 ft., China, and its varieties flore-pleno (double) and lutea (yellow); arvensis
(Ayrshire Rose), white or rose, 10 to 15 ft., Europe (Britain); blanda (Syn. R.
lucida), rose, June, 4 to 6 ft., N. America; bourboniana (Bourbon Rose), one of
the parents—the other indica—of the Bourbon class of roses; bracteata (Macartney Rose), white, July, 10 to 20 ft., China; canina (Dog Rose), pink, June, 6 ft.,
Britain; carolina, purplish rose, June to Aug., 4 to 6 ft., Eastern N. America;
centifolia (Cabbage Rose), rosy purple, June, 6 ft., Europe; centifolia muscosa
(Moss Rose), rose, June, 4 to 6 ft.; centifolia provincialis (Provence Rose), rose,
June, 4 to 6 ft.; cinnamomea (Cinnamon Rose), red, May, 6 to 9 ft., N. Temp.
Zone, and its variety flore-pleno (double); damascena (Damask Rose), white to
red, June, 4 to 8 ft.; Dupontii, white and pink, July, 6 to 8 ft., hybrid; Ecæ,
buttercup yellow, 3 to 4 ft., Afghanistan; Fargesi, rose, May to June, 4 to 8 ft.,
hybrid; gallica, dark red, June to July, 3 to 4 ft., Europe; hispida, pale yellow,
May to June, 5 to 6 ft., habitat unknown; Hugonis, yellow, summer, 8 ft., W.
China; indica (China or Monthly Rose), red, June to Sept., 6 to 10 ft., China;
indica fragrans (Syn. R. odorata), Tea Rose, various colours; indica minima
(Fairy Rose), Syn. R. lawrenceana, pink, etc., June, 1 to 2 ft.; indica sanguinea
(Crimson China Rose), crimson, summer, 6 to 10 ft.; lutea (Austrian Briar),
yellow, June, 3 to 5 ft., Orient, and its varieties punicea (Austrian Copper) and
Harrisoni (double yellow); lævigata (Cherokee Rose), white, June, 6 to 10 ft.,
China; macrantha, blush pink to white, June, 4 to 6 ft., Europe; moschata
(Musk Rose), yellow to white, summer, 15 to 30 ft., S. Europe; Moyesii, dark red,
succeeded by large red bottle-like heps, 6 to 10 ft., W. China; multiflora (Polyantha
Rose), white, June, 10 to 12 ft., China and Japan, and its varieties grandiflora,
platyphylla (Seven Sisters Rose), and flore-pleno (Bramble Rose); noisettiana
(Noisette Rose), white, July to Aug., 8 to 10 ft., hybrid; sericea, creamy white, May
to June, 10 to 12 ft., N. India, and its variety pteracantha (blood-red spines); pomifera (Apple Rose), Syn. R. villosa, pink, June, 4 to 6 ft., Europe; Rouletti, pink,
summer, 6 in., habitat unknown; rubiginosa (Sweet Briar), pink, June, 6 to 8 ft.,
Europe; rubrifolia, deep red, June to July, 5 to 7 ft., Central Europe; rugosa
(Japanese Rose), purplish rose, June, 6 ft., Japan; sempervirens (Evergreen Rose),
white, June, S. Europe; setipoda, purplish rose, June to July, 6 to 10 ft., Central
China; simplicifolia (Syn. R. berberifolia), yellow and crimson, 2 to 3 ft., Orient,
rather tender; spinosissima (Scotch or Burnet Rose), Syn. R. pimpinellifolia, white
to pale pink, May to June, 3 to 4 ft., Europe (Britain), and its varieties altaica and
lutea; wichuraiana, white, summer, 6 to 10 ft., Japan, parent of the trailing type
such as Dorothy Perkins; Willmottiæ, purplish rose, June to July, 5 to 10 ft.,
W. China; xanthina, pale yellow, June to July, 5 to 8 ft., Persia and Afghanistan.

Rosary Pea (*Abrus precatorius*)—See Abrus.

Roscœa—Ord. Scitamineæ. Dwarf hardy perennials of great charm and beauty.
First introduced 1820.

CULTURE : Soil, sandy loam and leaf-mould. Position, woodland gardens or half-
shady, sheltered borders. Plant the fleshy tuberous roots 6 in. deep in March.

PROPAGATION : By division of the roots in spring, or seed sown in warm greenhouse
in Feb. or March.

SPECIES CULTIVATED : R. cautleoides, pale yellow, summer, 9 to 12 in., China;
purpurea, purple, autumn, 1 ft., Himalayas.

Rose—See Rosa.

Rose Acacia (*Robinia hispida*)—See Robinia.

Rose Apple (*Eugenia Jambos*)—See Eugenia.

Rose Bay (*Nerium Oleander*)—See Nerium.

Rose Bay Willow-herb (*Epilobium angustifolium*)—See Epilobium.

Rose Box (*Cotoneaster microphylla*)—See Cotoneaster.

Rose Campion (*Lychnis coronaria*)—See Lychnis.

Rose Mallow—See Hibiscus.

Rosemary (*Rosmarinus officinalis*)—See Rosmarinus.

Rose of Heaven (*Lychnis Cæli-rosa*)—See Lychnis.

Rose of Jericho (*Anastatica Hierochuntica*)—See Anastatica.

Rose of Sharon (*Hypericum calycinum* and *Hibiscus syriacus*)—See Hypericum and Hibiscus.

Rose Pink (*Sabbatia campestris*)—See Sabbatia.

Rose Root (*Sedum roseum*)—See Sedum.

Rose-scented Geranium (*Pelargonium capitatum*)—See Pelargonium.

Rosette Mullein (*Ramondia pyrenaica*)—See Ramondia.

Rosin-weed (*Silphium laciniatum*)—See Silphium.

Rosmarinus (Rosemary)—Ord. Labiatæ. Hardy evergreen shrub. First introduced 1548. Leaves, highly fragrant.
CULTURE : Soil, ordinary, freely mixed with old mortar. Position, dryish sunny border or shrubbery. Plant, April. Water freely in summer.
PROPAGATION : Green-leaved kind by seeds sown ½ in. deep in sunny border outdoors in April ; green and variegated sorts by cuttings 6 in. long, removing leaves from lower half, inserted in shady border in spring or summer ; also by layering strong shoots in summer.
SPECIES CULTIVATED : R. officinalis, purple, Feb., 6 to 7 ft., S. Europe, and its variety prostratus (trailing).

Rosy-flowered Bramble (*Rubus spectabilis*)—See Rubus.

Rouen Lilac (*Syringa sinensis*)—See Syringa.

Rouen Violet (*Viola rothamagensis*)—See Viola.

Rouge Berry (*Rivina humilis*)—See Rivina.

Rouge Plant (*Rivina humilis*)—See Rivina.

Roupala—Ord. Proteaceæ. Greenhouse evergreen shrubs. Orn. foliage and flowering. First introduced 1802. Leaves, simple or feather-shaped, covered with brownish wool.
CULTURE : Compost, equal parts fibrous loam, leaf-mould, peat, and little sand. Position, large pots or tubs in lofty sunny greenhouse or conservatory. Pot, Feb. or March. Water freely April to Sept., moderately afterwards. No syringing required. Temp., Sept. to March 45° to 50° ; March to Sept. 55° to 65°. May be stood outdoors in sunny position, June to Sept.
PROPAGATION : By cuttings of firm shoots inserted in pure silver sand in well-drained pots under bell-glass in temp. 55° to 65°, summer.
SPECIES CULTIVATED : R. elegans, 6 to 10 ft., and Pohlii, 6 to 15 ft., Brazil.

Rowan-tree (*Pyrus aucuparia*)—See Pyrus.

Royal Brunswick Lily (*Brunsvigia Josephinæ*)—See Brunsvigia.

Royal Fern (*Osmunda regalis*)—See Osmunda.

Royal Palmetto Palm (*Thrinax parviflora*)—See Thrinax.

Royal Water Lily (*Victoria regia*)—See Victoria.

Rubus (Raspberry ; Blackberry ; Dewberry ; Loganberry ; Wineberry)—Ord. Rosaceæ. Hardy fruit-bearing and flowering shrubs and perennials.
CULTURE OF RASPBERRIES : Soil, deep, rich, moist loam, light ordinary or peaty ; clay soils unsuitable. Position, open, sunny or partially shady one. Plant, Oct. to March. Distances for planting : Singly 2 ft. apart in the row and 5 ft. between the rows for training to wire trellis ; in groups of three canes, 3 ft. apart in row and 5 ft. between rows ; singly 1 ft. apart in rows 4 ft. asunder for field culture. Pruning : Cut canes off to within 6 in. of ground first year ; succeeding years cut off old canes immediately after fruiting close to ground and reduce the number

of young canes at each root or stool to three or four of the strongest. Remove tips of latter in Nov. or Dec. Apply decayed manure annually in Nov., forking it in 3 in. deep only. Mulch with littery manure in April on dry soil. Water copiously with liquid manure during bearing period. Remove suckers appearing away from base of " stools." Avoid deep digging. Chemical manures : (1) 1½ oz. each of superphosphate of lime and kainit per square yard forked in 2 in. deep in Nov. and 1 oz. of nitrate of soda per square yard applied in March. (2) Two parts by weight of nitrate of soda, 1 part superphosphate, 1 part kainit—to be applied at the rate of 2 lb. per 100 canes in Oct. or Nov. (Griffiths).

PROPAGATION : By seeds sown outdoors in a shady border as soon as ripe ; by division of roots in autumn.

CULTURE OF BLACKBERRIES : Soil, deep, rich loam liberally dressed with old mortar. Position, trained to sunny fences, or in rows in open garden, with shoots trained to a rough trellis. Plant in autumn, 1 ft. apart in rows 4 ft. asunder. Prune in autumn, cutting away shoots that have borne fruit directly after fruiting and removing tips off remaining shoots in Dec. Top-dress annually in winter.

PROPAGATION : By layering shoots in summer or dividing the roots in summer.

CULTURE OF LOGANBERRY AND WINEBERRY : Soil as for raspberries. Plant, 4 ft. apart each way in autumn. Shorten shoots well back first season. Place four stakes around each plant, at a distance of 3 ft. from the base, and train growths spirally around these. Prune after fruiting, cutting away shoots that have borne fruit and removing soft tips of remaining shoots in Dec. Top-dress with decayed manure in winter.

PROPAGATION : By layering shoots in summer or dividing the roots in autumn.

CULTURE OF HARDY HERBACEOUS SPECIES : Soil, sandy peat. Position, shady rockery. Plant, autumn or spring. Water freely in dry weather.

PROPAGATION : By division in spring.

CULTURE OF HARDY SHRUBBY SPECIES : Soil, good ordinary. Position, sunny or shady borders. Plant in Oct. Prune after flowering, cutting away old shoots.

PROPAGATION : By division in autumn.

FRUIT-BEARING SPECIES : R. Idæus (Raspberry), white, May, berries red or yellow, 3 to 6 ft., Europe ; Idæus Loganii (Loganberry), a cross between the Raspberry and Blackberry, berries purple, 8 to 12 ft., hybrid ; innominatus, pink, fruit orange-red, to 10 ft., China ; laciniatus (American Blackberry), white, summer, berries black, 8 to 12 ft. ; phœnicolasius (Wineberry), pink, summer, berries crimson, 10 to 20 ft., Japan ; rosæfolius (Strawberry-raspberry), white, fruits red, 5 to 8 ft., E. Asia, a plant of no value in this country.

HERBACEOUS SPECIES : R. arcticus, pink, June, 3 to 4 in., N. Europe ; cæsius (Dewberry), white, summer, 4 to 6 in., Britain.

HARDY SHRUBBY SPECIES : R. australis (Lawyer Vine), white, pink, or yellow, ever-green, 10 to 20 ft., New Zealand ; bambusarum, pink, evergreen, fruits black, 3 to 6 ft., China ; biflorus, white, May, 8 ft., Himalayas ; deliciosus, white, May, 6 to 10 ft., Rocky Mountains ; flagelliflorus, white, June, evergreen, 5 to 6 ft., China ; giraldianus, purple, 8 to 10 ft., white stems, China ; lasiostylus, reddish purple, 4 to 6 ft., white stems, China ; leucodermis, white, June, 4 to 8 ft., bluish-white stems, Western N. America ; nutkanus (Nootka Sound Bramble), white, summer, 6 ft., N. America ; odoratus (Virginian Raspberry), purple and red, summer, 6 ft., N. America ; spectabilis (Salmon Berry), rosy red, May, 6 ft., California ; tricolor (Syn. R. polytrichus), white, prostrate, W. China ; ulmifolius (Daisy-flowered Bramble), rosy red, summer, 8 to 12 ft., Europe, and its variety bellidiflorus (Syn. flore-pleno), double-flowered.

Ruby Grass (*Tricholæna rosea*)—See Tricholæna.

Rudbeckia (Cone-flower)—Ord. Compositæ. Hardy herbaceous perennials. First introduced 1699.

CULTURE OF ANNUAL SPECIES : Soil, ordinary. Sow in boxes in cold frame in March, pricking seedlings out when large enough to handle into deeper boxes for hardening off and planting out in May ; or sow in open ground where desired to flower in April, thinning the seedlings to 9 in. apart.

CULTURE OF PERENNIAL SPECIES : Soil, ordinary. Position, sunny well-drained borders. Plant, Oct., Nov., March, or April. Mulch with decayed manure annually, Feb. or March. Lift, divide, and replant in fresh position triennially. PROPAGATION : By seeds sown ⅛ in. deep outdoors in ordinary soil and sunny position, March or April, transplanting seedlings into flowering positions following autumn ; by division of roots, Oct., Nov., March, or April.
ANNUAL SPECIES CULTIVATED : R. amplexicaulis, yellow and maroon, summer, 1 to 2 ft., N. America ; bicolor, yellow and maroon, July to Sept., 1 to 2 ft., N. America ; hirta, yellow and dull brown, summer, 1 to 3 ft., N. America, biennial or annual ; triloba, deep yellow and brown, summer, 2 to 5 ft., N. America, biennial or annual.
PERENNIAL SPECIES CULTIVATED : R. californica, yellow and brown, July to Sept., 4 to 6 ft., California ; fulgida, yellow and dark purple, July to Sept., 1 to 2 ft., N. America ; grandiflora, yellow and purple, autumn, 3 ft., N. America ; laciniata, yellow, summer, 3 to 6 ft., N. America, and its variety Golden Glow (double) ; maxima, yellow and blackish brown, late summer, 7 to 9 ft., N. America ; nitida, yellow, late summer, 4 ft., N. America ; speciosa (Syn. R. Newmannii), orange yellow, summer, 1½ to 3 ft., N. America ; subtomentosa, yellow and purple, late summer, 3 to 5 ft., N. America. See also Echinacea and Lepachys.

Rue (*Ruta graveolens*)—See Ruta.

Rue-anemone (*Thalictrum anemonoides*)—See Thalictrum.

Rue-leaved Spleen-wort (*Asplenium Ruta-muraria*)—See Asplenium.

Ruellia (Christmas Pride)—Ord. Acanthaceæ. Stove perennial herbs or shrubs. First introduced 1879.
CULTURE : Compost, equal parts fibrous loam, leaf-mould, peat, and silver sand. Pot, Feb. or March. Position, pots in shady part of stove. Water freely March to Oct., moderately afterwards. Syringe twice daily March to Sept., once daily other times. Apply weak stimulants during flowering period to perennial species. Temp., Sept. to March 55° to 65° ; March to Sept. 65° to 75°.
PROPAGATION : By cuttings inserted in above compost in well-drained pots under bell-glass or in propagator in temp. 75° to 85°, spring or summer ; perennial species by seeds sown in sandy soil in temp. 70° to 75°, Feb. or March.
SPECIES CULTIVATED : R. macrantha, rosy purple, winter, to 6 ft., shrubby, Brazil ; Portellæ, rose pink, winter, 1 ft., annual or perennial, Brazil. See also Strobilanthes.

Rumex (Herb Patience ; Sorrel)—Ord. Polygonaceæ. Hardy perennial herbs.
CULTURE OF HERB PATIENCE : Soil, ordinary moist. Remove flower stems directly they appear and gather leaves frequently.
PROPAGATION : By seeds sown in March 1 in. deep in drills 18 in. apart, thinning seedlings to 1 ft. apart in row in April ; division of roots in March.
CULTURE OF SORREL : Soil, ordinary rich moist. Position, open borders. Plant, 1 ft. apart in rows 15 in. asunder in March. Gather leaves frequently. Remove flower stems. Water freely in dry weather.
PROPAGATION : By seeds ½ in. deep in drills 15 in. apart in March, thinning seedlings to 12 in. apart in April ; division of roots in March.
CULTURE OF AQUATIC SPECIES : Soil, ordinary. Position, margins of water. Plant in spring. Increased by division in spring.
SPECIES CULTIVATED : R. acetosa (Garden Sorrel), green, summer, 18 in., leaves edible, Europe (Britain) ; hydrolapathum (Water Dock), 4 to 6 ft., Europe (Britain) ; Patientia (Herb Patience), 4 ft., leaves used as substitute for spinach, S. Europe ; scutatus (French Sorrel), 1 to 2 ft., leaves edible, Europe and Asia.

Runner Bean (*Phaseolus multiflorus*)—See Phaseolus.

Rupture-wort (*Herniaria glabra*)—See Herniaria.

Ruscus (Butcher's Broom ; Knee Holly)—Ord. Liliaceæ. Hardy evergreen shrub. Orn. leaved and berry-bearing. Male and female flowers borne on separate plants. Leaves (cladodes), oval, dark green. Berries, round, red ; winter.
CULTURE : Soil, ordinary. Position, shady or sunny shrubberies, borders, or woods. Plant, Sept., Oct., or April. Prune, April.

PROPAGATION : By suckers removed from parent plants in Sept. or Oct. ; division of roots in Oct.
SPECIES CULTIVATED : R. aculeatus (Butcher's Broom), green, May, 3 ft., Britain. The Alexandrian Laurel, frequently known as Ruscus racemosus, is correctly Danæ racemosa, *q.v.*

Rush—See Scirpus.

Rush Broom (*Spartium junceum*)—See Spartium.

Rush-leaved Daffodil (*Narcissus juncifolius*)—See Narcissus.

Rush Lily (*Sisyrinchium grandiflorum*)—See Sisyrinchium.

Russellia—Ord. Scrophulariaceæ. Stove evergreen shrubs. Flowering. First introduced 1812. Pretty plants for hanging baskets.
CULTURE : Compost, equal parts sandy loam, leaf-mould, and silver sand. Position, in light part of stove. Pot, Feb. or March. Water freely April to Sept., moderately afterwards. Prune, Feb. Apply weak stimulants when in flower only. Syringe twice daily April to Oct., except when in flower. Temp., Sept. to March 55° to 65° ; March to Sept. 65° to 75°.
PROPAGATION : By cuttings inserted in silver sand in temp. 75° in spring ; layering shoots at any time.
SPECIES CULTIVATED : R. juncea, red, July, 3 to 4 ft., Mexico ; sarmentosa, red, July, 4 ft., Trop. America. R. Lemoinei and R. elegantissima are hybrids between R. juncea and R. sarmentosa.

Russian Kale—A variety of Borecole or Kale—See Brassica.

Russian Knap-weed (*Centaurea ruthenica*)—See Centaurea.

Ruta (Rue)—Ord. Rutaceæ. Hardy evergreen shrub. First introduced 1562. Leaves, finely divided, bluish green ; used for medicinal purposes.
CULTURE : Soil, ordinary. Position, sunny border. Plant, March, 8 in. apart in rows 18 in. asunder. Prune the plants closely in April.
PROPAGATION : By seeds sown ⅛ in. deep in drills outdoors in April ; cuttings or slips inserted in shady border in summer.
SPECIES CULTIVATED : R. graveolens, yellowish green, summer, 3 ft., S. Europe.

Sabal (Fan or Thatch Palm ; Cabbage Palm)—Ord. Palmaceæ. Greenhouse orn.-leaved palms. First introduced 1810. Leaves, fan-shaped, green.
CULTURE : Compost, two parts rich loam, one part decayed leaf-mould and sand. Position, well-drained pots in greenhouse or sheltered well-drained beds outdoors in S. of England. Pot, March. Plant, April. Temp., Sept. to March 45° to 55° ; March to Sept. 55° to 65°. Water moderately in winter, freely in summer.
PROPAGATION : By seeds sown 1 in. deep in light soil in temp. of 80° in Feb. or March ; suckers removed from parent plant in April or Aug.
SPECIES CULTIVATED : S. Adansoni, 3 ft., S.U. States ; blackburniana (Fan Palm), 20 ft., Bermuda ; Palmetto (Cabbage Palm), 20 to 40 ft., S.U. States.

Sabbatia (American Centaury ; Rose Pink)—Ord. Gentianaceæ. Hardy biennial flowering herb. First introduced 1855.
CULTURE : Soil, equal parts good fibrous loam and finely-sifted leaf-mould and little sand. Position, moist, partially shaded borders or bogs. Sow seeds thinly in April where required to grow, lightly cover with soil, thin to 3 or 4 in. apart when an inch high, to flower following summer ; or sow seed ⅟₁₆ in. deep in well-drained pots or shallow pans filled with equal parts sandy peat and leaf-mould ; place in a pan partially filled with water and placed in cold frame or greenhouse. Transplant seedlings when an inch high, three in a 2 in. pot, in similar compost, keep in cold frame till following March, then plant out.
SPECIES CULTIVATED : S. campestris, rose, summer, 6 to 12 in., N. America.

Saccharum (Sugar Cane)—Ord. Gramineæ. Stove and hardy perennial grasses, flowering and orn. foliage. Inflorescence, silky, borne in pyramidal panicles, July. Leaves, ribbon-like, green, covered with silky hairs. First introduced 1597.
CULTURE OF SUGAR CANE : Two parts rich loam, one part leaf-mould or rotten manure, and little sand. Position, large pots or tubs in lofty stoves. Pot, Feb. or March. Water freely April to Sept., moderately afterwards. Syringe twice daily during spring and summer. Shade from mid-day sun essential. Temp., March to Oct. 70° to 85° ; Oct. to March 55° to 65°.
PROPAGATION : Sugar cane by cuttings of stems inserted in light soil in temp. of 70° to 80° in spring, or by suckers removed in Feb. or March and potted singly in above compost. S. spontaneum by division of roots in March or April.
SPECIES CULTIVATED : S. officinarum (Sugar Cane), white, summer, 10 to 15 ft., Tropics ; officinarum violaceum, stems violet tinted.

Saccolabium—Ord. Orchidaceæ. Stove epiphytal orchids. First introduced 1837. Ht., 1 to 4 ft.
CULTURE : Compost, sphagnum moss, charcoal, and broken potsherds. Position, hanging baskets, or attached to pieces of wood, or in pots filled to rim with charcoal and potsherds and remainder living sphagnum moss. Grow near glass always. Pot or fix to blocks in Jan. or Feb. Water plants grown on blocks copiously twice daily March to Sept., once daily afterwards ; those in baskets copiously April to Sept., moderately afterwards. Shade from mid-day sun. Temp., March to Oct. 70° to 85° ; Oct. to March 60° to 70°. Avoid allowing moisture to fall on leaves in winter. Moist atmosphere essential. Growing period, March to Nov. ; resting period, Nov. to March. Flowers appear in axils of leaves near the top after resting period.
PROPAGATION : By offsets any time.
SPECIES CULTIVATED : S. ampullaceum, magenta rose, June, India ; bellinum, green, brown, white, and yellow, Jan. to March, Burma ; Blumei, white, rose, and magenta, July to Aug., India and Java ; curvifolium, orange-scarlet, May and June, N. India ; giganteum, cream and purple, fragrant, Dec. to March, Burma ; hendersonianum, rosy red and white, spring, Borneo ; miniatum, orange-red, spring, Java ; violaceum, white and mauve, Jan. and Feb., Philippines.

Sacred Bean (*Nelumbium luteum*)—See Nelumbium.

Saddle-tree (*Liriodendron tulipifera*)—See Liriodendron.

Sadleria—Ord. Filices. Stove tree fern. First introduced 1877. Fronds, feather-shaped.
CULTURE : Compost, two-thirds peat and loam and abundance of sand. Position, large pots or tubs, well-drained, in shady stove or warm conservatory. Repot, Feb. or March. Water moderately Oct. to March, freely afterwards. Syringe trunks daily March to Sept. Temp., Sept. to March 55° to 65° ; March to Sept. 65° to 75°. Shade in summer essential.
PROPAGATION : By spores sown at any time on surface of finely sifted loam and peat in shallow, well-drained pans. Cover with sheet of glass and keep moist in shady position in temp. 75° to 85°.
SPECIES CULTIVATED : S. cyatheoides, 5 to 8 ft., Sandwich Islands.

Safflower (*Carthamus tinctoria*)—See Carthamus.

Saffron Crocus (*Crocus sativus*)—See Crocus.

Saffron Thistle (*Carthamus tinctorius*)—See Carthamus.

Sage (*Salvia officinalis*)—See Salvia.

Sagina (Pearl-weed ; Pearl-wort)—Ord. Caryophyllaceæ. Hardy perennial herbs. Orn. foliage and flowering ; evergreen. Leaves, narrow, green, or golden yellow. Stems, creeping. S. glabra used as a substitute for grass for forming lawns on sandy soils ; golden-leaved variety used for carpet bedding.
CULTURE OF S. GLABRA ON LAWNS : Soil, sandy. Position, sunny. Plant small tufts 3 in. apart each way in March or April. Keep free from weeds and roll frequently. Requires frequent renewal.

CULTURE OF GOLDEN-LEAVED VARIETY : Soil, ordinary. Position, sunny beds, borders, or rockeries. Plant small tufts in March, 2 in. apart, in lines, designs, or masses.

PROPAGATION : By seeds sown in sandy soil in sunny position outdoors in March ; by division in March or April.

SPECIES CULTIVATED : S. glabra, white, summer, 2 in., Europe ; glabra pilifera aurea (Syns. Arenaria cæspitosa aurea and Spergula pilifera aurea), leaves golden yellow.

Sagittaria (Arrow-head)—Ord. Alismaceæ. Hardy perennial aquatic herbs.

CULTURE : Compost, two parts strong, rich loam, one part well-decayed manure. Position, borders of open, sunny ponds or lakes for hardy species. Tender species in pots in warm greenhouse, Sept. to May ; sunk in borders of ponds outdoors, May to Sept. Depth of water, 6 to 12 in. Plant, March to Oct. Methods of planting : (1) Place plant in small wicker basket containing above compost and lower to the bottom of pond or lake. (2) Inclose roots with soil and large stone in piece of canvas or matting, tie securely, and immerse as above. (3) Place large hillock or mound of compost at bottom of pond when dry and plant roots in centre, afterwards submerging with water.

PROPAGATION : By seeds sown ¼ in. deep in rich soil in shallow basket and immersed in ponds or lakes in spring ; division of plants, March or April.

SPECIES CULTIVATED : S. latifolia (Syn. S. variabilis), white and purple, summer, 2 to 3 ft., N. America ; lancifolia, white, summer, 2 to 5 ft., America, tender ; montevidensis, white and purple, summer, 4 to 6 ft., S. America, tender ; sagittifolia (Syn. S. sinensis), white and purple, summer, 2 ft., Europe (Britain), and its variety flore-pleno (double), frequently erroneously named S. japonica.

Sago Palm (*Cycas circinalis*)—See Cycas.

St. Anthony's Nut (*Staphylea pinnata*)—See Staphylea.

St. Anthony's Turnip (*Ranunculus bulbosum fl.-pl.*)—See Ranunculus.

St. Bernard's Lily (*Anthericum Liliago*)—See Anthericum.

St. Bruno's Lily (*Paradisea Liliastrum*)—See Paradisea.

St. Dabeoc's Heath (*Daböecia polifolia*)—See Daböecia.

St. John's Wort (*Hypericum calycinum*)—See Hypericum.

St. Julian's Cherry (*Prunus communis* var.)—See Prunus.

Saintpaulia (African Violet)—Ord. Gesneriaceæ. Warm greenhouse perennial. First introduced 1894.

CULTURE : Compost, equal parts of loam, leaf-mould, peat, and sand. Pot, Feb. to May. Size of pots, 3 in. for small and 4½ in. for large plants. Pots to be well drained. Water freely from April to Sept., moderately afterwards. Apply weak liquid manure occasionally during flowering season. Temp., Oct. to April 53° to 60° ; April to Oct. 65° to 75°.

PROPAGATION : By seeds sown thinly on surface of a compost of equal parts peat, leaf-mould, loam, and sand in well-drained pots or shallow boxes. Cover seeds with a sprinkle of fine sand ; shade from sun and place in temp. of 65° to 75° in spring.

SPECIES CULTIVATED : S. ionantha, violet, June to Oct., 3 to 4 in., Central Africa, and its varieties albescens (white), purpurea (purple), and violescens (deep violet) ; kewensis, violet, summer, 3 to 4 in., Tropical Africa.

Salisburia—See Gingko.

Salix (Willow ; Sallow ; Osier ; Withy)—Ord. Salicaceæ. Hardy deciduous trees and shrubs. Orn. foliage. Male and female flowers borne on separate trees in spring. Bark, yellow, purple, red, whitish, or orange coloured. Shoots more or less drooping.

CULTURE OF ORNAMENTAL SPECIES : Soil, ordinary heavy or moderately heavy ; light soils not suitable. Position, damp, near margins of ponds, etc., for all species. Plant, Oct. to March. Prune, Nov. to Feb.

OSIER CULTURE : Soil, alluvial or sandy. Position, moist, low-lying land or margins of water. Trench soil deeply and add 30 tons of manure per acre. Plant cuttings 18 in. long, 15 in. apart in rows 18 in. asunder in Oct. Insert cuttings slantwise and 1 ft. deep. Number of cuttings to plant an acre, 23,000. Cut shoots for first time three years after planting. Time to cut, spring. Tie in bundles and immerse upright in water till bark readily peels off. Market peeled osiers in bundles of 50 lb. each. Average yield per acre, 1800 to 2000 lb. Soil should be cultivated annually between plants and given a dressing of 10 to 15 tons of manure per acre. Osiers of one year's growth used for making hampers and baskets ; those of two years' growth for ribs of hampers ; older wood for butter kegs.

TIMBER CULTURE : S. Caprea (Goat Willow), suitable for damp coppices, its wood being valuable for hoops, poles, crates, etc. S. alba (White or Huntingdon Willow) also suitable for damp soils, coppices, etc. Branches used for making scythe and rake handles ; timber for lining carts and barrows. Wood of the Bat Willow (Salix cœrulea) used for making cricket bats. Plant in autumn. Time to pollard willows, Feb. Weight of timber (cubic ft.), 33 lb.

PROPAGATION : By cuttings of shoots or stems of any age or size inserted in moist soil, Oct. to March ; choice kinds by budding on the Goat Willow (S. Caprea) in July, bandaging the bud with damp moss, or by grafting on a similar stock in March.

SPECIES CULTIVATED : S. alba (White or Huntingdon Willow), 50 to 60 ft., Europe, Asia, and N. Africa ; alba argentea, silvery foliage ; Arbuscula, 1 to 3 ft., Europe and Siberia ; babylonica (Weeping Willow), 30 to 50 ft., China ; Bockii, 3 to 4 ft., W. China ; cœrulea (Bat Willow), kind used for cricket-bat making ; Caprea (Goat Willow), 15 to 20 ft., Europe (Britain) ; Caprea pendula (Kilmarnock Willow) ; daphnoides, 30 to 40 ft., Europe and Asia, shoots covered with plum-coloured bloom ; fragilis (Crack Willow), 60 to 70 ft., shoots yellow and brown, Europe and N. Asia ; fragilis basfordiana, shoots orange-red ; herbacea, 2 to 4 in., N. Temperate Zone (Britain) ; incana (sometimes erroneously named S. rosmarinifolia, 8 to 12 ft., Europe and Asia Minor ; lanata, 2 to 3 ft., N. Europe ; magnifica, 6 to 20 ft., W. China ; pentandra, 20 to 50 ft., Europe (Britain) and N. Asia ; phylicifolia (Tea-leaved Willow), 8 to 10 ft., N. Europe ; purpurea (Purple Willow), shoots reddish purple, 10 to 18 ft., Europe ; purpurea pendula, weeping ; repens, 2 to 8 ft. Europe (Britain) and N. Africa ; reticulata, 6 to 12 in., Europe (Britain) and Labrador ; retusa, 4 to 8 in., Europe ; Salamonii, to 60 ft., semi-weeping, hybrid ; viminalis (Osier Willow), the species grown to yield osiers, 12 to 20 ft., Russia and N. Asia ; vitellina (Golden Osier), 60 to 65 ft., hybrid, shoots bright yellow, and its variety britzensis (brilliant red bark).

Sallow—See Salix.

Sallow-thorn—See Hippophæ.

Salmon-berry (*Rubus spectabilis* and *R. nutkanus*)—See Rubus.

Salpiglossis (Scalloped Tube-tongue)—Ord. Solanaceæ. Half-hardy annual. First introduced 1820.

OUTDOOR CULTURE : Soil, sandy loam or good ordinary rich. Position, sunny beds or borders. Sow seeds in well-drained pots, pans, or shallow boxes filled with compost of equal parts loam, leaf-mould, and sand placed in temp. of 65° to 75°, Feb. or March. Cover seeds with thin sprinkling of fine soil. Transplant seedlings when three leaves have formed ½ in. apart in well-drained pots or shallow boxes of above compost. Keep in temp. of 55° to 65° till May, then place in cold frame to harden and plant out in June. Water freely in dry weather. Apply weak stimulants occasionally to plants in flower.

INDOOR CULTURE : Compost, two parts sandy loam, half a part each of leaf-mould and decayed cow manure and silver sand. Sow seeds as advised above for summer flowering ; in Aug. or Sept. for spring flowering. Transplant seedlings when three leaves have formed, three in a 2½ in. pot, and place on shelf close to glass in temp. 55° to 65°. When well rooted in small pots shift into 5 in. size. Water moderately until plants are well established. Apply stimulants—¼ oz. each of kainit, superphosphate of lime, and nitrate of soda to 2 gall. of water—once a week during

flowering period. Nip off points of main shoots when 6 in. high to induce bushy growth. Place in cool greenhouse or window whilst in bloom.
SPECIES CULTIVATED : S. sinuata, various colours, 2 ft., Chile, parent of the beautiful strains grown in gardens.

Salsify (*Tragopogon porrifolius*)—See Tragopogon.

Salt-tree (*Halimodendron argenteum*)—See Halimodendron.

Salvia (Sage ; Clary)—Ord. Labiatæ. Greenhouse and hardy annuals and herbaceous perennials and evergreen shrubs.
CULTURE OF ANNUAL SPECIES : Soil, ordinary rich. Position, sunny borders. Sow seeds ¼ in. deep in April where required to flower and thin to 4 or 6 in. apart when 2 in. high.
CULTURE OF GREENHOUSE SPECIES : Compost, equal parts loam and decayed manure, little sand. Position: greenhouse, Sept. to June ; cold frame, June to Sept. Pot, March. Water freely March to Oct., moderately afterwards. Apply stimulants occasionally a month after repotting until flowers expand, then cease. Temp., Sept. to March 45° to 55° ; March to June 55° to 65°. Cut down shoots to within 3 in. of their base after flowering. Young plants : Insert cuttings, 3 in. long, of young shoots in light, sandy soil in temp. 65° in Feb. or March. When rooted place singly in 3½ in. pots. Nip off points of main shoots, also of succeeding shoots when 3 in. long. Shift into 5 or 6 in. pots when former pots are filled with roots. Water freely. Apply stimulants occasionally. Place in cold frame, June to Sept.
OUTDOOR CULTURE : Soil, rich ordinary. Position, sunny sheltered beds or borders. Plant, June. Lift in Sept., place in pots to flower in greenhouse in autumn. Water freely in dry weather. Apply stimulants once a week. Lift tuberous roots of S. patens in Oct. and store in sand in frost-proof place. Start in heat in March and plant out in May.
CULTURE OF HARDY SPECIES : Soil, ordinary rich. Position, sunny borders. Plant, Oct., Nov., March, or April. Mulch annually with decayed manure in March. Cut down stems close to ground in Oct. Lift, divide, and replant every third year.
CULTURE OF CLARY : Hardy biennial. Leaves used for flavouring soups. Pretty border plant also. Soil, ordinary. Position, sunny. Sow seeds 1 in. deep in drills 18 in. apart in April. Thin seedlings when 2 in. high to 12 in. apart in row. Gather leaves in summer and dry for use following year.
CULTURE OF SAGE : Soil, ordinary rich, light, dryish. Position, sunny. Plant, March or April, 12 in. apart in rows 18 in. asunder. Nip off points of shoots first year to induce bushy growth. Water freely in dry weather first year after planting. Renew plantation every four years.
PROPAGATION : Greenhouse species by cuttings 2 to 3 in. long of young shoots inserted in sandy soil in temp. 65° in spring ; sage by seeds sown ⅛ in. deep in light soil in temp. 55° to 65° in March, transplanting seedlings outdoors in May or June ; also by slips, *i.e.* young shoots pulled off the old plants in April and inserted in a shady border or under a hand-light, or in a cold frame, and kept moist until rooted ; miscellaneous hardy species by division in March or April.
GREENHOUSE SPECIES : S. azurea, blue, winter, 6 ft., N. America ; coccinea, scarlet, autumn, 2 to 3 ft., N. America ; fulgens, scarlet, summer, 2 to 3 ft., Mexico ; Grahami, scarlet, July to Oct., 4 ft., Mexico ; Greggi, carmine, Aug. to Nov., 3 ft., Mexico ; Heeri, scarlet, winter, 2 to 3 ft., Peru ; involucrata Bethelli, crimson, autumn, 3 to 4 ft., Mexico ; patens, blue, summer, 2 to 3 ft., Mexico ; rutilans, red, winter, 2 to 3 ft., origin uncertain ; splendens, scarlet, autumn, 2 to 3 ft., Brazil, and its varieties Harbinger, Pride of Zurich, and Simonsi.
HARDY SPECIES : S. argentea (Silver Clary), white, summer, 3 ft., foliage silvery, Mediterranean Region ; azurea grandiflora (Syn. S. Pitcheri), sky blue, summer, 3 ft., Mexico ; bicolor, bluish violet and white, summer, 3 ft., Spain and N. Africa ; carduacea, lilac blue, July to Aug., 1 to 2 ft., California, perennial but often grown as an annual ; dichroa, blue and white, summer, 4 to 6 ft., N. Africa ; glutinosa, pale yellow, July to Sept., 3 ft., Europe ; nutans, blue, July, 2 ft., S.E. Europe ; officinalis (Sage), blue, summer, 3 ft., S. Europe ; pratensis (Meadow Sage), violet, May, 3 ft., Britain, and its variety Tenori (deep blue) ; Sclarea (Clary), Syn. S.

Sedum lineare variegatum

Sedum spectabile

Selaginella Kraussiana
(Creeping Moss)

Selenipedium hybridum

Sempervivum calcareum
(House-leek)

Sempervivum tectorum
(House-leek)

Senecio macrophyllus
(Ragwort)

Sidalcea hybrida

Silene Armeria
(Catchfly)

Silene Hookeri
(Catchfly)

Sinningia speciosa
(Gloxinia)

Sisyrinchium bermudianum
(Satin-flower)

Skimmia Fortunei

Solanum capsicastrum

Solanum crispum

Soldanella alpina
(Blue Moon-wort)

Solidago Virgaurea
(Golden Rod)

Sophro Lælia hybrida

bracteata, bluish white, summer, 2 ft., Mediterranean Region ; turkestanica, lilac and pale blue, June to July, 3 ft., habitat unknown, possibly a variety of S. Sclarea ; uliginosa, azure blue, Aug. to Sept., 3 to 5 ft., Brazil ; virgata (Syn. S. nemorosa), violet blue, July to Sept., 3 ft., Europe.

ANNUAL SPECIES : S. farinacea, lavender, summer, 2 to 3 ft., Mexico ; Horminum (Horminum Clary), purple, summer, 18 in., S. Europe, and its variety Blue Beard.

Salvinia—Ord. Salviniaceæ.   Tender floating aquatic.

CULTURE : Soil, not necessary. Position, tanks of water in warm greenhouse or in indoor aquariums.   Temp., March to Sept. 65° to 75° ;   Sept. to March 55° to 60°. Place in tanks any time.

PROPAGATION : By division.

SPECIES CULTIVATED : S. auriculata (Syn. S. brasiliensis), small pea-green foliage, Tropical America.   This plant is sometimes erroneously named S. natans.

Sambucus (Elder ; Dane-wort)—Ord. Caprifoliaceæ.   Hardy deciduous shrubs and herbaceous perennials.   Berries, black or scarlet.   Leaves, feather-shaped, green, golden, or white.

CULTURE OF HERBACEOUS SPECIES : Soil, ordinary. Position, dry banks or shrubberies in sun or shade.   Plant, Oct. to Feb.   Cut down stems in Nov.

CULTURE OF SHRUBBY SPECIES : Soil, ordinary. Position, open shrubbery or hedge-rows for common species ; moist, sunny borders for variegated kinds.   Plant, Oct. to March.   Prune into shape, Nov. to Jan.   Nip off points of young shoots of golden and silver elders during summer ;   also cut shoots closely back in March to insure dwarf growth and rich colouring in foliage.

PROPAGATION : Herbaceous species by division, Oct. to March ; shrubby species by cuttings of branches or shoots inserted in moist soil outdoors, Oct. to March.

HERBACEOUS SPECIES : S. Ebulus (Dane's Blood), white and pink, summer, 3 ft., Europe (Britain).

SHRUBBY SPECIES : S. canadensis, white, July, to 12 ft., Eastern N. America, and its variety laciniata (leaves deeply dissected) ; nigra (Common Elder), white, June, 20 ft., Britain ; nigra foliis-aureis, leaves golden (Golden Elder) ; nigra laciniata, leaves finely cut (Cut-leaved Elder) ; racemosa (Scarlet Berried Elder), white, April, scarlet berries in June to July, 8 to 12 ft., Europe, and its varieties plumosa aurea (toothed, golden-yellow foliage) and tenuifolia (leaves finely dissected).

Samolus (Tasmanian Water Pimpernel)—Ord. Primulaceæ.   Hardy herbaceous perennial.   First introduced 1800.

CULTURE : Soil, sandy peat. Position, moist bog or rockery. Plant, March or April.   Water freely in dry weather in summer.

PROPAGATION : By division of the roots in spring.

SPECIES CULTIVATED : S. repens, white, Aug., 6 in., Australia.

Samphire (*Crithmum maritimum*)—See Crithmum.

Sanchezia—Ord. Acanthaceæ.   Stove flowering and orn. shrub.   First intro-duced 1866.

CULTURE : Compost, two parts peat and loam, one part decayed manure and sand. Position, light part of stove in winter ; shady part in spring and summer.   Pot, March.   Syringe twice daily April to Oct., once daily afterwards.   Water freely March to Oct., moderately other times.   Apply weak stimulants occasionally during summer.   Temp., Sept. to March 55° to 65°, March to Sept. 75° to 85°.

PROPAGATION : By cuttings of young shoots inserted under bell-glass in fine soil, March to July.

SPECIES CULTIVATED : S. nobilis, yellow and red, March to Oct., 3 to 4 ft., Ecuador, and its variety variegata (leaves striped white or yellow).

Sandersonia—Ord. Liliaceæ.   Stove climbing tuberous-rooted herb.   First introduced 1852.

CULTURE : Compost, sandy loam with a little leaf-mould and well-decayed manure. Position, well-drained pots, with shoots trained to roof or trellis.   Pot, Feb., placing tubers 2 in. deep, one in a 6 in. pot or several in an 8 or 12 in. pot.   Water moderately till growth is well advanced, then freely.   After flowering gradually withhold water and keep soil quite dry till potting time. Temp., Feb. to Sept. 70° to 85°; Sept. to Feb. 55° to 65°.

PROPAGATION : By seeds inserted singly ¼ in. deep in 3 in. pots filled with light soil in temp. 75° in Feb. or March ; offsets removed from large tubers at potting time.

SPECIES CULTIVATED : S. aurantiaca, orange yellow, July and Aug., 3 to 6 ft., Natal.

Sand Leek (*Allium Scorodoprasum*)—See Allium.

Sand Myrtle (*Leiophyllum buxifolium*)—See Leiophyllum.

Sand Pear (*Pyrus sinensis*)—See Pyrus.

Sand Pink (*Dianthus arenarius*)—See Dianthus.

Sand Verbena (*Abronia umbellata*)—See Abronia.

Sand-wort (*Arenaria balearica*)—See Arenaria.

Sanguinaria (Blood-root)—Ord. Papaveraceæ. Hardy perennial herb. First introduced 1680.

CULTURE : Soil, sandy loam or peat. Position, sunny borders or rockeries. Plant, Oct., Nov., March, or April. Water freely in dry weather. Top-dress annually with decayed cow manure in Feb. or March. Should be interfered with as little as possible.

PROPAGATION : By seeds sown 1/16 in. deep in equal parts leaf-mould, peat, and sand in cold frame or cool greenhouse in early autumn or spring, transplanting seedlings outdoors when large enough to handle ; by division of roots in Oct. or March.

SPECIES CULTIVATED : S. canadensis, white, April, 6 in., N. America.

Sanseviera (Bow-string Hemp ; Angola Hemp)—Liliaceæ. Stove herbaceous perennials. Orn. foliage. First introduced 1690. Flowers, white, green, yellowish ; insignificant. Leaves, narrow, ridged, green, long, margined or spotted with white.

CULTURE : Compost, equal parts loam, leaf-mould, and sand. Position, pots in shady part of stove. Pot, Feb. to April. Water copiously March to Oct., moderately afterwards. Syringe freely in summer. Temp., March to Sept. 65° to 75°; Sept. to March 55° to 65°.

PROPAGATION : By division of plants, Feb. to April.

SPECIES CULTIVATED : S. cylindrica, white, Aug., 2½ to 5 ft., leaves banded dark green, Trop. Africa ; thyrsiflora (Syn. S. guineensis), greenish white, Sept., 1 to 1½ ft., leaves banded pale green, S. Africa ; trifasciata Laurentii, greenish white, 2 ft., leaves striped golden yellow, W. Trop. Africa ; zeylanica, greenish white, 2 to 2½ ft., leaves banded light green, Ceylon.

Santolina (Lavender Cotton)—Ord. Compositæ. Hardy evergreen shrubby plants. First introduced 1573.

CULTURE : Soil, ordinary sandy. Position, sunny borders or rockeries. Plant, Sept., Oct., March, or April.

PROPAGATION : By cuttings of shoots, 2 to 3 in. long, pulled off with portion of stem attached and inserted in pots of sandy soil in cold frame, Sept. or Oct., or in sheltered position outdoors same time.

SPECIES CULTIVATED : S. Chamæcyparissus (S. incana), yellow, July, 1 to 2 ft., S. Europe, leaves covered with cottony grey down ; rosmarinifolia, yellow, July, 2 ft., Spain and Portugal ; viridis, yellow, summer, 2 ft., leaves green, S. Europe.

Sanvitalia—Ord. Compositæ. Hardy annual. First introduced 1798.

CULTURE : Soil, ordinary. Position, margins of sunny borders or rockeries. Sow seeds 1/16 in. deep in light soil in temp. 55° to 65° in March. Harden off seedlings in cold frame in April and plant outdoors in May ; or in lines or patches in open ground end of April, thinning seedlings when 1 in. high to 2 or 3 in. apart. Water freely in dry weather and apply weak stimulants occasionally in summer.

SPECIES CULTIVATED : S. procumbens, yellow and purple, summer to late autumn, trailing, Mexico ; procumbens flore-pleno, flowers double.

Sapodilla Plum (*Achras sapota*)—See Achras.

Saponaria (Soap-wort ; Fuller's Herb ; Hedge Pink)—Ord. Caryophyllaceæ. Hardy annuals and perennials. First introduced 1596.

CULTURE OF ANNUAL SPECIES : Soil, ordinary. Position, margins of sunny borders

or in beds.   Sow seeds in lines or patches ⅓ in. deep in April for summer flowering ; in Sept. for spring flowering.   Thin seedlings when 1 in. high to 2 or 3 in. apart. Water freely in dry weather and apply stimulants occasionally.
CULTURE OF PERENNIAL SPECIES :   Soil, deep, rich loam.   Position, sunny rockeries or borders for S. ocymoides ;   large sunny or shady shrubbery borders or wild garden for S. officinalis.   Plant, Oct. to April.   Top-dress annually in Feb. with decayed manure.   Water freely in dry weather.
PROPAGATION :   Perennial species by seeds sown in shallow boxes of sandy soil in temp. of 55° to 65° in March, hardening seedlings in a cold frame in April, and planting out in May or June ;   or outdoors in April, transplanting seedlings in June and July ;   by cuttings inserted in sandy soil in cold frame, Sept. to Oct. ;   division of roots, Oct. to March.
ANNUAL SPECIES :   S. calabrica, rose, July to Sept., 6 to 12 in., Italy ;   Vaccaria, pink, summer, 2 to 3 ft., Europe, and its variety alba.
PERENNIAL SPECIES :   S. bellidifolia, pale yellow, June to Aug., 9 to 12 in., E. Europe ; cæspitosa, rose, June to Aug., 4 in., Pyrenees ;   lutea, yellow, June to Aug., 3 to 6 in., Europe ;   ocymoides (Rock Soap-wort), rosy purple, summer, trailing, Europe ;   officinalis flore-pleno (Bouncing Bet), pink, Aug., 2 to 3 ft., Europe (Britain) ;   pulvinaris, rose pink, spring and early summer, 1 in., Asia Minor.

Sarcococca—Ord. Buxaceæ.   Hardy evergreen shrubs.   First introduced 1820. Natives of China.
CULTURE :   Soil, ordinary.   Position, moist and shady.   Thrives well under trees. Plant, Sept. to Oct. and April to May.
PROPAGATION :   By cuttings of ripened wood in sandy soil in cold frame during Sept. and Oct.
SPECIES CULTIVATED :   S. humilis, white, early spring, 1 to 1½ ft. ;   ruscifolia, milk white, winter, 2 ft. ;   saligna (Syn. Buxus saligna), greenish white, winter and spring, 2 to 3 ft.

Sarmienta (Chilian Pitcher-flower)—Ord. Gesneraceæ.   Greenhouse evergreen creeper.   First introduced 1862.
CULTURE :   Compost, soft peat, charcoal, and chopped sphagnum moss.   Position, teak baskets or pans suspended from roof, or in pots with shoots growing up stems of dead tree ferns.   Pot or plant, March.   Water copiously April to Oct., moderately afterwards.   Syringe freely daily March to Oct.   Shade from sun.   Temp., March to Sept. 60° to 70° ;   Sept. to March 45° to 55°.
PROPAGATION :   By division of plants in March.
SPECIES CULTIVATED :   S. repens, scarlet, summer, creeping, Chile.

Sarracenia (Huntsman's Horn ;   Indian Cup ;   N. American Pitcher-plant ; Side-saddle Flower)—Ord. Sarraceniaceæ.   Half-hardy herbaceous perennials. First introduced 1752.   Leaves, tubular, pitcher-shaped, reticulated.
INDOOR CULTURE :   Compost, equal parts fibry peat and chopped sphagnum moss. Position, cool, moist corner of greenhouse or fernery, cold frame, or Wardian case in dwelling-room.   Pot, March.   Pots to be two-thirds full of drainage.   Place pot containing plant inside another pot two sizes larger and fill space between with sphagnum moss.   Water freely April to Oct., very little in winter.   Syringe foliage gently daily in summer.   Shade from bright sun.   Top-dress in summer with a little decayed manure.
OUTDOOR CULTURE OF S. PURPUREA :   Compost, equal parts peat and sphagnum moss.   Position, fully exposed bog garden or moist rockery.   Plant, March or April.   Keep surface of soil covered with layer of moss.   Water freely in summer.
PROPAGATION :   All the species and hybrids by division in March or April.
SPECIES CULTIVATED :   S. Drummondii, flowers purple, June, leaves white, green, and purple, 2 ft., N. America ;   flava (Trumpet Leaf), yellow, June, 2 ft., N. America ; psittacina, flowers purple, leaves veined red or purple, N. America ;   purpurea, flowers purple, spring, leaves veined purple, N. America ;   rubra, flowers reddish, leaves veined purple, N. America ;   variolaris, flowers yellow, leaves spotted with white, N. America.   There are many hybrids such as Chelsoni, tolliana, and mitchelliana.

Sarsaparilla—See Smilax.

Satin-flower—See Sisyrinchium and Lunaria.

Satin Poppy (*Meconopsis Wallichii*)—See Meconopsis.

Satureia (Summer and Winter Savory)—Ord. Labiatæ. Hardy annual and perennial evergreen herbs and subshrubs. First introduced 1562. Aromatic shoots used for flavouring soups and salads and for boiling with peas and beans.

CULTURE OF SUMMER SAVORY: Hardy annual. Soil, ordinary. Position, sunny. Sow seeds ½ in. deep in drills 12 in. apart. Thin seedlings when 2 in. high to 6 in. apart. Water freely in dry weather. Pull plants up when in flower and dry for winter use.

CULTURE OF WINTER SAVORY: Hardy evergreen shrub. Soil, ordinary. Position, sunny. Plant, March or April, 12 in. apart in rows 15 in. asunder. Prune in closely in Oct. and top-dress with manure. Renew plantations every fourth year.

PROPAGATION: By seeds sown as advised for annual species; also by cuttings of young shoots inserted in shady border in April; division of roots in March.

ANNUAL SPECIES: S. hortensis (Summer Savory), lilac, July, 6 to 8 in., Mediterranean Region.

PERENNIAL SPECIES: S. montana (Winter Savory), purple, June, 6 to 12 in., Europe, and its variety illyrica (Syn. S. pygmæa), pale purple. See also Calamintha.

Sauromatum (Monarch of the East)—Ord. Aroideæ. Half-hardy perennial with tuberous roots and arum-like flower spathes. First introduced 1830.

CULTURE: Purchase tubers in autumn, place them in a dry saucer in a warm room, and in a few weeks the flower spathe will appear. No soil or water needed. After flowering plant the tuber in a moist place outdoors to make its leaf growth. Lift in Aug., keep in a cool place, and again place in a saucer indoors. Repeat the operation year by year.

SPECIES CULTIVATED: S. guttatum, purple, yellow, and green, winter or spring, 1½ to 2 ft., Central Asia.

Saururus (Lizard's Tail)—Ord. Piperaceæ. Hardy aquatic perennials. First introduced 1759.

CULTURE: Soil, heavy loam with peat and leaf-mould. Position, margins of ponds. Plant, April to May.

PROPAGATION: By division at planting time.

SPECIES CULTIVATED: S. cernuus, white, summer, 1 to 2 ft., N. America; Loureiri, creamy white, summer, 1 to 2 ft., N. America.

Saussurea (Saw-wort)—Ord. Compositæ. Hardy perennial herbs. First introduced 1816.

CULTURE: Soil, ordinary. Position, sunny rockeries. Plant, Oct., Nov., March, or April.

PROPAGATION: By seeds sown ¼ in. deep in ordinary soil in sunny position outdoors, April, transplanting seedlings when three or four leaves have formed.

SPECIES CULTIVATED: S. alpina, purple, Aug., 6 in., Northern and Arctic Regions (Britain); pygmæa, purple, July, 4 in., Europe.

Savin-tree (*Juniperus sabina*)—See Juniperus.

Savory (*Satureia hortensis* and *montana*)—See Satureia.

Savoy—See Brassica.

Saw-wort (*Saussurea japonica*)—See Saussurea.

Saxifraga (Rockfoil; London Pride)—Ord. Saxifragaceæ. Hardy and tender perennials. Interesting plants for rockeries and borders. Classes: (1) Encrusted Saxifrages, leaves silvery, borne in rosettes; (2) Mossy Saxifrages, leaves green and moss-like; (3) Megasea Saxifrages, leaves large and leathery; (4) Cushion (Kabschia) Saxifrages, small pointed leaves forming close cushions; (5) Porphyrion Saxifrages, leaves small, habit trailing; (6) Robertsonia Saxifrages, fleshy spathulate leaves in rosettes ; (7) Trachyphyllum Saxifrages, leaves thickish and linear ; (8) Miscellaneous type, leaves varied in form.

CULTURE OF ENCRUSTED SECTION : Soil, loam, leaf-mould, sand, and limestone chippings in about equal parts. Position, ledges or fissures of sunny rockeries or old walls. Plant in spring. S. Cotyledon pyramidalis a good plant for cool greenhouse. Grow in compost of two parts loam and one part of equal proportions of old mortar, leaf-mould, and sand ; 5 in. pots suitable. Place in cold frame till March, then remove into greenhouse. Water moderately in winter.

CULTURE OF MOSSY SECTION : Soil, ordinary moist loam. Position, ledges of rockeries for choice kinds, edgings to borders for commoner ones ; or carpeting surface of beds of choice bulbs. Plant in autumn or spring.

CULTURE OF MEGASEA SECTION : Soil, ordinary. Position, sunny or shady borders. Plant in autumn or spring. Good town and suburban garden plants.

CULTURE OF CUSHION SAXIFRAGES : Soil, loam, leaf-mould, sand, and stone chippings in about equal parts. S. lilacina and its hybrids thrive best in a lime-free soil. Position, slopes or ledges in the rock garden sheltered from the sun during the hottest part of the day. Plant in spring. Top-dress in winter with a mixture of leaf-mould, sand, and stone chippings.

CULTURE OF PORPHYRION SAXIFRAGES : Soil, loam, leaf-mould, and fibrous peat with a liberal addition of sharp river sand. Position, open parts of the rock garden with an abundant supply of moisture during the growing season. Plant in spring.

CULTURE OF ROBERTSONIA SAXIFRAGES : Soil, ordinary loamy. Position, edges of borders or open places in the rock garden. Plant in spring.

CULTURE OF TRACHYPHYLLUM SAXIFRAGES : Soil, loam, leaf-mould, fibrous peat, and sand. Position, open, sunny but moist parts of the rock garden. Plant in spring.

CULTURE OF MISCELLANEOUS SECTION : Soil, ordinary for S. umbrosa and Geum ; moist loam for other species. Position, shady borders for S. umbrosa, Geum, and granulata fl.-pl. ; moist, shady rockery for Andrewsii, cuneifolia, oppositifolia, and rotundifolia ; sunny rockery for apiculata, burseriana, and sancta ; margins of water-courses or damp borders for peltata ; damp walls or rockeries for Sibthorpii ; sunny walls for sarmentosa. Plant in autumn or spring.

CULTURE OF TENDER SPECIES : Soil, equal parts loam, peat, leaf-mould, and silver sand. Position, pots or baskets suspended near roof of greenhouse, or close to sunny window. Pot in spring. Water very moderately in autumn and winter. Temp., Oct. to March 55° to 60° ; March to Oct. 65° to 70°.

PROPAGATION : Encrusted saxifrages by seeds sown in sandy soil in well-drained pans in cool greenhouse or frame during Feb. and March, and by division immediately after flowering ; mossy saxifrages by seeds treated in the same way and by division in March or April ; megasea saxifrages by seeds in spring, or by division after flowering ; cushion saxifrages by seeds treated in the same way as those of encrusted saxifrages, and by division after flowering ; porphyrion saxifrages by seeds sown in cool, open soil in spring in shady frame or house, or by division of plants immediately after flowering ; miscellaneous saxifrages by seeds in Feb. and March, or by division in spring ; tender saxifrages by careful division in spring.

ENCRUSTED SPECIES : S. Aizoon, creamy white, June, 3 to 6 in., Arctic Regions, and its varieties baldensis (very minute), carinthiaca (white), la graveana (snowy white), lutea (yellow), notata (white), punctatissima (white and red), rosea (rose pink), and rosularis (creamy white) ; altissima, white and red, June, 18 in., Europe ; Burnati, white, June, 6 to 9 in., hybrid ; cartilaginea, pink, June, 9 in., Caucasus, and its variety kolenatiana ; cochlearis, white, June, 4 in., S. Europe, and its variety minor ; Cotyledon, white, June, 1½ to 2 ft., Europe, and its varieties pyramidalis (white) and caterhamensis (white and red) ; crustata (Syn. S. incrustata), creamy white, summer, 1 ft., Alps ; florulenta, rose-purple, June, 2 ft., Maritime Alps ; Hostii, creamy white, May to June, 1 ft., Europe ; lingulata, white, June, 9 in., S. Europe, and its varieties australis (broad-leaved), Alberti (white, a hybrid), Bellardii (narrow, silver-margined leaves), and lantoscana (leaves in full rosettes) ; longifolia, white, July, 12 to 18 in., Pyrenees ; macnabiana, white and crimson, May and June, 12 to 18 in., hybrid ; mutata, orange, June, 1 ft., Europe ; paradoxa,

cream, June, 6 in., hybrid ; pectinata, creamy white, June, 6 in., hybrid ; rocheliana, white, May, 3 in., Austria ; valdensis, white, June, 3 in., S. France.
CUSHION SPECIES (INCLUDING ENGLERIAS) : S. aretioides, yellow, April to May, 2 in., Pyrenees ; apiculata, yellow, Feb. to March, 2 to 3 in., hybrid ; arco-valleyi, pink, March, 1 to 2 in., hybrid ; Boydii alba, white, Feb. to March, 2 in., hybrid ; burseriana, white, March, 2 in., E. Europe, and its varieties crenata (petals crimped), Gloria (large white), major (large white), tridentina (white), and sulphurea (pale yellow, a hybrid) ; cæsia, milk white, 3 to 4 in., Alps ; diapensioides, white, April to May, 1 to 2 in., Alps, and its variety primulina (citron yellow) ; Elizabethæ, yellow, March, 3 in., hybrid ; Faldonside, yellow, March, 2 in., hybrid ; Federici-Angusti, claret, March to April, 4 in., Europe ; Ferdinandi-Coburgi, yellow, March, 4 in., Macedonia ; Griesbachii, crimson bracts, March, 9 in., Balkans ; Haagii, yellow, March to April, 2 to 3 in., hybrid ; Irvingii, pink, March, 1 to 2 in., hybrid ; Kellereri, carmine, March, 4 to 6 in., hybrid ; Kotschyi, yellow, March, 3 to 4 in., Asia Minor ; lilacina, lilac, March, 2 in., Himalayas ; marginata, white, March, 3 in., Italy, and its varieties coriophylla and rocheliana ; media, crimson, March, 3 to 4 in., Pyrenees ; Obristi, white, March, 3 in., hybrid ; Paulinæ, yellow, March 2 to 3 in., hybrid ; Petraschii, white, March, 2 to 3 in., hybrid ; porophylla, claret, March, 3 in., S. Europe ; sancta, yellow, March, 2 to 3 in., Macedonia ; scardica, white, March, 5 to 6 in., Macedonia, and its variety obtusa (white) ; Striburyi, reddish purple, March, 6 to 8 in., Balkans ; tombeanensis, white, April, 3 in., Maritime Alps ; Vandellii, white, April, 4 to 5 in., Tyrol, etc.
MOSSY SPECIES : S. aquatica, white, May, 12 to 18 in., Pyrenees ; cæspitosa, white, summer, 3 in., Arctic Regions (Britain) ; cuneata, white, May to June, 8 to 9 in., Spain ; decipiens, red, pink, or cream, May, 4 to 8 in., Europe, and many varieties and hybrids such as bathoniensis (red), Clibrani (large red), Red Admiral (scarlet), sanguinea superba (scarlet), and Guildford Seedling (bright red) ; exarata, creamy yellow, May to June, 3 in., S. Europe ; geranioides, white, May, 6 to 8 in., Pyrenees ; hypnoides (Dovedale Moss), creamy white, June, 9 in., Europe, and its varieties Whitlavei compacta (very dwarf), densa (medium height), and Kingii (dwarf) ; mixta, creamy white, May to June, 2 to 3 in., Alps ; moschata (frequently erroneously known in gardens as S. muscoides), creamy white, rose or red, May, 1 to 2 in., Europe, and its varieties Rhei (white, loose habit), atropurpurea (red), Miss Stormonth (pink), and Wild Rose (pink) ; muscoides, white, May, 2 in., Alps ; pedemontana, white, May, 2 in., S. Europe, and its varieties cervicornis, dwarf, Corsica ; sponhemica, greenish white or cream, May to June, 4 to 6 in., Europe ; trifurcata (Stag's-horn Rockfoil), Syn. S. ceratophylla, white, summer, 6 in., N. Spain ; Wallacei, white, June, 4 to 6 in., garden origin.
MEGASEA SPECIES : S. cordifolia (Syn. Megasea cordifolia), pink, spring, 1 ft., Siberia, and its variety purpurea (crimson) ; crassifolia (Syn. Megasea crassifolia), pink, early spring, 1 ft., Siberia, and its variety gigantea (purple) ; ligulata, white or pink, Jan. to Feb., 1 ft., and its varieties ciliata (leaves finely toothed) and speciosa (rose pink) ; Milesi, white, March to April, 1 ft., Himalayas ; Stracheyi, white or blush, March to April, 1 ft., Himalayas.
PORPHYRION SPECIES : S. oppositifolia, rosy crimson, March to April, 1 in., Northern and Arctic Regions, and its varieties alba (white), latina (rosy red), murithiana (purple), and splendens (purple) ; retusa, ruby red, April to May, 1 in., Pyrenees and Alps.
ROBERTSONIA SPECIES : S. Andrewsii, pink and purple, May to June, 6 in., hybrid ; cuneifolia, white, May to June, 3 to 4 in., Europe, and its variety capillipes ; Geum, pink, May, 9 to 12 in., W. Europe, and its varieties crenulata, dentata, and hirsuta ; umbrosa (London Pride), pink, May to June, 12 in., W. Europe, and its variety primuloides.
TRACHYPHYLLUM SPECIES : S. aizoides, yellow, late summer, 2 to 3 in., Northern and Arctic Regions, and its variety atrorubens (red) ; aspera, pale yellow, summer, 4 to 6 in., Europe ; bronchialis, cream and orange, summer, 4 to 6 in., Northern Asia and America ; tenella, white, summer, 4 in., Tyrol ; tricuspidata, cream and yellow, late summer, 4 in., Northern and Arctic Regions.
MISCELLANEOUS SPECIES : S. ajugifolia, white, July, Pyrenees ; granulata (Meadow

Saxifrage), white, May, 6 to 10 in., Europe (Britain), and its variety flore-pleno (double) ; peltata (Umbrella Plant), pink, April, 3 ft., California ; rotundifolia, white and pink, May to June, 1 to 2 ft., Europe ; sarmentosa (Mother of Thousands), white and pink, summer, Japan and China ; Sibthorpii (Syn. S. Cymbalaria), yellow, summer, trailing, Greece, annual ; tellimoides, white, July to Aug., 18 in., habitat unknown.

TENDER SPECIES : S. sarmentosa tricolor, leaves creamy white and red.

Scabiosa (Scabious ; Pincushion Flower ; Mournful Widow ; Sweet Scabious)— Ord. Dipsaceæ. Hardy biennial and perennial herbs. Flowers, useful for cutting. CULTURE OF BIENNIAL SPECIES : Soil, good rich ordinary. Position, sunny beds or borders. Sow seeds $\frac{1}{16}$ in. deep in light, sandy soil in temp. of 60° to 70° in Feb. or March and plant out in May to insure plants flowering same year, or outdoors in June or July, transplanting again following March to flowering position. In cold districts lift the seedlings in Aug. and place in small pots ; winter in cold frame and plant out in April.

CULTURE OF PERENNIAL SPECIES : Soil, ordinary deep rich. Position, sunny well-drained borders for S. caucasica ; sunny rockeries for S. graminifolia ; ordinary borders for S. columbaria, etc. Plant, Oct., Nov., March, or April. Top-dress annually in Feb. or March with decayed manure. Lift, divide, and replant every three or four years.

PROPAGATION : By division of roots, Oct. or March.

BIENNIAL SPECIES : S. atropurpurea (Sweet Scabious or Mournful Widow), various colours, single and double, July, 1 to 3 ft., S. Europe.

PERENNIAL SPECIES : S. caucasica (Caucasian Scabious), blue, June, 1 ft., Caucasus ; caucasica alba, white ; ochroleuca webbiana, yellow, July, 6 in., Europe ; ptero-cephala, purple, July, 3 to 4 ft., Greece. See also Cephalaria.

Scale Fern (*Asplenium Ceterach*)—See Asplenium.

Scallion (*Allium ascalonicum*)—See Allium.

Scalloped Tube Tongue (*Salpiglossis sinuata*)—See Salpiglossis.

Scarborough Lily (*Vallota purpurea*)—See Vallota.

Scarlet Avens (*Geum coccineum*)—See Geum.

Scarlet-berried Elder (*Sambucus racemosa*)—See Sambucus.

Scarlet Bindweed (*Ipomœa coccinea*)—See Ipomœa.

Scarlet Clematis (*Clematis coccinea*)—See Clematis.

Scarlet-flowered Orchid—See Sophronitis.

Scarlet Fritillary (*Fritillaria recurva*)—See Fritillaria.

Scarlet-fruited Thorn (*Cratægus coccinea*)—See Cratægus.

Scarlet Fuchsia (*Fuchsia macrostemma corallina*)—See Fuchsia.

Scarlet Lobelia (*Lobelia cardinalis*)—See Lobelia.

Scarlet Lychnis (*Lychnis chalcedonica*)—See Lychnis.

Scarlet Maple (*Acer rubrum*)—See Acer.

Scarlet Martagon Lily (*Lilium chalcedonicum*)—See Lilium.

Scarlet Mexican Sage (*Salvia fulgens*)—See Salvia.

Scarlet Mitre-pod (*Mitraria coccinea*)—See Mitraria.

Scarlet Monkey-flower (*Mimulus cardinalis*)—See Mimulus.

Scarlet Musk (*Mimulus cardinalis*)—See Mimulus.

Scarlet Oak (*Quercus coccinea*)—See Quercus.

Scarlet Root-blossom.—See Agalmyla.

Scarlet Runner Bean (*Phaseolus multiflorus*)—See Phaseolus.

Scarlet Sage (*Salvia coccinea* and *S. splendens*)—See Salvia.

Scarlet Skull-cap (*Scutellaria mociniana*)—See Scutellaria.

Scarlet Twin-flower (*Bravoa geminiflora*)—See Bravoa.

Scarlet Wind-flower (*Anemone fulgens*)—See Anemone.

Scarlet Wound-wort (*Stachys coccinea*)—See Stachys.

Schinus—Ord. Anacardiaceæ. Half-hardy evergreen shrubs. First introduced 1597.
CULTURE : Soil, ordinary, rather poor. Position, sunny sheltered borders in the open for S. dependens ; well-drained borders or pots in cool greenhouse or conservatory for S. molle and S. terebinthifolius. Plant or pot, Sept. or April to May. Water indoor plants freely during summer months, moderately other times.
PROPAGATION : By cuttings of nearly ripened wood inserted in sandy soil under bell-glass in gentle bottom heat during Aug.
SPECIES CULTIVATED : S. dependens, yellow, May, purple berries, 10 to 15 ft., Chile ; molle (Peruvian Mastic Tree, Pepper Tree), yellowish white, early summer, red berries, 15 to 20 ft., S. America ; terebinthifolius (Christmas Berry Tree), greenish white, early summer, red berries, 15 to 20 ft., Brazil.

Schismatoglottis—Ord. Aroideæ. Dwarf stove perennial herbs. Orn. foliage. First introduced 1862. Leaves, oblong or heart-shaped, green or striped with silver grey, purple, or yellow.
CULTURE : Compost, equal parts sandy loam, fibrous peat, leaf-mould, and silver sand. Position, well-drained pots in shady part of stove. Pot, Feb. or March. Water copiously April to Sept., moderately afterwards. Syringe daily April to Sept. Apply stimulants occasionally during summer. Temp., Sept. to March 60° to 65° ; March to Sept. 75° to 85°.
PROPAGATION : By division, Feb. or March.
SPECIES CULTIVATED : S. asperata, leaves deep green dotted white above and black beneath, Borneo, and its variety albo maculata (Syn. S. crispata), leaves silvery above ; concinna (Syn. S. Lavellei), leaves mottled with grey, Borneo ; neoguineensis, leaves blotched with yellow, New Guinea ; pulchra, leaves spotted with silvery white, Borneo. S. siamensis is a name frequently applied in catalogues to an unidentified plant having leaves spotted with white and requiring the same treatment as schismatoglottis.

Schizandra—Ord. Magnoliaceæ. Hardy deciduous climbing shrubs. First introduced 1860. Leaves, large and handsome. Berries, scarlet.
CULTURE : Soil, loam and peat. Position, sunny walls or arbours. Plant, Sept. and Oct. or April. Prune straggly shoots, April.
PROPAGATION : By cuttings of firm shoots inserted in sandy peat under bell-glass in cold frame, July to Oct.
SPECIES CULTIVATED : S. Henryi, white, April to May, climbing, W. China ; rubrifolia, red, April to May, climbing, W. China ; sinensis, rose, summer, 15 to 20 ft., China ; sphenanthera, yellow, April to May, climbing, W. China.

Schizanthus (Butterfly or Fringe Flower)—Ord. Solanaceæ. Half-hardy annual herbs. First introduced 1822. Natives of Chile.
OUTDOOR CULTURE : Soil, good ordinary rich. Position, sunny beds or borders. Sow seeds thinly in pots, pans, or boxes filled with light soil and place in temp. 65° to 75° in Feb. or March. Cover slightly with fine mould. Transplant seedlings when 1 in. high (four in a 3 in. pot), harden off in frame, and plant out in May. Sow also similarly in Aug., transplant three in a 3 in. pot, and place on shelf in light, airy greenhouse until following May, then plant out. Sow likewise outdoors end of April where required to grow.
POT CULTURE : Compost, one part loam, half a part each of decayed manure and leaf-mould, little sand. Sow seeds thinly in above compost in cool greenhouse or frame in Aug. Transplant seedlings singly in 3 in. pots and grow on shelf in greenhouse (temp. 45° to 55°) until Jan., then transfer to 6 in. pots and grow in

Sparaxis tricolor
(African Harlequin Flower)

Sparmannia africana
(African Hemp)

Spiræa japonica
(Meadow Sweet)

Spiræa prunifolia flore-pleno
(Meadow Sweet)

Stachys lanata
(Lamb's Ear)

Stanhopea devoniensis

Stapelia variegata
(Carrion Flower)

Staphylea colchica
(Bladder Nut)

Stephanotis floribunda
(Clustered Wax-flower)

Stevia ovata

Stokesia cyanea
(Stokes' Aster)

Strelitzia Reginæ
(Bird of Paradise Flower)

Streptocarpus hybridum
(Cape Primrose)

Styrax japonicum
(Storax)

Swainsonia galegiefolia
(Darling River Pea)

Symphoricarpus racemosus
(Snow-berry Tree)

Symphyandra pendula
(Pendulous Bell-flower)

Syringa vulgaris
(Lilac)

light position. Water moderately in winter, freely other times. Apply weak stimulants occasionally whilst flowering. Support plants with stakes. For summer flowering sow seeds in temp. 55° to 65° in. Feb or March, transplanting when 1 in. high to 3 in. pots, then into 5 in. pots.
SPECIES CULTIVATED : S. Grahami, lilac and orange, summer, 12 to 18 in., and many selected colour forms ; pinnatus (Syn. S. papilionaceus), rose, purple, and yellow, summer, 12 to 18 in., and many selected colour forms ; retusus, rose, crimson, and orange, summer, 18 in., and several selected colour forms ; wisetonensis, pink, white, and brown, summer, 1 ft., hybrid between S. pinnatus and S. Grahami. The strain known as S. hybridus grandiflorus contains many fine colour forms, while a further improvement upon this is known as Dr. Badger's strain.

Schizocodon—Ord. Diapensiaceæ. Hardy perennial herb suitable for rockery culture.
CULTURE : Soil, equal parts sandy peat and leaf-mould. Position, partially shady border, rhododendron bed, or cold frame. Plant, April. Water freely in dry weather. Protect with thick layer of cocoanut-fibre refuse and dry bracken.
PROPAGATION : By division of roots in April.
SPECIES CULTIVATED : S. soldanelloides, rose, March, 4 in., Japan.

Schizopetalon—Ord. Cruciferæ. Half-hardy annual. First introduced 1821.
CULTURE : Sow seeds in light, warm, rich soil in open border, April or May. Cover seeds lightly with fine soil. Thin seedlings when 1 to 2 in. high to 3 or 4 in. apart. Support plants when 6 to 12 in. high with small bushy twigs. Water freely in dry weather. Sow also thinly in well-drained pans filled with compost of loam, peat, and sand placed in temp. of 55° to 65°, Feb. or April, transplanting seedlings three or four in 3 in. pots filled with above compost ; harden off in cold frame and plant out in May.
SPECIES CULTIVATED : S. Walkeri, white, almond scented, summer, 6 to 9 in., Chile.

Schizophragma (Climbing Hydrangea)—Ord. Saxifragaceæ. Hardy deciduous self-clinging climbing flowering shrub. First introduced 1879.
CULTURE : Soil, ordinary. Position, sunny wall in warm districts only. Plant, Oct. or April. Prune straggly shoots into shape, April.
PROPAGATION : By cuttings inserted in sand under a bell-glass in temp. 55° in spring.
SPECIES CULTIVATED : S. hydrangeoides, yellowish white, July, 20 to 30 ft., Japan ; integrifolia, white, July, to 40 ft., China.

Schizostylis (Caffre Lily ; Crimson Flag)—Ord. Iridaceæ. Hardy bulbous or rhizomatous-rooted perennial. First introduced 1864.
OUTDOOR CULTURE : Soil, moist, loamy. Position, warm, sunny border. Plant, Oct. to March. Protect in severe weather by covering of dry litter. Water freely in dry weather in summer and apply stimulants occasionally.
POT CULTURE : Compost, two parts loam, one part decayed manure, little sand. Pot, Nov. to March. Position: cold frame, Dec. to April ; plunged to the rim of pots in sunny border, April to Sept. ; cold greenhouse, Sept. to Dec. Water copiously in summer, moderately other times. Apply stimulants occasionally in summer. Repot annually.
PROPAGATION : By division of rhizomes or roots in March or April.
SPECIES CULTIVATED : S. coccinea, crimson, Oct. and Nov., 1 to 3 ft., S. Africa, and its variety Mrs. Hegarty (pink).

Schomburgkia—Ord. Orchidaceæ. Stove epiphytal orchids. First introduced 1834.
CULTURE : Compost, sphagnum moss and fibrous peat. Position, on blocks suspended from roof or in well-drained pots or pans. Pot or reblock, Feb. or March. Water freely during growing period. Keep dry after growth has completed until flowers appear. Shade from sun. Moist atmosphere essential during growing period. Temp., March to Sept. 75° to 85° ; Sept. to March 60° to 70°. Resting period, winter ; growing period, March to Oct. Flowers appear at apex of new pseudo-bulbs.
PROPAGATION : By division

SPECIES CULTIVATED : S. Humboldti, rosy purple and yellow, Venezuela ; Lyonsii, white, brown, yellow, and purple, 1 ft., Jamaica ; tibicinis (Cow-horn Orchid), crimson, purple, orange, and white, summer, 1 ft., Honduras.

Schubertia—See Araujia.

Schyphanthus—See Grammatocarpus.

Sciadopitys (Parasol Fir Tree ; Umbrella Pine)—Ord. Coniferæ. Hardy evergreen conifer. First introduced 1861. False leaves, long, tapering, borne in tufts at the end of shoots, parasol-like ; green, with yellow groove on their lower surface. CULTURE : Soil, rich, moist, lime-free loam. Position, sheltered from piercing winds. Plant, Sept., Oct., March, or April.

PROPAGATION : By imported seeds sown ⅛ in. deep in pots filled with moist, sandy loam and placed in cold frame or greenhouse, transplanting seedlings outdoors following spring ; or ¼ in. deep outdoors in April in moist bed of sandy loam, transplanting seedlings next year.

SPECIES CULTIVATED : S. verticillata, 80 to 120 ft., Japan.

Scilla (Squill ; Blue Bell)—Ord. Liliaceæ. Greenhouse and hardy bulbous plants. OUTDOOR CULTURE : Soil, deep, sandy loam. Position, sunny beds, borders, in grass on lawns, or rockeries. Plant, Aug. to Nov., in lines or masses. Depth for planting : Small bulbs 2 in. deep and 2 in. apart ; large bulbs 4 in. deep and 3 to 4 in. apart. S. peruviana 4 to 6 in. deep in sheltered spot. Mulch with decayed manure, Nov. Lift, divide, and replant every third year.

POT CULTURE : Compost, two parts sandy loam, one part leaf-mould or well-decayed cow manure, one part river sand. Pot, Aug. to Nov., placing small bulbs, 1 in. apart, in a 5 in. pot ; or three to five large-sized bulbs 1 in. deep in similar pots. Position, under layer of cinder ashes from time of potting till growth commences, then in cold frame, cool greenhouse, or window till past flowering, afterwards in sunny spot outdoors. Water moderately from time growth commences till foliage fades, then keep dry. Repot annually. Apply weak stimulants once or twice during flowering period.

PROPAGATION : By seeds sown 1/16 in. deep in light, sandy soil in boxes or cold frame or outdoors in Sept. ; offsets from old bulbs removed when lifting and planted, as advised for full-sized bulbs. Seedlings flower when three to four years old.

SPECIES CULTIVATED : S. amœna (Star Hyacinth), indigo blue, March to May, 6 to 9 in., Europe ; autumnalis, rosy lilac, Aug. to Sept., 6 in., Europe (Britain) ; bifolia, blue, March, 6 in., Europe ; bifolia alba, white ; bifolia rosea, rose ; chinensis, rose, Aug. to Sept., 6 in., China ; hispanica (Spanish Squill), Syns. S. campanulata and S. patula, blue, May, 1 to 1½ ft., Europe ; hispanica alba, white ; hispanica rubra, red ; nonscripta (Bluebell), Syns. S. festalis and S. nutans, blue, April, 8 to 15 in., W. Europe (Britain) ; peruviana, lilac, May, 6 to 12 in., Algeria, and its variety alba (white) ; pratensis, lavender, April to May, 6 in., E. Europe ; sibirica (Siberian Squill), blue, Feb., 3 to 6 in., Asia Minor ; sibirica alba, white ; verna (Spring-flowering Squill), lilac blue, May, 3 in., W. Europe.

Scindapsus—Ord. Aroideæ. Stove evergreen climbers. Orn. foliage. CULTURE : Compost, equal parts rough peat, sphagnum moss, and coarse sand with a little broken charcoal. Position, pots, with shoots trained to trunks of tree ferns or walls. Pot, Feb. or March. Water copiously March to Oct., moderately at other times. Syringe freely at all seasons. Temp., Sept. to March 60° to 65° ; March to Sept. 80° to 85°. Shade from sun.

PROPAGATION : By division of roots at potting time.

SPECIES CULTIVATED : S. aureus (Syn. Pothos aureus), leaves blotched with pale yellow, 20 ft., Solomon Islands ; pictus, leaves glaucous, spotted dark green, 20 ft., E. Indies, and its variety argyreus (silver-spotted leaves).

Scirpus (Club Grass ; Rush)—Ord. Cyperaceæ. Greenhouse and hardy perennial marsh or water plants. CULTURE OF HARDY SPECIES : Soil, ordinary. Position, margins of lakes, streams, and ponds. Plant, Oct. to April.

PROPAGATION : By division, Oct. to April.

CULTURE OF GREENHOUSE SPECIES : Compost, equal parts loam, leaf-mould, and little sand. Position, small pots arranged along front of staging or in hanging baskets. Pot, Feb. or March. Water abundantly March to Oct., moderately other times. Temp., March to Oct. 55° to 65° ; Oct. to March 45° to 55°.
PROPAGATION : By division of plants in March.
HARDY SPECIES : S. lacustris (Porcupine Rush), inflorescence reddish, 4 to 5 ft., Britain, and its variety Tabernœmontani zebrina (stems ringed with yellow); maritimus, inflorescence golden brown, 3 to 5 ft., cosmopolitan.
GREENHOUSE SPECIES : S. cernuus (Syn. Isolepis gracilis), the Club Rush, 6 to 12 in., stems slender and drooping, cosmopolitan. Really hardy but almost invariably cultivated as a greenhouse pot plant.

Scolopendrium (Hart's-tongue Fern)—Ord. Filices. Hardy evergreen fern. Fronds, strap-shaped, crested, or contorted.
OUTDOOR CULTURE : Soil, one part each of fibrous peat and loam and one of sand, broken oyster shells, and limestone or mortar rubbish. Position, shady borders, rockeries, chinks of old stone or brick walls, or banks. Plant, April. Water copiously in dry weather.
INDOOR CULTURE : Compost, as above. Position, pots in cold frame, greenhouse, or dwelling-room. Shade from sun essential. Pot, Feb. or March. Water freely March to Oct., moderately afterwards.
PROPAGATION : By spores sown on surface of fine peat in well-drained pans placed in temp. of 75° any time ; division of plants, March or April.
SPECIES CULTIVATED : S. vulgare, 6 to 18 in., Europe (Britain), etc., and its numerous varieties, as crispum, cristatum, grandiceps, Kelwayi, marginatum, omnilacerum, ramosum, undulatum, variegatum, etc. See trade lists for other forms.

Scolymus (Spanish Oyster Plant ; Golden Thistle)—Ord. Compositæ. Hardy biennial and perennial herbs. First introduced 1653.
CULTURE : Soil, ordinary. Position, sunny borders. Plant perennial species Oct. to April. Sow seeds of biennial species ⅛ in. deep where required to grow, in March or April. Thin seedlings to 8 or 12 in. apart when 2 in. high.
PROPAGATION : Perennial species by seeds sown as above or by division of roots in April.
BIENNIAL SPECIES : S. hispanicus (Spanish Oyster or Golden Thistle), yellow, Aug., 2 to 3 ft., roots edible, Europe.
PERENNIAL SPECIES : S. grandiflorus, yellow, May, 3 ft., N. Africa.

Scorpion Grass (*Myosotis dissitiflora*)—See Myosotis.

Scorpion Iris (*Iris alata*)—See Iris.

Scorpion Senna (*Coronilla Emerus*)—See Coronilla.

Scorzonera (Viper's Grass)—Ord. Compositæ. Hardy herbaceous perennial with edible roots. First introduced 1576. Roots, carrot-shaped, white with dark skin, sweet-flavoured.
CULTURE : Soil, ordinary fine, rich, deeply trenched, free from stones. Position, sunny, open. Sow seeds in groups of three or four, 12 in. apart, in drills ½ in. deep and 18 in. apart in April. Thin seedlings when 3 in. high to one in each group. Remove flower heads as soon as seen. Lift the roots in Oct., twist off their leaves, and store in layers with sand or soil between in cellar or outhouse until required for cooking. Artificial manures for: 2½ lb. kainit, 1 lb. sulphate of ammonia, 2½ lb. of guano, mixed, per square rod (30¼ square yards) applied before sowing in spring. Requires to be raised from seed annually for producing roots for culinary purposes. Seeds germinate in seven to twelve days and retain their vegetative powers for two to three years. Crop reaches maturity in eighteen weeks.
SPECIES CULTIVATED : S. hispanica, yellow, June to Sept., 2 to 3 ft., S. Europe.

Scotch Crocus (*Crocus biflorus*)—See Crocus.

Scotch Elm (*Ulmus montana*)—See Ulmus.

Scotch Fir (*Pinus sylvestris*)—See Pinus.

Scotch Heather (*Erica cinerea*)—See Erica.

Scotch Kale—See Brassica.

Scotch Laburnum (*Laburnum alpinus*)—See Laburnum.

Scotch Rose (*Rosa spinosissima*)—See Rosa.

Scotch Shamrock (*Trifolium repens purpureum*)—See Trifolium.

Scotch Thistle (*Onopordon acanthium*)—See Onopordon.

Screw Pine—See Pandanus.

Scurvy Pea—See Psoralea.

Scutellaria (Helmet Flower; Skull Cap)—Ord. Labiatæ. Stove and herbaceous perennials.

CULTURE OF STOVE SPECIES : Compost, two parts loam, one part of equal proportions of leaf-mould, decayed manure, and sand. Position, light part of stove Sept. to June; sunny, cold frame remainder of year. Pot, Feb. or March. Prune shoots directly after flowering (Feb.) to within 3 in. of base. Good drainage essential. Nip off points of main shoots when 3 in. long, also of lateral shoots when of similar length, to induce bushy growth. Water freely Sept. to April, moderately afterwards. Syringe daily April to Sept. Apply stimulants once a week May to Dec. Temp., Sept. to March 55° to 65° ; March to June 70° to 80°.

CULTURE OF HARDY SPECIES : Soil, ordinary. Position, open, sunny borders or rockeries. Plant, March or April. Lift, divide, and replant only when overgrown.

PROPAGATION : Stove species by cuttings of firm shoots, 2 to 3 in. long, inserted in light, sandy soil under bell-glass in temp. 75° to 85° in spring; hardy species by seeds sown outdoors in April ; division of roots in March or April.

STOVE SPECIES : S. coccinea, scarlet, summer, 1 to 3 ft., Colombia ; costaricana, scarlet and yellow, June, 1½ to 3 ft., Costa Rica ; mociniana, scarlet and yellow, summer, 2 to 3 ft., Mexico.

HARDY SPECIES : S. alpina, purple, Aug., 6 to 8 in., S.E. Europe ; baicalensis, blue, July to Sept., 6 to 12 in., E. Asia, and its variety cœlestina (bright blue) ; indica japonica, lavender, summer, 1 ft., Japan.

Scuticaria—Ord. Orchidaceæ. Stove epiphytal orchids. First introduced 1834. CULTURE : Compost, sphagnum moss. Position, teak blocks suspended from the rafters in warm greenhouse. Change to new blocks when new growth commences. Water freely from March to Nov., little Nov. to March. Syringe once or twice daily whilst making growth. Ventilate freely May to Sept. Temp., April to Oct. 65° to 75° ; Oct. to April 55° to 60°. Growing period, Feb. to March ; resting period, Oct. to Feb.

PROPAGATION : By division of pseudo-bulbs immediately after flowering.

SPECIES CULTIVATED : S. Hadwenii, greenish yellow, white, and rose, May to Sept., 9 to 18 in., Brazil ; Steelii, yellow, chocolate, creamy white, and purple, Aug. to Sept., British Guiana.

Scyphanthus—See Grammatocarpus.

Sea Buckthorn (*Hippophæ rhamnoides*)—See Hippophæ.

Sea Bugloss—See Anchusa.

Sea Daffodil (*Pancratium maritimum*)—See Pancratium.

Sea Eryngo (*Eryngium maritimum*)—See Eryngium.

Seaforthia—See Archontophœnix.

Sea Heath (*Frankenia lævis*)—See Frankenia.

Sea Holly (*Eryngium maritimum*)—See Eryngium.

Seakale (*Crambe maritima*)—See Crambe.

Seakale Beet (*Beta Cicla*)—See Beta.

Sea Lavender (*Limonium vulgare*)—See Limonium.

Seal Flower (*Dicentra spectabilis*)—See Dicentra.

Sea Oat (*Uniola latifolia*)—See Uniola.

Sea Pink (*Armeria maritima*)—See Armeria.

Sea Poppy (*Glaucium luteum*)—See Glaucium.

Sea Rocket (*Cakile maritima*)—See Cakile.

Sea-shore Daffodil (*Narcissus odorus*)—See Narcissus.

Sea Spleenwort (*Asplenium marinum*)—See Asplenium.

Sedge—See Carex.

Sedum (Stonecrop)—Ord. Crassulaceæ. Greenhouse and hardy evergreen and herbaceous perennials, biennials, and annuals. Flowering and orn. foliage.
CULTURE OF GREENHOUSE SPECIES : Compost, two parts sandy loam, one part brick rubbish, one part of equal proportions of dried cow dung and sand. Position, pots or pans in sunny greenhouse. Pot, Feb. to April. Water freely April to Oct., very little afterwards. Temp., Oct. to March 40° to 50° ; March to Oct. 45° to 55°.
CULTURE OF HARDY PERENNIAL SPECIES : Soil, ordinary or sandy loam. Position, sunny or shady dryish rockeries and borders. Plant, Nov. to April.
CULTURE OF ANNUAL SPECIES : Soil, ordinary. Position, sunny dryish banks, rockeries, or borders. Sow seeds thinly in April where required to grow and lightly cover with fine soil. Thin 3 to 6 in. apart when 2 in. high.
PROPAGATION : Greenhouse species by seeds sown in well-drained pots or pans filled with fine compost of equal parts brick rubble, sandy loam, and sand and placed in temp. of 55°, Feb. to May; also by cuttings of shoots inserted in brick rubble, loam, and sand in temp. 45° to 55° in summer ; division of roots at potting time. Hardy species by seeds sown outdoors in April or division of the roots in March or April.
ANNUAL SPECIES : S. cæruleum, blue, July, 3 in., S. Europe.
HARDY PERENNIAL SPECIES : S. acre (Stonecrop), yellow, June, 3 in., Britain, and its varieties album (white) and majus (Syn. S. maweanum), yellow ; Aizoon, yellow, summer, 1 to 1½ ft., W. Asia ; album (Worm Grass), white, summer, 4 in., Europe (Britain), and its variety murale (pink) ; altissimum, whitish, late summer, 9 to 24 in., Mediterranean Region ; Anacampseros, dull purple, summer, 6 in., Tyrol and N. Spain ; anglicum, white and pink, June to July, 1 to 2 in., Europe (Britain) ; anopetalum, white or yellow, June to July, 6 to 9 in., Europe and Asia Minor ; brevifolium, white, June, 1 to 2 in., Mediterranean Region ; crassipes (often wrongly called S. asiaticum), yellowish white, June, 6 to 12 in., W. Asia ; dasyphyllum, pinkish white, summer, 1 to 2 in., Europe (Britain) and N. Africa ; ellacombianum, yellow, summer, 4 to 6 in., Japan ; Ewersii, pink, Aug., 6 to 12 in., W. Asia, and its variety homophyllum (miniature) ; hispanicum minus (Syn. S. glaucum), pink and white, July, 2 in., habitat unknown ; hybridum, yellow, spring and late summer, 6 in., Siberia and Mongolia ; kamtschaticum, orange yellow, autumn, 6 in., N.E. Asia, and its variety variegatum (leaves margined with white) ; lydium, white, Aug., 2 in., Asia Minor ; maximum, greenish white, Aug., 1 to 2 ft., Europe ; middendorffianum, yellow, July to Aug., 6 to 12 in., E. Asia ; moranense (often wrongly called S. liebmannianum), white, July, 3 to 4 in., S. Mexico ; multiceps, yellow, July, 3 to 4 in., Algeria ; Nevii, white, June, 3 to 4 in., Eastern U.S.A. ; oreganum (often wrongly called S. obtusatum), yellow, July to Aug., 6 in., Western N. America ; Palmeri, orange, May to June, 6 to 9 in., Mexico ; pilosum, rose, May to June, 2 to 4 in., Asia Minor and Caucasus, biennial ; populifolium, pink, Aug., 1 to 1½ ft., Siberia ; primuloides, white, Aug., 3 to 4 in., Yunnan ; pulchellum, rosy purple, summer, 4 to 6 in., N. America ; reflexum, yellow, summer, 8 to 10 in., Europe ; roseum (Rose Root), reddish purple, May,

6 to 10 in., N. Temperate Zone ; rupestre, yellow, July, 6 to 12 in., Europe (Britain) ; sarmentosum, yellow, summer, prostrate, China ; sempervivoides, crimson, June to July, 6 to 12 in., Asia Minor, biennial ; sexangulare, yellow, July, 1 to 2 in., Europe ; spathulifolium, yellow, May to June, 3 to 5 in., N. America, and its variety purpureum (deep purple foliage) ; spectabile, pink, autumn, 1 ft., Japan ; spurium, pink, July to Aug., 6 in., Caucasus ; stenopetalum, yellow, June, 4 to 6 in., N. America ; stoloniferum (sometimes wrongly called S. oppositifolium or S. spurium), pink, summer, 6 in., Caucasus ; telephium (Orpine or Live-long), reddish purple, summer, 1 ft., Northern Hemisphere.
GREENHOUSE SPECIES : S. Sieboldii medio-pictum, pink, summer, leaves blotched with white, 9 in., Japan ; lineare variegatum (Syn. S. carneum variegatum), leaves green striped with white, stems pink, China and Japan ; Stahlii, yellow, Aug. to Sept., 4 to 8 in., Mexico.

Selaginella (Creeping Moss ; Tree Club Moss)—Ord. Lycopodiaceæ. Stove and greenhouse orn. foliage plants. Evergreen. First introduced 1860. Fronds, creeping or erect ; branched ; green or variegated.
CULTURE : Compost, equal parts fibrous peat and chopped sphagnum moss. Position, pots, pans, or rockeries in shade. Pot or plant, Feb. or March. Water copiously April to Sept., moderately afterwards. Syringe daily April to Sept. Shade from sun. Temp., Sept. to March 55° to 65° ; March to Sept. 70° to 80° for stove species ; Sept. to March 40° to 50° ; March to Sept., 55° to 65° for greenhouse species.
PROPAGATION : By cuttings about 3 in. long inserted in above compost in well-drained pots and plunged in cocoanut-fibre refuse in a temp. of 80° at all seasons.
STOVE SPECIES : S. canaliculata, creeping, Trop. Asia ; cuspidata, W. Indies, and its variety emiliana ; erythropus, 10 to 12 in., W. Indies ; flabellata, 4 to 8 in., Tropics and Subtropics ; Galeottii, C. America ; grandis, 1½ to 2 ft., Borneo ; hæmatodes, 1 to 2 ft., W. Indies ; lepidophylla (Resurrection Plant), frequently sold as a curiosity, Texas ; Vogeli, 1 to 2 ft., Africa ; Wildenovi, climbing, Trop. Asia.
GREENHOUSE SPECIES : S. apus (Syn. S. apoda or densa), N. America ; Braunii, 12 to 18 in., China ; caulescens, 1 to 2 ft., Malay, China, and Japan ; kraussiana (Syn. Lycopodium denticulatum), creeping or trailing, S. Africa ; kraussiana aurea, foliage golden ; Martensii, 6 to 12 in., Mexico ; Martensii variegata, variegated ; uncinata (Syn. S. cæsia), trailing, China.

Selenipedium—Ord. Orchidaceæ. Stove terrestrial orchids allied to Cypripediums but differing from the latter in their long, narrow green leaves and bearing several flowers on a stem. The sepals, moreover, are mostly long and twisted.
CULTURE : Compost, two parts rough fibry peat, one part sphagnum moss and sand. Position, pots or pans drained one-third of their depth. Repot, March or April. Water freely March to Oct., moderately afterwards. Temp., March to Sept. 65° to 85° ; Sept. to March 60° to 65°. Shade desirable. Resting period, none. Flowers appear in centre of last-made growths after growth has finished.
PROPAGATION : All the species by division of the roots at potting or planting time.
SPECIES CULTIVATED : S. boissierianum, yellow, green, and white, autumn, Peru ; caricinum, white, rose, yellow, and green, various seasons, Bolivia ; caudatum, creamy white, crimson, bronze, and green, spring, Central America ; lindleyanum, green and red, winter, British Guiana ; longifolium, green, rose, yellow, and white, various seasons, Costa Rica ; Schlimii, white, rose, and yellow, all the year, Colombia. Also many hybrids, for which see trade lists. This genus is, by some authorities, referred to Paphiopedilum.

Self-heal—See Prunella.

Sempervivum (House-leek)—Ord. Crassulaceæ. Greenhouse and hardy succulent-leaved perennials. Leaves, fleshy ; green or variegated. All occasionally produce pinkish-white flowers in summer on stiff stems from 6 to 12 in. in length. The figures in the descriptions of species refer to the approximate diameter of the rosettes.

CULTURE OF HARDY SPECIES : Soil, ordinary light, sandy, containing a little old mortar. Position, open and sunny ; chinks, crevices, or ledges of rockeries ; edgings to borders. Plant, March to June. If used for edgings, plant close together in single or double rows. Top-dress annually in March with old and dried cow dung. Common House-leek (S. Tectorum) adapted for growing on sunny roofs or in crevices of old walls. Plant in a mixture of cow dung and clay in March or April.

CULTURE OF GREENHOUSE SPECIES : Compost, equal parts sandy loam, leaf-mould, and brick rubbish. Position, well-drained pots or pans in sunny part of greenhouse or window. Pot, March. Water moderately April to Oct., keep nearly dry remainder of year. No stimulants, shading, or syringing needed. Temp., March to Oct. 55° to 75° ; Oct. to March 40° to 50°.

PROPAGATION : By seeds sown in spring in a compost of equal parts sandy loam, leaf-mould, and old mortar in well-drained, shallow pans, slightly covered with fine mould, and placed in temp. 55° to 65° ; cuttings of shoots or leaves dried for a day or so after removal from the plant and inserted in above compost in summer ; division of offsets in March.

HARDY SPECIES : S. arachnoideum (Cobweb Houseleek), reddish rosettes covered with white filaments, $\frac{1}{2}$ to $\frac{3}{4}$ in., S. Europe, and its variety Laggeri (larger) ; arenarium, bright green rosettes, 1 to 1$\frac{1}{4}$ in., Tyrol ; boutignyanum, green and reddish-brown rosettes, 2 to 2$\frac{1}{2}$ in., Pyrenees ; calcareum, glaucous blue rosettes, 2 to 3 in., France ; dœllianum, reddish rosettes with white filaments, $\frac{1}{2}$ to $\frac{3}{4}$ in., Tyrol ; fimbriatum, green rosettes, 1 to 2 in., Tyrol ; glaucum, glaucous green rosettes, 2 to 3 in., Alps ; Greeni, glaucous green and red-brown rosettes, 1$\frac{1}{2}$ in., Eastern Alps ; Funckii, green rosettes, 1$\frac{1}{4}$ to 2 in., S. Europe ; montanum, dull green rosettes, 1 to 2 in., Alps and Pyrenees ; Reginæ-Amaliæ, bronze-purple rosettes, 4 to 5 in., Eastern Europe ; Schottii, reddish-bronze rosettes, 2 to 3 in., Tyrol ; soboliferum, green rosettes, 1 to 1$\frac{1}{2}$ in., Austria ; tectorum, green rosettes, 3 to 4 in., Europe ; triste, purplish-brown rosettes, 3 to 4 in., hybrid, and its variety bicolor (reddish) ; Wulfeni, pale green rosettes, 3 to 4 in., Alps.

GREENHOUSE SPECIES : S. arboreum, yellow, summer, 4 to 6 ft., Mediterranean Region ; arboreum variegatum, leaves variegated ; tabuliforme, 1 ft., Madeira ; tabuliforme variegatum, variegated. Last species used for carpet bedding.

Senecio (Jacobæa ; Cineraria ; Ragwort)—Ord. Compositæ. First introduced 1700. Greenhouse and hardy annuals, evergreen herbs or climbers, herbaceous perennials and half-hardy evergreen shrubs.

CULTURE OF ANNUAL SPECIES : Soil, ordinary rich. Position, sunny beds or borders. Sow seeds in April $\frac{1}{4}$ in. deep in patches or lines where required to grow. Thin seedlings 3 to 6 in. apart when 1 in. high.

POT CULTURE : Compost, two parts sandy loam, one part leaf-mould or well-decayed manure, and one part sand. Place in 6 in. pots, well drained, press firmly, and sow seeds thinly in April, covering with fine mould. Stand pots in cold greenhouse, window, or frame. Thin seedlings when 1 in. high to 2 in. apart. Water moderately and apply stimulants when flowers show.

CULTURE OF CLIMBING SPECIES : Compost, two parts sandy loam, one part well-decayed manure or leaf-mould, and one part sand. Position, well-drained pots in sunny greenhouse or window ; dwarf kinds on staging or inside window sills ; tall kinds trained up roof of greenhouse or round window frames. Pot, March or April. Water freely April to Oct., very little afterwards. Apply stimulants occasionally in summer. Temp., March to Oct. 55° to 65° ; Oct. to March 40° to 50°.

CULTURE OF HYBRID CINERARIAS (S. cruentes) : Compost, two parts yellow loam, one part leaf-mould and coarse silver sand. Sow seeds during May and June $\frac{1}{16}$ in. deep in well-drained pans or pots of above finely sifted compost. Cover top of pot with square of glass, keep soil moist, and shade from sun. Transplant seedlings when three leaves are formed singly in small pots ; keep in cold frame and shaded. Shift into 4$\frac{1}{2}$ in. pots in July, 6 in. size in Aug. Remove to greenhouse in Oct., near glass. Apply weak liquid manure twice weekly from Sept. onwards. Liquid cow manure best for cinerarias. Fumigate frequently to destroy aphis. Temp.,

Oct. to time plants have ceased flowering, 45° to 50°. Sow in May for winter flowering ; June for spring flowering. Double-flowered or choice single sorts may be increased by cuttings.

CULTURE OF S. CINERARIA : Compost, same as above. Pot, March. Plant outdoors in June. Lift in Sept. Water moderately if grown in pots.

CULTURE OF HARDY SPECIES : Soil, deep, rich loam. Position, partially shady, moist border. S. uniflorus on sunny banks in the rock garden. Plant, March or April. Mulch with decayed manure annually in March. Water freely in dry weather.

CULTURE OF SHRUBBY SPECIES : Soil, ordinary. Position, warm, sunny borders sheltered from cold winds. Plant, Sept. to Oct. or April to May.

PROPAGATION : Greenhouse species by seeds sown in March or April $\frac{1}{16}$ in. deep in a compost of equal parts loam, leaf-mould, and sand in well-drained pots or pans in temp. 65° to 75° ; by cuttings inserted in similar soil and temp. in spring or early summer. Hardy species by seeds sown $\frac{1}{4}$ in. deep outdoors in April ; division of the roots in March or April. Shrubby species by cuttings of nearly ripe wood in sandy soil under bell-glass in July or Aug.

ANNUAL SPECIES : S. elegans (Syn. Jacobæa elegans), various colours, single and double, summer, 1 to 2 ft., S. Africa.

GREENHOUSE SPECIES : S. cineraria (Syn. Cineraria maritima), the " Dusty Miller," yellow, summer, leaves silvery, 1 to 2 ft. (used also for carpet bedding), Mediterranean Region ; cruentus (Syn. Cineraria cruenta), parent of the well-known cinerarias, purple, summer, 1 to 2 ft., perennial but grown as an annual, Canaries ; macroglossus (Cape Ivy), yellow, summer, climber, S. Africa ; mikanioides (German Ivy), yellow, winter, climber, S. Africa.

HARDY SPECIES : S. abrotanifolius, orange, July to Aug., 1 ft., Europe ; adonidifolius, yellow, July to Aug., 8 to 12 in., Europe ; campestris (Syn. S. aurantiacus), orange yellow, summer, 1 to 1$\frac{1}{2}$ ft., Europe ; clivorum, orange yellow, July to Sept., 4 to 5 ft., China and Japan ; Doronicum (Leopard's Bane), yellow, summer, 1 ft., Europe ; incanus, silver-grey cushions of foliage, Europe ; japonicus (Syn. Ligularia japonica), orange yellow, autumn, 4 to 5 ft., Japan ; macrophyllus (Syn. Ligularia macrophylla), golden yellow, summer, 4 to 5 ft., Caucasus ; pulcher, red-purple, late summer, 2 to 4 ft., Uruguay and Argentina ; stenocephalus, orange yellow, late summer, 4 ft., China and Japan ; tanguticus, golden yellow, July to Sept., 6 to 7 ft., W. China ; uniflorus, yellow, July, 3 in., S. Europe ; veitchianus, yellow, summer, 3 ft., W. China ; wilsonianus, golden yellow, summer, 3 to 5 ft., China.

SHRUBBY SPECIES CULTIVATED : S. Greyi, yellow, summer, 3 ft., New Zealand ; laxifolius, yellow, June to Aug., 2 to 4 ft., New Zealand.

Senna Plant—See Cassia.

Sensitive Fern (*Onoclea sensibilis*)—See Onoclea.

Sensitive Plant (*Mimosa sensitiva*)—See Mimosa.

Sequoia (Mammoth Tree ; Californian Red-wood)—Ord. Coniferæ. Hardy evergreen coniferous trees. First introduced 1853.

CULTURE : Soil, deep loamy. Position, sunny sheltered. Plant, Sept., Oct., April, or May.

PROPAGATION : By seeds sown $\frac{1}{4}$ in. deep in well-drained pans of sandy loam placed in cold frames in spring, transplanting seedlings when large enough to handle 6 in. apart in nursery rows 6 in. asunder ; variegated kinds by grafting on common species in spring.

SPECIES CULTIVATED : S. gigantea (Syn. Wellingtonia gigantea), Mammoth Tree of California, 250 to 325 ft., California, and its variety aurea (golden-leaved) ; sempervirens (California Redwood), 200 to 300 ft., California.

Serapias (Tongue-flowered Orchid)—Ord. Orchidaceæ. Hardy terrestrial orchids. First introduced 1786.

CULTURE : Compost, calcareous loam or clay mixed with pieces of limestone. Position, sunny, deep, well-drained borders. Plant, Aug. to Nov., placing tubers

2 in. below surface. Water freely during growing period. Mulch with decayed manure annually in March or April. Lift and replant when unhealthy only.
PROPAGATION : By division of tubers, Aug. to Nov.
SPECIES CULTIVATED : S. cordigera, lavender and brown, summer, 1 ft., Europe , lingua, red and brown, spring, 1 ft., Europe.

Seratula—See Saussurea.

Sericographis—See Jacobinia.

Serpent Cucumber (*Trichosanthes Anguina*)—See Trichosanthes.

Serpent's-tongue (*Erythronium americanum*)—See Erythronium.

Service-berry (*Amelanchier canadensis*)—See Amelanchier.

Service-tree (*Pyrus Sorbus*)—See Pyrus.

Seven Sisters Rose (*Rosa multiflora platyphylla*)—See Rosa.

Seville Orange-tree (*Citrus aurantium bigarardia*)—See Citrus.

Shaddock-tree (*Citrus decumana*)—See Citrus.

Shaggy-fruited Rose (*Rosa villosa*)—See Rose.

Shaggy-leaved Primrose (*Primula villosa*)—See Primula.

Shaggy Lychnis (*Lychnis haageana*)—See Lychnis.

Shaggy Windflower (*Anemone vernalis*)—See Anemone.

Shallon Shrub (*Gaultheria Shallon*)—See Gaultheria.

Shallot (*Allium ascalonicum*)—See Onion.

Shamrock Pea (*Parochetus communis*)—See Parochetus.

Shanghai Jasmine (*Trachelospermum jasminoides*)—See Trachelospermum.

Shasta Daisy (*Chrysanthemum maximum*)—See Chrysanthemum.

Sheep's-bit Scabious (*Jasione montana*)—See Jasione.

Sheep Laurel (*Kalmia angustifolia*)—See Kalmia.

Shell-bark Hickory (*Carya alba*)—See Carya.

Shell-flower (*Chelone obliqua* and *Molucella lævis*)—See Chelone and Molucella.

Shepherdia (Beef Suet Tree ; Rabbit Berry ; Buffalo Berry)—Ord. Elæagnaceæ. Hardy deciduous shrubs. Orn. foliage and fruiting. First introduced 1759.
CULTURE : Soil, ordinary. Position, open or shady shrubberies and inland or seaside gardens. Plant, Oct. to Feb.
PROPAGATION : By seeds sown ½ in. deep outdoors in Nov. or Dec. ; by cuttings of roots inserted in Feb. or March in ordinary soil outdoors ; layering shoots in autumn.
SPECIES CULTIVATED : S. argentea (Beef Suet Tree, Rabbit Berry, Buffalo Berry), greenish, spring, scarlet fruits, 8 to 10 ft., N. America ; canadensis, greenish, spring, yellowish-red fruits, 3 to 6 ft., N. America.

Shield Fern (*Aspidium aculeatum*)—See Aspidium.

Shield-leaved Saxifrage (*Saxifraga peltata*)—See Saxifraga.

Shingle-plant (*Monstera deliciosa*)—See Monstera.

Shirley Poppy—See Papaver.

Shoe-black-plant (*Hibiscus rosa-sinensis*)—See Hibiscus.

Shooting Stars (*Dodecatheon Meadia*)—See Dodecatheon.

Shortia—Ord. Diapensiaceæ. Hardy perennial herb. First introduced 1888.
CULTURE : Soil, equal parts sandy peat and leaf-mould. Position, partially shady border, rhododendron bed, or cold frame. Plant, April. Water freely in dry weather. Protect with thick layer of cocoanut-fibre refuse and dry bracken.
PROPAGATION : By division of roots in April.
SPECIES CULTIVATED : S. galacifolia, white, spring, 3 to 6 in., N. Carolina ; uniflora, pink, spring, 6 in., Japan.

Shrubby Althæa (*Hibiscus syriacus*)—See Hibiscus.

Shrubby Cinquefoil (*Potentilla fruticosa*)—See Potentilla.

Shrubby Goosefoot (*Atriplex Halimus*)—See Atriplex.

Shrubby Horsetail (*Ephedra distachya*)—See Ephedra.

Shrubby Meadow-sweet (*Spiræa discolor*)—See Spiræa.

Shrubby Star Wort (*Microglossa albescens*)—See Microglossa.

Siberian Iris (*Iris sibirica*)—See Iris.

Siberian Lady's-slipper (*Cypripedium macranthum*)—See Cypripedium.

Siberian Larkspur (*Delphinium grandiflorum*)—See Delphinium.

Siberian Orange Lily (*Lilium dauricum*)—See Lilium.

Siberian Squill (*Scilla sibirica*)—See Scilla.

Siberian Pea Tree—See Caragana.

Siberian Wallflower (*Erysimum asperum*)—See Erysimum.

Sibthorpia (Cornish Money-wort)—Ord. Scrophulariaceæ. Greenhouse **and** hardy creeping perennial herb. A pretty plant for hanging baskets.
CULTURE : Compost, equal parts loam, leaf-mould, and little sand. Position, moist, partially shady borders or rockeries outdoors, or in pots or pans in cold frame, **or** cool, shady indoor fernery or greenhouse under bell-glass. Pot or plant, March or April. Water copiously in dry weather outdoors ; also indoors April to Sept. ; moderately other times. Moist atmosphere essential for indoor culture.
PROPAGATION : By cuttings inserted in pots of light soil placed under bell-glass **in** cold greenhouse or frame in summer ; division of plants in April.
SPECIES CULTIVATED : S. europæa variegata, golden-green foliage, N. Europe.

Sidalcea—Ord. Malvaceæ. Hardy perennial herbs. First introduced 1838.
CULTURE : Soil, ordinary. Position, sunny borders. Plant, Oct. to April. **Lift,** divide, and replant every three or four years.
PROPAGATION : By seeds sown ⅛ in. deep in light soil in April, transplanting seedlings when 1 in. high ; division of roots, Oct. to April.
SPECIES CULTIVATED : S. candida, white, summer, 3 ft., Rocky Mountains ; malvæflora, lilac, summer, 3 ft., N.W. America, and its varieties atropurpurea (purple) and Listeri (pink) ; spicata, rosy purple, July to Sept., 3 ft., California. There **are** numerous varieties and hybrids such as Rose Queen and Sussex Beauty.

Side-saddle-flower (*Sarracenia purpurea*)—See Sarracenia.

Sikkim Cowslip (*Primula sikkimensis*)—See Primula.

Silene (Catchfly)—Ord. Caryophyllaceæ. Hardy annuals, biennials, and herbaceous perennials.
CULTURE OF ANNUAL AND BIENNIAL SPECIES : Soil, ordinary light or sandy. Position, sunny beds or borders. Sow seeds in Aug. or Sept., ⅛ in. deep in a bed of light, rich soil, transplanting seedlings when 1 in. high 2 to 3 in. apart ; and plant 6 in. apart in flowering position in March for spring blooming. Sow also in similar depth and position in April, transplanting when 1 in. high to flowering positions for summer blooming. Or sow where required to grow and flower in April, thinning out seedlings in May or June to 6 in. apart.
CULTURE OF PERENNIAL SPECIES : Soil, sandy loam enriched with decayed cow dung. One-third loam, one-third peat, one-third stones for S. Elizabethæ, acaulis, and rupestris ; ordinary soil for other kinds. Position, sunny crevices or ledges of rockeries for S. acaulis, S. alpestris, S. rupestris, S. virginica, S. pennsylvanica, and S. Elisabethæ ; open borders for S. maritima fl.-pl. Plant, March or April. **Lift** and replant only when absolutely necessary.
PROPAGATION : Perennials by seeds sown in pans or boxes of sandy loam and leafmould, lightly covered with fine mould, and placed in cold frame in March or **April ;**

by cuttings of young shoots inserted in sandy loam in cold frame in summer ; by division in March or April.

ANNUAL SPECIES : S. Armeria, pink, summer, 1 to 2 ft., S. Europe ; Asterias, pink, summer, 12 to 18 in., Macedonia and Roumania ; pendula, pink, spring, 6 in., Mediterranean Region, and many varieties.

BIENNIAL SPECIES : S. compacta, pink, summer, 18 in., Asia Minor ; rupestris, white, May, 4 to 6 in., Alps.

PERENNIAL SPECIES : S. acaulis (Cushion Pink ; Moss Campion), pink, June, 2 in., N. Temperate Zone, and its variety alba (white) ; alpestris (Alpine Catchfly), white, May, 6 in., Alps ; californica, deep scarlet, late summer, 9 to 12 in., California ; Elisabethæ, crimson-magenta, summer, 6 to 9 in., Tyrol ; Fortunei, pink, June to Sept., 1½ ft., China ; Hookeri, pink and white, summer, 2 in,, California ; laciniata, scarlet, summer, 8 to 10 in., N.W. America ; maritima flore-pleno (Witch's Thimble), white, double, summer, trailing, Europe ; pennsylvanica (American Wild Pink), pink, spring, 6 to 8 in., U. States ; pumilio, rose pink, summer, 2 to 3 in., Tyrol ; pusilla, white, summer, 2 to 3 in., habitat unknown ; quadrifida (Syn. S. quadridentata), white, summer, 2 to 6 in., Europe ; Saxifraga, white and brown, summer, 6 in., S. Alps ; Schafta, purple, summer, 4 to 6 in., Caucasus ; vallesia, white and brownish red, summer, 3 to 4 in., Europe ; virginica (Fire Pink), crimson, June, 12 to 18 in., N. America.

Silk-bark Oak (*Grevillea robusta*)—See Grevillea.

Silk-vine (*Periploca græca*)—See Periploca.

Silk-weed (*Asclepias tuberosa*)—See Asclepias.

Silphium (Compass Plant ; Cup Plant)—Ord. Compositæ. Hardy perennials.
CULTURE : Soil, ordinary. Position, suuny borders. Plant, Oct. to April. Lift, divide, and replant every two or three years.
PROPAGATION : By division of roots, Oct. to April.
SPECIES CULTIVATED : S. laciniatum (Compass Plant), yellow, Aug. to Sept., 6 to 8 ft., N. America ; perfoliatum (Cup Plant), yellow, Aug. to Sept., 6 to 8 ft., N. America.

Silver Bell Tree (*Halesia carolina*)—See Halesia.

Silver-edged Primrose (*Primula marginata*)—See Primula.

Silver Fern (*Gymnogramme calomelanos peruviana argyrophylla*)—See Gymnogramme.

Silver Fir—See Abies.

Silver Grass (*Phalaris arundinacea variegata*)—See Phalaris.

Silver-leaved Beech (*Fagus sylvatica argenteo variegata*)—See Fagus.

Silver Maiden-hair Fern (*Adiantum æthiopicum scabrum* and *Nothochlæna nivea*)—See Adiantum and Nothochlæna.

Silver Maple (*Acer dasycarpum*)—See Acer.

Silver Rod (*Asphodelus ramosus*)—See Asphodelus.

Silver Thatch-palm (*Thrinax argentea*)—See Thrinax.

Silver-tree (*Elæagnus argentea*)—See Elæagnus.

Silver Vine (*Pothos argenteus*)—See Pothos.

Silver Wattle (*Acacia dealbata*)—See Acacia.

Silvery Clary (*Salvia argentea*)—See Salvia.

Silvery-leaved Oleaster (*Elæagnus argentea*)—See Elæagnus.

Silvery-leaved Sage (*Salvia argentea*)—See Salvia.

Silvery Tree Fern (*Cyathea dealbata*)—See Cyathea.

Silvery Reed Grass—See Cortaderia.

Silybum (Milk Thistle)—Ord. Compositæ. Hardy annual or biennial herb. Orn. foliage. Leaves, large, variegated with broad white veins. CULTURE : Soil, ordinary. Position, open borders. Sow seeds ⅛ in. deep in March where plants are to grow, thinning or transplanting seedlings to 2 ft. apart when large enough to handle. SPECIES CULTIVATED : S. Marianum (Blessed, Holy, Our Lady's, or Milk Thistle), rose-purple, summer, 1 to 4 ft., Mediterranean Region.

Simpson's Hardy Hedgehog Cactus (Echinocactus Simpsoni)—See Echino-cactus.

Sinningia (Gloxinia)—Ord. Gesneriaceæ. Stove tuberous-rooted flowering plant. Deciduous. First introduced 1815. Plants better known under the name of Gloxinia. CULTURE : Compost, equal parts fibrous peat, fibrous loam, leaf-mould, well-decayed manure, and a little silver sand. Position, well-drained pots close to glass in plant stove while growing ; greenhouse or conservatory when in flower. Pot, Jan., Feb., or March. Place tubers singly, and just below surface, in 3 or 4 in. pots, shifting into 5 or 6 in. pots when tubers have started growth. Water moderately till growth is well advanced, then freely. Apply weak liquid manure when flowers show. After flowering gradually withhold water till foliage dies down, then keep quite dry till potting time. Temp., Jan. to Oct. 65° to 75° ; Oct. to Jan. 50° to 55°. PROPAGATION : By seeds sown on surface of fine sandy peat and leaf-mould in well-drained pots or pans in temp. 65° to 75° in March ; cuttings of shoots, 1 to 2 in. long, inserted in small pots of sandy peat under bell-glass in temp. of 65° to 75° ; young leaves with stalk inserted in small pots of sandy soil treated as cuttings ; matured leaves with midribs cut and laid on surface of sandy peat in temp. 55° to 75°. SPECIES CULTIVATED : S. speciosa (Gloxinia), violet, autumn, 6 to 12 in., Brazil. Parent of the lovely strains of Gloxinias grown in gardens.

Sisal Hemp (*Agave sisalana*)—See Agave.

Sisyrinchium (Satin-flower ; Rush Lily ; Spring Bell)—Ord. Iridaceæ. Hardy and half-hardy perennials. First introduced 1693. CULTURE : Soil, two parts sandy loam, one part peat. Position, sunny, sheltered rock gardens. S. californicum does best in moist soil. Plant, Oct. or May. PROPAGATION : By offsets, removed and potted in March. SPECIES CULTIVATED : S. angustifolium (Syn. S. anceps), blue, summer, 6 to 8 in., N. America, and its variety bellum (violet purple) ; bermudianum, blue, summer, 12 to 15 in., Bermuda ; californicum, yellow, June, 12 in., California, rather tender ; chilense, white and mauve, June, 9 in., America ; filifolium (Pale Maidens), white, May, 6 in., Falkland Islands ; grandiflorum (Spring Bell), purple, spring, 1 ft., N.W. America, and its variety album (white) ; striatum, yellow, veined purple, June, 1 to 2 ft., Argentina.

Sitcha Water-leaf (*Romanzoffia sitchensis*)—See Romanzoffia.

Sium (Skirret)—Ord. Umbelliferæ. Hardy esculent-rooted perennial. First introduced 1548. Roots, cylindrical, clustered, white, sweet-flavoured. CULTURE : Soil, ordinary fine, rich, deeply trenched, free from stones. Position, sunny, open. Sow seeds in groups of three or four, 12 in. apart, in drills ½ in. deep and 18 in. apart in April. Thin seedlings when 3 in. high to one in each group. Remove flower heads as soon as seen. Lift the roots in Oct., twist off their leaves, and store in layers with sand or soil between in cellar or outhouse until required for cooking. Artificial manures : 2¼ lb. kainit, 1 lb. sulphate of ammonia, 2¼ lb. of guano, mixed, per square rod (30¼ square yards), applied before sowing in spring. Requires to be raised from seed annually for producing roots for culinary purposes. SPECIES CULTIVATED : S. Sisarum, white, Aug., 1 ft., E. Asia.

Skimmia—Ord. Rutaceæ. Hardy evergreen berry-bearing and orn. foliage shrubs. First introduced 1845. Flowers, fragrant. Male and female flowers form on separate plants. Berries, scarlet ; autumn.

CULTURE : Soil, stiff loam or loam and peat. Position, partially shady or open, sheltered borders. Plant, Sept., Oct., March, or April.
PROPAGATION : By seeds sown when ripe in sandy loam and peat in cold frame ; by cuttings of firm shoots inserted under bell-glass in temp. 55° to 65° in spring or summer ; layering shoots in autumn.
SPECIES CULTIVATED : S. Fortunei, white, spring, 2 ft., China, and its variety argentea (leaves variegated with silver) ; japonica, white, spring, 4 ft., Japan. S. Formani and S. Rogersi are considered to be hybrids between the two species.

Skirret (*Sium Sisarum*)—See Sium.

Skull Cap—See Scutellaria.

Slipper Flower —See Calceolaria.

Slipper Spurge (*Pedilanthus tithymaloides*)—See Pedilanthus.

Slippery Elm (*Ulmus fulva*)—See Ulmus.

Sloe (*Prunus spinosa*)—See Prunus.

Smilacina (False Spikenard)—Ord. Liliaceæ. Hardy perennials. Nat. N. America and Sikkim. First introduced 1633.
CULTURE : Soil, ordinary light deep, rich. Position, partially shady, moist shrubberies, woodlands, banks, or borders. Plant, Oct. to March.
PROPAGATION : By division of roots, Oct. to March.
SPECIES CULTIVATED : S. racemosa (False Spikenard), white, May, 3 ft., N. America ; stellata (Star-flowered Lily of the Valley), white, May, 2 ft., N. America. See also the genera Maianthemum and Clintonia.

Smilax (Sarsaparilla Plant ; Prickly Ivy)—Ord. Liliaceæ. Hardy, half-hardy, and stove evergreen and deciduous climbers. Shrubby and herbaceous. Orn. foliage. First introduced 1648.
CULTURE OF STOVE SPECIES : Compost, light loam, leaf-mould, and sand. Position, well-drained pots or borders in warm greenhouse, with shoots trained up wall or rafters. Water freely during growing season, moderately other times. Temp., March to Sept. 70° to 80° ; Sept. to March 60° to 65°. Pot, Feb. or March.
CULTURE OF SHRUBBY SPECIES : Soil, ordinary. Position, sunny walls, arbours, trellises, or banks. Plant, Sept. or Oct. : March or April.
CULTURE OF HERBACEOUS SPECIES : Soil, ordinary. Position, sunny borders, with shoots trained to fences or rustic poles. Cut back dead shoots in autumn. Plant, March or April.
PROPAGATION : By division of roots at planting or potting time.
STOVE SPECIES CULTIVATED : S. argyræa, bright green leaves with white spots, climber, Peru ; officinalis, shining green leathery leaves, climber, Colombia. The sarsaparilla of commerce is yielded by the tuberous roots of several Tropical American species.
SHRUBBY SPECIES CULTIVATED : S. aspera (Prickly Ivy), pale green, fragrant, July, 10 to 15 ft., evergreen, Mediterranean Region, and its variety maculata (leaves blotched white) ; China (China Root), greenish yellow, red berries, deciduous, 20 to 30 ft., China and Japan ; glauca, green, black berries, tall climber, semi-evergreen, Eastern U.S.A. ; rotundifolia, greenish yellow, black berries, to 25 ft., nearly evergreen, Eastern N. America. For greenhouse Smilax see the genus Asparagus.
HERBACEOUS SPECIES CULTIVATED : S. herbacea, greenish, bluish-black fruits, twining or semi-erect, N. America.

Smith's Tree Fern (*Hemitelia Smithii*)—See Hemitelia.

Smoke-tree (*Rhus cotinus*)—See Rhus.

Snail-flower (*Phaseolus caracalla*)—See Phaseolus.

Snake Fern (*Lomaria Spicant*)—See Lomaria.

Snake Gourd (*Trichosanthes anguina*)—See Trichosanthes.

Snake-root (*Cimicifuga racemosa*)—See Cimicifuga.

Snake's-beard (*Ophiopogon japonicus*)—See Ophiopogon.

Snake's-head Fritillary (*Fritillaria meleagris*)—See Fritillaria.

Snake's-tongue Fern (*Lygodium japonicum*)—See Lygodium.

Snapdragon (*Antirrhinum majus*)—See Antirrhinum.

Sneeze-wort or Sneeze-weed.—See Helenium.

Snow-ball-tree (*Viburnum Opulus*)—See Viburnum.

Snow-berry-tree (*Symphoricarpus racemosus*)—See Symphoricarpus.

Snowdrift (*Arabis alpina fl.-pl.*)—See Arabis.

Snowdrop (*Galanthus nivalis*)—See Galanthus.

Snowdrop Anemone (*Anemone sylvestris*)—See Anemone.

Snowdrop-tree (*Halesia carolina*)—See Halesia.

Snowdrop Windflower (*Anemone sylvestris*)—See Anemone.

Snowflake (*Leucojum vernum*)—See Leucojum.

Snowflower (*Chionanthus virginica*)—See Chionanthus.

Snow-in-Summer (*Cerastium tomentosum*)—See Cerastium.

Snow Pear-tree (*Pyrus sinensis*)—See Pyrus.

Snow Plant (*Cerastium tomentosum*)—See Cerastium.

Snow-tree (*Pyrus nivalis*)—See Pyrus.

Snow-white Primrose (*Primula nivalis*)—See Primula.

Snow Wood Lily (*Trillium nivale*)—See Trillium.

Snowy Mespilus (*Amelanchier canadensis*)—See Amelanchier.

Soap Plant (*Chlorogalum pomeridianum*)—See Chlorogalum.

Soap-tree (*Gymnocladus chinensis*)—See Gymnocladus.

Soap-wood (*Clethra alnifolia*)—See Clethra.

Soap-wort (*Saponaria officinalis*)—See Saponaria.

Sobralia—Ord. Orchidaceæ. Stove terrestrial orchids. First introduced 1836. CULTURE : Compost, peat and fibrous loam with a little sphagnum moss and coarse sand. Position, light part of house at all seasons. Pot, Feb. or March, filling pot one-third of its depth with coarse crocks, then adding a layer of sphagnum moss and sufficient compost to fill pot to within 1 in. of its rim. Press soil moderately firm. Water copiously April to Sept., moderately other times. Apply weak stimulants to established plants in summer. Shade from sun unnecessary. Repot only when soil is overcrowded with roots. Temp., Oct. to April 55° to 65° ; April to Oct. 65° to 75°. Growing period, all the year round. PROPAGATION : By division at potting time. SPECIES CULTIVATED : S. leucoxantha, white and golden yellow, summer, 1½ to 2 ft., Costa Rica ; Lowii, purple, summer, 12 to 18 in., Colombia ; lucasiana, white, rose, purple, and yellow, June, Tropical America ; macrantha, purple and yellow, May to July, 4 to 7 ft., Mexico, and its variety kienastiana (white) ; Ruckeri, mauve, crimson, and white, May, New Granada, and its variety Charlesworthi ; sandersiana, white, rose, purple, and yellow, summer, Central America ; sessilis, yellow and rose pink, Oct. to Jan., 1 to 2 ft., British Guiana ; xantholeuca, yellow, June to July, Central America.

Soft Grass—See Holcus.

Soft-leaved Azalea (*Rhododendron sinense*)—See Rhododendron.

Soft Prickly Shield Fern (*Aspidium aculeatum angulare*)—See Aspidium.

Solandra—Ord. Solanaceæ. Stove climbing flowering shrubs. First introduced 1781. CULTURE : Compost, two parts sandy loam, one part equal proportions fibrous peat and dry cow manure, and little sand. Position, pots or beds, with shoots trained up rafters or round trellises. Pot or plant, Feb. or March. Water freely

April to Oct. Keep almost dry remainder of time. Syringe daily April to Sept. Prune weak shoots in moderately close and remove tips of stronger ones in Feb. Temp., Oct. to March 50° to 55° ; March to Oct. 65° to 85°.

PROPAGATION : By cuttings inserted in light soil in cocoanut-fibre refuse in temp. of 65° to 75° in spring.

SPECIES CULTIVATED : S. grandiflora (Peach Trumpet Flower), cream and purple, spring, 10 to 15 ft., Trop. America ; longiflora, white and purple, autumn, 4 to 6 ft., W. Indies.

Solanum (Potato ; Egg Plant, etc.)—Ord. Solanaceæ. Greenhouse and half-hardy flowering, berry-bearing, and orn.-leaved plants or shrubs, including the Potato. Potato first introduced 1597 ; Egg Plant in 1597.

CULTURE OF THE POTATO : Classification : Kidney—oblong, white or coloured ; round—roundish, white or coloured ; pebble-shaped—flattish oblong, white or coloured. First earlies : varieties maturing in June ; second earlies : varieties maturing in July and Aug. ; late or main crop : varieties maturing in Sept. and Oct. Soil, deep, rich loam, or any kind except very heavy clay or bog land. Light soils best for very early crops. Position, sloping borders facing south for earlies and open garden for second early and main crops. Manures : (1) 1½ cwt. farmyard dung and 1 lb. of muriate of potash per square rod (30¼ sq. yards) applied in autumn ; 3 lb. of superphosphate per sq. rod applied at planting time and 1 lb. of nitrate of soda applied per sq. rod when shoots are 6 in. high. (2) 3½ lb. kainit, 3½ lb. nitrate of soda, 1 lb. iron sulphate, and 7 lb. superphosphate per sq. rod applied at planting time. (3) 3 lb. of superphosphate and 1½ lb. of sulphate of potash per sq. rod applied at planting time and 1 lb. of nitrate of soda per sq. rod applied when shoots are 6 in. high. (4) Special for heavy, damp soils : 9 lb. of basic slag and 4 lb. kainit per sq. rod applied in autumn and 1 lb. of sulphate of ammonia per sq. rod applied when shoots are 6 in. high. Sour or old garden soils should also be dressed with 3 bushels of fresh lime per sq. rod in Feb. Never plant sets direct on farmyard manure in drills. If applied in spring, cover slightly with soil. Sea-weed an excellent manure if dug in in autumn. " Sets " for planting : Best average size, 1½ to 2 in. wide and 3 in. long ; weight, 2 to 3 oz. Larger tubers to be divided into three or four parts, each furnished with one good " eye." Rub cut surfaces of sets in lime and expose a few hours before planting. Treatment of sets : Place tubers close together, " eyed " ends uppermost, in shallow boxes in a cool, light spot early in the year, and allow each tuber to develop two strong shoots only, rubbing off all others. Plant early sorts in Feb. ; second earlies in March ; late ones in April. Draw drills 6 in. deep on heavy and 7 in. deep on light soils. Rows to run N. and S. if possible, and be 15 in. apart for first earlies ; 2 ft. 6 in. for second earlies ; and 3 ft. 6 in. for late kinds. Distances apart for early kinds, 6 to 8 in. ; 12 in. for medium growers ; and 18 in. for robust kinds. Never plant with a dibble. Fork or stir up soil between rows when shoots are 6 in. high ; mould up when 6 to 8 in. high. Lift crop when haulm assumes a yellowish tinge. Avoid exposing tubers for eating too long to the light. Store in clamps in the open air or in cool cellars or dark sheds. Tubers for seed store in boxes as above advised in light, frost-proof position. Quantities of seed required : from 8 to 14 lb. per 100 ft. row, according to variety.

CULTURE IN POTS : Compost, two parts loam and one part leaf-mould. Place one large crock over drainage hole, then add 2 in. of turf and enough compost to half fill a 10 in. pot. Place one tuber in centre and fill pot to rim with soil pressed down moderately firm. Place pots in temp. of 55°. Water carefully till shoots appear, then keep soil uniformly moist. When shoots are 6 in. high fill up remaining space in pot with compost. Increase temp. to 65° and feed twice a week with liquid manure. Expose plants fully to light. Time to plant, Jan. Crop ready for use in April or May.

CULTURE IN FRAMES : Early crops may be grown in frames on hotbeds or without heat. Compost, good loam two parts, well-rotted manure or leaf-mould one part, with a little wood ashes and bonemeal added. Depth of compost, 1 ft. Surface of soil from glass, 1 ft. Plant sets 1 ft. apart in rows 15 in. asunder ; tubers 4 in. deep. Time to plant, Feb. Earth up when 6 in. high. Give air when sun is shining. Keep soil uniformly moist, using tepid water. Protect frames at night in cold weather by means of mats or litter. Crop ready for use in May.

CULTURE OF THE EGG PLANT : Soil, light rich. Position, in pots in sunny greenhouses (temp. 65° to 75°). Sow seeds in light soil in temp. 75° to 85° in Feb. or March. Transplant seedlings to 3 in. when third leaf forms, and into 6 in. pots in May. Syringe foliage twice daily and water freely. When fruit forms give weak liquid manure occasionally. Fruit ready to gather when fully coloured.

CULTURE OF BERRY-BEARING SPECIES : Compost, equal parts loam, leaf-mould, and silver sand. Pot, Feb. or March. Syringe daily, water freely, and grow in temp. of 55° to 65°. Pinch off points of shoots when 3 in. long. Transfer to cold frame in June, syringe morning and evening, and keep well watered. When berries set give liquid manure twice a week. Admit air freely after first week. Remove to greenhouse middle of Sept. and grow in a temp. of 55°. Prune shoots back to 2 in. in Feb., and when new growth begins repot and grow as before. May also be planted outdoors in rich soil early in June, points of shoots removed early in July, and plants carefully lifted, placed in pots, and stood in shady, cold frame for a fortnight, then removed to greenhouse.

CULTURE OF CLIMBING SPECIES : Soil, loam, leaf-mould, and silver sand. Position, pots, beds, or tubs, shoots trained up rafters of greenhouse. S. crispum will grow on a south wall in sheltered districts, while S. jasminoides will also thrive in the open in the south-west. Plant or pot in March. Prune away weak growths and shorten soft points of other shoots in Feb. Water indoor plants freely in spring and summer, moderately in autumn and winter. Temp., S. seaforthianum and S. Wendlandi, Sept. to March 55° to 60°, March to Sept. 65° to 75°. S. crispum and S. jasminoides only require protection from frost.

CULTURE OF ORNAMENTAL-LEAVED SPECIES : Soil, ordinary. Position, sunny beds or borders. Plant out in June. Sow seeds annually in light soil in temp. of 75° in spring, grow seedlings on in pots in heat till May, then harden for planting out in June.

PROPAGATION : Berry-bearing species by seeds sown in temp. 65° to 75° in Feb., transplanting seedlings into small pots and removing points of shoots when 3 in. high and later transferring to 5 in. pots. When shoots are 3 in. long remove their points, then allow them to grow naturally. From June onwards treat as advised for plants. Also increased by cuttings inserted in sandy soil in temp. of 65° in spring, afterwards treating rooted cuttings as advised for seedlings. Climbing species by cuttings of young shoots in sandy soil under bell-glass in gentle heat during late spring and early summer. Ornamental-leaved species by seeds as above.

TUBEROUS-ROOTED SPECIES : S. tuberosum (Potato), white, violet, etc., summer, S. America. First introduced 1597. Perennial.

FRUIT-BEARING SPECIES : S. Melongena (Aubergine or Egg Plant), Lowers blue, summer, 2 to 3 ft., fruit egg-shaped, white, yellow, or purple, Tropics, annual.

BERRY-BEARING SPECIES : S. capsicastrum (Star Capsicum), flowers white, summer, fruits scarlet, winter, 1 to 2 ft., Brazil ; pseudo-capsicum (Jerusalem Cherry), white, summer, fruits scarlet or yellow, 2 to 4 ft., habitat uncertain. Greenhouse evergreen shrubs. Wetherill's hybrids are the result of crosses between the two species.

CLIMBING SPECIES : S. crispum, bluish purple, fragrant, June to Sept., 15 to 25 ft., Chile ; jasminoides (Jasmine Nightshade), blue and white, summer, 15 to 20 ft., Brazil ; seaforthianum, blue or purple, summer, 10 to 15 ft., Tropical America ; Wendlandii, lilac and blue, summer, 15 to 20 ft.

ORNAMENTAL-LEAVED SPECIES : S. atropurpureum, stems purplish, midribs white, leaves prickly, Brazil ; marginatum, stems woolly and prickly, leaves prickly, white beneath, green above and margined with white, N. Africa and Costa Rica ; robustum, stems woolly, leaves velvety above, woolly beneath, and spiny, Brazil ; Warscewiczii, stems red, hairy, and prickly, leaves green, midribs prickly, S. America. Shrubs, but best grown as half-hardy annuals.

Soldanella (Blue Moon-wort)—Ord. Primulaceæ. Hardy perennial herbs. First introduced 1656.

CULTURE : Compost, equal parts peat and loam and sharp sand. Position, sheltered, open, moist rockery. Plant, March or April. Mulch surface of soil in dry weather with layer of cocoanut-fibre refuse.

PROPAGATION : By seeds sown in well-drained pans filled with equal parts sandy loam, peat, and sand and lightly covered with fine soil and placed in a cold, shady frame, March or April ; division of plants in March or April.

SPECIES CULTIVATED : S. alpina, blue, April and May, 3 in., Alps ; Ganderi, palest lilac, March, 2 in., hybrid ; hybrida, pale lilac, April, 2 in., hybrid ; minima, lilac and purple, April, 2 in., Europe ; montana, lavender, April, 6 to 9 in., E. Europe ; pusilla, pale lilac, April, 2 to 4 in., Alps.

Solidago (Golden Rod)—Ord. Compositæ. Hardy herbaceous perennials.

CULTURE : Soil, ordinary. Position, sunny or shady borders or banks or margins of water. Plant, Oct. to April. Lift, divide, and replant every three or four years.

PROPAGATION : By division of roots, Oct. to April ; seeds sown outdoors in April.

SPECIES CULTIVATED : S. brachystachys, yellow, autumn, 6 to 12 in. ; canadensis, yellow, Aug., 4 to 6 ft., N. America ; graminifolia (Syn. S. lanceolata), yellow, Sept., 2 to 4 ft., N. America ; missouriensis (Syn. Aster luteus), lemon yellow, Aug., 3 ft., N. America ; virgaurea (Common Golden Rod), yellow, Aug., 2 to 3 ft., Europe (Britain).

Sollya (Australian Bluebell Creeper)—Ord. Pittosporaceæ. Greenhouse ever-green twining shrubs. First introduced 1830.

CULTURE : Compost, two parts peat, one part turfy loam, and half a part silver sand. Position, well-drained pots or beds, with shoots trained to wire trellis or up rafters or pillars. Pot, Feb. or March. Water freely April to Sept., moderately after-wards. Syringe daily April to Aug. Shade not necessary. Temp., March to Sept. 55° to 65° ; Sept. to March 40° to 50°.

PROPAGATION : By cuttings of shoots inserted in sand under bell-glass in temp. 65° to 75° in spring or summer.

SPECIES CULTIVATED : S. heterophylla, blue, July, 4 to 6 ft., Australia : parviflora (Syn. S. Drummondi), blue, July, 4 to 6 ft., Australia.

Solomon's Seal—See Polygonatum.

Sonerila—Ord. Melastomaceæ. Stove perennial. Flowering and orn. foliage. First introduced 1854. Leaves, ovate or lanceolate, green or spotted with silvery white.

CULTURE : Compost, equal parts fibry peat, chopped sphagnum, charcoal, and sand. Position, well-drained pots or pans fully exposed to light. Pot, Feb. or March. Water freely April to Sept., moderately afterwards. Shade from sun and moist atmosphere highly essential. Temp., March to Sept. 70° to 85° ; Sept. to March 55° to 65°.

PROPAGATION : By seeds sown in above compost and lightly covered with fine mould, Jan. to April, in a temp. of 75° to 85° ; cuttings inserted in small pots under bell-glass in temp. 75° to 85°, Jan. to May.

SPECIES CULTIVATED : S. margaritacea, rose, summer, leaves white and green above, purplish beneath, Burma, and its variety argentea, leaves silvery grey. There are numerous varieties such as F. Marchand, Mdme. van Langenhove, and Victoria.

Sophora (Chinese Pagoda Tree ; New Zealand Laburnum)—Ord. Leguminosæ. Hardy and half-hardy evergreen and deciduous trees and shrubs. Flowering and orn. foliage. First introduced 1739.

CULTURE OF HALF-HARDY SPECIES : Compost, two parts loam, one of leaf-mould, and little sand. Pot, Oct. to Feb. Position, in pots or tubs in light, airy part of greenhouse, Oct. to May ; or against S. walls outdoors in warm districts. Protect in cold weather with mats. Water freely April to Oct., very little afterwards. Prune, Feb. or March. Temp., Oct. to April 40° to 45° ; April to May 50° to 65°.

CULTURE OF HARDY SPECIES : Soil, deep, rich loam. Position, open, sheltered lawns. Plant, Oct. to Feb. Prune into shape, Jan. or Feb.

PROPAGATION : By seeds sown ¼ in. deep in light soil in temp. of 55° in April ; cuttings taken with a heel and inserted in sandy soil in gentle bottom heat during July and Aug. S. japonica pendula by grafting on common species in March.

HALF-HARDY SPECIES : S. tetraptera (New Zealand Laburnum), Syn. Edwardsia grandiflora, yellow, May, 15 to 40 ft., deciduous in the open, evergreen in a greenhouse, New Zealand, and its varieties grandiflora (large-flowered) and microphylla (narrow-leaved).
HARDY SPECIES : S. japonica (Chinese Pagoda Tree), creamy white, Sept,. 50 to 80 ft., deciduous, China, and its variety pendula (weeping) ; viciifolia, bluish white, June, 6 to 8 ft., deciduous, W. China.

Sophro-Cattleya—Ord. Orchidaceæ. A race of bigeneric hybrid orchids, the result of a cross between Sophronitis grandiflora and several species of Cattleyas. Habit, dwarf. Flowering in winter.
CULTURE : Compost, two parts coarse fibry peat, one part chopped living sphagnum moss, charcoal, and sand. Position, well-drained pots, hanging baskets, blocks. Pot, Feb. or March. Keep plants well above rim of pot. Partial shade desirable. Water three times weekly March to Aug., once weekly Aug. to Nov. and Feb. to March, once a month other times. Syringe freely in summer. Temp., March to Sept. 65° to 85° ; Sept. to March 60° to 70°. Growing period, March to Sept. ; resting period, winter. Flowers appear at top of new growth.
PROPAGATION : By division of pseudo-bulbs at potting time.
HYBRIDS CULTIVATED : S. batemanniana, rose, scarlet, crimson, and white ; Calypso, rosy purple and yellow ; Chamberlainii triumphans, rosy purple and yellow ; hardyana, red, purple, and yellow ; eximia, purple, rose, and yellow ; Queen Empress, rose, crimson, and purple. Many more varieties to be found in trade lists.

Sophro Lælia—Ord. Orchidaceæ. Another race of bigeneric hybrid orchids, the result of crossing Sophronitis grandiflora with several species of Lælias. Habit, dwarf.
CULTURE : Compost, two parts coarse fibrous peat, one part living sphagnum moss, charcoal, and sand. Position, pots, pans, or hanging baskets, or on blocks with moss only. Pot or reblock, Feb. or March. Fill pots two-thirds with broken crocks and keep plants well above rim of pot. Secure plants and moss to blocks by means of copper wire. Water pot and basket plants three times weekly March to Aug., once weekly Aug. to Nov. and Feb. to March, once a month other times. Plants on blocks daily March to Aug., twice a week Aug. to Nov. and Feb. and March, once a week other times. Syringe freely in summer. Temp., March to Sept. 75° to 85° ; Sept. to March 60° to 70°. Resting period, none. Flowers appear at top of new pseudo-bulb.
PROPAGATION : By division of pseudo-bulbs at potting time.
HYBRIDS CULTIVATED : S. Læta, pink, rosy purple, and yellow ; Marriottii, orange yellow and scarlet, and many others to be found in trade lists.

Sophronitis (Scarlet-flowered Orchid)—Ord. Orchidaceæ. Dwarf evergreen epiphytal orchids. First introduced 1827.
CULTURE : Compost, equal parts peat, sphagnum moss, and charcoal. Position, shallow small pans or baskets suspended from roof. Pot, Feb. or March. Shade from sun most essential. Water freely April to Oct., moderately afterwards. Temp., Oct. to April 55° to 65° ; April to Oct. 65° to 75°. Growing period, May to Feb. ; resting period, March to May. Flowers appear at apex of new pseudo-bulb.
PROPAGATION : By division of pseudo-bulbs, Feb. or March.
SPECIES CULTIVATED : S. cernua, rosy red and yellow, winter, 3 in., Brazil ; grandiflora, scarlet, winter, 3 to 6 in., Brazil.

Sorrel—See Rumex.

Sour Sop (*Anona muricata*)—See Anona.

South African Hare-bell (*Roella ciliata*)—See Roella.

South African Thistle—See Berkheya.

South American Button Flower (*Gomphia decora*)—See Gomphia.

Southern Beech—See Nothofagus.

Southernwood (*Artemisia Abrotanum*)—See Artemisia.

South Sea Myrtle (*Leptospermum scoparium*)—See Leptospermum.

Sow-bread (*Cyclamen europæum*)—See Cyclamen.

Spanish Bayonet (*Yucca aloifolia*)—See Yucca.

Spanish Broom (*Spartium junceum*)—See Spartium.

Spanish Chestnut (*Castanea vesca*)—See Castanea.

Spanish Fennel-flower (*Nigella hispanica*)—See Nigella.

Spanish Furze (*Genista hispanica*)—See Genista.

Spanish Gorse (*Genista hispanica*)—See Genista.

Spanish Hyacinth (*Hyacinthus amethystinus*)—See Hyacinthus.

Spanish Iris (*Iris Xiphium*)—See Iris.

Spanish Moss (*Tillandsia usneoides*)—See Tillandsia.

Spanish Oyster-plant (*Scolymus hispanicus*)—See Scolymus.

Spanish Poppy (*Papaver rupifragrum*)—See Papaver.

Spanish Potato (*Ipomæa batatus*)—See Ipomæa.

Spanish Squill (*Scilla hispanica*)—See Scilla.

Spanish-tuft (*Thalictrum aquilegifolium*)—See Thalictrum.

Sparaxis (African Harlequin Flower)—Ord. Iridaceæ. Half-hardy bulbous plants. First introduced 1758.
OUTDOOR CULTURE: Soil, light, rich, sandy. Position, sunny well-drained border. Plant, Sept. to Jan., placing bulbs 4 in. deep and 2 in. apart. Mulch surface of bed in March with cow manure. Cover with litter during winter months if not planted in sheltered border.
POT CULTURE: Compost, two parts sandy loam, one part leaf-mould or decayed cow manure. Pots, 4½ in. in diameter, well drained. Place five bulbs, 3 in. deep, in each pot in Nov. and cover with cocoanut-fibre refuse in cold frame or under cool greenhouse stage until growth begins. Water moderately from time bulbs begin to grow until flowers fade, then gradually cease, keeping bulbs dry till Jan. Temp., Sept. to March 40° to 50°; other times 50° to 60°.
PROPAGATION: By offsets, treated as advised for bulbs.
SPECIES CULTIVATED: S. grandiflora, violet purple, spring, 1 to 2 ft., S. Africa; tricolor (Syn. Ixia tricolor), orange yellow and black, May, 1 to 2 ft., S. Africa. For varieties see trade lists. See also the genus Dierama.

Sparmannia (African Hemp)—Ord. Tiliaceæ. Greenhouse evergreen shrub. First introduced 1790.
CULTURE: Compost, two parts loam, one part peat, and little sand. Position, pots in light, airy greenhouse Sept. to June; sunny spot outdoors remainder of time. Pot, Feb. or March. Prune moderately close Nov. to Dec. Water copiously April to Oct., moderately afterwards. Apply stimulants April to Sept. No shade or syringing required. Temp., March to Sept. 55° to 65°; Sept. to March 40° to 50°.
PROPAGATION: By cuttings inserted singly in small pots filled with sandy soil under bell-glass in temp. 55° to 65°, spring or summer.
SPECIES CULTIVATED: S. africana, white, summer, 10 to 15 ft., S. Africa; africana flore-pleno, double flowered.

Spartium (Spanish Broom)—Ord. Leguminosæ. Hardy deciduous flowering shrub. First introduced 1548.

CULTURE: Soil, ordinary. Position, sunny, open borders or dry banks. Plant, Oct. to March.

PROPAGATION: By seeds sown ¼ in. deep in drills in fine soil in sunny position outdoors, autumn or spring. S. junceum flore-pleno by grafting in April or May upon seedlings of the common kind.

SPECIES CULTIVATED: S. junceum (Yellow Spanish Broom), yellow, summer, 6 to 10 ft., S. Europe; junceum flore-pleno, double flowered.

Spathiphyllum—Ord. Aroideæ. Stove evergreen perennials. First introduced 1874.

CULTURE: Compost, leaf-mould and peat with a little loam, sand, and charcoal. Water freely during growing season, moderately at other times. Maintain a humid atmosphere throughout the year, using the syringe freely. Temp., March to Sept. 75° to 85°; Sept. to March 65° to 70°.

PROPAGATION: By seeds sown in temp. 85° during Feb.; or by division, Feb. or March.

SPECIES CULTIVATED: S. cochlearispathum, white, large leaves with waved margins, 2 to 3 ft., Central America; floribundum, white and yellowish, foliage rich green, 1 ft., Colombia; Patini, white and greenish, pale green foliage, 1 ft., Colombia.

Spathoglottis—Ord. Orchidaceæ. Stove terrestrial orchids. First introduced 1837.

CULTURE: Compost, equal parts leaf-mould and fibrous loam or equal parts of leaf-mould, peat, sphagnum moss, and silver sand. Repot in spring. Grow in partial shade. Water freely April to Oct., little at other times. Growing period, spring and summer; resting period, winter. Flowers appear at top of last-made pseudo-bulb. Temp., March to Oct. 75° to 85°; Oct. to March 55° to 65°.

PROPAGATION: By division in spring.

SPECIES CULTIVATED: S. aurea, yellow and red, autumn, Malacca; Fortunei, yellow and red, autumn, Hong Kong; Lobbii, sulphur yellow and red, autumn, Burma; plicata, rosy purple, summer, Malaya; Viellardii, white, rose, and red, autumn, New Caledonia. There are several hybrids, of which S. kewensis is one of the best.

Spatlum (*Lewisia rediviva*)—See Lewisia.

Spear-flower (*Ardisia crenata*)—See Ardisia.

Spear Grass—See Aciphylla.

Spear Lily (*Doryanthes Palmeri*)—See Doryanthes.

Spear Mint (*Mentha viridis*)—See Mentha.

Spear-wort (*Ranunculus lingua*)—See Ranunculus.

Spectral Flowered Orchid (*Masdevallia chimæra*)—See Masdevallia.

Specularia—See Legonsia.

Speedwell—See Veronica.

Speik (*Valeriana celtica*)—See Valeriana.

Spergula—See Sagina.

Sphæralcea—Ord. Malvaceæ. Half-hardy perennial and greenhouse shrub. First introduced 1780.

CULTURE OF PERENNIAL SPECIES: Soil, ordinary. Position, sunny, dryish, sheltered banks or sheltered rock gardens. Plant, autumn or spring.

CULTURE OF SHRUBBY SPECIES: Compost, loam, leaf-mould, and sand. Position, well-drained pots or borders in unheated greenhouse. Water freely during growth.

PROPAGATION: Perennial species by division at planting time; shrubby species by cuttings of young shoots inserted in sandy soil under bell-glass in gentle bottom heat.

PERENNIAL SPECIES CULTIVATED : S. munroana, bright scarlet, May to Nov., 1 to 2 ft., N. America.

SHRUBBY SPECIES CULTIVATED : S. angustifolia, pink, Aug. to Sept., 3 to 4 ft., Mexico.

Sphenogyne speciosa—See Ursinia pulchra.

Spice-bush (*Lindera Benzoin*)—See Lindera.

Spider Fern (*Pteris serrulata*)—See Pteris.

Spider-flower—See Cleome.

Spider Orchis (*Ophrys aranifera*)—See Ophrys.

Spiderwort (*Tradescantia virginiana*)—See Tradescantia.

Spigelia (Carolina Pink ; Maryland Pink-root)—Ord. Loganiaceæ. Hardy herbaceous perennial. First introduced 1694.

CULTURE : Soil, equal parts loam, leaf-mould, peat, and sand. Position, partially shady border containing 2 ft. in depth of above compost. Plant, March or April. Water copiously during summer.

PROPAGATION : By division of roots, March or April.

SPECIES CULTIVATED : S. marilandica, red and yellow, summer, 1 ft., N. America.

Spignel (*Meum athamanticum*)—See Meum.

Spinach (*Spinacia oleracea*)—See Spinacia.

Spinach Beet—See Beta.

Spinacia (Spinach)—Ord. Chenopodiaceæ. Hardy annual. Esculent-leaved vegetable. First introduced 1568.

CULTURE : Soil, deep, rich, moist ordinary for summer spinach ; rich, moderately dry for winter kind. Position, sunny. Sow seeds of summer spinach at intervals of a fortnight, Feb. to Aug., in drills 1 in. deep and 12 in. apart ; winter spinach, Aug. and Sept., in drills 1 in. deep and 15 in. asunder. Thin winter spinach to 6 in. apart when three leaves form. Manures : 1¼ lb. kainit, 1½ lb. sulphate of ammonia, 2 lb. superphosphate per sq. rod, applied when plants are 2 in. high. Seeds germinate in ten to fifteen days ; retain their germinating powers for five years. Crop reaches maturity eleven weeks after sowing.

SPECIES CULTIVATED : S. oleracea glabra (Summer Spinach), 2 ft., S.E. Europe ; oleracea spinosa (Prickly or Winter Spinach).

Spindle-tree (*Euonymus europæus*)—See Euonymus.

Spinovitis Davidii—See Vitis Davidii.

Spiræa (Meadow Sweet)—Ord. Rosaceæ. Hardy deciduous flowering shrubs and herbaceous perennials.

CULTURE OF HARDY HERBACEOUS SPECIES : Soil, ordinary rich, well manured. Position, moist, partially shady, or sunny borders ; margins of streams, etc. for S. Ulmaria, astilboides, palmata, camtschatica, and aruncus ; moist rock gardens for S. cæspitosa, decumbens, and Hacqueti. Plant, Oct., Nov., March, or April. Top-dress annually in April with decayed manure. Water copiously in dry weather. Lift, divide, and replant every three or four years.

CULTURE OF DECIDUOUS SHRUBS : Soil, good ordinary or loamy. Position, open, sunny borders or shrubberies. Plant, Sept. to March. Prune straggly shoots moderately close directly after flowering.

CULTURE OF S. ASTILBOIDES IN POTS : Compost, equal parts loam and leaf-mould. Pot roots, Oct. or Nov., singly in 5 or 6 in. pots. Place in cold frame until required for forcing, or remove to ordinary heated greenhouse in Jan., cold house in Feb. Temp. for forcing, 55° to 65°. Water moderately when first brought into forcing or greenhouse ; freely when growth begins. Apply weak stimulants—½ oz. of guano to gall. of water—when flower spikes show. Remove to cold frame after flowering and plant out in sunny position in June. Let plants remain thus for two years, then lift, place in pots, and use for forcing.

PROPAGATION : Herbaceous kinds by division of the roots, Oct. to March ; shrubby ones by cuttings of young shoots inserted in sandy soil under hand-light or in frame in shade, summer ; also by offsets, removed and planted in autumn.

HARDY HERBACEOUS SPECIES : S. aruncus (Goat's Beard), white, summer, 4 to 6 ft., N. Temperate Regions, and its variety Kneiffi (leaflets deeply cut) ; astilboides (Syn. Astilbe astilboides), white, June, 2 ft., Japan, and its variety floribunda (free flowering) ; cæspitosa, white, summer, 3 in., N.W. America ; camtschatica (Syn. S. gigantea), white, June, 6 to 8 ft., Kamtschatka ; decumbens, white, May, 3 to 8 in., Tyrol ; digitata, rosy red, July to Aug., 2 ft., Siberia, and its variety nana (dwarf) ; Hacqueti, white, summer, 6 in., Tyrol ; lobata (Queen of the Prairies), (Syn. S. venusta), carmine rose, July to Sept., 4 to 6 ft., N. America, and its variety magnifica (red) ; palmata, crimson, June, 2 to 3 ft., Japan, and its varieties alba (white), elegans (pale pink), and purpurea (purple-leaved). See also Filipendula.

HARDY DECIDUOUS SHRUBS : S. Aitchisoni, white, July to Aug., 8 to 10 ft., Afghanistan, etc. ; arborea, white, July to Sept., 20 to 30 ft., W. China ; arguta, white, April to May, 6 to 8 ft., hybrid ; bella, red, July, 3 to 6 ft., Himalayas ; bracteata, white, June, 4 to 8 ft., Japan ; bullata, deep rose, July, 12 to 15 in., Japan ; canescens, creamy white, June, 6 to 15 ft., Himalayas ; cantoniensis (Syn. S. reevesiana), white, April, 4 to 6 ft., China and Japan ; discolor (Syn. S. ariæfolia), creamy white, July, 8 to 12 ft., N.W. America ; Douglasii, rose, Aug., 3 to 6 ft., N.W. America ; Henryi, white, June, 6 to 8 ft., China ; japonica (Syn. S. callosa), rose, June, 3 to 6 ft., Japan, and its varieties alba (white), Bumalda (carmine), and Anthony Waterer (bright carmine) ; lindleyana, white, July to Sept., 15 to 20 ft., Himalayas ; Margaritæ, pink, July to Sept., 4 to 5 ft., hybrid ; media, white, April to May, 4 to 6 ft., E. Europe to Japan ; Menziesii, purplish rose, July to Aug., 3 to 5 ft., N.W. America ; millefolium, white, July, 3 to 5 ft., N.W. America ; pectinata, white, 3 to 6 in., N.W. America ; prunifolia flore-pleno, white, double, April to May, 4 to 6 ft., China and Japan ; salicifolia, white or rose, June to July, 3 to 6 ft., E. Europe to Japan, and its variety paniculata (large panicles) ; Thunbergi, white, March to April, 3 to 5 ft., China ; Van Houttei, white, May to June, 4 to 6 ft., hybrid ; Veitchi, white, June, 10 to 12 ft., China ; Wilsoni, white, June to July, 6 to 8 ft., W. China. See also Neillia and Astilbe.

Spire Lily (*Galtonia candicans*)—See Galtonia.

Spleenwort—See Asplenium.

Spondias—Ord. Anacardiaceæ. Warm greenhouse trees. Cultivated for edible fruits. First introduced 1739.
CULTURE : Compost, fibrous loam and sand. Position, well-drained borders in heated greenhouse or conservatory. Water freely during growing season, moderately at other times. Temp., March to Sept. 65° to 75° ; Sept. to March 50° to 55°.
PROPAGATION : By cuttings of half-ripened shoots inserted in sandy soil under bell-glass in temp. 75°.
SPECIES CULTIVATED : S. dulcis (Otaheite Apple), Syn. S. cytherea, fruits 3 in. long, golden yellow, to 60 ft., Society Islands ; lutea (Hog Plum), Syn. S. Mombin, fruits 1 to 2 in. long, yellow, to 60 ft., Tropics.

Spotted Dead-nettle (*Lamium maculatum*)—See Lamium.

Spotted Laurel—See Aucuba.

Spotted Orchis (*Orchis maculata*)—See Orchis.

Spotted Winter Green (*Chimaphila maculata*)—See Chimaphila.

Spraguea—Ord. Portulacaceæ. Half-hardy perennial herb. First introduced 1858.
CULTURE : Soil, ordinary. Position, edges of sunny well-drained borders or rockeries. Plant, April or May.
PROPAGATION : By seeds sown, Feb. or March, in well-drained pots or pans in above compost in temp. of 55° to 60°, transplanting seedlings an inch apart in 3 in. pots when large enough to handle, and afterwards hardening off in cold frame and planting out in May ; cuttings of shoots inserted in sandy peat under bell-glass in temp. of 55° to 65° in spring.
SPECIES CULTIVATED : S. umbellata, white, summer, 1 to 2 in., New Mexico.

Spreading Wood Fern (*Nephrodium patens*)—See Nephrodium.

Sprekelia (Jacobean Lily)—Ord. Amaryllidaceæ. Warm house deciduous bulb. First introduced 1658.

CULTURE : Compost, two parts turfy loam, one part river sand, and a few crushed bones. Position, well-drained pots in light part of stove. Pot, Feb., burying bulb about two-thirds of its depth. Water freely from time growth begins (about Feb.) until Sept., when keep quite dry. Apply liquid manure when flower spike shows. Top-dress large bulbs annually and repot every three or four years only. Temp., Feb. to Sept. 65° to 75° ; Sept. to Feb. 50° to 55°.

PROPAGATION : By seeds sown $\frac{1}{16}$ in. deep in well-drained pots of sandy loam in temp. 65° to 70° in March, placing seedlings singly in 2 in. pots, and keeping them moderately moist all the year round for three years ; by offsets, treated as old bulbs. Seedlings are six to seven years before they flower.

SPECIES CULTIVATED : S. formosissima (Syn. Amaryllis formosissima), crimson, June, 2 ft., Mexico and Guatemala.

Spring Beauty (*Claytonia virginica*)—See Claytonia.

Spring Bell (*Sisyrinchium grandiflorum*)—See Sisyrinchium.

Spring Bitter Vetch (*Lathyrus vernus*)—See Lathyrus.

Spring Crocus (*Crocus vernus*)—See Crocus.

Spring-flowering Squill (*Scilla verna*)—See Scilla.

Spring Gentian (*Gentiana verna*)—See Gentian.

Spring Meadow Saffron (*Bulbocodium vernum*)—See Bulbocodium.

Spring Satin-flower (*Sisyrinchium grandiflorum*)—See Sisyrinchium.

Spring Snowflake (*Leucojum vernum*)—See Leucojum.

Spring Star-flower (*Brodiæa uniflora*)—See Brodiæa.

Spruce (*Picea excelsa*)—See Picea.

Spurge—See Euphorbia.

Spurge Flax (*Daphne mezereum*)—See Daphne.

Spurge Laurel (*Daphne laureola*)—See Daphne.

Spur Valerian (*Centranthus ruber*)—See Centranthus.

Squash—See Cucurbita.

Squaw-root (*Caulophyllum thalictroides*)—See Caulophyllum.

Squill—See Scilla and Urginea.

Squinancy-wort (*Asperula cyananchica*)—See Asperula.

Squirrel's-foot Fern (*Davallia bullata*)—See Davallia.

Squirrel-tail Grass (*Hordeum jubatum*)—See Hordeum.

Stachys (Woundwort ; Chinese Artichoke)—Ord. Labiatæ. Hardy and half-hardy perennials and tuberous-rooted vegetables. First introduced 1782.

CULTURE OF CHINESE ARTICHOKE : Soil, ordinary, deeply dug. Position, sunny. Plant tubers 9 in. apart, 4 in. to 6 in. deep in rows 18 in. asunder in March or April. Stir surface of soil between rows frequently. No earthing up required. Lift tubers in autumn as required for use. Cover surface of ground in severe weather.

CULTURE OF HARDY PERENNIALS : Soil, ordinary. Position, warm, sheltered border for S. coccinea ; edgings to borders or beds for S. lanata ; well-drained sunny rock gardens for S. corsica and S. lavandulæfolia. Plant, autumn or spring.

PROPAGATION : By division in autumn or spring.

SPECIES CULTIVATED : S. coccinea, scarlet, summer, 2 ft., Mexico ; corsica, cream and pink, summer, 1 in., Corsica and Sardinia ; grandiflora (Syn. Betonica grandiflora), violet, May to July, 1 ft., Asia Minor ; lanata (Lamb's Ear), leaves white and woolly, 1 ft., Caucasus ; lavandulæfolia, purplish rose, July to Aug., 6 in., Caucasus and Asia Minor ; Sieboldii (Syn. S. tuberifera), pink, summer, 1 ft., roots white, spiral in shape, and edible, Japan (Chinese Artichoke).

Stachyurus—Ord. Ternstromiaceæ. Half-hardy deciduous flowering shrubs. First introduced 1864.

CULTURE : Soil, peat, leaf-mould, and loam. Position, sheltered shrubberies. Plant, Nov. to Feb.

PROPAGATION : By cuttings with a heel removed in July and inserted in sandy soil under bell-glass in gentle bottom heat.

SPECIES CULTIVATED : S. chinensis, pale yellow, Feb. to March, 6 to 12 ft., China ; træcox, pale yellow, Feb., 5 to 10 ft., Japan.

Staff-tree (*Celastrus scandens*)—See Celastrus.

Stag's-horn Fern (*Platycerium alcicorne*)—See Platycerium.

Stag's-horn Moss (*Lycopodium clavatum*)—See Lycopodium.

Stag's-horn Rockfoil (*Saxifraga trifurcata*)—See Saxifraga.

Stag's-horn Sumach (*Rhus typhina*)—See Rhus.

Stanhopea—Ord. Orchidaceæ. Stove epiphytal orchids. First introduced 1824.
CULTURE : Compost, two parts fresh sphagnum moss, one part lumps of turfy peat and charcoal. Position, teak baskets suspended from roof. Plant, Feb., March, or April. Water copiously March to Sept., moderately Sept. to Nov., keep almost dry remainder of year. Syringe foliage daily, summer. Shade from sun. Temp., May to Sept. 70° to 85° ; Sept. to May 60° to 70°. Growing period, spring and summer ; resting period, winter. Flowers appear at base of matured pseudo-bulbs.

PROPAGATION : By division of pseudo-bulbs in spring.
SPECIES CULTIVATED : S. bucephalus, yellow and crimson, very fragrant, Aug., 1 to 2 ft., Peru and Mexico ; devoniensis, cream, yellow, purple, and crimson, fragrant, July, Peru ; eburnea, white and purple, June, Brazil ; insignis, yellow and purple, fragrant, Aug., S. America ; oculata, yellow, lilac, purple, white, and crimson, summer, Mexico ; tigrina, orange, yellow, and purple, fragrant, summer, Mexico ; Wardii, yellow, orange, and crimson, fragrant, summer, Guatemala.

Stanleya—Ord. Cruciferæ. Hardy perennial herb. First introduced 1816.
CULTURE : Soil, ordinary. Position, sunny border. Plant, Oct. or April.
PROPAGATION : By seeds sown in gentle heat in spring, planting out in May or June ; also by division of the roots in Oct. or March.
SPECIES CULTIVATED : S. pinnatifida, yellow, summer, 4 ft., California.

Stapelia (Carrion Flower ; Toad Flower ; Star-fish Flower)—Ord. Asclepiadaceæ. Greenhouse evergreen succulent-stemmed plants. First introduced 1790. Flowers, disagreeably scented.

CULTURE : Compost, two parts sandy loam, one part broken rubbish or old mortar, and one part sand. Position, well-drained pots close to glass in light, sunny green-house. No shade required. Pot, March or April. Water moderately April to Oct., keep nearly dry remainder of year. Temp., Oct. to March 40° to 50° ; March to Oct. 55° to 75°. Repot only when absolutely necessary. Top-dress annually in March with compost of two parts well-decayed cow dung and one part sandy loam.

PROPAGATION : By cuttings of stems exposed to air on shelf in greenhouse for two or three days, then inserted singly in 2 in. pots half filled with drainage, remainder with sand and brick rubbish ; spring.

SPECIES CULTIVATED : S. Asterias (Star-fish Flower), violet, yellow, and purple, summer, 6 in ; bufonia (Toad Flower), orange and brown, summer, 6 in. ; gigantea, yellow, red, brown, and purple, summer, 6 in. ; grandiflora, purple, autumn, 1 ft. ; variegata, greenish yellow and purplish brown, Aug., 4 to 6 in. All natives of S. Africa.

Staphylea (Bladder Nut)—Ord. Staphyleaceæ. Hardy deciduous flowering shrubs. First introduced 1640.
CULTURE : Soil, moist, loamy. Position, sunny borders or shrubberies. Plant, Oct. to Feb. Prune straggling shoots moderately close immediately after flowering. CULTURE OF S. COLCHICA FOR FORCING : Compost, two parts sandy loam, one part leaf-mould. Pot, Oct. to Jan. Place in sheltered position outdoors, or in cold frame until Jan., then remove into forcing house, or end of Jan. into cold green-house. Temp., 65° to 75°. Water moderately when first placed in heat, afterwards more freely. Syringe daily until leaves expand. Transfer to cold frame after flowering. Harden and stand outdoors, May to Oct.
PROPAGATION : By seeds sown in sandy soil in sheltered position outdoors in Sept. or Oct. ; cuttings of firm shoots, 6 to 8 in. long, inserted in sandy soil in cold frame or in sheltered corner outdoors in Sept. ; layering shoots, Sept. or Oct. ; suckers removed and planted, Oct. to Feb.
SPECIES CULTIVATED : S. colchica, white, summer, 6 to 10 ft., Caucasus ; Coulom-bieri, white, May, 8 to 12 ft., hybrid, and its variety grandiflora (large flowered) ; pinnata (St. Anthony's Nut), white, May, 8 to 15 ft., S. Europe.

Star Aniseed-tree (*Illicium anisatum*)—See Illicium.

Star Apple (*Chrysophyllum Cainito*)—See Chrysophyllum.

Star Capsicum (*Solanum capsicastrum*)—See Solanum.

Starch Hyacinth (*Muscari racemosum*)—See Muscari.

Star-fish Flower (*Stapelia Asterias*)—See Stapelia.

Star-flower (*Trientalis europæa*)—See Trientalis.

Star-flowered Lily of the Valley (*Smilacina stellata*)—See Smilacina.

Star Grass—See Hypoxis.

Star Hyacinth (*Scilla amœna*)—See Scilla.

Star of Bethlehem (*Ornithogalum umbellatum*)—See Ornithogalum.

Star Pine (*Pinus Pinaster*)—See Pinus.

Star Tulip—See Calochortus.

Star Windflower (*Anemone hortensis*)—See Anemone.

Star-wort—See Aster.

Statice—See Limonium.

Stauntonia—Ord. Berberidaceæ. Half-hardy evergreen climbing shrub. First introduced 1876.
CULTURE : Soil, deep, sandy loam. Position, S. wall or trellis in southern counties ; trained up trellis in conservatories or unheated greenhouses. Plant, Sept., Oct., March, or April. Prune trailing shoots not required to produce flowers following season back to two-thirds of their length in autumn.
PROPAGATION : By cuttings of firm young shoots inserted in sandy soil under bell-glass in shady position outdoors in summer.
SPECIES CULTIVATED : S. hexaphylla, white, tinged violet, April, 10 to 20 ft., China and Japan. See also the genus Holbœllia.

Steeple Bells (*Campanula pyramidalis*)—See Campanula.

Stellaria—Ord. Caryophyllaceæ. Hardy perennial with golden foliage ; used for carpet bedding.
CULTURE : Soil, ordinary. Position, as edgings to or bands in summer beds. Plant in May.
PROPAGATION : By division in autumn.
SPECIES CULTIVATED : S. graminea aurea, 3 in.

Stenactis—See Erigeron speciosus.

Stenandrium—Ord. Acanthaceæ. Stove flowering perennial. Orn. foliage. First introduced 1891.
CULTURE : Compost, equal parts peat, leaf-mould, loam, and sand. Position, well-drained pots in light stove Sept. to June, sunny frame June to Sept. Pot, March or April. Water moderately in winter, freely other times. Temp., Sept. to March 55° to 65°; March to June 65° to 75°. Prune shoots to within 1 in. of base after flowering. Apply liquid manure occasionally to plants in flower.
PROPAGATION : By cuttings of young shoots inserted in sandy peat under bell-glass in temp. 75°, March to July.
SPECIES CULTIVATED : S. Lindeni, yellow, leaves dark green above veined with white or yellow-purple beneath, 6 to 12 in., Peru. See also Eranthemum.

Stenanthium—Ord. Liliaceæ. Hardy perennials. First introduced 1846.
CULTURE : Soil, sandy loam and peat. Position, well-drained partially shaded beds or borders. Plant, Oct. to Nov. or March to April.
PROPAGATION : By seeds sown in pans in cool greenhouse or frame during March or April; offsets, detached at planting time.
SPECIES CULTIVATED : S. angustifolium, greenish yellow, June to July, 2 to 3 ft., N. America; occidentale, purple, summer, N.W. America; robustum, white, summer, 4 to 5 ft., N. America.

Stenotaphrum (Variegated Grass)—Ord. Gramineæ. Greenhouse orn.-leaved grass. First introduced 1874. Leaves, narrow, grass-like, striped with yellow.
CULTURE : Compost, equal parts peat, loam, leaf-mould, and sand or Jadoo fibre. Position, warm and moist part of greenhouse. Pot, March. Water copiously March to Sept., fairly freely Sept. to March. Temp., Sept. to March 50° to 55°; March to Sept. 55° to 65°.
PROPAGATION : By cuttings of shoots or by division of roots in spring.
SPECIES CULTIVATED : S. glabrum variegatum, 1 ft., Carolina.

Stephanandra—Ord. Rosaceæ. Hardy deciduous orn.-leaved shrubs. First introduced 1872.
CULTURE : Soil, moist loam. Position, in groups on the lawn, in the wild garden, or in the shrubbery. Plant in autumn.
PROPAGATION : By suckers or divisions; also by cuttings in summer under bell-glass.
SPECIES CULTIVATED : S. flexuosa, greenish white, June, fern-like foliage, 4 to 8 ft., Japan and Corea; Tanakæ, yellowish white, June to July, foliage turns orange in autumn, 4 to 6 ft., Japan.

Stephanotis (Clustered Wax-flower; Madagascar Chaplet Flower; Madagascar Jasmine)—Ord. Asclepiadaceæ. Stove evergreen twining shrubs. First introduced 1839.
CULTURE : Compost, equal parts good, light, fibrous loam and peat and one part equal proportions leaf-mould, well-decayed manure, and coarse silver sand. Position, pots, tubs, or beds, well drained, with shoots trained to wire trellis or up rafters of stove. Pot or plant, Feb. or March. Shade from sun. Water copiously March to Oct., moderately afterwards. Syringe daily March to Oct., except when in bloom. Apply stimulants once a week to healthy established plants between May and Sept. Prune straggling shoots in moderately close and thin out weak shoots freely, Jan. or Feb. Temp., March to Oct. 70° to 85°; Oct. to March 55° to 65°.
PROPAGATION : By cuttings of the shoots of the previous year's growth inserted singly in 2 in. pots, filled with equal parts sand, peat, and loam, placed under bell-glass in temp. 65° to 75° in spring.
SPECIES CULTIVATED : S. floribunda, white, fragrant, spring and summer, 10 to 15 ft., Madagascar, and its variety Elvastoni, a dwarfer and more free-flowering form.

Sterculia—Ord. Sterculiaceæ. Half-hardy orn. tree. Evergreen. First introduced 1757.
CULTURE : Soil, deep, loamy. Position, as specimens in sheltered gardens in

southern counties or planted in borders in large conservatories. Plant, Nov. to Feb.
PROPAGATION : By cuttings of ripened wood in frame during Sept. or Oct.
SPECIES CULTIVATED : S. platanifolia, yellow, handsome lobed foliage, to 60 ft.,
China.

Sternbergia (Winter Daffodil ; Yellow Star-flower)—Ord. Amaryllidaceæ.
First introduced 1596. Leaves produced usually late in autumn or early in spring
after flowering.
CULTURE : Soil, deep, fairly dry, good ordinary. Position, sunny sheltered border.
Plant bulbs, Oct. or Nov., 4 to 6 in. deep and 2 or 3 in. apart. Plant surface of
soil over bulbs with Saxifraga hypnoides or Sedum acre to form green carpet and
afford protection. Lift and replant when bulbs show signs of deterioration. May
also be grown in pots in cold greenhouse as advised for Amaryllis belladonna.
PROPAGATION : By offsets, removed and planted Oct. or Nov.
SPECIES CULTIVATED : S. lutea (Syn. Amaryllis lutea), yellow, Oct., 6 to 8 in.,
Mediterranean Region.

Stevensonia—Ord. Palmaceæ. Stove orn. foliage palm. First introduced 1865.
Leaves, once divided, wedge-shaped, green.
CULTURE : Compost, two parts fibrous peat, one part equal proportions charcoal,
turfy loam, and sand. Position, moist, shady part of stove. Pot, Feb. or March.
Syringe freely twice daily Feb. to Oct., once daily afterwards. Water freely at all
times. Shade and moist atmosphere essential. Temp., March to Oct. 70° to 85° ;
Oct. to March 65° to 75°.
PROPAGATION : By seeds sown 1 in. deep in peat and loam in small pots in temp.
75° to 85°, spring.
SPECIES CULTIVATED : S. grandiflora, 20 to 40 ft., Seychelles.

Stevia—Ord. Compositæ. Half-hardy herbaceous perennials. First introduced
1816.
CULTURE : Soil, sandy loam. Position, well-drained sheltered borders. Protect
with litter during the winter. Plant. Oct. to Nov. or March to April.
PROPAGATION : By division in spring.
SPECIES CULTIVATED : S. ovata, white, Aug., 2 ft., Mexico ; ivæfolia, deep rose,
summer, 1½ to 2 ft., Mexico. The plant commonly listed as S. serrata is Piqueria
trinervia, *q.v.*

Stewartia—See Stuartia.

Stigmaphyllon (Golden Vine)—Ord. Malpighiaceæ. Stove evergreen climbing
shrubs. First introduced 1796.
CULTURE : Compost, equal parts loam, leaf-mould, peat, and sand. Position, well-
drained pots, with shoots trained up roofs or round trellis. Pot, Feb. or March.
Prune away weak growths and shorten strong ones moderately, Jan. Water
freely March to Sept., moderately afterwards. Syringe daily in summer. Temp.,
March to Sept. 70° to 85° ; Sept. to March 55° to 65°.
PROPAGATION : By cuttings of firm shoots inserted singly in small pots of sandy
soil under bell-glass in temp. 65° to 75°, spring or summer.
SPECIES CULTIVATED : S. ciliatum, yellow, June to Sept., 8 to 10 ft., Brazil ; littorale,
yellow, autumn, 15 to 20 ft., Brazil.

Stingless Nettle—See Pilea.

Stinking Cedar (*Torreya taxifolia*)—See Torreya.

Stinking Gladwyn (*Iris fœtidissima*)—See Iris.

Stinking Hellebore (*Helleborus fœtidus*)—See Helleborus.

Stipa (Feather Grass)—Ord. Gramineæ. Hardy perennial flowering grasses.
Inflorescence borne in feathery panicles ; summer.
CULTURE : Soil, ordinary. Position, dryish sunny borders for S. pennata and
S. tenacissima ; pots in unheated greenhouse for S. elegantissima. Plant or pot,
March or April. Gather inflorescence for drying for winter decoration in July.
PROPAGATION : By seeds sown ¼ in. deep in shallow boxes or pots filled with light

soil placed in temp. of 55° to 65°, Feb. or March, hardening off seedlings, and planting outdoors, May or June ; or by sowing similar depth in ordinary soil in sunny position outdoors in April ; also by division of roots in March or April.
SPECIES CULTIVATED : S. elegantissima, 3 ft., Australia ; pennata, 2 ft., Europe ; tenacissima (Esparto Grass), 3 ft., Spain and N. Africa.

Stock Gilliflower (*Matthiola incana*)—See Matthiola.

Stokesia (Stokes' Aster)—Ord. Compositæ. Hardy perennial herb. First introduced 1766.
CULTURE : Soil, ordinary. Position, sunny well-drained borders. Plant, April. Protect in winter by covering with hand-light in cold districts. Plants may be lifted in Sept., placed in pots, and removed to greenhouse for flowering during autumn and winter, afterwards planting outdoors following April.
PROPAGATION : By division of roots, March or April.
SPECIES CULTIVATED : S. cyanea, blue, Aug., 18 in., N. America.

Stonecrop (*Sedum acre*)—See Sedum.

Stone Fern (*Asplenium Ceterach*)—See Asplenium.

Stone Pine (*Pinus cembra*)—See Pinus.

Storax-plant (*Styrax officinalis*)—See Styrax.

Stranvœsia—Ord. Rosaceæ. Half-hardy evergreen trees and shrubs. First introduced 1828.
CULTURE : Soil, sandy loam. Sheltered shrubberies in southern gardens or pots and borders in greenhouses or conservatories.
PROPAGATION : By cuttings of half-ripened shoots in sandy soil under bell-glass in gentle bottom heat.
SPECIES CULTIVATEI : S. glaucescens, white, July, 15 to 20 ft., Himalayas ; davidiana, white, June, to 20 ft., China, and its variety undulata (leaves waved at margins).

Stratiotes (Water Soldier ; Crab's Claw)—Ord. Hydrocharidaceæ. Hardy aquatic perennial.
CULTURE : Soil, ordinary. Position, shallow lakes or ponds. Plant, March or April, enclosing roots and small quantity of mould in pieces of old sacking tied securely round base of stem and dropped into water where required to grow.
PROPAGATION : By division in spring.
SPECIES CULTIVATED : S. aloides, white, June, 1 to 2 ft., Britain.

Strawberry—See Fragaria.

Strawberry-raspberry (*Rubus rosæfolius*)—See Rubus.

Strawberry Tree (*Arbutus unedo*)—See Arbutus.

Strelitzia (Bird of Paradise Flower ; Bird's Tongue Flower)—Ord. Musaceæ. Greenhouse orn. foliage and flowering perennials. First introduced 1773.
CULTURE : Compost, two parts loam, one part peat, and half a part silver sand. Position, pots or bed in sunny part of warm greenhouse. Pot or plant, Feb. or March. Water copiously April to Sept., moderately Sept. to Nov., keep nearly dry afterwards. No shade required. Temp., March to Oct. 65° to 75° ; Oct. to March 55° to 65°.
PROPAGATION : By seeds sown in compost of leaf-mould, peat, and loam in temp. of 65° to 75°, spring ; offsets or division of old plants, Feb. or March.
SPECIES CULTIVATED : S. augusta, white and purple, spring, to 18 ft., S. Africa ; Nicolai, white and blue, May, to 25 ft., S. Africa ; Reginæ, orange and blue, spring, 3 to 4 ft., S. Africa ; Reginæ citrina, yellow and blue.

Streptocarpus (Cape Primrose)—Ord. Gesneriaceæ. Greenhouse herbaceous perennials. First introduced 1824.
CULTURE : Compost, two parts loam, one part of equal proportions of leaf-mould, decayed manure, and silver sand. Position, pots in light greenhouse. Pot, March

or April. Temp., 40° to 50° Oct. to April ; 55° to 65° April to Oct. Shade from sun. Water freely April to Oct., keep nearly dry afterwards. Apply weak stimulants when plants are in flower. Admit air freely in summer. Cold, shady frame good position for young plants during summer.

PROPAGATION : By seeds sown in well-drained pots, pans, or boxes with equal parts of finely-sifted loam, leaf-mould, peat, and sand. Cover the seeds thinly with a sprinkle of fine silver sand. Moisten the soil by holding the pot, pan, or box nearly to its rim or edge in tepid water. Place a pane of glass over top of pot, pan, or box and put in a temp. 55° to 65°. Transplant seedlings as soon as large enough to handle 1 in. apart in above compost, in pans or pots, and when seedlings touch each other place them singly in 3 in. pots, and ultimately into 5 or 6 in. pots. Seeds sown in Feb. will produce plants for flowering following July ; in March or April, following Aug. or Sept.

SPECIES CULTIVATED : S. Dunnii, rose, summer, 12 to 18 in., S. Africa ; Rexii, blue, summer, 6 to 12 in., S. Africa ; Wendlandii, blue, spring, 18 to 30 in., S. Africa. Practically all the varieties cultivated to-day are hybrids between these species.

Streptosolen—Ord. Solanaceæ. Greenhouse evergreen flowering shrub. First introduced 1847.

CULTURE : Compost, two parts sandy loam, one part leaf-mould, and half a part silver sand. Position, well-drained pots close to glass in light, sunny greenhouse. Pot, Feb. to April. Prune shoots moderately close after flowering. Water freely April to Oct., moderately afterwards. Apply weak stimulants occasionally during summer. Shade only from bright sunshine. Temp., March to Oct. 60° to 70° ; Oct. to March 50° to 60°.

PROPAGATION : By cuttings inserted in light, sandy soil under bell-glass in temp. 55° to 65°, spring or summer.

SPECIES CULTIVATED : S. Jamesoni, orange, summer, 4 to 6 ft., Colombia.

Striped Squill (*Puschkinia scilloides*)—See Puschkinia.

Strobilanthes (Cone-head)—Ord. Acanthaceæ. Stove evergreen flowering shrubs. First introduced 1825.

CULTURE : Compost, equal parts loam and leaf-mould with a little silver sand. Pot, March or April. Position, well-drained pots in moist, light part of humid greenhouse. Temp., March to Sept. 75° to 85° ; Sept. to March 60° to 65°. Prune shoots in closely, Feb. Water moderately Sept. to April, freely other times. Use syringe frequently during the growing season. Apply liquid manure twice a week to plants in flower.

PROPAGATION : By cuttings of moderately firm shoots, 2 to 3 in. long, inserted in light, sandy compost under bell-glass in temp. 80°, Feb. to April.

SPECIES CULTIVATED : S. anisophylla (Syn. Goldfussia anisophylla), lavender blue, Oct. to March, 1 to 3 ft., Himalayas ; dyerianus, violet and blue, autumn, 3 ft., Burma ; isophyllus (Syn. Goldfussia isophylla), blue and white, winter, 2 to 3 ft., India. See also Ruellia.

Struthiopteris—See Onoclea.

Stuartia—Ord. Ternstrœmiaceæ. Hardy deciduous flowering shrubs. First introduced 1785.

CULTURE : Soil, two parts moist, sandy loam, one part peat. Position, open, sunny borders sheltered on N. and E. by walls, trees, or shrubs. Plant, Oct. to Feb.

PROPAGATION : By cuttings of firm shoots inserted in sandy soil under hand-light in sheltered position outdoors in autumn ; layering shoots in Sept. or Oct. ; seeds sown ½ in. deep in sandy peat in temp. 75° in March.

SPECIES CULTIVATED : S. Malachodendron (Syn. S. virginica), white, purple anthers, July to Aug., to 15 ft., South-eastern U.S.A. ; pentagyna, cream, summer, to 15 ft., Southern U.S.A. ; pseudo-camellia, white, orange anthers, July to Aug., to 50 ft., Japan ; sinensis, white, fragrant, July to Aug., to 30 ft., China.

Stud-flower (*Helonias bullata*)—See Helonias.

Sturt's Desert Pea (*Clianthus Dampieri*)—See Clianthus.

Stylophorum (Celandine Poppy)—Ord. Papaveraceæ. **Hardy perennial herb.** First introduced 1854.

CULTURE : Soil, ordinary moist. Position, partially shaded beds or borders. **Plant,** March or April.

PROPAGATION : By seeds sown ¼ in. deep in ordinary soil in sunny position outdoors, March or April ; division of roots, March.

SPECIES CULTIVATED : S. diphyllum, yellow, June, 12 to 18 in., N.W. America.

Styrax (Storax)—Ord. Styracaceæ. Hardy deciduous flowering shrubs. **First** introduced 1597.

CULTURE : Soil, light, peaty. Position, sunny borders or shrubberies, or against S. walls. Plant, Oct. to Feb.

PROPAGATION : By layering shoots in spring or autumn.

SPECIES CULTIVATED : S. dasyantha, white, July, 15 to 20 ft., W. China ; obassia, white, June, 20 to 30 ft., Japan ; japonicum, white, June, 10 to 25 ft., Japan.

Sugar Cane (*Saccharum officinarum*)—See Saccharum.

Sugar Maple (*Acer saccharinum*)—See Acer.

Sugar Pea (*Pisum japonicum* var.)—See Pisum.

Sumach—See Rhus.

Summer Cypress (*Kochia scoparia*)—See Kochia.

Summer Heliotrope—See Tournefortia.

Summer Pheasant's-eye (*Adonis æstivalis*)—See Adonis.

Summer Savory (*Satureia hortensis*)—See Satureia.

Summer Snowdrop (*Leucojum æstivum*)—See Leucojum.

Summer Snowflake (*Leucojum æstivum*)—See Leucojum.

Sun Cress—See Heliophila.

Sundew (*Drosera rotundifolia*)—See Drosera.

Sun-drops (*Œnothera fruticosa*)—See Œnothera.

Sunflower (*Helianthus annuus*)—See Helianthus.

Sun-plant (*Portulaca grandiflora*)—See Portulaca.

Sun-rose—See Helianthemum.

Supple Jack (*Berchemia volubilis*)—See Berchemia.

Surinam Tea-plant (*Lantana Camara*)—See Lantana.

Sutherlandia (Cape Bladder Senna)—Ord. Leguminosæ. **Half-hardy** evergreen flowering shrub. First introduced 1683.

CULTURE : Compost, equal parts loam, peat, and silver sand. Position, against S. walls outdoors S. and S.W. England only, or in pots in cold greenhouse any part of kingdom. Plant, Sept., Oct., or April. Pot, March. Water plants in pots freely April to Sept., moderately afterwards. Prune, April, shortening straggling shoots only.

PROPAGATION : By seeds sown in compost of equal parts peat, loam, leaf-mould, and sand, lightly cover with fine soil, and place in temp. of 45° to 55° in spring ; by cuttings of young shoots in May under bell-glass or hand-light.

SPECIES CULTIVATED : S. frutescens, scarlet, June, 4 ft., S. Africa.

Swainsonia (Darling River Pea)—Ord. Leguminosæ. Greenhouse evergreen flowering shrubs. First introduced 1800.

CULTURE : Compost, two parts fibrous loam, one part peat, and half a part silver sand. Position, well-drained pots in light, sunny greenhouse. Pot, Feb. or March. Water freely March to Oct., moderately afterwards. Apply weak stimulants occasionally in summer. Remove to cold frame or pit, June ; replace in greenhouse, Sept. Temp., Sept. to March 35° to 45° ; March to June 55° to 65°.

PROPAGATION : By seeds soaked for about an hour in tepid water, then sown ⅛ in. deep in light soil in temp. 55° to 65°, March or April ; cuttings of young shoots, 2 to 3 in. long, inserted in silver sand under bell-glass in cool, shady part of greenhouse in summer.

SPECIES CULTIVATED : S. galegiefolia, reddish purple, summer, 3 to 4 ft., Australia, and its varieties alba (white), coronillifolia (violet), and rosea (pink).

Swainson's Pea—See Swainsonia.

Swallow-wort (*Chelidonium majus* and *Asclepias tuberosa*)—See Chelidonium and Asclepias.

Swamp Bay (*Magnolia glauca*)—See Magnolia.

Swamp Dogwood (*Ptelea trifoliata*)—See Ptelea.

Swamp Globe-flower (*Cephalanthus occidentalis*)—See Cephalanthus.

Swamp Hellebore (*Veratrum viride*)—See Veratrum.

Swamp Honeysuckle (*Rhododendron viscosum*)—See Rhododendron.

Swamp Laurel—See Kalmia.

Swamp Lily (*Lilium superbum*)—See Lilium.

Swamp Sunflower (*Helenium autumnale*)—See Helenium.

Swan River Daisy (*Brachycome iberidifolia*)—See Brachycome.

Swan River Everlasting (*Helipterum Manglesii*)—See Helipterum.

Swan River Fern Palm (*Macrozamia Fraseri*)—See Macrozamia.

Swan's Neck Orchid—See Cycnoches.

Swede (*Brassica campestris napobrassica*)—See Brassica.

Swedish Turnips—See Swede.

Sweet Alyssum (*Alyssum maritimum*)—See Alyssum.

Sweet Amber (*Hypericum Androsæmum*)—See Hypericum.

Sweet Basil (*Ocimum Basilicum*)—See Ocimum.

Sweet Bay-tree (*Laurus nobilis*)—See Laurus.

Sweet Briar (*Rosa rubiginosa*)—See Rosa.

Sweet Buck-eye (*Æsculus octandra*)—See Æsculus.

Sweet Cicely (*Myrrhis odorata*)—See Myrrhis.

Sweet Fennel (*Fœniculum officinale*)—See Fœniculum.

Sweet Fern (*Comptonia asplenifolia*)—See Comptonia.

Sweet Flag (*Acorus calamus*)—See Acorus.

Sweet Gale (*Myrica Gale*)—See Myrica.

Sweet Gum-tree (*Liquidambar styraciflua*)—See Liquidambar.

Sweet John (*Dianthus barbatus*)—See Dianthus.

Sweet Marjoram (*Origanum marjorana*)—See Origanum.

Sweet Maudlin (*Achillea Ageratum*)—See Achillea.

Sweet Orange-tree (*Citrus aurantium*)—See Citrus.

Sweet Pea—See Lathyrus.

Sweet Pepper Bush (*Clethra alnifolia*)—See Clethra.

Sweet Potato (*Ipomæa batatus*)—See Ipomæa.

Sweet Rocket (*Hesperis matronalis*)—See Hesperis.

Sweet Scabious (*Scabiosa atropurpurea*)—See Scabiosa.

Sweet-scented Bramble (*Rubus odoratus*)—See Rubus.

Sweet-scented Clematis (*Clematis flammula*)—See Clematis.

Sweet-scented Crab (*Pyrus coronaria*)—See Pyrus.

Sweet-scented Olive-tree (*Osmanthus fragrans*)—See Osmanthus.

Sweet-scented Tobacco (*Nicotiana alata grandiflora*)—See Nicotiana.

Sweet-scented Verbena (*Lippia citriodora*)—See Lippia.

Sweet-scented Water Lily (*Nymphæa odorata*)—See Nymphæa.

Sweet Sedge (*Acorus calamus*)—See Acorus.

Sweet-sop (*Anona squamosa*)—See Anona.

Sweet Sultan (*Centaurea moschata*)—See Centaurea.

Sweet Vernal Grass (*Anthoxanthum odoratum*)—See Anthoxanthum.

Sweet Violet (*Viola odorata*)—See Viola.

Sweet William (*Dianthus barbatus*)—See Dianthus.

Sweet William Catchfly (*Silene armeria*)—See Silene.

Sweet Woodruff (*Asperula odorata*)—See Asperula.

Swertia (Marsh Fel-wort)—Ord. Gentianaceæ. Hardy perennial herb.
CULTURE : Soil, equal parts peat and leaf-mould. Position, moist rockeries or damp places. Plant, March to April. Water copiously in dry weather.
PROPAGATION : By seeds sown in well-drained pans filled with moist peat, placed in shady, cold frame, March or April, transplanting seedlings outdoors in June, and division of roots in March.
SPECIES CULTIVATED : S. perennis, blue, greyish purple, and black, 1 ft., N. Europe.

Swietenia (Mahogany Tree)—Ord. Meliaceæ. Stove evergreen tree of economic interest only. First introduced 1734.
CULTURE : Soil, sandy loam. Position, well-drained borders in heated greenhouse. Temp., March to Sept. 70° to 80° ; Sept. to March 55° to 60°. Water freely during growing season, moderately at other times. Plant, April.
PROPAGATION : By cuttings of ripened shoots under bell-glass in temp. 75°.
SPECIES CULTIVATED : S. Mahagoni, to 75 ft., W. Indies and S. Florida.

Swiss Chard, a variety of Leaf or Spinach Beet—See Beta.

Swiss Stone Pine (*Pinus Cembra*)—See Pinus.

Sword Lily—See Gladiolus.

Sycamore Tree (*Acer pseudo-platanus*)—See Acer.

Sydney Golden Wattle (*Acacia longifolia*)—See Acacia.

Symphoricarpus (Snow-berry Tree)—Ord. Caprifoliaceæ. Hardy deciduous shrubs. Flowering and berry-bearing. First introduced 1730. Flowers much sought after by bees. Berries, white, red ; autumn.
CULTURE : Soil, ordinary. Position, sunny or shady borders, copses, or woodlands. Plant, Oct. to Feb. Prune, Oct. to Feb., simply thinning out old or decayed wood.
PROPAGATION : By cuttings, 6 to 8 in. long, of firm wood inserted in ordinary soil in shady position outdoors, Oct. to Feb. ; suckers removed and planted, Oct. to Feb.
SPECIES CULTIVATED : S. occidentalis (Wolf Berry), pink, July, berries white, 4 to 6 ft., N. America ; orbiculatus, white, Aug. to Sept., berries purplish red, 3 to 7 ft., Eastern U.S.A. ; racemosus (Snow-berry), pink or rose, July, berries white, 8 to 10 ft., N. America.

Tacca cristata

Tagetes erecta hybrida
(African Marigold)

Tamarix pentandra
(Tamarisk)

Taxus baccata
(Common Yew)

Thalictrum aquilegifolium
(Meadow Rue)

Thalictrum dipterocarpum
(Meadow Rue)

Thalictrum minus adiantifolium

Thuya occidentalis

Thuya orientalis
(Chinese arbor-vitæ)

Thymus lanuginosus
(Garden Thyme)

Tigridia Pavonia
(Tiger Flower)

Trachelium cæruleum
(Blue Throat-wort)

Trachycarpus Fortunei
(Chusan Palm)

Tradescantia virginiana
(Spider-wort)

Trollius japonicus
(Globe Flower)

Tropæolum aduncum
(Canary Creeper)

Tulipa clusiana
(Lady Tulip)

Tulipa hybrida
(Cottage Tulip)

Symphyandra (Pendulous Bell-flower)—Ord. Campanulaceæ. Hardy perennials. First introduced 1823.
CULTURE : Soil, ordinary rich. Position, sunny well-drained borders or rockeries. Plant, Oct., Nov., March, or April.
PROPAGATION : By seeds sown $\frac{1}{16}$ in. deep in ordinary light, sandy soil outdoors, April to May ; cuttings of young shoots inserted in sandy soil in cold frame, March or April ; division of roots, March.
SPECIES CULTIVATED : S. Hofmani, white, summer, 1 to 2 ft., Bosnia ; pendula, straw yellow, summer, 9 to 12 in., Caucasus ; Wanneri, blue, summer, 6 in., S.E. Europe.

Symphytum (Comfrey)—Ord. Boraginaceæ. Hardy herbaceous perennials. Common Comfrey (S. officinale) not adapted for garden culture. First introduced 1799.
CULTURE : Soil, ordinary. Position, sunny or shady, moist borders or margins of water-courses or streams. Plant, Oct., Nov., March, or April. Lift, divide, or replant every three or four years.
PROPAGATION : By division of roots in spring.
SPECIES CULTIVATED : S. asperrimum aureo-variegatum, leaves variegated with yellow and green, 4 ft., Caucasus ; caucasicum, blue, May, 1½ to 3 ft., Caucasus ; officinale bohemicum, crimson, June, 3 ft., Europe ; officinale luteo-marginatum, leaves bordered with yellow.

Synthyris—Ord. Scrophulariaceæ. Hardy herbaceous perennial. First introduced 1885.
CULTURE : Soil, loamy. Position, partially shady beds or rock gardens. Plant, Oct. to Nov. or March to April. Water freely during summer months.
PROPAGATION : By division in spring or by seeds sown in sandy soil in pans in cold greenhouse or frame during March and April.
SPECIES CULTIVATED : S. reniformis, violet blue, May to June, 6 in., N. America.

Syrian Silk-plant (*Periploca græca*)—See Periploca.

Syringa (Lilac)—Ord. Oleaceæ. Hardy deciduous flowering shrubs. First introduced 1597.
CULTURE : Soil, ordinary good. Position, sunny borders or shrubberies. Plant, Oct. to Feb. Prune moderately after flowering (June), removing or shortening shoots that have flowered only. Allow no suckers to grow from roots. Apply house slops or liquid manure in summer to plants growing in poor soils.
POT CULTURE FOR FORCING : Compost, two parts good sandy loam, one part leaf-mould, and little sand. Pot, Oct. or Nov. Place plants after potting in sheltered corner outdoors, protecting pots from frost with litter until required for forcing. Transfer to temp. of 55°, Nov. to Feb. Syringe daily. Water moderately. Directly buds burst place in temp. of 60° to 65° ; when expanded replace in temp. of 55°. Prune shoots that have flowered to within 2 in. of base directly after blooming. Keep plants in heat until May, then gradually harden and plant outdoors. Plants must not be forced two years in succession. Lilacs may be grown in cold greenhouse for flowering in April and May. Place in greenhouse in Nov.
PROPAGATION : By seeds sown in sunny position outdoors in autumn or spring ; suckers removed and planted from Oct. to Feb.; layering shoots in spring ; choice varieties by budding on common species in July, or by grafting on common species in March or April ; by cuttings of nearly ripe shoots inserted in sandy soil in cold frame during Aug.
SPECIES CULTIVATED : S. chinensis (Rouen Lilac), violet, May, 10 to 15 ft., hybrid ; Emodi (Himalayan Lilac), purplish or white, June, 10 to 15 ft., Himalayas; japonica (Japanese Lilac), white, June to July, 20 to 30 ft., Japan ; Josikæa (Hungarian Lilac), bluish purple, May, 10 to 12 ft., Hungary ; Julianæ, violet, May, 4 to 6 ft., W. China ; Komarowi, lilac, May, 10 to 15 ft., China ; oblata, pale lilac, April to May, 10 to 12 ft., N. China ; pekinensis, white, June, to 20 ft., N. China, and its variety pendula (weeping) ; persica (Persian Lilac), lilac, May, 4 to 6 ft., Afghanistan, and its variety alba (white) ; reflexa, pink, June, to 12 ft., China ; Swenginzowi, pinkish lilac, June, to 10 ft. China, and its variety superba ; vulgaris

(Common Lilac), lilac, May, 15 to 20 ft., E. Europe; Wilsoni (Syn. S. tomentella), lilac or white, May, to 10 ft., China, requires sheltered position; Wolfii, lilac, May, to 20 ft., Manchuria and Corea. Also many charming varieties, for which see trade lists.

Syringa (*Philadelphus coronarius*)—See Philadelphus.

Tabernæmontana (Adam's Apple; East Indian Rose Bay)—Ord. Apocynaceæ. Stove evergreen flowering shrubs. First introduced 1770.
CULTURE: Compost, two parts sandy loam, one part fibry peat, half a part silver sand. Position, well-drained pots in light stove. Pot, Feb. to April. Prune straggling shoots moderately close immediately after flowering. Water freely March to Oct., moderately afterwards. Syringe daily March and until flowers appear. Temp., March to Sept. 70° to 80°; Sept. to March 65° to 75°.
PROPAGATION: By cuttings of ripe shoots, 2 to 3 in. long, inserted in small pots filled with sand under bell-glass in temp. 65° to 75° in Feb.
SPECIES CULTIVATED: T. coronaria, white, summer, 4 to 8 ft., India, and its varieties crispa (crisp petalled) and flore-pleno (double); grandiflora, yellow, summer, to 6 ft., Venezuela and Guiana; recurva (Syn. T. gratissima), yellowish white, June, 6 ft., Chittagong and Tenasserim.

Table Mountain Orchid (*Disa grandiflora*)—See Disa.
Table-shaped Houseleek (*Sempervivum tabuliforme*)—See Sempervivum.

Tacca—Ord. Taccaceæ. Stove perennial herbs. First introduced 1793.
CULTURE: Compost, equal parts loam, peat, and sand. Position, well-drained pots in warm greenhouse. Water freely during summer months, very little during winter. Temp., March to Sept. 75° to 85°; Sept. to March 60° to 65°. Pot, Feb. or March.
SPECIES CULTIVATED: T. cristata (Syn. Ataccia cristata), brownish purple, summer, purplish-green foliage, 2 ft., Malaya; pinnatifida, green and purple, June, 3 to 4 ft., Tropical Asia, Africa, and Australia. The tuberous roots of the latter species yield arrowroot.

Tacsonia (Blood-red Passion-flower; Van Volxem's Passion-flower)—Ord. Passifloræ. Greenhouse evergreen flowering climbers. First introduced 1815.
CULTURE: Compost, equal parts fibrous loam and peat, one fourth silver sand. Pot or plant, Feb. or March. Position, well-drained tubs or pots, or beds 18 in. deep and 2 ft. wide; shoots to be trained up rafters or walls; sunny. Prune, Feb., thinning out weak shoots and shortening strong ones one-third. Water copiously March to Sept., moderately afterwards. Syringe twice daily April to Sept. Apply stimulants occasionally to healthy plants when in flower only. Temp., March to Oct. 60° to 70°; Oct. to March 40° to 50°.
PROPAGATION: By seeds sown in pots of sandy soil in temp. 65° in Feb. or March; by cuttings of young shoots inserted in sandy soil under bell-glass in temp. 70°, June to July.
SPECIES CULTIVATED: T. exoniensis, red and pink, summer, 20 to 30 ft., hybrid; manicata, scarlet, autumn, 30 ft., Peru; mollissima, rose, summer, 20 to 30 ft., Andes; Van Volxemii, crimson, autumn, 30 ft., Colombia.

Tagetes (African Marigold; French Marigold; Mexican Marigold)—Ord. Compositæ. Half-hardy annuals. First introduced 1596.
CULTURE: Soil, ordinary, well enriched with decayed manure. Position, sunny borders for African Marigold; sunny beds or borders for French and Mexican Marigold; edgings to beds or borders for T. signata pumila. Sow seeds ⅛ in. deep in light soil in temp. 55° to 65° in March, or in unheated greenhouse in April. Transplant seedlings when three leaves form 3 in. apart in light soil in shallow boxes, or in bed of rich soil in cold frame, gradually harden off in May, and plant out in June. Plant African Marigolds in groups of three or six, or 16 in. apart in rows; French Marigolds singly, or in groups in borders, or 12 in. apart in rows; Dwarf Marigolds (T. signata pumila) 6 in. apart in rows. African Marigold for

exhibition to carry four blooms only. Thin shoots to four on each plant, each carrying one bloom. Water freely in dry weather. Apply stimulants occasionally to plants in flower. Suitable stimulants : (1) 1 oz. of Peruvian guano to a gallon of water. (2) ¼ oz. sulphate of ammonia to a gallon of water.
SPECIES CULTIVATED : T. erecta (African Marigold), yellow, summer, 2 to 3 ft., Mexico ; lucida (Mexican Marigold), yellow, summer, 1 ft., Mexico ; patula (French Marigold), orange, red, and brown, summer, 1 to 1½ ft., Mexico, and its variety nana (dwarf) ; signata, yellow, summer, 1 to 1¼ ft., Mexico, and its variety pumila (dwarf).

Tail Flower—See Anthurium.

Tamarind-tree (*Tamarindus indica*)—See Tamarindus.

Tamarindus (Tamarind Tree ; Indian Date)—Ord. Leguminosæ. Stove evergreen flowering tree. First introduced 1633.
CULTURE : Compost, two parts fibrous loam, one part sand. Position, large well-drained pots or tubs in lofty stove. Pot or plant, Feb. Water copiously April to Oct., moderately afterwards. Syringe daily April to Sept. Shade from sun. Temp., April to Oct. 70° to 85° ; Oct. to April 60° to 70°.
PROPAGATION : By seeds steeped for a few hours in tepid water and then sown ¼ in. deep in light soil in temp. 75° to 85° in spring ; cuttings of shoots inserted singly in small well-drained pots placed under bell-glass in temp. 65° to 75°, March to Aug.
SPECIES CULTIVATED : T. indica, pale yellow, summer, 40 to 80 ft., Tropics.

Tamarisk (*Tamarisk anglica*)—See Tamarix.

Tamarix (Tamarisk ; Manna Plant)—Ord. Tamaricaceæ. Hardy evergreen and deciduous shrubs. Flowering and orn. foliage.
CULTURE OF EVERGREEN AND DECIDUOUS SPECIES : Soil, ordinary or sandy. Position, shrubberies or hedges in seaside gardens, S. and S.W. England ; sunny banks or sheltered shrubberies in inland gardens south of the Trent. Plant, Sept. to April. Prune, Oct. to March, shortening straggling shoots only.
PROPAGATION : By cuttings of shoots, 4 to 6 in. long, inserted in sandy soil in sheltered position under hand-light or in cold frame, Sept. or Oct.
EVERGREEN SPECIES CULTIVATED : T. anglica (Common Tamarisk), white and pink, Aug. to Oct., 3 to 10 ft., Europe (Britain) ; gallica, pink, late summer and autumn, 10 to 30 ft., S. Europe.
DECIDUOUS SPECIES CULTIVATED ; T. hispida, pink, Aug. to Sept., 3 to 4 ft., Caspian Region, rather tender ; juniperina (Syn. T. chinensis), bright pink, May, 10 to 15 ft., N. China and Japan ; pentandra (Syn. T. hispida æstivalis), rosy pink, July to Aug., 12 to 15 ft., S.E. Europe and Asia Minor ; tetandra, pink, May, 10 to 15 ft., Mediterranean Region. See also Myricaria.

Tanacetum (Tansy ; Alecost)—Ord. Compositæ. Hardy herbaceous perennials.
CULTURE : Soil, ordinary. Position, sunny beds for T. vulgare ; open rock gardens for T. argenteum and T. Herderi. Plant T. vulgare 12 in. apart in rows 18 in. asunder in March or Oct. ; remove flower stems as they form ; replant every three or four years ; leaves aromatic, used for flavouring puddings, etc. and for garnishing.
PROPAGATION : By seeds sown outdoors in spring ; division of the roots in Oct. or March.
SPECIES CULTIVATED : T. argenteum, yellow, summer, silvery foliage, 9 in., Asia Minor ; Herderi, yellow, summer, silvery-white foliage, 9 in., Turkestan ; vulgare crispum, yellow, summer, 3 ft., Britain.

Tanakæa (Japanese Foam Flower)—Ord. Saxifragaceæ. Dwarf evergreen perennial with leathery-fringed rich green leaves.
CULTURE : Soil, light, containing plenty of humus. Position, woodland or partially shaded cool border. Plant in colonies in spring.
PROPAGATION : By division of tufts in March.
SPECIES CULTIVATED : T. radicans, white, April to June, 6 to 9 in., Japan.

Tangerine Orange-tree (*Citrus nobilis tangerana*)—See **Citrus.**

Tangerine Iris (*Iris tingitana*)—See Iris.

Tangier Pea (*Lathyrus rustingitana*)—See Lathyrus.

Tansy (*Tanacetum vulgare*)—See Tanacetum.

Tansy-leaved Hawthorn (*Cratægus tanacetifolia*)—See **Cratægus.**

Tape Grass (*Vallisneria spiralis*)—See Vallisneria.

Taraxacum (Dandelion)—Ord. Compositæ. Hardy perennial herb. Cultivated solely for its blanched leaves for saladings.

CULTURE : Soil, ordinary deep, free from recent manure. Position, sunny. Sow seeds 1 in. deep in drills 12 in. apart in April. Thin seedlings to 6 in. apart in rows in May Remove flower stems directly they form. Lift roots in Nov. and store in sand in cool place. Plant roots almost close together in boxes or large pots in ordinary soil. Cover pots, etc. to exclude light. Place in warm greenhouse between Nov. and April. Keep soil moist and cut leaves when 3 to 6 in. long for salads. Destroy roots afterwards. Make a fresh sowing annually.

SPECIES CULTIVATED : T. officinale, yellow, spring, Britain.

Taro-root—See Colocasia.

Tarragon (*Artemisia Dranunculus*)—See Artemisia.

Tartarian Honeysuckle (*Lonicera tartarica*)—See Lonicera.

Tasmanian Currant (*Coprosma Baueri*)—See Coprosma.

Tasmanian Heath—See Epacris.

Tasmanian Laurel (*Anopterus glandulosa*)—See Anopterus.

Tasmanian Tree Fern (*Dicksonia antarctica*)—See Dicksonia.

Tasmanian Water Pimpernel (*Samolus repens*)—See Samolus.

Tassel Cotton-grass (*Eriophorum polystachyon*)—See Eriophorum.

Tassel-flower (*Emilia flammea*)—See Emilia.

Tassel Hyacinth (*Muscari comosum*)—See Muscari.

Tawny Day-lily (*Hemerocallis fulva*)—See Hemerocallis.

Taxodium (Deciduous Cypress)—Ord. Coniferæ. Hardy deciduous coniferous trees. Orn. foliage. First introduced 1640. Leaves, feather-shaped, deciduous, bright green, changing to dull red in autumn. Habit, pyramidal when young ; broad, cedar-like when full grown.

CULTURE : Soil, moist loam. Position, margins of ponds and rivers or in damp places. Dry position quite unsuitable. Plant, Oct. to Feb.

PROPAGATION : By seeds sown ½ in. deep in pans of light soil in cold frame in April, transplanting seedlings singly into small pots following spring, and planting outdoors the year after ; cuttings of ripened shoots in shady, cold frame and sandy soil in Sept. or Oct., and kept moist ; layering branches in spring.

SPECIES CULTIVATED : T. distichum, 70 to 100 ft., S.W. States, and its variety pendulum (branches pendulous).

Taxus (Yew Tree)—Ord. Coniferæ. Hardy evergreen trees. Orn. foliage. Timber used for cabinet making, but too slow in growth to cultivate for that purpose. Leaves poisonous to cattle. Estimated average age, 1000 to 2000 years.

CULTURE : Soil, good deep ordinary, moist. Position, sunny or shady shrubberies for common kinds ; sunny shrubberies, lawns, or borders for variegated and Irish yews. Plant, Sept. to Nov., Feb. to May. Prune, April.

WINTER BEDDING : Variety best adapted for the purpose—T. baccata elegantissima. Plant, Oct. or Nov. Lift and replant in reserve border in May.

POT CULTURE : Most suitable kind—T. baccata elegantissima. Pot, Oct. or Nov. Compost, two parts good ordinary mould, one part leaf-mould. Water moderately Nov. to April, freely afterwards. Keep in cold greenhouse, balcony, or corridor, Oct. to May ; outdoors afterwards, pots plunged to rims in cinders or soil.

HEDGE CULTURE : Suitable kinds—Common, gold and silver striped, upright

English and Irish yews. Position, sunny. Soil, good moist ordinary, previously trenched three spits deep and 3 ft. wide. Plant, Oct., Nov., March, or April. Distance for planting : 12 in. for trees 18 in. high ; 18 in. for trees 3 ft. high ; 2 ft. for trees 3 ft. 6 in. to 5 ft. high. Prune, trim, or clip in April or Sept.

PROPAGATION : By seeds sown 1 in. deep in light soil outdoors in March, or ¼ in. deep in pans or boxes of light soil in cold frame or greenhouse in March, transplanting seedlings in nursery bed when large enough to handle ; by cuttings of shoots inserted in sandy soil under hand-light or in cold frame in Sept. ; grafting variegated kinds on common yew in March ; layering in Sept.

SPECIES CULTIVATED : T. baccata (Common Yew), 50 ft., Europe and N. Asia ; brevifolia, 20 to 50 ft., Western N. America ; canadensis (Canadian Yew), 4 to 6 ft., Canada ; cuspidata (Japanese Yew), 20 to 50 ft., Japan, and its variety compacta (shrubby). The following are varieties of the Common Yew : adpressa (8 ft.), aurea (leaves golden), Golden Yew ; Dovastoni (branchlets pendulous), and its variegated form aureo-variegata ; elegantissima, leaves edged with creamy white ; erecta (Fulham Yew), erect habit ; fastigiata (Irish Yew), columnar habit, and its variegated forms aurea and variegata ; nana, very dwarf ; and variegata (argentea), leaves variegated with white.

Tea-berry (*Gaultheria procumbens*)—See Gaultheria.

Teak (*Tectona grandis*)—See Tectona.

Tea-leaved Willow (*Salix phylicifolia*)—See Salix.

Tea-plant (*Camellia theifera*)—See Camellia.

Tea-scented Rose (*Rosa indica fragrans*)—See Rosa.

Tea Tree (*Lycium barbarum*)—See Lycium.

Tecoma (Trumpet Flower ; Moreton Bay Trumpet Jasmine)—Ord. Bignoniaceæ. Greenhouse and hardy evergreen climbing flowering shrubs. First introduced 1640.

CULTURE OF GREENHOUSE SPECIES : Compost, two parts loam, one part peat and silver sand. Position, large well-drained pots, or beds 3 ft. square, 18 in. deep, for one plant, in light, sunny greenhouse ; shoots trained up roof. Pot or plant, Feb. or March. Good drainage absolutely necessary. Prune away one-third of strong shoots, two-thirds of weak shoots, in Feb. Water copiously April to Oct., keep nearly dry Oct. to April. Apply weak stimulants occasionally to healthy established plants in summer. No shade required at any time. Admit air freely during summer and early autumn to thoroughly ripen wood for insuring abundance of flowers. Temp., April to Oct. 55° to 65° ; Oct. to April 40° to 50°.

CULTURE OF HARDY SPECIES : Soil, two parts loam, one part peat and silver sand. Position, well-drained border against S. wall. Plant, Sept. to March. Prune as for greenhouse species in March.

PROPAGATION : All species by cuttings of firm young shoots, 3 in. long, inserted in well-drained pots of sandy soil placed under bell-glass in temp. of 55° to 65° in summer ; cuttings of roots, 1 to 2 in. long, planted an inch deep in sandy soil in temp. of 55° to 65°, spring ; layering shoots in March, April, Sept., or Oct.

GREENHOUSE SPECIES : T. australis, yellowish white and purple, summer, 10 to 20 ft., Australia, and its variety rosea (pale rose) ; capensis, orange-scarlet, summer, 10 to 20 ft., S. Africa ; jasminoides, white and red, Aug., 10 to 20 ft., Australia ; Smithii, yellow, tinged orange, autumn, 2 to 3 ft.

HARDY SPECIES : T. grandiflora (Syn. Bignonia grandiflora), orange and red, Aug. to Sept., 20 to 30 ft., China and Japan ; radicans (Syn. Bignonia radicans), scarlet and orange, Aug. to Sept., 30 to 40 ft., South-eastern U.S.A.

Tecophilæa (Chilean Crocus)—Ord. Hæmodoraceæ. Half-hardy bulbous plant. First introduced 1872.

CULTURE : Soil, two parts sandy loam, one part decayed cow manure. Position, well-drained bed in cold frame or at foot of south wall, or pots in cool greenhouse. Plant bulbs 3 in. deep and 6 in. apart, Aug. to Nov. Pot, singly in 3¼ in. pots or three in a 5 in. pot and 2 in. deep. Cover pot with ashes or fibre refuse till growth

begins. Water moderately ; keep dry after foliage turns yellow until growth recommences. No artificial heat required. Admit air freely to plants in pots and frames after Feb.
PROPAGATION : By offsets, removed at potting time.
SPECIES CULTIVATED : T. cyanocrocus, blue and white, fragrant, spring, 6 in., Chile, and its variety Leichtlinii, blue.

Tectona (Teak)—Ord. Verbenaceæ. Stove tree of economic interest only. First introduced 1777.
CULTURE : Soil, loam, leaf-mould, and sand. Position, large well-drained tubs or borders in heated greenhouse. Temp., March to Sept. 75° to 85° ; Sept. to March 60° to 65°. Plant or pot, March or April.
PROPAGATION : By seeds sown in sandy soil in temp. 85° during Feb. or March.
SPECIES CULTIVATED : T. grandis, to 150 ft., India and Malaya.

Telanthera (Joy-weed)—Ord. Amarantaceæ. Half-hardy perennials. Orn. foliage. Better known under the generic name of Alternanthera. Used for carpet bedding. Foliage, crimson red. First introduced 1862.
CULTURE : Soil, ordinary. Position, sunny beds outdoors, May to Sept. Plant, May, 2 in. apart. Lift in Sept. ; store in pots or boxes in temp. 55° to 65° during winter.
PROPAGATION : By cuttings inserted in sandy soil, temp. 75°, March.
SPECIES CULTIVATED : T. amœna (Syn. Alternanthera amœna), leaves green, red, and orange, 3 in., Brazil, and its varieties amabilis (Syn. T. ficoidea), leaves orange-scarlet, spectabilis, and rosea ; bettzichiana (Syn. Alternanthera paronychoides), pale yellow and red leaves, 2 to 3 in., Brazil, and its varieties aurea, aurea nana compacta, magnifica, and spathulata ; versicolor, leaves coppery red, 3 in., Brazil.

Telegraph-plant (*Desmodium gyrans*)—See Desmodium.

Telekia—See Bupthalmum.

Tellima—Ord. Saxifragaceæ. Hardy herbaceous perennial. First introduced 1826.
CULTURE : Soil, ordinary. Position, open or partially shady borders or wild gardens. Plant, autumn or spring.
PROPAGATION : By division in spring.
SPECIES CULTIVATED : T. grandiflora, greenish, April to June, 2 ft., N. America.

Telopea (Waratah)—Ord. Proteaceæ. Greenhouse evergreen shrub. First introduced 1789.
CULTURE : Soil, sandy loam. Position, well-drained pots or tubs in greenhouse. Water very freely during summer, sparingly in winter. Dryish atmosphere essential at all seasons. Temp., March to Sept. 55° to 65° ; Sept. to March 45° to 55°.
PROPAGATION : By cuttings of young shoots inserted in sandy soil under bell-glass in gentle bottom heat during May or June.
SPECIES CULTIVATED : T. speciosissima, red, June, 8 ft., Australia.

Tenore's Candytuft (*Iberis Tenoreana*)—Iberis.

Ten-week Stock (*Matthiola annua*)—See Matthiola.

Ternstrœmia—Ord. Ternstrœmiaceæ. Half-hardy evergreen flowering shrub.
CULTURE : Soil, ordinary, well drained. Position, sheltered shrubberies in southern counties or borders in conservatories and unheated greenhouses. Plant, Sept. to Oct. or April to May.
PROPAGATION : By cuttings of young shoots inserted in sandy soil under bell-glass in gentle bottom heat during May, June, or July.
SPECIES CULTIVATED : T. japonica, yellowish white, fragrant, July to Aug., to 20 ft., Japan.

Testudinaria (Hottentot's Bread ; Elephant's Foot)—Ord. Dioscoreaceæ. Greenhouse deciduous climber. First introduced 1774.
CULTURE : Compost, equal parts fibrous loam, turfy peat, and sand. Position, well-drained in sunny greenhouse. Pot, Feb. or March. Water moderately April

to Sept., keep nearly dry afterwards. No shade required. Temp., March to Sept. 55° to 65°; Sept. to March 40° to 50°.
PROPAGATION: By cuttings of firm side shoots inserted in sandy loam under bell-glass in temp. 45° to 55° in spring, or cuttings of young shoots when 1 to 2 in. long inserted in sandy loam under bell-glass in similar temp., spring or summer.
SPECIES CULTIVATED: T. elephantipes, yellow, summer, 5 to 10 ft., S. Africa. This species has a remarkable tuberous root, frequently as much as 3 ft. in diameter. It is sometimes cooked and eaten by natives.

Tetracentron—Ord. Trochodendraceæ. Deciduous orn. tree. Hardy. Elegant foliage. First introduced 1901.
CULTURE: Soil, well-drained loam. Position, as specimens on lawns or in similar open places. Requires shelter from early spring frosts. Plant, Nov. to Feb.
PROPAGATION: By seeds sown ½ in. deep in Feb. or March in well-drained pans of sandy soil in a cold frame or greenhouse; layering in spring; grafting in heat in July or Aug.
SPECIES CULTIVATED: T. sinense, 50 to 90 ft., W. China.

Tetragonia (New Zealand Spinach)—Ord. Ficoideæ. Hardy annual. Cultivated in gardens as a substitute for summer spinach, especially on light, dry soils. First introduced 1772. Leaves, large, thick, succulent.
CULTURE: Soil, ordinary. Position, sunny. Sow seeds, previously soaked for 24 hours in tepid water, singly 1 in. deep in 2 in. pots filled with light soil in March. Place pots in temp. 55° to 65° and keep soil moist. Transfer seedlings to 5 in. pots when seedlings form four leaves, harden off in cold frame, and plant out 3 ft. apart in rows 4 ft. asunder. Gather the leaves only for cooking. Water freely in dry weather. Seeds may be sown in open ground in May if unable to sow them in heat.
SPECIES CULTIVATED: T. expansa, yellow, summer, 3 in., New Zealand.

Tetramicra—See Leptotes.

Tetrapanax—See Fatsia.

Tetratheca—Ord. Tremandraceæ. Greenhouse evergreen flowering shrub. First introduced 1820.
CULTURE: Compost, two parts fibrous peat, one part turfy loam, one part equal proportions charcoal, broken pots, and silver sand. Position, well-drained pots in light, airy greenhouse. Pot, Feb. or March. Water moderately at all seasons; rain water only to be used. Shade from sun June to Sept. Temp., Oct. to April 40° to 50°; April to Oct. 50° to 65°.
PROPAGATION: By cuttings of side shoots inserted in sand under bell-glass in shade in temp. 55° to 65°, summer.
SPECIES CULTIVATED: T. ericifolia, rose, summer, 1 ft., Australia.

Teucrium (Germander; Cat Thyme)—Ord. Labiatæ. Hardy perennials and half-hardy shrub.
CULTURE OF PERENNIAL SPECIES: Soil, ordinary. Position, sunny borders; sunny, dryish rockeries or old walls for T. marum, etc. Plant, March or April.
CULTURE OF SHRUBBY SPECIES: Soil, light, well drained. Position, at base of sunny wall in sheltered gardens. Plant, Sept. to Oct. or April to May.
PROPAGATION: Shrubby species by cuttings of half-ripened shoots inserted in sandy soil under bell-glass during July or Aug.; perennial species by division in March or April.
PERENNIAL SPECIES CULTIVATED: T. Chamædrys, rosy purple, July to Sept., 1 ft.; Europe; marum (Cat Thyme), purple, summer, 1 ft., S. Europe; polium (Syn. T. aureum), yellow, July, 4 to 6 in., Mediterranean Region; pyrenaicum, cream and lilac, June to July, 1 to 2 in., Pyrenees; Scorodonia variegatum, variegated foliage, 1 ft., Britain.
SHRUBBY SPECIES CULTIVATED: T. fruticans, purple or lavender, summer and autumn, 7 to 8 ft., S. Europe.

Thalia—Ord. Marantaceæ. Half-hardy aquatic perennials. First introduced 1791.
CULTURE: Soil, peaty loam. Position, tub in shallow pond of water. Plant in

March. Requires a warm, sheltered spot. Place tubs in ponds in open from May to Sept. Remove tubs to frost-proof greenhouse, Sept. to May.
PROPAGATION : By division in spring.
HARDY SPECIES : T. dealbata, blue, July, 6 ft., S. California.

Thalictrum (Meadow Rue ; Tufted Columbine)—Ord. Ranunculaceæ. Hardy herbaceous perennials. Leaves, finely divided, green.
CULTURE : Soil, ordinary. Position, sunny borders for tall species, T. aquilegifolium, etc. ; sunny rockeries for dwarf species, T. anemonoides and T. minus. Plant, Oct. to March. Top-dress annually in Feb. or March with decayed manure. Lift, divide, and replant only when absolutely necessary.
PROPAGATION : By division of roots in March or April.
SPECIES CULTIVATED : T. alpinum, yellowish green, summer, 4 to 6 in., Northern and Arctic Regions ; aquilegifolium, lilac, summer, 3 ft., Europe, and its varieties purpureum (purple) and album (white) ; Chelidoni, rosy lilac, summer, 6 in., Himalayas, requires sheltered position ; Delavayi, lilac, June to July, 1½ to 3 ft., E. China ; dipterocarpum, rosy lilac, summer, 5 to 7 ft., W. China, and its variety album (white) ; Fendleri, yellowish white, July, 2 to 3 ft., N. America ; flavum, yellow, summer, 3 to 4 ft., Europe ; glaucum, yellow, summer, 3 to 4 ft., S. Europe ; majus, greenish yellow, summer, 3 to 4 ft., Europe and Asia ; minus, yellow, summer, 1 ft., Europe, and its variety adiantifolium ; petaloideum, white, June to Aug., 1½ ft., N. Asia.

Thelesperma—Ord. Compositæ. Hardy annual. Flowers suitable for cutting.
CULTURE : Soil, ordinary. Position, sunny borders. Sow seeds outdoors in April where plants are required to grow.
SPECIES CULTIVATED : T. Burridgeanum (Syn. Cosmidium Burridgeanum), yellow and red-brown, summer, 18 in., Texas.

Theobroma (Cocoa Tree ; Chocolate Tree)—Ord. Sterculiaceæ. Stove evergreen tree. First introduced 1739. Fruit, oval, yellow, or reddish.
CULTURE : Compost, equal parts fibrous loam and sand. Position, well-drained pots in moist, warm stove. Pot, Feb. Water freely March to Oct., moderately afterwards. Syringe daily April to Sept. Shade from sun. Prune into shape, Feb. Temp., Oct. to March 55° to 65° ; March to Oct. 70° to 85°.
PROPAGATION : By cuttings of half-ripened shoots inserted in sand under bell-glass in temp. of 75° to 85°, April to Aug. ; seed sown in Feb. to March in temp. 80°.
SPECIES CULTIVATED : T. cacao, rose and yellow, summer, 15 to 20 ft., Trop. America. It is the seeds of this species which yield cocoa.

Thermopsis—Ord. Leguminosæ. Hardy herbaceous perennials. First introduced 1818.
CULTURE : Soil, ordinary. Position, open, sunny borders. Plant, March or April.
PROPAGATION : By seeds sown ⅛ in. deep in light, rich soil in sunny position outdoors in April, transplanting seedlings when large enough to handle ; division in spring.
SPECIES CULTIVATED : T. caroliniana, golden yellow, summer, 4 to 5 ft., N. America ; fabacea, yellow, June to July, 2 to 3 ft., Siberia ; montana, golden yellow, summer, 1 to 2 ft., N. America.

Thimble Weed (*Rudbeckia laciniata*)—See Rudbeckia.

Thistle Oil-plant (*Argemone mexicana*)—See Argemone.

Thlaspi—Ord. Cruciferæ. Hardy perennials. Suitable for rock garden.
CULTURE : Soil, ordinary. Position, sunny rock gardens. Plant, spring or autumn.
PROPAGATION : By seed sown in pans of sandy soil in cold frame or greenhouse during March or April ; division at planting time. First introduced 1759.
SPECIES CULTIVATED : T. alpinum, white, spring, 3 to 4 in., Europe ; bellidifolium, rose-purple, summer, 2 to 3 in., Macedonia ; rotundifolium, rosy lavender, summer, 2 to 3 in., Alps.

Thong Lily (*Clivia miniata*)—See Clivia.

Thorn—See Cratægus.

Thorn Apple (*Datura Stramonium*)—See Datura.

Tulipa hybrida
(Darwin Tulip)

Tulipa hybrida
(Early Double Tulip)

Tulipa hybrida
(Early Single Tulip)

Tulipa hybrida
(Parrot Tulip)

Tulipa hybrida
(Triumph Tulip)

Tulipa Kaufmanniana

Typha angustifolia
(Reed Mace)

Ulex europæus flore-pleno
(Double Gorse)

Ulmus campestris Louis van
Houtte (Golden Elm)

Ursinia anethoides

Vallota purpurea
(Scarborough Lily)

Vanda Kimballiana
(Cowslip-scented Orchid)

Venidium
calendulaceum

Verbascum hybridum
(Mullein)

Verbena hybrida
(Vervain)

Veronica Andersonii variegata
(Speedwell)

Veronica salicifolia
(Speedwell)

Veronica Teucrium
(Speedwell)

Three-sided Mercury—See Acalypha.

Thrift (*Armeria maritima*)—See Armeria.

Thrinax (Silver Thatch Palm)—Ord. Palmaceæ. Stove orn. foliage plant. **First** introduced 1778. Leaves, fan-shaped, green.

CULTURE : Compost, two parts loam, one part peat, and little sand. Position, well-drained pots in moist part of stove. Water copiously April to Oct., moderately afterwards. Syringe daily April to Sept. Moist atmosphere highly essential. Shade from sun. Temp., March to Oct. 70° to 85° ; Oct. to March 55° to 65°. PROPAGATION : By seeds soaked for a few hours in tepid water and then sown ½ in. deep in sandy loam in temp. of 75° to 85° any time.

SPECIES CULTIVATED : T. argentea (Broom or Silver Thatch Palm), 15 to 30 ft., W. Indies ; excelsa, 6 to 8 ft., Panama ; Morrisii, 3 to 4 ft., W. Indies ; multiflora, 6 to 10 ft., Dominica ; parviflora (Royal Palmetto Palm), 25 to 30 ft., W. Indies.

Thuja—See Thuya.

Thujopsis—See Thuya.

Thunbergia—Ord. Acanthaceæ. Stove and greenhouse evergreen flowering shrubs and perennials, mostly of climbing habit. First introduced 1796.

CULTURE OF T. ALATA AND T. GIBSONI : Compost, two parts loam, one part leaf-mould or decayed manure, and one part sand. Sow seeds thinly in light compost in a well-drained pot, pan, or box in temp. 65° to 75° in Feb. or March. Transplant seedlings when three leaves form singly in 3½ in. pots, and later on into 5 in. size. Place pots afterwards alongside of staging and let shoots hang down; or in baskets suspended from roof. May also be planted outdoors in June against sunny walls, in window boxes, or in vases. Water freely. Apply weak stimulants occasionally when in flower.

CULTURE OF OTHER SPECIES : Compost, equal parts leaf-mould or well-decayed manure, peat, fibrous loam, and silver sand. Position, well-drained pots in shady part of stove during growing period ; light part during the resting period for T. erecta ; well-drained beds, with shoots trained up roof, for T. mysorensis, etc. Pot, Feb. or March. Prune moderately, Feb. Water freely March to Sept., moderately Sept. to Nov., keep nearly dry Nov. to March. Syringe daily March to Sept. Apply stimulants occasionally May to Sept. Temp., Feb. to Oct. 65° to 75° ; Oct. to Feb. 55° to 65°.

PROPAGATION : By seeds sown 1/16 in. deep in sandy peat and leaf-mould in temp. 75° to 85° Jan. to May ; cuttings of firm young shoots, 2 to 3 in. long, inserted in leaf-mould, peat, and sand under bell-glass in temp. 75° to 85°, Feb. to June.

SPECIES CULTIVATED : T. alata, cream and dark purple, summer, 4 to 6 ft., Trop. Africa, and several colour forms ; coccinea, scarlet, summer, 8 to 10 ft., India ; erecta (Syn. Meyenia erecta), purple and pale yellow, summer, 6 ft., Trop. Africa, and its variety alba (white) ; fragrans, white, fragrant, summer, 8 to 10 ft., Trop. Asia ; Gibsoni, orange, summer, 10 to 15 ft., Trop. Africa ; grandiflora, blue, July to Sept., 10 to 15 ft., India, and its variety alba (white) ; Harrisii (Syn. T. laurifolia), light blue and white, July to Sept., 10 to 15 ft., India ; mysorensis (Syn. Hexacentris mysorensis), yellow and purple, spring, 10 to 15 ft., S. India.

Thunberg's Lily (*Lilium elegans*)—See Lilium.

Thunia—Ord. Orchidaceæ. Stove epiphytal and terrestrial orchids. First introduced 1836.

CULTURE : Compost, equal parts rough peat and sphagnum moss. Position, well-drained pots in moist part of stove. Water freely during the growing season and maintain a humid atmosphere ; sparingly at other times. Resting period, winter. Repot in spring. Temp., March to Sept. 75° to 85° ; Sept. to March 60° to 65°.

SPECIES CULTIVATED : T. alba, white, yellow, and purple, summer, 2 ft., India ; Bensoniæ, white, purple, and yellow, summer, 2 ft., Burma ; brymeriana, white, crimson, and yellow, summer, 2 ft., Burma ; marshalliana, white, yellow, and orange, early summer, 2 ft., Burma. **T. veitchiana is a fine hybrid between T. Bensoniæ and T. marshalliana.**

Thuya (*Arbor-vitæ*)—Ord. Coniferæ.   Hardy evergreen trees and shrubs.   Orn. foliage.   First introduced 1596.   Leaves, small, scale-like.   Habit, pyramidal.
CULTURE : Soil, deep, moist loam.   Position, open, sunny shrubberies, lawns, banks, or margins of water.   Plant, Sept. to Nov. and Feb. to April.   Prune, April or Sept.   Depth for planting roots, 6 to 8 in.
IN POTS : Compost, two parts loam and one part leaf-mould.   Pot, Sept. or Oct. Position, cold frame, window sill, or cold greenhouse, Nov. to May ; plunged to rim of pots in ashes or fibre refuse in sunny spot outdoors afterwards.   Water freely April to Oct., moderately afterwards.
HEDGE CULTURE : Suitable kinds—T. plicata, T. occidentalis, and T. orientalis. Soil, ordinary moist, previously trenched three spits deep and 3 ft. wide.   Plant, Sept., Oct., March, or April.   Distance apart for planting : 15 to 18 in.   Height of trees, 18 in. to 4 ft.   Prune, trim, or clip, April or Sept.
PROPAGATION : By seeds sown ¼ in. deep in sandy soil in temp. 55° in spring, transplanting seedlings in open ground when large enough to handle ; by cuttings of shoots, 2 to 3 in. long, inserted in sandy soil under bell-glass or in cold frame in Sept. ; grafting in March.
SPECIES CULTIVATED : T. dolobrata (Syn. Thuyopsis dolobrata), 30 to 50 ft., Japan, and its varieties nana (Syn. Thuyopsis lætevirens), dwarf and variegata (leaf tips white) ;   japonica (Syn. Thuya Standishii), Japanese Arbor-vitæ, 20 to 30 ft., Japan ;   occidentalis (American Arbor-vitæ), 50 to 60 ft., N.E. America, and its varieties aureo-variegata (yellow), ellwangeriana (dwarf form), ericoïdes (dwarf habit), lutea (ends of branches yellow tinted), pendula (branches drooping), Spathii (branchlets clustered), vervæncana (branchlets tinged with yellow or brown), and wareana (dwarf, dense growing) ;   orientalis (Chinese arbor-vitæ), Syn. Biota orientalis, 30 to 40 ft., China, and its varieties argenteo-variegata (variegated with white), aurea (golden), decussata (dwarf form), elegantissima (dwarf, graceful habit), and pendula (branches drooping) ; plicata (Syns. T. gigantea and T. Lobbii), 100 to 200 ft., N.W. America, a very handsome tree, and its varieties aurea (young growths yellow), fastigiata (Syn. pyramidalis), columnar, and zebrina (foliage with patches of yellow).

Thyme (*Thymus vulgaris*)—See Thymus.

Thyme-leaved Harebell (*Wahlenbergia serpyllifolia*)—See Wahlenbergia.

Thymus (Garden and Lemon-scented Thyme)—Ord. Labiatæ.   Hardy aromatic shrubby perennial.
CULTURE OF GARDEN THYME : Shoots used largely for culinary purposes.   Soil, light, rich ordinary.   Position, sunny, warm border.   Plant, 4 in. apart in rows 8 in. asunder, March or April.   Replant every three or four years.   Gather shoots when blossoms appear and dry for winter use.
CULTURE OF OTHER SPECIES : Soil, ordinary.   Position, sunny rockeries.   Plant, Oct. or March.   Excellent plants for carpeting bare spots over spring bulbs.
PROPAGATION : By seeds sown ¼ in. deep in lines 8 in. apart in April, thinning seedlings to 4 in. apart in May or June ; by division of the plant in March or April, each portion being furnished with a few roots ; gold and silver kinds by cuttings in cold frames in summer.
SPECIES CULTIVATED : T. azoricus, purple, summer, prostrate, Azores ; citriodorus (Lemon-scented Thyme), pink, June, 6 to 9 in., Europe, and its varieties argenteus (silver variegated) and aureus (golden variegated) ; carnosus, white, Aug. to Sept., 9 in., Spain ; Chamædrys, light purple, summer, 3 in., Europe ; Herba-barona, light purple, summer, foliage scented like carraway seed, 6 in., Corsica ; nitidus, rosy lilac, June, 9 in., Sicily ; odoratissimus, pale purple, summer, 2 in., Russia ; serpyllum, rosy purple, June, prostrate, Europe (Britain), and its varieties albus (white), coccineus (carmine), lanuginosus (woody-leaved), and micans (tufted) ; vulgaris (Garden Thyme), purple, June, 6 in., S. Europe.

Thyrsacanthus (Thyrse Flower)—Ord. Acanthaceæ.   Stove evergreen flowering shrubs.   First introduced 1851.
CULTURE : Compost, equal parts peat, loam, leaf-mould, and sand.   Position, well-

drained pots in light stove, Sept. to June ; sunny frame, June to Sept. Pot, March or April. Water moderately Sept. to March, freely other times. Temp., Sept. to March 55° to 65° ; March to June 65° to 75°. Prune shoots to 1 in. of base after flowering. Nip off points of young shoots occasionally, May to Aug., to induce bushy growth. Apply liquid or artificial manure twice a week to plants in flower. PROPAGATION : By cuttings of young shoots inserted singly in small pots of sandy soil under bell-glass in temp. 75°, March to July. SPECIES CULTIVATED : T. rutilans (Syn. Odontonema Schomburgkianum), crimson, winter, 3 to 6 ft., Colombia.

Tiarella (False Mitre-wort ; Foam Flower)—Ord. Saxifragaceæ. Hardy perennial herb. First introduced 1731. CULTURE : Soil, ordinary. Position, cool, shady beds or rock gardens. Plant, March or April. PROPAGATION : By division of roots in March or April. SPECIES CULTIVATED : T. cordifolia, white, June, 1 ft., N. America ; polyphylla, white, summer, 1½ ft., Himalayas ; unifoliata, creamy white, summer, 2 ft., N. America.

Tibouchina (Brazilian Spider-flower)—Ord. Melastomaceæ. Greenhouse flowering shrubs. Evergreen. First introduced 1864. CULTURE : Compost, two parts turfy loam, one part peat, and one part charcoal and sand. Position, well-drained pots, tubs, or beds. Pot or plant, Feb. or March. Prune into shape, Feb. Water freely April to Sept., moderately afterwards. Apply stimulants once a week May to Sept. Temp., March or Sept. 60° to 70° ; Sept. to March 50° to 60°. PROPAGATION : By cuttings of firm side shoots, 3 in. long, inserted singly in small pots of sandy soil under bell-glass or in propagator in temp. of 70° to 80°, Feb. to Sept. SPECIES CULTIVATED : T. elegans, purple, June, 6 ft., Brazil ; semidecandra (Syn. Lasiandra or Pleroma macranthum), purple, summer, 10 ft., Brazil.

Tick-seed (*Coreopsis tinctoria*)—See Coreopsis.

Tick Trefoil (*Desmodium canadense*)—See Desmodium.

Tidy-tips (*Layia platyglossa*)—See Layia.

Tiger-chop (*Mesembryanthemum tigrinum*)—See Mesembryanthemum.

Tiger Flower (*Tigridia Pavonia*)—See Tigridia.

Tiger Iris—See Tigridia.

Tiger Lily (*Lilium tigrinum*)—See Lilium.

Tigridia (Tiger Flower ; Tiger Iris)—Ord. Iridaceæ. Half-hardy or greenhouse bulbs. First introduced 1796. Blooms last in perfection but one day only. OUTDOOR CULTURE : Soil, equal parts rich loam and leaf-mould with a liberal addition of sand, in partially shaded bed prepared by digging out soil to depth of 24 in. ; place 6 in. of brickbats or clinkers in bottom and remainder compost ; or for ordinary culture an open, sunny border and any good soil. Plant bulbs 3 in. deep, 5 to 6 in. apart, placing little sand under and around each in April. Mulch with decayed manure and cocoanut-fibre refuse when 3 in. high. Water freely in dry weather. Lift bulbs in Oct., tie in small bundles, and suspend in cool, airy, frost-proof place until following April. POT CULTURE : Compost, two parts sandy loam, one part peat, and one part sand. Pot the bulbs singly in 4½ in. pots in March or April. Cover pots with cinder ashes or cocoanut-fibre refuse in cold frame or under stage in cold greenhouse until growth begins, then remove to light. Water moderately after growth begins ; freely when well advanced. Apply weak stimulants occasionally when flower stems show. Position when in flower, light, airy greenhouse or cold, sunny frame. After flowering gradually withhold water until foliage turns yellow, then keep quite dry. Remove bulbs from soil, tie into bundles, and suspend in cool place until potting time the following April.

PROPAGATION : By seeds sown ⅛ in. deep in light compost in temp. 55° to 65°, spring ; by offsets, removed and treated as advised for old bulbs in April.
SPECIES CULTIVATED : T. Pavonia, red, yellow, and purple, summer, 1 to 2 ft., Mexico, and its varieties alba (white), aurea (yellow), and conchiflora (rich yellow) ; violacea, rose, purple, and white, May, 1 ft., Mexico. See also Cypella.

Tilia (Lime Tree ; Linden Tree ; Bass Wood)—Ord. Tiliaceæ. Hardy deciduous trees. Orn. foliage. Flowers, white, yellow ; fragrant ; summer ; good for bees. Leaves, heart-shaped, green or variegated.
CULTURE : Soil, good ordinary or loamy, moist. Position, sunny ; as specimen trees on lawns or as screens. Also adapted for training over arches to form a shady path in summer. Plant, Oct. to March. Prune, Nov. to Feb. Not suitable for dry soils or exposed places. Timber, soft, pale yellow or white, used chiefly for toy making, carving, leather cutting boards, musical instruments, etc. Weight of cubic foot of timber, 28 lb. Number of seeds to a pound, 5000. Age at which timber reaches maturity, 30 years. Average life, 800 to 1000 years.
PROPAGATION : By layering shoots in autumn ; choice kinds by grafting on common species in March.
SPECIES CULTIVATED : T. americana (Bass Wood), 60 to 70 ft., N. America ; cordata, 50 to 80 ft., Europe ; euchlora (often wrongly named T. dasystyla), 40 ft., hybrid ; Moltkei, 40 ft., hybrid ; mongolica, 30 ft., N. China and Mongolia ; petiolaris 50 to 80 ft., E. Europe ; platyphyllos, 80 to 120 ft., Europe, and its variety asplenifolia (leaves deeply lobed) ; tomentosa (Syn. T. argentea), 60 to 100 ft., E. Europe ; vulgaris (Common Lime), 80 to 100 ft., hybrid.

Tillandsia (Old Man's Beard ; Spanish Moss)—Ord. Bromeliaceæ. Stove epiphytal perennials. Bracts, rosy crimson, pink, purplish green.
CULTURE : Compost, equal parts fibrous loam, rough peat, silver sand, and leaf-mould. Pot, Feb. or March. Water copiously March to Oct., moderately afterwards. Shade from sun. Syringe daily April to Sept. Moist atmosphere essential in summer. Temp., Sept. to March 60° to 70° ; March to Sept. 70° to 80°.
PROPAGATION : By offsets, inserted in small pots of sandy peat in temp. 75° to 85° in spring. T. usneoides may be grown suspended from roof by a wire or fastened to a piece of wood ; no soil required.
SPECIES CULTIVATED : T. circinnata (Syn. T. streptophylla), lilac, 1 ft., W. Indies and Central America ; duvaliana, yellow and green, 1 ft., Brazil ; fasciculata, blue, 2 ft., W. Indies and Central America ; lindeniana, bluish purple, summer, 1 ft., Peru ; usneoides, greenish red, July, stems slender and pendant, to 20 ft. (Old Man's Beard ; Spanish Moss). See also Cryptanthus, Vriesia, and Guzmannia.

Tithonia (Mexican Sunflower)—Ord. Compositæ. Tender shrub usually grown as half-hardy annual. First introduced 1833.
CULTURE : Soil, ordinary. Position, sunny beds or borders. Sow in boxes of sandy soil in greenhouse in temp. 60° during March. Prick out seedlings as soon as large enough to handle and gradually harden off for planting out in May.
SPECIES CULTIVATED : T. speciosa (Syn. T. rotundifolia), orange yellow, Aug. to Sept., 3 to 6 ft., Mexico and Central America.

Toad-cup Lily (*Marica cærulea*)—See Marica.

Toad-flax—See Linaria.

Toad-flower (*Stapelia bufonia*)—See Stapelia.

Toad Lily (*Tricyrtis hirta*)—See Tricyrtis.

Toad-root—See Actæa.

Tobacco Plant—See Nicotiana.

Tobago Cane Palm (*Bactris caryotæfolia*)—See Bactris.

Toddy Palm (*Caryota urens*)—See Caryota.

Todea (Crape Fern)—Ord. Filices. Greenhouse evergreen ferns. First introduced 1861. Fronds finely or coarsely divided ; dark green ; mostly semi-transparent.

CULTURE : Compost, equal parts peat, loam, leaf-mould, charcoal, sandstone, and silver sand. Position, moist, shady, in damp recesses of rockeries, under bell-glasses or in cases. Plant, March. Water freely March to Oct., moderately Oct. to March. Syringing unsuitable. Moist atmosphere and shade most essential. Temp., 55° to 65° March to Sept. ; 45° to 55° Sept. to March. T. superba and T. hymenophylloides suitable for cold houses.

CULTURE IN CASES : Compost, as above. Position, shady window, not exposed to sun. Pot or plant, March. Top-dress with fresh compost annually in March. Water freely April to Sept., moderately afterwards. Ventilate case few minutes daily. Suitable kinds, T. superba and T. hymenophylloides.

PROPAGATION : By spores sown on surface of sandy peat in shallow pan covered with bell-glass in temp. 65° to 75° at any time ; by division of plant at potting time.

SPECIES CULTIVATED : T. barbara, S. Africa, Australia, and New Zealand ; hymenophylloides, New Zealand ; superba (Prince of Wales' Feather Fern), New Zealand ; Fraseri wilkesiana, Fiji and New Hebrides.

Tollon—See Heteromeles.

Tolmiea—Ord. Saxifragaceæ. Hardy perennial herb. First introduced 1812. Flowers, green ; April. Calyx, purple-nerved.

CULTURE : Soil, ordinary. Position, shady beds or rock gardens. Plant, March.

PROPAGATION : By division of roots, March or April.

SPECIES CULTIVATED : T. Menziesii, 1 to 2 ft., N. America.

Tolpis (Yellow Garden Hawkweed)—Ord. Compositæ. Hardy annuals. First introduced 1620.

CULTURE : Soil, ordinary. Position, sunny beds or borders. Sow seeds $\frac{1}{8}$ in. deep in patches or lines where required to grow ; thin seedlings when 2 to 3 in. high to 6 or 8 in. apart.

SPECIES CULTIVATED : T. barbata (Syn. Crepis barbata), yellow, June, 1 to 2 ft., S. Europe.

Tomato (*Lycopersicum esculentum*)—See Lycopersicum.

Tom Thumb Lily (*Lilium tenuifolium*)—See Lilium.

Tongue-flowered Orchid—See Serapias.

Toothache-tree—See Zanthoxylum.

Tooth-wort—See Dentaria.

Torch Lily (*Kniphofia aloides*)—See Kniphofia.

Torch Thistle—See Cereus.

Torenia—Ord. Scrophulariaceæ. Greenhouse annuals. First introduced 1811.

CULTURE : Compost, loam, leaf-mould, and sand. Position, small pots, with shoots trained to sticks, or in baskets suspended from roof. Sow seeds thinly in boxes filled with sandy soil in temp. 60° from Feb. to April. Prick out seedlings when large enough to handle into the pots or boxes in which they are to flower. Nip off point of main shoot when 3 in. long, also of side shoots when 2 in. long, to induce bushy growth. Water freely.

SPECIES CULTIVATED : T. asiatica, purple, summer, 1 ft., Trop. Asia ; flava (Syn. Bailloni), yellow and red-purple, summer, 1 ft., Trop. Asia ; Fourneri, blue, purple, yellow, and black, summer, 1 ft., Cochin China, and its varieties grandiflora and speciosa.

Toringo Crab (*Pyrus Toringo*)—See Pyrus.

Torreya (Stinking Yew ; Stinking Cedar ; Californian Nutmeg)—Ord. Coniferæ. First introduced 1840.

CULTURE : Soil, light, sandy loam. Position, sheltered, sunny, well-drained shrubberies. Plant, Sept., Oct., March, or April. Seldom grown in England; too tender.

PROPAGATION : As advised for Taxus.

SPECIES CULTIVATED : T. californica (Californian Nutmeg), 40 to 70 ft., California ; grandis, 50 to 75 ft., China ; nucifera, 50 to 80 ft., Japan ; taxifolia (Stinking Cedar), 30 to 40 ft., W. Florida.

Totara Pine-tree (*Podocarpus Totara*)—See Podocarpus.

Toxicophlæa—See Acokanthera.

Trachelium (Blue Throat-wort)—Ord. Campanulaceæ. Half-hardy herbaceous perennial. First introduced 1640.

CULTURE : Compost, two parts sandy loam, one part leaf-mould. Position, sunny rock gardens or dry walls or as cool greenhouse pot plant, and for summer bedding. Plant, March or April. Protect in severe weather by covering of dry fern fronds.

PROPAGATION : By seeds sown in above compost lightly covered with fine light mould, placing in temp. of 55° to 65°, spring, transplanting seedlings when large enough to handle, hardening in cold frame and planting out, May or June ; cuttings of young shoots inserted in sandy soil under bell-glass in April or Sept. When grown as greenhouse pot plant or for bedding it is best raised annually from seed.

SPECIES CULTIVATED : T. cæruleum, blue, Aug., 2 ft., S. Europe, and its variety album (white).

Trachelospermum (Chinese Jasmine ; Chinese Ivy)—Ord. Apocynaceæ. Half-hardy evergreen climbing shrub. Flowering. First introduced 1846.

CULTURE : Compost, equal parts peat, loam, and silver sand. Position, well-drained pots or borders in unheated greenhouse or borders against west walls in the open in sheltered districts. Train shoots up trellis or walls. Pot or plant, April or May. Water pot plants freely April to Oct., moderately afterwards. Prune moderately after flowering. Shade from sun essential.

PROPAGATION : By cuttings of firm young shoots, 2 to 3 in. long, inserted in well-drained pots of sandy peat placed under bell-glass in temp. 65° to 75°, spring or summer.

SPECIES CULTIVATED : T. divaricatum, yellowish white, fragrant, July to Aug., to 15 ft., Corea and Japan ; jasminoides (Syn. Rhyncospermum jasminoides), white, fragrant, summer, 10 to 15 ft., China, and its variety variegatum.

Trachycarpus (Chusan Palm)—Ord. Palmaceæ. Greenhouse orn.-leaved plant. Hardy in southern parts of the kingdom. First introduced 1849. Leaves, fan-shaped and green.

CULTURE : Compost, two parts rich loam, one part decayed leaf-mould and sand. Position, well-drained pots in sunny greenhouse ; sheltered place outdoors in the south. Pot, March. Temp., Sept. to March 40° to 50° ; March to Sept. 50° to 60°. Water freely in spring and summer, moderately other times. Repotting only necessary every four or five years.

PROPAGATION : By seeds sown an inch deep in a temp. of 75° to 80° ; also by suckers removed from base of parent.

SPECIES CULTIVATED : T. Fortunei (Syn. Chamærops excelsa), 25 to 30 ft., China.

Trachymene (Blue Lace Flower)—Ord. Umbelliferæ. Half-hardy annual. Makes a pretty edging to beds or borders in summer. First introduced 1827.

CULTURE : Soil, ordinary. Position, sunny. Sow in temp. of 55° in March, transplant seedlings 2 in. apart in pots or boxes, harden off in cold frame in April, and plant out in May.

SPECIES CULTIVATED : T. cærulea (Syn. Didiscus cærulea), blue, summer, 8 in., Australia ; pilosa, blue, summer, 6 in., Australia.

Tradescantia (Spider-wort ; Flower-of-a-Day)—Ord. Commelinaceæ. Hardy herbaceous and stove perennials. First introduced 1629.

CULTURE OF HARDY SPECIES : Soil, ordinary. Position, partially shady or sunny borders or beds. Plant, Oct., Nov., March, or April. Lift, divide, and replant every three or four years. Excellent plants for town gardens.

CULTURE OF STOVE SPECIES : Compost, equal parts loam and leaf-mould with liberal addition of sand. Position, well-drained pots in warm greenhouse. Pot, March or April. Water freely March to Sept., moderately at other times. Temp., March to Sept. 65° to 75° ; Sept. to March 55° to 60°.

PROPAGATION : Hardy species by division in spring ; stove species by cuttings inserted in sandy soil under bell-glass in temp. 75°, April to Aug.

HARDY SPECIES CULTIVATED : T. virginiana, violet purple, May to Sept., 1 to 2 ft., N. America, and several colour forms.

STOVE SPECIES CULTIVATED : T. Reginæ, leaves purplish crimson and silver above, purple beneath, 1 ft., Peru. See also Rhœo and Zebrina.

Tragacanth Gum-plant (*Astragalus Tragacantha*)—See Astragalus.

Tragopogon (Salsify ; Vegetable Oyster)—Ord. Compositæ. Hardy biennial esculent-rooted vegetable. Roots, long, tapering, white.

CULTURE : Soil, ordinary fine, rich, deeply trenched, free from stones. Position, sunny, open. Sow seeds in groups of three or four, 12 in. apart, in drills ½ in. deep and 18 in. apart in April. Thin seedlings when 3 in. high to one in each group. Remove flower heads as soon as seen. Lift the roots in Oct., twist off their leaves, and store in layers with sand or soil between in cellar or outhouse until required for cooking. Artificial manures : 2½ lb. kainit, 1 lb. sulphate of ammonia, 2½ lb. of guano, mixed, per square rod (30¼ square yards), applied between sowing in spring. Requires to be raised from seed annually.

SPECIES CULTIVATED : T. porrifolius, purple, May and June, 2 to 3 ft., Europe.

Trailing Azalea—See Loiseleuria.

Trailing Fuchsia (*Fuchsia procumbens*)—See Fuchsia.

Transvaal Daisy—See Gerbera.

Trapa (Water Caltrops ; Water Chestnut ; Jesuit's Nut)—Ord. Onagraceæ. Hardy aquatic floating herbs.

CULTURE : Soil, rich, loamy. Position, sunny ; shallow pots or tubs in cool greenhouse. Plant, April or May.

PROPAGATION : By seeds sown in loamy soil in water in temp. of 65° to 75° in spring.

SPECIES CULTIVATED : T. natans (Syn. T. bicornis), reddish white, summer, fruits edible, 2 in. in diameter, Europe.

Traveller's Joy (*Clematis vitalba*)—See Clematis.

Traveller's Tree (*Ravenala madagascarensis*)—See Ravenala.

Treasure-flower (*Gazania Pavonia*)—See Gazania.

Tree Carnation—See Dianthus.

Tree Celandine (*Bocconia cordata*)—See Bocconia.

Tree Club Moss—See Selaginella.

Tree Ferns—See Cyathea and Dicksonia.

Tree Groundsel (*Baccharis halimifolia*)—See Baccharis.

Tree Heath (*Erica arborea*)—See Erica.

Tree Lupin (*Lupinus arboreus*)—See Lupinus.

Tree Mallow (*Lavatera arborea*)—See Lavatera.

Tree-of-Heaven (*Ailanthus glandulosa*)—See Ailanthus.

Tree of the Gods (*Ailanthus glandulosa*)—See Ailanthus.

Tree Onion (*Allium Cepa proliferum*)—See Allium.

Tree Pæony (*Pæonia Moutan*)—See Pæonia.

Tree Poppy (*Romneya Coulteri*)—See Romneya.

Tree Primrose—See Œnothera.

Tree Purslane (*Atriplex Halimus*)—See Atriplex.

Tree Rhododendron (*Rhododendron arboreum*)—See Rhododendron.

Tree Tomato (*Cyphomandra betacea*)—See Cyphomandra.

Tremandra verticillata—See Platytheca galioides.

Trembling-fern (*Pteris tremula*)—See Pteris.

Trevesia—Ord. Araliaceæ. Stove flowering shrub. First introduced 1818.
CULTURE : Compost, equal parts loam, leaf-mould, and sand. Position, large well-drained pots in warm greenhouse. Temp., March to Sept. 70° to 80° ; Sept. to March 60° to 65°. Moist atmosphere essential during the summer months. Shade from strong sun. Water freely during growing season, moderately at other times. Pot, Feb. or March.
PROPAGATION : By cuttings of half-ripened shoots inserted in sandy soil under bell-glass in temp. 80°.
SPECIES CULTIVATED : T. palmata (Syn. T. sundaica), yellowish white, spring, to 20 ft., Himalayas.

Tricholæna (Ruby Grass)—Ord. Gramineæ. Half-hardy annual grass.
CULTURE : Soil, ordinary. Sow seeds ¼ in. deep and 1 in. apart in light, rich soil in well-drained pots or boxes in temp. 55° to 65°, Feb. or March ; transfer seedlings when 2 in. high singly into 2 in. pots, then into 4½ in. pots. Place in cold frame to harden in May and plant outdoors in June. May also be grown in pots in compost of equal parts good loamy soil and leaf-mould and little sand. Water freely.
SPECIES CULTIVATED : T. rosea, 3 to 4 ft., S. Africa.

Trichomanes (Killarney Fern ; Bristle Fern)—Ord. Filices. Greenhouse filmy ferns. Fronds, more or less divided, semi-transparent.
CULTURE : Compost, equal parts peat, loam, leaf-mould, charcoal, sandstone, and silver sand. Position, moist, shady, in damp recesses of rockeries, under bell-glasses or in cases. Plant, March. Water freely March to Oct., moderately Oct. to March. Syringing unsuitable. Damp atmosphere and shade most essential. Temp., 55° to 65° March to Sept. ; 45° to 55° Sept. to March. The Killarney Fern is best grown in a cool house or frame in complete shade. Provide plenty of sandstone for rhizomes to cling to. Constant moisture most essential.
CULTURE IN CASES IN ROOMS : Compost, as above. Position, shady window, not exposed to sun. Plant, March. Top-dress with fresh compost annually in March. Water freely April to Sept., moderately afterwards. Ventilate case few minutes daily. Species most suitable, T. radicans.
PROPAGATION : By spores sown on surface of sandy peat in shallow pan covered with bell-glass in temp. 65° to 75° at any time ; by division at potting time.
SPECIES CULTIVATED : T. alatum, W. Indies ; auriculatum, Trop. Asia ; Colensoi, New Zealand ; exsectum, Chile ; parvulum, Tropics ; radicans (Killarney Fern), Tropical and Temperate Regions ; reniforme, New Zealand ; trichoideum, W. Indies.

Trichopilia—Ord. Orchidaceæ. Greenhouse evergreen epiphytal orchids. First introduced 1821.
CULTURE : Compost, equal parts fibrous peat and fresh sphagnum moss with a little charcoal and clean crocks. Position, baskets suspended from roof of light greenhouse close to glass. Pot, Feb. or March, or immediately new growth begins. Water moderately March to Sept., very little afterwards. Moist atmosphere essential in summer. Shade from sun. Growing period, March to Sept. ; resting period, Sept. to March. Temp., May to Sept. 55° to 65° ; Sept. to Feb. 45° to 55° ; Feb. to May 50° to 60°.
PROPAGATION : By division of pseudo-bulbs at potting time.
SPECIES CULTIVATED : T. coccinea, crimson and white, May and June, 6 in., Central America ; fragrans, greenish white and yellow, almond scented, summer, Colombia ;

PROPAGATION : By seeds soaked for a few hours in tepid water and then sown ¼ in. deep in sandy loam in temp. of 75° to 85° any time.
SPECIES CULTIVATED : T. acanthocoma, 10 to 15 ft., Brazil ; brasiliensis, 10 to 15 ft., Brazil.

Tritoma—See Kniphofia.

Tritonia—Ord. Iridaceæ.   Half-hardy deciduous bulbous plants.   First introduced 1758.
OUTDOOR CULTURE : Soil, equal parts sandy loam, leaf-mould, and decayed manure. Position, sunny well-drained borders.   Plant 3 in. deep and 2 in. apart in groups during March or April.   Water occasionally in very dry weather.   Apply stimulants occasionally during flowering period.   Lift plants in Oct., place in shallow boxes filled with dry soil, and stand in an unheated frame or greenhouse until planting time.   Practically no water required until growth recommences in Feb. In sheltered gardens corms may be left in the open ground but should be protected with covering of dry litter during winter.
POT CULTURE : Compost, two parts sandy loam, one part leaf-mould or decayed cow manure.   Pots, 4½ in. in diameter, well drained.   Place five bulbs 3 in. deep in each pot in Nov. and cover with cocoanut-fibre refuse in cold frame or under cool greenhouse stage until growth begins.   Water moderately from time bulbs begin to grow until flowers fade, then gradually cease, keeping bulbs dry till Jan. Temp., Sept. to March 40° to 50° ; other times 50° to 60°.
PROPAGATION : By offsets, treated as advised for bulbs.
SPECIES CULTIVATED : T. crocata (Syn. Ixia crocata), orange, summer, 2 ft. ; crocosmiæflora, orange-scarlet, summer, 2 to 3 ft., hybrid ; Pottsii, orange yellow, Aug., 3 ft. ; rosea, red and yellow, summer, 1½ ft.   Natives of S. Africa and formerly known as Montbretias.   A fine strain is known as " Earlham Hybrids."

Trochodendron—Ord. Trochodendraceæ.   Hardy evergreen flowering shrub.
CULTURE : Soil, moist, peaty loam.   Position, large shrubberies, or as specimens on lawns.   Plant, Sept. to Oct. or April to May.
PROPAGATION : By cuttings of half-ripened shoots inserted in sandy soil under bell-glass in slight bottom heat during July or Aug.
SPECIES CULTIVATED : T. aralioides, bright green, April to June, 15 to 30 ft., Japan and Corea.

Trollius (Globe Flower)—Ord. Ranunculaceæ.   Hardy herbaceous perennials.
CULTURE : Soil, deep, moist ordinary, or preferably loam.   Position, partially shady borders or margins of ponds or streams.   Plant, Oct. to April.   Water freely in dry weather.   Lift, divide, and replant every three or four years.
PROPAGATION : By seeds sown in moist, loamy soil in shady position outdoors in Sept. or April ; division of roots, Oct. to April.
SPECIES CULTIVATED : T. asiaticus, orange, May, 18 in., Siberia ; caucasicus, yellow, May to June, 2 to 3 ft., W. Asia ; chinensis, yellow, May to June, 2 to 3 ft., N. China ; europæus, lemon yellow, May to June, 1½ to 2 ft., Europe ; japonicus, yellow, May to June, 6 to 8 in., Japan, and its variety flore-pleno (double) ; Ledebouri, yellow, May to June, 1½ to 2 ft., Siberia ; patulus, golden yellow, May to June, 8 to 12 in., W. Asia ; pumilis, yellow, May to June, 8 to 12 in., Himalayas, and its variety yunnanensis (taller).

Tropæolum (Nasturtium ; Indian Cress ; Flame Flower ; Canary Creeper)— Ord. Geraniaceæ.   Greenhouse or hardy perennial dwarf or climbing herbs.   Several treated as annuals.
CULTURE OF CANARY CREEPER : Soil, good ordinary mould or sandy loam.   Position, against sunny or shady wall, fence, arbour, or trellis ; does well on a north aspect.   Sow seeds ¼ in. deep in light soil in temp. 55° in March, harden off seedlings in cold frame in April, and plant outdoors in May ; or ¼ in. deep outdoors in April where required to grow.   Water freely in dry weather.
CULTURE OF NASTURTIUM : Climbing kinds : Soil, ordinary.   Position, sunny or shady walls, fences, arbours, or window boxes.   Sow seed 1 in. deep in April where plants are required to grow.   Remove seed pods as they form to insure

free flowering. Dwarf kinds : Soil, ordinary, not over rich. Position, sunny or shady borders or beds. Sow seeds 1 in. deep and 3 in. apart in lines or masses in April. Thin seedlings to 6, 9, or 12 in. apart when 3 in. high if fine plants are desired. Remove seed pods unless seed is required.

POT CULTURE : Sow seeds ½ in. deep and 2 in. apart in 5 in. pots filled with a compost of two parts good mould and one part decayed manure in April. Place pots in window or cold frame. Water moderately at first, freely when in full growth. Apply stimulants occasionally when in flower. Double varieties propagated by cuttings in temp. 55° in spring. Plant outdoors in May or June. May be grown in pots in a compost of two parts loam, one part leaf-mould, and little sand. Pot in March or April. Water freely in summer, moderately other times. Temp., Oct. to March 40° to 50° ; March to June 55° to 65°.

CULTURE OF T. LOBBIANUM : Sow seeds in light soil in temp. 55° in March, harden seedlings off in cold frame in April, and plant out in June in sunny position against walls, fences, arbours, or in borders, placing tree branches to support the shoots ; or outdoors ½ in. deep in April where required to grow.

INDOOR CULTURE : Compost, two parts sandy loam, one part leaf-mould or decayed manure, and half a part sand. Position, well-drained pots or beds, training shoots up rafters. Water moderately Sept. to April, freely afterwards. Temp., Sept. to March 50° to 60° ; March to Sept. 65° to 75°.

CULTURE OF GREENHOUSE TUBEROUS-ROOTED SPECIES : Compost, equal parts turfy loam, leaf-mould, peat, and silver sand. Position, well-drained pots in light, airy greenhouse. Pot, Aug. to Nov. Place one tuber only in a pot and bury this about 1 in. Water very little till plants grow freely, then give an abundant supply. Withhold water entirely when foliage turns yellow and until growth recommences. Apply stimulants occasionally when plants are in flower. Train shoots to wire trellis fixed in pots or up rafters. Temp., Nov. to Feb. 40° to 50° ; Feb. to June 55° to 65°. After growth ceases store pots in cool place till potting time.

CULTURE OF HARDY SPECIES : Soil, light, sandy loam for T. pentaphyllum ; ordinary mould for T. polyphyllum ; equal parts loam, peat, leaf-mould, and sand for T. speciosum ; poorish mould for T. tuberosum. Position, south wall or fence for T. pentaphyllum ; sunny bank for T. polyphyllum ; shaded wall or hedge facing north for T. speciosum ; sunny border for T. tuberosum. Plant T. tuberosum in March or April ; T. polyphyllum, Aug. to Nov. ; T. speciosum and T. penta-phyllum, Oct. or March. Water freely in dry weather. Mulch with decayed manure in Oct. Lift tubers of T. tuberosum in Oct. and store in sand in frost-proof place till March ; leave others undisturbed.

PROPAGATION : T. lobbianum by cuttings of shoots 2 to 3 in. long inserted in sandy soil in temp. 60° in spring. Greenhouse tuberous-rooted species by seeds sown in light, sandy soil in temp. 60° in spring ; cuttings of shoots inserted in sandy soil and similar temp. in spring or summer. Hardy species by seeds sown in loam, leaf-mould, and sand in cold frame in April ; division of roots at planting time.

ANNUAL SPECIES : T. aduncum (Syns. T. canariense and T. peregrinum), Canary Creeper, yellow, summer, 3 to 10 ft., Peru ; Majus (Tall Nasturtium), orange and brown, summer, 5 to 10 ft., Peru, and its variety nanum (Tom Thumb Nasturtium). All these are strictly perennials but are best grown as annuals.

GREENHOUSE SPECIES : T. azureum, blue, green, and white, Oct., 3 to 6 ft., tuberous rooted, Chile ; lobbianum, orange-scarlet, summer and winter, 6 to 10 ft., S. America ; minus, yellow and red, summer, trailing, S. America ; pentaphyllum, vermilion and purple, summer, climbing, tuberous rooted, Buenos Ayres ; tricolor, vermilion, purple, and yellow, summer, climbing, Chile. There are several double-flowered climbing tropæoleums such as Hermann Gnashoff (scarlet) and Double Yellow which may be grown in the greenhouse or bedded out during the summer.

HARDY PERENNIAL SPECIES : T. polyphyllum (Yellow Rock Indian Cress), yellow, June, trailing, Chile ; speciosum (Flame Flower), crimson, summer, 10 ft., Chile ; tuberosum, yellow and red, Sept., climbing, tuberous rooted, Peru.

Tropical Duck Weed—See Pistia.

Trumpet-flower—See Datura, Tecoma, and Bignonia.

Trumpet Gourd (*Lagenaria vulgaris*)—See Lagenaria.

Trumpet Honeysuckle (*Lonicera sempervirens*)—See Lonicera.

Trumpet Leaf (*Sarracenia flava*)—See Sarracenia.

Trumpet Lily (*Lilium longiflorum* and *Richardia africana*)—See Lilium and Richardia.

Trumpet Weed (*Eupatorium purpureum*)—See Eupatorium.

Tsuga—Ord. Coniferæ. Hardy evergreen coniferous trees. Habit of growth handsome and elegant. First introduced 1736.

CULTURE : Soil, deep, rich loam. Position, elevated, well-drained sites in parks or pleasure grounds. Plant in autumn.

PROPAGATION : By seeds sown in sandy soil outdoors in April or in pans in gentle warmth in March ; cuttings of ripened shoots inserted in sandy soil in cold frames during Sept. or Oct.

SPECIES CULTIVATED : T. albertiana, 100 to 200 ft., Western N. America ; brunoniana, to 120 ft., Himalayas ; canadensis (Syn. Abies canadensis), Hemlock Spruce, 60 to 80 ft., N.E. America, and its varieties nana (dwarf), pendula (branches weeping), and Sargenti (weeping) ; caroliniana, 40 to 50 ft., South-eastern U.S.A. ; diversifolia, 70 to 80 ft., Japan ; mertensiana (Syn. Abies albertiana), 100 to 140 ft., N.W. America ; pattoniana (Californian Hemlock Spruce), Syns. T. mertensiana and T. hookeriana, 100 to 150 ft., N.W. America ; Sieboldii (Japanese Hemlock Spruce), 80 to 100 ft., Japan.

Tuberose (*Polianthes tuberosa*)—See Polianthes.

Tube-tongue (*Salpiglossis sinuata*)—See Salpiglossis.

Tufted Columbine—See Thalictrum.

Tufted Pansy—See Viola.

Tulip—See Tulipa.

Tulipa (Tulip)—Ord. Liliaceæ. Hardy bulbous-rooted plants. First introduced 1577.

CLASSIFICATION OF FLORISTS' TULIPS : Breeders or Selfs : Flowers of a more or less uniform colour. Feathered : Having a light, heavy, or irregular dark-coloured edge to the petals. Flamed : Having a dark candle-flame-like spot in the centre of each petal. Bizarres : Yellow petals marked with another colour. Byblomens : White, marked with shades of black, violet, or purple. Roses : White, marked with red.

CLASSIFICATION OF ORDINARY TULIPS : Early : March to April. Late or Cottage : Flowering in May. Darwin : A superior strain of self-coloured tulips. Rembrandt : Same as Darwins but striped. Parrot : Curiously-coloured blooms with large, feathery-edged petals.

CULTURE OF ORDINARY TULIPS : Soil, light, ordinary, previously liberally enriched with well-decayed manure. Position, sunny well-drained beds or borders. Plant bulbs 4 in. deep and 6 in. apart Oct. to Nov. Mulch surface of bed with decayed manure or cocoanut-fibre refuse. Lift bulbs directly after flowering and replant them in sunny reserve border to finish their growth ; or leave until July, then lift, dry, and store away in cool place till planting time. Bulbs may be left in ground altogether if desired, lifting, dividing, and replanting every three years.

POT CULTURE : Compost, two parts loam, one part decayed manure, and little sand. Pot, Sept. to Nov., placing three bulbs in a 5 in. or four in a 6 in. pot and burying bulbs just below the surface. Pot firmly. Cover pots with cinders or cocoanut-fibre refuse in cold frame. Remove to window, frame, or greenhouse when growth begins and water freely. Temp. for forcing, 55° to 65°.

CULTURE FOR EXHIBITION : Compost, four parts good turfy loam, one part leaf-mould, one part decayed cow manure, and one part sand mixed together and allowed to remain in a heap for one year. Position, well-drained sunny bed containing about 18 in. of above compost. Plant bulbs 3 to 4 in. deep and 6 in. apart end of Oct. or beginning of Nov. Surround each bulb with sand. Protect blooms

with canvas awning. Lift bulbs when leaves turn brown. Store in cool shed to dry, after which remove loose skins and place in drawers till planting time.
CULTURE OF HARDY SPECIES : Soil, light, rich, ordinary. Position, sunny borders, rockeries, or naturalised in grass. In latter case plant permanently ; no lifting required. Plant, Sept. to Nov., 3 in. deep and 6 in. apart. Lift, divide, and replant every four years.
PROPAGATION : By seeds sown in Feb. in light, sandy soil in a cold frame, transplanting following year in bed of rich soil outdoors ; by offsets removed from parent bulb and planted 3 in. deep in a bed of light, rich soil in a sunny position outdoors in Nov. Seedling bulbs flower when four to six years old ; offsets when three to four years old.
SPECIES CULTIVATED : T. acuminata, yellow and red, 1 to 1½ ft., May ; australis (Syn. T. celsiana), yellow and red, April, 1½ ft., S.W. Europe ; Batalinii, yellow, May, 5 to 6 in., Asia Minor ; biflora, cream and purplish rose, March, 3 to 4 in., Caucasus ; billiettiana, yellow, May, 2 ft., Europe ; chrysantha, yellow and cherry red, April, 6 to 8 in., Persia ; clusiana, white, red, and black, April, 12 to 18 in., S. Europe ; dasystemon, yellow, white, and green, April, 5 to 6 in., Turkestan ; Didieri, crimson and purplish black, 8 to 12 in., S. Europe, and its variety mauriana ; Eichleri, scarlet and blue-black, April, 9 to 12 in., S.W. Asia ; elegans, red and yellow, May, 1 ft., hybrid ; fosteriana, scarlet, yellow, and black, April, 12 to 18 in., Turkestan ; fragrans, yellow, April, 8 in., Algiers ; gesneriana, scarlet and black, fragrant, May, 2 ft., S. Russia and Asia Minor, parent of florists' tulips, and its varieties fulgens and spathulata ; Greigi, scarlet, yellow, and black, April, 6 to 9 in., Turkestan ; Hageri, copper-red and olive, April, 4 to 6 in., Greece ; ingens, vermilion and purplish black, April, 10 to 12 in., Bokhara ; kaufmanniana, white, red, and yellow, March, 6 in., Turkestan ; kolpakowskyana, yellow and rose, 5 to 6 in., April, 2 ft., Central Asia ; Leichtlinii, pink and white, May, 1½ ft., Kashmir ; linifolia, crimson and blue-purple, May, 6 to 8 in., Bokhara ; macrospeila, crimson and black, fragrant, May, 2 ft., hybrid ; montana, crimson and black, June to July, 6 to 8 in., Persia, etc. ; oculis-solis, red, yellow, and black, April, 18 in., S. Europe ; orphanidea, dark orange, April, 8 to 10 in., Greece ; persica, yellow, tinged green and red, May, 6 to 9 in., probably horticultural form of T. australis ; polychroma, white, yellow, and grey, April, 4 in., Persia ; præcox, red and black, April, 1½ ft., S. Europe ; præstans, light scarlet, April, 10 to 12 in., Bokhara ; primulina, yellow and red, spring, 6 in., Algiers ; pulchella, reddish mauve and yellow, March, 4 to 6 in., Cilicia ; retroflexa, yellow, May, 1½ ft., hybrid ; saxatilis, lilac and yellow, May, 9 to 12 in., Crete ; Sprengeri, orange-scarlet and buff, June, 10 to 12 in., Armenia ; suaveolens, scarlet and yellow, fragrant, May, 6 in., Crimea ; sylvestris, yellow, May, 18 in., Europe ; tubergeniana, vermilion and purplish black, May, 8 to 10 in., Bokhara ; undulatifolia, crimson, yellow, and black, 9 in., Asia Minor ; violacea, mauve, spring, 6 in., N. Persia.

Tulip Poppy (*Papaver glaucum*)—See Papaver.

Tulip Tree (*Liriodendron tulipifera*)—See Liriodendron.

Tunbridge Filmy Fern (*Hymenophyllum tunbridgense*)—See Hymenophyllum.

Tunica—Ord. Caryophyllaceæ. Hardy perennial.
CULTURE : Soil, ordinary light. Position, sunny well-drained rock gardens or dry walls. Plant, Oct. or March.
PROPAGATION : By seed sown in sandy soil in boxes in cold frame during March or by division at the same time.
SPECIES CULTIVATED : T. Saxifraga, pink, June to Sept., 6 in., Europe, and its varieties alba (white) and flore-pleno (double).

Tupelo-tree (*Nyssa aquatica*)—See Nyssa.

Turban Bellflower (*Campanula turbinata*)—See Campanula.

Turban Lily (*Lilium pomponium*)—See Lilium.

Turfing Daisy (*Pyrethrum Tchihatchewi*)—See Pyrethrum.

Turkey Oak (*Quercus Cerris*)—See Quercus.

Turkey Rhubarb (*Rheum palmatum*)—See Rheum.

Turkey's-beard (*Xerophyllum asphodeloides*)—See Xerophyllum.

Turk's-cap Cactus (*Melocactus communis*)—See Melocactus.

Turk's-cap Lily (*Lilium Martagon*)—See Lilium.

Turk's-head Grass (*Lagurus ovatus*)—See Lagurus.

Turmeric—See Curcuma.

Turnip—See Brassica.

Turnip Fern (*Angiopteris evecta*)—See Angiopteris.

Turnip-rooted Celery—See Apium.

Turnsole (*Heliotropium peruvianum*)—See Heliotropium.

Turpentine Tree (*Pistachia Terebinthus*)—See Pistachia.

Turquoise-berried Vine (*Vitis heterophylla*)—See Vitis.

Turtle-head—See Chelone.

Tutsan (*Hypericum Androsæmum*)—See Hypericum.

Tweedia—See Oxypetalum.

Twin-flower (*Linnæa borealis*)—See Linnæa.

Twin-leaf (*Jeffersonia binnata*)—See Jeffersonia.

Twin-leaved Lily of the Valley (*Maianthemum convallaria*)—See Maianthemum.

Tydæa—See Isoloma.

Tyerman's Groundsel (*Senecio pulcher*)—See Senecio.

Typha (Reed Mace)—Ord. Typhaceæ. Hardy aquatic perennials. Inflorescence, brown ; July.
CULTURE : Soil, ordinary. Position, margins of shallow rivers or ponds. Plant, Oct. or March, by division.
SPECIES CULTIVATED : T. angustifolia, 8 to 10 ft. ; latifolia, 6 to 8 ft. ; Laxmani (Syn. T. minima), 2 ft. All natives of the North Temperate Region (Britain).

Ulex (Furze ; Gorse ; Whin)—Ord. Leguminosæ. Hardy evergreen shrubs.
CULTURE : Soil, ordinary. Position, sunny banks, rockeries, or woodlands. Plant, Sept. to April.
HEDGE CULTURE : Plant 18 in. apart in single row. Trim sides in moderately close in April.
PROPAGATION : By seeds sown ¼ in. deep in light soil outdoors in April ; cuttings inserted in sandy soil in cold frame during Aug. and kept close.
SPECIES CULTIVATED : U. europæus flore-pleno, yellow, double, 6 ft., spring, Europe (Britain) ; nanus, yellow, Sept., 1 to 2 ft., W. Europe.

Ulmus (Elm ; Wych Elm)—Ord. Ulmaceæ. Hardy deciduous trees. Flowers, insignificant. Leaves, green or variegated.
CULTURE : Soil, ordinary for common species (U. campestris) ; deep, rich, loamy with gravelly subsoil for Wych Elm (U. montana) ; moist, loamy for American Elm (U. americana). Position, open and sunny woodlands, parks, or shrubberies for all species and varieties. Plant, Oct. to Feb. Timber, fine, hard grain and brown in colour. Used for coffin making, cart and wagon making, furniture, etc. Average weight of timber per cubic ft., 43 lb. Average life of tree, 400 to 500 years. Altitude to which elm will thrive, 1500 ft.
PROPAGATION : By suckers removed and planted Oct. to Nov. ; layering shoots in Sept. ot Oct. ; budding choice kinds on common species and choice variegated kinds on U. montana in July, or by grafting similarly in March ; seeds gathered as soon as ripe and sown in light soil in shady position outdoors.
SPECIES CULTIVATED : U. alata (Winged Elm), 30 to 40 ft., S.U. States ; americana (American Elm), 100 to 120 ft., N. America ; campestris (Common Elm), 70 to

120 ft., habitat uncertain, and its varieties australis (thicker leaves), Louis van Houtte (yellow leaves), and variegata (leaves blotched creamy white) ; fulva (Slippery Elm), 60 to 70 ft., N. America ; montana (Wych Elm), Syn. U. glabra, 100 to 125 ft., Europe, and its varieties Camperdowni (weeping), crispa (Syn. urticæfolia), fastigiata (upright growing), and pendula (branches stiffly drooping) ; nitens, to 100 ft., Europe (Britain) and W. Asia, and its varieties Berardi (small foliaged) and suberosa (Cork Barked Elm) ; parvifolia, to 40 ft., China and Japan ; pedunculata (Syn. U. lævis), to 100 ft., Europe ; pumila, 10 to 30 ft., N. Asia ; stricta (Cornish Elm), 80 to 100 ft., S.W. England and France, and its variety Wheatleyi (Jersey and Guernsey Elm) ; viminalis, 40 to 60 ft., probably a hybrid. Three natural and distinct hybrids between U. montana and U. nitens are known as U. belgica, U. major, and U. vegeta. See also Zelkowa.

Umbellularia—Ord. Lauraceæ.   Half-hardy evergreen flowering tree.   First introduced 1829.
CULTURE : Soil, loamy, well drained. Position, against sheltered walls or in protected places in the open.   Plant, Sept. to Oct. or April to May.
PROPAGATION : By seeds sown in pans of sandy soil in cool greenhouse during Feb. or March ; by layering in spring.
SPECIES CULTIVATED : U. californica (Syn. Oreodaphne californica), yellowish green, April, 20 to 80 ft., California and Oregon.

Umbilicus—See Cotyledon.

Umbrella Fern—See Gleichenia.

Umbrella Fir (*Sciadopitys verticillata*)—See Sciadopitys.

Umbrella Leaf (*Diphylleia cymosa*)—See Diphylleia.

Umbrella Palm (*Hedyscepe canterburyana*)—See Hedyscepe.

Umbrella Pine (*Pinus pinea*)—See Pinus.

Umbrella Plant—See Saxifraga and Cyperus.

Umbrella Tree (*Magnolia tripetala*)—See Magnolia.

Unicorn-plant—See Martynia.

Unicorn-root (*Veltheimia viridifolia*)—See Veltheimia.

Uniola (Sea Oat)—Ord. Gramineæ.   Hardy perennial grass.   Orn. flowering. Inflorescence borne in large loose panicles, July and Aug.
CULTURE : Soil, ordinary. Plant, March or April. Position, open, sunny borders. Gather inflorescence and dry for winter use in Aug.
PROPAGATION : By seeds sown in light, rich soil outdoors in April ; by division of roots in March.
SPECIES CULTIVATED : U. latifolia, 5 ft., N. America.

Urceolina (Golden Urn-flower ; Drooping Urn-flower)—Ord. Amaryllidaceæ. Greenhouse deciduous bulbous plants.   First introduced 1836.
CULTURE : Compost, two parts turfy loam, one part river sand, and a few crushed bones. Position, well-drained pots in light part of house. Pot, Feb., burying bulb about two-thirds of its depth. Water freely from time growth begins (about Feb.) until Sept., when keep quite dry. Apply liquid manure when flower spike shows. Top-dress annually and repot every three or four years only. Temp., Feb. to Sept. 55° to 65° ; Sept. to Feb. 40° to 50°.
PROPAGATION : By seeds sown $\frac{1}{16}$ in. deep in well-drained pots of sandy loam in temp. 65° to 70° in March, placing seedlings singly in 2 in. pots, and keeping them moderately moist all the year round for three years ; by offsets, treated as old bulbs.
SPECIES CULTIVATED : U. pendula (Syn. U. aurea), yellow, summer, 1 ft., Peru.

Urginea—Ord. Liliaceæ.   Half-hardy bulbous plant.   Source of the " squill " of commerce.   First introduced 1829.
CULTURE : Soil, light loam, leaf-mould, and sand. Position, well-drained pots in unheated greenhouse. Pot, Oct. to Nov. Water freely during the growing season.

Viburnum Carlesii

Viburnum fragrans

Viburnum Lantana
(Wayfaring Tree)

Viburnum lobophyllum

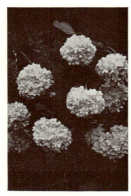

Viburnum Opulus sterile
(Snowball Tree)

Vinca major
(Periwinkle)

Viscum album
(Mistletoe)

Vitis hybrida
(Ornamental Vine)

Waldsteinia trifolia
(Barren Strawberry)

Wistaria floribunda
(Kidney-bean Tree)

Wistaria sinensis
(Kidney-bean Tree)

Xanthoceras sorbifolia

Xanthoceras sorbifolia
(Fruit)

Xeranthemum annuum
(Immortelle)

Yucca gloriosa
(Adam's Needle)

Zea Mays japonica
(Indian Corn)

Zenobia speciosa pulverulenta

Zephyranthes candida
(Peruvian Swamp Lily)

PROPAGATION : By offsets, removed at potting time.
SPECIES CULTIVATED : U. Scilla (Syn. U. maritima), whitish, late summer, to 3 ft., S. Europe and S. Africa.

Ursinia—Ord. Compositæ.   Half-hardy annuals.   First introduced 1774.
CULTURE : Soil, ordinary.   Position, sunny beds or borders.   Sow seeds, Feb. or March, in ordinary light mould in pots, pans, or boxes in temp. 55° to 65° and transplant seedlings when an inch high to 3 in. apart in shallow boxes ; place in cold frame in April ; harden off and plant outdoors, May or June.   Also sow seeds in open ground in April where required to grow and thin seedlings to 4 or 6 in. apart when 1 to 6 in. high.
SPECIES CULTIVATED : U. anthemoides, yellow and purple, summer, 1 ft., S. Africa ; pulchra (Syn. Sphenogyne speciosa), yellow and brown, summer, 1 to 2 ft., S. Africa.

Utricularia (Bladderwort)—Ord. Lentibulariaceæ.   Hardy aquatic herb.   Interesting as a carnivorous plant.
CULTURE : Soil unnecessary.   Position, ponds or tubs in about 2 ft. of water. Plant, April to May.
PROPAGATION : By division at planting time.
SPECIES CULTIVATED : U. vulgaris, yellow, Aug., floating, Europe (Britain).

Uvularia (Bell-wort)—Ord. Liliaceæ.   Hardy plants.   First introduced 1710.
CULTURE : Soil, moist peat.   Position, partially shaded border.   Plant, Oct. and Nov.
PROPAGATION : By division of roots in Oct.
SPECIES CULTIVATED : U. grandiflora, yellow, May, 1 ft., N. America ; perfoliata, yellow, May, 1 ft., N. America ; sessilifolia (Syn. Oakesia sessilifolia), greenish yellow, May, 1 ft., N. America.

Vaccinium (Whortleberry;   Bilberry;   Huckleberry)—Ord. Vacciniaceæ. Hardy deciduous and evergreen flowering or berry-bearing shrubs.   Berries, red, bluish black ; edible ; Aug. to Oct.
CULTURE OF DECIDUOUS SPECIES : Soil, boggy peat.   Position, moist rock gardens and shrubberies.   Plant, Oct. to March.
CULTURE OF EVERGREEN SPECIES : Soil and position, as above.   V. glauco-album and V. Mortinia are rather tender and require some winter protection.   Plant, Sept. to Oct. or April to May.
PROPAGATION : By seeds sown in shallow boxes or pans filled with moist, sandy peat in temp. of 55° to 65° in spring, transplanting seedlings outdoors in summer ; cuttings of shoots inserted in sandy, moist peat under hand-light in shade in summer ; layering shoots in autumn ; division of plants, Sept. ot March.
DECIDUOUS SPECIES CULTIVATED : V. canadense, white, tinged red, May, 1 ft., Eastern N. America ; corymbosum, pinkish, May, 4 to 12 ft., Eastern N. America, and its variety pallidum ; erythrocarpum, pale red, June, 3 to 6 ft., South-eastern U.S.A. ; hirsutum, white, tinged pink, May, 2 ft., N. Carolina, etc.; Myrtillus (Bilberry or Whortleberry), pale pink, May, 6 to 18 in., N. Hemisphere (Britain) ; padifolium, yellow, tinged purple, June, 6 to 8 ft., Madeira ; parviflorum, pinkish white, 2 to 6 ft., Western N. America ; pennsylvanicum, white, tinged red, April to May, 1 to 2 ft., N. America.
EVERGREEN SPECIES CULTIVATED : V. glauco-album, pinkish white, 2 to 4 ft., Himalayas ; Mortinia, rosy pink, June, 2 to 4 ft., Ecuador ; ovatum, white, Sept., 10 to 12 ft., Western N. America ; Vitis-Idæa (Cowberry), pink, May to June, 6 to 10 in., N. Hemisphere (Britain).

Valerian (*Centranthus ruber*)—See Centranthus.

Valeriana (Cretan Spikenard)—Ord. Valerianaceæ.   Hardy perennial herbs.
CULTURE : Soil, ordinary.   Position, sunny borders for V. Phu aurea ; sunny rock gardens or the front of borders for other species.   Plant, Sept. to April.   Cut down flowering stems of V. Phu aurea in Oct. and pick off flower buds as they form.

PROPAGATION : By seeds sown $\frac{1}{16}$ in. deep in light soil in sunny position outdoors in April ; division of roots in March or April.
SPECIES CULTIVATED : V. arizonica, pink, March, 2 to 3 in., habitat unknown ; celtica (Nard or Speik), brownish yellow, June, 4 to 5 in., Europe ; Phu aurea, white, Aug., 2 ft., Caucasus ; supina, rose pink, spring and early summer, 3 to 4 in., Europe.

Valerianella (Corn Salad ; Lamb's Lettuce)—Ord. Valerianaceæ. Hardy annual salad vegetables. Leaves, largely used in winter and spring for salads.
CULTURE : Soil, ordinary. Position, sunny, dryish border. Sow seeds in drills, 1 in. deep and 6 in. apart, fortnightly during Aug. and Sept. Thin seedlings when three leaves form to 6 in. apart in the row. Gather leaves either separately or by cutting off the entire plant.
SPECIES CULTIVATED : V. eriocarpa (Italian Corn Salad), light blue, April, 6 in., S. Europe ; olitoria, blue, April, 6 in., Europe (Britain).

Vallisneria (Eel Grass ; Tape Grass)—Ord. Hydrocharitaceæ. Half-hardy aquatic herb. First introduced 1818. Flowers, white ; minute ; July. Leaves, long, narrow.
CULTURE : Soil, rich loam. Position, deep tubs, cisterns, or aquariums filled with water. Plant in small pot or in heap of compost in bottom of tank, etc., March or April. Temp., Sept. to March 45° to 50° ; March to Sept. 60° to 75°.
PROPAGATION : By seeds sown in moist loam in water, spring ; division, spring.
SPECIES CULTIVATED : V. spiralis, S. Europe, and its variety magnifica.

Vallota (Scarborough Lily)—Ord. Amaryllidaceæ. Greenhouse evergreen bulbous plants. First introduced 1774.
CULTURE : Compost, equal parts good fibrous loam, leaf-mould, and sand. Position, well-drained pots in light, sunny greenhouse or window. Pot imported bulbs, Oct., Nov., March, or April. Repot established plants in June or July. Place bulbs with points just below the surface ; pot firmly. Water moderately Sept. to March, freely March to June, keep nearly dry June to Sept. Apply stimulants once or twice a week March to June. Established plants do best placed in sunny, cold frame, or on layer of cinder ashes or slate, tile, or board in open air, May till flowering period. Repotting necessary every three or four years only. Temp., Sept. to March 40° to 50° ; March to June 55° to 65°.
OUTDOOR CULTURE : Soil, light, sandy loam. Position, warm, well-drained border at foot of S. wall. Plant bulbs, Oct., Nov., March, or April, 6 in. deep and surround with sand. Press soil firmly round bulbs. Protect in winter with a covering of dry litter or fern fronds.
PROPAGATION : By offsets, removed at potting or planting time.
SPECIES CULTIVATED : V. purpurea, red, Aug., 2 to 3 ft., S. Africa ; purpurea eximia, white and crimson ; purpurea magnifica, large-flowered. Hybrida is a hybrid between V. purpurea and Cyrtanthus sanguineus and bears vermilion-coloured flowers.

Vancouveria—Ord. Berberidaceæ. Hardy perennial. First introduced 1827.
CULTURE : Soil, rich loam. Position, cool, shady beds or borders. Plant, Oct. to Nov. or March to April.
PROPAGATION : By division in spring.
SPECIES CULTIVATED : V. hexandra, white, spring, 12 to 18 in., N. America.

Vanda (Cowslip-scented Orchid)—Ord. Orchidaceæ. Stove epiphytal orchids. First introduced 1810.
CULTURE : Compost, clean potsherds and fresh sphagnum moss only. Position, teak baskets suspended from roof or pots filled three parts of their depth with potsherds, remainder sphagnum moss ; or on rafts of teak wood. V. teres does best with its stems secured to a branch of apple or oak fixed firmly in a pot. Pot, place in baskets or on rafts in March. In potting or basketing insert the roots carefully among the potsherds and finish off with a layer of fresh sphagnum moss. Water copiously daily March to Oct., moderately afterwards. Plants on rafts require

to be dipped for a few moments daily in water.   Expose plants fully to the sun all the year round.   Moist atmosphere highly essential March to Oct.   Growing period, March to Oct.   Temp., Oct. to March 60° to 70° ;   March to Oct. 75° to 85°.

PROPAGATION :   By cutting tops, furnished with one or two roots, off tall plants or by removing young growths with roots attached from base of plants in Feb. or March and potting or placing in baskets as advised for old plants.

SPECIES CULTIVATED :   V. amesiana, white, rose, and magenta, various seasons, fragrant, India ;   Bensoni, white, violet, and pink, various seasons, Burma ;   cærulea, lavender blue, autumn, N. India ;   cærulescens, purplish blue, March to May, Burma ;   cristata, greenish yellow and brown, winter, N. India ;   denisoniana, white and yellow, summer, Burma ;   hookeriana, white, rose, and magenta-purple, autumn, Malaya ;   insignis, brown, chocolate, yellow, white, and rose, winter, Timor ;   kimballiana, white, rosy purple, yellow, and brown, autumn, Burma ;   lamellata, yellow, brown, and white, autumn and winter, Philippines, and its variety Boxallii ;   Parishii, yellow, brown, magenta, and violet, fragrant, summer, Burma ;   Roxburghii, green, brown, purple, and white, summer, India ;   sanderiana, pink, yellow, and crimson, summer, Philippines ;   suavis, white, purple, and rose, fragrant, winter and spring, Java ;   teres, white, rose, orange, and magenta, spring, India ;   tricolor, yellow, white, magenta, and purple, various seasons, Java.

Vanilla—Ord. Orchidaceæ.   Stove climbing orchid.   First introduced 1800. Seed pods form the vanilla of commerce.

CULTURE :   Compost, equal parts peat, sphagnum moss, and clean potsherds. Position, well-drained pots, pans, or narrow bed, with shoots trained up wall or rafter or logs of wood.   Pot or plant, Feb. or March.   Water copiously March to Oct., moderately afterwards.   Shade from sun.   Syringe foliage daily in summer. Temp., March to Sept. 75° to 85° ;   Sept. to March 60° to 70°.

PROPAGATION :   By cuttings of climbing stems cut into 2 or 3 in. lengths and imbedded in sphagnum moss and peat in temp. of 75° to 85° in spring.

SPECIES CULTIVATED :   V. planifolia (Vanilla Orchid), greenish yellow, summer, 10 to 20 ft., Central America.

Vanilla Orchid (*Vanilla planifolia*)—See Vanilla.

Variegated Grass—See Stenotaphrum.

Vegetable Fire-cracker (*Brevoortia Ida-Maia*)—See Brevoortia.

Vegetable Marrow (*Cucurbita Pepo ovifera*)—See Cucurbita.

Vegetable Oyster (*Tragopogon porrifolius*)—See Tragopogon.

Vella—Ord. Cruciferæ.   Evergreen or deciduous flowering shrubs.   Hardy or half-hardy.   First introduced about 1759.

CULTURE :   Soil, ordinary light.   Position, sheltered and rather dry border for V. pseudocytisus ;   sunny position in rock garden for V. spinosa.   Plant, Oct. to Nov.

PROPAGATION :   By cuttings of half-ripened wood inserted in sandy soil under bellglass in gentle bottom heat from June to Aug.

SPECIES CULTIVATED :   V. pseudocytisus, yellow and purple, May to July, 1 to 2 ft., evergreen, Central Spain ;   spinosa, yellow and brown, June, 1 ft., deciduous, Spain.

Veltheimia—Ord. Liliaceæ.   Greenhouse bulbous plants.   First introduced 1768.

CULTURE :   Compost, two parts sandy loam, one part well-decayed cow manure, and little sand.   Position, light, sunny greenhouse or window Sept. to June ;   sunny, cold frame remainder of year.   Pot bulbs of V. viridifolia Aug. to Nov. ;   those of V. glauca Oct. to March.   Place bulbs with point just below surface of compost.   Press compost firmly in pots.   Water moderately when new growth commences, freely when in full growth, keep nearly dry when leaves die off. Apply stimulants occasionally when the plants are growing freely.   Temp., Sept. to March 40° to 50° ;   March to June 55° to 65°.

PROPAGATION :   By offsets removed from parent bulbs, placed in small pots, and treated as advised for large bulbs ; by leaves removed close to bulbs and inserted singly in pots of sandy soil in spring or summer.

SPECIES CULTIVATED : V. glauca, yellow, tinged red, March, 1 to 1½ ft. ; viridifolia (Unicorn-root), yellow, tinged red, Aug., 1 to 1½ ft.   Both natives of S. Africa

Velvet Flower—See Amaranthus.

Venetian Sumach (*Rhus Cotinus*)—See Rhus.

Venidium—Ord. Compositæ.   Half-hardy annuals and perennials.   All treated as half-hardy annuals.

CULTURE : Soil, ordinary.   Position, sunny borders.   Sow seeds in light soil in temp. 55° to 65°, March or April, transplanting seedlings outdoors May or June.

SPECIES CULTIVATED : V. decurrens calendulaceum (Syn. V. calendulaceum), yellow and purplish brown, summer, 2 ft., S. Africa, perennial treated as annual ; fastuosum, orange and purplish black, summer, 1½ to 2½ ft., S. Africa.

Venus's Fly Trap (*Dionæa muscipula*)—See Dionæa.

Venus's Looking-glass (*Legonsia speculum-veneris*)—See Legonsia.

Venus's Navel-wort (*Omphalodes linifolia*)—See Omphalodes.

Veratrum (False Hellebore)—Ord. Liliaceæ.   Hardy herbaceous perennials. First introduced 1548.   Leaves, large, much ribbed, green.   Roots, poisonous.

CULTURE : Soil, light ordinary or peaty.   Position, partially shady, moist borders. Plant, Oct. to April.

PROPAGATION : By seeds sown in peaty soil in deep pans in cool greenhouse during Feb. or March ; division of roots, Oct. or April.   Seed frequently takes several months to germinate.

SPECIES CULTIVATED : V. album, white, July, 3 to 4 ft., Europe ; californicum, greenish white, summer, to 6 ft., California ; nigrum, maroon, summer, 4 to 5 ft., Europe ; viride, yellowish green, July, 5 to 8 ft., N. America.

Verbascum (Mullein ; Aaron's Rod)—Ord. Scrophulariaceæ.   Hardy biennial and perennial herbs.

CULTURE OF BIENNIAL SPECIES : Soil, ordinary.   Position, sunny borders.   Sow seeds in light, rich soil in sunny position outdoors in April, transplanting seedlings when three or four leaves form 6 in. apart in sunny position until following April, then plant where required to flower.

CULTURE OF PERENNIAL SPECIES : Soil, deep, light, rich ordinary.   Position, sunny borders.   Plant, Oct., Nov., March, or April.

PROPAGATION : By seeds, as advised for biennial species ; by division of roots in March or April.

BIENNIAL SPECIES : V. olympicum (Olympian Mullein), yellow, summer, 6 ft., Bithynia ; Thapsus, yellow, summer, to 6 ft., Europe (Britain) and Asia.

PERENNIAL SPECIES : V. Chaixii (Nettle-leaved Mullein), yellow, summer, 3 ft., S.W. Europe ; longifolium, yellow, July to Aug., 4 to 6 ft., Europe, and its variety pannosum ; nigrum (Dark Mullein), Syn. V. vernale, yellow, summer, 3 ft., Europe (Britain) ; phœniceum (Purple Mullein), violet and red, summer, 3 ft., Europe ; thapsiforme (Syn. V. densiflorum), yellow, summer, to 5 ft., Europe ; wiedemannianum, blue and purple, summer, to 3 ft., Asia Minor.   There are numerous hybrids such as Caledonia, Cotswold Queen, Miss Willmott, and Harkness Hybrid.

Verbena (Vervain)—Ord. Verbenaceæ.   Greenhouse half-hardy perennials. Present race of bedding verbenas originally derived from V. teucrioides and other species.   First introduced 1774.

CULTURE OF V. HYBRIDA AND V. TEUCRIOIDES : Compost, two parts good turfy loam and one part of equal proportions of decayed manure, leaf-mould, and sharp silver sand.   Position, pots in light greenhouse ; or cold frames in summer. Pot, Feb. to May.   Water freely April to Oct., moderately afterwards.   Apply stimulants two or three times weekly to plants in flower.   Nip off points of shoots during spring to induce bushy growth. Discontinue nipping off points of shoots six weeks before plants are required to flower. Young plants struck from cuttings or raised from seed best adapted for pot culture. Temp., Oct. to March 40° to 50° ; March to June 55° to 65°. Shade from sun.

OUTDOOR CULTURE : Soil, good ordinary liberally enriched with decayed manure. Position, sunny beds or borders. Plant 12 in. apart each way in June. Water freely in dry weather. Peg shoots to surface of bed as they grow, and when they meet each other nip off their points.

CULTURE OF V. CANADENSIS, V. ERINOIDES, AND V. TENERA : Soil, ordinary. Sow seeds in pans of sandy soil in temp. 60° during Feb. or March, transplanting seedlings to deep boxes when large enough to handle and hardening off for planting outdoors in sunny beds or borders during May. Really perennials but are best treated as half-hardy annuals.

CULTURE OF V. VENOSA AND V. BONARIENSIS : Soil, ordinary rich. Position, sunny beds or borders. Plant, May. Lift roots in Oct., store in ordinary soil in boxes in frost-proof place until March, then place in temp. 55°, and when new shoots form remove these with portions of old roots, place in small pots, harden off, and plant out 12 in. apart in May ; or plant old roots, dividing them, if necessary, direct into beds in April. Peg shoots of V. venosa down as they grow. May be grown outdoors altogether in well-drained soils in sheltered districts.

CULTURE OF V. CHAMÆDRYFOLIA : Soil, ordinary. Position, sunny beds or rock gardens. Insert cuttings of current year's growth in Aug. and Sept. in boxes filled with sandy soil and place in frost-proof frame or greenhouse until May, then plant in the open. Plants may survive outdoors in a mild winter.

PROPAGATION : Garden verbenas by seeds sown $\frac{1}{16}$ in. deep in pots, pans, or boxes filled with a compost of equal parts loam and leaf-mould and little sand, placed in a temp. 65° to 75° in Jan., Feb., or March, transplanting seedlings when third leaf forms in boxes or pans, placing these on shelf near glass in temp. 55°, transferring when fairly strong singly to 2½ in. pots, and later on to a larger size ; by cuttings inserted in a bed of sandy soil in cold frame in Aug., lifting cuttings when rooted and planting 2 in. apart in boxes or pans and storing in shelf in greenhouse until March, then potting off singly in small pots ; or young shoots taken off in Feb. or March and inserted in damp sand under bell-glass in temp. 65°.

SPECIES CULTIVATED : V. bonariensis, purplish lilac, summer, 4 to 5 ft., S. America ; canadensis (Syns. V. Aubletia and V. Drummondi), purple or lilac, summer, 1 ft., N. America ; chamædryfolia, scarlet, summer and autumn, trailing, Brazil, Peru, etc. ; erinoides (Syn. V. laciniata), lilac, summer, trailing, Peru ; hybrida, various colours, summer, 1 ft., hybrids ; tenera (Syn. V. pulchella), blue or lilac, summer, trailing, Southern S. America, sometimes wrongly named V. ericoides ; teucrioides, yellowish white or pink, summer, 1 ft., Brazil, etc. ; venosa, claret-purple, summer, 2 ft., Argentina.

Vernonia (Ironweed)—Ord. Compositæ. Hardy herbaceous flowering plants. First introduced 1710.

CULTURE : Soil, rich, sandy loam. Position, sunny borders. Plant, March or April. Top-dress with decayed manure in spring.

PROPAGATION : By seeds sown in sandy soil in a cold frame in March or April, or outdoors in a sunny border in April ; also by division of the roots in March or April.

SPECIES CULTIVATED : V. altissima, purple and violet, autumn, 4 to 10 ft., U. States ; arkansana (Syn. V. crinita), purple, autumn, 4 to 12 ft., N. America ; novebora-censis, purple, summer, 4 to 9 ft., U. States.

Veronica (Speedwell)—Ord. Scrophulariaceæ. Half-hardy and hardy evergreen flowering shrubs and hardy herbaceous perennials.

CULTURE OF SHRUBBY SPECIES : Soil, ordinary, or loam and peat. Position, sunny rockeries, borders, or beds near the sea coast, or in inland sheltered districts south of the Trent. Plant, Sept. or April. Protect in very severe weather. Prune straggly plants into shape in April.

POT CULTURE : Compost, two parts loam, one part peat, and little sand. Position, sunny greenhouse, windows, corridors, porches, or balconies. Pot, Sept. or

March. Water freely April to Oct., moderately other times. Apply stimulants occasionally to healthy plants during summer. Plants put out in rich soil in sunny position in May, kept well watered, lifted, and placed in pots in Sept., will usually flower freely in the greenhouse during autumn.

CULTURE OF HARDY PERENNIAL SPECIES : Soil, ordinary rich. Position, sunny borders or rockeries. Plant, Sept. to Nov. or Feb. to May. Lift, divide, and replant triennially. Water freely in dry weather.

PROPAGATION : Shrubby species by cuttings of young growth inserted in sandy soil under bell-glass in gentle bottom heat in June to July ; cuttings of nearly ripened growth under hand-light or in cold frame in summer ; perennials by division of roots in autumn or spring ; seeds sown in light soil in shade outdoors in April.

SHRUBBY SPECIES : V. Andersonii variegata, foliage margined with white, 2 to 3 ft., hybrid ; amplexicaulis, white, July to Aug., 1 to 3 ft., New Zealand ; angustifolia, white, July to Sept., New Zealand ; anomala, white or pale pink, July to Aug., 3 to 5 ft., New Zealand ; Armstrongi, white, July to Aug., 1 to 1½ ft., New Zealand ; Astoni, heath-like bronzy-green foliage, 6 to 12 in., New Zealand ; Bidwillii, white, veined pink, summer, 6 to 12 in., New Zealand ; Buchananii, white, July to Aug., 1 ft., New Zealand ; carnosula, white, July to Aug., 1 to 3 ft., New Zealand ; Catarractæ, white and pink, summer, 6 to 9 in., New Zealand ; chathamica, purple, summer, 1 to 1½ ft., New Zealand ; Colensoi, white, July to Aug., 1 to 1½ ft., New Zealand ; cupressoides, pale blue, summer, 1 to 6 ft., New Zealand ; darwiniana, white, July to Aug., 2 to 3 ft., New Zealand ; decumbens, white, July to Aug., to 3 ft., New Zealand ; diosmæfolia, white or pale blue, July to Aug., to 5 ft., New Zealand ; elliptica (Syn. V. decussata), white, summer, to 20 ft., New Zealand ; glauco-cœrulea, purplish blue, July to Aug., 1 ft., New Zealand ; Hectori, white or pink, July to Aug., 6 to 24 in., New Zealand ; hookeriana, white, summer, 8 to 12 in., New Zealand ; hulkeana, lilac, 4 to 6 ft., New Zealand ; Lewisii, pale blue, summer, 4 to 6 ft., New Zealand ; loganioides, white, July to Aug., 4 to 12 in., New Zealand ; Lyallii, white, veined pink, summer, 6 to 9 in., New Zealand ; lycopodioides, white, July, 1 to 2 ft., New Zealand ; Matthewsii, white and pink, July to Aug., 2 to 3 ft., New Zealand ; pimeleoides, purplish blue, June to Aug., 1 to 1½ ft., New Zealand ; pinquifolia, white, July to Aug., 1 to 3 ft., New Zealand ; salicifolia, white, summer, 6 to 10 ft., New Zealand ; speciosa, reddish purple, July to Sept., to 5 ft., New Zealand ; Traversii, white, summer, 4 to 6 ft., New Zealand ; vernicosa, white, June to Aug., 1 to 2 ft., New Zealand.

PERENNIAL SPECIES : V. Allionii, violet blue, June to July, 2 in., S.W. Europe ; cæspitosa, pink, May to June, 1 to 2 in., Greece and Asia Minor ; canescens, pale blue, July, prostrate, New Zealand ; cinerea, pink, July to Aug., 3 to 4 in., Asia Minor ; filiformis, china blue, May to June, 3 in., Asia Minor ; gentianoides, blue, June, 8 to 12 in., S.E. Europe, and its variety variegata (leaves variegated with white) ; incana, blue, summer, 18 in., S. Europe ; kotschyana, pink, May to June, 2 to 3 in., Cilicia ; linifolia (frequently erroneously named V. filifolia), pale blue or pink, June, 6 to 9 in., New Zealand ; longifolia, lilac blue, Aug., 18 in. to 2 ft., Europe, and its variety subsessilis (deep blue) ; orientalis, pink, summer, 6 to 8 in., Asia Minor ; pectinata, pale blue, May to June, 6 in., Greece and Asia Minor ; peduncularis, pearly white, May to June, 6 in., Caucasus ; pyrolæfolia, lavender, June, 6 in., China ; repens, pale blue, summer, 2 to 3 in., Corsica ; satureoides, deep blue, April, 3 in., Dalmatia ; saxatilis (Syn. V. fruticans), blue, July, 6 in., Europe ; spicata, blue, July, 12 to 18 in., Europe, and its varieties alba (white), corymbosa (blue), and rosea (pink) ; Teucrium, blue, May to June, 1½ ft., Europe, and its varieties dubia (Syns. V. rupestris and V. prostrata), dwarf, and Trehane (golden-leaved) ; virginica, bluish white, July, 4 to 6 ft., N. America, and its varieties alba (white) and japonica (pale purple).

Verschaffeltia—Ord. Palmaceæ. Stove palm. Orn. foliage. First introduced 1864. Leaves, roundish, divided at tips, bright green.

CULTURE : Compost, two parts fibrous peat, one part equal proportions charcoal, turfy loam, and sand. Position, moist, shady part of stove. Pot, Feb. or March. Syringe freely twice daily Feb. to Oct., once daily afterwards. Water freely at

all times. Shade and moist atmosphere essential. Temp., March to Oct. 70° to 85° ; Oct. to March 65° to 75°.
PROPAGATION : By seeds sown 1 in. deep in peat and loam in small pots in temp. 75° to 85°, spring.
SPECIES CULTIVATED : V. splendida, 12 to 80 ft., Seychelles.

Vervain—See Verbena.

Vesicaria—Ord. Cruciferæ. Hardy perennial. First introduced 1730.
CULTURE : Soil, ordinary. Position, sunny borders or rock gardens. Plant, autumn or spring.
PROPAGATION : By division or seed sown in spring.
SPECIES CULTIVATED : V. utriculata, yellow, May to June, large, inflated seed pods, to 1½ ft., Europe.

Vetch, Kidney—See Anthyllis.

Viburnum (Guelder Rose ; Laurustinus ; Wayfaring Tree ; Snowball Tree)—Ord. Caprifoliaceæ. Hardy deciduous and evergreen flowering shrubs.
CULTURE : Soil, rich, deep, rather moist loam. Position, open, sunny shrubberiest Plant, Oct. to March. Thin out weak growths in winter, but otherwise do no. prune.
CULTURE OF LAURUSTINUS : Soil, deep, sandy loam. Position, warm, sheltered shrubberies, etc. Plant, Sept., Oct., or April. Prune, April. This species also suitable for pot culture for flowering in cold greenhouses in winter. Pot, spring. Position, outdoors in semi-shady position, May till Oct. ; in cold greenhouse, Oct. to May. Water freely while outdoors, moderately in winter.
PROPAGATION : By cuttings of half-ripened shoots inserted in sandy loam under bell-glass in gentle bottom heat during July and Aug. ; or by layering shoots in Sept. or Oct.
DECIDUOUS SPECIES : V. acerifolium, white, June, fruits bright red to black, 3 to 6 ft., Eastern N. America ; alnifolium, white, May to June, fruits red to black, 6 to 10 ft., Eastern N. America ; bitchuense, white, fragrant, May to July, to 5 ft., Japan ; betulifolium, white, fruits red, to 12 ft., W. China ; buddleifolium, white, fruits black, to 6 ft., Central China ; Carlesii, pink to white, fragrant, April, 3 to 4 ft., Corea ; cassinoides, yellowish white, June, fruits blue-black, 6 to 12 ft., Eastern N. America ; dentatum (Arrow Wood), white, June to July, fruits blue-black, to 15 ft., Eastern N. America ; dilatatum, white, May, fruits red, 6 to 10 ft., China and Japan ; fragrans, pinkish white, fragrant, autumn and winter, to 10 ft., China ; hupehense, white, June, fruits red, to 6 ft., China ; Lantana (Wayfaring Tree), white, May to June, berries red, 12 to 15 ft., Europe (Britain) ; Lentago, creamy white, May to June, 20 to 30 ft., Eastern N. America ; lobophyllum, white, May to June, fruits red, to 15 ft., China ; macrocephalum, white, May to June, 12 to 20 ft., China, partially evergreen, and its variety sterile (all flowers sterile) ; Opulus (Wild Guelder Rose), white, June, 8 to 15 ft., Europe (Britain) ; Opulus sterile, sterile-flowered (the Garden Guelder Rose or Snowball Tree) ; prunifolium, white, June, fruits dark blue, 20 to 30 ft., Eastern N. America ; pubescens, white, June, fruits dark purple, 3 to 5 ft., Eastern N. America ; Sieboldi, creamy white, June to July, fruits pink to blue-black, 6 to 10 ft., Japan ; theiferum, white, May to June, fruits red, to 12 ft., China ; tomentosum, white, June, 6 to 10 ft., China and Japan, and its varieties Mariesii (large sterile flowers) and plicatum (flowers sterile) ; Veitchii, white, May to June, fruits red to black, 5 ft., Central China ; venosum (frequently wrongly named V. pubescens), white, June to July, fruits blue, 10 to 12 ft., Eastern U.S.A. ; Wrightii, white, May, fruits red, 6 to 10 ft., China and Japan.
EVERGREEN SPECIES : V. cinnamomæfolium, white, fruits blue-black, to 20 ft., China ; cylindricum (Syn. V. coriaceum), white, July to Sept., to 40 ft., China and Himalayas ; Davidii, white, June, fruits deep blue, 2 ft., W. China ; fœtidum, white, June, fruits red, 6 to 10 ft., China ; harryanum, white, fruits black, 6 to 8 ft., W. China ; Henryi, white, summer, fruits red to black, to 10 ft., China ; japonicum (Syn. V. macrophyllum), white, June, 4 to 6 ft., Japan ; propinquum, greenish white, fruits blue-black, 3 to 5 ft., China ; Tinus (Laurustinus), white and pink, winter, 8 to 10 ft., Mediterranean Region ; utile, white, May, 5 to 6 ft., China.

Vicia (Vetch ; Broad Bean)—Ord. Leguminosæ. Hardy annual and perennial herbs, including the well-known vegetable called the Broad Bean.
CULTURE OF BROAD BEANS : Soil, rich, well-manured, moist loam for main crops ; lighter, rich soil for early ones. Position, south borders for early crops ; open garden for main or late ones. Sow early longpod varieties in Jan. and Feb., main crop sorts in March and April. Distances : Drills 3 in. deep and 2½ ft. apart for early ; 3 in. deep and 3 ft. apart for main crops. Seeds to be 4 to 6 in. apart in drills. Soak seeds in water for a few hours before sowing. Nip off points of plants when first flowers open. Mulch late crops with decayed manure, especially on light soils. Manures : Kainit, 2 lb. ; superphosphate, 9 lb. ; nitrate of soda, 5 lb. ; sulphate of iron, 1 lb. Apply these quantities per square rod when young plants are above ground. Crop ready for use 18 weeks after sowing. Seeds take 12 to 14 days to germinate. Seeds retain their germinating powers one year. Quantity of seeds to sow a row 50 ft. long, 1 pint.
CULTURE OF PERENNIAL SPECIES : Soil, ordinary. Position, sunny rock gardens or front of borders. Plant, Oct. to Nov. or March to April.
PROPAGATION : Perennial species by seed sown in cold frame in March.
ANNUAL SPECIES : V. faba (Broad Bean), white, June and July, 3 ft., East.
PERENNIAL SPECIES : V. oroboides (Syn. Orobus lathyroides), white or yellow, summer, 2 ft., Europe ; Orobus, purplish white, summer, 1 ft., Europe (Britain) ; unijuga, violet purple, summer, 1½ ft., Siberia.

Victoria (Royal Water Lily ; Queen Victoria's Water Lily)—Ord. Nymphaceæ. Stove aquatic plant. Orn. foliage. First introduced 1838. Leaves, roundish, flat, with turned-up edges ; bronzy green ; 4 to 6 ft. diameter ; floating.
CULTURE : Compost, two parts good, rich turfy loam, one part decayed cow manure. Position, large tank 6 ft. deep and 20 to 25 ft. wide. Plant, May. Temp. of water, 80° to 85°. Temp. of atmosphere, March to Sept. 75° to 85° ; Sept. to March 65° to 70°. No shade required.
PROPAGATION : By seeds sown in pot of sandy loam submerged in water heated to temp. of 85° and placed near glass in light position, Jan. When seedlings appear above surface transplant singly in small pots and place in water again until May, then plant out as above advised. The Victoria regia is strictly a perennial, but thrives best treated as an annual in this country.
SPECIES CULTIVATED : V. regia, white, rose, and purple, summer, Trop. America.

Victorian Snow-bush (*Olearia Haastii*)—See Olearia.

Victoria Water Lily (*Victoria regia*)—See Victoria.

Victor's Laurel (*Laurus nobilis*)—See Laurus.

Vieussexia—See Moræa.

Villarsia—See Limnanthemum.

Vinca (Periwinkle ; Madagascar Periwinkle)—Ord. Apocynaceæ. Hardy herbaceous perennials and stove evergreen shrubs.
CULTURE OF STOVE SPECIES : Compost, two parts fibrous loam, one part decayed manure, and little silver sand. Position, well-drained pots in stove Sept. to June ; sunny, cold frame or greenhouse remainder of year. Pot, Feb. or March. Prune shoots of old plants to within 1 or 2 in. of their base in Jan. or Feb. Water freely April to Oct., moderately afterwards. Apply weak stimulants occasionally during summer and autumn. Nip off points of shoots in young or old plants once or twice during July and Aug. to insure bushy habit. Temp., March to June 65° to 75° ; Sept. to March 55° to 65°. Alternatively the plant may be treated as a tender annual, sowing seeds in temp. 70° during Feb. or March and transplanting seedlings to small pots as soon as large enough to handle.
CULTURE OF HARDY SPECIES : Soil, ordinary. Position, shady borders, rockeries, or shrubberies under trees. Plant, Oct. to April. Lift, divide, and replant only when absolutely necessary.
POT CULTURE : Compost, two parts sandy loam, one part leaf-mould, and little sand. Pot, Oct. to March. Position, pots suspended in wire baskets in cold or cool

greenhouses, balconies, or windows. Water freely April to Sept., moderately afterwards. Repot annually.

PROPAGATION : V. rosea by cuttings of young shoots removed when 2 or 3 in. long in spring and inserted in sandy soil under bell-glass in temp. 65° to 75° ; by seeds sown in temp. 70° during Feb. Hardy species by division in March or April.

STOVE SPECIES : V. rosea (Madagascar Periwinkle), rose, summer, 1 to 2 ft., Tropics, and its variety alba (white).

HARDY SPECIES : V. difformis (Syn. Media), lilac blue, Nov. to Dec., trailing, S.W. Europe ; major (Large Periwinkle), bright blue, May to Sept., trailing, Europe (Britain) ; major variegata, variegated ; minor (Lesser Periwinkle), blue, summer, trailing, Europe (Britain), and its varieties flore-pleno (double), argenteo variegata (leaves silver variegated), and aureo variegata (leaves golden variegated).

Vine—See Vitis.

Viola (Violet ; Tufted Pansy ; Pansy ; Heart's-ease)—Ord. Violaceæ. Hardy perennial herbs.

CLASSIFICATION : Pansies in General.—Any free-growing or free-flowering strain, self-coloured or variegated. Show Pansy.—Blooms circular, flat, and smooth, without wavy or crinkled edges ; petals thick, velvety, and lying closely over each other ; principal or ground colour of three lower petals pure white or yellow ; dark circular blotch in centre of blooms, orange eye ; dark narrow belt to three lower petals ; same colour as upper petals ; diameter 1½ in. Fancy Pansy.— Blooms circular, flat, and smooth, with wavy or crinkled edges ; petals thick and velvety, lying closely over each other ; solid, bright orange eye ; large blotches of colour, with narrow belt or margin of another colour on three lower petals ; top petals same colour as blotches or margins ; colour, sometimes suffused ; size, 1½ in. to 2 in. in diameter. Tufted Pansy.—A name applied to a class of pansies commonly called " violas," hybrids of the ordinary pansy and the Horned Violet (V. cornuta). Blooms smaller than those of ordinary pansies. Colours varied, chaste, and delicate. Habit, dwarf, not spreading as in the pansy. Violetta.—A strain of very dwarf pansies, the result of a cross between a pansy and Viola cornuta. Flowers, small, rayless, and fragrant.

CULTURE OF SHOW, FANCY, AND TUFTED PANSIES : Soil—(a) deep, rich, moist loam enriched with well-decayed cow manure ; (b) two parts loam, one part of equal proportions of leaf-mould and sand ; (c) ordinary light mould enriched with cow manure ; (d) clayey or heavy soils with decayed horse or cow manure. Soil best manured and dug previous autumn. Position, open, light, sheltered, away from roots and branches of trees, and shaded from mid-day sun. Plant pansies in Sept., Oct., or April, 12 in. apart each way ; tufted pansies, March or April, 10 in. apart each way. Mulch with cow manure and leaf-mould in May or June. Stir the surface frequently. Water copiously in dry weather, applying it in the evening. Remove all flower buds until plants are established. If exhibition blooms are desired allow only one bloom to grow on each shoot. Manures : (1) 1 oz. guano to a gall. of water ; (2) ¼ oz. sulphate of ammonia, ¼ oz. superphosphate of lime, ¼ oz. sulphate of iron to 2 gall. of water (Griffiths) ; (3) liquid soot, prepared by enclosing a peck of soot and a heavy stone in a canvas bag and immersing this with a few crystals of sulphate of iron in 30 gall. of water, used undiluted ; (4) liquid cow or sheep dung, prepared by placing a peck of dung in 30 gall. of water, keeping mixture stirred at intervals for a week, then applying liquid in a clear state undiluted. All the foregoing may be applied every ten days or so during growing and flowering season. Violettas best grown as edgings to beds or in patches on rockeries. Plant in May.

CULTURE OF VIOLET : Soil, ordinary, previously well enriched with well-decayed manure. Clay soils require plenty of grit, decayed vegetable refuse, and manure incorporated with them. Light and gravelly soils need a liberal amount of cow manure and loam or clay mixed with them. Position, border or bed on north or north-east side of hedge or under the shade of fruit trees. Full exposure to hot summer sun undesirable. Plant " crowns " 9 in. apart in rows 12 in. asunder, April. " Crowns " are portions separated from parent plant, each furnished with roots.

Water when first planted and shade from sun. Apply manures recommended for pansies at intervals of three weeks during summer. Remove runners, *i.e.* shoots that issue from the " crowns," as they form during summer and keep plants free from weeds. Lift plants for winter blooming in Sept. and replant, 6 to 8 in. apart, in equal parts good soil and leaf-mould in a cold, sunny frame. Water freely in fine weather. Protect from frost. In case of deep frames decayed manure may be used to fill up space to within 12 in. of light, putting 6 in. of above soil on this. Replant annually.

POT CULTURE : Compost, two parts loam, one part leaf-mould, and one part sand. Pot, April, placing six " crowns " in a 6 in. pot. Place in a shady frame and water moderately. Plunge pots to their rims outdoors in shade in May and let them remain till Sept., when remove to greenhouse. Water freely outdoors, moderately in winter. Winter temp., 40° to 50°.

CULTURE OF OTHER SPECIES : Soil, ordinary rich. Position, moist, partially shaded rockeries, beds, or borders. Plant, March or April, 3 to 6 in. apart.

PROPAGATION : By seeds sown in light, sandy soil in boxes or pans in cold, shady frame in July or Aug., transplanting seedlings into flowering positions in Sept. ot Oct. ; by cuttings inserted in cold, shady frames in Aug. or Sept. ; divisions in Sept. or Oct. ; violets by runners in April.

SPECIES CULTIVATED : V. alpina, purple, May, 3 in., E. Europe ; altaica (Altaian Violet), lilac purple or yellow, May, 6 in., Taurus and Asia Minor ; arborescens, lavender blue, 6 to 8 in., S. France ; Beckwithi, purple and pale lilac, 3 to 4 in., California ; biflora (Twin-flowered Violet), yellow, June, 3 in., Europe and N. Asia ; bosniaca (Syn. V. declinata), rosy mauve, May to June, 4 in., S.W. Europe ; calcarata (Spurred Violet), violet or variable, May to June, 4 in., Europe ; canadensis, white, yellow, and violet, 12 in., N. America, and its variety Rydbergi ; canina (Dog Violet), blue or white, May, 3 to 4 in., Europe, and its variety elatior (violet) ; cenisia (Syn. V. Bertoloni), violet purple, 3 to 4 in., Alps ; cornuta (Horned Violet), blue, summer, 6 in., Pyrenees, one of the parents of the Garden Viola or Tufted Pansy ; cornuta alba, white ; cucullata (Hollow-leaved Violet), violet, spring, 3 to 4 in., N. America ; gracilis (Olympian Violet), violet purple, June, 4 to 6 in., Macedonia and Asia Minor ; hederacea (Syn. Erpetion reniforme), purple and white, summer, 2 to 3 in., Australia ; lutea (Mountain Violet), yellow, June, 3 in., Europe (Britain) ; munbyana (Munby's Violet), violet or yellow, spring, 6 to 12 in., Mediterranean Region ; nummulariæfolia, blue and blackish violet, summer, 3 to 4 in., Maritime Alps ; odorata (Sweet Violet), blue, spring, 6 in., Europe (Britain), and its varieties alba (white), pallida plena (Neapolitan Violet), lavender double, and sulphurea (sulphur yellow) ; palustris (Marsh Violet), pale lilac to white, May, 3 to 4 in., N. Europe (Britain) ; pedata (Bird's-foot Violet), violet and lilac, May, 6 in., N. America, and its variety alba (white) ; pedunculata, orange yellow, summer, 6 to 8 in., California ; pinnata, rosy lilac, May to June, 2 to 3 in., Europe ; rothamagensis (Rouen Violet), lilac, summer, 6 in., Europe ; sylvestris (Wood Violet), blue, spring, 6 in., Europe ; tricolor (Heart's-ease), yellow, purple, and white, summer, 6 in., Europe (Britain), one of the parents of the Pansy.

Violet—See Viola.

Violet-flowered Cress (*Ionopsidium acaule*)—See Ionopsidium

Violet-scented Orchid—See Odontoglossum.

Viper Gourd—See Tricosanthes.

Viper's Bugloss (*Echium vulgare*)—See Echium.

Viper's Grass—See Scorzonera.

Virgilia lutea—See Cladrastis tinctoria.

Virginian Bird Cherry (*Prunus virginiana*)—See Prunus.

Virginian Cowslip (*Mertensia virginica*)—See Mertensia.

Virginian Creeper—See Vitis.

Virginian Poke (*Phytolacca decandra*)—See Phytolacca.

Virginian Raspberry (*Rubus odoratus*)—See Rubus.

Virginian Snow-flower (*Chionanthus virginica*)—See Chionanthus.

Virginian Spiderwort (*Tradescantia virginiana*)—See Tradescantia.

Virginian Stock (*Malcomia maritima*)—See Malcomia.

Virginian Willow (*Itea virginica*)—See Itea.

Virgin's Bower—See Clematis.

Viscaria—See Lychnis.

Viscum (Mistletoe)—Ord. Loranthaceæ. Hardy evergreen parasitical plant. Fruit, white, roundish, viscid ; winter.
CULTURE : Cut a notch in bark on under side of branch and press ripe berry gently thereinto. Time for insertion, March. Trees adapted for mistletoe culture : Apple, hawthorn, poplar, lime, maple, mountain ash, cedar, larch, and oak ; two first most suitable.
SPECIES CULTIVATED : V. album, green, March, Europe (Britain).

Vitex (Chaste Tree ; Tree of Chastity)—Ord. Verbenaceæ. Hardy evergreen flowering shrub. First introduced 1570.
CULTURE : Soil, ordinary. Position, sheltered, warm border or against S. wall. Plant, Oct. to Feb. Prune into shape moderately after flowering.
PROPAGATION : By cuttings of shoots inserted in ordinary light, sandy soil under bell-glass in cool greenhouse or cold frame, Sept. or Oct.
SPECIES CULTIVATED : V. Agnus-castus, lilac or white, Sept. to Oct., to 10 ft., S. Europe.

Vitis (Grape-vine ; Virginian Creeper)—Ord. Ampelideæ. Hardy and half-hardy deciduous climbing shrubs. Ampelopsis is now included in the genus.
CULTURE OF GRAPE VINE : Compost, five parts of top spit turfy loam from an old pasture chopped into small pieces, one part old lime rubbish, one part equal proportions of charcoal and wood ashes, and one part half-inch bones. Position, sunny, fairly dry subsoil. Borders : Inside for early forcing ; outside for late or ordinary culture. Width, 10 to 16 ft.—that is, equalling width of house. Depth, 3 ft. On cold clayey soils surface of border best raised 18 in. above ordinary ground level and bottom covered with layer of concrete. Place brick rubbish and old mortar 2 ft. deep at back, sloping to 18 in. in front, in bottom of border. On this put a layer of turves, grass side downwards, then fill the remaining space with above compost. A drain along the bottom of border is advisable. Plant, end of Jan. or beginning of Feb. ; or in the case of young plants raised from eyes in spring, June or July. Distance for planting, 5 ft. apart.
PRUNING : Newly planted canes should be cut back before growth starts. Those planted outside should be cut to the first eye inside the house. Those planted inside to the first eye above ground. Allow one strong shoot only to grow and form future stem ; rub all others off when they first form. Prune this following Dec. half-way back. Second year : Allow side shoots to form 18 in. apart and one young shoot to grow at end of each rod ; rub off remainder in a young state. Nip off points of side shoots at second joint beyond bunch, if any, otherwise at fourth joint. Prune side shoots following Dec. close to basal bud. Shorten the year's extension of main rod by one-half. Third year : Allow side shoots to form at spurs, and on youngest portion of rod. Confine extension of main root to one growth. If more than one shoot forms at a spur, select strongest and rub off (disbud) remainder. Nip off points of shoots as before advised. Following Dec. shorten all growth of the current year as previously described, and shorten leader to the length decided upon for permanency. Future pruning to consist of rubbing off (disbudding) all side shoots except one at each spur, nipping off (stopping) points at second joint beyond bunch or fourth from base, cutting back, Dec. or Jan., side shoots to last bud or eye from their base.
STARTING TEMPERATURE AND WATERING : Time for starting vines : Nov. to ripen

first in April; Dec. for May; Jan. for June; March for July. Vines started in March without artificial heat will ripen in Aug. or Sept. Temp. by night: 35° to 40° until buds break; 40° to 50° from then until flowers expand; 50° to 55° during flowering period; 60° to 70° from then until berries are ripe. Temp. by day: 60° on cold and 70° to 75° on sunny days until buds break; 65° on cold and 75° to 80° on sunny days until vines flower; 75° on cold and 85° to 90° on sunny days onwards till grapes are ripe. Watering inside borders: Apply water heated to temp. 60° at the rate of 4 to 5 gall. per square foot when vines are started; again when shoots are 6 in. long; also just before flowers expand; lastly, when berries begin to swell for second time. Watering outside borders: Apply water similar temp. and quantity just before flowering and when berries begin to swell second time. Syringe morning and afternoon daily until vines flower, then cease. Moisten floors, staging, walls, and borders several times daily from start until berries colour, then discontinue. Ventilation: Open the ventilators tentatively on fine days when the sun rises and close again early in afternoon or when sun disappears. Ventilate freely night and day during ripening period.

MANURES FOR GRAPE VINES: Drainings from stable or manure heap diluted with three times the volume of water. Apply when berries first form, and again when they commence to colour. Special manures for various soils—(a) Sandy soils not containing much humus: 2 lb. of guano, 3 lb. kainit mixed together and latter crushed fine; apply at the rate of 2 oz. to a square yard once a week from time berries form until they change colour. (b) Sandy soils containing much humus: 1 lb. nitrate of soda, 2 lb. superphosphate, 3 lb. kainit, applied at the rate of 1½ oz. per square yard as advised for (a). (c) Calcareous soils: 1 lb. dried blood, 2 lb. superphosphate, 1 lb. sulphate of potash, applied at the rate of 1 oz. to a square yard as recommended for (a). (d) Peaty soils: 1 lb. nitrate of soda, 3 lb. basic slag, 2 lb. sulphate of potash; apply 1 oz. to a square yard once a fortnight. Potash and soda to be crushed fine; mixture to be well washed in by a copious watering. Top-dressing: Apply 2 in. of horse or cow manure to surface of border when vines commence to grow. Also compost of two parts loam, one part of equal proportions of wood ashes and bone shavings or ground bones applied in autumn, first removing loose, inert soil from surface. Cropping: Average weight of fruit per foot run of rod, 1 lb. Average weight of a fair-sized bunch, ¾ lb. Average number of bunches borne by a rod 12 ft. long, about twelve. Allow one bunch only to each spur for heavy crop; one to every alternate spur for moderate crop. Thin berries when size of radish seeds, and again later on, finally allowing a space of 1 in. between berries to enable them to fully develop. Avoid touching berries with hand or head. Temp. for grapes when ripe, 40° to 45°.

POT CULTURE: Two-year-old plants established in 10 or 12 in. pots best adapted for fruit in pots. No repotting required. Place in temp. 60°, Nov. to Feb. Give little water till buds break, then apply freely. Increase temp. to 65° after buds break, and to 75° when in flower; lower to 68° afterwards until stoning is completed, when again raise to 70°. Allow above temp. to be increased 5° to 10° by sun-heat. Syringe daily until vines flower. Thin berries when size of radish seeds. Apply one of above liquid stimulants three times weekly after berries form and until they are ripe. Top-dress with Standen's manure at the rate of a tablespoonful to each pot; or with two parts loam and one part Thomson's vine manure when berries form. Allow each vine to carry six to eight bunches—8 to 10 lb. altogether.

OUTDOOR CULTURE: Soil, two parts sandy loam, one part of equal proportions of wood ashes, old mortar, half-inch bones, and rotten manure. Position, against a south sunny wall. Plant, 2 ft. apart, Nov. or March. Prune, Jan. or Feb., precisely as advised for indoor culture. Disbud also in a similar manner. Manures advised for indoor vines equally applicable for outdoor ones.

CULTURE OF HARDY ORNAMENTAL VINES: Soil, good ordinary enriched with decayed manure. Position, walls or fences for Virginian Creepers; arbours, trellises, poles, pergolas, etc. for others. Plant in autumn. Prune away straggling shoots of Virginian Creepers in winter; shorten previous year's shoots of other kinds not required to form new branches to 1 in. from base in Feb.

PROPAGATION : Grape vine by seeds sown in sandy soil in temp. 55° to 65° in spring ; by " eyes " inserted in similar compost in temp. 65° to 75° in Jan., Feb., or March ; by cuttings of shoots, 6 in. long and having a " heel " of older wood attached to the base, inserted in shady position outdoors in Oct. or Nov. ; layering shoots in spring or summer ; inarching in spring ; grafting when the vines are in flower. Ornamental vines by seeds sown in heat in spring ; cuttings of shoots, 6 to 8 in. long, inserted in pots of sandy soil in cold frame in Sept. or Oct. ; layering the shoots in spring or summer.

SPECIES CULTIVATED : V. æstivalis (American Summer Vine), climber, U.S.A. ; arborea (Syn. V. bipinnata), deeply toothed foliage, climber, Southern U.S.A. ; californica (Californian Vine), climber, leaves crimson-tinted in autumn, California ; Coignetiæ (Japanese Vine), climber, leaves crimson-tinted in autumn, Japan ; cordifolia, vigorous climber, Eastern U.S.A. ; Davidi (Syns. V. armata and Spinovitis Davidi), fine autumn colour, Central China ; doaniana, foliage turns bronzy crimson, climber, hybrid ; flexuosa, climber, leaves richly tinted in autumn, China and Japan, and its variety Wilsoni (small foliage) ; henryana, leaves velvety green, white and pink, changing to crimson, Central China ; heterophylla (Turquoise Berry Vine), climber, blue berries, China and Japan ; inconstans (Syn. Ampelopsis Veitchii), Veitch's Virginian Creeper, climber, stems self-clinging, Japan and China, and its variety Lowi (small leaved) ; indivisa (Syn. Ampelopsis cordata), large leaves turning crimson in autumn, Southern U.S.A. ; Labrusca (American Fox Grape), climber, N. America ; megalophylla, very large foliage, climber, W. China ; Pagnucci, foliage turning blood red, slender climber, Central China ; pulchra (frequently wrongly named V. flexuosa major), foliage turning crimson, habitat unknown ; quinquefolia (Syn. Ampelopsis hederacea, and sometimes wrongly named V. Engelmanni), the true Virginian Creeper, climber, stems self-clinging, N. America ; V. striata (Syn. Ampelopsis sempervirens), climber, Chile and Brazil ; Thunbergi, deeply lobed foliage, slender climber, Japan ; Thompsoni (Syn. Parthenocissus Thompsoni), claret-purple foliage, slender climber, China ; vinifera, parent of the cultivated Grape Vines, Orient, and its variety purpurea (purple leaved) ; vitacea (Common Virginian Creeper), foliage turning red, climber, N. America ; vulpina, heart-shaped foliage, climber, Eastern N. America ; watsoniana (Syn. V. leeoides), green and claret-purple foliage, climber, W. China. See also Cissus.

Vittadenia triloba—See Erigeron mucronatus.

Vriesia—Ord. Bromeliaceæ. Stove epiphytal perennials. Showy red or green bracts.

CULTURE : Compost, equal parts fibrous loam, rough peat, silver sand, and leaf-mould. Pot, Feb. or March. Water copiously March to Oct., moderately afterwards. Shade from sun. Syringe daily April to Sept. Moist atmosphere essential in summer. Temp., Sept. to March 60° to 70° ; March to Sept. 70° to 80°.

PROPAGATION : By offsets inserted in small pots of sandy peat in temp. 75° to 85° in spring. T. usneoides may be grown suspended from roof by a wire or fastened to a piece of wood ; no soil required.

SPECIES CULTIVATED : V. fenestralis, yellow, leaves marked brown, to 1½ ft., Brazil ; hieroglyphica, yellowish, leaves banded dark green and brown, Brazil ; psittacina, greenish, yellowish-green leaves, 1 to 1½ ft., Brazil ; splendens (Syn. V. zebrina), yellowish white, leaves banded dark brown, to 3 ft., Guiana, and its variety major ; tessellata, yellowish, leaves marked with green and yellow, Brazil. See also Tillandsia.

Wachendorfia—Ord. Hæmodoraceæ. Half-hardy tuberous-rooted plants. First introduced 1700.

OUTDOOR CULTURE : Soil, light, rich sandy. Position, sunny well-drained border. Plant, Sept. to Jan., placing bulbs 4 in. deep and 2 in. apart. Lift and replant bulbs annually. Mulch surface of bed in March with cow manure.

POT CULTURE : Compost, two parts sandy loam, one part leaf-mould or decayed cow manure. Pot, 4½ in. diameter, well drained. Place five bulbs, 3 in. deep, in

each pot in Nov. and cover with cocoanut-fibre refuse in cold frame or under cool greenhouse stage until growth begins. Water moderately from time bulbs begin to grow until flowers fade, then gradually cease, keeping bulbs dry till Jan. Temp., Sept. to March 40° to 50° ; other times 50° to 60°.
PROPAGATION : By offsets, treated as advised for bulbs.
SPECIES CULTIVATED : W. paniculata, yellow, April, 3 ft. ; thyrsiflora, yellow, May, 2 ft. Natives of S. Africa.

Wahlenbergia (Bell-flower)—Ord. Campanulaceæ. Hardy perennial herbs.
CULTURE OF HARDY SPECIES : Soil, gritty, well drained, containing plenty of well-rotted leaf-mould. Position, sunny rockeries well supplied with moisture during the summer months. Protect Australasian species with hand-light during the winter. Plant, Oct. to April.
PROPAGATION : By seeds sown in a temp. of 55° in March or April ; cuttings in summer ; division in spring.
HARDY SPECIES : W. albo-marginata, white or blue, summer, 3 to 6 in., New Zealand, frequently wrongly named W. saxicola ; dalmatica (Syns. W. caudatus and Edraianthus caudatus), purple, summer, to 6 in., Dalmatia ; dinarica (Syn. W. pumiliorum), purple, summer, 2 in., Eastern Europe ; graminifolia (Syn. Edraianthus graminifolia), blue, summer, 4 in., Italy ; hederacea (Syn. Campanula hederacea), Creeping Harebell, blue, summer, trailing, Britain ; Kitaibelli (Syn. Edraianthus Kitaibelli), blue, summer, 4 to 6 in., S.E. Europe, and its variety croatica ; Pumilio, lavender, June, 1 to 2 in., Dalmatia ; serpyllifolia (Thyme-leaved Harebell), purple, May, 2 to 3 in., Dalmatia ; serpyllifolia major, flowers rich violet blue, summer, 6 ins., Serbia ; tenuifolia, blue, violet, and white, summer, 6 in., Dalmatia ; vincæflora, light blue, summer, 1 ft., New Zealand.

Wake Robin (*Trillium grandiflorum*)—See Trillium.

Waldsteinia (Barren Strawberry)—Ord. Rosaceæ. Hardy perennial herbs. **First** introduced 1900.
CULTURE : Soil, ordinary rich. Position, on sunny rockeries. Plant, Oct. to April. Cut away flower stems in Sept.
PROPAGATION : By seeds sown ¹⁄₁₆ in. deep in shallow boxes or well-drained pots of light soil in cold frame, April or July, or in sunny positions (similar depth and soil) outdoors, April or Aug. ; division of plants, Oct. to April.
SPECIES CULTIVATED : W. fragarioides, yellow, June, 6 in., N. America ; trifolia, yellow, summer, 3 to 4 in., Europe.

Wall Cress (*Arabis albida*)—See Arabis.

Wallflower—See Cheiranthus.

Wallichia—Ord. Palmaceæ. Stove palms. Orn. foliage. Leaves feather-shaped. First introduced 1825.
CULTURE : Compost, two parts rich loam, one part leaf-mould, little sand. Position, well-drained pots in moist part of stove. Pot, Feb. Water copiously Feb. to Oct., moderately afterwards. Syringe daily in summer. Shade from sun. Temp., March to Oct. 75° to 85° ; Oct. to March 55° to 65°.
PROPAGATION : By suckers removed with roots attached, Feb. or March ; seeds sown in temp. 80° in Feb. or March.
SPECIES CULTIVATED : W. caryotoides, 6 to 9 ft., India ; disticha, 10 to 15 ft., Himalayas.

Wall Pepper (*Sedum acre*)—See Sedum.

Wall Rue Fern (*Asplenium Ruta-muraria*)—See Asplenium.

Walnut (*Juglans regia*)—See Juglans.

Wandering Jew (*Saxifraga sarmentosa*)—See Saxifraga.

Wandflower (*Dierama pulcherrima*)—See Dierama.

Wand Lily (*Chamælirion luteum*)—See Chamælirion.

Wand Plant (*Galax aphylla*)—See Galax.

Warscewiczella—Ord. Orchidaceæ. Stove epiphytal orchids.
CULTURE : Compost, equal parts rough fibrous peat and sphagnum moss and charcoal. Position, well-drained pots, or on blocks of wood (roots being covered with sphagnum moss) or in baskets suspended from roof. Pot, etc., Feb. or March. Water freely April to Sept., moderately Sept. to Dec. Give very little Dec. to April. Shade from sun in summer. Moist atmosphere essential. Temp., March to June 58° to 65° ; Dec. to March 53° to 60°. Growing period : All the year round. Resting period : None. Flowers appear at base of new growth.
PROPAGATION : By division any time.
SPECIES CULTIVATED : W. discolor, white, yellow, and purple, May to June, Costa Rica ; Lindeni, white and purple, habitat unknown ; Wendlandi, yellowish green, violet, and white, Aug. to Sept., Costa Rica. See also Zygopetalum.

Washingtonia—Ord. Palmaceæ. A genus of ornamental warm greenhouse plants or palms. Leaves, roundish and fringed with filaments.
CULTURE : Compost, equal parts peat, loam, and silver sand. Position, pots in partial shade. Repot, Feb. Water moderately Oct. to April, freely afterwards. Temp., Sept. to March 55° to 65° ; March to Sept. 65° to 75°.
PROPAGATION : By seeds sown in above compost in temp. 85° in spring.
SPECIES CULTIVATED : W. filifera (Syn. Brahea or Pritchardia filamentosa), 20 to 80 ft., California.

Water **Arum** (*Calla palustris*)—See Calla.

Water **Caltrops** (*Trapa natans*)—See Trapa.

Water **Chestnut** (*Trapa natans*)—See Trapa.

Water **Cress** (*Nasturtium officinale*)—See Nasturtium.

Water **Dragon** (*Calla palustris*)—See Calla.

Water **Elm**—See Zelkowa.

Water **Gowan** (*Caltha palustris*)—See Caltha.

Water **Hyacinth**—See Eichornea.

Water **Lettuce** (*Pistia stratiotes*)—See Pistia.

Water **Lily**—See Nymphæa and Nuphar.

Water **Locust** (*Gleditschia aquatica*)—See Gleditschia.

Water **Melon** (*Citrullus vulgaris*)—Not grown in Britain.

Water **Oat** (*Zizania aquatica*)—See Zizania.

Water **Plantain** (*Alisma Plantago*)—See Alisma.

Water **Rice** (*Zizania aquatica*)—See Zizania.

Water **Shield** (*Brassenia Schreberi*)—See Brassenia.

Water **Soldier** (*Stratiotes aloides*)—See Stratiotes.

Water **Violet** (*Hottonia palustris*)—See Hottonia.

Watsonia (Bugle Lily)—Ord. Iridaceæ. Half-hardy bulbous plants. First introduced 1750.
OUTDOOR CULTURE : Soil, deep, rich, liberally manured. Position, sunny, sheltered, well-drained beds or borders. Plant, March to May. Place corms 4 in. deep and 6 in. apart in groups of three, six, or twelve ; put a little silver sand under each corm. Protect in winter with layer of manure. Apply liquid manure when flower buds form. Fix stakes to spikes when 2 or 3 in. high. Lift corms in Sept. and store in cool place till planting time.
POT CULTURE : Compost, two parts loam, one part well-decayed manure and river sand. Position, pots in cold frame, cool greenhouse, or window. Pot, Oct. to March, placing five corms 1 in. deep in a 6 in. pot. Place pots in cold frame till flower spikes show, then remove to greenhouse or window. Water moderately at first, freely afterwards. Apply liquid manure when flower spikes show. After flowering gradually withhold water till foliage dies, then keep quite dry till repotted.
PROPAGATION : By seeds sown ¼ in. deep in pans of light, rich soil in Feb. in temp.

55° to 65° ; by bulbils planted 2 in. deep and 6 in. apart in sunny border outdoors, April.

SPECIES CULTIVATED : W. angusta, scarlet, to 4 ft. ; coccinea, scarlet, 1 ft. ; densiflora, rosy red, June, 1 ft. ; Meriana (Syn. W. iridifolia), pink, to 4 ft., and its variety Ardernei (O'Brieni), white ; rosea (Syn. Gladiolus pyramidatus), rose, 3 to 6 ft. All are natives of S. Africa and flower in the summer.

Wattle—See Acacia.

Wax Flower (*Hoya carnosa*)—See Hoya.

Wax Myrtle (*Myrtus cerifera*)—See Myrtus.

Wayfaring Tree (*Viburnum Lantana*)—See Viburnum.

Weather Plant (*Abrus precatorius*)—See Abrus.

Wedding Flower (*Moræa robinsoniana*)—See Moræa.

Weeping Ash (*Fraxinus excelsior pendula*)—See Fraxinus.

Weeping Beech (*Fagus sylvaticus pendula*)—See Fagus.

Weeping Birch (*Betula verrucosa pendula Youngii*)—See Betula.

Weeping Elm (*Ulmus glabra* vars. *Camperdowni* and *pendula*)—See Ulmus.

Weeping Myall (*Acacia pendula*)—See Acacia.

Weeping Oak (*Quercus pedunculata pendula*)—See Quercus.

Weeping Willow (*Salix babylonica*)—See Salix.

Weigela—See Diervilla.

Weevil-plant (*Curculigo recurvata*)—See Curculigo.

Weinmannia—Ord. Saxifrageæ. Half-hardy evergreen orn. shrubs or trees. First introduced 1815.

CULTURE : Soil, light, rich. Position, sheltered walls in southern counties or well-drained borders in unheated greenhouse or conservatory. Plant, Sept. to Oct. or April to May. Water indoor plants freely during growing season.

PROPAGATION : By cuttings of half-ripened shoots inserted in sandy soil under bell-glass in gentle bottom heat during July and Aug.

SPECIES CULTIVATED : W. racemosa, white or pink, June, 20 to 80 ft., New Zealand ; trichosperma, creamy white, May to June, Chile.

Wellingtonia—See Sequoia.

Welsh Onion—See Allium.

Welsh Polypody (*Polypodium vulgare cambricum*)—See Polypodium.

Welsh Poppy (*Meconopsis cambrica*)—See Meconopsis.

Welwitschia—Ord. Gnetaceæ. A curious hothouse plant of mushroom-like habit of growth with leaves fringed with ribbon-like filaments. A difficult plant to grow. First introduced 1862.

CULTURE : Equal parts brick rubble and coarse sand. Position, a well-drained bed in a hot, dry corner. Scarcely any water required. Full exposure to sun essential. Temp., 55° in winter ; 75° in summer.

PROPAGATION : Exceedingly difficult.

SPECIES CULTIVATED : W. mirabilis, Trop. Africa.

Western Plane (*Platanus occidentalis*)—See Platanus.

West Indian Jasmine (*Ixora coccinea*)—See Ixora.

West Indian Kale (*Colocasia esculenta*)—See Colocasia.

Westringia—Ord. Labiatæ. Half-hardy evergreen flowering shrub. First introduced 1791. Native of Australia.

CULTURE : Soil, light, rich loam. Position, sheltered shrubberies in southern gardens or unheated greenhouses and conservatories. Plant, Sept. to Oct. or April to May. Water indoor plants freely during the summer months.

SPECIES CULTIVATED : W. rosmariniformis, pale blue, July to Aug., 3 to 5 ft.

Weymouth Pine (*Pinus Strobus*)—See **Pinus.**

Whangee Cane—See Phyllostachys.

Whin—See Ulex.

White Alder (*Clethra acuminata*)—See **Clethra.**

White Beam-tree (*Pyrus Aria*)—See Pyrus.

White Fir (*Abies amabilis*)—See Abies.

White Hellebore (*Veratrum album*)—See Veratrum.

White Spanish Broom (*Cytisus albus*)—See Cytisus.

White Willow (*Salix alba*)—See Salix.

Whitlavia—See Phacelia.

Whitlow Grass—See Draba.

Whorl-flower—See Morina.

Whortleberry (*Vaccinium myrtillus*)—See Vaccinium.

Widdringtonia (African or Milanji Cypress)—Ord. Coniferæ. Tender evergreen coniferous trees, suitable only for greenhouse cultivation in this country. Habit, elegant and graceful. First introduced 1756.
CULTURE : Compost, two parts sandy loam and one part leaf-mould with a liberal amount of silver sand. Position, pots in light, sunny greenhouse. Pot in March. Water freely March to Oct., moderately afterwards. Temp., March to Oct. 55° to 65° ; Oct. to March 45° to 55°.
PROPAGATION : By seeds sown in gentle heat in spring, transferring seedlings singly to small pots as soon as large enough to handle.
SPECIES CULTIVATED : W. cupressoides, to 12 ft., S. Africa ; juniperoides, to 60 ft., S. Africa ; Whytei, leaves glaucous and graceful, to 140 ft., Central Africa.

Wigandia—Ord. Hydrophyllaceæ. Stove orn. foliage plants. First introduced 1836. Height, 3 to 10 ft. Leaves, large, very wrinkled, more or less downy.
CULTURE : Soil, ordinary. Position, sunny sheltered beds outdoors May to Oct. ; warm greenhouse remainder of year. Plant, May or June. Lift, Sept. or Oct.
PROPAGATION : By seeds sown in light soil in temp. 65° to 75° in Feb. ; cuttings inserted in sandy soil under bell-glass in temp. 75° in spring. Usually treated as an annual ; seldom preserved during the winter.
SPECIES CULTIVATED : W. caracassana (Syn. W. macrophylla), 8 to 10 ft., Mexico, and its variety imperialis (vigorous) ; Vigieri, 4 to 6 ft., silvery foliage, origin uncertain.

Wig Tree (*Rhus Cotinus*)—See Rhus.

Wild Balsam Apple (*Echinocystis lobata*)—See Echinocystis.

Wild Rosemary—See Andromeda.

Wild Sweet William (*Phlox maculata*)—See Phlox.

Willow—See Salix.

Willow Herb—See Epilobium.

Windflower—See Anemone.

Wine-berry (*Rubus phœnicolasius*)—See Rubus.

Winged Elm (*Ulmus alata*)—See Ulmus.

Winter Aconite (*Eranthis hyemalis*)—See Eranthis.

Winter Cherry—See Physalis and Solanum.

Winter Cress (*Barbarea præcox*)—See Barbarea.

Winter Daffodil—See Sternbergia.

Winter Flax (*Reinwardtia trigyna*)—See Reinwardtia.

Winter Green (*Pyrola minor*)—See Pyrola.

Winter Hawthorn (*Aponogeton distachyon*)—See Aponogeton.

Winter Heath (*Erica carnea*)—See Erica.

Winter Heliotrope (*Petasites fragrans*)—See Petasites.

Winter Savory (*Satureia montana*)—See Satureia.

Winter Sweet (*Acokanthera spectabilis* and *Chimonanthus fragrans*)—See Acokanthera and Chimonanthus.

Wistaria (Grape-flower Vine ; Kidney-bean Tree)—Ord. Leguminosæ. Hardy deciduous climbing flowering shrubs. First introduced 1724.
CULTURE : Soil, deep, rich, sandy loam. Position, well-drained borders against S. or S.W. walls ; or on sunny pergolas ; or as standards in shrubbery or on lawns in sheltered districts. Plant, March or April. Prune, Jan. or Feb., shortening shoots not required for extending branches to within 1 in. of base.
PROPAGATION : By layering young shoots during spring and summer.
SPECIES CULTIVATED : W. floribunda, purplish blue, May to June, climber, Japan, and its variety macrobotrys (Syn. W. multijuga), long racemes ; frutescens (American Kidney-bean Tree), lilac purple, June to Aug., vigorous climber, U.S.A., and its variety alba ; japonica, pale yellow, July to Aug., climber, Japan ; macrostachya (Syn. W. frutescens magnifica), lilac purple, May to June, climber, N. America ; sinensis (Chinese Kidney-bean Tree), mauve, May, China, and its varieties alba (white) and flore-pleno (double) ; venusta, white, May to June, climber, China and Japan.

Witch Hazel—See Hamamelis.

Witch's Thimble (*Silene maritima flore-pleno*)—See Silene.

Witloof—See Cichorium.

Witsenia—See Aristea.

Wolf-berry (*Symphoricarpus occidentalis*)—See Symphoricarpus.

Wolf's-bane (*Aconitum lycoctonum*)—See Aconitum.

Wood Anemone (*Anemone nemerosa*)—See Anemone.

Woodbine (*Lonicera periclymenum*)—See Lonicera.

Wood Lily—See Trillium.

Woodruff (*Asperula odorata*)—See Asperula.

Woodsia—Ord. Filices. Greenhouse and hardy ferns. Deciduous and evergreen. Fronds, feather-shaped.
CULTURE OF GREENHOUSE SPECIES : Compost, equal parts peat and loam with little silver sand and charcoal. Position, well-drained pots or beds in shady greenhouse. Pot or plant, Feb. or March. Water freely March to Oct., moderately afterwards. Syringing not required. Shade from sun. Temp., Sept. to March 45° to 50° ; March to Sept. 50° to 60°.
CULTURE OF HARDY SPECIES : Compost, equal parts peat and loam. Position, shady borders or banks. Plant, April. Water copiously in dry weather. All the hardy species are suitable for greenhouse culture.
PROPAGATION : By spores sown on surface of fine peat in well-drained pans placed in temp. of 75° at any time ; division of plants, March or April.
GREENHOUSE SPECIES : W. obtusa, 1 ft., N. America ; polystichioides, 6 to 9 in., Japan ; p. Veitchii, China.
HARDY SPECIES : W. glabella, 6 in., N. America ; ilvensis, 4 in., Arctic and N. Temperate Zone (Britain) ; hyperborea (Syn. W. alpina), 6 in., N. Temperate Zone ; scopulina, 8 in., N. America.

Wood Sorrel—See Oxalis.

Wood Tongue Fern (*Drymoglossum carnosum*)—See Drymoglossum.

Wood Violet (*Viola sylvestris*)—See Viola.

Woodwardia (Chain Fern)—Ord. Filices. Greenhouse evergreen ferns. First introduced 1774.
CULTURE : Compost, equal parts loam and leaf-mould or peat. Position, in well-drained pots, or on rockeries in cool greenhouse or fernery. Water freely in summer, moderately other times. Syringe daily in summer. W. radicans and W. r. cristata suitable for suspending in baskets. Greenhouse species will also grow outdoors in sheltered positions, and with the protection of litter in winter.
PROPAGATION : By spores sown on surface of fine peat in well-drained pans placed in temp. of 75° any time ; division of plants, March or April ; by bulbils removed from fronds and placed in small pots in temp. of 65° to 70° until roots form.
SPECIES CULTIVATED : W. areolata, 12 to 18 in., U. States ; Harlandii, 18 in., Hong Kong ; japonica, 18 in. to 2 ft., China and Japan ; orientalis, 4 to 8 ft., Japan ; radicans, 3 to 8 ft., N. Temperate Zone ; radicans Brownii (Syn. Radicans cristata), fronds crested.

Woolly Beard Grass (*Erianthus Ravennæ*)—See Erianthus.

Worm Grass (*Sedum album*)—See Sedum.

Wormwood (*Artemisia Absinthium*)—See Artemisia.

Woundwort—See Stachys and Anthyllis.

Wulfenia—Ord. Scrophulariaceæ. Hardy perennial herb. First introduced 1817.
CULTURE : Soil, light, rich, sandy loam. Position, partially shady rockeries. Plant, March or April.
PROPAGATION : By seeds sown in light, sandy soil in shallow boxes in cold frame in March or April, transplanting seedlings when large enough to handle on to rockery ; by division of plants in March or April.
SPECIES CULTIVATED : W. carinthiaca, blue, July, 1 ft., Carinthia.

Wych Elm (*Ulmus montana*)—See Ulmus.

Wych Hazel (*Hamamelis virginica*)—See Hamamelis.

Xanthisma—Ord. Compositæ. Hardy annual. First introduced 1877.
CULTURE : Sow seeds in gentle heat in spring, harden off seedlings in May, and plant out in June, a foot apart, in bold groups in sunny borders.
SPECIES CULTIVATED : X. texanum (Syn. Centauridium Drummondi), yellow, summer, 2 to 4 ft., Texas.

Xanthoceras—Ord. Sapindaceæ. Hardy deciduous flowering tree. First introduced 1870. Leaves, feather-shaped.
CULTURE : Soil, ordinary. Position, sunny borders or shrubberies. Plant, Oct. to Feb.
PROPAGATION : By seeds sown in light soil outdoors in autumn or spring, or by root cuttings inserted in pans of sandy soil in cool greenhouse in Feb. or March.
SPECIES CULTIVATED : X. sorbifolia, white and red, May, 15 ft., China.

Xanthosoma—Ord. Aroideæ. Stove perennial herbs. Orn. foliage. First introduced 1710. Leaves, arrow head-shaped.
CULTURE : Compost, equal parts turfy loam, peat, leaf-mould, decayed manure, and silver sand. Position, well-drained pots in shade. Pot moderately firm in pots just large enough to take tubers in Feb. or March ; transfer to larger pots in April or May. Water moderately Feb. to April and Sept. to Nov., freely April to Sept., keep quite dry Nov. to Feb. Temp., Feb. to Sept. 70° to 80° ; Sept. to Nov. 65° to 75° ; Nov. to Feb. 55° to 65°.
PROPAGATION : By dividing the tubers in Feb. or March.
SPECIES CULTIVATED : X. atrovirens, leaves dark green above, greyish beneath, Venezuela ; Lindenii (Syn. Phyllotænium Lindenii), bright green leaves with white veins and midribs, Colombia ; violaceum, leaves green with purplish veins, W. Indies.

Xeranthemum (Immortelle)—Ord. Compositæ. Hardy annuals. First introduced 1570. Flowers, single and double ; suitable for winter decoration.
CULTURE : Soil, ordinary. Position, sunny beds or borders. Sow seeds in light soil in March in temp. 55° to 65°, planting out in June, or in open ground end of April. Gather flowers for winter decoration directly they are fully expanded.
SPECIES CULTIVATED : X. annuum, purple, etc., summer, 2 ft., S. Europe, and its varieties ligulosum (Syn. X. imperiale), double, and perigulosum (Syn. X. superbissimum), very double.

Xerophyllum (Turkey's Beard)—Ord. Liliaceæ. Hardy perennial subaquatic herb. First introduced 1765.
CULTURE : Soil, moist, sandy peat. Position, boggy places near the margin of ponds or lakes or damp spots in the wild garden. Plant, March or April.
PROPAGATION : By seeds sown in moist, peaty soil in April where required to grow or by division of roots in March or April.
SPECIES CULTIVATED : X. asphodeloides, white, May, 3 to 5 ft., N. America.

Xylobium—Ord. Orchidaceæ. Stove epiphytal orchid.
CULTURE : Compost, equal parts fibry peat and chopped sphagnum moss with little sand and charcoal. Position, well-drained pots, pans, or baskets in light part of greenhouse. Pot when new growth commences. Water deciduous species freely from time new growth begins until Nov., then occasionally ; evergreen species freely from March to Nov., moderately Nov. to March. Syringe once or twice daily whilst making growth. Ventilate freely May to Sept. Temp., April to Oct. 55° to 65° ; Oct. to April 45° to 50°. Growing period, Feb. to March ; resting period, Oct. to Feb. Plants may be grown in sitting-room or cool conservatory when in flower.
PROPAGATION : By division of pseudo-bulbs immediately after flowering.
SPECIES CULTIVATED : X. leontoglossum, yellow and red, spring, Peru.

Xylophylla—See Phyllanthus.

Xylosma—Ord. Bixaceæ. Hardy evergreen flowering tree.
CULTURE : Soil, ordinary. Position, open, sunny shrubberies or borders. Plant, Sept. to Oct. or April to May.
PROPAGATION : By cuttings of half-ripened growth inserted in sandy soil under bell-glass in gentle bottom heat during July and Aug.
SPECIES CULTIVATED : X. racemosa pubescens, yellow, fragrant, summer, to 80 ft., Japan, Corea, and China.

Yam (*Dioscorea Batatas*)—See Dioscorea.

Yarrow—See Achillea.

Yellow Adder's Tongue (*Erythronium americanum*)—See Erythronium.

Yellow Asphodel (*Asphodeline lutea*)—See Asphodeline.

Yellow Centaury—See Chlora.

Yellow Garden Hawkweed—See Tolpis.

Yellow Ox-eye—See Bupthalmum.

Yellow Pimpernel (*Lysimachia nemorum*)—See Lysimachia.

Yellow Rock Indian Cress (*Tropæolum polyphyllum*)—See Tropæolum.

Yellow Root (*Zanthorhiza apiifolia*)—See Zanthorhiza.

Yellow Star of Bethlehem (*Gagea lutea*)—See Gagea.

Yellow Star Flower—See Sternbergia.

Yellow Water Flag (*Iris pseudacorus*)—See Iris.

Yellow Water Lily (*Nuphar advena*)—See Nuphar.

Yellow Wood Anemone (*Anemone ranunculoides*)—See Anemone.

Yellow-wood Tree—See Cladrastis.

Yellow-wort—See Chlora.

Yerba Mansa (*Anemonopsis macrophylla*)—See Anemonopsis.

Yew—See Taxus.

Youth-and-old-age—See Zinnia.

Youth-wort—See Drosera.

Yucca (Adam's Needle; Mound Lily; Spanish Bayonet)—Ord. Liliaceæ. Greenhouse and hardy evergreen perennials. First introduced 1596.
CULTURE OF HARDY SPECIES : Soil, ordinary light, well drained. Position, sunny banks, mounds, rockeries, raised borders, or singly lawns. Plant, Oct. or April. Protect in severe weather with mats.
CULTURE OF GREENHOUSE SPECIES : Compost, two parts sandy loam, one part leaf-mould, and little sand. Position, light greenhouse Sept. to June ; sunny position outdoors, pots plunged to rims in soil, June to Sept. ; or may be grown entirely in greenhouse. Pot, March. Water freely April to Sept., very little afterwards. Repotting only necessary when root-bound. Temp., Sept. to March 40° to 50° ; March to Sept. 55° to 65°.
PROPAGATION : By division in March ; offsets or suckers in March or April ; cuttings of roots inserted in sand in temp. 55° in spring.
GREENHOUSE SPECIES : Y. aloifolia, creamy white, summer, 15 to 25 ft., S.U. States and W. Indies, and its varieties Draconis (leaves drooping), quadricolor (leaves reddish), tricolor (leaves variegated with white, green, and yellow), and variegata (leaves striped with white) ; baccata, creamy white, summer, to 3 ft., Colorado and Texas ; Whipplei, creamy white, summer, to 12 ft., California and Arizona.
HARDY SPECIES : Y. filamentosa, creamy, July to Aug., 3 to 6 ft., S.U. States, and its variety variegata (leaves variegated yellow or white) ; flaccida, creamy, July to Aug., 3 to 4 ft., South-eastern U.S.A. ; glauca (Syn. Y. angustifolia), creamy, July, S.U. States ; gloriosa (Adam's Needle), creamy, July, 6 to 9 ft., S.U. States ; recurvifolia, leaves recurving, creamy, summer, to 6 ft., S.U. States.

Yulan (*Magnolia conspicua*)—See Magnolia.

Zaluzianskya—Ord. Scrophulariaceæ. Half-hardy annuals. First introduced 1776.
CULTURE : Soil, rich, sandy loam. Position, warm, sunny borders or rockeries.
PROPAGATION : By seeds sown on surface of fine light mould and slightly covered with silver sand and placed in temp. 55° to 65° in March, transplanting seedlings outdoors in June ; or sow seeds $\frac{1}{16}$ in. deep outdoors in May where plants are required to flower. Water freely in dry weather. Mulch with layer of cocoanut-fibre refuse in June.
SPECIES CULTIVATED : Z. capensis (Syn. Nycterinia capensis), white and purple, spring and summer, fragrant, 1 to 1½ ft., S. Africa ; selaginoides (Syn. Nycterinia selaginoides), white and lilac, summer, 8 to 12 in., S. Africa.

Zamia (Jamaica Sago Tree)—Ord. Cycadaceæ. Stove or greenhouse orn. foliage plants. Leaves, feather-shaped. First introduced 1691.
CULTURE : Compost, equal parts loam and peat, little silver sand. Position, well-drained pots in shady part of stove. Pot, Feb. or March. Water copiously March to Oct. Syringe daily April to Sept. Moist atmosphere essential. Shade from sun. Temp., March to Oct. 70° to 75° ; Oct. to March 55° to 60°.
PROPAGATION : By seeds sown in light soil in temp. 75° to 85°, spring ; by offsets removed and placed in small pots under bell-glass in propagator in spring ; by division, Feb. or March.
SPECIES CULTIVATED : Z. furfuracea (Jamaica Sago Tree), 3 ft., W. Indies ; integrifolia, 3 ft., W. Indies ; Lindenii, 8 ft., Ecuador ; Wallisi, Colombia.

Zanthorhiza (Yellow Root)—Ord. Ranunculaceæ. Hardy deciduous flowering shrub. First introduced 1766.
CULTURE : Soil, moist loam. Position, thin woodlands or partially shady shrubberies. Plant, Nov. to Feb.
PROPAGATION : By division in Feb.
SPECIES CULTIVATED : Z. apiifolia, purple, March to April, 1 to 2 ft., Eastern U.S.A.

Zanthoxylum—Ord. Rutaceæ. Hardy deciduous shrubs or trees. First introduced 1740.
CULTURE : Soil, deep, loamy. Position, open shrubberies, or as specimens on lawns. Plant, Nov. to Feb.
PROPAGATION : By seeds sown in cool greenhouse in Feb. ; by cuttings of half-ripened shoots in July under bell-glass ; by root cuttings in cool greenhouse in Feb.
SPECIES CULTIVATED : Z. alatum, yellowish, spring, to 12 ft., Himalayas ; americanum (Prickly Ash or Toothache Tree), yellowish green, spring, 10 to 25 ft., Eastern U.S.A. ; piperitum, green, 10 to 20 ft., China and Japan ; planispinum, yellowish, spring, to 12 ft., China and Japan.

Zanzibar Balsam (*Impatiens Sultani*)—See Impatiens.

Zauschneria (Californian Fuchsia)—Ord. Onagraceæ. Half-hardy shrubby perennial. First introduced 1847.
CULTURE : Soil, sandy loam. Position, well-drained rockery or old wall. Plant, March or April.
PROPAGATION : By seeds sown in light, sandy soil, lightly covering with fine mould, placing in temp. 55° to 65°, March, transplanting seedlings outdoors end of May or beginning of June ; by cuttings of young side shoots inserted in pots of sandy soil under bell-glass or hand-light in shady position outdoors in Sept., protecting cuttings in heated greenhouse until following April, then planting out ; by division of old plants in April.
SPECIES CULTIVATED : Z. californica, scarlet, autumn, 1 ft., California, and its varieties microphylla (narrow leaves) and mexicana (bright coloured).

Zea (Maize ; Indian Corn)—Ord. Gramineæ. Half-hardy annual. Orn. foliage. First introduced 1562. Leaves, narrow, grass-like ; green or variegated with white.
CULTURE : Soil, ordinary. Sow seeds ½ in. deep and 1 in. apart in light, rich soil in well-drained pots or boxes in temp. 55° to 65°, Feb. or March ; transfer seedlings when 2 in. high singly into 2 in. pots, then into 4½ in. pots. Place in cold frame to harden in May and plant outdoors in June. May also be grown in pots in compost of equal parts good loamy soil and leaf-mould and little sand. Water freely.
SPECIES CULTIVATED : Z. Mays, 3 to 12 ft., habitat uncertain, and its varieties gracillima (dwarf, narrow leaved), japonica (striped yellow, white, or pink), japonica quadricolor (striped), and japonica variegata (variegated).

Zebra Plant—See Calathea.

Zebra-striped Rush (*Miscanthus sinensis zebrinus*)—See Miscanthus.

Zebrina—Ord. Commelinaceæ. Greenhouse herbaceous trailing perennial. Orn. foliage. First introduced 1849. Leaves, oval oblong ; dark green, striped white above, purplish beneath. Stems creeping.
CULTURE : Compost, equal parts loam, leaf-mould, and sand. Position, in pots or baskets suspended from roof, or in beds under stage or on rockeries. Pot or plant, Jan. to April. Water freely March to Oct., moderately afterwards. Shade from strong sunshine. Temp., 40° to 50° Oct. to April ; 55° to 65° April to Oct. May be grown in windows as a pot or basket plant. Protect from frost in winter.
PROPAGATION : By cuttings of young shoots inserted in light soil under a bell-glass in above temp., March to Oct.
SPECIES CULTIVATED : Z. pendula (Syn. Tradescantia zebrina), foliage striped white above, purple beneath, Mexico, and its variety quadricolor (foliage striped with red and white).

Zelkowa (Water Elm ; Siberian Elm)—Ord. Urticaceæ. Hardy deciduous trees
of no special merit. Closely allied to the elms. Sometimes spelt Zelkova.
CULTURE : Soil, deep, moist loam. Position, side of water-courses and in similar
damp places. Plant, Oct. to Feb.
PROPAGATION : By seeds sown outdoors in autumn or spring ; grafting in March.
SPECIES CULTIVATED : Z. acuminata (Syn. Ulmus Keaki), 40 to 120 ft., Japan and
Corea ; crenata (Syn. Planera Richardi), to 100 ft., Caucasus ; Verschaffeltii (Syn.
Ulmus Verschaffeltii), 30 ft., E. Asia.

Zenobia—Ord. Ericaceæ. Hardy evergreen flowering shrub. First introduced
1800.
CULTURE : Soil, peat or sandy loam. Position, moist sheltered borders. Plant,
Sept., Oct., March, or April.
PROPAGATION : By cuttings of half-ripe shoots inserted in sandy soil under bell-glass
in gentle bottom heat during July.
SPECIES CULTIVATED : Z. speciosa, white, summer, 4 to 6 ft., Eastern U.S.A., and its
variety pulverulenta (blue-grey foliage). See also Pieris.

Zephyranthes (Zephyr Flower ; Atamasco Lily ; Peruvian Swamp Lily ;
Flower of the West Wind)—Ord. Amaryllidaceæ. Hardy and half-hardy deciduous
bulbous flowering plants. First introduced 1629.
CULTURE OF HALF-HARDY SPECIES : Soil, light, sandy loam. Position, well-drained
sunny beds, borders, or rockeries. Plant, Aug. to Nov., placing bulbs 3 to 4 in.
deep and 4 in. apart. Protect in winter by a layer of cinder ashes. Lift and replant
only when bulbs show signs of deterioration.
CULTURE OF HARDY SPECIES : Compost, two parts loam, one part peat, leaf-mould,
and silver sand. Position, well-drained pots in cold frame or greenhouse. Pot,
Aug. to Nov., placing one bulb 2 in. deep in a 5 or 6 in. pot. Water very little till
growth begins, then freely. Withhold water when flowers fade and keep soil quite
dry till potting time.
PROPAGATION : By offsets, planted and treated as advised for large bulbs, Aug. to
Nov.
HALF-HARDY SPECIES : Z. Andersoni, golden yellow, summer, 6 in., Monte Video ;
Atamasco (Atamasco Lily), white, tinged purple, May, 1 ft., N. America ; carinata,
pink, summer, 6 to 12 in., Central America and West Indies.
HARDY SPECIES : Z. candida (Peruvian Swamp Lily), white, Sept., 6 to 12 in.,
La Plata.

Zephyr Flower (*Zephyranthes candida*)—See Zephyranthes.

Zingiber (Ginger)—Ord. Zingiberaceæ. Stove perennial. Roots furnish the
ginger of commerce. First introduced 1605.
CULTURE : Compost, equal parts loam, peat, and sand. Position, pots in shady,
moist part of stove. Pot, Feb. Water copiously March to Oct., keep nearly dry
Oct. to March. Temp., March to Oct. 75° to 85° ; Oct. to March 55° to 65°.
Stems die down in autumn.
PROPAGATION : By division of the rhizomes in Feb.
SPECIES CULTIVATED : Z. officinale, yellowish green and purple, July, to 3 ft.,
Tropical Asia.

Zinnia (Youth-and-old-age)—Ord. Compositæ. Half-hardy annuals. First
introduced 1770.
CULTURE : Soil, deep, loamy liberally enriched with decayed manure. Position,
sunny beds or borders. Sow seeds $\frac{1}{16}$ in. deep in light soil in temp. 55° early in
April. Transplant seedlings when third leaf forms 2 in. apart in shallow boxes
filled with light mould. Place box near the glass in temp. 55° until seedlings are
established, then remove to a cooler house, and if possible plant out 4 in. apart in
good rich soil in cold frame early in May. Shade from sun, keep moist, and
gradually expose to air, end of month. Plant out 8 to 12 in. apart second week in
June. Sow also outdoors middle of May. Prepare bed of rich soil in sunny
position, sow three or four seeds at intervals of 12 in., and thin seedlings to one at

each place when third leaf forms. Mulch all zinnias with decayed manure after planting. Water liberally in dry weather. Apply stimulants when the plants commence to flower. On dry soils take out mould to depth of 12 in., put 3 in. of decayed manure in, then replace former.
SPECIES CULTIVATED : Z. elegans, various colours, summer, 2 to 3 ft., Mexico ; haageana, orange-scarlet, summer, 1 ft., Trop. America ; pauciflora, yellow or purple, summer, 1 ft., Mexico ; tenuiflora (Syn. Z. multiflora), scarlet, summer, 2 ft., Mexico.

Zizania (Water Rice ; Water Oats ; Canadian Rice ; Indian Rice)—Ord. Gramineæ. Hardy aquatic perennial grass. First introduced 1886.
CULTURE : Soil, ordinary. Position, margins of shallow ponds or lakes. Plant, April or May.
PROPAGATION : By seeds sown in heat in spring, growing seedlings on under glass until May, then hardening off in cold frame.
SPECIES CULTIVATED : Z. aquatica, green and brown, summer, 6 to 10 ft., N. America.

Zizyphus (Jujube)—Ord. Rhamnaceæ. Hardy deciduous tree. Fruits edible. First introduced about 1640.
CULTURE : Soil, good loamy. Position, sheltered and sunny. Plant, Nov. to Feb.
PROPAGATION : By seeds sown in boxes of sandy soil in Oct. to Nov. and placed in the open to become stratified by frost ; by cuttings of the roots in cool greenhouse in Feb.
SPECIES CULTIVATED : Z. sativus, yellowish, fruits dark red, to 30 ft., South-east Europe to China.

Zonal Geranium (Pelargonium zonale)—See Pelargonium.

Zygadenus—Ord. Liliaceæ. Hardy bulbous-rooted plants. First introduced 1758.
CULTURE : Soil, peat, leaf-mould, and sand. Position, partially shady, moist border or bed. Plant, autumn. Lift and replant triennially.
PROPAGATION : By division of offsets in autumn ; seeds sown in sandy soil in a cold frame in spring.
SPECIES CULTIVATED : Z. angustifolius (Syn. Helonias angustifolia), white and purple, June, 18 in., N. America ; elegans, green and white, July, 2 to 3 ft., N. America ; glaberrimus, white, July, 2 to 3 ft., N. America ; muscitoxicus, green, July, 2 ft., N. America ; Nuttallii, white, June, 18 in., N. America.

Zygocolax—Ord. Orchidaceæ. A race of bigeneric hybrid orchids obtained by crossing species of Zygopetalum with those of Colax. Habit, intermediate between the two genera. Flowers, large. Require similar culture to Zygopetalums.
HYBRIDS CULTIVATED : Z. amesianus (Zygopetalum brachypetalum × Colax jugosus), green, purple, violet, and white ; leopardinus (Colax jugosus × Zygopetalum maxillare), white, purple, and blue ; Veitchii (Z. crinitum × C. jugosus), yellow, purple, violet, and white ; wiganiana (Z. intermedium × C. jugosus), green, purple, white, and violet.

Zygopetalum—Ord. Orchidaceæ. Stove epiphytal orchids. First introduced 1825.
CULTURE : Compost, equal parts rough fibrous peat and sphagnum moss and charcoal. Position, well-drained pots, or on blocks of wood (roots being covered with sphagnum moss) or in baskets suspended from roof. Pot, etc., Feb. or March. Water freely April to Sept., moderately Sept. to Dec. Give very little Dec. to April. Shade from sun in summer. Moist atmosphere essential. Temp., March to June 58° to 65° ; Dec. to March 53° to 60°. Growing period : All the year round. Resting period : None. Flowers appear at base of new growth.
PROPAGATION : By division any time.
SPECIES CULTIVATED : Z. Burkei, green, chocolate brown, white, and purple, winter, 12 to 18 in., Guiana ; Burtii, white, yellow, brown, crimson, and purple, summer,

1 ft., Costa Rica; cerinum (Syn. Pescatorea cerina), straw and yellow, various seasons, 1 ft., Chiriqui; cœleste (Syn. Bollea cœlestis), blue, mauve, white, and violet, summer, Colombia; crinitum, green, white, and purple, spring, 18 in. to 2 ft., Brazil; intermedium, green, brown, white, and violet purple, autumn, Brazil; Lalindei (Syn. Bollea Lalindei), rose and yellow, various seasons, 1 ft., Colombia; Mackaii, green, yellow, brown, and violet, winter, 18 in. to 2 ft., Brazil; maxillare, green, brown, violet, and blue, winter, 1 ft., Brazil, and its variety Gautieri; rostratum (Syn. Zygosepalum rostratum), white and rosy purple, May and June, 8 in., British Guiana; stapelioides (Syn. Promenæa stapelioides), green, yellow, brown, and purple, summer, 3 in., Brazil; xanthinum (Syn. Promenæa xanthina), yellow, red, and crimson, summer, 3 in., Brazil. See also Warscewiczella.

Zygosepalum rostratum—See Zygopetalum rostratum.

AECHMEA. — Stove flowering plants. (also CANISTRUM) . Brazil
× RHODOCYAMEA. ×.
× ROSE-ROBINIA. ×. (Acacia?).

ANASTATICA — Rose of Jericho (Dried). Withers in dry weather —
but picks up again (even from dry) when watered. Often called Resurrection
plant.

PENSTIMON. ✓

CISTUS. (white with Maroon blotch). ✓

Triteleia Uniflora or IPHEION. leaves like long grass. flowers
starry shaped. (Bulbous) Pretty Blue - See. Brodiaea (page 62) -

NOTES

NOTES

NOTES